CorelDRAW! 5
The Professional Reference

Deborah Miller

Gary David Bouton

Giuseppe De Bellis

John R. Faunce

June Kanai Reeder

Ken Reeder

John J. Shanley

Full-color art by:
Steve Bain
Joe Donnelly
Deborah Miller
Phillip Williams

NRP
NEW RIDERS
PUBLISHING

New Riders Publishing, Indianapolis, Indiana

CorelDRAW! The Professional Reference

By Deborah Miller, Gary David Bouton, Giuseppe De Bellis, John R. Faunce, June Kanai Reeder, Ken Reeder, and John J. Shanley

Published by:
New Riders Publishing
201 West 103rd Street
Indianapolis, IN 46290 USA

Printed in the United States of America 1 2 3 4 5 6 7 8 9 0

Library of Congress-in-Publication Data

CorelDRAW! the Professional Reference / Deborah Miller ... [et al.].
    p. cm.
    Includes index.
    ISBN 1-56205-297-7 : $50.00
    1. CorelDraw! 2. Computer graphics.   I. Miller, Deborah, 1952-

    T385.C664 1994   94-39835
    006.6'869—dc20   CIP

Warning and Disclaimer

This book is designed to provide information about the CorelDRAW! computer program. Every effort has been made to make this book as complete and as accurate as possible, but no warranty or fitness is implied.

The information is provided on an "as is" basis. The author and New Riders Publishing shall have neither liability nor responsibility to any person or entity with respect to any loss or damages arising from the information contained in this book or from the use of the disks or programs that may accompany it.

Publisher	*Don Fowley*
Associate Publisher	*Tim Huddleston*
Product Development Manager	*Rob Tidrow*
Marketing Manager	*Ray Robinson*
Director of Special Projects	*Cheri Robinson*
Managing Editor	*Tad Ringo*

About the Authors

Deborah Miller is co-owner, with her husband, Mike, of Miller Graphic Consulting, Ltd. in Mesa, Arizona. She has been a computer graphics artist for over 25 years and has been using CorelDRAW! since 1989. She has served as the technical editor for several CorelDRAW! books published by New Riders Publishing and has contributed to the New Riders title *CorelDRAW! Special Effects.*

Gary David Bouton was born in Auburn, New York, in 1953. Gary, although denying that he's "grown up," spent his school years in Syracuse, New York, where he studied advertising design at Syracuse University.

After graduating with a bachelor's degree in fine art, he moved to New York City, where he became an art director. Dozens of television commercials and magazine ads later, Gary relocated to a suburb of his hometown in 1991 to start his own company. Exclamat!ons is a company that "polishes rough ideas," he explains. Together with his wife, Barbara, and a loose collection of people they call a "staff," Gary takes other people's print and desktop video ideas and gives them shape and impact. He hopes that more sophisticated software will continue to be written for computers, because he loves to experiment and adopt new looks into his work. Exclamat!ons is responsible for designing several regional publications and logos.

Gary's books for New Riders Publishing include *CorelDRAW! 5 for Beginners, CorelDRAW! for Non-Nerds, Photoshop NOW!,* and *Inside Adobe Photoshop,* which he coauthored with his wife.

Editor of *NewsBytes,* the Central NY PC Users Group, Gary also has been writing reviews about image-editing and illustration software since 1992. *NewsBytes* won first prize in the *InfoWorld/Lotus International Newsletter Competition* in June 1993.

In his spare time, Gary likes to collect coffee mugs, rubber stamps, and wind-up toys.

Giuseppe De Bellis was born in Taranto, Italy on November 23, 1959. He spent his early years in this city, on the coast of the Mediterranean Sea.

After completing the artistic liceo and graduating in fine arts, at the age of 16 he went off to the University of Florence School of Architecture. He remained there after completing his doctorate, and started to work as a free-lance graphic artist for *Vogue* magazine and other local companies.

In 1986, he married an American, Rome Chiarello, who has been very supportive and invaluable in her help and relocated to the New York metropolitan area. He has since been very busy working for the New York City Board of Education as an architect, and free-lancing for many companies and corporations needing his artistic talent.

He has recently established "New Design Concepts," a company that offers computer and graphic consulting services. He has won numerous awards for his artwork, and can name quite a few big companies as clients.

Giuseppe currently resides in New Jersey, heading his newly established company, writing and publishing his work in specialized graphic magazines and books in his free time.

John R. Faunce discovered an interest in computers in the early '60s. He worked for Travelers Insurance Company operating UNIVAC mainframes, then as an IBM System/360-Systems programmer. He joined IBM in 1968 in marketing and spent six years selling System/370s to Aetna Life & Casualty.

In 1975, to bring up four daughters in Vermont, he left IBM and bought a farm supply business. He ran this business until 1986, then returned to computers. He has built, sold, programmed, taught, and used PCs since then, including one year with Macintoshes.

June Kanai Reeder and **Ken Reeder** are the owners of Ideas to Images, a training company specializing in the needs of graphics and desktop-publishing professionals. They have traveled throughout the United States and Europe presenting printing and publishing seminars to groups of up to 500.

Ken has worked as a computer/graphics designer at ad agencies for two years; as a communications manager for a large municipality for three years, doing video, broadcasting, print production, computer graphics, photography, and multimedia work; and as a communications consultant to a legal professor. He has spent three years in computer training and writing.

June worked for two years for MUSA Systems as a product development specialist, writing, directing, and producing video and print productions. She has spent three years in computer training and writing.

John J. Shanley is president of Phoenix Creative Graphics, a Somerset, New Jersey, graphics design firm. John is a traditionally trained designer and illustrator who has been working in the graphic art and advertising fields since 1975. He has been a CorelDRAW! user since version 1.

John's positions with design studios, agencies, and commercial printing companies introduced him to the computer via typesetting. In 1988 he recognized that the combination of the IBM PC and Windows would have a profound impact on the graphics and business worlds. He focused his newly formed Phoenix Creative Graphics' computer resources on this platform. Merging traditional skills and computer innovations has proved to be a successful strategy.

Over the years, Phoenix Creative Graphics augmented its design and production services with desktop-publishing consulting services. These services focus on utilizing in-house, computer-based functions more effectively with outside design and production services. John's real-world experience has been instrumental in helping corporate clients set up and maintain their own DTP departments.

Readers are invited to contact John by telephone at (908) 873-5757 or through CompuServe at 76535,3443.

Trademark Acknowledgments

Dedication

From Deborah Miller:

This book is dedicated to the memory of my father, Calvin H. Posey, who never failed to believe during my lifetime. I regret he passed away before this book could be completed.

Wa-do'

Acknowledgments

From Deborah Miller:

I am privileged to have a wonderful family and a wealth of talented friends. I never would have completed this book without their inspiration, support, suggestions, and tolerance. My husband Mike held home, hearth, and soul together, while serving as my resource person, sounding board, and chief techie guru. He managed to keep the computers running despite my abusing them. My thanks go to my family of young adults, Bevin, LaRae, and Matt, who managed to put up with me, and do without me, during the long hours.

The images of a number of photographers and artists grace the pages of this book. Richard Morris, friend and photographer, donated his extraordinary genius. Phillip Williams, Gary Bouton, Robert Naeyaert, and Bevin Mallory generously allowed me to use fruits of their varied talents. Small glimpses of the lifetime collection of LaResta Posey are sprinkled throughout this book. It was difficult to choose from the tens of thousands of images that represent her passion for photography.

Sections of this book are the result of the literary talents of their authors. Ken and June Reeder authored the chapters on CorelSHOW, CorelCHART, and CorelMOVE. The bitmap magic of CorelPHOTO-PAINT was written by Gary Bouton. Giuseppe De Bellis and John Shanley were gracious enough to author the chapters on creating your own font and working with service bureaus, respectively. John Faunce lent his enthusiasm and expertise with publishing packages to the section on CorelVENTURA.

The following friends were constant in their support, even during my more crazed moments: Robert Beckwith, Leonore Cash, James Karney, Jennifer Lambert, and Maryann Watkins.

A number of corporations provided information and assistance during the course of writing this book. They are listed in the Resource Appendix, and have my gratitude.

William Schneider lent his technical expertise to the editing of this book. My thanks go out to him, even if he does buy cheap pepperoni.

Corel Corporation lent their generous support to this book. Bill Cullen, John Senez, Mike Bellefeuille, and Kelly Grieg answered questions and tolerated my being a pest throughout the project.

A special thanks goes to the staff of Seiko Instruments, USA. The color composite images for this book were printed on their Professional Color Point II hybrid printer. The printer (and sometimes their staff) kept my hours and consistently helped me produce color images of incomparable quality. Throughout the project their continued, patient support and assistance helped make this book possible.

The staff of NRP assisted in helping get this book into print, against occasionally formidable odds. This was a "morphed" book. The humor and extraordinary talents of Cheri Robinson, Stacey Beheler, Steve Weiss, John Kane, and Alicia Krakovitz provided a flow toward completion despite network crashes and other natural disasters. Thank you all for your patience and input.

From John Shanley:

Without the help of many, the information for this chapter could not have been compiled and verified. Special thanks goes out to:

Geoff Holmes at Persimmon Software in England. Geoff was invaluable in deciphering the maze of the PostScript driver, its relationship to CorelDRAW!, and also for plenty of technical information on high- resolution imagesetters and RIPs.

Rob Miller of Artco Graphics in Elizabeth, NJ. Rob's experience running a slide service bureau contributed greatly to the slide portions of this chapter.

The personnel of ColorLogic in Parsippany, NJ and Pulsar Graphics Inc. in Manalapan, NJ for their assistance with high-resolution image issues.

Product Director
Cheri Robinson
Production Editors
John Kane
Steve Weiss
Editors
Amy Bezek
Fran Blauw
Laura Frey
Sarah Kearns
Mary Ann Larguier
Rob Lawson
Cliff Shubs
John Sleeva
Lillian Yates
Acquisitions Editor
Stacey Beheler
Technical Editors
Giuseppe De Bellis
William Schneider
Lisa AgnesWindham
Editorial Assistant
Karen Opal
Cover Designer
Roger S. Morgan
Book Designer
Roger S. Morgan
Kim Scott
Graphics Image Specialists
Clint Lahnen
Dennis Sheehan
Production Imprint Manager
Juli Cook
Production Imprint Team Leader
Katy Bodenmiller
Production Analysts
Angela D. Bannan
Dennis Clay Hager
Mary Beth Wakefield
Production Team
Carol Bowers, Don Brown, Michael Brumitt, Elaine Brush, Stephen Carlin, Kim Cofer, Lisa Daugherty, Judy Everly, Roberto Falco, Kimberly K. Hannel, Ayanna Lacey, Elizabeth Lewis, Shawn MacDonald, Erika Millen, Vic Peterson, Casey Price, Brian-Kent Proffitt, Susan Shepard, SA Springer, Jacqueline Thompson, Jill Tompkins, Scott Tullis, Suzanne Tully, Jeff Weissenberger, Dennis Wesner, Holly Wittenberg, Donna Winter
Indexer
Greg Eldred

Contents at a Glance

Table of Contents

Introduction

*T*he world of graphics is undergoing one of the most exciting evolutions in its history. Powerful computers and software are emerging that enable the creative mind to soar with almost infinite possibilities. The computer is rapidly replacing the drawing board as the standard tool for graphics design and illustration. The rapid growth of computers and software has created large programs with increasing complexity and lengthy learning curves. In the midst of this evolution is the graphics professional, with a growing need for a thorough understanding of these extraordinary tools.

Since its inception, Corel Corporation has endeavored to keep pace with the expanding demands of the graphics industry. Released in May 1994, CorelDRAW version 5.0 is the most powerful graphics suite in today's market. Far more than just a drawing package, it provides graphics, publishing, and presentation solutions to meet the variety of needs required by the design industry.

This introduction covers:

- How to use this book
- How this book is organized
- Conventions used in this book
- Special text used in this book
- Information about New Riders Publishing
- Artist credits for the 16-color insert

How To Use This Book

CorelDRAW! The Professional Reference is designed as a reference for the graphics professional. Although basics are considered, its focus is far more encompassing. Attention has been paid to detail in issues of concern to anyone who requires professional-quality output. Because of the concentration on advanced use of the CorelDRAW suite of applications, this book presumes experience with Windows and graphics software.

For ease of use, this book has been organized into sections. Each section discusses an application or a facet of the suite as a whole. This enables you to easily find the information you require.

How This Book Is Organized

CorelDRAW! The Professional Reference is designed to be a reference book for the experienced user. The book is divided into eight clearly defined parts:

- Part One, "CorelDRAW," serves as your complete reference to the drawing module of version 5. From the basics, such as learning the tools and menus, to working with fills and color, Part One details every aspect of creating professional-quality drawings.

- Part Two, "CorelVENTURA," introduces the newest module of

this graphics suite of applications, VENTURA desktop publisher. You learn the essentials to creating and using tags, style sheets, and tables. You also learn to add graphics to your documents by fully integrating VENTURA with all the other modules.

- Part Three, "CorelPHOTO-PAINT," provides thorough coverage of the concepts behind pixel-based graphics. This section covers working with objects, masks, and filters, as well as color specification and output.

- Part Four, "CorelCHART," focuses on the aspects of creating quality graphical charts. You learn to create and enhance charts, and about what types of charts are best to use in different situations.

- Part Five, "Creating Presentations," focuses on the CorelMOVE and CorelSHOW modules. Complete coverage of creating actors and props and building animations is provided.

- Part Six, "Advanced Topics," covers color management and color calibration. Tips and techniques are provided on working with service bureaus to obtain quality output. Also covered are cross-platform concerns and using the OLE features of CorelDRAW.

- Part Seven, "Managing Your System and Files," provides the advanced-level information you need on customizing your computer setup and font management, and what to do when you have problems with CorelDRAW.

■ Part Eight, "Appendixes," provides instructions on installing CorelDRAW, a resource list of service providers, and information about using the *CorelDRAW! The Professional Reference* companion CDs.

Many of the images included in the color insert pages appear on the CDs as well, enabling you to examine them more closely. You should note, however, that the purpose of these images is illustrative, and that they are the copyrighted property of the respective artists. As such, you can use them for experimentation purposes, but they are not clip art and cannot be used in any publication without the express written permission of the artist.

Conventions Used in This Book

Most New Riders Publishing books use similar conventions to help you distinguish between various elements of the software, Windows, and sample data. This means that after you purchase one New Riders book, you'll find it easier to use all the others.

Before you continue, you should spend a moment examining these conventions. Key combinations appear in the following formats:

■ **Key1+Key2.** When you see a plus sign between key names, you should hold down the first key as you press the second key. Then release both keys.

■ **Key1, Key2.** When a comma appears between key names, you should press and release the first key, and then press and release the second key.

Windows underlines one letter in all menus and menu items, and most dialog box options; for example, the File menu is displayed on-screen as **<u>F</u>ile**. This book sets off such hot keys as follows: <u>F</u>ile. The underlined letter indicates which letter you can type to choose that command or option.

Text you type is in a special **bold** typeface. This applies to individual letters and numbers, as well as text strings. This convention, however, does not apply to command keys, such as Enter, Esc, and Ctrl.

New terms appear in *italic*.

Text that appears on-screen, such as prompts and messages, appears in a `special typeface`.

Special Text Used in This Book

This book features *sidebars,* special text that is set apart from the normal text by icons. These sidebars include the following:

T I P

A Tip marks a shortcut or idea that helps you get your work done faster or better.

N O T E

A Note includes extra information you should find useful, but which complements the discussion at hand, instead of being a direct part of it.

W A R N I N G

A Warning tells you when a procedure may be dangerous. Warnings tell you how to avoid data loss, system lockups, and damage to files or software.

New Riders Publishing

The staff of New Riders Publishing is committed to bringing you the very best in computer reference material. Each New Riders book is the result of months of work by authors and staff who research and refine the information contained within its covers.

As part of this commitment to you, the NRP reader, New Riders invites your input. Please let us know if you enjoy this book, if you have trouble with the information and examples presented, or if you have a suggestion for the next edition.

Please note, though: New Riders staff cannot serve as a technical resource for CorelDRAW or for related questions about software- or hardware-related problems. Please refer to the documentation that accompanies

CorelDRAW or to the applications' Help systems.

If you have a question or comment about any New Riders book, there are several ways to contact New Riders Publishing. We will respond to as many readers as we can. Your name, address, and phone number will never become part of a mailing list or be used for any purpose other than to help us continue to bring you the best books possible. You can write us at the following address:

New Riders Publishing
Attn: Associate Publisher
201 W. 103rd Street
Indianapolis, IN 46290

If you prefer, you can fax New Riders Publishing at (317) 581-4670.

You can send e-mail to New Riders from a variety of sources. NRP maintains several mailboxes organized by topic area. Mail in these mailboxes will be forwarded to the staff member who is best able to address your concerns. Substitute the appropriate mailbox name from the list below when addressing your e-mail. The mailboxes are as follows:

ADMIN	Comments and complaints for NRP's publisher
APPS	Word, Excel, WordPerfect, and other office applications
ACQ	Book proposals and inquiries by potential authors

CAD	AutoCAD, 3D Studio, AutoSketch, and CAD, products
DATABASE	Access, dBASE, Paradox, and other database products
GRAPHICS	CorelDRAW, Photoshop, and other graphics products
INTERNET	Internet
NETWORK	NetWare, LANtastic, and other network-related topics
OS	MS-DOS, OS/2, all operating systems except UNIX and Windows
UNIX	UNIX
WINDOWS	Microsoft Windows (all versions)
OTHER	Anything that doesn't fit the previous categories

If you use an MHS e-mail system that routes through CompuServe, send your messages to:

mailbox @ NEWRIDER

To send NRP mail from CompuServe, use the following to address:

MHS: *mailbox* @ NEWRIDER

To send mail from the Internet, use the following address format:

mailbox@newrider.mhs.compuserve.com

New Riders Publishing is an imprint of Macmillan Computer Publishing. To obtain a catalog or information, or to purchase any Macmillan Computer Publishing book, call (800) 428-5331.

Thank you for selecting *CorelDRAW! The Professional Reference*.

Artist Credits for the Color Insert

Image 1 ....Joe Donnelly

Image 2 ....Steve Bain

Image 3 ....Steve Bain

Image 4 ....Deborah Miller

Image 5 ....Joe Donnelly

Image 6 ....Joe Donnelly

Image 7 ....Phillip Williams

Image 8 ....Steve Bain

Image 9 ....Joe Donnelly

Image 10 ....Joe Donnelly

Image 11 ....Deborah Miller

Image 12 ....Deborah Miller

Image 13 ....Deborah Miller

Image 14 ....Phillip Williams

Image 15 ....Deborah Miller

Image 16 ....Deborah Miller

Part I

CorelDRAW

- **Print Merge.** Similar to mail merge options available in most word processors, this command enables you to print a form document, replacing selected artistic text with text created in a word processor. Print **M**erge prompts you for the path and file name of your prepared text.

- **Print Setup.** Accesses the Print Setup dialog box. The options available vary according to the active printer.

- **Color Manager.** Enables you to calibrate your monitor, scanner, and printer for color correction. For more information, see Chapter 38, "Color Management."

- **Exit.** Exits the program. Keyboard shortcut = Alt+F4.

N O T E

CorelDRAW keeps track of the last four documents you opened. This allows you to access these documents quickly by clicking on the number beside the document, or by depressing the respective number on your keyboard.

The Edit Menu

The **E**dit menu (see fig. 1.4) contains the commands for the step, Clipboard, and most OLE functions. The following list details the commands within the Edit menu.

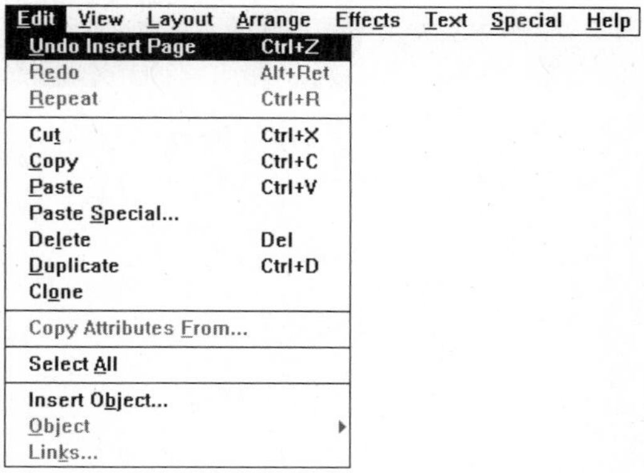

Figure 1.4
The Edit menu.

Edit	View	Layout	Arrange	Effects	Text	Special	Help

Undo Insert Page .... Ctrl+Z
R**e**do .... Alt+Ret
Repeat .... Ctrl+R

Cu**t** .... Ctrl+X
Copy .... Ctrl+C
Paste .... Ctrl+V
Paste **S**pecial...
De**l**ete .... Del
Duplicate .... Ctrl+D
Cl**o**ne

Copy Attributes **F**rom...

Select **A**ll

Insert O**b**ject...
Object ▸
Links...

- **Undo.** Cancels the last command performed and returns the selected object(s) to their previous appearance. CorelDRAW supports multiple levels of Undo. The number of levels available is determined by the settings you select in the **P**references command. The default number of Undo levels is four. You can set the program for up to 99 levels of undo. Keyboard shortcuts = Ctrl+Z or Alt+Backspace.

- **Redo.** Repeats the last command applied prior to Undo. Keyboard shortcut = Alt+Ret.

- **Repeat.** Reproduces the last command applied to a selection. Repeat is helpful when applying the same command to several different selections, such as **G**roup, **A**lign, or Move. Most of the special effects commands cannot be repeated. Use Cop**y** from the Effe**c**ts menu instead. Keyboard shortcut = Ctrl+R.

███████ N   O   T   E ███████

The Windows Clipboard is for temporary storage of a selection. The selection can be viewed with the Clipboard viewer, or placed in other documents. When you exit CorelDRAW, the program asks you if you want to retain data stored in the Clipboard for use in other application.

■ **Cut.** Copies the selected object(s) to the Windows Clipboard and removes them from your image. The objects can then be pasted into other documents, created in a Windows application. Keyboard shortcut = Ctrl+X.

■ **Copy.** Places a copy of the selected object(s) in the Windows Clipboard. Unlike Cu**t**, **C**opy leaves the selected object(s) in the image. Keyboard shortcut = Ctrl+C.

■ **Paste.** Places data stored in the Windows Clipboard into another document, graphic, or speedsheet. Text pasted in a CorelDRAW image from a word processor is treated as a document object, and cannot be edited with CorelDRAW's text-editing features. Double-clicking on the text starts the associated word processing application, enabling you to edit the text. Double-clicking on a graphic object, created in an application other than CorelDRAW, starts the associated application. This allows you to edit the object in the originating application. Keyboard shortcut = Ctrl+V or Shift+Insert.

■ **Paste Special.** An OLE function that enables you to link or embed an object into a CorelDRAW file by pasting it from the Windows Clipboard.

■ **Delete.** Removes the selected object(s) from your document. Keyboard shortcut = Del.

■ **Duplicate.** Reproduces the selected object(s). Placement of the duplicate in your document depends upon the settings in **P**references. Keyboard shortcut = Ctrl+D.

■ **Clone.** Is similar to **D**uplicate in that it creates a copy of the selection within your document. Changes made to the original or master object, however, are duplicated in the clone object. If you make changes to a cloned object, future changes of that attribute, made to the master object, will no longer apply to the clone. Example: If you change the fill of a cloned object, changes made to the fill of the master object will not change the clone.

■ **Copy Attributes From**. Accesses the Copy Attributes dialog box (see fig. 1.5), enabling you to apply the attributes of one object to a selected object. After selecting the attribute(s) you want to copy, an arrow appears with the word From, prompting you to click on the object containing the desired attributes. If you select **R**epeat after applying Copy Attributes **F**rom, the dialog box does not appear. The selected object, instead, gains the same attributes as the last object selected.

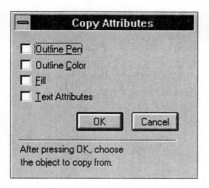

Figure 1.5
The Copy Attributes dialog box.

■ **Select All.** Selects all of the objects contained on active layers within your document. Objects contained on locked layers cannot selected.

■ **Insert Object.** Accesses the Insert Object dialog box, enabling you to insert an OLE object in your document. Objects can be embedded or linked. The dialog box offers you the option of inserting an object from a pre-existing file, or creating a new object in the selected application.

■ **Object.** Opens the associated server application for the selected OLE object, enabling you to edit the object. When you finish the editing process and close the associated server application, your CorelDRAW document is updated to reflect the changes. Alternatively, double-click on a linked or embedded object.

■ **Links.** Opens the Links dialog box, permitting you to update, change, or cancel links of OLE objects. It also enables you to open the server application associated with the object.

For more information about OLE, see the section called, "Understanding and Using OLE2," found later in this chapter.

The View Menu

The **V**iew menu (see fig. 1.6) enables you to customize the appearance of your workspace. The following list describes the commands found in the View menu.

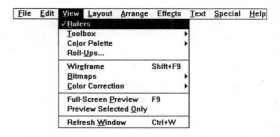

Figure 1.6
The View menu.

■ **Rulers.** Switches the display of rulers on and off within the drawing window.

■ **Toolbox.** Accesses the Toolbox Options fly-out. Select **V**isible to display the toolbox. When **F**loating is enabled, the toolbox can be repositioned within the drawing window.

■ **Color Palette.** Enables you to choose the on-screen palette from the fly-out menu. CorelDRAW offers a variety of palettes for your selection. For more information on the available palettes, see Chapter 6, "Working with Fills."

■ **Roll-Ups.** Accesses the Roll-Ups dialog box (see fig. 1.7), enabling you to select the appearance of the roll-up menus in the drawing window. Roll-ups can be configured individually, and the configuration saved for future CorelDRAW sessions. The options can be customized to the way you work.

Figure 1.7
The Roll-Ups dialog box.

W A R N I N G

Roll-ups require a large amount of system resources. To prevent system slowdowns and memory error messages, avoid the temptation to keep more roll-ups on your workspace than you need.

■ **Wireframe.** CorelDRAW offers two editing views: editable preview and wireframe. Editing in wireframe view lowers the screen refresh time. This is useful when creating and editing large or complex files. Keyboard shortcut = Shift+F9.

■ **Bitmaps.** Accesses a fly-out menu, enabling you to choose to hide or display bitmaps when working in wireframe view. If **V**isible is disabled, bitmaps appear as empty rectangles. The fly-out menu also enables you to lower the display resolution of bitmaps. For more information, see Chapter 13, "Working with Bitmaps."

■ **Color Correction.** Accesses a fly-out menu, enabling you to alter the display of your monitor to compensate for color variations between your display and your printer. This increases your ability to predict the color output of your file with greater accuracy. Color correction is dependent upon choices you make in the Color Manager. For more information, see Chapter 44, "Customizing Your Computer for CorelDRAW."

■ **Full-Screen Preview.** Switches the display to Full-Screen Preview, hiding the tools and the menus. Objects cannot be edited in Full-Screen Preview. Keyboard shortcut = F9.

■ **Preview Selected Only.** Displays only the selected object(s), when Full-Screen Preview is enabled. This is useful for viewing the results of editing applied to an object or group of objects.

■ **Refresh Window.** Redraws the image in the drawing window and removes any residual screen trash leftover from previous editing. Keyboard shortcut = Ctrl+W.

The Layout Menu

The Layout menu (see fig. 1.8) enables you to customize document pages, and contains aids that assist in making document creation easier. The following list describes the commands found in the Layout menu.

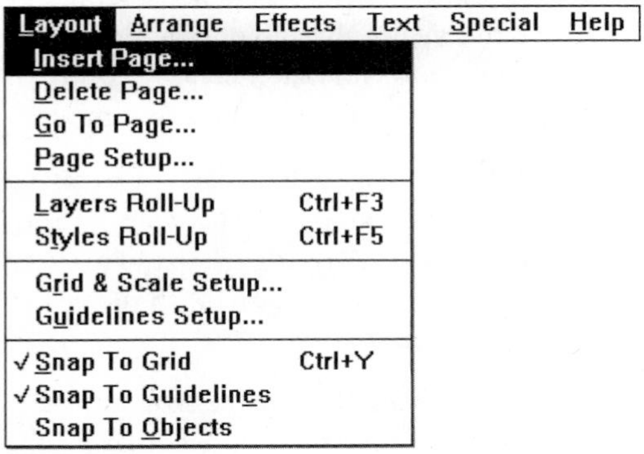

Layout	Arrange	Effects	Text	Special	Help
Insert Page...					
Delete Page...					
Go To Page...					
Page Setup...					
Layers Roll-Up		Ctrl+F3			
Styles Roll-Up		Ctrl+F5			
Grid & Scale Setup...					
Guidelines Setup...					
√Snap To Grid		Ctrl+Y			
√Snap To Guidelines					
Snap To Objects					

Figure 1.8
The Layout menu.

■ **Insert Page.** Enables you to add new page(s) before or after the current page.

■ **Delete Page.** Used to delete pages from your document.

■ **Go To Page.** Changes the view, in multiple page documents, to the page you select.

■ **Page Setup.** Displays the Page Setup dialog box. The property sheets, accessed by clicking on the tabs, enable you to set the size, layout, and display options for your document (see fig. 1.9). The bitmap at the top of the dialog box reflects the changes you make.

The Size property sheet allows you to choose from an assortment of sizes, set the size to your printer, or specify custom page sizes up to 30×30 inches. Choose Portrait orientation if the vertical dimension of your drawing exceeds the horizontal dimension. Choose Landscape if the horizontal dimension of your drawing exceeds the vertical dimension.

N O T E

The page size options are not device-dependent. The printable image size available for your printer may vary from the size options. These options do not allow for margins required by your printer. If you choose a larger page size than your printer permits, part of your image may be lost during printing.

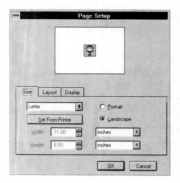

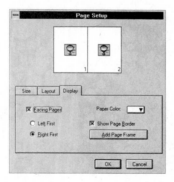

Figure 1.9
The three property sheets in the Page Setup dialog box.

The Layout property sheet enables you to choose full page or from a selection of popular page layouts.

The Display property sheet permits you to choose **F**acing pages and the page that is displayed first, for multipage documents. You can also disable the Show Page **B**order feature in CorelDRAW within this box. The page border in CorelDRAW's drawing window provides a visual reference for the printable page.

W A R N I N G

Exercise caution when disabling Show Page **B**order—elements of your drawing could fall outside the printable page without this visual reference.

Choosing a paper color enables you to add a background color to the view of your document while you are in color preview mode. This color is a representative view only, and does not print. This allows for better creative control if your final output is on colored paper.

Adding a **P**age Frame places a rectangle in your drawing with the same dimensions as your page size. This printable frame appears with the default outline and fill.

■ **Layers Roll-Up.** Enables you to place various elements on different layers. This is especially useful when creating complex drawings. You can lock layers, making selection of a single object easier. Making a layer invisible speeds screen refresh time, while enabling you to edit objects on active visible layers. Printing can be toggled off and on for each layer if desired. Various options available with the Layers roll-up make manipulation of large files easier. Keyboard shortcut = Ctrl+F3. For more information, see Chapter 10, "Using Layers in Documents."

- **Styles Roll-Up.** Enables you to define and apply formatting instructions to text and graphics. For more information, see Chapter 12, "Working with Layouts."

- **Grid & Scale Setup.** Grids are one of many alignment tools available in CorelDRAW. The Grid Setup dialog box lets you set the units of measurement used in CorelDRAW and place an adjustable grid on your page as an alignment reference. You can also define global units of measurement, permitting easier scaling of objects.

- **Guidelines Setup.** Enables you to specify the placement of non-printing guidelines on your page as an alignment reference. These guidelines permit the precise placement of objects on the page. Alternatively, you can click on either of the rulers and drag a guideline into place manually. Double-clicking on a guideline accesses the Guidelines dialog box.

- **Snap To Grid.** Forces objects to align with a grid. Keyboard shortcut = Ctrl+Y.

- **Snap To Guidelines.** Forces objects to align with guidelines you have placed on a page.

- **Snap To Objects.** Makes objects behave like magnets, forcing objects to snap to control points of other objects.

N O T E

For more information regarding grids, guidelines, and snap to features, see Chapter 9, "Using Alignment Aids."

The Arrange Menu

The Arrange menu (see fig. 1.10) enables you to alter the relationship of objects to one another, or change the characteristics of an object. The following list describes the commands found in the Arrange menu.

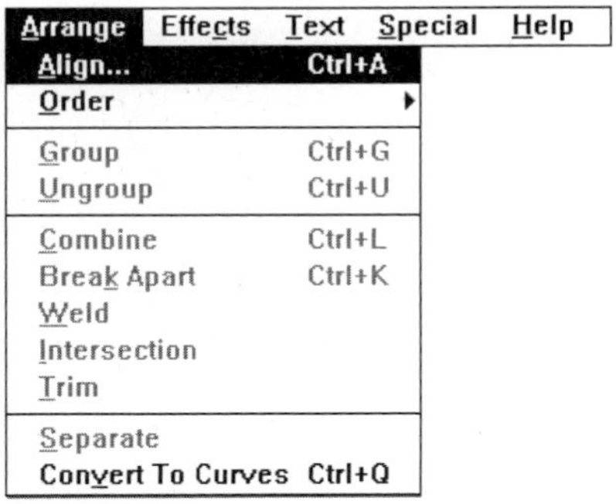

Arrange	Effects	Text	Special	Help
Align...			Ctrl+A	
Order			▶	
Group			Ctrl+G	
Ungroup			Ctrl+U	
Combine			Ctrl+L	
Break Apart			Ctrl+K	
Weld				
Intersection				
Trim				
Separate				
Convert To Curves			Ctrl+Q	

Figure 1.10
The Arrange menu.

■ **Align.** Arranges objects horizontally or vertically in relationship to one another. Horizontal alignment enables the left, right, or center alignment of objects. Vertical alignment allows the top, bottom, or center alignment of objects. The last object selected provides the guide for alignment. The align command also enables you to center selected objects on the printable page. Keyboard shortcut = Ctrl+A.

■ **Order.** When you choose **O**rder, a fly-out menu appears enabling you to adjust the stacking order of objects on a layer. Objects can be moved up one, brought to the front, moved down one, moved to the back, or reversed. Selections of multiple objects or blend groups can have their order reversed. Keyboard shortcuts: Shift+PgDn = To Bottom; Shift+PgUp = To Top; Ctrl+PgDn = Back One; Ctrl+PgUp = Forward One.

■ **Group.** Enables you to package multiple objects together by selecting them and applying the **G**roup command. Grouped objects retain their individual attributes, but function as a single object when manipulated. Any changes applied to grouped objects, such as fill or outline changes, apply to all the objects within the group. Grouped objects cannot be edited with the shape tool. Keyboard shortcut = Ctrl+G.

N O T E

Individual objects within a group are called Child Objects, and can be selected for individual editing by depressing the Ctrl key and clicking on the object.

■ **Ungroup.** Reverses the **G**roup command, allowing objects to be manipulated individually. Keyboard shortcut = Ctrl+U.

■ **Combine.** Used primarily to create masks and clipped holes. When two or more overlapping objects are combined, they become a single multipath object. The areas of overlap become transparent, allowing objects placed underneath to show through the transparent areas. The combined object assumes the attributes of the last object selected before applying the command. Unlike grouped objects, combined objects can be edited using the shape tool. Objects need not be overlapping to combine them. Keyboard shortcut = Ctrl+L.

N O T E

Combining objects significantly reduces the file size of your drawing.

■ **Break Apart.** Separates combined objects into individual objects. The individual objects retain the attributes of the combined object. Keyboard shortcut = Ctrl+K.

- **Weld.** **W**eld is like **C**ombine in that it creates a single object from two or more objects. It differs from **C**ombine, however, in that the resulting object's intersecting paths are removed. A welded object assumes the attributes of the last object selected.

- **Intersection.** Creates a new object from the area of two or more overlapping objects. The new object assumes the attributes of the last object selected. If the objects are marquee-selected, the new object assumes the attributes of the bottom object. The intersection command cannot be applied to grouped objects.

- **Trim.** Cuts out the section common to two or more overlapping objects. The last object selected is the object that is trimmed. If objects are marquee-selected, the bottom object is trimmed. It retains all fill and outline attributes.

- **Separate.** Used to separate a control object from a dynamically linked group. Dynamically linked groups are created by the application of one of the special effects, such as blend, contour, extrude, or text to path.

- **Convert To Curves.** Changes text as well as rectangular and elliptical shapes to curved objects, allowing the object to be edited using the shape tool. Keyboard shortcut = Ctrl+Q.

The Effects Menu

The Effects menu (see fig. 1.11) provides a number of options for altering the shape or characteristics of objects and text. The following list describes the commands found in the Effects menu.

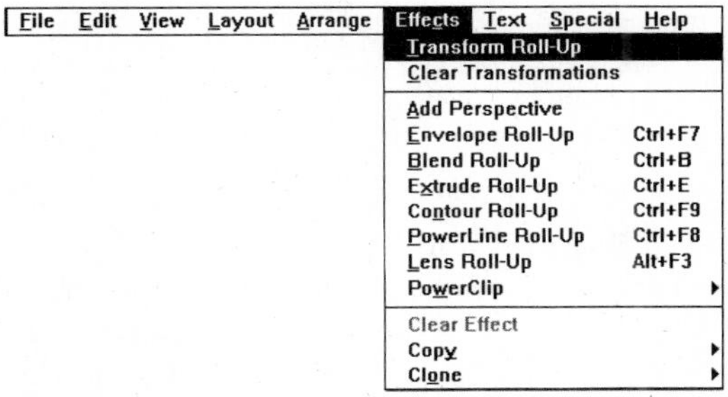

File	Edit	View	Layout	Arrange	Effects	Text	Special	Help

Transform Roll-Up
Clear Transformations

Add Perspective
Envelope Roll-Up   Ctrl+F7
Blend Roll-Up   Ctrl+B
Extrude Roll-Up   Ctrl+E
Contour Roll-Up   Ctrl+F9
PowerLine Roll-Up   Ctrl+F8
Lens Roll-Up   Alt+F3
PowerClip   ▶

Clear Effect
Copy   ▶
Clone   ▶

Figure 1.11
The Effects menu.

- **Transform Roll-Up.** Accesses the Transform roll-up, enabling objects to be moved, skewed, rotated, scaled, resized, stretched, or mirrored.

- **Clear Transformations.** Clears any changes made by applying options available in the Transform roll-up. **C**lear Transformations restores an object to its original shape, size, and orientation. When applied to a grouped object, only the changes made to the group are cleared; any changes made to individual objects within the group are not cleared.

- **Add Perspective.** Enables you to create one- and two-point perspective views of a selection.

- **Envelope Roll-Up.** Alters the shape of objects. CorelDRAW offers a variety of preset envelope shapes, as well as the ability to create your own using objects you have created or by editing an envelope. The envelope editing tools include single line, single arc, two curves, and unconstrained. Keyboard shortcut = Ctrl+F7.

- **Blend Roll-Up.** Changes one object's shape, fill, and outline into those of another object via a series of transitional steps. The resulting blend group is dynamically linked. Changes made to either of the original control objects affect the entire blend group. Objects can be blended together along a path, which forces the blend to follow a defined contour. Keyboard shortcut = Ctrl+B.

- **Extrude Roll-Up.** Gives an object or group of objects a 3D appearance. Dynamic linking enables you to modify the control object later by changing the extrusion to conform. The Extrude roll-up enables you to add light and gradient fills to the extrusion, further enhancing an object's 3D feel. Keyboard shortcut = Ctrl+E.

- **Contour Roll-Up.** Creates a blend of a single object via a definable series of transitional steps. You can contour an object to the inside, outside, or to its absolute center. The resulting contour group is dynamically linked. Modifications made to the control object affect the entire group. Applying contour to an object can give the object a feeling of depth. Keyboard shortcut = Ctrl+F9.

- **PowerLine Roll-Up.** Accesses a series of options useful for creating calligraphic effects. You can set PowerLines to support pressure-sensitive tablets and speed, affording even more dramatic effects. CorelDRAW includes a number of preset shapes for your use. Keyboard shortcut = Ctrl+F8.

- **Lens Roll-Up.** Offers shortcuts for simulating various filter-style effects. For more information, see Chapter 11, "Creating with Special Effects." Keyboard shortcut = Alt+F3.

- **PowerClip.** Accesses a fly-out menu, enabling you to place one or more objects inside another object. PowerClip can be used to place bitmaps inside irregularly shaped objects, eliminating the white rectangular bounding box common to imported bitmap images.

N O T E

If an object is placed in an open path, the contents will not appear until the path is closed.

- **Clear Effect.** Clears the last effect applied to the selection. Clear Effect does not clear other transformations, nor will it clear multiple effects previously applied to an object.

■ **Copy.** Copies a special effect from one object to the selected object. Clicking on this command accesses a fly-out menu, enabling you to choose the effect you want to copy. After choosing the effect, CorelDRAW prompts you to identify the object whose effect you want to copy.

■ **Clone.** Similar to copying an effect. It differs in that changes made to the original master object are applied to the clone. For more information, see Chapter 11, "Creating with Special Effects."

The Text Menu

The **T**ext menu (see fig. 1.12) enables you to access the Text roll-up, formatting commands and an assortment of text aids. The following list describes the commands found in the Text menu.

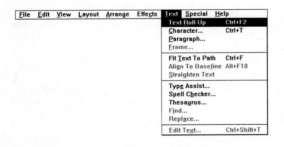

Figure 1.12
The Text menu.

■ **Text R<u>o</u>ll-Up.** Enables you to rapidly access text formatting commands. Alignment, font, style, type size, and

paragraph formatting commands can be applied using the Text roll-up. Keyboard shortcut = Ctrl+F2.

The Text roll-up can also be accessed by double-clicking on the text icon in the toolbox.

■ **Character.** Enables you to change the character attributes of a text object. The character attributes include the font, type size, style, and placement of the text. Choosing this command when no objects or multiple objects are selected enables you to change the default text attributes of artistic text, paragraph text, or both. Keyboard shortcut = Ctrl+T.

■ **Paragraph.** Accesses the paragraph text formatting dialog box.

■ **Frame.** Enables you to select the number of columns and the gutter width between them.

■ **Fit Text To Path.** Constrains artistic text to fit the contour of a line or object. Editing controls in Fit Text To Path allow for horizontal displacement on the path, as well as adjusting the distance from the path. Keyboard shortcut = Ctrl+F.

■ **Align To Baseline.** Realigns text to the baseline of the selected text string. Ensures that text modified using interactive kerning is evenly aligned vertically. Align To Baseline does not

affect any horizontal shift previously applied to the text. Keyboard shortcut = Alt+F10.

■ **Straighten Text.** Removes any horizontal or vertical distortions previously to text by rotation or shifting. When **S**traighten Text is used in conjunction with Align To Baseline, the selected text regains its original appearance. **S**traighten Text does not remove any skewing distortions applied previously to the text.

■ **Type Assist.** Enables the automatic replacement of commonly misspelled words, capitalization errors, or abbreviations. Clicking on Typ**e** Assist accesses a dialog box, permitting you to customize this command.

■ **Spell Checker.** Checks the spelling of a selected word or text string. Spell Checker also enables you to add words to the dictionary and create custom dictionaries.

■ **Thesaurus.** Suggests synonyms for a selected word or phrase.

■ **Find.** Searches for a selected word or phrase within paragraph text.

■ **Replace.** Accesses a dialog box that enables you to search for a selected word or phrase within paragraph text, and then replace it.

■ **Edit Text.** Accesses the Text Edit dialog box, permitting you to alter the wording of a string of text. The Text Edit dialog box is also used to change the font, type size, alignment, or style

of the text. When you choose the **S**pacing option, a dialog box appears that enables you to alter the spacing of the individual characters, lines, or paragraphs. Selecting **I**mport and **P**aste gives you the option of importing and placing ASCII text within your document. Keyboard shortcut = Ctrl+T.

The Special Menu

Commands found under the **S**pecial menu (see fig. 1.13) enable you to modify text and some of CorelDRAW's features. The following list describes the commands found in the Special menu.

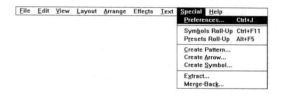

Figure 1.13
The Special menu.

■ **Preferences.** Accesses the Preferences dialog box, enabling you to configure various features and options in CorelDRAW. For more information, see "Setting Preferences," later in this chapter. Keyboard shortcut = Ctrl+J.

■ **Symbols Roll-Up.** Displays the Symbols roll-up, enabling you to add symbols to your document. Symbols are added by selecting the desired shape and dragging it into the drawing window. Keyboard shortcut = Ctrl+F11.

■ **Presets Roll-Up.** Enables you to quickly re-create a multiple step effect. Presets function as a visual macro recorder to permit you to select or create an effect, and apply it to a selected object. Presets can only be applied to single objects. Keyboard shortcut = Alt+F5.

■ **Create Pattern.** Creates custom two- and full-color fills from created images and adds them to the available fills for future use. Two-color fills are added to the bitmap fills. Full-color fills are added to the vector fill patterns.

■ **Create Arrow.** Creates custom arrowheads from drawn objects and adds them to the arrowhead library for future use.

■ **Create Symbol.** Creates custom symbols from selected drawn objects and enables you to add them to symbol libraries.

■ **Extract.** Permits you to save artistic and paragraph text in a text file for editing in a word processor. Text can be edited in any word processor that accepts ASCII text format.

■ **Merge-Back.** Reintegrates text that has been edited using Extract.

The Help Menu

The **H**elp menu (see fig. 1.14) offers a series of ways to obtain help and get information. The following list describes the commands found in the Help menu.

Figure 1.14
The Help menu.

■ **Contents.** Contains a list of categories of help topics available. The list has icons to assist you in choosing a category. Clicking on one of the icons displays the associated topic help files. Keyboard shortcut = F1.

■ **Screen/Menu Help.** Is a context-sensitive help aid. When you choose Screen/**M**enu Help, a help selection cursor appears. Clicking on a tool, menu item, or other screen element displays the associated help file. Keyboard shortcut = Shift+F1.

■ **Search For Help On.** Displays a search dialog box, enabling you to search for the desired help topic by inputting key words. Keyboard shortcut = Ctrl+F1.

■ **Tutorial.** Accesses a context-sensitive tutorial, enabling you to learn to use CorelDRAW.

■ **About CorelDRAW!.** Displays a comment box that contains information about CorelDRAW, registration, your document, and available drive space.

Examining Other On-Screen Features

You will use several other on-screen features of CorelDRAW in your everyday work. These include the ribbon bar, the horizontal and vertical scroll bars, the toolbox, the color palette, the status line, the page counter, and the drawing window.

The Ribbon Bar

The ribbon bar (see fig. 1.15) allows access to CorelDRAW's most common features. All of the commands shown on the ribbon bar can also be accessed from the menus. If you want, you can choose to hide the ribbon bar by disabling Show Ribbon Bar in the View section of the **P**references dialog box.

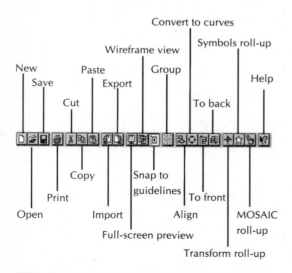

Figure 1.15
The ribbon bar.

Horizontal and Vertical Scroll Bars

The Scroll bars enable you to pan through your work. Auto-**P**anning can be enabled or disabled in the View section of the Preferences dialog box.

The Toolbox

The toolbox contains the basic tools used in CorelDRAW (see fig. 1.16). The tools introduced in this overview are discussed in detail throughout this book. The default location for the toolbox is on the left side of the drawing window. Reposition the toolbox by selecting the Floating Toolbox command from the **V**iew menu, or by double-clicking on the gray area at the bottom of the toolbox. Drag the toolbox to the location you desire. To return the toolbox to its default location, deselect Floating Toolbox from the Display menu, or double-click on the toolbox's control menu button.

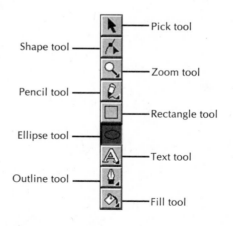

Figure 1.16
The toolbox, with the Ellipse tool selected.

The following list describes the tools accessed through the toolbox.

- **The Pick tool.** Used for selecting and transforming objects.

T I P

Depressing the spacebar is a quick way to toggle from other tools to the Pick tool. To toggle to the Pick tool from the text tool, depress Ctrl+Space. Depress the spacebar again to return to the last tool used.

- **The Shape tool.** Used for altering the shape of objects by editing the nodes of a selected object.

- **The Zoom tool.** Enlarges or reduces the view of your document. When you choose the Zoom tool, a fly-out menu appears allowing you to select the type of zoom you desire.

- **The Pencil tool.** Used to create lines, curves, PowerLines, dimension lines, and callouts.

- **The Rectangle tool.** Creates rectangles and squares.

- **The Ellipse tool.** Creates ellipses and circles.

- **The Text tool.** Adds artistic and paragraph text to your document.

- **The Outline tool.** Enables you to select outline attributes and access the Outline roll-up via the fly-out menu.

- **The Fill tool.** Enables you to select fill attributes via the fly-out menu.

The Color Palette

The color palette, at the bottom of the drawing window, enables you to quickly apply fill and outline colors to objects. To choose the palette you want to be displayed on-screen, select **C**olor Palette from the **V**iew menu. The palettes contain more colors than can be displayed on one line in the drawing window. Click on the up arrow on the right side of the palette to display the full palette. Clicking on the arrow at either end of the palette scrolls through the balance of the available colors. To fill a selected object, click on the desired color with your left mouse button. Clicking on the X at the far left of the palette gives the object no fill, making it transparent. Similarly, using the right mouse button selects the outline color or no outline.

The Status Line

The status line has information about your drawing, and any selected object(s). The numbers at the far left indicate the position of your cursor. If any of CorelDRAW's Snap To features are active, their active status is displayed just below the position indicator. The center portion of the status bar has information about the object selected. If you have Show Menu & Tool Help enabled in the View property sheet of the **P**references dialog box, it appears in the lower left corner of the status line. The status line by default appears at the bottom of the screen. You can choose to hide the status line or move it to the top when you configure your preferences. For more information see "Setting Preferences," later in this chapter.

The Page Counter

The Page Counter box, located in the bottom left corner of the drawing window, indicates the number of pages contained in your document. To page through your document, click the page forward or page back arrows to the left of the Page Counter. Alternatively, you can use the Page Up or Page Down keys on your keyboard, or select the **G**o To Page command in the **L**ayout menu.

The Drawing Window

The drawing window is the large white rectangle in the center of the screen. The drawing window is composed of two main parts. The printable area is the rectangle in the center, which resembles a piece of paper with a drop shadow. The balance of the drawing window is the desktop. The size and orientation of the printable area changes with the settings you make using the **P**age Setup command under the **L**ayout menu. Generally, only objects that fall within the printable area are printed. The desktop is a useful temporary holding area for elements of your design, when working with complex drawings.

Using MOSAIC

MOSAIC (see fig. 1.17) is a file manager that enables you to visually manage bitmap, vector, sound, and text files. Files are represented by small thumbnail images. The file name is located below each thumbnail. This enables you to view and select files from directories or collections. Files are selected by clicking on them. To select a batch of files, depress the Shift or Ctrl key while clicking on the desired thumbnails.

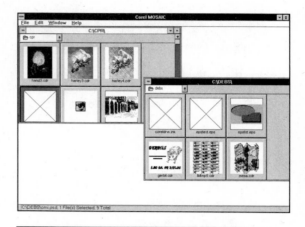

Figure 1.17
The MOSAIC screen.

The File Menu

The following list describes the commands found in MOSAIC's File menu.

- **New Collection.** Creates a new collection. A collection can be either a library or catalog. Files that are moved or copied to a library are compressed, unless they are already in a compressed format. A catalog contains a bitmap thumbnail of the file and stores the path information for the file, rather than the file itself. Catalogs are useful when you need to associate a file with more than one group of files. If you have a number of catalogs, you will find it helpful to attach a description to the catalog. Keyboard shortcut = Ctrl+N.

■ **Open Collection.** Enables you to view a directory or collection. You can have multiple directories and collections open. MOSAIC enables you to move or copy files from one collection or directory in the view screen to another by dragging and dropping the thumbnail. The default is to copy files. To move a file, copy it to the desired collection, then delete the thumbnail from the original collection. Keyboard shortcut = Ctrl+O.

■ **Delete Collection.** When you click on Delete Collection, the program prompts you for the collection you want to delete. Select the collection and click on OK.

■ **Convert.** Enables you to convert one or more files to another format. To convert a file, click on Convert. Select the file format from the drop-down list box and rename the file if desired. Click on OK.

■ **Print Files.** Prints one or more files to the selected printer.

■ **Print Thumbnails.** Prints the selected thumbnails.

■ **Print Setup.** Enables you to select a printer and configure print options.

■ **Color Manager.** Enables you to calibrate your monitor, scanner, and printer, and adjust color correction. See Chapter 38, "Color Management," for more information.

■ **Color Correction.** Accesses a fly-out menu, enabling you to enable color correction.

■ **Preferences.** Enables you to configure the MOSAIC display and enable confirmation options. MOSAIC enables you to display collections in two view sizes, either as text only or as thumbnails. Keyboard shortcut = Ctrl+J.

■ **Exit.** Closes the program. Keyboard shortcut = Alt+F4.

N O T E

MOSAIC allows for batch operations on multiple selections. Options selected for the first file apply to all selected files. Batch operations include: Printing, Importing, Converting, and Extract/Merge-back.

The Edit Menu

The following list describes the commands found in MOSAIC's Edit menu.

■ **Select by Keyword.** Enables you to select files and thumbnails by keyword.

■ **Select All.** Selects all the thumbnails in a window.

■ **Clear All.** Deselects all the currently selected thumbnails.

■ **Update Catalog.** Updates thumbnails and file information in a catalog.

■ **Expand Library Files.** Uncompresses the selected files of a library.

■ **Edit.** Opens the selected file in its associated application.

■ **Import into CorelDRAW.** Starts CorelDRAW and imports the selected file(s).

- **Delete.** Deletes the thumbnail and the associated file.

- **Extract Text.** Permits you to save artistic and paragraph text in a text file for editing in a word processor. Text can be edited in any word processor that accepts ASCII text format.

- **Merge-Back Text.** Reintegrates text that has been edited using Extract.

- **Keywords.** Enables you to add or delete keywords associated with files.

- **Edit Description.** Enables you to add or edit a catalogue description.

- **Get Info.** Provides information about the selected file.

The Window Menu

The Window menu enables you to organize your view. It conforms to standard Window view operations, and includes a listing of the last four directories opened in MOSAIC. You can reopen these directories by clicking on the entry.

The Help Menu

The Help menu contains the commands to get assistance from the help files, as well as get information about CorelMOSAIC.

Understanding and Using OLE2

A great deal of CorelDRAW's power comes from OLE (Object Linking and Embedding). OLE routinely takes two forms. The first is application-specific, and is the hidden power that enables you to create macros such as presets and styles. Its linking ability creates the relationships in commands such as Extrude and Blend. The second form or usage of OLE allows you to integrate applications. By using DDE (Dynamic Data Exchange), it enables you to share data between OLE-compatible applications that may or may not have common file formats. Using OLE eliminates the need to switch back and forth between applications to share data. Lengthy exporting and conversion time are no longer necessary; OLE reduces compatibility problems between applications. Data exchanged in this way is known as an *OLE object.*

OLE-compatible applications can function as servers or clients. CorelDRAW is capable of functioning as both a server and a client. A server application is one that contains the original information in the source document. A client application receives the OLE object in a destination document. As a server, CorelDRAW enables you to create a graphic in your source document and then link or embed it in the destination document of a client, such as Microsoft Word for Windows. A bitmap image scanned in an application, such as ImagePals2, could be placed in CorelDRAW, functioning as a client.

> **N O T E**
>
> In order to use OLE, SHARE or VSHARE must be installed in your \Windows\System directory. CorelDRAW automatically installs VSHARE during setup.

Embedding versus Linking

When you embed an OLE object, you copy the object and all of its associated information from the source document into the destination document. The embedded object becomes a part of the document, and the connection to the source document ceases to exist. Later changes made in the source document will not automatically change the embedded object. Because the embedded object becomes part of the document, the file size increases and more memory is required to open the document. You can, however, choose to edit the embedded object and update your destination document. Embedding an OLE object is the best choice when you do not need to share identical information with other files, but still need editing ability.

Linking an OLE object does not copy the object from the source document to the destination document. Instead, it includes the path and application information. The source document must be saved prior to creating the OLE link. Unless otherwise specified, any future changes made to the

OLE object in the source document automatically update the object in the destination document. This is useful if you create information in a source document that you want included in numerous destination documents. It eliminates the need to switch back and forth between applications to update information.

> **N O T E**
>
> OLE links are adaptable if the paths are relative. This means that if you store both the source and destination documents in the same directory, you can move them to another directory later. As long as you store both files in the same location, the link will be maintained. Should the files become separated, however, the link will cease to exist. This is important to remember if you are transferring a destination document to disk or another computer. Both the source and destination document must be moved.

Using OLE

There is more than one way to embed an object into a CorelDRAW document. Objects copied or cut to the Clipboard in a server application can be embedded in your CorelDRAW document by selecting **P**aste or Paste **S**pecial from the **E**dit menu. The server application can be minimized, but cannot be closed until after the object is embedded. Alternatively, to embed an OLE object in a CorelDRAW document, follow these steps:

1. Select Insert O**b**ject from the **E**dit menu to display the Insert O**b**ject dialog box.

2. Choose Create **N**ew, and select the application or the description of the type of object you want to embed.

3. Choose OK to open the server application.

4. In the server application, select or create the object you want to embed in your CorelDRAW document.

5. Depending upon the server application, choose one of the following to embed the object and return to your CorelDRAW document:

   ■ Exit

   ■ Exit and Return

   ■ In the dialog box asking if you want to update, choose OK or Yes

6. The embedded OLE object appears centered in your destination document.

If you use Paste Special to insert an object into your document, select Embed and the type of data you want to add to your document. Click on OK to complete the operation.

N O T E

By choosing Create from File in the Insert O**bj**ect dialog box, you can embed or link an OLE object in your CorelDRAW document. Click on OK and follow the prompts to complete the operation.

To use Paste **S**pecial or Insert O**bj**ect to link an object with your CorelDRAW document, follow these steps:

1. Select Insert O**bj**ect from the **E**dit menu to display the Insert O**bj**ect dialog box.

2. Choose Create New, and select the application or the description of the type of object you wish to embed.

3. Choose OK to open the server application.

4. In the server application, select or create the object you want to link in your CorelDRAW document.

5. Depending upon the server application, choose one of the following to embed the object and return to your CorelDRAW document:

   ■ Exit

   ■ Exit and Return

   ■ In the dialog box asking if you want to update, choose OK or Yes

6. The linked OLE object appears centered in your destination document.

To edit an embedded or linked OLE object, follow these steps:

1. Select the object you want to edit in your CorelDRAW document.

2. Choose Linked **O**bject from the **E**dit menu, and **E**dit from the fly-out menu. Alternatively, choose Open Source in the Links fly-out of the **E**dit menu or double-click on the object.

3. The source document is opened in the server application, enabling you to edit the object.

4. Exit the server application, as shown previously.

5. The edited object appears in your CorelDRAW document.

Using Drag-and-Drop Functions

CorelDRAW supports drag-and-drop OLE functions, enabling you to drag objects to or from CorelDRAW across windows containing other OLE applications. Objects placed in this way are cut from the source document and embedded into the client file. If the destination document is a printer or other device, the object is copied rather than cut, unless you depress the Alt key while dragging the object.

If you want to use drag-and-drop to copy the object to another document, depress the Ctrl key while dragging the object. This embeds a copy of the object in the destination file.

If you want to link an object in a destination document, depress the Shift+Ctrl keys while dragging the object from one window to the other.

Updating OLE Links

Links are updated either automatically or manually. The default setting is for automatic updating. To select the update method, click on Links from the **E**dit menu. Choose the update style you want and click on OK to return to the drawing window.

To manually update a link, select the object(s) you want to update. Select Link from the **E**dit menu, and click on Choose Update Now from the fly-out menu. You can also choose the links you want to update from the Link list in the fly-out menu.

Your CorelDRAW document reflects any changes made in the source document(s) since the last update. This is useful if you need to edit a number of object or if the OLE objects have a number of different source documents. This enables you to update all the links at one time.

Changing a Link

CorelDRAW enables you to alter the server and type of source document. To change a link, select the object in your CorelDRAW document and select Links from the **E**dit menu. Click on Change Source to display the Change Source dialog box. Select a new source document and click on OK. If the link needs to be updated, click on Update Now. Click on Close to return to the drawing window.

WARNING

If you change a link and the source document changes substantially, the appearance of your CorelDRAW document can alter dramatically.

Setting Preferences

CorelDRAW enables you to customize its appearance and the way it operates to meet your requirements. The **P**reference command from the **S**pecial menu is one way of customizing CorelDRAW. The Preference settings you make can be changed at any time to correspond with your requirements. When you exit CorelDRAW, changes you have made are saved and remain active for future CorelDRAW sessions, or until you change them. When you access the Preferences dialog box (see fig. 1.18), a series of property sheets are displayed. To access a property sheet, click on its respective tab.

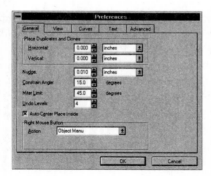

Figure 1.18
The Preferences dialog box.

The General Property Sheet

Clicking on the General property sheet tab enables you to configure the following settings:

- **Placing Duplicates and Clones.** The first time you use CorelDRAW, the default setting for Place Duplicates and Clones is 0.25", **H**orizontal and **V**ertical. To change this setting, select the units of measurement you desire from the drop-down list, and enter the desired value in the Horizontal and Vertical numeric entry boxes. The units of measurement need not be the same. This feature is handy for placing duplicates and clones with accuracy. Set the value in both the Horizontal and Vertical numeric entry boxes to 0, if you want copies placed directly on top of one another.

- **Nudge. N**udge enables you to use the cursor keys to move an object, a specified amount, in the direction of the arrow on the cursor key. Select the unit of measurement from the drop-down list. Next, enter a value in the numeric entry box by either using the scroll bars or by highlighting the value and then typing a new value into the box. The smallest value possible using nudge is .001. The largest value possible is 2.0. When using node edit, you can select a node with the shape tool and nudge it as you would an object. This enables you to maintain finer control over editing.

■ **Constrain Angle.** When you skew or rotate objects, holding down the Ctrl key constrains the angle of motion. Constrain angle also applies to drawing straight lines in freehand mode, and to adjusting the control points of a Bézier curve. The constraint applied is in increments you set within the Preferences dialog box. The default angle, set in the Constrain **A**ngle numeric entry box, is 15 degrees. Change the angle by clicking the up or down arrows, on the scroll bar beside the value. This changes the degree of angle one increment at a time. To change the angle more quickly, click on the button between the arrows and drag up or down as desired. You can also highlight the value and type the desired value in the box.

■ **Miter Limit.** When you draw objects that contain small angles, the line might appear to extend well beyond the actual corner of the angle. The Miter **L**imit option of the Preference dialog box prevents this occurrence. The default setting is 10 degrees. The available setting range is between 0 and 45 degrees. Angles that fall below the set amount are beveled at the corner, giving your drawing a cleaner appearance. To change the setting, highlight the value in the numeric entry box and type in the desired value. Alternatively, click the up or down arrows, or use the scroll button to change the value.

■ **Undo Levels.** CorelDRAW supports multiple levels of Undo—up to 99 levels. The default setting is four levels of Undo. The value entered here also equals the number of levels of Redo available. To change the levels of Undo, highlight the value in the numeric entry box and type in the desired number of levels. Using the scroll bar beside the numeric entry box also changes the levels of Undo. The number of levels of Undo is limited by your system's memory resources and hard disk space. When editing complex or large files, maintaining a limited number of Undo levels will help prevent running out of memory.

An understanding of how Undo works should help you determine how many levels of Undo are appropriate for your system. For each level of Undo you have, CorelDRAW writes a temporary file containing the contents of your original file, plus the change you just made. These temporary files are stored in your Windows Temp directory. Each level of Undo also reserves RAM, Windows swap file space, and buffer handles. When you select Undo from the **E**dit menu, CorelDRAW restores the last temporary file.

The amount of space Undo requires varies greatly with the size of the file you are editing. Other applications and printing also place demands on your system resources. The calculations for deciding the optimum levels of Undo

are rather complex. The following system examples will give you an idea of the required system resources and the effect of Undo on those resources:

- 386/33, with 8MB of RAM and 64 KB cache

- Running Windows, optimized with no TSRs (Terminate-and-Stay-Resident applications)

- 20MB permanent swap file

- Approximately 700MB hard disk, with a dedicated 50Mb Temp drive

The preceding system had difficulty when editing a 1.5MB file with 8 levels of Undo. After a period of time, it would slow down and get out of memory errors, at 10 levels of Undo. Compare this with the following system:

- 486/DX2-66, with 16MB RAM and 512KB cache

- Running Windows, optimized with no TSRs (Terminate-And-Stay-Resident applications)

- 60MB permanent swap file

- Approximately 1.1GB hard disk, with Temp directory space limited to hard disk space

This system handled 16 levels of Undo, manipulating a 4MB file with ease. There was no noticeable slow down and no memory error messages. The system started to slow down, appreciably, at 50 levels of Undo.

Many variables affect the demands placed on system resources. The preceding examples are only guides. Experimentation will tell you what your particular system is capable of handling.

- **Auto-Center Place Inside.** Enables or disables the centering of objects in a PowerClip.

- **Right Mouse Button.** CorelDRAW enables you to assign a function to the right mouse button of your mouse. Regardless of what function you assign, you will still be able to leave a copy of an object being moved while continuously depressing the right mouse button. You also will be able to assign outline colors using the right mouse button.

  To assign a function to your right mouse button, click the down arrow and select the function you desire.

- **Object Menu.** If you select this function, the **O**bject menu appears when you click the right mouse button. The **O**bject menu contains commands that pertain to styles, overprinting, and attaching notes to objects. If you assign another function to the right mouse button, you must right click on an object to display the **O**bject menu.

- **2x Zoom.** Zooms the area your cursor is pointing at by a factor of two each time you click the right mouse button. The portion of your drawing residing under the cursor will be centered in the page when you zoom. Double-clicking on the secondary button returns to the view prior to the last zoom. If you reach the maximum magnification allowable by your display, zoom out before zooming again. To zoom out, select the Zoom Out icon from the fly-out menu of the Zoom tool, double-click the secondary mouse button, or depress F3.

■ **Edit text.** After selecting a text string, this function displays the Text Editing dialog box.

■ **Full Screen Preview.** Switches the screen between Full Screen Preview and the editable drawing window.

■ **Node Edit.** Activates the Shape tool.

The View Property Sheet

The View property sheet (see fig. 1.19) enables you to configure the following settings:

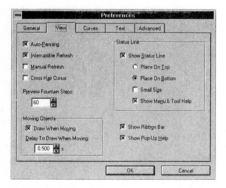

Figure 1.19
The View property sheet.

■ **Auto-Panning.** To activate Auto-Panning, select the checkbox beside it. Auto-Panning enables you to scroll the view by dragging the cursor beyond the drawing window.

■ **Interruptible Display.** When Interruptible Display is enabled, you can stop the screen redraw temporarily to edit an object or choose a command. To interrupt the screen redraw, click with the mouse or depress a key when the object you want to edit appears. Clicking on a menu to perform a command also interrupts the screen. Once the command or edit is complete, redraw will automatically resume, within a few seconds. You can force an immediate redraw by selecting Refresh Window (Ctrl+W) from the Display menu.

If redraw is drawing an object to the screen when you interrupt the display, it will finish drawing that object before the display is interrupted. Fountain and texture fills can take time drawing to the screen, so it may take a moment.

You can select objects even though they have not appeared on the screen, though it may be difficult to discern which object you have selected. Objects in CorelDRAW are drawn from back to front. When editing complex files, it could take time for the front objects to appear on the screen. When using wireframe view, the selected object is drawn first regardless of its order, unless it is part of a group.

■ **Cross Hair Cursor.** Selecting this box changes the cursor to a pair of cross hairs that extend horizontally and vertically to the edges of the drawing window. The cursor reverts to the default pointer when outside the drawing window.

■ **Preview Fountain Steps.** Preview Fountain Steps enables you to select the number of stripes displayed in fountain fills. The default is 20. While 20 or lower greatly improves the screen refresh time, the results are a fountain fill with noticeable banding. The maximum number of steps you can set is 256. A setting of 60–80 produces good results, without slowing screen refresh time, on most computers.

Unless you are exporting your finished drawing as a SCODL file, the display preferences you select will have no effect on output. It can have a dramatic effect on design choices you make, however. The number of fountain steps used for printing is controlled by settings made in the Print dialog box.

The Steps option in the Fountain Fill dialog box overrides both the settings made in the Preferences \ Display dialog box, and those in the Print dialog box. This enables you to adjust the number of fountain steps for individual objects.

■ **Draw When Moving.** Enables you to display the wireframe of an object while moving it. The default delay is .500 seconds. This feature can slow the program down, because as it forces the screen to constantly refresh. Consider setting a higher number, or disabling this command, if speed is a consideration.

■ **Show Status Line.** Enables you to enable or disable the display of the Status line and Show Menu & Tool Help. You can also select the location and appearance of the status line.

W A R N I N G

If you have Show Menu and Tool Help enabled and the Status line is placed at the top of the drawing screen, the help text will be hidden when you open a menu.

■ **Show Ribbon Bar.** Switches the display of the ribbon bar.

■ **Show Pop-Up Help.** Switches the display of the pop-up help.

The Curves Property Sheet

The Curves property sheet (see fig. 1.20) enables you to configure the following settings:

Figure 1.20
The Curves property sheet.

■ **Freehand Tracking.** Freehand Tracking directs how closely CorelDRAW follows the movement of your mouse when creating Bézier curves. The lower the number, the more tracking conforms to your mouse movements. This increases the number of nodes in the curve. The result is a curve with a jagged appearance. The higher the number, the smoother your curve will appear. To set Freehand Tracking, highlight the value in the numeric entry box and type in the value you desire, or use the scroll bar next to the box to change the value. If you are using a mouse to create your drawings, setting Freehand Tracking to 7 or 8 will yield smoother results. Making smoother curves is much easier if you use a digitizer pad, such as a SummaSketch or Kurta. The default setting, or lower, yields the best results for digitizers.

■ **Autotrace Tracking.** Autotrace Tracking directs how closely CorelDRAW follows the edges of the bitmap when creating Bézier curves. If the number is lower than 4, the curves will contour closely to the bitmap you are tracing, resulting in more nodes and a rougher appearance. If the value is higher than 6, the Bézier curves will loosely flow around the bitmap you are tracing, yielding smoother curves, which contain fewer nodes.

■ **Corner Threshold.** Corner Threshold controls how CorelDRAW senses changes of direction you make with your mouse when using freehand drawing or Autotrace. Values lower than the default create more cusp corners and curves, making changes in direction more pronounced. Values higher than the default create smoother curves and corners, and follow the contours more smoothly.

■ **StraightLine Threshold.** Controls whether line segments made using freehand drawing or Autotrace are drawn as curves or straight lines. Lower values result in more curves and less straight lines. Higher values result in more straight lines and fewer curves. This should be altered to suit your own particular drawing style and your input device. Mice are harder to control than digitizers, and may require higher settings.

■ **AutoJoin.** AutoJoin sets the sensitivity of the program to your mouse movements. Line segments drawn with lower settings require more precise control over the movement of your mouse. However, fewer lines are automatically joined at their end nodes. Higher settings require less precision, but may cause unintentional AutoJoins at the node endings.

■ **Auto-Reduce.** Auto-Reduce controls the amount a curve changes when you use the Auto-Reduce function from the Node Edit menu. Auto-Reduce eliminates extraneous nodes. The higher the value, the more a curve's shape will be affected.

■ **Min. Extrude Facet Size.** Enables you to set the minimum extrusion you can create. Smaller sizes produce smoother rendering.

The Text Property Sheet

The Text property sheet (see fig. 1.21) enables you to configure the following settings:

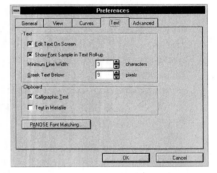

Figure 1.21
The Text property sheet.

■ **Edit Text On Screen.** Enables or disables your ability to edit text on-screen.

■ **Show Font Sample in Text Roll-Up.** Enables or disables the font sample display. You can configure the Minimum Line Width and Greek Text Below to a specified size.

Minimum Line Width specifies the minimum number of characters required before a word is placed on a

new line. This only pertains to paragraph text that is placed in an envelope. The default number of characters is three. Increasing or decreasing this number can affect the way paragraph text appears.

Greek Text Below enables you to speed the screen refresh by displaying paragraph text containing small font sizes as small rectangles. The text information stays intact and does not affect printing. The larger the setting you select, the faster the screen refresh time will be. This does not affect drawings that contain no text. If you want to view or edit the text on-screen, zoom into a portion of the text. The largest setting available for this option is 500. This is not the font size, but rather the number of pixels, and is resolution-dependent. Due to variations in monitors and video cards, the actual effect on your screen might vary.

■ **Calligraphic Text.** Enables support for calligraphic text. If this feature is disabled, calligraphic pen effects are ignored when the object is placed on the Clipboard, or exported using any of the vector formats. Some calligraphic effects such as powerlines are not affected. Disabling this feature can help reduce the file size, but can substantially change the image's appearance.

■ **Text in Metafile.** Enables support for placing text on the Clipboard. If this feature is disabled, text is placed as curves, and cannot be edited as text.

- **P<u>A</u>NOSE Font Matching.** Enables font substitution and mapping. For more information, see Chapter 4, "Working with Text and Symbols."

The Advanced Property Sheet

The Advanced property sheet (see fig. 1.22) enables you to configure the following settings:

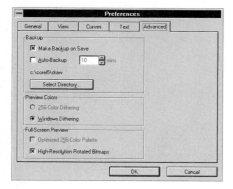

Figure 1.22
The Advanced property sheet.

- **Make Bac<u>k</u>up on Save.** Causes the program to make a backup of your file when you save. The backup file has the same name as your file, but with a BAK extension. Unless hard disk space is limited, this feature should be enabled. Being able to restore a backup file can save hours of work recreating an image. To restore a BAK file, rename the file with a CDR extension using the Windows File Manager.

- **Auto-Backup.** Forces the program to make a backup of the file at regular intervals. The default time is 10 minutes. You can reset this time to reflect your personal working style. Click on Select Directory to choose the storage location for these backup files.

- **Preview Colors.** Determines how colors are displayed on your screen. They do not affect printing. The default is for 256 Color Dithering. This option is automatically selected if you are using a video card that supports this option.

  The **W**indows Dithering option is the only one available if your video card only supports 16 colors. If you are using a graphics adapter that does not support paletted colors or does not have special drivers, colors are displayed using the screen default driver. This option uses 15 colors to create the colors within the palette, and has a grainy appearance. Some high resolution graphics accelerator cards, such as Matrox MGAII or STB Pegasus, override CorelDRAW's color display options by displaying their own palettes. If you are using one of these cards, **W**indows Dithering is automatically selected, and the other Preview Color options are grayed.

- **Full-Screen <u>P</u>review.** Selecting Optimized Palette for Full-Screen **P**review causes CorelDRAW to optimize the colors. When you display your drawing in Full-Screen Preview, CorelDRAW will render your drawing

in up to 256 pure, undithered colors.
This option requires that your video
card and monitor support this option.

Summary

An understanding of the menu structure
provides sufficient information for the basic
operation of many of the commands used in
CorelDRAW. The program provides
flexibility in its command structure and
configurable options to permit the program
to be customized for most uses. Other
customization issues are addressed in Part
VII, "Managing Your System and Files."

OLE reduces many of the incompatibility
problems that have existed in the past
between various applications. Sharing of data
between applications has become both easier
and quicker, without compromising the
quality of images. MOSAIC makes use of
this ease, both through its stand-alone
application and its roll-up, to make the
importing of images a relatively painless
operation.

CorelDRAW's toolbox is deceptive. Instead
of the enormous number of tools common to
other applications, CorelDRAW has only a
few tools. Each tool has increased functionality and flexibility, while retaining ease of
operation. Chapter 2, "Using Graphic
Tools," discusses each of these tools in more
depth.

Using Graphic Tools

CorelDRAW offers three basic graphic or drawing tools: the Pencil tool, the Rectangle tool, and the Ellipse tool. The power of the three drawing tools comes from their versatility. By using each tool in conjunction with the keyboard, you can create an unlimited number of shapes and objects. When you create an object with any of the graphic tools, default outline and fill characteristics are applied to the object. For information on changing the default outline and fill, see Chapter 6, "Working with Fills."

This chapter covers:

- Using the Freehand Pencil tool
- Using the Bézier Pencil tool
- Using dimension lines
- Using callouts
- Drawing ellipses and circles
- Drawing rectangles and squares

All three graphic tools enable you to temporarily activate the Pick tool by depressing the spacebar. When you depress the spacebar a second time, you return to the graphic tool you selected last.

The graphic tools are shown in figure 2.1.

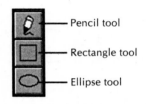

- Pencil tool
- Rectangle tool
- Ellipse tool

Figure 2.1
The graphic tools.

Exploring the Pencil Tool

The Pencil tool is the most flexible of the graphic tools. When you click on the Pencil tool and continue to depress the mouse button, a fly-out menu appears (see fig. 2.2). This fly-out menu displays the following Pencil tool options: the Freehand Pencil tool, the Bézier Pencil tool, the Vertical Dimension tool, the Horizontal Dimension tool, the Diagonal Dimension tool, and the Callout tool. The default Pencil tool is the Freehand Pencil tool. When you select one of

the alternative tools, the function and icon of the Pencil tool changes to those of the selected option. The status line displays information about the angle and distance of the line from its point of origin.

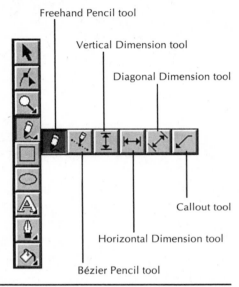

Freehand Pencil tool
Vertical Dimension tool
Diagonal Dimension tool
Callout tool
Horizontal Dimension tool
Bézier Pencil tool

Figure 2.2
The Pencil Tool fly-out menu.

You use the Freehand and Bézier Pencil tools to create both open and closed objects. An *open object* is a line or shape that has a definite starting point and ending point. The endpoints of the path or line do not meet. Outline characteristics (such as color and width) apply to open path objects. If you apply a fill to an object that has an open path, the fill does not appear until the path is closed. By contrast, a *closed object* is a shape whose ends meet at a single point. Both outline and fill characteristics are applied to closed objects.

CorelDRAW enables you to trace bitmapped images using either the Freehand or Bézier Pencil tool. Although CorelTRACE is useful for tracing entire bitmaps or large sections of a bitmap, you might want to trace only a small portion of a bitmap. The Pencil tools enable you to trace these small portions with ease.

The Pencil tools are also used to create *PowerLines*, a special-effect feature that gives your lines a calligraphic or 3D feel. For more information about PowerLines, see Chapter 11, "Creating with Special Effects."

N O T E

The keyboard shortcut F5 activates the active Pencil tool.

Understanding the Freehand Pencil Tool and the Bézier Pencil Tool

Deciding whether to use the Freehand Pencil tool or the Bézier Pencil tool is largely a matter of understanding how each tool works. You use the Freehand Pencil tool much as you would use a drawing pencil or pen on paper. When you are drawing a curve, for example, the result of your efforts depends on the steadiness of your hand and, to some degree, on the speed of your movement. After you have drawn a curve, you can adjust it or eliminate extra nodes to give the curve a smoother appearance. When you are using the Freehand Pencil tool, the line appears as it is created. Straight lines appear as you move the cursor. In this way, you can change the direction or angle of a line before setting the endpoint of a line segment.

Lines created with the Bézier Pencil tool are a series of plotted points connected by line segments. You adjust Bézier curves as they are drawn, which gives them a smoother appearance. Bézier lines have precise mathematical equations attached to them. Although you don't need to understand the mathematical nature of Bézier lines, this quality makes the Bézier Pencil tool ideal for precision drawing. Lines created with the Bézier Pencil tool appear after you set each succeeding segment endpoint. When you draw a straight line, the line does not appear during cursor movement.

Using the Freehand Pencil Tool

You use the Freehand Pencil tool to create a variety of shapes. The movement of the mouse defines the contour or path of the shape. To use the Freehand Pencil tool, select it from the Pencil tool fly-out menu. When you move the cursor back to the drawing window, the cursor changes to cross hairs. The cross hairs cursor enables you to place the starting point of a line precisely. If you make a mistake, you can delete the last line segment by selecting **U**ndo from the **E**dit menu (Ctrl+Z or Alt+Backspace).

Drawing Straight Lines

To create a straight line using the Freehand Pencil tool, follow these steps:

1. Click on the desired starting point of the line.

2. Release the mouse button.

3. Move the cursor to the location for the endpoint of the line, and click to set the endpoint (see fig. 2.3).

Click to set the first point

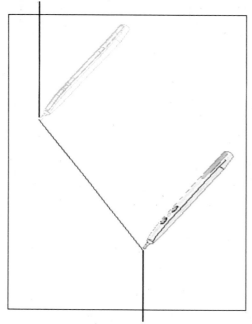

Click to set the second point

Figure 2.3
Drawing a straight line using the Freehand Pencil tool.

Constraining Lines

A line can be forced to maintain the incremental degree of angle that you have specified using the Preferences command. For more information on this topic, see the section in Chapter 1 titled "Setting Preferences." The default angle constraint is 15°. To constrain a line to a specific angle, follow these steps:

1. Click on the desired starting point of the line.

2. Release the mouse button.

3. Hold down the Ctrl key, and move the cursor to the desired endpoint. Note that the cursor and line appear to jump to stick to the desired degree of angle.

4. Click to set the endpoint (see fig. 2.4).

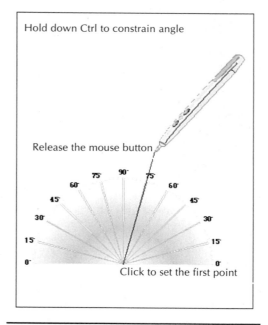

Hold down Ctrl to constrain angle

Release the mouse button

Click to set the first point

Figure 2.4
Drawing constrained lines. The compass used illustrates the default angle of constraint.

Drawing Polygons

CorelDRAW enables you to create multi-segment lines or polygons with the Freehand Pencil tool by double-clicking at intermediate points on the line or object. To create a multisegment line, follow these steps:

1. Click to set the starting point.

2. Move the cursor to the location for the next point, and double-click.

3. Continue moving and double-clicking to set the intermediate points.

4. Move the cursor to the desired endpoint, and click once to end the multisegment line (see fig. 2.5).

When you hold down the Ctrl key while setting the points, the line segments are constrained to specific angle increments.

To create a polygon or closed object, click on the starting point of the line when you set the endpoint.

Creating Curved Lines

You create curves with the Freehand Pencil tool by clicking and dragging the cursor to form the curve you want. CorelDRAW places a node on the line wherever the line makes a sharp turn or the inflection changes (see fig. 2.6).

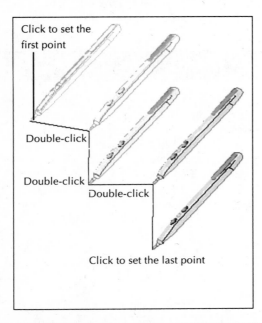

Figure 2.5

Creating a multisegment line using the Freehand Pencil tool.

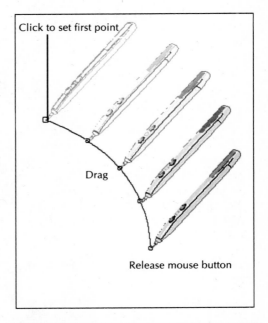

Figure 2.6

Creating a curved line using the Freehand Pencil tool.

When you are using a mouse, freehand curves are somewhat difficult to control. The result can be a curve with a jagged appearance. Use the Shape tool to remove extraneous nodes. For information on using the Shape tool, see Chapter 5, "Shaping Objects."

Tracing Bitmaps Using the Pencil Tool

You cannot directly edit bitmaps in CorelDRAW. By tracing small sections of a bitmap, you can enhance an image and apply special effects to specific areas. This technique is useful if you want to include only parts of a bitmap in your drawing or to emphasize small portions of it. On the other hand, if you want to trace a large part or all of a bitmap, you might want to use CorelTRACE. For information on using CorelTRACE, see Chapter 13, "Working with Bitmaps."

In CorelDRAW, traced portions of a bitmap are treated as graphic objects. The default fill and outline are applied to the objects as they are traced. You decide how closely an object's outline is followed by adjusting the **A**utotrace Tracking option in the Preferences dialog box. For more information, see the section titled "Setting Preferences" in Chapter 1.

To trace portions of a bitmap, follow these steps:

1. Import the bitmap by selecting **I**mport from the **F**ile menu. Choose the file type from the drop-down list, and enter the correct path and file name of the bitmap. Then click on OK.

2. Files imported into CorelDRAW automatically become the selected object. If the bitmap is not selected, use the Pick tool to select it.

3. Select the Pencil tool from the toolbox. When you move your cursor back to the drawing window, the cursor changes to small cross hairs with a dotted line.

4. Move the cross hairs cursor to the area you want to trace and click. The traced portion of the bitmap appears as an object in the drawing window. The object assumes the default fill and outline characteristics.

5. Repeat step 4 to trace other portions of the bitmap (see fig. 2.7).

N O T E

Tracing bitmaps with the Pencil tool might require a little practice. If you trace an undesired portion of the bitmap, depress the Delete key or apply the Undo command and try again. If you click on an area and CorelDRAW cannot find an object in the tracing range to trace, an error message appears telling you CorelDRAW cannot find anything to trace. Click on OK and try again.

Figure 2.7
Tracing a bitmap using the Pencil tool.

Using the Bézier Pencil Tool

The Bézier Pencil tool is useful for creating smooth curves and objects that require precise placement of points or nodes. You create lines and curves with the Bézier Pencil tool by plotting points and adjusting the angles of the curves to the desired shape. To use the Bézier Pencil tool, select the tool from the Pencil Tool fly-out menu. As with the Freehand Pencil tool, the cursor changes to cross hairs when you move back to the drawing window. If you make a mistake, you can delete the last line segment by selecting **U**ndo from the **E**dit menu (Ctrl+Z or Alt+Backspace).

N O T E

If you enable **S**nap To Grid (Ctrl+Y) when using the Bézier Pencil tool, you can place the points more easily.

Drawing Straight Lines

To draw a straight line with the Bézier Pencil tool, follow these steps:

1. Click on the drawing window to set a starting point for the line.

2. Move the cursor to the desired endpoint of the line and click. A line appears between the two points (see fig. 2.8).

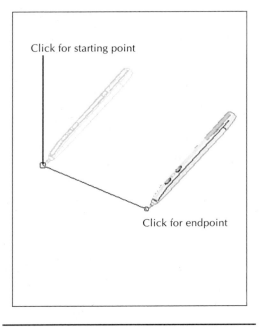

Figure 2.8
Drawing a straight line using the Bézier Pencil tool.

Drawing Polygons

As an illustration of how to draw a polygon, you create and save an arrowhead in this section that will be used in a later example. To draw a polygon with the Bézier Pencil tool, follow these steps:

1. Select the Grid & Scale Setup option from the Layout menu. In the Grid & Scale Setup dialog box, set both the horizontal and vertical grid frequency at 8 per inch. Enable Snap To Grid and Show Grid. With these options enabled, you can set the point of the arrowhead with greater ease and more precision.

2. If Show Rulers and Show Status Line are not enabled, select them from the Display menu to enable them.

3. Set the first point of the arrowhead at 4" horizontal and 8" vertical (4.0, 8.0) by clicking once at that point. The location of your cursor appears on the status line.

4. Release the mouse button, and reposition the cursor at 6" horizontal and 3" vertical (6.0, 3.0). Click to set the second point (see fig. 2.9a).

5. Repeat step 4 to place the rest of the points of the arrowhead. Set the third point at 4" horizontal and 5" vertical (4.0, 5.0) (see fig. 2.9b).

6. Set the fourth point at 2" horizontal and 3" vertical (2.0, 3.0) (see fig. 2.9c).

7. To close the arrowhead, click on the starting point (see fig. 2.9d).

8. Save the finished arrowhead as ARROW1.CDR.

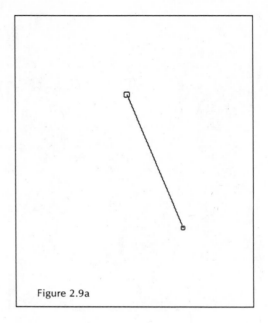

Figure 2.9a

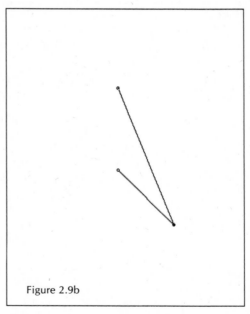

Figure 2.9b

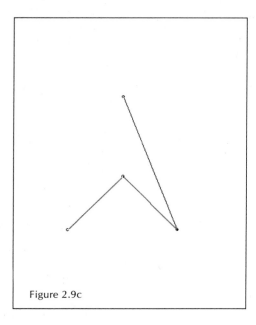

Figure 2.9c

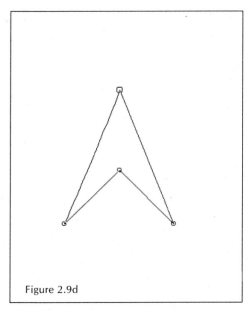

Figure 2.9d

Figure 2.9
Drawing a polygon with the Bézier Pencil tool.

Creating Bézier Curves

To draw a Bézier curve, follow these steps:

1. Click in the drawing window to set a starting point for your curve.

2. Drag the control points in the direction you want the curve to be drawn. If you drag the control point up and to the right, for example, the arc of the curve is at the top of the object, and the curve slopes to the right. The depth of the curve is determined by the distance of the control points from the point you set as the starting point of the curve (see fig. 2.10a).

3. Release the mouse button after you adjust the depth and slope of the curve. To set the second point of the curve, click on the location you want. The first line segment of the curve is displayed in the drawing window (see fig. 2.10b).

4. To draw the next line segment, drag the control point at the end of the last line segment to the depth and slope you want (see fig. 2.10c).

5. Release the mouse button, and click on the location you want for the next point. The next line segment of the curve is then displayed (see fig. 2.10d).

6. Repeat steps 4 and 5 to draw additional line segments. If you want to close the curve, click on the starting point of the curve.

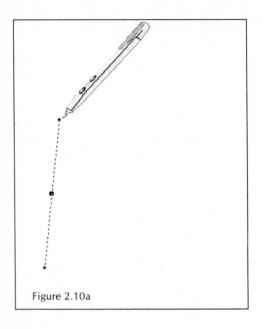

Figure 2.10a

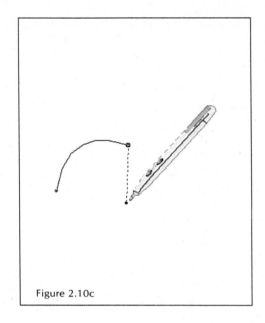

Figure 2.10c

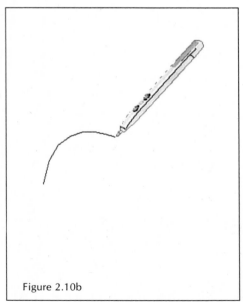

Figure 2.10b

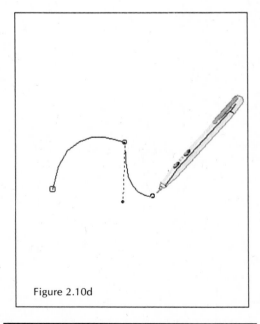

Figure 2.10d

Figure 2.10

Drawing a curve with the Bézier Pencil tool.

You can add line segments to a curve or line you have created earlier with either the Freehand or Bézier Pencil tool. For AutoJoin to work, you must first select the curve or line with the Pick tool. Then select the Pencil tool, and click on the endpoint to create additional line segments.

Understanding Points of Inflection

The point at which a curve or line makes a sharp change in direction is called a *point of inflection*. When you use the Freehand Pencil tool, CorelDRAW sets a node wherever it senses a radical change in direction. When you use the Bézier Pencil tool, you set the points of inflection. Normally, a line should contain as few nodes as possible. Lines created with a minimum of nodes have smoother curves, occupy less file space, and require less memory to create.

Lines that change direction radically, such as the line in figure 2.11, require a point of inflection at the *cusp* (or pointed part) where the two line segments meet.

Curved lines that change direction gradually have points of inflection where the direction change begins. CorelDRAW places nodes at the points of inflection (see fig. 2.12). You can edit these nodes using the Shape tool and the Node Edit roll-up.

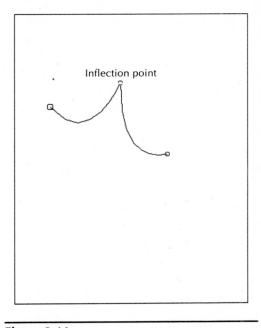

Figure 2.11

Point of inflection on a line segment with a cusp.

Closed objects or lines that move in a single direction (*monodirectional*) require a node or point of inflection approximately every 120°. If the object has either insufficient nodes or too many nodes, the result is a rough-looking curve (see fig. 2.13).

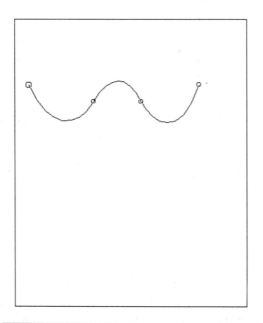

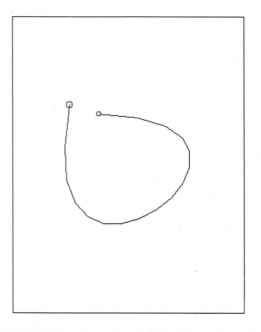

Figure 2.12

Points of inflection on a line segment with smooth curves.

Figure 2.13

Points of inflection on a monodirectional curve.

Using Dimension Lines

For anyone who creates technical illustrations, having the capability to add dimension lines to a drawing is important. Dimension lines can be linked to either an object or a group of objects; dimension lines also can be used as stand-alone rulers. Linked dimension lines are controlled by the snap points of the object to which they are linked. When you link a dimension line to an object, you can resize, skew, rotate, or reshape the object, and the dimension line updates accordingly. By contrast, nonlinked dimension lines do not update in relationship to an object. You also can link multiple dimension lines to an object. CorelDRAW offers you three dimension line tools:

- **Vertical Dimension.** The Vertical Dimension tool adds dimension lines to vertical lines of your drawings.

- **Horizontal Dimension.** The Horizontal Dimension tool adds dimension lines to horizontal lines of your drawings.

- **Diagonal Dimension.** The Diagonal Dimension tool adds dimension lines to angular lines of your drawings.

The preceding definitions do not imply that the three dimension line tools are used only for straight lines or objects. These tools also can measure the dimensions of irregular, curved, or grouped objects or the distance between two objects (see fig. 2.14). The status line in CorelDRAW does not indicate the dimensions of grouped objects. For this reason, the dimension line features of CorelDRAW can make sizing groups of objects easier.

Figure 2.14
Dimension lines added to an irregular or curved object.

N O T E

You cannot apply an extrusion, envelope, or perspective to an object that has a linked dimension line. If you want to apply these effects to an object, apply them before you add the dimension line.

To add a dimension line to a drawing, follow these steps:

1. Enable Snap To **O**bjects from the **L**ayout menu if you want to create a linked dimension line, and select the dimension line tool you want to use from the Pencil Tool fly-out menu.

2. Click at the point where you want the dimension line to start. As you move the cursor, a dimension line appears. To draw a straight line with the Diagonal Dimension tool, depress the Ctrl key while you move the cursor.

3. Click at the point where you want the dimension line to end.

4. Drag the dimension away from the objects to establish an extension line.

5. Drag along the dimension line to indicate the insertion point for dimension text, and click the mouse again to set the dimension text (see fig. 2.15).

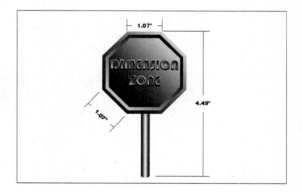

Figure 2.15
Inserting dimension lines.

N O T E

You must select the dimension line tool appropriate to the measurement you want to make. If you use the Vertical Dimension tool to measure a horizontal plane or the Horizontal Dimension tool to measure a vertical plane, the value in the dimension text will be 0.0".

If you are creating a nonlinked dimension line but want the ease and precision of one that is linked, drag guidelines to the edges of the object you want to measure. Enable Snap To Guidelines from the **L**ayout menu, and create your dimension line.

Working with Dimension Text

Dimension text appears either at the location of your last click on a dimension line or at the location you specify using the Dimension roll-up (see fig. 2.16). The Dimension roll-up is accessed by double-clicking on Dimension text or by pressing Alt+F2.

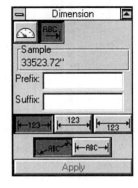

Figure 2.16
The Dimension roll-up.

The orientation and placement of dimension text depends on the following criteria:

- If none of the Dimension options are enabled, the text appears in-line with the same orientation as the dimension line, regardless of the Dimension tool chosen. In-line placement is the default. The text is placed at the location of your last click.

- If the Horizontal button is enabled, the text appears horizontally, regardless of the Dimension tool chosen. The placement is defined by the location of your last click.

- If the Center button is enabled, the text appears along the same path as the dimension line and is centered between the extension lines.

- If both the Horizontal and Center buttons are enabled, the text appears horizontally and is centered between the extension lines.

To select a format for the dimension text, choose the Format button in the upper left corner of the Dimension roll-up. The roll-up changes, enabling you to choose the format type you want by clicking on the down arrow beside Style and selecting from the style list. From the decimal list box, choose the appropriate measurement and the units of measurement you want. Click on Apply to complete the operation.

CorelDRAW enables you to edit the font and type size without changing the dimension line. The dimension line automatically spreads to accommodate the type size.

For more information on editing text, see Chapter 4, "Working With Text and Symbols."

By combining dimension lines with CorelDRAW's Use **D**rawing Scale and **W**orld Distance settings, you can add scaled dimension lines to your drawing. If you are drawing a landscape design or the blueprint of a house or other large object, scaled dimension lines are useful. To use dimension lines for scaling, select the G**r**id & Scale Setup option from the **L**ayout menu. In the Grid & Scale Setup dialog box, enable Use **D**rawing Scale, and enter the values you want in the **P**age Distance and **W**orld Distance measurement entry boxes. If you have Show Rulers enabled, the rulers change to reflect the values set in the global units. Adjust the settings in the Dimension roll-up, choosing the style and appearance you want. Then click on Apply to complete the operation (see fig. 2.17).

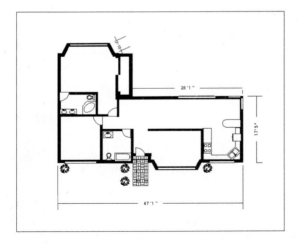

Figure 2.17
Adding scaled dimension lines to a house plan.

Editing Dimension Lines

Most of CorelDRAW's editing capability is available when you edit dimension lines. You can change the text fill color or the outline color of the dimension line as you would for any object. You can add arrowheads to dimension lines if you choose. Some editing operations behave differently, however, depending on the method employed in the editing:

- **Delete.** You can select the dimension line and delete it without deleting the linked object. If you delete a snap point on a control object, the associated dimension line is also deleted.

- **Duplicate.** You can duplicate the control object separately from the linked dimension line; however, you cannot duplicate a linked dimension line without also duplicating the control object. To duplicate both the control object and its associated dimension line, you must select both objects.

- **Separate.** You can select **S**eparate from the **A**rrange menu to break the link between a linked dimension line and its control object. A link that has been broken cannot be re-established. You can apply the Undo command to restore the link, provided that you do not exceed the number of Undo levels you have set.

- **Node edit.** Any editing that affects a snap point node also affects any dimension lines linked to that node. If you move a snap point node, for example, the dimension lines linked to that node reflect the difference in measurement.

- **Rotate.** Horizontal and vertical dimension lines do not rotate; they maintain their appearance. If you select the control object or both the control object and the dimension line, only the control object appears rotated.

- **Skew.** Horizontal and vertical dimension lines do not skew; they maintain their appearance. If you select the control object or both the control object and the dimension line, only the control object appears skewed. The dimension text updates to reflect any changes in measurement.

- **Stretch.** If you stretch a control object or its linked dimension line or both, the control object and the dimension line stretch, and the dimension text reflects any changes in measurement. Note that the dimension text remains at the specified font size and must be edited separately. In addition, the outline size does not reflect any changes, even if **S**cale to Image is enabled in the Outline dialog box.

When you are creating a linked dimension line, be sure that your line snaps to two points on the object you want to measure. If only one end of a dimension line is linked to an object, the other end links to a fixed point on the page (see fig. 2.18). During editing, this condition causes the measurement to update inaccurately in relation to the object.

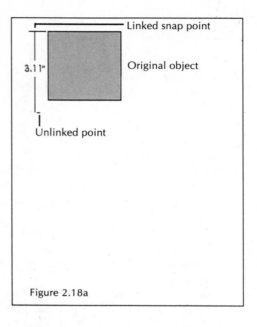

Figure 2.18a

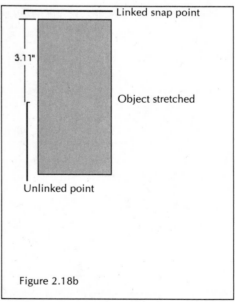

Figure 2.18b

Figure 2.18

Linking a dimension line to only one point of a control object.

Unlinked dimension lines can be stretched, and the dimension text reflects the change. Unlinked dimension lines cannot be skewed, however, and only diagonal dimension lines can be rotated. If the object(s) being measured is modified, the dimension is not updated unless it is linked.

Using Callouts

Callouts are used to label parts of a drawing. CorelDRAW enables you to create linked callouts (see fig. 2.19). With this linking capability, you can move or edit the control object and the callout moves accordingly. Callout lines can have one or two segments. The default font, type size, arrowhead, fill, and outline of the callout can be edited as you choose.

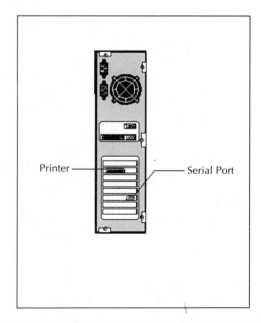

Figure 2.19
An image with callouts.

To create a callout, follow these steps:

1. Choose the Callout tool from the Pencil Tool fly-out menu (refer to fig. 2.2), and enable Snap To **O**bjects from the **L**ayout menu. If Snap To **O**bjects is not enabled, the callout does not link with the object.

2. Click a starting point for the callout. If you are creating a linked callout, the starting point should be the snap point of the control object.

3. For a one-segment callout, click a second point where you want to place the text. For a two-segment callout, drag to the point where you want the second segment to begin and click. Then drag again to the point where you want to place the text and click once more.

4. The text cursor appears, enabling you to enter the desired text.

Examining the Geometric Drawing Tools

Most real or imagined objects are made of basic geometric shapes. These shapes are the skeletal frame upon which a design evolves. CorelDRAW offers two versatile tools for creating geometric shapes: the Ellipse tool and the Rectangle tool (refer to fig. 2.1). You use the Ellipse tool to create ellipses and circles; similarly, you use the Rectangle tool to create rectangles and squares. The shapes these two tools create are also the basis for

other symmetrical shapes when they are edited with the Shape tool. Chapter 5, "Shaping Objects," provides information on editing shapes with the Shape tool.

To use the Ellipse or the Rectangle tool, select the tool from the toolbox by clicking on it. When you move the cursor back to the drawing window, it changes to cross hairs. With this cross hairs cursor, you can easily position the beginning and ending points of the object.

Drawing Ellipses and Circles

Ellipses are surrounded by invisible rectangular bounding boxes. The corners of the bounding box identify the height and width of the ellipse. Normally, the starting point for an ellipse is one of these corners. In figure 2.20, the dotted rectangle and square represent these imaginary bounding boxes and do not appear when you draw an ellipse or a circle. If you depress the Shift key while drawing an ellipse, the ellipse is drawn from the center point.

N O T E

The keyboard shortcut for the Ellipse tool is F6.

To draw an ellipse, follow these steps:

1. Click on the location in the drawing window where you want to begin the ellipse.

2. Continue to depress the mouse button

while you drag away from the starting point. As the ellipse appears, you can modify it by dragging the mouse in different directions.

3. Once the ellipse is the shape and size you want, release the mouse button.

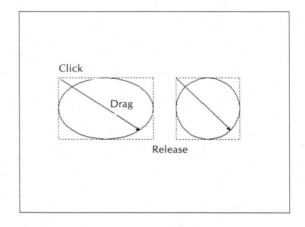

Figure 2.20
Drawing an ellipse and a circle.

You follow the same steps to draw a circle, but you hold down the Ctrl key to constrain the shape of the ellipse. If you depress both the Shift and Ctrl keys while drawing an ellipse, a circle is drawn from its center point. After you release the mouse button, release the Ctrl or Shift keys or both. The status line then displays the height and width of the ellipse or circle.

Drawing Rectangles and Squares

To draw a rectangle, follow these steps:

1. Click on the location in the drawing window where you want to begin the rectangle.

2. Continue to depress the mouse button while you drag away from the starting point. As the rectangle appears, you can modify its shape and size by dragging the mouse in different directions.

3. Release the mouse button to complete the rectangle.

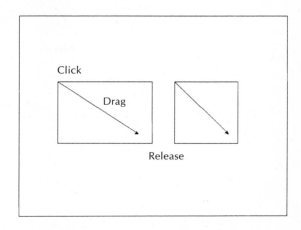

Figure 2.21

Drawing a rectangle and square.

N O T E

The keyboard shortcut for the Rectangle tool is F7.

You follow the same steps to draw a square, but you hold down the Ctrl key while you drag to constrain the rectangle to a square (see fig. 2.21). If you depress both the Ctrl and Shift keys continuously while using the Rectangle tool, the square is drawn from its center point. After you release the mouse button, release the Ctrl or Shift keys or both. As with the Ellipse tool, the status line then displays the height and width of the rectangle or square.

Summary

In CorelDRAW, the drawing tools are essential elements in the creation of any design. This chapter explored the use of each of the drawing tools. At first glance, they might seem limited; in reality, however, each one is powerful yet easy to use. The capabilities of the drawing tools, when used in conjunction with CorelDRAW's other tools and commands, are limited only by your imagination. The next chapter, "Working with Objects," discusses how to combine the drawing tools with some of the object commands to create more complex objects.

Working with Objects

*C*orelDRAW offers a number of methods of working with simple shapes to create more complex objects. The exercises in this chapter illustrate some of the commands that enable you to modify the basic shape of an object. Most of the steps in this chapter use the mouse rather than roll-ups or menus to complete the operation. When precision is not required, using the mouse to move and place objects is faster than using menus or roll-ups.

This chapter covers:

- Creating a pizza slice
- Creating a pierced image
- Using the Clone command

Creating a Pizza Slice

Although the pizza slice that you create in this exercise is not the most exotic piece of art, it illustrates the use of CorelDRAW's most powerful object commands. The commands highlighted in this exercise include the following:

- Repeat
- Duplicate
- Nudge
- Weld
- Trim

Before you start this exercise, you should configure the Place Duplicates and Clones setting in the Preferences dialog box. Set both the horizontal and vertical values to 0.0". Set the Nudge value to .01". For ease, the exercise is worked in landscape origin on a letter-size page. To change the orientation of the page, select **P**age Setup from the **L**ayout menu. From the Size property sheet select Landscape, and choose Letter from the drop-down size list box.

CorelDRAW is capable of creating huge and complex files that can create problems at printing time. The Weld and Trim commands used in creating the pizza slice reduce the complexity of a drawing by minimizing overlapping objects. To create the pizza slice, use the following steps:

1. Select the Bézier pencil from the Pencil tool fly-out menu.

2. Click at 3" horizontal and 6" vertical (3",6") to set the starting point for a line. Depressing the Ctrl key to constrain the line, double-click at 3", 2" to set the second point. Release the Ctrl key.

3. Click at 9", 4" to set the third point. Click a last time at the beginning point to finish the triangle, as shown in figure 3.1.

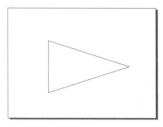

Figure 3.1
Creating a triangle with the Bézier pencil tool.

N O T E

CorelDRAW's AutoJoin feature enables you to adjust the maximum distance where two line endings automatically join together as a continuous shape. To configure autojoin for the way you work, see "Setting Preferences" in Chapter 1, "Features of CorelDRAW."

4. From the **L**ayout menu, enable Snap to **O**bjects, and select the Ellipse tool from the toolbox.

5. Starting at a point near the top left point of the triangle, click and drag the Ellipse tool down to the bottom left point and release the mouse button. The ellipse automatically snaps to the node or snap point of the object, as shown in figure 3.2. Disable Snap to Objects to proceed.

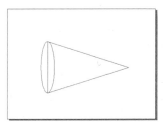

Figure 3.2
Placing the ellipse.

6. Using the Pick tool, depress the Shift key and select both the ellipse and the triangle by clicking on them.

Double-clicking on the Pick tool selects all of the objects in the drawing window.

7. Select the **W**eld command from the **A**rrange menu to complete the wedge shape shown in figure 3.3. The **W**eld command merges two or more superimposed objects so that the resulting object has the outline shape of the selected objects. Interior lines are deleted automatically. The resulting

objects attain the attributes of the last object selected. If objects from different layers are selected, the resulting object is placed on the active layer, as shown in the Layers roll-up, and attains the attributes of the last object selected on that layer.

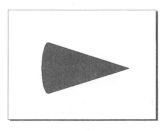

Figure 3.3
Using the Weld command to create a wedge.

8. With the wedge selected, choose the **D**uplicate command from the **E**dit menu (Ctrl+D). Though it is not visibly apparent, there are two wedges superimposed one over the other. The object handles belong to the duplicate. Holding the Shift key down, drag one of the corner handles toward the center slightly to scale the duplicate wedge, as shown in figure 3.4. Using the color palette at the bottom of the drawing window, fill the top wedge with yellow by clicking on the color. Click on the bottom wedge to select it, and fill it with orange.

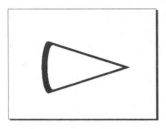

Figure 3.4
Duplicating and scaling the wedge.

N O T E

Scaling an object with the mouse differs from stretching an object. Holding the Shift key constrains the object and forces it to scale equally from the center on all sides.

9. Select the Ellipse tool and, depressing the Ctrl key, create a .5" circle on top of the yellow wedge. Fill the circle with black.

10. Click and drag the circle to another location on the yellow wedge. While dragging the circle, click the right mouse button to leave a copy of the circle behind. Note that you now have two pieces of pepperoni. The right mouse button enables you to move an object leaving a duplicate behind. You can also duplicate an object by using the + key on the numeric keypad of your keyboard. With one of the circles selected, click the + key to create a duplicate and drag it to another location on the yellow wedge. Using the method with which you are most

comfortable, continue until you have four or five circles. Place one circle near the tip of the wedge but not overlapping the outlines (see fig. 3.5). If you want to resize one or more of the circles, click the corner handle of a circle with the pick tool, and drag the handle to resize the circle.

Figure 3.5
Using the right mouse button or the + key to create duplicates.

11. Using the Pick tool, marquee-select the circles by clicking and dragging a bounding box to contain them. Be careful not to include the wedges. As you drag the cursor, a dotted box appears outlining the area you are selecting. Release the mouse button. The control handles mark the boundaries of the objects selected. Fill the objects with black.

12. Duplicate the circles and, using the cursor keys, nudge the circles up and to the right .04 ". Nudge, from the **P**references dialog box, enables you to move objects small distances with precision using the cursor keys. The nudge value can be set in increments of .001" to 2.0" (see fig. 3.6).

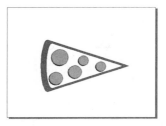

Figure 3.6
Using the Nudge command to move objects.

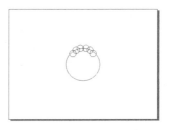

Figure 3.7
Placement of the smaller circles.

13. In another part of the drawing window, draw a circle approximately 2.5" in diameter. The status line displays the size of the circle as it is being drawn.

14. Select the Pick tool by depressing the spacebar. Duplicate the circle. Using one of the corner handles of the duplicate circle, click and drag toward the center of the circle. Stretch the circle until it is .5" in diameter.

T I P

You can switch quickly to the Pick tool by depressing the spacebar. To return to the last tool selected, depress the spacebar again. Depress Ctrl+spacebar to switch to the Pick tool when using the Text tool.

15. Create five duplicates of the smaller circle and arrange them on the larger circle, as shown in figure 3.7.

16. Marquee-select the overlapping circles. The status line shows seven objects selected. Apply the **W**eld command to create the shape shown in figure 3.8.

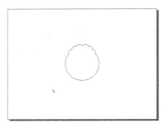

Figure 3.8
Using the Weld command to create an irregular shape.

17. Drag the object, positioning it over the pointed edge of the wedge. Be sure that the point of the wedge is covered by the object.

18. Click a second time on the object to display the rotation and skewing handles. The circle in the center of the handles is the center of rotation. You can move the center of rotation by dragging it to another location.

Depressing the Ctrl key while dragging the center of rotation forces it to snap to one of the handles. For this exercise, depress the Ctrl key and drag the center of rotation to the extreme side handle, away from the wedge.

19. Click and drag one of the corner handles to rotate the object until it appears as shown in figure 3.9.

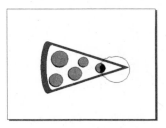

Figure 3.10
Using the Trim command to modify objects.

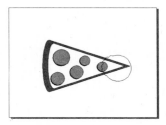

Figure 3.9
Rotating a shape.

20. Depress the Shift key and click on the red circle that is covered partially by the irregular object. The status line shows two objects selected. Choose the **T**rim command from the **A**rrange menu to cut away a portion of the red circle and reveal the black circle below. The **T**rim command enables you to cut away a portion of one of two selected objects. The object trimmed is always the last object selected. This is useful for creating cut-away drawings (see fig. 3.10).

```
T  I  P
```

When working with the **T**rim, **W**eld, and **I**ntersection commands, it is sometimes easier to work in wireframe view or with objects that have no fill. This enables you to position superimposed objects more easily.

21. Select the irregular object and the black circle. Choose the **R**epeat command from the **E**dit menu (Ctrl+R) to cut away a portion of the black circle.

22. Repeat Step 21 to trim away pieces from both wedges. Delete the bite-shaped irregular object. The final pizza slice appears with a bite out of it, as shown in figure 3.11.

Figure 3.11
The final appearance of a pizza slice.

Creating a Pierced Image

In previous versions of CorelDRAW, creating an object that appeared to be pierced by another object was a time-consuming and tedious operation. The pierced effect creates the illusion of one object passing through another. This exercise uses the following commands to create the illusion:

■ Intersection

■ Duplicate

■ Combine

■ Break Apart

Before you start this exercise, configure the horizontal and vertical values of the Place Duplicates and Clone setting in the Preferences dialog box to 0.0".

1. Create a circle with a diameter of 3.0" and fill it with red from the on-screen palette. Using the right mouse button, click on the X at the left of the palette to change the outline to none.

T I P

You don't have to toggle back to the Pick tool to apply a color to the fill or outline of an object immediately after you create it. Move the cursor to the on-screen color palette and click on the desired color. If you want to remove a fill, click on the X. You can quickly apply color to an outline or remove an outline with the right mouse button. Click on a color in the on-screen palette to use that color as the outline for your object. Right clicking on the X removes the outline. When you return the cursor to the drawing window, the tool remains the last tool you selected.

2. In another location of the drawing window, create an ellipse 4" wide and 2" tall. Duplicate the ellipse and scale the duplicate down slightly. Nudge the duplicate .02" toward the top of the original ellipse, as shown in figure 3.12.

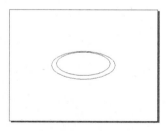

Figure 3.12
Superimposed ellipses.

3. Select the two ellipses and choose the **C**ombine command from the **A**rrange menu (Ctrl+L). The **C**ombine command is used to create masks and

clipped objects. For more information about using the **C**ombine command, see Chapter 8, "Transforming and Arranging Objects." Fill the resulting ring with black (see fig. 3.13).

Figure 3.13
Using the Combine command to create a ring.

4. Click on the selected ring to display the rotation and skewing handles. Click and drag the left skewing handle upward to tilt the ellipse. Place the ellipse over the circle, as shown in figure 3.14.

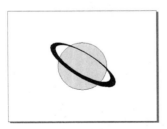

Figure 3.14
A skewed ellipse.

N · O · T · E

Depressing the Ctrl key while using rotate or skew constrains the movement of the object to specific increments configured in the Preference dialog box. The default amount is 15 degrees. Similarly, if you depress the Ctrl key while moving an object, it is constrained to move horizontally or vertically in a straight line.

5. Select the ring and circle. Choose the **I**ntersection command from the **A**rrange menu (see fig. 3.15).

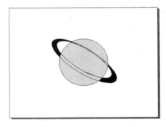

Figure 3.15
Using the Intersect command.

6. Select the center intersected portion of the ring, which appears as a red section of the ring with a black outline. Click on Brea**k** Apart from the **A**rrange menu (Ctrl+K). The Brea**k** Apart command separates combined objects with multiple paths. For more information about using the Brea**k** Apart command, see Chapter 8.

7. Depress Esc to deselect both objects. Select the front red portion of the ring and fill it with black. Press Tab

repeatedly until the back portion of the ring is the selected object. The Tab key is useful for cycling through the objects of a drawing. It makes superimposed objects easy to select if they are hidden by another object. Choose the De**l**ete command from the **E**dit menu (Del) to erase the back ring segment.

8. Select the circle and choose the **O**rder command from the **A**rrange menu. Click on Forward **O**ne to bring the circle up one level. The **O**rder command enables you to rearrange objects on your screen. For more information about using the **O**rder command, see Chapter 8. The final planet with its ring appears, as shown in figure 3.16.

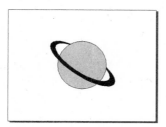

Figure 3.16
The completed pierced image.

Using the Clone Command

The Cl**o**ne command enables you to create a duplicate of an object. It differs from the **D**uplicate command in that the cloned object is linked to the originating or source object. The cloned object takes on the attributes of the source object. If you change the attributes of the source object, the attributes of the cloned object change as well. The Cl**o**ne command is useful when you need several copies of an object and need to manipulate all of them in the same manner. The following exercise illustrates the various aspects of using the Cl**o**ne command.

Before you start this exercise, configure the Place Duplicates and Clones setting of the Preferences dialog box for a horizontal value of 2.0" and a vertical value of 0.0".

1. Draw a rectangle on the left side of the printable page. Fill the rectangle with black.

2. Select the Cl**o**ne command from the **E**dit menu to place a clone of the rectangle.

3. Change the color of the source object. (Note the color of the clone object changes.)

4. Stretch the source object vertically, and then click on the source object again to display the skew and rotation handles. Try rotating and skewing the source object.

5. Mirror the source object. To apply mirror, depress the Ctrl key and drag one of the side or corner handles across the object. For example, drag the top handle toward the bottom of the object and slightly beyond. The object flips or mirrors. Movement is constrained to 100% increments, making it easier to maintain the same size and aspect ration. Note that the clone object is mirrored as well.

You can move the cloned object or change its color without breaking the link between the objects. If you change the color, however, future color changes applied to the source object will not affect the clone. Stretching, scaling, rotation, or skewing manipulations applied to the source object will still affect the clone. Other changes applied to the clone, such as rotate or skew, break the link between the objects, and the objects will no longer be affected by changes made to the source object.

Some commands also affect cloned objects. If you apply the Con**v**ert to Curves, **A**dd Perspective, **E**nvelope, or **L**ens commands to a source object, they are applied to the cloned object as well. Commands that create dynamically linked objects, such as E**x**trude, **P**owerline, **B**lend, or Co**n**tour, can be applied to clone objects created using the Cl**o**ne command from the **E**dit menu. Applying these effects, however, partially breaks the link between the source object and the clone. Resizing or recoloring applied to the source object is applied to the clone, but Special Effects applied to the source objects are not applied to the clone. For more information about cloning or copying special effects, see Chapter 11, "Creating with Special Effects."

enables you to choose the way you work best and to configure the program to meet those needs. For basic operations, you can manipulate objects with either the mouse or the Transform roll-up. The Transform roll-up offers precision difficult to achieve with a mouse and is discussed in Chapter 8, "Transforming and Arranging Objects."

Summary

The ability to manipulate simple shapes to create objects is critical to speed and efficiency in your work. Commands such as **W**eld, **T**rim, **D**uplicate, Cl**o**ne, and **I**ntersect increase productivity by making objects easier to create. One of CorelDRAW's most powerful features is its flexibility, which

Chapter 4

Working with Text and Symbols

CorelDRAW is rich in text and symbol features. This chapter introduces these features and describes the basic operations associated with them. CorelDRAW 5.0 provides strong text-handling capability by offering two types of text options. You can choose from the options available with Paragraph text or those with Artistic text. Both text types offer benefits to the professional designer.

Symbols function as bullets beside your text or as stand-alone objects within your document. CorelDRAW's symbol libraries contain symbols that are popular for a broad variety of applications.

This chapter covers:

- Entering and editing Artistic text
- Understanding Artistic text limitations
- Converting text to curves
- Creating a frame with Paragraph text
- Editing Paragraph text
- Using the Text roll-up
- Using CorelDRAW's text aids
- Using CorelDRAW's symbol libraries

Artistic Text versus Paragraph Text

If you want to enliven your documents and add a creative touch, Artistic text and symbols enable you to turn plain text into word art. CorelDRAW treats Artistic text strings as text objects, so you can apply transformations and special effects to the text. You can, for example, change the fill and outline of the text as you do for other objects. On the other hand, if you want to create a text-intensive document, Paragraph text enables you to use a wide array of formatting options, such as columns, tabs, and indents. Note the differences between the following toolboxes.

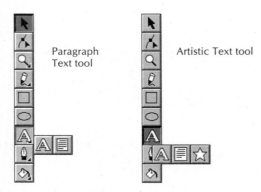

Paragraph Text tool

Artistic Text tool

Entering and Editing Artistic Text

You can add Artistic text to your documents by using one of four methods: typing text directly on-screen, typing text in the Edit Text dialog box, pasting text from the Clipboard, and importing text from other applications. Artistic text does not have the word-wrap feature, so you must press Enter at the end of each line to place multiple lines of text. The typed or pasted text appears in the drawing window with the default font and character attributes. The default attributes are 24 points, normal style, left aligned, and Avalon (Avantgarde BK BT); however, you can change the default font and character attributes. For more information, see the section later in this chapter titled "Changing Default Attributes."

T I P

By default, CorelDRAW *greeks* text under 9 pixels in size. Greeked text appears as small rectangles in full-page view. If you zoom in on the text, you can see the real characters. Text-greeking conserves memory and speeds screen refresh time. If you prefer to work in full-page view, however, you can adjust the default pixel size with the **G**reek Text Below setting in the Text property sheet of the Preferences dialog box.

Entering Text On-Screen

By entering text on-screen, you can quickly add text objects. This method is especially helpful when you are adding numerous short text strings to a document, such as object labels on a technical illustration.

The procedure is simple. With the Artistic Text tool selected, click an insertion point in the drawing window. A bar appears, which indicates the insertion point for your text. You can then type the text string (see fig. 4.1).

Figure 4.1
On-screen text entry.

Note that on-screen text is easier to enter and edit if you enlarge your view by using the Zoom tool. To zoom in on only the text, select the Zoom To Selected Objects tool from the Zoom fly-out menu.

Entering Text Using the Edit Text Dialog Box

By entering text in the Edit Text dialog box, you can change the attributes of the text before you return to the drawing window. Text that has been rotated or skewed is easier to edit in the Edit Text dialog box. Moreover, text that has been transformed by special effects (other than Blend) must be edited in the Edit Text dialog box.

To enter text using the Edit Text dialog box, follow these steps:

1. Place an insertion point about 1" below the string of text you typed earlier.

2. Select Edit Te**x**t from the **T**ext menu, or use the keyboard shortcut

Ctrl+Shift+T. The Edit Text dialog box opens, with a blinking cursor in the text-entry box.

3. Type **Entering Artistic Text Using The Dialog Box**, and click on OK to return to the drawing window (see figs. 4.2 and 4.3).

4. Save the document as ARTTXT1.CDR. Throughout the exercises in this chapter, you create a series of files with similar names. In the Save Drawing dialog box, type **Enter** in the **K**eywords entry box; then add a note describing this file to the Not**e**s entry box. This information makes the file easier to locate later.

Figure 4.2
Entering text in the Edit Text dialog box.

In version 4.0, the Edit Text dialog box is called the Artistic Text dialog box.

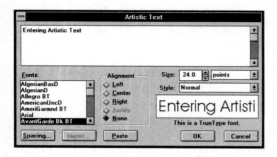

Figure 4.3

Entering text in version 4.0's Artistic Text dialog box.

Copying, Cutting, and Pasting Text

You can quickly add and edit text in CorelDRAW documents by using the basic operations of copying, cutting, and pasting. Text from a CorelDRAW document or other word processing application can be copied or cut to the Windows Clipboard and then pasted into the destination document. Copying text to the Clipboard leaves the original text in the source document, whereas cutting text removes the text from the source document. (In effect, cutting enables you to move blocks of text.) The copied or cut text can then be pasted either directly on-screen or in the Edit Text dialog box. When you paste text without selecting an insertion point, the text is centered on the page as Paragraph text and cannot be transformed as Artistic text (see fig. 4.4).

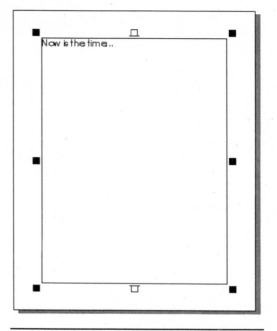

Figure 4.4

Text pasted without an insertion point.

N O T E

The Text property sheet in the Preferences dialog box enables you to specify how you want CorelDRAW to place text on the Clipboard. Chapter 7, "Working with Outlines," discusses calligraphic pen effects that can be applied to objects (including text). If you want these calligraphic effects to be copied to the Clipboard with a text selection, you enable the Calligraphic **T**ext feature. By default, this feature is enabled, requires more memory, and slows Clipboard functions. If your system configuration requires conservation of resources, consider disabling this feature.

You also can specify whether you want text placed as text or as curves. When you enable the Te**x**t in Metafile feature, text attributes are copied with the text to the Clipboard and can be edited in the destination document as text. Text placed as curves cannot be edited as text after it is pasted into a document. By default this feature is disabled. If you are working between various applications, consider enabling this feature to ensure that you can edit the text as needed.

Copying Text

To copy text to the Clipboard from a CorelDRAW document, you do the following: Swipe the text with the Text tool by clicking and dragging the text cursor over the desired text to highlight it. Then choose **C**opy from the **E**dit menu. The keyboard shortcut is Ctrl+C or Ctrl+Insert.

Cutting Text

To cut text to the Clipboard from a CorelDRAW document, you do the following: Swipe the text with the Text tool by clicking and dragging the text cursor over the desired text. Then choose Cu**t** from the **E**dit menu. The keyboard shortcut is Ctrl+X or Shift+Del.

Pasting Text

To paste text as a new text object, follow these steps:

1. Place an insertion point with the Artistic Text tool in the drawing window, or choose Edit Te**x**t from the **T**ext menu.

2. Select **P**aste or Paste **S**pecial from the **E**dit menu (see fig. 4.5). The keyboard shortcut is Ctrl+V or Shift+Insert.

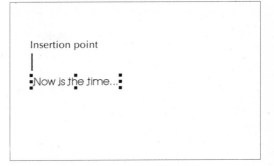

Figure 4.5
Using the Paste command to add new text.

Adding Text

To add text to an existing text string, follow these steps:

1. Select the text with the Pick tool.

2. Using the Artistic Text tool, place an insertion point where you want to add the text.

3. Select **P**aste or Paste **S**pecial from the **E**dit menu (see fig. 4.6). The keyboard shortcut is Ctrl+V or Shift+Insert.

Now is the timel——Insertion point

Now is the time for all good men

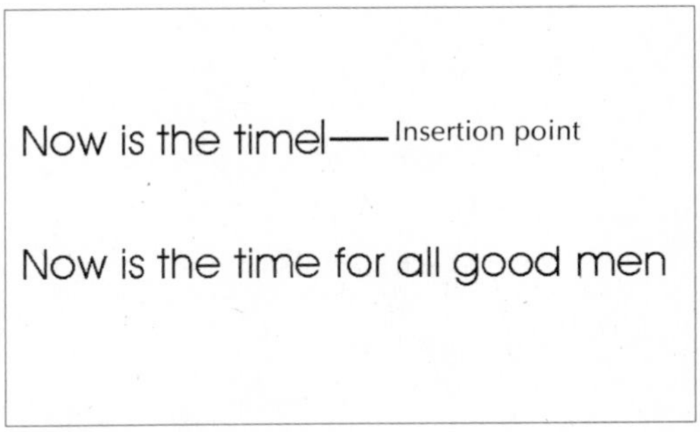

Figure 4.6
Using the Paste command to add text to an existing text string.

Professional Reference Series
New Riders

Replacing Text

To replace text with the contents of the Clipboard, follow these steps:

1. Highlight the text by clicking and dragging the Text tool over the desired text, either on-screen or in the Edit Text dialog box.

2. Select **P**aste or Paste **S**pecial from the **E**dit menu (see fig. 4.7). The keyboard shortcut is Ctrl+V or Shift+Insert.

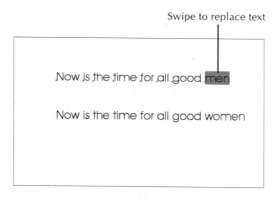

Swipe to replace text

Now is the time for all good men

Now is the time for all good women

Figure 4.7

Using the Paste command to replace existing text.

Paste versus Paste Special

CorelDRAW, as well as a number of other Windows applications, is OLE-compliant. The OLE feature enables documents to share information in a manner that makes editing and updating easy. CorelDRAW functions as both a server application and a destination application. When you copy text between OLE applications, the Paste and Paste Special commands enable you to edit the text in the source document and update the destination

document. Choosing the **P**aste option embeds the text in the destination document, whereas selecting the Paste **S**pecial option links the file information for the text with the source file. For more information about the OLE functions of the Paste and Paste Special commands, see Chapter 40, "Importing and Exporting."

Understanding Artistic Text Limitations

An Artistic text string can have a maximum of 8,000 characters. Special effects such as Envelope, however, can be applied only to text strings that are under 250 characters. In fact, this number might be even lower because of variations in font descriptions. If the number of characters in your text object exceeds the allowable number for a given font, a message is displayed telling you that your text may be truncated.

N O T E

An Artistic text object in version 4.0 can have a maximum of 250 characters.

To prevent text from truncating, you can shorten the text string in one of two ways. One method is to split the text string into multiple strings. CorelDRAW doesn't have a limit to the number of Artistic text objects in a document. Another method is to enter the text using the Paragraph Text tool. Most of CorelDRAW's special effects commands, however, cannot be applied to Paragraph text.

Figure 4.8 shows a string of unmodified text. When the Envelope special effect was applied to the text (see fig. 4.9), it was truncated because it exceeded the character limit for that font. To avoid the truncation, the text was entered as four strings of text that were aligned and grouped to make a single grouped object. A two-curve envelope was then applied to the grouped object. The effect was completed by copying the envelope to a rectangle and modifying the rectangle to resemble a sheet of paper with a drop shadow (see fig. 4.10). For more information about Envelope and other special effects, see Chapter 11, "Creating with Special Effects."

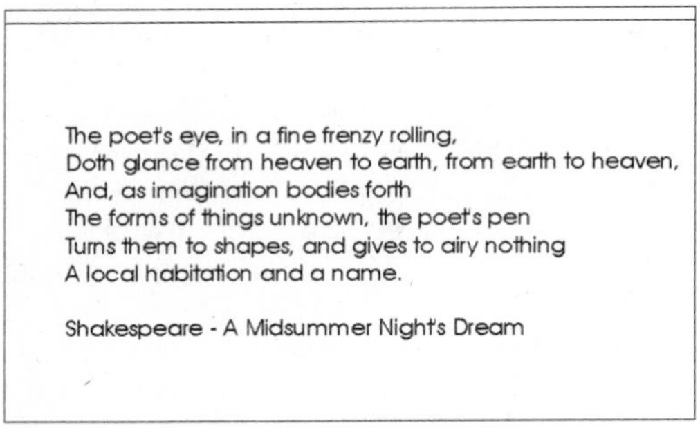

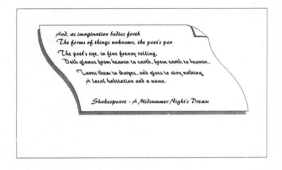

Figure 4.10
Fixing the truncated text.

Figure 4.8
A string of unmodified text.

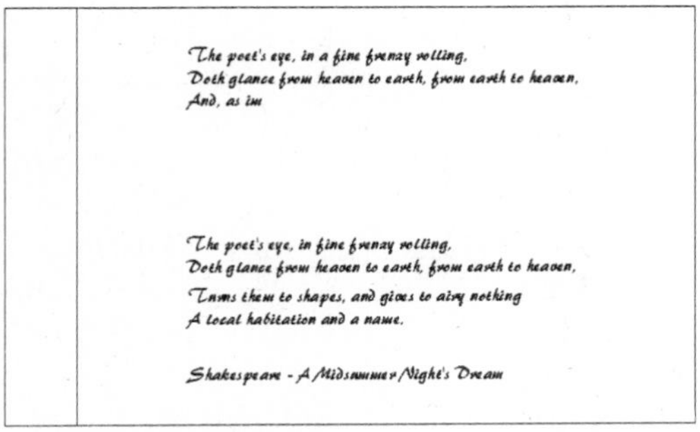

Figure 4.9
Applying the Envelope effect causes the text to be truncated.

Using Extended or Special Character Sets

Extended and special characters are used as bullets to call attention to text, or they are used to add a required symbol (such as a copyright symbol) to a string of text. CorelDRAW supports both ANSI and ASCII extended character sets. The following exercise demonstrates the use of special characters by adding a copyright symbol to the text you created earlier:

1. Open the ARTTXT1.CDR file.

T I P

CorelDRAW keeps track of the last four documents that were opened. When you click on the **F**ile menu, the associated file names appear at the bottom of the menu. If the document you want is one of the four, you can open the file by clicking on it or by typing its number on the keyboard. This feature is helpful when you have a number of similarly named files in a single directory. If you have

difficulty finding a file that has keyword notations, you can click on **O**ptions in the Open Drawing dialog box. Then select **F**ind and enter the keyword. The program searches for files containing that keyword.

2. Select the text `CorelDRAW! Artistic Text` by clicking on it with the Pick tool.

3. Select Edit Te**x**t from the **T**ext menu to display the Edit Text dialog box, or select the Artistic Text tool from the toolbox.

4. Place an insertion point directly after the last "t" in text.

5. While you depress the Alt key, type **0169**. (You must include the zero in the entry.)

6. Release the Alt key, and the copyright symbol (©) appears in the text string (see fig. 4.11).

7. Click on OK to return to the drawing window if you entered the special character in the Edit Text dialog box.

8. Save the file as ARTTXT2.CDR, using the Save **A**s option from the **F**ile menu.

Insertion point

CorelDRAW! Artistic Text|

CorelDRAW! Artistic Text©

Figure 4.11
Adding an extended character to text.

The extended and special characters that are available vary from one font to another. In addition, some characters may appear in the text entry window of the Edit Text dialog box as a small rectangle, but these characters appear in the drawing window as the correct characters.

T I P

The Windows Character Map provides a reference detailing the extended characters that are available for any installed font and their associated code numbers. The Character Map is located in the Accessories group in Program Manager. To use the Character Map, select the font you want from the **F**ont drop-down list box. The available characters for that font are displayed in the window below the box. When you click on the character you want, the keyboard code number for that character is displayed in the bottom-right corner of the window. For more information on the Character Map, see the *Microsoft Windows User's Guide.*

Editing Artistic Text

CorelDRAW offers two methods of editing Artistic text. You can edit text on-screen as well as from within the Edit Text dialog box. Editing text on-screen enables you to add or modify the existing text string. When you edit text in the Edit Text dialog box, you also can change the attributes of the text.

Editing Text On-Screen

The following exercise demonstrates on-screen text editing:

1. Open the ARTTXT1.CDR file.

2. Select the Artistic Text tool from the toolbox, and click to choose an insertion point at the beginning of the top text string.

3. Add the word **Editing** to the text string. The text object appears, as shown in figure 4.12.

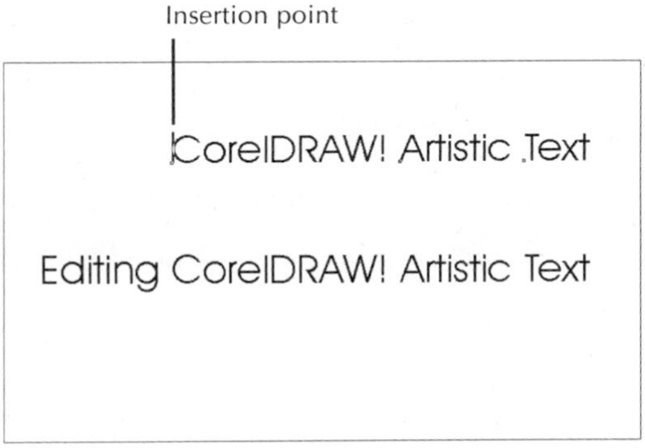

Insertion point

CorelDRAW! Artistic Text

Editing CorelDRAW! Artistic Text

Figure 4.12
On-screen text editing.

N O T E

To edit text on-screen, the **E**dit Text On Screen option in the Text property sheet of the Preferences dialog box must be enabled. By default this feature is enabled.

Editing Text Using the Edit Text Dialog Box

In the following exercise, you use the Edit Text dialog box to edit a text string:

1. Select the top text string with the Pick tool, and choose Edit Te**x**t from the **T**ext menu. The Edit Text dialog box appears, enabling you to modify the text string.

N O T E

You also can access the Edit Text dialog box by using the right mouse button. To configure the right mouse button to access the Edit Text dialog box, see Chapter 1, "Features of CorelDRAW."

2. In the text-entry box, click and drag the cursor over the word Entering to highlight it.

3. Type **Editing** to replace the highlighted text (see fig. 4.13).

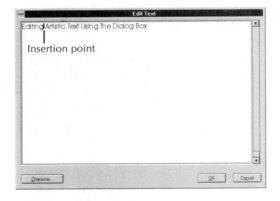

Figure 4.13
Editing text in the Edit Text dialog box.

Changing Character Attributes

The *character attributes* of a text string refer to the font, type size, style, alignment, spacing, and placement of the text. The Character Attributes dialog box (see fig. 4.14) and the Text roll-up enable you to change these attributes. In addition, you can quickly create underline, overline, and strikeout text.

Figure 4.14

The Character Attributes dialog box.

In the following exercise, you use the Character Attributes dialog box to change some character attributes:

1. Click on **C**haracter under the **T**ext menu, to open the Character Attributes dialog box.

2. Click on the down arrow, or click and drag the scroll bar until Swiss721 BT appears in the **F**onts selection box.

Select this font by clicking on its name. The selected font is highlighted, and a sample of the text appears in the text box.

3. Change the type size to 72 points, either by using the scroll arrows or by highlighting the number in the text-entry box and typing **72**. Although points and picas are the standard units of type measurement throughout the publishing and printing industry, you can change the units of measurement to inches or millimeters if you want.

N O T E

The procedure for stretching and scaling Artistic text is the same as that used for other objects. With the mouse, you drag the handles of the selected text string. The status line displays the new size.

4. Select Bold from the **S**tyle drop-down list to change the style of the font. The **S**tyle list enables you to choose from the available styles for that font. Depending on the font you select, the style options include normal, italic, bold, or bold italic. Some fonts have limited styles available.

5. Click on the arrow beside **P**lacement. The options available on the **P**lacement drop-down list include Normal, Superscript, and Subscript. The default placement is Normal. For this example, leave the placement setting at Normal.

6. Change the alignment by clicking on the radio button beside **C**enter. Placement of a text string is in relation

to the location you choose as an insertion point. The Character Attributes dialog box offers five alignment options:

- **Left.** The **L**eft option aligns the beginning character of the text string with the insertion point.

- **Center.** The **C**enter option centers the text string with the insertion point.

- **Right.** The **R**ight option aligns the last character of the text string with the insertion point.

- **Justify.** The **J**ustify option aligns multiple lines of text evenly, thereby reducing the ragged right edge normally associated with text that has been left-aligned.

- **None.** The **N**one option enables you to align text freely in relation to the insertion point. Unless the alignment option is **N**one, spaces placed at the beginning or end of a text string are ignored (see fig. 4.15).

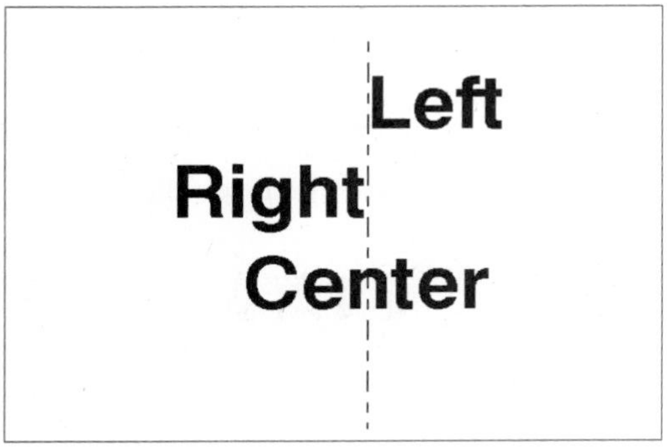

7. CorelDRAW enables you to alter the spacing between characters (*kerning*), words, and lines (*leading*). You modify text by changing the values of these three spacing options. In so doing, you can balance the appearance of your documents and create interesting effects. Adjust the character spacing by changing the Charact**e**r setting to 300%. This value spreads the letters apart. Increase the spacing between the words in your text string by changing the **W**ord setting to 200% (see fig. 4.16). Finally, you can change the spacing between lines by altering the setting in the L**i**ne entry box; however, leave that setting at the default. For more information about spacing, see the section later in this chapter entitled "Editing and Formatting Paragraph Text." Click OK to return to the drawing window.

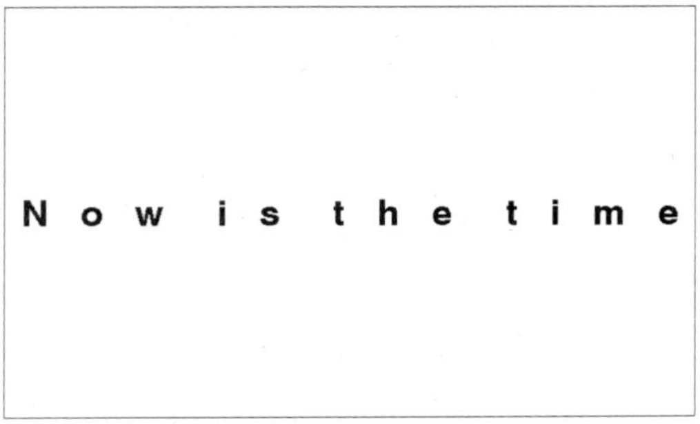

Now is the time

Figure 4.16
Text string after editing.

Left
Right
Center

Figure 4.15
Text alignment.

Using Underline, Overline, and Strikeout

CorelDRAW enables you to emphasize text by adding underlines, overlines, and strikeouts (see fig. 4.17). In the Character Attributes dialog box, click on the arrow beside the **U**nderline, **O**verline, or S**t**rikeout option to display a list box showing the available text emphasis lines. You can choose from Single Thin, Single Thin Word, Single Thick, Single Thick Word, Double Thin, or Double Thin Word. If you choose one of the Word options, the line applies to the words only and not to the spaces between the words. The options in the list boxes affect the function, as follows:

- **Underline.** The **U**nderline option places a single or double line below a text selection. Underlining is linked to the baseline of the individual characters. If you have modified the baseline of individual characters in a text string, the result is a noncontinuous line.

- **Overline.** The **O**verline option places a single or double line above a text selection. Overlining is linked to the height of the text string. If you have modified the size or baseline of individual characters in a text string, the result is a noncontinuous line.

- **Strikeout.** The S**t**rikeout option places a single or double line through the text selection. If you have modified the size or baseline of individual characters in a text string, the result is a noncontinuous line.

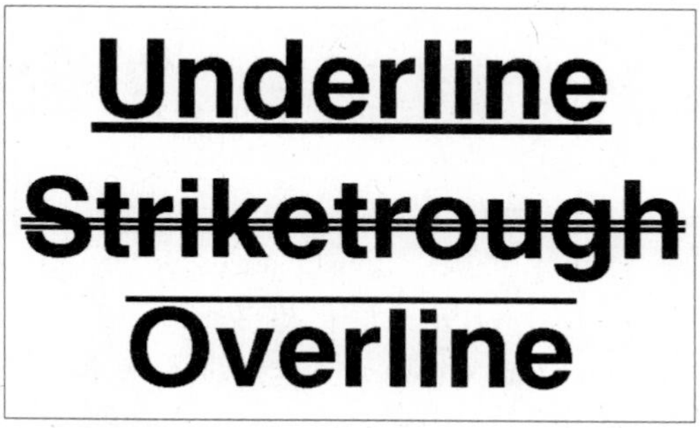

Figure 4.17
Examples of text emphasis lines.

Changing Default Attributes

You can change the default character attributes used in CorelDRAW by following these steps:

1. Deselect all the objects in the drawing window. To deselect all the objects, click on the white space in the drawing window, or depress the Esc key.

2. Choose **C**haracter from the **T**ext menu. The Character Attributes selection box appears, with both Artistic and Paragraph text preselected. You can leave them both selected, or you can deselect either of them by clicking on the selection box beside the text type. Then click on OK.

3. The Character Attributes dialog box appears, enabling you to make the selections you want. Click on OK to return to the drawing window.

The changes you make are permanent. The CORELDRW.INI file is modified, and the new defaults are available for future documents until you choose to change the defaults.

Altering Text Interactively

In addition to altering text by using the spacing options of the Character Attributes dialog box, you also can interactively alter text by adjusting character (kerning) and line spacing with the Shape tool. When you select the text you want to change with the Shape tool, two arrow handles appear. You drag the right arrow to adjust the kerning. After interactive kerning, use the Align To Baseline command from the **T**ext menu to ensure proper alignment of the characters. Similarly, you drag the down arrow to adjust the space between lines of text (see fig. 4.18).

Figure 4.18
Adjusting kerning and line spacing interactively.

N O T E

Dragging the down arrow on a single line of text does not affect the text string.

Shifting Characters

The Shape tool enables you to alter the position of individual characters in a text string. You can shift characters interactively or by using the Character Attributes dialog box.

To shift characters interactively, follow these steps:

- **Vertical Shift.** Select the nodes of the characters you want to move. Depress the Ctrl key to constrain the movement, and drag the nodes vertically.

- **Horizontal Shift.** Select the nodes of the characters you want to move. Depress the Ctrl key to constrain the movement, and drag the nodes horizontally (see fig. 4.19).

Figure 4.19
Shifting characters interactively.

To shift characters using the Character Attributes dialog box, follow these steps:

- **Vertical Shift.** Select the nodes of the characters you want to move. Double-click on one of the selected nodes to display the Character Attributes dialog box. Enter the desired positive or negative value in the **V**ertical Shift entry box, and click on OK to return to the drawing window.

- **Horizontal Shift.** Select the nodes of the characters you want to move. Double-click on one of the selected nodes to display the Character Attributes dialog box. Enter the desired positive or negative value in the **H**orizontal Shift entry box, and click on OK to return to the drawing window.

- **Angle.** Select the nodes of the characters you want to change. Double-click on one of the selected nodes to display the Character Attributes dialog box. Enter the desired positive or negative value in the **A**ngle entry box and click on OK to return to the drawing window (see fig. 4.20).

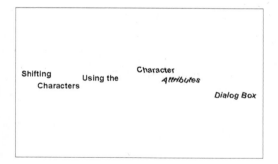

Figure 4.20

An example of shifting characters using the Character Attributes dialog box.

Using Straighten Text and Align To Baseline

The Straighten Text command enables you to remove any placement shifts or angle changes previously applied to a string of text. You can straighten individual characters or an entire string of text. To straighten individual characters, use the Shape tool to select the characters, and then choose the **S**traighten Text option from the **T**ext menu. To straighten an entire string of text, use the Pick tool to select the text, and then apply the Straighten Text command.

The Align To Baseline command resets the vertical shift to 0 percent. This command does not affect any horizontal shift or angle changes previously applied to the text. You can align individual characters or an entire string of text to the baseline. To align individual characters to the baseline, use the Shape tool to select the characters, and then click on the Align To Base**l**ine option from the **T**ext menu. To align an entire string of text to the baseline, use the Pick tool to select the text, and then apply the Align To Baseline command.

To force characters to the baseline interactively, use the Shape tool to select the characters. Depress the Ctrl key while you drag the text. Characters that have been moved vertically are constrained to the baseline.

Modifying a Text Object

You can change the fill or outline color of a portion of a text string in two ways:

- Use the Shape tool to select the nodes of the characters you want to change. Then choose the new fill or outline color.

- Use the Text tool to select the text you want to change. Then choose the new fill or outline color.

Converting Text to Curves

Converting text to curves enable you to alter the shape of the characters in a string of text. Text that has been converted to curves becomes a graphic object and can no longer be edited as text. To convert a string of text to curves, use the Pick tool to select the text. Then click on Con**v**ert To Curves from the **A**rrange menu. If you want to modify the characters as individual objects, select Brea**k** Apart from the **A**rrange menu. Characters that are pierced, such as the letters D or P, are broken into two objects. The pierced area seems to disappear because both objects have the same fill and outline attributes. You can combine the two objects to regain the pierced effect, or you can change the color of either the main object or the clipping hole. The objects can then be reshaped as graphic objects (see fig. 4.21). For more information about shaping objects, see Chapter 5, "Shaping Objects."

Figure 4.21
Text converted to curves and modified.

Fitting Text to a Path

Words become art when text is fitted to a path. The *path* can be a line, a geometric shape, a letter, or another text string. The Fit Text To Path roll-up enables you to fit Artistic text to a path (see fig. 4.22).

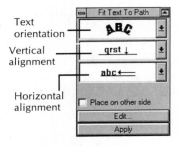

Figure 4.22
The Fit Text To Path roll-up.

Using Fit Text To Path

The Fit Text To Path roll-up contains the commands and options that allow you to bend artistic text along a path. This roll-up has two views: one for fitting text to most open paths and irregular shapes and one for fitting text to a geometric path such as an ellipse or rectangle.

To fit text to a path, follow these steps:

1. Select the text and the object. Then choose the Fit **T**ext To Path option from the **T**ext menu. The keyboard shortcut is Ctrl+F.

2. Select the options you want in the Fit Text To Path roll-up, and click on Apply.

If you want to use a letter as the path, you must first convert the letter to curves.

Vertical Alignment

In the Fit Text To Path roll-up, click on the down arrow beside Vertical Alignment to display the list box with the available alignment options (see fig. 4.23).

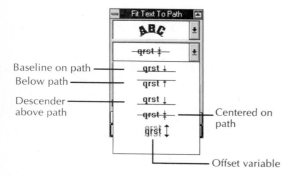

Baseline on path
Below path
Descender above path
Centered on path
Offset variable

Figure 4.23
Vertical Alignment options.

Horizontal Alignment

Click on the down arrow beside Horizontal Alignment to display the list box with the available alignment options (see fig. 4.24). See figure 4.25 for examples of vertical and horizontal alignment.

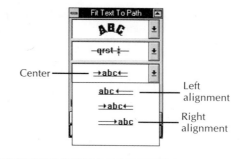

Center
Left alignment
Right alignment

Figure 4.24
Horizontal Alignment options.

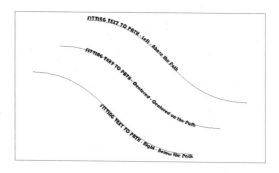

Figure 4.25
Effects of vertical and horizontal alignment.

Text Orientation

The Text Orientation options in the Fit Text To Path roll-up enable you to choose the way text lies on the path. You can choose from four options (see fig. 4.26):

- **Rotate Letters.** Choose the Rotate Letters option if you want the letters to follow the contour of the path.

- **Vertical Skew.** Choose the Vertical Skew option if you want the letters to be vertically skewed in orientation to the path.

■ **Horizontal Skew.** Choose the Horizontal Skew option if you want the letters to be horizontally skewed in orientation to the path.

■ **Upright Letters.** Choose the Upright Letters option if you want to force the letters to remain vertically oriented.

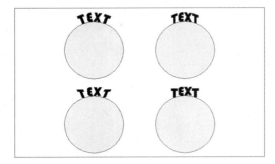

Figure 4.26
Text orientation.

horizontal alignment of the text placed on the triangle is left-aligned, and the horizontal offset is .65". The **D**istance From Path value was modified to place a gap of .10" between the path of the arc and the text. The horizontal alignment is set to align center.

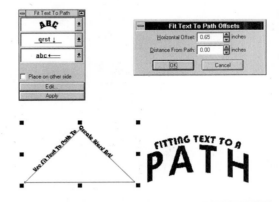

Figure 4.27
Horizontal Offset and Distance From Path.

Adjusting Text on a Path

The text follows the outline of the control object. By default, the first character is placed at the first node of a path if horizontal alignment is set to align left. If you want to adjust the text to lie a set distance from the path or to be shifted along the path, click on Edit in the Fit Text To Path roll-up. The Fit Text To Path Offsets dialog box appears, from which you can edit the placement of the text with precision.

The value you enter in the **H**orizontal Offset numeric entry box is in relation to the horizontal alignment. The horizontal offset in figure 4.27 was modified to balance the appearance of the text on the triangle. The

You can interactively adjust the text on a path. To change the distance between the text and the path, depress the Ctrl key while you click on the text to select it. Click and drag to adjust the distance between the path and the text. If you pause in the movement briefly, a representation of the path appears. This representation indicates the distance between the baseline of the text and the path. To shift the text along the path, select the Shape tool. Marquee-select all the nodes in the text string, and drag them along the path to move the text. If you want to move only a portion of the text string, select the nodes that represent that portion. With the nodes selected, you can use nudge to move the text in the direction you want.

Fitting Text to a Circle or Rectangle

When you select a circle or rectangle as the path for your text string, a quadrant icon appears that enables you to choose how the text is placed on the path (see fig. 4.28). The center point of the text string is aligned with the center point of the quadrant you select.

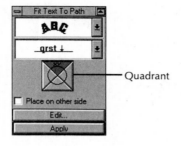

Quadrant

Figure 4.28
Fit Text To Path roll-up quadrant.

Choosing Place on Other Side

When you enable Place on other side, the text shifts to the opposite side of the path. Text appears mirrored horizontally and vertically. Offsets and other options you have selected are observed after you click Apply.

If Place on other side is enabled, selecting left or right horizontal alignment from the quadrant reverses the alignment. If you want to reverse the text but have it remain on the same side of the path as it originally was, choose the opposite alignment.

The example in figure 4.29 shows text fitted to a circle. Both the top and bottom text

were placed by selecting the top quadrant. To move the bottom text string below the path, the distance from the path was edited.

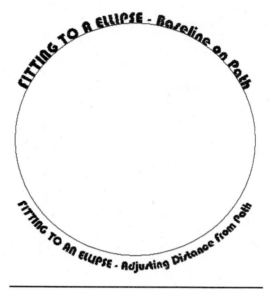

Figure 4.29
Text fitted to a circle.

Editing Text on a Path

To edit text that has been placed on a path, depress the Ctrl key while you select the text. Then choose Edit Text from the **T**ext menu to access the Edit Text dialog box.

You can change the fill or outline color of either the text or the path as you do for any other object. You also can change the character attributes if you want. When the control object has an irregular shape, changing the character and word spacing gives the text a balanced appearance.

Editing the Control Object

Editing the control object affects the text linked to it. You can scale, stretch, rotate, or skew the control object, and the text moves with it to reflect the changes you make. If you want to change the center of rotation, either group the text and control object, or move the center of rotation of the control object. Grouping the two objects speeds screen refresh time while maintaining the relationship between the text and the path. Changing the center of rotation for the text alone might cause undesirable results when rotation is applied. If this situation occurs, select the Undo command.

After you are satisfied with the appearance of the text along the path, you can detach the control object and delete it if you want. To detach the text from the control object, select **S**eparate from the **A**rrange menu. This option breaks the link between the text and the control object. After the link is broken, the text can no longer be edited using the Fit Text To Path roll-up. Apply **S**traighten Text from the **T**ext menu if you want to straighten the baseline of the text.

Using Paragraph Text

You can create text-intensive documents in CorelDRAW by using the Paragraph text options. These options are useful when you design brochures, booklets, and catalogs. In addition to the editing features available for Artistic text, CorelDRAW offers enhanced formatting features for use with Paragraph text. The enhanced formatting enables you to use bullets, indents, tabs, and columns and to flow text between frames. Unlike Artistic text, Paragraph text automatically word-wraps.

Working within Paragraph Limits

Paragraph text supports a maximum of 8,000 characters per paragraph. This restriction does not limit your capability to create large documents, however, because you can have up to 16,000 paragraphs in a set of linked frames and up to 16,000 sets of linked frames. Thus it is theoretically possible to have 256 billion paragraphs or 2.048^{12} characters. These numbers are somewhat unrealistic because you can have a maximum of 999 pages in a CorelDRAW document. The likelihood of approaching the maximum number of paragraphs is remote. Memory considerations suggest that you use applications such as CorelVENTURA for extremely large documents, unless you have a considerable amount of resources.

N O T E

Print Merge cannot be used with Paragraph text.

Creating a Frame

Paragraph text is flowed into a text frame. Text frames can be stretched, scaled, rotated, and skewed in the same manner as objects. When you scale or stretch a text frame, however, the size of the text within the frame does not change. To create a text frame,

select the Paragraph Text tool from the Text tool fly-out menu (Shift+F8). Click on the printable page to create a page-size frame that is centered on the page (see fig. 4.30). If you click outside the printable page, a page-size frame is created, but the upper left corner of the frame appears at the location where you clicked. Click and drag the cursor to create a text frame that is larger or smaller than page size.

Figure 4.30

The Paragraph text frame.

If you have on-screen editing enabled, you can enter the text you want in the frame. If you want to import text into the text frame, you must use the Edit Text dialog box. For more information about importing text, see the section later in this chapter titled "Editing and Formatting Paragraph Text."

Flowing Text between Frames

Multiple-page frames can be linked together. This option enables text to flow naturally from one frame to another. The linked frames can be on the same page or on different pages. When you resize a linked frame, the text automatically flows into the appropriate linked frame. For example, if you resized the first frame of a linked set of three frames by making it smaller, the overflow text would move to the second and then to the third frame. Similarly, if you enlarged the first frame, the text would flow into it from the second frame.

To flow text between multiple frames on the same page, follow these steps:

1. Create a page frame, and fill it with text. Resize the frame as you want.

2. Use the Pick tool to select the frame, and click on the hollow handle at the bottom of the paragraph frame.

3. Click and drag another frame to automatically create a linked frame. Alternatively, you can click on an existing frame to create a linked frame manually. With either method, the overflow text flows into the second frame.

To flow text between multiple frames on different pages, you must change to the page on which you want the linked frame to appear before creating the second frame. The location of the plus (+) sign indicates the direction of the text flow. If the plus sign is in the top hollow handle, text flows from the preceding frame; if the plus sign is in the bottom hollow handle, text flows to the subsequent frame (see fig. 4.31).

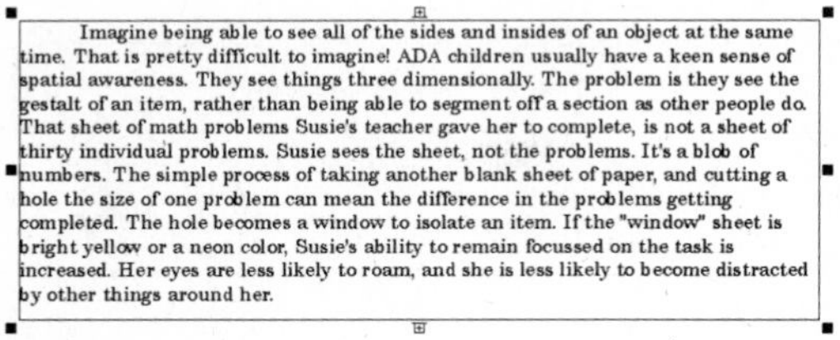

Imagine being able to see all of the sides and insides of an object at the same time. That is pretty difficult to imagine! ADA children usually have a keen sense of spatial awareness. They see things three dimensionally. The problem is they see the gestalt of an item, rather than being able to segment off a section as other people do. That sheet of math problems Susie's teacher gave her to complete, is not a sheet of thirty individual problems. Susie sees the sheet, not the problems. It's a blob of numbers. The simple process of taking another blank sheet of paper, and cutting a hole the size of one problem can mean the difference in the problems getting completed. The hole becomes a window to isolate an item. If the "window" sheet is bright yellow or a neon color, Susie's ability to remain focussed on the task is increased. Her eyes are less likely to roam, and she is less likely to become distracted by other things around her.

Figure 4.31

Linked Paragraph text frames.

To break the links between frames, you select the frame from which you want to remove the link and choose **S**eparate from the **A**rrange menu. Any text contained in that frame flows into the other frames, and the selected frame is cleared. If you want to break the link between two frames but have the existing text remain in its respective frame, you select both frames and apply **S**eparate to complete the operation.

Shaping a Frame

You can shape a text frame by skewing, rotating, or applying an envelope to the frame. The Paragraph text follows the contour of the frame while retaining its justification and other attributes. You skew or rotate a text frame as you skew or rotate any object (see fig. 4.32).

To apply an envelope to a page frame, use the Pick tool to select the page frame. Choose the **E**nvelope Roll-Up option from the Effe**c**ts menu. Select the options you want from the roll-up, adjust the envelope, and then click on Apply (see fig. 4.33). For more information about using the Envelope roll-up, see Chapter 11, "Creating with Special Effects."

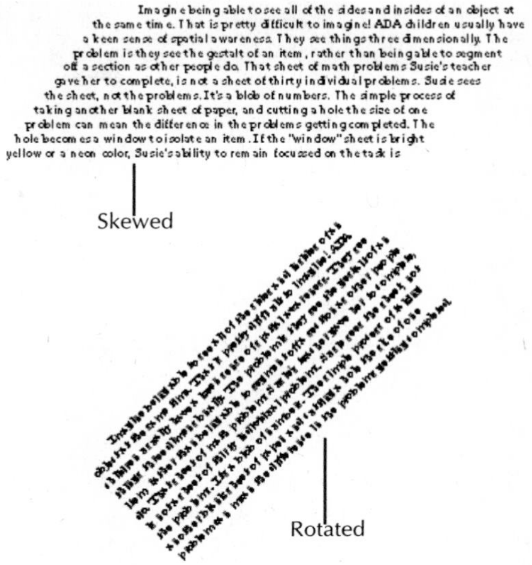

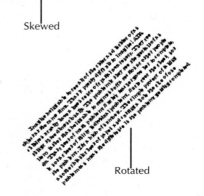

Imagine being able to see all of the sides and insides of an object at the same time. That is pretty difficult to imagine! ADA children usually have a keen sense of spatial awareness. They see things three dimensionally. The problem is they see the gestalt of an item, rather than being able to segment off a section as other people do. That sheet of math problems Susie's teacher gave her to complete, is not a sheet of thirty individual problems. Susie sees the sheet, not the problems. It's a blob of numbers. The simple process of taking another blank sheet of paper, and cutting a hole the size of one problem can mean the difference in the problems getting completed. The hole becomes a window to isolate an item. If the "window" sheet is bright yellow or a neon color, Susie's ability to remain focussed on the task is

Skewed

Rotated

Figure 4.32

Skewed and rotated text frames.

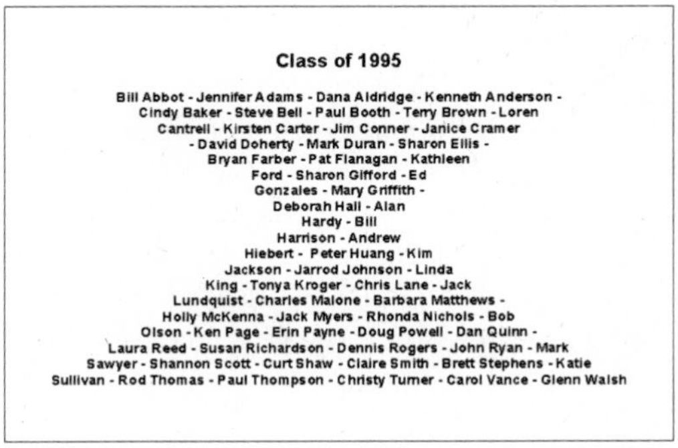

Class of 1995

Bill Abbot - Jennifer Adams - Dana Aldridge - Kenneth Anderson - Cindy Baker - Steve Bell - Paul Booth - Terry Brown - Loren Cantrell - Kirsten Carter - Jim Conner - Janice Cramer - David Doherty - Mark Duran - Sharon Ellis - Bryan Farber - Pat Flanagan - Kathleen Ford - Sharon Gifford - Ed Gonzales - Mary Griffith - Deborah Hall - Alan Hardy - Bill Harrison - Andrew Hiebert - Peter Huang - Kim Jackson - Jarrod Johnson - Linda King - Tonya Kroger - Chris Lane - Jack Lundquist - Charles Malone - Barbara Matthews - Holly McKenna - Jack Myers - Rhonda Nichols - Bob Olson - Ken Page - Erin Payne - Doug Powell - Dan Quinn - Laura Reed - Susan Richardson - Dennis Rogers - John Ryan - Mark Sawyer - Shannon Scott - Curt Shaw - Claire Smith - Brett Stephens - Katie Sullivan - Rod Thomas - Paul Thompson - Christy Turner - Carol Vance - Glenn Walsh

Figure 4.33

An envelope applied to a page frame.

If an envelope has been applied to a paragraph frame, the text contained in the frame cannot be edited interactively. To edit the text, you must use the Edit Text dialog box.

Editing and Formatting Paragraph Text

You can edit Paragraph text interactively or by using the Edit Text dialog box. The process of editing Paragraph text on-screen is identical to that of editing Artistic text on-screen. After you select the text with the Paragraph Text tool, the screen changes to reflect that you have entered the Paragraph text-editing mode (see fig. 4.34). In addition to adding and editing text using the Clipboard, you can import text from other applications. CorelDRAW supports many popular text formats, including WordPerfect, Microsoft Word, and Ami Pro. When you import text from one of the supported formats, formatting information is retained. If you import ASCII text, the page frame is sized according to the page dimensions and margins of the current CorelDRAW document.

To import text, select **I**mport from the **F**ile menu, choose the file you want to import, and click on OK. The text appears in a frame placed on top of any other objects that are on the page. Reposition either the objects or the text frame. Subsequent frames are placed on additional pages, as required by the size of the imported document. For more information about importing, see Chapter 40, "Importing and Exporting."

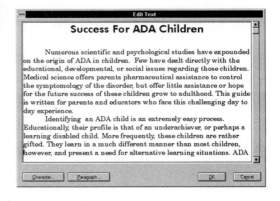

Figure 4.34
The Paragraph text editing window.

Formatting Options

You access the Paragraph text formatting options by clicking on the **P**aragraph option from the **T**ext menu. The Paragraph dialog box opens with four property sheets—Spacing, Tabs, Indents, and Bullets. You access each of these property sheets by clicking on the respective tab.

Spacing

The Spacing property sheet (see fig. 4.35) enables you to enter values for characters, words, and lines, as well as for the spacing before and after paragraphs. You also can set alignment and hyphenation options.

The following list briefly describes the options in the Spacing property sheet:

- **Character.** The Character setting determines the percentage of space between characters within a word. Character spacing is based on the letter m. The exact amount of space depends on the font you select and the way it kerns. CorelDRAW version 5.0 includes CorelKERN, which enables you to adjust the way an individual font kerns.

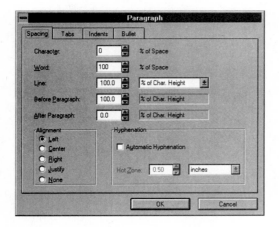

Figure 4.35
The Spacing property sheet.

- **Word.** The Word setting determines the percentage of space between words. Word spacing is proportionate to character spacing and uses that information to calculate the space.

- **Line.** The Line setting defines the space between lines of text. The way CorelDRAW calculates this space depends on the selection you make in the drop-down list box beside the entry. The default is a percentage of the character height. If you use the default, the program adds the percentage of the first line's descender and the second line's ascender. If you specify a point size, the program subtracts the font's point size from the value you set

here to yield the amount of space. If you choose percentage of point size, the program bases the calculation on the point size of the largest letter in the second line.

- **Alignment.** The Alignment section enables you to select from five alignment options—Left, Center, Right, Justify, or None.

- **Hyphenation.** The Hyphenation option enables you to set automatic hyphenation. When Automatic Hyphenation is checked, you can set the value for the *hot zone*. Select inches, millimeters, picas/points, or points from the drop-down list box, and enter the value you want in the entry box. A larger hot zone value results in less hyphenation and a more ragged right margin; a smaller hot zone value results in more hyphenation and a smoother right margin (see fig. 4.36).

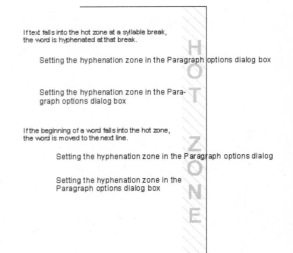

Figure 4.36
The hyphenation hot zone.

Tabs

The Tabs property sheet (see fig. 4.37) enables you to set the tab stops for your document. You can change the tab interval from the default increment of .5", or you can add individual tab stops. You also can move tabs interactively in the drawing window.

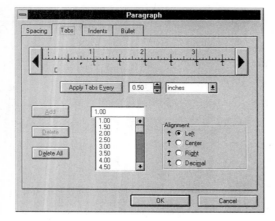

Figure 4.37
The Tabs property sheet.

To change the preset tab increments, follow these steps:

1. Use the Paragraph Text tool to select a paragraph.

2. Choose **P**aragraph from the **T**ext menu, and select the Tabs property sheet.

3. Select a unit of measurement from the drop-down list box. (The default is inches.)

4. Type the new value in the box next to Apply **T**abs Every, and then click on OK.

To add individual tab stops, follow these steps:

1. Use the Paragraph Text tool to select a paragraph.

2. Choose **P**aragraph from the **T**ext menu, and select the Tabs property sheet.

3. Choose an Alignment option.

4. Click on the ruler at the position you want the new tab stop. You can drag the tab stop to the desired location. A tab icon appears in the ruler window, indicating the position of the new tab. Alternatively, you can type the position you want in the Tabs entry box and click on **A**dd. The left margin of the document is 0".

To move tab stops interactively, follow these steps:

1. Use the Paragraph Text tool to select a paragraph.

2. On the paragraph ruler at the top of the drawing window, click and drag a tab stop icon to a new location.

The Tabs property sheet offers four options for setting alignment (see fig. 4.38):

■ **Left Alignment.** The left edge of the text aligns with the tab stop and continues to the right. The Le**f**t alignment option is the default tab alignment.

■ **Center Alignment.** The Ce**n**ter alignment option centers the text on the tab stop.

■ **Right Alignment.** The Right alignment option extends the text left from the tab stop and then right when the tab space is filled.

- **Decimal Alignment.** The Decimal alignment option centers the decimal point in the text on the tab stop. If the text has no decimal points, the text extends to the left from the tab stop.

This text has left tab alignment, set at one-half inch intervals.

This text has center tab alignment, set at one-half inch intervals.

This text has right tab alignment, set at one-half inch intervals.

1.0 This text has decimal tab alignment, set at one-half inch intervals.

Figure 4.38
Tab alignment.

Indents

The Indents property sheet (see fig. 4.39) enables you to set indenting values for your document. Indents can be set for the whole document or for individual paragraph frames. CorelDRAW also enables you to set indents interactively. The following indenting options are available:

- **First Line.** The First Line option indents the first line of the text.

- **Rest Of Lines.** The Rest Of Lines option indents the balance of the lines in the paragraph frame.

- **Left Margin.** The Left Margin option sets the indent from the left margin of the paragraph frame. If you have bullets enabled, the Bullet Indent option replaces the Left Margin indent. Bullet Indent enables you to set the indent for bullets in your document.

- **Right Margin.** The Right Margin option sets the indent from the right margin of the paragraph frame.

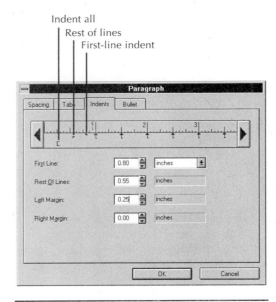

Figure 4.39
The Indents property sheet.

To set indents, you enter the values you want in the entry boxes. You also can drag the left bracket on the ruler in the Indents property sheet to indent the entire paragraph. Drag the top arrow to indent the first line; drag the bottom arrow to indent the rest of the lines (see fig. 4.40).

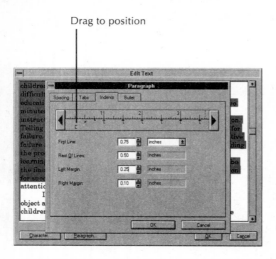

Drag to position

Figure 4.40
Setting indents interactively in the Indents property sheet.

When you first set a paragraph frame in CorelDRAW, the program sets default margins and tabs (see fig. 4.41). You can click and drag the margins on the paragraph formatting ruler in the drawing window to reset them. You are limited, however, by the size of the frame. If you want to set the margins beyond the default frame size, you need to stretch or scale the frame. You also can click and drag the indent markers for the first line and subsequent lines.

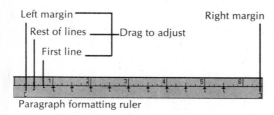

Left margin
Rest of lines — Drag to adjust
First line
Right margin
Paragraph formatting ruler

Figure 4.41
Modifying margins and indents in the drawing window.

Bullets

The Bullet property sheet (see fig. 4.42) enables you to activate and add bullets to your document. You can select bullets by symbol numbers or by small thumbnail images. The library list box remains grayed out until you enable bullets by checking the Bullet On box. To display the associated thumbnails, select the library you want. CorelDRAW offers you a selection of thousands of symbols that you can use as bullets. You can add a bullet to the beginning of any paragraph.

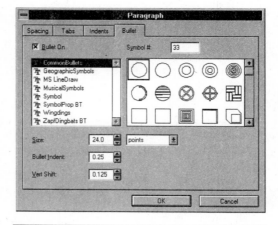

Figure 4.42
The Bullet property sheet.

You select a bullet by clicking on it. Enter the size you want in the Size entry box, and set the amount of indention you want. When bullets are enabled, the text following the bullet is indented by the amount specified in the First Line indent. The amount of the indention must be less than or equal to the values set for the First Line and Rest Of Lines options. To indent all the lines by the same amount, enter an identical value for the First Line and Rest Of Line indents. When you enter a value in the Vert Shift entry box, you can position the bullet up or down in relation to the text. Click on OK to return to the drawing window.

Setting Frame Attributes

CorelDRAW enables you to set Paragraph text in columns. You can have a maximum of eight columns of text, and the columns don't have to be the same width. To format a paragraph frame with columns, you select the frame and then choose Frame from the Text menu. The Frame Attributes dialog box appears (see fig. 4.43). From this dialog box, you can set the following options:

- **Number of Columns.** Enter the number of columns you want in the Number of Columns box.

- **Equal Column Widths.** The Equal Column Widths option forces all the columns to be the same width.

- **Column #.** Enter the number of the column you want to format in the Column # box. The Column # option remains grayed out unless Equal Column Widths is disabled.

- **Width.** If Equal Column Widths is enabled, set the width for all columns in the Width box. When you are formatting individual columns, set the value associated with the Column #. The default value is the width of the paragraph frame.

- **Gutter.** If Equal Column Widths is enabled, set the width for all gutters in the Gutter box. When you are formatting individual columns, set the value

associated with the Column #. The default value is 0.0", but you can set any value up to 2.0".

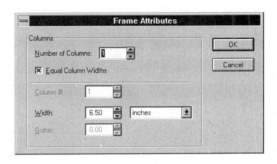

Figure 4.43
The Frame Attributes dialog box.

The sum of the gutter value plus the column width cannot exceed 30 inches. A column must be a minimum of .25 inches wide.

Using the Text Roll-Up

The Text roll-up (see fig. 4.44) enables you to apply formatting and character attributes on-screen. The Text roll-up is an alternative to the separate menus normally used for formatting and character attribute options. To display the Text roll-up in the drawing window, choose the Text Roll-Up option from the Text menu. The keyboard shortcut is Ctrl+F2.

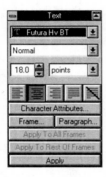

Figure 4.44
The Text roll-up.

The Text roll-up offers the following formatting and character attribute options:

- **Typeface list box.** The Typeface list box enables you to choose a typeface by clicking on the down arrow beside the box. Hold the mouse button down on the typeface name to display a sample (see fig. 4.45).

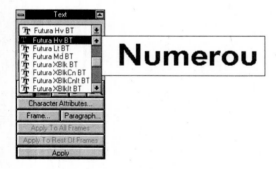

Figure 4.45
A typeface sample.

- **Style list box.** The Style list box enables you to choose one of the type styles available for the selected typeface. The styles available vary for different typefaces.

- **Type Size.** The Type Size option enables you to set the size and select the unit of measurement.

- **Alignment.** The Alignment option enables you to choose from left, center, right, justified, or no alignment.

- **Character Attributes.** The Character Attributes option accesses the Character Attributes dialog box.

- **Frame.** The Frame option accesses the Frame Attributes dialog box.

- **Paragraph.** The Paragraph option displays formatting options available for Paragraph text.

- **Apply To All Frames.** The Apply To All Frames selection applies the options you set to the selected paragraph frame and to all subsequent linked frames.

- **Apply To Rest Of Frames.** The Apply To Rest Of Frames selection applies the options you set to the selected frame and to all previous or subsequent linked frames.

- **Apply.** The Apply selection applies the options you set to an Artistic text selection or to a selected frame.

Using Styles for Formatting

Applying formatting options to individual Paragraph text frames can be a tedious and time-consuming operation. CorelDRAW enables you to create formatting styles. A *style* contains all the formatting choices you have selected, and it can be applied to multiple paragraphs in a single step. You also can use styles to update paragraph formatting by making the formatting changes in the style and then applying the style to those paragraphs tagged with that style. For more information on using styles, see Chapter 12, "Working with Layouts."

Using Extract and Merge-Back

The Extract command enables you to save selected Artistic or Paragraph text in an ASCII text file for editing in a word processing program. After you have made the editing changes you want, the Merge-Back command reinserts the text in the original location (see fig. 4.46). Extract and Merge-Back should be used only for major edits of large quantities of text. You can make minor revisions either in CorelDRAW or by using OLE functions to move the text between applications.

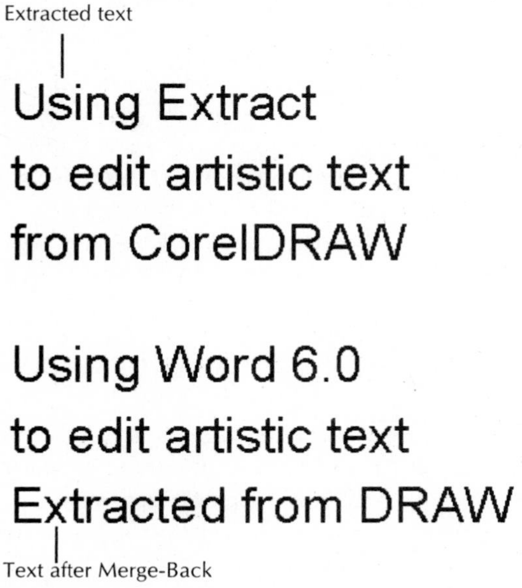

Extracted text

Using Extract
to edit artistic text
from CorelDRAW

Using Word 6.0
to edit artistic text
Extracted from DRAW

Text after Merge-Back

Figure 4.46
An example of Extract and Merge-Back.

When you apply the Merge-Back command, the text that originated in CorelDRAW retains the attributes that were assigned to it. These attributes include typeface, point size, spacing, and so on. On the other hand, text added in the word processing application may or may not conform to these attributes. You may have to apply these attributes after you issue the Merge-Back command.

W A R N I N G

Extract and Merge-Back are not designed for use with Artistic text that has been modified with one of the special effects, such as Extrude or Blend. This type of use can cause unexpected results. At the least, kerning and other character attributes can be lost. More seriously, the program can crash or your computer can lock up, requiring that you reboot your system. Before you attempt to use the Extract and Merge-Back commands, therefore, be certain to save the file.

To use the Extract and Merge-Back commands, follow these steps:

1. Save any changes you have made to the document. Do not apply changes to the file after you select Extract, or Merge-Back may fail.

2. Select Extract from the Special menu to display the Extract dialog box (see fig. 4.47). Enter the file path and file name for the extracted text, and then click on OK.

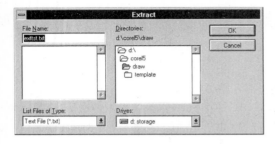

Figure 4.47
The Extract dialog box.

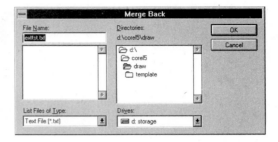

Figure 4.48
The Merge-Back dialog box.

3. Close or minimize CorelDRAW.

4. Open the file in your word processing application. Note that when you edit Artistic text, the text strings are listed individually from the most recent to the least recent. Paragraph text appears as blocks of text in the original order, with paragraph code numbers at the start of every paragraph. Do not change the order of the text strings or paragraphs.

5. Make the editing changes you want, taking care not to delete or modify any of the string codes. If you make changes to the string codes, Merge-Back will fail.

6. Save the changes in ASCII format, and close the application.

7. Restore CorelDRAW, or reopen the original CDR file in CorelDRAW.

8. Select Merge-Back from the Special menu to display the Merge-Back dialog box (see fig. 4.48). Enter the file path and file name for the text you saved in step 6, and click on OK.

9. The document, including the changes you made in your word processing application, appears on the screen. You can save the file or continue to work with your document.

Using Text Aids

CorelDRAW provides text aids to make the process of creating documents easier. You can use these text aids with both Artistic and Paragraph text. The Spell Checker and the Thesaurus are among the CorelDRAW text aids that help you to proof and edit your text. This section describes five text aids you can use to create professional-quality documents in CorelDRAW.

Type Assist

The Type Assist dialog box (see fig. 4.49) enables you to automatically correct common typing, spelling, and capitalization errors. You can customize the Type Assist option to meet your personal needs. If you enter words or phrases you frequently misuse, Type Assist can replace them with the proper forms of the words or phrases. Perhaps you have a tendency to write contractional words such as "don't" and "can't"; you can have the program automatically replace these words with "do not" and "cannot." Abbreviations (such as info for information) can be replaced automatically. Type Assist also supports extended characters and punctuation marks.

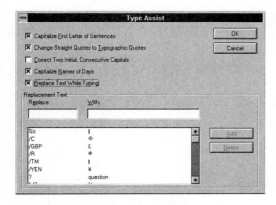

Figure 4.49
The Type Assist dialog box.

To use Type Assist, follow these steps:

1. Select Type Assist from the Text menu to display the Type Assist dialog box.

2. Enable the options you want by clicking on the check boxes.

3. To add text that you want Type Assist to insert automatically, enable the Replace Text While Typing option, and type a name for the replacement text. Be sure to type the word exactly as you would in a document. If you commonly misspell a word, type the word misspelled in the Replace box. If you commonly type "thier" instead of

"their," for example, type "thier" in the Replace box. Be careful not to enter homonyms or actual words in the box, or the program will use the replacement text every time you type the word. You can use up to 64 characters, but no spaces, in the Replace box.

4. In the With box, type the replacement text (that is, the text you want to replace the text in the Replace box with). You can insert up to 255 characters, including spaces and punctuation. To insert an extended character, depress the Alt key while you enter the character's four-digit code number.

5. Click on the Add button, and then click on OK to return to the drawing window. You can remove entries by selecting the entry and clicking on Delete.

Type Assist includes a list of common abbreviations and replacement suggestions in the list box. Any additions you make to the list are stored for future CorelDRAW sessions. If you need to reinstall CorelDRAW at any time, be sure to make a backup of CORELDRW.TPA in the custom directory of CorelDRAW.

Spell Checker

The Spell Check dialog box (see fig. 4.50) enables you to check your document for spelling errors. If an unrecognized word is found, you can either add the word to a custom dictionary or correct the spelling of the word.

Figure 4.50
The Spell Check dialog box.

Spell Checker is always available. You can use it to check the spelling of any word, including words not in your document. To check the spelling of a word, choose the Spell Checker option from the **T**ext menu, enter the word you want to check in the **U**nknown Word box, and click on **B**egin Check.

To use the Spell Checker, follow these steps:

1. Select the text you want to check. You can select multiple strings of text or paragraph frames if you want.

2. Choose Spell Ch**e**cker from the **T**ext menu to display the Spell Check dialog box.

3. Click on the **R**ange button to select from the available options: Check Word, Text Block, Highlighted Text, or All Document Text.

4. Click on **B**egin Check.

5. If the Spell Checker finds an unrecognized word, you have the following options:

- Correct the spelling by choosing one of the words from the list box or by entering the correct spelling in the Change **T**o box. Then click on the **C**hange button to continue.

- Click on **S**kip to leave the word unchanged.

- Click on Sk**i**p All to leave the word and subsequent occurrences of the word unchanged.

- Click on **A**dd Word to add the word to a custom dictionary.

- Click on Close if you want to cancel the spell checking process before its completion.

- A dialog box appears informing you that the spell checking process is complete. Click on OK to return to the drawing window.

Creating a Custom Dictionary

CorelDRAW enables you to create a custom or personal dictionary to which you can add words. To create a custom dictionary, open the Spell Check dialog box. Click on Cr**e**ate, and then enter a name for the dictionary. The name can have up to eight characters. When a word is displayed that you want to add to a custom dictionary, select the dictionary from the **D**ictionary list box, and click on **A**dd Word. When all the words have been checked, choose OK to return to the drawing window.

When you create a custom dictionary, a file with the eight-character name and a DIC extension is stored in the Custom directory of CorelDRAW. Be sure to create a backup of this file. If for any reason you need to delete CorelDRAW from your hard disk, this backup ensures that the dictionary will be available for use when you reinstall CorelDRAW.

Thesaurus

The Thesaurus dialog box (see fig. 4.51) enables you to find and choose synonyms for selected words. To assist you in the appropriate selection of a word, the thesaurus allows you to select from a list of definitions. This is especially helpful when a word has more than one definition, or when you want to look up a definition for a word.

Figure 4.51
The Thesaurus dialog box.

To use the Thesaurus, follow these steps:

1. With the Text tool, highlight the word for which you want to find synonyms.

2. Select Thesaurus from the **T**ext menu to display the Thesaurus dialog box with the selected word in the Looked

Up box. If the word is also in the dictionary, its definition appears in the **D**efinitions box. If the word has multiple definitions, all known definitions appear in the box.

3. Choose the definition that most closely approximates your use of the word, and a list of possible synonyms appears in the R**e**place With list box. Click on **P**revious, if you want to go back to the previous definition you selected.

4. Choose a synonym to replace the selected word, and it appears in the Replace With box. Click on **R**eplace, and then click on Close to return to the drawing window.

5. If you don't find an appropriate synonym, click on Close without choosing **R**eplace to return to the drawing window.

Thesaurus is always available. You can search for synonyms and definitions of words not contained in your document by accessing the Thesaurus dialog box and entering the word in the Looked **U**p box. After you have entered the word, follow steps 3-5 as previously described.

Find and Replace

The Find and Replace commands enable you to search for words and phrases in your document. The Find command locates the word or phrase, and the Replace command substitutes another word or phrase.

T I P

You can use Replace to delete text by leaving the Replace With box empty.

The Match **C**ase option enables you to force the search to be case-sensitive and to ignore words that do not match exactly. If Match **C**ase in enabled, however, words might be ignored that you want replaced. If you want to replace occurrences of the word "this" with the word "that," for example, and you enter these words in lowercase letters, the words are ignored if they fall at the beginning of a sentence. If Match **C**ase is disabled, the replacement word matches the case of the word being replaced.

The text cursor indicates the beginning location of the search. When CorelDRAW reaches the end of the text, it asks if you want to continue searching from the beginning of the text. If you are searching for Paragraph text, all the associated linked frames are searched. If you are searching multiple strings of Artistic text, the line that contains the word is selected by the search.

To find text, follow these steps:

1. Select F**i**nd from the **T**ext menu to display the Find dialog box (see fig. 4.52).

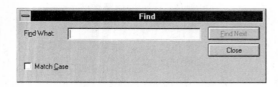

Figure 4.52
The Find dialog box.

2. In the Fi**n**d What box, enter the text you want to find. You can enter a maximum of 100 characters, including spaces and punctuation marks.

3. Enable Match **C**ase if you want, and then click on **F**ind Next to begin the search. CorelDRAW highlights the first occurrence of the text in the Paragraph text frame. Choose **F**ind Next again to continue searching through the remaining text.

4. To edit the text you find, return to the drawing window by clicking on Close.

To replace text, follow these steps:

1. Choose Repl**a**ce from the **T**ext menu to display the Replace dialog box (see fig. 4.53).

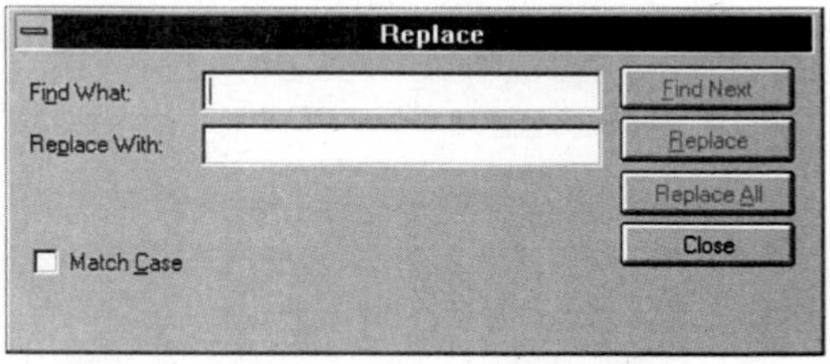

Figure 4.53
The Replace dialog box.

2. In the Fi**n**d What box, enter the text you want to find. You can enter a maximum of 100 characters, including spaces and punctuation marks.

3. Enter the text you want to replace in the Re**p**lace With box.

4. Enable Match **C**ase if you want, and then click on **F**ind Next to begin the search. CorelDRAW highlights the

first occurrence of the text in the Paragraph text frame. Choose **F**ind Next again to continue searching through the remaining text.

5. Select **R**eplace to confirm the replacement of each occurrence of the text. To change all occurrences of the word in the document, select Replace **A**ll.

> ### W A R N I N G
>
> Selecting Undo after you apply the Find and Replace commands undoes the changes made; however, it also undoes all changes made since you last entered the text-editing mode.

PANOSE Font Matching

With the PANOSE Font Matching feature, you can substitute fonts that appear in the drawing but are not installed on your system. By default, P**A**NOSE Font Matching is enabled in the Text property sheet of the Preferences dialog box. For more information about PANOSE Font Matching, see Chapter 46, "Font Management."

Using Symbols

CorelDRAW offers you a collection of over 5,000 symbols. Each symbol is a vector-format graphic object and can be edited as you edit other graphic objects. The symbols are categorized by type and use in smaller symbol libraries. To access the symbol libraries, you use the Symbols roll-up (see fig. 4.54). You can open the Symbols roll-up by clicking on the Symbol button on the

ribbon bar or by choosing the Sym**b**ols Roll-Up option from the **S**pecial menu. The keyboard shortcut is Ctrl+F11.

Figure 4.54
The Symbols roll-up.

To use symbols in your document, follow these steps:

1. Select a symbol library from the library list box in the Symbols roll-up, and choose a symbol by clicking on it. Alternatively, you can use the clip art and symbols catalog to choose a symbol. Select the corresponding category in the Symbols roll-up, and enter the associated index number in the # box.

2. Select or enter an initial size for the symbol in the Size box of the Symbols roll-up. The units of measurement correspond with those of the vertical ruler in the drawing window. If necessary, the symbol can be scaled or stretched in the drawing window.

3. Click on the symbol and drag it onto the drawing page.

Tiling Symbols

CorelDRAW enables you to use symbols to create a tiled pattern. This option is useful for creating an overall background pattern behind other objects or text (see fig. 4.55). After you create the pattern in the drawing window, you can edit the symbols individually. To edit the symbols as a single unit, either group or combine them to create an object group or a single object. Click Tile in the Symbols roll-up to enable the tiling option, and then select the **O**ptions button to set the spacing between the symbols. The spacing is relative to the horizontal and vertical rulers, respectively. If you enable **P**roportional sizing, you need to enter only one value.

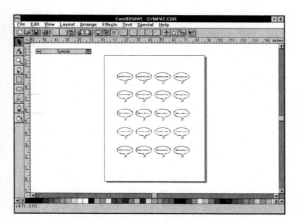

Figure 4.55
Symbol tiling.

N O T E

To avoid having symbols overlap, select a symbol size that is either larger or smaller than the grid size.

Adding Symbols to a Library

You can create and add symbols to existing libraries. To add a symbol to a library, follow these steps:

1. Create or import the object you want for a symbol. Note that you cannot create a symbol from grouped objects. Also, the object must be a single object. The symbol shown in figure 4.56 was created by applying the Combine command to a selection of objects to create a single object. The object can be any size, because it is automatically scaled to match the symbols in the libraries.

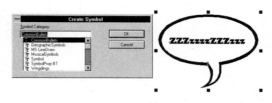

Figure 4.56
Creating a symbol.

2. With the object selected, choose the Create **S**ymbol option from the **S**pecial menu to display the Create Symbol dialog box.

3. Enter the name of the library to which you want to add the symbol. Alternatively, you can click on a category name from the **S**ymbol Category list.

4. Choose OK to return to the drawing window. The symbol appears at the end of the list in the associated library category of the Symbols roll-up.

You also can create entire new custom symbol libraries. For more information about creating new libraries, see Chapter 46, "Font Management."

Summary

The extensive Paragraph and Artistic text features of CorelDRAW offer you excellent creative control of the text in your documents. You can create both large and small documents that combine text and graphics. CorelDRAW also offers font management, including the capability to create your own typefaces. For more information about font management, see Chapter 46. In addition to the text-editing features discussed in this chapter, you also can edit text with the Shape tool, which provides a flexibility that is unavailable in other programs. In the next chapter, the Shape tool and its editing capabilities are discussed in greater detail.

Chapter 5

Shaping Objects

*O*ne of the advantages of using a vector based
graphics package is the ability to edit the shape of
objects individually. Each object, unless it is
linked to another object, behaves as a self-
contained unit with no inherent relationship to
the other objects in the drawing. An object's shape
is based upon path segments calculated mathematically rather than being pixel-based. Bitmap
packages rely on anti-aliasing to create smooth
curves. CorelDRAW allows you to create and edit
curves, adjusting the smoothness to your needs.

Chapter 4 discussed using the Shape tool to
interactively kern text. Its primary use, however,
is to edit the basic shape of curved objects. The
Shape tool is used in conjunction with the Node
Edit roll-up. The commands available in the
Node Edit roll-up are not available via any of
the menus. This makes the use of the Shape tool
totally interactive.

This chapter covers:

- Working with rectangles
  and circles

- Shaping objects

- Working with bitmaps
  and traced images

Working with Rectangles and Circles

Rectangles and ellipses are geometric objects. Their vector descriptions are different from those of curved objects. The Shape tool interacts in another manner with rectangles and ellipses. The Shape tool allows you to round the corners of a rectangle and create arcs and wedges from ellipses. Creating these shapes in another manner would be a tedious operation.

To round the corners of a selected rectangle:

In each corner of a rectangle is a node. Using the Shape tool, click and drag the node as shown in figure 5.1. Note that all four corners are rounded evenly. The status line displays the radius of the curve, allowing you to control the amount of the curve.

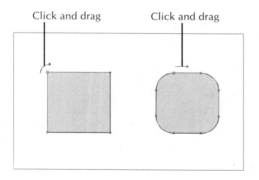

Click and drag   Click and drag

Figure 5.1
Rounding the corners of a rectangle.

If you stretch or skew a rectangle with rounded corners, the corners become elliptical.

To create an arc or wedge from a selected ellipse:

At the top of an ellipse is the control node. Click and drag the node around the ellipse, as shown in figure 5.2, to create an arc or wedge. Dragging from the inside of the ellipse creates a wedge; dragging from the outside of the ellipse creates an arc. The total number of degrees of the angle are displayed in the status line. The new shape is still called an ellipse on the status line, even though it has been modified.

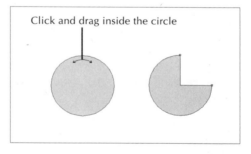

Click and drag inside the circle

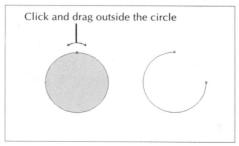

Click and drag outside the circle

Figure 5.2
Creating arcs and wedges.

N O T E

Depressing the Ctrl key when editing a rectangle or ellipse with the Shape tool allows you to constrain the degree of change. The default increment is 15 degrees. This number may vary according to constrain setting in the General property sheet of the Preferences dialog box.

Editing rectangles and ellipses with the Shape tool is restricted to creating arcs, wedges, and rounded corners on rectangles. If you want to make other editing changes, you must first convert the rectangle or ellipse to a curve using the Con**v**ert to Curves command from the **A**rrange menu. Alternatively, click the Convert to Curves button on the ribbon bar (Ctrl+Q). Once you apply Con**v**ert to Curves to a rectangle or ellipse, the action cannot be reversed. You can apply Undo only if the program is configured with sufficient levels of undo to include the point when you converted the geometric object to curves.

Shaping Objects

Every object in CorelDRAW consists of at least one path. Paths provide the framework that describes the shape of the object. A path can be closed or open. An open path, such as a line, cannot display a visible fill; a closed path, such as a geometric object, can display a visible fill (see fig. 5.3).

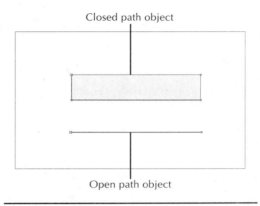

Closed path object

Open path object

Figure 5.3
Closed and open path objects.

W A R N I N G

CorelDRAW will allow you to apply a fill to an open path. If you close the path later, the fill you chose becomes visible. If you leave the path open, however, it can cause PostScript printing errors. This most often occurs accidentally as the result of filling a marquee-selection of objects.

Selecting Elements of a Path

Unlike the Pick tool, you can only select a single object at one time with the Shape tool. Clicking on an object displays the paths of the object. The paths are made of line segments separated by small hollow squares called nodes (see fig. 5.4). Each path, even if it is closed, has a starting and ending node. The starting node appears slightly larger than the balance of the nodes. If you want to close an open path you need to select the starting

and ending nodes. If a path is selected with the Shape tool, you can identify the starting node by pressing the Home key; you can find the ending node by pressing End.

When you select a node, the segment preceding it is also selected. Selecting a single node from a curved line segment displays two small squares attached to the node by dashed lines. These small squares are control points that manipulate the segment on either side of the node. Nodes that are associated with straight line segments do not have control points. The Shape tool allows you to select multiple nodes by pressing the Shift key while clicking on the nodes. You can also marquee-select nodes.

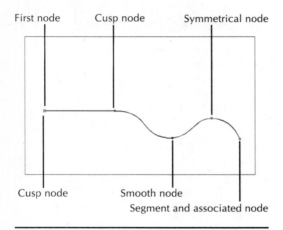

Figure 5.4
Elements of a path.

When you need to select most of the nodes of an object, it is easier to select all of the nodes and then deselect the ones you do not want to include in your selection. To deselect individual nodes, press the Shift key while clicking on them. To deselect all of the nodes, click outside the drawing in a white space or press Escape.

Some objects contain multiple subpaths. The strawberry shown in figure 5.5 is a single object, although it appears to be a group of individual objects. When you select multiple nodes with the Shape tool the status line indicates whether the nodes lie on multiple subpaths.

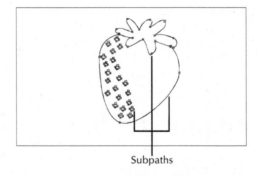

Figure 5.5
Object with multiple subpaths.

Types of Nodes and Segments

The status line displays the type of node and its associated segment when you select a single node. Segments are either a curve or straight line. There are three types of nodes. Each type behaves differently, allowing you better control when reshaping an object. To change a node's type, double-click on the node to display the Node Edit roll-up, and select the type of node you want (see fig. 5.6).

- **Cusp nodes:** Are used to make radical changes in direction. A cusp node has two control points that move independently of one another, allowing you to reshape the segment on either side of the node.

- **Smooth nodes:** Are used to make smooth transitional curves between segments. A smooth node has two control points that lie on a straight line. When you move one of the control points the other point moves proportionately, maintaining the smoothness at the node. Smooth nodes are frequently used to make the transition between a straight line and a curve. When used in this way, only the curved side of the node has a control point and movement of the node is restricted to bidirectional movement along the same plane as the line.

- **Symmetrical nodes:** Are used to join two curve segments while maintaining a symmetrical curve at the node. A symmetrical node has two control points that lie on a straight line equidistant from the node. The two control points move as one. Symmetrical nodes cannot be used to join straight line segments with curved segments.

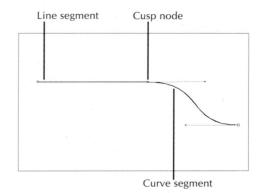

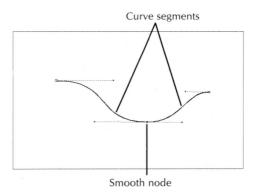

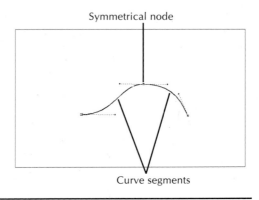

Figure 5.6
Types of nodes and segments.

The Node Edit Roll-Up

The Node Edit roll-up as seen in figure 5.7, contains all the editing commands for curve objects. You can configure the right mouse button to access the Node Edit roll-up in the Preferences dialog box. To open the roll-up, double-click on a node. Double-clicking on the Shape tool also displays the Node Edit roll-up (Ctrl+F10). If you find yourself using the Node Edit roll-up a great deal, you might consider leaving it on your screen since there are no menu equivalents for the commands. You can configure the appearance of roll-ups in the Roll-Ups dialog box, from the View menu.

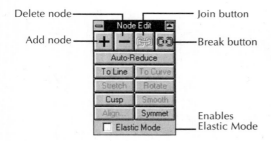

Delete node — Add node — Join button — Break button — Enables Elastic Mode

Figure 5.7
The Node Edit roll-up.

Moving Segments, Nodes, and Control Points

Segments, nodes, and control points offer varying degrees of fine tuning to a shape. Moving segments allows for crude shaping of a curve. Repositioning a node allows for finer control; moving a control point allows for minute adjustments to a curve.

When you click on a curve segment with the Shape tool, a round handle appears, allowing you to move the segment by dragging the round handle. As the segment moves, the control points, associated with the nodes at either end, move with it. Note that you cannot move a straight line segment in this manner.

To move a node, click and drag it to the desired location. As the node is moved the control points and the segment associated with the node move with it. When you move a node, the degree of curvature remains constant at the point of the node. You can move multiple nodes by selecting them and dragging one of the selected nodes to the location you want.

T I P

You can use CorelDRAW's *nudge* feature to move nodes and control points by pressing the cursor key in the direction you want the node and control points to move.

Moving a control point changes the degree of curvature at the node. The further a control point is from a node, the gentler the curve. A control point can lie on top or below a node, making it difficult to select. If it is above the node click and drag to move it off the node. If it is below the node, depress the Shift key while clicking and dragging to move the control point. Because of the size of the nodes and control points, it may be hard to tell whether it is above or below the node. You may have to try both methods to move the control point.

Using Elastic Mode

When elastic mode is enabled in the Node Edit roll-up, nodes behave differently when they are moved. If a single node is selected, elastic mode has no effect; if multiple nodes are selected, the control points move in proportion to the nodes. This gives the curves an elastic feel. The nodes move incrementally in relationship to the node being dragged. The further away a node is from the node being dragged, the less it will move in relationship to the node.

In some cases the nodes may behave as if they are anchored to a location. In figure 5.8 the solid lines represent the original identical lines. The dashed lines represent the lines as the nodes were moved. In both cases, the two right-hand nodes were selected and the center node was moved down while depressing the constrain key. Note the difference in the result between having Elastic Mode enabled or disabled. Elastic Mode is also used to edit envelopes. For more information see Chapter 11, "Creating with Special Effects."

Elastic Mode enabled

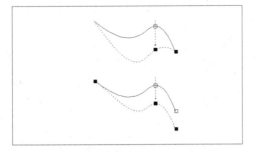

Elastic Mode disabled

Figure 5.8
Elastic Mode vs. normal.

NOTE

When you use the Pick tool to select an object, it is possible for the handles to appear farther away from the object than the object's visible edges. This is because the handles encompass not only the object's visible edges, but also the control points that define the object. This can cause the edges of two objects to not align properly when the Align command is used. It can also cause the bounding box for EPS exports to be considerably larger than the object itself. For more information see Chapter 9, "Using Alignment Aids."

Changing Segments to Lines or Curves

Changing a segment to a line or curve changes the characteristics of the segment. A curved segment has two control points extending from the nodes at either end. Curved segments can be stretched or moved by either clicking on the segment itself or on one of its associated nodes. A straight line segment does not have any control points. Moving the node at either end of the segment changes the angle of the segment, but the line remains straight.

To change a segment from one type to the other, select the segment or the node associated with it and click To Line or To Curve in the Node Edit roll-up. When you change a line to a curve, its appearance initially remains the same. If you select the segment, two control handles appear equidistant from the nodes at either end of the segment, allowing you to modify the

shape of the segment. Figure 5.9 shows two paths, with one curved and one line segment each. The types of segments have been swapped from one path to the other for illustration purposes.

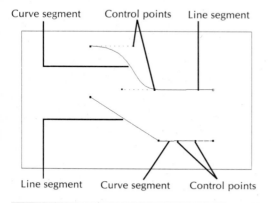

Figure 5.9
Converted segments.

Transforming Curves

CorelDRAW allows you to transform a curve as much as you would an object. You can stretch, scale, rotate, or skew a curve. You must select multiple nodes to perform this operation.

To transform a curve:

■ **Stretch:** Select the nodes of the segments you want to stretch. Click on Stretch in the Node Edit roll-up to display the transformation handles. Drag one of the handles in the direction you want to stretch the curve. See figure 5.10a.

■ **Scale:** Select the nodes of the segments you want to stretch. Click on Stretch in the Node Edit roll-up to display the

transformation handles. Drag one of the corner handles while depressing the shift key in the direction you want to scale the curve. See figure 5.10b.

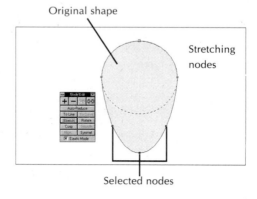

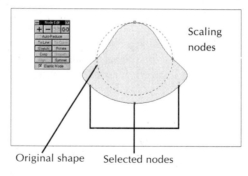

Figure 5.10
Stretching and scaling a curve.

■ **Rotate:** Select the nodes of the segments you want to rotate. Click on Rotate in the Node Edit roll-up to display the transformation handles. Drag one of the corner handles in the direction you want to rotate the curve. See figure 5.11a.

■ **Skew:** Select the nodes of the segments you want to skew. Click on Rotate in the Node Edit roll-up to display the transformation handles. Drag one of the side handles in the direction you want to skew the curve. (See fig. 5.11b.)

Rotating node

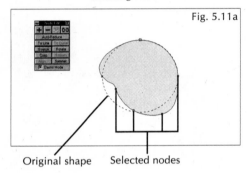

Fig. 5.11a

Original shape   Selected nodes

Original shape

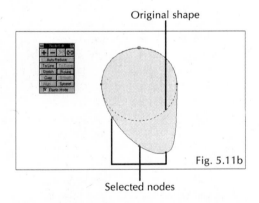

Fig. 5.11b

Selected nodes

Figure 5.11
Rotating and skewing a curve.

Creating Symmetrical Curves

Choosing the type of node and adjusting the control points allows you to create smooth shapes such as a symmetrical curve. When

you create a symmetrical curve, you adjust the control points for three nodes. The center node should be symmetrical and its control points should be stretched outward and perpendicular to the adjacent segments. The control points for the adjacent nodes are aligned and adjusted as straight extensions from their respective nodes. The Snap to Guidelines feature is helpful in creating symmetrical curves. For more information about using guidelines, see Chapter 10, "Using Layers in Documents."

To create a symmetrical curve:

Drag guidelines from the rulers to the adjacent nodes, and enable snap to guidelines. Press the Ctrl key to constrain the motion in the horizontal direction while dragging the control points toward the guidelines. (See fig. 5.12.)

Guidelines

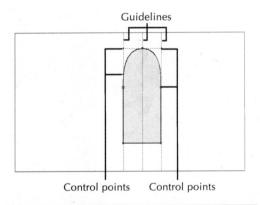

Control points   Control points

Figure 5.12
Creating a symmetrical curve.

Adding Nodes

Adding nodes to a curve can assist in maintaining the smoothness of the curve. There should be a node for about every 120

degrees of change in a path. If there are insufficient nodes on a curve, the appearance is adversely affected. By adding nodes, you can also edit the basic shape of the object by creating a new inflection point on a curve. For more information about curve inflection, see Chapter 2, "Using Graphic Tools." There are several ways to add nodes to an object:

- If you want to add a node in the middle of a segment, select the node at the end of that segment and click the + button in the Node Edit roll-up.

- To place a node at another location on a segment, click on the location for the node and then click on the + button on the roll-up. A node appears at the location you clicked.

- To add several nodes at once, select the nodes adjacent to the segments where you want to add nodes and click on the + button on the roll-up.

T I P

You can also press the + key, instead of the + button on the Node Edit roll-up. If you continue to press the + key, the number of nodes doubles each time. This is helpful when you need to place several evenly spaced nodes.

Deleting Nodes and Segments

Just as not having enough nodes on a path can create a rough appearance, having too many can also make the path jagged looking.

This is common when using the Freehand Pencil tool and with traced images imported into CorelDRAW. In addition to increasing the file size, excess nodes also increase the complexity of an object. This is a common cause for PostScript printing errors. There are two methods of deleting nodes: you can either delete the node manually or by using the Auto-Reduce feature of the Node Edit roll-up.

To delete nodes manually:

Select the nodes you want to delete and click on the minus button on the Node Edit roll-up or press the Delete key on your keyboard. Use caution when selecting nodes for deletion. Deleting nodes can dramatically alter the appearance of an object.

To delete nodes using Auto-Reduce:

Select the nodes you want to reduce. Click the Auto-Reduce button. The amount of reduction is controlled by the Auto-Reduce setting on the Curve property sheet of the Preferences dialog box. The minimum value is 0.000" (no reducing); the maximum value is 1.0". Lower settings reduce fewer nodes, but have the least effect on a curve's shape. Higher values delete more nodes, but can have an undesirable effect on the curve's shape. Because you can apply Auto-Reduce more than once to a selection of nodes, it is suggested to leave the value at a lower setting. The totems shown in figure 5.13 both had too many nodes. The top totem was auto-reduced using a setting of .01", allowing it to retain its shape. The bottom totem was auto-reduced using a setting of 1.0", causing a distortion in shape.

Auto-Reduce setting = 0.01"

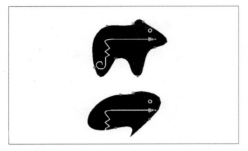

Auto-Reduce Setting = 1.0"

Figure 5.13
The effect of deleting nodes.

Working with Paths

Joining nodes allows you to splice together two segments, or close an open path. You can only join two nodes together on one subpath. You can also join the end nodes of multiple subpaths in a single step as long as the subpaths are combined as a single object. Nodes at the end of a segment can be joined. Intermediate nodes cannot. Sometimes nodes are superimposed, hiding other nodes underneath. This is common when using the Freehand Pencil tool because it is extremely difficult to move a mouse smoothly.

If multiple nodes are superimposed on one end of a segment, press the Home or End key to locate the last node of a segment. Then use nudge to move it away from the cluster. Before joining two nodes, it is a good idea to move them so that they are in close proximity to one another, and adjust the curves as needed. The join feature will join nodes even if they are inches apart. This can have some undesirable effects on the appearance of the object.

To close a path on a single subpath:

1. Select the two nodes to be joined and click on the join button on the Node Edit roll-up. If you select multiple nodes of a subpath, the program will automatically join the end nodes, ignoring the others.

2. Adjust the curve as necessary (see fig. 5.14).

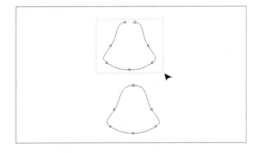

Figure 5.14
Joining nodes on a single subpath.

To close the paths of multiple subpaths of a single object:

1. Select the nodes to be joined and click the join button. If you select multiple nodes, the program will automatically join the end nodes of each subpath.

2. Adjust the curves as necessary (see fig. 5.15).

N O T E

If two paths are not combined into one object, you cannot join their nodes together. Select **A**rrange, **C**ombine to make separate paths into one object.

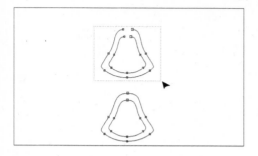

Figure 5.15
Joining nodes on multiple subpaths.

Breaking a Curve into Subpaths

Breaking a curve into subpaths allows you to separate sections of a curve without them becoming individual objects. The program still treats them as a single object though they may appear to be separate objects. This is useful for creating hatching and other line effects. Multiple subpaths are more memory-efficient than individual objects or a group of objects and conserve hard disk space. If you break a closed object into subpaths any fill applied to the object disappears, though the program still recognizes its presence. Be sure to remove this fill unless you intend to reclose the paths later to prevent printing errors.

To break a curve:

1. Select the node or nodes you want to break. Note that you cannot break a curve at an end node.

2. Click on the break button on the Node Edit roll-up. This leaves two nodes superimposed at each break. Move them independently as desired.

Aligning Nodes

The ability to butt two objects together can be important when printing separations. It improves the quality of registration and reduces other printing problems that overlapping objects can cause. If you are aligning two objects with matching straight lines, aligning the edges is effortless. If, however, you want to align the edges of two irregularly shaped objects, the process is more involved.

Visually moving and aligning nodes can be tedious and quality results are difficult to achieve. CorelDRAW offers you the ability to align nodes seamlessly by first combining the two objects. You can break the objects apart later and apply separate fills if you want. Before aligning two edges, make sure that the objects are approximately parallel and that the two edges contain the same number of nodes. This ensures that the two edges will align without significant distortion of the shape of the two objects (see fig. 5.16).

To align nodes:

1. Select the object with the Shape tool and choose the two nodes you want aligned.

N O T E

The first node selected is the node that moves to align with the second node. This can affect the final shape of the two objects and should be taken into consideration when aligning nodes. If the two nodes are marquee-selected, the node of the bottom object aligns with the node of the top object. The most recently created objects are on top unless their order has been changed.

2. Click on the Align button on the Node Edit roll-up to display the Node Align dialog box.

3. The Node Align dialog box offers you three options: Align **H**orizontal, Align **V**ertical, and Align **C**ontrol points. By default all three options are selected. Deselect any options you do not want. If you want to align both nodes and curves, all three options must be selected.

4. Choose OK.

5. Repeat steps as needed to align the edges.

T I P

Using Align can cause lines to overlap and leave gaps unless you break apart the resulting object. This is because the three types of nodes respond differently to the align command. One way to minimize overlapping is to convert the nodes of the edges you want to align into cusp nodes before attempting to align them.

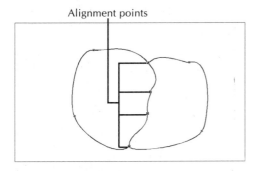

Alignment points

Figure 5.16
Aligning nodes.

Working with Bitmaps and Traced Images

CorelDRAW allows minimal editing of bitmap images. In addition to transforming the bitmap, you can crop the image in the drawing window using the Shape tool. Cropping is confined to a rectangular shape. If you require greater editing ability of the image, consider tracing the image before importing. You can then use the Shape tool to reduce the number of nodes and edit the traced image.

To crop a bitmap:

1. Select the bitmap with the Shape tool to display the cropping handles.

2. Drag a handle toward the center of the bitmap to crop the image. Cropping a bitmap in this manner merely hides some of the image. DRAW maintains the original bitmap in its entirety, allowing you to readjust the cropping later.

N O T E

You can also crop an image when importing the file. For more information about importing files, see Chapter 40, "Importing and Exporting."

A traced import is edited in the same manner as you would any other curve object. The amount of editing necessary within CorelDRAW varies with the quality of the

traced import. The logo in figure 5.17 shows a tracing of a bitmap image. The top image is the raw import. The bottom image is after editing with the Shape tool. The image was scanned, edited in PHOTO-PAINT, and imported as a CorelTRACE .EPS. For more information regarding bitmaps and CorelTRACE, see Chapter 13, "Working with Bitmaps."

Raw trace import

After editing

Figure 5.17
Editing a traced bitmap.

Summary

Using the Shape tool allows for almost infinite editing of the basic shape of objects. By adding, delete, moving, and editing nodes and segments, you can refine the shape of an object. The resulting object becomes a framework for the finished image. By applying fill, outline, and special effects enhancements to the framework, you can further refine your documents. Using fills, as discussed in the next chapter, allows you to add definition to objects.

Working with Fills

*T*he previous chapters have dealt primarily with creating objects as frameworks for final images, with almost no mention of applying fills. The topic of fills could easily take up an entire book. Using color, in its almost infinite diversity, grants definition to images and documents. The wide variety of fill types available in CorelDRAW offers you alternatives for almost any application. Each one of the types has a separate set of options, expanding the possibilities even more.

This chapter covers:

- Process fills
- Spot color fills
- Fountain fills
- Two-color patterns
- Full-color patterns
- Bitmap texture fills

Viewing Your Work

Whenever there is a discussion regarding graphics and color, one of the primary topics is WYSIWYG (what you see is what you get). For years, graphics software companies have touted this as a feature. Actually, it is just now becoming close to reality, because too many factors interfered with color matching.

Understanding the variables involved can help you choose a palette and help ensure the success of the final output. The primary factor in working with color and graphics software is the relationship between your monitor and your output device. Monitors use RGB display, whereas most printers use CMYK values for output. The spectrum of RGB and HSB colors available is much broader than CMYK. The result is that the colors you see on the screen may not match the output colors.

CorelDRAW offers comprehensive color management features. The first step toward successful color output is calibrating the software for your monitor and printer. Once these calibrations are complete, you can enable Color Correction from the View menu. The Color Correction command enables you to choose from None, Fast, and Accurate. You can also choose Simulate Printer. When you select Fast or Accurate, the palettes change to reflect the color correction profile for your monitor. By enabling Simulate Printer, the palettes change to correspond with your printer. This allows the display on the screen to more closely match your output. For more information on color management and color calibration, see Chapters 38 and 39.

N O T E

Enabling Color Correction is memory-intensive and affects the refresh rate.

Choosing a Fill Method

The method you choose to fill objects is determined both by the type of fill and your personal preference. The basic procedure for filling objects is the same, regardless of your choice. You can also change the fill of an object at any time. To apply a fill, select the closed objects you want to fill, and then apply the fill. You can use three methods to select a fill.

The On-Screen Palette Method

You can apply uniform spot and process colors by using the on-screen palette method. The colors displayed correspond with the default palette and reflect your color correction settings.

To change the on-screen palette, select Color Palette from the View menu and choose from the palettes listed in the fly-out. If you want to hide the on-screen palette, select None.

You can scroll through the palette one color at a time by clicking on the right or left arrow beside the palette. Alternatively, you can expand the on-screen palette by clicking on the up arrow on the right side of the palette to display other colors in that palette (see fig. 6.1). After you select a color, the expanded palette reverts to a single line of colors. Clicking on a color fills the selection with that color; clicking on the X at the left end of the color palette removes the fill and leaves objects transparent.

Figure 6.1
The expanded on-screen color palette.

The Fill Dialog Boxes Method

When you select the Fill tool, a fly-out menu appears (see fig. 6.2). You can choose the fill type or select from a series of grayscale colors, including black and white. You can also choose to leave objects transparent by clicking on the X. Clicking on one of the fill types displays the corresponding dialog box, which enables you to choose from the options available for that type of fill.

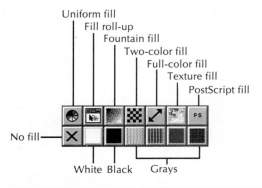

Figure 6.2
The Fill Tool fly-out menu.

The Fill Roll-Up Menu Method

If you select the Fill roll-up icon from the Fill Tool fly-out, the roll-up appears and remains on-screen until you close it (see fig. 6.3). You can access the various fill dialog boxes or apply uniform colors by using this roll-up.

Figure 6.3
The Fill roll-up.

The appearance of the Fill roll-up changes to correspond with the selected fill type. This is useful, as it enables you to edit objects without having to access the dialog boxes repeatedly.

Changing the Fill Type

When you draw a new object in CorelDRAW, it is automatically filled with the default fill. You can change the default fill whenever you choose. To change the default fill, deselect all of the objects in the drawing window. Select the Fill tool to display the Fill fly-out menu, and select the fill type you want. A dialog box appears, and you are asked to choose to which object types

you want the new fill to apply. Make the selections you want and click on OK. The Fill dialog box that corresponds with the fill type you selected appears. Choose the new default fill and any options you want. Click on OK to return to the drawing window. The default fill applies to any new objects drawn. This fill remains the default fill for future CorelDRAW sessions until you change it.

Understanding Color Models

CorelDRAW enables you to choose between three different color models and four brand-name color matching systems to fill objects. Choosing a color model or color matching system is dependent on your final output. If you are creating on-screen presentations, the RGB or HSB color models are the ideal choice.

Print shops use CMYK and spot colors for final output, however. If you are creating a document that ultimately will go to press, selecting CMYK or one of the color matching systems is a better choice for successful output.

To ensure consistency, it is a good idea to use one color model or matching system for an entire document, if possible. For the purposes of illustration, this section uses the Uniform Fill dialog box method. To access the Uniform Fill dialog box, click on the color wheel in the Fill tool fly-out or press Shift+F1. The color selection procedure is the same for all fill types.

RGB and HSB color models are automatically converted to CMYK equivalents when you print the file. If you are creating an on-screen presentation that will be printed as well, it is important to remember that conversions to CMYK are approximations only. You can convert individual objects filled with one color model to another. CorelDRAW calculates the closest approximation automatically when you select another color model.

The RGB Model

The RGB color model adds red, green, and blue light to simulate colors. This additive color model starts with a black screen or a base of zero for each color. A value of 255 for each of the colors represents white.

N O T E

RGB (Red, Green, Blue) uses phosphor values to represent color on your monitor. These values vary from monitor to monitor. To compensate for these differences, calibrate your monitor. For more information regarding calibration, see Chapter 39.

Select the color wheel from the Fill Tool fly-out to display the Uniform Fill dialog box. Clicking on Sho**w** displays a drop-down list of the various color models, palettes, and color matching systems. Select one from the list to display the corresponding color options.

To use the RGB model, follow these steps:

1. From the Sho**w** box, choose the RGB color model (see fig. 6.4).

2. Click on a color in the visual selector.

   You can drag the markers in the visual selector to increase or decrease the amount of each color. The top marker controls the red, the left marker the green, and the right marker the blue. Drag the vertical bar to adjust the brightness of the color.

   You also can enter values between 0 and 255 in each of the RGB boxes below the visual selector. The new color appears to the right, below the current color.

3. Click on OK to apply the color and return to the drawing window.

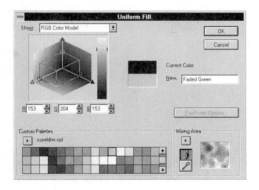

Figure 6.4
The RGB color model.

The CMYK Model

The CMYK color model uses percentages of ink colors, common to the printing industry, to simulate color. This is considered a subtractive process, because it starts with white and works toward black by layering cyan, magenta, and yellow ink colors. Theoretically, 100-percent values of all three inks should equal black. The color they actually make is an off-black that reads as a dark brown when a colorimeter is used to measure the color. To obtain the density of a true black, a K or black value is added.

To select a CMYK color, follow these steps:

1. From the Sho**w** box, choose the CMYK color model (see fig. 6.5).

2. Next, do one of the following:

   ■ Click on a color in the visual selector or from the palette at the bottom of the dialog box.

   ■ Drag the markers in the visual selector to increase or decrease the amount of each color. The top marker controls the cyan; the left marker the magenta; the right marker the yellow. Drag the vertical bar to adjust the amount of black in the color.

   ■ Enter values between 0 percent and 100 percent in each of the CMYK boxes below the visual selector. The new color appears to the right, below the current color.

3. Click on OK to apply the color and return to the drawing window.

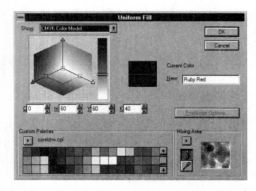

Figure 6.5
The CMYK color model.

N O T E

Color wax thermal and dye sublimation printers are generally CMYK printers. They use either three- or four-color inksheets to lay color on paper. Three-color inksheets produce more vibrant color; however, they are manufactured to compensate for the lack of the black component. The result is denser color that can have a tendency to be dark. Be sure to compensate for color variation by either calibrating your printer, or by following manufacturer recommendations.

The HSB Model

The HSB color model uses three components—hue, saturation, and brightness—to simulate color. *Hue* represents the name of a color in the color spectrum. The color spectrum has 360 degrees. Each of the 360 degrees of the circle represents a color, with 0 degrees denoting red. The colors range through the spectrum with 60 degrees denoting yellow, 120 degrees denoting green, 180 degrees denoting cyan, 240 degrees denoting blue, and 300 degrees denoting magenta.

The *saturation* of a color refers to its intensity, with 0 representing white and 255 representing the maximum intensity. *Brightness* refers to the purity of a color. Black corresponds to 0, while 255 represents pure color.

To select an HSB color, follow these steps:

1. From the Sho**w** box, choose the HSB color model (see fig. 6.6).

2. Choose one of the following techniques:

   ■ Click on a color in the visual selector.

   ■ Drag the marker in the color wheel to change the hue of the color. Moving the marker in or out from the center adjusts the saturation of the color. The perimeter of the wheel represents the greatest intensity of a color. Drag the vertical bar to adjust the amount brightness.

■ Enter values between 0 and 255 in each of the HSB boxes below the visual selector. The new color appears to the right, below the current color.

3. Click on OK to apply the color and return to the drawing window.

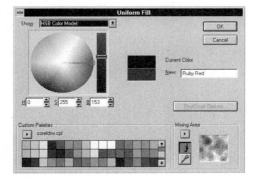

Figure 6.6
The HSB color model.

Grayscale Palettes

The grayscale palette is based on 256 levels of gray. It is similar to the brightness value of the HSB model, where 0 corresponds to black and 255 corresponds to white.

From the Show box, select Grayscale (see fig. 6.7). To select a gray, click on the visual selector or slide the bar up and down. The gray scale moves in increments of one and displays the color number in the gray level entry box.

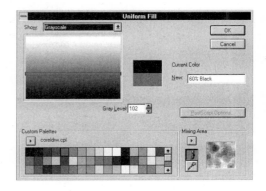

Figure 6.7
The Grayscale color palette.

A sample of the gray appears in the box beside the visual selector. You can also enter a value in the gray level entry box to select one of the 256 levels of gray. If you click on a color in the palette at the bottom of the window, the resulting fill is a CMYK color. You can create a custom palette containing the shades of gray you commonly use. Click on OK to apply the fill and return to the drawing window.

The Uniform Color Palette

The Uniform color palette is based on the RGB model. It provides you with a palette of pure colors. After selecting Uniform Colors from the Show box, choose a color by clicking on one of the color samples in the visual selector (see fig. 6.8). A sample of the new color appears, along with a sample of the current color in the boxes beside the visual selector.

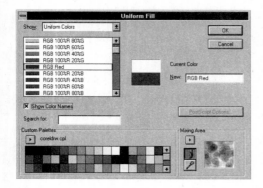

Figure 6.8

The Uniform color palette.

The RGB values of a color are displayed in the **N**ame box. If you enable Sh**o**w Color Names, the visual selector changes to display smaller samples with the names beside them. The S**e**arch for box enables you to search for a color by entering the name in the entry box. Once your color is selected, click on OK to apply the fill and return to the drawing window.

Understanding Color-Matching Systems

CorelDRAW offers you a selection of four-color matching systems. These palettes are generated to correspond with inks available to the printing industry. You can purchase swatch books for each of these proprietary palettes to help ensure the success of your printed output. The swatch books enable you

to select colors from the swatch books, and then choose the corresponding color from the palette. Consult your printer to decide what types of matching systems are employed in his business.

To choose colors from these proprietary palettes, follow these steps:

1. Select a brand-name palette from the Sho**w** list box.

2. Scroll through the color swatches to locate the color you want, and click on that color. The new color is displayed, along with the current color in the boxes beside the visual selector. The name of the color is displayed in the adjacent box.

3. Click on OK to apply the fill and return to the drawing window.

If you enable Sh**o**w Color Names, the visual selector changes to display small samples of the color with the names beside them. You can search for a color by entering a name in the S**e**arch for entry box.

N O T E

CorelDRAW provides for automatic conversion from the proprietary palettes to any of the three color models. To convert an object's fill to one of the color models, select the color model you want and click on OK to return to the drawing window.

FOCOLTONE Process Colors

The FOCOLTONE palette is unique in that each color has at least 10 percent of a process color in common with any other color (see fig. 6.9). This minimizes problems associated with trapping and overprinting. The FOCOLTONE system is primarily used in Europe and is generally not supported by commercial printers outside of that area.

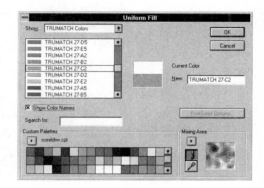

Figure 6.10
TRUMATCH process colors.

PANTONE Process Colors

The PANTONE process color palette is a proprietary conversion of PANTONE spot colors. It is designed to approximate process colors as closely as possible with their spot equivalents. To match spot colors, you must use swatch books, as CorelDRAW does not support direct conversion from one Color Matching system to another. Choosing PANTONE Process Colors from the Sho**w** list box displays the color choices (see fig. 6.11).

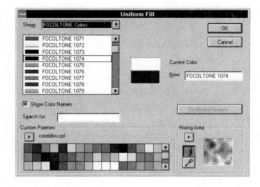

Figure 6.9
FOCOLTONE process colors.

TRUMATCH Process Colors

If you choose TRUMATCH Colors from the Show list box, you see the TRUMATCH colors displayed (see fig. 6.10).
TRUMATCH is designed specifically for digital output. Using the HSB color model as its base, TRUMATCH colors still rely upon CMYK conversion for final output.

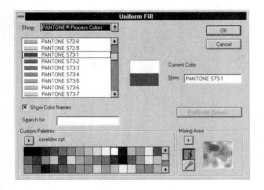

Figure 6.11
PANTONE process colors.

PANTONE Spot Colors

The PANTONE spot color system has been an industry standard since 1963. A given spot color is consistently uniform across a variety of media. If you specify a spot color for ink, film, coated papers, or any of the other PANTONE spot media, the color will always be the same.

Spot colors separate differently than process colors, unless you specify that spot colors should be converted to CMYK values when you go to print. Because each ink is specific, when you separate a file containing spot colors, the separations are sent as the specific ink color rather than as a CMYK mix. The result is more object-oriented separations. This is ideal for industries that rely upon spot colors, such as the screen printing industry. For more information regarding printing separations, see Chapter 14, "Printed Output."

You can use tints of a spot color as opposed to pure color. To choose a tint, select the spot color from the visual selector. In the **T**int entry box, enter the percentage of the color you want. A value of 0 percent corresponds with white, while a value of 100 percent is the pure color (see fig. 6.12).

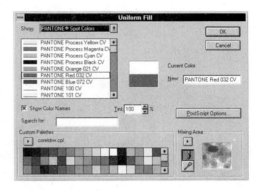

Figure 6.12
PANTONE spot colors.

PANTONE spot colors support halftone screening. This is only available with PostScript output. For more information, see "Working with Halftones" in Chapter 11, "Creating with Special Effects."

Spot versus Process Color Inks

The decision to choose spot or process inks at press time is one of budget versus exacting standards. Each ink color requires its own plate, and can require multiple passes through a press. Spot inks are opaque reflective inks, and require tighter trapping because they are not designed to be mixed.

Overlapping spot inks can cause unpredictable and unpleasant color mixing at the adjoining edges of objects. Spot colors are ideal for one- to four-color jobs that require exacting color. Because of the time required for commercially printed spot colors, they are cost-prohibitive for full-color jobs when a design has many colors.

Process color inks are transparent. They produce color by layering percentages of cyan, magenta, yellow, and black inks on paper. A maximum of four plates are required, regardless of the number of colors in a design. For more information, see Chapter 14, "Printed Output," and Chapter 41, "Working with Service Bureaus."

Customizing Color

You can add colors to existing palettes and create customized palettes in a variety of ways. Custom colors are useful for reproducing fills and outlines within a drawing. To create a new palette, click on the arrow in Custom Palettes in the Uniform Fill dialog box, and select New. The Custom Palettes area clears, enabling you to add colors.

CorelDRAW enables you to customize palettes by doing one of the following:

- **Creating colors using the visual selector.** Adjust the markers of any of the color models or color matching systems to choose a color. Note that if you select a color matching system, the new color will not be added to the system—it is added to a custom palette only. The new color appears in the box adjacent to the visual selector. Click on OK to apply the fill and return to the drawing window.

- **Creating colors using the parameter entry boxes.** Select the color model you want to use as a base. In the parameter entry boxes, enter the values for the color you want to create. The new color appears in the box adjacent to the visual selector. Click on OK to apply the fill and return to the drawing window.

- **Mixing colors from the visual selector or custom palette.** Click on the arrow in the mixing area, and select Clear to create a clean mixing area. Choose a color model from the Show List box. Alternatively, open a custom palette by clicking on the arrow in the Custom Palettes box, and selecting **O**pen. Choose the PAL (version 4.0) or CPL (version 5.0) file you want to use, and click on OK.

  Choose the eyedropper, and move over the color you want. Click to pick up the color. Move back to the mixing area and select the paintbrush (see fig. 6.13). Paint the color in the mixing area. Continue to pick up colors in this manner, mixing the colors as you desire. Choose the eyedropper (see fig. 6.14), and click on the color in the mixing area that you want to add to the palette. The new color appears in the box adjacent to the visual selector. Click on OK to apply the fill and return to the drawing window.

  You can save the mixing area by clicking on the arrow and selecting Save. Enter a file name, and click on OK.

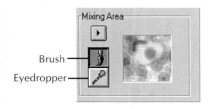

Figure 6.13
The Paintbrush and Eyedropper tools in the Mixing Area.

Figure 6.14
Selecting the Eyedropper tool in the Mixing Area.

If you choose the paintbrush in the mixing area, it changes to the eyedropper when you leave the mixing area, enabling you to pick up colors. It will revert back to the paintbrush when you reenter the mixing area.

- Extracting colors from .BMP images: Click on the arrow in the mixing area, and select Load. Select the .BMP file from which you want to extract colors, and click on OK. You can either use the paintbrush to custom mix the colors further, or use the eyedropper to select a color from the image. Click on OK to apply the fill and return to the drawing window.

- Creating tints of spot colors: Select the PANTONE Spot color palette from the list box. Click on the color from which you want to create tints. Enter a value between 0 percent and 100 percent in the tint box. Add the tint to your palette.

Adding Colors to an Existing or New Palette

Click on the arrow in the Custom Palettes box, and select **A**dd. Enter a name for the color, for future reference. Continue adding colors, and then save the modified palette, if you want to use it for future CorelDRAW sessions. It is a good idea to use Save **A**s and rename the palette.

Using Fountain Fills

Fountain fills enable you to apply gradients of one or more colors to objects. Figure 6.15 displays the four types of fountain fills:

- **Linear.** Creates a straight line gradient.

- **Radial.** Creates a gradient of concentric circles.

- ■ **Conical.** Creates a gradient in a clockwise or counterclockwise direction.

- ■ **Square.** Creates a gradient of concentric squares.

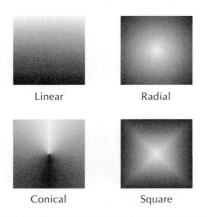

Linear   Radial

Conical   Square

Figure 6.15
Types of fountain fills.

All fountain fills are applied using the following basic method:

1. Select the object(s) you want to fill.

2. Select the Fountain Fill icon from the Fill tool fly-out or the Fill roll-up, or by pressing F11.

3. Choose the options you want, and click on OK or Appl**y** to apply the fill and return to the drawing window.

Specifying a Color

A fountain fill requires a minimum of two colors or two spot color tints to define the fill. Define the colors as shown earlier in the chapter. If you define tints, both colors

should be tints of the same spot color. A gradient between a spot color and a process color yields a process gradient, and will not separate as a spot color. Specifying spot colors allows you to modify halftone screens and use them in your fountain fill. For more information about halftone screens, see "Working with Halftone Screens," in Chapter 11.

About Fountain Steps and Banding

Clicking on the lock icon beside the Steps box allows you to reset the number of steps. A small number of 20 can cause banding (see fig. 6.16). The value you enter here overrides printer controls, forcing the printer to print the number of steps you set. This makes the file larger and increases the complexity threshold of the file. Increasing the number of steps also lengthens printing time.

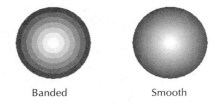

Banded   Smooth

Figure 6.16
Eliminating banding.

Ideally, you should set the number of fountain steps in relationship to your output device. If you are using a desktop printer, the number of steps that will make a visible difference is finite, depending upon your printer. Most laser printers create smooth transitions at a setting of 60–90. Imagesetters

require higher settings. A setting of 120–150 for a 1,270 dpi imagesetter and 200 for a 2,540 dpi imagesetter is recommended. You can reset the default values for fountain steps. For more information, see Chapter 47, "Troubleshooting."

N O T E

You can set the number of fountain steps that appear in your drawing window on the View property sheet of the Preferences dialog box.

Creating Highlights

The radial, conical, and square fountain fills enable you to offset the center of the gradient. This enables you to quickly create highlights, as shown in figure 6.17. To offset the center, follow these steps:

1. Click on the preview box and drag the crosshair to reposition the center. The fill redraws, displaying the offset center.

2. Enter the percentage of offset you want in the Offset Center entry boxes.

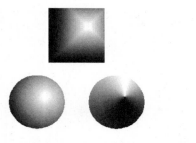

Figure 6.17
Creating highlights.

Changing the Angle

The linear fountain fill enables you to change the angle of the fill, as shown in figure 6.18. To do this, follow these steps:

1. Click on the preview box, and drag the crosshair around to reposition the angle.

2. Enter the desired degree of angle in the Angle entry box.

Figure 6.18
Changing the angle of a linear fill.

Creating Custom Fountain Fills and Using Presets

CorelDRAW has three methods of calculating a fountain fill: Direct, Rainbow, and Custom (see fig. 6.19). The **D**irect method is the default method for fountain fills. It calculates a straight line across the color wheel. The **R**ainbow method moves logically through the color spectrum in either a clockwise or counterclockwise direction. The number of colors displayed in the fill are dependent upon the direction of the fill and the spread between the two colors. The

<u>C</u>ustom method enables you to specify intermediate colors in the fountain fill, and their position on the fill. You can specify up to 99 colors. Custom fountain fills are capable of creating metallic and other special effect fills.

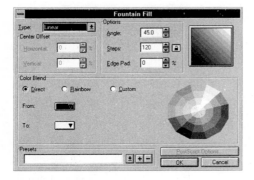

Figure 6.19

The Fountain Fill dialog box, showing the Direct, Rainbow, and Custom options in the Color Blend group.

To create a custom fountain fill, follow these steps:

1. Click on the Custom button.

2. Position the cursor in the custom blend preview window, and double-click to set the first intermediate marker.

3. Drag the marker to the desired location, or choose a location by entering a percentage in the Position entry box.

4. Click on the color box to choose a color.

5. Continue adding markers and choosing colors to create the effect you want. A rough representation appears in the preview box.

6. You can edit the intermediate or end colors by clicking on the markers and choosing a new color from the color box.

7. You can save the fill for future use by clicking inside the Presets box. A text cursor appears, enabling you to enter a name. Click on the + button to add the fill to the available presets.

8. Click on OK to apply the fill and return to the drawing window (see fig. 6.20).

Figure 6.20

Using custom fountain fills makes it possible to add authentic effects to this CD-ROM image.

A variety of color preset fountain fills are provided with CorelDRAW. To access the Presets, click on the down arrow to display the list, and select a preset. Selecting a preset and clicking on the - button will delete the preset.

Applying Two-Color and Full-Color Patterns

Two- and four-color patterns enable you to add a variety of bitmap fills to objects. CorelDRAW provides a selection of patterns for your use. In addition, you can import, create, or edit your own. Both fills are applied in a similar manner.

Two-Color Pattern Fills

Two-color fills enable you to change the background and foreground color. Simple fills can be created using the bitmap editor. More elaborate fills can be created in either CorelPHOTO-PAINT or CorelDRAW, and then saved as a pattern.

To apply a two-color fill, follow these steps:

1. Select the two color fill icon from the Fill Tool fly-out to display the Two-Color Pattern dialog box, as shown in figure 6.21.

2. To display the palette of patterns, click on the preview box. Select a fill and click on OK. Alternatively, double-click on a fill to select it.

3. Select a background and foreground fill by clicking on the color buttons and choosing a color. The default colors are a white background with a black foreground.

4. Click on OK to apply the fill and return to the drawing window (see fig. 6.22).

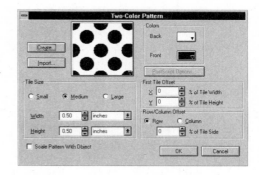

Figure 6.21
The Two-Color Pattern dialog box.

Figure 6.22
Using two-color pattern fills.

Full-Color Pattern Fills

Full-color pattern fills enable you to use any bitmap image as a fill, and retain the color of the original image.

To apply a full-color fill, follow these steps:

1. Select the full-color fill icon from the Fill Tool fly-out to display the Full-Color Pattern dialog box, as shown in figure 6.23.

2. To display the palette of patterns, click on the preview box. Select a fill and click on OK. Alternatively, double-click on a fill to select it. If you want to import a bitmap to use as a pattern, click on **I**mport and select the file you want to use.

3. Click on OK to apply the fill and return to the drawing window (see fig. 6.24).

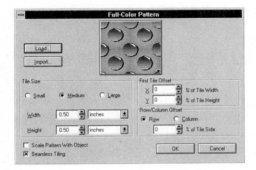

Figure 6.23
The Full-Color Pattern dialog box.

Figure 6.24
Using full-color pattern fills.

Choosing a Tile Size

CorelDRAW uses tiling to fill an object with a pattern. The size of the pattern is adjustable. If you use the preset sizes, Small is .25", Medium is .50", and Large is 1.0". If you need another size, select **T**iling, and enter a size in the size entry boxes. Making a tile too large can cause a jagged image. If the tile is too small, the pattern may disappear into the background or become blurred.

Offsetting Tiles

Offsetting tiles allows you to adjust their orientation in your object (see fig. 6.25). Offsets are based upon percentages of the tile size. To adjust the tiling, click on the **T**iling button in the dialog box. The tile adjustments and their effect on the fill are as follows:

■ First Tile Offset: Adjusts the placement of the first tile in the pattern. The X Offset parameter adjusts the horizontal shift; the Y Offset parameter adjusts the vertical shift. Entering a value of 25 percent in both boxes would shift the first tile of a 1" tile to the right .25" and down .25".

■ Row/Column Offset: Adjusts the placement of a row or column in relationship to the adjacent row or column. Entering a value of 50 percent would shift the row one half the width of a tile.

0% Offset   50% Row Offset

Figure 6.25
Offsetting tiles.

Using the Fill Roll-Up to Edit and Apply Patterns

Accessing pattern editing dialog boxes and tools is slightly different from the way they are accessed using the Fill Tool fly-out.

To apply a pattern fill, follow these steps:

1. Select the object to be filled, and click on the two- or full-color pattern icon. The first pattern in the pattern library appears in the roll-up (see fig. 6.26).

Click here and drag to move file 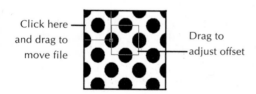 Drag to adjust offset

Figure 6.26
Applying patterns with the Fill roll-up.

2. Select the preview box to display the patterns, and click on a pattern to select it.

3. Choose Apply.

To interactively resize and adjust tile offset, use the following steps:

1. Select the object containing the pattern you want to edit.

2. Click on Update in the Fill roll-up to display the fill in the roll-up.

3. Clicking on Tile displays two tiles in your object.

4. To resize the tile, drag the handle in the bottom corner of the left square. To adjust the offset, drag the right square downward to change the row offset. Dragging the right square down as far as it can move enables you to move it horizontally, in relationship to the left square. This adjusts the column offset. To shift the entire pattern, drag the left tile.

5. Click on Apply. The edited pattern appears in the drawing window.

Creating Patterns

Creating a pattern allows you to expand the existing collection of patterns. When you create a two-color pattern, the tile is added to the existing library. Full-color patterns are saved as files, and you are prompted to name the file and specify the path where you want the pattern stored. To create a pattern, follow these steps:

1. Create the graphic from which you want to make a pattern. The graphic can be created in CorelDRAW, CorelPHOTO-PAINT, or another application. When creating a graphic for a pattern, keep the following in mind:

■ If the graphic is going to be used as a two-color pattern, it will be converted to a black and white image. Using extensive coloring can have an undesirable effect on the finished pattern.

■ The overall width and height should be roughly equal.

■ The pattern is going to be tiled to achieve the fill effect. Overdesigning can result in a muddy or busy pattern. For example, the polka dot pattern in the two-color pattern library was created as a single filled circle.

2. Open or import the file in CorelDRAW.

3. Select Create Pattern from the Preferences menu to display the Create Pattern dialog box (see fig. 6.27).

4. Select the type of pattern you want to create and the resolution you desire. Higher-resolution patterns require more storage space, and require more memory to load and for screen refresh. Click on OK.

5. A set of crosshairs appears, enabling you to marquee-select the area from which to create the pattern. Drag to make the selection. If there is significant white space surrounding your selection, the pattern will appear smaller when tiled.

6. A message box appears, requesting verification to create the pattern. Click on OK.

7. If you created a full-color pattern, a dialog box appears, prompting you for a file name and path for the new pattern. Enter the information, and click on OK.

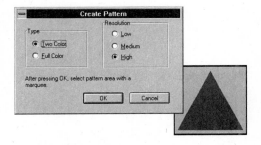

Figure 6.27

Creating a pattern.

Using the Two-Color Pattern Editor

You can use the two-color pattern editor to create a pattern (see fig. 6.28). This is useful for geometric patterns, as it provides a grid to assist in keeping the dimensions uniform.

To use the two-color pattern editor, follow these steps:

1. Click on the two-color pattern icon to open the dialog box, and choose Create. The Two-Color Pattern Editor appears with a grid to assist you in creating your pattern.

2. Select the bitmap size with which you want to work. The choices are in pixels. The grid changes in size to correspond with the bitmap size. Working with a 64 × 64 pixel grid allows for finer detail.

3. Select the pen size. The size is measured in pixels.

4. Draw the design you want in the grid window. The left mouse button fills squares; the right mouse button erases squares.

5. Click on OK to return to the Two-Color Pattern dialog box. The new pattern is saved with the library, and appears in the Preview box.

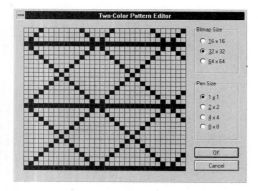

Figure 6.28
The two-color pattern editor.

Working with Texture Fills

Bitmap texture fills use a random number generator to allow you to choose from millions of fractal fills. The libraries of textures contain more than 100 different base fills. You can accept them as they are, or regenerate new ones within the parameters available for the individual fill. Fractal imaging is very memory-intensive and creates large files. To minimize this problem, avoid filling large objects with a texture fill.

N O T E

The default screen resolution for a texture fill is 127 dpi. This may make textures appear jagged on-screen. The lower screen resolution does not affect printing. You can change this value in the Corelapp.ini. Changing the value causes slower screen refresh rates, and requires more memory. Consider your system resources before changing this value. For more information regarding editing the Corelapp.ini, see Chapter 47, "Troubleshooting."

To apply a bitmap texture using the Texture Fill dialog box, follow these steps:

1. Select the object and then choose the bitmap texture icon from the Fill Tool fly-out.

2. Choose a library from the Texture Library box to display the textures in that library.

3. Select the texture you want to display a sample of in the preview box.

4. Modify the parameters for the texture, if desired; select the preview box to view the results of your modifications.

5. Click on OK to apply the fill and return to the drawing window.

To apply a bitmap texture using the Fill roll-up, use the following steps:

1. Select the object and then choose the bitmap texture icon from the Fill roll-up.

2. Click on the preview box to view the pop-up Texture Fill palette. Choose a texture from the palette, or load another library from which to select a texture. To load another library, click on the Style box or Load from the File menu of the pop-up palette.

3. Click on Edit to access the Texture Fill dialog box, if you want to edit the texture (see fig.6.29). Set the desired parameters.

4. Click on Apply to fill the object with the selected texture.

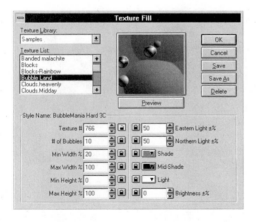

Figure 6.29
The Texture Fill dialog box.

T I P

The default print resolution of a texture fill is unacceptable for high resolution output. There is a way to work around this problem, however. Before filling an object with a texture fill, scale the object 200–400 percent. Fill the object and then scale it back to normal size. This increases the effective resolution to acceptable levels. Note that this also increases the file size.

Modifying the Texture Parameters

Selecting a texture displays the various parameters available for that texture. Not all of the parameters are available for every texture, however. To change the parameters, enter the new value in the entry boxes. You can change the colors by clicking on the color boxes and choosing new colors. If you continue clicking on the Preview button, a slightly different version of the fill is displayed in the preview box. Examples of modified parameters are displayed in figure 6.30. In the top row, from left to right, are 100% Softness, 50% Softness, 60% Eastern/ 50% Northern, and –60% Eastern/50% Northern. In the second row are 25% Density, 100% Density, 100% Grain, and 0% Grain. In the third row are 0% Phase Origin, 100% Phase Origin, 0% X Origin/ 0% Y Origin, and 25% X Origin/25% Y Origin. In the fourth row are 100% Volume, 0% Volume, 50% Brightness, and 0% Brightness. In the bottom row are 80% Contrast, 10% Contrast, 0% Perspective, and 100% Perspective.

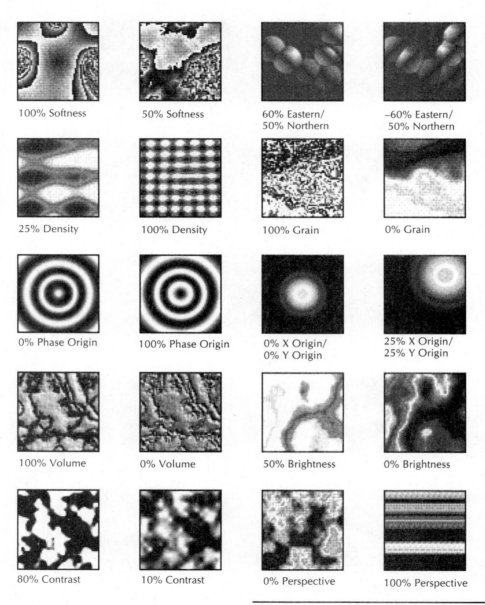

100% Softness	50% Softness	60% Eastern/ 50% Northern	−60% Eastern/ 50% Northern
25% Density	100% Density	100% Grain	0% Grain
0% Phase Origin	100% Phase Origin	0% X Origin/ 0% Y Origin	25% X Origin/ 25% Y Origin
100% Volume	0% Volume	50% Brightness	0% Brightness
80% Contrast	10% Contrast	0% Perspective	100% Perspective

Figure 6.30
Parameter modification examples.

Beside each of the parameters is a lock icon. CorelDRAW can randomly generate any or all of the parameters, including color. To randomly generate a parameter, click on the lock icon into the unlocked position. Click on the Preview button until the fill you want is displayed.

- **Texture Number.** By default, this parameter is unlocked, enabling you to view different versions of similar textures. You can enter a number between 0 and 32,768 to select a particular texture.

- **Softness.** Blurs the edges of the colors. The parameter can be set from 0 percent to 100 percent.

- **Density.** Increases or decreases the amount of chaos, with 100 percent corresponding with the greatest amount of chaos.

- **Lighting.** Enables you to modify Eastern and Northern lighting effects. Lighting effects give a 3D effect to fills.

- **Grain.** Increases or decreases the intensity of the color. Higher values increase the intensity; lower values decrease the intensity.

- **Rainbow Grain.** Enables you to create a rainbow effect by altering the color's intensity and shifting the color value. Higher values increase the effect of this parameter.

- **Phase Offset or Origin.** Determines how rings are displayed for circular textures. The origin determines the placement of the center. Modifying this parameter alters the illusion of depth.

- **X or Y Origin.** Affects circular textures by modifying the horizontal and vertical offset.

N O T E

Not all of the parameters are available for every texture. Some textures have other parameters that are specific to only that texture.

Saving and Deleting Texture Fills

There are two types of texture fills: style textures and user textures. A *style texture* is a model from which other textures are generated; you can save the modified texture as *user texture* without overwriting the original. Click on the Save As button, and enter a name for the texture in the Texture Name box. The name can have up to 32 characters and spaces. Choose a library in which to save the texture. You cannot save it to the Styles library, however. If you want to create a new library, enter a name in the Library Name Box.

When you select a user texture from one of the libraries, the original style name appears below the texture list. User textures can be modified and then saved, overwriting the file. Alternatively, you can select Save As, and add the texture to one of the libraries.

Summary

Using color and fills effectively is a matter of understanding the way they work. This chapter illustrated the function of the color models and color matching systems available in CorelDRAW. The assortment of fill options enables you to enhance your documents. Chapter 7 uses the color information detailed in this chapter to enhance the use of the Outline tool.

Working with Outlines

*O*utlines are far more than containers for fills; they describe an object. Outlines add depth to an image, creating a three-dimensional appearance. For many objects, it is appropriate to have no visible outline. Other objects require not only an outline, but they also need a color outline of variable width. The outline features in CorelDRAW provide the ability to create pen and ink and calligraphic effects, as well as use arrowheads and dashed lines. PowerLines take calligraphic effects one step further by enabling you to utilize pressure-sensitive tablets, and create a variety of special effects outlines.

This chapter covers:

- Choosing outline attributes
- Working with arrowheads
- Creating calligraphic effects
- Using PowerLine effects

Choosing Outline Attributes

Using the Outline Pen and Pen roll-up enables you to adjust the color, style, and width of lines. Outlines can be of uniform or variable width. Variable-width lines are *calligraphic lines*, and are discussed later in this chapter. The Pen tool fly-out (see fig. 7.1) enables you to access the following outline features:

- The Outline Pen dialog box

- The Pen roll-up

- The Outline Color dialog box

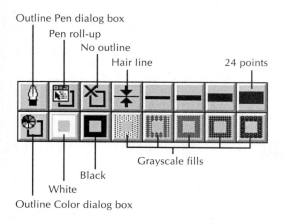

Figure 7.1
The Pen tool fly-out.

The Pen tool fly-out also enables you to do the following:

- Apply a variety of preset line weights, ranging from 1/4 point to 24 points

- Apply a 0 line weight to an outline, making the outline transparent in editable preview mode

- Apply white, black, and a small assortment of grayscale colors

In wireframe mode, all lines appear to have the same width. Working in editable preview mode is helpful if you have lines of varying widths that overlap one another.

Using the Outline Pen Dialog Box

The Outline Pen dialog box provides access to every attribute control available for an outline. You can apply the changes to any selected outline by making the changes you want. Click on OK to apply the changes and return to the drawing window.

T I P

You can access the Outline Pen dialog box by clicking on Edit in the Pen roll-up. F12 also opens the Outline Pen dialog box.

Changing a Color

Clicking on the color box accesses the color palette, enabling you to choose a color. If you select the More button, the Color Outline dialog box appears, enabling you to choose from all of the available color options and even to mix your own colors.

Setting a Line Weight

You can set the width of a line from .001" to 4.0". To set the line width, use the scroll buttons or enter the value you want in the entry box. Change the units if desired by clicking the down arrow and choosing from the unit list. The value in the entry box is automatically converted to the corresponding unit of measurement.

W A R N I N G

Very fine outlines may disappear when printing, depending upon the output device. It is generally not a good idea to choose a line width smaller than .003", unless you are going to output your artwork on a high-resolution printer.

Selecting Corner Styles

CorelDRAW offers three corner styles: mitered, rounded, and beveled (see fig. 7.2). Corner styles apply when an outline takes a sharp turn in direction, and do not apply to curved line segments. Each of the corner styles offers a different aesthetic appeal. At larger outline widths, the different styles can have an enormous impact on the appearance of your design. Choose a corner style by clicking the radio button beside it.

| Mitered | Rounded | Beveled |

Figure 7.2
Corner styles.

The following list explains CorelDRAW's three corner styles:

- **Mitered.** Choosing this option creates a sharp pointed corner. This can be problematic if two line segments meet at more than a 90 degree angle. At larger line widths, the line extends beyond the node and can cause an undesirable appearance (see fig. 7.3). You can prevent this problem by either choosing another corner style, or by increasing the Miter Corner value in the Preferences dialog box.

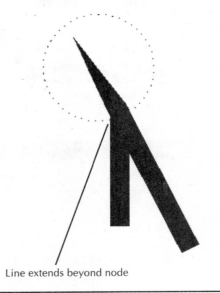

Line extends beyond node

Figure 7.3
Miter corner problems.

- **Rounded.** Choosing a rounded corner provides a smooth, curved corner where two line segments meet. The radius of the corner is dependent upon the line width and angle of the corner.

■ **Beveled.** Choosing a beveled corner cuts the corner off at an angle, where two line segments meet. The degree of the angle is equal to 50 percent of the angle of the corner.

Selecting Line Cap Styles

You can choose from three line cap styles: square, rounded, and extended (see fig. 7.4). To choose a line cap, click the radio button beside it.

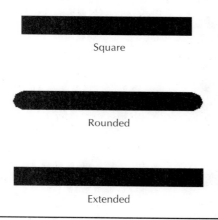

Figure 7.4
Line cap styles.

The following list explains the three line cap styles:

■ **Square.** Cuts the line off at the end nodes of a line. This provides a clean, precise line.

■ **Rounded.** Creates a semicircular end point on a line. The diameter of the end is equal to the width of the line.

■ **Extended.** Extends the line beyond the end nodes. The amount of the extension is equal to 50 percent of the line width.

Selecting an Arrowhead Style

You can add arrowheads to any open path. For more information about adding, creating, and editing arrowheads, see the section "Working with Arrowheads," later in this chapter.

Selecting a Line Style

Click on the down arrow to display a list of line styles (see fig. 7.5). Choose a line style by clicking on the style. Line cap styles apply both to the ends of the line and the dashes or dots between them. You can add your own line styles by editing the Coreldrw.dot file. For more information about editing configurable files, see Chapter 45, "Customizing CorelDRAW for Optimum Performance."

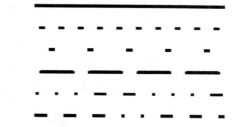

Figure 7.5
An example of line styles offered by CorelDRAW.

Using Calligraphy

The calligraphy section of the dialog box enables you to alter the angle and vary the width of a line. For more information about using calligraphic effects, see "Creating Calligraphic Effects" later in this chapter.

Using Behind Fill

The **B**ehind Fill option enables you to place the outline behind the fill of an object (see fig. 7.6). The default location for an outline is in front of an object, making the entire width of the outline visible. If Behind Fill is enabled, only one-half of the outline will be visible; the balance will be behind the fill. This is useful when working with outlined text. If you apply an outline to text, particularly the more scripted typefaces, the outline may conceal some of the finer details of the typeface. By enabling Behind Fill, the detail of the typeface is preserved, while still allowing an outline. You can use this feature to create bold text when a bold style is not available.

Above fill   Behind fill

Figure 7.6
Using Behind Fill.

Behind Fill can also be of assistance when minute trapping is required. Selecting a color that corresponds to the fill color of the object underneath ensures a tight trap on small objects, without eliminating the detail.

Using Scale With Image

Enabling **S**cale With Image causes the outline width to increase or decrease as you scale the associated object (see fig. 7.7). This is useful when a finished design is going to be

output at various sizes. It also enables you to create an object at a greatly increased size, and then reduce the size, maintaining the detail. If Scale With Image is disabled, the outline remains the same width and may seem to disappear at larger sizes. A wide outline can conceal most or all of an object, if the object is reduced to a very small size. If you rotate an object with Scale With Image enabled, the angle and width adjust with the angle of the object to maintain its appearance. This helps reduce a jagged-looking effect.

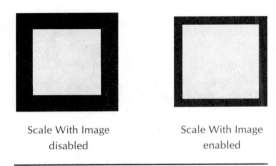

Scale With Image   Scale With Image
disabled   enabled

Figure 7.7
Examples of Scale With Image.

Changing Default Outline Attributes

To change the default outline attributes, deselect all the objects by either clicking on the white space in the drawing window or by pressing the Escape key. Choose the Outline Pen Dialog icon from the Pen fly-out menu. A dialog box appears, asking to which object types you want the new outline to apply. Select the options you want, and click on OK. The Outline Pen dialog box is displayed, enabling you to make the changes you want. Select the new options, and click

on OK to return to the drawing window. Note that any changes you make will only apply to new objects, not to existing ones.

Copying an Outline

The Copy Attributes From command, under the **E**dit pull-down menu, enables you to apply the attributes of one object to a selection. When you click on the command, a dialog box appears, enabling you to choose which attributes you want copied. Make the selections you want, and click on OK. When the cursor changes to an arrow, click on the object whose attributes you want to copy. The attributes are applied to the selection. If you want to copy all the attributes of an object to a selection, just click on Update From in the Pen roll-up. Pick the selection, and then click on Apply.

Using the Pen Roll-Up

The Pen roll-up (see fig. 7.8) enables you to apply outline attributes to a selection. Keeping this roll-up on-screen is useful when you are editing a number of objects.

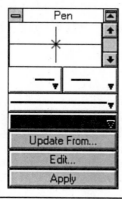

Figure 7.8
The Pen roll-up.

To apply Outline Pen attributes using the Pen roll-up, follow these steps:

1. Select the object(s) you want to outline or edit.

2. Click the Outline Pen Roll-Up icon from the Pen tool flyout.

3. Choose the attributes you want to apply to the selection, and click on Apply to apply them to the selection.

Clicking on Edit accesses the Outline Pen dialog box. If you are editing an existing outline, click on Update From to display the current outline in the preview box.

Applying Color Outlines

Outlines have the same color options as fills, except they are restricted to uniform colors, PostScript textures, and halftone effects. You cannot apply gradient color to an outline. For information about using PostScript textures and halftone effects, see Chapter 11, "Creating with Special Effects."

Using the On-Screen Palette

The on-screen palette is the easiest way to choose outline colors. Make sure the palette you want is displayed in the drawing window. If you need to change the palette, select Co**l**or Palette from the **V**iew pull-down menu, and choose the palette you want. To apply an outline color, select the object and click on the color with the right mouse button.

Using the Outline Color Dialog Box

The Outline Color dialog box enables you to access the various color models and color matching systems. These colors can be applied to any outline. If you select a color for an object that has no outline, the hair line width will be applied to the object. To apply a color, choose a palette from the Sho**w** list box, and choose a color. Click on OK to apply the outline color, and return to the drawing window. For more information about the various color models and color matching systems, see Chapter 6, "Working with Fills."

Simulating a Gradient Line

You can simulate a gradient line. It takes a bit of effort, but for some applications it is well worth it. The following instructions are for a straight line, but you can alter them to create curves as well.

1. Draw a straight line, and apply the line width you desire.

2. Using the Shape tool, select both nodes. Click on the + button of the Node Edit roll-up, or the + key on the keyboard, multiple times to add evenly spaced nodes. The number of nodes you add is dependent upon the length of the line, and the number of gradient steps you want. The example shown in figure 7.9 has a total of four nodes for both line segments. This is an approximate amount and can be adjusted to meet your needs.

3. Select all the nodes, and click on the Break button in the Node Edit roll-up to break the line into segments.

4. Select Brea**k** Apart from the **A**rrange menu to make the line segments individual objects.

5. Delete segments to leave the two end segments.

6. Color the two line segments.

7. Blend the two segments together. For more information on using Blend, see Chapter 11, "Creating with Special Effects."

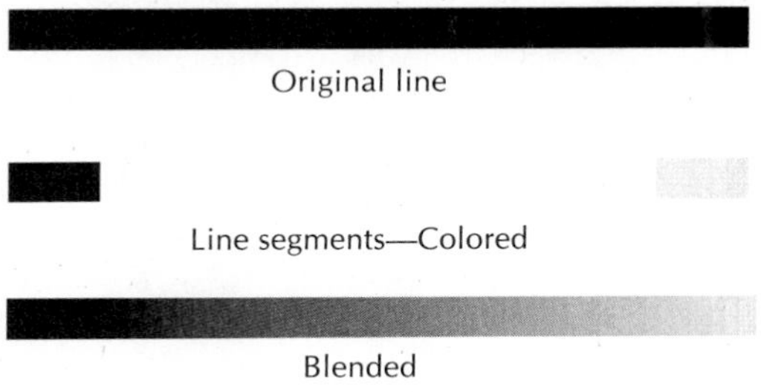

Original line

Line segments—Colored

Blended

Figure 7.9
Gradient outline illusion.

With some adjustment this illusion can be used with curved lines. If applying this effect to a closed object, copy a duplicate of the object to the Clipboard without an outline. Select no fill for the object in the drawing window. Complete the gradient line effect, and paste the object with no outline back over the top of it. Group the resulting image to prevent it from being accidentally shifted.

Working with Arrowheads

Arrowheads (see fig. 7.10) can be applied to any open path. They are especially useful for dimension lines and callouts. An assortment of arrowheads are included with

CorelDRAW. You can also edit an arrowhead or create your own. To apply an arrowhead to the start of a line, click on the left box in the Arrows section of the Outline Pen dialog box, or in the Pen roll-up. Click on the right box to place an arrowhead at the end of a line. In addition to arrowheads, special end caps are available in the selection boxes.

box (see fig. 7.11). The selected arrowhead appears in the editing window. The solid black line in the window is the reference line. This enables you to see how the arrowhead will be placed in relationship to the line.

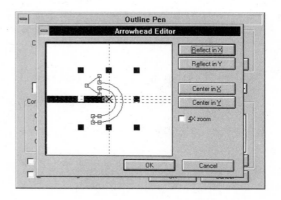

Figure 7.11
The Arrowhead Editor dialog box.

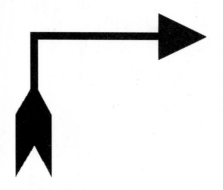

Figure 7.10
An example of a CorelDRAW arrowhead.

Using the Arrowhead Editor

The arrowhead is sized in proportion to the line width. You can resize or edit the shape of an arrowhead. To edit an arrowhead, follow these steps:

1. Select the arrowhead you want to edit, and click on the **O**ptions button in the Arrows section of the Outline Pen dialog box.

2. From the drop-down menu, select **E**dit to display the Arrowhead Editor dialog

3. You can drag the handles to scale or stretch the arrowhead, as you would with any object. To center the head over the X, click on one of the Center buttons. Center in X centers the arrowhead vertically; center in Y centers the arrowhead horizontally. To flip the arrowhead horizontally, click on Reflect in X; vertically, click on Reflect in Y.

You can remove an arrowhead from the list by selecting the arrowhead you want to remove in the arrowhead list box. Click on the **O**ptions button, and select Delete From List.

Creating Arrowheads

CorelDRAW enables you to create custom arrowheads in the drawing window, and then add them to the arrowhead list. To create a custom arrowhead, follow these steps:

1. Open ARROW1.CDR, created earlier in Chapter 2. The arrowhead appears, as shown in figure 7.12.

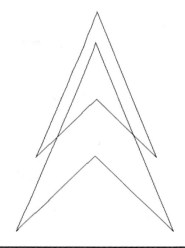

Figure 7.13
Adding the second section.

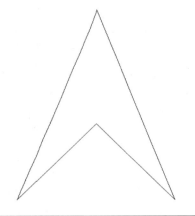

Figure 7.12
ARROW1.CDR.

2. Duplicate the shape, move it up about one inch, and scale it, as shown in figure 7.13, to add a second object.

3. Select the two objects and apply the Weld command.

4. Open the Contour roll-up in the Effe**c**ts pull-down menu. Select Inside, Offset to .20 inches and set steps to one. Click on Apply.

5. In the **A**rrange menu, select **S**eparate.

6. Deselect the outermost arrowhead by clicking on it while depressing the Shift key. This leaves the innermost arrowhead as selected. Press Ctrl+U to ungroup it.

7. Select the two objects and combine them. Fill the resulting object with black.

8. Rotate the arrowhead –90 degrees (see fig. 7.14).

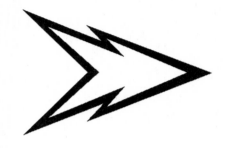

Figure 7.14
The arrowhead after combining and rotating.

9. With the arrow selected, choose Create **A**rrow from the **S**pecial menu. A dialog box appears, asking for confirmation to create the arrowhead. Click on OK. The arrowhead is added to the Arrows list.

Creating Calligraphic Effects

CorelDRAW enables you to add calligraphic effects to outlines. These effects alter the appearance of an object by varying the line width according to the orientation of the line. The default shape of the pen nib is square; the configuration is 100-percent stretch and 0-degrees angle. The default pen orientation is horizontal. This gives lines an equal width, regardless of the angle of the line.

Altering the stretch and angle of the pen nib changes the orientation and width of the nib. The value here is a percentage of the pen width setting. You can change the orientation and stretch interactively by clicking in the preview box of the calligraphic effects section, and dragging the pen nib. If you would like a rounded pen nib, click on the radio button beside the rounded corner option.

Using calligraphic pen effects (see fig. 7.15) is mostly a matter of experimentation. The affect of any amount of stretch or orientation depends upon the selected object.

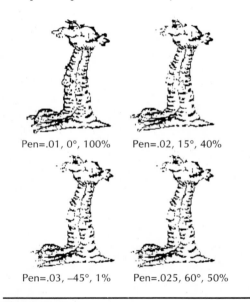

Figure 7.15
Using calligraphic pen effects.

Using PowerLine Effects

PowerLines allow for additional pen type effects. Although the appearance of a PowerLine is that of a line, it is not strictly an outline. It is a dynamically linked group of objects. Objects of varying or tapered widths are calculated and linked to a line. Unlike calligraphic pen effects, PowerLines can have a fill, as well as an outline. If you use a pressure-sensitive tablet, PowerLines can respond to the tablet, allowing your stylus to behave much like an artist's pen. All PowerLine effects are accessed via the PowerLine roll-up (see fig. 7.16). To display the roll-up, select PowerLine Roll-Up from the Effects menu. Keyboard Shortcut = Ctrl+F8.

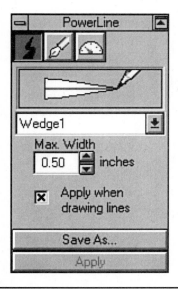

Figure 7.16
The PowerLine roll-up.

Examining the PowerLine Roll-Up

The PowerLine roll-up contains 24 preset effects that can be applied either as lines are drawn, or afterwards. Click on Apply when drawing lines to apply PowerLines to every object drawn. To apply a preset to a selected object, choose the Preset from the list box. To remove a PowerLine from an object, select the object and click on None from the Preset list. Adjust the maximum width, and click on Apply. The chart in figure 7.17 shows the various presets applied to the same line.

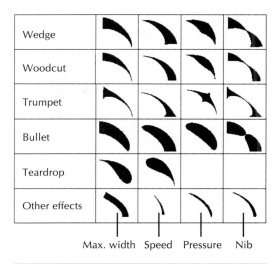

Figure 7.17
Preset PowerLine styles.

N O T E

PowerLines create large files and are memory-intensive. Consider either working in wireframe view or applying PowerLines after drawing an object, to prevent long refresh times.

Adjusting the Maximum Width

You can adjust the maximum line width that is applied to a PowerLine. A PowerLine can be any width between .01" and 16.0". The default line width is .50". The effect the maximum width has on a PowerLine is dependent upon the line width set in the Outline Pen dialog box (see fig. 7.18).

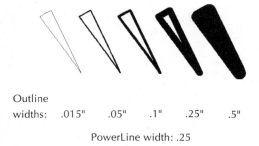

Outline
widths: .015"   .05"   .1"   .25"   .5"

PowerLine width: .25

Figure 7.18
Outline width and PowerLine width.

N O T E

If you are creating a PowerLine of uniform width, the resulting line can appear to have chunks removed from it, where the control line takes a sharp change in direction. To correct this problem, adjust the node control points.

Adjusting Speed, Spread, and Ink Flow

Clicking on the configuration button in the PowerLine roll-up enables you to adjust the speed, spread, and ink Flow (see fig. 7.19). Speed and spread are reliant upon one another for information to achieve an effect. Ink Flow operates independently.

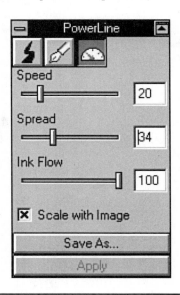

Figure 7.19
The PowerLine roll-up Speed, Spread, and Ink Flow settings.

The following list describes the Speed, Spread, and Ink Flow settings:

- The speed setting adjusts the response of the PowerLine at a sharp curve. The program takes into consideration the amount of the curve. Higher speed settings produce wider lines at sharp curve; lower settings create narrower lines. The response is less dramatic for moderate curves (see fig. 7.20).

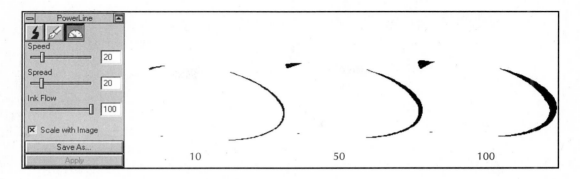

Figure 7.20

The effect of Speed settings on a curve.

- Spread adjusts the response to Spread to smooth a curve, when the Speed is set at a value greater than 0. Lower settings create more segmented and rougher lines; higher settings create more continuous and smoother lines (see fig. 7.21).

- Ink Flow adjusts the amount of ink in the pen. Higher values produce more continuous lines; smaller values more segmented lines (see fig. 7.22).

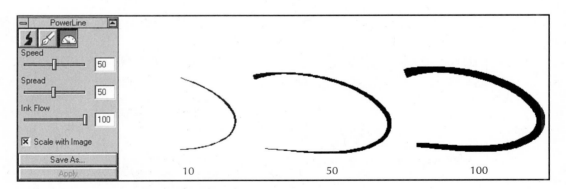

Figure 7.21

The effect of Spread settings on a curve.

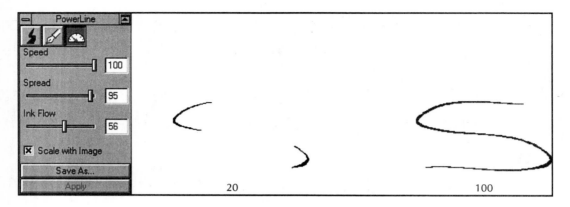

Figure 7.22
The effect of Ink Flow settings on a curve.

Using Scale With Image

Scale With Image operates much like it does with outlines. You should select this as a default, unless the specific application requires it be disabled. When Scale with Image is enabled, the width of the PowerLine is scaled in proportion to the object.

Using the Pressure Preset

The Pressure Preset applies to lines as they are drawn. If you are using the Pressure Preset to take advantage of a pressure-sensitive tablet, the Pencil tool appears when the preset is enabled. You can mimic a pressure-sensitive tablet by using the up and down keys, while drawing to adjust pressure.

When you draw a line with the Pressure Preset, the line responds to the amount of pressure you apply. This may require some experimentation to achieve the effect you want. If your tablet is configurable, you may want to adjust the pressure sensitivity.

N O T E

Use of a pressure-sensitive tablet can increase the number of nodes in a line. Use Auto-Reduce from the Node Edit roll-up to eliminate superfluous nodes.

Modifying the Nib Shape

You can change the width and angle of a nib, allowing the pen nib to behave as a croquis pen. The effect of the changes alters the appearance of the PowerLine by allowing the line to vary in width as it is drawn (see fig. 7.23). To change the nib's shape, click on the Nib button in the PowerLine roll-up. Click and drag the nib in the preview box to adjust the angle. Dragging away from the box makes a thinner nib; closer to the box creates a wider nib. Adjusting the Intensity changes the response of the angle and shape to a curve. Higher values create more dramatic effects.

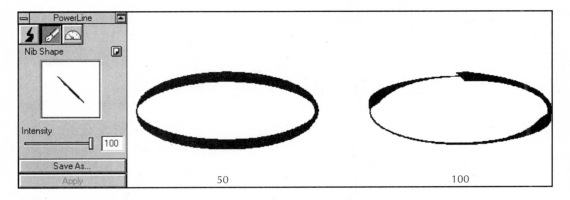

Figure 7.23
The effect of adjusting the nib.

N O T E

Nib and Speed controls affect one another—this changes the appearance of a PowerLine. If neither of the controls are active, no change is made, and acute corners and curves are triangular. If the Speed controls are active, acute curves and corners are rounded. When the Nib is active, acute corners and curves are trimmed at the nib angle. If both controls are active, Nib is dominant, and the acute corners and curves are trimmed.

Saving Custom PowerLines

When you create a PowerLine, the wrench icon appears in the window if the line does not represent one of the presets. This indicates that the PowerLine has been customized. You can save a custom PowerLine by clicking on the Save As button near the bottom of the PowerLine roll-up. A dialog box appears, enabling you to name the

PowerLine. Click on OK to save the PowerLine for future use, and return to the drawing window.

Cloning a PowerLine

You can clone the attributes of a PowerLine from one object to a selected object. The attributes of a clone cannot be edited directly. The master object must be edited to affect changes in the clone. You can change the fill and outline color of a clone, as well as stretch, scale, or transform a clone.

You cannot undo a PowerLine clone unless you have sufficient Undo levels configured in the Preferences dialog box. You must either select Clear PowerLine from the Effects pull-down menu, or None from the roll-up. This clears the PowerLine effect from the master object, as well as any clones. One way around this is to copy the clones to the Clipboard, and then delete the clone(s) and paste the objects back into the drawing window, You can then edit the objects individually.

Copying a PowerLine

Selecting PowerLine, located in the Copy fly-out of the Effects menu, enables you to copy the PowerLine attributes from one object to a selected object. Unlike with Clone PowerLine, you retain full editing ability.

Editing PowerLines Using the Node Edit Roll-Up

Using the Shape tool, you can edit a PowerLine much as you would any other curved object. To edit a PowerLine, double-click on the core line with the Shape tool to display the Node Edit roll-up (see fig. 7.24).

You can move the control points of a node on the core line to adjust the angle of the ends of a PowerLine. You can also use any of the other node edit commands.

When a PowerLine is selected, the Node Edit roll-up changes to include Pressure Edit. Pressure Edit enables you to uniformly resize portions of a Pressure PowerLine. Enable Pressure Edit to resize a Pressure PowerLine, as shown in figure 7.25. To edit a portion of the line uniformly, select two Pressure Edit Handles. Drag the handles to adjust the line. If you want to adjust just one side of a PowerLine, use Ctrl+click to select all the handles on one side; use Shift+Ctrl+click to select all the handles on the other side.

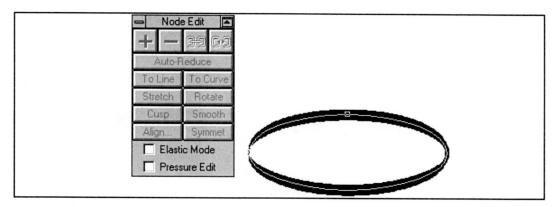

Figure 7.24
Node Edit roll-up with a selected PowerLine.

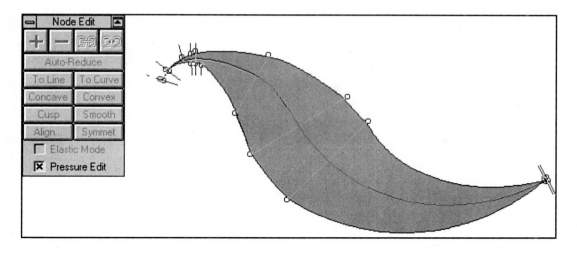

Figure 7.25
Editing a Pressure PowerLine.

Editing Multiple Subpaths

When a PowerLine has multiple subpaths, the response to editing changes is dependent upon whether the line is a Pressure PowerLine or one of the presets. If the PowerLine is one of the presets, you can edit each subpath as desired. When editing a Pressure PowerLine, editing changes for one subpath are applied to all subpaths.

If you apply Pressure features to a PowerLine created with a preset, either the Pressure feature or the preset becomes dominant, as follows:

- Pressure is dominant in wider portions of the line.

- Preset is dominant in narrower portions of the line.

Summary

Using outlines and PowerLines to define an image enables you to add depth, and make a powerful statement with your document. The variety of calligraphic effects possible enable you to give your image a three-dimensional appearance. The previous chapters have dealt with creating individual objects. Chapter 8, "Transforming and Arranging Objects," discusses the relationship between objects.

Transforming and Arranging Objects

*T*ransforming, arranging, and establishing the relationships between objects is critical to document layout. Chapter 5, "Shaping Objects," discussed using the mouse to move and transform objects. Mice lack the precision required for some documents.

The Transform roll-up offers precision that is difficult to achieve with a mouse. Using the Transform roll-up, objects can be moved, sized, stretched, scaled, rotated, skewed, and mirrored with accuracy.

The *A*rrange menu enables you to establish the relationship between objects. You can change the order or group objects, allowing them to be transformed as a single unit.

This chapter covers:

- Using the Transform roll-up
- Using anchor points
- Clearing transformations
- Arranging objects

Using the Transform Roll-Up

The Transform roll-up is actually five roll-ups in one. The view changes according to the command icon chosen. Regardless of the command chosen, the basic method for applying the command is the same—select Apply to Duplicate, copy the objects, and apply the command to the copy.

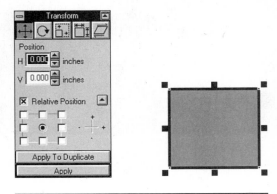

Figure 8.1

The Position view of the Transform roll-up.

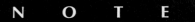

N O T E

There are multiple ways of accessing the Transform roll-up. Most of the transformation commands have individual keyboard shortcuts associated with them.

Moving Objects

The Transform roll-up enables you to position objects in either a relative or absolute manner (see fig. 8.1). Relative movement considers the object's current location, and moves the object respective to that location. Absolute movement places the object relative to the printable page. When the relative position is not checked, then the absolute position takes place.

To move an object a specific distance, follow these steps:

1. Select the object you want to move, and access the Transform roll-up by selecting it from the Effects menu or from the ribbon bar. Keyboard shortcut = Alt+F7.

2. Click on the down arrow to display the entire roll-up, and enable Relative Position.

3. Click on the position icon, if not already selected.

4. Enter the distance you want to move the object in the Horizontal and Vertical entry boxes. Positive values move the object up and to the right; negative values move the object down and to the left. Alternatively, click on the anchor point around which you

want the object to move. For more information about anchor points, see "Using Anchor Points," later in this chapter.

5. Click on Apply to complete the operation.

To move an object relative to the page, follow these steps:

1. Enable Show Rulers, if they are not already displayed.

2. Disable Relative Position in the Transform roll-up.

3. Enter the coordinates for the new position where you want the object placed. Click on the alignment location you want. Clicking the upper-left square would position the upper-left corner of the object at the selected coordinates.

4. Click on Apply to complete the operation.

Rotating Objects

Each object in CorelDRAW has a center point, or center of rotation. When you rotate an object, it pivots on its center, either clockwise or counterclockwise. You can change the center of rotation either with the mouse, or by entering values in the Center of Rotation offset boxes (see fig. 8.2). In addition, you can use the anchor points to define how the object will rotate in relation to its center.

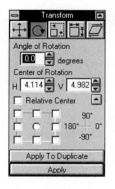
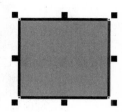

Figure 8.2
The Rotation view of the Transform roll-up.

To rotate an object, follow these steps:

1. Select the object you want to rotate, and access the Transform roll-up by selecting it from the Effects menu or from the ribbon bar. Keyboard shortcut = Alt+F8.

2. Click on the down arrow to display the entire roll-up.

3. Click on the Angle of Rotation button on the Transform roll-up.

4. Enter the value in the Angle of Rotation box, or use the scroll bars to change the value. Negative values rotate the object clockwise; positive values rotate the object counterclockwise.

5. Click on one of the anchor points to define how you want the object to pivot around its center of rotation.

6. Click on Apply to complete the operation.

Moving the Center of Rotation

To move the center of rotation to an exact location, follow these steps:

1. Leave the Angle of Rotation at 0 degrees. Enter the desired location in the Center of Rotation entry boxes. The current center of rotation is displayed both in the Center of Rotation entry boxes and in the Status Line.

2. Click on Apply to move the center of rotation to the new location.

To move the center of rotation using relative center and the anchor points, follow these steps:

1. Enable Relative Center and leave the Angle of Rotation at 0 degrees.

2. Click on one of the anchor points, or enter the relative center offset in the entry boxes.

3. Click on Apply to move the center of rotation to the new location.

Rotating and Skewing Bitmaps

Bitmaps are rotated or skewed as other objects. Rotated or skewed bitmaps are displayed at a lower resolution, however, to increase refresh speed. The resolution is equal to a fractional amount of the original resolution. A 300 dpi bitmap is displayed at approximately 96 dpi; a 1200 dpi bitmap is displayed at approximately 300 dpi. This amount is device dependent. The resolution of your monitor affects the display.

N O T E

A rotated or skewed bitmap cannot be copied and pasted via the Clipboard into other applications. You can, however copy and paste a rotated or skewed bitmap within CorelDRAW.

Scaling and Stretching Objects

Scaling and stretching differ in that an object that is stretched does not necessarily maintain its aspect ratio. Scaling an object maintains the aspect ratio, as it is increased in length and width by the same amount. The Transform roll-up enables you to scale and stretch objects with precision (see fig. 8.3).

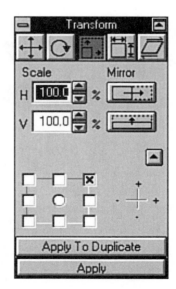

Figure 8.3
The Scale and Stretch view of the Transform roll-up.

To stretch an object, follow these steps:

1. Select the object to be stretched, and access the Transform roll-up by selecting it from the Effects menu or from the ribbon bar. Keyboard shortcut = Alt+F9.

2. Click on the Scale button in the Transform roll-up.

3. Click on the down arrow to display the entire roll-up, and enter the percentage of horizontal and/or vertical stretch you want in the entry boxes.

4. Click on an anchor point to define the direction you want the object to be stretched. Click on Apply to complete the operation.

To scale an object, follow these steps:

1. Select the object to be scaled, and access the Transform roll-up by selecting it from the Effects menu or from the ribbon bar. Keyboard shortcut = Alt+F9.

2. Click on the down arrow to display the entire roll-up, and enter the percentage of horizontal and vertical scaling you want in the entry boxes.

3. Click on an anchor point to define the direction you want the object to be scaled. Click on Apply to complete the operation.

Mirroring Objects

You can flip an object horizontally or vertically. This is useful when you want to print part of an image emulsion down, such

as text, but want the rest of the image to maintain its current orientation. Figure 8.4 highlights the Mirror settings in the Transform roll-up.

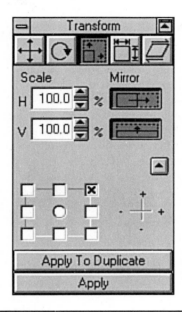

Figure 8.4

The Mirror view of the Transform roll-up.

To mirror an object, follow these steps:

1. Select the object to be mirrored, and access the Transform roll-up by selecting it from the Effects menu or from the ribbon bar. Keyboard shortcut = Alt+F9.

2. Click on the down arrow to display the entire roll-up, and click on the horizontal and/or vertical mirror button(s).

3. Click on an anchor point to define the direction you want the object to be mirrored. Click on Apply to complete the operation.

Sizing Objects

Sizing an object or image to specific dimensions is useful when creating precision drawings. This command enables you to size an image to page, but it does not automatically maintain the aspect ratio. The dimensions must be calculated manually. Figure 8.5 shows the Size settings in the Transform roll-up.

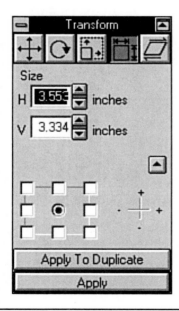

Figure 8.5
The Size view of the Transform roll-up.

To size an object, follow these steps:

1. Select the object to be sized, and access the Transform roll-up by selecting it from the Effe**c**ts menu or from the ribbon bar. Keyboard shortcut = Alt+F9.

2. Click on the Size button in the Transform roll-up.

3. Click on the down arrow to display the entire roll-up, and enter the horizontal and vertical dimensions you want in the entry boxes.

4. Click on an anchor point to define the direction you want the object to be sized. Click on Apply to complete the operation.

Skewing Objects

Skewing objects modifies the shape of objects by slanting them. The Transform roll-up enables you to skew objects with precision (see fig. 8.6).

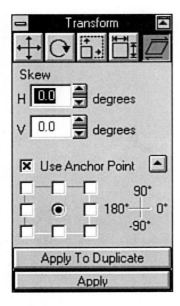

Figure 8.6
The Skew view of the Transform roll-up.

To skew an object, follow these steps:

1. Select the object to be skewed, and access the Transform roll-up by selecting it from the Effects menu or from the ribbon bar. Keyboard shortcut = Alt+F12.

2. Click on the down arrow to display the entire roll-up, and enter the percentage of horizontal and/or vertical skew you want in the entry boxes. Positive values skew the object counterclockwise; negative values skew the object clockwise.

3. Click on an anchor point to define the direction you want the object to be skewed. Click on Apply to complete the operation.

Using Anchor Points

Anchor points enable you to change the point of origin, around which an object will be transformed. The anchor point functions as a locked pivot for the operation. All transformation, with the exception of Positioning, work with anchor points in the same manner. In figure 8.7, the hands were rotated 45 degrees, with Relative center disabled. Each hand was rotated around its respective anchor. The white hands represent the original position of the hands.

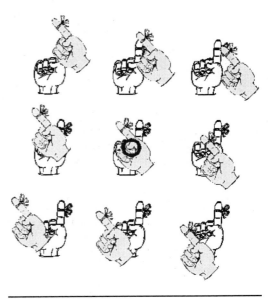

Figure 8.7
Using anchors to modify rotation.

When used with the Position command, the object is moved according to whether the object is being moved with absolute positioning or relative positioning. When combined with absolute positioning, the selected anchor aligns on the page with the coordinates you have selected. When combined with relative positioning, the object moves relative to the anchor. If you were to select the right anchor, the object would use that anchor as the starting point for the move. The object would move the amount you entered in the horizontal and vertical entry boxes. It would use the anchor point, rather than the object's current location, as the starting point for the move.

Clearing Transformations

Clearing transformations enables you to reset any rotation, skewing, stretching, scaling, and sizing changes that have been made to an individual object. It will not undo any repositioning of the object. When you apply clear transformations to a group of objects, only the transformation made to the group is cleared. Changes made to individual objects are not cleared. This is useful when you have made several transformations to an object and want to clear them.

Arranging Objects

Establishing the relationship between objects provides control over images. When working with complex images, these relationships can help speed creation, layout, and printing

time. CorelDRAW offers the ability to arrange objects, as follows:

- Ordering overlapping objects
- Grouping and ungrouping objects
- Aligning objects with one another
- Centering objects on the page
- Combining objects to create clipping holes and masks

Ordering Objects

When you draw, import, or paste an object in CorelDRAW, the object is automatically placed on top of all the other objects. CorelDRAW creates objects on levels of position. Each object or group of objects occupies its own level. These levels are somewhat like sheets of paper, each with a line or group of lines on it, stacked on top of one another. Choosing **O**rder from the **A**rrange menu allows you to change the stacking order of objects (see fig. 8.8). When you select Order, a submenu appears, enabling you to choose from the following commands:

- **To Front.** Places the selection on top of all other objects.
- **To Back.** Places the selection behind all other objects.
- **Forward One.** Moves the select forward one position.
- **Back One.** Moves the selection back one position.
- **Reverse Order.** Reverses the order of the selected objects.

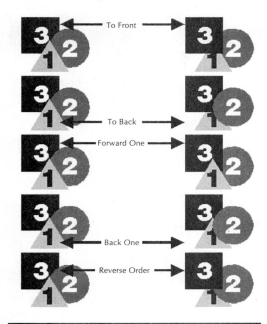

Figure 8.8
Reordering objects.

N O T E

If you import or paste an object from another application, the objects appear centered on the page.

A group of objects all occupy a single level in the stacking order. When you group a selection of objects, all of the objects move to the level of the last object selected. When you apply the command to a group, all of the objects of the group move together. They do maintain their relationship to one another, however.

Sometimes it is difficult to establish the stacking order of a number of objects that overlap or are superimposed. This is a particular problem when you are working in wireframe view. You can use the tab key to move through the stack of objects. The tabbing order in CorelDRAW is from front to back. By repeatedly pressing the Tab key, you can move through the stack to select a particular object. This is also useful for applying the same command to a series of objects. For example, if you wanted to change all the black objects to red, you could select one black object and fill it with red. Then you could tab through the objects to identify all the black objects, and apply the Repeat command until all the black objects are changed. The Status Line shows you the fill and outline color of an object.

Reversing the order of a selection of objects is used not only with individual objects. The Reverse Order command enables you to change the order of a blended group of objects. For more information about blending objects, see Chapter 11, "Creating with Special Effects."

Grouping and Ungrouping Objects

Grouping enables you to collect multiple objects together in a set. The objects can then be manipulated as a single unit. This is useful when working with large graphic images, if you want to arrange a number of objects in the same manner. Each object retains its individual attributes, unless you change the attributes of the group. The stack order of the objects cannot be changed without ungrouping the set. To create a group of objects, follow these steps:

1. Select the objects to be grouped. Be sure the stacking order is the way you want it before grouping them. Hold the Shift key down and select each object, or marquee-select the objects. Remember that all the objects will be placed on the same level as the last object selected. If you marquee-select the objects, all objects will move to occupy the same level as the bottommost object.

2. Select **G**roup from the **A**rrange menu to complete the operation. The group can now be manipulated as a unit. Keyboard shortcut = Ctrl+G.

When creating a group of objects from multiple layers, the objects move to the layer of the object selected last. If you marquee-select the objects, they move to the same layer as the bottommost object.

Selecting a Child Object

If you want to edit a single object in a group, you do not have to ungroup the set of objects. Hold down the Ctrl key, and select the child object. If you have created groups of groups, you may have to click multiple times to select the individual object. You can then transform or edit the object.

When creating a short string of artistic text, select Center alignment. This enables you to change the text later, without having to reposition the text. It will automatically center itself into the same position as the old text. This is helpful when the text is part of a group, or has been aligned in relationship to other objects. It can also take the work out of merging text and inserting text into templates.

Ungrouping Objects

Groups can either be a temporary or permanent method of maintaining the relationship between a set of objects. If you want to ungroup a set of objects, click on any of the objects to select the group, and choose **U**ngroup from the **A**rrange menu. Keyboard shortcut = Ctrl+U.

Aligning Objects

The Align command enables you to align selected objects or groups of objects with one another. When you select Align from the ribbon bar or the **A**rrange menu, the Align dialog box appears (see fig. 8.9), enabling you to select your alignment choices.

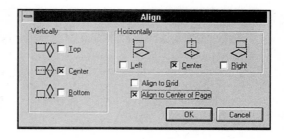

Figure 8.9
The Align dialog box.

To align a selection, follow these steps:

1. Select the objects to be aligned. The objects will align with the last object selected.

2. Choose **A**lign from the **A**rrange menu. Keyboard shortcut = Ctrl+A.

3. Select the alignment options you want, and click on OK to complete the operation and return to the drawing window. Figure 8.10 shows the effect of the various alignment options.

Align Left Horizontal & Top Vertical	Align Center Horizontal & Top Vertical	Align Right Horizontal & Top Vertical
Align Left Horizontal & Center Vertical	Align Center Horizontal & Center Vertical	Align Right Horizontal & Center Vertical
Align Left Horizontal & Bottom Vertical	Align Center Horizontal & Bottom Vertical	Align Right Horizontal & Bottom Vertical

Figure 8.10
Alignment options.

N O T E

Sometimes objects will appear not to align. This is usually because the bounding area of an object includes any control points on a node. If a control point is stretched well beyond the object, the object will not align correctly. To prevent this problem, add a node to define the shape, rather than use a control point.

Centering Objects on the Page

You can center one or more objects on the page by clicking Align to Center of Page, in the Align dialog box. This is useful when you

are getting ready to print your image. By selecting all the objects and temporarily grouping them to hold their place, you can align the entire image on the page. You can ungroup the objects after aligning them.

Using Combine and Break Apart

The Combine command offers a method of group objects for special purposes. It differs from Group in that objects that are combined assume the attributes of the last object selected. If you marquee-select the objects, the resulting object assumes the attributes of the bottommost object. Instead of having a set of objects, it merges the objects together into a single object. The objects need not overlap to be combined.

Because Combine creates a single object, the program stores it differently. This saves hard disk space, conserves memory, and speeds screen refresh. This is useful when creating an image that contains many curved objects, such as a heavily rendered drawing. Combining the cross-hatching in such a drawing would speed the screen refresh and create a smaller file.

To use Combine, follow these steps:

1. Select the objects to be combined.

2. Choose Combine from the **A**rrange menu. Note that grouped objects cannot be combined.

Combine can also be used to create clipping holes or masks. This creates interesting effects in an image (see fig. 8.11).

Figure 8.11
Using Combine to create a mask.

Using Break Apart

The Break Apart command separates an object with multiple subpaths into individual objects. This enables you to undo a combined object. It is also useful when applied to text objects that have been converted to curves. The subpaths become individual objects, and enable you to edit their attributes and transform them separately. When you break apart an object, all of the individual parts assume the same attributes. Since they all have the same fill and outline, this can make it impossible to edit them in Editable Preview. You might find it easier to edit the objects in Wireframe View.

Using Separate

Separate is used to separate dynamically linked groups into their individual elements. Using the Separate command enables you to edit the objects individually.

Use the Separate command to do the following:

- Separate text that has been fitted to path

- Detach the control objects from extruded objects, blends, contours, or PowerLines

Summary

This chapter discussed some of the more commonly used methods of ordering, relating, and aligning objects. Using the Transform roll-up enables you to move and align objects on the page. In the next chapter, grids, guidelines, and other alignment aids will be discussed.

Chapter 9

Using Alignment Aids

*A*lignment aids help give your document a balanced appearance by enabling you to organize the various elements of your document on the page. CorelDRAW provides a set of interrelated precision alignment aids for your use. They ensure consistency when measuring or positioning objects. This set of alignment aids includes rulers, grids, and guidelines.

These alignment aids provide a visual reference for your document. By enabling the Snap To commands, discussed later in this chapter, you can turn grids, guidelines, and objects into virtual magnets. This enables you to position objects with precision and ease.

This chapter covers:

- Setting up rulers
- Moving the rulers
- Setting the grid frequency
- Setting the grid origin
- Setting the drawing scale
- Examining the Guidelines Setup dialog box
- Using Snap To Grid
- Using Snap To Objects and Guidelines

Using Rulers

CorelDRAW's rulers make measuring and positioning objects while drawing easier. When **R**ulers from the **V**iew menu is enabled, the rulers appear at the top and left of the drawing window, as shown in figure 9.1. The dotted lines on the rulers indicate the current position of your cursor, and move as your cursor moves across the drawing window.

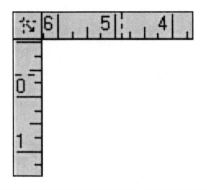

Figure 9.1

CorelDRAW's rulers.

N O T E

CorelDRAW saves the configuration of alignment aids, both in its INI files and with the files created in CorelDRAW. This makes them available for future sessions. When you start a new drawing, grid and ruler settings are the same as for the last file that was saved or opened in the program. If you open an existing drawing, the ruler, grid, and guideline settings for that file are displayed. The grid and ruler settings become the new default until you change them, or open a file with different settings.

Enabling the Cross H**a**ir Cursor, on the View property sheet of the Preferences dialog box found in the **S**pecial pull-down menu, turns the cursor into crosshairs (see fig. 9.2). The crosshairs extend across the drawing window and rulers, both horizontally and vertically. This enables you to measure and align objects more easily. Crosshair cursors behave like the arrow cursor as a selection tool, but revert back to the arrow when you move the cursor outside the drawing window.

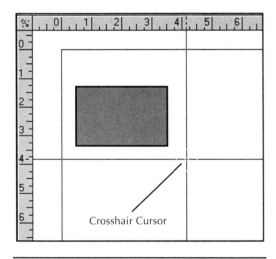

Crosshair Cursor

Figure 9.2

The crosshair cursor (center figure at the line intersection).

The unit of measurement displayed on the status line and the rulers corresponds to the Grid Frequency settings. For information on setting the Grid Frequency, see "Setting the Grid Frequency," later in this chapter.

Setting Up Rulers

The zero position on the rulers equals the coordinates of the grid origin. One way to change the zero points on the rulers is to change the settings for the Grid origin, using the G<u>r</u>id & Scale Setup from the <u>L</u>ayout menu.

N O T E

Double-clicking on either ruler displays the Grid & Scale Setup dialog box.

Alternatively, click on the crosshairs where the rulers meet in the upper left corner of the drawing screen, and drag the crosshairs onto the screen. Once you are satisfied with the position of the cross hairs, release the mouse button. This resets the rulers' zero points at the new location. Changing the zero points resets the grid origin to the new location, as shown in figure 9.3. To return the zero points and grid origin to the default location, double-click on the gray box where the rulers meet.

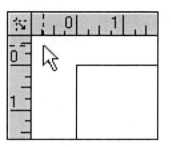

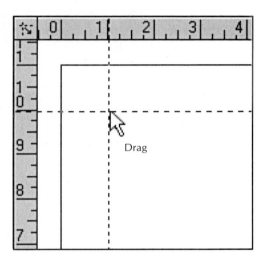

Drag

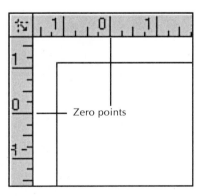

Zero points

Figure 9.3

Resetting the zero points and grid origin.

Moving the Rulers

When manipulating objects that require precise measurement, it is useful to move rulers onto the printable page. To detach rulers from their default location on the page, do one of the following:

■ To move a single ruler, depress the Shift key and click on the ruler. Continue to depress the Shift key while dragging the ruler to reposition it. To move the ruler back to its default location, depress the Shift key and double-click on the ruler.

■ To move both rulers onto the printable page together, depress the Shift key and drag from the gray box where the rulers meet (see fig. 9.4). To move the rulers back to their default location, depress the Shift key and double-click on the gray box where the rulers meet.

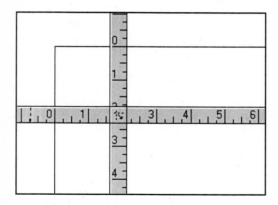

Figure 9.4
Moving rulers onto the printable area.

Using Grids

Displaying a grid furnishes you with a visual reference. This assists in positioning objects in relationship to one another and to the printable area. To configure the grid for your document, select Grid & Scale Setup from the Layout menu. The Grid & Scale Setup dialog box appears, permitting you to adjust the grid frequency, units of measurement, and origin (see fig. 9.5). When you are satisfied with the settings you have made in the Grid & Scale Setup dialog box, click on OK to return to the drawing window.

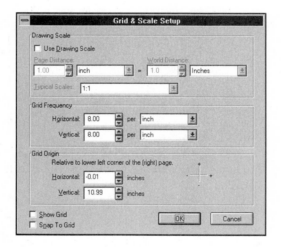

Figure 9.5
The Grid & Scale Setup dialog box.

Setting the Grid Frequency

Clicking on the down arrow beside the unit of measurement lets you select inches, millimeters, picas, or points. The default unit of measurement is an inch. To select the unit of measurement you desire, click on its name.

> **N O T E**
>
> CorelDRAW does automatic conversion of measurement. If you set the value in the entry box for inches and later change it to millimeters, the program will update the value in the entry box to correspond with the new unit of measurement.

CorelDRAW enables you to set the frequency for up to 72 units per inch, 12 per pica, 1 per point, or 2.8 per millimeter. To prevent screen clutter, large settings are not visible when displayed unzoomed. If you choose 8 units per inch, the visible grid will be displayed every half inch. If you zoom in on a section of the printable area, a larger number of the units become visible. Select the box beside **S**how Grid to display the grid within your drawing.

Setting the Grid Origin

The Grid origin is the point where the horizontal and vertical coordinates intersect at (0,0). The default location is in the lower left corner of single page documents, and the lower left corner of the right page in multiple page documents. The most popular setting for the grid origin is either at the center of the page or at its default location. If your printer's image size is less than the current page size, setting the origin for the required margins is helpful. This gives you a visual printing boundary.

> **N O T E**
>
> The grid frequency and units of measurement affect the behavior of some of CorelDRAW's special effects. Fine adjustment of an extrusion, for example, might be difficult if the current grid frequency is too large.

Setting the Drawing Scale

CorelDRAW enables you to create scaled images. This is useful when creating a landscaping or other design that calls for precision scaling. Note that the Grid Frequency updates to reflect the settings in the Drawing Scale section.

> **N O T E**
>
> The values entered in the Page Distance and World Distance entry boxes affect measurement when using dimension lines. For more information about dimension lines, see Chapter 2, "Using Graphic Tools."

To set the drawing scale, follow these steps:

1. Access the Grid & Scale Setup dialog box, and enable Use **D**rawing Scale.

2. Select the units of measurement for Page Distance and World Distance. Enter the desired values in the entry boxes. Alternatively, select a unit of measurement from one of the unit boxes, and click on the down arrow to display the Typical Scales.

N O T E

Generally, grids and guidelines are for on-screen reference and are non-printable. You can choose to print them within your document by using the Layers roll-up. Double-click on the Grid or Guidelines layer name, and select Printable. You can change the color by clicking on the color box and choosing a new color. For more information about layers, see Chapter 10, "Using Layers in Documents."

Using Guidelines

Guidelines offer you another method of aligning objects. You can place as many guidelines as you desire anywhere within the drawing window. To place a guideline, click and drag from either ruler toward the drawing window. Use the top ruler to place horizontal guidelines; use the side ruler to place vertical guidelines. Double-clicking on a guideline accesses the Guidelines Setup dialog box, as shown in figure 9.6.

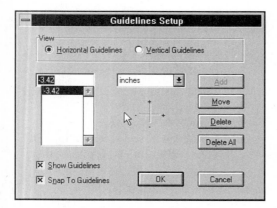

Figure 9.6
The Guidelines Setup dialog box.

Examining the Guidelines Setup Dialog Box

The Guidelines Setup dialog box enables you to precisely place guidelines within your document. To place a guideline, choose either **H**orizontal or **V**ertical, and enter the desired location. Click **A**dd to place the guideline, and click on OK to return to the drawing window.

If you want to move a guideline, click on the guideline and drag it to the new location. Alternatively, access the Guideline Setup dialog box by either double-clicking on the guideline or selecting G**u**idelines Setup from the **L**ayout menu. Select Horizontal or Vertical, then choose the desired guideline from the list box. Enter the new location in the text entry box and select **M**ove to reposition the guideline, and then return to the drawing window.

You can also delete guidelines in the Guidelines Setup dialog box. It is easier, however, to click on the guideline and drag it back to the ruler.

Using Snap To Commands

The Snap To commands allow guidelines, grids, and objects to behave like magnets, attracting objects that are drawn or moved near them. The positions of objects already on the screen do not change when one of the Snap To commands is enabled.

To enable a Snap To command, select it from the **L**ayout menu. You can also enable Snap To Grid and Snap To Guidelines in the

Grid & Scale Setup or Guidelines Setup dialog boxes, respectively. A message appears in the status line, indicating when Snap To commands are enabled.

Using Snap To Grid

When Snap To Grid is enabled, your cursor is constrained to stay on the grid points, which enables you to draw objects with a great deal of precision. This is useful when the measurement of objects is critical, or when drawing dimensioning lines. There are a few instances when the cursor is not constrained to the grid lines, as in the following:

■ Using the Pick tool or Shape tool to select an object.

■ Using Copy Style From.

■ Drawing a curve in freehand or Bézier mode.

■ Using the Zoom tool.

■ Rotating or skewing an object using the Pick tool.

N O T E

Snap To Grid can also be enabled or disabled using the keyboard shortcut, Ctrl+Y.

When moving an object with Snap To Grid enabled, how Snap To Grid behaves is determined by the type of object being moved. There are basically two types of objects in CorelDRAW: graphics objects and text objects. The two object types react to Snap To Grid differently.

N O T E

When an object is moved, a marquee box appears around the object, defining its editing boundaries. It is possible that an object's editing boundaries might appear to be well beyond the actual shape of the object. This occurs when a control point defining the Shape of the object extends beyond the object, or when an ellipse has been edited with the Shape tool. CorelDRAW uses the control points, which define the editing boundaries, to align graphics objects. Aligning objects whose boundaries exceed the actual shape of the object can yield unexpected results.

The corner handles of graphic objects are forced to the nearest grid point. The handle that snaps to the grid is determined by the direction in which you are moving the object, and which corner of the object you use to initiate the move. If you were moving a rectangle down and to the right, clicking and dragging the upper left corner would force the upper left handle to the grid (see fig. 9.7).

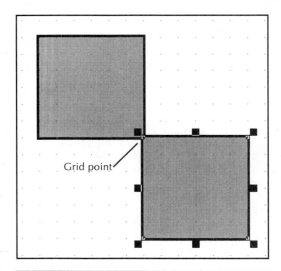

Grid point

Figure 9.7

Using Snap To Grid to align graphics objects.

N O T E

If the edge of a rectangle lies on a grid point, you must disable Snap To Grid in order to edit the rectangle with the Shape tool. This is because the corner node of the rectangle is attracted to the grid.

When moving artistic text vertically with Snap To Grid enabled, the baseline of the text is forced to the grid. When moving the text horizontally, the justification of the artistic text string determines the behavior, as follows:

- **Left Justified.** The left edge of the text snaps to the grid.

- **Center Justified.** The center point of the text snaps to the grid.

- **Right Justified.** The right edge of the text snaps to the grid.

- **No Justification.** If the text justification is None, the position of the starting point of the text string snaps to the grid. A text string, with two spaces at the beginning of the string and no justification, snaps at the left edge of the first space when moved horizontally.

CorelDRAW treats paragraph text like a graphics object when Snap To Grid is enabled. The side of the bounding box of the text snaps to the closest grid point. The side that snaps to the grid is determined by the direction of the move. If paragraph text is moved to the right, the right side of the bounding box snaps to the grid. The justification of the text has no effect on the way paragraph text snaps to the grid.

Using Snap To Guidelines

Snap To Guidelines behaves like Snap To Grid. Objects created or moved with Snap To Guidelines enabled follow the same constraints as Snap To Grid. When both Snap To Grid and Snap To Guidelines are enabled, Snap To Guidelines takes precedence. Regardless of the location of the guideline, an object will snap to the guideline before it will snap to a grid. Snap To Guidelines is enabled by selecting it from the **L**ayout menu.

Using Objects as Guide Objects

CorelDRAW enables you to place objects on the Guidelines layer of a drawing. Objects placed on this layer become Guide Objects, and behave like guidelines. An object on the guideline layer has no fill. The object appears as a dotted outline with the same color attributes as the guidelines.

N O T E

For more information about Layers, see Chapter 10, "Using Layers in Documents."

Every object created in CorelDRAW has snap points. These snap points are the nodes that define the shape of the object, or the baseline nodes of a string of text. When you select an object you want to move, the location of your cursor becomes the selection point. If Snap To commands are enabled, objects being moved on layers other than the Guideline layer behave as follows:

- Snap To Guidelines Enabled and Snap To Objects Disabled: The selection point of the moving object snaps to the snap points of the guide object. This occurs even if the selection point of the moving object is near one of its own snap points (see fig. 9.8).

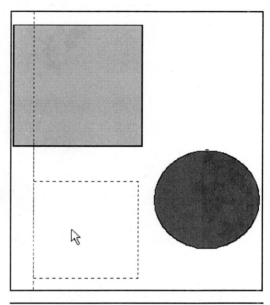

Figure 9.8

Using objects as guides—Snap To Guidelines Enabled & Snap To Objects Disabled.

- Snap To Guidelines Enabled and Snap To Objects Enabled: If the selection point on the moving object is near one of its snap points, the snap point takes priority. The snap point of the moving object snaps to that of the guide object (see fig. 9.9).

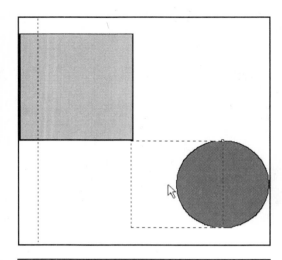

Figure 9.9
Using objects as guides—Snap To Guidelines Enabled and Snap To Objects Enabled.

Use the Shape tool and node edit on a stationary object to control the point to which moving objects will snap. Add nodes, at the desired location, to the stationary object.

Using Snap To Objects

Enable Snap To **O**bject by selecting it from the **L**ayout menu. Select the object you desire to move. Take care to select it at the point you want to snap to the stationary object. Drag the object toward the stationary object. When the moving object is within the gravity range of a snap point, the moving object will snap to it. If the point you select is within the gravity range of the object's own snap points, the snap point of the moving object will snap to that of the stationary object.

Resizing Objects Using Snap To Objects

Using Snap To commands, objects can be accurately resized in relationship to a given measurement or another object. Enable the desired Snap To command by selecting it from the **L**ayout menu.

To resize an object using Snap to Grid or Snap To Guideline, follow these steps:

1. Enable Snap To Grid or Snap To Guideline.

2. Choose the object to be resized, and click on the handle you want to use to resize the object.

3. Drag the handle toward the desired guideline or grid point until the handle snaps to that point.

To resize an object in relationship to another object, as shown in figure 9.10, follow these steps:

1. Enable Snap To Object.

2. Select the object you want to resize.

3. Click on the handle you desire to use to resize the object, and drag your cursor toward the snap point of the stationary object. When your cursor comes within the gravity range of the desired snap point, the cursor will snap to it. The stationary and moving objects may or may not come in contact with one another.

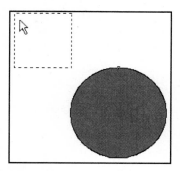

Figure 9.10

Resizing an object using Snap To commands.

Summary

The alignment aids in CorelDRAW provide precision controls for measuring, positioning, and resizing objects. The Grid & Scale dialog box enables you to set the units of measurement for your drawing. By enabling and configuring world units, you can create scaled drawings and include accurate dimension lines.

The Snap To features in the program enable you to use grids, guidelines, and objects as positioning controls. Other control features are available for working with grids, guidelines, and guide objects. These controls are accessed from the Layers dialog box, discussed in Chapter 10, "Using Layers in Documents."

Using Layers in Documents

*L*ayers are like a stack of transparent sheets of media. Each sheet has its own image but allows images below it to show through where that sheet is blank. CorelDRAW enables you to create documents with multiple layers. You can have as many layers as you want. Layers are useful when creating multipage and complex drawings. You can turn individual layers off, making them invisible. This enables you to edit the individual layers without waiting for long refresh cycles. Other layer commands make this a versatile tool for image management. All of the layer controls and options are accessed through the Layers roll-up. To open the Layers roll-up, select it from the **L**ayout menu. Keyboard Shortcut = Ctrl+F3.

This chapter covers:

- Examining the Layers roll-up

- Creating layers

- Editing layers

- Working with image layers

- Using layers to create multiple views of a document

- Working with multipage documents

The number of layers available is not an infinite number. It is limited by the amount of system resources you have available, although systems with limited resources can still employ a large number of layers. On a system with limited resources, the most noticeable effect of a large number of layers is refresh speed. The speed difference is less significant than that of creating a complex document on a single layer, however.

Examining the Layers Roll-Up

The Layers roll-up (see fig. 10.1) offers you a means of image control to assist in the creation and editing of your document. When you first open the roll-up, a list of four layers appears: Grid, Guides, Desktop, and Layer 1. By default, every document has these four layers. Using the Layers roll-up, you can edit and control the elements of this list by doing the following:

- Adding and deleting layers

- Toggling the visibility of individual layers

- Making individual layers nonprintable

- Locking individual layers to prevent accidental changes

- Showing or hiding guidelines and grids, and switching their printability

- Changing the order of layers

- Moving or copying objects between layers

- Creating Master layers for multipage documents

Figure 10.1
The Layers roll-up.

The Grid Layer

The Grid layer contains the grid you set for your document. When Snap to Grid is enabled, objects snap to the grid points, even though it resides on its own layer. The layer remains locked, and you cannot add objects to the grid layer. You can make the grid printable, change the color of the grid, and toggle its visibility.

Double-clicking on the Grid layer name in the Layers roll-up, and then S**e**tup in the Edit Layers dialog box, displays the Grid & Scale Setup dialog box, enabling you to edit the grid.

The Guides Layer

The Guides layer contains the guidelines you set for your document. When Snap to Guidelines is enabled, objects snap to the guidelines, even though they reside on their own layer. You can make guidelines printable and change their color. Using the Guides layer, you can temporarily disable the guidelines and guides. This enables you to retain them for later use.

Double-clicking on the Guides layer name in the Layers roll-up, and then clicking on S**e**tup, displays the Guidelines Setup dialog box, enabling you to edit the guidelines.

The Desktop Layer

Any object residing out of the printable page is automatically inserted into the Desktop layer. This layer is used when working with a multipage document. Objects in the Desktop layer are also shown on each page of the document. To insert any of the Desktop objects into another layer, simply drag the object into the printable page.

Layer 1

When you first start a new drawing, all objects are placed on Layer 1. Unless you add layers to create a multilayer document, your entire image will be placed on this layer.

Creating Layers

You can add layers to your document by clicking on the arrow pointing to the right in the Layers roll-up. Selecting New displays the New Layer dialog box. In the Na**m**e entry box, enter the name you want to call your layer (see fig. 10.3). The program numbers layers, by default: Layer 1, Layer 2, Layer 3, and so on. This is not a very descriptive method of naming layers. You can use up to 32 characters to name a layer. Choosing a name that relates to the objects placed on the layer will better assist you in the selection, editing, and printing of objects. Figure 10.2 shows several layer names that correspond to the "castle" graphic.

Figure 10.2

An example of a Layers roll-up with custom names.

When you add a layer, it becomes the active drawing layer. New, pasted, or imported objects are always added to the active drawing layer. You cannot add an object to a locked layer. To change the active layer, click

on the layer name in the Layers roll-up. If a locked layer is active, you cannot add new objects to the drawing. Select an active layer, or unlock the layer, to continue drawing.

To delete a layer, make the layer you want to delete the active layer. Click on the arrow pointing right, in the Layers roll-up, and select Delete.

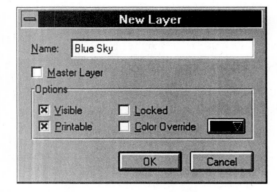

Figure 10.3
The New Layer dialog box.

![WARNING]

When you delete a layer, all of the objects on the layer are deleted with it. Be sure to copy or move objects you want to retain to other layers.

Editing Layers

The Edit Layers dialog box enables you to select the options you want for all layers. To edit a layer, click on the arrow pointing right in the Layers roll-up and select Edit to display the Edit Layers dialog box (see fig. 10.4), or just double-click on any layer name in the Layers roll-up.

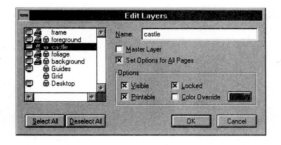

Figure 10.4
The Edit Layers dialog box.

Using the Edit Layers dialog box, highlight the layer you want to edit in the layers list box. To select consecutive layers, click on the individual layer names while depressing the Shift key. Alternatively, click and drag over the desired consecutive layers. To select multiple nonconsecutive layers, click on the individual layer names while depressing the Ctrl key. Once you have made the layer selections you want, you can set multipage options and toggle various options on and off. When you are satisfied with the options you have selected, click on OK to return to the drawing window.

To change the name of a layer, select the layer. Swipe the current text in the entry box, and enter the new name. Deleting the current name and leaving the entry box blank displays a missing layer name message. The program requires that every layer have a name.

Switching Visibility

Enabling **V**isible allows the layer to be displayed in your image. When working with complex drawings, it is sometimes desirable to make a layer invisible. This enables you to edit other layers more easily and reduces the screen refresh time. Making a layer invisible does not affect printing. The objects on that layer will still print. Figure 10.5 shows one layer of the rather complex drawing shown in figure 10.2. Each of the 3,584 blocks on this layer were created individually. The use of layers and toggling the visibility were used extensively to create this drawing.

Figure 10.5
Making layers invisible.

Locking Layers

The Edit Layers dialog box enables you to lock layers. Locking layers prevents accidental changes from being made to layers that you are not currently editing. Objects on locked layers cannot be edited or selected.

Switching Printability

The **P**rintable option in the Edit Layers dialog box enables you to print select layers of a drawing. This option is enabled by default for all layers, except the Desktop, Grid, and Guides layers. This is an important proofing tool. By enabling only the layers you want to proof, you can speed printing time. To make the Grid and Guides layers printable, select the layer and check the Printable box.

T I P

When working with large complex files, printing to PostScript devices can be problematic. You can reorganize your drawing so that only one color prints per layer. By printing the individual layers one at a time, you can alleviate some printing problems.

Using Color Override

Switching the **C**olor Override enables you to temporarily change the outline color of all objects on a selected layer. This is useful for identifying objects on a single layer. The objects appear in the drawing window, with the specified outline color and no fill. Using this feature enables you to see the objects below that layer and assists in the editing of complex drawings.

Follow these steps to enable Color Override:

1. Choose an outline color by clicking on the color swatch box, and selecting a color from the palette.

2. Enable Color Override by clicking the box beside it.

When working in Wireframe view, the color you select for the Color Override is the color displayed in the drawing window. This is the color used for that layer, even if Color Override is not enabled.

For the color override to be visible in Editable Preview, Color Override must be enabled.

The little symbols beside the layer names are a graphic representation of the various options given to a specified layer. The monitor symbol means that the layer is visible. The printer symbol tells you that the layer can be outputted to a printer. The lock symbol is self-explanatory, meaning that the layer is locked.

Working with Image Layers

The Layers roll-up enables you to manipulate the order of layers. When you move a layer to a different position, all the objects on that layer move with it. To reorder a layer, click the layer name and drag it up or down to the desired position. You can also arrange individual objects using the Layers roll-up.

Arranging Objects Using the Layers Roll-Up

CorelDRAW enables you to move and copy objects from one layer to another. You can also group and combine objects that reside on different layers.

To move or copy objects from one layer to another, follow these steps:

1. Unless Multilayer is enabled, make the layer active—this contains the object(s) you want to move or copy.

2. Select the objects to be moved or copied.

3. Click on the arrow pointing right on the Layer roll-up, and select either Move or Copy.

4. An arrow appears, enabling you to select the layer in the roll-up where you want to place the objects. Click on the name. The objects are either moved or copied to that layer.

You can group, combine, and arrange objects on different layers. To group or combine objects on multiple layers, follow these steps:

1. Make sure that the layers that contain the objects are unlocked.

2. Select the layer where you want the group or combined object to be placed, to make it the active layer.

3. Select the objects to be grouped or combined, and apply the command. The resulting group or object is moved to the active layer. If you marquee-select the objects, the resulting object or group is moved to the layer that contains the most recently created object.

For more information about using the Group and Combine commands, see Chapter 8, "Transforming and Arranging Objects."

Using Layers To Create Multiple Views of a Document

Suppose you ran a small business and wanted to create a flyer or ad with information that changed only once a month. There are a number of ways to approach this situation. You could create a template, style sheet, or even separate documents. Another approach would be to create the document on different layers.

The example shown in figure 10.6 is a single document created on multiple layers. The bulk of the flyer was placed on a layer named Main Ad. The Regular layer contains the normal pricing and the footer for the ad. The Month End Specials and the discount pricing were placed on the third layer.

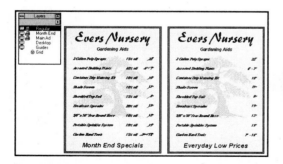

Figure 10.6
Using layers to create multiversion documents.

Toggling visibility and printing allows for the ad to be created in a single document with multiple views. The views can be printed as needed. When creating simple ads and documents with multiple versions, this is a quick way of producing the document. This also assists in file management, because there is only one document to track.

Working with Multipage Documents

Using the layering features in CorelDRAW, you can create Master layers to work in conjunction with multipage documents. Objects placed on Master layers appear on every page of the document, unless you hide them for a given page. You can have more than one Master layer. This enables you to place different information on each of the Master layers. You can then hide or display the information on various pages according to your requirements.

N O T E

For more information regarding multipage documents, see Chapter 12, "Working with Layouts."

To create a Master layer, follow these steps:

1. From the Layers roll-up, choose the layer you want to become the Master layer, or create a new layer.

2. Open the Edit Layers dialog box, and enable the **M**aster Layer option.

The information on that layer appears on every page of the document. If the Master layer contains facing pages, objects contained on the left page are repeated on all left pages of the document; objects contained on the right page are repeated on all right pages of the document. It is important to create facing pages before creating Master layers. Information contained on Master layers is oriented to the drawing window, and not to the page. If you select facing pages after creating a Master layer, objects will appear in the wrong location. For more information regarding facing pages, see Chapter 12, "Working with Layouts."

To hide Master layer information on a selected page, follow these steps:

1. Display the page from which you want to remove the Master layer information.

2. In the Layers roll-up, double-click on the Master layer you want to hide, and disable Set Options for **A**ll Pages. Once you have disabled this function, the Master layer information must be enabled in the individual layers to be visible.

3. Disable the **V**isible option, and click on OK to return to the drawing window.

Summary

CorelDRAW provides you with enormous document control over objects and layers. You can arrange the elements of your document in an almost infinite variety of ways. This chapter and the preceding chapters discussed the basics of object and image control. Chapter 11 takes basic objects and adds a new dimension to your image by adding special effects.

Creating with Special Effects

*C*orelDRAW's versatility lies in the range of the program's abilities. A number of effects are created with outlines, fills, and basic manipulation of text and objects. The Effects menu expands those abilities by enabling you to add another dimension to your images.

Many of the effects illustrated in this chapter appear in the color insert and are contained on *the* CorelDRAW! The Professional Reference companion CDs, enabling you to take a closer look.

This chapter covers:

- Perspective
- Envelope
- Extrude
- Blend
- Contour
- Lens
- PowerClip

Working with Perspective

Applying perspective to objects allows you to create the illusion of depth to an image. On a two-dimensional plane, such as a piece of paper or a monitor screen, objects can appear to float. Adding one- and two-point perspective to objects lends a sense of realism to an image by "grounding" elements of the image. When you select **A**dd Perspective from the Effe**c**ts menu, a bounding box appears around the object or group of objects.

To add one-point perspective to a selection, as displayed in figure 11.1, follow these steps:

1. Select the objects to which you want to apply perspective.

2. When you move the cursor over one of the handles, the cursor changes to a small set of crosshairs.

3. While depressing the Ctrl key, click and drag the handles either vertically or horizontally.

4. Release the mouse button and Ctrl key to complete the operation.

N O T E

The images on the *CorelDRAW! The Professional Reference* companion CDs are the property of their respective artists, and are not clip art. Their owners have graciously donated their use for illustrative purposes only. You must obtain permission to use the illustrations for any other purpose.

To add two-point perspective to a selection, as shown in figure 11.2, follow these steps:

1. Select the objects to which you want to apply perspective.

2. When you move the cursor over one of the handles, the cursor changes to a small set of crosshairs.

3. Click and drag the handles diagonally, either toward or away from the selection.

4. Release the mouse button to complete the operation.

Figure 11.1

Using one-point perspective.

Figure 11.2
Using two-point perspective.

Understanding Vanishing Points

When you add perspective to a selection, one or two vanishing points appear on the screen, represented by an X. If you are applying one-point perspective, one vanishing point is displayed; if you are applying two-point perspective, both a vertical and horizontal vanishing point are displayed.

N O T E

You may have to zoom out to see the vanishing points.

You can move the vanishing point by dragging it to a new location. Moving a vanishing point toward an object makes the closest edge smaller; dragging a vanishing point away from an object makes the closest edge larger. If you drag the vanishing point parallel to the bounding box, the far edge is anchored to its position, and the near edge moves with the vanishing point. If you move a vanishing point too close to an object, the perspective disappears and the object regains its original shape. Use the Ctrl key to constrain the movement of vanishing points to horizontal or vertical movement.

N O T E

Applying **C**lear Transformations from the Effe**c**ts menu clears any perspective applied to a selection, returning it to its original appearance.

Aligning Vanishing Points

You can align the vanishing points of two or more objects, by using the Snap to Guidelines command from the **L**ayout menu. To mark the vanishing point and align the vanishing points, as shown in figure 11.3, follow these steps:

1. Drag a horizontal and vertical guideline to the desired location. The point where the guidelines intersect will be the snap point for the vanishing points.

2. Enable Snap to Guidelines. Drag the horizontal or vertical vanishing point of one object to the intersection until it snaps into place.

3. Repeat step 2 for the other objects.

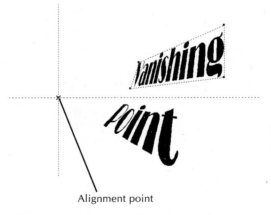

Alignment point

Figure 11.3
Aligning vanishing points.

Using Envelopes

Envelopes enables you to change the shape of an object without altering its attributes. Envelopes works like a container. When you change the shape of the container, the shape of the object changes correspondingly. There are four envelope editing modes that enable you to alter the shape of an object. In addition, there is a collection of preset envelopes that you can apply to objects.

All envelopes are applied using the **E**nvelope roll-up (see fig. 11.4) from the Effe**c**ts menu. To apply an envelope, use the following steps:

1. Select the object or group to which you want to apply an envelope.

2. Choose the **E**nvelope roll-up from the Effe**c**ts Menu.

3. Click on the icon for the editing mode you want to use, and click on Add New.

4. Drag the handles to alter the shape of the object, as you would with the Shape tool, and click on Apply to complete the operation.

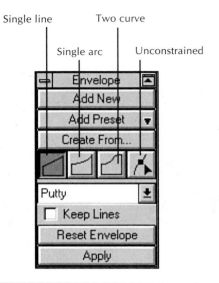

Figure 11.4
The Envelope roll-up.

You can control the way an envelope behaves when you drag the handles, as follows:

■ Depressing the Ctrl key while dragging a handle moves the opposite handle in the same direction.

■ Depressing the Shift key while dragging a handle moves the opposite handle in the reverse direction. For example, if you drag a handle toward the object, the opposite handle moves toward the drag handle. If you drag the handle away from the object, the opposite handle moves away from the drag handle.

- Depressing both the Ctrl and Shift keys, move the handles in opposite directions.

N O T E

You must click on Apply for any changes to take effect.

Selecting an Editing Mode

Each of the four editing modes creates an entirely different effect. The functions of the editing nodes are described in the following list.

- **Single line.** Enables you to apply a slanted or beveled appearance to an object (see fig. 11.5).

Figure 11.5
A single-line envelope.

- **Single arc.** Applies a single convex or concave curve to an object (see fig. 11.6).

Figure 11.6
A single-arc envelope.

- **Two curves.** Applies a bidirectional curve or two curves to an object (see fig. 11.7).

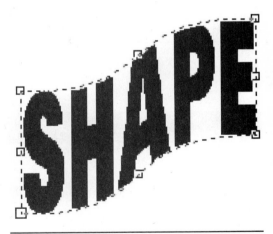

Figure 11.7
A two-curve envelope.

■ **Unconstrained.** Enables you to edit an envelope in a freeform manner. You can use Node Edit with the Unconstrained roll-up to add, delete, or modify the nodes, much like you would with any object (see fig. 11.8).

Figure 11.8

An unconstrained envelope.

N O T E

If you want to use the Shape tool to further edit an object to which an envelope has been applied, you must either clear the envelope or convert the object to curves.

Changing Editing Modes and Adding Envelopes

While editing an envelope applied to an object, you can change editing modes to combine the effects of two or more different envelopes (see fig. 11.9). To change editing modes, click on Apply between the changes. Then select the icon for another editing mode to further edit the object.

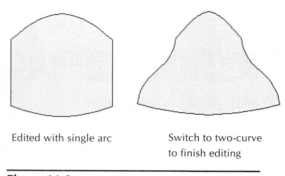

Edited with single arc   Switch to two-curve to finish editing

Figure 11.9

Changing editing modes.

You can also add a new envelope to an object to which an envelope has already been applied, as shown in figure 11.10. Select an editing mode, and click on Add New. Edit as desired, and click on Apply to complete the operation.

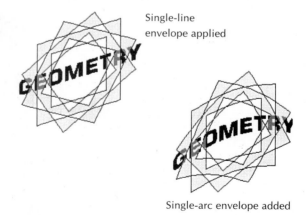

Single-line envelope applied

Single-arc envelope added

Figure 11.10

Applying a new envelope to an existing one.

Applying Envelopes to Text

Adding an envelope to text enables you to create special effects, while retaining the ability to edit the text. When you apply an envelope to Paragraph text, the effect is like pouring the text into the shape. All of the character attributes are retained, but the margins conform to the shape of the envelope (see fig. 11.11).

The envelope feature enables you to create banners and headlines with Artistic text (see fig. 11.12). Choosing Center alignment in the character attributes before applying an envelope to Artistic text allows you to change or edit the text later, and ensures proper alignment in an envelope.

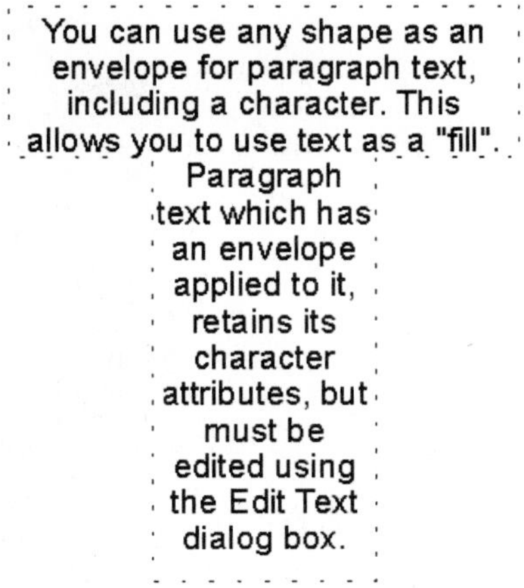

You can use any shape as an envelope for paragraph text, including a character. This allows you to use text as a "fill". Paragraph text which has an envelope applied to it, retains its character attributes, but must be edited using the Edit Text dialog box.

Figure 11.11

Applying an envelope to Paragraph text.

Creating A Banner With Artistic Text

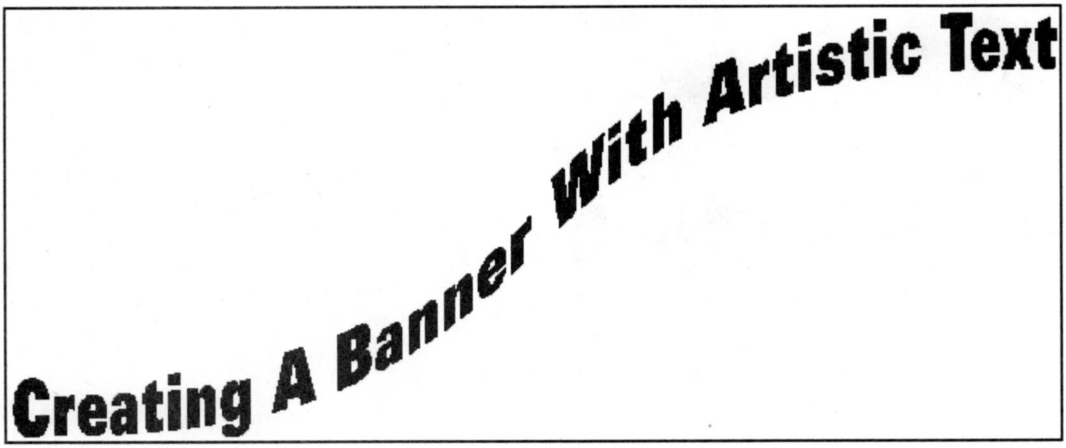

Figure 11.12

Creating a banner by applying an envelope to Artistic text.

You can use the envelope feature to force a space restriction on text, as shown in figure 11.13. For example, if you are creating a template using Artistic text, the envelope command enables you to ensure that a replacement text string will fit into the same space. To force a space restriction, enter a string of text that fits the dimensions you want to preserve. Make sure you select Center Alignment for the text. Apply a single line envelope to the text, but do not modify the envelope by dragging the handles. Later, when you change the text, the new text will be forced into the same space. Figure 11.13 shows the word "SPACE," to which a single line envelope was applied. The text was changed to "FORCED SPACE" in the bottom text. Note that the text occupies the same amount of space.

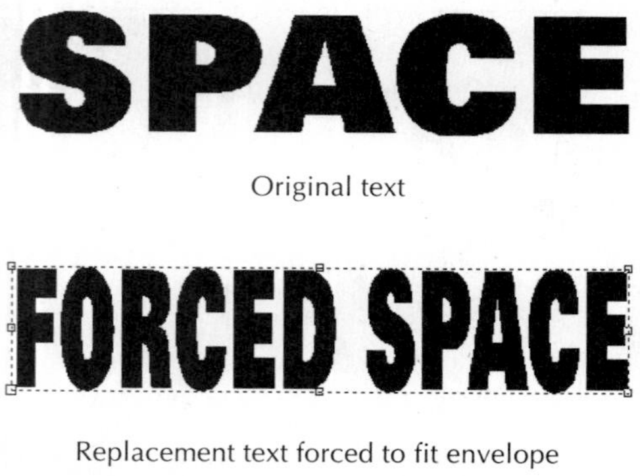

SPACE

Original text

FORCED SPACE

Replacement text forced to fit envelope

Figure 11.13

Using an envelope to force a space restriction.

Editing Enveloped Text

When you apply an envelope to text, you can no longer edit the text on-screen. You can change the character attributes of the text, but you cannot change the text itself. The text must be edited using the Text Edit dialog box.

Using Mapping Options

Mapping options enable you to choose how an object behaves when an envelope is applied. When you click the down arrow, CorelDRAW enables you to choose from the following five modes:

- **Original.** Maps the corners of the bounding box of a selection with the envelope corners. Interior nodes are mapped using Bézier arcs. This mapping method has been in use since version 3.0, and should be used when importing 3.0 objects that have used envelope effects.

- **Putty.** Ignores Bézier arcs and interior nodes. The object is mapped using the bounding box corners only. This method creates smoother and less distorted effects. The two shapes in figure 11.14 are identical envelopes. Only the mapping option was changed.

Original · Putty

Figure 11.14
Original vs. putty mode.

■ **Vertical.** Stretches the object to fill the bounding box, and then stretches the object to vertically fill the envelope. Figure 11.15 shows the effect when applied to text.

Original · Vertical

Figure 11.15
Original vs. vertical mode.

■ **Horizontal.** Works similar to vertical mode, except it stretches objects on the horizontal plane. Figure 11.16 shows the difference between original and horizontal modes.

Original · Horizontal

Figure 11.16
Original vs. horizontal mode.

■ **Text.** Applies only to Paragraph text. Other mapping options are not available for envelopes applied to paragraph text.

Using Presets

CorelDRAW packages a number of preset envelope shapes that you can apply to objects and text (see fig. 11.17). To apply a preset, select the object to which you want to apply the envelope, and click on the down arrow to display the available shapes. Choose the shape you want, and click on Apply to complete the operation. When you select a preset envelope, the envelope is stretched non-proportionally to fit the bounding box of the object, unless the object is paragraph text. If you apply a preset to paragraph text, the envelope is stretched proportionately.

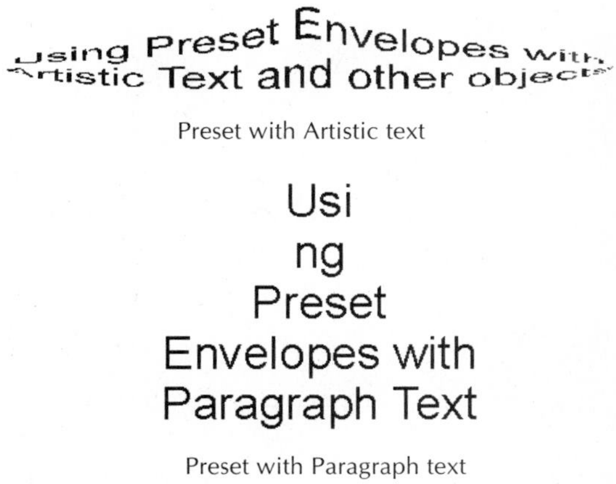

Using Preset Envelopes with Artistic Text and other objects

Preset with Artistic text

Usi ng Preset Envelopes with Paragraph Text

Preset with Paragraph text

Figure 11.17
Using presets.

Creating an Envelope

Any object, other than Paragraph text, can serve as an envelope. This is especially useful when applying an envelope to Paragraph text, because it enables you to flow Paragraph text into unusual shapes. When you use one object to create an envelope for another object, CorelDRAW uses the four nodes closest to the source object's bounding box to calculate the envelope. The distance of the nodes from the source object's bounding box determines how closely the destination object will resemble the envelope. The greater the distance, the less the object will resemble the envelope. Add nodes to the source object, if needed, to place nodes as close as possible to the bounding box of the source object (see fig. 11.18).

To create an envelope from an object, use the following steps:

1. Create a source object to use an envelope.

2. Select the destination object or group, and click on Create From in the Envelope roll-up.

3. A dotted line will appear around the destination object, showing the new envelope shape.

4. Click on Apply to complete the operation.

Using Keep Lines

When you apply an envelope to an object, the program maps straight lines as Bézier curves to fit the envelope. If you enable Keep Lines, straight lines are retained (see fig. 11.19). An object may not conform closely to the shape of the envelope with Keep Lines enabled, however.

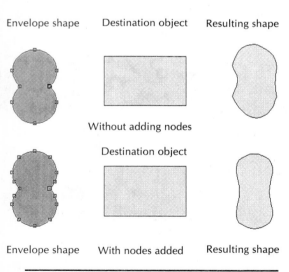

Envelope shape   Destination object   Resulting shape

Without adding nodes

Destination object

Envelope shape   With nodes added   Resulting shape

Figure 11.18
Add nodes to control the conformity to an envelope.

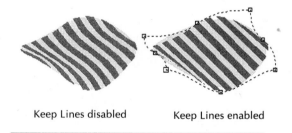

Keep Lines disabled   Keep Lines enabled

Figure 11.19
Using Keep Lines.

Resetting and Clearing Envelopes

You can clear an envelope from an object, and return it to its original shape, by selecting Clear Envelope from the Effects menu. Selecting Clear Envelope clears the last envelope applied. To clear more than one envelope, you need to apply this command repeatedly. If you want to clear all of the envelopes simultaneously and return the object to its original appearance, select Clear Transformations from the Effects menu. If, while editing an envelope, you have applied more than one envelope to an object and want to clear the last envelope (and return to the previous envelope), select Reset Envelope from the Envelope roll-up. You can continue to clear envelopes by reselecting Reset Envelope, if you have applied more than two envelopes to an object. Reset Envelope will not remove envelopes that have been applied. It is intended to reset envelopes during editing only.

Copying an Envelope from One Object to Another

Applying the Copy Envelope command from the Effects menu enables you to copy the envelope from one object to another. To copy an envelope, follow these steps:

1. Select a destination object or group.

2. Choose Copy Envelope from the Effects menu.

3. An arrow appears, enabling you to select the source object whose envelope you want to copy to the destination object.

N O T E

If you apply another effect, such as Perspective, to an enveloped object, you must first clear that effect before you can apply Clear Envelope.

Working with Blends

The blend command enables you to transform the shape, fill, and outline of one object into those of another object, via a series of intermediate shapes. This enables you to create highlights, contour objects, create painted effects, and add depth to your image. You can also evenly place objects on another object by blending two objects along a path.

The image shown in figure 11.20 was created using a number of blends to add depth and contour to the various elements of the drawing. The highlighted veins in the center of the flowers were created by drawing a Bézier curve, and breaking it into segments. The segments were assigned different outline colors, and then blended together. (See the full-color section of this book for hummingbird image.)

Figure 11.20
Using blends to contour objects.

CorelDRAW enables you to blend objects and fills from different palettes, including spot tints. Objects can have open or closed paths. As with most special effects, blends can only be applied to Artistic text with a maximum of 250 characters.

You cannot blend Paragraph text, lens effects, or dynamically linked groups to which extrude, contour, PowerLine, or PowerClip effects have been applied.

Applying a Blend

All blends are created using the Blend roll-up, as shown in figure 11.21. To apply a blend to two objects, use the following steps:

Figure 11.21
The Blend roll-up.

1. Select the objects you want to blend. Choose **B**lend Roll-Up from the Effe**c**ts menu to display the roll-up, or press Ctrl+B.

2. Enter the number of steps you want in the blend.

3. Select any other options you want to use, and click on Apply. The blend group appears with the two control objects and the intermediate shapes.

N O T E

Blending objects with an unequal number of subpaths can cause unexpected results. The intermediate shapes may appear as open paths and may not print, or may print as lines with no fill. This is common when blending Artistic text characters that are pierced, such as the letters P and D, with a single path object. To minimize this effect, avoid blending two objects with an unequal number of paths.

Understanding Blend Behavior

The appearance of the intermediate shapes in a blend is dependent upon the fills of the starting and ending objects. The following behavior applies when blending objects:

- If either control object has no fill, the intermediate shapes will have no fill.

- When blending two objects with uniform fills, the intermediate shapes will have a process fill.

- If one object contains a spot fill, and the other object contains a process fill or a different spot color, the intermediate shapes will have a process fill.

- If one object contains a tint of a spot fill, and the other object contains a tint of the same spot color, the intermediate shapes will have incremental tints of the spot color.

- If one control object has a fountain fill, and the other has a uniform fill, the intermediate shapes will blend from one type of fill to the other.

- Fountain fills are always dominant. They have the following order of dominance: radial, square, conical, and linear. When blending objects containing two different fountain fills, the order of dominance is observed. If you are blending a radial-filled object with an object containing any other fountain type, the intermediate shapes will have a radial fill.

If one object contains a fountain fill, the intermediate shapes will also have a fountain fill. The fill type of the other object is ignored. For example, if you blend a fountain-filled object with one containing a uniform fill, the intermediate shapes will all have a fountain fill. The program will blend the color, shape, and outlines of the two objects, with the exception of those fills that are pattern or texture fills. The colors of pattern or texture fills are ignored, and only the shapes and outlines, if any, are blended.

- If one control object has a pattern and the other has a uniform fill, the intermediate shapes will have a uniform fill.

- If you are blending two objects with different pattern fills, the top or starting object is dominant. The intermediate shapes will contain the fill of the dominant object.

- Texture fills are the least dominant of all fills. If you blend two objects together and only one object contains a texture fill, the resulting intermediate steps will contain the fill of the other object.

If both objects contain the same texture fill, the intermediate objects will be a blend between the two fills. CorelDRAW will map the colors, shape, and outlines of the two objects. This occurs even if the two objects contain different colors.

If the objects contain different texture fills, the starting or top object becomes dominant, and the intermediate shapes will have that fill.

Reversing a Blend

Reversing a blend enables you to reverse the stacking order of the intermediate shapes, as shown in figure 11.22. By default, CorelDRAW blends two objects from the starting or top object to the end or bottom object. You can reverse the order by selecting **O**rder and then **R**everse Order from the **A**rrange menu.

Figure 11.22
Reversing a blend.

Selecting Blend Options

CorelDRAW enables you to select the options you want to apply to a blend. Each of these options affect the behavior and appearance of the blend group or compound object.

Steps

Specifying the number of steps in a blend can alter the smoothness of a blend. The greater the number of steps in a blend, the smoother a blend appears (see fig. 11.23). Enter the number of steps you want in the numeric entry box. The complexity of the file increases as the number of steps increase, slowing refresh time and creating a larger file.

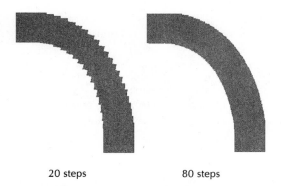

20 steps   80 steps

Figure 11.23
Smoothing a blend by increasing the steps.

Spacing

If you click on the down arrow beside the Steps, you can adjust the spacing between intermediate objects. Spacing corresponds with the units of measurement on the horizontal ruler. This option is only available if you are blending objects along a path.

Rotation

If you want to rotate the intermediate shapes between the control objects, enter the degree of rotation you want in the entry box (see fig. 11.24).

10-degree rotation

Figure 11.24
Applying rotation to a blend.

Loop

When you enable Loop, the intermediate objects rotate around the halfway point between the starting and ending objects' centers of rotation. The image in figure 11.25 has a 200 degree rotation, with Loop enabled.

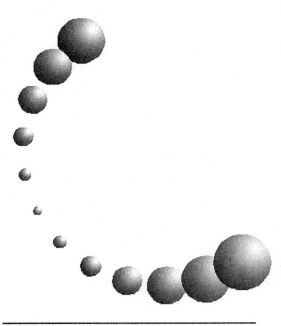

Figure 11.25
Using Loop to alter the center of rotation.

Start and End

When a blend group is selected, these icons become active, enabling you to select or change the starting and ending objects. To change the start or end object, select the blend group and click on the appropriate

icon. When you move your cursor back over the drawing window, the cursor changes to an arrow, enabling you to select the new start or end object.

Path Icon

Blending along a path enables you to force a blend to follow a specific path you designate. The path can be an open or closed object. To blend two objects along a path, select the two objects, and then click the path icon. When you move your cursor back over the drawing window, an arrow appears, enabling you to select the path along which you want the objects to blend. Figure 11.26 shows a series of gears. The image was created by drawing one gear, duplicating it, and blending it along the path shown in the figure. The blend was split, and the center gear was shifted to the top, by selecting **O**rder and then To **F**ront from the **A**rrange menu.

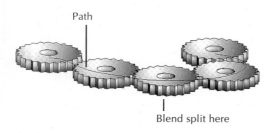

Figure 11.26
Creating a blend along a path.

Choosing a path that contains a greater or lesser number of subpaths can cause unexpected results. If this occurs, break the path apart by selecting Brea**k** Apart from the **A**rrange menu, and then apply the blend.

You can then separate the blend from the path and recombine the subpaths of the object.

Blending objects along a path enables you to evenly space a set of objects on a path, as shown in figure 11.27. When combined with rotate, you can achieve a number of interesting effects.

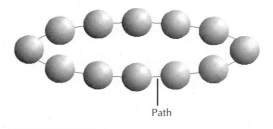

Figure 11.27
Using a blend to evenly space objects along a path.

Mapping Nodes

CorelDRAW uses the first node of an object to map the blend between two objects. When you are blending groups of objects, the program uses the first node of each object in the group to map the blend. This method may not yield the appearance you want, however. You override the program and map the nodes as you choose by selecting the object control icon from the roll-up, and choosing Map Nodes. When you move your cursor back over the drawing window, an arrow appears, enabling you to choose mapping node on the starting object. After you select the node, the arrow reverses, enabling you to choose the mapping node for the end object. Clicking on Apply finishes the operation, and the blend group appears in the drawing window (see fig. 11.28).

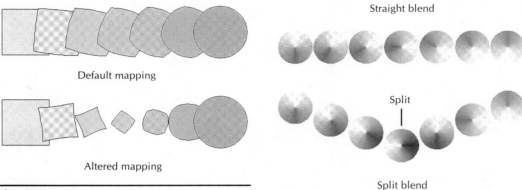

Default mapping

Altered mapping

Figure 11.28
Mapping nodes to alter the appearance of a blend.

Straight blend

Split

Split blend

Figure 11.29
Splitting a blend.

Splitting Blends

The attributes of a blend group are determined by those of the control objects. If you make changes to either of the control objects, the blend updates correspondingly. You cannot directly alter or edit the intermediate shapes of a blend group.

If you want to change the attributes of an intermediate shape, you can convert the shape to a control object by splitting the blend at that location, as shown in figure 11.29. The resulting blend groups become compound objects because they share a control object. The new control object serves as both the beginning of one blend group and the end of another. If the blend is not applied along a path, you can move it to another location, causing the compound object to deviate from a straight line.

To split a blend, click on the Split button, and then select the intermediate shape where you want the blend to split. Click on Apply to complete the operation.

Fuse Start and Fuse End

Using Fuse Start and Fuse End enables you to recombine blend groups that have been split. If the blend groups do not lie on a straight path, they are reformed along a straight line. To fuse a split blend, depress the Ctrl key while selecting an intermediate shape from either blend group. Click on the Fuse button, and then click on Apply to complete the operation.

Color

By default, CorelDRAW maps color in a straight line between the fills and outlines of the two control objects. Select the color icon, and click on Rainbow to alter the color

mapping of the intermediate objects. When you enable Rainbow, two icons appear, enabling you to specify clockwise and counterclockwise mapping on the color wheel. A curve appears on the color wheel, displaying the range of colors that will be included in the mapping. Choose the direction you want the mapping to follow, and click on Apply to complete the operation.

Working with Dynamically Linked Groups

When you blend two objects, a dynamically linked group is created. The attributes of a dynamically linked group are defined by those of the control objects. If you change the shape, fill, or outline of either or both of the control objects, the intermediate shapes are updated to reflect the changes.

To separate the elements of a dynamically linked group, select **S**eparate from the **A**rrange menu. This breaks the OLE2 link between the blend group, leaving three elements. The control objects revert to curved objects, and the intermediate shapes become a group. The number of objects in the group is defined by the number of steps in the blend. Once the link is broken, intermediate shapes are no longer updated when the original control objects are edited.

When you select the starting or ending object of a dynamically linked group, the status line reflects that selection by displaying the type of object, and identifying it as a control

object (see fig. 11.30). If you select the group by clicking on an intermediate shape, or by marquee-selecting the group, the status line displays the type of group.

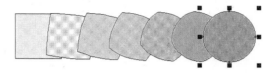

Figure 11.30
The status line display, with a control object selected.

The status line display shows a compound object, if you select two or more interrelated linked groups. It also shows the number of elements in the compound object. Interrelated linked groups share a control object in common. It becomes both the start of one group as well as the end of another group. If, for example, you blended two objects together and then created a blend group between one of the control objects and a third object, the result would be a compound object. The compound object would have five elements: the start and end control objects, the common control object, and the two blend groups.

Editing a Blend Group within a Compound Object

When you click on a compound object, the entire compound object is selected, and you cannot edit the individual blend groups. You can edit the individual control objects, however. To select and edit a single blend group from a compound object, depress the Ctrl key while clicking on the blend group you want to edit. This is useful if you want to reverse or split a single blend group within a compound object.

T I P

Using the Tab key makes selecting individual control objects in compound objects easier. Select the compound object, and then press the Tab key once to select the next object. Depressing the Shift key while pressing Tab again tabs back to one of the control objects. Continue using Shift+Tab to select the control object you want to change.

Chaining a Blend

Chaining blends enables you to use the intermediate shapes of a blend to create new blend groups. Figure 11.31 shows chains of blend groups, created by splitting and fusing individual blend groups together.

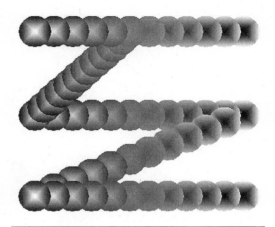

Figure 11.31
Chaining blend groups.

Creating Highlights

The blend feature in CorelDRAW enables you to create highlights and the feeling of texture in your drawings. Keywine, by Phillip Williams, displayed in figure 11.32 and in the color insert, shows the power of the blend features in CorelDRAW. Phil used blends extensively in this drawing. By choosing subtle color variations and restricting the number of steps in each blend, he was able to create the woodgrain of the piano. The highlights in the glass employed more blend steps to produce smooth transitions from dark to light.

Figure 11.32
Keywine, by Phillip Williams.

To create a highlight and shadow using blends, as shown in figure 11.33, follow these steps:

1. Draw the object you want to highlight, and apply the fill and outline you want to use.

2. Draw the highlight areas and apply the same fill as the original object.

3. Create smaller highlight shapes, within the highlight area, by either drawing them, or by duplicating the highlight area and adjusting the size and position of the highlight shape. Apply a lighter color to the highlight shape.

4. Select the highlight area and shape, and apply a blend.

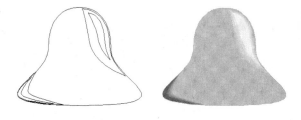

Figure 11.33
Creating highlight and shadow areas on an object.

Blending Artistic Text

Blending Artistic text can create some interesting effects. As mentioned earlier in this chapter, some Artistic text characters such as P and D are multipath objects. Blending objects with an unequal number of paths can yield unsatisfactory results, or may not print. You blend Artistic text as you would any other object. It is most effective when you blend duplicate strings of text, as shown in figure 11.34.

Figure 11.34
Blending Artistic text.

If you are blending Artistic text containing multipath characters with a single path object, convert the text to curves first. Then apply Brea**k** Apart from the **A**rrange menu. Blend the main portion of each object with a single path object. Fill the pierced area of the text with another color, and bring it to the front to give the illusion of text. In figure 11.35, the main portion of each character was blended with a square.

Figure 11.35
Blending Artistic text characters with multiple subpaths.

Copying and Cloning Blends

When you choose Cop**y** and then **B**lend From, under the Effe**c**ts menu, the blend options are copied from one object to another. The fill and outline of the selection are unaffected, however. To copy a blend,

choose a starting and ending object, then select Copy - Blend From. The cursor changes to an arrow as you move back over the drawing window. Click on the source object from which you want to copy the blend.

Cloning a blend is similar to copying a blend. Fill and outline attributes are retained, unless you select the Rainbow color option from the Blend roll-up. Clone differs from copy in that cloned blends are linked to the source or master blend. Any changes you make in the master blend's options will cause a corresponding change in the clone blend. Cloned blends cannot be edited. You must edit the master blend to effect a change. To clone a blend, choose Clone from the Effects menu, then select **B**lend From, from the flyout menu. The cursor changes to an arrow as you move back over the drawing window. Click on the source object from which you want to clone the blend.

Clearing a Blend

You can clear a blend by choosing Clear Blend from the Effects menu. The starting and ending objects remain in the drawing window. The path remains, as well, if the blend was along a path.

Using Contour

When you apply a contour to an object, concentric shapes are created. You can choose whether you want the shapes to be inside, outside, or at the absolute center of an object. Contour behaves similarly to blend, as it

enables you to create highlights, shadows, and transitions between an object with one color to another. Contour enables you to work with single objects, however. All contours are applied using the Contour roll-up, from the Effects menu, or by pressing Ctrl+F9 (see fig. 11.36).

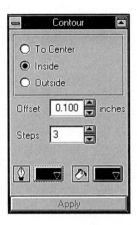

Figure 11.36
The Contour roll-up.

To apply a contour, use the following steps:

1. Select the object to which you want to apply the contour, and then access the Contour roll-up.

2. Choose the options you want and click on Apply.

Choosing Contour Options

CorelDRAW enables you to choose the mapping method the program uses to create the contour group. You can select from the following mapping options:

■ **To Center.** This option creates concentric steps mapped to the absolute center of the object, as shown in figure 11.37. When you select To Center and enter an offset, CorelDRAW automatically determines how many steps it requires to redraw the object to the center.

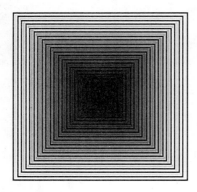

Figure 11.37
Center mapping.

■ **Inside.** This option enables you to draw concentric shapes inside the object, as shown in figure 11.38. You specify the number of steps and the offset you want. If the steps you enter exceed the number that can be contained inside the object, the

program automatically draws the number of steps possible. The number of possible steps is determined by the dimensions of the object and the offset.

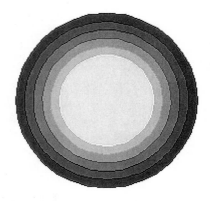

Figure 11.38
Inside mapping.

■ **Outside.** This option enables you to draw concentric shapes outside the object, as shown in figure 11.39. You specify the number of steps and the offset you desire.

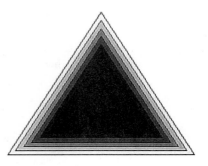

Figure 11.39
Outside mapping.

Specifying Steps

You can specify up to 999 steps, if the size of the object and the offset will accommodate them. To set the steps, use the scroll bar or enter the number of steps in the numeric entry box.

Setting the Offset

The offset entry box enables you to specify a spacing value between zero and 10 inches. The offset value overrides any step value you set, unless you have selected an outside contour. The smaller the offset value, the smoother the blend.

Setting the Outline and Fill Colors

Set the outline and fill colors by clicking on the color box, and choosing the color you want. In order for the contour group to have a color, the control object must have a fill. If you want to simulate a smooth blend without an outline, remove the outline on the control objects before applying the contour. The image shown in figure 11.40 and the color insert utilizes the contour feature to create the symmetrical shapes in the egg. The contour was separated, and then blended to create the glow effect.

Figure 11.40
Using Contour to simulate a blend.

Working with Dynamic Links

One of the similarities between the contour and blend features is that they both create a dynamically linked group. The fill, outline, and shape of the control object determine the contour group. If you edit the control object, the contour group is updated to reflect the changes you make. You cannot edit the contour itself. If you want to edit the individual shapes of the contour group, you must first break the dynamic link by selecting **S**eparate from the **A**rrange menu. This operation yields the original object and a group of objects. Apply the **U**ngroup command to edit the individual shapes.

Copying and Cloning a Contour Group

When you choose Cop**y** and then **C**ontour From, under the Effe**c**ts menu, the contour options are copied from one object to another. The fill and outline of the selection are unaffected, however. To copy a contour, choose an object, then select Cop**y** - **C**ontour From. The cursor changes to an arrow as you move back over the drawing window. Click on the contour source object that you want to copy.

Cloning a contour is similar to copying a blend. Fill and outline attributes are retained. Clone differs from copy in that cloned contour groups are linked to the source or master contour. Any changes you make in the master contour's options will cause a corresponding change in the clone contour group. Cloned contour groups cannot be edited. You must edit the master contour to effect a change. To clone a contour, choose Cl**o**ne from the Effe**c**ts menu, then select **C**ontour From, from the flyout menu. The cursor changes to an arrow as you move back over the drawing window. Click on the contour source object that you want to copy.

Using PowerClip

The PowerClip features in CorelDRAW enable you to place objects inside one another. One object behaves as a container for other objects. The container can be any closed path object or group of objects. You can place bitmaps, text, or other objects or groups of objects inside a container. You can also nest containers inside one another.

To apply a PowerClip, use the following steps:

1. Select the contents for the PowerClip (see fig. 11.41).

2. Choose PowerClip from the Effe**c**ts menu, and select **P**lace Inside Container.

3. Click on the Container Object. The completed effect is displayed in figure 11.42.

Figure 11.41
Grouped Rose bitmap images to be placed in text container.

Figure 11.42
The finished effect.

The ability to place objects inside a container is extremely useful when incorporating a bitmapped image into a drawing. When you import a bitmapped image into CorelDRAW, it appears as a rectangle. If the objects in the bitmapped image do not occupy the full space of the rectangle, there is white space around them. This white space hides any objects it overlaps. Before version 5.0, it was difficult to place a bitmap on any but the bottommost layer for this reason. Using the PowerClip feature enables you to use an irregular-shaped object as the container. This means you can mask any superfluous white space in an imported bitmap. The PowerClip can overlap other objects, enabling more seamless integration of bitmaps in CorelDRAW.

The image shown in figure 11.43 was created as follows:

1. A circle was drawn, and a copy of it was placed on the Clipboard.

2. The photo image was cropped during importing, and placed inside the circle using PowerClip.

3. The circle was pasted into the drawing.

4. The text was created as two individual text strings and fitted to the path of the circle. The distance from the path was adjusted for the bottom text.

5. The text was then separated from the circle, and both text strings were copied to the Clipboard.

6. The pasted circle was used to trim the two text strings, and a .015" outline was applied to the resulting curved objects.

7. The Clipboard text was pasted into the image and placed behind the trimmed text.

N O T E

After text has been trimmed, it becomes a curved object and can no longer be edited as text.

8. The top text attributes were changed to have no fill and a .015" black outline. The bottom text attributes were changed to have no fill and a .015" white outline.

Figure 11.43
Bridal Veil: photography by Richard Morris.

N O T E

CorelDRAW will enable you to place the contents into an open path; however, the contents will not be displayed until the path is closed.

Editing a PowerClip

When you apply a PowerClip, the contents are automatically centered in the container. You can reposition or edit the contents of a PowerClip by selecting PowerClip and **E**dit Contents from the Effe**c**ts menu. When you are finished editing, select **F**inish Editing This Level.

Editing a PowerClip temporarily creates a PowerClip contents layer and container layer. Although these layers are visible in the Layers roll-up, they are not related to the drawing layers. Normal layer functions are not available until the PowerClip editing is complete. The temporary layers are listed as Level 1, 2, 3, and so on when you edit nested PowerClips. Click on the contents of a PowerClip level to edit that level. When the editing for that level is complete, select Finish Editing This Level to move up a level. As you complete the editing for lower levels, the status line is updated, displaying the current editing level. If you are finished editing all the levels, repeatedly click on Finish Editing This level until the editing level in the status line is no longer displayed.

To create a nested PowerClip, use the following steps:

1. Create the first PowerClip by placing a selection inside a container, as detailed earlier in this section.

2. With the PowerClip selected, repeat Place Inside Container to place a PowerClip inside a container, creating a second PowerClip level.

3. Continue until you are satisfied with the results. The book cover shown in figure 11.44 (and included in the full-color insert) uses grouped and nested PowerClips to create the checkerboard and graphics effects.

Figure 11.44
Using nested PowerClips.

Extracting the Contents of a PowerClip

You can extract the contents of a PowerClip by selecting the PowerClip and choosing E**x**tract Contents from the Effe**c**ts menu.

Nesting PowerClips creates increasingly complex images. This can place a strain on resources, and creates large files. Nesting PowerClips can also create printing problems, as the complexity threshold of the image is increased.

Locking and Unlocking the Contents of a PowerClip

Locking and unlocking the contents of a PowerClip enables you to determine the behavior of the contents when a PowerClip is transformed. If the contents are locked, the contents will be transformed with the container. If the contents are unlocked, you can reposition the container over the contents directly, without using the editing command. If the contents are unlocked, and you rotate or skew the PowerClip, only the container is transformed. The contents must be locked for them to rotate or skew with the container. To lock or unlock a PowerClip, right-click on the PowerClip and either enable or disable the lock.

Using Group and Ungroup with PowerClips

Because a PowerClip container can be a group of objects, you can create interesting effects by ungrouping the PowerClip after placing the contents. Ungrouping a PowerClip creates a new set of PowerClips. Each of the PowerClips contains that portion of the contents that were contained in that portion of the group. The individual pieces of the group can be moved or rotated as desired.

Using PowerClip Features with Other Special Effects

CorelDRAW enables you to combine the effects created with PowerClips with any of the other special effects. The effect will vary, depending upon the other effect chosen. The results of some effects are also dependent upon whether the effect is applied before or after the PowerClip. All of the effects can be placed inside a PowerClip.

The effects behave as follows:

- **Perspective.** When you apply perspective to a PowerClip, the result is the same as for any other object.

- **Envelope.** When you apply an envelope to a PowerClip, the result is the same as for any other object.

- **Extrude.** If you place the contents in an extruded PowerClip, the contents appear in the control object of the extrusion. If you extrude a PowerClip, the contents appear draped over the sides of the extrusion when Drape Fills is enabled.

■ **Blend.** When you blend a PowerClip with another object, the PowerClip is always the start object. The start object is dominant, and the intermediate shapes assume the contents of that object. If you separate and ungroup blended PowerClips, you can create multiple PowerClips. This can create large and complex files, especially if the content of the PowerClip is a bitmap.

■ **Contour.** This behaves in a manner similar to Blend. The contour shapes contain the contents of the PowerClip. If the contents of the PowerClip fill the entire area of the container, or the container has no fill applied to it, the program will ignore any fill you designate for the contour shapes.

■ **Lens.** You can apply lens effects to both the contents and the container of a PowerClip.

Copying and Cloning a PowerClip

When you choose Copy and then PowerClip From, under the Effects menu, the PowerClip options are copied from one object to another. The fill and outline of the selection are unaffected, however. To copy a PowerClip, choose an object, and then select Copy, PowerClip From. The cursor changes to an arrow as you move back over the drawing window. Click on the contour source object that you want to copy.

When you clone, the fill and outline attributes are retained. Clone differs from copy in that cloned PowerClips are linked to the source or master PowerClip. Any changes you make in the master PowerClip's options will cause a corresponding change in the clone PowerClip. Cloned PowerClips cannot be edited. You must edit the master PowerClip to effect a change. To clone a PowerClip, choose Clone from the Effects menu, and then select PowerClip From from the flyout menu. The cursor changes to an arrow as you move back over the drawing window. Click on the PowerClip source object that you want to copy.

Using Extrude

Extruding objects enables you to add a 3D feel to objects. This produces the illusion of depth. You can apply an extrusion to most objects and groups in CorelDRAW, with the exception of bitmapped images and Paragraph text. If you want to apply an extrusion to a dynamically linked group, you first need to apply Group from the Arrange menu.

When you apply an extrusion, you create a dynamically linked group. The shape, fill, and outline determine the default attributes of the extrusion. You can change the fill and outline if you want. Both closed and open path objects can be extruded. All extrusions are applied using the Extrude roll-up, or by pressing Ctrl+E (see fig. 11.45).

Figure 11.45
The properties view of the Extrude roll-up.

N O T E

The view of the Extrude roll-up corresponds to the control icon selected at the top of the roll-up.

To apply an extrusion, follow these steps:

1. Select the object you want to extrude, and access the Extrude roll-up by selecting it from the Effects menu.

2. Click on the 3D icon to apply a wireframe to the object.

3. Select the extrusion options you want, and click on Apply to complete the operation.

Choosing an Extrusion Type

CorelDRAW displays a representation of each extrusion type in the view window of the roll-up to assist you in choosing an extrusion type. The arrows on the wireframe shown in the view window indicate the direction of the extrusion. There are two basic extrusion types: parallel and perspective.

The parallel extrusion enables you to select whether you want the extrusion in front of your source object or behind it (see fig. 11.46). If you choose Back Parallel, the extrusion is created behind the source object; if you choose Front Parallel, the extrusion is created in front of the source object.

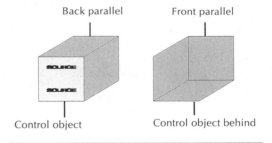

Figure 11.46
Using parallel extrusions.

Perspective extrusions include Small Back, Small Front, Big Back, and Big Front (see fig. 11.47). The names indicate the extruded face and the relationship to the source object, as described in the following:

- **Small Back.** The source object is in front, and the extrusion is drawn to the smaller back extruded face.

- **Small Front.** The source object is in back, and the extrusion is drawn to the smaller front extruded face.

- **Big Back.** The source object is in front, and the extrusion is drawn toward the larger back extruded face.

- **Big Front.** The source object is in back, and the extrusion is drawn toward the larger front extruded face.

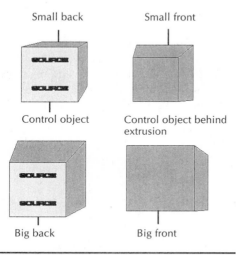

Small back   Small front

Control object   Control object behind extrusion

Big back   Big front

Figure 11.47
Perspective extrusions.

Adjusting the Depth and Vanishing Point of an Extrusion

When you select a perspective extrusion, you can adjust the depth of the extrusion, as well as the vanishing point. You can select a depth value from 1 to 99. The higher the value, the further away the extrusion extends from the source object (see fig. 11.48).

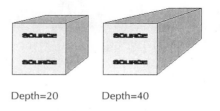

Depth=20   Depth=40

Figure 11.48
Adjusting the depth of an extrusion.

N O T E

The depth control is disabled for parallel extrusions. Any adjustments you want to make to the extrusion are made by dragging the X, or entering precise coordinates on the vanishing point coordinates page of the roll-up.

The vanishing point is adjusted either interactively on-screen by dragging the X, or by entering coordinates on the vanishing point coordinates page of the roll-up. The coordinates correspond to the horizontal and vertical rulers in the drawing window. To

enter precise coordinates, click on the page icon in the roll-up. When an object is first extruded, the vanishing point is set to the center of the page. When you adjust the vanishing point, the new vanishing point becomes the default. If you extrude another object, the initial vanishing point is that of the last object extruded. This value is saved with the file only; it will not affect future CorelDRAW sessions.

N O T E

You can make fine adjustments to an extrusion by using the cursor keys to nudge the X in the direction you want.

Choosing Vanishing Point Options

The vanishing point options control the way an extruded object behaves if you reposition it in your image, as described in the following list. To select the vanishing point option, click on the down arrow and choose from the drop-down list.

- **VP Locked to Object.** Choosing this option locks the vanishing point to the object. If you move the object, the vanishing point stays relative to the object.

- **VP Locked to Page.** Choosing this option creates an absolute vanishing point by locking it to the page. As you move an extruded object on the page, the extrusion is adjusted according to its position, relative to the coordinates of the vanishing point.

- **Copy VP From.** This enables you to copy the current vanishing point and apply it to a new extrusion. Both vanishing points can still be edited independently. If the vanishing point is locked to the object, the vanishing point is relative and will be adjusted as you reposition the extruded object. If the vanishing point is absolute, the extrusion will adjust as the source object is repositioned.

- **Shared Vanishing Point.** If you select shared vanishing point, the current vanishing point is applied to the new extrusion. As you adjust the vanishing point, the extrusions of any object sharing the vanishing point will be redrawn accordingly.

Using the Color Options

By default, the fill and outline attributes of the control object are passed to an extrusion. CorelDRAW provides the following three choices to control the fill of an extrusion through the color view of the Extrude roll-up (see fig. 11.49).

Figure 11.49
The color view of the Extrude roll-up.

■ **Use Object Fill.** This is the default option (see fig. 11.50). If the control object is filled with a bitmap, pattern, fountain, or texture fill, you can select Drape Fill. Draping a fill smoothly applies the fill to the combined surface of the extruded area. If Drape Fill is disabled, the fill is applied individually to each of the extruded surfaces, creating a rougher appearance. Drape Fill has no affect when selected with uniform fills.

Figure 11.51
Using Solid Fill.

Figure 11.50
Using Object Fill.

■ **Solid Fill.** Choosing this option enables you to apply a solid fill, using a different color or tint, from the control object (see fig. 11.51). Click on the color box to select a fill. If you click on more, you can change the color model used for the fill.

■ **Shade.** Choosing this option applies a fill similar to a linear fountain fill to the extruded area of the object (see fig. 11.52). The fill is applied along the length of the extrusion. Click the From color box to select the color that will be applied closest to the control object. Click the To color box to select the fill that will be applied most distant from the control object.

Figure 11.52
Using a shaded fill.

Setting the Minimum Facet Size

The facet size determines how the shaded fills are displayed and printed. The Minimum Extruded Facet Size is set in the Curves tab of the Preferences dialog box, found in the **S**pecial menu. You can select any value between .01 inches and .5 inches. The default setting is .125 inches. Lower settings create smoother shading. Larger values create a banded appearance. Settings you make here affect the memory requirements, file size, and print time of the image. Smaller settings are more resource intensive, and require longer print times.

Setting Light Sources

Settings made in the light sources control view of the Extrude roll-up control the color and shading effects of an extrusion (see fig. 11.53). CorelDRAW enables you to assign three lights to an extrusion. You can reposition the lights and adjust the intensity of each light independently. If the shaded extrusion of an object appears too dark, increasing the number and intensity of the lights will lighten the rendering of the object. If you do not specify a light source for an extruded object, all the colors of the extrusion will appear to be the same.

The view window displays a sphere in a cube to represent your extruded object. To place a light source (see fig. 11.54), click on the light icon. The light number appears in the view window. You can drag the light to any intersection point of the cube. Use the slide bar to adjust the intensity of the light. You can select any value between 0 and 100; the color appears lighter as values approach 100. If you use multiple light sources, the higher the light intensity value, the more reflective the extruded fill appears. Enabling Use full color range enables the program to use the full range between the two colors you have selected to render the extrusion. Disabling this feature limits the available range, and creates stark transitions between colors.

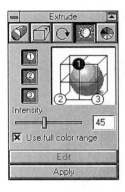

Figure 11.53
The light source view of the Extrude roll-up.

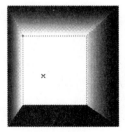

Figure 11.54
Using light sources to create effects.

When you select a light source, the marker icon appears as black with white lettering, indicating the light source is being edited. When a marker icon is deselected, the color of the icon indicates the intensity of the light. White indicates more intense lighting; gray indicates a lower intensity of light.

N O T E

The effect of lighting may not be noticeable if the control object is hidden by an extrusion—the light sources always focus directly on the control object. This occurs most commonly when a control object has been rotated.

Rotating an Extrusion

The 3D rotation icon accesses the rotation view of the Extrude roll-up (see fig. 11.55). CorelDRAW enables you to rotate the extrusion of a control object along three planes by clicking on the arrows located on the sphere in the view window. Each time you click on an arrow, the extrusion rotates in the prescribed direction by five degrees. Clicking on the X in the center of the sphere removes any rotation you have applied.

You can rotate perspective extrusion only (see fig. 11.56). If the vanishing point has been locked to the object, once the extrusion is rotated, you can no longer adjust the vanishing point on-screen. You must remove any rotation prior to adjusting the vanishing point. If the vanishing point of an extrusion is shared or has been locked to the page, you cannot rotate the extrusion.

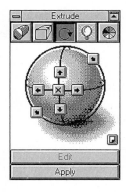

Figure 11.55
The rotation view of the Extrude roll-up.

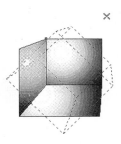

Figure 11.56
Rotated extrusion.

N O T E

If you need to rotate the extrusion with greater precision, click on the page icon to enter precise rotation values. To change the center of rotation for an extrusion, you must group the extrusion first by selecting **G**roup from the **A**rrange menu. Once the extrusion and control object are grouped, you can change the center of rotation as you would for any object.

Editing Extruded Text

You can apply an extrusion to Artistic text; however, once an extrusion has been applied, the text can only be edited in the Edit Text dialog box (see fig. 11.57). If you alter the fill of the individual characters in a text string, the extrusion will use those fills to shade the extrusion. Any color changes you make in the Extrude roll-up are applied to all of the characters in a text string.

Figure 11.57
Extruded text.

Editing the Nodes on a Control Object

The control object of an extrusion can be edited using the Shape tool, as you would any object. You cannot, however, edit the nodes of an extrusion that has been rotated. You must first remove the rotation before you can edit the nodes of the control object.

Copying and Cloning Extrusions

You can copy the extrusion options from one object to another. To copy the extrusion options, select the control object to which you want to copy the extrusion. Choose Copy, and then Extrude From, from the Effects menu. The cursor changes to an arrow when you move back to the drawing window. Click on the extrusion you want to copy. Be sure to click on the extruded area of the object, and not the control object. The fill and outline attributes of the destination object are retained, and the extrusion settings are copied from the source extrusion.

When you clone an extruded object, the object from which you are copying becomes the master object. Fill and outline attributes of the destination object are retained, but the extrusion settings of the master or source object are transferred to the destination extrusion. You cannot edit a cloned extrusion directly—you must edit the master object. Any changes you make in the extrusion settings of the master object cause the program to automatically update the clone object.

Separating and Clearing an Extrusion

You can clear an extrusion by selecting Clear Extrude from the Effects menu. The control object reverts to a curved object or text, and the extrusion is removed from the image.

Extrusions, like other special effects objects, are dynamically linked groups. The control object determines the basic attributes of the extrusion. When you apply **S**eparate from the **A**rrange menu, the link is broken, leaving the original object and a group of objects that constituted the extrusion. Separating an extrusion enables you to edit the individual elements. Once a dynamic link has been broken, it cannot be relinked.

Using and Creating Preset Extrusions

A set of extrusion presets comes packaged with CorelDRAW. You can apply these standard presets instead of creating an extrusion. All of the presets are editable. In addition to using the packaged presets, you can add to the set by creating and saving your own extrusions. Using and creating preset extrusions are done through the preset view of the Extrude roll-up (see fig. 11.58).

Figure 11.58
The preset view of the Extrude roll-up.

To apply a preset extrusion, use the following steps:

1. Select the object to which you want to apply the Preset extrusion.

2. Access the Extrude roll-up, and click on the Preset icon to display the preset view.

3. Click on the down arrow to display a list of preset names. Some of the extrusion presets have notes attached to them that describe the effect in more detail.

4. When you click on a name, a thumbnail of the preset appears in the view window. Select a preset and click on Apply to complete the operation.

Creating a Preset Extrusion

When you create a custom preset, you can specify the fill, depth, rotation, color, extrusion type, lighting, vanishing point coordinates, and whether the vanishing point is locked to an object or page. You cannot specify if an extrusion has a shared vanishing point or copies a vanishing point from another object.

To create a custom preset, follow these steps:

1. Create the extrusion effect you want to save and, with the extrusion group selected, click on the Preset icon.

2. Click on Save As to display the Save Extrude Preset dialog box, as shown in figure 11.59. By default, the next incremental preset name appears in the

name entry box. You can either accept the default or replace it with a name you choose. The name can have up to 32 characters. If you want to add more information about the effect, you can enter notes in the Notes entry box. If you want to include the fill and outline in the extrusion preset, click on the boxes beside the notation to enable them.

Figure 11.60
The Delete Preset dialog box.

Figure 11.59
The Save Extrude Preset dialog box.

3. Click on OK to save the preset and return to the drawing window. A thumbnail of the new preset will appear in the preset view window.

Deleting Presets

There are two methods of deleting a preset. If a preset is selected in the drawing window, you can click on Save As, and then the Delete button. If no preset is selected, click on the Delete button in the Preset view of the Extrude roll-up to display a list of the presets in the Delete Preset dialog box (see fig. 11.60). Select the preset you want to delete, and click on OK to complete the operation and return to the drawing window.

Using Lens Effects

Paint and photo-editing packages have long been able to add lens effects to images. Vector packages have always created hard-edge drawings. Filter effects that softened the edges or simulated transparency were normally tedious and time-consuming special effects, which required a number of objects to create the illusion. CorelDRAW has added the ability to create special color filtering effects simply by using the lens command. Lenses can be used alone, stacked, or used in conjunction with other effects.

Lens effects are applied to the fill area of an object. If you do not want an apparent outline on the lens, select no outline color from the Outline tool flyout, or right-click on the X on the color palette. You can apply lenses to single objects only. You cannot apply a lens effect to a grouped or dynamically linked object. If you want lens effects to be apparent in these objects, apply the lens prior to creating the group. An exception to this is PowerClip effects. You can apply a lens either before or after creating the PowerClip.

You can apply lens effects to open or closed path objects, with the exception of Invert, Magnify, Brighten, and Heat Map. These lenses can only be applied to closed objects. If you do not specify a fill for an object prior to applying the lens, the current lens color displayed in the roll-up is applied. All lens effects are applied using the Lens roll-up, accessed by selecting it from the Effects menu or by pressing Alt+F3 (see fig. 11.61).

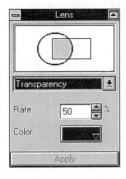

Figure 11.61
The Lens roll-up.

To apply a lens, use the following steps:

1. Select an object to serve as a lens, and access the Lens roll-up.

2. Select a Lens type from the drop-down list. A thumbnail image appears in the view window of the roll-up to illustrate the effect of the lens.

3. Select from the options available for the lens you have chosen.

4. Click on Apply to complete the operation and return to the drawing window.

N O T E

Lens effects are memory-intensive and create large files. This can slow loading and refresh times. Because lenses increase the complexity threshold, you may experience printing difficulties. Complexity threshold printing problems occur most often when complex objects are superimposed over one another. To minimize this problem, simplify the lens object and any objects underneath the lens. You can simplify objects in a number of ways. Using the **T**rim, **W**eld, and **I**ntersect commands from the **A**rrange menu enables you to reduce the number of objects that are superimposed to create an image. Reducing the number of nodes also decreases the complexity threshold of an object.

The Brighten Lens

Adding a Brighten lens to an image brightens or darkens the image underneath the lens (see fig. 11.62). The program disregards any fill in the lens object when it creates this effect. Brightness and darkness are created by adjusting the rate value of the lens. You can enter values from −100 percent to 100 percent, with −100 percent creating the maximum amount of darkness, and 100 percent creating the maximum amount of brightness. Values are entered by either using the arrow keys to change the value in 5 percent increments, or by entering them directly into the numeric entry box.

Figure 11.62
Using the Brighten lens.

Color Add

The Color Add lens enables you to simulate an additive light model (see fig. 11.63). When equal amounts of color from the color spectrum are added together, the result is white light. If you superimpose a colored lens over an object filled with color, the two colors are added together to create the illusion of colored light. To create a Color Add lens, select a color and adjust the rate value of the lens. The rate value is adjustable between 0 percent and 100 percent. A value of 0 percent results in no color being added; a value of 100 percent adds the maximum amount of color. Values are entered by either using the arrow keys to change the value in 5 percent increments, or by entering them directly into the numeric entry box.

N O T E

For this lens to be effective, the object below the lens cannot be white. Any Color Add lens placed above a white fill yields the results of adding white light to the object, and will not be visible.

Figure 11.63
Using the Color Add lens.

Color Limit

Superimposing a Color Limit lens over an object is similar to using a color filter on a camera (see fig. 11.64). All of the colors of the object below are filtered out, except for black and the color you specify. If you superimposed a blue lens over a group of objects, all the colors with the exception of blue and black would be reduced. White objects would be filled with the color of the lens. You control the amount of filtering to be applied by adjusting the rate value. A rate value of 0 percent adds no filtering; a rate value of 100 percent filters out all color other than the lens color and black. Values are entered by either using the arrow keys to change the value in 5-percent increments, or by entering them directly into the numeric entry box.

Figure 11.64
Using the Color Limit lens.

Heat Map

Applying a Heat Map lens to an image produces the illusion of an infrared image by converting the colors of the object below the lens to those of a limited palette. The palette contains red, blue, orange, yellow, violet, cyan, and white. Though the color wheel is not visible in the roll-up, the colors of the heat map are controlled by adjusting the rotation of the color wheel. The resulting color is dependent upon the color of the object below the lens and the amount of rotation you select. It may require some experimentation to discover the effect of the lens on the object below. To add a Heat Map to an image, select a color for the lens, and then adjust the rotation value of the color palette. Values are entered by either using the arrow keys to change the value in 5 percent increments, or by entering them directly into the numeric entry box.

Invert

The Invert lens replaces the colors of the object below the lens with the respective complimentary color (see fig. 11.65). Complimentary colors are those that lie directly opposite a given color on a color wheel. When an Invert lens is superimposed over a bitmapped photo image, the result is the illusion of a photo-negative. The Invert lens disregards any color fill you have applied to the object prior to converting it to a lens.

Figure 11.65
Using the Invert lens.

Magnify

Superimposing a Magnify lens over an object creates the illusion of magnifying the object or portion of object below the lens (see fig. 11.66). This lens is most effective when it does not completely cover an object, as it allows the contrast in size to be most apparent. The lens object can have a color fill or no fill. Magnify lenses disregard any color information that was previously applied to the lens object. You adjust the Magnify lens to the degree of magnification you want. Values can be set between 1.0× to 10.0×

magnification. Values are entered by either using the arrow keys to change the value in 0.1× increments, or by entering them directly into the numeric entry box.

using the arrow keys to change the value in 5-percent increments, or by entering them directly into the numeric entry box.

Figure 11.66
Using the Magnify lens.

Figure 11.67
Using the Transparency lens.

Tinted Grayscale

The Tinted Grayscale lens enables you to quickly convert a colored image to grayscale or sepia tones. Tinted Grayscale lenses are applied by choosing a color from the color box in the roll-up. Any color you select is added to gray to create the illusion. If you select a shade of brown from the color box, a sepia effect is created.

Transparency

The Transparency lens creates the illusion of glass or plastic being superimposed over an object (see fig. 11.67). You can adjust the rate of transparency, creating an effect that can range from opaque to completely clear. The default rate value is 50 percent. When you select an object to convert to a lens, the color of the object appears automatically in the color box. You can accept this color or change it by clicking on the color box and selecting a color. Values are entered by either

N O T E

If you save a file that contains special effects, such as lens effects, as a version 4.0 file, the effect may not appear if it is a nonsupported effect. The object containing the effect will appear as it would without the effect, however.

Copying and Cloning the Lens Effect

You can copy the lens effect from one object to another. To copy the lens effect, select the object to which you want to copy the effect. Choose Copy, and then Lens From, from the Effects menu. The cursor changes to an arrow when you move back to the drawing window. Click on the lens effect you want to copy. The fill and outline attributes of the destination object are retained.

When you clone a lens effect, the object from which you are copying becomes the master object. Fill and outline attributes of the destination object are retained, but the lens settings of the master or source object are transferred to the destination object. You cannot edit a cloned lens effect directly—you must edit the master object. Any changes you make in the lens settings of the master object cause the program to automatically update the clone object.

Removing a Lens

To remove a lens effect, select the object and choose None from the lens menu in the roll-up. Click on Apply to complete the operation and return to the drawing window.

Adding PostScript Textures

Though not technically a special effect, PostScript effects can enhance the appearance of a document. These effects are memory intensive and create large files. You control the effect by adjusting the parameters in the PostScript Texture dialog box (see fig. 11.68). For more information about this feature, consult the CorelDRAW user's manual.

Figure 11.68
The PostScript Texture dialog box.

PostScript fills are extremely complex, and can take a long time to print. If you increase the complexity too much by setting the frequency parameter at a high value, the image may not print. If this occurs, decrease the values for that object.

Summary

CorelDRAW enables you to stretch the limits of your imagination by providing the tools required to create a number of special effects. These effects enhance your documents, and enable you to create high impact documents.

Working with Layouts

*L*ayout is the foundation of any well-designed document. Many graphic designers and artists are tempted to jump in and create a drawing, saving the issue of layout for later. Although there is a great deal to be said for spontaneity, there is also much to be said for the frustration of having to back up and rethink a design to make it fit the space. Planning the final appearance of a document is an important first step toward creating a professional-looking document.

This chapter covers:

- Setting up a new page layout

- Working with multipage documents

- Using styles and templates

- Using presets

Setting Up a New Page Layout

Choosing a layout style and page setup creates the foundation for the elements of a document. If your document is going to have a new layout, select **P**age Setup from the **L**ayout menu. The Page Setup dialog box contains the controls for designing your layout. It enables you to adjust the layout for specific output and provides a visual on-screen reference for your design. Unlike paint programs, CorelDRAW enables you to change the layout at any time, without compromising your drawing.

The Page Setup Dialog Box

The options available within the Page Setup dialog box are organized on tabbed property sheets. The options available on the property sheets enable you to set the page size, layout, and display for your document. Above the property sheets is a preview box that enables you to preview the results of the options you select.

Double-click on the page frame in the Drawing Window to display the Page Setup dialog box.

The Size Property Sheet

The Size property sheet enables you to set up the page size and the orientation of your document (see fig. 12.1). CorelDRAW offers 19 paper sizes for your selection. You can also specify custom page sizes up to 30 × 30 inches. To view the available sizes, scroll through the Paper Size list box. Select one of the preset sizes. Note that when you select one of the preset sizes, the numeric entry boxes are grayed out and cannot be changed.

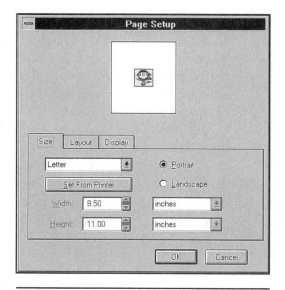

Figure 12.1
The Page Setup dialog box.

If you do not see the paper size you want, select Custom. Choosing the custom setting enables you to specify the units of measurement and the width and height values in the numeric entry boxes.

You choose the page orientation of a document by clicking on one of the orientation radio buttons. Choose Portrait orientation if the vertical dimension of your drawing exceeds the horizontal dimension. Choose Landscape if the horizontal dimension of your drawing exceeds the vertical dimension.

To select the paper size appropriate for your printer setup, click on **S**et From Printer. Some printers also allow for additional sizes not listed in the box.

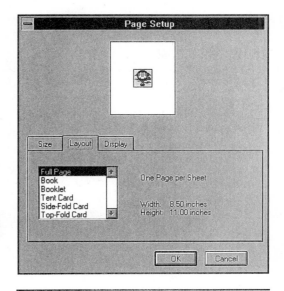

Figure 12.2
The Layout property sheet.

N O T E

Choosing **S**et From Printer sets a page size only. The printable image size may vary from the size options, which do not allow for margins required by your printer. If you choose a larger page size than your printer permits, part of your image may be lost during printing.

The Layout Property Sheet

You can choose from a number of preset page layout options on the Layout property sheet. To view the available options, scroll through the Page Layout list box (see fig. 12.2). Beside the box is a brief description of the number of pages and the dimensions for that selection. The way the page folds appears in the preview area, along with the default printing order.

N O T E

The page layout image that appears in the drawing windows contains only one page of multipage layouts. You must insert the remaining pages for the layout.

CorelDRAW automatically calculates the printing location of the pages in multipage documents. The pages may not print in the order they appear on the screen. Figure 12.3 illustrates the printing order for a 16-page booklet. The illustration on the left shows the order the pages print on a large format printer or offset press. On a standard laser printer, pages 1 and 16 print on the same

page, as do pages 2 and 15, and so on. The page shown on the left prints on the back side of the right page, with the side edges matching as indicated by the arrows. The illustration on the right shows how the booklet would fold and trim.

Corners match back-to-back

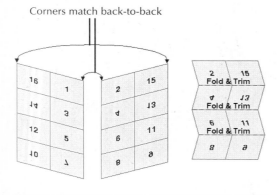

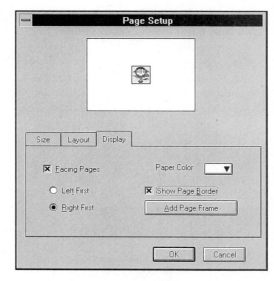

Figure 12.4
The Display property sheet.

Figure 12.3
Typical printing layout for a booklet.

The Display Property Sheet

The Display property sheet contains various options you can choose to alter the appearance of your document in the Drawing Window. Figure 12.4 shows the Display property sheet.

The Display options from which you can choose are as follows:

■ **Paper Color.** You can add a nonprintable color to the screen view of your document so that you can visualize the final appearance of a document once it is printed on colored paper. The default paper color is white. The active palette in this window is the same as the active palette at the bottom of the drawing window. The color you select becomes the active default color for other documents and CorelDRAW sessions until you change it. To select a paper color, click on the color indicator beside Paper Color. A color palette appears, enabling you to scroll through the available colors and make your selection.

■ **Show Page Border.** When Show Page Border is enabled, a non-printable page with a drop shadow appears in the drawing window. Show Page Border is enabled by default. This is a visual representation of the printable area of the drawing window, sized accordingly with the paper size you selected. Generally, objects that fall on the printable area are printed; however, the actual printed image area is device dependent. Most laser printers do not print a full bleed to the edge of the paper; they normally require a margin on all sides. The amount of the margin varies from printer to printer, but usually it is approximately 1/2 inch. To find the image sizes your printer supports, consult your printer manual.

■ **Add Page Frame.** Adding a Page Frame places a rectangle in your drawing, with the same dimensions as your page size. This printable frame appears with the default outline and fill. Since the frame is an object, the fill and outline can be changed.

You can use **A**dd Page Frame to place a visual guideline of the actual image area your printer supports in your document. This enables you to ensure that all the objects in your drawing fall within the area supported by your printer.

To add a printing frame to your document, select the image size your printer supports from the Paper Size list box. If the paper size is not listed, select Custom. Choose the units of measurement you want, and enter the correct value into the numeric entry boxes. Select **A**dd Page Frame, and a frame appears on the page.

Go back to Paper Size and select the paper size your printer uses. Click on OK to return to the drawing window. A page frame appears on the page, which represents the image area your printer supports. If you do not want the page frame to print, you can either delete it later, or place it on the guideline layer using the Layers roll-up.

T I P

If you double-click on the Rectangle tool, the program automatically adds a page frame.

■ **Facing Pages.** Selecting **F**acing Pages enables you to view two pages, which face one another, when working with a multipage document. If you want your document to start on the left page, select Lef**t** First. Choosing **R**ight First starts the document on the right page. Facing pages enable you to create graphics that flow across the two pages. Because objects will not print in the gutter between two pages, portions of your drawing will not disappear when the page is folded.

After you have finished making your page layout selections, click on OK to return to the drawing window. If you selected a single page document and have Show Page Border enabled, a representative page appears in the drawing window. Page one of your layout is displayed if you selected a multipage layout for your document.

You do not have to draw or place an object on the page to save a file. You can save a file with a blank drawing surface. This is useful if you want to create a master file or template, which contains layout information that will be used multiple times.

Working with Multipage Documents

You can create documents that contain up to 999 pages with CorelDRAW. By using Styles and Master Layers, you can quickly lay out multipage documents with ease. Using the Page Setup dialog box to set up a multipage document, you can select one of the preset layout styles. When organizing objects on multipage documents, it is sometimes useful to move objects off into the drawing window, outside the printable page. This places the objects on the Desktop layer, and makes them accessible from every page of your document.

Although CorelDRAW enables you to create documents that contain up to 999 pages, this size is limited by the amount of system resources and hard disk space in your computer. Documents containing a large number of pages can become unwieldy and cause your system to slow. If you plan on creating large multipage documents, CorelVENTURA is better suited to handle the large file size.

Setting Up a Multipage Document

To add pages to your document, choose **I**nsert Page from the **L**ayout menu. Use the scroll bar beside the Insert box to select the number of pages you want to add (see fig. 12.5). Alternatively, highlight the number in the box and type the desired number of pages in the box. Click on OK. The Page Counter in the lower left corner of the drawing window shows the number of pages in your document, and the current number of pages in the drawing window.

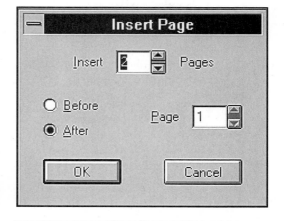

Figure 12.5
The Insert Page dialog box.

To delete pages, select **D**elete Pages from the **L**ayout menu, and enter the number of pages you want to delete in the numeric entry box (see fig. 12.6). Click on OK to return to the drawing window.

Figure 12.6
The Delete Page dialog box.

Remember that when you delete pages, the contents of those pages will also be deleted. No confirmation message appears for this action. Be certain to move any objects you want to keep to other pages to prevent data loss *before* choosing to delete pages.

Moving through a Multipage Document

To move forward through your document, click on the Page Forward or Page Backward icons in the Page Counter, or use the Page Up and Page Down keys on your keyboard. Clicking on the Page Forward or Page Backward icon with the right mouse button changes the view forward or backward five pages—ten pages, if you have facing pages enabled. If you want to move to a specific page, select **G**o To Page from the **L**ayout menu, and enter the page desired in the numeric entry box (see fig. 12.7). Click on OK to return to the drawing window.

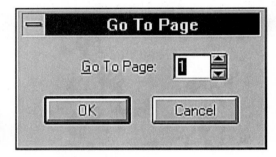

Figure 12.7
The Go To Page dialog box.

By using various mouse movements, you can quickly navigate through a multipage document. Table 12.1 illustrates these shortcuts.

Table 12.1
Mouse Shortcuts for Moving through a Multipage Document

Mouse Movement	Action
Click on the + in the Page Counter	Provides access to the **I**nsert Page dialog box.
Click on the gray area	Accesses the **G**o To Page dialog box.
Press the Ctrl key and click on the page forward icon	Goes to the last page in the document.
Press the Ctrl key and click on the page backward icon	Goes to the first page in the document.

Using Styles and Templates

Styles are a set of formatting instructions that you can apply to graphic and text objects. Using styles can reduce layout time by automating repetitive layout procedures. You can define styles to include fill and outline attributes, as well as special effects. By saving styles in sets, as templates, they are available for future CorelDRAW sessions. The Styles roll-up (see fig. 12.8) is used to apply styles and templates. You access the S**t**yles roll-up by selecting it from the **L**ayout menu or by pressing Ctrl+F5.

Figure 12.8
The Styles roll-up.

The Styles Roll-Up

CorelDRAW comes with a default template that contains styles you can apply to objects in your document. The top of the Styles roll-up displays the name of the selected template. Below that are three styles format buttons: Artistic Text, Paragraph Text, and Graphic. When you select a button, the Styles List displays the available styles for that format. You can choose any or all of the buttons.

To apply a style, follow these steps:

1. Select the object to which you want to apply a style.

2. Choose the style from the list you want to apply, and click on Apply.

N O T E

You can only apply a designated style to a corresponding type of object. For example, you cannot apply a graphic style, such as perspective, if the perspective style was created as a graphic style. To apply perspective to Artistic text, you would need to create a perspective style, and designate it as an Artistic Text style.

Clicking on the right arrow in the Styles roll-up accesses the following styles management controls:

- **Load Styles.** Loads a new template. If you have made changes to the current template, you will be prompted to save the changes.

- **Save Template.** Saves the current template, including any changes you have made. A dialog box appears, prompting you for the path and file name.

- **Set Hot Keys.** Designates hot keys to apply styles.

- **Delete Style.** Deletes the selected style. You are prompted for confirmation before the style is deleted.

- **Find.** Searches and finds objects to which the selected style has been applied. Once it finds an object that matches the style, the command name changes to Find Next, enabling you to continue the search for objects associated with the style.

Assigning Hot Keys

Assigning hot keys enables you to quickly apply styles to paragraph text. To assign hot keys, follow these steps:

1. Click on the right arrow in the Styles roll-up, and select Set Hot Keys to display the Set Hot Keys dialog box.

2. Select the options you want. The following options are available:

   - **New Hot Key.** Enables you to assign a new hot key.

   - **Unassigned.** Enables you to clear the hot key for the selected style.

   - **Auto Assign.** Automatically assigns hot keys to all the styles in one step.

   - **Sort By.** Sorts the styles alphabetically by name or type size.

   - **Cluster Bullet.** Groups styles that contain bullets.

3. Click on OK to return to the drawing window.

The Object Menu

The Object menu accesses the following controls for performing a number of commands associated with styles:

- Save As Style
- Update Style
- Revert to Style
- Apply Style
- Overprint Outline
- Overprint Fill
- Object Data roll-up

Creating and Saving a New Style

Creating and saving styles enables you to preserve the attributes of a text or graphic object. To create a new style, follow these steps:

1. Select the object with the right mouse button to display the Object menu (see fig. 12.9). If you do not have the right mouse button programmed for the Object menu, you might have to hold the mouse button down for a moment.

N O T E

You can program the right mouse button to open the Object menu within the Preferences dialog box.

2. Select Save As Style. The Save Style As dialog box appears, enabling you to enter a name for the style (see fig. 12.10). Choose any other attributes you want included in the style, and click on OK.

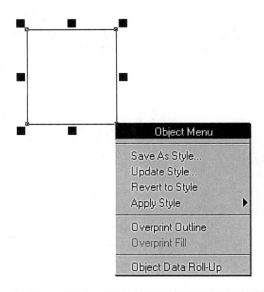

Figure 12.9
The Object Menu roll-up.

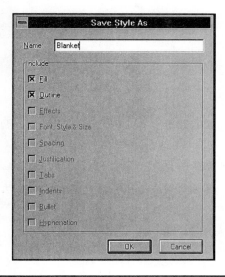

Figure 12.10
The Save Style As dialog box.

CorelDRAW automatically loads the appropriate Save Style As dialog box, along with its corresponding list of options. Each dialog box contains a list of options specific to the selected style format.

Editing Styles

The Object menu also enables you to edit existing styles. To edit and update a style, follow these steps:

1. Make the editing changes to the object associated with the style.

2. Select Update Style from the Object menu to display the Update Style dialog box (see fig. 12.11).

3. Choose the options you want to apply to the updated style, and click on OK.

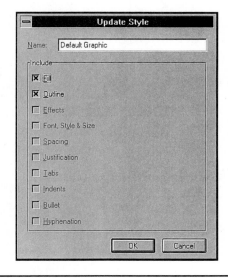

Figure 12.11
The Update Style dialog box.

Reverting to Style

Selecting this choice in the Object Menu roll-up clears any changes you have made to an object that are associated with the style attached to that object.

Applying Style

To apply a style using the Object menu, follow these steps:

1. Select the object with the right mouse button to display the Object menu.

2. Click on Apply Style, and choose the style you want applied to the object.

Overprinting Outline and Fill Attributes

Selecting the Overprint options from the object menu enables you to set overprinting for the selected objects. For more information regarding overprinting, see Chapter 14, "Printed Output."

Using the Object Data Roll-Up

Choosing this option accesses the Object Data roll-up, enabling you to create or append a database with information about your image. For more information about Object Data, see Chapter 38, "Color Management."

Using Presets

Presets are visual representations of macros, which can be applied to artistic text and graphic objects. Some presets can be applied to paragraph text. CorelDRAW comes packaged with a library of presets. You can apply these presets, or you can create your own. Presets are accessed via the P**r**esets roll-up (see fig. 12.12). To open the roll-up, select it from the **S**pecial menu, or press Alt+F5.

Figure 12.12
The Presets roll-up.

To apply an existing preset, follow these steps:

1. Select the object to which you want to apply the preset, and access the Presets roll-up.

2. Click on the down arrow to scroll through the available presets. An example of the preset appears in the preview box above the list (see fig. 12.13).

3. Select a preset and click on Apply.

N O T E

Presets cannot be applied to multiple selections or groups of objects.

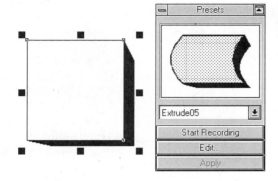

Figure 12.13

An example of a preset.

> **N O T E**
>
> Presets appear in the drawing window in a grouped format. This is applicable whether you use one of the available presets or create your own.

Selecting the Edit button from the Presets roll-up displays the Edit Preset dialog box. This enables you to change the name, add notes, or delete the preset. Changing the name does not create a new preset—it only renames the existing preset, and overwrites it. Make the changes you want, and click on OK to return to the drawing window.

Creating a Preset

To create a preset, perform the following steps:

1. Create or select an object.

> **N O T E**
>
> This object will not become part of the recording session. The preset will be applied to it, but the object will not become part of the playback. If you want the object to become part of the playback, skip this step. Note that you must pre-create artistic and paragraph text, as well as open paths and irregular objects. They cannot be created during the recording session.

2. Open the Presets roll-up.

3. Select Start Recording, and apply one or more of the following transactions:

   ■ Create (rectangles and ellipses only)

   ■ Delete

   ■ Duplicate and clone

   ■ Copy attributes

   ■ Transformations, using the mouse or the Transform roll-up

   ■ Clear Transformation

   ■ Align and Order

   ■ Group, combine, weld, intersect, and trim

   ■ Add, copy, edit, or clear a perspective

   ■ Create, copy, clone, or clear a blend

   ■ Create, copy, clone, or clear an extrusion

- Create, copy, clone, or clear a contour

- Create, copy, or clear a lens

- Edit artistic or paragraph text

- Convert to curves

- Change fill and outline attributes

- Overprint fill and outline

The first object to which you apply a transaction is the seed object. When you play back the preset or apply it to an object, all transactions will be relative to the size and location of the seed object.

N O T E

Not all presets are designed for all objects. Some presets may not preset a pleasing appearance when applied to another type of object, other than the type for which the preset was originally designed.

During recording, you can select multiple objects and apply supported transactions to them if they were created during the recording.

4. Click on Stop Recording.

5. The Edit Preset dialog box appears, enabling you to enter a name and any notes you want attached to the preset. If you do not enter a name, a default name starting with the word Preset and a sequential number are assigned to the new preset. Click on OK.

6. A thumbnail is automatically generated and saved with the Preset list.

Understanding Transaction Sequence

When recording a Preset, if the first transaction is the creation of an object, size and placement of objects become absolute. For example, if you create a preset in this manner, and an ellipse is the first transaction, an ellipse will be created when you play back the transaction later. The ellipse will be positioned on the page and sized as it was during the recording session.

If the first transaction is other than the creation of an object, the effect of the playback will be proportional to the size and location of the seed object. This allows a Preset effect to be applied to objects of other shapes.

Summary

Predetermining layout, and using templates, styles, and presets, can save hours of creation time. They are ideally suited for production work, such as newsletters, catalogs, and other documents that require frequent updating. These documents often require bitmap images, such as photos, to complete the document. Chapter 13 discusses the use of bitmap images in CorelDRAW documents.

Working with Bitmaps

*C*orelDRAW enables you to import bitmaps into the drawing window. The editing you can perform is rather limited, however. Although you can scale a bitmap in CorelDRAW, bitmapped images degrade when they are resized in CorelDRAW. Most paint- and bitmap-editing packages enable you to resize a bitmap while maintaining the aspect ratio and resolution, which helps prevent distortion and pixelation of the image.

Paint- and bitmap-editing applications also enable you to apply special effects, such as brushes, distortion, and channel adjustments, to a bitmapped image. These effects cannot be applied to bitmapped images within CorelDRAW.

When you import a bitmap into CorelDRAW, you can move and crop the bitmap. You can also transform the bitmap by skewing, scaling, or rotating the bitmap. If the bitmap is monochrome, you can apply color to the bitmap.

This chapter covers:

- Understanding bitmaps
- Importing bitmapped images into CorelDRAW
- Exporting bitmap images
- Understanding display considerations
- Editing bitmaps
- Tracing bitmaps in CorelDRAW
- Using CorelTRACE

Understanding Bitmaps

The characteristics of a bitmap graphic are quite different than those of a vector graphic. A bitmap has four descriptive characteristics: dimension, resolution, bit depth, and color model.

N O T E

Vector images are described by their outline and fill attributes. Because of the mathematical nature of the outline description, the final output resolution is dependent upon the output device rather than the image itself.

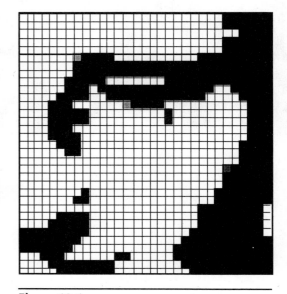

Figure 13.1
The dimensions of a bitmap graphic as measured in pixels.

- **Dimension.** Bitmap images are basically grids. Each square represents a pixel. The image is comprised of pixels that are either turned on or off. The grid of pixels that represents the display on your computer screen might be 640×480, but that does not designate the actual measurement of the image. The dots on one screen may be closer together than on another screen. The number of pixels (usually measured in *ppi*, or *pixels per inch*) represents the dimension of the image. It is better to describe an image in numbers of dots, rather than by physical size. Figure 13.1 shows a portion of a graphic divided into pixels.

- **Resolution.** The resolution of an image output to a printer is described in dots per inch, dpi. An image that is 100 dpi and has 100 dots on each side would also be one inch on each side. If you changed the dpi to 50 dpi, the image would become two inches on each side. You still have the same total number of dots, but now each one is twice as large.

Increasing the resolution of a bitmapped image increases the file size geometrically. If you double the resolution of an image, the file size increases by a factor of four. An increase of three times the original resolution would enlarge the file by a factor of nine.

■ **Bit depth.** Each dot in a bitmapped image can be black, white, gray, or a color. A bit is the smallest unit of computer data. It can either be a 0 or a 1. A zero is white; a one is black. An image that is described as being 1-bit color only has two possible combinations, black or white. If the image was 2 bits, there would be four possible combinations: black, white, and two grays. An 8-bit image has 256 levels of gray, and a 24-bit image has over 16 million possible colors.

N O T E

A 24-bit image actually has three 8-bit values. Each 8-bit value represents one of the RGB values: red, green, or blue.

CorelDRAW can only apply color to bitmaps that are 1-bit color, or bilevel. The greater the number of bits in an image, the larger the resulting file. This is important to remember when importing bitmap images into CorelDRAW. Large files take longer to import, and may be larger than required for optimum output.

■ **Color model.** The fourth characteristic of a bitmapped image is the color model. When you create or scan an image on the computer, the color is displayed in a format the monitor understands. Monitors use RGB to display color. If you choose another color model for a bitmapped image, the color will still be displayed in RGB. Your computer interprets the values for the color model you choose, and adjusts the RGB values accordingly. Printers and the printing industry use spot or process colors. This difference is important to remember when creating an image. Color management, as described in Chapter 38, can make the difference between a realistic display and one that varies greatly from printed output.

Resizing a bitmapped image causes distortion, because it has a fixed resolution. If you display and print a bitmap at its original size and resolution, this does not present a problem. If you enlarge a bitmap, the space between the pixels becomes greater, causing jaggies. When you reduce the size of a bitmap, pixels are stripped from the image, which also produces a rough appearance, because information is lost (see fig. 13.2).

Figure 13.2

Vector versus bitmapped images at different resolutions.

Another factor in resizing bitmaps is interpolation. When you reduce a bitmap, the pixels that surround those being removed interpolate, or average; this can create a blurred image.

One solution to the problems that bitmapped images present is to use vector images, which can be resized and manipulated without any degradation of quality. CorelDRAW allows you to turn bitmap images into vector images by either tracing the image in CorelDRAW, or by using CorelTRACE. For more information about using CorelTRACE, see "Using CorelTRACE," later in this chapter.

Importing Bitmapped Images into CorelDRAW

When you import a graphic image into CorelDRAW, it centers the file on the page and places it on top of any other object in the drawing. CorelDRAW supports the following bitmapped image formats: WPG, BMP, CPT, CT, GIF, PCX, PCC, TGA, TIF, JPG, JFF, JFT, and PCD.

Cropping and Resampling Images

Cropping an image allows you to reduce the file size and loading time of the image. To crop an image when you import it into CorelDRAW:

1. Choose **F**ile, **I**mport and select the file you want to import.

2. Instead of selecting Full Image, click on the down arrow and choose Crop. Click on OK. The Crop Image dialog box appears, enabling you to decide how you want the image cropped (see fig. 13.3).

3. Resize the marquee by dragging the boxes to the image you want to display. You can also enter values in the entry boxes to specify the cropping. If you want to move the marquee frame, click in the center of the frame and move it to the desired location.

4. Click on OK. The image appears in the drawing window, cropped to the selection you made.

N O T E

When you crop an image using the shape tool, it does not reduce the file size of the bitmap. The original bitmap is still intact. You can change the cropping at any time. Cropping on import, however, reduces the size of the file, allowing you to save hard disk space when you save the CorelDRAW file.

Cropping handles

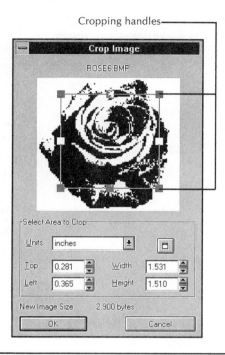

Figure 13.3
Cropping an image on import.

Resampling an image allows you to resize the image and change the resolution. You can resample bitmapped images when importing them into CorelDRAW. To resample an image, do the following:

1. Select **I**mport from the **F**ile menu and choose the file you want to import.

2. Instead of selecting Full Image, click the down arrow and choose Resample. When you click on OK the Resample dialog box appears, enabling you to resize or change the resolution of the image.

3. Click on OK. The image appears in the drawing window, resampled according to the values you entered.

Using PhotoCD Images

You can import PhotoCDs into CorelDRAW by selecting the .PCD format for your import and specifying the path of the file you want. When you click on OK after selecting a file, the Photo CD Options dialog box appears (see fig. 13.4). To import the image into CorelDRAW, follow these steps:

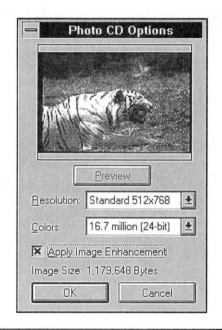

Figure 13.4
The Photo CD Options dialog box.

1. Choose a resolution for the image. You can choose from an assortment of resolutions. To make a selection, click on the down arrow and highlight the resolution you want.

2. Choose a color depth from the drop down box. For more information about color depth, review the Understanding Bitmaps section earlier in this chapter.

3. Either choose OK or enable **A**pply Image Enhancement.

T I P

When you install CorelDRAW, it includes a file called PCDLIB.DLL. Various other programs install this file, as well. If multiple versions of this file are on your system, it could cause the import of a PhotoCD file to fail. To prevent this problem, use the Windows File Manager to locate all the files with this name. Rename all the matching files, with exception of the most recent file. Exit the File Manager and restart Windows. PhotoCD files should now import without a problem.

When you enable **A**pply Image Enhancement and click on OK, the Photo CD Image Enhancement dialog box appears (see fig. 13.5). You can choose between GamutCD or Kodak color correction.

Figure 13.5
Using GamutCD color correction.

Applying GamutCD Color Correction

Follow these steps to apply GamutCD color correction:

1. Select the preview speed you want. The preview speed does not affect the image being imported. Selecting Best Preview requires more time to process the preview, but yields a better quality preview upon which to base your color correction.

2. Enable White in Image if white appears in the image. Enter a value to represent the white in your image (255 represents the purest white possible on your monitor). If there is no white in your image, disable White in Image unless you need to lighten the image.

3. Enable Black in Image if black appears in the image. Enter a value to represent the Black in your image (0 represents the purest black possible on your monitor). If there is no black in your image, disable Black in Image unless you need to darken the image.

4. Select Set **A**ctive Area and marquee-select the area upon which you want to base the image enhancement calculations. Do not include the black border or any area that will be cropped out of the image.

5. Choose Set **N**eutral Colors and select any colors that should be neutral in order to remove color casts from the image. To select neutral colors, click in the preview window on gray, black, and white; these colors should not receive a color cast.

   The most successful image enhancement sets neutral colors that encompass the range of lightness in an image. For example, if you selected a black and gray as neutral, but not a white, a color cast would be applied to the white. This would yield unsatisfactory results. If your image contains no neutral colors, do not select Set **N**eutral Colors.

6. Select **P**review to display the updated enhancement in the preview box, and click on OK to continue the import.

Applying Kodak Color Correction

Clicking on the **K**odak Color Correction option displays a new set of options (see

fig. 13.6). The following steps explain how to apply Kodak color correction:

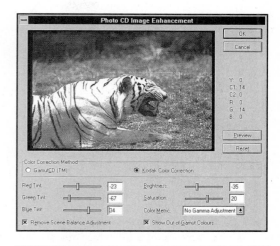

Figure 13.6
Using Kodak color correction.

1. Adjust the red, green, and blue tints by sliding the bars or by entering a value for each in the values box next to each option.

2. Adjust the brightness level and saturation. Select **P**review to display the updated enhancement.

3. Choose No Gamma Adjustment, or a Contrast Level, from the Color **M**etric list box. The Scene Balance Adjustment was made when the CD was created. You can either accept this setting or remove it by clicking in the Re**m**ove Scene Balance Adjustment check box.

4. Enabling Show Out-of-**G**amut Colors allows you to check the adjustments you have made. If you have overcorrected, or the adjustments are inaccurate, the pixels that are Out-of-Gamut will be displayed as pure red or blue.

5. When you are satisfied with the results of your enhancement, click on OK to continue the import.

Exporting Bitmap Images

CorelDRAW allows you to save images in a variety of vector and bitmap formats. These allow you to choose an export format appropriate for the application and platform that will be using the file. Each of the formats has limitations as well as points that recommend it for a particular use. For more information about export formats, see Chapter 40.

To export a file or selection, follow these steps:

1. If you are going to export a specific selection of your image, make the selection prior to exporting.

2. Select **E**xport from the **F**ile menu to display the Export dialog box (see fig. 13.7).

3. Enter a name you want to use for your export. If the name appears on the list, select it.

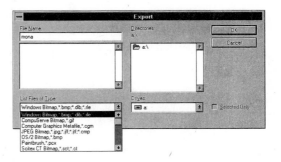

Figure 13.7
The Export dialog box.

4. Enable **S**elected Only, if desired. Enabling **S**elected Only enables you to save a portion of a drawing under another name. This is useful if you want to incorporate portions of one image into another.

5. From the List Files of **T**ype box, select an export format. CorelDRAW automatically enters the appropriate extension for the file format you choose.

6. Choose OK to start the export and return to the drawing window. Some file formats display an additional dialog box when you return to the drawing window. Select any options that apply to your export and click on OK to continue.

Understanding Display Considerations

Unless you are creating an on-screen presentation, displaying bitmapped images at a high resolution offers limited value, at the expense of speed and efficiency. You might want to increase the resolution, however, when you check the image on-screen before running printer proofs. When you select high resolution either from the **V**iew menu or in the Preferences dialog box, your image is displayed at the resolution it was created.

When high resolution is disabled, a thumb-nail of the image is displayed in Editable Preview. This is usually sufficient for positioning and manipulating the object. If you are working in Wireframe View, disabling high resolution and visible enables you to edit your image more easily by displaying the bitmap as an empty rectangle (see fig. 13.8). Should you select the bitmap, the status line indicates your selection.

Selected object is bitmap

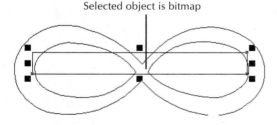

Figure 13.8
A wireframe view of a bitmapped image.

> **N O T E**
>
> Rotated or skewed bitmaps always display at a reduced resolution. This does not affect the output of your image when it is printed.

Editing Bitmaps

CorelDRAW allows you to edit bitmapped images in a limited manner. You can rotate, skew, or scale a bitmap as you would other objects in CorelDRAW. You can also color monochrome images.

> **N O T E**
>
> A rotated bitmap cannot be placed in other applications with the Clipboard. You can place the rotated bitmap in another CorelDRAW image. For information about transforming bitmaps, see Chapter 8, "Transforming and Arranging Objects."

Applying Color and Halftone Screens to Monochrome Images

If the image is a black and white bitmap, you can apply color to the background and foreground of the image. You color the background using the Fill tool and color the foreground using the Outline tool. You can also apply PostScript halftones to both the foreground and background of the bitmap. This allows you to create some interesting effects.

To apply a halftone screen to a monochrome bitmap, follow these steps (see fig. 13.9 for an example of the result):

1. Select the bitmap.

2. To apply a halftone screen to the background, select the Uniform Fill dialog box from the Fill flyout menu or press Shift+F11. You can also apply a fountain halftone screen to a background.

3. In the dialog box, choose a Pantone Spot color from the **S**how list box, and enter the amount of tint you want in the **T**int entry box.

4. Click on **P**ostScript Options and select the type of halftone screen you want from the list box.

5. Enter the frequency and angle of the screen and click on OK to complete the operation and return to the Uniform Fill dialog box. Click on OK again to return to the drawing window.

To apply a halftone screen to the foreground, access the outline color dialog box and repeat steps 3–5.

Figure 13.9

Applying halftone screens to monochrome bitmaps.

While you cannot add color to a grayscale bitmap, you can create a number of effects by applying a Lens to an object and superimposing it over the bitmap. Using this procedure, you can create sepia effects or apply a tint over the entire bitmap. For more information about using Lens effects with bitmaps, see Chapter 11, "Creating with Special Effects."

Tracing Bitmaps in CorelDRAW

Using the Pencil tool, you can auto-trace bitmapped images in the drawing window. To trace an image, select the bitmap and click on the Pencil tool. When you return the cursor to the drawing window, it turns into a plus sign shape with a small dotted line after it. Move to the bitmap and click to trace a portion of the bitmap. This is useful for tracing small portions of a bitmapped image, but is not designed to trace entire bitmaps.

Auto-trace is designed to be used with monochrome bitmaps. The auto-trace function treats every bitmap as monochrome, whether it is or not. You can trace color bitmaps, but the trace may not be successful; any tint of a color will be disregarded as white.

Figure 13.10 shows a bitmap image of a rose with the shaded section auto-traced.

Figure 13.10
Using auto-trace in the drawing window.

Using CorelTRACE

CorelTRACE enables you to trace bitmapped images and save them in a vector format so that you can edit the images in CorelDRAW. The program supports any bitmap format supported by CorelDRAW and is capable of OCR recognition as well. It provides a number of different tracing methods, enabling you to choose different effects.

Figure 13.11 shows the CorelTRACE screen.

To use CorelTRACE, follow these steps:

1. Open a bitmap by selecting **O**pen from the **F**ile menu and entering the path and file name for the bitmap you want to trace. If the bitmap is not a .BMP, the program will convert the bitmap to that format.

2. Select the portion of the image you want to trace by using the Pick tool to marquee-select. If you want to trace the entire image, skip to step three.

3. Click on the color box on the ribbon bar to select a color for the traced image. You can use the eyedropper in the toolbox to pick up a color from the bitmap.

4. Select a tracing method from the Trace menu. The program will trace the image.

5. If you are satisfied with the results, save the traced output. CorelTRACE saves traced images as .EPS files and automatically adds that extension to any file you save.

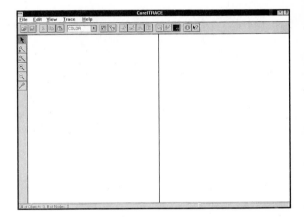

Figure 13.11
The CorelTRACE screen.

Tracing Methods

When you choose a tracing method, you can select the final effect you want. Not all tracing methods are available for every type of bitmap. The centerline method, for example, only supports monochrome images. The tracing methods available in CorelTRACE are as follows:

■ **Outline.** Supports color, grayscale, and monochrome bitmaps. It traces the outline of each element in an image and fills it with a corresponding color (see fig. 13.12). Color bitmaps are filled with the various colors that are associated with the bitmap.

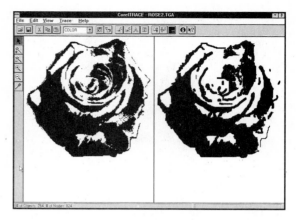

Figure 13.13
An image traced using Centerline format.

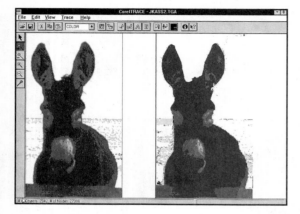

Figure 13.12
An image traced using Outline format.

■ **Centerline.** Supports only monochrome bitmaps. You can convert an image to monochrome in the Edit Options dialog box. The centerline method treats lines as objects, and traces the line. It does not trace the outline of an object. Figure 13.13 shows an example.

■ **Woodcut.** Creates a carved woodblock effect as it traces (see fig. 13.14).

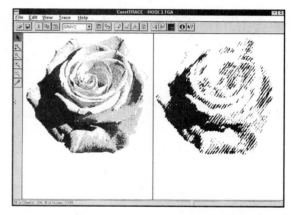

Figure 13.14
An image traced using Woodcut format.

■ **Silhouette.** Supports only monochrome bitmaps. Silhouette traces the outline of the image and fills it with a single color (see fig.13.15). To use silhouette, you must first select a portion of the image.

Figure 13.15
An image traced using Silhouette format.

- **OCR.** Converts scanned text into artistic text so it can be edited within CorelDRAW.

- **Form.** Is used for scanning and converting forms into an editable format. It traces the text, lines, and other objects to create a form that can then be used or modified in CorelDRAW.

Regardless of the tracing method, you can choose various options to modify the way CorelTRACE behaves. To edit the tracing options, select **E**dit Options from the **T**race menu.

Selecting Trace Options

When you select **E**dit Options, the Tracing Options dialog box appears. The five property sheets in the dialog box allow you to modify the way your image is traced. The settings for each option will vary from one image to another, and may require experimentation on your part to get the effect you want.

The Image Property Sheet

The Image property sheet allows you to change the color information of the image you are tracing. These options are not permanent, and have no effect on the original image unless you choose to save the image with the new information. You can modify the following options, as shown in figure 13.16:

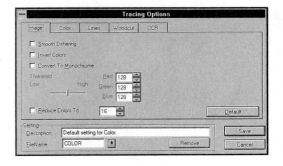

Figure 13.16
The Image property sheet.

- **S**mooth Dithering. Enables you to choose the dithering method for the image. If you have opened a 24-bit image, this changes the colors to 256 dithered colors.

- **I**nvert Colors. Reverses the coloration of the image. When used with monochrome bitmaps, black portions of the drawing become white; white portions of the image become black.

- **Convert to M**onochrome. Converts color and grayscale images to black and white. Silhouette and Centerline tracing methods require monochrome images. When Convert to **M**onochrome is enabled, you can adjust the

threshold for the red, green, and blue values individually. If an image has a dominant color, this allows for a more successful trace that has more detail.

- **Reduce Colors To.** Enables you to reduce the number of colors in an image. Colors are averaged to create the resulting image. Reducing colors makes tracing some images more successful.

The Color Property Sheet

The Color property sheet (see fig. 13.17) enables you to adjust the sensitivity to a range of colors when using the tracing wand. Selecting a low number will isolate a smaller range of colors; a setting of 255 might select more colors than you want to trace. Because CorelTRACE allows you to "build" trace output, using a low setting can allow you to build a more accurate trace. Using the slide bar changes the sensitivity for all channels equally.

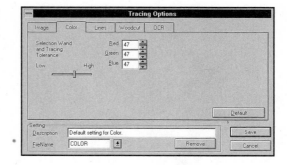

Figure 13.17
The Color property sheet.

The Lines Property Sheet

The Lines property sheet adjusts the way CorelTRACE responds to the image you are tracing (see fig. 13.18).

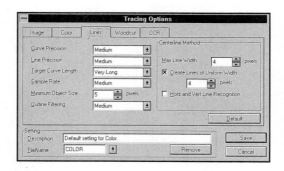

Figure 13.18
The Lines property sheet.

The following options are available:

- **Curve Precision.** Determines how closely the trace follows the original curve.

- **Line Precision.** CorelTRACE tries to convert all the trace lines to straight line segments. This control enables you to decide how straight a line must be before it is converted into curves. Medium, the default setting here, is the best setting to capture the most detail in a trace.

- **Target Curve Length.** Controls the length of lines in the output trace image. Shorter settings create more detail in the trace but create a larger and more complex image.

- **Sample Rate.** Controls how much of the original image is used to calculate the traced output. A fine setting forces the program to look at most of the image, creating a more detailed trace. A coarse setting uses an averaging method to create smoother curves. The finer settings create larger and more complex files.

- **Minimum Object Size.** A larger setting here enables CorelTRACE to eliminate smaller objects from the trace. This is useful when tracing a scanned image that may contain scan trash. Scan trash is extra pixels that might appear in your scanned image. These pixels can be caused by dust, displacement of pixels in the scanning process, or very small lines. The pixels detract from your image and need to be deleted to provide a clean trace.

- **Outline Filtering.** Enables you to decide how smooth you want the traced image. Choosing smooth creates more smooth points and reduces the number of jaggies in the image.

- **Max Line Width.** Applies to the Centerline tracing method. This setting determines the widest line to be created in the trace.

- **Create Lines of Uniform Width.** Forces the program to create the trace using one line weight. You can adjust the line width in the entry box.

- **Horz and Vert Line Recognition.** Enables the program to rotate the image if the lines are not perfectly horizontal or vertical.

The Woodcut Property Sheet

The Woodcut property sheet enables you to set woodcut options, including angle of cut and the sample width (see fig. 13.19).

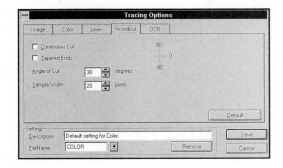

Figure 13.19
The Woodcut property sheet.

The options in the Woodcut property sheet are described in the following list:

- **Continuous Cut.** When this option is enabled, the cut line is continuous, without breaks. If the option is disabled, the lines are separate. All lines are drawn from left to right.

■ **Tapered Ends.** Allows for the lines to narrow at the end, simulating a chiseled effect.

■ **Angle of Cut.** Specifies the angle of the lines. The setting here must be between –90° and 90°.

■ **Sample Width.** Enables you to set the width of the lines, in the trace output. Lower settings create more lines and therefore larger and more complex files.

The OCR Property Sheet

The OCR property sheet enables you to choose settings for OCR and form tracing only (see fig. 13.20).

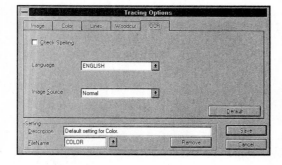

Figure 13.20
The OCR property sheet.

The options in the OCR property sheet are described in the following list:

■ **Check Spelling.** Enables the spelling checker. If the program finds a word that is misspelled, it will not trace the word.

■ **Language.** Enables you to choose a language dictionary to use with the trace. To choose a dictionary, you must have a CD-ROM. The dictionaries are located on the CD-ROM.

■ **Image Source.** Selecting a source ensures more successful OCR output. Select Normal for 300 dpi documents. If the scan source is a dot matrix printer, the processing will take more time because of the lower quality of dot matrix output. Select Fax Fine if the source image is a standard scanned fax.

N O T E

Clicking on the **D**efault button resets the settings to the default for trace file listed in the Setting box at the bottom of the dialog box.

Summary

Using bitmapped images in CorelDRAW can greatly enhance documents. Catalogs and newsletters frequently call for the use of photographs, and CorelDRAW easily enables you to use them in your work. If you can, try to use PhotoCDs as the source for photographic material. Services are available that process your film and place the images on CD.

CorelTRACE enables you to trace images when the bitmapped format does not meet your needs. The images it creates are frequently complex and should be simplified in CorelDRAW to ensure successful printing.

Chapter 14

Printed Output

*W*hen most people talk about outputting a file, they are referring to their in-house printer. The reality is that more types of output equipment exist than this chapter can begin to address. In addition to all the online output choices that include on-screen presentation, discussed in Part Five of this book, a long list of other nonprinted output exists. Today, CorelDRAW is used to create designs that are output directly on engraving, embroidery, etching, and signage equipment, among other media. The printed output choices are even more extensive. All of the output choices have one thing in common, however—they address a specific audience.

This chapter covers:

- Planning for output
- Preparing to print
- Using the Print dialog box
- Printing a file
- Examining printing options
- Using Print Merge

Previewing Printing

This chapter considers printed output in its varied forms. The key to successful output is planning. The results of this planning should begin before the design is initiated. Designing for specific requirements is much easier than adapting an already created design for those requirements. Planning must consider the audience and any restrictions involved in the final output. Screen printing requirements are very different from the those of the corporate newsletter or of publishing-quality output. Screen printing needs can be more restrictive than publishing needs.

The Corel suite of applications can print to any device supported by Windows drivers, including a number of printers and imagesetters that support various resolutions of output.

Planning for Output

What will be the final product of your design? Frequently, the overall design, color choices, and other factors are determined by the final product. Screen printing and similar industries are restricted to spot colors. Generally, these industries require only dense 150 dpi output; higher resolutions would be wasted. High-quality publishing uses more CMYK colors and requires resolutions frequently in excess of 2,400 dpi.

Choosing an Output Device for Resolution

Generally, resolution is dictated by the job you're doing. You should not allow a device to dictate the resolution if the job has more demanding requirements. Budget, paper choices, and quality should determine the resolution and the device you use for output. Your in-house laser printer might be fine for newsletters, flyers, or other one-color quick-press jobs. It is not adequate, however, for a full-color print on glossy-coated paper stock.

T I P

One way to maintain a budget when printing is to use halftones to produce one-color jobs on colored stock. This option can produce an excellent appearance at a fraction of the cost of full-color.

Commercial printers measure resolution in lines per inch (lpi). For most printing, including a monochrome output, a good rule of thumb to use is that the dpi output should be twice the lpi. A good quality laser printer can produce adequate results for this application.

The success of your job is increased if you print to film as opposed to hard copy. The most frequent problem with laser output that is to be commercially printed is tone density. Most lasers do not produce sufficient toner density. The result is a copy that cannot stand up to a camera. When the film is shot, it contains fading and holes where the toner was thin. Dye sublimation and wax thermal printers produce a better quality print for these types of jobs.

If you are creating a high-quality job for a catalog or book your requirements will be greater. To create the highest quality possible, you need to span as much of the 256 grayscale levels as possible. This is especially critical if photographs or other bitmapped images are going to be included in the document. When determining the resolution for high-quality output, consider the chart in figure 14.1.

Resolution of laser printer or imagesetter in dpi	Screen Ruling in lpi									
	60 lpi	65 lpi	80 lpi	85 lpi	100 lpi	110 lpi	120 lpi	133 lpi	150 lpi	175 lpi
300	25	21	14	12	9	7	6	5	4	3
400	44	38	25	22	16	13	11	9	7	5
600	100	85	56	50	36	30	25	20	16	12
800	178	151	100	89	64	53	44	36	28	21
1000	278	237	156	138	100	83	69	57	44	33
1270	448	382	252	223	161	133	112	91	72	53
1700	803	684	452	400	289	239	201	163	128	94
2540	1792	1527	1008	893	645	533	448	365	287	211
3250	2943	2500	1650	1462	1056	873	734	597	469	345

Figure 14.1

Optimum printing resolutions.

The values in each column represent the maximum levels of gray obtainable for resolution of various devices at specific screen rulings. The grayed area indicates the optimum combinations to achieve the best quality final output. Consult your printer to determine the lpi available on presses he or she uses. You might need to output your document to a service bureau to achieve the results you want. For more information about using a service bureau, see Chapter 41, "Working with Service Bureaus."

Preparing To Print

Many of the problems normally encountered in printing can be avoided. If you keep in mind your final output while designing your document, and check the document before printing, you can realize an enormous savings in time and frustration. If you are using a service bureau, ruined film can be a costly lesson. Checking the following items before you begin printing can help ensure the success of your printed output:

- If you are printing an image that is not going to be tiled, make sure it falls within the printed page. Take into consideration any margins the printer requires. Most laser printers require a half-inch border on the top of a sheet of paper to grip the paper. Also, they generally cannot print full bleed and require margins on the sides as well. Consult your printer manual to find out what your specific printer requires.

- Check the palettes for your colors. Do not mix spot and process palettes, unless the document you are printing needs both. A document might need to

mix the two palettes to create halftone screens. If you send your document to a printer or service bureau, each spot color requires its own film and plate. Images created from CMYK palettes require a maximum of four plates, one for each channel.

■ CorelDRAW offers you the ability to calibrate your monitor, printer, and the program to help eliminate color accuracy problems. For more information on color management, see Chapter 38, "Color Management."

■ Take into consideration the stock on which you are printing. The paper you use determines the amount of dot gain and the halftone frequency.

■ If your image requires a full bleed, make sure the image extends one-eighth inch to one-fourth inch beyond the paper surface. Use the Shape and Pick tools to even any edges. If you mask the drawing to create clean edges, it adds complexity to the drawing that could interfere with printing.

■ Make sure the font you choose is available at your service bureau or print shop. If it is not available, either download the fonts with the print job or convert the text to curves prior to printing.

■ Eliminate unnecessary or extremely small objects. These might contain a number of nodes that could cause PostScript Errors.

Using the Print Dialog Box

When you are ready to print your document, select **P**rint from the **F**ile menu to display the Print dialog box (see fig. 14.2). The Print dialog box contains the basic controls for printing.

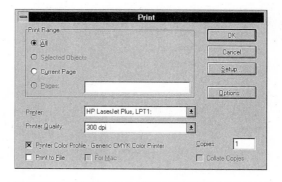

Figure 14.2
The Print dialog box.

Setting a Print Range

Within the Print Range area of the Print dialog box, select the pages of the document you want to print. You can choose to print the entire document by selecting **A**ll. If you need to proof a selection from your document, click on S**e**lected Objects. Select the objects before accessing the Print dialog box. Selecting C**u**rrent Page prints the page currently displayed in the Drawing window. You also can select a range of pages by entering the page numbers separated by a hyphen in the **P**ages entry box. Use a comma between page ranges to specify more than one page range.

Selecting a Printer

The printer listed in the Printer box is the default printer specified in the Windows Control Panel. You can activate another printer temporarily by clicking the down arrow and selecting a printer from the list box.

You do not have to physically have a printer to choose that printer, if you are printing to file. You must have installed the driver for that printer, however, for the printer to appear in the list box. This feature enables you to print files for output at a service bureau.

Choosing Print Quality

Choosing printer quality sets the resolution of your print job. Click on the down arrow in the Printer Quality field to display the available resolutions for the printer specified in the Printer list box. The default resolution for the printer appears in the box.

If you want to use the color correction profile you generated for color calibration, enable the Printer Color Profile that matches the printer you specified by clicking on the box next to the option name.

Preparing a File for a Service Bureau

By enabling Print to File, you can create a PRN or EPS file that can be output at a service bureau or other site. These files do not depend on CorelDRAW being present at the actual printer site. They contain all the information required for printing, and print

independently. If you are outputting for Macintosh, enable For Mac.

Printing a File

To print a file, follow these steps:

1. Select the Print Range.

2. Select a Printer.

3. Choose the Printer Quality.

4. Choose the checkboxes for Printer Color Profile, Print to File, or For Mac as needed.

5. Select the number of copies you want to print in the Copies box.

6. Enable Collate Copies, if desired, when printing multipage documents by clicking on the checkbox.

7. If you need to set up the printer listed in the Printer box, click Setup. If you want to select other options such as separations or custom halftone screening, select Options.

8. After you specify all the print options, click OK to print the document.

Examining Printing Options

When you click on Options in the Print dialog box, the Print Options dialog box appears, with the Layout property sheet displayed on top. The Print Options dialog

box contains a series of reference tools and the property sheets that control options for layout, separations, screening, and PostScript output (see fig. 14.3). The Separations and Options property sheets are displayed by clicking on their respective tabs.

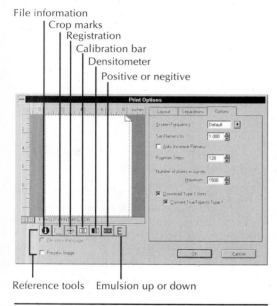

Figure 14.3
The Print Options dialog box.

Reference Tools

CorelDRAW offers a number of reference tools that enable you to include reference information on your document proofs. Professional printers and service bureaus use the information provided to ensure the quality of the print job. In addition, some types of output require the capability to print emulsion down or print a negative of your image. The capability to create this type of

output in-house can save darkroom time and expense. The trend toward color dye-sublimation printers has made it possible to imprint a variety of materials with designs output on these printers. This heat transfer process requires emulsion down output, to ensure that the orientation of the design and text is not printed backwards. These tools expand your printing options, and assist you in achieving the results you desire. The reference tools are described in more detail in the following list:

- **File information.** If you specified a printable page smaller than the physical paper size, you can print information regarding your document and the print job. If you are printing a composite image, the information includes the file name, date, time, and tile number (if applicable). If you are printing separations it includes information regarding CMYK screen frequencies, angles, and plate numbers. Selecting **F**ile info within page forces the program to write the information within the printable page. Be sure your artwork is positioned so that this information doesn't overlap the art.

- **Crop marks.** You can add crop marks to documents. This enables you to indicate how you want your document trimmed. If you want the color of your image to run up to the edge of the trim, you need to set the image to run as full bleed.

- **Registration marks.** These guides assist in the aligning of separation film sheets. CorelDRAW prints these guides outside the printable page. For registration marks to be printed, the printable page area must be smaller than the paper size.

- **Calibration bar.** When you enable the Calibration Bar, a bar of six RGB and CMYK colors is printed on the side of the printout. This enables you to check the color of your job.

- **Densitometer scale.** When you enable the Densitometer Scale, a grayscale bar is printed beside your drawing, enabling you to check the accuracy, quality, and density of the output with a densitometer.

- **Positive or negative.** Choosing this option enables you to print a positive or negative image from your in-house printer. Check with your commercial printer or service bureau before using this option. They might use equipment that creates a negative, causing the film output to be reversed from what you want.

- **Emulsion up or down.** This option enables you to print your image in reverse. Generally, you use this option in one of two circumstances. The first is when the lpi of the output is under 133. Check with your service bureau to see what it requires. This option is also used when printing to transfer media on a wax thermal or dye sublimation printer. Toggling this option ensures that your image does not appear reversed when pressed onto other media, such as a T-shirt.

- **Preview Image.** When this option is enabled, your image appears in the preview window as it does on the printed page. You can scroll through multipage documents by clicking the arrows at the bottom of the preview

window. The dotted line around the image indicates the default margins required by your printer.

The Layout Property Sheet

The Layout property sheet enables you to adjust the position, size, and layout of your image (see fig. 14.4). The top portion of this property sheet contains the options for position and size. The bottom portion of the sheet contains options for the actual layout of your work.

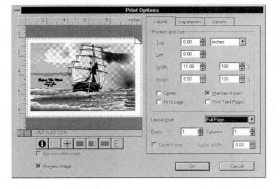

Figure 14.4

The Layout property sheet.

The Position and Size options include the following:

- **Top.** This option indicates the distance from the top of the paper to the image. You can change the unit of measurement by clicking the down arrow and selecting a new unit of measurement from the list box.

■ **Left.** This option indicates the distance from the left side of the paper to your image.

■ **Width.** This option indicates the width of your image at its widest point. The entry box beside width enables you to adjust the printed size of the image. If **M**aintain Aspect is enabled, both dimensions of the image will be adjusted. You might need to reposition the image on the page when you adjust this amount. You can either click the image in the preview window or enable C**e**nter to move the image to the location you want.

■ **Fit to Page.** If Fit to Pa**g**e is enabled, the image is adjusted to the size the program calculates as the best to fit both dimensions of the paper.

■ **Print Ti**led Pages.** This option enables you to enlarge the image beyond the printable area of the paper. The image is tiled onto multiple pieces of paper.

■ **Layout Style.** This option displays the current layout selection. Choices you make here enable you to override the current page layout setting in the drawing window and choose another layout (see fig. 14.5). You also can choose to place more than one image on a page. By entering values in **R**ows and C**o**lumns, you indicate how many copies of the same image you want on a page. You can specify the G**u**tter Width you want between images. Choose Clo**n**e Frame to fill the sheet with the same images.

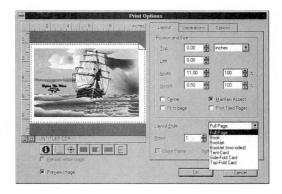

Figure 14.5
Layout Style options.

The Separations Property Sheet

The Separations property sheet enables you to specify how you want your job separated when it goes to press (see fig. 14.6). The list that follows describes the options available within the Separations property sheet:

Figure 14.6
The Separations property sheet.

■ **Print Separations.** Print Separations enables you to print the sheets of paper or film that represent your drawing when you go to press. If you are printing CMYK colors you will have up to four sheets for the drawing. If you are printing PANTONE spot colors you will have one sheet per color.

■ **in Color.** Selecting in Color enables you to print color proofs of each channel. If you print the color proofs on transparency film, you can use the film to create overlays from which you can check registration.

■ **Convert Spot Color to CMYK.** When you choose this option the program calculates the closest CMYK values for the spot colors you used in your image and substitutes them into the printed image.

■ **Colors.** This box contains a list of the channels in your drawing. If your drawing contains a number of channels, you might need to create a separate .PRN file for each channel. For more information on outputting to file, see Chapter 41, "Working with Service Bureaus." To print a single channel, highlight the channel you want to print.

Trapping

The Auto Trapping options control the trapping on separations. When an image is trapped, either manually or by enabling Auto Trapping, adjoining objects overlap one another to prevent white space due to registration shifts that occur when a document is printed. This shift occurs with every press job for a number of reasons. Slipping, stretching, and slight misregistration are some of the most common causes. Even the smallest shift can create undesirable white space.

The best method of trapping is object to object, which is performed during the creation of each object. You can choose to overprint the fill, which ensures there are no trapping problems, or you can overprint the outline. When you overprint the outline, you must set the trap amount to ensure proper registration. Because the outline of an object lies half inside and half outside the physical boundary that describes the object, the amount of trap is equal to half the line width of the outline. Trapping objects with white fills or outlines that overlap other objects isn't necessary.

N O T E

The effects of Auto Trapping do not appear on-screen. They are displayed in the printout of your document.

Selecting Always **O**verprint Black forces the program to print any object that contains 95-percent-or-more black on top of other objects (see fig. 14.7). This procedure works well with black text. You should be careful trapping text by any other method because of the fine detail usually found in text objects. Other trapping methods can cause the detail of the text to disappear in the trap.

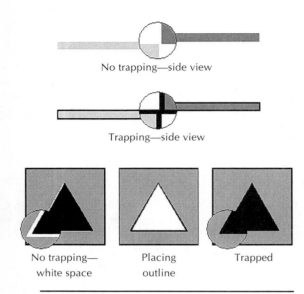

Figure 14.7
Trapping objects.

To trap an open path, add an end cap to the line and increase the line width by at least .30 points. Use the same method for closed objects that have an outline but no fill.

Enabling **A**uto Spreading forces the program to spread any objects filled with a uniform fill that have not been set to overprint (refer to fig. 14.6). This applies only if the object has no outline. The program calculates an appropriate amount of spread based upon the color of the object and the maximum amount of spread you designate in the entry box. Auto Trapping is only supported by PostScript devices. If you are using another

type of device, you need to trap the objects individually.

Halftone Specifications

By enabling the **U**se Custom Halftone option you can control the halftone specifications for your document (refer to fig. 14.6). This method of designating halftones is global. You can create custom halftones on an object-by-object basis, when you create the object. When an object has a custom halftone assigned to it by this method, it overrides any global specifications you make. To edit the default setting for global Custom Halftones, click **E**dit. The Advanced Screening dialog box appears (see fig. 14.8).

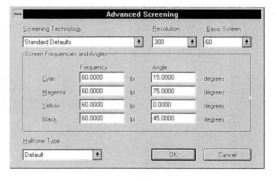

Figure 14.8
The Advanced Screening dialog box.

The Advanced Screening dialog box enables you to choose an imagesetter, the resolution, and the basic screen frequency (lpi), for your output. You also can change the angles and frequency of the individual channels and the halftone type. For more information regarding halftones, see Chapter 38, "Color Management."

The Options Property Sheet

The Options property sheet enables you to adjust the way CorelDRAW's print engine responds to PostScript output (see fig. 14.9). The Options property sheet is designed for use with PostScript devices and is not available for other types of output.

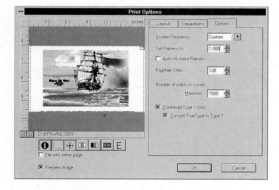

Figure 14.9
The Options property sheet.

The Options property sheet includes the following features:

- **Screen Frequency.** The default value in this entry box corresponds with the default value of your specific printer. You can change the frequency by selecting any frequency from the list box that is supported by your printer. Consult your service bureau or commercial printer for guidance in setting this option.

- **Set Flatness to.** The default value in this entry box is 1.0. You can change

that value to reduce the complexity of the curves in your image. Higher settings ensure greater printability, but might distort your image. If you enable **A**uto Increase Flatness, the program continues to decrease the complexity of curves until the document prints. If the complexity exceeds the value in the Set Fla**t**ness to box by a factor of 10, the print engine skips that object and goes on to the next object in the print sequence. To simulate printing on a 1,270-dpi imagesetter, use a setting of .2 on your in-house PostScript printer. A better method of reducing the complexity of objects is editing your image in the drawing window. Problems with these settings usually generate a Limitcheck error. For information about reducing the complexity of objects see Chapter 5, "Shaping Objects."

- **Fou**ntain Steps.** This global setting increases or decreases the number of steps that are used to print fountain fills. A high setting helps eliminate banding, but increases printing time. The default setting is 128. This value corresponds with the recommended settings for printing documents at 1,270 dpi. Increase the number to 200 for optimum printing at 2,540 dpi.

Your in-house printer can display only a maximum number of steps. Consult your printer's user manual for more information. You can change the settings of individual objects when you apply a fountain fill to them. The **S**teps setting in the Fountain Fill

dialog box overrides any setting you make in the Options property sheet if you engage the lock on the number of steps.

- **Number of points in curves.** The value in this box counts the number of segments on a path. The value can be between 200 and 20,000. The default value is 1,500 and is suitable for most printing. Entering a value of 3,000 usually disables this function, enabling you to have more segments per path. If a path has fewer segments but contains complex fills, such as texture or fountain fills, you might need to lower this value to 600 or less. Problems with these settings usually generate a Limitcheck error.

- **Download Type 1 fonts.** By enabling the text features in the Options property sheet, you can control how text is handled when printing your document. If the fonts in your document are not resident in the printer, you need to enable **D**ownload Type 1 fonts. Check with your service bureau or commercial printer to see what fonts are resident on their imagesetter.

- **Convert to TrueType to Type 1.** This option forces CorelDRAW to make the appropriate font substitutions at print time. Both the TrueType and Type 1 fonts must be installed on your system for you to use this feature.

Using Print Merge

If you find that you must print documents that are nearly identical except for their names, the Print **M**erge option (found in the **F**ile menu) can reduce your work. Print **M**erge enables you to create documents, such as customized certificates or mass mailings, that include different names and addresses.

To use Print **M**erge, follow these steps:

1. Create your document. To ensure success when the text is substituted during printing, select Center alignment for each string of Artistic text you are replacing.

2. Using the Windows Notepad or another ASCII text editor, create a text file using the following format:

3	(number of text strings to be replaced)
David Smith\\	(first text string to be replaced)
Advanced\\	(second text string to be replaced)
August 1, 1994\\	(third text string to be replaced)
John Ackers\\	(first text string replacement)
Intermediate\\	(second text string replacement)
September 5, 1994\\	(third text string replacement)

```
\Sandra Monahan\
\Beginning\
\June 10, 1994\

\Sean Brown\
\Advanced\
\October 7, 1994\
```

3. Save the text, making sure to use a .TXT extension on the file. CorelDRAW does not recognize ASCII text files with other extensions.

All text, whether replacement or original text, must appear in the text file as it appears in the original document. Capitalization, spaces, and line spaces must be the same. Set off each entry with a backslash as shown. Consider using numbers instead of text characters to avoid confusion.

To print merged text, follow these steps:

1. Open the original document, and select Print **M**erge from the **F**ile menu.

2. The Print Merge dialog box appears prompting you to enter the path and file name for the replacement text file. Enter the information and click OK to continue.

3. The Print dialog box is displayed, enabling you to select any options you want. Click on OK to print. CorelDRAW then replaces the designated text with the replacement text (see fig. 14.10).

N O T E

You cannot use Print **M**erge with Paragraph text.

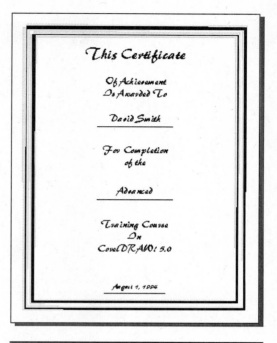

Figure 14.10
*A certificate created using Print **M**erge.*

Summary

The printing features available in CorelDRAW provide a wide range of options for all types of documents. Your service bureau and commercial printer can offer invaluable information. Using this advice to tailor your document creation and printer options ensures a quality print job. Understanding halftone application and various color management issues also can help you achieve the results you want. For more information about color management and color calibration, see Chapters 38 and 39.

Part II

CorelVENTURA

Chapter 15

CorelVENTURA Essentials

Since prehistoric times, mankind has tried to communicate with the written word, and the objective has always been to get the thought on paper as fast as possible, while making it look nice. Our first printed materials were hand-lettered by scribes with the best calligraphy on the best parchment. Each copy was laboriously and tediously rendered by hand.

Today, documents of all types can be quickly produced with desktop publishing programs. CorelVENTURA has evolved into a strong candidate in the arena of desktop publishing.

This chapter covers:

- The evolution of VENTURA

- CorelVENTURA's interface

- Understanding publications

- Opening an existing publication

- Starting a new publication

- Setting up a page layout

The Evolution of VENTURA

VENTURA, the brain child of Xerox, was the first successful attempt to utilize the prolific growth of personal computers in what grew to be called "desktop publishing." Any page layout program needs to be able to show what the output will look like on the computer monitor, but VENTURA Publishing arrived long before the advent of Microsoft Windows. The only choice available was GEM, by Digital Research. GEM provided the first *Graphic User Interface* (GUI) for the PC.

The Macintosh computer owes its success to its integrated operating system, which exploited the ability to show a user on the monitor what would print on the printer. Design Studio, PageMaker, and QuarkXPress were the three programs that made the Macintosh the preferred vehicle for publishing. VENTURA Publishing languished as the Macintosh took over the publishing business.

When Windows on the PC became a success, both platforms could offer the user visual confirmation of the look of the printed piece before printing. Both also could offer the programmer a rich set of built-in routines that would accomplish this graphic user interface with simple requests to the operating system.

Corel Corporation Buys VENTURA Publishing

In 1994, Corel Corporation purchased VENTURA Publishing from VSI, and proceeded to give it the financial and the marketing strength to be a potential contender in the publishing world. Almost immediately, Corel repackaged VENTURA into CorelVENTURA release 4.2 for Windows at an attractively low price, pushing it onto the bestselling list.

Version 4.2 was evolutionary, moving VENTURA's interface toward Windows standards. Corel fixed many bugs, speeded font loading, and added support for Adobe Acrobat, a portable document system that allows a document created on one type of computer to be viewed on another. Corel also added its normal packaging extravaganza—600 typefaces, 75 style sheets, 10,000 pieces of clip art, and support for Kodak PhotoCD Photos.

Corel also announced its intention to perform a major overhaul of CorelVENTURA 5, and to move it completely away from its GEM base. This restructured version was to be distributed with CorelDRAW 5, but was delayed at the last minute, in concert with the opinions of the beta testers. Since then, Corel has poured enormous efforts into producing a better program.

Installation of CorelVENTURA 5

After several delays, Corel is now shipping VENTURA 5 in several packages, as follows:

■ CorelDRAW! 5 users will automatically receive VENTURA, along with a maintenance update for all DRAW-related programs, if they sent their registration card and VENTURA coupon to Corel.

- Corel will also market a stand-alone VENTURA product that includes CorelPHOTO-PAINT 5.

- Both products are available on CD-ROM or disk.

Your best choice is to buy VENTURA 5 as part of the complete DRAW package on CD-ROM and load it onto your hard drive. There are many advantages, including the following:

- If you have CorelDRAW installed along with VENTURA, you will be able to load any DRAW file into VENTURA.

- If you have a CD-ROM reader, you will be able to access Corel's huge clip art library. There is only a limited amount of clip art on the disks.

- Having VENTURA loaded on your hard drive with the rest of CorelDRAW leaves your CD-ROM free to access other material while you work.

Installing to Your Hard Drive

The installation procedure for Corel VENTURA is fairly straightforward and simple. Complete the following steps:

1. Place the CD labeled "ONE" in your drive and locate, with Windows File Manager, the file "setup.exe" in the root directory.

2. Double-click on the setup.exe file to begin installation.

3. Choose Minimum or Custom Installation. If you choose Full Installation, you will not have control over where Corel installs and what it installs.

N O T E

VENTURA must be installed in a subdirectory of COREL50/PROGRAMS. VENTURA shares many files with DRAW, including filters and common DLLs. If you have already installed DRAW and some of its related programs, choose to reinstall them. Many problems have been solved since the initial release and the products are more stable. Reinstalling will update and replace the original release.

4. Choose the drive where you want VENTURA/DRAW installed. Depending on the options you choose, it can require up to 50 megabytes of space. The installation program will calculate the space requirements for you.

5. The rest of VENTURA's installation is very easy—you need only choose how much of VENTURA you want.

The Strength of CorelVENTURA 5

Broadly speaking, CorelVENTURA uniquely provides you with the ability to bring in text and graphics from almost any source, position the imported material with precision, and output it to any printer supported by Windows. This capability virtually

replaces the traditional paste-up board and provides you with precision, quality, and speed. In fact, the metaphor of a paste-up board is an important concept to keep in mind as you learn VENTURA. This is what you see on the screen and where you place all your text and illustrations.

Consider the following capabilities of CorelVENTURA:

- Documents can be one to hundreds of pages long.

- Documents can be single sheet format, of many dimensions, or one of many reformatted layouts, including books, booklets, and greeting cards.

- Documents, or a publication, can contain one or many chapters, as well as portable subsections.

- Templates automate repetitive publications and can be created dynamically.

- Styles and tags, preformatted paragraph attributes, predefine layout choices. Tags, long considered the major strength of previous versions of VENTURA, speed the formatting of body text, footnotes, titles, picture captions, and the overall look and feel of the document. Tags can be overridden within a paragraph and these overrides can be managed with built-in tools.

- Menus, dialog boxes, tools, and roll-ups—the user interface—provide complete and flexible control over every aspect of the publication design.

N O T E

CorelVENTURA in version 5 has adopted the new look of tabbed dialog boxes. With this architecture, the program designer can organize dialog information into sections selectable by clicking on the tabs at the top of the box. IBM's OS/2 has this style, and it is slated for implementation in the next release of Windows, Microsoft Windows™ 95.

- Text can originate in a variety of external word processors—31 in all—can be formatted in or tagged in Techman or SGML and translated by Tagwrite, or be created by using VENTURA's Copy Editor. In each case, full spelling, thesaurus and Type Assist tools are available. Chapter 16, "Adding and Editing Text," details the handling of text.

- Graphics can be imported from almost any source. This capability is usually very restricted in most page layout programs, but VENTURA shares filters with CorelDRAW, giving it the ability to import any format that DRAW can. VENTURA is the only page layout program that can import a native DRAW file format! Chapter 18, "Adding Graphics," gives the techniques for the control of illustrations.

- Printing in VENTURA is highly flexible. It borrows DRAW's print engine and prints to any printer supported in Windows, including dot matrix, laser, and bubblejet printers, and imagesetters. Accurate color can be managed throughout Corel's products and separated with full pre-press controls. This print engine alone may well provide sufficient justification to choose VENTURA over other programs.

When you first start CorelVENTURA, it is possible to be overwhelmed by the complexity of the program. The thousands of specifications available in VENTURA can be confusing, but most have built-in default values that may require little or no adjusting. The program contains 129 menu items, 103 shortcut keys, 86 dialog boxes, 35 ribbon bar functions, 10 roll-ups, and several context-sensitive pop-up menus.

If you are a CorelDRAW user who is unfamiliar with VENTURA, or even to desktop publishing, building a document in the following sequence may simplify the process for you:

1. Start VENTURA and begin, or select a publication.

2. Choose the major layout design in Chapter Settings.

3. Lay out your base page frame by using Frame Settings to specify margins, number of columns, and the way in which your text will flow.

4. Create or bring in your text (see Chapter 16) and, using tags, format it by using Paragraph Settings (see Chapter 17).

5. Add graphics and size and position them (see Chapter 18).

6. Add tables, indexes, and tables of contents to your publication (see Chapter 19).

7. Fine-tune your publication with a handful of special-purpose specifications (see Chapter 20).

8. Print your document (see Chapter 20).

CorelVENTURA's Interface

Figure 15.1 shows the structure of the CorelVENTURA workspace window. Not unlike most modern Windows screens, VENTURA has a menu and ribbon bar across the top, with a workspace consisting of the large central portion, bordered by rulers and scroll bars. Like CorelDRAW, VENTURA's tools are in a fixed tool bar (also called a toolbox) at the left, or as a floating tool bar (not shown). If a publication is open, the current chapter and its style will be shown as status information at the very bottom left of the screen. To the right of the horizontal scroll bar are controls for navigating to different pages.

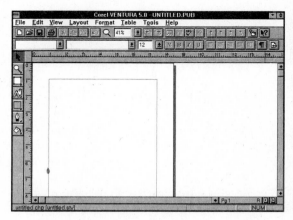

Figure 15.1
An initial view of CorelVENTURA.

> ### N O T E
>
> This view of VENTURA is shown at 640 x 480 resolution, thus showing only the top half of an 8.5" x 11" piece of paper. If your screen is set to 800 x 600, you will see the full size.

The workspace *is* the paste-up board. Objects, text, and graphics can be moved around either on or off the page. You can use the Zoom tool at the left or the Zoom function in the ribbon bar to view more or less of the paste board. Pressing Shift+F4 displays the entire page.

> ### N O T E
>
> CorelVENTURA is frame-dependent. A *frame* is a container that holds objects, either text or graphics. It can be drawn with the Frame tool or will automatically be drawn when you load an object. Objects do not exist outside a frame, so when you move an object you are actually moving the frame containing the object.

Understanding Publications

When you start CorelVENTURA, your first decision is whether to operate on an existing publication or to start a new one. Corel uses the publication concept to describe a whole document comprised of all the chapters, style definitions, text, and illustrations that are used in the entire finished product. Chapters are more managable pieces that can be added or deleted from or rearranged in the publication.

In VENTURA, a chapter contains the same information and pieces as does a chapter in this book—text, illustrations, and formatting specifications. Because you can have up to 128 chapters in a publication (the limit will be raised in version 6), you can create very long documents and manage them in smaller parts.

It is important to understand that you must use the publication framework as the holding concept for all the pieces of a finished document, regardless of the type of work or its size. A publication can be as simple as a business card on one page or as complex as a 1,000-page book. You will have a publication file that contains one or more chapters. Corel believes that as we move toward more object-oriented operating systems, this publication concept will not only be desirable but also necessary.

Publication File Structure

A PUB file, designated with a file extension of ".pub," is the highest-level file in your document. It is a binary file (you can't read it with a text editor) and contains the following:

- The version number of VENTURA

- Miscellaneous publication information

- Temporary storage for table of contents, index, and cross reference data

- The names of all chapters

- The locations of all chapters

- The sequence of chapters

Chapter File Structure

The chapter files have always been the basic foundation of VENTURA; chapter files contain the same information as previous releases and have a file extension of .chp. Chapter files are also binary, and contain the following information:

- The version number of VENTURA
- Miscellaneous chapter information
- The names and locations of text files
- The names and locations of graphic files
- The name and location of the chapter style sheet
- Storage for text and graphics that have been copied into a chapter from the Windows Clipboard

Style (Style Sheet) File Structure

Styles (extension of ".sty") hold all the formatting information for a chapter. Several chapters can use the same style sheet but can use only one per chapter. Style sheet files have the following information:

- The version number of VENTURA
- The layout of all of the chapters and the base frame settings
- All Tags with their paragraph settings

N O T E

If you are just curious or need documentation of style sheets, you can print them from the Manage Tags List option under the Format menu. This function produces a ".gen" file, containing all text.

Opening an Existing Publication

If you want to work on a publication you have already started, you can click on the Open Publication button or select one of the publications listed at the bottom of the File menu (see fig. 15.2). Pressing Ctrl+O is the shortcut to opening a publication.

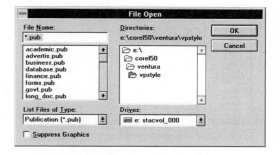

Figure 15.2

The File Open dialog box.

Starting a New Publication

If you are just starting VENTURA and have not previously created a publication, or if you want to start a new publication, you have several options. You can choose **N**ew from the **F**ile menu, press Ctrl+N, or click on the left-most button ribbon bar. You see the New Publication dialog box (see fig. 15.3).

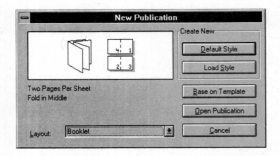

Figure 15.3
The New Publication dialog box.

The Default Publication

When you first start CorelVENTURA, you will see an almost-empty paste board with some defaults set (page size, orientation, margins, type font, style, and so forth). Every specification has a default value that is set by Corel when the product was shipped, or set by you the first time you used VENTURA.

With this default set up as a beginning, you can immediately start loading text or graphics or start changing the underlying specifications that you wish to use to control your publication.

At any time, you can save your new publication with a new name by choosing **F**ile/Save **A**s. Before exiting VENTURA you will be prompted to save the publication, if you haven't already.

Selecting Load Style

If you want a style other than default, click on the **L**oad Style Sheet option under the **L**ayout menu. The Open Style Sheet dialog box enables you to choose which of the previously saved styles you want. Only styles will be listed in the file list.

Selecting Base on Template

Basing a new publication on a template is more complicated than simply loading a style or another publication. The idea is to glean selected settings and data from an existing publication and to transplant them to your new publication. This operation is accomplished in a series of steps.

This process is straightforward, but the second dialog box you encounter is complex. The following exercise shows this operation in detail.

Exercise: Specifying a Template

1. Click on File/New.

   The New Publication dialog box opens.

2. Click on Base on Template.

   The Base on Template dialog box is displayed (see fig. 15.4).

3. Choose EXAMPLE.PUB in COREL50/VENTURA/TYPSET directory (assuming you have loaded the sample files at installation time).

4. Click on OK.

   The Specify Template Destination dialog box opens.

   At the bottom of the box is a list of all the files contained in EXAMPLE.PUB. Notice that the chapter files (.chp) have a circle with a diagonal line; the other files have a check mark.

   In the upper portion are controls for specifying the name of your new publication and its directory location. Type in your new name, then select a new directory. Selecting a new directory changes the symbol before the chapter names from the circle to a check mark. The circle, a stop signal, means that you will not be able to select that chapter file without specifying a different directory. Allowing selection would mean having the same chapter name twice in the same directory.

   EXAMPLE.PUB contains many chapters. For this exercise, you will extract some files from SCOOP_2.CHP, namely the chapter itself, and MASTHD1.WMF and POT4.TIF.

5. Click on Omit All to deselect all files.

6. Press and hold down Ctrl as you click on the SCOOP 2.CHP, MASTHD1.WMF, and POT4.TIF.

7. Click on Include Files.

The files you selected are checked.

8. Click on OK.

A new publication is created and loaded.

Figure 15.4
The Base on Template dialog box.

Base on Template is a production feature that will speed up recurring documents like newsletters and specification sheets. The power of this function lies in the ability to select from a pre-existing publication only the parts that remain unchanged.

Regardless of which method you choose to start your publication, you can see how

simple it is to get going. With a few mouse clicks you can start a simple document and then expand upon it later as you learn more about VENTURA. Throughout this program, you can select many different routes to accomplish similar results. As you progress from selecting default style to selecting open publication, you should find that you will have less specifications to change, with open publication having the least. Utilizing the menu and the dialog boxes, you have complete control over everything in your publication.

Setting Up a Page Layout

Regardless of the method you select to start a VENTURA document, the next step is to check, and set, some specifications of your document. As with most layout programs, one of the first steps should be to set the page size and orientation.

Chapter Settings

The Chapter Settings dialog box contains five tabbed sections in which you can set the major specifications for the entire chapter, and only this chapter. Each chapter has its own settings which, therefore, can vary from chapter to chapter.

Exercise: Constructing a Booklet

Booklet production is a very powerful and handy feature of CorelVENTURA 5. This exercise will continue through the rest of the chapters on VENTURA and give you an opportunity to use many of the functions of this new version. Performing this exercise, you will create five "chapters":

1. Cover

2. Table of Contents

3. Chapter 1—Booklet Printing

4. Chapter 2—What They Didn't Tell Me About Film

5. Index

On the accompaning CD are the files you will need. To prepare for this exercise:

1. Create a subdirectory on your hard drive called EXERCISE.

2. Copy all the files from the CD in directory Chapter 15 to your new directory—EXERCISE.

3. The finished exercise booklet is on the CD in directory Chapter 15. You may want to copy this subdirectory to your hard drive as well if you want to see what it will look like.

To begin this exercise, start VENTURA. You will start to create Chapter 1 and its Style Sheet.

1. Choose **F**ile/**N**ew (Ctrl + N) to start a new publication.

2. Select Booklet in the drop-down list next to **L**ayout.

3. Choose **D**efault Style.

At this point, you have an unsaved publication and are ready to specify some chapter settings before you save.

N O T E

Chapter Settings, like many of the functions in VENTURA, can be accessed many ways:

- From the menu: **L**ayout/**C**hapter Settings

- From the keyboard: Alt+L+C

- From the hotkeys: F5

- From the pop-up menu: right-click the mouse and choose Chapter

The method you choose is completely up to you, but you will probably find that for most functions, right-clicking the mouse is the fastest and easiest.

Layout Tab

The Layout Tab is the first stop for you in Chapter Settings (see fig. 15.5). Come here to set up your page size and layout. Normally, you will select your layout settings, use the default settings of the other taps, and close Chapter Settings, returning to them later in your design work.

Booklet Exercise—Continued

1. Open Chapter Settings with F5.

2. Check to see that Lay**o**ut is booklet (you set this in New Publication).

3. Set Page Size to Letter and Orientation to **L**andscape.

4. Set Sides to **D**ouble.

5. Set Start On to **R**ight Side.

   See fig. 15.5 to compare your settings.

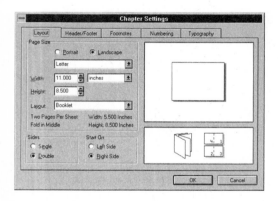

The page size drop-down list box enumerates 34 fixed dimensions. Clicking on a choice will put the measurements in the width and height boxes. The following table lists these sizes, with the native unit of measure in bold.

Figure 15.5
The Chapter Settings dialog box—Layout tab.

Table 15.1
Fixed Page Sizes

Size	Width— in	Height— in	Width— mm	Height— mm
Letter	8.50	11.00	216	279
Legal	8.50	14.00	216	356
Tabloid	11.00	17.00	279	432
Statement/Half	5.50	8.50	140	216
Executive	7.25	10.50	184	267

Size	Width—in	Height—in	Width—mm	Height—mm
Fan Fold	11.00	14.88	279	378
Double	11.00	17.00	279	432
Broad Sheet	18.00	24.00	457	610
A2	16.54	23.39	420	594
A3	11.69	16.54	297	420
A4	8.27	11.69	210	297
A5	5.83	8.27	148	210
A6	4.13	5.83	105	148
B4	9.84	13.90	250	353
B5	6.93	9.84	176	250
C3	12.76	18.11	324	460
C4	9.06	12.76	230	324
C5	6.38	12.60	162	320
C6	4.53	6.38	115	162
RA2	16.93	24.02	430	610
RA3	12.01	16.93	305	430
RA4	8.46	12.01	215	305
SRA3	12.60	17.72	320	450
SRA4	8.86	12.60	225	320
Envelope # 9	8.88	3.88	226	99
Envelope # 10	9.50	4.13	241	105
Envelope # 11	10.38	4.50	264	114

continues

Table 15.1, Continued
Fixed Page Sizes

Size	Width— in	Height— in	Width— mm	Height— mm
Envelope # 12	11.00	4.75	279	121
Envelope # 14	11.50	5.00	292	127
Envelope Monarch	7.50	3.88	191	99
Envelope Check	8.58	3.88	218	99
DL	4.33	8.66	110	220
German Fan Fold	8.50	12.00	216	305
German Legal Fan Fold	8.50	13.00	216	330

When you select custom page size, you can select the unit of measure and specify sizes.

T I P

Instead of selecting Custom page size, select the size closest to your choice and either type in sizes or use scroll controls to change values. This action will force the Custom designation, add the dimensions after Custom in the page size box, and change the preview example.

Header/Footer Tab

Open the Header/Footer tab by double-clicking on the tab's title (see fig. 15.6). Initially, all headers and footers (and page numbering) are turned off.

Constructing headers/footers is a two step process, first to design the header or footer, and second to enable it (turn it on). In the

upper left of the dialog box is a drop-down list of all four items: left and right, header and footer. Selecting one of these choices will enable the three text boxes labeled **L**eft, **C**enter, and **R**ight. You may type directly into these boxes or use the buttons below them, or a combination of both. Information is inserted in order, from left to right.

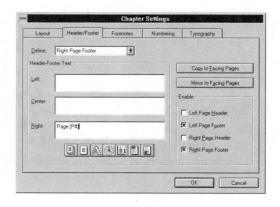

Figure 15.6

The Chapter Settings dialog box—Header/Footer tab.

Booklet Exercise—Continued

To finish the exercise for this chapter, you will set up page numbering.

1. Open Chapter Settings and move to the Headers/Footers tab.

2. Choose **D**efine Right Page Footer.

3. Choose Enable R**i**ght Page Footer.

4. Click in the space—**R**ight. Enter "Page" and click on the page number icon below (second from the left).

5. Click on Mirror to F**a**cing Pages to duplicate page numbering on the left page also.

This exercise represents the most common use of the header/footer function. With page number, you can choose to place on the left, center, or right–top or bottom of the page. If you have a left/right document, you can create the header/footer on one side and copy or mirror it to the other side. In this exercise, you created a page number on the left bottom of the left hand page. If you click on Mirror to Facing Pages, your page numbers will be on the outside (clicking on Copy to Facing Pages would cause page numbers to be on the left on both pages).

- Chapter numbers

- Page numbers

- Text Attributes—opens Selected Text Attributes dialog box

- Current time

- Current date

- Insert paragraph text from *first* paragraph formatted with first paragraph tag

- Insert paragraph text from *last* paragraph formatted with first paragraph tag

Footnotes Tab

Footnotes in VENTURA come in two varieties: Custom and Numerical. Footnotes are defaulted to Off when you click on this tab (see fig. 15.7).

Numerical Footnotes

Choose the **N**umerical radio button to enable footnotes. Normally, this will be sufficient for the most common footnotes, and all you have to do—the default values will do the rest.

N O T E

Remember to enable a footer/header before formatting. After formatting you can disable the headers or footers to increase screen redraw speed, enabling it again just before production.

Below the Header-Footer Text boxes are seven icon buttons that can be used in any order. They are, from left to right as shown in figure 15.6:

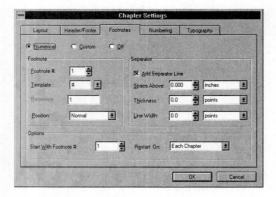

Figure 15.7
The Chapter Settings dialog box—Footnotes tab.

With Numerical footnotes, you have several other options. In the options section you can choose to start at a number other than 1 (Start with Footnote #) and start the numbers over either by page or chapter (Repeat On). **P**osition offers normal, superscript, or subscript placement of the footnote in the text.

Custom Footnotes

Custom footnotes allows for more control over the appearance and implementation of footnotes; however, each footnote must be individually defined. **F**ootnote # and **T**emplate, options grayed out with numerical footnotes, are used together to format each footnote. **F**ootnote # determines which **T**emplate is used. Using the **T**emplate drop down list, type in how you want your footnote to be formatted, using "#" as a place holder for the footnote number.

Separators

With both custom and numerical footnotes, you can instruct VENTURA to place a line

above the footnote. Three controls format this line:

- **S**pace Above—the distance from the line to the text
- **Th**ickness—point size of the line
- **L**ine Width—the length of the line

Numbering Tab

Numbering tab, Chapter Settings, has two sections: Counters and Automatic Paragraph Numbers (see fig. 15.8).

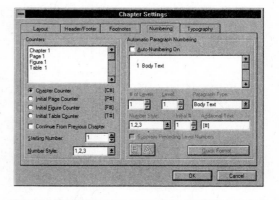

Figure 15.8
The Chapter Settings dialog box—Numbering tab.

Counters

Four internal counters are maintained by VENTURA: chapter, page, figure, and table. The default settings for each counter are:

- Continue counting from the previous chapter
- Format the counter in simple digits (1, 2, 3 . . .)

Selecting the radio control next to each counter enables you to change these values. If you turn off the check box by Continue from previous chapter, the counter will reset at the start of each new chapter and from the number you specify in the Starting Number box (normally 1).

With each counter you can choose the formatting of the number in the **N**umber Style drop-down list. Choose:

- 1, 2, 3
- A, B, C
- a, b, c
- I, II, III, IV
- i, ii, iii, iv
- One, Two, Three
- ONE, TWO, THREE
- one, two, three

N O T E

The format in this book is:

- Chapter counter—unchanged (continuous numbers from the first chapter to the end).

- Page counter—unchanged and not restarted at each chapter.

- Figure counter—restarted with each chapter and appended to the chapter number, separated by a period.

- Table counter—same as figure counter.

- Number style is 1, 2, 3.

Automatic Paragraph Numbering

Paragraph numbering is an extremely powerful feature to employ when you desire to have levels of paragraphing numbered. In many technical and governmental publications the format of the final document follows an outline structure. Each paragraph can have a superior or inferior position in relation to paragraphs of other types. As in common outlining, the number or letters preceding the text indicate its relative position and importance.

Automatic Paragraph Numbering is covered in detail in Chapter 20, "Fine-Tuning and Printing with VENTURA."

Typography Tab

The final tab of Chapter Settings deals with the typography of the chapter. Please refer to Typography in Chapter 20, "Fine-Tuning and Printing with VENTURA."

Frame Settings

Frames are an integral part of VENTURA and are used to contain all text and illustrations. Frames are analogous to the pieces of paper that are glued to the paste up board manually. By placing all text and graphics in frames, each can be moved and resized independently. Every page automatically has a page frame—other frames are created by the Frame tool or by loading text or graphics.

General Tab

The General tab of the Frame Settings dialog box contains settings for dimensions, origin, and locking; flow text around; repeating frames; and caption format (see fig. 15.9).

Dimensions, Origin, and Locking

The General tab handles dimensions. You can place and size, precisely, a frame on a page with the Dimensions and Frame Origin sections. Origin dimensions are calculated from the topmost left corner of the page with positive numbers indicating downward and rightward. Once positioned and sized, the Lock Frame check box will protect the frame from accidental adjustment.

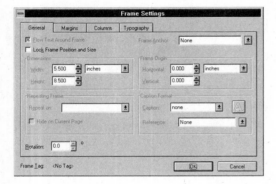

Figure 15.9
The Frame Settings dialog box—General tab.

Flow Text Around

The default, when creating a frame, has text flowing around the frame. The option check box, Flow Text Around Frame, when off, allows the frame to appear above the text, without interrupting it. If you had a graphic that you wanted to appear as a watermark, you could turn off Flow Text Around, and the text would appear over the illustration (the graphic frame would have to be drawn before the text frame in order to be behind the text).

Repeating Frames

Once you have set the dimensions and size of a frame, you can also automatically duplicate them to every page by selecting All Pages in the drop-down list. The other options are: All Left Pages, and All Right Pages. In booklet form, repeating frames to all pages properly mirrors the frame throughout the document.

Caption Format

Caption formatting is not available for repeating frames. Under **C**aption select above, below, left, right, or none (the default) for placement of a caption that will be attached to the frame, and move with it. The Reference list box provide four formats for the caption, or you may create your own by typing in your changes.

Rotation

Frames can be rotated counter clockwise in 10th-of-a-degree increments up to 360°.

Frame Tags

Frames can have tags (see Chapter 17) and the tags can be applied by selecting Frame **T**ag from the drop-down list box. You can apply a frame tag from any place in the Frame dialog box; it is below the tabbed sections.

Margins Tab

The Margins tab is used most frequently to set the margins for the base page frame, but can be used for any frame (see fig. 15.10).

Booklet Exercise—Continued

In this part you will set the frame margins for the base frame. If you look inside most books, including this one, you will see that the outside margins are smaller than towards the inside.

1. Click anywhere on the page selecting the base frame.

2. Right-click the mouse and choose Frame, and then Margins.

3. At **P**ages, choose Right.

4. Set **R**ight to .5 inches.

5. Set **L**eft to .75 inches.

6. Click on **M**irror to Facing Page.

Because you are finished for this chapter, save your publication. Before you do, go to Preferences under **T**ools and turn on **V**erbose Save.

1. Choose **F**ile/Save **A**s and point to the EXERCISE directory.

2. Name your Publication "PRINTING."

3. Name your Chapter "CHP-1."

4. Name your Style "PRINTSTY."

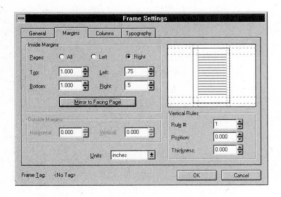

Of the two sections, Inside Margins and Outside Margins, outside margins are unavailable for page base frames and rotated frames. Choose All, Left, or Right page and set the margins. In either book or booklet layout, you can **M**irror to Facing Page to create the margins in reverse on the facing page. This technique was used to set margins in figure 15.11, to allow for more space in the center binding than on the outside edge.

Figure 15.10

The Frame Settings dialog box—Margins tab.

Notice that as you adjust the margins, the thumbnail picture of the page in the upper right will change to show the effects.

Columns Tab

The Columns tab is probably the most intuitive of all the controls in VENTURA (see fig. 15.11). Utilizing the thumbnail picture on the right side when you enter values, you will have visual confirmation of your actions.

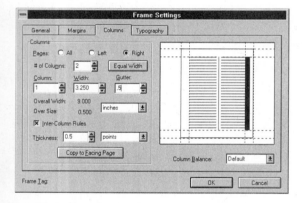

Figure 15.11
The Frame Settings dialog box—Columns tab.

Two methods are available to set columns: by equal width and by unequal width.

Equal Width

In # of Columns, either enter a value or use the spin control to increment the value. Clicking on Equal Width will balance the columns and then you can adjust the Gutter, the space between the columns, to create your target column width.

Unequal Width

The controls—**C**olumn, **W**idth, and **G**utter—allow for setting of columns of non-equal sizes. As you change each value, VENTURA will report Overall Width and Excess Space amounts below the controls. If the overall width is less than the frame width, the difference will be stated as excess space. The excess space will be applied to the right of the rightmost column. If this is undesirable, you can adjust the excess space to zero by increasing a column width or increasing a gutter width.

Inter-Column Rules

A vertical line can be placed between columns by clicking on the **I**nter–Column Rules check box. Just below, enter the thickness of the rule.

Copy to Facing Pages

If you have facing pages, clicking on this button will duplicate your column setup to the opposite page.

Column Balance

If you have two columns and the text you load into the frame is less than enough to fill both, setting Column **B**alance to on will place an equal number of lines of text in each column.

Typography Tab

The final tab of Frame Settings deals with the typography of the chapter. Please refer to Typography in Chapter 20.

Using CorelVENTURA's Tools

If you are familiar with CorelDRAW's tools, you will find that VENTURA's tools are very similar. Figure 15.12 shows VENTURA's toolbox.

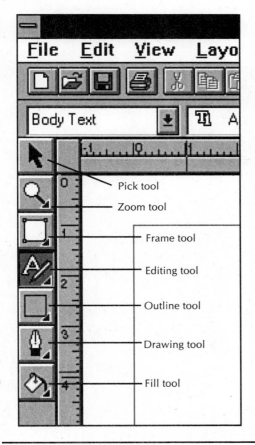

Figure 15.12
VENTURA's toolbox.

Pick Tool

The Pick tool, the only tool without a fly-out, is used to select, adjust, resize, and move objects. It's the arrow-shaped icon at the top of the toolbox.

Zoom Tool

There are six functions contained within the Zoom tool, as shown in figure 15.13.

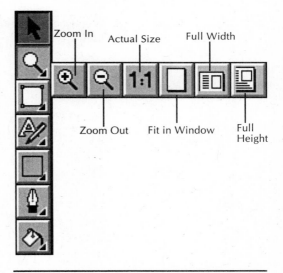

Figure 15.13
VENTURA's Zoom tool.

From left to right, the Zoom tool functions are:

- **Zoom In.** After selecting this tool, marquee-select the area you want to zoom and that area will fill the screen. F2 is the shortcut.

- **Zoom Out.** Selecting this tool and clicking on the page will cause a zoom out of twice the area, or return to the view before the last zoom in. F3 is the shortcut.

- **Actual Size.** Displays the page to a close approximation of the printed page.

- **Fit in Window.** Depending on the size of your monitor and the resolution set in your video driver, this tool will fit the whole page to your monitor. Shift + F4 is the shortcut.

- **Full Width.** Maximizing the width of the page, this tool will show as much of the page as possible.

- **Full Height.** Maximizing the height of the page, this tool will show as much of the width as possible.

Frame Tool

The Frame Tool fly-out contains two tools: the Frame tool and the Node Edit tool (see fig. 15.14).

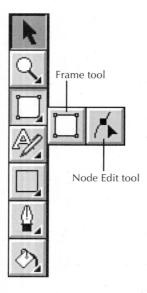

Frame tool

Node Edit tool

Figure 15.14
VENTURA's Frame Tool fly-out.

The Frame tool is used to marquee–select an area to be a frame.

The Node Edit tool is used to adjust nodes in curves and the wraps around a graphic.

Editing Tools

In this tool fly-out, as shown in figure 15.15, you see two tools: the Freeform Text tool and the Tagged Text tool (the tool with the little tag is also nicknamed "Minnie Pearl" by some users).

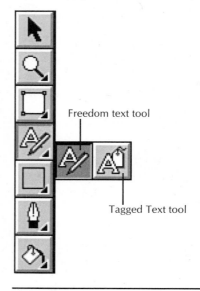

Freedom text tool

Tagged Text tool

Figure 15.15
VENTURA's Editing tool.

Briefly, each tool can either swipe text (highlight it) or be "planted" (clicked anywhere in a paragraph). The four conditions are shown in table 15.2, as follows:

Table 15.2
VENTURA's Text Tools

Tool	Action	Result
Freeform Text tool	Swipe	Selected text can be changed and have no effect elsewhere.
Tagged Text tool	Swipe	Selected text will be an override to the paragraph's tag.
Freeform Text tool	Planted	Overrides paragraph tag.
Tagged Text tool	Planted	Changes the tag of the paragraph and every other paragraph with the same tag.

Drawing Tools

VENTURA's Drawing tools, as shown in figure 15.16, contain: squares and rectangles, straight lines, curved cornered squares and rectangles, ellipses and circles, and box text. See Chapter 18, "Adding Graphics," for details.

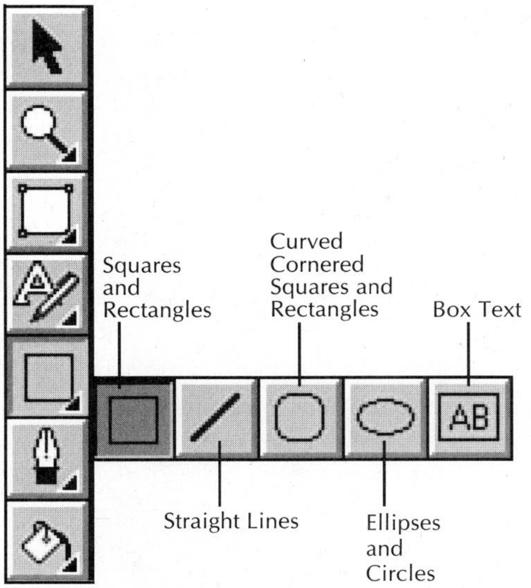

Outline Tool

The Outline Tool fly-out is essentially transplanted from CorelDRAW and has the same functions (see fig. 15.17). You can choose colors, line styles, and varieties of pen functions including line width and pen shape. Pausing your cursor over each of these boxes causes an identifier label to appear.

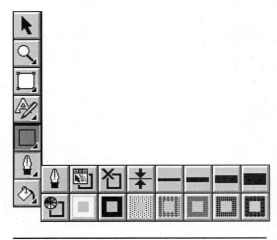

Figure 15.17
VENTURA's Outline Tool fly-out.

Figure 15.16
VENTURA's Drawing tools.

Fill Tool

The Fill Tool fly-out is virtually the same one used in CorelDRAW(see fig. 15.18). You use it to fill objects with pattern fills, texture fills, fountain fills, or preset fill colors.

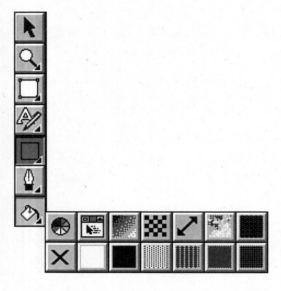

Figure 15.18
VENTURA's Fill Tool fly-out.

Summary

The information in this chapter provides the basic starting point for you to understand the use of CorelVENTURA. With these techniques and tools, you can open and start a publication and specify its layout. The next two chapters detail how to load and manipulate text and graphics in a CorelVENTURA publication.

Adding and Editing Text

*C*hapter 15 covered how to start up VENTURA and begin, or select, a publication; how to choose the major layout design in Chapter Settings; and how to lay out your base page frame using Frame Settings where you specify margins, number of columns and how your text will flow.

Chapter 16 explains the basics of adding and editing text in your VENTURA document.

This chapter covers:

- Choosing text options
- Loading text
- Using TagWrite
- Using Copy Editor
- Using Page Layout mode
- Using Draft mode
- Using the Box Text tool

Choosing Text Options

Text usually (and fairly obviously) represents the biggest portion of most documents. CorelDRAW has always provided a superior tool with which to create illustrations, but has until now been a sometimes mediocre performer with text. Text creation and use has improved in DRAW 5, especially with TrueType in Paragraph text, but as you use VENTURA, you will come to appreciate the speed, options and tools now available to CorelDRAW users.

If you own both CorelVENTURA and CorelDRAW, you have a choice when you design a document. Most functions can be done in either, but you will find it faster and easier to control text in VENTURA, leaving DRAW for the small jobs, particularly where you need to add effects to text. When you are choosing which path to take, consider the following:

- **Length of document.** The longer the document, the more the reason to choose VENTURA. VENTURA's strength lies in producing long documents—even documents up to the size of books. A one-page publication, however, makes your decision less obvious.

- **Proportion of text to graphics.** Given that VENTURA is good at text, and DRAW at illustrations, the balance of the composition may make the difference. If the document is heavy in graphics, stick to DRAW; if graphics are incidental to the text, use VENTURA and place the graphics.

VENTURA is a serviceable word processor in its own right with many tools to assist you, but historically, text has originated from outside the program. As with so much of the architecture of CorelVENTURA, it provides you with many options for placing text into your document:

- Load Text
- TagWrite
- Copy Editor
- Layout mode
- Draft mode
- Box Text tool

Loading Text

Using the **F**ile, Load **T**ext (Shortcut Key = F9) is the most common way to enter text into a document in CorelVENTURA. Most prefer to use their favorite word processing program to compose long batches of text. Reasons vary, but this preference generally arises from familiarity with a program or that the text may have been already created for another purpose.

You can load text into either the page frame or another frame you have drawn. If you load into the page frame, additional pages will be automatically created to fit the length of the text being imported. If you do not select a frame before asking VENTURA to load text, the text will be loaded, but not placed. At this point, the text file will be listed in the drop-down list in the ribbon bar, and in the File roll-up.

The following exercise, introduced in Chapter 15 and running throughout Part II of this book, demonstrates some of the text control commands in VENTURA.

T I P

After you bring in text with Load Text, be sure that VENTURA does not change your original file (remember that VENTURA will place formatting codes into the text file). You can prevent any changes by renaming your text file (**F**ile, Rena**m**e). A new file will be created, in any supported formated. The old file will be deleted from VENTURA's file list and replaced with your new one.

Booklet Exercise—Continued

If you have closed VENTURA, restart it and **O**pen your EXERCISE publication. In these brief steps, you load text for your first chapter.

1. Choose **F**ile, **L**oad Text.

2. Select the file "booklet.txt" and click on OK.

3. Select the base frame by clicking anywhere on the page.

4. From the drop-down file list in the ribbon bar choose booklet.txt.

Notice that this text flows through this current page and to enough other pages to contain it. Use PageUp and PageDown to view the rest of the text.

Since you only have Chapter 1 started, you need to start a new chapter to house Chapter 2.

1. Choose **L**ayout, Add Ne**w** Chapter.

2. Repeat the steps above for the file "film.txt."

3. Save your publication with **F**ile, **S**ave and you will be prompted for a chapter name—choose "CHP-2."

This part of the exercise, above, shows the ease of adding a chapter to a publication.

N O T E

The list of text files in the ribbon bar is not active unless a frame is selected. Its function is to either display the name of the file when a text frame is selected, or to place the text file into a selected frame. Either way, a frame must be selected first.

Table 16.1 is a list of all the load text filters supported by CorelVENTURA. The filter name and suffixes are those that will show in the Load Text dialog box. These are either Corel internal filters or external ones written by Mastersoft. As you can see, it is a very extensive list and provides support for most of the major word processing programs.

T I P

As is the case with DRAW, if you use the file filter designation "All files" with the file type of "*.*" you may find that you occasionally receive an error. It is more efficient to specify the particular filter for the type of text you are loading, rather than use the generic *.* type. This will also, by restricting the files displayed in the file list to only those of the specified suffix, reduce the number of files through which you have to search to find the right one.

Table 16.1
Text Import Filters

Filter Name	Suffixes	Filter DLL	Filter Author
All Files	*.*		Corel
Ami Pro 2.0, 3.0	.sam	W4W33F.DLL	Mastersoft
ASCII Text	.txt	IMPTXT	Corel
ASCII Text (8 bit)	.txt	IMPTXT8	Corel
Excel for Windows 3.0, 4.0	.xls	W4W21F.DLL	Mastersoft
Lotus 123 1A, 2.0	.wk?	W4W20F.DLL	Mastersoft
Lotus 123 3.0	.wk?	W4W20F.DLL	Mastersoft
Lotus/Excel Print Table	.prn	IMPPRN	Corel
MS Word 5.0, 5.5	*.*	W4W05F.DLL	Mastersoft
MS Word for Mac 4.0	*.*	W4W54F.DLL	Mastersoft

Filter Name	Suffixes	Filter DLL	Filter Author
MS Word for Mac 5.0	*.*	W4W54F.DLL	Mastersoft
MS Word for Windows 1.x	*.*	W4W44F.DLL	Mastersoft
MS Word for Windows 2.x	.doc	W4W44F.DLL	Mastersoft
MS Word for Windows 6.0	.doc	W4W49F.DLL	Mastersoft
Rich Text Format	.rtf	IMPRTF	Corel
Tag Write - SGML/Custom Template	*.*	IMPSGML	Corel
Tag Write - Style Match RTF	.rtf	IMPRWRTF	Corel
VENTURA Generated File	.gen	IMPGEN	Corel
WordPerfect 5.0	*.*	W4W07F.DLL	Mastersoft
WordPerfect 5.1	*.*	W4W07F.DLL	Mastersoft
WordPerfect 6.0	*.*	W4W48F.DLL	Mastersoft
WordStar 3.3, 3.31	*.*	W4W04F.DLL	Mastersoft
WordStar 3.45	*.*	W4W04F.DLL	Mastersoft
WordStar 4.0	*.*	W4W04F.DLL	Mastersoft
WordStar 5.0	*.*	W4W04F.DLL	Mastersoft
WordStar 5.5	*.*	W4W04F.DLL	Mastersoft
WordStar 6.0	*.*	W4W04F.DLL	Mastersoft
WordStar 7.0	*.*	W4W04F.DLL	Mastersoft
WordStar for Windows 1.x, 2.0	*.*	W4W37F.DLL	Mastersoft
XyWrite for Windows 1.0	*.*	W4W17F.DLL	Mastersoft
XyWrite III	*.*	W4W17F.DLL	Mastersoft
XyWrite III Plus	*.*	W4W17F.DLL	Mastersoft
XyWrite IV	*.*	W4W17F.DLL	Mastersoft

If you are missing a filter you need, you may have left it out during install. To add a filter, you can either reinstall, or open up corelflt.ini with a text editor. Using table 16.1, locate the missing filter and find it in the corelflt.ini file (it should be preceded by ";" to indicate a comment). If you remove the comment character and manually copy the filter name from the table to the COREL50\PROGRAMS directory from the corresponding directory on the CD, the filter name will appear in the Load Text list next time.

Using TagWrite

TagWrite is a utility program provided with VENTURA and accessible from the desktop, or from within using **T**ools, Extensions. TagWrite must be selected as an option when you are installing CorelVENTURA.

TagWrite has a very strange interface which proves a bit confusing. Its function, however, is clear: it converts RTF and SMGL formats to VENTURA Tags. This utility in conjunction with a word processor that supports RTF (such as Microsoft Word and WordPerfect) allows you to pretag text before bringing it to VENTURA.

Using Copy Editor

The Copy Editor is well named. Come here if you want either to edit existing text, or to create new. Selecting a text file from the file drop-down list box in the ribbon bar, or the File roll-up, will make it available to the Copy Editor when you switch modes. If no text files have been loaded, Copy Editor will provide a clean screen to create a new text file. Any graphics in your document are excluded from the Editor to increase speed. Text is not formatted on the screen as it is in Page Layout mode.

When you select Copy Editor, Alt+F10, or **V**iew, Copy **E**ditor, the normal VENTURA screen is replaced with a two-column layout. The left column will show the tag applied to the text in the right column.

The Preferences dialog box, shown in figure 16.1, provides two options for appearance (T**o**ols, Pre**f**erences or Ctrl+J). Choosing a font and font size here does not change your main document but gives you a font for editing. Try selecting either System, Courier, or a TrueType font—these will increase the screen draw speed. As in CorelDRAW, Panose font matching system is available to substitute a font on your system instead of a font specified by the incoming text file.

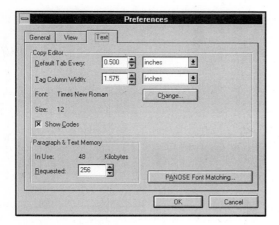

The other option, Show **C**odes, is a check box which, when on, displays the formatting characters that VENTURA places in your text. Notice in figure 16.2 the words "by Joseph Smith," with the formatting codes <W7> and <W15> on either side.

Figure 16.1

The Text sheet of the Preferences dialog box.

Copy Editor Exercise

1. Open VENTURA.

2. Choose **F**ile, **L**oad Text.

3. Select from the Corel50/VENTURA/Typeset directory the file "MAGAZINE.TXT."

4. Press Alt+F10 to activate the Copy Editor.

5. With the Text tool, swipe the third line down "by Joseph Smith."

6. Click on the Bold button on the ribbon bar.

Notice that the phrase is now surrounded by control characters that tell VENTURA when to start using bold and when to stop. (See fig. 16.2.)

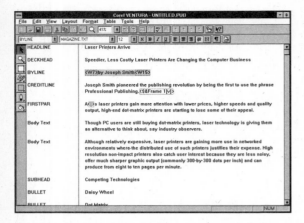

Figure 16.2
The VENTURA Copy Editor screen.

Both text tools, Tagged Text and Freeform Text, are available for the Copy Editor. Whichever tool that was selected last will be active in the editor, but you can switch them. When the editor is active, the toolbox is not. Use Shift+F8 with use for the other tool (the one not active) and F8 to switch back. Both have the same appearance on the screen, but if you move the cursor up to the ribbon bar, the "Minnie Pearl" tag will appear if the text tool is the Tagged Text tool.

W A R N I N G

Be very careful in choosing which tool to use. This choice will determine whether your editing affects the tag for the text or overrides it. Because in editor mode you cannot see formatting changes in tags, it may not be apparent what kinds of changes you are making. Until you are comfortable with tags, you might use Page Layout mode to apply tags, for visual confirmations of your changes.

Using Page Layout Mode

Page Layout mode gives you the closest appearance of your printed output. It is the richest in detail, and therefore, places the heaviest burden on screen drawing. Graphics that you have placed in your document, depending on their complexity, slow down the performance of VENTURA.

To access Page Layout mode, select **V**iew, **P**age Layout, or Alt+F12.

Using Draft Mode

Draft mode overcomes the graphic problem in Page Layout mode by hiding graphics with an outline representation and by omitting color.

To access Draft mode select **V**iew, **D**raft, or Alt+11.

Using the Box Text Tool

The Text tool is part of the drawing tools and is located in the drawing tools fly-out. This method of entering text is very handy if you need only a small amount. You can, after selecting this tool, draw a box by clicking anywhere on the page and, while holding down the mouse button, marquee-select the area you want the box to cover. After releasing the button, VENTURA automatically switches to the Text tool so that you can begin typing.

You might consider using this method for small legends on graphics and other incidental text where frames and tags may be unnecessary.

Summary

This chapter introduced CorelVENTURA's text-handling capabilities. You learned how to load text, use the TagWrite and Copy Editor functions, operate in Layout and Draft modes, and practice using the Box Text tool.

The information provided here serves as a springboard for Chapter 17, "Tags, Style Sheets, and Layout."

Chapter 17

Tags, Style Sheets, and Layouts

*I*n Chapter 15 you set up your document with Chapter Settings and Frame Settings to give you a basic layout. You either composed (with Copy Editor) or loaded text in the previous chapter. This chapter discusses the hard-core formatting capabilities of CorelVENTURA. They are rich and many.

This chapter covers:

- Understanding and using tags
- Using style sheets
- Using paragraph settings
- Understanding layouts

Tags

If you are new to VENTURA, you may find the formatting concepts difficult to grasp. Longtime VENTURA users are loyal to this program because of their appreciation of the power of quickly applying attributes to text. This power is nested in *tags*.

Simply stated, a tag is a collection of all the attributes applied to a paragraph. This includes font, font size, font style (bold, italic, bold italic, normal), justification (left, right, centered, justified), and so forth. The attributes of a tag are applied with the Paragraph Settings dialog box and *number over 50.*

N O T E

A "Paragraph" is defined as a portion of text ending with a carriage return. (Enter is used on computer keyboards.)

All paragraphs must have tags; they can't be avoided. Even if you load text into a new, blank chapter or publication, VENTURA will apply the default "Body Text" tag.

Think of a tag as shown on the Tagged Text tool. A VENTURA tag is similar to the tags used at lawn sales or auctions to describe the article to which it is attached. It is supplementary information. It is analogous to a description in a catalog listing all the features of a product.

"Tag" is used both as a noun and as a verb. The noun refers to a specific name in the tag list which, in turn, contains the formatting information. As a verb, it is the action of applying a tag to a paragraph. "VENTURA

tags all paragraphs with Body Text Tag in the Default Style Sheet."

The simple answer to the question "Why use tags?" is that tags are a very easy and quick way to format your text. Each of the attributes for each of your paragraphs could be applied one at a time. With a tag, you define a set of specifications once and then make it available to reapply often. Tags provide a consistent way to ensure that your publication follows your rules for how it will finally look. This consistency is contained in the restriction of the number of tags you make available in a publication as demanded by good design.

Making a Tag

CorelVENTURA allows flexibility in the creation of tags. Tags can come from the outside world embedded in the text, or they can be created and applied within VENTURA itself.

Tagging within VENTURA

There is always a style sheet (the home of tags) active in VENTURA, and only one. If you omit specifying a style sheet, you will get the "untitled.sty" default style sheet.

N O T E

VENTURA internally creates an unnamed style sheet called "untitled.sty", identical to the default style when you select **F**ile/**N**ew/**D**efault Style. It does this so you won't accidently overwrite the "default.sty" and forces you to do a Save **A**s, instead.

Tagging within VENTURA is automatic to the extent that when you load text, VENTURA applies the default "BodyText" tag to everything. From this tagged position, you can add or change tags.

Changing Existing Tags

Select the Tagged Text tool from the toolbox. It is the tool with the icon of the little tag off to the right. If it is not visible, click and hold the mouse button down until the flyout tools appear, showing both tools. (Shift+F8 is the keyboard shortcut.)

N O T E

"The Tagged Text tool" is a bit of a mouthful. One beta tester of CorelVENTURA thought it looked like entertainer Minnie Pearl's signature hat (a hat with a price tag still attached) and coined the expression: "the Minnie Pearl" tool. It stuck. Many users use the term almost exclusively.

If your cursor does not have the tag, go to Tools/Preferences/View and Enable Tagged Cursor. Plant (click between any letters) the "I-bar with tag" cursor in a paragraph. With this action you have chosen a paragraph and its tag's name will appear in the ribbon bar, at the left.

It's important to remember that having selected this paragraph and tag, any change you make to this paragraph's specifications will not only change this paragraph, but also its tag *and any other paragraph* with the same tag.

Thus, when you select Format/Paragraph, you are really specifying with the tag. And, by dealing with the tag you are changing all of the text having this tag!

Changing the Default Style Sheet Tags

As mentioned previously, if you utilize the basic default style sheet, the Body Text tag is automatic. The Body Text tag attributes were set by Corel when they shipped VENTURA; however, you can change them.

If you want a different set of specifications, do the following:

1. Plant the Tagged Text tool marker in a paragraph.

2. Set the new settings in Paragraph Settings or Manage Tags (more about this later in this chapter).

3. Save the changes using Layout/Save Style Sheet As.

At this point you can change the default by saving with the file name default.sty, or you can give your new style a different name, leaving the old default style in place.

N O T E

Consider for a moment the different possibilities of dealing with a paragraph and the effects of the tools.

- ■ **Planting the Tagged Text tool.** Result: The tag is changed and the changes are automatically applied to every paragraph with this tag. When you save your publication or save the style sheet, these changes will go along with the save.

■ **Planting the Freeform Text tool.** Result: An override to the tag is created by VENTURA, keeping all the specifications of the original tag except those that you have changed. See the following section on overrides.

■ **Swiping text with either tool.** Result: The action has no effect on the tag; it only affects the selected text. You'll probably save this action for changing emphasis styles, such as italics, bold, and underlining.

Overrides

Overrides are not necessarily a good thing. Although Corel has gone to lengths to make sure you are given clues that you are creating an override, it is still pretty easy to change an existing style accidentally. Good practice dictates that instead of creating an override, you should take the time to create a new tag. It is much simpler and cleaner to keep track of tags than it is to control overrides.

Notice that if you plant the Freeform Text tool and select Format/Paragraph, the Paragraph dialog box opens with a new title of "Override Paragraph Settings," another reminder that you are in override mode.

Tagging Paragraphs

Tagging is quite easy, as you will see when you continue the exercise series that runs through the VENTURA section of *CorelDRAW! The Professional Reference.*

Tagging is basically a two-step process:

1. Plant the Tagged Text tool in the paragraph to be tagged.

2. Choose the tag from the ribbon bar.

If you need to tag more than one paragraph, hold down the Alt key and click on each paragraph (the paragraphs need not be in sequence).

T I P

If you have a long document to tag, you might want to assign shortcut keys to your tags. Go to the For**m**at menu and choose Ma**n**age Tag List, choose Set Hotkeys, and either let VENTURA automatically assign keys or do it yourself. All hotkeys are Ctrl+0-9 (thus a 10-hotkey-per-tag limit).

Continuing with the Booklet Exercise, it is time to apply tags to all your text. The exercise will use Arial and Times TrueType fonts because Corel installs them automatically. Try it with your own choice of fonts, if you desire.

Booklet Exercise—Continued

If you have closed VENTURA, restart it and **O**pen your EXERCISE publication.

1. Choose Chp-1 when asked by the Open Publication function.

2. Select the Tagged Text tool. If it is not visible in the toolbox, double-click on the Text tool and it will change to Tagged Text.

3. All paragraphs in your Chapter 1 have the tag of "Body Text," by default. In this exercise section you will modify the tags in your style sheet and add some new ones.

4. Plant the Tagged Text tool in the first line.

5. Select "MainHeading" from the drop-down tag list in the ribbon.

6. Right-click the mouse, select For**m**at/**T**ext. Change the font to Arial and the type size to 18 points, bold.

7. Plant the Tagged Text tool in the second line and choose "SubHeading" as a tag.

8. Change the font to Arial and the type size to 15 points, bold/italic.

9. Plant the Tagged Text tool in the third paragraph and leave it as "Body Text."

10. From the ribbon bar, select Justified. (If you don't know which button this is, pass your cursor slowly over each button and a small yellow sign will appear to tell you its function.)

11. Using PageDown, look at the rest of the chapter and apply the "SubHeading" tag to the small section phrases (you should find six of them).

12. Choose **V**iew/G**o** to Chapter and go to Chp-2. Repeat the tagging as above.

N O T E

As soon as you plant the Tagged Text tool, the lower half of the ribbon bar immediately reflects the attributes of the tag of that paragraph. If you change any of these attributes, you change them in the tag, also.

Creating a New Tag

Creating a new tag is also quite easy. Under For**m**at/Ma**n**age Tag List (Shift+F9) is the Manage Tag List dialog box, which contains **A**dd Tag (see figs. 17.1 and 17.2). Name your new tag, then choose the tag that comes closest to the specifications you want in the new one from the list in **C**opy Attributes From. Click on OK and you now have a second, identical tag. Select this tag from the list and choose **E**dit Tags. This action takes you directly to Paragraph Settings.

Professional Reference Series
New Riders'

Figure 17.1
The Manage Tag List dialog box.

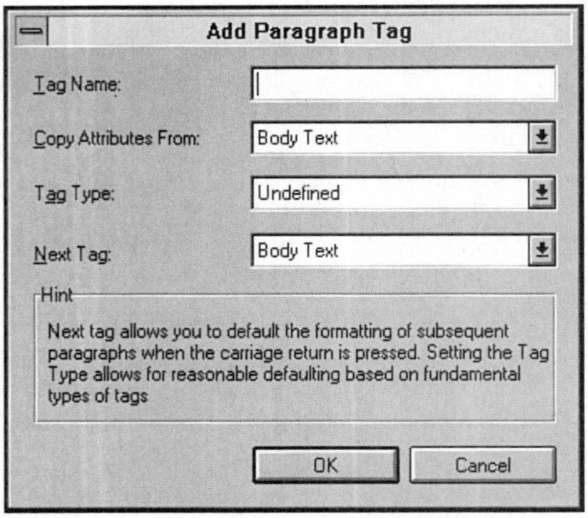

Figure 17.2
The Add Paragraph Tag dialog box.

T I P

While you are in the Add Paragraph Tag dialog box, if you specify a Next Tag for the tag you are creating, you can speed formatting. Suppose you have just created a headline tag and body text always follows. By choosing body text as next tag, as soon as you enter a carriage return the body text tag becomes active.

N O T E

You can also tag text outside of VENTURA. TagWrite is the vehicle for applying tags on text before it reaches VENTURA. You can also insert your own tags in any word processor.

Managing Tags

The Managing Tag List dialog box in figure 17.1 displays options to add, delete, rename, merge, and edit tags for paragraphs, frames, and borders. You can also assign your own shortcut keys (hotkeys) to each tag. At the completion of your efforts, save your changes with **S**ave Stylesheet.

Style Sheets

Style Sheets in VENTURA are files (using an .sty extension) that contain the formatting commands for a chapter. In addition to parameters from Chapter Settings and Frame Settings, they contain all the tags in the chapter.

All chapters must have a style sheet, if none other than the "default.sty," which contains five tags:

- Body Text
- Bullet
- MainHeading
- MinorHeading
- SubHeading

You can have two style sheets, with different names, containing the same tags (tag names), but having different specifications. By substituting the second style sheet, you automatically change the effect of the formatting of the chapter.

Using Paragraph Settings

Most of the text properties in VENTURA are controlled in the Paragraph Settings dialog box. It can be reached by choosing Format/Paragraph or using the Ctrl+T shortcut. The Paragraph Settings dialog box contains five tab sheets, each of which offers control options for a different aspect of VENTURA text:

- Character
- Alignment
- Spacing
- Defaults
- Typography

Clicking on a sheet's "tab" brings that sheet to the front of the Paragraph Settings dialog box.

Character Tab Settings

The Character settings tab, shown in figure 17.3, contains font, font style (bold, italic), and font size controls along with text color. Check boxes turn on underlining, overscoring, and strike-thru. This same dialog box appears if you swipe text and choose Format/Selected Text. Here is another example where VENTURA's interface is context-sensitive to help you navigate through its many options.

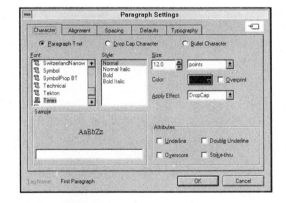

Figure 17.3
The Paragraph Settings dialog box—Character tab.

Alignment Tab Settings

The Alignment settings tab is next (see fig. 17.4). Justification and alignment of text can be specified here. Choices are left, right, centered, full justified, and table. The second section sets tabs and tab types.

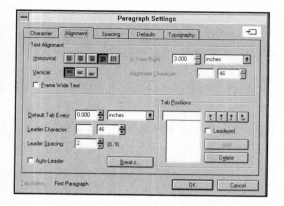

Figure 17.4

The Paragraph Settings dialog box—Alignment tab.

Spacing Tab Settings

You have total control over text spacing and can precisely set it in VENTURA's Spacing tab (see fig. 17.5). Please see Chapter 20 for more information on spacing. In CorelVENTURA, text can be rotated in increments of 90 degrees (0, 90, 180, 270).

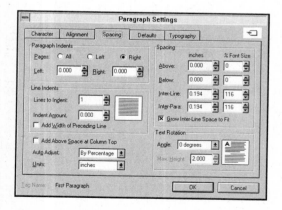

Figure 17.5

The Paragraph Settings dialog box—Spacing tab.

Defaults Tab Settings and Typography Tab Settings

By using the Defaults tab settings, you can alter the default settings for underscore, strikethrough, overscore, small caps, superscript, and subscript text attributes. These settings take place within the Text tool as well, and will affect any changes you make to text using the Text tool.

Typography settings, including spacing, are covered in detail in Chapter 20 for Chapter, Frame, and Paragraph Settings dialog boxes.

Layouts

VENTURA provides six standard page designs or layouts. The two you will probably use the most are Full Page and Booklet. Layouts are simply preorganized shortcuts to various Chapter and Print settings. The six are:

- Full Page (the default)
- Book
- Booklet
- Tent Card
- Side-Fold Card
- Top-Fold Card

These layouts can be selected either in **F**ile/**N**ew or in **L**ayout/**C**hapter Settings. Go to **F**ile/**N**ew to see pictures of each type.

Summary

VENTURA has long been known for its tagging capability. Experienced users claim enormous productivity gains with its formatting advantages. Corel, in version 5, has enhanced tags with override capacity and changed the cursors and dialog boxes to give you a visual reminder of the actions you are taking.

The next chapter introduces you to VENTURA's graphics-implementation capabilities.

Chapter 18

Adding Graphics

*Y*ou add visual impact to your documents with graphics: pictures, illustrations, cartoons, graphs, charts, almost every non-text object. Obviously, one of the main features and requirements of desktop publishing is to integrate graphics with text to construct the most effective communication tools possible.

Now that VENTURA is bundled and fully integrated with the CorelDRAW graphics suite, combining text and graphics has never been easier—or more effective—for desktop publishers.

This chapter covers:

- Importing graphics with Load **G**raphics

- Dragging and dropping graphics with CorelMOSAIC

- Linking and embedding files with OLE2

- Accessing illustrations from PhotoCDs

- Resizing, moving, and cropping graphics

- Wrapping text around graphics

Understanding Graphic File Formats

Of all the page layout programs, CorelVENTURA has the richest set of import filters for graphics. VENTURA commands the lead with its Corel file format filters—specifically the proprietary .CDR file type. It is this last ability which may make VENTURA the choice for all CorelDRAW users.

Graphic files are of two types—bitmap and vector. These two very different formats are both available to VENTURA and each has advantages.

Graphics as Bitmaps

Illustrations using the bitmap format are composed of collections of small points or dots. Each dot has a color or a shade of gray. The density of these dots, dpi (dots per square inch), describes the quality of the bitmap. A bitmap with a dpi of 300 would generally be richer in detail than one with 75 dpi.

Multiplying the dpi by the size of the bitmap gives the total number of dots in the file. Clearly, file size is dependant on these two factors and will vary proportionately. Full color photographs in bitmap format can run to millions of dots.

When bitmaps are resized, dots must be either added or subtracted. Reduction of size does not affect quality because some dots are discarded and the image is retained. However, when a bitmap is expanded, new dots have to be created, which usually lowers the quality of the picture. A good rule is to never increase a bitmap size—but it can be safely reduced. Manipulation of bitmaps—resizing and changes of dpi—should be performed with a program like CorelPHOTO-PAINT and then imported into VENTURA. Use VENTURA only to crop the image or to position it.

For further discussion of bitmaps, see the section on "Using PhotoCD Images" later in this chapter.

Graphics as Vectors

CorelDRAW produces vector illustrations. Vector-based graphics take a different approach to image creation than do bitmaps. Vectors are line segments and are expressed mathematically. For example, a vector might be described as a line drawn between point A and point B of a thickness of one half a centimeter and black in color. A rectangle would be four vectors of specified length, joined at right angles and filled with, perhaps, red. Curves are defined in Bézier notation, a mathematical formula with which the position of four points shapes the curve.

Vector drawings are very precise. High-quality typefaces are vector drawings. Once the formulas are stated, the drawing can be reproduced exactly. The major advantage of vectors is the ability to resize them and retain accuracy. Because they are formulas, their dimensions can be multiplied and divided without loss of accuracy.

Choosing Vectors or Bitmaps

Bitmaps have high detail and complex color effects, but are rather rigid in size. They are excellent for photographs. PHOTO-PAINT should be used to modify these images and then export them as TIFF files.

Vector drawings can be imported into VENTURA in any size and freely resized within VENTURA. These include CorelDRAW files (CDRs) and Corel clip art (CMXs). Files from Adobe Illustator and other line-based programs fit in this category.

Importing Graphics

You can load graphics into either the page frame, another frame you have drawn, or just into VENTURA's file list. In all cases, use the File/Load Graphic command (F10).

You can choose whether the graphic will be loaded into a frame and the file list or just the file list. This action is controlled by Add File to List check box that is found under Options in the Load Graphic or Load Text dialog boxes (see fig. 18.1).

■ If this option is checked, the graphic will be placed *only* in the file list. It will not be visible on your screen until you select a frame and choose the graphic from the drop-down file list.

■ If this option is unchecked, the graphic will be placed in the file list *and* placed into a frame, if one is currently selected.

N O T E

The Add File to List option is shared by Load Graphic and Load Text. Checking in one will also change it in the other.

Table 18.1 lists all the valid file types from the dropdown list entitled List Files of Type.

Table 18.1
Import Filters

Types of Files	Extension
Adobe Illustrator 1.1, 88, 3.0	.ai .eps
All Files	*.*
AutoCad DXF	.dxf
CompuServe Bitmap	.gif
Computer Graphics Metafile	.cgm

continues

Table 18.1, Continued
Import Filters

Types of Files	Extension
Corel Presentation Exchange	.cmx
CorelCHART Chart	.cch
CorelDRAW! Graphic	.cdr .pat
CorelTRACE	.eps
EPS (Placeable)	.eps .ps .ai
GEM File	.gem
GEM Paint File	.img
HPGL Plotter File	.plt
IBM PIF	.pif
JPEG Bitmap	.ijp .jff .jft .cmp
Lotus PIC	.pic
Macintosh PICT	.pct
Micrographic 2*x*, 3*x*	.drw
Paintbrush	.pcx
Scitex CT Bitmap	.sct .ct
Targa Bitmap	.tga .vda .icb .vst
TIFF Bitmap	.tif .sep .cpt
Windows Bitmap	.bmp .dib .rle
Windows Metafile	.wmf
WordPerfect Graphic	.wpg

N O T E

This large selection of file types is impressive, but some are quite out-of-date. Their inclusion helps support old documents and existing graphics. Today, graphic designers rely on a few.

Shown in figure 18.1 is the Load Graphic dialog box—extended view (obtained by clicking on **O**ptions). **P**review will show a thumbnail representation of the graphic you are about to load. The preview of Corel's clip art files are almost instantaneous, but views of large color TIFF files can take much longer to appear.

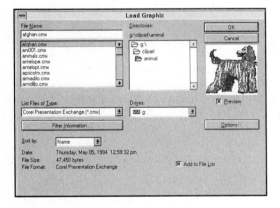

Figure 18.1
The Load Graphic dialog box.

The example in figure 18.1 shows loading of a piece of clip art from the Corel CD. Notice that the filter chosen was the specific Corel Presentation Exchange module rather than the non-specific All Files. VENTURA's

Corel Presentation Exchange (.cmx) filter opens the door to Corel's enormous clip art collection on the CDs. Choosing All Files is not always reliable and declines to import some otherwise-valid files.

T I P

Multiple files of the same type (extension) and in the same directory can be loaded by pressing Shift and clicking on the first and last file (for multiple contiguous files), or by pressing Ctrl and clicking on any file for selecting non-contiguous ones.

If multiple files are loaded, they are placed in the Files List and must be placed on the page individually.

Loading Graphics by Dragging from the MOSAIC Roll-Up

The MOSAIC roll-up is a handy, built-in viewer of graphic files, allowing you to find files by seeing a thumbnail (a small bitmap view) of your files without needing to remember their names.

To start MOSAIC, press Alt+F1 (it can also be started from the ribbon bar—second button from the right). Change directories by selecting the file folder icon in the upper right of the roll-up. (The MOSAIC roll-up always opens showing the VENTURA\Typeset directory.) Figure 18.2 shows the MOSAIC view of a clip art directory.

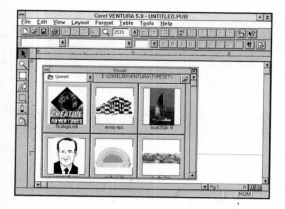

Figure 18.2
The Corel MOSAIC roll-up.

The MOSAIC roll-up will show thumbnails of most graphics, and icons of text files. It provides a very good road map of your working directory.

MOSAIC is an exciting and powerful tool to quickly search Corel's vast clip art library. Rather than leafing through the clip art manual, you can see the files on screen. With release 5 of DRAW, Corel switched formats for clip art from the normal file structure (.CDR) to the new Presentation Exchange (.CMX). The speed increase is dramatic.

One you have located an appropriate file, you need not search for its location in the libraries, as you would when using the manual; all you need to do is drag the thumbnail from MOSAIC on to your VENTURA page. This action imports the image, creates its frame, and adds the file to the file list.

Using OLE2 to Import Graphics

Graphics imported into VENTURA are static. You import them and VENTURA creates a direct link to the graphic file and places it in your document. Should you want to alter it, you must return to the program that created it. Because VENTURA stores this graphic as a separate file, any changes to the file will automatically be reflected in the publication or chapter the next time you open it, but no changes are possible directly from within VENTURA.

With both version 4 and 5, Corel has made a large investment in Microsoft's OLE2 (Object Linking and Embedding, version 2) technology. OLE2 provides dynamic access to the linked or embedded graphic through the program that created it. This process is initiated by double clicking on the graphic while in VENTURA. The creating program immediately starts, overlaying VENTURA, and displays the double-clicked illustration.

The linking part of OLE2 creates a pointer to the current location of the graphic file, whereas embedding creates a new file copy. Changes can be made outside of VENTURA to a linked file but *must* be made through VENTURA for an embedded one.

OLE2 technology may be quite complex, but its implementation is quite simple. Follow these steps to try OLE2:

1. Choose **E**dit/I**n**sert Object. The Insert Object dialog box appears (see fig. 18.3). Regardless of the vendor of the program, all OLE2 dialog boxes are very similar.

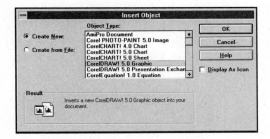

Figure 18.3
The Insert Object dialog box.

2. From the list of OLE2–registered programs (all programs that are OLE2–compliant must submit their information to the Windows program—Regedit), select your choice of program.

3. Choose to create a new file or load an existing file.

4. Choose link or embed (not checking the Link option causes embedding).

5. Choose to see the graphic on the screen or to have it represented by the creating program's icon.

The decision of how to obtain your graphics—OLE2 link, OLE2 embed, or load graphic—depends on who needs access to the file.

■ If the graphic will be maintained and updated by another person, consider OLE2 link.

■ If you want complete control of the graphic, use OLE2 to embed it within VENTURA. Access can then only be obtained by double-clicking in VENTURA.

■ If you will not need to edit the illustration, just use Load Graphic.

Importing Graphics from the Clipboard

As with most Windows programs, the Clipboard is a handy temporary pasteboard to transfer images. Any graphic from another program that is either cut or copied can be pasted into VENTURA. When you paste, the image is stored in the Chapter file (.chp), not as a separate file.

This method prevents editing. Once pasted into VENTURA, the image is fixed. If the image is large or complex, it would be better to use one of the other methods to transfer the image. Storing the image in the chapter file would slow down load time.

Considerations for Choosing Graphic Formats

All graphic formats are not equal in utility. The following sections indicate some points of difference.

Using CDRs for Vector Drawings

CorelDRAW formats give you the most flexibility within VENTURA. Because both products share common code groups (DLLs), they are tightly coupled. If you have DRAW installed on the same system, you can import

DRAW 3, DRAW 4, and DRAW 5 files directly. Without DRAW installed on the same system, utilize the CMX (Corel Presentation Exchange) format, which limits you to DRAW 5 files (or 3 and 4 files recycled through DRAW 5). Table 18.2 outlines your choices.

Table 18.2
Requirements for CorelDRAW files

Import	Format
DRAW 3, 4, 5 (.cdr)	DRAW 5 must be installed to place them in VENTURA.
DRAW 5 plus CMX	Created in DRAW 5 with CMX checked. No current need for this format, but Corel says it will have future merit communicating outside Corel products.
Corel Presentation Exchange	Exported from DRAW 5, but DRAW 5 need not be installed on the same system with VENTURA. The clip art on the CD reflects this approach.

Using TIFF for Bitmaps

Today, the most popular format for bitmap files is TIFF (Tagged Image File Format); with its many varieties, you can vary the quality, and therefore, the size, of your images. Most graphics programs support this file type, at various levels, so you can be assured that you will have portability.

Using PhotoCD Images

An obvious missing player from the list of import filters is Kodak's new PhotoCD file format. With this technology, and for around $20, photographs are processed by Kodak and up to 100 images placed on the normal-sized CD. To read them, your CD reader must be Kodak–format-aware; the recording of proprietary PCDs requires special circuitry, especially for multi-session PhotoCDs, which allows pictures to be added to an existing CD. Non-multi-session CD readers should be considered obsolete.

PhotoCDs bring to the computer (and your TV) digitized full color pictures of reasonable quality, depending on the skill of the photographer controlling focus, lighting, backgrounds, and camera speed. This format bypasses traditional scanning (Kodak does the scanning for you), and produces files ready for adjusting and separating.

Corel, responding to beta testers who noticed lack of support for PCDs, has indicated that PhotoCD images would probably need adjusting before use in VENTURA. With CorelPHOTO-PAINT included with VENTURA, the logical process would be to

open the PCD in PHOTO-PAINT, adjust
the image, and save it as a TIFF (or JPEG, if
you need compression).

NOTE

Corel's PHOTO-PAINT 5 has a very extensive
interface for PhotoCD that pops right up when
you open a PCD. PHOTO-PAINT provides
high-precision tools to adjust color levels,
curves, and other image components. See
figure 18.4.

On the PhotoCD you will find each image
recorded in five sizes (see table 18.3). Use the
smallest size for positioning the image during
design, and then replace it with a high-
quality, adjusted picture just before production.

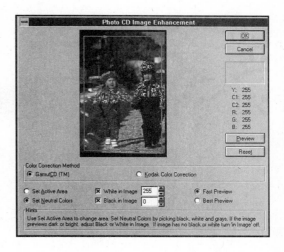

Figure 18.4
*PHOTO-PAINT's PhotoCD Image Enhancement dialog
box.*

Table 18.3
PhotoCD Specifications

Image Size Type	Pixels	Inches	File Size Bytes
Poster	2048 × 3072	28.444 × 42.667	18,874,368
Large	1024 × 1536	14.222 × 21.333	4,718,592
Standard	512 × 768	7.111 × 10.667	1,179,648
Snapshot	256 × 384	3.556 × 5.333	294,912
Wallet	128 × 192	1.778 × 2.667	73,728

Experiment with the different sizes of images, and pick one large enough so that you can reduce (never enlarge) after you crop it and adjust for the screening. Your picture's dpi should equal exactly twice the line screen at which you will print. For example, if you print at 133 screen (fairly standard), then choose 266 dpi.

Compressing Graphics

JPEG image compression has become the standard for both video and still-picture files. Large, 24-bit color files require incredible amounts of storage space. JPEG methods severely reduce this size requirement, without distortion of the picture, by eliminating or coding redundant information.

Captions

Captions are special text frames attached to a graphic frame either above, below, to the left, or right. They move with the picture, and if the picture's width is changed, so is the width of the caption. Turn on captions in For**m**at/**F**rame/General dialog tab by choosing the position in the drop-down list.

Working with Graphics in VENTURA

Once you understand the basic principles behind using graphics in CorelVENTURA— file formats and file importing—you're ready to use graphics in your work. The next section covers the basics of working with graphic images in VENTURA.

Sizing Graphics

When a graphic is placed in a frame, it is constrained by the inside margins of that frame. Without distorting its measurements, VENTURA will place the largest size possible within these confines. If you change the size of the frame, either through the Frame Settings dialog box or by dragging the frame handles, the graphic will automatic follow the frame size change.

The default value of a graphic frame is **F**it in Frame, causing it to be automatically resized. If you uncheck this choice in the Graphic tab of the Frame Settings dialog box, the graphic will revert to its original size. If the size of the graphic is larger than the inside margins of the frame, the graphic is cropped and only part of it is visible.

Sizing control of your graphic is in the **F**ormat/**G**raphic menu. Uncheck **F**it in Frame to resize and use **W**idth to control your adjustments (see fig. 18.5).

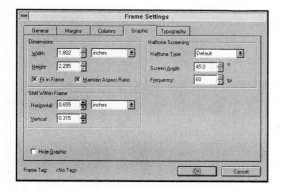

Figure 18.5

Frame graphic settings are set in the Graphic tab of the Frame Settings dialog box.

With the two check boxes, **F**it to Frame and **M**aintain Aspect Ratio, you have four choices:

- **F**it to Frame and **M**aintain Aspect Ratio. When both are active (checked) neither **H**eight nor **W**idth are selectable.

- **M**aintain Aspect Ratio, only. With **F**it to Frame unchecked, you can change the size of the graphic by changing **W**idth. **H**eight will change by the same ratio, although you cannot change **H**eight directly.

- **F**it to Frame, only. Neither **H**eight nor **W**idth are selectable and the graphic will redraw to fit the frame. By moving the sizing handles of the frame, you can manually proportion the graphic and produce some interesting effects.

- Neither checked. Both **H**eight and **W**idth can be manipulated to give you complete control over the graphic dimensions.

These controls are most appropriate for vector drawings, but may severely distort bitmaps. Use CorelPHOTO-PAINT to resize bitmaps.

Wrapping Graphics around Text

Adding graphics to documents allows you to illustrate information contained in the document, as well as create points of interest to guide the eye through the page. When you add graphics to a document, you need to balance the appearance of the page. Creating an irregular text wrap frame around an image can assist you in producing a balanced appearance. CorelVENTURA enables you to wrap text around graphics using one of three methods. The flexibility offered by these methods enables you to easily control the appearance of text within your document. The three methods include:

- Auto Wrap

- Preset Wrap Shape

- Creating a Custom Path

When you wrap text around a graphic you are actually wrapping the text around a frame that surrounds the graphic. This frame provides space around the graphic to prevent the text from lying too close to the image. To wrap text around a graphic using either Auto Wrap or Preset Wrap Shape:

1. Select the graphic frame, then right-click the mouse button to display the Frame Options menu.

2. Choose either Auto Wrap or Preset Wrap Shapes.

The next two sections each outline the specifics of using Auto Wrap and Preset Wrap Shapes.

Using Auto Wrap

When you select Auto Wrap, VENTURA determines the shape to place around the image, automatically. The shape may or may not be an irregularly shaped frame, depending upon the contour of the graphic. The wrap frame is a complex curve, with nodes, that you can edit using the Node Edit tool. When you apply Auto Wrap, the program toggles to the Node Edit tool allowing you to modify the shape of the wrap frame as desired. The Node Edit tool in VENTURA functions like that in CorelDRAW. Drag the nodes or node handles to the desired shape. If you need to add or subtract nodes, double-click on one of the nodes to display the Node Edit roll-up. For more information about using the Node Edit tool, see Chapter 5, "Shaping Objects."

The first two frames of figure 18.6 show Auto Wrap applied to a Windows Metafile format illustration of an egg carton. If you've used the Node tool in CorelDRAW, the second frame (showing nodes) will be quite familiar—and Auto Wrap works the same way. The text that you see within the frame shows you the approximate results of Auto Wrap if you just accepted Auto Wrap's initial shape.

The third frame shows the container with some adjustment and the last frame shows the result. After adjusting, choose the Pick tool; the container outline disappears and the text flows to its new shape. If the text wrap is unacceptable, you can repeat the process often by reselecting the Node tool. The container reappears for readjustment.

Using Preset Wrap Shape

When you select Preset Wrap Shape, a flyout list appears allowing you to choose one of eleven popular preset wrap frame shapes. These shapes include: Oval, Diamond, Heart, Inverted Rounded Rectangle, Octagon, Rectangle, Rounded Rectangle, Left Trapazoid, Right Trapazoid, Teardrop, and Star. All of the Preset Wrap Shapes are symmetrical and can save valuable time spent customizing a shape around a graphic. As with Auto Wrap, these shapes are complex curves and can be edited using the Node Edit tool.

N O T E

Auto Wrap and Preset Wrap Shape do not support OLE objects. To apply a frame to an OLE object, you must either create a custom frame or use the default graphic frame for wrapping text around the image.

Creating a Custom Frame

The third method of wrapping text around a graphic enables you to create a custom frame. If your image has an irregular shape, or you only want to frame a portion of the image, consider using this method. Interesting effects can be achieved by allowing the text to flow over a portion of an image, yet be masked or prevented from flowing over the balance of the graphic.

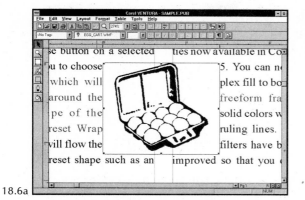

18.6a

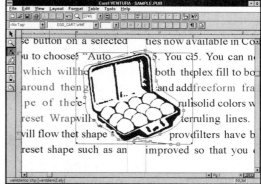

18.6b

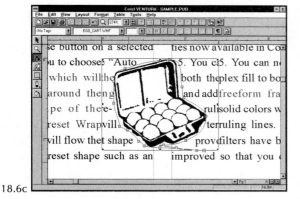

18.6c

18.6d

To create a custom frame around a graphic, select the graphic frame. Choose the Node Edit tool from the Frame Tool fly-out menu. You can either draw a freehand frame around the area you want to mask, or you can click points around the area. If you choose to click points, VENTURA will automatically join those points, to create the frame.

Figure 18.6

VENTURA's Auto Wrap function lets you quickly and easily wrap text around a graphic.

W A R N I N G

If you import an graphic saved as an EPS (Encapsulated PostScript) file, the wrap frame will be generated based upon the file header, rather than the image itself. This can cause a disparity between the screen representation and the actual printer output.

If you want to return a wrap frame to its default shape, right-click the mouse button after selecting a graphic to which a wrap frame has been applied. Choose Regenerate Wrap from the Frame Options menu. The wrap frame will return to the shape you initially assigned. If you applied a Preset Wrap Shape it will return to that shape; if you applied Auto Wrap it will return to the default shape the program applied to the graphic. This is useful if you are disatisfied with editing you have applied to a frame wrap.

The frame options available on the menu function as toggles. They are either enabled or disabled. To remove a wrap frame of any variety from a graphic, reselect the graphic and right-click to display the frame options menu. Select the option you previously selected to remove the wrap frame.

Using Clip Graphic

VENTURA offers another valuable tool in creating custom wrap frames around graphics. The Clip Graphic option from the Frame Options menu enables you to irregularly crop a graphic to fit the contour of the wrap frame. To use the Clip Graphic option:

1. Select the graphic, to which you have applied a wrap frame, and then right-click the mouse button to display the Frame Options menu.

2. Choose Clip Graphic. The graphic is clipped to fit the contour of the frame. Until you disable Clip Graphic by selecting it again from the menu, the graphic will conform to the frame, regardless of any frame editing you apply.

Using Size Frame to OLE Object

VENTURA allows you to resize and crop OLE objects within your documents. If you want to return an OLE object to its original size and apply a wrap frame to the object, select the object. Right-click the mouse button to display the frame options menu, and choose Size Frame to OLE Object. The wrap frame will follow the contours of the original object. You can edit this wrap frame using the Node Edit tool as described previously in this section.

Adjusting and Moving Frames

In VENTURA you have the normal control over a graphic frame as with any frame elsewhere in CorelDRAW. Selecting a frame will show six handles that you can drag to change its shape, or you can move the entire frame by dragging. Precise positioning of the graphics frame is better controlled by the Frame Settings dialog box where you can enter the exact origin position and size.

The best approach to frame creation is to first draw the frame with the frame tool and then size and then position it exactly with the Frame Settings dialog box.

Panning and Cropping Frames

With the frame size and position set, you can visually move the graphic within the frame if the **F**it in Frame option is unchecked. Panning allows you to slide the image around the inside of the frame and, if the image is moved beyond the inside margins, it will be cropped or hidden.

Hold down Ctrl, click on the graphic, *and while holding the mouse button down* release Ctrl. VENTURA will spend a few seconds doing some calculations, then the cursor will turn to a hand icon. This grabber tool is used to pan the graphic within its frame. When you release the mouse button, the graphic will stay in the position but can be readjusted by repeating the process.

Panning and cropping allows you to use a frame as a view port to show part of an image. If this feature were not available, you would have to resize or cut the image itself in the program that created it.

The following exercise can help you become familiar with the graphic arrangement and text-wrapping functions covered so far in this chapter.

Graphic Exercise

1. Choose File, New.

2. Draw a large frame on the page.

3. Without a frame selected, choose File/Load Graphic. Using the Corel Presentation Exchange filter and with Add to File List turned off, select and load BALLOON1.CMX.

4. Select the frame by clicking anywhere on the balloon, and right-click the mouse.

5. From the popup menu, choose Frame/General. Enter these values:

Dimensions, Width:	3.0
Dimensions, Height:	4.0
Frame Origin, Horizontal:	0.75
Frame Origin, Vertical:	1.0

6. Click on OK and notice the new positioning.

7. Again, right-click the balloon and select Frame/Graphic. Deselect Fit in Frame and enter 4.0 into Width.

8. Click on OK and notice the new positioning.

9. Press Ctrl and click in the balloon frame. Holding down the mouse button, release Ctrl. When the cursor turns to a hand shape, move the graphic up toward the top left, cropping the left and top of the balloon (see fig. 18.7).

10. Load any text file in the base frame and try Auto Wrap on the balloon.

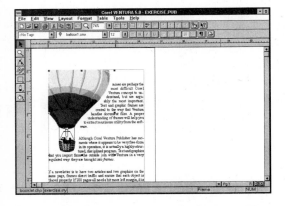

Figure 18.7
*Graphic Frame Exercise Results showing balloon with
text in the base frame. Notice the handles on the balloon
frame.*

Graphics can add great appeal to your
document. CorelVENTURA gives you more
options, more control, and more formats
than any other page layout program. Try the
various methods for placing and adjusting
your graphics, and you will discover the
power of VENTURA's document-generation
capabilities.

Summary

There are several approaches to obtaining
graphics in VENTURA:

- Load Graphics, the most common
  method, places an illustration into your
  document without editing capability.

- Linked OLE2 allows you to edit the
  file in its original location and will
  reflect changes made outside of
  VENTURA.

- Embedded OLE2 allows you to edit
  the file from within VENTURA *only*
  because it is now part of your
  document.

- Dragging from the MOSAIC roll-up is
  a short cut and time saving method
  particularly for Corel's clip art.

- Pasting from the Clipboard is quick
  and easy but lacks flexibility.

Chapter 19

Adding Indexes, Tables, and Tables of Contents

Normally, the last jobs in preparing a publication are organizational. You have designed your document, loaded text and graphics, and have most of the content ready. To help your audience, you may want to add features that make it easier to navigate through your publication. Tables organize data for better presentation; tables of contents tell the reader what is in the publication—VENTURA automates this function; and an index shows how to find information. VENTURA will create indexes for words, sections, tags, figures, and tables. CorelVENTURA helps you implement any or all of these features quickly and effectively.

This chapter covers:

- Constructing a table within VENTURA

- Pasting a table from another application into VENTURA

- Using OLE2 and DDE to embed and link tables from other applications into VENTURA

- Building a table of contents

- Generating an index

Using Tables

Tables are integral parts of many documents, especially technical publications. They provide, in rows and columns, concisely organized data, both text and numbers. Properly designed tables also have visual impact, attract the reader's attention, and show the relationships of the entries. Included with the sample files shipping with CorelVENTURA 5.0 is a chapter file called "PARTSLST.CHP," which can be found in the VENTURA/Vpstyle directory. This is an excellent example of a large table–a price list (see fig. 19.1). To view this chapter in its entirety, select **L**ayout, Add E**x**isting Chapter and choose VENTURA/VPSTYLE/PARTSLST.CHP.

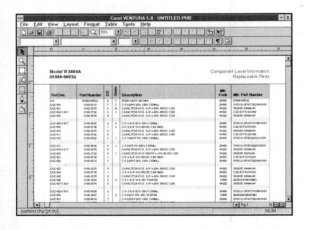

Figure 19.1

An example of a VENTURA table—PARTSLST.CHP in the Vpstyle directory.

We find tables in use everywhere in daily life: airline schedules, tax forms, annual reports, and even restaurant menus. They all have common elements—data that can be made more meaningful when placed in cells in horizontal rows and vertical columns. The cells are bounded by rules or lines of specifiable thickness and color. Cells can be colored and shaded for emphasis.

In concert with the rest of Corel's application architecture, VENTURA has support for numerous ways of inserting tables:

- Use VENTURA's Table feature to create a table within VENTURA

- Copy a table through the Clipboard

- Use Dynamic Data Exchange (DDE)

- Use Object Linking and Embedding (OLE2) to access table-building capabilities of spreadsheet programs

VENTURA's Tables

VENTURA 5.0 has a built-in table facility which should handle most of your needs. It is very interactive and can use the full range of VENTURA's tagging system. Each cell, the rectangular area where you place data, can be filled and outlined using the line and fill tools.

Creating a Table

Creating a table in VENTURA is quite straightforward. Plant either (tagged or freeform) Text tool cursor in a frame and select **T**able/Creat**e** Table. The seventh button from the right on the ribbon bar also creates a table.

T I P

Rather than creating a table in the base frame, draw a separate free frame, just for the table. There are several advantages:

1. A table in its own frame can be easily moved, but a table in the base frame is fixed.

2. If you need to delete the table, just delete the frame, which deletes the table at the same time.

3. A free frame with a table has outside margins to create a border area between the frame and text. A base frame has no outside margins.

4. A free frame table can be drawn over another frame so that the table could be superimposed over, for example, a graphic.

5. A free frame can have a caption.

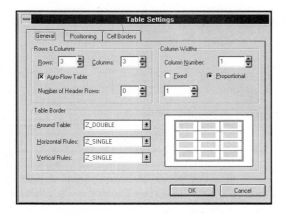

Figure 19.2
The Table Settings dialog box.

With the Table Settings dialog box, shown in figure 19.2, choose the number of **R**ows and **C**olumns you need. Because you can always add and delete rows and columns if you make a mistake or if your table grows, you can estimate the need at this point.

Rows are horizontal cells and **C**olumns are vertical, and the intersection of a row and column is a cell.

Remember to allow an extra row on the top for column titles and a column on the left for row descriptions. You are limited to 32 columns, but to no practical limit to rows.

If your table is apt to span more than one page, the A**u**to-Flow function, if checked, will duplicate the top row(s) when the table continues on the next page. Specify in Nu**m**ber of Header Rows how many rows are occupied with column titles. In figure 19.1 the top row, in dark gray with "Part Number," is an Auto-Flow row.

Formatting with Quick Format

One of the functions within the Quick Format roll-up is table formatting. The Quick Format roll-up applies certain built-in values to various attributes of objects, like tables (see fig. 19.3). The shading of cells, for example, applies a fill to cells that would normally be filled with VENTURA's Fill tool. Quick Format has no effect on the numbers of rows and columns, so don't be concerned if the preview is either larger or smaller than your table. You can always reapply Quick Format if you add or subtract rows or columns.

Selecting Table in the **T**ype list displays 13 reformatted table images. Use the steps in the following exercise to apply Quick Formats.

In each cell, you can enter either free form text or tagged text with the appropriate Text tool. Each cell is treated as a paragraph, so you can use all the text formatting tools, and Paragraph Settings, with cells.

With the Tagged Text tool, you can apply various tags to each cell in the same manner as you would apply them to regular text.

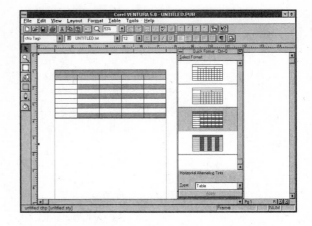

Figure 19.3
Quick Format for tables.

Table Quick Format Exercise

1. With either the Tagged Text tool or the Freeform Text tool, click on (plant the cursor in) the base frame or a free frame.

2. Select **T**able, Creat**e** Table and the Table Settings dialog box opens (see fig. 19.2).

3. Enter 10 for **R**ows and 5 for **C**olumns and click on OK.

4. Open the Quick Format roll-up by pressing Ctrl+Q.

5. Move the roll-up off the page to the right so that it does not interfere with your view (see fig. 19.3).

6. Choose Table from the list labeled **T**ype.

7. Select the Pick tool, the first one, and click anywhere in the table. This action selects the table.

8. Choose any of the preformatted table selections or choose the one shown in figure 19.3.

9. Press apply. Notice that your table is now quite similar to the preview you chose in the Quick Format roll-up.

Using the Clipboard

The Windows Clipboard will store tables as well as text and images. If a table already exists in another application you can copy it to the Clipboard and paste it into VENTURA. Use these steps:

1. Select all the cells of the table in the other application.

2. Choose **E**dit, **C**opy from the menu.

3. Without exiting from the source program, start VENTURA.

4. Draw a free frame.

5. Choose **E**dit, **P**aste.

NOTE

You must leave the other application running during this transfer through the Clipboard; otherwise the table will be lost.

Tables copied and pasted into VENTURA are static; their data cannot be edited nor format changed. They are treated by VENTURA as a graphic brought in by **F**ile/ Load **G**raphic.

TIP

You can use this technique of copying tables to create an image in VENTURA of the table, then in a frame below it create a VENTURA table with the same information. This way you do not have to switch back and forth between VENTURA and the other program. When the new table is completed, delete the old one.

Using OLE2 and DDE Tables

Corel Corporation has supported OLE2 and DDE from its inception, and now it's payoff time. VENTURA can communicate with any other application that has been registered with Windows as an OLE2- or DDE-compliant program. This group of programs is represented by most of the current Windows applications, including CorelDRAW, Microsoft Word and Excel, and Lotus 1-2-3. Figure 19.4 shows a Microsoft Excel 5.0-created worksheet pasted into a VENTURA frame (the frame has outside margins of .25 inches).

- Linked files are left with the application that created them and saved them. A link is established from VENTURA pointing to the creating application and the location of the file.

- Embedded files are brought into VENTURA, stored with VENTURA files, and are no longer accessible to the originating application without going through VENTURA.

- Linked and embedded files are both accessible in VENTURA by double-clicking on the table on VENTURA's page.

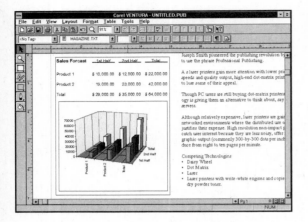

Figure 19.4

An Excel table embedded into VENTURA.

You can link or embed tables into VENTURA using the methods described in the following sections.

Using the Clipboard and DDE Link

For this DDE method, use the same procedure as previously described (Using the Clipboard), but select **E**dit/Paste **S**pecial (instead of **E**dit/**P**aste), and then check the link box. The file, containing the table you have pasted, remains where it was saved by that application, and is not physically part of your VENTURA publication's files.

By using the DDE Paste Special command, and keeping a link, you retain editing capabilities. At any time, you can double-click on the table to edit it.

This marvelous feature immediately starts the program that created the table, loads the table into it, and passes control to you. Complete your edit, save the file, and exit. When you return to VENTURA, the table is automatically updated.

Using the Clipboard with a DDE Link provides you with an alternative to creating a table with VENTURA's internal tools. Consider using this method if the following criteria apply to you:

■ You have a favorite spreadsheet program that you know well

■ You have already created the table in your spreadsheet program

To review the steps to transfer a table with a DDE Link, complete the following steps:

1. Start your spreadsheet program.

2. Create your spreadsheet or load one you have previously created.

3. Select the table and choose **E**dit, **C**opy (or that program's equivalent of these commands).

4. Leaving your spreadsheet program running, return to VENTURA.

5. Select **E**dit, Paste **S**pecial and check Paste **L**ink (see fig. 19.5).

6. Choose OK and your table is placed in VENTURA.

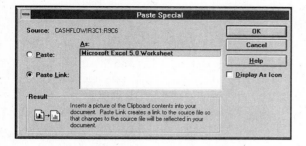

Figure 19.5
VENTURA's Paste Special DDE dialog box.

Using OLE2

OLE2 presents even another approach to tables in VENTURA. While using VENTURA 5.0, you can use OLE2 to operate other OLE2-compliant applications. The major difference between the Clipboard and DDE and OLE2 is operation. With OLE2, you stay in VENTURA and, with **E**dit/**In**sert Object, you run another application program.

Creating an OLE2 table, you have four options:

- **New and Embed.** Starts the other OLE2 application to create a new file that will become part of your publication's file structure and will only be accessed through VENTURA and OLE2.

- **New and Link.** Starts the other OLE2 application to create a new file that will *not* become part of your publication, and can be accessed without VENTURA.

- **Existing File and Embed.** Starts the other OLE2 application with the specified file loaded. At the completion of this operation, this file will be placed in your publication and only accessed through VENTURA from then on. The original file will still exist but will not reflect any changes you make through VENTURA.

- **Existing File and Link.** Starts the other OLE2 application with the specified file loaded. This file will *not* be included within your publication and will be accessable from either within VENTURA or from the outside in the other OLE2 application.

The decision whether to embed or link is based upon control. If you want to prevent modification of the file outside VENTURA, then *embed*. If you want access given to others, then *link*.

At first, OLE2 sounds quite complicated, but in practice it is very easy to operate. For example, while you are working on a document, you might think, "I have already prepared a table that might fit here. I'll go get it." The procedure is easy:

1. Select **E**dit, **In**sert Object.

2. Click Create from **F**ile, and press **B**rowse.

3. Using the controls in **B**rowse, locate your file.

4. Choose OK.

That's all there is to it. The table is placed into VENTURA and you can move it, resize it, and if you double-click on it, you will restart the source application so that you can edit it.

If you need to create a new table:

1. Select **E**dit/**In**sert Object. The Insert Object dialog box opens (see fig. 19.6).

2. Select Create **N**ew (this is the default).

3. Make a selection from the list of registered applications, and a small window from that program will open in VENTURA and replace VENTURA's menu with its own.

4. When you have finished creating your table, click anywhere outside the other application's window. This simple action closes the tie, and VENTURA's menu returns with your table pasted into VENTURA.

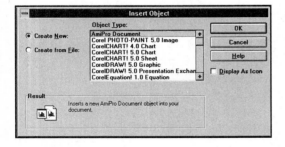

Figure 19.6
The Insert Object dialog box.

Using OLE2 and Create from File and Link

Choose **E**dit/**In**sert Object and Create from **F**ile. After the dialog box is repainted, check the Link box and click on **B**rowse (see fig. 19.7). By selecting a file, the file extension tells Windows which program to start.

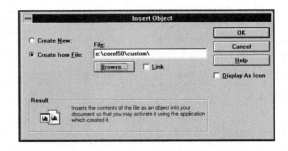

Figure 19.7
Creating from an existing file in the Insert Object dialog box.

The other application runs behind the scenes —out of view. Once you click on OK after selecting the file, the OLE2 application opens, loads your file, and sends it to VENTURA. VENTURA then places it into your document—without further actions. When this process is complete, the table will appear on the screen; you now can move it and use Frame specifications with it.

Because this file is linked, it can be updated outside of VENTURA, but VENTURA will reflect the changes. You can, however, edit the file from VENTURA by simply double-clicking on the table, and the original application will open with the table loaded into it.

Using OLE2 to Embed

Choose **E**dit/**In**sert Object and Create from **F**ile. Follow the same steps as with OLE2 and Link, described previously, but do not check the **L**ink check box.

The only difference with Embed is that the entire file is embedded within your chapter file and becomes inaccessible from the original application. You can edit it from within VENTURA at any time with a double-click.

Tables Summary

How to create your tables is a judgment call based on several factors. Does the table already exist? Do you have a spreadsheet program you really like and know? Where is the data for the table? Will you need to change it later? Does someone else have to change it? With the previous discussions of each method, choose the one that seems to fit your needs best.

Creating a Table of Contents and Index

In medium-to-large publications, you will need to provide your readers with a table of contents and an index. These are roadmaps to tell them what they will find inside and where to find it easily.

A table of contents will normally include the names of all your chapters, the names of sections within the chapters, and other relevant information that will help the readers understand the content of your publication.

Likewise, an index at the back of your publication is an important reference tool for the reader. Especially with technical documents, your readers will expect to be able to use an index to find just the subject and specific reference they need. The Index lists topics in your publication followed by page numbers.

Choosing the tags to include in your table of contents and the words and phrases to include in your index is a subjective process which, in VENTURA, is interactive. Because VENTURA creates a text file in both cases, you can always add, subtract, and reformat entries. You can also regenerate them at any time. For example, if you decide to add (or delete) a level to the table of contents, just add (or delete) the tag and choose **G**enerate.

N O T E

You can only make tables of contents and indexes within a publication structure. If you have not created a publication yet, the **G**enerate button in the TOC and Inde**x** dialog box will remain inactive until you do so. To create the publication, select **F**ile, **S**ave and choose a name for your document.

Creating a Table of Contents

Many documents are created using an outline, which in turn, is the basis for creating tags. Chapter titles, section heads, and figure names will all have different tags.

VENTURA provides a powerful mechanism for organizing your list of tags into a table of contents. It works like this:

- You tell VENTURA which tags to use.

- VENTURA collects all the text in the document with these tags.

- VENTURA creates a tagged text file with this information.

- You can load this file and edit it like any other text file.

Many publications, including this book, started as an outline. Following this organized approach, it is quite easy to create a TOC (table of contents) from the tags applied to each level of the outline. See the example below.

Figure 19.8 shows a five-level table of contents with level two using the Chapter Subheading tag. The instructions for the entry include the tagged subhead, several tab characters and a page number symbol.

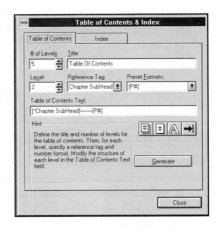

Figure 19.8
The Table of Contents & Index dialog box.

Example: Five-level TOC outline

I. Level One	Chp Heading Tag
II. Level One	Chp Subheading Tag
A. Level Two	Section Heading Tag
1) Level Three	Subsection Tag
a) Level Four	Major Subject Tag
i) Level Five	Example Tag
III. Level One	Chp Heading Tag

When you choose **G**enerate, VENTURA searches for all occurrences of the selected tags, extracts the text tagged by them, and writes a file containing all the tagged text in the order encountered.

N O T E

Before writing the file, VENTURA will ask you for a file name and enable you to select a directory; choose the same directory as your publication. There is no need to add a suffix. VENTURA will automatically add .GEN.

Next, you should open a new chapter, **L**ayout/Add Ne**w** Chapter, and Load **T**ext. Select—VENTURA Generated File (.GEN)—as the import filter. With this text loaded, you can begin to format and modify your table of contents as you would any other text file in VENTURA.

You can also create lists of tags to show the following:

- List of figures
- List of tables
- List of illustrations
- Table of contents
- List of maps
- List of footnotes
- Any other collection of items formatted with specific tags

Each one of these examples of lists can be created by using the TOC and Index dialog box. With it, you select the numbers of levels of a list (similar to levels in normal outlining).

Creating an Index

Creating an index can be a laborious process, but it provides the reader with a more detailed map of locations of subjects than the table of contents. The TOC outlines the document in document order, but the index follows alphabetical order of key words and phrases, regardless of the location. Properly constructed, it is an asset to your publication. The art of this construction lies in forecasting the entries for which your reader may seek. A good index is invaluable for longer, technical documents, and a poorly implemented one detracts from the document's utility.

To construct an index, use the following steps:

- Starting at the beginning of your publication, make a list of all the words and phrases to include in your index, and their page location. Also include major subjects, particularly if they span a page or more.

- Sort the entries into alphabetical sequence.

- Compose the actual index and attach it to the publication.

- Ensure that changes in your document are reflected in the index.

These steps describe roughly the process of creating an index by hand, but the same procedure is followed when using VENTURA. VENTURA provides tools to help automate the index creation, enabling you to concentrate on the content.

To make a list of index words and phases for your index, open the **T**ools/Inde**x** Entries roll-up (Alt F7), shown in figure 19.9.

In figure 19.9, notice that the word "Tagged" is highlighted and selected, and also is listed in the preview section of the Index roll-up. The steps to add this entry are:

1. Select the word or phrase you want to index—in this case, "Tagged."

2. Click on the Index Entries roll-up to make it active. When the roll-up first opens, it does not have focus until you click on it; thereafter, just click on the appropriate button.

3. Choose **M**ain Entry or S**u**b Entry—subentries are maintained alphabetically below their main entry and move to the correct position as you add them.

4. Click on **A**dd to Index List.

You may create the index at any time during this process by pressing **G**enerate. Repetitive generations can be either to the same file to update, or you can create different versions and multiple indexes.

As with TOCs, **G**enerate produces a text file (.GEN) that you will load into a chapter and format in the same manner that you would format any text file.

Figure 19.9

The Index Entries roll-up.

Summary

These supporting files—tables of contents, tables, and indexes—give industrial publishing strength to CorelVENTURA. Once you have set up your table, indexes, and table of contents, VENTURA can update them with ease as your publication grows or is edited.

These publishing tools are relatively independent of the actual content of your document, due to the nature of tagging, so once created, they will apply to future versions of your publication. For example, a magazine or a journal, could be published every month and the table of contents would be automatically generated without redesign.

Fine-Tuning and Printing with VENTURA

*S*o far, this VENTURA-oriented part of CorelDRAW! The Professional Reference *has covered the basic essentials of CorelVENTURA. However, once you've dealt with the generalities of creating a publication, you still will need to make adjustments and attend to details—fine-tuning, in other words.*

Finally, no desktop publication is truly complete until it has been printed out. VENTURA features a wide variety of printing options and output capabilities that are covered in this chapter.

This chapter covers:

- General typography
- Widows and orphans
- Balancing columns
- Spacing and kerning
- Justified type
- Publication manager
- Printing
- Output options

Using Typography

With VENTURA's typography tools, you can precisely tune text. Typically, you apply typography in VENTURA to change either the amount of space your text occupies or how it appears. The space issue is a mechanical one, but the appearance of the type requires some subjective decisions that bring in the "art" of typesetting. VENTURA gives you the interactive ability to take something that looks funny and make it look right. As you work more and more with typography, you may find yourself noticing mistakes in printed material by others.

Once you have placed your frames in position and loaded them with text and graphics, fine tuning begins. Even the most well-planned project can present design problems at this point. In reviewing your document, you may find anomalies such as these:

- The text takes up *more* room than you have space.

- The text takes up *less* room than you have space.

- The next column or page starts with one line.

- Columns have unbalanced amounts of text.

- You have loose lines (too much spacing between words).

These challenges can be quickly answered with VENTURA's advanced typographical controls.

Typographical Controls

Before proceeding, you should familiarize yourself with the key terms relating to typography (if you're not already aware of them).

Typography has special terms to describe spacing of text:

Kerning—Adjusting the space between, usually, two letters. Depending on the shape of letters, the space between them must be adjusted so that it looks right. Typical examples show "AV" and "ML" where you need to move the "V" closer to the "A" to give the same appearance of spacing as between the "M" and "L."

Ems—Pronounced like the letter "M," this is a unit of measure representing a width of space equal to the height of the typeface you are using. It is approximately equal to the width of the letter "M," thus its name. In VENTURA, the size of an "M" is equal to the type size.

Ens—Same as Ems, only half the space.

Tracking—The spacing of letters horizontally. By controlling tracking you can increase or decrease the amount of space a word, line, or paragraph takes. The word "Space" could be: "S p a c e" or "S p a c e".

Leading—Pronounced "ledding," this is the amount of interline space. It is derived from the old printing industry technique where thin strips of lead were inserted between lines of type. If some text occupied 2 inches of space and needed to take up 2.5 inches, the typesetter would increase the leading to make up the difference.

Loose Lines—Occurring only in justified text, lines become "loose" when the spacing between words exceed the Maximum Word Spacing setting in the Paragraph/Typography tab. Generally, this happens because VENTURA has been unable to hyphenate words in your text and must fill in with extra space between words.

Controls for typography are found in three dialog boxes: Chapter, Frame, and Paragraph (both tagged and untagged).

- Chapter Settings contain the highest level of controls for all the frames and all the paragraphs in a chapter.

- Frame Settings can either accept the default values from Chapter Settings or override them in each frame.

- Paragraph Settings respond to the choice of tools—tagged or freeform. It is here that you find the fundamental controls for adjusting the fine spacing between lines, paragraphs, words, and letters.

N O T E

Loose lines will appear in red on your screen if you check L**o**ose Lines in the **T**ools/**P**references dialog box.

VENTURA is designed to allow you to start adjusting your publication at a high level of view, the chapter, and continue down to smaller and smaller segments, ending with a couple of characters. This approach is similar to zooming in with a microscope on a laboratory specimen. The closer you get, the less you see, but you have finer control.

N O T E

With this top-down method, you need only go as far as necessary to resolve the problem. A minor adjustment at the chapter level may, for example, solve a problem of too much space at the end of a column. This saves you from adjusting each frame.

W A R N I N G

Remember! With the Tagged Text tool, changes affect all paragraphs with the same tag, while with the Freeform Text tool changes apply only to the selected paragraph. VENTURA gives you visual clues so that you know what mode is active:

- The tool bar shows the active tool.

- The cursor, when moved over the ribbon bars, shows a tag when the Tagged tool is active.

- The Paragraph Settings dialog box will have a tag icon in the upper right if the Tagged tool is active.

In the following three sections, you will find the options for setting typography controls.

Widows and Orphans

When a paragraph splits across two columns or pages, the part of the text left in the first column is called a *widow*, and the remainder in the next column or page is an *orphan*.

You can control the number of lines allowed in each column by increasing or decreasing the values: **W**idows and Orp**h**ans, in **L**ayout/**C**hapter Settings, Typography tab.

Enter a value from 1 to 5 for **W**idows and Orp**h**ans to specify exactly the number of lines that must remain in the column to prevent widows and orphans. For example, if you always want at least two lines on either side of a column break, enter the value of 2. Likewise, for three lines, enter 3. These two numbers need not be equal.

With these values you dictate how the paragraph can break. You can override these controls on a frame-by-frame basis in Frame Settings. Each frame will accept a value from 1 to 5 or "default," which copies the value set in **C**hapter Settings.

Widows and Orphans Exercise

In this exercise, you will load text into VENTURA and study the effect of widows and orphans controls. First, you will need to set up two frames, one with two columns.

1. Start CorelVENTURA, and in **L**ayout/**C**hapter Settings, choose these settings:

2. Set page size to 8.5 x 11 inches.

3. Set to portrait orientation.

4. Set margins one inch on top, bottom, left and right.

5. Draw two frames, as shown in figure 20.1.

6. Set width to 6.5 inches.

7. Set height to 2.0 inches. Adjust dimensions in Frame Settings.

8. Set the top frame with 2 columns—see figure 20.2.

9. Spin to two columns and gutter of .25 inches.

10. Click on Equal Width to balance the two columns.

11. Turn on **I**nter-Column Rules.

12. Type .05 points into T**h**ickness.

13. Press F2 to zoom and marquee around the two frames to fill the window.

14. Next, you will load in some of the text in Corel's samples. Any text would do, but using this file, your screen will look the same as the figure 20.3.

15. Using **F**ile/Load **T**ext find ABOOK.TXT in Corel50/VENTURA/Typset and load it.

16. Using the Pick tool, click anywhere in the first frame to select it.

17. Choose ABOOK.TXT from the dropdown list in the ribbon bar.

18. Repeat for frame two.

Your screen should look like figure 20.3. Notice how the text automatically flowed through the two columns in frame one, and began again in frame two.

Notice in frame one, column two, that the text stops about two lines from the bottom of the frame but continues into frame two. This white space was caused by the setting of Widows and Orphans (set at 2). Without adjusting inter-line or inter-paragraph spacing, there was not enough room for two more lines and the space between paragraphs.

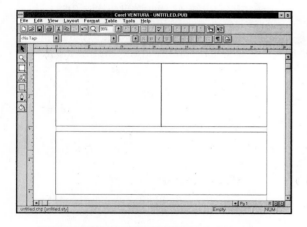

Figure 20.1

Exercise—Layout of blank frames.

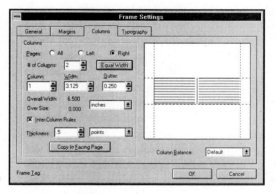

Figure 20.2

Exercise—Frame settings for top frame.

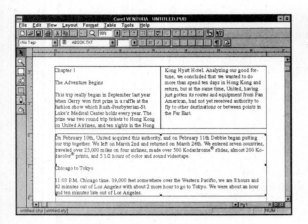

Figure 20.3
Exercise—Two frames with text.

Vertical Justification

Vertical justification controls leading, the space between lines in a paragraph. Almost every printed document runs into this issue—too much or too little text to fill the space. Certainly, you can adjust the size of the type to increase or decease the room your text takes, but usually this is not the best answer. Subtle or small changes to interline spacing can increase or decrease the area occupied by text.

T I P

The objective in vertical justification is to make the text fit the space allotted *without* destroying its appearance. It is better to adjust spacing across large amounts of text with very small increments than to put in larger space between a small number of lines. In the latter case, this would be noticeable and appear to the reader to be a mistake. Therefore, make your spacing adjustments at the highest level that works. Start at the chapter level and work down.

Vertical justification reflects VENTURA's top-down approach. Start with Chapter Settings, then go to Frame and Paragraph.

- In Chapter Settings you dictate the overall look of the entire chapter. In many cases, these controls are sufficient to achieve proper justification without the need for further action.

- In Frame Settings you can adjust vertical justification for a specific frame rather than the whole chapter.

- In Paragraph Settings, you specify the maximum amount of space you will allow VENTURA to apply before and after your paragraphs and the amount of space between the lines of the paragraph. Paragraph Settings also has controls for inter-word and inter-letter spacing.

Using Chapter Vertical Justification

In Chapter Settings, you turn on automatic vertical justification. In the section, Vertical Justification—Within Frame is a drop-down list giving you a choice of Off, Feathering, or Carded.

- Carded justification forces spacing between lines in exact multiples of the interline space specified in Paragraph Settings. For example, if you set 12 points for interline spacing, then VENTURA will add 12, 24, 36 , etc. points of space between lines.

- Feathering, though, allows more flexibility. Using four constraints— Maximum **A**bove, **B**elow, **I**nter-line (Paragraph Settings) and Maximum **J**ustification (Chapter or Frame Settings), VENTURA will attempt to space out your text to fill the space exactly to the bottom of the frame.

N O T E

If VENTURA is unsuccessful with the justification operation and cannot fill the space without exceeding your maximums, then it will not adjust at all. Should this happen, you will need to either readjust your maximums or manually adjust the leading.

Adjusting First Baseline

The First Baseline setting dictates the amount of space between the top of the frame and the top of the first line of text. This option has two choices:

- **Cap-Height**—Aligns the top of the first line (capital height) of the first paragraph with the top of the frame.

- **Inter-Line**—Adds an amount of space, equal to the paragraphs inter-line space, to the top of the first line of the first paragraph.

Normally, you will leave First Baseline in the default position at Cap-Height, but this feature is a good example of VENTURA's attention to typographical controls. Following is the technical explanation of the use of Inter-Line calculation used in professional typesetting.

First Baseline also affects the formula that VENTURA uses for calculating space between paragraphs.

```
Paragraph Spacing = Above/Below +
Inter-paragraph + Inter-line
```

The following conditions apply:

- In all cases, take either the space Above value for the second paragraph or the space Below value for the first paragraph, whichever is *greater*, **PLUS**

- In all cases, add the Inter-Paragraph spacing *if* it is the same for the first and second paragraph, (otherwise—zero) **PLUS**

- One of the four following amounts:

  1) **Cap-Height**—the Inter-Line spacing of the *second* paragraph

  2) **Inter-Line** *and* **type is the** *same* **size in paragraph one and two**—the Inter-Line spacing of the *first* paragraph

  3) **Inter-Line** *and* **type in paragraph one is** *larger* **than paragraph two**—the Inter-Line spacing of the first paragraph *plus* the difference between the type sizes

  4) **Inter-Line** *and* **type in paragraph one is** *smaller* **than paragraph two**—the Inter-Line spacing of the first paragraph *minus* the difference between the type sizes

While this is a very complicated formula, it does illustrate the complete control you have over spacing with VENTURA.

Balancing Columns

VENTURA can automatically balance the text in columns for you with this control. In a multi-column frame, if there is not sufficient text to fill all the columns, then this feature will make the bottom of each column even horizontally across the page.

N O T E

If you have modified **W**idows and Orp**h**ans to other than one line, you may not be able to balance. To force column balance, change the **W**idows and Orp**h**ans setting to 1.

Kerning Letters

Kerning of text refers to adjusting the amount of space between two characters. Because letters have different shapes, two adjoining letters may have a fixed space between them but appear to be farther apart. In figure 20.3 the letters "A" and "W" need to be placed closer to each other than the "W" and the "N". This is caused by the complimentary slopes of "AW".

VENTURA will apply automatic kerning of type if **P**air Kerning is checked. Make note of the following kerning characteristics:

- Kerning of large paragraphs will slow down screen redraw.

- Kerning will affect spacing of paragraphs.

- Kerning amounts can be changed with CorelKERN, a utility program accompanying CorelVENTURA, and are applied font by font.

TIP

Turn on automatic kerning until just before you need to do final vertical justification. Leaving it off until then will increase the speed of screen redraws.

At any time, you can adjust the kerning of any two characters in your document. To manually kern, select the two characters and use the shortcut keys:

- Ctrl+Alt+I to increase kerning
- Ctrl+Alt+K to decrease kerning

You can repetitively apply these keystrokes and watch the movement of the kerning process on the screen. Notice that it is the right character that moves, not the left.

Using Discretionary Hyphenation

A discretionary hyphen, represented by the characters <-> placed in text, gives VENTURA additional ways to hyphenate words. This is useful in fixing loose lines caused by a lack of finding a word in VENTURA's hyphenation dictionary. A discretionary hyphen overrides entries in VENTURA's hyphenation dictionary.

VENTURA will not hyphenate a word that does not occur in its hyphenation dictionary, but you can override this by adding a discretionary. "The Only **u**se Discretionary Hyphens if present" checkbox turns off all other hyphenation, except discretionaires (see fig. 20.4).

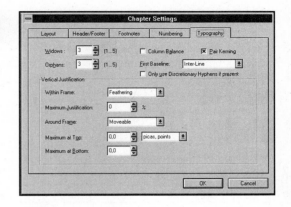

Figure 20.4
The Chapter Settings dialog box—Typography tab.

To place a discretionary hyphen in a word, place a text cursor at that point and press Ctrl+Shift+H. This word will only hyphenate if it is the last word in a line. To verify this action, switch to the Copy Editor (Alt+F10), and you will see the <-> characters that VENTURA placed at the hyphenation point within the word.

Using Frame Vertical Justification

The controls in Frame Settings, as shown in figure 20.5, are normally set to Default, enabling the setting at the chapter level to flow through to frames. The three sections—Widows & Orphans, Text Positioning (First Baseline and Pair Kerning) and Vertical Justification—are duplicated from Chapter Settings but can be overridden here. They will have the same effect on your text as at the chapter level, but only apply to the selected frame.

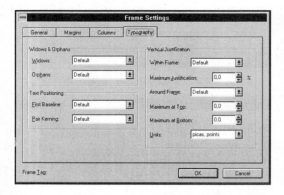

Figure 20.5
The Frame Settings dialog box—Typography tab.

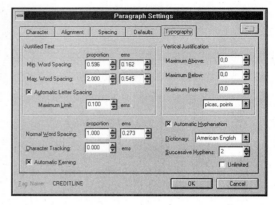

Figure 20.6
The Paragraph Settings dialog box—Typography tab.

Using Paragraph Vertical Justification Settings

The typographical controls in Paragraph Settings, in turn, override setting in both Frame and Chapter Settings. The three sections—Widows & Orphans, Text Positioning (First Baseline and Kerning) and Vertical Justification—are duplicated from Frame Settings but can be overridden here (see fig. 20.6). They will have the same effect on your text as at the frame level, but only apply to the selected tag. As a cautionary note, remember that changes to Paragraph Settings apply to *all* paragraphs that have the same tag.

N O T E

Notice the icon of tag in the upper right-hand corner of figure 20.6. This icon indicates that you are in tag mode (you have planted the Tagged Text tool), and that any changes you make here will be reflected in the tag. The name of the tag is in the bottom left corner.

If this icon is not present (you have planted the Freeform Text tool), you will affect this paragraph only as an override, and the tag will remain unchanged.

Vertical Justification Exercise

Use the page layout and text from the previous exercise.

1. Select **L**ayout/**C**hapter Settings/Typography tab.

2. Set Vertical Justification Within Frame to Feathering.

3. Set Maximum Justification to 100% (see fig. 20.7).

4. Plant the Tagged Text tool in one of the paragraphs in first frame.

5. Select **F**ormat/**P**aragraph Settings/Typography tab.

6. Set all three controls in Vertical Justification to 12 points (see fig. 20.8).

Notice the text in frame one. Because you have set typography controls to allow for adjusting spacing of lines, two lines that were in frame two are now in frame one. The bottom lines in each column now touch the bottom for frame one and show equal line spacing (leading). Compare your results with figure 20.9.

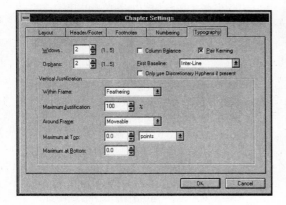

Figure 20.7

Exercise—The Chapter Settings dialog box, Typography tab.

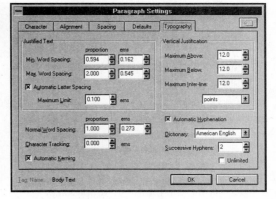

Figure 20.8

Exercise—The Paragraph Settings dialog box, Typography tab.

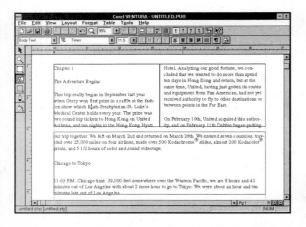

Figure 20.9
Exercise—final results.

Using Word Spacing

Paragraph Settings include controls not found in either Frame or Chapter levels. These determine the spacing of words within a paragraph.

Justified text (text with even margins on both the left and the right) is spaced across the line to fill the space set by the columns or margins.

With settings in the Paragraph Settings dialog box, you limit the proportional amount of space VENTURA can add between words and characters to obtain justification.

- **M**in. Word Spacing—The smallest space VENTURA can put between words.

- **Ma**x. Word Spacing—The largest space VENTURA can put between words.

- Aut**o**matic Letter Spacing—Allows VENTURA to add space between letters.

- Maximum **L**imit—The largest space allowed between letters.

N O T E

Once VENTURA has applied the maximum word and letter spacing, it will try to hyphenate the last word in the line, if possible. If unsuccessful, VENTURA will mark the line as a loose line and display that line in red on the screen. This display can be turned off in the View tab of Preferences, but the line remains loose.

Unjustified text, right-, center-, or left-aligned, does not need the controls of justified text. You can specify the Normal **W**ord Spacing and **C**haracter Tracking to change the space between words and letters.

Typography Summary

VENTURA is an industrial-strength typesetting program. It contains, at various levels, and in an organized progression, all the controls you need to precisely and easily place type.

The following exercise illustrates many of the controls you will use to balance text within a frame:

Publication Manager

When you create a publication in CorelVENTURA, you will probably also create many files. Within VENTURA, you have the following:

- **PUB.** A Publication file is the controlling, high-level file of a VENTURA document that contains pointers to chapter files (see table 20.1).

- **CHPs.** Chapter files contained in the publication with pointers to their style sheets.

- **STYs.** Style Sheet files that list the specifications for all the tags in that style.

- **GENs.** Generated text files—indices, lists, and tables of contents.

Table 20.1
VENTURA File Content

File Type	File Content
Publication (.PUB)	Root Entry CVP Version CV Pub Xref Data CVP Publication Info CVP Pub Index Data Pointers to Chapters
Chapter (.CHP)	Root Entry CVP Version CVP Fill Objects CVP IR Text Data CVP Chapter Info Pointers to Style, Text & Graphic files
Style Sheet (.STY)	Root Entry CVP Version CVP AI Objects CVP Style Sheet Tag List and Specifications
General Text (.GEN)	Indices Lists Tables of Contents

Part of the power of VENTURA is its capability of assembling objects—text, graphics, and tags—located in many files in many locations. Once you point VENTURA to a publication file (.PUB), then VENTURA can find all the files (objects) that comprise it. VENTURA locates files through use of pointers, made up of actual file locations (path and file name).

W A R N I N G

This flexibility and power has a price. The high-level publication file must be notified whenever one of its files is moved or deleted. *For the safety of your publication, always use VENTURA's Publication Manager to copy or move any of the files.*

The Publication Manager operates at two levels: Publication and File.

Using the Publication Level

Shown in figure 20.10, the Publication Manager shows a list of all the publications in your scanned directories. At the right is a list of all the chapters within the selected publication.

Figure 20.10
Publication Manager—Pub Level.

Using the Chapter Level

If you double-click on any publication in the list, its chapters will be enumerated below it. Selecting a chapter will show all the files associated with it in the preview window to the right.

You can drag a chapter in the list to a different position to change the order of chapters in a publication (see fig. 20.11). Chapters may be added or deleted from a publication—but their files will not be deleted from your drive.

If you change the order of your chapters, do not forget to renumber the publication.

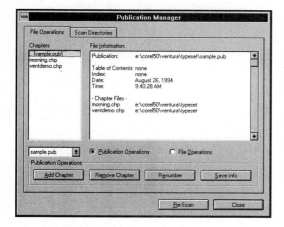

Figure 20.11
Publication Manager—Chapter Level.

Using the File Operations

Switching to File Operations allows you to physically move, copy, and delete files in "Smart Mode." The Publication Manager will insure that pointers are correctly maintained and prevent any file from being deleted that is used by another publication (see fig. 20.12).

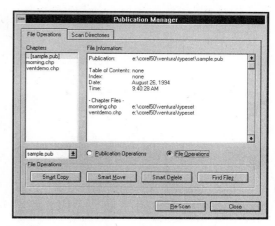

Figure 20.12
Publication Manager—File Operations.

Scanning Directories

By default, the Publication Manager will scan all directories on all your drives looking for publications and chapters. With this tab of the dialog box, you can restrict this search to only those directories that you know contain VENTURA files (see fig. 20.13).

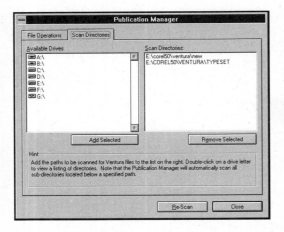

Figure 20.13
Publication Manager—Scan Directories.

Using CVP Fix

The file structure of VENTURA, and its use of pointers to files, has been part of the program through previous releases. Information within the Publication (.PUB) file indicates the locations (drive and directory) of all the chapter (.CHP) files, which in turn have locations of style sheets and all the files that have been loaded into the chapter.

If you move any file with the Windows File Manager instead of VENTURA's Publication Manager, the information stored within VENTURA's files becomes obsolete. The next time you load the publication or one of the chapters, an error will occur when VENTURA can not find all of its files.

CPVFIX.EXE will repair the publication by relocating the files and updating the internal pointers. Run CPVFIX.EXE from Tools, Extensions, or as a standalone program.

T I P

With proper use of the Publication Manager, you should not have to use CPVFIX.

If you do not find an icon for this program installed on your desktop, you can find it in Corel50/Programs directory cvpfix.exe.

Corel has greatly improved the Publication Manager in VENTURA 5.0. It is a very sophisticated program that can be relied upon to perform all file management functions for publications within CorelVENTURA 5.0. Use it with confidence.

Printing with VENTURA

Everything up to this point has been in preparation for the final act: printing. The whole purpose of using VENTURA has been to use its tools to assemble a document that will end up being printed.

You may have selected CorelVENTURA solely on its printing capabilities; VENTURA can print to any device you can hook up to Microsoft Windows. This includes the full range—from the slowest dot-matrix printers right up to the newest stochastic imagesetters. From 10 dpi to 3000. From black-ink only to full color—either composite or complete separations.

This power is brought to VENTURA with CorelDRAW's print engine. When you select **P**rint in VENTURA, you automatically load this unique facility—one that is now shared by all the major Corel applications.

Most documents in CorelDRAW are single pages, although DRAW has long had the capacity for multiple pages. Some consider DRAW an illustration program and VENTURA a page layout application, but the line between them is blurry. The major difference rests in their ability to handle large amounts of text on the design side. VENTURA is engineered for this purpose, but paragraph text in DRAW is challenging.

Planning Your Output Layout

Before you print to a device, it is critical to know its capabilities. If it is your own printer attached to your computer, you probably already have the necessary information. However, if the device belongs to someone else, as on a network, service bureau, or at your commercial printer, you may need to seek advice. Things you need to know include:

- Output paper sizes
- Printable area
- Various DPI settings
- Default screenings
- Standard settings

When your output is headed for a service bureau or a commercial printer, find someone on its staff who can assist you. If the sales staff is a little short of knowledge, ask to speak to someone in production.

N O T E

Over the years, the author has spent much time with production people at commercial printers. They have all been very helpful and more than willing to share their knowledge. Press operators take intense pride in their work and can do some adjusting of colors by controlling ink flow. Strippers, the people who assemble film, can guide you in designing impositions (multiple pages on one piece of film).

Finally, most printers now have computer staffs who will output files to film. The best print professionals have helped the author enormously, providing the right drivers for their imagesetters, proper screening values, and so forth. If you plan to do a lot of film work, get to know the people who will handle your output—they can be a big help.

Using Print Setup

<u>F</u>ile, P<u>r</u>int Setup creates a conversation with your printer driver, the part of Windows that links your printer to an application program. A printer driver translates the print output of a program by adding the specific commands that the printer needs and that are device-dependent. It is critical that you use the correct and most-up-to-date driver, particularly with PostScript printers.

It is in this printer driver that you set device-dependent controls that vary from printer to printer. Common parameters are page size, orientation, screening values (LPI), resolution (DPI), and color variables.

T I P

Many CorelDRAW users have, by practice, used the Windows Control Panel (Print Manager) to change settings in the print drivers. Previous bugs in DRAW printing were fixed with this workaround, and the habit stayed. Today, users continue this practice as an extra piece of insurance and consider it safer than changing the setting from within DRAW. Because VENTURA uses the same print engine, consider following this method.

Using the Print and Print Publication Commands

VENTURA provides two print commands: <u>F</u>ile, <u>P</u>rint and <u>F</u>ile, Print Pub<u>l</u>ication. Print Publication is available only if you have created a publication and desire to print the entire publication at once.

N O T E

In VENTURA's version 5, all selections of printing anything other than the whole publication have been disabled, including booklet printing, but print publication has great promise for the future.

The normal <u>P</u>rint command, which is chapter-oriented, however, does have flexibility. You can choose to print the entire chapter (Curren<u>t</u> Chapter), the current page, or select pages.

Single-page output is easy. Just set printing to C<u>u</u>rrent Page or select certain pages by entering the page numbers. VENTURA recognizes three characters and numbers to choose pages:

- The dash "–" means all pages between two numbers, as in 1–14 means all pages, starting with page 1 and ending with page 14.

- The comma "," is used to separate selection. 1–2,5–6 will print pages 1, 2, 5, and 6.

- The tilde "~" indicates every other page. 1~ will print all odd-numbered pages. 2~ will print all even-numbered pages. 2~8 gives you pages 2, 4, 6, and 8.

Pages are selected in the Print (Ctrl+P) dialog box—see figure 20.14.

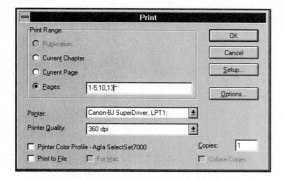

Figure 20.14
The Print dialog box.

Notice in figure 20.14 that pages to print have been entered as "1-5,10,13~". In a 23-page document, this will produce pages 1, 2, 3, 4, 5, 10, 13, 15, 17, 19, 21, and 23.

Using the Options in Printing

Advanced settings for print can be found in the Print Options dialog box. With these options, you have complete control over your printed output.

N O T E

Settings made in the Print Options dialog box are not retained when you exit VENTURA. They do remain, however, while VENTURA is running so you can count on them between print jobs in the same session.

Checking Position

The left hand side of the Print Options dialog box (see fig. 20.15) contains a large thumbnail preview of the placement of your VENTURA page upon the page of the printer (as determined by the page size you set in Print Setup or through the Control Panel's Print Manager).

You have a choice of two views: the default, no preview, displays a gray box proportionate to your VENTURA page size (see fig. 20.16). The other view choice is a detailed preview showing actual text and graphics. This second display, obtained by checking Preview Image, takes considerable time to draw on the screen.

Use this preview in conjunction with its rulers to verify the position and orientation of the image to be printed. A quick look here can save wasted print time.

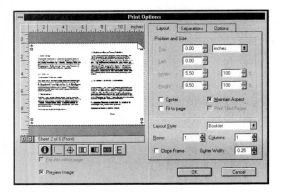

Figure 20.15
The Print Options dialog box—Layout tab.

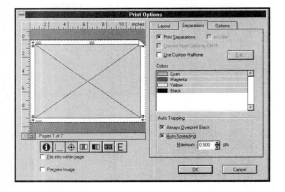

Figure 20.16
The Print Options dialog box—Separations tab.

Using Positioning Controls

The right side of the Print Options dialog box is tabbed. The first tab, Layout, has all the controls for positioning and resizing your printed image, but because they were designed to print files from CorelDRAW, most are usually not needed in VENTURA.

Fit to page, however, can be used to reduce larger pages to fit a desktop printer for proofing.

Using Crop Marks and Registration Marks

Crop marks, registration marks, and file information will be turned on when you select print as separations. They provide enough guides to line up one separation upon another.

Printing Calibration Bars and Densitometer Scales

Choose this button if you are printing full color pictures. This option will place these bars and scales on each separation.

Creating Positives or Negatives

Unless your commercial printer or service bureau tell you otherwise, leave this option strictly alone. The imagesetter will already have this setting made, and if you change it here, you may reverse their setting.

Using Separation Options

If you are printing to a composite color printer (one of the many desktop color laser and bubblejet printers now available) you will print all the colors on one sheet of paper and need not use Separations.

Under the Separations tab (Print **S**eparations) you can choose to print your document as separations. This means that you will get a separate piece of film (for an image setter) or paper (for a laser printer) for each color in your job. The colors that will be produced are listed in this tab and highlighted.

If you are printing a four-color job (CMYK), you should see Cyan, Magenta, Yellow, and Black listed.

Converting Spot Colors to CMYK

The colors listed here are all the colors VENTURA finds in your document. If you have specified spot colors, they too will be listed. You can print these either as spot separations, or have them combined or translated into process colors by checking **C**onvert spots to CMYK. This might occur if, in addition to color pictures, you have chosen a spot color elsewhere. In this case, you would see five colors listed, and if you are producing film, you will get five pieces. Checking the convert option will back the number of colors down to four.

You can also print one separation at a time by unchecking the other colors.

If you have a color printer, you can elect to print your separations in color. Use In Co**l**or found next to Print **S**eparations.

Trapping Your Document

Trapping is a complex subject in printing and worthy of a book by itself. When one image is printed on top of another image, slight misalignment of the paper for one of the images will cause a gap. One type of trapping technique prints one image slightly over the other to close this gap. Spreading is another type of trap.

NOTE

Before attempting any trapping efforts, talk to your commercial printer to find out what, if anything, they want you to do. Some printers will ask you not to trap unless you thoroughly understand the process and their requirements.

The author has frequently had good success using both Always **O**verprint Black and **A**uto-Spreading for most jobs.

Using Options in Print Options

Screen frequency is device-dependent. Some printing devices have fixed screening, while others, notably image setters have frequencies than can be changed. Even though VENTURA will allow you to change this specification in the Print Options dialog box, it is best to change it in your print driver from the Windows Control panel. For most work, do not change it unless your commercial printer or service bureau recommends it.

In the Options tab you can check **A**uto-Increase Flatness if you have some extremely complex images that are producing PostScript errors when you are printing (see fig. 20.17).

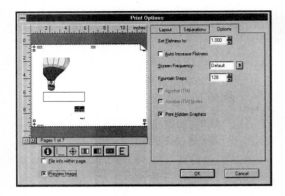

Figure 20.17
The Print Options dialog box—Options tab.

Printing Booklets

Multiple pages printed in combination require planning because sequential pages may not be printed on the same output page.

VENTURA's print engine minds these details for you. Under Options in the **P**rint dialog box, choose Booklet from Layout **S**tyle, and VENTURA will print the pages in the correct order.

N O T E

If you have a duplex printer (one that is capable of printing on both sides of a sheet of paper), booklet printing should produce the pages in the proper order. If you do not, you will have to print all the pages, reshuffle the sheets, turn them over, and print the backs. This will take some experimenting, but first try exchanging sheets 1 and 2, 3 and 4, 5 and 6 and so forth through the end. This process should produce two copies.

N O T E

Printing booklets has been very, very difficult with any page layout program before VENTURA release 5.

Unfortunately, due to time constraints, Corel had to remove booklet printing at the publication level but retained it for chapters. The foundation is in place to build complete publication booklet printing in the next release.

Exercise: Page Sequencing

Suppose your document is designed to contain 16 pages, each 5.5 by 8.5 inches, such that two pages fit exactly on letter-size paper (landscape). Further, the paper is to be printed on both sides, on your laser printer, so that when the result is folded in half, the pages are in order.

1. To better understand page sequencing, take four sheets of letter size paper and fold them together to obtain a cover size of 5.5 inches wide by 8.5 inches high.

2. Next, starting with the cover, number each page in order as they would appear in a booklet.

3. Unfold the sheets and separate them. They should be numbered as in table 20.2. Notice that the only two pages with sequential numbers are pages 8 and 9 in the center of the booklet.

Table 20.2
Booklet Page Order

Sheet	Side	Left Page	Right Page
1	Front	16	1
2	Front	14	3
3	Front	12	5
4	Front	10	7
1	Back	15	2
2	Back	13	4
3	Back	11	6
4	Back	9	8

This method gives you a way to determine page order for any size booklet.

Printing from VENTURA to an Imagesetter

"Going to film" is the common term used to describe printing from VENTURA to an imagesetter. Imagesetters are very high resolution devices that use laser beams to expose film to light and thus write an image. The film is then developed and used to create plates, sheets of metal that are wrapped on the cylinders of the press to produce the printed piece.

Most printers and service bureaus are very Macintosh-oriented. The good outfits recognize that they can accept PostScript files (*.PRN) from the PC community. Steer clear of the ones who seem hesitant with PC files. The major difference between a Mac and a PC PostScript file has to do with Control + D characters in the PC files. This problem is eliminated by checking the For Mac check box in the Print dialog box. Otherwise, the files are functionally identical.

While procedures vary, the following is a good list of steps to take produce your film output:

- Obtain from your service bureau or printer the Windows printer driver for their brand and model of imagesetter. Common imagers are Lino 230, 330, and Afga 7000.

- Ask them also for a list of the specifications they want you to use. These include DPI, screening LPI, dot gain, emulsion up or down, and others. See Chapter 14, "Printed Output," for more information on these controls.

- Install the driver in your system and under Setup and Options configure it for default values given by the list above.

- When you are ready to print from VENTURA, select **F**ile/**P**rint, choose the new driver under printer, and check Print to **F**ile and for **M**ac (if it indeed is going to end up on a Mac).

NOTE

Printing to file is the bridge you need if you do not have the printing device physically attached to your computer. Loading the file on the computer that *is* attached to the device completes the bridge, and the process continues as though there was no interruption.

- Click on Options in the Print dialog box and select the Separations tab. All of the colors in your publication will be highlighted and selected under Colors. If you are doing two-color work, then two colors should be highlighted. Four-color work requires Cyan, Magenta, Yellow, and Black to be highlighted.

- Unless your printer or service bureau prefers each separation to be in a file by itself, clicking on OK here tells VENTURA to print all the separations in one file; otherwise you can choose to print one color per pass.

- Click on OK back in the Print dialog box, and your last step is to choose a file name for your PostScript file.

VENTURA will automatically add .PRN as an extension to your PostScript output. If you view these files with a file editor (MS Write will work), you will see that they contain some rather abstruse text. These are commands to a PostScript interpreter and are quite precise. Very few people in the industry can "read" PostScript and you certainly do not need this skill. If there is a problem with the file, you will rerun, not edit, the file.

Because PostScript is text, it compresses nicely. Most PC-friendly service bureaus and printers are equipped to handle ZIP files produced by PKZip. WINZIP, a very handy utility written by Nico Mak, is a Windows program that will quickly compress your files.

Over the years, Corel has fine-tuned their printing engine for speed, particularly with PostScript. PostScript is the industry standard and wherever possible you should select PostScript printing and PostScript Type 1 fonts.

Obtaining Professional Output

If you are publishing a large document, it will probably take the form of a book. The normal process, in the publishing industry, is to print each page of a book on a high-resolution laser printer (600 dpi or greater). Series of pages are laid out on a table, in the proper page sequence and orientation, and photographed.

The alternative to printing to a laser printer first is to output each page directly to film. These pieces of film are combined to produce larger sheets through a process called *stripping*.

N O T E

You may hear the term *signature*. A signature refers to the layout of pages that will fit a commercial printer's printing press. The size of the press will determine how many pages it can print at a time. This book, for example, is made up of 16-page signatures, bound together to create the book you're reading.

Imposition is the term for placing multiple pages, in the proper orientation, on the output media.

Currently, sophisticated page layouts, which impose multiple pages on large output sheets with signatures of three or more pages, exceed VENTURA's internal capabilities.

Many service bureaus and commercial printers charge for image making by the piece of film. Significant money can be saved by pre-imposing your page output to larger film sizes, reducing the film charges and, possibly, stripping charges (the charge for assembling the film pieces into the size the printer needs).

One product, "Double Up" by Legend Communications, provides professional-level imposition for PostScript files. This program offers you complete control over your output and the signatures it produces. It has many predefined layouts but also provides the tools to customize your own (see fig. 20.18).

Check with your commercial printer to find out what savings are available if you provide imposed film.

For further information on "Double UP," contact them at:

Legend Communications, Inc.
54 Rosedale Avenue West
Brampton, Ontario L6X 1K1
Canada
(905) 450-1010
FAX (905) 455-9702

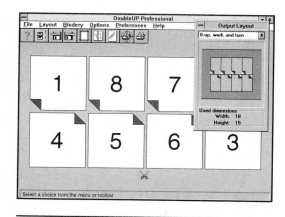

Figure 20.18
View of "Double Up" screen.

Summary

Experienced VENTURA users should find CorelVENTURA version 5 every bit as powerful as they had expected it to be. This is true globally, but especially in fine tuning and printing publications. Today, CorelVENTURA can print to any device that you can attach to Windows. The tweaking features have been automated to the point where users can spend more of their time creating the actual document and less time executing it.

The future holds promise for more sophisticated layouts, among other developments, and Corel is positioning VENTURA to remain the most powerful desktop publishing program of its kind. While this section of the *CorelDRAW! The Professional Reference* has tried to give you a solid foundation of information about VENTURA, you may also want to read New Riders Publishing's comprehensive *Inside CorelVENTURA 5*, to be published in January, 1995.

Part

CorelPHOTO-PAINT

Essential Concepts of Pixel-Based Graphics

This chapter contains very little about the core features and tools of CorelPHOTO-PAINT; instead, it concentrates on a thorough examination of the bitmap format of computer graphics. Unlike CorelDRAW, PHOTO-PAINT doesn't yield artistic results "straight out of the box"; photo-realistic, magnificent designs that are uniquely bitmap in format all contain properties of resolution, gamma, pixels, color depth, and other qualities you have to understand before you can manipulate them.

This chapter provides the ground rules for working with photographic-quality images. In the following chapters, you develop a working methodology to incorporate PHOTO-PAINT into your design life as a creative alternative to CorelDRAW. By exploring the world of raster graphics that PHOTO-PAINT offers, you expand your own abilities to include all types of computer graphics in your professional repertoire.

This chapter covers:

- Raster versus vector images
- Resolution dependence and pixels
- Color depth
- Scanning images
- PhotoCD images
- Anti-aliasing

Understanding Raster versus Vector Format

Today computer graphics are created with two distinctly different file formats; traditionally, they have been created using entirely different sets of tools. Version 5.0 of PHOTO-PAINT is a contrapuntal complement to CorelDRAW's vector design tools; *raster imaging* is the yin to the vector's yang, and the two graphics formats complete a range of design expression for the PC graphics professional.

PHOTO-PAINT 5.0 may come as a surprise for users upgrading from CorelDRAW 3, because it bears almost no resemblance to the former version in interface or in capability. Even PHOTO-PAINT 4.0 had creative limitations that Corel has virtually eliminated in the present version. Because CorelDRAW has been marketed as the star attraction of the Corel bundle, many experienced users may initially have side-stepped PHOTO-PAINT as a valuable creative tool. An unfamiliarity with the bitmap format of computer graphics is often the reason for users overlooking PHOTO-PAINT's rich feature set. PHOTO-PAINT's tools and interface operate similarly to those of CorelDRAW, but you necessarily achieve different effects because bitmaps are not the same as vectors.

The good news is that PHOTO-PAINT is now part of a tightly integrated software suite. The more familiar you become with CorelDRAW, the more your skills can be ported to PHOTO-PAINT to produce outstanding effects and editing work in a unique medium.

Much of the mystique that shrouds digital photography and the creation of realistic (and surrealistic) images has to do with concepts and procedures that fundamentally differ from vector designs produced in CorelDRAW. To produce excellent work in PHOTO-PAINT, you need an understanding of display and memory requirements, as well as a grasp of how a raster (or *bitmap*) imaging program writes a file format.

Most people stick with what works best for them. When you are conditioned to expect immediate results, you may quickly lose interest in a "different" program, such as PHOTO-PAINT. If you spend some time experiencing the flip side of computer graphics with PHOTO-PAINT, however, you discover a medium of expression that is more subtle and delicate, more demanding of your creative talents, and ultimately more rewarding.

Examining Raster Graphics Terminology

Before diving into the whys and wherefores of the bitmap images you can manipulate in PHOTO-PAINT, you need to learn some of the terminology that is associated with pixel graphics. When you are seeking direction, an understanding of the local language is always important. The following list briefly defines some terms used in raster imaging:

- **Pixel.** A *pixel* is a unit of light and the basic building block of a raster graphic. Although a pixel can be displayed on the monitor as a collection of RGB phosphor groups, it cannot be divided any smaller than one whole unit. Pixels are also referred to as "dots," but this terminology is quite confusing and imprecise. PHOTO-PAINT measures raster images in dots per inch (dpi); strictly speaking, pixels per inch is a better phrase of measurement, especially when you are dealing with a service bureau or commercial printer for output.

- **Raster graphic.** A *raster graphic* is also called a bitmap graphic or a pixel-based graphic. All three terms refer to the technology behind a specific type of computer graphic. Bits of color information (expressed as pixels) are mapped to a fixed dimension background. Raster graphics are quite unlike vector graphics in that raster graphics are resolution-dependent; in

other words, bitmap images cannot be increased in size without distorting the original image information.

- **Sampling.** *Sampling* is a term used to describe the digitizing process a scanner or digital camera performs on a source image. Scanner manufacturers frequently refer to the incremental measurement of a digitized image as dots per inch (dpi) or pixels per inch. In this chapter's discussion about the resolution of a scanned image, the dpi terminology is used, as well as the more accurate terminology of samples per inch.

- **Resampling.** When you stretch or shrink a pixel-based image using PHOTO-PAINT's features, you are changing the number or size of the samples/inch of the original image. The process is called *resampling*, which means you are respecifying the sample ratio and/or size with which an image was originally acquired or created.

Mapping Bits of Color Information

The fundamental difference between work produced in a vector design program (such as CorelDRAW) and work created with the raster imaging program PHOTO-PAINT is in the way in which graphical information is arranged on-screen and written to a file format. To oversimplify for a moment, vector graphics are saved to a file format as a

description of the geometry you design in the workspace along with the color properties you assign to the geometry. Vector images are stored in files as mathematical equations—no actual, visible image is saved.

The Basis of a Vector Image

Suppose you draw a Desert Blue ellipse in CorelDRAW in the upper left of the Printable Page, and this ellipse has a .028" Moss Green outline. If you save this image, only the essential information is written to file: namely, the center of the ellipse relative to the Printable Page, the distance the ellipse extends along the X and Y coordinates of the page, the breadth of the outline, and (by default in CorelDRAW) the CMYK values for Desert Blue and Moss Green.

If a vector graphic seems like a neat, succinct bundle you can open later and get exactly the same design again, that's because it is. Vector designs are also called *resolution-independent* designs because they can be scaled up or down with no loss of image detail. If you were to make the Desert Blue ellipse twice its original size on CorelDRAW's Printable Page, the values of its X and Y coordinates would be multiplied by a percentile, its center relative to the Printable Page would be reassigned, but almost everything that mathematically describes the essence of the ellipse would remain a constant.

Vector Images Made Tangible

A vector design would therefore seem to be not actually palpable; it appears for a fleeting moment as you create it, only to become a string of mathematical references and values stored in a file format. To make a vector design something visible, malleable, and workable, Corel Corporation decided to *rasterize* a vector design to the screen and to continue to update the raster screen display as you continue to design and edit.

Rasterizing and raster graphics are achieved with pixels (units of light values) that are arranged across a figurative grid (or map) across the screen, generally in sequence from top to bottom and from left to right. On a computer with a 386 processor and less than 8MB RAM, you may actually view the rasterizing of a vector graphic in CorelDRAW as it redraws the screen after an edit.

Raster graphics belong to the "paint" family of computer graphics (such as PHOTO-PAINT), in which a pixel of color information with a color capability (*bit depth*) is mapped to a grid so that it has a special coordinate relative to the background. Thus the term *bitmap* was coined. CorelDRAW shows you a bitmapped representation of a vector design so that you can see it and edit it on-screen; however, the saved vector design contains no actual raster information, only mathematical values. This distinction is a constant source of confusion among users who expect a screen capture of a

CorelDRAWing to be editable within CorelDRAW, and who anticipate that a Shape tool would naturally be included in PHOTO-PAINT's feature set.

To date, the best analogy computer graphics people have been able to formulate about vector and raster design programs is as follows: a vector is analogous to a pencil—sharp, precise, and constant; whereas a raster is analogous to a paintbrush—soft, flexible, and dependent on a canvas (imaginary bitmap grid) to render design work.

Raster Image Dependence on a Background

In the earlier example of the Desert Blue ellipse, you may have noted that the term "background" was absent. Vector images have no background as such; objects you draw in CorelDRAW have special coordinates relative to the page, but the page and the size of the ellipse can be changed at whim. Vector images have no background grid coordinates and therefore no pixels and no constraints. By contrast, raster images must by definition contain a foreground element (one pixel or several) and a background on which the pixel is precisely located. This necessity of having a background is the reason that bitmapped images typically have larger file sizes than do vector graphics—much larger sizes. A small photo-realistic bitmap can easily be 4MB, and 40MB files are not unheard of. If your design consists of a single dot on a large background, the *entire* background must be stored in a bitmap-based file.

Raster Images and Resolution

The natural question arises about how to reduce the size of a bitmap file: If I make the dimensions of my virtual canvas smaller, won't the overall file size also become smaller? The answer is yes, but at the expense of *resolution*. Raster images are resolution-dependent; a raster image (or photograph) occupies a height and width of fixed dimensions that a finite number of pixels fills. If you change the dimensions of a bitmapped image by resampling it, you change the design—sometimes obviously and sometimes unpleasantly.

The resolution of a raster image is measured in pixels per inch. A *pixel*, or unit of light, is the building block of a raster image, and yet pixels have no fixed dimensions until they are determined when you scan an image or create a new image in PHOTO-PAINT. Resolution is inversely proportional to a raster image's dimensions in inches. In effect, a 2" by 2" raster image with a resolution of 300 dpi is identical to the same image at 4" by 4" with a 150-dpi resolution. PHOTO-PAINT can change image dimensions while maintaining resolution, but the price you pay is in the quality of the image itself. The reason is that an image is scanned or created in PHOTO-PAINT with a fixed amount of information contained within it that can't be altered without destroying or distorting the image.

The best way to demonstrate a raster image's dependence on resolution is to open a new file in PHOTO-PAINT, create a simple design, and then change the dimensions by

resampling while maintaining image resolution. In the following example, you see an effect called pixelation. *Pixelation* is the loss of image quality when the "building blocks" of a raster image are forced to display more visual information than they were originally designed to portray.

1. Choose **F**ile, then **N**ew (or press Ctrl+N, or use the New button on the ribbon bar).

2. Choose 24-bit Color in the **C**olor Mode drop-down list, choose inches for both the width and height, and enter **2** in the **W**idth and **H**eight fields for your new "canvas."

3. In the Resolution field, enter **96** for both the H**o**rizontal and **V**ertical dpi values; then click on OK.

4. Click and hold down the Rectangle tool to reveal the menu flyout, and then choose the Polygon tool. This tool creates polygonal shapes consisting of straight lines with fill and outline attributes. For this example, you need to see the visible effects of the outline surrounding the polygonal shape, so set the **S**ize field on the Tool Settings roll-up at least 4 pixels. The color of the fill is unimportant, but make sure that the color of the outline is dark. Press Ctrl+F2 to display the Colors roll-up, and select a dark color for the outline.

5. Design a triangle by clicking once to start the polygon, moving the cursor to the second corner location and clicking, then double-clicking where the third corner of the triangle should

be to make PHOTO-PAINT rasterize the design. As you see in figure 21.1, there's nothing extraordinary or harsh-looking about the outline, because 72 to 96 dpi is the average resolution of monitors. Simply put, you can't view stairstep (jaggy) edges in the pixels of the design at 100-percent viewing size because your monitor basically matches the resolution of the image.

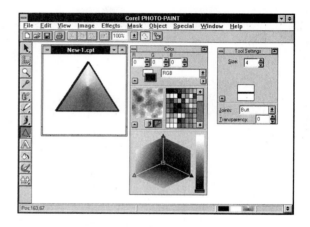

Figure 21.1
When image resolution matches that of your monitor, pixel stairsteps are not apparent.

6. Choose R**e**sample from the **I**mage menu. In the Resample dialog box, choose inches from the **U**nits drop-down list. In the **W**idth and **H**eight fields, choose 200 percent for the resampled image size. In the **P**rocess field, choose Stretch/Truncate. Notice that the New Image Size is four times the Original Image Size. The reason is

that you're mapping twice the horizontal and twice the vertical dimensions of your original design. Your screen should look like figure 21.2.

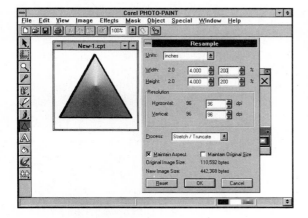

Figure 21.2

Resampling an original image can change pixel sizes and image file sizes.

7. Click on OK. By default, PHOTO-PAINT does not perform alterations on an original image but creates a new image instead. You can now compare the original image with the resampled image.

8. Chances are you see a noticeable harshness in the resampled image along the diagonal outlines on your own monitor. Figure 21.3 shows both images zoomed in at 200 percent, so that you can get a good view of what has happened.

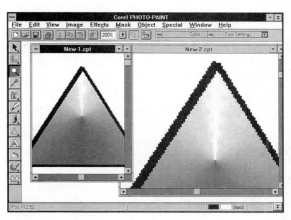

Figure 21.3

Pixelation is the visible deterioration of image quality due to resampling.

Bitmap image programs have a difficult time representing diagonal lines (like those that make up the triangle in the preceding example), because the grid that a raster program uses to map pixels is made up of "lines" that intersect at right angles. Right angles are infrequently found in nature, however, and a naturalistic design usually contains an angle anywhere between 0 degrees and 90 degrees, but not *exactly* a right angle. The bitmapped pixels can fit into the grid only by filling the horizontal and vertical matrices. The difficulty in displaying non-right-angle designs becomes more apparent when you "sample up" a raster image; the pixels (of which there are a fixed number per inch in the preceding example) are forced to represent the same image at greater physical dimensions. The pixels become enlarged, and their square-ish property is apparent.

Similarly, when you increase the number of pixels per inch and maintain image dimensions, PHOTO-PAINT must create new pixels in the image based on information about the pixels presently occupying image areas. In either situation, pixelation can become evident. Pixelation is an effect equivalent to holding a photograph so close to your eyes that you see more film grain than image detail.

N O T E

Anti-aliasing can help to soften the harsh, stairstep effect of pixelation. The way in which anti-aliasing is used in PHOTO-PAINT is explained toward the end of this chapter.

Optimal Resolution for Images

Determining the best resolution for acquiring an image through scanning, or for creating a new image destined for commercial presses, is a matter that requires input from whoever is performing your output. As odd as it might seem, you're typically better off starting a design *after* you know what resolution your final output is capable of handling.

Operators of a commercial press can usually tell you the lines per inch (lpi) value used to screen a continuous-tone photo to make camera-ready art, as well as the angle used on color separations to prevent moiré patterning in the printed image. You should adopt the

values of a commercial press's and any additional information concerning what percentage of black can be used in an image. Chapter 27 discusses the details of outputting your work. If you need ballpark estimates immediately, however, the following are recommendations for image resolutions based on the assumption that you will print an image at 100 percent of its original dimensions:

- For newsletter-quality publications, scan or create an image in PHOTO-PAINT at 150 dpi. This value yields an image whose commercial press resolution is approximately 75 lpi and that renders to the printed page at 1200 dpi.

- For magazines, books, or other high-quality publications, use 300- to 350-dpi sampling. These values yield a line-screen value of about 133 to 150 lpi and that renders to the printed page at approximately 2540 dpi.

- For most laser printers, a 75- to 100-dpi raster image fits the bill more than adequately. Laser printers of 300 to 600 dots per inch cannot render more than about 50 to 60 lines per inch without visible degradation of image quality; such laser printers are therefore unsuitable for reproducing camera-ready images. If your intended output is a laser printer, or if you want an image for display on your monitor as part of a presentation, your resolution does not need to exceed 100 dpi.

Color Capability of Pixels

The pixels that make up a bitmapped image have color capability; that is, you have a selection of how wide a range of color expression an image file has when you open a new file. Color capability is qualified in bits per pixel (bit depth), and several standards have been established for raster image graphics that have more colloquial, familiar names.

If you have used the Windows 3.*x* Paintbrush utility, for example, you have probably noticed that the range of color values you can use is limited. The reason for this limited range is that Windows itself has native support for only 16 unique colors. You can access additional colors only by using a video card and monitor that support enhanced color modes and by using a program that can handle more than 16 colors, such as PHOTO-PAINT.

Color Modes and Image Formats

If you are scanning an image to edit in PHOTO-PAINT, you can choose from several color-capability modes that the scanner manufacturer builds into the hardware. Both hand-held and flatbed scanners are color-capable today; and although options vary from model to model, most TWAIN-compliant scanners support at least one color and one monochrome mode with which you can acquire a digital sampling of a source image.

A scanning session in PHOTO-PAINT differs from a session in which you open a new file from within the program. A scanning session produces an image possessing the color mode you specify at the time you scan the image. The color modes that a middle-of-the-road scanner offers roughly correspond to the **C**olor Mode options found in both PHOTO-PAINT's Create a New Image dialog box menu and the **I**mage, Con**v**ert To command on the menu. In table 21.1, you see the name of a color-capability mode, the bit depth of the mode, and the maximum number of unique color values the mode accepts.

Most physical things that you can fit beneath a scanner platen can be digitally sampled in one or more of these color modes to produce a faithful reproduction. PHOTO-PAINT and some scanners offer a screen or halftone mode that cannot truly be considered a color mode. Instead, halftone screens are used to prepare an image for a commercial printer. Halftone screens arrange the pixels of a digital image into a pattern of dots that commercial printers can successfully use when they reproduce the image with dots of ink on paper. You can't really perform any editing on a halftone image in PHOTO-PAINT, because the source information has been digitized into patterns of dots.

Table 21.1
Color Modes

Common Name of Mode	Bit Depth	Maximum Number of Unique Colors
Line art (black-and-white)	1 bit/pixel	2
Halftone	1 bit/pixel	2
Grayscale	8 bits/pixel	256
HiColor	15 bits/pixel	32,768
HiColor	16 bits/pixel	65,536
RGB	24 bits/pixel	16.7 million

Black-and-White (Line Art) Color Mode

Black-and-white, 1-bit/pixel, color-capable images are the lowest mode of digital images. A black-and-white image represents a design through either turning a pixel on (white) or turning a pixel off (black). This is the maximum amount of information one binary digit (bit) can represent for a single pixel. The Black-and-White color mode obviously has severe limitations and usefulness in serious image editing work, and a 1-bit/pixel scan is best used only to acquire pen and ink drawings. Valuable color information in an original is discarded when the color threshold of a scanner is set to acquire in Black-and-White color mode. Furthermore, the information discarded by scanning an image in black and white cannot be retrieved by PHOTO-PAINT.

In addition, some of PHOTO-PAINT's tools do not work with a 1-bit/pixel black-and-white image. When a 1-bit/pixel image mode is assigned to the active window, for example, the Smear and the Paintbrush tool icons appear dimmed, and gradient and texture fills appear as a mass of dithered pixels instead of a recognizable image element.

Grayscale Color Mode

A *continuous tone* black-and-white photograph can be represented as a digital image using 8 bits/pixel. As shown in table 21.1, a pixel containing 8 bits of information can express 256 unique color values. In the case of a grayscale image, all the unique color values are various intensities of neutral gray colors from 0 (absolute black) to 255 (absolute white). If you want to add a color to a digital image that has Grayscale color mode, you must use PHOTO-PAINT's **I**mage, Con**v**ert To command to change the image mode to one of color capability.

Indexed Color

The Indexed color mode is not a color mode scanners support. Indexed color doesn't exist in real life; instead, it is a color-mapping scheme you can use with images already acquired or with new images you create in PHOTO-PAINT. *Indexing* an image is a process carried out by PHOTO-PAINT and other imaging programs in which a limit is set to the number of unique colors contained in a saved file format. The most common formats for indexed color images are .PCX, .GIF, and .BMP; any of these formats save indexed color information faithfully.

Generally, the purpose of an indexed color image is for PC presentations or online service downloads. Most designers who save to an Indexed color mode also save a copy of the original image with its full color capability intact. A designer might want to take a full-color image and reduce the number of colors to an indexed format for the following three reasons:

- Indexed color images occupy less space on the hard disk or floppy disk. Full-color, RGB images (explained in the following "RGB Color Mode" section) can take up massive amounts of disk space because of their color capability. In contrast, indexed color images display a fair to good amount of original color information in some-times a third of the file space.

- Indexed color images are ideal for display in other programs that lack the color capability of PHOTO-PAINT. Consider the following examples. An image that's a candidate for Windows wallpaper must be saved in the .BMP format and must have a color index of no more than 256 unique values; an indexed color image is an ideal candidate. Although CorelSHOW accepts RGB color images, an indexed color image inserted in a frame redraws much faster, because an indexed color format contains less information than an equivalent RGB image. When you are creating electronic slide shows with CorelSHOW, Microsoft PowerPoint, or other programs, keep in mind that the image must not only display but also animate as it dissolves to the next frame. Computer animation requires a hefty amount of RAM and free hard disk space; therefore, the less you ask your PC to process, the quicker the animation occurs.

- Your client might not have a system as color-capable as yours. A full-color image can display poorly on a system whose video driver is capable of handling only 256 colors. When you are designing a logo, presentation, or other graphics for businesses, you often have to "play to the cheap seats." The business community has a kernel of imaging experts whose professions demand high-quality images. Outside of desktop publishing, filmmaking, service bureaus, commercial printers, and digital photography, however, there is a severe drop-off in the quality of color that businesses are accustomed to or can handle. Indexed color is a happy middle ground in color capability that suits the general needs for many businesses.

RGB Color Mode

RGB color needs to be discussed in tandem with indexed color, because you usually start with an RGB image and then create an indexed image from the RGB image.

An RGB image consists of three color channels; the level of intensity of each primary color component is expressed as a range from 0 to 255 in a Red, Green, and Blue color channel. You generally view an RGB image from a composite view of these three color channels. Because each color channel is capable of 256 unique shades, 8 bits/pixel is the expression used to define color capability within each channel. Three channels multiplied by 8 bits/pixel produces the 24-bit RGB image. An RGB color mode image is capable of displaying 16.7 million unique color values; this number is arrived at by multiplying 2 to the 24th power (256 colors is 2 to the 8th power, and so on).

At present, display systems for PCs are capable of rasterizing 24-bit color using an appropriate driver. TrueColor (spellings vary from manufacturer to manufacturer) is the name most video card manufacturers and others use to describe RGB, 24-bit color capability.

When you are working with images in PHOTO-PAINT, RGB color is the mode of preference for many reasons. The primary reasons are as follows:

■ Color scanners generally sample sources in the RGB mode.

■ RGB images, when edited and viewed using a 24-bit color video driver, display no screen dithering (an annoying phenomenon covered in the next section).

■ You have more control over color reduction when you convert an RGB image to another color mode.

RGB images can be quite large if the image dimensions and resolution are high. Before you create a graphically sumptuous, high-resolution image, you should make sure your PC has sufficient RAM and free hard disk space. The best file formats for saving RGB images are Targa (.TGA), .TIF, and PHOTO-PAINT's proprietary .CPT. The .CPT file format cannot be read by other applications. The .CPT format is designed to accommodate CorelDRAW's Layers feature, and you cannot save discrete image objects from session to session in any other format. .TIF and .TGA formats are especially useful when you are working with a service bureau that doesn't own CorelDRAW 5. Because .TIF and .TGA images are device-independent formats, they can be opened and printed from any program and any kind of computer that understands these formats.

Indexed Color Images

PHOTO-PAINT offers three tiers of color capability for images converted to indexed color: black-and-white, 16 colors, and 256 colors. When an RGB image undergoes color reduction to qualify for the Indexed color mode, a custom color lookup table can be created for the image. This color lookup table (referred to by Corel as a *color palette*) contains the exact color formula (example: R=255, B=137, G=239) for each color present in an image. In a 256-color mode,

256 color registers are filled with unique colors intended to represent an RGB original image. In a 16-color mode, 16 colors are applied from a lookup table to color the pixels in an image.

Color reduction from RGB to indexed obviously creates inaccurate portrayals of original image areas. Tens of thousands of unique colors are present in an average RGB scan of a photo, and a 256-color indexed image must simulate the "missing" colors through a process called *dithering*.

Uniform Palette and Dither Options

PHOTO-PAINT offers two lookup table schemes (color palettes) and two methods of dithering an image from a greater color capability to a lesser one. When you are converting an image, you shouldn't automatically accept PHOTO-PAINT's defaults, because the results may be less than aesthetic.

By default, PHOTO-PAINT won't touch your original RGB file; instead, it creates a New-*n*.CPT image when you change the color modes of a file. This New-*n*.CPT image enables the PHOTO-PAINT user to experiment with the conversion options and greatly reduces the possibility of ruining an original file.

To convert images to different color modes, you need to examine the content of each image on a case-by-case basis to decide which color reduction options will provide the best-looking indexed image. In figure 21.4, you see an RGB image whose theme is tropical. The picture has a bright, contrasting

assortment of colors—somewhat like evenly dispersed spectral confetti. This .TIF image has over 51,000 unique color values.

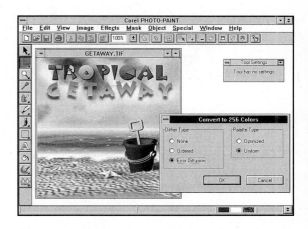

Figure 21.4
PHOTO-PAINT offers color palette and dithering options for converting between image color modes.

When you cram 51,000 colors into an index containing only 256 registers, scores of unique color values are discarded. The rest of the original values are either lost or approximated, depending on which options you choose.

The Palette Type field in the Convert to 256 Colors dialog box (see fig. 21.4) refers to the type of lookup table PHOTO-PAINT builds for the image. A Uniform palette consists of a lookup table in which all 256 of the indexed colors represent the visible spectrum with an equal amount of frequency; in other words, as much color space is given to red as to blue, and so on. Uniform is generally the best choice of palettes when an image is made up

of many different colors. Photos of beach balls, rainbows, and crowd scenes fare better when they are converted to 256 colors using a Uniform palette. No particular emphasis is given to any range of the color spectrum.

By default, PHOTO-PAINT offers None in the Dither Type section of the Convert to 256 Colors dialog box. *Dithering* is the interlacing of color values found in a limited color palette to simulate a color not present. If an indexed image has no color register for orange, for example, red and yellow pixels are dispersed in equal amounts across an image area to simulate orange.

PHOTO-PAINT offers two dithering options: Ordered and Error Diffusion. Ordered dithering (also called *pattern dithering*) produces a latticework of color pixels in an image to represent most of the original values of an RGB image. Error Diffusion dithering spreads alternating color pixels across an indexed image to simulate the color values found in the original. The way you want dithering to occur in a color conversion is a matter of personal preference. Error diffusion takes more time to process, but it often produces more eye-pleasing results.

In figure 21.5, an RGB image has been dithered down to 256 indexed colors using Ordered dithering. Note that the most glaringly unpleasant effects occur when you are dithering an image of a gradient fill.

Gradient fills consist of subtle tonal changes within an image, and 256 colors aren't enough to represent the gradient.

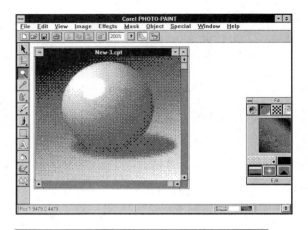

Figure 21.5
An ordered dither produces patterns of colors to represent the eliminated original colors.

In figure 21.6, Error Diffusion dithering has been applied to the same image. Neither type of dithering can compensate for color reduction during conversion. If you choose None, however, sharp banding appears in an image where gradients were found in the original, because PHOTO-PAINT assumes that you want the colors reduced to the nearest ones found in the color palette.

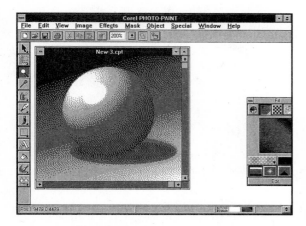

Figure 21.6
Error diffusion spreads pixels across an indexed image in a random pattern.

When To Use an Optimized Palette

In the last section, a Uniform palette was specified for reducing the number of colors in an RGB image. At times, however, an Optimized palette produces better-quality, limited palette images.

An Optimized palette is actually a custom lookup table. When you check Optimized as the Palette Type in the Convert to 256 Colors dialog box, PHOTO-PAINT "weighs" the color table for the image with colors most frequently found in the original RGB image. Pictures with one predominant color value, such as sunsets or the ocean, are good candidates for an Optimized palette. In figure 21.7, you see an RGB illustration of fading twilight behind some lettering.

Because a twilight doesn't have a lot of different colors, PHOTO-PAINT can create an Optimized palette that gives more registers to shades of blue than to colors like yellow or green that fail to appear in this design.

Figure 21.7
Choose Optimized palette when your image contains much more of one single hue than others.

In PHOTO-PAINT, the 256 (Indexed) color mode is the only truly reasonable alternative to multichannel, high-color design color capabilities. A color palette of 16 or fewer colors cannot express images with any sense of photo-realism. This fact notwithstanding, software authors and people compiling online documents such as Windows Help files are obliged to use a 16-color palette owing to Windows 3.*x*'s native color support of only 4 bits/pixel for the interface.

CMYK Modes

PHOTO-PAINT 5 offers on-the-fly CMYK color conversion. *CMYK* (Cyan, Magenta, Yellow, blacK) is a four-channel color model used to produce color separations for camera-ready, commercial color printing. CMYK is a 32-bit color model, which is usually not found as an acquisition option on inexpensive scanners because of the additional processing and resolving power necessary to create the four channels.

Additionally, each color channel in an image adds substantially to overall file size and RAM requirements. PHOTO-PAINT needs at least three times an image's file size in available system RAM to offer editing capabilities and multiple Undo commands. After editing an RGB image, CMYK is the color mode you would choose last. Few people work in this mode, except to perform last-minute color corrections.

PHOTO-PAINT automatically corrects out-of-gamut colors in an RGB image when you convert from RGB to CMYK. You will notice a dullness to a CMYK image when you compare it to the same image as an RGB, because CMYK colors more closely resemble the result of color inks printed to paper. Naturally, this CMYK representation that PHOTO-PAINT displays on-screen uses the red, green, and blue phosphors of your monitor, but PHOTO-PAINT offers a fairly accurate representation of CMYK inks on an RGB monitor nonetheless. Ink on paper does not have the luster and life that excited phosphors on your monitor have, and there are simply some colors you can view on-screen that won't reproduce as four inks

laid on top of each other on a page will. Light is additive, and pigment is subtractive; PHOTO-PAINT intelligently estimates how much a given color in an image has to be "pulled in" to be a color that can be accurately printed.

HiColor Mode

HiColor is not exactly a color mode, but it is a color *capability* that video card and scanner manufacturers offer. HiColor was developed as a trade-off between 24-bit color and indexed color. Depending on the manufacturer of your video card or scanner, HiColor can be either 15-bit (32,768 colors) or 16-bit (65,536 colors).

As mentioned earlier, neither of the figures in the dithering/color palette experiment contains more than 65,000 unique values, and yet they both required a 24-bit/pixel, 16.7 million color mode and file format to save every color value represented in the design accurately. In such figures, the HiColor scheme becomes a valuable option for viewing and perhaps even for scanning full-color, continuous-tone images. Unless you're scanning a photo of the Mardi Gras, your average snapshot may have only tens of thousands of unique colors. If your scanner supports 15- or 16-bit/pixel sampling, try out HiColor sometime. You might be surprised by the clarity and richness with which an image is acquired. Additionally, a video card running a 16-bit/pixel driver can display a 24-bit/pixel RGB image with nearly total fidelity, if the driver isn't required to map more than 65KB of unique colors to the monitor.

The advantage of viewing your editing work in HiColor display mode is that you're not taxing your video system as much as when you use a 24-bit driver and therefore you'll be able to work a little quicker with your present hardware investment. As far as PHOTO-PAINT is concerned, it "sees" a 15- or 16-bit image as a 24-bit/pixel file. A file acquired with a 16-bit scan takes up the same hard drive space as a 24-bit image when it is saved, and all of PHOTO-PAINT's tools can be used to edit a HiColor image.

Monitor Calibration and PHOTO-PAINT

Color Manager is a new feature of PHOTO-PAINT 5 as well as of the other CorelDRAW modules. Before you begin serious image editing work, you owe it to yourself to pay a visit to this utility. Monitors should display the same color capability as your image mode, and they should accurately reflect the values on-screen as they are saved to an image file format. Service bureaus and other imaging centers aren't paid to care whether their system reads your PHOTO-PAINT image as too dark or too light; you'll simply receive mismatched output. All the color modes discussed earlier also apply to your monitor, and matching color capability is the first step toward accurately viewing and editing your work.

Video Resolution and Color Capability

Table 21.2 shows a sampling of video drivers available for a typical VESA adapter card with 1MB of VRAM. The video card you use may have different resolutions and color depths available, but most vendors offer the following standard capabilities:

Table 21.2
Video Driver Configurations

Configuration	Standard Name	Ideal for Viewing/Editing
640×480/16 colors 800×600/16 colors 1024×768/16 colors	VGA	Screen captures
640×480/256 colors 800×600/256 colors	SVGA	Indexed color images
640×480/65KB colors 800×600/65KB colors	HiColor	RGB images
640×480/16MB colors	TrueColor	RGB images

As the number of pixels displayed across the monitor increases, your options for color depth decrease. This limitation is mathematical: 1MB video cards don't have the power to offer panoramic screen displays and pixel color depth simultaneously. For TrueColor display at high screen resolutions, you need a video adapter (card) with more than 1MB of memory.

When you run a display at a resolution higher than the standard 640×480, you gain screen real estate. PHOTO-PAINT has 25 roll-ups available, and although you may not need every one rolled down in one editing session, elbowroom is at a premium in the confines of a standard viewing resolution. Figure 21.8 is a view of PHOTO-PAINT's workspace using a 640×480/16MB-color video driver. Figure 21.9 displays the same layout of PHOTO-PAINT roll-ups with an 800×600/65KB-color video driver running.

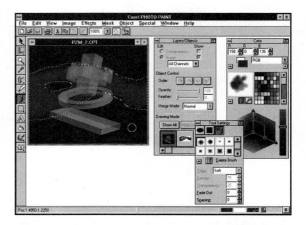

Figure 21.9
An 800×600 viewing resolution creates more room on PHOTO-PAINT's workspace.

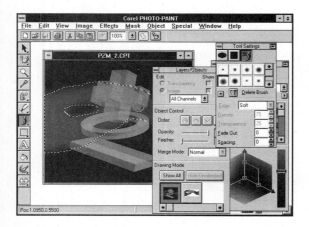

Figure 21.8
With more than three roll-ups extended, workspace for an image is reduced on a 640×480 screen.

Corel Color Management

The interrelationship between your monitor, the images you produce in PHOTO-PAINT, and the method of acquiring images through a scanner or PhotoCD is based on color accuracy. To this end, CorelDRAW 5 offers a comprehensive Color Manager in each Corel module that you can use to adjust inconsistencies in color values you might view or scan.

Perhaps you have been sending your finished images to a service bureau or other imaging service, and you have been disappointed with the results. A leading cause of poor-quality images is that your system isn't calibrated to the same specifications as those of the service bureau you use. Imaging centers earn their living producing printed images on film and paper. If your images are coming back washed out or too dense, chances are that the problem lies with your system and not theirs.

Monitor Calibration

PHOTO-PAINT installs with a default system profile of how images are displayed on-screen, how the information is sent to a printer, and how PHOTO-PAINT reads information from a scanner. If images you send to a service bureau are coming back too light or too dark, or if an image a co-worker hands you on disk looks wrong when you view it in PHOTO-PAINT, you can correct the color-casting and gamma display on your screen by following these steps:

1. Choose **F**ile, then **C**olor Manager.

2. In figure 21.10, you see the System Color Profile dialog box. By default, the profile after installing CorelDRAW is read from DEFAULT.CCS. DEFAULT.CCS contains general information applicable to most PCs, but it is not necessarily ideal for your own setup. Start calibrating with the generic profile for your monitor by clicking on the down arrow next to the drop-down list in the **M**onitor field.

3. Twenty-two of today's most popular monitors are listed in the **M**onitor drop-down list. If your model is listed, you may have a shorter calibration session than you expect, because the color characteristics of your monitor are already stored in a PHOTO-PAINT information file.

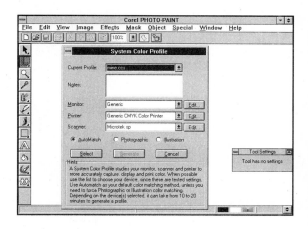

Figure 21.10
The System Color Profile dialog box offers calibration for your monitor, printer, and scanner.

4. If your monitor does not appear on the list, consult the documentation for your monitor. You can manually enter several of the parameters that describe your monitor's operating characteristics in the entry fields in Corel's Color Manager. Increasingly, monitor manufacturers are including their products' gamma, chromacity, and color temperature specifications in their documentation.

5. Click on the **E**dit... button next to the **M**onitor field, or choose Other from the **M**onitor drop-down list. With either method, you move to the Monitor Calibration dialog box. If you choose Other, you can name your monitor so that it appears in the System Color Profile dialog box in subsequent sessions (in case you switch monitors sometime and then want to switch back).

6. If your monitor appears on the list, the entries in the fields are already filled in for you. You can change these entries, however, if you believe that they are not correct for your monitor. No two monitors are ever exactly the same. If the entry boxes in the Monitor Calibration dialog box (see fig. 21.11) are displaying default values, click in each text field and enter the value from your monitor documentation. You won't damage the monitor if you enter the wrong data, but you won't improve your system calibration either.

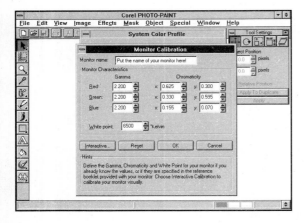

Figure 21.11

Use the data about your monitor's color characteristics to complete the calibration for use with PHOTO-PAINT.

7. Interactive calibration is perhaps the most forgiving of all Color Manager's options. If you don't have the data about your monitor's chromacity or white point, click on the Interactive...

button, and you can visually tune the relationship between PHOTO-PAINT and your monitor.

8. Take a moment or two to adjust the lighting in your work environment. Do you have a glaring fluorescent lamp reflecting into your screen? Such a condition can throw off your fine-tuning, so arrange your lights to a comfortable reading level, with no light source reflecting directly onto your screen. On the other hand, if you have no lights on in the room and the only source of illumination is your monitor, turn on a light or two to create average lighting conditions.

9. Clean your monitor, if you haven't done so earlier. Dust, smoke, and other airborne particles dim your view of the screen over time without your realizing it. In addition, don't run the calibration unless your monitor has been turned on for more than a half hour. Monitors need a little time to reach a consistent color display.

10. In figure 21.12, you see the Interactive Monitor Calibration dialog box. As the legend at the bottom of the dialog box suggests, don't tamper with the chromacity settings unless the Preview image shows noticeable color-casting. Owners of monitors that have been in constant use for three or more years might want to adjust chromacity, because the screen phosphors tend to change nonuniformly over a period of time.

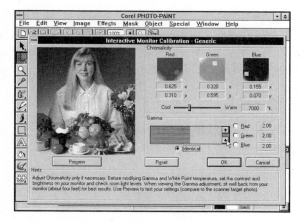

Figure 21.12

You have visual guides for adjusting monitor chromacity, gamma, and color temperature in the Interactive Monitor Calibration dialog box.

11. Your monitor's gamma is probably the parameter that causes the greatest difference in image viewing and editing. *Gamma* is the breadth of contrast in the midtones within an image; the higher the gamma value, the more brilliant the visual detail appears in an image. The best gamma setting for any one monitor is up to each user. Some users find a 2.0 setting to be a little high for imaging work, and they prefer a 1.78 gamma setting. If you exchange images with Macintosh imaging people, you may find their images are too brilliant, because gamma for a Macintosh is typically set higher than that for IBM/PCs.

12. This next step is not necessary, but it might provide greater color accuracy when you are working in PHOTO-PAINT. First use the spin buttons next to the Gamma field to adjust the **I**dentical (color value) gamma setting, which is a combination of the three color channels. At the bottom of the Interactive Monitor Calibration dialog box, Corel suggests that you "sit well back (about four feet)" from the monitor to view the comparison between the striped pattern in the Gamma window on the left and the solid gray pattern on the Gamma window's right. The idea is to make the two perceived values in the Gamma display box match. When the two patterns look alike, you have attained an Identical gamma correction for all three color channels. If you are like most users, your arms aren't four feet long; instead of sitting well back, you can squint a little to make a good comparison between both patterns in the Gamma display box.

13. If you think that areas of the sample image at the left of the calibration menu are blocked in and image detail is hard to discern, try clicking on one of the RGB (**R**ed, **G**reen, **B**lue) radio buttons to adjust the gamma for an individual channel up or down.

14. If you have performed the last step, a good final procedure is to click once more on the **I**dentical gamma value radio button. Check again to see whether the midtones of the sample image show enough detail and whether the two sample patterns align in value.

You have now calibrated your monitor for use in PHOTO-PAINT. By typing a name in the Current Profile field of the System Color Profile dialog box and clicking on Generate, you save a profile of the adjustments you've made to hard disk as a *.CCS file. You can retrieve the profile from the System Color Profile dialog box any time you get a new monitor or want to update the profile.

Scanner Calibration

Most people who perform digital image editing for a profession own a scanner, a PhotoCD player, or both. Either means enables you to sample real-world images and bring them into PHOTO-PAINT for corrections and modifying. The next section covers PhotoCD technology. Now it's time to address scanning considerations before you get too deeply into acquiring images that might not be calibrated correctly.

If you haven't purchased a scanner for your PC yet, you should know that Corel directly supports certain models by means of a proprietary TWAIN interface. If you've purchased a TWAIN-compliant scanner other than the ones in the following list, manual calibration of your scanner can be performed rather painlessly. PHOTO-PAINT is "aware" of the following scanners:

- AVR 800CLX
- Canon CJ-10
- Epson ES600
- HP ScanJet 2C
- Kodak 2035
- Microtek 300Z and 600Z

If your scanner is on the preceding list, scanner calibration is as simple as choosing the appropriate scanner from the Scanner drop-down list in the Scanner field of the System Color Profile dialog box. Choose an *.SCN file from the ones provided by PHOTO-PAINT for your make and model of scanner. PHOTO-PAINT then asks you which .SCN file you want it to use for the calibration. After you specify an .SCN file, PHOTO-PAINT calibrates. To append your system profile so that it includes your scanner, choose your scanner and then click on Generate in the System Color Profile dialog box.

With today's sophisticated scanners, you might be able to select the generic scanner calibration from the System Profile and never notice anything wrong with your digital acquisitions. To create a calibration for your scanner that guarantees that a digitized photo looks the same on-screen as it does when printed to film or paper, you must install your scanner software and make sure the scanner hardware is properly connected to your PC.

Many scanners are Mac/PC compatible, which means that they are probably *Small Computer Standard Interface* (SCSI, pronounced "scuzzy") devices. SCSI devices are not always the easiest kind to install correctly. Be sure that you have carefully read all the documentation. If you are adding the scanner to a chain of SCSI devices, pay special attention to the issue of termination.

The first (usually the SCSI interface card in your computer) and the last device in the chain must be properly terminated. SCSI devices do not work properly and can be permanently damaged if they are not terminated correctly.

Many scanners offer their own calibration routines, TWAIN setup, and sometimes explicit instructions on how to edit your CONFIG.SYS file to add an exclude statement to protect the upper memory regions the scanner subsystem uses. For example, X=D400-D7FF is the region of upper memory that needs to be excluded for a Microtek IISP scanner to work properly when using the supplied Microtek interface card. Refer to your scanner documentation for the proper memory address to exclude, and check your memory manager's documentation for the proper syntax and procedure for establishing excluded memory areas.

If you're using an accelerated video card, you may also have to exclude an address that the video card uses. Check your video card documentation for the address that the video card uses. If you don't exclude the areas of memory that the scanner interface card and the video card use, Windows uses the areas for its own purposes, which causes conflicts. Upper memory conflicts are the most common reason that scanners fail to operate in Windows, and you must have your scanner in operational order before you can calibrate it.

PHOTO-PAINT's link to TWAIN (the common interface between scanners and applications) is found under the File menu. You need to scan a target image for PHOTO-PAINT to calibrate. Choose File, Acquire Image; then choose Select Source. The Select Source dialog box provides a list of installed TWAIN interfaces. If you have more than one TWAIN device listed (such as a digital camera or a scanning device you've upgraded from), choose the correct scanner, and then click on Select.

Find the calibration card that came with the Corel documentation. If you have lost it, a second good choice for a target scan is the card that came with your scanner. Failing that, you can purchase an IT8 target from a camera or electronics store, or you can create your own target card by using a brilliant white piece of paper and many colorful markers.

In the Special, Preferences, General tab menu, make sure that Scanner Calibration is turned *off*. You do not want PHOTO-PAINT to automatically correct an image that itself is going to be used to calibrate the automatic correction. Choose File, Acquire Image; then choose Acquire.

As you see in figure 21.13, the Microtek TWAIN interface has popped over PHOTO-PAINT's workspace, and a target card is cropped in the scanner window. The resolution (Resolution) and the dimensions of the target image are not critical, but you should select RGB from the Scan Mode drop-down list so that the image you acquire is something you can use to calibrate with the Color Manager.

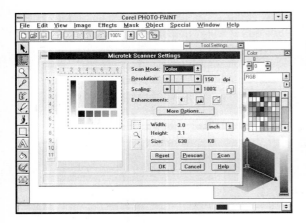

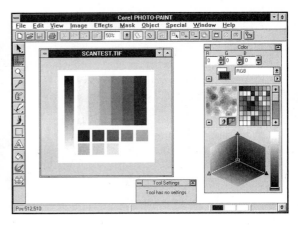

Figure 21.13

Although TWAIN interfaces vary from manufacturer to manufacturer, they share most of the common features.

Figure 21.14

Once you have your target scan, choose *.TIF from the List Files of Type drop-down list when you save the image.

W A R N I N G

If your TWAIN interface offers color correction, *don't* use it for this calibration image unless you intend to repeat prescanning adjustments every time you scan. (Hint: You won't. Every image is photographically unique.)

Launch the scan, and save the image with a *.TIF extension, as shown in figure 21.14. Tagged Image File (TIFF) format is the only format PHOTO-PAINT's Color Manager can use for calibration. You should not convert a .PCX or some other image to .TIF as a shortcut here, because Color Manager needs *original* scanner information to perform calibrations.

Choose **F**ile, then **C**olor Manager. From the Sca**n**ner drop-down list, choose Other.

In the S**c**anner name field, type whatever your choose. Mixed-case letters and spaces are valid characters, so you can enter the exact name of the scanner. Click on **I**mage in the Scanned Target field, then click on **B**rowse to locate the image you scanned as the target for calibration. Click on **S**canned target in the Scanner Calibration dialog box (see fig. 21.15).

In figure 21.16, you see the menu PHOTO-PAINT moves you to after selecting a homemade calibration target. You need to click and drag the four corners of the boundary box to the edges of the scanned image to indicate to PHOTO-PAINT that this is the entire target area it should calibrate against its reference file.

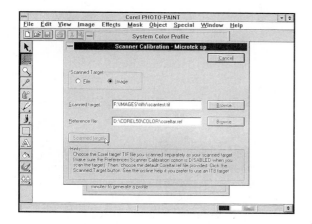

Figure 21.15

If you don't have a scanner that PHOTO-PAINT directly supports, use an image you've scanned for the calibration target.

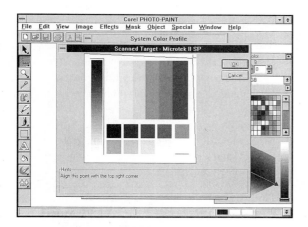

Figure 21.16

Align the boundary box to the edges of the preview window of your scanned target image.

Click on **O**K. Enter a legal DOS file name for the calibration file in the File Name box. The file should end with the proprietary *.SCN extension.

Click on **O**K, and PHOTO-PAINT creates a scanner calibration for your scanner. When you are returned to the System Color Profile menu, select a *.CCS profile name (you can append the one used for the monitor) with your scanner highlighted in the Sca**n**ner field, then click on **G**enerate to create the profile.

Printer Calibration

Unless you won the state lottery, you probably depend on a commercial printer or service bureau for your output. Chapter 27, "Color Specification and Output," addresses pre-press considerations and the ins and outs of your PHOTO-PAINT image at an imaging center; however, you might want to pay attention to one or two items in the **P**rinter calibration field of the System Color Profile dialog box.

Applications frequently rely on a specified printer driver, whether you ever output to one or even have one connected to your PC. A good example is PostScript printing, a technology and page-description language created by Adobe Systems, Inc. A PostScript printer renders image information passed from the print driver in a completely different way than non-PostScript-based printers do. Similarly, a film recorder doesn't calculate dots per inch but instead looks at image file size for its rendering information.

If you want your service bureau to thank you when you bring in an image, you should know what printer driver they use, try to obtain the same one, and use it in your **P**rinter calibration specification. With this approach, PHOTO-PAINT builds a system profile that displays an image the way your intended output will be. Suppose, for example, your service bureau uses a Genigraphics print driver to run their film recorder. Whenever you need a 35mm transparency of your work, you would use a PHOTO-PAINT profile that indicates that Genigraphics is the intended output device, even though you don't personally own the $65,000 machine.

More expensive and more accurate means of calibrating monitors, scanners, and output devices are available, most of which involve hardware such as suction cups and meters. Nevertheless, for a software calibration program as thorough as Color Manager (which essentially comes free with CorelDRAW), you can't beat the price or the involvement of a few minutes of time.

Working with PhotoCD Images and PHOTO-PAINT

In April 1992, Kodak unleashed a technological wonder called the PhotoCD that is making professionals rethink conventional image acquisition. The PhotoCD is gaining such widespread acceptance in publishing and photographic circles that many designers may never again use their scanners to acquire photographs. PHOTO-PAINT is not only capable of reading PhotoCD images but is also actually optimized to give PC users photographic images with unprecedented clarity, detail, and color.

PhotoCDs can hold an average of 100 images in Kodak's proprietary *.PCD format. A .PCD file consists of five different resolutions of the same image. When you open a .PCD file in PHOTO-PAINT, you have a choice of opening an image in one of the five sizes that range from 500KB to 18MB. PhotoCDs are not like conventional CDs because you must use an XA, PhotoCD-compatible CD-ROM drive to read the disk. Fortunately, most computers that come with a CD-ROM drive meet PhotoCD standards, and the CD-ROM drives in most multimedia add-on kits also meet the standards.

You can have your photographic images written to a PhotoCD as easily as you can drop off a roll of film at the photofinisher. Additionally, any negatives you already have (black-and-white or color) can be put on a PhotoCD. Kodak's PCD writers scan film negatives at high resolutions; for this reason, a PCD image is one generation less removed from an original source image.

PhotoCDs are inexpensive, they hold much more image detail and resolution than you could possibly fit on an average hard disk, and they are an absolute pleasure to work with in PHOTO-PAINT. PhotoCD images exhibit almost none of the digital "grit" and heavy grayscale mottling that scanned photographs sometimes exhibit.

How MOSAIC Works with PhotoCDs

You can preview images on a PhotoCD in two ways, and you should choose one if you're ever going to retrieve images quickly from a PhotoCD. All the images contained on a PhotoCD are numbered sequentially, and all PhotoCD disks look identical, with the exception of minute etchings somewhere on their surface. If you make a guess at the image you want from the PhotoCD and load the wrong image, the mistake can cost you a fair amount of time, particularly if you are loading an 18MB file. On the cover of each PhotoCD case is a collection of thumbnail images with the corresponding number of the file next to the image. This is a convenient way to pick the images you want to load into PHOTO-PAINT, if you can avoid the common errors of misplacing the case or misfiling the Photo-CDs in their case.

Fortunately, Kodak writes an overview file on the PhotoCD along with the images, and this overview file is where CorelMOSAIC proves indispensable in PHOTO-PAINT's workspace. If you installed CorelMOSAIC during the CorelDRAW setup, you have a very powerful cataloging software that can show you previews of an entire PhotoCD. As in all the other CorelDRAW modules, CorelMOSAIC provides drag-and-drop support for .PCD images.

In the following steps, you see how easy it is to load a .PCD-format image; and in the next section, you learn to perform preloading color correction so that you can begin to edit an image.

1. Have a PhotoCD loaded in your CD-ROM drive.

2. In PHOTO-PAINT, click on the CorelMOSAIC icon on the ribbon bar. By default, CorelMOSAIC immediately starts taking "snapshot" thumbnail pictures of everything in your last-accessed directory (frequently this directory is Windows, if you start PHOTO-PAINT directly after starting Windows). This process works great if you've established a working directory in which you store all your digital images, but CorelMOSAIC doesn't always locate your CD-ROM drive on the first try.

3. Click on the folder icon on the right of CorelMOSAIC, and choose the CD-ROM drive from the Dri**v**es drop-down list. Under List Files of Type, choose Kodak PhotoCD (*.PCD).

4. Click on OK, and CorelMOSAIC displays thumbnail images, in sequence, of the images contained on the PhotoCD (see fig. 21.17).

5. Scroll through the visual catalog of images until you arrive at one you'd like to edit or at least to view with a little more detail. Expanding CorelMOSAIC's window to see more than three or four previews at a time, however, is not recommended. CorelMOSAIC requires many processing cycles to get the next row of images ready for display. If you maximize CorelMOSAIC's workspace to reveal 12 or more images at once, you may wind up looking at the hourglass for a long time.

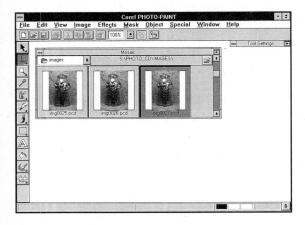

Figure 21.17
CorelMOSAIC can read a PhotoCD's overview file and display miniature previews of all the images on the CD.

6. You are not required to open a new file in PHOTO-PAINT's workspace to load a .PCD image, as you are with other image formats. Having no active image windows, you can click and drag on an image you like, and CorelMOSAIC eventually places the file on the workspace in its own image window. *Eventually* means that you need to make some decisions about the image you choose before it rasterizes on-screen.

How Large Do You Want a PCD Image?

As mentioned earlier, the .PCD format contains five images of different sizes, which gives you incredible flexibility in cropping and sizing an image. After selecting and

dragging a thumbnail preview into PHOTO-PAINT, you must decide how large you want your image to be. All .PCD images are saved to 72 dpi; the larger image dimensions are quite hefty, but you may ultimately want to trade file dimensions for resolution by accessing the Resample command.

The file size you choose depends on the image quality you need and your system capabilities. If you have 8MB of system RAM installed, your life in PHOTO-PAINT is not going to be an easy one. You should therefore not attempt to load an image larger than the 1.3MB BASE (Standard) image. You and your system will be much more comfortable and productive if you stick to the BASE/4-size image. PHOTO-PAINT calls this a Snapshot image, and the file size for a 24-bit Snapshot image is a comfortable 294KB.

When you work with small file sizes such as 294KB, there is a limit on the final output size you can achieve and still maintain an adequate resolution for the image. The only solution to this problem is to get more RAM for your computer. PHOTO-PAINT requires additional RAM to perform filter effects, and the Windows environment claims at least 2MB on startup. Although 294KB seems like a pittance, you cannot work with large, magazine-quality images on a fast 486 machine without at least 16MB RAM. Many professional imaging stations sport no less than 32MB RAM, and some have as much as 128MB RAM.

Additionally, CorelDRAW offers you options for the color capability of the .PCD image to be loaded. Corel Corporation is sometimes accommodating to a fault in trying to provide every user with alternatives to processor and memory-intensive editing work; however, choosing a color mode less than 24 bit is a professional mistake. Only 24-bit color mode (while viewing with a 24-bit color driver) provides pure (not dithered) colors with which you can perform editing work. You will experience frustration with any color mode lower than RGB 24-bit, 16.7MB color, and your work will show photographic-quality inadequacies when it is viewed and printed to more color-capable equipment.

Naturally, if you have a PhotoCD with only monochrome (grayscale) images, you would want to choose grayscale as the **C**olors selection in the Photo CD Options dialog box. Grayscale images can't contain any more than 256 unique shades, so choosing to load a grayscale as a 24-bit color image is analogous to ordering a moving van to transport a single chair. Figure 21.18 shows the Photo CD Options dialog box you receive after you click and drag a thumbnail image onto the workspace.

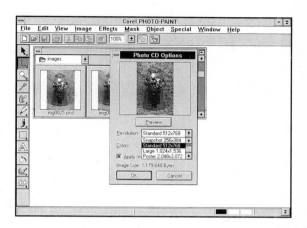

Figure 21.18

Choose the color mode and image size of the .PCD file in the Photo CD Options dialog box.

High PCD Gamma and YKK Color Space

The Photo CD Options dialog box has an **A**pply Image Enhancement check box that Kodak should have thought about when they first merchandised PhotoCDs. If you have been working with PhotoCD images before you purchased CorelDRAW, you might have noticed that the .PCD images appear a little washed out and that they require gamma correction before you can perform serious image editing work. .PCD images are over-brilliant before correction because they are balanced for television sets, not PC monitors. Kodak was hoping that a large installed base

of consumers would be drawn to the new photo technology for home use; people would get a roll finished to PhotoCD, rent a player, and watch their pictures on a home television set. Since 1992 the phenomenon has still not happened to any appreciable extent. In all probability, digital imaging professionals (not average consumers) will fund future Research and Development on the PhotoCD format.

.PCD images have a gamma of 2.2 and are written to a color space called YCC. The Y component of a .PCD color model refers to the luminosity of an image from 0 to 200 percent. On a television set, this produces startling whiter-than-whites; but on a PC screen, a .PCD image looks washed out. The YCC color space, however, does translate to both additive color models (such as RGB) and subtractive color models (such as the CMYK space commercial printers image to the printed page).

Preloading Image Correction

To correct the off-balanced gamma of .PCD files, users of this format have been forced to resort to adjusting gamma manually (and occasionally to sending hate mail to Rochester, New York). Corel Corporation had the foresight in CorelDRAW 5 to include auto and manual correction features in PHOTO-PAINT; therefore, it's less fuss to open a perfect tonally balanced .PCD image than to scan a perfect photograph. Corel has licensed

GamutCD, a program by Candela, Ltd., to be run directly from PHOTO-PAINT. You'll find that simply by checking the Gamut**C**D box in the Photo CD Image Enhancement dialog box, you're 90 percent of the way to a perfect picture in PHOTO-PAINT's workspace.

In the Photo CD Image Enhancement dialog box, Corel also offers tonal adjustments for black-and-white points in an image (when necessary) and a choice between Candela/ Corel or Kodak image adjustment.

Corel documentation on using the Photo CD Image Enhancement dialog box to perform image enhancement is not very robust. For this reason, the following list provides an explanation (cause and effect) of each option available in the menu. Because no two images are alike, you should treat each image you correct as a unique case. In other words, there is really no one setting that can always be recommended in image enhancement.

If you click on the Gamut**C**D radio button in the Photo CD Image Enhancement dialog box (see fig. 21.19), you are necessarily *not* working with Kodak's color correction. The next section covers the **K**odak Color Correction options, which offer different, and perhaps better, features to bring the image into alignment with PC display characteristics rather than with those of television.

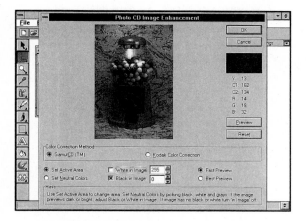

Figure 21.19
You have tonal balance controls over a .PCD image yet to be loaded with the GamutCD options.

- **Set Active Area.** Set Active Area and Set Neutral Colors are toggling radio buttons; in other words, you select one, then the other, but not both simulta- neously. When you click on the Set Active Area radio button, your cursor becomes a marquee selection tool, and you can choose a part of an image to balance tonally. This option is useful when you plan to crop a full-frame image to use only an area. The corrections affect the entire .PCD image, but the critical corrections are made based on the area you've marqueed with the cursor. Imagine an image of a light-colored sparrow flying across a dark sky—if you intend to crop the image so that the sparrow occupies most of the image area, tonally balancing the entire image is not worthwhile.

- **Set Neutral Colors.** The Set Neutral Colors option is a way to remove color-casting from an image. After you click on this radio button, you can then click on any area in the entire image with the cursor and "tell" PHOTO-PAINT that the area you clicked over should contain equal amounts of Red, Green, and Blue—a neutral shade. To see what effect this adjustment has on your overall image, click on the Preview button after you do this. If your image becomes too light or too dark, try clicking in a lighter area that you think should be neutral. When the value of an area is dark, it's harder to tell whether an image area is truly neutral or contains a color-cast. Look at the sample swatch below the Cancel button, and check the RGB values before you click on a neutral area. If the values displayed on the upper right of the dialog box are approximately equal, yet the neutral area displays a color-cast, clicking on the area tells PHOTO-PAINT that this area has identical R, G, and B values.

- **White in Image and Black in Image.** The White in Image and Black in Image buttons don't necessarily have to be active at the same time. In figure 21.19, the gum-ball machine has dark shadows cast across its surface while the rest of the image is vibrant and light. Because there are no whiter-than-whites in this image, the White in Image option is not checked: instead, concentration is on the Black in Image adjustment.

YCC color has its equivalence in the RGB color model (although the RGB color space is smaller than YCC), and both models are displayed as changing values when you move your cursor over the image area. In a nutshell, the Y value is luminescence, and a value of 8 represents only 1 percent reflection of light on a surface. This corresponds to a value of R=11, G=11, and B=11 in the RGB color space for PCs. By moving the cursor over what appears to be the darkest areas of the image, you can see that the lowest value found in this image is 13. The course of action, then, is to leave the Black in Image spin box next to the radio button as it is at 0. The preview image isn't flawless in its representation, but your own eyes can generally tell you when relative improvements have been made to an image. If you create a tonal rearrangement with the image that you don't like, you can always press the Reset button.

N O T E

The upper limit to the Y value, the way a surface reflects light in an image, is 200 percent. The RGB color space cannot express this value; a Y value of 188 is equivalent to R=255, G=255, B=255. If you move your cursor over a white area that produces a Y reading greater than 188, you should definitely tune the White in Image spin buttons down to within the RGB color space's tolerance. The result of not knocking some highlight off the image is a glaring void in the image file with no image detail.

■ **Fast Preview and Best Preview.** Fast Preview is an option you should select before clicking on the **P**review button. Fast preview shows changes you propose to make in the tonal scheme of an image before you press the OK button to actually load the .PCD file. The Best Preview option, although not truly representative of the changes, can make you wonder whether your machine is processing at all as it creates a more refined representation

Kodak Color Correction

The other radio button in the Photo CD Image Enhancement dialog box (**K**odak Color Correction) offers a different set of tonal corrections for a .PCD image, and this set necessitates explaining the PC color wheel a little. Because pixels represented by phosphors on your screen are made of light, *hue* (the definitive component of color) is evaluated in an *additive* way; red plus green plus blue add up to white because these are the components of light as displayed on a RGB-phosphor monitor. Red, green, and blue have their complementary colors, and they are expressed on a digital color wheel as Yellow, Cyan, and Magenta, as shown in figure 21.20.

Kodak's method for removing color-casting in an image is to offer plus/minus settings for red, green, and blue. In figure 21.21, you see the sliders labeled Re**d** Tint, Gree**n** Tint, and Bl**u**e Tint on the left of the **K**odak Color Correction option. If you think your image is displaying too much overall red, for example, you slide the Re**d** Tint control to the left to lessen the Red component. As you see in figure 21.20, this shifts the color to more Cyan. Whenever you lessen a hue, you necessarily shift the image's color to a complementary color.

Figure 21.20

The spectrum of color for the RGB color space.

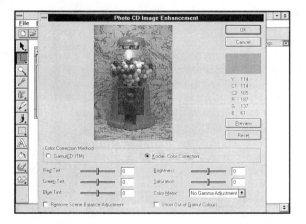

Figure 21.21

PHOTO-PAINT offers Kodak color correction for PhotoCD images.

The Kodak options cover the following additional color correction features:

- **Remove Scene Balance Adjustment.** Within each PhotoCD is a mapping curve unique to the roll of film you sent to Kodak to be digitized. The operator of the PCD writer looks at your roll before digitizing it. He or she might see an overall bluish tint to your pictures and punch in a correction before digitizing to PhotoCD; the correction curve is called the *Scene Balance*. Similarly, if you took pictures with 400ASA film that you want developed at 1600ASA, the Scene Balance curve changes how the .PCD image loads with the corrections compensated for. With the Remove Scene Balance Adjustment box unchecked, each .PCD image is undergoing minor refinements as it is presented to you. If you want to disable the Scene Balance adjustment, check this box before you load a .PCD image.

- **Brightness and Saturation.** *HSB* (Hue, Saturation, and Brightness) is a color model frequently used in imaging programs to express the same values as RGB. HSB is a little easier to use in your imaging work, because the HSB components isolate color characteristics in an image rather than present them as values of Red, Green, and Blue.

  Saturation refers to the relationship between neutral colors and pure ones in an image. If you increase saturation, you force a predominance of pure color

found in an image to the surface. Too much saturation, however, can turn an ordinary image into a "dayglo" poster, with original colors displayed like the hues found on a detergent box. Conversely, too little saturation reveals the neutral tones in an image and suppresses any one predominant hue, thereby making an image appear to be grayscale.

Brightness refers to the amount of light reflected off (or passed through) a surface depicted in an image. Use your own artist's eye to evaluate how brightly an original PCD image should be illuminated.

■ **Color Metric.** Color Metric is Kodak's control for gamma display in an image. The higher the value you select from the drop-down list, the more contrast in the midtones of an image appear. After you select a gamma adjustment, it's useful to click on the **P**review button. You'll usually find no more or less than a value of 2 corrects an average image.

■ **Show Out-Of-Gamut Colors.** CMYK, the color space of process color printing, is narrower than the YCC color space. Having the Show Out-Of-**G**amut Colors box checked is important, especially when you are adjusting gamma, because Kodak color correction displays areas where colors simply can't be expressed with printing inks, and the color correction utility displays flat red or blue colors in these image areas in the preview window.

The flat color areas indicate that you have reached a saturation in an image area that cannot be expressed with a combination of cyan, yellow, blue, and black pigments. If you see splotches of red or blue in the preview window after adjusting the controls, adjust the controls so they are closer to the default settings. Then click on **P**review again to see if Kodak's indicator colors have disappeared from the preview.

In figure 21.22, the OK button has been clicked in the Photo CD Image Enhancement dialog box, and PHOTO-PAINT has loaded a Standard resolution of the image, which measures 512 pixels by 768 pixels at 72 pixels/inch and takes up a saved file size of 1.17MB.

Figure 21.22
You can view and edit a .PCD image exactly as you would a scanned photo.

When you load a .PCD file using CorelMOSAIC, PHOTO-PAINT assumes that this is an image in a volume of read/write files—but it's not because .PCD images reside on CD-Read-Only Memory media. Consequently, once the PCD image appears in the workspace, you get an error warning that PHOTO-PAINT cannot save this image or the editing work you perform on it.

After the image loads and you get the error warning, your recourse is to save the .PCD image you want to work on to your hard disk in a .TIF or other file format. Naturally, when you save a copy of the original .PCD file, you have the opportunity to name it something a little more evocative than IMGxxxx.PCD. This descriptive name adds the benefit of later locating your file more easily to those of overall ease of use and quality of the .PCD image.

Anti-Aliasing

Color capability and anti-aliasing go hand in hand; without an RGB color mode that offers 16.7 million unique color values in its format, true anti-aliasing cannot take place. *Anti-aliasing* is the resampling of an image area (or an entire image) to produce semi-transparent pixels along the edges in a design to soften the "jaggy" characteristic of pixel images. PHOTO-PAINT interpolates in-between values for pixels it creates when you make vacancies in the grid of a bitmap (raster) image. *Interpolation* is the intelligent creation by a software program of pixels that are transitionally correct between neighboring pixels of different color or tonal values.

These transitional, interpolated pixels must have unique colors assigned to them. Moreover, the only successful way to enable PHOTO-PAINT to create unique, anti-alias pixel values is to begin with a color mode for an image that has the color capability to hold millions of unique values, such as the 24-bit, RGB mode.

By trying a simple experiment, you can see the effects of PHOTO-PAINT's anti-aliasing and better understand why this is the resampling mode of preference. The following steps outline the experiment:

1. Choose **F**ile, then **N**ew. Select a 2-inch-by-2-inch image area in 24-bit RGB color mode with a resolution of 96 pixels/inch. Ordinarily, you would want a new image to have greater resolution if the design were destined for a commercial printer or service bureau, but this is only an experiment.

2. Select the Line tool, click and drag a line on the image background, then click and drag a second line next to it.

3. Choose **S**pecial, then **P**references. Select Anti-alias from the **S**tretch Mode for Objects drop-down list in the General tab options box. Click on OK to return to the workspace.

4. Click and hold down the Object Picker tool to reveal the flyout menu of tools; then choose the Rectangular tool. If you are in doubt as to a specific tool, PHOTO-PAINT provides pop-up Help by default—if you let your cursor linger over a tool icon, the tool name appears on-screen.

5. Marquee-select the tip of one of the lines you drew, then release the Rectangular tool, and click and drag on an object handle. By default, all the other object selection tools revert to the Object Picker tool after an action has been completed.

6. Choose **O**bject, then **M**erge (or press Ctrl+G) after you've stretched the end of the line 200 to 300 percent of its original size.

Figure 21.23 is a 600-percent zoom of the end of the line. As you can see, anti-aliasing has placed a number of gray pixels around the periphery of the black line to create a smooth transition between foreground black and background white.

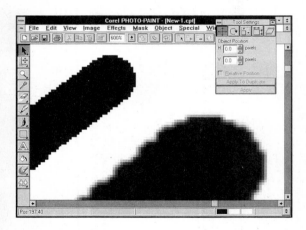

Figure 21.23
Anti-aliasing can smooth the transition between original pixels and new ones PHOTO-PAINT creates when you stretch something.

You necessarily lose some edge detail in an image when you stretch a selected object and the Anti-alias preference has been activated. In the grand scheme of things, however, the purpose of PHOTO-PAINT's tools is to enable you to create lifelike images from pixels and to edit them. Try enabling the Stretch/Truncate preference and performing the same last steps; then try performing a *stretch* (resampling an image area) on an object selection whose color mode is less than 24 bit. You'll find that jagged, stairstep pixel edges become more prominent and that dithering is required by PHOTO-PAINT to carry out the command.

Summary

As you move into PHOTO-PAINT's advanced feature set in the following chapters, you should keep in mind that the purpose of a raster image editing program is to modify and correct pixel-based graphics while making the work undetectable. Keeping image areas from displaying pixelation is a task that goes hand in hand with your work. When you start with the right set of tools, conditions, and source material (as described in this chapter), the imaging work you perform later happens with less effort, and you can concentrate on the core of your goals—producing fantastic bitmap graphics.

Working with Objects

Pixel-based computer graphics have traditionally adopted the convention of applying a foreground color to a background image (or canvas). But recently, software developers have given bitmap-based computer graphics applications the vector graphic–based option of assigning no fill to a selected area—not a white background, not a black one. When empty space, made up of totally vacant grids that normally would hold color pixels, is a designer's option, a whole new world unfolds for creative manipulation of bitmap images. Layers and objects present the PHOTO-PAINT user with flexibility and power over image control that parallels CorelDRAW, except you can perform sophisticated editing work with photographic-quality pixels rather than vector shapes.

This chapter covers:

- Understanding basic object manipulation

- Exploring drag-and-drop object support

- Using distortion handles to create dimensionalism

- Feathering and distorting

- Creating a new background image

- Merging objects

- Combining and reordering objects

Using PHOTO-PAINT's .CPT image format, areas from different images can be kept discrete, which means each object can be rearranged and modified indefinitely. The objects can be rearranged in different layer orders, or *hierarchies,* using the Layers/Objects roll-up. PHOTO-PAINT 5 also supports drag-and-drop between image windows, so quickly arranging a graphically sumptuous piece has never been easier. Once everything is exactly where you want it and you have finished modifying all the objects, components can be merged seamlessly into a single image that can be saved in traditional file formats such as .TIF or .TGA.

Understanding Basic Object Manipulation

PHOTO-PAINT has seven tools for selecting an image area you want to change into an object, one tool for moving the object, and the Object Node Edit tool for refining an object's outline. If you know you are going to be creating a multi-object image in advance, some preplanning can save you a lot of effort when defining an object.

Using the Magic Wand Object Tool To Define an Area

When used in its default mode, the Magic Wand Object tool defines an area within an image based upon color similarities and turns the area into an object. After the area

becomes an object, it can be copied, pasted, edited, and repositioned in an entirely different image.

The Magic Wand Object tool is extremely useful for quickly and precisely selecting areas of an image with a single mouse click. When creating images that are destined to become object-oriented, you can take advantage of the Magic Wand Object tool's capabilities if you make the background around the soon-to-be object a solid color not found in other image areas. Similarly, when taking photos that will be used in PHOTO-PAINT creations, try to place a solid background behind your model and light the scene evenly. Selecting a background area that contains little tonal variation makes selection with the Magic Wand Object tool in PHOTO-PAINT an easy task.

The following series of steps demonstrates the usefulness of the Magic Wand Object tool in creating a composite image, one made up of several objects from different sources. You will find the sample images used in these steps in the CHAP22 subdirectory of the *CorelDRAW! The Professional Reference* companion CDs. The example images were preplanned a little, and you will see that by investing a few moments to set up your raw materials to work better with PHOTO-PAINT's tools, producing a professional composition is a snap.

1. Open the DOORKNOB.TIF image from the *CorelDRAW! The Professional Reference* companion CDs. Because CD-ROMs are read-only, PHOTO-PAINT will flash you a Warning dialog box: *File X is Read-Only. Save is disabled.* Click on OK; you can work

with a CD image while it's stored in system RAM, but you have to save the finished image to your hard disk, or to removable media such as a floppy or a Bernoulli disk.

2. Click and hold on the Object Picker tool (on top of the toolbox) to reveal the Object Menu fly-out.

3. Click on the Magic Wand Object tool, release the left mouse button, then double-click on the tool.

4. As you can see in figure 22.1, the Color Comparison Tolerance menu is where the breadth of color range the Magic Wand Object tool will use to make a selection is set. Because this image has a uniform color background, the default settings for Color Comparison Tolerance can be used with DOORKNOB.TIF.

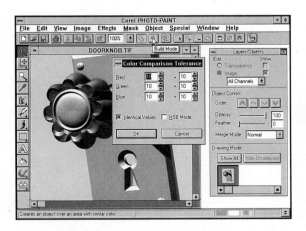

Figure 22.1

The Color Comparison Tolerance menu can make the Magic Wand Object tool select a wide or narrow range of colors.

However, if your image is of a subject photographed against a seamless background, you might find minute variations in the solid background. In this situation, specify different values (from 0 to 255) in the Color Comparison Tolerance settings so that the Magic Wand Object tool will include the additional variations on the color present in the background.

Additionally, you can uncheck the **I**dentical Values check box if the area you want to select contains more of one primary color than another. Identical values of 255 will enable the Magic Wand to select everything in an image (a fairly useless setting), whereas a low setting of 5–10 can pick uniquely colored pixels out of an image area.

5. Click on the Build button on the ribbon bar (or choose **O**bject, **B**uild Mode). Build mode enables the user to select an area, then continue adding to the selected area with any of the other Object tools. This feature is most useful when defining noncontiguous areas in an image, such as the keyhole and background in this example.

W A R N I N G

Don't change your Zoom setting while in Build mode. If you begin selecting an image area and switch to another PHOTO-PAINT tool, you will lose your selection area and have to start over. As an alternative to the Zoom tool, type a viewing resolution in the Zoom level box on the ribbon bar, or click on the down arrow to the right of the Zoom level to choose a pre-set field of viewing resolution.

6. The objective here is to isolate the green background from the doorknob and plate, but because the foreground image is composed of so many different color values, it is easier to select all the green background, then invert the selection of the object. Click on the green area outside the doorknob and plate, then click inside the round part of the keyhole. Finally, click inside the oblong part of the keyhole.

7. Click on the Invert button on the ribbon bar or choose **O**bject, **I**nvert, as shown in figure 22.2. Now everything except the green background is selected. However, the doorknob image area is not an object yet, and your selection work can come undone if you select a different tool before performing the next step.

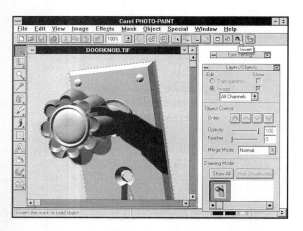

Figure 22.2

Invert the areas you have selected with the Magic Wand Object tool to select everything except the original selection areas.

T I P

By default, a selection created in Build mode that hasn't been saved as an object has a red and white marquee running around it. A saved object has a blue and white marquee around it. This visual guide can save you a lot of grief as you build increasingly complex layer/object designs.

If you'd like to specify colors for the marquees other than red or blue, use the Advanced tab settings in the **S**pecial, **P**references menu to define other colors.

---

8. Click on the Create button on the ribbon bar (or choose **O**bject, **C**reate). The image of the doorknob will eventually be used in a different background image, and it makes no difference whether you choose **C**opy or Cu**t** from the **C**reate menu. By default, clicking on the Create button copies a selection area to make an object. Either of the **C**opy or Cu**t** commands will make a permanent object (blue and white marquee outline) of the door-knob within the DOORKNOB.TIF image. After the Create command has been made, the image area inside the marquee becomes a permanent object—you can move on to other PHOTO-PAINT tools without the risk of losing the object selection.

In Build mode, it is important to use the **O**bject, **C**reate command as the final step to making an object. If you try to *move* the red and white marqueed area with the Object Picker tool before issuing the Create command, you are only moving the marquee and not the *contents* of the image area surrounded by the marquee. This can lead to some interesting design possibilities, especially when you want to move the marquee to other image areas before creating the object, but you cannot copy an "empty" object marquee, so multiple marquees cannot be made from an original selection.

Exploring Drag-and-Drop Object Support

Although the doorknob image is now an object and can be moved around within the DOORKNOB.TIF image window, the goal is to make this an interesting part of a different image file. Moving an object from one image file to another and assigning it a position in a stack of PHOTO-PAINT layers is the next step, and the next section.

PHOTO-PAINT's drag-and-drop option of moving an object from one open image file to another is due in part to PHOTO-PAINT's *Multiple Document Interface* (MDI). Because of the MDI capability of PHOTO-PAINT, you can have as many open image windows as your system RAM can handle.

Before You Drag and Drop

Before covering how to move objects between images, it is worthwhile to reinforce the reality that PHOTO-PAINT does

exceptional things at the price of pushing your system to its limits on occasions. Dynamic operations, such as dragging and dropping objects, performing global color corrections on PhotoCD images, and previews (Open image, Filters, and so on) can push your PC beyond its capability to move information in and out of RAM, and to and from temp space on your hard disk. When working in PHOTO-PAINT, it is best not to have screen savers running in the background, have too many TrueType or Type 1 fonts installed, try to download files from online services in the background, or have a large document in queue for printing. PHOTO-PAINT needs all the resources your system can provide; don't handicap your work or PHOTO-PAINT's by running resource-stealing background applications, or by cheating on adequate system configurations.

The Layers/Objects Roll-Up

By default, a new object is automatically created from a copy of a selection area when the Build mode is switched off. Although Build mode necessitates the Create step to make a permanent object, in PHOTO-PAINT's default non-Build mode, every selection you create becomes a discrete object.

The Layers/Objects roll-up provides excellent object management within complex documents. The function of the Layers/Objects roll-up is to keep tab on all the objects and their corresponding layers present in an

image window, as well as assigning objects an opacity and a mode in which they eventually will be merged into the background image. Objects exist on layers, and each layer contains an object (although several image areas can be defined as a single layer/object). Due to the relationship between image layers and objects, you cannot simply create a blank layer to paint on or otherwise edit. You can, however, use the regular object mode to create a copy of a layer upon which you can add or remove design elements. In the next exercise, you will see how to prepare a background image to receive an object.

1. Make sure the Build mode is disabled by either clicking on the Build Mode button on the ribbon bar or unchecking the **O**bject, **B**uild Mode command on the menu.

2. Open the SKY.TIF image file from the *CorelDRAW! The Professional Reference* companion CDs.

3. To demonstrate some of the other properties objects can have, you will copy the sky image so that it becomes an object, leaving the original sky image as a painting surface (canvas) for the final background layer in the composition. Click on the Zoom tool, right-click over the SKY.TIF image, then click and drag the window frames outward so that the background to the image window is exposed. You cannot select anything from the image background, but PHOTO-PAINT enables you to use this space to make an edge-to-edge selection area of the image.

4. Click and hold on the Object Picker tool, then select the Rectangle Object tool from the menu fly-out.

5. Click and diagonal-drag from above and to the left of the sky image to below and to the right of it.

6. Press Ctrl+F7 to display the Layers/Objects roll-up if you haven't already done so (or double-click on the Object Picker tool). As you can see in figure 22.3, the icons on the Layers/Objects roll-up indicate that there are two identical objects on separate layers within the SKY.TIF image file.

Figure 22.3
Automatically create a copy of a selection area using the Object tools.

7. Resize the SKY.TIF image window so that you can see the DOORKNOB.TIF image. Reposition the two images so that you have a clear view of both images, then click on the title bar of DOORKNOB.TIF to make it the active image window.

8. Click and drag the doorknob object from the DOORKNOB.TIF image window into the SKY.TIF image window, as shown in figure 22.4. This command might take PHOTO-PAINT a moment or two to process. You actually have moved the object from one image to another. If you want to leave a copy behind, hold the Ctrl key down while you click and drag the doorknob.

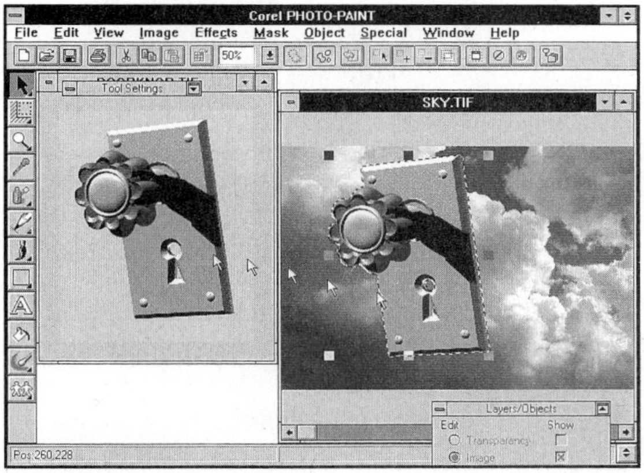

Figure 22.4

You can drag and drop objects between image windows in PHOTO-PAINT.

9. Save the SKY.TIF image as SKYKNOB.CPT. Choose the PHOTO-PAINT (*.CPT) format from the Save File as **T**ype field in the Save an Image to Disk menu. The .CPT format is the only image type available that will accept discrete objects between PHOTO-PAINT sessions; all other image types such as .TIF and .TGA will be automatically

merged to create a standard pixel image file.

In non-Build, regular object Create mode, clicking and dragging automatically produces a copy of the area you marqueed over as an independent object. Right-clicking and dragging, however, cuts the image area out from the background, leaving whatever background color you have defined at the moment to show through when you move the object.

T I P

Although marquee lines are a useful visual reminder of a selection area, the lines can sometimes be a distraction and hinder your view of an image area. The Activate/Deactivate Marquee button (also known as the Marquee Visible button, also found as the Marquee Visible command on the **O**bject menu) hides marquee lines around an object, although the selection will still be an active selection. A good visual hint that an object still exists when the marquee is turned off are the selection handles surrounding the border of the object.

Understanding the Modes of a Selected Object

Besides the capability to decide (and redecide) on a permanent location within an image for objects, PHOTO-PAINT provides the option to edit both the rotation and the boundary of an object. As with CorelDRAW, clicking on an active object displays rotate/skew handles around the four corners of an object. However, clicking a third time on an object produces a set of distortion handles. These distortion handles are very useful for changing an object to produce a sense of perspective within an image.

As you have seen in the previous figures, the doorknob object is rotated in such a way that it won't look right if it is applied to a door that is slightly open and swinging away from the viewer. In the surrealistic composition created in this series of exercises, the sky will be the door upon which the doorknob is affixed. The "skydoor" with its doorknob will be cast slightly open to reveal a background that has not yet been created. This might not be a run-of-the-mill graphics assignment, but it is a very good example of how objects can be edited in PHOTO-PAINT without disturbing objects on other layers. In the following steps, the doorknob will be rotated to a more appropriate angle.

1. Either minimize the DOORKNOB.TIF image or close it. The image used in the rest of the examples is SKYKNOB.CPT. With fewer image windows open, more system resources are available and PHOTO-PAINT will run faster and more predictably.

2. Resize the SKYKNOB.CPT image window so that you have a clear view of the entire image. Roll-ups always remain as the top item in the Drawing Window, so they need to be shuffled around when they obscure your view of an image area.

3. With the doorknob object selected in the SKYKNOB.CPT image, click once on it. This switches the object's mode to rotate/skew, and arrows reminiscent of those found in CorelDRAW surround the object.

4. Click and drag on a corner rotation handle until the Status Line at the bottom of the screen reads about Angle: 8, as shown in figure 22.5. Counterclockwise rotation is measured in positive degrees. Alternatively, you can press Ctrl+F8 to display the Tool Settings roll-up and enter the angle of rotation manually.

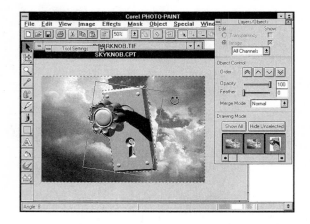

Figure 22.5
PHOTO-PAINT's Status Line will indicate the degree of rotation of an object until you release the mouse button.

As with CorelDRAW, a center of rotation is apparent when a selected object is in rotate/skew mode, and clicking and dragging the bull's-eye center marker with the cursor will change the axis along which an object can be rotated.

Using Distortion Handles To Create Dimensionalism

As mentioned earlier, there is a distort mode available when working with objects. Clicking a second time on an object that is already displaying rotate/skew handles produces a new set of handles used for distorting the object. Clicking and dragging on any of the distortion handles changes the object's boundary and consequentially its shape. Holding the Ctrl key down while clicking and dragging constrains the movement of a distortion handle to the straight line direction in which you first begin to move.

The distort mode is often used to give a sense of dimension and perspective to an object. In the next example, the distort mode is used on the sky object to make it appear as though it is a cosmic doorway, slightly open. No more than one object can be edited at a time, so the exercise starts with selecting the sky object.

Before you begin, make certain that under the **S**pecial, **P**references, General tab, the **S**tretch Mode for Objects is set to Anti-alias/average, and not Stretch/Truncate. See Chapter 21, "Essential Concepts of Pixel-Based Graphics," for a complete explanation of how these two modes of interpolating pixels differ.

1. Click on the sky object in the SKYKNOB.CPT image to select it. This deselects the doorknob object, and you can safely edit the sky object

without disturbing the doorknob. Sometimes you might want an unobstructed view of the layer/object you have selected. You can hide all other objects in the image by clicking on the Hide Unselected button above the Drawing mode window on the Layers/Objects roll-up. Clicking on an individual object's button in the Drawing Mode field will turn the view of that object on or off. The background image of the sky can interfere with your view of the next steps, so why not switch this object view off for a while?

2. Click on the sky to display the rotate/skew handles, then click once more to display the distort handles. The amount you stretch the image by clicking and dragging a corner is not confined to the image area, or even the image window; you can click and drag a distort handle clear off your monitor if you so choose, which is handy for creating extreme effects.

3. Click and drag the top left distort corner down about 1/4 screen inch, then click and drag the bottom left distort corner straight up by the same amount. Although this is not a precision exercise, you might want to choose **V**iew, **R**ulers as an option for other assignments. Rulers steal viewing and working area from the Drawing Window space, so it usually is helpful to have this option off most of the time. The increments the rulers display can be changed in the General tab of the **S**pecial, **P**references menu.

4. Click and drag the top- and bottom-right distortion corners out of frame, as shown in figure 22.6, so that the sky object appears to be viewed in perspective. If you've dragged too far, press Ctrl+Z to Undo your editing move, and try again. It is not recommended that you readjust a distort corner too many times—the Anti-alias interpolation that takes place when you stretch an object degrades image quality, and it cannot be restored by successive distort handle edits.

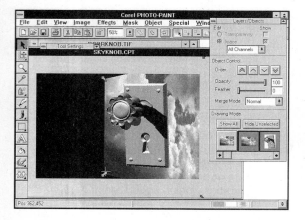

Figure 22.6

Use PHOTO-PAINT's distort handles on objects to create perspective within a design.

It is important to note here that distort and skew/rotate edits performed on an object force PHOTO-PAINT to recalculate pixel assignments within an image, and although it's a sophisticated calculation, something of the original image quality is always lost. If you are stretching an object's side, PHOTO-PAINT creates "in-between" pixels where there's a gap in the fabric of the bitmap grid,

and when you shrink a side, pixels are eliminated from the original object.

Bitmap edits are performed progressively; you make relative changes to a bitmap, not absolute ones you can undo by performing a counter move. If you stretch a side of an object by 100 percent, then shrink it by 50 percent, you have altered the bitmap object twice; you have not restored it to its original state. Use the **E**dit, **U**ndo command if you are unhappy with an editing move; don't try to restore it manually.

Unlike CorelDRAW, there is only one level of Undo under the Edit command. This is why remembering the Ctrl+Z shortcut and using it as second nature will get you out of many potentially disastrous situations.

Feathering and Distorting the Doorknob

In the next set of steps, you will use the distort mode again, this time to create a matching perspective for the doorknob so it appears to be attached to the sky door.

If you are working through this experiment, you might have noticed that the selection area created with the Magic Wand Object tool was not flawless; you might have an edge pixel or two around the outline of the doorknob that is brilliant chartreuse. There are several ways to correct fringing around object outlines. The first (and perhaps most tedious) is to use PHOTO-PAINT's brushes to retouch the offending areas. The second method is to create the object again, except this time specifying a higher Color Comparison Tolerance value for the Magic Wand Object tool.

The disadvantage of setting too high a color tolerance is that RGB pixel images tend to have indistinct edges; one of the 16.7 million colors usually has a neighboring pixel of approximately the same value. The result of setting too high a value when selecting with the Magic Wand Object tool is a border that looks chipped-away. A far better solution is to use the Layers/Objects roll-up's Feather control to soften and remove unwanted colors from the edges of an object.

The first stop in the following exercise is to feather the border of the doorknob, then to use the distortion handles to give the object a perspective similar to the sky object. Feathering is not a permanent edit until you merge layers in a design, so you can choose to increase or decrease feathering at any time in your image-editing work.

1. Click on the doorknob object in the SKYKNOB.CPT image, then click and drag the Feather slider on the Layers/Objects roll-up slightly to the right. Depending on the image size, 3 or 4 pixels, tops, is all one needs to smooth the edge of an object. You also can enter the value manually in the text entry field to the right of the Feather slider, as shown in figure 22.7.

2. Click on the doorknob selection, then click again to display the distort handles. Alternatively, you can select **O**bject, **D**istort to immediately go to this object mode.

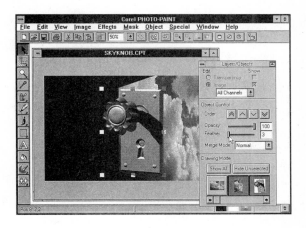

Figure 22.7
Use the Feather slider to soften the edges of an object.

3. Click and drag the edges of the doorknob object so that the horizontal edges of the selection are parallel to those of the sky object, as shown in figure 22.8. The distort boundary box is a good visual guide for duplicating perspectives within an image.

The distort mode basically has no limits. You can choose to actually click and drag one distort boundary over another to create an effect. By giving two distort handles a negative value, you are in effect mirroring an object. Unfortunately, extreme distortions degrade the image quality of certain pixel-based designs, most noticeably photographic images. However, an object consisting of a PHOTO-PAINT fill (texture or fountain) can be distorted significantly without noticeable loss of the quality of the fill.

Figure 22.8
The amount of distortion you apply to an object can be seen as boundary boxes before you finalize an edit.

Creating a New Background Image

The black background you have seen in earlier examples should not be confused with a background image. The background image, the main image an original design is composed upon, can be edited, whereas the black background cannot. If you deselect the image you began with and try to merge objects to the black background, you will lose the object.

However, you occasionally will want to create a layer to serve as a background canvas, upon which you can edit or even replace in its entirety. This is why the sky that was distorted earlier was a copied object; you now have the original background image to modify.

In the next exercise, you will modify the original sky image so that it becomes another element in the design.

1. Click on the icons of the distorted sky and doorknob objects in the Drawing Mode window to hide them, then click on the background sky to make it visible/editable.

2. Double-click on the Rectangle tool on the toolbox. This selects the tool and displays the Tool Settings roll-up.

3. You need to select a fill and an outline attribute before using the Rectangle tool. In its default settings, the Rectangle tool produces a conic fill with a black, rounded outline. Lose the outline entirely by entering **0** in the Size field on the Tool Settings roll-up. Corner Roundness will become irrelevant and the preview box will contain an *x*.

4. Press Shift+F6 (**V**iew, F**i**ll Roll-Up) or double-click on the Current Fill icon (far right swatch) on the Status line to display the Fill roll-up. Choose the fountain fill, and then click on the Radial fill button.

5. To add a little drama within this design, make the main layer, the original image of the sky, a dark background with a hint of light peeking out from the corner. Click on the Edit button on the Fill roll-up to display the Fountain Fill dialog box, and then pick black from the From color palette and a persimmon color from the To color palette.

6. In the Steps field in the upper middle of the Fountain Fill dialog box, unlock the field by clicking on the lock icon, and set the value to about 85 or so. Although the Fountain Fill options box is similar to CorelDRAW's, PHOTO-PAINT needs at least this many in-between steps to produce fountain fills without noticeable banding.

7. Set the **E**dge Pad value to 25. This will produce a highlight of transitional color rather than a smooth transition across the background layer. Click on OK.

8. Click and drag the preview box of the Fill roll-up so that the light Radial highlight is in the lower left corner of the preview box.

9. In the Drawing Window, click an initial point with the Rectangle tool to the upper left on the window background, outside of the active image, and then drag to the lower right, releasing the mouse outside of the active image. The sky background should now look like figure 22.9.

The trick in the last exercise can also be used on objects, but the object marquee is not a constraining border for the Rectangle tool—wherever you click and drag with the Rectangle tool, the object and anything else that falls within the Rectangle tool marquee will be reassigned the specified fill. If you want to fill an object without disturbing other objects, hide everything except the desired object by clicking on the Hide Unselected button in the Layers/Objects roll-up Drawing Mode field.

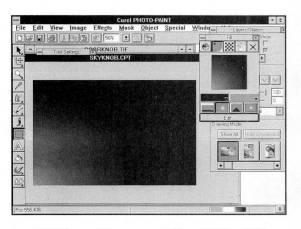

Figure 22.9

Cover an entire image area with a pattern or fill using the Rectangle tool.

Merging Objects

The three components of the design can stay independent of one another in PHOTO-PAINT's proprietary .CPT format. But the .CPT format is not very portable. A .TIF or .TGA format, on the other hand, can be sent to other PCs that don't have PHOTO-PAINT, and even to Macintosh and UNIX platforms. The most obvious disadvantage to letting the composition stand as is, is the reality that these objects can still accidentally be moved around!

To conclude this section on object manipulation, there's one or two rules to be followed in merging the objects that make up an image.

■ Objects have hierarchical order; that is, the object furthest to the right in the

Drawing Mode window is on top of all the other objects. Make certain that your layers of objects are in the right sequence. In the past exercise, layers were not reordered, so you are in good shape at this point, but there will be occasions (as in the next section) where the order of object layers will be shifted. Before you use the Merge command, make sure your layers are in the order you want.

- Objects are merged one at a time. Although you can merge the topmost object to the Background while it overlaps an object on Layer 1, doing this truncates the lower object (Layer 1 object) where image areas overlap. This means that if, for instance, you merge Layer 2 onto the background layer while Layer 2 is still a floating object, any area that Layer 2 overlaps on Layer 1 will be carved out of Layer 1 as a function of the merge. Therefore, it's usually a good idea to decide on a final position for all the object elements before using the Object, Merge (Ctrl+G) command, and not to reposition objects after you've begun the merging process.

In figure 22.10, the conic fill object was merged to the background. The pattern object was in between the background and the conic fill at the time of the merge, and it's now been repositioned. This is an interesting artistic effect, but not always a pleasant one.

Figure 22.10

Don't merge a top object that partially overlaps a lower object that hasn't been merged.

Sequentially, here's how to create a finished image from all the objects in this example:

1. Click on the distorted sky in the image to select it. If the doorknob image is in the way, click on its icon in the Drawing Mode window to hide it for the moment.

2. With the distorted sky object selected, press Ctrl+G (or **O**bject, **M**erge from the menu). The icon of the distorted sky in the Drawing mode window disappears, and the distorted sky and gradient background become one image.

3. Display the doorknob image by clicking on its icon in the Drawing mode window, then press Ctrl+G. There are no more free objects in the image, and you now can save the file as SKYKNOB.TIF, as shown in figure 22.11.

Figure 22.11

A composite image will display only a single Drawing mode window icon.

Creating composite images, as described in the previous sections, is a relatively simple operation when you have single objects to work with and they are in sequential order. When a composition calls for reordering and combining object selections, however, a different approach is called for, and the following section shows how to make the best use of other PHOTO-PAINT selection tools.

Combining and Reordering Objects

At times you will have two objects in precisely the overlapping arrangement that suits a design need and you want to lock the relationship together for final placement in a background other than the one you began

with. The Lasso Object tool fits this particular need because of its unique selection capability. There is no equivalent to the Lasso Object tool in CorelDRAW; the Lasso Object tool is used to freehand-select an area, then a border is created around the encompassed area that excludes the color value where you initially click with the tool. This means you can eliminate a color field from your selection the same as with the Magic Wand Object tool, but the added benefit here is that you can select and copy multiple objects in one fell swoop.

In the following exercise, the letter *P* and the number *5* have been saved as objects within the .CPT file format. The P5.CPT image has a white background, and the image was prepared using the steps outlined earlier for creating objects. The goal in this example is to place the *P* so that it overlaps the *5* in sort of an aesthetic way, create a composite copy of the arrangement, and then place it as a single object upon a different background.

1. Open the P5.CPT image from the *CorelDRAW! The Professional Reference* companion CDs, located in the CHAP22 subdirectory.

2. Choose the Object Picker tool, then click and drag the *P* to overlap the *5*. If you look at the Layers/Objects roll-up, you will see that this is an impossible feat; the *5* is to the right of the *P*, which indicates that it is on a higher layer than the *P*.

3. Click on the *5* to select it, then click on the single down arrow on the Layers/Objects roll-up to demote the *5* one layer, as shown in figure 22.12.

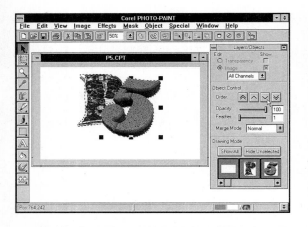

Figure 22.12

Use the arrow buttons to promote or demote an object by one or all layers.

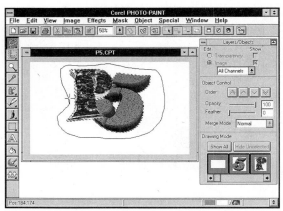

Figure 22.13

Use the Lasso Object tool to encompass the P and 5 with an outline.

4. Click on the Build Mode button on the ribbon bar (or choose **O**bject, **B**uild Mode from the menu). The outline of these shapes can be selected as objects, but the "counters" in the *P* and *5* will need to be deselected, and noncontiguous image areas require the **B**uild Mode to create.

5. Click and hold on the Object Picker tool to reveal the menu fly-out, then click on the Lasso Object tool.

6. Click and drag an outline that encompasses both the *P* and *5,* as shown in figure 22.13, then release the mouse button. In Build mode, you cannot deliberately cut a selection area away to become an object by right-clicking. Don't do this now, but for example, the cut action is performed by choosing **O**bject, **C**reate, Cu**t**. The ribbon bar's Create button cannot cut out an object.

7. Click and hold on the Object Picker tool, then select the Magic Wand Object tool. The inside "counter" areas of the *P* and *5* are solid white, which makes them more easily selected with the Magic Wand Object tool.

8. Click on the Remove from Selection button on the ribbon bar (or choose the **S**pecial, **R**emove from Selection command), then click inside the *P* and the *5* where white areas are still included in the selection, as shown in figure 22.14.

9. Now that only the solid portions of both objects are selected, click on the Create button on the Button Ribbon (or choose **O**bject, **C**reate from the menu). The Layers/Objects Drawing mode window can display only three objects without scrolling, but if you scroll to the right, you will see that an

amalgam of the *P* and *5* has been added to the layers of objects within this image. The original, discrete objects still exist, but you have reordered them and made a composite that now can be copied to another background.

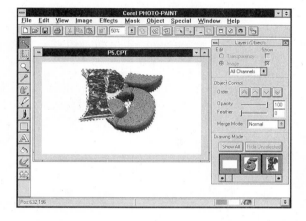

Figure 22.14
In Build mode, complex shapes can be subtracted or added to one another to create an object.

10. Choose **F**ile, **N**ew (or click on the New button on the ribbon bar) and specify a Width 4" by Height 3", at 150 dpi resolution, and 24-bit color, then click on OK. These specifications were designed when the P5.CPT image was created, and will nicely hold the new object you have created. For more information about determining file dimensions and resolution, refer to Chapter 21, "Essential Concepts of Pixel-Based Graphics."

11. Use the Rectangle tool to create an interesting background for the new object in this new image file. PHOTO-PAINT's texture collection is identical to CorelDRAW's, except that textures within an image might appear a little more refined. This is because Corel textures belong to the bitmap family of computer graphics, and CorelDRAW doesn't include editing and viewing support as complete as its paint-oriented sibling.

12. Resize and reposition the two image windows, then click and drag the *P5* object into the P5_BACK.TIF image window, as shown in figure 22.15.

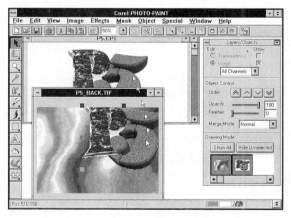

Figure 22.15
A composite of objects retains their relative positions and can be copied and moved without fear of messing up stuff.

The Modes of the Merge Command

When two objects are merged, by default the topmost pixels replace the underlying pixels. You can change the default, however, by selecting one of the many modes on the Layers/Objects roll-up prior to using the Merge command. Sometimes you might be looking for an artistic effect, whereas other times a special merge mode can eliminate some unwanted foreground pixels in an object altogether when the command is made. In figure 22.16, the Invert mode has been chosen for the *P5* object. Invert changes the object to the chromatic opposite of its original color values; blue becomes yellow, green becomes magenta, and so on. You can preview on-screen and change your mind about any Merge mode before making the Merge command.

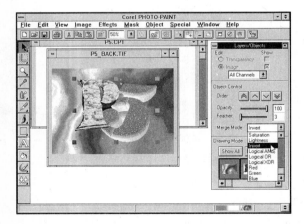

Figure 22.16

Choose a mode for an object to be merged to create different effects.

The following is a brief description of what to expect from each Merge Mode:

■ **Normal.** This retains the color values of the objects; pixels in the background object are replaced with the topmost object's pixels where they overlap.

■ **Add.** Combines the values of the object with underlying values of the background. A blue object on top of a white background will be merged as white; against a black background it would merge blue; and against a colored background, the object would lighten the background toward a white color.

■ **Subtract.** Removes color from the background. A light object darkens a light background, whereas a dark object usually turns background areas it's merged into a very dark or black color.

■ **Difference.** Changes the object's color to the chromatic opposite when placed on a white background, and changes colored areas in the background to black when merged.

■ **Multiply.** The object retains original color values when merged against white, and will decrease brightness of colored background areas when merged. This is a key mode you'll want to use in lots of situations in the future.

■ **Divide.** Changes the object color to white when merged to a white background; changes colored background areas to the chromatic opposite of the original.

■ **If Lighter.** This mode causes colors in an object to retain color value if the underlying background is darker than the object area above it, and colors lighter than the background in the object merge transparent.

■ **If Darker.** If an object is darker than the corresponding underlying background, the object merges with its original color values. If object color is lighter than background, the object area merges as transparent.

■ **Texturize.** All colors except white in an object merge as grayscale against a background. The amount of grayscale texturize merge produces depends on how dark the object color is. Texturize produces a similar effect to Multiply, except that object color values are discarded during the merge.

■ **Color.** Changes color values in an object to a tint of the predominant primary color. Merging in Color mode produces an effect similar to placing colored sunglasses over a background area. White values in the object become transparent.

■ **Hue.** The object color changes the background image to reflect the object's hue without disturbing Saturation or Brightness values in the background. Try this mode as a more subtle variation than Color merge mode.

■ **Saturation.** The object saturates the color background areas with original background color values that vary

according to how saturated the object is. With dull objects containing high grayscale (little saturation) values, the object will bleach the background toward white. This mode is best used with pure color objects merged to photographic image backgrounds. Very little object detail is retained in a Saturation merge.

■ **Lightness.** The object bleaches the entire background area it covers toward pure, light colors, with no grayscale content. Try using the opacity slider in combination with Lightness merge to highlight a background area.

■ **Invert.** The object has no effect over the background it's merged to, but instead adopts the chromatic opposite of original object color values. Invert produces an effect similar to viewing a color film negative of an original object.

■ **Logical AND.** Accommodates color values found in both the original background and the object merged to it. This is a useful mode when the object is a pure color and the background is of a scene or other image of visual interest. Merging two such images produces a heavy tint of the background image.

■ **Logical OR.** Retains only color values unique to the object to be merged; all other colors common to the background are replaced by background color. This merge mode tends to bleach the object into the background, keeping only lighter object details.

■ **Logical XOR.** The object to be merged retains color values unique to the object but not found in the background, and multiplies colors found in both the object and background, producing both darker and lighter values in the merge. This effect can produce a solarized effect, depending on the object's visual content. Try using a photographic object on a solid background as a test for this merge mode.

■ **Red.** Emphasizes the red component of the object, and turns other color areas transparent. In Red mode, the object colors the underlying background to a complementary color; for example, Red over a green area produces yellow.

■ **Green.** Emphasizes the green component of the object, and turns other color areas transparent.

■ **Blue.** Emphasizes the blue component of the object, and turns other object colors transparent.

The Red, Green, and Blue merge modes act like selective color filters when merged to the background. When a primary color is present in the object and the same color merge mode is selected, the effect is a combination of bleaching and tinting. If a color value is not present in the object when a specific color merge mode is selected, a mild tint or no effect at all will be performed on the background upon merging.

Merge modes can serve as a valuable set of special effects filters within PHOTO-PAINT. Experiment with a mode in combination with the Opacity slider before you issue the Merge command, and you might achieve a pleasing effect as an added bonus to your compositing work.

Editing an Object Outline

Accurate definition of an object outline can be critical to a piece. The examples earlier in this chapter were set up to demonstrate a capability of some of the Object selection tools, but often an image area you need as an object is not surrounded by pristine white or other solid colors. Photographic images often contain distracting background elements that are a mixture of different color values, and the Magic Wand Object tool would prove to be a poor one to trim the object outline.

The Freehand Object tool creates irregular outlines that can be turned into an object border, and its operation is as versatile and unconstrained as CorelDRAW's Pencil tool. If you're using a mouse as input hardware, however, a lot of tools don't have the precision required to accurately use them. This is why PHOTO-PAINT features an Object Node Edit tool. When you define an object in Build mode, you can switch to the Object Node Edit tool to convert a Build mode marquee outline to a path with repositionable nodes. The path the Object Node Edit tool makes can be handled with the finesse and precision of outline paths you make in CorelDRAW. After your refining work is done on the path, you can convert the path back to a marquee outline and use the Create command to finish building an object.

The example to follow illustrates the procedure for selecting an image area to become an object using the Freehand Object tool in combination with the Object Node Edit tool.

1. Open the EFF.TIF image from the *CorelDRAW! The Professional Reference* companion CDs, then click on the Build Mode icon (**O**bject, **B**uild Mode), as shown in figure 22.17. Then select the Freehand Object tool from the Object tools menu fly-out, also shown in figure 22.17. With Build mode active, you can switch between a marquee and path description of the outline you'll create.

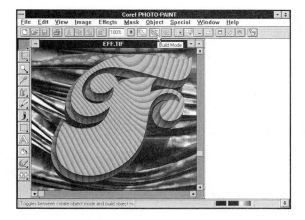

Figure 22.17
Use Build mode when you want to perform editing work on a selection before it defines an object.

2. Click and drag an outline with the Freehand Object tool that roughly describes the wooden *F*, as shown in figure 22.18. Precision is not important

because you'll refine the border next. All the Freehand Object tool does is outline an area; it doesn't create a selection area based on color similarities as does the Lasso Object tool.

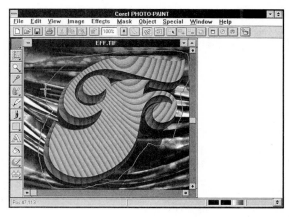

Figure 22.18
The Freehand Object tool creates freeform selection areas.

If you let go of the mouse button while drawing an outline with either the Freehand or Lasso Object tool, PHOTO-PAINT automatically closes the outline, taking the shortest direction between the outline beginning and where you left off. This path is a straight line, and sometimes this is desired. Most of the time, however, a straight line is unwelcome, and you must be in Build mode to compensate for any truncated selection outline.

3. Click and hold on the Freehand Object tool to reveal the Object tools menu fly-out, and select the Node Edit Object tool. As you can see in figure 22.19, PHOTO-PAINT automatically calculates nodes for the outline and creates a path very similar in its properties to a shape created in CorelDRAW with the Freehand Pencil tool. What is unique about this Node Edit Object tool path is that it lies on top of the image and doesn't physically react to the image in any way. The path is an intermediate step to creating an object from the image that the outline describes.

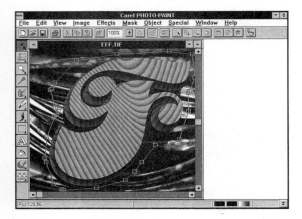

Figure 22.19

Cusp-property nodes and curved line segments represent the path you drew using the Freehand Object tool.

4. You most likely have more nodes than you need to manipulate in order to perfectly describe the outline of the *F*.

If you click on a node, then press Del, you'll remove a node from the path. Don't get overly ambitious in deleting superfluous nodes, however, because you cannot add nodes to an outline path. Keep a node at about every 120 degrees of an arc, and leave a node where you want sharp turns in the path.

5. Manipulating the nodes is a process identical to working with them in a CorelDRAW shape, except you cannot change node properties—PHOTO-PAINT has no Node Edit roll-up.

6. When you have a path outline that fits the *F* snugly, it's time to convert the path back into a selection marquee. Click and hold on the Object Node Edit tool, then select any tool except the Object Picker. When an object tool is active, the path will revert to a marquee outline.

7. Press the Create button on the ribbon bar (or choose **O**bject, **C**reate), then Cu**t** or **C**opy. You now have an object within the EFF.TIF file.

8. If you're getting up to stretch at this point, choose Save **A**s, then choose CorelPHOTO-PAINT (*.CPT) in the Save File as **T**ype box, and save your work to hard disk. If a native TIF image with an object in it is accidentally closed, PHOTO-PAINT will automatically merge all layers.

N O T E

Whenever you use the Save or Save **A**s command, you have the option to check the **B**ackup box. The Backup option saves an identical copy of the image, but places a dollar sign ($) as the last letter of the file extension. Most image viewing and editing programs won't be able to understand this extension, so the backup copy cannot accidentally be opened and modified. If you want the backup copy to become available on your or someone else's PC, rename the file using Windows File Manager or another third-party Windows utility.

The capability to modify an object outline as a path obviously holds a lot of attraction for experienced CorelDRAW users. Every object tool in PHOTO-PAINT calls for a situation that best suits a tool's unique properties. You must consider the nature of what you're selecting before doing any editing. In the next section, you'll add the *F* to a different background image and examine the background for an opportunity to use an object tool that suits the task and the theme of the design.

Editing Natural, Random Image Areas

The composition in this section is based on the theme of Fall. The *F* object is the first letter of "FALL," and the other three letters will be added by importing a CorelDRAW design. These elements, plus a realistic shadow, will be added to the FALL.TIF image (in the CHAP22 subdirectory on the *CorelDRAW! The Professional Reference*

companion CDs). All the objects can be composited easier and quicker than you imagine if you bear in mind some of the techniques covered earlier in this section.

Before getting into a technique for selecting random, natural patterns such as the leaves in the FALL.TIF image, add the *F* object to the FALL.TIF image by first opening the FALL.TIF image, repositioning and resizing it in PHOTO-PAINT's workspace so both EFF.CPT and FALL.TIF can be seen, then clicking and dragging the *F* object into the FALL.TIF image window.

As you can see in figure 22.20, the EFF.CPT image has been closed, and the image zoomed to 100% (double-clicking on the Zoom tool takes the active image window to 1:1 viewing resolution). The *F* object is on top of the background FALL.TIF image, but by hiding it, you can create objects out of the FALL.TIF image areas that then become the topmost layer in the object composition. For an experiment, follow the next steps to isolate leaves in the background image. They then can be merged on top of the wooden *F* so that the effect of the *F* being surrounded by leaves in a dimensional scene is created.

The wonderful aspect about organic, natural patterns found in wood, leaves, sand, and other materials is that the edges aren't as pronounced as you'd find in the *F* object or another sharp geometric shape. This means precision isn't as critical in selecting an object that is easily recognized by its visual content and not necessarily its outline. In essence, when you create a leaves object in the next exercise, accurately trimming around each leaf's outline won't necessarily contribute to the overall finished image.

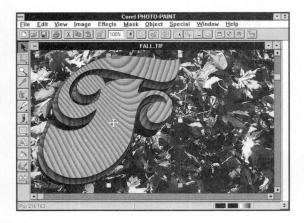

Figure 22.20

Click and drag the object across to a new background, then close the first background image to conserve system resources.

1. Switch the wooden *F* object off on the Layers/Objects roll-up's Drawing Mode window. The object becomes invisible and impervious to the editing work you'll perform next.

2. Click and hold on the Object Picker tool to display the menu fly-out, then select the Freehand Object tool.

3. Click on the Build Mode button on the ribbon bar.

4. Trace around a leaf in the fall background image. Pay attention to the outline of the leaf—that is, you won't be converting the leaf selection to a path as you did earlier, so strive for precision, but don't sweat it if the outline is off by a pixel or two here and there.

5. Click on the Add to Selection button on the ribbon bar (or choose **S**pecial, **A**dd to Selection). Now, subsequent closed selections you draw will be added to the original leaf selection, and a group of noncontiguous areas can be defined as one object when the Create command is made.

N O T E

The four buttons grouped on the ribbon bar, of which Add to Selection is one, are for adding to and eliminating contiguous or noncontiguous image areas as part of a selection. On the far left of this group is the Select command, which returns you to a new selection mode after using one of the other three buttons. Use the Select button when you're finished adding to or subtracting from a selection and want to begin defining a new, discrete object within an image area. The XOR command on the far right of the group of four buttons enables you to add background or object areas to a selection except the areas where two marquees overlap. This is an interesting capability that can be used to produce checkerboard objects and other "peek through" areas. The XOR selection provides a similar effect to combining overlapping, filled shapes in CorelDRAW.

6. After you have selected a few leaves, use the Create command to turn the selections into objects (duplicates of the image areas they surround). In figure 22.21, you can see that the selected leaves are scattered around the periphery of where the *F* will finally be merged.

Figure 22.21

Noncontiguous (areas that don't touch) selections can make up a single object using the Build Mode, Add to Selection, and Create commands.

Figure 22.22

Use the object property of the image areas to compose an aesthetic design.

7. Click on the F icon on the Layers/ Objects Drawing Mode window to display it and make it an active part of the image.

8. Select the leaves object within the image, then click and drag the object so that it covers areas of the wooden *F,* as shown in figure 22.22. Because the leaves object was created after the wooden *F,* its order in the layers of the design is on top and requires no reassignment to a lower layer.

Do not use the merge command yet. You need to add the letters *all* to the composition, and depending on your own artistic tastes, you might want to reposition all the elements in different locations before merging them. Don't deprive yourself of some of the power of PHOTO-PAINT's object layers by merging elements before all the players have been added to a scene.

Working with CorelDRAW, EPS Images, and PHOTO-PAINT

The Text tool in PHOTO-PAINT is a rudimentary tool for adding words to your images. It is not nearly as capable or flexible as CorelDRAW's Text tool, and for this reason you'll take an excursion to CorelDRAW in the next section to create the letters *all* to complete the design. PHOTO-PAINT's Text tool will place floating object text on an image, but you cannot resize text without noticeable pixelation, and you cannot use creative transformations such as individual character rotation or envelopes on PHOTO-PAINT text per se.

CorelDRAW has a bevy of import/export filters that cover most bitmap and vector image types, and Encapsulated PostScript (EPS) usually is the best format for creating

and exporting text to pixel-based programs. .EPS images contain a mathematical (vector type) description of the image contents, and for this reason .EPS images are resolution independent. You can import an .EPS image into PHOTO-PAINT at any size, and the edges of the EPS design are clean and smooth.

Because CorelDRAW offers a type of .EPS export format for a CorelDRAWn image as grayscale information, you can export text that's clean and has no native color values that require correction in PHOTO-PAINT. After PHOTO-PAINT rasterizes the vector information to the size of your choosing, the information is then pixel-based and can be edited to have any color or texture you choose.

To create lettering to accompany the design in this section, follow these steps:

1. Choose **F**ile, Save As, then choose PHOTO-PAINT (*.CPT) in the Save File as **T**ype field and save the piece as FALL.CPT to your hard disk.

As mentioned earlier, most other graphics-capable applications cannot recognize this format. However, CorelDRAW will import a .CPT image, so you can use a copy as a reference within CorelDRAW's Drawing window. The only disadvantage in importing an object/layer bitmap is that CorelDRAW ignores objects that haven't been merged to the background; CorelDRAW will display only the original background image, which is okay for our purposes. The FALL.CPT image is used in CorelDRAW to size up the positioning of the *all* lettering you'll create in CorelDRAW, where it fits and what size it should be in the final composition. You

already have a fair idea of where the wooden *F* will be within the final image design. If this was a placement-critical design, you might decide to merge the *F* and the leaves before importing a copy to CorelDRAW, and save a Backup copy of the design unmerged.

2. Start CorelDRAW, click on the Import button, and choose the drive and directory where the FALL.CPT image is located.

3. When the image is placed on the Printable Page, choose the Rectangle tool and click and drag a rectangle that more or less matches the image dimensions of the FALL.CPT import, as shown in figure 22.23. This will be used as a background for the fore-ground lettering you'll create next. PHOTO-PAINT will need a field of reference for its import of the CorelDRAW .EPS export, and it's best if the background upon which you add text is roughly the same size as the image you're working on in PHOTO-PAINT.

4. With the Text tool, type **all**, then use your creative instincts as to the appearance, rotation, and font of each character. In figure 22.24, Bodoni Poster (italic) has been used, the Shape tool has scattered the characters off the baseline somewhat, and the **T**ext, **C**haracter command has been used to rotate the letters a little. Because most users prefer the default style of black text, the *all* letters might not be readily visible on top of the imported bitmap, and you might want to fill the text with white until your design of them is finalized.

Figure 22.23

Create a background of similar dimensions to the image you imported.

Figure 22.24

The "all" lettering, with its font, appearance, and rotation changed.

5. After the lettering is the way you want it, give the rectangle a white fill with no outline, and make the text black. If you intend to save the design as a

.CDR file in addition to exporting it, you might consider deleting the copy of FALL.CPT from the file, because bitmaps take up a lot of hard drive space and you don't really need the bitmap for further reference. In figure 22.25, you can see the wireframe view of the design. This might be an easier view to recolor the text and background, because white text on a white rectangle is hard to select and change to black.

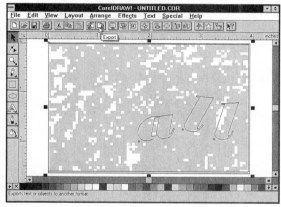

Figure 22.25

The rectangle background and text are the only objects to be exported to .EPS format.

6. Click on the rectangle, Shift+click on the text to select both objects, then click on the export button on CorelDRAW's ribbon bar (or choose **F**ile, **E**xport).

7. Choose Adobe Illustrator, *.ai, *.eps in the List Files of **T**ype drop-down list, and name the file **FALL.EPS**. The .AI

extension also works as an Encapsulated PostScript export, but is not as universally accepted with programs other than those made by Adobe and Corel.

N O T E

By default, Adobe Illustrator v1.1 is selected in the EPS Export dialog box. Leave this setting this way. Adobe Illustrator was a "classic" version, and the format, the arrangement of image information, is the de facto standard for most other imaging and drawing programs.

8. Check the **S**elected Only box before clicking on OK. You do not want the copy of the FALL.CPT image to travel along with the lettering and rectangle background.

9. Close CorelDRAW and restart PHOTO-PAINT. Use the File, Open command to import the newly created .EPS file.

10. PHOTO-PAINT doesn't work directly with an .EPS image, but instead converts the information to a new bitmap-type image. In figure 22.26, you can see the Import Into Bitmap dialog box PHOTO-PAINT displays after an .EPS image is chosen to load. Image resolution is an important consideration here; the FALL.TIF image is 150 dpi (pixels/inch), and the .EPS import should have matching resolution for it to have the same image dimensions. If you're in doubt as to the resolution of a host image, use the **I**mage, **I**nfo command to check before importing a resolution-independent component of your design.

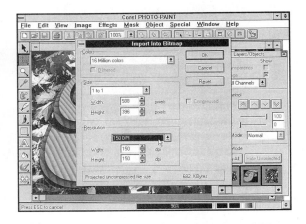

Figure 22.26
Choose the same image resolution for an EPS as the image you'll be adding it to.

11. Choose 24-bit color as the mode for the imported .EPS image. The color mode doesn't affect the property of the lettering; it's still made up of a grayscale color space. But you'll be coloring the lettering in PHOTO-PAINT, so a 24-bit color mode will enable you to use all of PHOTO-PAINT's texture, fill, and other tools to edit the import.

Creating a Gaussian Blur Drop Shadow Object

Because object tools can be used to create an object as a duplicate of an original area, there's untold amount of design possibilities for the 24-bit color .EPS import at present. One of the photo-realistic effects PHOTO-PAINT offers is the *Gaussian Blur,* a distortion of image area that creates lifelike shadows from grayscale designs. Gaussian Blurs display a bell-shaped curve to the area to which they are applied; center areas are densest, and the edges gently fall off into a haze. An effect such as this cannot be achieved in CorelDRAW with as much realism as you'd find a shadow in real life.

Before coloring the text, you need to create a selection area around it to create an object that will be Gaussian-blurred. Because Gaussian Blurs spread out, you do not want a tight selection border created around the lettering, but instead want plenty of white space to take up the bleed from the Gaussian Blur. Before merging the blurred selection, you'll use the multiply mode on the Layers/ Objects roll-up to eliminate the lighter, white portions of the object.

Here's how to make a convincing digital shadow for the text you'll add shortly:

1. Click on the Select button to deactivate the Build and Add to Selection modes, then with the Freehand Object tool, click and drag a rough area around the *all* text.

2. Choose Effe**c**ts, Fancy, then choose Gaussian Blur.

3. Increasing the **R**adius of the Gaussian Blur effect heightens the blurring and speeds the fall-off across a selection area. As you can see in figure 22.27, a Radius value of 13 creates a good blurry shadow in this instance. Click on the Pre**v**iew button to confirm your

settings for the effect. You might have to put the cursor inside the Preview window, where it becomes a hand tool, and scroll the active Preview view around until you see the lettering with the future blur applied.

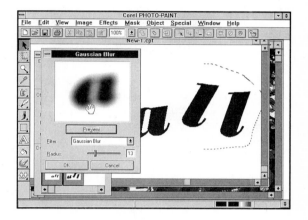

Figure 22.27

The Preview window shows the entire active image; place your cursor inside and scroll until you see the desired image area.

4. Click on OK. The Gaussian Blur effect (and several others) are processor-intensive; expect to wait 5–10 seconds on even a fast 486 machine with plenty of RAM. Load the FALL.CPT image next. It should be the first on the four last-saved list under the **F**ile command.

5. Reposition and resize the two image windows, then click and drag the blurry *all* object into the FALL.CPT image window, as shown in figure 22.28.

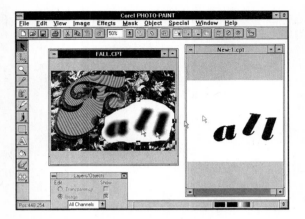

Figure 22.28

The blurred "all" text will become a shadow beneath regular text in the finished image.

Figure 22.29

Multiply merge mode turns lighter shades within an object transparent.

6. You don't need to merge the blurred text yet, but it would be helpful if the white background within the object would disappear at this point! Click on Multiply Mode with the blurred object selected. As you can see in figure 22.29, the lighter (white) value within an object becomes transparent, while the darker areas intensify the areas covering the background image.

If you wanted to do something extraordinary with the two contrasting shades in the *all* object, other modes, as described earlier, would do the trick. The goal, however, is to create a surrealistic image, not an unrealistic one, so Multiply mode helps make a shadow for which you now need to create some autumnal text.

Painting over an Object That Has No Background

The beginning of the chapter discusses the peculiar structure of a bitmap-type image that has no background. In PHOTO-PAINT, when you hide all the object layers in a multilayer image, you are presented with a black image area. This is not a background; you cannot paint over it, and you cannot copy a selection out of it. The black area is not featured as a layer on the Layers/Objects roll-up, and the only way to make it appear is by hiding the original background image.

The advantage to having an inky void readily accessible is that it gives you some place over which to fill an object. If you paint outside the lines of a selected object, the paint simply disappears into the black image space, and you have a neatly recolored object to later position against an original image background and other objects.

In the next exercise, you'll see how to recolor another copy of the *all* selection in one or two mouse clicks and make this object fit into the FALL.CPT composition as if it was painstakingly hand-colored with a painting tool.

1. With the New-1.CPT (the FALL.EPS import copy) active, select the Magic Wand Object tool from the Object Tool fly-out, then click on the Build Mode button on the ribbon bar.

2. Click on the letter *A*, then on *L*, then the last letter *L*. The Magic Wand Object tool selects only the black image areas, so the white counter within the *A* is not part of the complex object, as shown in figure 22.30.

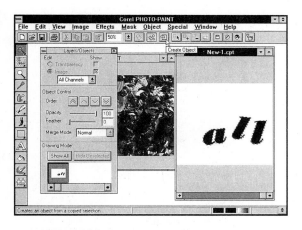

Figure 22.30
Use the Magic Wand Object tool to select just the black areas in the image.

3. Click on the Create button. You'll notice that the Drawing mode window on the Layers/Objects roll-up now sports an object in addition to the original background image.

4. Hide the original background image by clicking its icon off in the Drawing Mode window.

5. Terrific. You now have a black object surrounded by a black void with black selection handles around the object. You must use faith at this point to proceed with the conviction that there's something in the image you can color! Press Shift+F6 to display the Fill roll-up, then click on the Rectangle tool.

6. Select a fountain fill that steps from orange to gold. In the example in the figures, a Radial type fountain fill works nicely.

7. Click and drag the Rectangle tool to marquee the image area you believe where the *all* object is located. In figure 22.31, you can see that instant, fountain-filled lettering now appears. You haven't altered the original background image because it was hidden, so it can be reused again in case you want to try different color variations.

8. Click and drag the *all* object onto the FALL.CPT image window, then reposition it so it is to the left and above the blurred all text, as shown in figure 22.32.

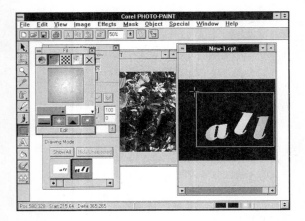

Figure 22.31

The Rectangle tool covers image objects, but won't affect the blank area behind images.

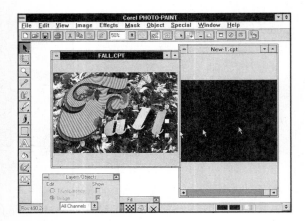

Figure 22.32

The blurred object beneath the fountain-filled lettering suggests a light source and direction within the image.

Pixel-based lettering never quite displays as lifelike a quality as other visual detail because

we commonly perceive lettering as smooth, and—let's face it—text is a man-made invention. To soften the edges of the fountain fill text, and to allow it to blend a little into the background areas, increase the Feather value on the Layers/Objects roll-up to 1, as shown in figure 22.33.

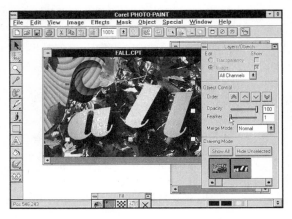

Figure 22.33

A very small Feather value helps blend objects into the background scene.

You should merge each object to the background image in order of its layer once you're happy with the composition of the image. Figure 22.34 is a full-screen display of the image. Press F9 to clear the screen of menus, tools, and roll-ups, then press Esc when you've previewed enough. You will find that many commands are identical to CorelDRAW's in PHOTO-PAINT, while others have small variations.

Figure 22.34
The finished, merged image.

Summary (Moving from Objects to Masks)

Users who are new to version 5 of PHOTO-PAINT (which means everyone) experience exasperation on occasion when they mistake PHOTO-PAINT's Object tools with Masking tools. The tools are strikingly similar in appearance, and the menu fly-outs are located right next to each other.

Applying a mask to an area is not the same as making an object from it, although masks can be used as the basis for objects you create. The similarities overlap and the differences are quite pronounced, and Chapter 23 is an introduction to the capability masking provides in your imaging set of tools.

Masks

Masks serve a different design function than PHOTO-PAINT objects, but the way you create, manipulate, and modify them is almost identical to working with the Object tools, as described in Chapter 22. So why a chapter on masks? Masks are a complement to the editing capabilities of Layers Objects; they help you isolate image areas so that you can modify portions of an existing image. Additionally, selections made from masks can be converted to objects—you have a lot of artistic flexibility when you tap into the power of Masks in PHOTO-PAINT.

How often has the color cast been off in only a section of a photo? What do you do when you want to paint over an image area instead of replacing it with an object? How can you change a single color value within an image? You use masks.

This chapter covers:

- Creating and working with an Opaque mask

- Using Color masks

- Spot and process color

- Using Transparency masks

- Saving and editing masks

- Using special effects and masks

Masks come in three varieties in PHOTO-PAINT, and you can exchange one type for another and continue your editing work with masks for different purposes. This chapter explores the creative uses of masks in a variety of situations you probably encounter in your own work. You also learn by way of example some of the outstanding things you can do with masks that only happen when you perform digital imaging in the world of CorelPHOTO-PAINT.

Types of PHOTO-PAINT Masks

PHOTO-PAINT offers the following three different types of masking features, each of which suits a particular imaging need:

■ A *Regular* mask is defined by using the suite of masking tools on the toolbox fly-out menu. Regular masks are general-purpose masks, whose function is to isolate an image area for editing purposes, while protecting unmasked image areas from change. Regular masks are 100-percent opaque—they completely protect (or expose) image areas, and the boundary of a Regular mask is hard-edged. A Regular mask has properties of 1 bit/pixel information; areas in an image that contain a Regular mask are either "on" or "off." Regular masks can be saved to an image file format and can be recalled and reused when you want to isolate an identically sized, shaped, and placed image area in the original image or another image. When active in an image, a Regular mask is easily identified by a marquee outline.

■ A *Transparency* mask can be designed above an image to partially protect image areas from editing. Unlike a Regular mask, a Transparency mask operates at 8 bits/pixel in protecting or exposing image areas. This capability of a Transparency mask can lead to some interesting design possibilities, such as allowing partial editing of an image with a 50-percent Transparency mask active. Unlike Regular masks, a Transparency mask is not viewed on-screen by a marquee outline, but instead by a transparent color overlay that indicates the percentage of masking an image area has. Transparency masks are edited with paint and fill tools, not the Masking tools on the menu fly-out. Transparency masks can be saved to an 8-bit/pixel grayscale image format. Additionally, you can convert a Transparency mask into a Regular mask and vice versa.

■ A *Color* mask selects an image area based on its color range, not by any specific geometric constraints within an image. Color masks are most useful for replacing original colors in an image, and Color masks can also be converted to a Regular mask.

Because these three mask types are interchangeable, you may decide to begin isolating an image area based on color range, convert the selection to a Regular mask and refine the selection with a Masking tool, then change the mask to a Transparency mask so you can take advantage of the Transparency mask's partial selection property. In the next section, you'll explore the best usage of the PHOTO-PAINT workhorse, the Regular mask, and how to define and edit one.

Defining a Regular Mask

Although the Rectangle, Ellipse, and other geometric shape-producing tools in PHOTO-PAINT are useful sometimes, very few photographic images you'll come by in your imaging experiences will contain only straight or curved lines. Most image areas you want to protect from editing (or allow to be edited while protecting an image background) are composed of an irregular outline. Using a combination of Masking tools therefore is the best methodology to adopt from the beginning of an assignment. When masking a bicycle from a background, for example, use the Freehand Mask tool for some areas, click on the Add To or Subtract From selection buttons, then continue to refine the mask border with the Mask Node Edit tool and the Mask Brush tool.

The following steps should help you understand how to work with a custom mask selection border. An image of a picnic meal is perched on a table. Imagine

that it's a bright day, so the picture was taken with a high F-stop; as a result, the background of the picnic feast is in sharp focus. Pictures get too busy when the background detail encroaches on (or even overwhelms) the foreground action. In this example, you diminish the visual interest of the background in the PICNIC.TIF image while retaining the foreground detail of the feast.

A prudent first step in refocusing this picture is to protect the foreground so that the background area can be altered. To use a combination of PHOTO-PAINT's Mask tools to enhance the picnic picture, follow these steps:

1. In PHOTO-PAINT, choose **F**ile, **O**pen (or click on the Open button on the ribbon bar). Then select the PICNIC.TIF image from the *CorelDRAW! The Professional Reference* companion CDs. It's located in the CHAP23 subdirectory.

2. Click on OK to ignore PHOTO-PAINT's warning that PICNIC.TIF is a read-only file; save it under the same name to your hard disk to avoid future warnings.

3. After the image is displayed in the drawing window, click-and-drag the window frame so that the window background is visible beyond the image area. You need to mask parts of the picnic scene right up to the image edge. Expanding the window makes the edges easy to select.

4. Click-and-hold on the Rectangle Mask tool to reveal the fly-out menu of Mask tools. Click on the Polygon Mask tool (the icon with the pair of shears). You're going to create a rough outline around the background of the PICNIC image and refine it in a moment.

5. Click outside the upper right corner of the PICNIC image. Then click again where the background meets the picnic table along the right edge of the image. It's okay to click outside of the live image area with the Polygon (or any other) Mask tool; when a marquee is made from the outline you've defined, it will shrink to fit the image border.

6. Continue tracing a rough counter-clockwise outline around the background area, excluding the top of the frankfurter, but touching the edge of the picnic table.

In figure 23.1, you can see a polygon outline in its early stages. Because you cannot accurately trace around the top curve of the frankfurter with a Mask tool that produces straight lines, click points of inflection around the curves. Image in the way you would trace a curve using the Freehand tool in CorelDRAW—create straight-line segments that overlap (or miss) the edge of a curve, and then convert the

segments to curves and adjust them to fit whatever you're tracing. You will modify the straight segments of the polygon mask later, so it's okay to change directions by clicking a corner on an area that you will adjust later.

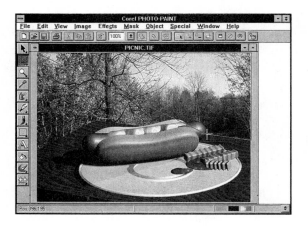

Figure 23.1

Click on a point where you come to a sharp change in direction within the area you want to isolate with the Polygon Mask tool.

7. After you define the entire outline of the background area, double-click on the last point with the Polygon Mask tool. A mask marquee appears in place of the polygon lines, and areas outside the live-image area have snapped inward to perfectly frame the edges, as shown in figure 23.2.

Figure 23.2
Polygon Mask lines can be shaped with as many facets as you need.

Now you need to modify the mask marquee because the curved areas of the top of the frankfurter have been sliced through by straight marquee lines, and the intention here is to create an accurate mask around the background that excludes all foreground image areas.

Unlike object marquees, once a mask marquee has been defined, it remains in place above an image even if you select a different tool after completing the selection. Only if you click on an image again with a Mask tool (or by using the **M**ask, **R**emove command) will a mask disappear.

The image area inside the marquee is *live* now, because only the area within the marquee is capable of being affected by any editing or other modifications you make. Additionally, Regular masks (the one of three types of masks discussed in this chapter and the kind that is now in place) can be repositioned. If you want to reposition the mask, you can choose the Mask Picker tool and reposition, resize, or distort the mask (none of these options is recommended for this example, but they are featured later in this chapter). Repositioning a Regular mask of a design, for example, provides a quick way to make a repeat "stencil" pattern.

Refining a Regular Mask Border

Like the suite of Object tools in PHOTO-PAINT, the Mask tools include a Mask Node Edit tool, which is identical in operation and very similar in functionality to the Object Node Edit tool.

The Mask Node Edit tool is used in the next example to create a more accurate outline around the background area. However, the Object tools and the Mask Node Edit tool share a similar weakness: If you choose the Zoom tool between Mask Node edits, the selection reverts to a marquee outline, spoiling the Node editing session. If you do this and then select the Mask Node Edit tool again, PHOTO-PAINT re-evaluates where nodes belong on the curve of the selection. The inability to use the Zoom tool within an editing session with the Mask Node Edit tool is an annoying quirk of the program, but there's a trick in the following example to how to work around it:

1. Click-and-hold on the Polygon Mask tool, then choose the Mask Node Edit tool. A node appears at every point of inflection around the background.

2. Start reshaping the Node segments so that they conform to the outline of the picnic table and frankfurter top. Click on a node, and then click-and-drag on the control points as you would on an object in CorelDRAW using the Shape tool.

3. To get a closer view of your work, *do not* click on the Zoom tool; instead, click on the Zoom level area on the ribbon bar and type a value of magnification. Alternatively, you can use the hot key commands (Alt+V, Z, and then an arrow key to choose a preset magnification) or simply click on the menu command. As shown in figure 23.3, the curves around the frankfurter can be edited in a very precise, comfortable viewing resolution by entering a value in the Zoom field and using the window scroll bars to move to the appropriate image area.

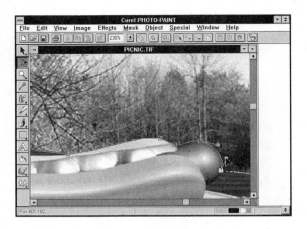

Figure 23.3
Use the Zoom levels field on the ribbon bar instead of the Zoom tool to zoom in and retain the editable mask nodes.

N O T E

None of the Effe**c**ts menu options (or any other image editing command) will work on any part of an image, including an area in Mask Node Edit mode, while a mask exists in Node Edit mode. Also, by selecting a painting or other tool, the nodes that define the mask selection automatically convert to a marquee selection.

Therefore, the best use of the Mask Node editing capabilities is to get the mask refined in one session with the Mask Node Edit tool.

4. The last step before converting the mask segments back into a mask marquee is to make sure that the image edges are covered. The conversion of a marquee into a mask requires some approximating on PHOTO-PAINT's part, and the clean edge work you originally did with the Polygon tool might have come a little undone in the conversion process. Press Ctrl+1 or use the Zoom level field on the ribbon bar to choose a 100-percent view of the PICNIC image. Then adjust the nodes in the mask so the node's segments fall outside of the live area. In figure 23.4, you can see that PHOTO-PAINT enables you to place segments as well as polygon lines on the window background.

5. Click-and-hold on the Mask Node Edit tool, then choose any Mask tool (you might want to pick the far left tool, the Mask Picker tool, because it's in easy reach). You now should have an accurate, Regular mask defined by a marquee around the background of the image.

A Regular mask protects the exterior of a marquee created with a Masking tool. The area inside the mask marquee is subject to change, and the area outside the marquee is protected from change. It's similar to the usage of the term mask as when used in the context of house painting and video editing. In the next section, you edit the masked area to create less visual interest in the background area of the image's composition.

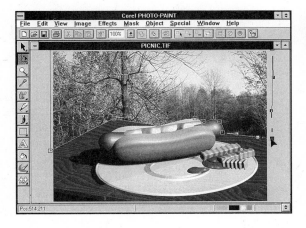

Figure 23.4

Position the selection segments outside the live image area to create a marquee flush with the image edges.

N O T E

If you intend to take a short break now, remember *not* to click in the image with a Mask tool again; put on a screen blanker or choose the Zoom tool. You learn how to make a mask permanent in "Saving a Regular Mask," later in this chapter. At the moment, however, the mask is temporary and can be lost forever if it is deselected accidentally. If you need to use your machine for another task for a period of time, read the aforementioned section to learn how to save the mask.

Using PHOTO-PAINT Effects on a Masked Area

The Gaussian Blur filter can be used in many situations where you want a naturalistic blurring of an area or an entire photo. This effect can create lifelike shadow, it can smooth an area that has an unsightly dent or seam, and it can throw an image area out of focus exactly like someone's relative does at a wedding with a cheap camera.

In the following example, you apply PHOTO-PAINT's Gaussian Blur to the area you defined with the Masking tools earlier. Blurring the background effectively draws attention away from the glorious park scene and directs all eyes to the feast on the picnic table. By using Gaussian blurring on an image area, you can compensate for elements in an image that compete for attention. Using a Gaussian Blur is a good way to achieve an effect that should have been created within a photo at the time it was taken. Follow these steps:

1. Choose Effe**c**ts, Fancy, and then Gaussian Blur.

2. The Gaussian Blur dialog box appears. This box contains a preview window and, as with any powerful effect, it's usually a good idea to click on Pre**v**iew before clicking on OK. Place your cursor inside the preview window and drag the image so that your view matches the masked area in the image.

For some reason, PHOTO-PAINT is unaware that a mask exists and previews the entire image blurred—not just the masked area. Regardless of the preview, however, the only area actually blurred is the masked area.

3. Set the Gaussian Blur to a radius of **5** pixels. The Gaussian Blur effect is quite concentrated, and you usually never need a setting greater than 5 to blur an area into unrecognizability, as shown in figure 23.5.

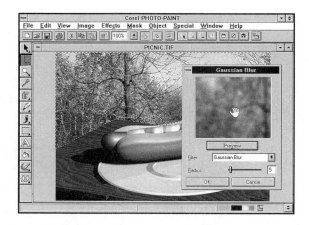

Figure 23.5

Preview what you're going to blur and by how much in the Gaussian Blur dialog box.

If you are using an Effect Preview dialog box and cannot get the exact effect you're looking for, PHOTO-PAINT features all the other options within that specific command in the **F**ilter drop-down box. Edge Detect, Emboss, Invert, Despeckle, Motion Blur, and Outline are available for you to preview and apply to the image from within the Gaussian Blur dialog box if you decide that one of the these effects is more appropriate.

4. Click on OK. As you can see in figure 23.6, the focal attraction of the PICNIC image is now the meal. The marquee outline was removed from this figure so that you can get a good look at the effect, but *you* should not use the remove command at this point, because the mask has not been saved yet.

There are other creative possibilities for modifying a masked area of an image besides blurring it. In the next section, you see an inventive mask option used with one of PHOTO-PAINT's painting tools.

Figure 23.6

The Gaussian Blur effect can diminish the importance of any area you have defined with a Regular mask.

As of the October 31, 1994 release of Corel version 5.00.E2, the Marquee Visible button applies only to object selections, not masked selections. For this reason, you always should assume that if you design a Regular mask, get sidetracked with something else around the office, and then return to find no mask marquee, it's gone, and it's not due to a coworker clicking on a nonexistent Hide Mask Marquee button.

Transparency masks and Color masks display on-screen much differently than Regular masks, and they are covered in later sections of this chapter.

The lack of a Visible Marquee button for masks could change if there is enough user feedback to Corel Corporation. There have been several "silent updates" to the initial commercial release version of Corel 5, with each one containing more enhancements and fixes. Frequently requested changes and enhancement suggestions do not go unnoticed by Corel Corporation. Send them a letter if you would like something changed, and you may be pleasantly surprised when you take a look at the next update.

Using Fractal Textures and Masks

The same set of fractal textures available in CorelDRAW are featured in PHOTO-PAINT. You might find working with fractal textures even more rewarding in PHOTO-PAINT than in DRAW! Bitmap manipulation is PHOTO-PAINT's forte, and you can use all the effects, painting tools, and filters to modify the fractal textures.

Fractal textures are mathematical formulas that, when mapped to color pixels, do an amazing imitation of lifelike organic materials. Because fractal textures are so photogenic, they are ideal candidates to replace an area you have masked in a photographic image. You can apply a texture fill in two ways: First, you can use the Fill tool by adjusting the Color Tolerance (from the Special menu) to plus/minus 255 to include all color values in a masked area. You can also delete the masked area by pressing the

Delete key when a Masking tool is selected, to expose background image color and then fill at any Color Tolerance. If you have a tool other than a Masking tool active, this last trick doesn't work; if you have the Mask Picker tool active, the mask marquee is deleted, but not the image contents the mask marquee surrounds.

If this scenario sounds like something less than the shortest distance between two points, you're right. The Rectangle tool flood fills any area you define with the same fill options as the Fill tool. In the next example, you see how to add a beautiful, unobtrusive fractal sky to the PICNIC image in less time than you can imagine.

Here's how to fill a masked area with texture:

1. The mask still should be present in the PICNIC image (the marquee lines should be visible). If you don't have a mask now, you will not be able to create the following effect. Why not create one, if this is the case?

2. Double-click on the Current fill icon on the Status line (far right color swatch), or choose View, Fill Roll-up, and press Shift+F6, then choose the Rectangle tool (F6) from the toolbox.

3. Click on the Texture Fill button (fourth from the left on the top of the roll-up) and then click on Edit. More than 32,000 variations of a fractal preset can be chosen, and every color component of a texture can be modified almost infinitely.

4. Choose Samples from the Texture **L**ibrary drop-down list, choose Clouds.heavenly from the **T**exture List, and then use the spin control next to the Texture # field to find a pleasant variation on the clouds for the PICNIC image.

5. You can reassign colors within the texture. In figure 23.7, the Atmosphere color has been reassigned to add a little peach to Texture #9759, and the **P**review window displays these changes. Click on OK after you've made any changes.

7. Click above the upper left corner of the active image (on the window background) and then drag to the far right of the image, below where the mask marquee ends within the image.

Fractal textures can take some time to process before they appear; the larger the image file size, the longer PHOTO-PAINT needs to map the texture to the masked area. As you can see in figure 23.8, the fractal cloud is unobtrusive and provides the sort of nondescript visual support to the PICNIC scene to let the picnic table and meal become the main visual attraction.

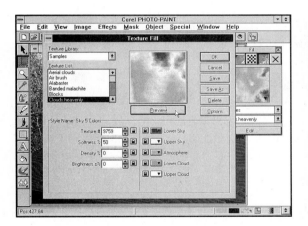

Figure 23.7
Create your own look for a fractal texture fill by specifying variations and different color values.

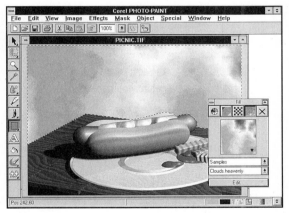

Figure 23.8
Use the Rectangle tool to force a fill into a masked image area, regardless of the present visual content within the mask.

6. Double-click on the Rectangle tool in the toolbox. The Tool Settings roll-up appears. Make sure that **S**ize is set to 0.

Saving a Regular Mask

When you have a Regular mask you're happy with, you can save it indefinitely as a separate image file. The following section explains how to edit masks and how to use the mask files as different mask types.

By saving the mask you created for the background of the PICNIC image, you can come back to the PICNIC.TIF image again and again, and substitute other backgrounds to make the image suitable for a variety of graphics needs. Follow these steps:

1. Choose **S**ave from the **M**ask menu.

2. By default, PHOTO-PAINT offers you the CPT file format for your saved mask. You can use this format or choose a different format, such as TIF. The file format does not affect PHOTO-PAINT's capability to read the mask file back into the PICNIC image. Select a directory on your hard disk to store the mask. As you can see in figure 23.9, you have the option of compressing the mask file. Compressing the mask helps conserve hard disk space, but it will take PHOTO-PAINT a little longer to decompress the mask the next time you want to use the mask.

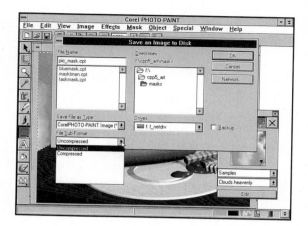

Figure 23.9

Save your mask in CPT format (or as another format), just as you save an image file.

> ## T I P
>
> If you frequently need to save and recall masks, you should organize your hard disk accordingly. Create a subdirectory for an assignment, or collection of assignments, and store your masks in the subdirectory.
>
> You also might want to consider reserving PHOTO-PAINT's CPT format for masks and keeping your images in TIF or TGA format. This way, your mask can have the same name (with a different extension) as the image to which it corresponds.

Creating Non-Contiguous Masks

Although you can use any of the Masking tools to create a geometric mask, an irregularly shaped one, or select an area with the Mask Wand tool based on similar color values, the selection of non-contiguous areas—areas that are scattered about an image—requires the use of the Selection modes PHOTO-PAINT offers. As shown in figure 23.10, there is a group of buttons on the ribbon bar—Selection Mode buttons—that are a quick alternative to the choices under the Special menu when working with the Masking tools.

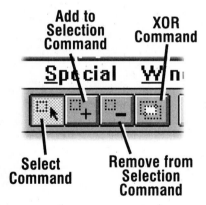

Figure 23.10
Use the Selection mode buttons as an alternative to the Special menu commands.

The Selection Mode buttons serve a dual purpose in PHOTO-PAINT, but their function is identical when working with objects or masks. The following is a brief list of what each button does, and a suggestion of when you would need to use it. You will see an example in the next section of working with complex masks built by using the Selection Modes.

- The Select button is the default setting when using a Masking tool. While in this mode, a Masking tool can be used to define an image area. While in the Select mode, a mask can be moved (but not the underlying image area it defines) by choosing the Mask Picker tool. If you click a marquee with a geometric Masking tool (Rectangle, Circle, Freehand, Polygon, or Lasso), the marquee is deselected when in Select Mode. If you click outside a marquee while the Magic Wand Mask tool is active, the selection will be redefined when in Select Mode.

- The Add to Selection Mode preserves original mask marquees, and enables you to add to the selection with any of the Masking tools. This is a particularly useful mode for selecting different image areas that have no neighboring pixels.

■ The Subtract from Selection Mode serves the inverse function of Add to Selection. If you wanted to create a mask shaped like a crescent moon, for example, you would first create an ellipse with the circle Mask tool, click on the Subtract from Selection mode button, and then create a second ellipse that partially overlaps the first. The second ellipse would then subtract the overlapping area in the resulting marquee, in a manner similar to that of the Trim command in CorelDRAW.

■ The XOR Selection is not commonly used in mainstream design tasks; it is useful, however, for eliminating the overlapping portions of two masks from the area the overlapping masks define. When In XOR mode, you can add non-contiguous, non-overlapping areas to your mask selection using any Masking tool. If you overlap a mask marquee with one you've defined earlier, however, the areas that overlap will be excluded from the resulting marquee.

The XOR Selection mode can also be used to define the intersection of two marquee masks. To do this, draw two mask marquees that overlap while the XOR Selection mode is active, choose Mask, Invert, and then choose the Subtract from Selection mode to remove image areas that don't belong to the intersection.

The Selection Mode button is always used to reset the selection properties you've chosen while using Masking tools. Quite often, users choose the Add to Selection mode and forget it's active after they're done with it. This leads to interesting, albeit unwanted, marquee masks. By choosing the Selection Mode button after you've accessed one of the other modes, you're assured that no further modification of an existing marquee mask can occur. You can switch between any of the four Selection modes while you have an active mask marquee on an image.

In the next section, you'll see a practical working example of how the Selection modes can be used to accurately define non-contiguous image areas.

Using the Add to Selection Mode

The reason for creating one mask to cover many non-adjacent image areas is not immediately apparent in its usefulness. Why not simply create several regular masks, one at a time to accomplish the same effect?

Suppose you've created a traditional-looking window as a design element, built of four squares representing the window panes which are divided by mullions. If you were to use a radial fountain fill to represent light peeking though the window, you would need to apply the fill four times, one for each division of the window. The appearance of lighting would be unconvincing, because light doesn't begin each time it hits a mullion; instead, you see a division of one continuous tone through each window pane. The solution to this hypothetical design element in CorelDRAW would be to use the Combine command to make the four window elements one, non-contiguous selection, and then add one fountain fill to the compound object. Think of mask marquees as "linked" when you define non-contiguous image areas using the Add to Selection Mode.

If you would like to experiment with the materials shown in the following figures as you walk through creating non-contiguous masks, the HALOWEEN.TIF image is in the CHAP23 subdirectory of the *CorelDRAW! The Professional Reference* companion CDs.

Here's the concept: It would be nice if one of the foreground pumpkins in the HALOWEEN.TIF image reflected more of the holiday spirit commonly associated with the vegetable. One of the pumpkins in the image could benefit from some virtual carving.

Here's how to use Add to and Subtract from Selection modes in a design.

1. Click-and-hold on the Masking tool to display the fly-out menu, then choose the Polygon tool (the shears-shaped icon). This tool can be used to create a closed, straight-line marquee mask.

2. By default, marquees are created starting with the Selection Mode active. Click on the Add to Selection button.

3. Click a starting point, click beneath it, then double-click to the left of both points to create a triangular marquee. This is the pumpkin's right eye (camera left), as shown in figure 23.11.

Figure 23.11
The Polygon tool creates straight-line selections; double-click a finishing point to close the polygon.

4. Decide where the other eye should go, then repeat step 3. You'll notice that because Add to Selection is the active mode, the first eye you defined is still displayed by a marquee—it didn't become deselected when you finished creating the second polygon.

5. Give the pumpkin a nose by using the method described in step 3.

For the pumpkin's smile to look authentic, accurate, and traditional, you need a Masking tool that can define areas that contain curves, so you need to trade the Polygon tool for the Freehand Mask tool. Also, traditional halloween pumpkins sport three teeth within their smile, so using a combination of Masking tools and a different Masking mode is in order.

Using the Subtract from Selection Mode

As described earlier, the Subtract from Selection Mode is useful for "carving" the geometry of one marquee from another (or several other) existing marquees where the marquees overlap. The Subtract from Selection Mode is useful for correcting an error in an existing Mask—for example, you might want to use the Freehand Mask tool to trim the corner of a rectangle to conform to the image area you want to mask around.

You create the smile on the pumpkin in this example by first defining the shape of the smile, then subtracting three straight-edge selections to create the appearance of a pumpkin that is happy, despite poor dental hygiene practices.

1. Click-and-hold on the Masking tool, then choose the Freehand Mask tool. This tool operates like a Pencil tool; you can "sketch" an unconstrained selection border that will auto-close to make a marquee if the end of your path doesn't meet at the beginning.

2. Draw a smile on the pumpkin, as shown in figure 23.12. Click+drag until the interior of the smile is defined, then let go of the mouse button when you've reached your starting point.

Figure 23.12
Use the Freehand Mask tool to define any irregular shape as a closed Mask Marquee.

N O T E

You can create a self-intersecting path with the Freehand Mask tool. This capability leads to some creative design possibilities; try drawing a "figure eight" using the Freehand Mask tool.

Better yet, draw an inward spiral and let go of the mouse button before you reach the center. With either suggestion here, you can then press the Delete key to expose a contrasting paper color.

Admittedly, the subject of this example lends itself to imprecision. If you wanted to create a perfect smile on the pumpkin, you could define the smile with the Freehand tool, convert the marquee to editable nodes by choosing the Mask Node Edit tool, then tighten up the design element a little more (see Chapter 21 on the use of the Node Edit tools in PHOTO-PAINT). But for anyone who has ever carved a pumpkin to make a lantern, you know that a crooked smile is perfectly acceptable.

3. Click on the Subtract From Selection Mode button on the ribbon bar, then click-and-hold on the Masking tools button to choose the Polygon Mask tool again.

4. Click-and-drag a tooth for the pumpkin's smile by clicking a four-sided polygon that bisects one of the sides of the crescent smile. See figure 23.13 for the location of the tooth along the crescent. This is the pumpkin's lower molar.

5. Repeat step 4 to create two other teeth at different locations along the crescent smile. Notice that when you're in Subtract from selection Mode, every area you define that overlaps an existing marquee creates negative space.

6. It's time to light the pumpkin. If you're taking a break at this point, save the mask you have defined by using the steps described in Saving a Regular Mask, found earlier in this chapter.

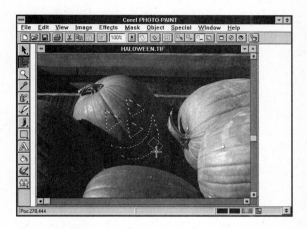

Figure 23.13
Click on the four-sided polygon that bisects one of the sides of the crescent smile.

Filling a Non-Contiguous Selection

PHOTO-PAINT considers the work performed in the last section to be one selection area; even though the eyes, nose, and toothy grin of the pumpkin selections appear to be discrete areas, they can be moved as one with the Mask Picker tool, and they can be filled simultaneously by flooding the exposed image areas with the Rectangle tool. The only instance where the components of this complex mask behave as individual areas is when they are clicked over with the Fill tool.

The Rectangle tool is a good choice for simulating a glow in the selected (unmasked) areas within the marquee, because this tool gets its color properties from the Fill roll-up, not the Colors roll-up. On the Fill roll-up, there are four different types of fill, of which the fountain fill is the most appropriate for this example. By specifying a light orange as the beginning color and dark sepia as the end of a radial fountain fill, you can suggest the glow of candlelight emanating from within the unmasked, selected areas that have been defined.

Here's how to make the HALOWEEN mask serve a creative and practical design purpose:

1. Double-click on the Current Fill icon on the status line (or choose **V**iew, **F**ill Roll-Up) to display the Fill roll-up, then click on the Fountain Fill button.

2. Click on the Radial fill type button (the first above the Edit button), then choose a dark brown from the left, ending color fly-out palette.

3. Choose a bright orange from the right, beginning color fly-out palette.

4. Click-and-drag inside the Fill roll-up's preview window to adjust the center of the radial fill. Because a candle inside the pumpkin would emanate light from a position toward the bottom, you need to position the center of the radial fountain fill a little to the south of its default location.

5. Double-click on the Rectangle tool to choose it, and to display the Tool Settings roll-up (Ctrl+F8 is also a shortcut to displaying the View, Tool Settings roll-up).

6. Type **0** (zero) in the Size field. When using the Rectangle tool, the size option refers to the width (measured in pixels) of a color outline that surrounds any rectangle you draw with the tool. When this option is set to zero, the roundness (of the outlined corners of the rectangle) setting is not available. This is okay because you don't want an outline around the rectangle fill.

7. Click above and to the left of the complex mask, then drag diagonally below and to the right of the mask, as shown in figure 23.14. If you didn't include all the selection areas that comprise the pumpkin's face, immediately press Ctrl+Z (**E**dit, **U**ndo).

As you can see in figure 23.15, the type of mask (Regular mask) created for this design suited the need to protect unselected image areas from the Rectangle tool's fountain fill. You only need to encompass the selected areas when you force-fill a color, fractal pattern, or fountain fill this way. Encompassing the entire image was unnecessary to produce the effect, because except for the face of the pumpkin, the entire HALOWEEN.TIF image is masked, and therefore protected from editing.

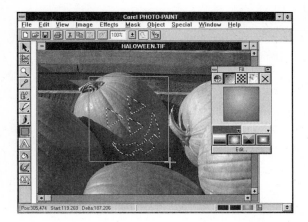

Figure 23.14

Completely surround the selection areas within the image with the Rectangle tool.

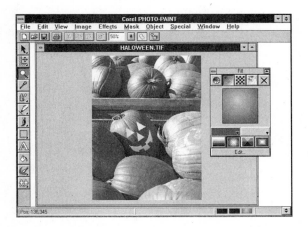

Figure 23.15

The use of the Regular mask to protect unselected image areas from the Rectangle tool's fountain fill.

Transparency Masks

Transparency masks enable you to take a large step toward more photorealistic image editing and toward producing special effects. Unlike its sibling, the 1 bit/pixel Regular mask, a Transparency mask is made of 8 bits/pixel of selection information. What this means to users is that masks can be assigned a partially transparent (or partially opaque) consistancy, allowing some, but not all color, fill, and filtering through to the underlying image. In this section, the creative uses of PHOTO-PAINT's Transparency masks is explored.

Comparing Different Types of Mask Information

In addition to Transparency masks and Regular masks displaying differently onscreen, there is also a fundamental difference in the *composition* of each mask, in their capacity to store information, and in how they are manipulated.

If you examine the mask you saved at the beginning of this chapter for the PICNIC image using the **I**nfo command from the **I**mage menu, you'll see that the image type of the mask file is black-and-white. As discussed in Chapter 22, a black-and-white image mode is expressed in 1 bit/pixel format (also called a *line art* image by some scanner

manufacturers), and its color capability is limited to black or white. PHOTO-PAINT sees black in a mask as an instruction to make the image pixels that are positioned under the black mask pixels "available for editing." Conversely, white pixels in the mask indicate to PHOTO-PAINT that underlying image pixels are masked.

It becomes immediately apparent, then, that it is not a good idea to change the resolution or dimensions of a mask file; PHOTO-PAINT would read the black and white areas and mismatch them to the original image areas you intended to mask. Figure 23.16 is the PICNIC.TIF image, with the mask file that corresponds to the editing work performed to isolate the sky area earlier. With both Regular and Transpaency masks, the white areas contained within the saved mask correspond to completely selected working image areas, and black areas represent completely masked image areas.

Transparency masks, on the other hand, open a whole new world to the imaging professional. Although a saved Transparency mask still must have the same dimensions as the image to which you're appling the Transparency mask, these kinds of masks have an 8 bit/pixel color capability. The 8 bit/pixel color capability means that a saved Transparency mask can be made up of 256 different shades of black. When a pixel in a Transparency mask file falls between absolute black (0, or "mask off") and white (255, or "mask on"), the corresponding area in the image that the mask is applied to is *partially* masked. The higher the number of the grayscale value in the mask (closer to white), the more completely the underlying image area is subject to editing changes.

The defining characteristic of Transparency masks—to protect and expose image areas to varying degrees—furnishes the designer with a powerful mechanism for producing sophisticated design work. In the next section, you see how to create a Transparency mask by working "backward." Creating a mask without PHOTO-PAINT's Masking tools can better show the relationship between grayscale selection information and the effect it has as a Transparency mask on an image. In the next example, you'll learn how to achieve an effect normally requiring countless hours in a chemical darkroom.

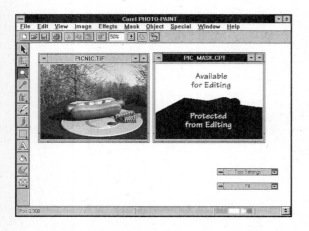

Figure 23.16

Black areas correspond to masked image areas, and white areas are selected when you load a mask.

How To Create a Transparency Mask

When a *Regular* mask is displayed on an image as a series of marquee lines, the information PHOTO-PAINT is using to calculate the areas selected and masked is represented by "ons" and "offs." When you use the **M**ask, **L**oad Mask command to load a Regular saved mask or a saved Transparency mask that is being used as a Regular mask, the resulting marquee defines underlying image areas that are 100-percent selected and 100-percent protected. A hard-edge border separates the selected and protected areas. The hard-edge characteristic of the border sometimes produces a harsh effect when you edit inside the marquee, particularly if your subject area has indistinct edges, such as a tree, or a person's hair.

The solution to seamless image editing lies in the use of a Transparency mask in PHOTO-PAINT as a saved Transparency mask and not as a Regular mask. You can create a Transparency mask in several ways:

■ You can choose **M**ask, Create Transparency Mask. This option provides you with a choice of saving any active mask on an open image in an 8 bit/pixel format, or *creating* one on top of the current image using PHOTO-PAINT's painting and filling tools. This is an option that is explored shortly that serves you in a wide variety of design situations.

■ You can **L**oad any grayscale image as a Transparency mask. That's right, you can use a scan of Uncle Fred as information PHOTO-PAINT reads onto an active image, as long as Uncle Fred's image is in Grayscale format and it was saved as a TIF, CPT, or TGA image. Using a grayscale image can produce a very strange Transparency mask because mask's selection information is based on the image detail in the grayscale image you used. But you can wind up with some fascinating abstract art this way.

■ You can open a new image file in grayscale format, and use PHOTO-PAINT's tools to apply paint. You'll see how to create a mask by painting in the next section, as well as observe how PHOTO-PAINT looks at varying degrees of brightness when it creates partial selection areas.

In figure 23.17, you can see the PIC_MASK.CPT image next to 2LIPMASK.CPT, an 8 bit/pixel grayscale image. Both images can be used for masks, but PIC_MASK.CPT can't handle a linear fountain fill because of the complexity of tonal information. PHOTO-PAINT creates pattern dithering in a 1 bit/pixel image when you use fountain fills, and while this is a close visual approximation of what a linear fountain fill should look like, the tonal information produces a Regular mask over an image that's simply too painful to look at.

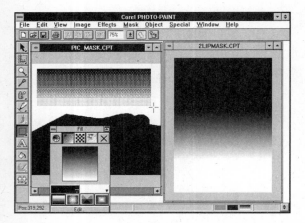

Figure 23.17
Regular mask information is only 1 bit/pixel. The black and white image format cannot be used to create partial masks.

In contrast, the 2LIPMASK image can be read by PHOTO-PAINT as a Transparency mask, and the areas of gray in the image will correspond to image areas that receive partial coloring or effects. The 2LIPMASK image is an original creation you'll design next, to see how a "cross fade" effect can be created by using a special-purpose Transparency mask.

Cross-Fading an Effect into an Image

Advertising and the motion picture industry get a lot of milage from soft edges around photographs, and this effect can be created quite easily in PHOTO-PAINT by using filters, which are the subject of Chapter 26.

However, when two or more images blend into *each other*, the effect is a provoking and eye-catching one, and requires a little more than the automated routine a filter provides.

The following is an advanced user trick disguised as an experiment. If you follow along, you'll learn the relationship between what you paint in a grayscale image, and what PHOTO-PAINT offers as a Transparency mask built around the image's tonal information. Here's how to design a "cross fade" effect, where one image appears to blend into another:

1. Open the TULIPS.TIF image from the *CorelDRAW! The Professional Reference* companion CDs. It's in the CHAP23 subdirectory; save a copy to your hard drive. This is the *base*, or background image, to which you'll add a second image.

2. Type **85** in the Zoom levels box on the ribbon bar. At this level of Zoom, you can see the entire image, as well as the window background outside of the image's border.

3. Choose **I**mage, Con**v**ert to, then choose **G**rayscale (8-bit). PHOTO-PAINT automatically creates a grayscale copy of TULIP.TIF, titled NEW-1.CPT. You now have a new image in which you'll design a Transparency mask for TULIP.TIF. NEW-1.CPT is of the same size and resolution as the TULIP image, which

makes it ideal for a 1 to 1 mapping of selection information within the original TULIP image. Creating a file exactly the same size as the image you intend to work with can be as simple as this. Alternatively, you could choose **I**mage, **I**nfo, then take down a list of original image specifications, then try to remember them while entering the details in the New Image dialog box. Why bother?

4. Save the NEW-1.CPT image as 2LIPMASK.CPT to your hard disk. You're not done with the image yet, so don't close it.

5. Double-click on the Current Fill icon on the status line if the Fill roll-up isn't on screen right now (or choose **V**iew, F**i**ll Roll-Up).

6. Click on the Fountain Fill button, then click on the left button above the Edit button to choose the linear fountain fill type.

7. Click-and-drag in the Fill roll-up's preview window to point the direction of the linear fountain fill from top to bottom, black to white. Refer to figure 23.17 for an illustration of how the preview box should look right now.

8. Click on the Edit button, click on the **E**dge Pad spin box until it reads 35 percent, then click on OK. Increasing the Edge Pad makes the fountain fill's transition from black to white occur with less space given to transitional

shades. The Transparency mask that is produced by the gradient you've specified here has large areas of pure white (selected) and pure black (totally masked), with a sharp–yet–smooth transition between the two areas.

9. Click-and-drag the Rectangle tool over the entire 2LIPMASK image. You should now have an image that looks like figure 23.18.

10. Press Ctrl+S (**F**ile, **S**ave).

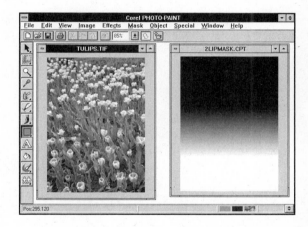

Figure 23.18

A Transparency mask can be created in a grayscale image file with the 256 available shades and any painting tool.

The Fill roll-up makes all the colors in the various color models available to you when you are working on a grayscale image. However, this doesn't mean it's a *good idea* to apply a color to a grayscale image! Grayscale images can only accept brightness values on a scale from 0 to 255; if you try to paint a color into a grayscale image, Hue and Saturation properties are discarded, and you'll be painting with the relative brightness component of the paint color you chose. This is an inaccurate approach to adding grayscale information to a Transparency mask file because most people can't perceive the unique brightness value in a color. When you paint with color in a grayscale image, you take a guess at the shade of gray you'll get.

The Colors roll-up, on the other hand, only displays values of black, and not display color in the Paint Selector at the bottom of the roll-up when the current image onscreen is a grayscale image.

Defining and Loading a Transparency Mask

When you choose to display a Transparency mask above an image as a tinted overlay, you have the option to decide on the overlay color the Transparency mask uses as a representation of protected image areas. When a Transparency mask is loaded and visible on an image, you can edit directly on the tinted mask with any of PHOTO-PAINT's painting tools, and apply effects to only the mask; the underlying image is unaffected when you edit the mask.

To accurately see and edit a Transparency mask that is being displayed over an image, it is best to choose a mask overlay color that contrasts the predominant underlying image colors. PHOTO-PAINT's default value for Transparency masks is brilliant red, and this works well most of time. However, the TULIP.TIF image has a lot of red in it, and a color other than red would be a better choice for the Transparency mask tint when working with this image.

Here's how to reset PHOTO-PAINT's default color value for displaying a Transparency mask:

1. Choose **S**pecial, **P**references, then click on the Advanced tab in the Preferences dialog box.

2. Click on the **T**ransparency Tint button, then click on the primary blue swatch on the drop-down palette, as shown in figure 23.19. Additionally, you can click on the More button on the bottom of the drop-down palette to custom blend a color for the Transparency tint.

3. Click on OK. If you perform these steps while a Transparency mask is loaded, the change in tint will immediately be reflected within the image. If a mask isn't already displayed, the change in preferences will appear the next time you create a Transparency mask. You don't have to restart PHOTO-PAINT for the preference change to become effective.

Now that the tint has been defined for the Transparency mask, it's time to load it with the following:

4. Choose **M**ask, L**o**ad Transparency Mask. This displays the Load a Transparency Mask from Disk dialog box.

5. Choose the location of the 2LIPMASK.CPT image, select the image, then click on OK. It doesn't matter that this image is presently onscreen; PHOTO-PAINT can read an image as a mask even if the file is open on the workspace. This gives you a good opportunity to compare the mask file to the tint displayed over the TULIPS.TIF image.

6. Press Ctrl+F7 (or choose **O**bject, **L**ayers/Objects Roll-Up from the menu). The options for displaying an active Transparency mask, and for editing the image while a mask is still displayed are located on the top of the Layers/Objects roll-up. This is a counter-intuitive place for options that have nothing to do with Layers/Objects, so it's good to remember that the Layers/Objects roll-up is also the Transparency mask options' location!

7. Click on the Image radio button on the Edit field on the Layers/Objects roll-up, and click on the Show check box next to Transparency. Now, the Transparency mask is loaded and visible, as shown in figure 23.20, but

cannot be edited. The image of the tulips beneath the Transparency mask can be edited, however, but only to the extent that it is beneath the tint.

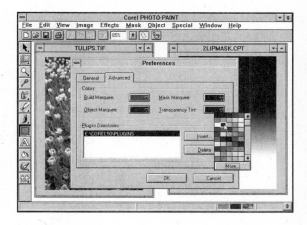

Figure 23.19

Choose a color for the tint of a Transparency mask.

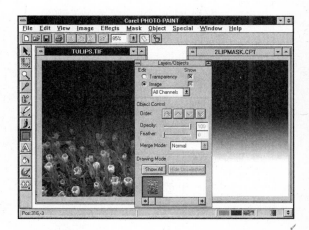

Figure 23.20

The amount of Transparency tint over the image corresponds to the amount of black in the Transparency mask file.

Again, it's important that you set up a Transparency mask file to have the same dimensions and resolution as the image you intend to mask. If you had created a grayscale file larger or smaller than the TULIPS.TIF image, the Transparency tint would display in a distorted fashion on the image. PHOTO-PAINT does not maintain the height–to–width aspect of a Transparency mask that is disproportionate to the image over which you load it, and stretches the shorter dimension of the mask to create a mask that covers the entire image.

Applying a Fill to a Transparency-Masked Image

When you have a Transparency mask defined over an image, you can do a number of things to the selected areas. You'll composite two images together shortly; compositing requires the use of both Transparency mask and the Layers/Objects features. You will start with a smaller project first, however. A PHOTO-PAINT fractal texture can be added to the TULIPS.TIF image now to create a surreal image. The technique described in the next set of steps shows how quickly to make a still life image a little more interesting. On occasion, abstract art is a legitimate alternative to *inspired* art! You can close the 2LIPMASK.CPT image at any time now—the only reason for its continued presence onscreen is to show the correspondance between grayscale information and the Transparency mask which is now visible on the TULIPS.TIF image.

Follow these steps to put the Transparency mask to creative use with the TULIPS image:

1. Double-click on the Current Fill icon on the status line to display the Fill roll-up if it isn't already on screen.

2. Click on the Texture button (the fourth button) on the top of the Fill roll-up.

3. Clicking on the preview window to display the visual representations of different textures is a processor-intensive process. If you know the exact texture fill you want, you might prefer to select the fill from the drop-down list beneath the Styles drop-down on the Fill roll-up. If you need to see thumbnails of the textures, click on the preview window. Choose "Mineral.Swirled 5 colors" for this example.

4. With the Rectangle tool, click-and-drag to create a rectangle that encompasses about the bottom 4/5th of the TULIPS.TIF image, as shown in figure 23.21. Because the Transparency mask totally masks the upper 1/5th of the TULIPS.TIF image, it's not necessary to draw a rectangle that completely encompasses the image. Creating fractal textures is a processor-intensive command, and the smaller the area you define, the quicker the process goes.

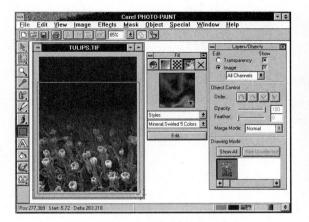
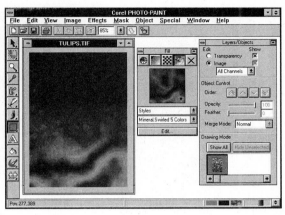

Figure 23.21

Don't click-and-drag to encompass a Transparency mask area of 100% coverage; the area is completely protected.

Figure 23.22

Areas are filled with texture to the percentage that the Transparency mask displays color.

5. As you can see in figure 23.22, the Mineral.Swirled 5 colors texture fill *partially* covers the TULIPS image. Areas that display the Transparency mask tint with the most color density protect the underlying image the most, while lighter areas of tint allowed the fractal texture to fill in.

6. Click on the Transparency Show check box on the Layers/Objects roll-up to uncheck the box, and to display the editing work.

7. Choose **M**ask, R**e**move Transparency Mask to remove the information PHOTO-PAINT calculated from the 2LIPMASK.CPT image—the mask isn't hidden; instead, the information is no longer active on the image.

8. Save this image as MISTULIP.TIF to your hard drive. You'll need the original, unedited TULIPS image in the next example.

Figure 23.23 is the finished image, without the distracting element of the Transparency mask tint above the tulips. Notice how the Mineral texture gently blends into the tulips, creating sort of a misty fog on the bed of flowers.

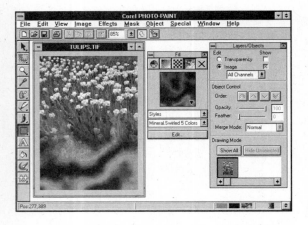

Figure 23.23
The visual detail of two different elements is blended together by using a fountain fill in the Transparency mask.

T I P

Because the color icons on the status line aren't clearly labeled, they are a little confusing to interpret. However, if you hover your cursor over each of the three color swatches on the Status Line, a message identifying each one will appear on the left of the Status Line.

Although the creation of a Transparency mask as a grayscale image is a sound way to define partially masked areas within an image, it's also the least direct route to more complex image editing. In the following section, you'll see how to create a Transparency mask directly upon an image, and how to blend a different photograph into the TULIPS.TIF file.

Composite Photography and Transparency Masks

Once you understand the relationship between tonal densities in an image mask and the degree to which this information is used to protect image areas, the sky's the limit with your imaging assignments. You can create "morphing" effects, and subtly alter the reality portrayed within an image. The next set of examples isn't as ambitious as, say, a Hollywood production, but they do give you the keys to producing stunning, fantastic work within PHOTO-PAINT.

RUFFROCK.TIF is a close-up of a rocky surface, and the image is on the the *CorelDRAW! The Professional Reference* companion CDs in the CHAP23 sub-directory. You'll use this image in addition to the TULIP.TIF image to create a composite of the two images, using a Transparency mask you create directly on the TULIPS image.

The following steps show how to blend two images together:

1. Open the TULIPS.TIF image from your hard disk. PHOTO-PAINT lists the four most recently accessed files, so you'll find TULIPS.TIF under the **F**ile command if you followed the steps in the last section.

2. Choose **M**ask, Create **T**ransparency Mask. If you had a Regular mask (one created with the Masking tools) defined over the image, the **F**rom Mask option would be available at this point. Choose **N**ew.

3. In figure 23.24, you can see the Transparency Mask Creation dialog box. You have two options here: you can begin a Transparency mask over the TULIPS image with a fountain fill by clicking on the **G**radient button, or start with a **U**niform intensity for the Transparency mask. Click on the **U**niform radio button, enter **255** in the field next to the button, then click on OK.

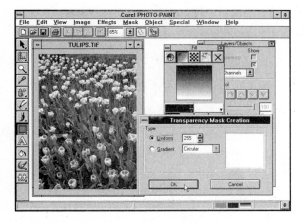

Figure 23.24
You have a choice of a pre-made Transparency mask (Gradient), or a Uniform fill for New Transparency masks.

Sometimes, you'll want to use the Gradient option for a new Transparency mask as a quick route to creating a special effect within an image. Gradient fills come in Linear, Circular, Conical, and Rectangular; these correspond to the types of Fountain fills you may choose in PHOTO-PAINT and

CorelDRAW, and Corel gives no explanation as to why these fills have different names when used as a Transparency mask. You'll create a custom Transparency mask in this example that is similar in effect to the Linear Gradient.

4. Make certain the Edit radio button on the Layers/Objects roll-up is presently set to Transparency and not Image, and the Show check box next to Transparency is checked. Because you chose 255 as the Uniform fill value for the new Transparency mask, you can't see any Transparency tint on the TULIP.TIF image now. You're starting with a "clean slate" upon which you'll design mask areas.

5. The finished design here will consist of a vertical crack in the TULIP image, and the tulips will peek through the RUFFROCK image areas. To do this, the center of the TULIPS image needs to be completely masked, with the Transparency mask fading to image areas that are completely selected (no tint) on both the left and right sides. Choose the Fountain Fill Mode button on the Fill roll-up, and click on the linear fill type on the bottom of the roll-up.

6. Click-and-drag inside the preview window to make the linear fountain run from black on the left to white on the right. Black and white should still be defined as the colors of the fountain fill from the last time the fountain fill was used in this chapter. If these are not your present colors, click on the drop-down palettes on the Fill roll-up to select them.

7. With the Rectangle tool, click-and-drag from the top, center of the TULIP.TIF image, to the bottom, about one screen inch to the right. This creates a Transparency mask area of blue tint that begins with black and ends in transparency from left to right.

8. Reverse the direction of the linear fountain fill in the preview window of the Fill roll-up, so it goes from white on the left to black on the right, then click-and-drag a rectangle starting from the top, center of the TULIPS image, to about one screen inch to the left, bottom of the image, as shown in figure 23.25.

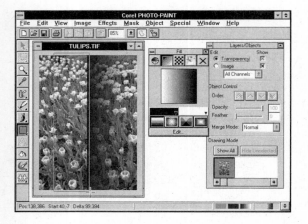

Figure 23.25

Create a narrow band of Transparency mask that fades to transparency at the left and right of the image.

You might want to save this Transparency mask for future use on images that have equal dimensions and resolution to that of the TULIPS image. You can save the mask now by choosing **M**ask, S**a**ve Transparency Mask, and then giving the Transparency mask a file name. In appearance, the mask image file will look similar to the 2LIPMASK image shown earlier. Heavily masked areas appear as darker regions in the image, while transparent regions of the mask are displayed as white, or light, areas.

"Sandwiching" a Transparency Mask between Two Images

You're now ready to add the RUFFROCK image to the TULIPS image. PHOTO-PAINT will merge two images as long as one of them is a background layer, and TULIPS.TIF qualifies as a background image. PHOTO-PAINT offers a quick, effortless way of adding an image from hard disk to an active image window; the **E**dit, Paste **F**rom File command provides an alternative to copying an entire image and pasting it into an active image window. As with most File and Edit dialog boxes in PHOTO-PAINT, you have the option to preview a file's contents before you paste it into a different image.

The mask is in place above the TULIPS image; however, you need to perform one more step before copying in the RUFFROCK image. The Layers/Objects roll-up currently has Transparency set as the Edit option, and this is not the currect mode for the Transparency mask. You need to switch the Editing mode to Image. By clicking on the Image radio button, you're indicating to PHOTO-PAINT that you want the mask to go into effect on top of the image, and that future changes will be made to the image, *not* the mask. This is not a straightforward procedure, or option, and for this reason, the next example is one you really should follow along and do. It's wiser to experiment with the example images provided on the companion CD than to possibly destroy an image of your own.

Here's how to blend the RUFFROCK image into the TULIP image, using areas defined by your custom Transparency mask:

1. Choose **E**dit, Paste **F**rom File (shown in fig. 23.26), then choose the CHAP23 subdirectory on the *CorelDRAW! The Professional Reference* companion CDs.

2. Choose RUFFROCK.TIF from the CHAP23 subdirectory. You can choose to preview this image before clicking on OK by checking the **P**review check box, but system performance slows while PHOTO-PAINT creates the thumbnail image.

RUFFROCK.TIF is of the same dimensions and resolution as the TULIP image, so it fits neatly over the background image as an independent, floating object. The example images on the *CorelDRAW! The Professional Reference* companion CDs are pre-measured

so you can get right to the point in these examples. When you apply the techniques presented in these chapters to your own PHOTO-PAINT work, you'll need to measure images prior to combining them.

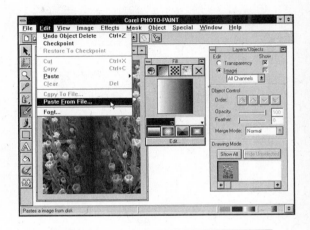

Figure 23.26
*Selecting Paste **F**rom File from the **E**dit menu.*

It's a little hard to see the composite image with the Transparency mask visible at this point, as shown in figure 23.27, but it's been made visible here to show how the RUFFROCK image will be merged (composited) into the TULIP image when you choose the merge command. The left and right sides of the RUFFROCK pasted image are clearly visible, which means they'll replace corresponding areas on the TULIPS image on the background layer. However, the area displaying the heaviest shade of Transparency tint will retain the TULIPS image areas when the two layers are merged.

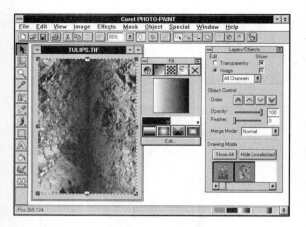

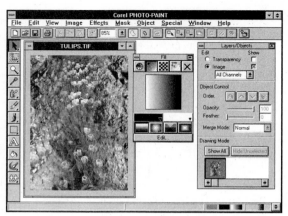

Figure 23.27

The Transparency mask only affects the image layer it is associated with.

Figure 23.28

A blend of two different images, created by masking the background image in specific areas.

3. Uncheck the Show check box next to Transparency on the Layers/Objects roll-up, to preview the composite blend of the two images.

4. To finalize the edits you've performed on the TULIPS image, press Ctrl+G (**O**bject, **M**erge).

5. A Transparency mask will remain on a merged image until you remove it. Choose **M**ask, R**e**move Transparency mask, and you should now have an image that looks pretty much like figure 23.28.

In this last section, you've seen solid, working examples of how a Transparency mask can be designed with a fountain fill to provide a smooth transition from one image element to a different one you add to the base image. But there are as many different effects you can create with a Transparency mask as there are creative ideas, and in the next section, you'll see how PHOTO-PAINT's Masking tools can be used in combination with painting tools to create a spotlight effect within an image.

Creating a Spotlight within an Image

There are many ways for a designer to call attention to an element of interest within an image. Of course, artistic expression (like all expression) can be performed with subtlety or with bluntness. For example, the attraction in the PICNIC image was redirected by manipulating the background element; you didn't need to paint a circle around the frankfurter to make it the star attraction!

Similarly, the image in this section's exercise has good composition, but suffers from flat lighting. A fictitious company, Altruist Airlines, has a poster composed of a headline and a logo. There is a design problem with this poster, however: The viewer's eye isn't attracted to any specific image element because everything is lit the same way—dull and flat.

To make the ALT_AIR.TIF image more powerful—so that it communicates and catches the viewer's eye—you create a spotlight effect within the image to point out the key element, which is the company's logo. You create a spotlight design from a New Transparency mask added to the image, then change the image's brightness while the mask is in place within the image.

This might sound involved, and it is, but it's not a complicated procedure. It involves the interchangeability of Regular and Transparency masks, a little inspired use of the Masking tools, and a filter applied to the Transparency mask design to make the edges appear soft and more photographic. With PHOTO-PAINT and a little effort, you can bring some movie-quality magic to your own work.

The mask in this example should enable you to change the background by using the spotlight effect, but the foreground logo shouldn't be completely defined within the selection area of the spotlight mask. Otherwise, the logo element would be "washed out" in addition to the areas on the background that receive the spotlight effect. The logo needs to be protected so that it contrasts with the washed-out background, and therefore the logo should not be included in the mask selection area.

To begin creating the Transparency mask for the airline poster, follow these steps:

1. Open the ALT_AIR.TIF image from the *CorelDRAW! The Professional Reference* companion CDs. It's located in the CHAP23 subdirectory. Click on OK after PHOTO-PAINT warns you that this is a read-only image, and then save a copy of it to your hard drive to avoid future warnings.

2. Maximize the image area by clicking on the up arrow on the top right of the image window. This exposes all the image window background of PHOTO-PAINT's drawing window. The spotlight you create will go out of frame in the bottom right corner, so you need to be able to access this area.

3. Choose the Circle Mask tool from the Mask Tool fly-out menu. Then click-and-drag an ellipse similar in size, shape, and location within the image (see fig. 23.29). The ellipse is not in position to highlight the airline logo, but you reposition and refine the selection in the next steps.

4. Click-and-hold on the Circle Mask tool. Then choose the Mask Picker tool from the Tool fly-out menu.

5. Click inside the ellipse to display the marquee selection in rotate/skew mode. Then click-and-drag the upper right corner selection handle downward until the status line reads about `Angle: 20`.

6. Click twice within the ellipse marquee selection to cycle through the selection modes back to normal selection handles. Then click-and-drag the ellipse so that it fits over the airline logo, as shown in figure 23.30.

Figure 23.29
Ellipses created with the Circle Mask tool can be repositioned and modified after creating them.

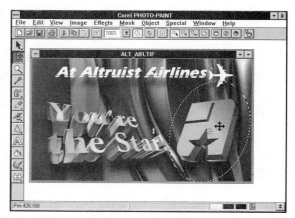

Figure 23.30
Move the marquee selection so it fits over the area to be highlighted.

N O T E

If you want to create an equilateral ellipse (a circle), press Ctrl while you click-and-drag diagonally. Within all the Corel modules, the Ctrl key usually means *constraining an action*—whether it's creating an equilateral selection or creating a line with an angle limited to a fixed number of degrees.

A mask marquee can be repositioned indefinitely, and if you position it so that it's partially off the image area (on the window background), you can continue to reposition the mask without losing the mask areas that have gone outside the image area. However, if you select a different tool (such as a Brush or Fill tool) while a marquee selection is outside the image border, the selection is truncated by the image border. So in a way, a marquee selection created with a Mask tool doesn't really become a mask until you switch PHOTO-PAINT tools.

Converting a Regular Mask to a Transparency Mask

The only reason why the mask in this example began its life as a Regular mask, is so the ellipse could be rotated. There is no facility in PHOTO-PAINT to rotate a Transparency mask tint, and Masking tools cannot be used on a tint displayed above an image. You could open a saved Transparency mask as an image file, then use a Masking tool to select the area you wish to rotate, but this is the long way around accomplishing the effect.

Rotating the ellipse mask to better represent a spotlight cast at an angle was the "hard part" of creating the spotlight effect, and now it's time to convert the regular ellipse mask to a Transparency mask, so that a shaft of light can be added to the image.

The following steps show how to convert the ellipse mask to a Transparency mask:

1. Choose **M**ask, Create **T**ransparency Mask, then choose From Mask. This displays the Transparency Mask Creation dialog box, but it contains different options when a mask marquee is active within an image file.

2. Choose 100 percent for the new Transparency mask **O**pacity, and Choose **0** for the **F**eather option, shown in figure 23.31. Although these are excellent options available for creating a soft, subtle mask, you need to append the mask with a light shaft, and the two mask areas should display the same degree of softness. You'll see how to accomplish manual adjustment of opacity and feathering for a Transparency mask shortly.

3. Click on OK.

4. Click on the Transparency radio button in the Edit field in the Layers/Objects roll-up. Bang! Areas that are masked outside the ellipse selection turn opaque blue (appearing as black in a black and white figure), as shown in figure 23.32.

Figure 23.31

Choose Opacity and Feathering characteristics for a Transparency mask based on an existing, Regular mask marquee.

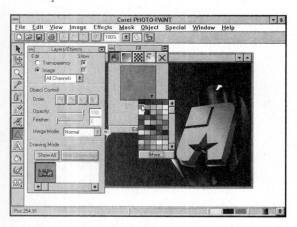

Figure 23.32

Opaque Transparency mask areas protect the underlying image from editing changes.

You might want to choose a different color for the Transparency mask because the purple background in the image is a little too close in hue to the Transparency mask. Use the steps described in "Defining and Loading a Transparency Mask," earlier in this chapter.

Adding Graphical Information to the Transparency Mask

As mentioned previously, the goal here is to attach a shaft of light to an elliptical spotlight within the ALT_AIR.TIF image. To do this, a second area must be defined in the present Transparency mask, that has a different tint opacity than the spotlight ellipse. At present, the ellipse shows the underlying image, which means this image area will be completely selected when an effect is applied to the overall image, while the completely opaque, tinted areas of the underlying image will be masked and protected from change.

Make the shaft of light 50-percent dense, so it will receive some, but not all, of the effect you eventually apply to the ALT_AIR.TIF image. To do this, you need to fill an area shaped like a shaft of light with 50-percent black. When the Transparency mask is visible and editable, application of 50-percent black to the mask will result in a semi-opaque tinted overlay.

The Polygon Shape tool is located on the fly-out for the Shape tools (the same suite of tools the Rectangle tool belongs to), and is a good choice for building the light shaft on the Transparency mask.

The following list shows how to create a shaft of light in the Transparency mask that will be used to slightly lighten the corresponding ALT_AIR.TIF image area:

1. Type **170** in the Zoom level field on the ribbon bar. This takes you to a comfortable viewing resolution of the ALT_AIR.TIF image. Scroll up and to the right in the image so you have a clear view of where the shaft of light will be designed on the Transparency mask.

2. Double-click on the Current Fill color swatch on the Status line if the Fill roll-up isn't currently on screen, then click on the Uniform Fill button on the top of the roll-up.

3. Choose **50%** black from the color palette drop-down. Like all the Shape tools, the Polygon tool fills the interior of the shape you define with color from the Fill roll-up, not the Colors roll-up.

4. Click a starting point for the polygon at the leftmost edge of the Transparency mask ellipse, then click again at the top edge of the image window. Click to the right of your last click, then click on the rightmost edge of the ellipse. This is the basic shape of the spotlight shaft, and you now need to

trace around the edge of the top portion of the ellipse, so shaft and ellipse touch, but don't overlap.

It's a mistake to overlap Transparency mask areas of different opacity when using a Shape tool. Shape tools "flood fill" the interior of the shape you design—in this example, this means a straight line across the top of the ellipse with a polygon line would create a hard straight edge where an area of 50-percent opacity meets the 100-percent transparent ellipse. Instead, do the following:

5. Click points along the top edge of the ellipse about every five degrees or so, as shown in figure 23.33, then double-click on the point where you began the polygon shape, as shown in figure 23.34.

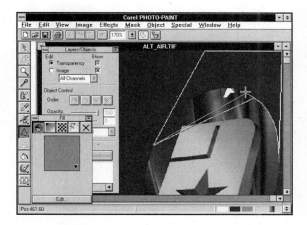

Figure 23.33
Single-click points along the curve of the ellipse shape to make the edges of the polygon meet the ellipse edge.

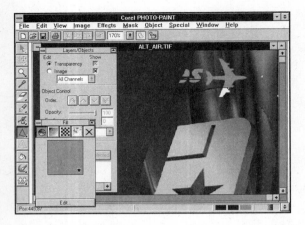

Figure 23.34

Once the polygon shape is closed, it will fill with opacity corresponding to the density of the fill you've specified.

The edge where the shaft meets the ellipse is a little rough, and there are a number of solutions to refining the edge now. First, you could choose white Paint color, then use the Paint Brush tool to carefully redefine this edge. Or you could set the Paint color to 50-percent black and try to refine the edge from the shaft side of the edge.

A far simpler method, however, is to use the Gaussian Blur filter on the Transparency mask. You need to soften the design of the Transparency mask anyway, to create a less hard-edged effect when you lighten these areas.

Applying an Effect to a Transparency Mask

Although you can't use Masking tools to alter a Transparency mask tint, using painting tools and all commands under the Effects menu are possible techniques for editing the mask.

In the next set of steps, you'll see how to make the Transparency mask a little less harsh. When you then edit the corresponding ALT_AIR image areas, the transition between original and edited image areas will be smooth and photographic in quality.

1. Choose Effects, Fancy, then choose Gaussian Blur...

2. Click-and-drag the **F**ilter slider to 7, as shown in figure 23.35. This is a mild amount of blurring to apply to the Transparency mask. You'll notice that the preview window displays a Transparency mask representation in grayscale. The brighter areas are the ones that allow the most painting or other editing through to the underlying ALT_AIR.TIF image. With your cursor inside the preview window, you can right-mouse click to zoom out and see more of the image in the preview window. You can also scroll your view within the preview window by click-and-dragging inside the window.

3. Click on OK.

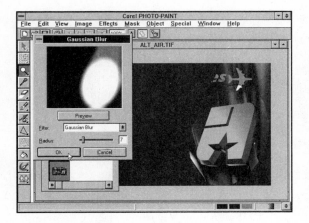

Figure 23.35

When editing a Transparency mask, Effects preview windows show the mask, not the underlying image.

Altruist's logo in the ALT_AIR.TIF image is currently set to receive the same spotlight treatment as the background areas, because the logo has not been protected with opaque mask. In the next section, you'll see how to further edit the Transparency mask to protect the logo from the spotlight effect.

Adding an Area to a Transparency Mask

Always plan ahead when designing an image that requires special effects or a Transparency mask because, as you've seen throughout the PHOTO-PAINT section of this book, there is a definite order, a sequence of editing techniques, that brings the best results. Procedurally, it now is the right time to mask the logo in the ALT_AIR.TIF image. The reason why it wasn't masked earlier is because

you want the logo to be cleanly and accurately masked away from the spotlight—applying the Gaussian Blur to the entire Transparency mask would have blurred the masked area over the logo had it been over the image. This would cause an interesting effect, but not one appropriate for this assignment.

Here's how to mask the logo in the image before applying a filter to the overall image:

1. Choose black from the Fill roll-up's drop-down palette. This color corresponds to total masking in areas you apply it on the Transparency mask.

2. Use the Polygon tool to define the edge of the logo in the ALT_AIR.TIF image, as shown in figure 23.36, then double-click to end the polygon at the point where you began. The polygon immediately fills with 100-percent opaque mask and covers the underlying logo.

Figure 23.36

Click points around the periphery of the logo area to add Transparency mask fill.

Because Uniform fill is one, solid color, there are now harsh edges around the logo area, which sort of defeats the advanced features of a Transparency mask. Chapter 24 covers PHOTO-PAINT's painting and editing tools in detail, and you'll use one, the Blend tool, in the next section to soften the edge of the logo's mask.

Using the Blend Tool on a Transparency Mask

Several effects and tools are available in PHOTO-PAINT for softening image areas or entire images. The most telltale aspect of the artificial nature of digital images are hard, pixelated lines. Stairstep, jaggy edges are particularly unwanted in photographic, digital images because they call attention away from the subject and toward the medium of creative expression. Using image modes of high color capability always should be your first step toward eliminating harsh image edge detail, and your second step should be the creative application of a little image blurring when stairstep pixel edges move into the scene.

The Transparency mask is capable of holding 256 unique shades of brightness values. This makes the polygon fill area on top of the logo area an ideal subject for experimentation with the Blend tool. The Blend tool is sort of a "Gaussian Blur in a Bottle" that can be applied selectively in this image to blend the edges of the mask over the logo area into the

clear areas of the ellipse within the Transparency mask. By blending the edges, you achieve a softer look for editing areas in the ALT_AIR.TIF image—a look that can be accepted more easily by the viewer as being natural, as though the image was photographed under spotlight lighting.

To add the finishing touches to a professional-quality Transparency mask, follow these steps:

1. Click-and-hold on the Special Tools button on the toolbox. By default, the Smear tool icon is on its face. Choose the Blend tool (the waterdrop-shaped icon).

2. Press Ctrl+F8 to display the Tool Settings roll-up if it isn't on-screen, and type **25** in the brush tip **S**ize field. Because the Tool Settings is a context-sensitive roll-up, options unique to the Blend tool are currently displayed. Click-and-drag the Blend slider until the Blend value is about **75**. The Blend slider controls how much paint color (in this case, the mask tint color) is blended into the paper color (in this case, this is the transparent area of the mask).

3. Click-and-drag on the edge of the masked area of the logo. As you can see in figure 23.37, the Blend tool doesn't produce a pronounced effect, but instead can be used to slightly soften the hard, pixelated edges.

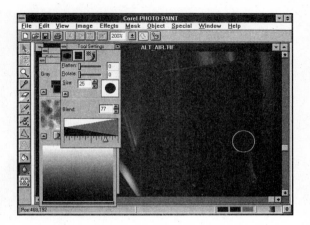

Figure 23.37

Click-and-drag on image edge areas with the Blend tool to soften the contrast between them.

4. Double-click on the Zoom tool to zoom out to 100-percent viewing resolution. If your image looks like figure 23.38, you're in good shape and all set to apply an effect to the areas exposed by the Transparency mask.

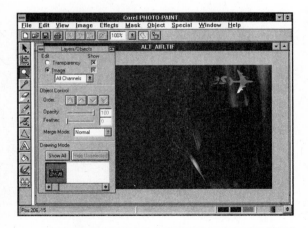

Figure 23.38

The finished Transparency mask.

Using the Transparency Mask for Image Editing

The mask contains all the necessary information for PHOTO-PAINT to read the transparent, opaque, and in-between mask areas into the ALT_AIR.TIF image.

It's time to apply the Transparency mask to the image and edit the image areas that contain the least mask tint. To add a realistic (or at least plausible) spotlight to the ALT_AIR.TIF image, follow these steps:

1. Click on the Image radio button on the Layers/Objects roll-up, and uncheck the Show check box next to the Transparency radio button. The mask is still in place, but by hiding it from view, you can now see the edits you're going to perform.

2. From the Effects menu, choose Color, then choose Brightness and Contrast. If you decide against using Brightness-Contrast-Intensity controls based on the preview image, you can also choose Gamma from the Filters list in the Brightness-Contrast-Intensity dialog box.

3. Click and drag the sliders in the Brightness-Contrast-Intensity dialog box to **B**rightness: **50**, **C**ontrast: **29**, and **I**ntensity: **73**, as shown in figure 23.39. The preview shows you the entire image with the effect, but the Transparency mask protects the areas you defined.

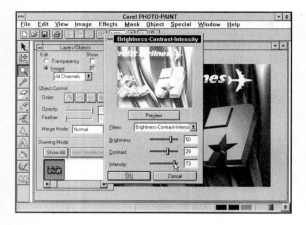

Figure 23.39
Use the Brightness/Contrast controls to simulate a brilliant spotlight in the ALT_AIR.TIF image.

Figure 23.40
A soft, realistic lighting effect is achieved through creative manipulation of a Transparency mask.

4. Click on OK. As you can see in figure 23.40, the spotlight effect is a big hit within the image, and by hand-crafting a Transparency mask, you achieve an effect *not* available on any application menu.

5. Save the finished image to your hard disk.

Using masks to create unusual image effects is not limited to artificial lighting, and the next section shows how to get quick, dramatic results using the tools and techniques discussed in this section.

Using Down-and-Dirty Special Effects with Masks

The examples in this section show how to prepare and apply manually created Transparency masks that you can use in a variety of theme-related digital photographs. Now that two types of PHOTO-PAINT masks have been covered, you'll see how to incorporate them and the color Mask feature in a free-form design experiment. By following along, you'll see the relationship between the different types of masks, what each one is best used for, and get a feeling for their interchangeable properties.

Designing a Transparency Mask in CorelDRAW

The capability to lighten selected masked areas in an image offers the opportunity to add text in an unusual way. Catalog manufacturers and department stores currently are using an effect to "emboss" a logo or name on an image. The lettering is lighter than the image, but the contents of the lettering are identical and contiguous with the rest of the photograph.

The following steps demonstrate how to lighten text out of an image so that it becomes another graphical element:

1. You need to leave PHOTO-PAINT for a moment and open CorelDRAW to create some custom text. First, create a black background rectangle that measures 2.84 inches wide by 2.4 inches high. These are the dimensions of the THREADS.TIF image used in this example, and the black rectangle represents a protected, masked area when the design is used in PHOTO-PAINT as a Transparency mask. If you're in a rush, THREADS.CPT is located in the CHAP23 subdirectory of the *CorelDRAW! The Professional Reference* companion CDs. THREADS.CPT is a copy of the finished mask created in CorelDRAW.

2. Type **THREADS** (in all uppercase letters), press Ctrl+spacebar to select the text, then press Ctrl+T to display CorelDRAW's Character Attributes dialog box.

3. Choose an extremely bold typeface such as Futura, Compacta Black, or Kabel Ultra from the Fonts list. Then click on OK.

4. Left-click on the white swatch on the color palette with the Artistic Text selected. The white color serves as an indicator that the entire text area is to be available for editing when it is used in a bitmap format as a PHOTO-PAINT Transparency mask.

5. Choose **T**ransform roll-up from the Effe**c**ts menu (or press Alt+F7). Then click on the Rotate button (second from the left at the top of the roll-up) and type **90** in the Angle of Rotation degrees field. Click on the Apply button.

6. Choose the Pick tool and resize the Artistic text so that it fits snugly inside the rectangle, touching the left side and the top and bottom borders.

7. Double-click on the Pick tool on the toolbox to Select **A**ll.

8. Click on the Export button on the ribbon bar (or choose **E**xport from the **F**ile menu). Then select Adobe Illustrator, *.AI, *.EPS as the file format from the List Files of **T**ype field. Name the selection THREADS.EPS. Check the **S**elected Only box and click on OK. Accept Corel's defaults for exporting the selected objects (click on OK).

9. Close CorelDRAW. You don't need to save UNTITLED.CDR, so you can click on No in the dialog box. Start PHOTO-PAINT.

10. Open the THREADS.TIF image from the *CorelDRAW! The Professional Reference* companion CDs, then choose **F**ile, **O**pen from PHOTO-PAINT's menu.

11. Choose the THREADS.EPS image you created in step 8, and change the List Files of **T**ype box to display Adobe Illustrator or CorelTRACE!,*.EPS images. Then click on OK. Unless you explicitly specify the *.EPS image type in the List Files of **T**ype box, PHOTO-PAINT cannot import the Encapsulated PostScript information into bitmap format. EPS images are not native bitmap-type graphics.

12. In the Import into Bitmap dialog box, choose 256 shades of Gray in the **C**olor field, and accept the rest of the defaults. Click on OK.

13. In figure 23.41, you can see the imported CorelDRAW design next to the THREADS.TIF image. Save the NEW-1.CPT image as THREADS.CPT so you can locate it in a moment, and then close the file. PHOTO-PAINT needs to *rasterize* (convert to bitmap) Encapsulated PostScript images before they can be used as a mask.

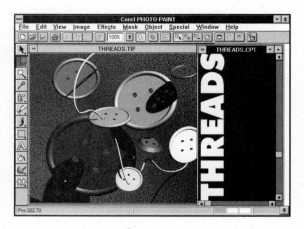

Figure 23.41

Create precise text designs in CorelDRAW and then import them for use as masks in PHOTO-PAINT.

In this section, you created a clean text element for use as a mask in PHOTO-PAINT that simply would have taken too long to create with PHOTO-PAINT's tools. Working between Corel modules is the preferred practice of graphics designers who have discovered the power of Corel. You must evaluate each module's strengths and use them as you would other business applications.

Creating a Lettering Effect with a Mask

Neither Transparency masks nor Regular masks have to be created using PHOTO-PAINT's Mask tools—or any of PHOTO-PAINT's tools, period—as the last section demonstrated. The lettering file you created now can be loaded onto the THREADS.TIF image as though it was designed in PHOTO-PAINT. Because there are no tonal values in the THREADS.CPT file, the file can be used as a Regular mask or a Transparency mask, although its use as a Transparency mask offers no advantages because there is no tonal information greater then 1 bit/pixel.

The THREADS.EPS image was rasterized to file format as a 256-grayscale (8 bit/pixel) mode, which means that if the file is loaded as a Regular mask, PHOTO-PAINT reads only the black-and-white areas. If the THREADS.CPT image contained any grayscale information and was loaded as a Regular mask, PHOTO-PAINT would read tonal values up to 128 and treat them as black, and those values from 128 to 255 would be read as white (*subject to change* areas, as displayed on top of an image as a mask).

You can edit the THREADS.CPT mask as a marquee selection or as a Transparency tint at any time, and because the saved file format is 8 bits/pixel, you can edit the THREADS.CPT image directly using painting and editing tools, as described earlier in this chapter. Saving masks to 256 grayscale format gives you the option of later loading the mask information either as a Regular mask or a Transparency mask.

In the following steps, you create an effect with the mask you created in CorelDRAW to make the lettering a design element in the THREADS.TIF image:

1. Choose **L**oad from the **M**ask menu, then click on the THREADS.CPT file. The advantage to loading a mask file as a Regular mask is that you can reposition it using the Mask Picker tool if the mask isn't aligned to the image area you want. A Transparency mask has no marquee, and the only way to reposition it is to edit the corresponding grayscale file directly.

2. Choose Color from the Effe**c**ts menu, then Brightness and Contrast.

3. Type 23 in the Brightness field. As you can see in figure 23.42, the Effects Pre**v**iew window displays only editable images areas (areas containing a mask). Although you cannot see the effect of the mask producing the lettering (the Preview window doesn't display unique masked area changes), you get a fair idea that a positive value of 23 lightens the masked area noticeably. Click on OK. PHOTO-PAINT processes the command for a moment, and then produces the effect within the masked area of the THREADS.TIF image.

4. Choose **R**emove from the **M**ask menu to get rid of the mask and the marquee lines. As you can see in figure 23.43, the visual detail in the image really hasn't changed, but a new graphical element has been added.

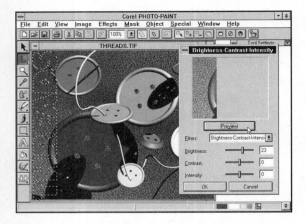

Figure 23.42

Increase the brightness in the masked area to create a lettering effect within the image.

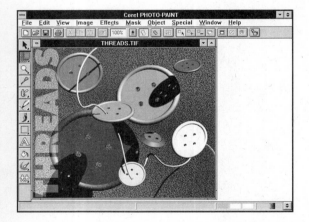

Figure 23.43

By editing tonal values within on a mask, you can create a multitude of variations on a single image.

The effect produced in this section can be spun off into a number of different themes. You can add to a picture logos, designs created using grayscale values, and anything else you can imagine as a different shade or hue when you load the selection as a mask.

Transparency-Masking a Limited Image Area

Earlier in this chapter, you saw how to use a linear fountain fill as the design of a Transparency mask to make a half-fractal texture and half-tulip abstract image. Fountain fills are terrific for creating gradual transitions between original image detail and fills, and can be used to combine images when the Layers/Objects roll-up is used in combination with a Transparency mask.

However, there's a "control issue" that needs to be addressed, and in the next series of steps, you'll see how to create a smooth transition between masked image areas and a very small selection area in an image. To confine an effect or another color to a limited area while producing a smooth transition between masked and selected areas, you'll use a combination of Fill roll-up settings.

To manually create a Transparency mask file with a custom gradient as mask information, follow these steps:

1. Choose **M**ask, Create **T**ransparency Mask, then choose **N**ew.

2. The Transparency Mask Creation dialog box retains settings within a single PHOTO-PAINT session, so click on OK to accept the **U**niform 255 value.

3. Press Ctrl+F7 to display the Layers/ Objects roll-up if it isn't already onscreen, then click on the Transparency radio button and check the Show check box. Now, you're editing the mask and not the image.

4. Choose black from the Fill roll-up, then click+drag a rectangle over the left half of the THREADS.TIF image, as shown in figure 23.44.

5. Click on the Fountain Fill button in the Fill roll-up, click on the Linear fill button, and choose (from the color drop-down palettes) black as the foreground color and white as the background color.

6. Click inside the preview window for the Linear fountain fill, and drag the fill preview so that, from left to right, the fill makes the transition from black to white.

7. Click-and-drag diagonally over the remaining image area in the THREADS.TIF image, as shown in figure 23.45. You've achieved a homemade gradient Transparency mask that is not offered as a preset from the New dialog box accessed through the Create **T**ransparency Mask command.

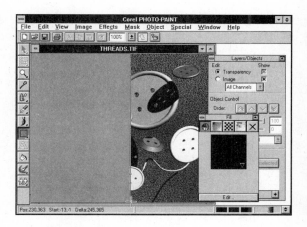

Figure 23.44
Give the left side of the THREADS.TIF image an opaque mask by filling it with black Uniform fill.

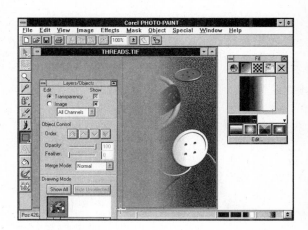

Figure 23.45
You can use any grayscale color, including Fountain fills, to create a custom Transparency mask.

Using Fractal Textures to Add Motion to an Image

The Transparency mask totally blocks the left two-thirds of the image from edits, while the right one-third makes a gentle transition from protected to editing availability.

In the next set of steps, you see a graphical result using a custom Transparency mask in combination with a special fractal texture. Unlike the example of the tulips and the mineral texture earlier in this chapter, you'll see how fading a fractal texture into a *small portion* of an image can add to the composition instead of simply producing abstract art. This is a lesson in choosing the right fractal design in addition to creating a custom Transparency mask.

The O's fractal texture is new to Corel 5, and it offers a stunning array of soft-edge circles that, when applied to the THREADS.TIF image with the Transparency mask loaded, become arcs that suggest motion and add to the visual interest of the image's composition.

The following steps show how to set the THREADS image into motion:

1. Uncheck the Show button on the Layers/Objects roll-up and click on the Image radio button. The image can be edited and seen in its entirety now, although the Transparency mask is still protecting the image in various areas to different degrees.

2. Click on the Texture button in the Fill roll-up. Then choose the Samples 5 collection from the top drop-down list and O's from the bottom drop-down list.

3. With the Rectangle tool, click-and-drag over the right half of the THREADS.TIF image. Because the left half of the image is completely (100-percent) masked, you're assured that every partially masked area is covered on the right side of the image, and it takes less time for PHOTO-PAINT to process the command when filling only half the image area compared to click+dragging a fill over the entire image. See the effect of the fractal texture on the partially selected areas in figure 23.46.

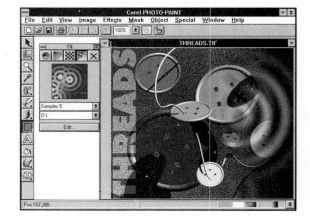

Figure 23.46

The amount of texture fill in the THREADS image corresponds to the amount of transparency in areas in the mask.

The more you experiment with creating custom Transparency masks, the more ideas you come across for original design work using any sort of image. That's the "Zen" of Corel; by knowing what the tools do, you can express almost any graphical concept, and the unique functions of Corel's feature set actually can create new ideas by experimenting with them.

Using Color Masks

Color masks are created around an image area without the use of Mask tools. You use the Color Mask roll-up to select ranges of colors that can be modified or protected. There are many uses for Color masks in everyday assignments; suppose that you need to change all the green fruit in a photo to a more ripe color, or change only the fashions depicted in a clothing catalog to colors more appropriate for a certain season.

Defining a Color Mask Area

A Color mask can make quick work of protecting or modifying image areas based on color value, but as you see in this section, a Color mask also can be converted to a Regular mask or a Transparency mask and saved as either mask type. After a Color Mask is converted, saved, or both, it can be edited to include or exclude other image areas.

To apply a Color mask to a button in the THREADS.TIF image, follow these steps:

1. Press Ctrl+F5 (or choose Color **M**ask Roll-Up from the **M**ask menu).

2. You want to change the pink button in the middle of the THREADS.TIF image to a different color. To mask the button, click on the first of the 10 buttons in the Color Mask roll-up and choose Modify Selected Colors from the drop-down list at the top of the roll-up.

3. Your cursor turns into an eyedropper after you click on a color button, and the button's face displays the areas of the image you move your cursor over. Put the cursor over the pink button in the THREADS image and click, as shown in figure 23.47. The color then is registered with the Color Mask roll-up as a color area that can be modified while all other areas are protected from editing.

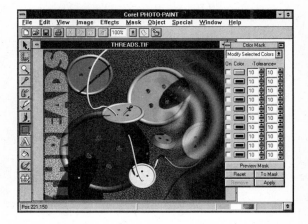

Figure 23.47

Select a color within an image with the Color Mask roll-up's eyedropper cursor.

4. THREADS.TIF is a 24-bit color image and, as such, contains a wide latitude of color values. Although the button in the image you clicked on appears to be completely pink, there are gradations of shadows and highlights within the button area. The Color Mask roll-up offers a plus/minus Tolerance for Color Mask selection. Use the spin controls in the Tolerance field next to the color selection button to increase the color tolerance to "give or take" **75**. This is a value based on a few "hit-and-miss" tries with the Tolerance setting. The range of color tolerance runs from 0 to 255, indicating that the *brightness* (the amount of light or dark attributed to a particular hue) is what the color tolerance actually takes into account when you specify a range for a selected color.

5. Click on the Preview Mask button on the Color Mask roll-up. As you can see in figure 23.48, the color tolerance of plus or minus 75 did pretty well in selecting most of the pink button in the image.

6. Click anywhere within the image with the cursor to remove the preview color.

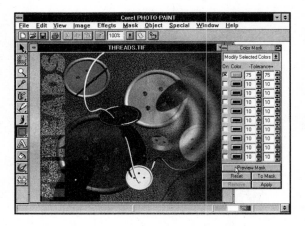

Figure 23.48

Adjust the color tolerance in the Color Mask roll-up to select more or less of a chosen color value in an image.

Refining Color Mask Selections

Closer examination of the Color mask preview shows that a plus minus tolerance of 75 selects the pink of the button better than imagined. You can see in figure 23.48 that the exposed areas of the pink button aren't really pink; some shadows and highlights are exposed, but these values don't actually contribute to what a viewer sees as being "a pink button." Forget about the unmasked regions of the pink button for the moment. If you need to mask completely a similar object for editing, you have four courses of action:

■ Increase the color tolerance to include the highlights and shadows.

■ Sample a second or third color from the pink button to include them as separate ranges. The Color Mask roll-up has 10 color registers available to which you can assign image color values. You select other colors exactly in the same way that you selected the initial pink sample.

■ Convert the Color mask to a Regular mask, and then use the conventional Mask tools to refine the selection area.

■ Use the **M**ask, Create **T**ransparency Mask option after the Color mask has been converted to a mask marquee. Next click on the Show check box near the Transparency option in the edit field on the Layers/Objects roll-up, and use a painting tool to refine the Transparency mask selection. In this case, you would want to choose **M**ask, **In**vert Transparency Mask as an intermediate step to editing not the selection but the mask areas. It's easier this way. You then choose to invert the mask again before applying changes to the image, so the button is a selected area, and the rest of the image is masked.

The first two options are good ones, but they both have unique disadvantages. If you specify a high color tolerance for the pink color mask selection, you probably will start to include other image areas you might not want included. The THREADS lettering you created earlier, for example, already is displaying some dark green tint overlay, as shown in figure 23.48.

The disadvantage of sampling other color values is primarily one of time and labor. The easiest solution to refining the pink button area and eliminating the Color mask over the THREADS lettering at this point is to convert the Color mask to a Regular mask, and use the Mask tools from the toolbox to quickly adjust things.

To refine the Color mask and make it readily available for use in some image editing, follow these steps:

1. Click on the To Mask button in the Color Mask roll-up. A marquee border now surrounds image areas in which color values were included in the tolerance range you specified when you switched on the Color mask for the pink values.

2. You probably will note a few areas in the image that have marquee lines that shouldn't have them. Check out the THREADS lettering, for example. To remove the marquee from the lettering, choose the Lasso Mask tool and click on the Remove from Selection button on the ribbon bar (choose **R**emove from Selection from the **S**pecial menu). Then click-and-drag with the Lasso Mask tool around any areas that should be removed from the selection.

3. When all extraneous marquees have been removed from the THREADS.TIF image, click on the Add to Selection button on the ribbon bar (or choose **A**dd to Selection from the **S**pecial menu).

4. Click-and-drag the Lasso tool around any areas you feel should be included in the selection of the pink button.

5. It's time to recolor the pink button when the marquee selection has been refined adequately. Choose Color from the Effects menu, and then choose Hue/Saturation. The Hue/Saturation settings effect changes in the basic color of a selection area, but they don't change the grayscale component. In effect, image detail is preserved, but the hue—the primary component of colors people recognize—is altered when you use Hue/Saturation to make adjustments.

6. Drag the Hue slider to -64. As you can see in figure 23.49, this changes the pink button to a more heliotrope color. Click on OK to make the change in hue to the button.

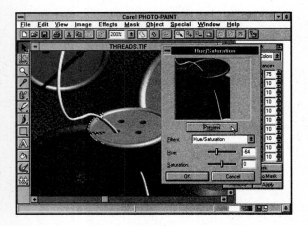

Figure 23.49

The Hue/Saturation effect changes the color, but not the image detail, of a selected area.

Hue and saturation make up two of the three components of an HSB color model (brightness is the third component). Chapter 27, "Color Specification and Output," goes into more detail about PHOTO-PAINT's use of color spaces, but for the moment, you should evaluate hue changes made in the Hue/Saturation command dialog box (Effects, Color, then Hue/Saturation) based on a simple primary and secondary color wheel—a color model used by many graphics applications. Hue is measured in PHOTO-PAINT in increments from 0 to 255; 0 represents pure red and violet is 255. The color wheel cycles counterclockwise in the order traditionally taught to schoolchildren: R, O, Y, G, B, I, V (red, orange, yellow, green, blue, indigo, and violet).

Therefore, a negative hue value in the Hue/Saturation command dialog box starts the progression through violet to indigo, blue, green, yellow, orange, and finally to red. This is why the pink button in the last example turned bluish when –64 was specified in the **H**ue field.

7. You didn't need to change the saturation of the selection in the last step because saturation is the adding or subtracting of the pure color component (the hue) of a selection. Saturation adjustment, therefore, doesn't change the color of something; instead, it removes or adds pre-existing color to a selected area. Choose **R**emove from the **M**ask menu and save the image in which you've performed color correction.

Use the Color Mask roll-up when you have an image that needs a color range, but not necessarily a geometric image area edited.

Summary

This chapter covered some of the practical uses for masks in PHOTO-PAINT, as well as some examples of how each of the mask types can be converted to another mask type. You can modify, create, and reposition masks, and you can convert a mask to an object selection as easily as copying the masked selection to the Clipboard. The only time you would want to define an object instead of a mask is when you want to composite two or more objects into a single image. Masks are for performing editing work within a single image, but the flexibility of masks can lead to exciting creative possibilities in your own work.

In summary, choose the following mask types in the corresponding situations:

- **Regular mask.** When you need a marquee outline to indicate an area where a mask is. Regular masks make the enclosed image area available for editing, and they can be inverted to edit outside the mask but not inside by using the **M**ask, **I**nvert command. Regular masks always display a marquee until they are removed, and while the marquee area is displayed, a masked area can be repositioned; the image area the mask defines is not moved, however. Regular masks are limited to 1 bit/pixel of selection

information, but can be converted to a Transparency mask (which can hold 256 levels of selection information) by choosing **M**ask, Create **T**ransparency Mask, **F**rom Mask. A Regular mask that has not been converted to 256-grayscale mode can be loaded as a Transparency mask, but it only provides 1 bit/pixel masking information. Mask tools can create only 1 bit/pixel mask information when you use them. A Regular mask only contains "modify area" and "protect area" information; there are no partial Transparency mask characteristics.

- **Transparency mask.** Used when you want to create an elegant, elaborate mask around image areas to make image areas *partially* protected. You can hide a mask from view by unchecking the Show check box on the Layers/Objects menu, and you can check the status of your image for the presence of a Transparency mask by looking at the right side of the Status Line; if you see a gradient icon, a Transparency mask is active within the document. By copying an image into an active image, you can merge the two images with a Transparency mask partially protecting the background image to create a cross-fade effect. A saved Transparency mask can be loaded as a Regular mask, but the grayscale information contained in it is only read as black (protected) or white (not protected), with the break point set at 128 (from grayscale values between 0 and 255).

■ **Color mask.** The best use of the Color Mask roll-up is in situations where you want to edit image areas that are similar in color. Color masks can be converted to Regular masks, which in turn can be saved as Transparency masks for further refining. Color masks usually tend to be more effective in isolating a color range in computer illustrations rather than photographic images, because illustrations tend to have more pure, absolute color values.

PHOTO-PAINT earns its name by providing tools for editing both computer graphics and photographic images. Earlier chapters in this book.are oriented toward photographic usage of PHOTO-PAINT, and for that reason, PHOTO-PAINT brushes and other tools have not been examined. The following chapter provides working examples of the brushes, painting, drawing, and other tools designers can use and modify to produce amazing paintings and illustrations.

Painting and Drawing

In the world of bitmap graphics, anything you imagine can be used as a brush to apply color to an image; painting and drawing tools are simply bitmap designs applied to bitmap backgrounds. The real value of PHOTO-PAINT's collection of color-application tools lies within the predefined set Corel offers and the user-definable controls with which you can create your own painting tools.

How you use the painting and drawing tools, and how you can customize PHOTO-PAINT's offerings, is the focus of this chapter. If you ever wanted to express yourself without the restrictions of hard-edge vector tools, PHOTO-PAINT is the key, and the following pages unlock some of the secrets to producing fascinating, provocative work.

This chapter covers:

- Tool settings for the Paint Brush tool

- Creating custom Paint Brush shapes

- Using combinations of brushes

- Using and building an Artist Brush

- Working with the Air and Spraycan Brushes

- Using the Pencil tools

- Options for the Canvas roll-up

- Creating a custom canvas

Getting Familiar with a Virtual Paint Brush

Corel Corporation put a lot of thought into the design of the paint-application tools you have available in PHOTO-PAINT; a lot of the functionality of the Paint Brush tool mimics the way an actual paint brush operates. In fact, PHOTO-PAINT has special terms for the foreground/background properties of bitmap images used in the program—*paint* is referred to as the application of foreground color, and *paper* is the background to which you apply the foreground color. Both sets of terms are used throughout this chapter so that both computer graphics people and traditional artists who are migrating to computer graphics can feel at home with the following discussions.

There are similarities and differences between traditional painting and the equivalents PHOTO-PAINT offers in its environment. Obviously, you do not have to clean a PHOTO-PAINT brush, but how deeply you dip the brush into paint, how thick a coat you want to apply, and how the tip is shaped all are user-defined. You can create a brush with characteristics to fit any task. The next section explores the user settings for the collection of brush tools.

Tool Settings for the Paint Brush Tool

The Tool Settings roll-up plays a heavy part in how color is painted onto an image background. As you might have noticed when working with various PHOTO-PAINT tools, the Tool Settings roll-up offers context-sensitive options for the active tool—the Object Picker tool has Tool Settings features that relate to moving objects, and by choosing the Rectangle or other geometric shape tool, the Tool Settings roll-up displays options relevant to the corresponding tool's capability.

The best tool to demonstrate the Tool Settings options for the category of brush tools is the standard Paint Brush. Because the Paint Brush tool produces a stroke without a fancy effect as the Impressionism and Pointillism Brushes do, it's easier to see the customizing work you can perform on the simple Paint Brush tool.

The examples in the following sections cover the brush characteristic settings in a sequence that makes sense for a designer, and not in the order you find them on the Tool Settings roll-up. All the variations you can create with the Tool Settings are covered here, but the idea here is to build on the understanding of the characteristics as you'd use them on an assignment, so, very naturally, they are a little out of order.

Fade Out and Spacing Brush Characteristics

There are three settings for brush tools found on the top of the Tool Settings roll-up that determine the shape of a brush tip—round, square, and custom. The next set of steps isn't so much an exercise as it is an opportunity to experiment with the Tool Settings roll-up controls for brushes in PHOTO-PAINT.

Here's how to give some variance to the Paint Brush tool as you apply color to an image:

1. Open the CHEKBORD.TIF image from the *CorelDRAW! The Professional Reference* companion CDs. It's located in the CHAP24 directory. The CHEKBORD image was designed to prominently display changes you make to brush characteristics when you paint. (Basically, it's an image file you can mess up without destroying work of your own.)

2. Double-click on the Paint Brush tool on the toolbox to display the Tool Settings roll-up (or press Ctrl+F8). You can also menu your way to display the Tool Settings by choosing **V**iew, Tool **S**ettings Roll-Up, if the roll-up is not visible upon startup of PHOTO-PAINT.

3. Click on the Round Shape setting at the top left of the Tool Settings roll-up. The Square and Round Shapes are self-explanatory as to the sort of brush tip they produce, but the other brush tip characteristics on the Tool Settings roll-up can modify the basic brush shape greatly.

4. Enter **50** in the **S**ize field. This makes the round brush tip 50 pixels in diameter, a good size for which to experiment on the CHEKBORD.TIF image.

5. The first characteristic to examine is the **F**ade Out setting. Fade out is measured in percentages, from 0 to 100, not according to amount of pixels. Before testing this characteristic, press Ctrl+F2 (**V**iew, C**o**lor Roll-Up) to make the color palette available, and choose a dark paint (foreground) color by clicking on the paint color box on the Colors roll-up to select the foreground color. The active box (paint or paper) has a double-line border around the box. Click on a dark color on the color palette.

6. Enter a **F**ade Out percentage of **0**, then click and drag the brush across the CHEKBORD.TIF image. You have an endless supply of color because the characteristic of the brush is to never fade.

7. Set the **F**ade Out amount to **70**, then click and drag the Paint Brush tool. As you can see in figure 24.1, the brush runs out of color before you reach the edge of the CHEKBORD image. Fade Out is the characteristic you want to adjust when painting one stroke onto another stroke to achieve a blend of the two colors in image areas.

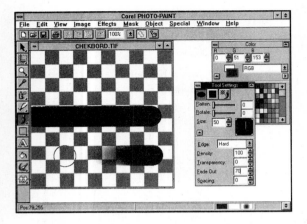

Figure 24.1

Use the Fade Out amount to control how far a painted stroke applies paint color.

The Fade Out setting determines the amount of "paint" a brush can hold in one stroke (on one click and drag). If you click in an area and hold without dragging, you deplete the amount of color, and dragging after holding produces a much shorter stroke. Try clicking and dragging with a Fade Out of 50, then try click/hold/dragging, and you will see that by immediately dragging the cursor, you can produce a longer stroke before the paint fades out completely.

Spacing

Spacing is a setting that determines how consistently a brush stroke is applied. With a Spacing of 1, a brush stroke is applied as a single, even stroke. When set at 100, a brush stroke has gaps in it, which produce a dotted line or intermittent effect. The shape of the stroke with which you paint is determined by

the shape of the brush tip you select. You might notice when painting with a Spacing value of 1 that brush strokes take an eternity to complete. This is because PHOTO-PAINT is placing consecutive brush strokes exactly 1 pixel away from each other along the route you took when you dragged the brush. When you click and drag a long stroke, PHOTO-PAINT performs incredible calculations to render multiple, virtually redundant painted areas.

However, you easily can accomplish smooth, even strokes by choosing 0 as the Spacing characteristic. 0 is the manual setting for brush spacing, unlike the preset values (from 1 to 100) that Corel offers. When you click and drag slowly with Spacing set at 0, you achieve smooth lines; when you drag quickly, you get a random "skip brush" effect.

Here's how to achieve two different effects using the same Spacing setting:

1. Set the Fade Out to 0 so that it doesn't affect the Spacing setting.

2. Set the Spacing to 0, then click and drag slowly across the CHEKBORD image toward the top of the image.

3. Click and drag quickly to make a brush stroke underneath the first one. As you can see in figure 24.2, the Spacing setting is the same for both strokes, but the speed with which you apply the paint produces different results.

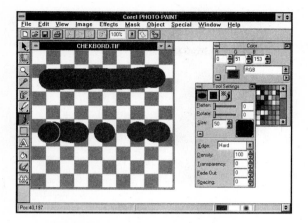

Figure 24.2

PHOTO-PAINT treats an abrupt brush stroke like that of actual paint—you skip strokes.

The **Sp**acing setting values (from 1 to 100) corresponds to an interval measured in pixels. Creative use of these settings can be used to easily produce pattern effects.

4. Set the **S**ize of the tip to 30, set the **D**ensity to 100, then set the S**p**acing to 60. Note that the spacing value is twice the diameter of the tip size, so this should leave a space of 30 pixels (60 spacing minus the stroke's own diameter) whenever you click and drag.

5. Open a new image file, 300 pixels in Height by 300 pixels in Width, 150 dpi Horizontal and Vertical Resolution with 24-bit Color Mode, then hold the Ctrl key (to constrain strokes to a straight line) and click and drag the cursor from left to right. You will get a dotted line.

6. Shift+click a new beginning point for the brush below the dotted line, between the first and second dot, then Ctrl+click+drag across the image. The Shift+click combination resets the angle to which you are constraining the brush stroke. If you don't press Shift before clicking and dragging to reset, you will paint over the previous line.

7. Repeat the last step below the second line. As you can see in figure 24.3, using a predetermined value of Spacing makes quick work of creating patterns.

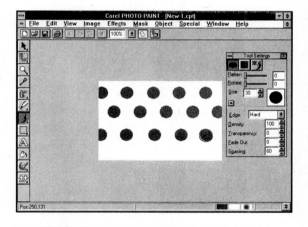

Figure 24.3

Use the Ctrl key in combination with the Spacing setting to create patterns in an image.

In figure 24.4, you can see how making the spacing narrower and changing the **R**otate setting to 45 (degrees) can turn overlapping skips in the Spacing into a more closely knitted pattern.

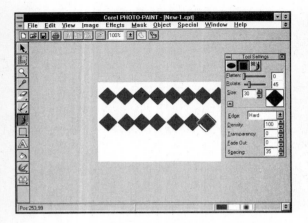

Figure 24.4

When the Spacing is less than the diameter of a brush tip, you can create patterns that seem woven together.

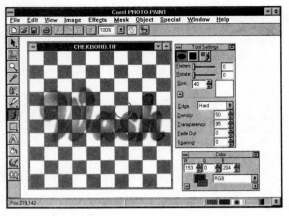

Figure 24.5

Use a high Transparency setting to "tint" a background image area.

Transparency

The **T**ransparency setting can be used to apply paint (foreground) color with a little more subtlety than a flat 100 percent-opaque setting. If you want to cast a tint over an area, set a high Transparency value for a brush tip. A highly transparent color does not create exactly the same effect as merging an object onto a background image in one of the various modes (described in Chapter 22), however; neither does using the Tint tool. If you repeatedly stroke an area, even with more than 90% **T**ransparency set, you eventually will arrive at an opaque, flatly colored image.

As shown in figure 24.5, an area has been stroked 3–4 times with paint (foreground) color having 95% Transparency, and both the checkered background and the foreground color are visible.

Figure 24.5 was created by loading a mask over the checkered image that contained the *Wash* lettering, and then the area was stroked over. See Chapter 23, "Masks," on the creative uses of masks in your work.

Edge and Density Characteristics

You have a choice of **E**dge characteristics of the brush tip: Hard, Medium, or Soft. These options are not that evident while painting unless the **D**ensity of the tip is adjusted. **E**dge characteristics treat the brush tip as though it is a ball: Hard is analogous to a baseball with a hard core covered by a more flexible material, whereas Soft is more like a ball of string, fairly consistent in its density.

In the next example, you will see how changing the **D**ensity of a brush tip in combination with the **E**dge characteristics can produce a look like aerosol paint:

1. Open a new copy of CHEKBORD.TIF (Ctrl+O).

2. On the Tool Settings roll-up, choose the Hard **E**dge setting and enter **2** in the **D**ensity field, and set the **T**ransparency to **0**. This creates a brush that is soft overall, but has a hard edge.

3. Click and drag to produce a stroke that has the shape of the letter *W* in the top half of the CHEKBORD image.

4. Choose the Soft **E**dge setting and keep the **D**ensity value the same. This creates a tip for the brush that produces a very soft stroke, with almost no buildup in the center of each stroke.

5. Click and drag to produce a similar letter *W* shape in the bottom of the CHEKBORD image. As you can see in figure 24.6, altering the **D**ensity of a Round brush tip creates a more "painterly" brush stroke, which resembles pastels and the markings found on metropolitan subways.

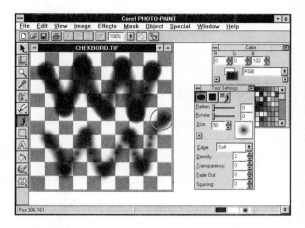

Figure 24.6

Adjust the Density of a brush tip to create soft, flowing strokes.

As mentioned earlier, by using a combination of settings, you can develop a custom brush that can create a unique effect when a situation in a design calls for it. In the next section, you will see how **D**ensity, **F**ade Out, and S**p**acing can be set to automatically create an element in an illustration.

Using Brush Characteristics in a Design

Users are frequently impressed with the number of options and the combinations of options a palette or roll-up offers in a graphics application. But the same basic question arises after a graphics tool has been examined and explained: What is it good for? If millions of creative applications for the Paint Brush tool and Tool Settings roll-up do

not immediately spring to mind, that's okay; if you design for a living, an assignment that cries out for a variation on a plain digital paint brush is just around the corner.

In the next exercise, the FIREWORK.TIF image was created using text and an intermediate fountain fill (discussed later in this chapter). Although it's a nice title for a television promotion or resort, it is static and does not represent a fireworks show. In a nutshell, the image needs some fireworks painted in. Use this exercise as a review of the Tool Settings roll-up's features, and complete the design.

Here's how to create fireworks using PHOTO-PAINT's Paint Brush tool:

1. Choose the Medium **E**dge, round shape tip from the Tool Settings roll-up, and set the **D**ensity to **1**, **T**ransparency to **0**, **F**ade Out to **70**, and S**p**acing to **0**. The Fade Out rate to achieve this effect is somewhat dependent on the speed of your processor; if you have a 386-class machine, set the Fade Out rate to a higher amount.

2. On the test image CHEKBORD.TIF, slowly paint an arc. Experiment with the feel the Paint Brush tool has with these settings.

3. Change the Spacing setting to 40, and repeat an arc. As you can see in figure 24.7, a simple change in S**p**acing creates two different kinds of fireworks displays.

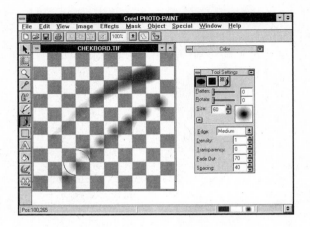

Figure 24.7

*Different S**p**acing settings used in combination with your brushstroke speed and angle produce different effects.*

4. When you are happy with the test run results and you have a feel for producing fireworks, open the FIREWORK.TIF image from the *CorelDRAW! The Professional Reference* companion CDs. Click on OK to confirm with PHOTO-PAINT that the image is read-only, and save the file to your hard drive under the same name and image type.

5. Select red from the color palette on the Colors roll-up, then make an arc in the FIREWORK.TIF image.

6. Create a few more arcs, changing the paint color on the Color roll-up, and changing the S**p**acing from 40 to 0.

7. Stop when you start humming Francis Scott Key songs. As you can see in figure 24.8, a working knowledge of the Tool Settings roll-up and the Paint

Brush tool can produce special effects that would take far longer to create in a vector drawing program.

Figure 24.8
Use the Paint Brush and Tool Settings roll-up to flesh out a graphical idea.

Because PHOTO-PAINT has no facility for remembering a particular tool setting, it's a good idea to write down a discovery you like. The Tool Settings roll-up will hang on to your last custom setting, but once you have changed it, the setting is gone forever.

The Custom Brush

The preceding section carefully skirted around the last of three brush shapes on the Tool Settings roll-up because the custom brush shape is unique and deserves coverage on its own. PHOTO-PAINT has the capability to sample an 8-bit/pixel grayscale image area. Corel has created 50 sample custom brushes, and this section shows how to create your own.

Using the Custom Brush Presets

A custom Paint Brush tip can be used like the round or square shapes to produce a pattern effect within an image. Because any bitmap area can be used to define a custom tip, you can paint with a design and achieve an effect similar to cloning an image area. In figure 24.9, the star-shaped custom tip has been selected, and by setting a **F**ade Out and S**p**acing value, "instant art" has been added to the background image.

Figure 24.9
Create a rubber-stamp effect by choosing a custom brush shape on the Tool Setting roll-up.

Some of the presets PHOTO-PAINT provides for the custom brush shape can be used to create complex background patterns, too. After you have filled an image window with a pattern, you can paint over it with paint (foreground) color, select areas as objects, or add effects.

In the following example, texture is created using a custom brush and the Emboss filter. Professional designers are in constant need for fresh background images to use in a composite design, and here's how to increase your stock of background images very quickly:

1. Choose File, New (Ctrl+N, or click on the New button on the ribbon bar).

2. Choose Color Mode, 24 Bit Color, choose white for the Paper color, type **450** in the Width field and **330** pixels in the Height field, choose 150 dpi resolution (check the Identical Values check box), then click on OK.

3. Select the "squiggle" custom brush, as shown in figure 24.10, enter **44** as the Spacing for the brush, and set the Fade Out to 90. Again, the optimal Fade Out value for this example is based on a 486 machine; 386-class PCs require that you specify a lower Fade Out rate. The squiggle pattern is about 44 pixels wide, so the pattern you will create will be edge-to-edge. You have no control over the Edge, Transparency, or Density of a custom brush, and notice that these fields are dimmed when a custom brush has been selected. Ctrl+click+drag the brush across the top of the NEW-1.CPT image, then using the steps outlined earlier, repeat the strokes until you have a page of alternating brush patterns similar to figure 24.10.

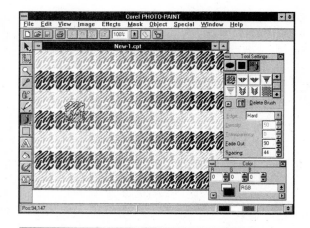

Figure 24.10

Fill the image window with a repeat pattern using the custom brush tip.

4. PHOTO-PAINT's features were designed to be used in combination with one another. The Emboss effect is perfect to use with an image of patterns, and because the patterns fade across the image, the Emboss effect will create the impression of protrusions and recesses based on how much paint (foreground) color it finds in a specific image area. When the image background is covered, choose Effects, Fancy, then Emboss.

5. Choose Gray from the Emboss Color drop-down list, and click on the 4 o'clock direction arrow. In your own assignments, you might want to create a new file with a solid background color, and use the Paint or Paper Color to achieve a color Emboss effect. Click on the Preview window to see the

Emboss effect, then click on OK. As you can see in figure 24.11, the Emboss Effect produces the most pronounced embossing where the paint (foreground) and background color contrast the greatest. You now have a perfect background to create a painting that illustrates fingerprints or Mayan architecture.

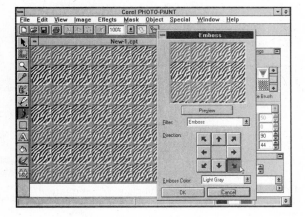

Figure 24.11
Create instant textured background images using custom patterns and PHOTO-PAINT's Effects filters.

Creating Your Own Custom Brush

There are some rules for creating a brush for the custom brush shapes feature. Although you can make your own brush shape quite easily, it's equally easy to clutter the custom brush shape field on the Tool Settings roll-up with shapes that are more fanciful than

functional. Here are some tips on creating brushes before you begin:

- A user-defined brush shape can be created in any color mode; RGB, Grayscale, and Black and White all are legitimate color modes for the image in which you create a tip. However, PHOTO-PAINT can use only 256-shade grayscale (8 bit/pixel) information about your brush shape design, so you might as well begin the brush shape with a new image in Grayscale Color Mode.

- Brush shapes have a fixed size, and the Corel presets do not exceed about 45 pixels across their wider side. Custom brush tips you create shouldn't be huge, unless you intend to paint with them on a gigantic image background. Set yourself an upper limit of about 72 pixels for the custom brush shape.

- A custom brush should be surrounded by white. This means you shouldn't create a grayscale shape for the custom brush that has a percentage of gray extending to the border of the tip, because it will be hard to paint with it without leaving an "edge." Custom brushes produce totally opaque design areas in areas where the shape is black (0 color brightness), and transparent design areas in areas that are white (255 color brightness). Areas of gray will partially apply color, and you might not want this effect when you paint with the custom brush shape.

Here's an example of how to create a custom brush tip of a sun, using the Weather True Type font that came with CorelDRAW! 5:

1. Choose **F**ile, **N**ew (Ctrl+N, or click on the New button on the Ribbon bar), choose white as the **P**aper color, make the **C**olor Mode Gray Scale, and make the **H**eight and **W**idth 200 pixels. You will need a little elbow room within the new image to create the brush shape. Click on OK.

2. Choose black from the Colors roll-up as the paint color.

3. Double-click on the Text tool to select it and to display the Font dialog box.

4. Choose Weather from the **F**ont list, or you can choose any other symbol font if you decided not to install Weather during Corel Setup. Choose 36 as the font **S**ize, then click on OK.

5. If you did not select Weather as the font in this example, you might want to use the Windows CHARMAP.EXE utility to find the keystroke that corresponds to the symbol you want to use. If you are using Weather, click an insertion point in the middle of the NEW-1.CPT image, and type a capital **I**, as shown in figure 24.12.

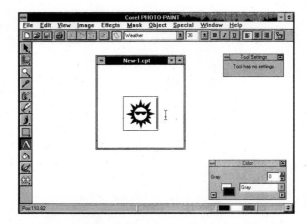

Figure 24.12

Choose a symbol or decorative font character as the shape of a custom brush.

6. Text entries remain editable as long as the Text tool is selected, so if you didn't type the character you want, backspace over the character and select a different key.

7. When you are happy with a symbol, click on the Object tool menu fly-out and choose any object tool. Text entries will become floating, repositionable objects in PHOTO-PAINT the moment you deselect the text tool.

8. Choose **O**bject, **M**erge (Ctrl+G) from the menu to affix the floating symbol to the background image.

9. Choose any Mask tool (the Rectangle Mask tool is probably the most straightforward in its use for selecting the symbol). Marquee-select the symbol, but try to crop as tightly around the symbol as possible without lopping off part of the design. PHOTO-PAINT measures the size of a new custom brush according to *the longest dimension of the rectangle* (or largest vertical/horizontal bounding box around an irregularly shaped mask), so don't leave too much air around the selection.

10. Choose **S**pecial, Create **B**rush.

11. As you can see in figure 24.13, the Create a Custom Brush options dialog box appears. Actually there is a singular option here: the size you want the area defined by the mask selection marquee to be. I recommend you accept the default size offered and click on OK. You can indeed reproportion the size at this point, but this would involve PHOTO-PAINT recalculating the selected area, and this sometimes results in hard pixelation displayed in the custom brush shape. I also recommend you write this default value down, because nowhere in PHOTO-PAINT can you find the custom shape size information after creating a brush tip.

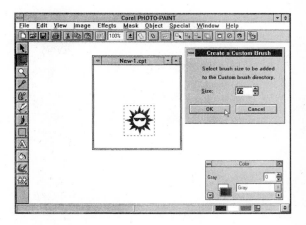

Figure 24.13

Stick with the default size PHOTO-PAINT offers for the custom brush size.

12. After clicking on OK, your custom brush is added to the end of PHOTO-PAINT's preset collection. You also can choose to delete existing brushes by clicking on the trashcan icon on the Tool Settings roll-up. PHOTO-PAINT will ask for a delete confirmation if you click on the trashcan, so accidentally deleting a custom brush is a little harder than most accidents in Windows! In figure 24.14, the custom sun shape has been selected, and a pattern design is created in a new image. You can see that the S**p**acing setting of **50** causes multiple sun images to slightly overlap, because the custom brush is 72 pixels across.

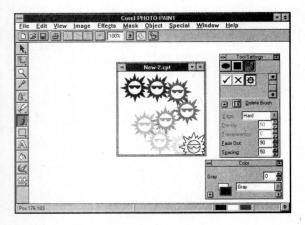

Figure 24.14
Use the information about the size of a custom brush you have created to decide on the Spacing setting.

Combinations of Brushes

The Paint Brush tool is only one of six paint application tools that use color from the Color roll-up (as opposed to the Fill roll-up), and the Paint Brush tool can be modified with the Tool Settings roll-up. PHOTO-PAINT "remembers" the settings you last specified for the Paint Brush tool; you can switch between different brushes, and even other tools, and the Tool Settings you made for the Paint Brush will reappear the next time you choose the tool.

This leads to some interesting possibilities: you can create an outline with one brush, create an effect with another, and then go back and refine a design indefinitely in the same PHOTO-PAINT session.

Understanding the Impressionist and Pointillist Brush Tools

The Impressionist and Pointillist Brush tools (located on the Brush tools menu fly-out) are so-named because they lend an effect to brush strokes similar to those found in the types of painting they are named after. Do not believe for a moment that you can create a Seurat- or van Gogh-inspired painting in PHOTO-PAINT using these tools, however. The effect these two brushes produce is that of random brush strokes that are almost impossible to guide without the use of a digitizing tablet.

However, if you divorce yourself from the notion that the Impressionist and Pointillist Brushes simulate real brush strokes against a physical canvas, you are free to explore the capabilities of the tools, and through inventiveness, create new situations wherein the brush tools can be used with great expression.

Tracing over a Design with Brush Tools

In the following example, the Paint Brush and Impressionist Brush are used in combination to create a design. You'll use the unique characteristics of the Impressionist Brush to add an element of freedom to the design, and the Paint Brush tool is used in areas of the design where you need more control over the brush strokes. To begin with, I've created a stylized outline of the face of a woman by sketching it on a piece of paper, scanning it at 24-bit color mode, then cleaning it up to serve as a guide for painting over. This is not cheating; if you don't use a digitizing tablet, a scanner is always a legitimate method for inputting graphical data, in the same sense that scanning a photograph is not compromising a design idea. It's a good idea to always scan original artwork, however. Copyright laws are getting stricter with the popularity and improved quality of scanners, and other artists probably feel the same way about people appropriating their artistic ideas as you do.

The next set of steps cover the use of a combination of PHOTO-PAINT tools to create a digital painting:

1. Open a copy of the FACE.TIF image from the *CorelDRAW! The Professional Reference* companion CDs. It is located in the CHAP24 subdirectory.

2. Click on the paint color (foreground) swatch on the Colors roll-up to select it, then click on the Twilight Blue color swatch (or enter R=**61**, G=**0**, B=**255** in the color value field). This is the paint color over the outline within the FACE.TIF image.

3. Choose the Paint Brush tool and set the Tool Settings characteristics to the round shape with **0** value for <u>F</u>latten and <u>R</u>otate, <u>S</u>ize: **12**, <u>E</u>dge: Soft, <u>D</u>ensity: **20**, <u>T</u>ransparency **0**, <u>F</u>ade Out: **1**, and S<u>p</u>acing: **1**.

These characteristics will produce a round edge to the beginning of a brush stroke trailing off to a point; a similar effect is produced when you lay real paint on a canvas with a large brush and lift the brush off the canvas as you complete the stroke. Therefore, you

must pay attention to which ends of a brushstroke are going to be wide and narrow.

4. Click at the bridge of the woman's nose and drag the cursor to trace upward along the woman's forehead line.

5. Click on the line of the woman's eyebrow closest to the bridge of the nose, and trace the eyebrow going left.

6. Continue creating brush strokes that cover the woman's outline. You can see the work in progress in figure 24.15.

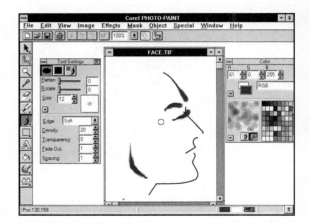

Figure 24.15

Decide which end of a brush stroke looks more appealing over the various outlines you trace over.

As Michaelangelo said to the Pope's emissary, you're done when you're done. At least with the facial portion of this design. Save your work, and in the next section you will conclude the design using the Impressionist Brush.

Examining the Settings for the Impressionist Brush

When you click on the Impressionist Brush, the Tool Settings roll-up automatically extends to offer additional settings and options that are not available with the other brushes. The Impressionist Brush produces not one, but several lines wherever you click and drag. Hue, Saturation, and Lightness (or Brightness) Variance can be specified for the brush, and these settings affect how the individual brush strokes differ from one another in chromacity. In addition, Brush Spread controls how far apart each component stroke wanders from the initial stroke, from a value of 1 (very close strokes) to 8 (strokes meandering all over the place). The number of individual lines produced with a single Impressionist Brush stroke can be set from 0 (with every different stroke placed directly on top of each other; skip this setting) to 8.

You can use anywhere from 1 to 20 lines to produce a single Impressionist stroke, and perhaps the most intriguing aspect of this brush is that you determine the shape of a brush stroke before PHOTO-PAINT applies the color.

In the next exercise, you will see how to define a path for Impressionist Brush strokes, and add a hairstyle to the woman in the painting:

1. Choose the Red Brown swatch from the Colors roll-up's color palette as the paint color (or enter R: **204**, G: **102**, B: **51** in the fields at the top of the roll-up).

2. Use these settings on the Tool Settings roll-up with the Impressionist brush active: round shape with **0** for both Flatten and Rotate, Size: **12**, Edge: Soft, Density: **75**, Transparency: **20**, Fade Out: **20** (set Fade Out to **1** if you have a 386), Spacing: **2**.

3. You don't want a lot of Variance in Hue, so set **H** Variance to **5**. Set the **S** Variance (Saturation) to **5**, and let variations of lightness (**L** Variance) show a lot of range by setting the value to **30**.

4. To keep the strands of hair you'll be painting far apart, set the Brush spread to **8** (the maximum), and try **5** as the # **of** Lines.

5. Click and hold the Impressionist Brush to make a wavy line from right to left, beginning at the top of the woman's forehead, as shown in figure 24.16. By clicking and holding simultaneously, you can set a path for Impressionist Brush strokes. PHOTO-PAINT will paint in the strokes only after you have released the left mouse button.

6. After making the line with the cursor, release the mouse button and sit back and watch! As you can see in figure 24.17, the Impressionist Brush will paint the number of strokes you have set, with variance in H, S, and L values and any other brush characteristic you have defined. Try making wide arcs, circles, and squares with the Impressionist Brush, too.

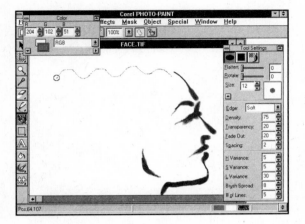

Figure 24.16

Create shapes with the Impressionist Brush that PHOTO-PAINT will follow in creating the effect.

Figure 24.17

PHOTO-PAINT completes the path you have drawn using the characteristics you have defined for the brush.

By using the Impressionist Brush a few times, you will realize that the quality of control does not head the list of brush attributes, and that you must create a line with either very little Brush Spread, or expect the randomness that comes with PHOTO-PAINT's autocreation of Impressionist strokes. The Impressionist strokes usually appear an equal distance away from where you define the shape of the line with the cursor.

There is a method, however, that involves using a mask to control where the Impressionist and Pointillist strokes distribute themselves, and another creative use of these tools can be found in the next section.

Using Masks and the Brush Tools

As described in Chapter 23, Transparency masks can be created and used in PHOTO-PAINT to protect and expose image areas. The lighter a grayscale shade in a mask file, the more the corresponding area in an active image is available to be edited. Because PHOTO-PAINT's features are designed to work together, and because Impressionist and Pointillist tools do not operate with the utmost precision, using masks with these brush tools can make a splendid working combination. Although the Pointillist Brush produces a stroke different in appearance from the Impressionist Brush, you use the same techniques as those described in the last section to paint with it.

In the next exercise, a mask of a simple design (shown in figure 24.18) was created in CorelDRAW and exported as a bitmap image for the purpose of masking an image so that the image can be painted over with the Impressionist and Pointillist Brushes. Both these design brushes produce enough character to be used as fill within defined areas of a background image. The effect is one of dimension and movement.

Figure 24.18
Use a mask to isolate image areas in which you want to paint with Impressionist and Pointillist Brushes.

Here's how to use the Impressionist and Pointillist effects as fills:

1. Copy the FISHBOWL.CPT image from the *CorelDRAW! The Professional Reference* companion CDs to your hard drive.

2. Choose **F**ile, **N**ew (Ctrl+N, or press the New image button on the Ribbon bar), and select the 24 Bit Color **C**olor Mode from the drop-down list.

3. Enter **338** (pixels) in both the **H**eight and **W**idth fields, choose black as the **P**aper color, then click on OK. This is going to be a somewhat stylized illustration, and a black background makes the Impressionist and Pointillist Brush effects appear more luminous. Click on OK.

4. Choose **M**ask, **L**oad, then select the FISHBOWL.CPT image from your hard disk.

5. Click on the Impressionist Brush. Don't touch the values on the Tool Settings roll-up, with the exception of the **H** (Hue) Variance and the # **o**f Lines. Flex your creative muscles and imagine the fish are tropical fish; set the **H** Variance at **50** (the maximum to produce lines that cycle through the visible spectrum) and change the # **o**f Lines to **20** (also the maximum value). Choose a light green paint color from the Colors roll-up, then start clicking and dragging the cursor across the marquee selections of the fish in the image.

Because the **H**ue Variance is set to the maximum value, you will get all sorts of colors running through the fish masks; it's more important that the color you choose is light rather than green, though, because the **L** Variance (brightness) is small and a dark color here would result in a spectrum of very dull colors.

6. The areas that correspond to black areas in figure 24.18's image of the mask cannot be painted over, and the white areas allow brush strokes. As you

can see in figure 24.19, horizontal strokes produce a wide variety of color stripes for the fish.

outside the fishbowl marquee, as shown in figure 24.20, to restore the background areas to black.

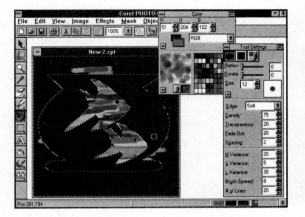

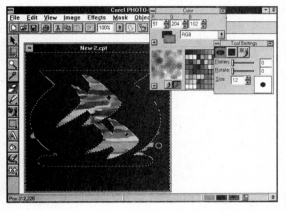

Figure 24.19

The mask defines the geometric areas in the image, and the Impressionist Brush adds character.

Figure 24.20

The Eraser tool removes paint color, replacing it with the currently defined paper color.

You will notice that it's very easy to "go outside the lines," and that some of the areas outside of the bowl marquee get painted as you color the fish. This is not good, because the area outside of the bowl will eventually be painted with the Pointillist Brush in this example.

7. Click and hold on the Local Undo tool (the correction fluid icon beneath the Eyedropper tool). Choose the Eraser tool, the middle tool on the menu fly-out. The Eraser tool removes paint (foreground) color and exposes paper (background) color. Assuming you haven't changed the background color on the Colors roll-up, it's still black, as you defined it when you opened a new image. Click and drag over the areas

N O T E

The Color Replacer tool is an eraser of a different sort; instead of replacing paint color with paper color, the Color Replacer tool removes any color in an image currently defined as the paint (foreground) color, and replaces it with the currently defined paper color. This means you can begin a new image with a black background, paint orange over it, switch the paper (background) color to white, then only erase the orange paint to white, while leaving the original background black untouched.

Be sure to click on the Color Tolerance button on the Tool Settings roll-up before using the

continues

Color Replacer tool, however. If you have been experimenting with Color Tolerance, as shown in other chapters, make sure the values are set at about plus/minus 10; otherwise, the Color Replacer tool will replace *more* than one paint color. At a plus/minus 255 setting, the Color Replacer tool will act exactly like the Eraser tool, which removes any paint color and substitutes the current paper color in image areas.

Double-clicking on the Color Replacer tool can remove part or all of an image design to expose the current paper color; the range of color values replaced depends upon your Color tolerance setting for the Color Replacer tool. At a tolerance of 255, the entire image is erased, for example. With a narrower color tolerance defined (like 50), however, only the current paint color found in the design will be replaced with paper color.

Using the Pointillist Brush

The Pointillist Brush covers an area with dots of color as opposed to the lines the Impressionist Brush produces. The Variance settings, amount of spread, and number of lines, however, are options that are similar to those available with the Impressionist Brush; the Pointillist Brush simply makes a different shape.

In the next exercise, you will fill the area outside the fishbowl with colored areas using the Pointillist tool. When a small variance in Hue and a close amount of Brush Spread are set, you can get an effect that suggests textures. Sand, stippling, carpeting, and other grainy surfaces can be painted using different tool settings for the Pointillist Brush.

Here's how to fill the background area of the fishbowl composition with some Pointillist texture:

1. Click and hold on the Impressionist Brush to display the Brush tool menu fly-out, and select the Pointillist Brush.

2. As mentioned earlier, the Tool Settings roll-up will retain unique settings you specify for each type of brush, so you now can choose different setting for the Pointillist Brush, and when you choose the Impressionist Brush in the future, the settings you made in the last exercise will still be there. Keep the 12 pixel diameter **S**ize, round tip and Soft **E**dge, but set the **D**ensity to **2**, set the **F**ade Out to **100**, and the S**p**acing to **0**. On the bottom of the roll-up, in the area that is displayed only when the Pointillist or Impressionist Brush is chosen, make **H** Variance: **5**, **S** Variance: **5**, **L** Variance: **30**, Br**u**sh Spread: **3**, and keep the # **o**f Lines at **20**.

3. Click on the paint (foreground) swatch on the Colors roll-up, then click on a sand-colored swatch (or enter R: **255**, G: **204**:, and B: **0** at the top of the Colors roll-up).

4. Paint a small stroke outside the bowl marquee to try out this new brush, then continue painting the black paper outside the marquee. As you can see in figure 24.21, you can achieve a random, organic effect by varying the direction of your strokes. Areas that are covered by multiple Pointillistic strokes don't become saturated with flat color, but instead appear as denser areas of texture.

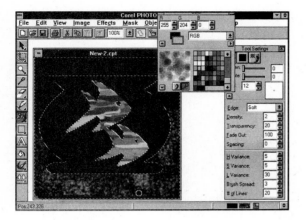

Figure 24.21
The Pointillism Brush can fill paper areas with dots of varying colors.

5. Try to make several passes around the edge of the bowl to make it more clearly defined. After you have painted over every area outside the bowl marquee at least once, you are done.

Inverting a Mask and Using the Fill Tool

As you saw in the last exercise, the distinction between lines and fills isn't all that clear when working with a bitmap application; tools used for creating strokes can be used to create fills.

PHOTO-PAINT's Fill tool can be used to cover image areas of the same color value, and this makes the Fill tool a good choice for putting the final touches on the fishbowl painting. When an image area is defined by contrasting colors, the Fill tool will spread a color, texture, bitmap pattern, or fountain fill within the area you first click it over. The

area that is filled is confined to adjacent areas that contain colors that fall within the range specified by the Color Tolerance settings on Tool Settings roll-up. If a high Color Tolerance is set, the fill will spread out across the entire image, whereas a low Color Tolerance setting will result in an area containing only a single shade being filled.

As you saw in figure 24.21, the edge of the bowl in this painting relies on the Pointillist strokes to define it. If the edges are completely defined with the paint color, you can use the **M**ask, **R**emove command at this stage, then choose a Fill from the Fill roll-up and click over the bowl area. However, the painting illustrated in these figures does not sport a bowl edge totally defined by Pointillist dots; clicking over the bowl area without a mask would result in a design like that shown in figure 24.22.

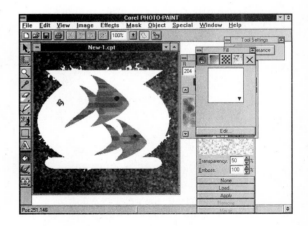

Figure 24.22
The Fill tool covers contiguous (pixels that touch on an edge) areas of color you define by Color Tolerance.

A mask clearly serves a purpose when edges in a design are not completely defined by one or more paint colors not found in the image area you click over with the Fill tool. When you have an incompletely defined edge, the Fill color or texture seeps through any gaps you have around a design edge.

However, the task of filling only the bowl with any paint (foreground) color or texture offered on the Fill roll-up is an easy one if you simply invert the mask presently protecting the bowl image area. Here's how to finish the design and add dimensional fill by using the intermediate steps feature of the fountain fill:

1. Choose **M**ask, **I**nvert (or click on the Invert button on the Ribbon bar with a Mask tool selected). The fish and background areas now are protected from painting over, and areas that were protected from painting over are now available. Conversely, the last image areas you used the brush tools over are now protected from editing.

2. Double-click on the fill icon (the far right one) on the Status line (or choose View, F**i**ll Roll-Up), and then click on the Fountain Fill button and choose the radial fill type.

3. Click on Edit on the Fill roll-up. From the Fountain Fill options box, click and drag in the preview window so that the highlight of the radial fill is in an 11 o'clock location, and choose **C**ustom in the Color Blend field.

4. Click on the left dot above the preview box (strip) in the Color Blend field and choose a medium green color, then

click on the right dot and choose a light green.

5. Double-click above the preview box between the left and right dots. This produces an arrow; it's an intermediate point in the radial fill you can specify with another color. You can add up to 100 intermediate steps to a fountain fill blend. Click on a dark green on the color palette, as shown in figure 24.23. You can see the effect on the radial fill in the upper right preview window. Additionally, you can click and drag the intermediate arrow marker to the left or right to create different effects. Double-clicking on an intermediate blend marker removes it. You've just created a radial fill for the fishbowl that contains a highlight. Click on OK when you are finished.

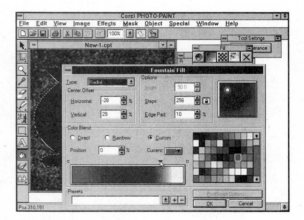

Figure 24.23

Create intermediate steps for fountain fills in the Fountain Fill options box.

6. Click the Fill tool anywhere within the black area of the fishbowl. As you can see in figure 24.24, the bowl has dimension and contrasts nicely with the impressionist fish.

Figure 24.24

The fountain fill is confined to the area described by the mask marquee.

7. It's a little difficult to get a good look at your handiwork with marquee lines running around the image. If you want to preview an image without the marquee lines and still be able to come back to them (and perhaps use the **U**ndo command if you don't like what you see), press F9 to see a full-screen preview of your work, without marquee lines (**V**iew, **F**ull-Screen Preview). Press Esc to return to PHOTO-PAINT's Design Window and your work, and to mask marquee lines.

8. Choose **M**ask, **R**emove (or click on the Remove button on the Ribbon bar when a Mask tool is selected) and save your work.

Design work using masks does not have to be limited to photographic image editing, as the last exercise demonstrates. Use masks whenever precision rendering cannot be achieved using a mouse or even a digitizing tablet. It's by taking the design skills you have learned in CorelDRAW and applying them when they are relevant for use in PHOTO-PAINT and the other Corel modules that you can work quickly to achieve effects in PHOTO-PAINT that are impossible to execute in a vector program.

The Artist Brush Tool

The Artist Brush tool is unlike any of the other brushes; you actually paint with a bitmap design that acts as a brush tip. PHOTO-PAINT offers 23 "packs" of brushes, charcoals, crosshatches, and other photo-realistic materials that can be used with the Colors roll-up to produce lifelike strokes on a background image.

Because the Artist Brushes actually are bitmap images, there is a limit to the strokes you use; you cannot produce a stroke longer than the bitmap used to define the brush. Additionally, the Artist Brush cannot be used to paint anything except a straight line. But you can increase the size of the Artist Brush stroke and create strokes in any direction, and you can specify a Fade amount, which makes Artist Brush strokes vanish into the paper at the end of a stroke.

In figure 24.25, you can see a basic application of the Artist Brush, using the FlatBrush setting. This tool is fun to experiment with, and you will find through experimenting that design ideas you never imagined suddenly sprout up.

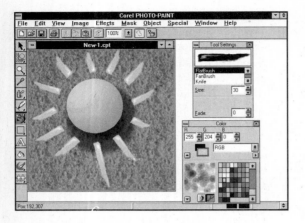

Figure 24.25
The Artist Brush tool creates realistic brush strokes.

After you try out the Artist Brush in its various settings a few times, you might not be satisfied with only the 23 different settings. It would be nice if you could stock up on new Artist Brushes, but new brushes are not purchased—they are created. In the next section, you will see how to build a new pack of Artist Brushes.

How Does an Artist Brush Work?

An Artist Brush can be defined as having between one and five individual bitmaps that compose the brush tip. Corel documentation refers to an Artist Brush as a "pack," but the Oil1 Artistic Brush, for example, is made up of five bitmap, grayscale images, with each image slightly different than the other. When the Oil1 Artistic Brush is used, PHOTO-

PAINT randomly selects one of the five bitmaps to apply paint (foreground) color. When you lay down several strokes within a design using the Oil1 brush, viewers get the impression that a real brush was used because the strokes vary in appearance.

Each bitmap image in a pack that comprises an Artist Brush needs to be 64 pixels wide by 128 pixels deep, at a resolution of 300 pixels/inch, and the image(s) must be in grayscale 8 bit/pixel color mode. In figure 24.26, you can see a 200 percent viewing resolution of one of the Oil8 Artistic Brushes, along with the corresponding bitmap preview on the Tool Settings roll-up. The actual bitmap image that produces the Artist Brush stroke is a negative of the way it appears on the roll-up and as you apply paint (foreground) color with it.

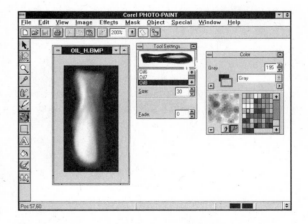

Figure 24.26
Artist Brushes are bitmap images PHOTO-PAINT evaluates for tonal densities as you apply color.

WARNING

I recommend against opening the *.BMP files that are used by PHOTO-PAINT as I did to create the last figure, however. None of these files has write-protection attributes, and if you open one up and modify it, you could lose an Artist Brush that has a characteristic you're fond of. Beyond the bitmap size and a few pieces of information to follow, you will have all the tips and tools you need to create your own Artist Brush without ever opening the Artist Brush *.BMP files to examine.

When you use an Artist Brush, PHOTO-PAINT evaluates the tonal densities of the brush's bitmap image. PHOTO-PAINT then assigns the values it finds within the brush to color brightness for the paint color you use with the brush. For instance, the black regions of the bitmap correspond to an image area that gets no color, the gray areas in the bitmap correspond to paint color areas, and white areas in the bitmap correspond to white highlights.

PHOTO-PAINT performs a lot of behind-the-scenes processing when you use an Artist Brush. PHOTO-PAINT transforms the bitmap information to shorten the brush shape image, change its degree of rotation, and switch between bitmaps at random when you make Artistic Brush strokes. And PHOTO-PAINT does all this pretty much on-the-fly although you may notice a split-second wait when you paint with an Artist Brush.

How To Build an Artist Brush

Suppose you want an Artist Brush not offered in PHOTO-PAINT's collection. A good place to start creating an Artist Brush is with some real ink, chalk, or materials lying around the house, a surface on which to design, and a scanner. In figure 24.27, you can see three bitmap images that began as ink blots on a paper towel. The blots were scanned in grayscale mode on a flatbed scanner, then the digitized images were resized using the **I**mage, **R**esample command (see Chapter 23, "Masks"). Next the blots were cropped to meet the 64 by 128 pixels criterion for Artists Brushes, and cleaned up a little in PHOTO-PAINT to remove any tonal values around the image edges.

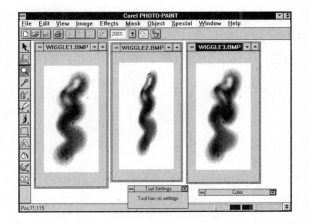

Figure 24.27
Scan or create original grayscale images to use as an Artist Brush.

The three "wiggle" images comprise a future three-pack of PHOTO-PAINT brushes; you can build as many as five variations, but your custom Artist's Brush can be only a single file.

The next step is to use the Effects, Fancy, Invert command on each of the bitmap images. This command will create a black paper (background) color (no information read), with the paint consisting of grayscale and white tones, which PHOTO-PAINT considers color and highlight values when you paint with an Artist Brush. Figure 24.28 is an example of how a pack of Artist Brushes look, as they are saved to the COREL50\PHOTOPNT\IMPRBRS subdirectory. If you are following along with this example, this is the subdirectory on your hard drive where the bitmap images must be stored as BMP files so that PHOTO-PAINT can recognize them as brushes.

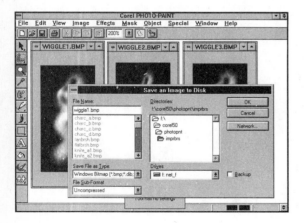

Figure 24.28

Light areas in the bitmap brush will consist of color and highlights when you paint; black will be read as clear (no paint).

W A R N I N G

Corel documentation for the Artist Brushes was incorrect as of version 5.00.E1 as to where the bitmap images must be located. Corel's Help line and accompanying literature was published in advance of the many changes Corel made to the program in the patch disks that bring users up to version E1.

After the bitmaps have been saved to hard disk, you need to close PHOTO-PAINT, because the next step is to edit the PHOTOPNT.INI file located in the COREL50\CONFIG subdirectory. Editing an INI file while the application is running is a little like stepping into an elevator that's not on your floor. Be sure to make backup copies of the INI files you intend to edit, and never have the application open that is controlled by the INI file when you perform the surgery.

Always use a plain ASCII or ANSI text editor—such as Windows' Notepad—when editing INI files; do not use a word processor. Word processors imbed formatting codes that corrupt INI files. Open PHOTPNT.INI in a text editor and scroll down until you reach the [ARTIST] section, then increase the NumBrushPacks= from 23 to 24. Don't leave a space after the equal sign; INI files are very sensitive to spaces within lines.

Next, scroll to the last line in the [ARTISTS] section. PHOTO-PAINT allows up to 32 packs of Artist Brushes, and if no one's touched your INI file, the last line should read:

```
Pack23=Oil8,1,OIL_H.BMP
```

On the next line, enter the specs for your brushes pack. In this example, call the name of the brush "WIGGLES"; it consists of three bitmaps, and the file names for the bitmaps are listed last. If you would like to try this example in PHOTO-PAINT, copy the WIGGLE*.BMP image from the *CorelDRAW! The Professional Reference* companion CDs in the CHAP24 subdirectory to the IMPRBRS subdirectory on your PC, and type the following:

```
Pack24=Wiggles,3,WIGGLE1.BMP,WIGGLE2.BMP,
➥WIGGLE3.BMP
```

Make sure there are no spaces in the line and that the section header that follows is at least one line below the line you typed. Figure 24.29 is an example of my line in the PHOTOPNT.INI to make the wiggles brush appear on the Tool Settings roll-up when the Artist tool is selected. Save the file, then close the text editor.

The Personal Pleasures of the Artist Brush

I have to admit that I had no concept already prepared to use with the "wiggles" brush; part of the fun of being a computer graphics-type person on the IBM/PC platform is that you get to tinker with stuff inside the operating system and applications, take a look at the results, then perhaps find inspiration in the results of the tinkering.

This was the case with the wiggles brush. If you followed the previous procedure, you now have a new slot on the Tool Settings roll-up at the end of the Artist Brushes, called Wiggles. And if you select the Artist tool, load an image of toast, pick a strawberry paint color, and set the **F**ade on the Tool Settings roll-up to **75**, you can paint break-fast, as shown in figure 24.30.

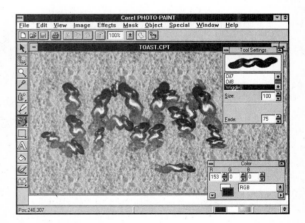

Figure 24.30
Let the effects you can create with a custom Artist Brush provide you with creative inspiration. Or a side of bacon.

Figure 24.29
The PHOTOPNT.INI file is a plain text file that tells PHOTO-PAINT where to locate user specifications before the program loads.

The Air Brush and the Spraycan Brush

The Air Brush and Spraycan Brushes are the last two brushes left to explore on the Brushes menu fly-out. Both are effects brushes that provide you with some control over the shape and flow of the paint as you click and drag them over your image. Of the two brushes, the Air Brush tool might serve as a more useful tool in paying assignments.

The Air Brush tool is so named because it mimics a conventional physical airbrush. The Air Brush tool is good for cleaning spots, lint marks, or unwanted edges from photographic images, but you also can adjust the Rate of Flow for the paint it holds.

Open a new image in PHOTO-PAINT, specify white as the **P**aper Color, and accept the rest of the default settings for the new image by clicking on OK. Here's a hands-on experiment to test the different looks you can achieve by changing only the **R**ate of Flow settings for the Air Brush tool:

1. Click on the Air Brush tool on the Brushes menu fly-out, then choose black as the paint color from the Color roll-up.

2. On the Tool Settings roll-up, choose the round shape. The bitmap shape on the Tool Settings roll-up does not offer **D**ensity and **T**ransparency controls. These two settings are key to adjusting the Air Brush so that it produces an effect like a real airbrush.

3. Set the **S**ize at **50**, **E**dge: Soft, **D**ensity: **30**, **T**ransparency: **90**, **F**ade Out: **0**, and make the **R**ate of Flow **5**. The **R**ate of Flow in this example mimics a fine mist. If you hold the Air Brush tool in one place over the image with these settings specified, almost no saturation occurs.

4. Slowly click and drag the cursor down the left side of the image.

5. Set the **R**ate of Flow to **100**, and try the same thing on the right side of the image. As you can see in figure 24.31, you have to keep the cursor moving all the time with a high **R**ate of Flow, or concentrated areas of color will appear. Of course, you can use this as a look in your work, but you know how to get the effect, and how to avoid it.

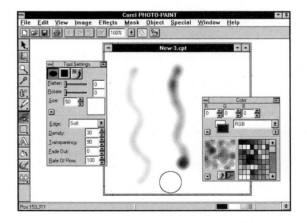

Figure 24.31

*The **R**ate of Flow is the setting that most influences the characteristics of color you apply with the Air Brush tool.*

Now you can put this knowledge about the Air Brush tool to a more practical use. In the CHAP24 subdirectory of the *CorelDRAW! The Professional Reference* companion CDs is IND_PARK.TIF. The image is a photo of a building taken on such a cloudless day that the sky has no character. By setting the **R**ate of Flow for the Air Brush to a small value, choosing an off-white paint color (photos of clouds are almost never pure white), and using an angled brush shape, you can add clouds that a viewer would never question as being authentic.

Keep the effect to a minimum—as soon as your retouching work calls attention to itself, you've tipped your hand. Here's how to add a little more character to a static image:

1. Click on the 10 gray swatch on the Color roll-up (or enter **229** in the R, G, and B fields at the top of the roll-up).

N O T E

You will notice in a lot of the figures in the PHOTO-PAINT section that roll-ups are rolled up. This is partially to provide readers with a view of the important elements, but it's mostly good PHOTO-PAINT working practice. Roll-ups can take up a lot of space on a 640×480 screen, so the best way to maximize the space left for an image is to keep roll-ups retracted when not in use.

2. Enter **48** for the **F**latten value (or use the slider), and set **R**otate at 50. This creates an angled brush that can produce clouds with a little more irregular shape (in other words, more believable clouds).

3. For the rest of the settings set them as follows: **S**ize: **100**, **E**dge: Soft, **D**ensity: **20**, **T**ransparency: **90**, **F**ade Out: **50**, and **R**ate of Flow: **20**. This combination of Air Brush characteristics was arrived at by trial and error. You should invest some time with the Tool Settings roll-up and invent Air Brush characteristics that suit special graphics needs of your own.

4. Click and drag over the blue sky, starting with quick, short strokes, then click and drag a little slower, and cover areas a second time to get a denser effect. As you can see in figure 24.32, a hint of clouds provides visual relief from the hard geometric lines that dominate the image.

Figure 24.32

*A low Air Brush **D**ensity removes the edge from areas you paint over; low **R**ate of Flow enables you to work quickly or slowly without color buildup.*

Notice in the last figure that the outline of the cursor for the Air Brush tool is positively flying saucer-sized, yet the strokes it painted were small and in proportion to other image elements. PHOTO-PAINT's cursor is not always an accurate indicator of the size of a brush stroke produced. The cursor outline is an indicator of the outside boundary of a brush, but when **D**ensity is set very low, the noticeable effects of painting are a fraction of the size of the cursor outline.

The Spraycan Tool

The Spraycan and Air Brush tool share similar names but produce entirely different effects. Perhaps the Spraycan tool would be more aptly named, "Spraycan with a clogged nozzle" tool, but then it would be too long to fit on a pop-up help balloon.

For as refined and diffuse a look as the Air Brush tool can produce, the Spraycan tool is coarse and harsh; it renders color as random, hard-edged single pixels as you click and drag across the paper. The Spraycan tool isn't of much use in retouching photographic-quality images, but it can be used to create interesting texture effects in an image area.

As with the Air Brush tool, the Tool Settings roll-up features a **R**ate of Flow whenever the Spraycan is the active brush. In figure 24.33, the effect of clicking and holding over the paper different lengths of time can be seen. Click briskly, and you have a texture; click and hold, and the paper area eventually becomes covered with flat paint (foreground) color.

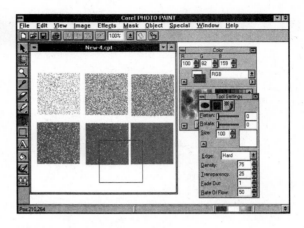

Figure 24.33
*The **R**ate of Flow for the Spraycan tool determines how much an image area is filled in with a random pattern of single pixels.*

Try creating an entire image with the Spraycan tool set at a low **R**ate of Flow, with a custom brush defined on the Tool Settings roll-up. You can get an effect that truly looks like a rubber stamp impression.

Exploring the Pencil Tools

Just as bitmaps are fundamentally different from vector graphics, PHOTO-PAINT has three open line tools, not brushes. These line tools work very much like their CorelDRAW counterparts, and the experienced CorelDRAW user will feel quite comfortable using the Pencil tools.

Note that the Line tool, Curve tool, and Pen tool do not produce closed shapes; the shape tools are designed to produce closed ellipses, rectangles, and irregular polygons. However, with very little effort, you can draw two or more lines with the Pencil tools that form an enclosed area that can be filled later using the Fill tool.

The Line Tool

There are not nearly as many options on the Tool Settings roll-up for Pencil tools as there are for Brush tools. In fact, only **T**ransparency and S**p**acing are the options for Pencil tool characteristics when a custom tip has been defined. If you choose a square or round shape, however, you can set **S**ize, **F**latten, and **R**otate values for a line.

The method for drawing a straight line with the Line tool is to click and hold, and then drag to set the direction and length of the line before releasing the mouse button. You will see a wireframe of the line at the center of the line's path as you click and hold and drag. You can change the direction and the length of the line at anytime before you release the mouse button. If you change your mind about drawing a line in mid-drawing, press the Esc key before releasing the mouse button.

In figure 24.34, two lines have been drawn with the Line tool. The top line was drawn with 0 (zero) S**p**acing set and a 20 pixel **S**ize. The bottom line was given 40 pixel S**p**acing, and as you can see, dotted lines are as easy to create as patterns with the Brush tools when you set the S**p**acing to a value greater than the **S**ize of the line.

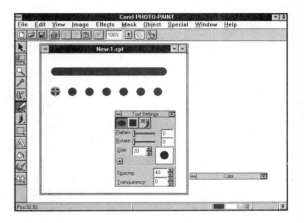

Figure 24.34
*Use S**p**acing in combination with line **S**ize to create patterns in a straight line.*

The Curve Tool

The Curve tool operates very similarly to the Object and Mask Node Edit tools, in that you can preview a curve indefinitely and adjust nodes along its path before finalizing the curve (Corel's terminology is *pasting* a curve). Corel has invented a unique method for defining not a single, but a series of curves along a path with the Curve tool.

Here's a simple exercise that demonstrates the properties of a line drawn with the Curve tool:

1. Click and hold on the Pencil tool's icon on the toolbox, then choose the Curve tool from the menu fly-out.

2. Click on the New button on the Ribbon bar (Ctrl+N or **F**ile, **N**ew also creates a new image).

3. Choose the white **P**aper Color, and accept the rest of the defaults by clicking on OK.

4. Click and drag an outline with the Curve tool. Make it bend and turn, and when you have run out of inspiration and room on the paper, release the cursor.

5. As you can see in figure 24.35, the curve isn't quite a bitmap line on the paper yet, nor does it become one until you click in an area of the image that is not part of the line. If the nodes on the outline seem familiar, it's because they belong to the Corel family of nodes and line segments; click and drag a node or a control point to adjust the curve while it still is in its outline phase.

N   O   T   E

An easy way to tell if your cursor is outside a curve that hasn't been finalized is by the shape of the cursor. If you are inside the boundary of the curve, the cursor is a crosshair. If you are outside the boundary of the line, your cursor is a crosshair with a circle. This is a good visual reminder so that you can avoid accidentally finalizing a curve you are working on.

6. When you are finished editing the curve, click outside the outline, and the curve will take on the size and color you have defined on the roll-ups, as shown in figure 24.36.

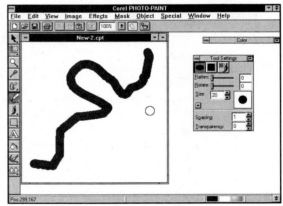

Figure 24.36
Click outside of a curve after you are done editing it to finish the effect.

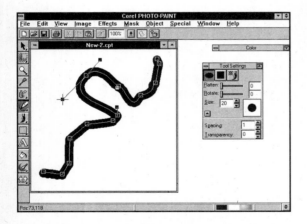

Figure 24.35
Treat the nodes and control points in the curve outline the same as you would a shape in CorelDRAW.

End of story, end of line.

The Pen Tool

Of all the Pencil tools, the Pen tool is the most straightforward in its use and functionality. Click and drag with the Pen tool to produce a flat, colored shape. There are no outlines that require special cursor moves to produce effects with the Pen tool, and you should use this tool when you need to highlight an image area with color that's consistent.

None of the Pencil tools have a soft edge, and for this reason they are best used for annotating photographic images, putting solid borders around image areas, and perhaps creating direction lines on maps. The Pencil tools would not be your first choice of tools for refining or retouching photos or other images with grayscale or higher color capability. The Pencil tools produce approximately the same effect in any Color Mode you have defined for a new image.

But because you can set a Transparency value for lines drawn with the Pencil tools, you can overlap lines of the same color value, and the lines retain all of their visual information. In figure 24.37, you can see a line designed with the Curve tool at 10% Transparency overlapped by a line produced with the Pen tool at 50% Transparency. Choose colors and degrees of Transparency with the Pencil tools to produce designs that weave lines together.

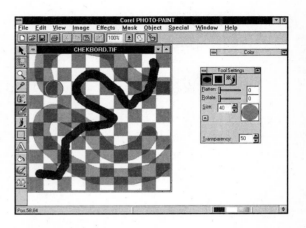

Figure 24.37
By varying the Transparency of lines, you can create an overlapping effect.

Exploring the Canvas Roll-Up

Although it's not a drawing or painting tool, the Canvas roll-up can provide a quick background for a design that might be missing an element of color or composition, or a touch of realism. PHOTO-PAINT is a place where the abstract and photo-realistic come together, and canvases can be anything the user defines.

The Options for the Canvas Roll-Up

PHOTO-PAINT installs with 10 premade canvases that are ready for use in the CANVAS subdirectory of PHOTO-PAINT. The premade canvases are seamless in that Corel took care to make the image files so that they tile to any paper size without the edges of the repeated tiles showing.

You can add a canvas to an image at any time, but it usually is better to begin a design with a canvas already merged to the paper. If you have a design already in progress and decide on adding a canvas, you will have to specify a percentage of Transparency on the Canvas roll-up to accomplish this; otherwise, the Canvas image will completely obscure your design when merged.

The Merge command is sort of a misnomer for the function the Canvas roll-up serves, in that the Canvas image is not an object. In fact, you can save an image to PHOTO-PAINT's CPT format with an unmerged canvas, and call it back weeks later with the canvas still waiting to be finalized within the image design. You cannot paint on a canvas that has not been merged, and the Eyedropper tool will pick up only the paper color. It's downright spooky, and I imagine life as an unmerged canvas to be an unpleasant one. However, if you choose a more conventional format for saving a file with an unmerged canvas, such as TIF or PCX, PHOTO-PAINT will automerge canvases when saving the image.

Selecting a canvas to apply to an image file is simple. The Canvas roll-up automatically finds the CANVAS subdirectory where canvas images are stored (unless you have specified an alternate directory). When you click on the Load button on the Canvas roll-up, you are offered a preview of the canvas image you selected from the subdirectory of files. It's as easy to remove an unmerged canvas as it is to load another one, and you can change your mind about canvas images, or even create new ones for a design until you click on the Merge button.

As of version 5.00.E1, the Emboss setting on the Canvas roll-up does not produce an effect, so there is little point in specifying Emboss settings before merging a canvas to the paper within an image.

How To Create a Custom Canvas

The larger the image you use for a canvas (in terms of dimensions and/or pixels/inch), the longer it will take PHOTO-PAINT to load and display a canvas. All of the 10 premade canvases measure 128 by 128 pixels at 300 pixels/inch, and I recommend you follow these image dimensions when creating an original canvas. Canvases you create have to be of at least 256 (8-bit/pixel) color capability, although you can define most any image type (TIF, PCX, BMP) as a canvas.

As with the custom Artist Brushes, a good place to start building your canvas is with a scanner and some patterned material; linen, confetti, even rocks can make interesting canvas designs. But before you begin piling interesting dusty, sticky, or abrasive stuff on top of the scanner glass, be sure to protect the glass and the platen on the scanner with a piece of acetate or other appropriate material.

Figure 24.38, is a scan of a cloth napkin. The scan was acquired through PHOTO-PAINT's TWAIN interface, and the dimensions and resolution were set through the scanner's features. The napkin is a good example of randomly distributed patterns; the weave is irregular, and when PHOTO-PAINT tiles the design to fit any size image, the edges will not be very evident.

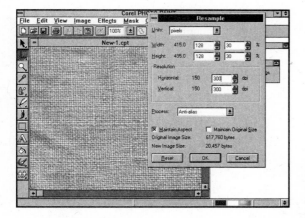

Figure 24.38

Acquire an image, or create one for use as a canvas that does not have a visible repeating pattern in it.

You also can create a canvas image; this chapter has shown several ways to generate a texture, and as long as it's a 256-color or greater RGB image, you're in business.

The next step in creating a canvas is to resample it if necessary. It's quite hard to get an area exactly 128 by 128 pixels at 300 pixels/inch with the precise image detail you want, so use PHOTO-PAINT's **I**mage, **R**esample command to perform adjustments. See Chapter 23, "Masks," for more information on the Resample command and image resolution.

After you have a correctly proportioned canvas image, save it to the COREL50\PHOTOPNT\CANVAS subdirectory on your hard drive as a PCX, TIF, or other color-capable image type. By saving the image file here, you won't have to search your hard drive the next time you want to load a canvas.

Creative Uses for a Canvas Image

In figure 24.39, you can see an image in need of a special effect. Quite often, painting and photography are thought to be interchangeable, but the biggest mistake a designer can make is by expressing an idea using the wrong medium.

Figure 24.39

Sometimes a composition makes a better painting than photograph.

The fruit in the STILLIFE.TIF image observes the century-old conventions for content and composition for classic still-life paintings. What's wrong with this image is

that it is photographic; the highly accurate medium has removed flowing lines and washes that only a painter's brush can lend to bring more feeling to the composition.

Short of painting over the image, the Canvas roll-up and the scan of the napkin can bring the feeling of needlepoint or painting to this image without so much as lifting a tool. Both the Canvas roll-up and Effects filters in PHOTO-PAINT can add a layer of interest as they remove a layer of reality in this image. Adding the cloth texture to the image in this case isn't so much of a cover-up as it is the creative use of an effect to make a viewer reevaluate an artistic composition.

In figure 24.40, you can see the cloth napkin scan applied as a canvas at 50% Transparency on top of the STILLIFE.TIF image. The image has lines it did not have before, and the illusion that the fruit image was created on a rough surface makes the composition more natural-looking and more aesthetically pleasing.

The example in this section was only one creative use of the Canvas roll-up. Certainly, you can begin an image with a canvas, and build upon it as you would a plain paper color. But PHOTO-PAINT's capabilities to repair a flawed image as well as create new ones should not be underestimated by the serious designer. There's more retouching work in business performed every day to photos and illustrations, and you should always look at the potential of a design or photo you are unhappy with before casting it aside.

Summary

PHOTO-PAINT's tools can serve a valuable function to restore, re-create, and enhance images you might think are unsalvageable. Chapter 25 covers image enhancement in PHOTO-PAINT: how to use the tools and the capabilities, and some fresh approaches to modern image editing.

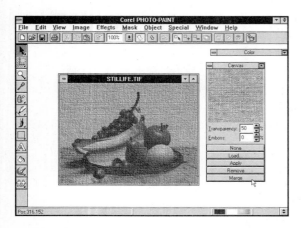

Figure 24.40
Add texture to an image by applying a canvas with a percentage of Transparency.

Image Enhancement

*T*raditionally, the world of chemical photography has been given a helping hand here and there through the art of photographic retouching. A few darkroom experimentalists produced imaginative distortions of real-life scenes, but for the most part, individuals who retouched images did so to correct a flaw in a piece of film. Today, however, photo retouching has become redefined as a subset of digital image enhancement.

It's easier than ever to bring a photo into the PC for retouching, and programs like Corel PHOTO-PAINT aren't restricted to real-world conventions. Correcting a photographic image is only the starting point in terms of PHOTO-PAINT's capabilities—you can take a perfect image or several image areas and weave, blend, resample, and generally create something new from something acquired.

This chapter covers:

- Removing unwanted image areas

- Restoring images

- Using the basic working set of tools for image enhancement

Removing Unwanted Image Areas

PHOTO-PAINT's Clone tool copies image areas and instantly merges them to other image areas, all with the convenience of a paintbrush metaphor. Whenever you have a sizable area within an image that has been damaged, and undamaged parts feature a similar pattern, the Clone tool becomes your first choice of tools in your virtual repair kit.

At other times, an image might not be damaged at all, but instead contains an image *area* you simply don't want. Because PHOTO-PAINT offers digital tools that operate with a computer's precision, the task of removing unwanted lint from a portrait photo is as easy as removing the top floor of a skyscraper.

Once you learn the techniques involved, retouching large areas becomes more a matter of investment of time than talent. Don't be put off by what appears to be a giant retouch undertaking when you use PHOTO-PAINT. If you have an image that appears to be unsalvageable, pore through this chapter before arranging another photographic session—appearances *can* be changed, as you'll see soon.

Using the Clone Tool

Image enhancement was performed on the EYESORE.TIF image shown in figure 25.1. A fire hydrant has been inserted in an absolutely grotesque place in this nice-looking landscape, creating a retouching

situation that cries out for help from PHOTO-PAINT's Clone tool. Before tackling an assignment like the one in this section, a creative assessment of how to go about retouching the image is advisable.

Figure 25.1
The Clone tool is perfect for removing a glaring mistake in the foreground of a photograph.

Three approaches to getting rid of the fire hydrant immediately spring to mind: Crop the photo to exclude the hydrant, put an object larger than the hydrant in front of it, or replace the area the hydrant occupies with material that matches the adjacent nonhydrant image areas.

Here's an example of how the Clone tool can be used to assist in the third option, as well as an opportunity to get hands-on experience with how the Clone tool works. Follow these steps:

1. Copy the EYESORE.TIF image in the CHAP25 subdirectory of the *CorelDRAW 5 Professional Reference Guide* Companion CDs to a location on your hard disk.

2. Open the image in PHOTO-PAINT, and use the Zoom tool to zoom into a 200-percent viewing resolution over the hydrant in the image.

3. Double-click on the Clone tool (the Paper Doll icon) in the toolbox to choose the tool, and to make the Tool Settings roll-up appear.

N O T E

In general, it's a good idea to keep the Tool Settings roll-up in the design window all the time; you can keep it rolled up to conserve space, but the Tool Settings roll-up constantly changes to reflect the options you have with each tool you select. If you need to customize a setting for the tool you're working with, all the characteristics and features available for a tool are found on the Tool Settings roll-up.

4. To operate the Clone tool, right-click on an image area. This is the *sample point*—the initial point in the image where PHOTO-PAINT begins capturing image information that is copied to another part of the image, or to a different image file altogether.

   The area in an image that receives the new image information is defined by holding down the left mouse button and dragging over an area with the Clone tool. The sample point that was set with the right-mouse click "shadows" the moves you make while painting with the Clone tool, so your sample point changes constantly and different image information is transferred.

5. Set the brush characteristics for the Clone tool. For this example, choose the round tip on the Tool Settings roll-up. Then choose the settings for the following options: **F**latten: **0**, **R**otate: **0**, **E**dge: **Soft**, **D**ensity: **20**, **T**ransparency: **50**, **F**ade Out: **0**, and S**p**acing: **0**. The low Density setting gives the areas you paint over extremely soft edges. You want soft edges for painting in background flora because hard edges leave distinct stroke marks that would show where the plants had been "propagated." Additionally, the 50% Transparency setting enables you to make several strokes over an area to further blend image areas together.

6. Right-click on an area of background leaves, as shown in figure 25.2. This is a good spot to begin sampling, because it's far enough away from the hydrant so that you can paint several strokes over the hydrant without resetting the sampling point.

Figure 25.2

Set a sampling point for the Clone tool that has the same visual detail with which you want to replace another area.

W A R N I N G

The biggest problem users have with the Clone tool is that they get so engrossed in applying the cloning effect that they lose track of where the sampling point has moved. If you do not pay careful attention to where the sampling point is set and where it travels as you move the Clone tool, you might accidentally sample and copy unwanted image areas.

7. Click and drag over the hydrant. Two cursor shapes now appear on-screen: the shape of the brush tip you defined on the Tool Settings roll-up marks the location where you're cloning, and the crosshair cursor shows from where the Clone tool is sampling.

   You'll notice that one stroke doesn't completely hide the hydrant. This gives you the opportunity to redefine the initial sampling point of the tool and to create a soft combination of image areas that covers the hydrant completely. Right-click on another area of vegetation when you want to start a new sampling point.

N O T E

Occasionally, you might discover that you've lost the sampling-point cursor; it may not be visible on top of every image area you sample. Right-clicking snaps the sampling cursor to directly under the Clone tool cursor where you can find it. This is a useless place for future sampling, however, so after you locate the cursor, reset the sampling point.

8. It's best not to *straight clone*—to set a sampling point and leave it that way throughout your retouching work. Cloning from a single sample point produces patterns within the image, and this produces phony-looking work. When you feel that enough brightly colored leaves have been cloned over the hydrant, sample some darker leaves above the hydrant and continue cloning, as shown in figure 25.3. This produces a realistic random variation of leafy background.

Figure 25.3

Change sampling points as the need arises to avoid static or pattern effects in the area you clone over.

9. Do not set a sampling point in an area you have cloned over; in other words, don't sample over where the hydrant used to be. PHOTO-PAINT has a weird rule about resampling samples, which is explained in the next section. When you have the top half of the hydrant cloned over with leaves, click on the Save button on the ribbon bar

(choose **S**ave from the **F**ile menu or press Ctrl+S). You finish off the hydrant in the next section.

Looking at the Atypical Properties of PHOTO-PAINT's Clone Tool

PHOTO-PAINT is very sensitive to users changing tools. Besides the Tool Settings roll-up constantly updating to offer different options as each new tool is selected, there are a few anomalies you need to watch for if you want to produce excellent work quickly.

In past chapters, you learned about workarounds for using the Zoom tool when in Object or Mask Node Edit modes; in general, you should not change tool categories when you haven't completed an edit or other effect. A different caveat is in effect when using the Clone tool—if you sample an area that has been cloned over and begin to paint with the tool, you'll be cloning with *original* areas of the image, not the new cloned-over image areas you see on-screen.

This strange recurrence of the original image happens if you *don't* change tools between cloning strokes. To avoid restoring the area that you are trying to get rid of, periodically switch to a different tool, and then switch back to the Clone tool.

Figure 25.4 shows a good example: The top of the hydrant was cloned over, the sampling point reset in the newly cloned area, and cloning resumed in a different area, producing the disembodied hydrant top to the right of the original.

Figure 25.4

Don't sample from an area you've cloned over until you deselect and then reselect the Clone tool.

Don't start cloning when the Clone tool sampling point is on an area you just cloned over *until* you select a different tool and then switch back to the Clone tool. This is the only method for continuing to resample cloned areas; choosing **S**ave from the **F**ile menu or choosing Checkpoint from the **E**dit menu are not alternatives.

In essence, when you clone, changes are displayed on-screen but they aren't *written* to the image until you select a different tool.

Cloning from Appropriate Image Areas

Note that in the EYESORE.TIF image the areas marred by the hydrant are not limited to the leaves in the garden; there is actually a peat moss trim around the edge of the garden, and a shadow is cast by the hydrant on the foreground grass. You always need to

pick a sample point for the Clone tool that is similar to the area surrounding the area you want to replace.

In the following steps, you clone over the hydrant completely, and then move on to a new technique for replacing the area of grass presently covered by the hydrant's shadow.

Here's how to remove all traces of this eyesore from the image:

1. Continue cloning over the hydrant until you reach the peat moss area of the image. Reset the sample point for the Clone tool as the need arises to cover the image areas you're replacing with a _variety_ of leaves, as you would see in an actual garden. Random texture is the most realistic in this situation; avoid creating patterns within the area.

2. Right-click over an area of peat moss directly to the right of the image area that the remaining hydrant area is covering. This sets the Clone tool's sample point.

3. Carefully left-click and drag in a near-horizontal direction to extend the area of peat moss to meet the leaves on the other side of where the hydrant was, as shown in figure 25.5.

Figure 25.5
Use the Clone tool to make original image areas blend together with the areas you have cloned.

4. After you finish cloning over the garden area, reset the Clone tool's sample point (right-click) over an area of foreground grass, and then clone over the very bottom of the hydrant. Stop when you have no evidence of the hydrant left, except its shadow. Press Ctrl+S (choose **S**ave from the **F**ile menu, or use the Save button on the ribbon bar).

Using the Freehand Mask Tool

In the previous exercises, you saw how the Clone tool is a valuable tool for replacing original image areas with not one, but several different image samples. The Clone tool is best used when you have a small area that requires editing, and that area's shape calls for the precision of a tool that has a brush tip.

The shaded area of grass in the EYESORE image has ill-defined borders and covers a large area, however. Additionally, there isn't much overall variation in tone or visual detail in this area, which makes it a perfect candidate for replacing by simply pasting over with another, unshaded area of grass. You could use the Clone tool, but that's not the quickest way to eliminate the shaded grass.

Use the Freehand Mask tool in this situation. By creating a marquee around the shaded grass area and then repositioning the mask to enclose an unshaded grass area within the image, you can copy the pristine area and then paste it back into the image as a new object that perfectly covers the shaded grass.

Here's how to professionally retouch an image so there's no trace of an unwanted image element:

1. Click and hold on the Mask tool button to display the menu fly-out, and then choose the Freehand Mask tool. This tool's use is not limited to straight lines or arcs.

2. Click and drag to create a border around the shaded grass area, as shown in figure 25.6. The border should enclose the entire shaded grass area.

Figure 25.6

Defining the shaded grass area with the Freehand Mask tool.

3. Click and hold on the Freehand Mask tool button, and then select the Mask Picker tool. This tool is used to reposition only the marquee mask, not the image area that lies underneath the marquee. You see eight selection handles around the boundary of the marquee when the Mask Picker tool is active.

4. Click and drag the mask selection area to the right of the image, as shown in figure 25.7, so that the marquee surrounds an area of unshaded grass. This is the area you'll copy to replace the shaded grass.

Figure 25.7
Choose an area of unshaded grass to copy and replace the shaded grass using the marquee mask you defined.

5. Choose **C**opy from the **E**dit menu (or press Ctrl+C, or click on the Copy button on the ribbon bar).

6. Click on the Remove button on the ribbon bar (or choose **R**emove from the **M**ask menu). This is not a necessary step, but when you paste the copy of the grass area back into the image, things will get a little cluttered and confusing with an active mask marquee *and* an active object marquee running around the image!

7. Choose **P**aste from the **E**dit menu, and then choose As New **O**bject (press Ctrl+V, or click on the Paste button on the ribbon bar). The Ctrl+V and button commands always paste a copy as a new object; you have no New Document option when you use them.

8. After the Paste command, the toolbox automatically activates the Object

Picker tool. Click and drag the floating object to the position over the shaded grass where you originally defined the mask, as shown in figure 25.8. Click on the Marquee Visible button on the ribbon bar to hide the marquee lines as you position the grass selection.

Figure 25.8
Position the floating object selection with the Object Picker tool.

9. Press Ctrl+G (or choose **M**erge from the **O**bject menu) and the object becomes part of the image. You might want to use the Clone tool once more to blend the object edges into the surrounding grass a little more.

10. Save the image as a CPT (or TIF) file to your hard drive.

The main eyesore in this image has been replaced, and it's a much better looking picture because you have the power of PHOTO-PAINT's Clone tool and Layers/Objects feature at your disposal. Now that you've had a taste of image enhancement with PHOTO-PAINT, you can see what other enhancements can be performed on this image using these tools.

Using the Mask and Clone Tools Together

The example of removing the hydrant was a fairly straightforward one, in that an area could be cloned over without having to pay attention to surrounding elements. The cloned areas and original areas simply needed to be blended together to create a continuous image area.

However, there will be occasions when you want to clone over an area, but visual elements are directly next to the area to be retouched that you need to keep intact. Rather than exercising a ridiculous amount of care and precision as you work, you can take advantage of PHOTO-PAINT's masking capability to protect only those areas you want to remain within the image as you remove others.

The next set of steps shows how to use the Magic Wand Mask tool to isolate the path in the image to protect it, leaving the picnic tables in the background available for editing. The picnic tables add unwanted visual interest to the image. There will be times when your own assignments call for removing only an element or two from an area that is otherwise fine, giving you an opportunity to experiment with the technique explained in the following steps:

1. Choose the Zoom tool and zoom in to a 400-percent viewing resolution of the picnic tables in the background of the image. The image displays some pixelation at this viewing resolution, but precise editing sometimes requires a view this close. You should adopt a practice of zooming in and out of an image while you work so that you can see the effects of the changes you are making at different perspectives.

2. Click and hold on the Mask Picker tool to display the fly-out menu, and then choose the Magic Wand Mask tool.

3. Make sure that the Tool Settings roll-up is rolled down, and then click on the Color Tolerance button. The Color Comparison Tolerance dialog box appears.

4. Choosing an area with the Magic Wand Mask tool is a matter of trial and error; your eyes can tell you that the path in this image looks like a fairly even shade of gray. However, the default color tolerance with which the Magic Wand Mask tool selects similar colors is plus/minus 10. This is not a great enough tolerance to accurately select the path for masking; a better setting is plus/minus 50. Type **50** in both the + and – fields of the Color Comparison Tolerance dialog box.

5. Click on a stone path, and then click on the Add to Selection button on the ribbon bar.

6. Click in other areas where you see the path. These areas need to be protected before you clone over the picnic tables, as shown in figure 25.9. Only the stone path directly next to the picnic tables needs to be masked; the rest of the image area should be available to clone over.

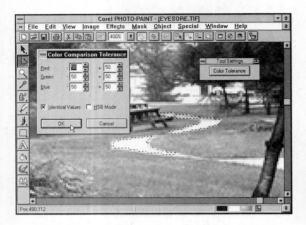

Figure 25.9
Select the areas next to the picnic tables to keep them apart from areas you want to clone over.

7. Areas marqueed by mask tools are available for editing, while areas outside the marquees are protected from change. You want the exact opposite of the present marqueed areas to be protected. Click on the Invert button on the ribbon bar (or choose **I**nvert from the **M**ask menu).

8. The area that is to be cloned over is very small, and the characteristic of the Clone tool should be equally small. Click on the Clone tool, and then in the Tool Settings roll-up choose **S**ize **4**: **F**latten: **0**, **R**otate: **0**, **E**dge: **Soft**, **D**ensity: **50**, **T**ransparency: **0**, **F**ade Out: **0**, and S**p**acing: **0**.

9. Right-click on a clear area of grass not too near the picnic tables with a similar color value as that found in the grass next to the picnic tables. Don't choose a shaded area, however.

10. Click and drag the Clone tool over the picnic tables, as shown in figure 25.10. You can be somewhat cavalier in your cloning strokes; the path area is protected from change because you inverted the mask that was created around the paths.

Figure 25.10
You can clone with broader strokes than usual because you have a mask protecting key areas of the image.

11. Reset the sampling point when necessary to completely clone over the picnic tables. If you need to sample from areas you've cloned over, choose a tool other than the Clone tool (to make cloning changes permanent within the image), and then select the Clone tool again. Then right-click over the previously cloned area to set a new sample point, and continue cloning.

12. When the picnic tables are gone, save your work, click on a Mask tool, and click on the Remove button (or choose **R**emove from the **M**ask menu). It

makes no difference whether you remove a mask before or after you save your work because masks have to be saved to a *separate* image file. The marquee selection created with Mask tools isn't permanent, and it does not become part of the image it is created in when the image is saved.

Don't be concerned that you've left areas with hard edges over the picnic table area. This cannot be avoided because there are light and shaded areas of the grass in the background, and you're bound to clip one of the shadows of the trees as you clone. In the next section, you see how to use a PHOTO-PAINT Special tool to correct any strokes you've made that don't look photo-realistic.

Using the Smear Tool and Image Editing

There is a very fine line to walk in image enhancement that has to do with visual content found in an image. Chemical photographs, by their nature, usually contain image areas that are sharp, and others that are ill-defined and fuzzy. When you retouch areas in a photo, you must take care not to disturb the overall focus of an area; if something is blurred, you do not want to make its surroundings sharp and clear.

Fortunately, in this example, the background grass near the picnic tables has little detail. The variations in colors suggest grass viewed from a distance and, although it has a textured feel, the grass gets most of its characteristics from the variation in color rather than from distinct visual detail.

This situation provides a perfect opportunity to use the Smear tool to correct any harsh background areas that are a result of cloned areas butting against original image areas. The Smear tool spreads color across an image area—it uses the color of the area you begin click and dragging in to apply color to other image areas. The Smear tool destroys image detail by performing this action but, as previously discussed, the image background has almost no image detail. In the next set of steps, you rearrange color values with the Smear tool to create a more believable background:

The following steps show how to use the Smear tool, and in this case to finish enhancing the EYESORE.TIF image.

1. Choose the Smear tool from the toolbox and choose the following settings from the Tool Settings roll-up: Round shape, **S**ize: **4**, **F**latten: **0**, **R**otate: **0**, **E**dge: **Soft**, **D**ensity: **75**, **T**ransparency: **25**, **F**ade Out: **0**, and S**p**acing: **0**. With a partial opacity and mostly solid (**D**ensity setting) characteristic, you'll find working with the Smear tool to be similar to actually working with a cotton swab, just as depicted on the tool's icon!

2. Depending on how you applied the clone strokes, you might have intruded on the tree's shadow, or perhaps the tree's shadow now extends farther than it should. In either case, the tree's shadow eventually needs to be rounded, so bear this in mind when you smear the background image area. Click and drag the Smear tool over any hard-edge areas that exist on the grassy background, as shown in figure 25.11.

Figure 25.11

The background is supposed to be slightly out of focus; the Smear tool assists in making the lack of focus consistent.

Figure 25.12

A retouched image should call attention to its composition, but not to image enhancements.

3. When you think you're finished, double-click on the Zoom tool to return to a 100-percent viewing resolution of the image. Check for any areas you missed. Bear in mind when using the Smear tool (or any other powerful editing tool) that "less is more." You generally need to apply color or an effect with less intensity than you think to create photo-realistic edits. Photos require a subtle approach, whereas you have more creative latitude with bitmap illustrations. Figure 25.12 shows the completed image.

Scenes of nature are a relatively easy genre of images to retouch, because they typically contain random composition of leaves, grass, and other textures. The staple of imaging professionals is the photographic portrait, however; it's not nearly as easy to retouch a person's face as a nature scene. In the next section, you see how to restore and enhance a photographic portrait that has been handled inexpertly, and now suffers cracks, chips, and other defects. In short, the next example contains most of the common challenges to photographic retouching.

Restoring Images

The Eastman Kodak Company estimates that the average life span of a photographic negative is less than 20 years. The deterioration of a photographic print however, begins the first time you hand it to someone else. If you've ever been in the position of needing to use an image in an assignment, only to find that it contains scuff marks, surface defects, lint, spots, or other natural disasters, now is a good time to invest in a scanner and some time with PHOTO-PAINT's features.

Setting Up the Acquisition of a Digital Image

A PhotoCD made from original negatives is usually the preferred format for the digital images you enhance, but when a negative is lost, a good color print is your second and only choice for acquiring a digital image. A PhotoCD image isn't subject to the variety of defects a color print is, because PhotoCD images aren't exposed to airborne materials, light, or abrasive surfaces. Kodak estimates that a PhotoCD will last 100 years before disintegrating.

Naturally, after an image has been digitized, the binary data can be preserved indefinitely on a number of computer-media formats. PhotoCD technology has its upper limits of resolution, however; after an image has been digitized, it contains a fixed amount of visual information. If not enough information has been captured, you need to go back to the source to acquire missing digital information.

When restoring a photograph, there are several things you must consider before you digitize the photo:

- Can color correction be performed on the image as you scan? It's better to take care of color-casting, brightness, and contrast at the acquisition phase of digitizing an image. If your scanner

supports color correction, use it before you bring the image into PHOTO-PAINT.

- How large should you scan the image you want to enhance? This is something that can be answered only by knowing what your final output will be. Is the image intended for publication? Will you have the finished digital image film recorded? In general, you want to oversample, not undersample, an image in need of enhancement so that you have as much original detail to work with as possible.

- Whatever the file size of the scanned image, PHOTO-PAINT will need two to three times that amount in system RAM and hard disk space for active storage as you work on the image. It's a good idea to free up as much hard drive space as possible for the sole purpose of letting PHOTO-PAINT use it as a temp file.

  Additionally, you should seriously consider buying 32MB to 64MB of RAM for your PC, or as much as the motherboard can support. Professional image editing and enhancing is a field relatively new to the IBM/PC platform, and the trade used Macintosh and UNIX-based workstations for imaging until very recently. Both these platforms address conventional RAM differently than the PC, and the only way to keep up is to stock up on RAM.

- PHOTO-PAINT can handle an image that is 18MB in file size; any larger file is opened automatically as a partial file

(see Chapter 27, "Color Specification and Output"). If you believe that an image is too ungainly to be handled as a single image with your PC's resources, you have the option in PHOTO-PAINT to open a portion of the image, and PHOTO-PAINT reassembles the whole image when you're done editing.

■ Gently remove any foreign materials from a print before you scan, and make sure that the image is at right angles to the face of the scanner. PHOTO-PAINT can rotate a crooked image, but the process involves interpolating the image. *Interpolation* is a series of calculations used to reassign pixels different color values to represent the changes you want made to the image, such as rotation, and other angular or size transformations.

When rotating a crooked image, PHOTO-PAINT uses interpolation to smoothly average the difference in pixel values between the location of a color in the original image, and the new position for the color, represented by a different pixel. The effect you see is that PHOTO-PAINT is rearranging pixels when you rotate an image (or image area); in reality, massive amounts of calculating and averaging are being performed to reassign color values. PHOTO-PAINT also uses interpolation to add or subtract pixels within an image when you increase or decrease the size or resolution of an image. Interpolation is a time-consuming process that inevitably results in loss of original image

information and moves the image one step further from the original image.

After considering all these issues, it's time to scan an image and restore it. In the next section, you use the DAVE.TIF image on the *CorelDRAW 5 Professional Reference Guide* Companion CDs. You learn the techniques for correcting bad exposure, surface flaws, and a little creative composition through some hands-on experience.

Setting Brightness, Contrast, and Exposure

Unlike transparencies and 35mm slides, a photograph is opaque and light bounces off the surface of the print. This makes it tougher to get a workable scan from a print that contains the luminosity and brilliance seen in slides and objects viewed in real life. Like your eyes, the scanner's "eye" sees the surface of an image as much as the image's visual content. Before performing any fancy editing and restoration work, it's a good idea to use PHOTO-PAINT to correct for brightness and contrast of the scanned image.

PHOTO-PAINT has three basic sets of controls that are used for correcting the tonal balance of an image—Brightness, Contrast, and Intensity. These controls are accessed by choosing the Brightness and Contrast command. This command, along with the Gamma, Hue/Saturation and Tone Map commands, is nested under the Color commands found on the Effects menu. Although these commands are found under the Color Effects category, none of these commands touches color values. Only the neutral density grayscale components displayed by the pixels are changed when the Brightness and Contrast controls are used.

Brightness is one of the three qualities of color (the other two are saturation and hue). Brightness is measured by the amount of light reflected (or passed through) an object. *Contrast* is the amount of tonal difference among the shadows, highlights, and midtones in an image. Increasing the overall contrast in a dull image often helps bring out visual detail. Intensity is a feature unique to PHOTO-PAINT; most imaging programs don't have an Intensity control. Intensity affects the brightness of the midtone and highlight values in an image.

In the following example, you see how to compensate for a scan's deficiencies. Here's how to set up an image for future editing and enhancing:

1. Open a copy of the DAVE.TIF image on the *CorelDRAW 5 Professional Reference Guide* Companion CDs found in the CHAP25 subdirectory. DAVE.TIF is the sample image used to explore image-restoration methods. Save a copy of it to your hard drive. As you can see in figure 25.13, the DAVE image suffers from all the *family shoebox* symptoms—cracked emulsion, lint, and poor exposure within the image. Scanning an image in this condition should be performed with as many preset color corrections as your scanner features.

Figure 25.13

Try to use your scanner's features to correct an image as much as possible before resorting to PHOTO-PAINT's features.

2. Choose Color from the Effects menu, and then choose Brightness and Contrast and use your own aesthetics for setting the values in the command. As you can see in figure 25.14, the Preview window displays changes that will be made if you decide to click on the OK button and make the changes to the image. A +4 Brightness setting with a +20 Intensity value brings out a lot of image detail without having to resort to increasing contrast. Enter these settings and click on OK to return to the image in the design window. In general, adjust Brightness before Contrast; the balance of tones within an image is hard to see and adjust if the overall image is too dark.

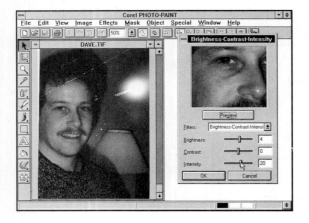

Figure 25.14
Clicking on the Preview button shows what your changes will look like when applied to the image.

3. Save the image as DAVE2.TIF to your hard drive. It's good practice to save variations of an image you're working on. If you make a mistake or want to use a different restoration strategy, saving different copies of the file gives you the option of going back to the original or to pick up again at one of the intermediate stages.

T I P

If you have more than 12MB RAM and hard disk space to spare, you might want to choose Checkpoint from the **E**dit menu at regular intervals in your imaging work. The Checkpoint command makes a copy of an image you're working on, and you can use the Restore to Checkpoint command to revert to a saved state of the image in case you made a mistake.

The Checkpoint and Restore to Checkpoint commands require a separate version of an image to be stored for quick retrieval by PHOTO-PAINT, so the larger the file you're working on, the more demands are made of your system. Checkpoint is a good alternative to saving multiple copies of an image, and you should familiarize yourself with the **E**dit, **U**ndo (Ctrl+Z) command and the Local Undo tool from the Eraser Tools fly-out on the toolbox. The Local Undo command erases part or all of your last edit, depending on how much you "paint" over an edited area with the Local Undo tool.

After the DAVE2 image is balanced tonally, it's time to address the surface flaws on the image. Always correct an image before restoring it. Anything you apply to an image (like foreground color or cloned image areas) responds to Brightness and Contrast adjustments a little differently than original image areas, and harsh, discolored areas where you've painted over something can be the result. This is because PHOTO-PAINT's colors don't contain photographic grain and random values of tones that a scanned image does.

Using the Clone Tool on a Human

Cracks in photographic emulsion are actually areas of a photo that are missing, and no tonal or color adjustment can retrieve them. The two most powerful tools you can use in PHOTO-PAINT to re-create missing image areas are the Eyedropper tool and the Clone tool. You'll see how the Eyedropper tool is a valuable assistant when color matching, but first you will use the Clone tool to replace cracked emulsion with duplicate areas within the DAVE2 image.

Unlike the EYESORE image, the Clone tool should not be used with imprecision when restoring a portrait. Always examine a portrait carefully, scouting for areas of undamaged image color and detail that are candidates for replacing the missing areas. In this section's example, Dave's forehead is unevenly lit, and the crack in the emulsion runs right across differently colored skin areas. Additionally, the crack runs through Dave's hair and has destroyed visual detail that needs to be restored without giving Dave the appearance of a bad haircut. In the next set of steps, you restore Dave's forehead using the Clone tool and discover a technique for making your work invisible.

To restore an image area that is missing completely, follow these steps:

1. Double-click on the Clone tool to select the tool and display the Tool Settings roll-up.

2. On the Tool Settings roll-up, set the Clone tool's characteristics to the round shape—**S**ize: **12**, **F**latten: **0**, **R**otate: **0**, **E**dge: **Soft**, **D**ensity: **5**, **T**ransparency: **0**, **F**ade Out: **50**, and S**p**acing: **0**. With a very soft "core" (**D**ensity), cloning strokes will blend seamlessly into original image areas, and the **F**ade Out value of 50 will limit the strokes to short ones. These are desired qualities in a retouching brush because photographic images are composed of "clumps" of color areas, and long strokes of sampled image area would create telltale evidence of the retouching work.

3. Click in the Zoom field on the ribbon bar, and type **200**. Then use the window scroll bars to get a good view of Dave's forehead. Many times, you'll find that entering a zoom value is quicker than deselecting the active tool, selecting the Zoom tool, and then selecting your tool once again.

4. Right-click on an area on the left side of Dave's forehead that is one-half inch below the crack in the photo. Click-and-drag a short stroke (about one-half inch) from left to right directly over the crack, as shown in figure 25.15.

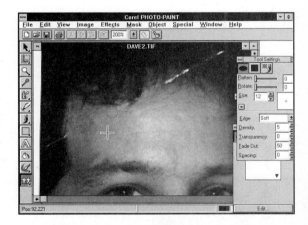

Figure 25.15
Keep the sampling point of the Clone tool close to the cloning area.

5. Only use the Clone tool to retouch the skin in the image; leave the areas where hair should be cloned in for later. Reset the sample point for the Clone tool often; you shouldn't use the same area for retouching different shades of skin. Try to right-click as close to beneath the emulsion crack as possible without

sampling the crack, and then click-and-drag a short stroke over the crack and reset the sample point. It's okay to deselect the Clone tool and then reselect it to make the cloned areas in the image permanent. You then can resample the cloned areas to continue removing the crack.

6. Once you've covered the crack with samples of other skin areas, it's time to address the hair that's damaged.

   Right-click to sample an area that has a few strands of hair and some forehead, and then click-and-drag across the area damaged by the crack, as shown in figure 25.16. Oddly enough, this is a phase of photographic retouching where accuracy is of little importance. Dave's hairline is not well-defined and, as such, you can clone over other areas of hairline, and regardless of which way the locks of hair go, it doesn't look "wrong."

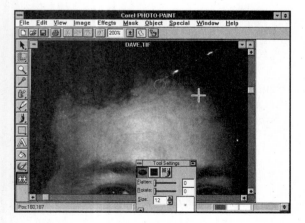

Figure 25.16

Areas with no distinctive pattern can be cloned over successfully by using different areas that have the same "feel."

7. After you've successfully cloned away the emulsion crack over all of Dave's forehead, leave the rest of his hair and the rest of the image alone. You get into another technique and a conceptual discussion in the next section on how to repair the whole photo. Save your work at this point.

If you consider the content of this image, you have to agree that there's nothing of visual interest besides the subject; the lamp and part of a cabinet don't really contribute to the visual interest of the image. Besides being boring, there is also a massive amount of physical damage ruining the background areas of the image. After the subject has been retouched thoroughly, there are creative options for image enhancement to take the picture way beyond simple retouching work.

Using the Eyedropper Tool

There is little point in using the Clone tool to clean up the rest of the subject in this image. The Clone tool is very useful in restoring complex image detail, but for lint and pinholes in a print, it's far better to use the Paint Brush tool and a selection of foreground color that precisely matches missing image areas.

The Eyedropper tool can choose a sample color of a single pixel; a 3×3 pixel area; a 5×5 pixel area; or a custom, user-defined area. The sample size option is set on the Tool Settings roll-up when the Eyedropper tool is selected. The technique for covering small areas is to click the Eyedropper tool over an area very close to the missing area, and then paint in the area with the Paint Brush tool.

This technique is very similar to spot-toning a chemical photo, except the guesswork of mixing up exactly the right replacement shade is foolproof. In fact, the Eyedropper tool is more convenient and takes up less space on the design window than the Colors roll-up, and the Eyedropper might be the only thing you'll need to accurately define foreground colors for painting image enhancements.

Here's how to perform some virtual spot-toning on the DAVE2.TIF image:

1. The biggest problem with the image of Dave is now on his left temple (the right side of the image); there's a white spot marring it. Click on the Eyedropper tool and then click on a hair area directly above the spot, as shown in figure 25.17. By default, the Tool Settings roll-up is set to Point Sample. This means that the pixel you click over determines the present foreground (paint) color for the painting tools. You don't need to increase the Eyedropper tool's sample size because the hair area is composed of almost identical color values. Also, there's no need to display the Colors roll-up—if you were to press Ctrl+F2 right now, you would lose valuable design-window space to the Colors roll-up, and it would only confirm that you selected the foreground color of Dave's hair.

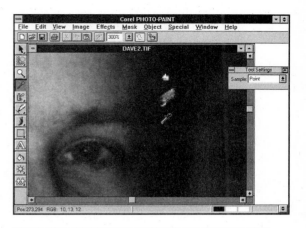

Figure 25.17

Select a color from the image that you want to paint with.

2. Click on the Paint Brush Tool on the toolbox. Then set the following brush characteristics: <u>S</u>ize: **12**, <u>F</u>latten: **0**, <u>R</u>otate: **0**, <u>E</u>dge: **Soft**, <u>D</u>ensity: **50**, <u>T</u>ransparency: **0**, <u>F</u>ade Out: **75**, and S<u>p</u>acing: **0**. All the settings for the tools used in this and other PHOTO-PAINT chapters were arrived at by trying different values and setting each for a specific task at hand. The tool settings for every image you retouch have to be defined on a case-by-case basis—there is no hard-and-fast rule for settings.

3. Click-and-drag a short stroke over the white area on Dave's temple. As in traditional retouching, don't linger over an area with your tool. Short, precise strokes make spot-toning in an image invisible. You might want to consider clicking over (don't drag) small flecks of discoloration within the image.

4. When you're done with the spot on the subject's temple, scroll over to other areas that need spot-toning. Click on the Eyedropper tool, sample an area close to the one that needs retouching, and then set the **S**ize of the Paint Brush to about 3 pixels. The smaller the area, the smaller the brush size should be.

5. You're done when the image looks like figure 25.18 or better. As mentioned earlier, there's a way to fix the background of this image without all the painstaking precision you normally would use on the main focal attraction in a photograph. Don't feel compelled to use the two techniques covered so far to turn a dull, flawed background into one that's simply dull.

Figure 25.18

Concentrate on retouching the important elements in an image.

T   I   P

An excellent method for evaluating a size for the Paint Brush tool is to take a good look at the size of the pixels when your viewing resolution is magnified from 300 percent to 400 percent. The **S**ize of the Paint Brush tip is absolute—the closer you view the image, the larger the brush cursor appears. It makes sense, then, that if you're retouching a spot on an image that appears to be no larger than one or two pixels on-screen, you don't need a Paint Brush size much larger than two or three pixels.

Replacing an Image Background

If you've read Chapter 22, you are familiar with the techniques used in isolating an image area and copying it or defining it as an object. This is the approach to be taken with the DAVE2.TIF image background—it's hopelessly damaged, and if it wasn't, it's still poorly composed.

Never underestimate the value of having a personal collection of stock photography. Whether you photograph it yourself or purchase it, a collection of multipurpose background scenes can get you out of a bad situation in a real assignment exactly like the one presented to you in this exercise.

Companies like Corel Corporation, Aris Entertainment, Image Club Graphics, and many others offer royalty-free CDs full of landscape photography taken by freelance photographers. Typically, stock photography images are of places you never would have an opportunity to visit. Having an image of a pyramid, a lush Polynesian garden, or other exotic locale can help make your tabletop or fashion-model work look a little more worldly.

Defining a Foreground Selection Border

For the task at hand, Dave needs a new background, so creating a selection border around him is the next step. You'll notice that the flash used to take this picture has cast an enormous shadow behind Dave's head on the wall. This makes accurately selecting the top of his head impossible. What you need to do in situations like this is to "guesstimate" where the top of the subject's head is, and trim around it with an appropriate selection tool. This always results in the "helmet hairdo" so commonly found in inexpert retouching work, but this problem can be resolved as a last step after transplanting the foreground image into a new background scene.

To create a selection border around an irregularly shaped image area, follow these steps:

1. Choose the 50-percent viewing resolution on the ribbon bar. This puts all the DAVE2 image within view in the design window.

2. Click-and-hold on the Mask tool to display the fly-out menu, and then choose the Freehand Mask tool. This tool is used to create a freeform selection area.

3. Click-and-drag a selection area around Dave, like the one shown in figure 25.19. This is a rough-out of the final selection border, so don't worry if the border isn't precise at this point.

Figure 25.19

Create an outline with the Freehand Mask tool of the area you want to transplant to a different background.

4. Click-and-hold on the Freehand Mask tool, and then select the Node Edit Mask tool. Make sure that the Tool Settings roll-up is extended now. You will see that this roll-up offers a number of drop-down options as to how many nodes it will fit to a path based on your Freehand selection. Choose Medium. Setting these options places a fair number of nodes along the path—approximately the number you need to accurately define the border of Dave.

5. Choose the 200-percent viewing resolution from Zoom level drop-down on the ribbon bar and begin fitting the outline to the border of the subject. As you can see in figure 25.20, a close viewing resolution provides you with adequate visual detail about where Dave ends and the background begins. The "easy" part is around Dave's face and sweater. Make sure that the left

and bottom edge of your selection path are flush with the edge of the image.

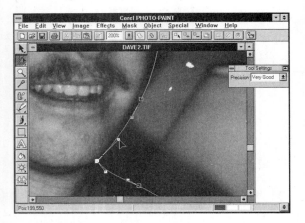

Figure 25.20

If you find that you have a node you have no use for, click on it and press the Delete key to remove it.

Figure 25.21

Create an outline around the hair that suggests the top of the head; you can refine the outline at the end of the retouching.

6. When you have fit the path to the border of the subject, click-and-hold on the Node Edit Mask tool, and select a different Mask tool. This action returns the path to a selection marquee, and you should have an image similar to that shown in figure 25.21.

7. Choose **S**ave from the **M**ask menu, and then choose PHOTO-PAINT! *.CPT as the file format in the Save File as **T**ype drop-down list and name the file DAVE2. By saving masks to the CPT format and keeping the corresponding RGB images in TIF format, you easily can find the masks that images correspond to.

Selecting Background Images

The image of Dave was taken using a flashbulb for the primary source of illumination, which is definitely not what the world of professional photography accepts or uses. However, the flat lighting provides an opportunity to reflect on the topic of matching source lighting in original and replacement image areas.

If your plan is to use a replacement background for an image, it's best to pick your stock photography with lighting in mind. For example, if your subject is lit from a source at a ten o'clock position, the background stock photography should contain similar lighting conditions.

There aren't many pleasing-looking background images available that contain flashbulb illumination, however. But if you think about this one for a second, flash photography taken outdoors toward dusk or at night illuminates foreground elements and leaves background areas more than three feet behind a subject alone. This is because flashbulbs don't have a tremendous amount of "throw" to them.

There's also the problem of color compatibility between the two images to consider. The colors in the DAVE2 photo are quite cold, but if the coloration in the background you want to use is much warmer, you'll have to make color adjustments. In real life, your subject Dave would have a warmer color cast than he now has regardless of the flashbulb lighting, because some of the warm natural background illumination would contribute to his overall hue. In the next set of steps, you overcome the problem of the different color environments by color correcting Dave before adding him to the new background.

Here's how to perform a little color comparison and color correction in PHOTO-PAINT:

1. Open a copy of the OUTDOORS.TIF image from the *CorelDRAW 5 Professional Reference Guide* Companion CDs. It's in the CHAP25 subdirectory. Save it to your hard disk under the same name.

2. Resize and reposition the DAVE2 and the OUTDOORS images in PHOTO-PAINT's design window so that you have an unobstructed view of both images. Figure 25.22 is in black and white, making it difficult to see subtle variations in color, but on-screen you

will be able to see that Dave needs a little more of a reddish cast to fit into the OUTDOORS image better.

Figure 25.22
Evaluate the relative color differences in images before you combine them.

N O T E

Comparing colors in images before you combine them is important, because as separate objects in the same image window, you cannot correct the color of one object without applying the same changes to the other. The only way to edit an object by itself in an image is to hide all the other layer objects. When objects are hidden, however, it becomes impossible to compare the colors within the objects.

3. Choose Color from the Effects menu, and then choose Hue/Saturation.

The Hue slider in the Hue/Saturation menu spans values from −180 to +180—360° of the visible spectrum modeled around a color wheel. Every 52 degrees or so represents a different additive primary and complementary light-frequency value. The color casts of the Hue command from −180 to 0 are Blue, Indigo, Violet, Red, Yellow, Green, and Blue. This sequence of colors is repeated as the hue changes from 0 to +180.

4. Dave needs a little more red, so click-and-drag the Hue slider to about −12. Then click on the Preview button, as shown in figure 25.23. You might want to choose a different value than −12, depending on your monitor's calibration. The important point is to reference the OUTDOOR image for color consistency before clicking on OK. Click on OK when Dave has a similar color cast to the OUTDOOR image.

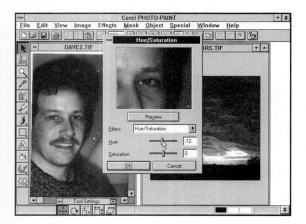

Figure 25.23
Keep the image with the color you're trying to match in plain view as you preview a different image in the Hue/Saturation dialog box.

5. Additionally, you might want to lighten or darken the tonal values of the subject now that you have decided on a new background. In the case of the photo you're working on, Dave's contrast needed to be heightened and the brightness also could come up a little so that he doesn't appear to be washed out when composited into the new background. To make more tonal adjustments, choose Color from the Effects menu, and then choose Brightness and Contrast. Preview any changes you propose, then click on OK.

W A R N I N G

Ctrl+F is the shortcut key command for applying the last Effects filter chosen, and this command appears at the top of the Effects drop-down menu after you've applied an effect in a single PHOTO-PAINT session. Don't use this command or shortcut key unless you want to apply the same values that you specified last. In other words, if you increased contrast by 12, and then pressed Ctrl+F (or chose Effects, Brightness-Contrast-Intensity), you would *not* get a preview box or a menu, and an additional 12 percent of contrast would be applied automatically.

Choose Effects commands carefully, and don't use the "last effect" shortcut key if you want to readjust Effects settings.

6. Choose Load from the Mask menu, and choose the DAVE2.CPT image from the File Name box. Then click on OK.

7. Choose **C**opy from the **E**dit menu (or press Ctrl+C or click on the Copy button on the ribbon bar). Then click on the title bar of the OUTDOORS.TIF image.

8. Click on the Paste button on the ribbon bar (or choose **P**aste from the **E**dit menu and choose As New **O**bject; or press Ctrl+V).

As you can see in figure 25.24, Dave has plenty of breathing room now in the great OUTDOORS image, and this is because the background image was chosen with image resolution and dimensions planned beforehand. In a real assignment, you should calculate the image dimensions of objects you define, and make certain that the image you're pasting into is of equal or greater dimensions. This planning gives you the freedom to reposition an object within the new image. Choose **I**nfo from the **I**mage menu when you need to spec an image for size.

Figure 25.24

Choose the background for an image selection that has greater or equal size as the object.

You always can resize an object or background and use "brute force" to make the two images compatible sizes, but this should be a last option. Resizing an image or object means resampling it, and resampling always degrades image quality somewhat. If you must resize, resize down rather than up. The loss of image detail is less noticeable when you lose pixels than when PHOTO-PAINT has to create extra pixels.

Considerations on Image Composition

The image of Dave was cropped poorly in the camera. Although PHOTO-PAINT has powerful imaging tools, trying to restore an image area not captured with the camera is a futile effort. Although a chair, part of a building, or another image area with a clear geometry or pattern can be faked successfully, you usually create a phony-looking image when you try to restore substantial areas of a portrait.

The best course of action with an image like Dave on the OUTDOORS background is to create an interesting foreground-background composition; cropping the image is a final step. You have no control over the crop to the left of the image—it must be flush with the area of the subject that was cropped originally in the camera.

In the next steps, you position the floating object image area so that some interesting background detail is visible within the cropped finished image. Bear in mind that the closer you position the top of Dave's head to dark background area, the more it blends into the background and the less work you need to do to refine the border that was "guesstimated" when you created the selection.

Here's how to position and composite the foreground object into the background image:

1. Minimize or close the DAVE2 image. You're done with it and you conserve system resources by having only the image(s) you need open within PHOTO-PAINT's design window.

2. Choose the 50-percent viewing resolution from the ribbon bar and maximize the OUTDOORS.TIF image window by clicking on the up arrow at the upper right corner of the window. Now you can see the image edges, and you can position the bottom edge of the floating foreground subject so that it's flush with the bottom edge of the OUTDOORS image if you think this would make a good composition.

3. Click on the Marquee Visible button on the ribbon bar to turn off the marquee. The object still is floating (you can see the eight selection handles around it), but you can reposition objects with greater accuracy when you're not visually distracted by marquee lines.

4. Regular masks are made of 1 bit/pixel information; a pixel is on (selected) or off (not selected). Therefore, the floating foreground object, Dave, displays harsh outline edges, reminiscent of a time when designers used utility blades to trim around image areas. Press Ctrl+F7 or choose **L**ayers/Objects Roll-Up from the **O**bject menu.

5. Type **5** in the Feather field. A foreground object can be feathered at any time before merging it to the background, and the amount of feathering can be reset as often as you want before the object is merged.

As you can see in figure 25.25, Dave's outline now blends into the background better, and the composition is becoming more realistic looking. Additionally, now that the feathering provides a more finished look for the overall image, you can reposition the foreground object and have an accurate view of how the composition is coming together.

Figure 25.25

Use the Feather option to smooth object edges into the background image.

6. Use the Object Picker tool from the toolbox to reposition the floating foreground object. You can position Dave anywhere you want within the OUTDOORS image because the

finished image can be cropped to accommodate the incomplete portrait of Dave.

7. When the foreground element looks good within the context of the background area, press Ctrl+G (or choose **M**erge from the **O**bject menu). The image of Dave becomes a permanent part of the OUTDOORS background, and the color pixels in the OUTDOORS image that the Dave selection covers are replaced.

8. Click-and-hold on the Mask tool on the toolbox to display the fly-out menu and select the Rectangle Mask tool.

9. Click-and-drag diagonally from the upper left to the lower right on the OUTDOORS.TIF image to define the area you want to crop out of the image.

10. If you don't have exactly the cropping area you want, click-and-hold on the Rectangle Mask tool, and then choose the Mask Picker tool from the fly-out menu. You can click-and-drag a side of the marquee selection border to stretch or shrink it. This doesn't affect the underlying image area in the least; you're only resizing the mask above the image.

11. When you're happy with the dimensions and placement of the crop marquee, choose Cro**p** Image from the **M**ask menu, as shown in figure 25.26. The Cro**p** Image command does not trim away areas outside the OUTDOORS image; instead, it creates a new image based on the area within the crop marquee you've defined. NEW-1.CPT should appear

in the design window after you issue the Cro**p** Image command, and the OUTDOORS.TIF image window will be behind the new image window.

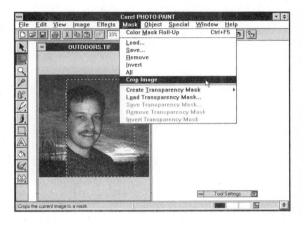

Figure 25.26

The Crop Image command produces a new image based on the crop area you specified in an original image.

12. Save the NEW-1.CPT image as DAVE_FIN.TIF to your hard disk. You have a choice to make about closing the OUTDOORS.TIF image now. If you save it in the TIF format, PHOTO-PAINT auto-merges the floating selection. If you want to play with this image in the future with the floating selection intact, save it as OUTDOOR.CPT. The *.CPT extension is proprietary to PHOTO-PAINT, and enables you to keep unmerged objects separate from one another indefinitely.

(Photo) Finishing Touches in Image Enhancement Using the Paint Brush Tool

Although the DAVE_FIN image now has better overall color and composition, there are one or two more things that need to be done to make the relationship between the merged foreground image and the new background a more realistic one. Dave's hair is still pretty roughly defined, and the best way to go about correcting this problem is through the creative use of the Paint Brush tool.

You've zoomed in and out of this image quite a few times in this chapter, and you've had a good, close look at what comprises most of the hair area at the top of Dave's head. There is no *image detail*—there are no clearly defined strands of hair; instead, there is only flat color.

This reality prompts a very simple correction technique for the area that presently needs retouching; create a soft Paint Brush tip, sample the color of Dave's hair in an area close to the edge, and paint in a few wisps of hair. It's a simple technique, but it produces a more realistic overall image.

Here's how to add color to create detail in an image:

1. Zoom to 100-percent viewing resolution of the DAVE_FIN image, and then use the window scroll bars to get a good view of the top of Dave's head.

2. Choose the Eyedropper tool and click on an area within Dave's hair.

3. Choose the Paint Brush tool, and then enter these settings in the Tool Settings roll-up for the characteristic of the brush tip: Round shape, **S**ize **2**, **F**latten: **65**, **R**otate: **65**, **E**dge: **Soft**, **D**ensity: **50**, **T**ransparency: **0**, **F**ade Out: **75**, and S**p**acing: **0**. It's small brush tip, but you'll be painting in individual strands of hair with it, and the short **F**ade Out distance will help in creating short strokes, which are ideal for suggesting hair.

4. Click-and-drag in random areas along the edge of Dave's hair. Use your creative instincts and add strands of hair in places where you think they would exist naturally, as shown in figure 25.27. The angled tip helps produce irregular strokes, and these tool settings are useful for producing similar effects in your own assignments.

Figure 25.27

Adding wisps of hair to the hard outline helps blend the subject into the background image.

5. "Less is more" is a phrase that should be tacked up next to every computer graphics artist's workstation. You only need to add a half dozen strands to the outline of Dave's hair to complete the effect and finish the image. When you think that you need one or two more strokes, you're most likely already finished! Save your work and then zoom out to the 50-percent viewing resolution to see the entire image. Choose **S**ave from the **F**ile menu at this point or click on the Save button on the ribbon bar.

One of the perks of saving the finished image to a new file name is that you can create your own "before and after" on-screen. In figure 25.28, you can see the original image and the dramatic difference you created in the finished image.

Figure 25.28

Use the techniques you learned in this chapter to add enhancements to portrait images of your own.

There are as many creative uses for PHOTO-PAINT's tools in image enhancement as there are different images in the world. No two pictures call for exactly the same tools or techniques to correct and enhance them, but you now have a good foundation on which to build with the techniques covered in this chapter.

Some PHOTO-PAINT tools are bound to have a greater effect on the images you enhance. The following section is a brief review of the situations under which you would use a tool, as well as some pointers on using them.

Working with the Basic Set of Tools for Image Enhancement

Unless your concept entails creating unusual or surrealistic effects, the best first step to image retouching is to begin with the best possible acquisition of the source image. PHOTO-PAINT offers basic tonal and color adjustments, but you shouldn't rely on them or expect miracles if a scan or other digital image is of poor quality in the first place.

Chapter 26, "Filters," covers some fine-tuning you can perform with the tonal balance of an image, but comprehensive color correction is not PHOTO-PAINT's forte. You do have global color adjustment capability with the Hue/Saturation effect, as well as local color adjustment tools such as the Hue and Saturation tools and the Color

Replacer tool, but your best chance for successfully manipulating an image is to begin with one that already is color balanced.

An approach to retouching or enhancing an image follows, with some suggestions about which effect or tool to begin with. Use this as a guide for image enhancing, but always rely on your own eye as the final judge of what an assignment calls for:

- **Begin with a concept.** Do you want to create something fantastic out of a set of ordinary images, or do you simply want to restore a damaged image? PC image editing is such a wonderful, plastic medium that many designers start tinkering with pixels without the slightest amount of planning. Sometimes a free-form image editing session produces ideas along the way, but if you get paid for designing things, it's best to have some pre-flight-of-fancy directions in mind.

- **Is any part of the image you're working on beyond repair?** Don't get caught in a bind by spending valuable time trying to fix the unfixable. If any part of an image demands replacement, measure this area by choosing **I**nfo from the **I**mage menu, and then hunt around for a suitable replacement image. If the size of the available replacement image area is too small, first consider shrinking the foreground element you intend to keep from the original image. If the size of the finished image is critical, pick a background that doesn't display a lot of image detail and choose R**e**sample from the **I**mage menu. Resampling an image necessarily destroys some image

detail, so pick a background image of nature, wallpaper patterns, textures, or anything that resists displaying distortion.

- **Avail yourself of stock photography.** Stock photography is a life saver in the image-editing business. Find collections that are thematically in synch with the types of image you work with on a daily basis, and catalog them so that you can retrieve quickly the specific images you need. PhotoCD and regular CD-ROM collections of stock photography are the best sources because they are typically of high quality, and the storage medium keeps dozens of megabytes of stock photography off your hard drive. CorelMOSAIC can make quick work of cataloging your stock images, and it's free when you buy the Corel bundle.

- **Use the Clone tool, but don't overuse it.** The Clone tool is a terrific alternative to copying and pasting objects to restore an image, but there are occasions when you want to stop using the tool and simply replace missing or damaged image areas with color instead. The Clone tool is prone to creating patterns in an image area, and for that reason, you constantly must reset the sampling point to make the best, most invisible, use of the tool.

Sometimes you want repeating patterns in an image; it depends on the effect you're trying to create. But if you're trying to create no effect at all, and only want to repair an image, sample an equivalent color/detail area within an image, and then clone over the area that needs to be replaced. For pinholes, dust, and lint marks that intrude on an image, it's best to sample an equivalent color from around the defect with the Eyedropper tool, and then apply the color to the missing area. The Clone tool is for restoring sizable areas, not pinholes, in an image.

■ **Use the Checkpoint and Restore to Checkpoint commands.** If you've invested more than 15 minutes in your image enhancement, you want to protect your investment. Accidents happen sometimes; however, you can choose Checkpoint from the **E**dit menu after completing a masterstroke within an image to go back to this point if you mess up the image later on. You also can save multiple copies of your work to have the freedom to go back and perform a variation to an effect. Large amounts of free hard drive space and adequate RAM ensure that your work always is backed up while it's in progress.

■ **When in doubt, smear it!** Bitmap images, and the continuous tone images they represent, don't always have clearly defined image details. Photographic images depend on the focal plane and f-stop of the camera and lens, and quite often foreground images are sharp while background areas are lacking in detail and focus. Use the Smear and Blend tools to soften harsh edges in your editing work, and zoom in and out of your work at regular intervals to get a scope on how the entire image looks.

Also, the Feather option on the Layers/Objects roll-up can soften the edge of an object before it's merged to the background. CorelDRAW and similar vector-drawing programs are the only ones that produce clean, sharp edges in all image areas. When you work with bitmap images, use the unique properties of the image format to your advantage, and blur something if it makes it fit better into the rest of the composition.

■ **Editing changes are *progressive* changes to an image.** Unlike vector artwork, bitmap images cannot be restored to their original conditions after you've made several edits. Each change you make to an area pushes color and tonal values farther in a direction. You cannot choose Hue: +50 and then choose Hue −50 and wind up with an image that appears untouched, for example. Whenever you make a change, the next change you make is based on the current state of the image. Edits, therefore, are relative, not absolute ones. For this reason, saving multiple copies of an image at various stages of completion is your best insurance that you can go back and fix something.

Summary

Image enhancement can be thought of as the creative manipulation of pixels within a bitmap image, and the result is as open-ended as your own imagination. This chapter focused on starting with realistic images and

producing realistic-looking images. However, if you need to express a graphical idea that cannot be captured with a camera, one that is a complete product of your imagination, The following chapter is an extension of this chapter; in it, you learn how to create photorealistic art that's simply impossible to photograph.

Chapter 26

Filters

*A*nything in the PC world that translates data is considered a filter. In Chapter 25, "Image Enhancement," you saw how the Brightness and Contrast effect helped bring out visual detail by filtering out tonal areas in an image that muddied the overall picture. Although some of PHOTO-PAINT's Effects filters serve as image enhancers, there is a wide assortment of filters for creative manipulation of images to serve a range of graphics needs.

This chapter is a comprehensive guide to PHOTO-PAINT's Effects commands—what a filter does, situations in which you want to use a filter, the types of filtering you can produce, and user-defined options for each filter. In addition, you see examples of plug-in effect filters, created by third-party manufacturers, that work within PHOTO-PAINT. The open architecture of PHOTO-PAINT is an invitation for software developers to offer unique filters, and it enables designers to use these separate plug-ins without leaving PHOTO-PAINT's design window.

This chapter covers:

- Mapping filters
- Special filters
- Transformation filters
- CorelMOSAIC and filters
- Tone filters
- All other filters
- Third-party plug-in filters

Making Advanced Tonal Corrections

In the last chapter, you adjusted a color image for brightness, contrast, and intensity to make detail within the image more pronounced. In most instances, the grayscale component of color in an image makes up the distinguishing characteristic of the image's detail. It is the tonal (grayscale) information, for example, that makes a portrait of a face recognizable—the skin is basically one hue that is shaded by various amounts of neutral-density or grayscale information.

Because good tonal balance can make or break an image, PHOTO-PAINT offers correction capabilities through Effects filters that are more sophisticated than the Brightness and Contrast setting. You will experience instances in your imaging career when an absolutely unusable image crosses your desk, and by understanding how tones are mapped to a digital image, you can perform some miraculous changes by manipulating the correct PHOTO-PAINT filter.

Histograms

In PHOTO-PAINT, a *histogram*, such as the one shown in figure 26.1, is a visual representation of the tonal regions within an image in the form of a graph. One axis of the graph plots the range of tonal values from 0 (black) to 255 (white), and the other axis displays the number of pixels within the image that fall at each tonal value.

The Effects, Tone, Equalize command in PHOTO-PAINT not only displays a histogram of an image, but offers hands-on control over how an image's pixels are distributed tonally. The Equalize command, like the Brightness and Contrast setting, doesn't affect the color in an image. You can bring out color as you redefine tonal values and enhance visual content within an image, however, by adjusting the number of pixels located at any specific brightness region. In figure 26.1, you can see an image of a stone ornament, PIPER.TIF, that has little visual detail because the "landscape" of pixel tones is crowded around the midrange of brightness values.

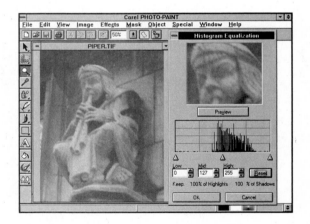

Figure 26.1
Images with little contrast between tonal regions often lack visual detail.

The Histogram Equalization dialog box provides control over remapping the tonal range of images in three regions: the white point, the black point, and the midrange. (The *midrange* is the tonal range in an image that usually holds delicately shaded image detail such as skin tones and the color values of natural textures.) Images with poor contrast, muddiness, or unacceptable visual detail need to have tonal values redistributed to better occupy these distinct ranges. The number of pixels in an original image is a fixed number, and by changing selective values with the Equalize command, you create gaps and peaks that correspond to contrasting areas in the image—hence, more detail.

In the next exercise, you adjust the PIPER.TIF image so that some midrange pixels are remapped to represent the black point and the white point in the image. You will see a vast improvement in the image because, in its present state, the tonal areas that represent highlights and shadows in the image are too close to the midrange. PIPER.TIF is a grayscale image, because the point to be observed here is how to manipulate tonal values without the added distraction of color. The Equalize command works exactly the same whether an image is in black and white or in color—tonal values are a component of every variety of bitmap-format image.

Here's how to use the Equalize command to restore an image with more finesse and precision than the Contrast and Brightness command:

1. Open a copy of the PIPER.TIF image found on the *CorelDRAW! The Professional Reference* companion CDs in the CHAP26 subdirectory, and then save it to your hard drive under the same name.

2. Choose Tone from the Effects menu, and then choose Equalize.

   In its original state, the PIPER image displays most of its total pixels around the midrange; nonetheless, your eyes tell you that clearly there are shadows in this image, and some of the shadow regions should serve as the *black point*—the darkest area within the image.

3. Click-and-drag the **L**ow triangle slider to a point just left of where the frequency of pixels is greatest, so that the new **L**ow value reads about 92 in the entry field. Notice that there are some pixels represented beneath this value. Because you cannot make a pixel vanish from within the image (the number of pixels in an original image is finite), the pixels that fall out of range of the new low (black) point are reassigned other tonal values when you complete your changes.

4. Similarly, you need to set a new white (high) point within the PIPER.TIF image. At present, there is no absolute white in the image, but your eyes tell you that there should be highlights in various areas, and there are only a few pixels above the midrange in the histogram representing highlights. Click-and-drag the **H**igh triangle slider to the left until it is located at the upper end of where most of the pixels are located on the midrange. The new **H**igh value in the text entry field now should be about 218.

   You'll notice that a status line in the Histogram Equalization dialog box tells you the amount of original highlights and shadows that will be retained after you click on OK to approve the edits. On a photo this bad, generally the status line tells you that even the drastic adjustments you've made will result only in a one-percent to two-percent shift in the original highlight and shadow values. This means that a negligible amount of pixels are falling out of the new tonal range and will be reassigned values within the new range.

5. Click on Pre**v**iew to see how the image is shaping up. PHOTO-PAINT updates the preview image if you don't make quick, successive edits. If you cannot see an image area in the Pre**v**iew window that you would like to, place the cursor inside the window and drag the area around until you find the right area. Additionally, left-clicking within the Pre**v**iew window zooms in the preview, and right-clicking zooms out the viewing resolution of the Pre**v**iew window.

6. The **M**id slider controls the brightness of the midrange of the image. You can think of the Mid slider as the equivalent of Gamma adjustment while in the Equalize command. You might need to adjust *gamma*, the contrast in the midrange of images, after specifying a new high and low for an image.

   Midtones are different in every image. As you can see in figure 26.2, a slightly higher midtone range was specified for the PIPER image, because the subject in the image—the stone piper—needs more contrast in the midrange. If this were a photo of an actual person, you might want to leave the midrange value alone; stone carvings look pleasing with a little harsh contrast in the midtone values, while images of people tend to display age lines and wrinkles if they have a high midtone contrast setting.

7. If you have a roll of film that displays consistent lack of good tonal balance, you might want to adjust one image using steps 1 through 6; write down the values in the **L**ow, **M**id, and **H**igh fields; and then enter these values for every picture from that roll of film.

Doing this takes a lot of the guesswork out of tonally correcting a dozen or so images that have the same flaw. Click on OK to confirm your changes, and then click on the Save button on the ribbon bar.

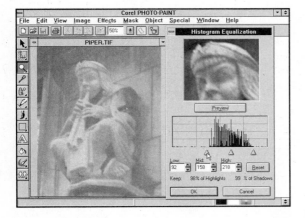

Figure 26.2

Reassign tone values to pixels by using the Equalize command to produce a sharper, crisper image.

N O T E

The values used in this and many of the other Effects dialog boxes were arrived at by trial and error in these examples. Each image is different and requires different settings. Use your eye, the preview box, and Ctrl+Z (**E**dit, **U**ndo) to determine settings that are appropriate for the image you are working on.

As you can see, the Equalize command offers superior handling over tonal mapping of entire images. In the event that only part of an image displays weak image detail, you can use any Mask tool to define an area within an image and perform similar histogram editing on only that portion of the image.

The overall effect created by the Equalize command is one of selectively adding contrast to an image; the Brightness and Contrast command basically compresses a histogram and decreases the number of available brightness levels that pixels in an image can occupy. Still, three controls (**L**ow, **M**id, and **H**igh) for tone adjustments aren't as good as four, and in the next section, you see how further adjustments can be made to create a better image through mapping tones.

The Tone Map

Actually, PHOTO-PAINT's Tone Map does not belong to color filters at all, but more closely relates to the Equalize command in functionality. Earlier, the Histogram Equalization filter was referred to as a "landscape" of the individual brightness levels of pixels in an image. The Tone Map offers more "points of interest" in an image's tonal landscape; between shadows and highlights are *quartertones*—regions at the bottom and top of the midrange in an image. By adjusting the quartertones through the Tone Map, you can give more or less emphasis to shadow detail and to the areas in

an image that are just short of actual high-lights. These two areas often can contain valuable image-detail information. In the next exercise, you learn how to restore the PIPER.TIF image to total, proper tonal balance.

Here's how to adjust the quartertones in an image:

1. Choose Color from the Effe**c**ts menu, and then choose Tone Map.

   Looking ahead to figure 26.3, PHOTO-PAINT's Tone Map displays a range of brightness values between the shadows and highlights, with three points along the curve to shape the flow of the brightness in the midrange of the image. You cannot change the top and bottom end of the response curve; use the Equalize command to respecify shadows and highlights within an image. The default **P**resets setting is Solarized Response Curve. This and the other preset curves are designed so that you can fix specific problems with images and add some fancy enhancements to distort tonal information. Because the PIPER image has been preadjusted to a certain extent, none of the **P**resets offer the subtlety with which you now need to approach the image.

2. Choose Default Response Curve from the **P**resets drop-down list box.

An S-shaped curve commonly is used by imaging professionals to add snap to a dull image. The ideal steepness of the S shape depends on how much the image is in need of filtering. In figure 26.3, you can see in the Pre**v**iew window that a mild S-shape increases the breadth of the upper highlights. You heighten the upper quartertone to diminish the contrast in highlight areas (providing smoother detail areas). Also, by suppressing the curve toward the bottom (shadow) of the midtones, you increase contrast in areas to sharpen the detail.

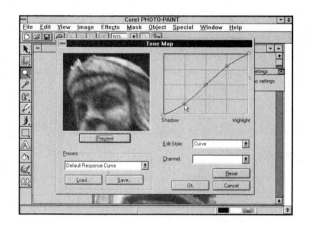

Figure 26.3

A Response curve in the midtones with an S shape helps snap an image up and make details clearer.

3. Click-and-drag the first and third nodes on the response curve to create a gentle S-shaped curve.

4. Click on OK to make the changes and return to the image.

In addition to displaying the Tone Map as a curve, you can use the Edit Style drop-down list to choose other ways to edit the response curve. The Gamma option for Edit Style is extremely useful for isolating only the midpoint in an image's brightness and broadening it or narrowing it to create more or less contrast in an underexposed image of someone's portrait, for example. You probably should not use the Freehand style, however, unless there is a tonal point within your image that you want to eliminate. This almost never happens in photography; "spikes" in a Tone Map can create unusual effects, but for the most part, severe changes in a Tone Map produce unflattering images. For photography in which the subjects are people, gentle curve edits in the Tone Map produce the most eye-pleasing results.

T I P

When working with color images, you have a choice in the Tone Map dialog box whether you want to adjust the RGB **C**hannel or the component Red, Green, and Blue channels. You can change the amount of contrast in a color image by selecting the All (RGB) **C**hannel setting; however, redefining the response curve of a single color channel creates color-casting in an overall image, and does not usually contribute to greater or lesser contrast. When you change the Tone Map of an individual color channel, you are specifying greater or lesser color component. A color image of a cloudy day, for example, is best rearranged tonally by using the All (RGB) **C**hannel setting. By creating an S-shaped curve in only the Blue channel, you lessen the cloudiness of the photo, but you also increase the amount of blue in the overall image to an unrealistic extent.

In figure 26.4, you can see a "before and after" of the PIPER image. Equalizing and creating a heightened response curve in the Tone Map dialog box brought out image detail and made an unusable image suitable for reproduction.

Figure 26.4

Bring out definition and detail in an image by using the Equalize and Tone Map filters.

You should remember that image information not present in the PIPER.TIF file has not been added mysteriously through the use of filters. Filters remove things and change values, but they cannot perform the impossible. The PIPER.TIF image now, in fact, has a lot of information missing when compared to the original image; the viewer doesn't mind the lack of information because the tones that have been kept and respecified now present a more aesthetic image. When you need to present an image with absolute fidelity in portraying a real-life scene, it is best to capture the image with the best lighting conditions and photographic equipment. PHOTO-PAINT can help "fake" good tonal characteristics, but it cannot replace tones that are missing from a poor scan or PhotoCD image.

Improving Sharpness in an Image

Focus and contrast are not identical image qualities, but in the digital world of imaging, filters that sharpen apparent focus often do so by selectively increasing an image's contrast.

With the exception of the Unsharp Mask filter, PHOTO-PAINT's features for sharpening an image essentially work in one of two ways:

- Neighboring pixels of similar or unequal tonal value are assigned more visibly different tonal values.

- Pixel values near the edge of a dark or light region in an image are assigned similarly dark or light tones.

In either case, increased image detail is the perceived result. The following sections contain descriptions of each Sharpen filter's function and the circumstances under which you should choose each filter.

Adaptive Unsharp

The Adaptive Unsharp filter accentuates edge detail only, and does not produce harsh, pixelated edges in the image or defined selection area. The term *unsharp* in this context means the same as *sharp*. Contrast between neighboring pixels is increased to create the Adaptive Unsharp effect.

Directional Sharpen

The Directional Sharpen filter creates a sharpening effect even more subtle than Adaptive Unsharp, and again it works best with a lot of image information (more than 100 pixels/inch; RGB images benefit most from Directional Sharpen). When you use Directional Sharpen on an image or image area, PHOTO-PAINT "looks" at the color values within the image to see in which direction (horizontal or vertical) sharpening needs to be applied most. Directional Sharpen does for image focus what Polaroid sunglasses do for glare; both directionally filter visual information. Don't be misled by the connotation of *directional*; no streaking or unwanted effects are produced by the filter. Generally, a value of less than 50-percent Directional Sharpen can improve an image without displaying obvious zones of harsh contrast.

Edge Enhance

Edge Enhance is a powerful filter that produces the most noticeable changes to an image. PHOTO-PAINT evaluates areas in an image based on color or tonal differences and accentuates them by creating contrast in those areas of color change. A negative side effect of Edge Enhance is the creation of unwanted dark or light pixels in isolated areas, when a percentage of greater than 50 is specified. Depending on your point of view, the effect of unwanted pixels is similar to either increasing the photographic grain of the image, or to the presence of lint or dust on a print. The best use of this filter is within images that clearly display different color and tonal areas, but whose focus (image detail) is weak.

Sharpen

The Sharpen filter simply adds contrast to the image to "fake" detail. Pixels of similar tonal and color value are reassigned much different values. The Sharpen filter is used best on an image that will be used at small dimensions in a publication. The unfortunate side effect of a large percentage of the Sharpen filter is in the creation of black and white pixels randomly dispersed over an image, creating an effect of grainy, high-speed photographic film.

Unsharp Mask

This Unsharp Mask filter creates a second image from the original, blurs zones of contrast, and then subtracts the values found in the copy from the original. This process helps preserve tonal integrity without displaying pixelation, while reinforcing light and dark isolated areas you perceive as image detail. The higher the resolution of the image and the greater the color capability, the more Unsharp Mask can assist in bringing out image detail gently and with a sensitivity toward the shortcomings of digital imaging.

Values for Sharpen Filters

The most typical result of specifying a high percentage when using Sharpen filters is the display of random pixels of extremely light or dark tonal value. This result is unavoidable because, as intelligently as applications can remap tonal regions, there is a random distribution of film grain in photographic images, and pixels too far from the "norm" in a tonal landscape are singled out in the sharpening process.

The next exercise shows the use of the Edge Enhance filter on the PIPER image after tone mapping and equalizing have been performed. Edge Enhance is the filter of choice because it moves pixels of similar values toward areas where PHOTO-PAINT detects

an edge. At a high percentage of Edge Enhance, pixels representing enhanced film grain also will be visible (and unwanted). The subject in the photo is a stone building ornament, however, and viewers of this image tend to accept "grit" in this kind of image as being part of the sandstone texture more readily than they would accept poor image focus. Always consider the content of the image you're sharpening to better choose a filter uniquely suited for the task.

Here's how to add apparent detail to the PIPER image by using the Edge Enhance Sharpen filter:

1. Choose Sharpen from the Effe**c**ts menu, and then choose Edge Enhance. The Edge Enhance dialog box appears.

2. Left-click on the Pre**v**iew window to zoom into the PIPER image, and scroll in the box to view some geometric areas within the image that need more defining. Leave yourself a view of some of the solid image areas, because the Edge Enhance will have some visible effect on areas that appear to be smooth.

3. Type **68** in the **P**ercentage field to begin with (see fig. 26.5). You've made tone map and equalize changes to the image so far, and all edits to bitmap images are relative changes. If the values you used with the first two filters were even slightly different than the ones outlined in this chapter, the filter setting for Edge Enhance of 68

might not be the best. Click on the Pre**v**iew button, and then change the **P**ercentage value by 3 or 4 to see whether you have a good balance between visible sharpening of the image and unwanted pixelation in the smooth image areas.

Figure 26.5

*Choose a **P**ercentage value for Edge Enhance that is a balance between good focus and an unwanted pixelation effect.*

4. Click on OK to apply the changes, and then click on the Save button on the ribbon bar.

For every filter in PHOTO-PAINT, there is a filter that will produce an opposite effect. Image sharpening doesn't necessarily have to produce sharp, pixelated images, and the next section discusses your filter options after an image has been mapped and enhanced tonally.

Dealing with Image Noise

Image noise is the 1990s euphemism for static when applied to the video medium. Random pixels of tone or color can appear at the scanning phase of imaging, or can be the result of using too much of a particular effect such as the Sharpen filter.

PHOTO-PAINT has the capability to both reduce and increase image noise. There will be instances in your own assignments when a "squeaky clean" image needs a little grit; at other times, the selective noise-reduction features of PHOTO-PAINT can rescue an image that is unusable in its present state. This section lists PHOTO-PAINT's Noise filters found on the Effects menu, what they do, and when you should use them.

Add Noise

The Add Noise filter has three options for applying a random pattern overlay to an image. With color images, pixels chosen at random from the color model of the image are dispersed; grayscale images display noise only from 0 to 255 brightness levels. You can use these three options:

- **Gaussian.** Creates a hard-grain effect within the image. At a high-**L**evel percentage, color images become unrecognizable, but when applied to selection areas, you can simulate textures.

- **Spike.** Creates exactly the effect you usually want to remove from images— that of lint and dust. This option is useful for creating effects on color images of low resolution (72 pixels/ inch and less).

- **Uniform.** Creates a pleasing effect when applied to grayscale images. In figure 26.6, you can see the effects of Gaussian noise and Uniform noise. Image quality naturally takes a nose-dive when you add noise to a picture. If you're looking for an effect, how-ever, noise definitely can liven up a flat photo, and "noisy" images print well when they are output to lower-resolution laser printers.

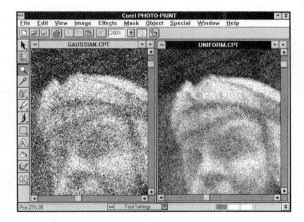

Figure 26.6
Gaussian noise (left) and Uniform noise (right) added to the same image.

Maximum Noise

The Maximum Noise command is a smoothing filter that reduces the number of unique colors in an image. Maximum Noise does not reduce color equally across values, but instead removes more lighter values than darker values. If you have a coarse, dark image, the Maximum Noise command can help restore it.

Minimum Noise

Minimum Noise is the opposite of Maximum Noise; take a grainy, overexposed image and pass it through the Minimum Noise filter to make an image more usable.

Median Noise

The Median Noise command turns hard-edged clumps of pixelated image areas into soft clumps of tone and color. The Median Noise command, like Minimum and Maximum, destroys focus in an image by softening the hard edges of video noise.

Remove Noise

Remove Noise is the most sophisticated and processor-intensive of the noise-reduction filters, but it also provides the most eye-pleasing results on scanned images where speckling is evident from lint or dust. The Remove Noise command also is useful in softening an image that has been through a Sharpen filter with too high a percentage

specified. Remove Noise compares any given image pixel to those surrounding it and then performs an averaging process to create more similarity in tonal values between pixels. This filter depends on tonal, rather than color, variations. You can specify the relative brightness values you want included in PHOTO-PAINT's comparisons by clicking-and-dragging the Levels slider to any value from 0 to 255 in the Remove Noise command.

Figure 26.7 shows the PIPER image after being sharpened excessively (on the left) and the result of the Remove Noise command on the same image (on the right). You lose image detail (focus) with the noise-reduction filters, but sometimes you must decide whether loss of sharpness is preferred to that of an image displaying pixels the size of golf balls.

Figure 26.7
The Remove Noise command softens the difference between tonal values in pixels.

Using Soften Filters

The Soften filters in PHOTO-PAINT basically correspond to the inverse functions of the Sharpen filters. Instead of heightening tonal and color differences between neighboring pixels, differences are averaged and loss of image sharpness creates soft blends of color and tone values. Note that sharpening, softening, and noise filters work best with images of high color capabilities—usually of grayscale and RGB mode.

You always should turn to at least 8 bit/pixel and higher color modes because PHOTO-PAINT requires a large color space in which to performs all the "in-between" averaging of pixel values. An image with 100,000 unique colors stored in a mode capable of displaying 16.7 million colors easily can expand to 200,000 unique colors after a Soften filter averages values. Color values are added and eliminated when you filter an image, and the image mode must be able to handle these changes.

Imagine pouring a 16-ounce beverage into a 12-ounce glass; something will be lost. You perform a similar act when filtering an image to produce extra values while the image mode is eight, four, or less bits per pixel.

PHOTO-PAINT offers four categories of softening filters: Diffuse, Directional, Smooth, and Soften. These filters are described in the following section.

Diffuse

The Diffuse filter provides a "ground glass" look. When a high-Level value for the effect is set, a look similar to the pebbled glass found in fancy hotel-room showers is produced. You determine how many shades of image brightness are affected (from 0 to 255) with the Levels slider. Colors are scattered, and the Diffuse filter can produce a pleasing, abstract image from a boring image.

Directional Smooth

When you apply the Directional Smooth filter, PHOTO-PAINT performs comparisons on the vertical and horizontal arrangement of pixels and performs averaging of tonal values along the axis that is coarser. Directional smoothing can help eliminate (or tone down) photos that have streaks in them from careless photo-finishing or a particle that was lodged in the film canister when you rewound a roll.

Smooth and Soften

The distinction between Smooth and Soften is lost on most users, except those who watch a lot of dishwashing-detergent commercials. Basically, the Smooth filter clips the overall tonal range of an image selection, eliminating harsh values of absolute black and white, and reassigns the clipped tonal values more moderate ones within the image. The effect is that of smoother areas of tonal transitions, and not much image detail is lost, although

Smooth can throw off focus when a high value is specified. Soften creates a less-harsh transition between shadows and brighter areas. Soften produces an effect similar to Smooth, except that no image detail is lost— hence, focus usually is unaffected.

All the Soften filters are good for producing stylized artwork from photographic images. Additionally, you can use the Soften filter to make artwork produced in PHOTO-PAINT a little less harsh and to reduce greatly the stairstep edges commonly associated with bitmap graphics.

Using Special Filters

Grouped under the category of Special in the Effects menu is a collection of creative, novelty filters that can produce images that are reminiscent of the 1960s or those of cutting-edge, stylized graphics. The Posterize command is of particular interest, because you can use it with a combination of techniques covered in earlier chapters to produce a silk-screen effect.

The filters found in the Special dialog box are Contour, Posterize, Psychedelic, Solarize, and Threshold. These filters, along with suggested applications and the effects that can be produced on an image or selected image area, are explained in this section.

Contour

By using the Contour filter, you can specify the tonal brightness values used to produce outlines around edges PHOTO-PAINT finds in an image. This filter is used best with color RGB images of high resolution. You can select the light and dark areas to which the contour is applied, but you have no control over the thickness of the contour lines or the color used for contouring.

Psychedelic

You probably will use the Psychedelic filter all of one time in your imaging profession. It's a nostalgic re-creation of 1960s blacklight posters and Richard Avadon's work with the Beatles, but the filter fails to produce effects you have control over. You can set the Psychedelic filter from 0 to 255 to affect various brightness areas within an image and to replace colors with brilliant, neon shades such as fuchsia, cyan, and other pure colors usually found on a tie-dyed garment.

Solarize

The Solarize filter is useful for creating partially reversed chroma in color images and inverted grayscale values in grayscale pictures. You can use a **L**evel setting of 255 to turn an entire image into a photographic negative. You can get this same effect by choosing Fancy from the Effe**c**ts menu, and then choosing Invert. Use the Solarize filter on scenes of nature such as flowers and autumn foliage to create interesting, stylized images.

Threshold

The Threshold filter enables users to set an artificial "fall off" in light within an image. Image areas beneath the **L**evel setting you define turn to black in both color and monochrome images. The Threshold filter is useful for "cleaning up" mottled image areas. You can make a dull picture crisp by replacing darker areas with a uniform shade of black.

Posterize

The Posterize filter is perhaps the command in PHOTO-PAINT's Special list that holds the greatest amount of creative possibilities for the imaging professional. The Posterize filter reduces the number of colors in an image, the number of color levels is user-controlled, and the method of color reduction is hard-edged with no dithering patterns evident. At higher levels, color and monochrome images display very little of the Posterize filter effect, but when you limit a picture that contains a great deal of tonal variation to less than 10 levels, the effect becomes apparent.

In the next section, you see how the Posterize filter can help set up the PIPER image for further, hands-on refinement (using PHOTO-PAINT tools covered in earlier chapters) in the creation of an authentic-looking silk-screen pattern.

Silk Screens from Posterized Images

The Posterize filter's unique capability to segment tonal image areas and assign them a flat color value offers several commercial possibilities. Besides presenting a stylized appearance, a posterized image takes the dullest, softest image and creates crisp color fields within it. Additionally, standard 300-dpi laser printers are incapable of printing true grayscale halftone images. Because laser-printed image resolution is inversely proportional to the number of digital halftone values that can be expressed, rendering more than 60 or so values at a decent 85 lines per inch is mathematically impossible. However, a posterized image falls well within the reproducing capabilities of a 300-dpi laser printer.

In figure 26.8, you can see the Preview window of the Posterize dialog box displaying six levels of posterization for the PIPER image. The image displays poor focus and uneven gradations of tone, but it becomes sharper and more of a graphic when edges are defined by a limited palette of unique shades. Image information definitely is lost; however, the geometry and composition of the image become more appealing by filtering out the elements, like shading, that don't work well in the original image.

Figure 26.8

The Posterize filter can create sharply defined edges in an image in which tonal variations are not pronounced.

In the following example, you create a color-posterized image from a grayscale original. Begin by converting the grayscale image to RGB Color (24-bit) by choosing Convert To from the Image menu. Save the NEW-1.CPT image to your hard drive as PIPER2.TIF.

To prepare for the next exercise, choose Special from the Effects menu, and then choose Posterize to create a PIPER2 image that has six levels of posterization.

Here's how to create a "silk-screen" print from a posterized image that contains no original color:

1. After you posterize a copy of the PIPER image to six different grayscale values, press Ctrl+F5 (or choose Color Mask Roll-Up from the Mask menu).

2. Sample each of the six posterized values. First, click on the Reset button in the Color Mask roll-up. This action clears color mask values you might have defined in another PHOTO-PAINT session.

3. Choose Modify Selected Colors from the drop-down list at the top of the Color Mask roll-up. You do not need to change the plus/minus tolerance of the selected values from the default value of 10 in this exercise. Posterized values are those of flat colors with no color and tone variation, so a latitude (tolerance) or color variation is not required to accurately select all the posterized areas.

4. Click on a color button, and then click the Eyedropper tool over a shade in the PIPER2 image. This action samples the shade.

5. Repeat step 4 for each posterized shade, clicking on a different button before you sample a shade, as shown in figure 26.9. You can preview the areas sampled by clicking on the On check box next to the color button, and then clicking on the Preview Mask button on the Color Mask roll-up. The Preview mask in an RGB image is a color tint (the same shade as your currently defined Transparency mask) above image areas that are to be included in the Color mask selection. To remove the Tint Preview mask, click anywhere inside the active image window.

Figure 26.9

Click with the Eyedropper tool on the image values one at a time to assign them to different color buttons on the Color Mask roll-up.

6. Double-click on the paint color swatch (the far left swatch) on the status line to display the Color roll-up (or choose Color Roll-Up from the **V**iew menu or press Ctrl+F2).

7. Click on the Paper (background) color swatch on the Color roll-up, and choose white. Click on the fly-out menu button (directly beneath the Color Model drop-down list that currently should display RGB), and choose Clear Paint Area. The square next to the color palette turns the background white, and you now have an area to define colors you will use to make the PIPER2 image silk-screen design.

8. Think of a color scheme for the design. Each color you choose to replace a grayscale value in the PIPER2 image should be of equivalent brightness. This example was designed with a "sepiatone" theme. Sample different colors from the color palette or use the RGB color model at the bottom of the Color roll-up to select a color, click on the Edit button in the Color roll-up (the paintbrush icon next to the paint area), and then brush a dot or two on the white paint area.

T I P

The HSB color model is a lot easier to work with than the RGB. If you would like to quickly specify color within the range of RGB values, you can click on the drop-down button above the color palette and choose HSB.

If you have a hard time getting the color you want from the RGB model, but still intend to use it for color definition, try clicking on an area of color you want (instead of clicking-and-dragging the wireframe cube in different directions), and then adjust the brightness on the slider to the right of the color model.

9. When you have the colors you want to use available as samples on the paint area, click on the background (paper) color swatch in the Color roll-up and choose the darkest color on the paint area with the Pick button (the

eyedropper next to the Edit button). After you have your colors chosen, you don't need the color model (the color wireframe) extension on the Color roll-up on-screen. This portion of the roll-up retracts by clicking on the triangle to the left of the Edit button.

10. On the Color Mask roll-up, click the On check box next to the shade you want to replace in the PIPER2 image, then click on the To Mask button. The chosen color area in the PIPER2 image becomes a regular mask marquee. Now, click on the Masking Tool button on the toolbox, so the ribbon bar offers menu commands that are relevant to mask marquees. Unlike a Color mask, a Marquee mask defines an area that can be deleted to the current paper color.

11. Press the Delete key, and then click on the Remove Mask button, shown in figure 26.10. The selected color area within the image has been replaced with the paper color you defined in step 10, and the Remove Mask button (which performs the same thing as the **M**ask, **R**emove command) removes the marquee around the area you've modified.

12. You don't need to uncheck the color button you used last in order to move on to replacing the next color value, because this color value no longer exists within the PIPER2.TIF image. Choose

a new Paper (background) color on the Color roll-up, click on the next color button on the Color Mask roll-up, click on the To Mask button, press Delete, and then click on the Remove Mask button on the ribbon bar.

Figure 26.10

Specify a background (paper) color, then delete the area you want to fill with the color.

13. Repeat steps 9 through 12 for the other shades in the image. When you're done, you've completed a colorizing process that would have taken hours, if not days, if performed manually. You now have the techniques at your disposal for creating stirring color images from a very humble original black-and-white snapshot. In figure 26.11, the colorizing of a grayscale image has been completed. Unfortunately, the Color Mask roll-up cannot

convert figure 26.11 from grayscale to color, but if you've followed the steps, you'll see a remarkable difference in PHOTO-PAINT running on your PC!

Figure 26.11
Color masks that have been converted to regular masks can be deleted, exposing background paper color.

In a chapter on filters, the CorelMOSAIC module shouldn't be overlooked. MOSAIC is a cataloging utility that recognizes 8,000 image formats; you can use it to bring bitmap images to PHOTO-PAINT's design window. You also can use MOSAIC to display CorelDRAW CDR and CMX images that are converted to a usable bitmap format when you drag-and-drop their thumbnails into PHOTO-PAINT. In the next section, you see how you can use PHOTO-PAINT's amazing Transformation filters on anything you design in CorelDRAW.

Creating a Photo-Illustration Using Filters

CorelDRAW's feature and tool set admittedly is a little easier to use than PHOTO-PAINT's. Vector designs are clean and crisp in their execution, and you don't stand much of a chance of "coloring outside the lines," as even experienced bitmap-imaging professionals do on occasion. Because of CorelDRAW's close links to its sister modules, you can bring a chart object into CorelSHOW, and you can design an Actor for CorelMOVE in CorelDRAW. Perhaps the most intriguing aspect of this cross-application compatibility, however, is the capability to import a CorelDRAW design into PHOTO-PAINT as a bitmap image and to apply filters and other enhancements to it to create a stellar design. The bridge between Corel applications is CorelMOSAIC, and this section explains how to use DRAW and PHOTO-PAINT to make an original design.

Dragging a Drawing into PHOTO-PAINT

The components in this next example consist of a photograph of clouds and a drawing of the Earth's continents. The concept is to create an image from a drawing of the Earth and then float the Earth between the photographed clouds. The MAP.CDR file on the *CorelDRAW! The Professional Reference*

companion CDs shows a careful rearrangement of the continents' positions as you normally would find them on a flat projection of the Earth; the Eastern and Western continents practically squeeze out the Atlantic Ocean... for a good reason.

The Map to Sphere filter in PHOTO-PAINT, as the name broadly implies, takes a flat projection, such as the MAP.CDR image, and creates a hemisphere from it. With PHOTO-PAINT's fractal texture fills and the use of objects and masks, you can create an image that would be tedious and imprecise using the features of CorelDRAW or PHOTO-PAINT alone.

The next example is task-oriented; filters play a heavy part in the creation of the design, but more emphasis is placed on integrating the techniques and tools covered in previous chapters. Here's how to spec a CorelDRAW design and import it for use as a bitmap in PHOTO-PAINT:

1. In PHOTO-PAINT, first close any open image windows, because MOSAIC's drag-and-drop capability creates objects on top of other images, not separate files, if an image window is active in the design window.

2. Click on the CorelMOSAIC button on the ribbon bar. CorelMOSAIC immediately begins updating graphical image files from the last-accessed hard drive location, which is usually WINDOWS.

3. Click on the Open File button at the upper right of MOSAIC, choose your CD-ROM drive, and then pick the CHAP26 subdirectory of the *CorelDRAW! The Professional Reference* companion CD that contains the chapter samples. Click on a file in this subdirectory to start MOSAIC's cataloging routine, then click on OK to exit the dialog box.

4. MOSAIC displays a low-resolution thumbnail of every graphical-type file in a specified path; even different graphics types can be cataloged in a single directory. Scroll down MOSAIC's window until you see MAP.CDR, and then click-and-drag the image onto the design window. Your cursor becomes an arrow with a tiny plus sign to its right. This signifies that the action you want MOSAIC to perform is to move the selected image to the design window.

5. In order to import a vector design into a bitmap-editing program, PHOTO-PAINT has to convert image formats, and requires input about the size and resolution of the image (because vector images are resolution-independent). Specify 16 Million colors in the **C**olors field, accept the 1-to-1 default size, specify 150 pixels/inch in the **R**esolution field, and then click on OK. The image of the sky that a selection area of the MAP.CDR image is composited into later has an image resolution that

corresponds to the size of the MAP image. Always measure two images for matching resolution and dimensions before beginning a complex assignment. See Chapter 21, "Essential Concepts of Pixel-Based Graphics," for detailed information on image resolution.

6. As you can see in figure 26.12, with the file specifications entered, PHOTO-PAINT completes the click-and-drag motion you made from MOSAIC moments before, and you now have an RGB copy of the MAP.CDR image as NEW-1.CPT in the design window. Save the image as MAP.CPT to your hard drive.

Figure 26.12
Even vector images such as CorelDRAWings can be imported into PHOTO-PAINT via MOSAIC.

W A R N I N G

CorelMOSAIC's function as a visual guide to images stored in a directory is only part of its power.

The thumbnail icons you see in MOSAIC's workspace are linked to the actual files they represent. Because the *CorelDRAW! The Professional Reference* companion CDs are a read-only medium, MOSAIC is directed to open a copy of an image you click on from the CDs' directories. Similarly, a vector image format such as CDR or CMX needs to be converted by PHOTO-PAINT to bitmap format; you also create a copy of the original file when you drag-and-drop a CDR or EPS image.

However, TIF, TGA, PCX, and all other members of the bitmap-graphics format are recognized by PHOTO-PAINT to have native support for the editing tools that PHOTO-PAINT features. Therefore, unless a bitmap-format image on your hard drive is read-only, you are indeed calling the original image when you drag-and-drop from MOSAIC to PHOTO-PAINT; you are *not* experimenting with a copy! An alternative way to make a copy of an image displayed in MOSAIC is to drag-and-drop an image file onto an existing open window, where the copy of the selected image or graphic becomes a floating object within the open image window.

The images on the CDs are safe to experiment with, but you *can* accidentally ruin an original image dragged in from your hard drive if you think that you're playing with a copy.

Using MOSAIC and Dynamic Links

As you've seen, CorelMOSAIC is not limited to drag-and-drop support of bitmap-type images in PHOTO-PAINT. MOSAIC is a near-universal cataloger of computer graphics, and it hooks into the Corel application from which you're calling it for import support. You even can access Corel's clip-art collection from the Corel CD-ROM from within PHOTO-PAINT. The clip-art collection is in the Presentation Exchange CMX format, virtually identical to DRAW's native CDR, except the information that dynamically links CorelDRAW's Blend and Contour objects has been broken.

The copy of the MAP image that was imported and converted with CorelMOSAIC is a bitmap and can be edited and filtered by using PHOTO-PAINT's tools. The only problem you might run into when using MOSAIC to import vector drawings is if you accidentally double-click on a MOSAIC image-file icon before clicking-and-dragging it into the design window. Images in CDR and CMX formats are registered in the OLE2 facility of Windows as belonging to the application in which they were created. This means that until the importation of a CDR file to CPT or other bitmap format is complete, the files are OLE objects, and double-clicking on them in the MOSAIC window launches CorelDRAW. At most, this "feature" will slow down your work, and

you'll have to close a session of CorelDRAW before continuing your work in PHOTO-PAINT. If your Windows resources are low, however, you will not have to close only CorelDRAW—your system will hang on an incompletely executed OLE link, and you'll have to restart your machine.

Make your selections from MOSAIC in one definitive click-and-drag motion.

Mapping Filters

Generally, when you create a bitmap image, you are mapping values to an invisible linear grid that holds color pixels forming a recognizable image. PHOTO-PAINT's Mapping filters, however, reorganize pixels arranged in rows to create nonlinear arrangements that can represent whirlpools, cylinders, and waves.

Map to Sphere

You use the Map to Sphere filter in the next exercise to map the flat bitmap image of the Earth to an imaginary pixel grid shaped like a hemisphere. The Map to Sphere filter analyzes an image (or a selection area), and distorts pixel information around a hemisphere, or a vertical or horizontal cylinder. When you choose **H**orizontal Cylinder or V**e**rtical Cylinder as the option in the Map to Sphere dialog box, distortion is performed along only one of the two axes found in the original image.

The Map to Sphere filter distortion multiplies the pixel information in the center of the selection to suggest that the center is closer to the viewer; the filter decreases the number of pixels that contain original image information toward the edge of a selection, suggesting that image areas are close to the horizon of the sphere. Because the filter emphasizes the center of the selection, the MAP.CDR file was built with continents closer to each other than you normally would find on a map. You see shortly why the continents were rearranged in the MAP.CDR file to compensate for the Map to Sphere's wide-angle view of selected image areas.

The best way to demonstrate the powers and usefulness of the Map to Sphere filter is by way of example as you continue to build this section's graphic. Here's how to use the Map to Sphere filter on a selection area of the MAP.CPT image:

1. Click-and-hold on the Mask tool to display the fly-out menu, then click on the Ellipse Mask tool.

2. Click-and-drag while pressing Ctrl to create a selection above the Western hemisphere like the one shown in figure 26.13. Readers in Europe might want to perform the same moves, except clicking-and-dragging over the Eastern hemisphere. In any event, because a viewer can see only half of the world at a time on a three-dimensional globe, you shouldn't try to include all the continents found in the

MAP.CPT image in the elliptical selection. Additionally, if you're unhappy with your present selection, click-and-hold on the Ellipse Mask tool, choose the Mask Picker tool, and click-and-drag the selection to reposition the mask marquee.

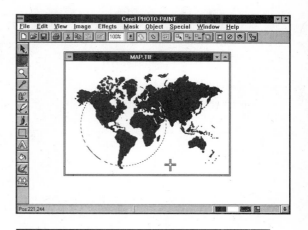

Figure 26.13
Pressing Ctrl constrains the ellipse mask to a perfect circle.

3. Choose Mapping from the Effects menu, and then choose Map to Sphere.

4. Click on the **S**pherical radio button, type **29** in the **P**ercentage field (a number chosen through trial-and-error experimentation), and then click on the Pre**v**iew button, as shown in figure 26.14. High **P**ercentage values tend to distort selections into an unrecognizable state; the Map to Sphere filter is a concentrated one, and a little of it goes a long way.

Figure 26.14
A low percentage setting in the Map to Sphere dialog box creates a noticeable effect on a selection area.

5. Click on OK. Then choose **S**ave from the **M**ask menu and name the saved mask MAP_MASK.CPT. Choose a directory that's easy to find later. In the next set of steps, you apply a Color mask to the Ellipse mask; by saving the ellipse selection, you easily can recall the mask in case you accidentally deselect it.

In the following figures, the continents that fall outside the ellipse selection have been removed so that you can clearly see the effects that will be applied to the ellipse selection. You also can remove the continents by choosing **I**nvert from the **M**ask menu, and then double-clicking on the Replace Color tool on the Erase tool's fly-out menu. The

selection marquee must be active while you perform this procedure to avoid erasing the entire MAP.CPT image. After erasing everything outside the mask, you can choose **L**oad from the **M**ask menu to restore the mask around the globe; or choose **I**nvert from the **M**ask menu once more to restore the mask to make changes available to only the area within the ellipse shape.

Using the Color Mask on the Globe

The spherized portion of the map looks dimensional now, but it lacks the shading and texture you would expect on Earth, and this is where the chapter departs for a moment from explorations of PHOTO-PAINT's filters. The map areas within the mask selection consist of black and white areas. You can use the Color Mask roll-up to isolate the black and white areas, while ignoring the white areas outside the ellipse marquee. This is an important quality to remember in your assignments: Color masks can protect or expose the areas inside a Regular mask. You use this mask-within-a-mask property to select only the continent regions within the image and apply a Texture fill. Then you select the ocean areas and add a fill that suggests the oceans.

Here's how to color the dimensional globe so that it is a more realistic compositional element:

1. Make sure that the Ellipse mask you defined earlier is active. Regular masks display a marquee, so if you have

deselected the Ellipse mask, choose **L**oad from the **M**ask menu and select the mask file you saved earlier.

2. Press Ctrl+F5 (or choose Color **M**ask Roll-Up from the **M**ask menu) if the Color Mask roll-up isn't in the design window.

3. Click on Reset in the Color Mask roll-up. Then click on the first color button and click the cursor (which turns into an eyedropper when over an image window) on a black area of the MAP.CPT image.

4. Click the On check box next to the first color button, and make sure that Modify Selected Colors is the mode in the drop-down list toward the top of the Color Mask roll-up. Then click on the Apply button. Now only the black areas of the MAP.CPT image within the Ellipse mask are available for modifying.

5. Double-click on the far right color swatch on the status line (or choose F**i**ll Roll-Up from the **V**iew menu, or press Shift+F6). Then double-click on the Rectangle tool (directly beneath the Brush tools on the toolbox). Double-clicking on the Rectangle tool selects it and displays the Tool Settings roll-up.

6. On the Tool Settings roll-up, set Size (of the outline) to 0. You then can click on the roll-up button to the right of its title bar to conserve screen space, but you will need to use it again in the following steps, so don't close it yet.

7. Select the Texture Fill button in the Fill roll-up. You have a wide selection of textures with which to fill the black continent areas; Mineral.Cloudy 3 Colors is used in the Styles collection in this exercise. You might want to click on the Collections and Texture Fills drop-down list buttons in the Fill roll-up to make a texture selection of your own. After you have a collection specified in the upper drop-down list, click on the image in the Pre**v**iew window to display a thumbnail collection for any selection. Then click on a thumbnail image you like, and click on OK to make your selection the active fill.

8. With the Rectangle tool, click-and-drag a marquee that encompasses the entire globe selection area. PHOTO-PAINT takes a moment to process the command; Fractal Texture fills have to be rasterized to file and on-screen, and the time it takes PHOTO-PAINT to calculate is proportional to the image dimensions you specify. As you can see in figure 26.15, the black areas within the image now look a lot more like continents.

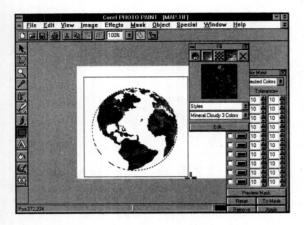

Figure 26.15

Use the Rectangle tool to quickly fill a defined area with color or texture.

9. Click on the Remove button in the Color Mask roll-up to remove the selection area within the Ellipse mask. Uncheck the On check box next to the first button, and then click on the second color button and sample a white area in the MAP.CPT image. Click the On check box next to the second button, and click on the Apply button. Regardless of whether you clicked on a white color sample inside or outside the Ellipse mask, only areas inside the Ellipse mask marquee that are white are now available for editing; in short, you can fill the oceans now.

10. Click on the Fountain Fill button in the Fill roll-up, and then click on the Radial Fill button. Select a medium blue from the drop-down color palette for the first color, and select white as the second color. Click-and-drag in the Fill roll-up's Preview window to move the white area of the Fountain fill to the upper right.

11. With the Rectangle tool, click-and-drag a marquee so that it surrounds the Ellipse mask. As you can see in figure 26.16, you've transformed the dimensional globe into an image selection that now has texture and lighting—two other valuable qualities in creating photorealistic illustrations.

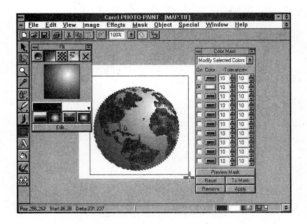

Figure 26.16

Use the Color Mask roll-up with Texture and Fountain fills to add realism to selection areas.

Although you can use the Radial fill to simulate highlights on rounded surfaces, the highlights might not be as pronounced as you would like them in certain cases where transitional (foreground/background) colors are similar. To create more of a visible highlight, click on the Edit button in the Fill roll-up, and increase the **E**dge Pad setting in the Fountain Fill dialog box.

To finish the design, you place the globe selection in a different image as an object and arrange foreground objects to give the dimensional image area some depth.

Combining Illustration and Photography

The globe image needs a background to support it compositionally, and the possibilities are endless if you have a good cache of stock-photography images available. The next set of steps uses a PhotoCD made by a photofinisher from images taken of clouds. You use the IMG00001.TIF image for this exercise, but copying the image is a little different when it's on PhotoCD.

You can use MOSAIC to copy PhotoCD images to a new image window (as discussed in Chapters 21, "Essential Concepts of Pixel-Based Graphics," and 25, "Image Enhancement"), but the importing process involves

specifying the image resolution because PCD images exist on PhotoCD as multiple-resolution files. This step is missing from the following exercise because the IMG00001.TIF file has been copied and saved to a non-PhotoCD format. Whether you access images from a PhotoCD or any other media, MOSAIC can provide you with a quick visual reference of the images in a specified path. Copying an image from read-only media is as easy as drag-and-drop when you use MOSAIC.

Here's how to create a background for the globe that consists of multiple objects built from a single image file:

1. Click on the Save button on the ribbon bar (or choose **S**ave from the **F**ile menu or press Ctrl+S to save the MAP.CPT image. With the Ellipse mask marquee still active, choose **C**opy from the **E**dit menu (or press Ctrl+C, or click on the Copy button on the ribbon bar). Close the MAP.CPT image by double-clicking on the control menu button (or choose **C**lose from the **F**ile menu).

2. Click on the MOSAIC button on the ribbon bar. MOSAIC remembers the last path you selected, which is the CHAP26 subdirectory on the *CorelDRAW! The Professional Reference* companion CDs (you last used it to copy the MAP.CDR image).

3. Scroll down the MOSAIC window until you see the IMG00001.TIF thumbnail, and then click-and-drag the thumbnail to the design window, as shown in figure 26.17.

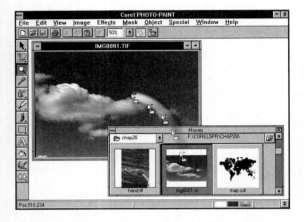

Figure 26.17
You can use CorelMOSAIC to drag copies of read-only images to PHOTO-PAINT's design window.

4. Double-click on the Object tool to display the Layers/Objects roll-up shown in figure 26.18 (or press Ctrl+F7, or choose Layers/Objects Roll-Up from the **O**bject menu).

5. Choose the Object Brush tool from the Object Tool fly-out menu, and select a custom brush shape from the Tool Settings roll-up. You want a soft, medium-sized tip, like the one shown in figure 26.18, so that you can paint

an object marquee around one or two cloud areas. Precision is not critical here, and it's okay if you select some of the blue sky along with cloud areas. Any blue sky areas disappear when the cloud objects are merged to the globe selection, because the globe features a lot of darker blue ocean areas.

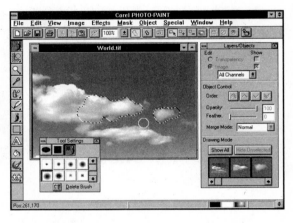

Figure 26.18
Every new area you select with the Brush Mask tool becomes an independent object—a copy of the original image area.

6. Click on the Paste button on the ribbon bar. This action pastes in the sphere you created and copied to the Clipboard from MAP.CPT. The Paste button on the ribbon bar performs the same action as choosing **P**aste from the **E**dit menu and choosing As New

Object. If you ever want to create a new document from the contents of the Clipboard, you should use the menu; in situations where you want to paste a new object, the ribbon bar performs the command in a single click.

7. The order of the objects in the IMG00001.TIF image is determined by the order in which you created them; the globe object currently is on top of the cloud selections because it was added most recently. With the globe object still selected, click on the down arrow on the Layers/Objects roll-up once or twice to move the globe beneath the cloud objects.

8. Position the globe so the clouds slightly obscure the view of the globe. Click on the Marquee Visible button on the ribbon bar to remove the marquee border if it hinders your positioning work with the clouds. Press Ctrl+G or choose **M**erge from the **O**bject menu to merge the globe to the IMG0001.TIF image.

9. Select the cloud objects one at a time, and assign them values of Opacity: 90 and Feathering: 5 (you can type the values in the fields or use the sliders on the Layers/Objects roll-up). As you can see in figure 26.19, the clouds composite beautifully (and seamlessly) over the globe image area.

Figure 26.19

Use the Opacity and Feathering sliders to specify how an object is merged into the background image.

10. Select the clouds one at a time, and then press Ctrl+G (or choose **M**erge from the **O**bject menu) to *composite* (merge) the clouds to the background image. With the selection handles and marquee lines gone, you now should have a photo-illustration similar to that shown in figure 26.20.

11. Save your finished image as GLOBE.TIF; choose the Tagged Image File Format, *.TIF from the Save File as **T**ype field in the Save an Image to Disk dialog box.

Figure 26.20
The finished image is a composite of PHOTO-PAINT illustration and photographic imagery.

The last exercise demonstrated the creative use of not one, but several, PHOTO-PAINT filters working with other features. The next section covers the other Mapping filters, with a few creative suggestions on how you can best use them. You also look at some imaging exercises to familiarize yourself with what the Mapping filters do.

Ripple

The Ripple filter belongs to the same variety of displacement filters as the Map to Sphere filter. Ripple takes linear pixel information in an image and maps it to horizontal, vertical, or a combination of waves. You can specify the Ripple type as well as the period and amplitude of the Ripple effect. The **P**eriod setting specifies how often the ripple occurs, and **A**mplitude is the intensity of the effect. You can apply a Ripple effect to an entire image, or only in a selection area made by any of the Mask tools.

The BRICKS.TIF image on the *CorelDRAW! The Professional Reference* companion CDs, under the CHAP26 subdirectory, is a good test image to experiment on using the Ripple filter. You can drag-and-drop a copy of the image from CorelMOSAIC, choose Mapping from the Effe**c**ts menu, and then choose the Ripple filter.

In figure 26.21, you can see the settings and preview of the Ripple effect used to turn the bricks in the image into soft, wavy bricks. You can achieve a wonderful sort of "cognitive dissonance" by applying this filter to images of static items that ordinarily are thought of as having a solid geometry and structure.

Figure 26.22 is a better look at the Ripple effect as applied to the entire BRICKS image. The Ripple filter is used best at high Period values and small Amplitude values. If you increase the Ripple **A**mplitude setting or use a small value for **P**eriod, image areas become unrecognizable.

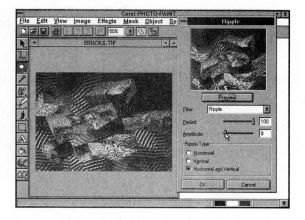

Figure 26.21

Specify the period (frequency of occurrence) and amplitude (strength of effect) for the Ripple filter to get different looks.

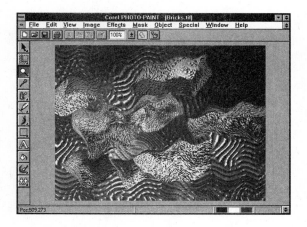

Figure 26.22

Use the Ripple filter and other filters sparingly to retain image detail.

Glass Block

The Glass Block filter maps image areas to create a splintered image, similar to a view through glass blocks found in buildings and ornamental facades on houses. You can specify Block **H**eight and Block **W**idth settings between 5 and 100 "shards," and the height and width can be specified independent of one another. You might find the most creative use of the Glass Block filter to be with selections of text and other hard-edged design elements. Try typing the word **caffeine** with the Text tool on a new image background, and then apply the Glass Block filter. Instant visual gestalt!

Pinch/Punch

Similar to the Map to Sphere filter, the Pinch/Punch filter offers two slightly milder distortions of selected image areas to create a dent or a bump. Unlike the Map to Sphere filter, a Pinch or Punch effect creates a soft transition between image areas not affected by the filter and areas of high-distortion mapping. Negative slider values result in a *punch* in an image (or selection area), while positive slider values create a *pinch*.

Try pinching or punching an image of textures such as stucco (or any of the Canvas roll-up images) to create depth in the image.

Pixelation

The Pixelation filter averages image areas to fewer pixels per inch, and therefore should be used on images of high resolution. Pixelation simulates an insect's view of an image in **R**ectangular mode, with coarse, hard-edged pixels representing greatly reduced image detail. In **C**ircular mode, the Pixelation filter performs the same image-detail reduction as Rectangular, except image areas are mapped to concentric circles; a polar projection of the globe with the latitude and longitude lines displayed looks similar to the circular Pixelation effect.

Additionally, you can set the Opacity option of the Pixelation effect from 0 to 100 percent to create a semitransparent overlay of a pixelated copy on top of the original image.

Smoked Glass

The Smoked Glass filter gives a view of an original image as seen through thick, tinted glass. The **T**int slider specifies how much the image or selection area is moved toward the foreground (paint) color specified on the Color roll-up, and **P**ercent specifies how much of the original image is blended into the tint.

Use the Smoked Glass filter to tint an object to a shade more harmonious with different image backgrounds. Specifying a white foreground color in the Color roll-up produces a smoked glass image that appears to be bleached.

Tile

The Tile filter creates mini-images from a selection or entire image. The Tile filter is useful for creating repeat patterns from a single image, and you can set **W**idth and **H**eight for the tiles separately, which produces distorted, tiled original images.

Wind

The Wind filter creates streaks of highlights on top of the original image, using highlights in the image for information about which areas display the most "wind." You can create the Wind effect only horizontally from left to right, but you always can use the **I**mage, **F**lip, or **R**otate command prior to using the Wind filter to create other wind directions in a finished image. The **O**pacity slider in the Wind dialog box controls how much the effect is applied to the original image, and you can adjust Wind **S**trength to control how long the streaks of wind appear in the image.

The Wind filter is a creative variation of blurring filters. You might find that the most creative use of the filter is for stylizing a design instead of a photographic image.

Swirl

Mapping an entire image with the Swirl filter can produce a funhouse mirror effect similar to the visual effect of dropping a stone in a pond. You can set **A**ngle of Swirl to an entire clockwise rotation (+360) or full counter-clockwise (–360). Unlike every other effect in PHOTO-PAINT, a positive value of Swirl followed by an equal, negative amount applied directly afterward, results in no effect on an image or selected area except a little image pixelation due to PHOTO-PAINT's Anti-Alias method of rearranging pixel values.

You can use the Swirl effect at small angle values to create effects that are costly to produce in the traditional darkroom. In figure 26.23, the PRETZHAS.TIF image (found in the CHAP26 subdirectory of the *CorelDRAW! The Professional Reference* companion CDs) has been swirled to –28 degrees. It's a fun filter of questionable use in professional design work, and a must to avoid with portraits. Use the Swirl filter on a friend's image, and he or she might use a traditional Punch filter on *you*.

Figure 26.23
Use the Swirl filter to bend well-defined geometric image areas.

Wet Paint

The Wet Paint filter has controls for **P**ercent, which controls the focus of paint drops made from image areas; and **W**etness, which controls how much the wet paint streaks downward in the image. The Wet Paint effect works best with an image that has clearly defined, contrasting areas of color. Use MOSAIC to drag-and-drop a copy of the PAINT.TIF image from the CHAP26 subdirectory to the design window; then choose Mapping from the Effe**c**ts menu and choose Wet Paint to experiment with the filter.

As you can see in figure 26.24, a **P**ercent value of 100 produces sharp, paint-like distortions in areas of contrasting color in the image. With **W**etness set to 30, the filter can be used to create a melting look, or simply to suggest an inept application of paint on a variety of surfaces.

Figure 26.25 is a closer viewing resolution of the PAINT.TIF image after applying the Wet Paint filter.

Try applying the Wet Paint filter to a photo of a skyscraper or another hard, geometric design to create a surreal effect.

Figure 26.24

Use the Wet Paint filter to simulate image areas melting.

Figure 26.25

*To soften the edge of the wet paint, use a lower **P**ercent value.*

Impressionist

Don't mistake this filter with the **A**rtistic, **I**mpressionism filter; the two bear no resemblance in effect. You see the use of the Impressionist filter every time you launch PHOTO-PAINT—the fruit still-life on PHOTO-PAINT's splash screen has been filtered with the Impressionist effect. Basically, the Impressionist filter provides a glass-distortion effect. It randomizes pixels in a selection area and creates a variety of effects, depending on the image to which you apply it.

In the next set of steps, you see how the Impressionist effect can simulate rust. The Impressionist effect is best applied to selected image areas; you achieve a striking look when part of an image has been filtered to show the viewer something like a "before and after" within the same image.

Here's how to make a fresh, clean digital graphic look a little rusty with the Impressionist filter:

1. Drag-and-drop the RUST.TIF image from CorelMOSAIC to the workspace. CorelMOSAIC should be pathed to the CHAP26 subdirectory on the *CorelDRAW! The Professional Reference* companion CDs from the preceding exercise. Be certain that no other image windows are active; if you drag-and-drop a MOSAIC thumbnail on top of an image window, the corresponding graphic lands within the active image as an object.

2. Choose **M**ask, Create **T**ransparency Mask, and then click on **N**ew.

3. Click on the **U**niform radio button, type **255** in the field, then click on OK. This creates a Transparency mask above the image, which you now need to apply color to in areas you want to mask from the Impressionist filter.

4. Double-click on the Current Fill icon. This displays the Fill roll-up. Click on the Uniform button (top left on the Fill roll-up), and then choose black from the drop-down palette.

5. Press Ctrl+F7 to display the Layers/Objects roll-up, and click on the Transparency radio button. Now, you can "paint" on the Transparency mask, but not the underlying image. The Transparency mask isn't visible right now, because the fill within the mask is currently 255, or completely transparent.

6. Double-click on the Rectangle tool on the toolbox. This makes the Rectangle tool the current painting tool, and displays the Tool Settings roll-up. Make sure **S**ize (of the rectangle's outline) is set to 0. You do not want an outline around the rectangle you'll create, because the Rectangle tool will be used to create masked areas on the Transparency mask. Double-click on the Tool Settings roll-up's control menu button to close it, and conserve screen real estate.

7. Click-and-drag with the Rectangle tool, starting at the upper-left corner and ending on the lower-left edge of the RUST image, so that the bottom of the rectangle bisects the RUST letters in the image (see fig. 26.26).

Figure 26.26

Marquee-select an area with the Rectangle Mask tool to make it available for the Filter effect.

8. The top of the image is now completely covered with the Opaque mask. The objective here is to partially expose the bottom of the RUST lettering with the Transparency mask, so click on the Fountain Fill button on the Fill roll-up, click on the linear type fill (the button above the Edit button), then select a black beginning and white ending from the drop-down palettes on

the roll-up. Click and drag inside the preview window to "point" the linear Fountain fill so that it travels top to bottom, from black to white.

9. With the Rectangle tool, click-and-drag around the unmasked area on the image, starting at the bottom of the Transparency mask tint and finishing at the bottom of the image, as shown in figure 26.27.

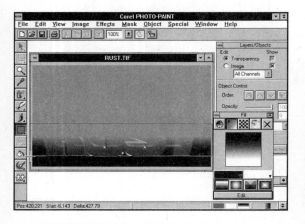

Figure 26.27

Create a transition between masked and unmasked areas on the image by using a linear Fountain fill.

10. Click on the Image radio button on the Layers/Objects roll-up, then uncheck the Show button next to Transparency. The mask is active, but invisible now. All future edits will affect the RUST.TIF image, and the areas of most Transparency mask color will be areas the Impressionist filter won't affect.

11. Choose Mapping from the Effects menu, choose Impressionist, and type **10** in both the **H**orizontal and V**e**rtical text boxes. As you can see in figure 26.28, this amount of Impressionist filter produces a noticeable effect, but not a completely distorted one over any image area that has less than 100% opaque Transparency mask; the bottom of the lettering will display the most pronounced Impressionist effect, which will fade into the original image detail at about the horizontal halfway point on the RUST lettering.

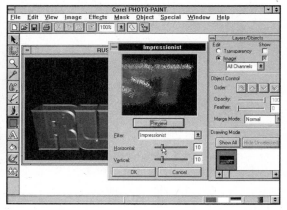

Figure 26.28

*The Pre***v***iew window in the Impressionist dialog box displays the effect over all the preview image, regardless of masked areas that are active.*

12. Click on OK to apply the filter. As you can see in figure 26.29, the word "rust" still is clearly defined, but it looks a tad

corroded. Save the image and consider using Transparency masks in your assignments to confine an effect to part of an image.

Figure 26.29

The Impressionist filter applied to a transparency-masked image area.

Vignette

You can use the Vignette Mapping filter to highlight an image area while obscuring other areas with white, black, or foreground paint color. This effect can lead to some interesting design prospects, particularly when you want to crop unwanted image areas away from a focal point without cropping an image's dimensions or resolution.

In the next set of steps, the MIKE.TIF image is the host for an experiment using the Vignette filter. The MIKE.TIF image is a handsome illustration of a microphone, but areas surrounding the microphone are littered with unwanted visual clutter. The Vignette filter is a quick way to clean up an image and direct attention wherever you want.

Unfortunately, the Vignette filter offers no options for determining the aperture of the vignette. There is a workaround for the filter's limitation, however, and you get hands-on experience using the Vignette filter in a practical exercise that follows.

Here's how to direct attention to an image element, while simultaneously getting rid of other elements, by using the Vignette filter:

1. Use CorelMOSAIC to drag-and-drop a copy of the MIKE.TIF image in the CHAP26 subdirectory of the *CorelDRAW! The Professional Reference* companion CDs to PHOTO-PAINT's design window.

2. The concept here is to Vignette the microphone using a color found in the MIKE image to replace all other image areas with solid color. Click on the Eyedropper tool, and then left-click over an area of the maroon backdrop in the MIKE image. You might want to double-click on the far left color swatch on the status line (Paint color) to display the Color roll-up and confirm that this is the exact shade you

want to use as image color outside the vignette, as shown in figure 26.30. You can fine-tune the shade using the controls on the Color roll-up, but the Eyedropper tool is generally the most fail-safe method for defining the exact shade found in an image.

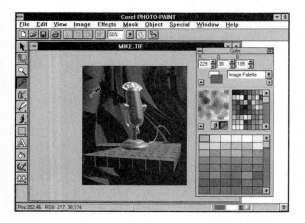

Figure 26.30

Use the Eyedropper tool to sample foreground color from the image to replace image areas outside the vignette.

Right-clicking with the Eyedropper tool over an image area defines the present Fill color that can be used with the Fill tool or any of the Shape tools (Rectangle, Ellipse, or Polygon).

Pressing Ctrl while left-clicking an image area with the Eyedropper tool defines the current paper color.

See Chapter 27, "Color Specification and Output," for more comprehensive information on color specification.

A manual technique is used to force the Vignette filter to create a soft spotlight around the microphone in the MIKE image. The Vignette filter evaluates an image's *total* width and height, and then defines the center of the vignette using the center of the image coordinates. The solution for redirecting the center of the Vignette effect is to mask only the area you want the filter to evaluate.

3. Using the Rectangle Mask tool, click-and-drag a marquee over the microphone image area, and use the Mask Picker tool to reposition the mask marquee so that the microphone is in the center of the selection.

4. Choose Mapping from the Effects menu, and choose Vignette to display the Vignette dialog box. Set **O**ffset to 0; this setting controls how wide the aperture of the Vignette is, but has no effect on the location of the aperture. Set the F**a**de amount to 65. Fade controls the contrast between vignetted and nonvignetted areas, and can be used to alter the sharpness of the edge of the Vignette effect. As you can see in

figure 26.31, by clicking on the Pen **C**olor and then on Pre**v**iew, the microphone is surrounded gently by an ellipse, and extraneous image areas in the image are replaced with the maroon color you sampled from the image backdrop.

tool, set **S**ize to 100, and then click-and-drag to apply foreground (Paint) color in the other image areas, as shown in figure 26.32.

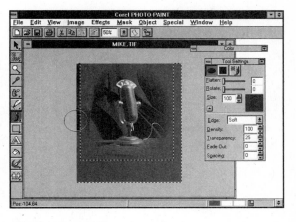

Figure 26.32
Use the Paint Brush tool and the present foreground (Pen color) to cover images areas that were protected earlier.

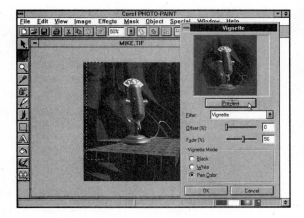

Figure 26.31
*Choose **B**lack, **W**hite, or Pen **C**olor for the image areas outside the Vignette effect.*

5. Click on OK to apply the effect.

6. The MIKE image is vignetted nicely now, except the unmasked areas still feature unwanted image areas. No problem. Choose **I**nvert from the **M**ask menu (or click on the Invert button on the ribbon bar) to make areas unaffected by the Vignette filter available for editing. Click on the Paint Brush

7. The MIKE image is now an asymmetrical composition, but as you can see in figure 26.33, this creates a perfect opportunity to add some text. A good lesson here is not to crop an image before you've explored its many possible uses with its original dimensions.

Figure 26.33
Use the Vignette filter to clear space in an image for the addition of text or other design elements.

8. Click on the Save button on the ribbon bar when you finish editing the image.

Transformations Filters

The most exotic of PHOTO-PAINT's effects can be accessed through the Transformations command. Although they are extremely limited in usability for everyday graphics, the effects are stunning and the results can be very eye-catching when you have selected the right image for the effect.

These are "once-in-a-while" effects that you might want to resort to when an image is absolutely boring or unusable in order to create some visual interest. The effects of Transformations filters often can speak more loudly within an image than its composition. In the next sections, you find some ideas and text images for use with the Transformations filters.

3D Rotate

The 3D Rotate effect provides users with a convenient graphical set of controls used to make a flat image seem as if it's being viewed at an angle of perspective. Imagine your image as one of six on a desktop photo cube; you can view the top photo from a variety of perspective angles; the 3D Rotate filter offers the same angled views.

In the exercise that follows, you create an image of an open book from two flat images using the 3D Rotate filter. The filter has two options for remapping an image or selection area. When you check the Best Fit box on the dialog box, PHOTO-PAINT reproportions the 3D-rotated image to as large as the selection area or entire image dimensions allow without clipping part of the image. If the Best Fit box is unchecked, PHOTO-PAINT scales the 3D-rotated image area so that it's centered with equal amounts of background color displayed on all four surrounding sides.

You almost never want to leave the Best Fit box unchecked, because it substantially reduces the size of the image area to which you applied the effect.

Here's how to use the 3D Rotate filter to create a dimensional look from two flat images:

1. Clear your design window of active image windows. Drag-and-drop the NUT&BOLT.TIF image from CorelMOSAIC to the design window.

   The paper size of an image is how much extra design space surrounds an image file. By default, the paper size of an image is the same as the image size, but you can adjust this in PHOTO-PAINT. The NUT&BOLT image plays the role of the left side of an open book, so it requires more paper (image background) to the right of it.

2. Select the Rectangle Mask tool and then marquee-select the entire NUT&BOLT image. The Marquee mask remains active even after changing the paper size, and it's easier to precisely select the image before changing the paper size.

3. Click on the Eyedropper tool, and then press Ctrl while left-clicking on the "Design Work" lettering in the NUT&BOLT image. This action sets the paper color to white. It's a down-and-dirty trick, but it works and saves a trip to the Color roll-up to specify background paper color.

4. Choose **P**aper Size from the **I**mage menu. The Paper Size dialog box appears (see fig. 26.34). Click on

Custom in the **P**lacement field and uncheck the **M**aintain Aspect check box. Click on the Increments drop-down list arrow to specify the paper dimensions in inches, not pixels.

5. Type **3.4** in the **W**idth field, and **2** in the **H**eight field. PHOTO-PAINT displays the current image dimensions to the left of the dimension fields.

6. Place your cursor in the Pre**v**iew window and position the NUT&BOLT image so that it's centered and on the left side of the paper, as shown in figure 26.34. Then click on OK. You can reposition an original image anywhere you want on a new paper size; you even can place the image partially off the page, thus clipping it, but you would need a compelling artistic reason to do so.

Figure 26.34

*Reposition the original image relative to the new paper size by clicking-and-dragging in the Paper Size Pre**v**iew window.*

7. Resizing paper, resampling an image, and changing color modes always results in PHOTO-PAINT creating a copy of the original image, so save the NEW-1.CPT image as MAGAZINE.TIF to your hard drive and close the NUT&BOLT.TIF image without saving changes.

8. Choose Transformations from the Effects menu, and then choose 3D Rotate. The 3-D Rotate dialog box appears. Type a value of **26** next to the horizontal slider and click on the Preview window. As you can see in figure 26.35, with the **B**est Fit check box checked, the nuts and bolts design appears to be angled away from the viewer—an effect you would see when holding an open book. Click on OK to apply the effect, and remember the value 26, because you'll want to create a facing page equally rotated in the opposite direction.

9. Choose **R**emove from the **M**ask menu (or click on the Remove button on the ribbon bar). Then minimize the MAGAZINE.TIF image.

10. Click on the MOSAIC button on the ribbon bar, and then drag-and-drop the METAL1.TIF image to the design window.

11. Type 33 in the Zoom level field on the ribbon bar, and then seriously resize the image window of the METAL1.TIF image so that the window's frames are almost flush with the image.

12. Choose Transformations from the Effects menu and then choose 3D Rotate to access the 3-D Rotate dialog box. Type **–26** for the horizontal perspective and click on OK. Negative values require a minus sign in front of them, but positive values do not need a plus sign in front of the value.

13. Select the Magic Wand Object tool and click on the Build Mode button on the ribbon bar. The Build mode enables you to further edit an object selection before creating an object. The Build mode is required because you'll select the white area in the METAL1 image window and invert the selection to include the 3D-rotated image. You cannot invert object selections in the standard (non-Build) object mode.

Figure 26.35

Selections can be rotated horizontally, vertically, or in both directions at once with the 3D Rotate filter.

14. Click on the white area of the METAL1 image, and then click on the Invert button on the ribbon bar (or choose **I**nvert from the **O**bject menu).

15. Click on the Create Object button on the ribbon bar (or choose **C**reate from the **O**bject menu and choose **C**opy).

16. Restore the MAGAZINE.TIF image and resize and reposition the image window so that you have a clear view of both images.

17. Click on the title bar of the METAL1.TIF image to make it the active window; then click-and-drag the object onto the MAGAZINE.TIF image, as shown in figure 26.36.

18. Reposition the object so that its left side is flush with the right side of the NUTS&BOLTS image area. You can unclick the Marquee Visible button to remove the marquee from view, and use the arrow keyboard keys to nudge the object so that it precisely meets the NUTS&BOLTS image area.

19. Press Ctrl+G (or choose **M**erge from the **O**bject menu) when the object is positioned correctly, and then click on the Save button on the ribbon bar.

You can use the 3D Rotate Transformations filter in many situations where you want to show perspective in an image that was not photographed with perspective. Use a combination of tools and features, like those described in the preceding exercise, to make filters a more valuable component of your design technique. Start with a concept, and then choose the PHOTO-PAINT features that can best assist in expressing the concept.

Perspective

You can accomplish perspective in one of two ways by using the Perspective filter. The Perspective command creates four nodes at the corners of a selection or entire image as viewed from the Pre**v**iew window in the command. You have your choice as to the direction in which to move the surrounding nodes to distort the image. The Perspective command is somewhat of a redundant feature; if you put an image object in Distort mode (click two successive times on a

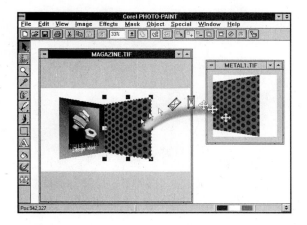

Figure 26.36

Click-and-drag an object between image windows using the Object Picker tool.

selected object; see Chapter 22, "Working with Objects"), both the Perspective filter and Distort mode can accomplish the same thing.

The Shear option in the Perspective filter performs an effect that can be manually created by using a Tool Settings roll-up option when an image exists as a floating object. You can use the Tool Settings roll-up's Object Skew settings to precisely move one side of an object away from the opposing side. Because the Shear option and the Object Skew settings produce the same artistic results, you can use them interchangeably.

Mesh Warp

The Mesh Warp transformation is the most flexible, precise method for distorting part of an image area. No selection masks or other PHOTO-PAINT features are required to reshape part, or all, of an image as though it were made of putty.

In a way, the Mesh Warp filter is, in advertising slang, "an execution in search of a concept." It's a totally engaging experience to tug and pull on images with the Mesh Warp filter, but the practical results of the filter are limited in most day-to-day design work.

The exercise that follows is based on an advertisement for a financial institution that's trying to make a point about straightening out clients' checking accounts. The

CHECKING.TIF image used in this example features a plain-looking pencil. The poster will benefit from the appropriate use of the Mesh Warp, and you'll have some fun creating an attention-getting, surrealistic image.

Here's how to use the Mesh Warp filter in a situation that requires "bending" only a portion of an image:

1. Use CorelMOSAIC to drag-and-drop a copy of the CHECKING.TIF image from the *CorelDRAW! The Professional Reference* companion CDs' CHAP26 subdirectory to the design window.

2. Choose Transformations from the Effects menu and choose Mesh Warp. The Mesh Warp dialog box appears (see fig. 26.37).

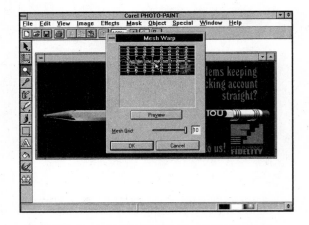

Figure 26.37
Click-and-drag on the nodes in the Preview window to alter the shape of the mesh.

3. The Mesh Warp filter offers a user-defined number of grids that intersect the Preview image and the corresponding image area. You can set a maximum of 10 transversals of an image by using the Mesh Grid slider; click-and-drag the slider to 10 for this exercise.

4. The mesh can be warped by clicking-and-dragging on any node that intersects the grid in the Preview window. Unfortunately, you cannot click inside the Preview window of this filter to zoom in or out. To bend the end of the pencil, but leave the rest of the image intact, for example, click-and-drag on the nodes that fall over the corresponding areas in the Preview window. When the nodes and mesh look similar to the image in figure 26.37, click on OK.

5. You're done! Save your image to the hard disk. As you can see in figure 26.38, the Mesh Warp effect bent only the pencil tip, which adds an element of exaggeration to the bank ad. The text and rest of the graphics in the image were undisturbed by the Mesh Warp because the nodes that corresponded to these areas weren't moved.

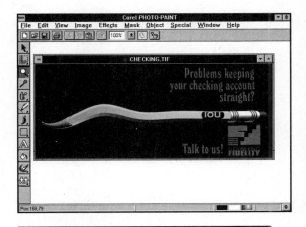

Figure 26.38
You have total control over which areas in an image are affected by the Mesh Warp filter.

There will be occasions in your design assignments when the Mesh Warp can be a secret weapon in your arsenal of PHOTO-PAINT filters. It's best to reserve this effect for special occasions, and use it only when a design clearly calls for powerful and strange effects.

Other Filters

This exploration of PHOTO-PAINT filters has not been structured identically to the way you find them on the menu. The time and

space in this chapter have been spent addressing the uses for the filters you'll use most in your work. The remaining PHOTO-PAINT filters are listed here, with explanations of how they work and what they do.

Artistic Filters

PHOTO-PAINT offers two Artistic filters that produce Pointillism and Impressionism effects identical to the Pointillism and Impressionism brushes found in the Brush tool fly-out menu. Because both Artistic effects are automated, PHOTO-PAINT must perform a huge number of calculations based on the image or selection area to which you apply Pointillism or Impressionism.

But don't hold your breath in anticipation of a Seurat or Van Gogh "original." And if you choose to apply either filter to a file larger than 150KB, you can tie up your machine for minutes on end only to receive a very sterile, unrecognizable collection of multicolored dots or strokes made from sample colors from the original image.

It would be patronizing to laud the Artistic filters as anything more than a complex feat of application programming that simply fails to enhance an image. Corel Corporation has packed a lot of incredible features and filters into PHOTO-PAINT; the Artistic filters aren't among them.

Fancy Filters

The Fancy filters affect image areas with variations on softening and sharpening an image, but the filters produce more stylized effects.

Edge Detect

The Edge Detect filter operates similarly to the Special, Contour command. It creates outlines around solid image areas in which the color is determined from your selection in the Edge drop-down box. Additionally, you can specify a color for nonoutlined areas within the image from the Color drop-down list. Sensitivity controls how detailed the edges within an image are enhanced with outlines and fills. The Edge Detect filter is best used on high-resolution images. Images of low resolution become unrecognizable when Edge Detect is applied.

Emboss

The Emboss filter creates a highlight and a dark copy, and slightly offsets them in any of eight directions to create the appearance of an embossed image. You can achieve particularly striking effects with color images, but original color is not retained when the Emboss effect is applied. You cannot control the depth of an Emboss effect, but you can specify paint color, paper color, or three shades of gray for the main, non-embossed part of the effect from the Emboss Color drop-down list.

Gaussian Blur

This effect is covered more thoroughly in Chapter 22, "Working with Objects." The Gaussian Blur effect produces a blur more intense toward the center of a selection, and gently tapers off toward the edge of a selection or entire image. Gaussian Blur produces a more realistic blurring effect when used to create shadows than any of the Soften filters.

Invert

The Invert filter creates the chromatic opposite of original color areas, producing a film negative from a positive image. You can use the Invert filter on grayscale images to produce a negative image.

Jaggy Despeckle

The Jaggy Despeckle filter is similar to the Soften filters in that it removes harsh areas of contrast within an image that are typically associated with bitmap images. The jagged stairstep effect is reduced by averaging tonal values in neighboring pixels of high tonal contrast, and slight image detail is lost through the use of this filter.

Motion Blur

The Motion Blur filter selectively blurs an image in any of eight user-definable directions. The filter features a **S**peed control, which affects the amount or intensity with which the Motion Blur effect is applied to an image. Motion Blur also can be achieved

without the use of PHOTO-PAINT by holding a cheap camera out the window of a speeding car, and you probably will find limited use of the Motion Blur filter in your assignments.

Outline

The Outline filter accentuates all image areas that have a fairly solid color fill by applying identical color values around the image area edges. Any image areas that are out of focus or have a mixture of values (like image backgrounds) receive evenly distributed grayscale pixels. The effect definitely sharpens even the poorest of images, but much visual detail is lost, and images that have been filtered with Outline are best printed at very small sizes.

Corel Corporation gave some foresight to the ever-changing face of computer graphics and made PHOTO-PAINT 5 capable of reading third-party plug-in filters that are written to be compliant with Adobe Systems' Plug-In standard for filters. The Effects menu doesn't end at Transformations if you want to purchase third-party add-ons and expand the capabilities of PHOTO-PAINT to provide exotic interpretations of original images.

Plug-In Filters

The effects you see in the following section are not part of PHOTO-PAINT's complement of Effects filters. PHOTO-PAINT was

designed with an open architecture that allows different manufacturers to design filters and effects that will work within the application. Industry-standard plug-in filters can be purchased and loaded quite easily into PHOTO-PAINT, where you immediately can gain access to them from PHOTO-PAINT's Effects menu.

Adobe Systems, HSC Software, Andromeda Software, and other imaging software companies have plug-ins that will work with PHOTO-PAINT at prices that typically are less than $200.

How you install a third-party plug-in, what some of the unique features do, and how you might benefit from them in your work are the topics covered in the conclusion of this chapter.

Installing a Plug-In Filter

For the purposes of the next example, Aldus Gallery Effects, Volume 2 from Adobe Systems was chosen. Gallery effects are filters that produce lifelike brush strokes and textures in an image such as watercolor, charcoal, and even a Photocopy filter that degrades an image with the familiar "low toner supply" characteristic.

You need to check with the filter manufacturer or read the documentation that comes with a filter set to make sure that the filters adhere to the Adobe Plug-In standard. Some

manufacturers offer stand-alone filters that can operate outside of PHOTO-PAINT as a separate application, but cannot be recognized by PHOTO-PAINT.

The following is a series of steps you need to follow if you want to use Aldus Gallery Effects within PHOTO-PAINT. The procedure for installing a filter set is similar for most plug-in filters, but be sure to follow the specific instructions that come with any filter set.

1. Install the plug-in filters using the setup routine described in the manufacturer's documentation. Generally, a plug-in filter requires a unique subdirectory, and you should name the subdirectory something you easily can locate later. PLUG-IN is not a good name, because this is also the name of the subdirectory PHOTO-PAINT installed its own filters to during Corel Setup.

2. Start PHOTO-PAINT. Then choose **P**references from the **S**pecial menu and click on the Advanced tab.

3. Click on the **I**nsert button to the right of the **P**lug-In Directories field.

4. Choose the plug-in directory you installed the third-party filters to in the Select Directory menu. As you can see in figure 26.39, the GALLERY subdirectory has been chosen. By clicking on the filter subdirectory, you've shown PHOTO-PAINT where

to locate and load them, and they will be immediately available for use after exiting the **P**references menu. You can have as many different directories for plug-in sets as you want.

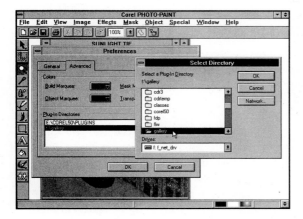

Figure 26.39

Select a directory where you want PHOTO-PAINT to search for third-party plug-ins.

5. Click on OK, and then click on OK in the **P**references menu to return to PHOTO-PAINT.

6. Additions then are made to the Effe**c**ts menu. In figure 26.40, you can see the Aldus Gallery Effects menu on the design window. The SUNLIGHT.TIF image on the *CorelDRAW! The Professional Reference* companion CDs in the CHAP26 subdirectory is being filtered to create Angled Strokes, an effect that adds realistic brushstrokes to an image.

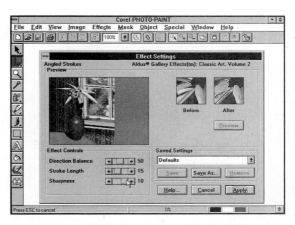

Figure 26.40

*Use the Effe**c**ts menu to access third-party filters you have added to PHOTO-PAINT.*

7. Click on OK to apply the effect.

Figure 26.41 is a better view of the Angled Stroke effect. It's important to note that additional plug-in filters can slow the performance of PHOTO-PAINT. If you have purchased several collections of filters, it's best to specify only one set at a time for use in PHOTO-PAINT.

Occasionally, a third-party filter might "disagree" with PHOTO-PAINT; your video driver could fail, or an effect might not function according to the manufacturer's instructions. Fortunately, additional plug-in directories can be uninstalled as easily as they are installed. To remove a set of filters, choose **P**references from the **S**pecial menu,

click on the path to the filters in the Plug-In Directories field, and click on the **D**elete button on the Advanced tab menu. You actually aren't deleting the filters you installed; you're deleting only the path to them so that PHOTO-PAINT will not offer them on the Effe**c**ts menu.

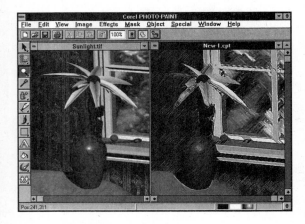

Figure 26.41
Third-party filters can provide effects beyond those of PHOTO-PAINT's native filters.

Using Kai's Power Tools for Windows

Kai's Power Tools originally was designed to work with Adobe Photoshop for the Macintosh. The suite of imaging tools was ported to the Windows environment in late 1993, and the Adobe Plug-In standard was adopted so that many imaging programs, including PHOTO-PAINT, could take advantage of these unique filters.

Kai's Power Tools is a set of filters broken into two categories: fractal, texture, and complex Gradient tools are available so that users can create unique color areas; and automated filters are available that are more similar to PHOTO-PAINT's filters in terms of execution.

Figure 26.42 is an example of Kai's Glass Lens Bright filter applied to an image area defined with the Ellipse Mask tool. Glass Lens Bright is similar to the Map to Sphere command, but it's a little more elegant in the effect it produces, and there is no preview offered for the one-click effect. You also will note that the submenu of filter effects practically runs off the display. This is another good reason for using an 800×600 video driver to create more screen space for your imaging work in PHOTO-PAINT.

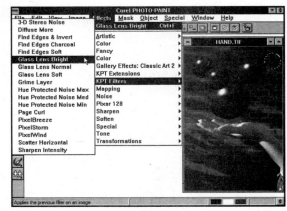

Figure 26.42
HSC's Kai's Power Tools offers more than 40 filters, with almost infinitely modifiable controls on some tools.

Kai's Power Tools is an investment in your career as an imaging professional. The interface for Kai's Extensions is definitely unintuitive, and the learning curve is steep for a lot of the effects, but Kai's has become the *de facto* plug-in for imaging professionals on both Macintosh and Windows computer platforms, and you take a step further into big-league imaging when you add the set to PHOTO-PAINT.

Figure 26.43 is of Kai's Page Curl filter. The only down side to having all the KPT filters commercially available for use in Windows imaging programs is the same as the availability of CorelDRAW clip art: the uniqueness of an image is diluted when every third computer designer uses the same third-party plug-in.

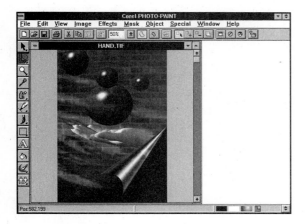

Figure 26.43
KPT's Page Curl filter is used—and perhaps overused— with magazines, music cassette covers, and billboards.

Plug-in filters can provide scores of useful effects within PHOTO-PAINT's design window, and more and more filters are being designed every day. But the question of which filters you should purchase, if any, for enhancing your work remains the same: What is a filter good for?

Summary

All good imaging work can benefit from having a collection of filters to correct and modify images. Creative license is the privilege of designers, but it doesn't require the improper or unaesthetic use of a filter to turn good design work into unsellable art.

The best approach to using PHOTO-PAINT's filters, or any digital filter, is to begin with a concept; if that concept calls for the creative use of an effect, then use it. However, as you've seen in this chapter, a filter sometimes can prove to be more useful when used with other PHOTO-PAINT features. Transparency masks can provide smooth transitions between filtered and unfiltered image areas. Inspired use of an effect can create a design that doesn't look like a filter was used at all; many of the exercise images on the *CorelDRAW! The Professional Reference* companion CDs were filtered, color corrected, and enhanced in advance so that you could see more clearly the effect of a PHOTO-PAINT filter.

Filters don't hold any particular charm, remedy, or mystical powers. It's only by exploring the filters and finding creative uses for them that you truly can evaluate their worth.

FRIENDS OF THE EARTH
LES AMI(E)S DE LA TERRE

protecting the earth for tomorrow

protégeons l'avenir de la terre

CorelDRAW!
PROFESSIONAL REFERENCE

CorelDRAW!
PROFESSIONAL REFERENCE

CorelDRAW!
PROFESSIONAL REFERENCE

CorelDRAW!
PROFESSIONAL REFERENCE

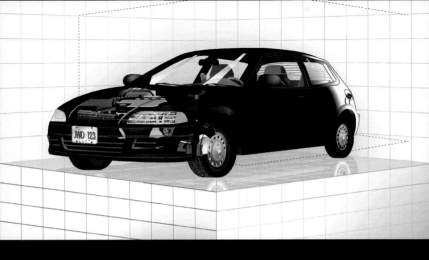

...and urge you to take immediate action.

Yours respectfully and sincerely,

J.D.

CorelDRAW!

PROFESSIONAL REFERENCE

CorelDRAW!
PROFESSIONAL REFERENCE

CorelDRAW!
PROFESSIONAL REFERENCE

The image to the left,
"Harley," by Phil Williams,
was generated in CorelDRAW.

The image at right was exported
to Adobe Photoshop, where the
lighting-enhancement effects
were added.

CorelDRAW!
PROFESSIONAL REFERENCE

CorelDRAW!
PROFESSIONAL REFERENCE

Arizona

Native Folkart

Exhibit

Arizona Center
May 23 - May 27

CorelDRAW!
PROFESSIONAL REFERENCE

Color Specification and Output

*U*nlike CorelDRAW, PHOTO-PAINT enables the designer to create a "mesh" of color. There are no discrete objects to be filled, but your finished PHOTO-PAINT creation can have thousands of unique colors that blend into one another. Because of the mathematics principle behind bitmap image types, making a print, press proof, or color slide requires more care and more understanding of how a computer pixel translates to a color dot of ink in the real world.

This chapter explains the color models in which you can specify paint for correcting and creating an image, how to convert a computer image to a color model that commercial presses can use, and how to finish a design to specifications for rendering at a service bureau. Output depends on what you put into a PHOTO-PAINT graphic, and the best physical representations of your labors should reflect your original concept.

This chapter covers:

- Color modes

- Color conversions

- Halftones

- Spot and process color

- Service bureaus and color slides

Defining Color Models for Painting

A *color model* is a man-made arrangement of a particular segment of the visible spectrum or range of values used for a specific purpose. The grayscale color model, for example, has a gamut that can be represented as a series of brightness values from 0 to 255. This gamut consists of the range of tones that are available when working with 8-bit/pixel neutral density (grayscale) images. PHOTO-PAINT offers two color models for working with RGB, 24-bit color images. You can use the RGB color model or the HSB color model when specifying paint colors for an RGB image; both achieve identical results.

The following sections describe the various color modes you use when painting an original image or retouching. Additionally, PHOTO-PAINT offers color modes that address press specifications for color; these modes and the situations in which you use them are discussed later in this chapter.

Using RGB Color

The default color model the Color roll-up offers for choosing a specific color is the RGB model for Red, Green, and Blue. The RGB color model accurately corresponds to phosphors that display pixels on your monitor, and the RGB *color space*—the boundary of expression of color—is confined to 16.7 million unique color values. The RGB color model is based on the principal of additive color—the three additive hues that, when combined, create white.

The basis of RGB color revolves around the principle that each color channel in an RGB image has 256 distinct shades of brilliance from 0 to 255. The center of the RGB color model on the Color roll-up is black—zero brightness values for all three color channels. You can click-and-drag any of the handles on the color model wireframe to specify a color; its exact RGB component values are listed at the top of the roll-up. Additionally, you can enter RGB values directly in the R, G, and B spin boxes if you've been given a color specification you need to reproduce.

By clicking-and-dragging on two of the wireframe handles, the two primary additive colors are combined to create shades of secondary additive colors. Clicking-and-dragging on both the G and the B handles to increase their brightness, for example, yields cyan. The purpose of the Brightness slider is to uniformly increase or decrease more than one color channel's brightness simultaneously. In figure 27.1, the Red wireframe handle has been dragged to the top of the model and the Blue wireframe handle has being dragged all the way to the right. When Red and Blue are set to their maximum values, the color displayed on the Brightness slider becomes magenta.

Although you can specify any one of the 16.7 million colors available in RGB color mode through the RGB color model, some techniques with PHOTO-PAINT's Color roll-up are quicker and easier than others. You can click on any area of the color space underneath the wireframe on the color model to specify a value if clicking-and-dragging on the wireframe doesn't work for you.

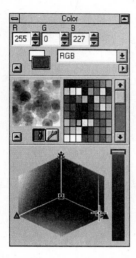

Figure 27.1

The center of PHOTO-PAINT's RGB color model represents black, moving outward to white.

RGB color directly relates the three individual color channels that make a composite RGB color image. In figure 27.2, you can see an original RGB image, US_FLAG.TIF, along with a copy in which Blue Channel is displayed by selecting it in the Layers/Objects roll-up. The more a particular primary color is present in an image, as are the sky and blue star field, the higher the brightness value appears in the corresponding color channel.

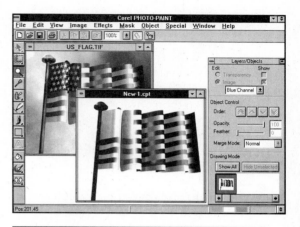

Figure 27.2

The more a primary color contributes to the overall image, the brighter the area is in its respective color channel.

Most designers are accustomed to working with physical, subtractive pigments, and are new to this additive color game. Figure 21.20 in Chapter 21, "Essential Concepts of Pixel-Based Graphics," is a figure of the primary additive color wheel along with the secondary colors; in a nutshell, these are the colors you will move to in an RGB color model when two or more primary values are added:

- Red plus green moves to yellow
- Red plus blue moves to magenta
- Green plus blue moves to cyan

A combination of all three color channels moves to white.

Although the RGB color model maps values in an identical fashion to how your monitor displays values, the Hue, Saturation, and Brightness color model is a more traditional and straightforward model to use to create color specifications.

Examining the HSB Model

Hue, Saturation, and Brightness (*lightness* and *value* also are used as synonyms to *brightness*) is the second color model the Color roll-up offers. This model, which can be chosen from the drop-down list on the Color roll-up, describes color according to its three main attributes rather than a collective sum of additive primary values. The HSB color model predates personal computers, and although it was created for evaluating the colors you see in real life, RGB values can be expressed accurately as HSB values with no loss of color information or switching the color mode of a digital image.

PHOTO-PAINT's HSB color model is a two-parter. The Hue component is expressed and modified by clicking-and-dragging in a clockwise or counterclockwise direction around a color wheel. You control Saturation by clicking-and-dragging the color-wheel handle closer or farther from the center of the wheel. Brightness is determined by a separate slider to the right of the color wheel. Every color you can define using the RGB model also can be specified with the HSB controls. If you specify a color for wood as being R=169, G=134, and B=125, for example, you also can specify this exact shade of brown as H=12, S=66, B=169.

Because the HSB color model was intended for use in the real world rather than the digital environment, many companies, including Corel Corp., have made minor adjustments to the *increments* found on the color space HSB color defines. Hue traditionally has been measured in degrees around a color wheel, from 0 degrees to 360 degrees. Additionally, Saturation has been measured in percentages from 1 to 100. However,

you'll find that every parameter within the HSB color (and other PHOTO-PAINT color models) is measured from 0 to 255. This anomaly doesn't really change the way you create colors, but because HSB measurements are nonstandard in PHOTO-PAINT, it's best not to quote H, S, and B values as a color specification to those who don't use PHOTO-PAINT.

Unlike the RGB color model, HSB is not arranged in color channels, so you cannot view only one aspect of an image's color composition. Like the RGB color model, however, HSB is additive color; the higher the value of Brightness, the closer you move a Hue and Saturation value to white.

Converting RGB to Grayscale

If you work for an average-sized company or have clients in a city of less than 1 million in population, chances are the bulk of your assignments will be for grayscale graphics.

Color is the way we see the world, however, and it is hard to conceive and execute an image in grayscale. And more often than not, you're asked to perform editing work on a color photograph; many photofinishers aren't even set up to process a roll of Tri-X or Pan-X film.

PHOTO-PAINT can convert a color image to black and white simply by using the Convert To command, but this command often produces less-than-perfect results. The reason why there is no straight port of an RGB image to grayscale has to do with *luminosity*—the amount of brilliance a color displays. RGB images are not made of equal parts of red, green, and blue, but instead display their respective components as a *weighted* palette. If you isolate only the brightness contributions of the RGB color components, you find that in a color-balanced image, red contributes 30 percent of the total luminosity, green contributes 60 percent, and blue contributes about 10 percent. This distribution is why photocopiers tend to display black-and-white renderings of color images poorly. The improper balance of luminosity when a color image is converted to grayscale using PHOTO-PAINT can lead to a darker, muddier image for reproduction than you intended. Figure 27.3 is of the image WOODWORK.TIF in the CHAP27 subdirectory of the *CorelDRAW! The Professional Reference* companion CDs. The original image is RGB 24-bit color, and the NEW-1.CPT image was created by choosing Con**v**ert To from the **I**mage menu. Although the figure is in black and white in this book, it's clear that a straight grayscale conversion of the image produces a copy that is far too dark and lacking in detail to be reproduced as a halftone black-and-white image.

Figure 27.3

The Convert To command has its limitations when reducing RGB information to grayscale.

PHOTO-PAINT offers an alternative to straight RGB-to-grayscale conversion with the **S**plit Channels To command. This command takes the color channels found in RGB and CMYK images and creates grayscale copies in a number of individual image windows. The capability to split channels is handy if you want to make last-minute adjustments to one specific color channel of an image without disturbing the other channels.

Another use of the **S**plit Channels To command is to split an RGB image to the YIQ color format. Like LAB color, the YIQ color model is based on one channel on luminosity and two hue channels. The YIQ model is used frequently in television when color film is being broadcast as black and white; only the Y channel of visual information is sent to receivers.

Because the Y channel contains only information about an image's brilliance, it can make a better grayscale representation of a color image you want to print from PHOTO-PAINT. In figure 27.4, the WOODWORK.TIF image has been split into channels by choosing **S**plit Channels To from the **I**mage menu and choosing **Y**IQ. If you compare figures 27.3 to 27.4, you'll have to agree that there is more contrast and detail in the Y-0.TIF image.

PHOTO-PAINT saves the new Y-0.TIF image in a number of 8-bit/pixel-capable formats such as TIF, PCX, BMP, and its native CPT format. After splitting channels of a copy of an RGB image, you can edit the file with PHOTO-PAINT tools to further enhance it, or you can use the Brightness and Contrast filters from the Effe**c**ts menu to further modify the image before printing. Additionally, you might want to try splitting the channels of an RGB image to HSB, and strongly consider using the Brightness composite component as your finished grayscale converted image.

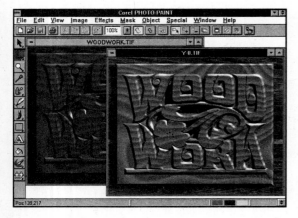

Figure 27.4
The Y channel of the YIQ color model only describes the brilliance found in an image—not color-value information.

Using LAB Color

LAB color is both a model and color mode for images, and was developed by the *Centre Internationale d'Eclairage* (CIE), an international organization that created in 1931 a standardized method for describing color the way the human eye perceives it. LAB color is described mathematically in a way that is device-independent, so LAB color can be displayed accurately on a Macintosh, IBM/PC, or UNIX-based graphics workstation.

PHOTO-PAINT does not offer LAB as a color mode for images, although LAB images can be saved in programs other than PHOTO-PAINT with LAB color channels.

In a LAB image, the L channel controls Luminance, hues from green to magenta are assigned to channel A, and hues from blue to yellow fall within the B channel.

Do not try to open a TIF or EPS image in PHOTO-PAINT that was saved to LAB color channels. PHOTO-PAINT only recognizes 24-bit RGB and 32-bit CMYK channel color images, and your system might crash if you attempt to open an image with LAB color channels.

LAB's usefulness to the PHOTO-PAINT user lies in the color model's unique structure. The LAB color model embraces both the RGB and CMYK gamut of color ranges, and if you're designing an illustration in PHOTO-PAINT, you can make certain the colors you use are "legal" for on-screen and printed media.

In figure 27.5, a color label is being created for printing. As you can see, the color model on the Color roll-up is L*a*b, and the outline within the color mode displays colors that exist within both the RGB and CMYK color gamut. The box inside the outline indicates the present foreground (paint) color. If you specify a color that cannot be reproduced with CMYK colors, the box turns into an x. To bring a color back into printable range, click-and-drag the x towards the interior of the area encompassed by the boundary. Keep an eye on the status line—when you've reached a legal (printable) color, the status line display in the lower left changes from Outside Gamut to Inside Gamut.

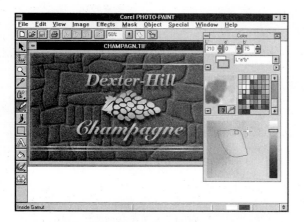

Figure 27.5
The LAB color model displays a gamut that includes both RGB and CMYK color.

The LAB color model is useful for specifying changes in only the *luminance* of a particular hue—the brightness of a color. Technically, luminance is not identical to the brightness component of the HSB color model; *brightness* is the measurement of how much light is reflected off (or passed through) an object, while *luminance* is how much apparent brightness an object displays. Brightness and luminance generally are synonymous terms in digital graphics; however, all the images you work with fail to match real-world light characteristics because they are photographic and illustrative representations.

Working with User- and PC-Defined Palettes

Corel understands the need for designers to work with both wide and narrow ranges of colors, and PHOTO-PAINT has two modes of color specification on the Color roll-up that pertain to how indexed color images are created. Indexed color images can represent only a limited range of unique, pure color values. Although you never want to specify color for an RGB image using a Uniform or Image palette, the two palettes can serve to match colors for special applications, such as adding a title to an indexed color image using a value found within the active image.

Image and Uniform palette colors have their color components listed as R, G, and B values at the top of the Color roll-up when selected, and these numerical values correspond exactly to the identical shade of color when the RGB color model is used. Uniform and Image colors are a subset of RGB and HSB color models; they occupy a smaller *color space*, or gamut of available colors.

Using the Uniform Palette

In addition to RGB and HSB color specifications, the Uniform palette enables you to access colors for painting or retouching an image. The Uniform palette displays 264 colors, regardless of the color mode of an active image. An indexed 256-color image can be painted into using the 264 uniform colors, just as a 16.7-million, color-capable image accepts uniform colors. The reason for

the disparity between the number of colors in the palette and the number of available color registers in an indexed image is because eight shades of black (measured in 10-percent increments) are included on the Uniform palette, along with black and white.

The Uniform palette earns its name due to the way it segments shades of color in the visible spectrum. Each hue found on a color wheel is represented in equal amounts on the Uniform palette—there are as many shades of red as there are orange, for example. The Uniform palette corresponds to the Windows 3.x system palette, so if you've used Uniform palette colors to create a design, you can count on each color value being supported by all applications that use system colors to define color values.

The Uniform color palette does not express the range of values the RGB and HSB color models do. The Uniform palette is useful to designers of application interfaces; and unlike programs that offer optimized indexed color palettes, the Uniform palette ensures that colors used will display properly with video drivers and other applications that comply with Microsoft's specifications.

When the color mode of an image exceeds the number of available colors on the Uniform color palette, the excess colors are represented as a dithered combination of available values. See Chapter 21 for information on dithered colors.

Using the Image Palette

The Image palette is a color model that constantly changes on the Color roll-up, depending on the active image window in PHOTO-PAINT. PHOTO-PAINT examines the active image when this color model is selected, and presents 256 of the

most commonly occurring shades found in the active image, regardless of whether the image is 256-color capable or 16.7 million RGB color. The Image palette is useful for selecting and using the same values as foreground (paint) colors as those found in the image. Figure 27.6 is a view of an RGB image with the Image palette selected in the Color roll-up.

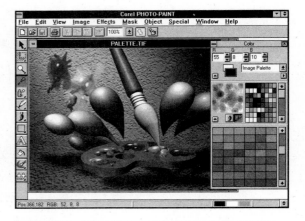

Figure 27.6
The Image palette color model presents the user with 256 of the most prevalent shades that PHOTO-PAINT finds in an image.

If an active image contains less than 256 unique values (such as screen capture performed while running a 16-color video driver), PHOTO-PAINT adds Uniform palette colors to the Image palette to offer more color selections.

Working in the User Paint Area

The paint area on PHOTO-PAINT's Color roll-up ships with some nice lilac blobs of samples, although you can remove these at any time and replace them with colors you're testing before applying them to an image. In addition to using the paint area for color testing, you can load a photographic or other image onto the paint area and use it as a source for paint colors. After the image is on the paint area, you can use the Color roll-up's Pick button to identify and specify paint colors.

In the next example, you see how to use the Resample command to copy part of an image to the paint area of the Color roll-up. You sample colors in the image in the paint area and paint with them in an entirely different image. This is a very useful technique when you need to create images that have common colors. The PICNIC.TIF image from Chapter 23, "Masks," is used in this example, and you can access the image file from the subdirectory of the same name on the *CorelDRAW! The Professional Reference* companion CDs.

Here's how to sample photographic colors for use in a different image:

1. Choose **O**pen from the **F**ile menu and select the PICNIC.TIF image from the CHAP23 subdirectory on the *CorelDRAW! The Professional Reference* companion CDs. You also can select one of your own images for this example; the image should be RGB color mode to provide the greatest number of unique color samples from within the image.

   The image that is copied to the Color roll-up paint area appears at maximum size if the horizontal and vertical dimensions are equal. Rectangular images used as paint-area images become distorted when sampled by

PHOTO-PAINT, and it becomes difficult to see accurately the different image color areas.

2. Choose the Rectangular Mask tool from the Mask Tool fly-out menu. Then press Ctrl while clicking-and-dragging a square marquee around the image area that features the colors you want to sample and paint with. As you can see in figure 27.7, most of the unique color values can be found in the center of the PICNIC image.

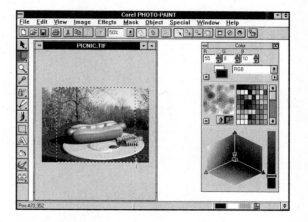

Figure 27.7

Pressing Ctrl constrains the rectangular marquee to that of a square.

3. If your square crop isn't in an ideal location, choose the Mask Picker tool and click-and-drag the square marquee to where you want it.

4. Choose Cro**p** Image from the **M**ask menu. PHOTO-PAINT creates a NEW-1.CPT image window containing the cropped image, and you can close the PICNIC image without saving it.

PHOTO-PAINT has two criteria for the images to be displayed on the paint area: they must be saved images in the BMP format, and they must be 72 pixels × 72 pixels high and at a resolution of 72 pixels/inch. PHOTO-PAINT resizes a copy of an image you specify as the paint-area image, but you might not be happy with the automatic pixel reduction it performs. This is why you should manually resample an image you intend to use as a color source.

5. Choose R**e**sample from the **I**mage menu. Then specify the following settings in the Resample dialog box: **U**nits: Pixels, **W**idth: 72, **H**eight: 72, and Resolution: 72 dpi (pixels/inch) for H**o**rizontal and **V**ertical measurements, as shown in figure 27.8. Choose **P**rocess: Anti-alias to ensure that color values are interpolated rather than simply being lost when the reduction occurs. Click on OK.

6. Save the image as PICNIC.BMP in the Save Files as **T**ype field, and then close the image.

7. On the Color roll-up, click on the fly-out menu (the button beneath the color model), and choose Save Paint Area if you want to save the colors on the paint area you have been using.

8. Click on the fly-out menu button again, choose Load Paint Area, and select PICNIC.BMP from your directory.

As you can see in figure 27.9, any color within the 24-bit PICNIC.BMP image now can be sampled with the Pick button, and color can be applied to an original composition. By specifying an image for the paint area, you more quickly can find a shade in an original for retouching purposes.

Figure 27.8

Resample an image area to conform to the dimensions of the paint area.

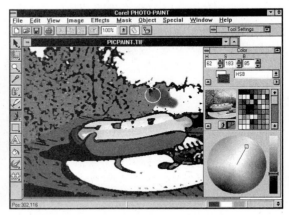

Figure 27.9

Sample paint-area colors for use in retouching or in an original composition.

Using the Color Palette

In addition to all the color modes you can use to specify colors, the color palette on the Color roll-up is there to provide a quick way to choose a color from a collection of colors. The color palette's colors are not unique; there is no formal organization of color values based on a color model, and these are the same colors as those offered in the last three versions of Corel.

You can rearrange the swatches on the color palette by clicking-and-dragging a swatch to a different location. If you drop a color swatch on top of another, the swatch you are moving will occupy the slot directly after the swatch you dropped it on.

In several instances in these PHOTO-PAINT chapters, you have shown how to use the Shape tools to fill an area with color rather than using the Color roll-up with a Brush tool. Although there is no automatic way to move a specific color value from the Fill roll-up to the Color roll-up (and vice-versa), you can use the Eyedropper tool to sample a color you have painted with in an image for the Color roll-up or the Fill roll-up.

Follow these steps to make the same color from PHOTO-PAINT's color palette available as a solid fill or as foreground (paint) color:

1. Click on the New button on the ribbon bar, choose **C**olor Mode: 24-bit Color, and accept the default settings by clicking on OK.

2. Choose any foreground (paint) color on the Color roll-up's color palette, click on the Paint Brush tool, and click-and-drag a solid stroke of color in the new image window.

3. Choose the Eyedropper tool from the toolbox, and then *right-click* over the color stroke you created.

4. You're done! Look at the status line; the same color used to indicate the present foreground color is also the color indicated on the swatches for fill color.

T I P

CorelDRAW's CORELDRW.CPL color palette contains the same color names and approximately the same values as the CORELPNT.CPL used as the Color roll-up default color palette. The only difference between the two color specifications is in the color model used to define the values. CorelDRAW's color palette is based on the CMYK color model, while PHOTO-PAINT's uses the RGB model.

Creating Your Own Color Palette

You have seen how to define an image as the paint area on the Color roll-up, but there will be occasions when you want a more permanent location for colors you're working with.

PHOTO-PAINT enables you to save a hypothetically unlimited number of custom colors to its default palette, and to rename the modified palette.

You add colors to the color palette by sampling a foreground color from an active image with the Eyedropper tool (on the toolbox), or by sampling the paint area with

the Pick button. Admittedly, the two cursors look identical, but the tools cannot be used for sampling the same areas.

In either case, a foreground color can be added to the default color palette by choosing Add Color from the Color roll-up fly-out menu. Unless you choose the Save Palette command from the fly-out menu after modifying the palette, however, your changes are not written to file and you can lose your custom colors. The best way to create a custom collection of color values for a specific assignment is by using the NRP_CDR5.CPL file, found in the CHAP27 subdirectory of the *CorelDRAW! The Professional Reference* companion CDs. This custom palette contains the RGB primary and secondary colors, black, and white, and that's it. You can experiment by adding colors to the NRP_CDR5.CPL palette or by using the Delete Color command to remove colors from the NRP_CDR5.CPL. Experimenting and building a custom color palette of your own when you have the NRP_CDR5.CPL loaded, helps keep the PHOTO-PAINT default palette intact.

To use the NRP_CDR5 palette, Choose Load Palette from the Color roll-up's fly-out menu, and then move to the CHAP27 directory on the *CorelDRAW! The Professional Reference* companion CDs. Click on NRP_CDR5.CPT, then click on OK. Click on the Color roll-up fly-out button again. Choose Save Palette and choose the COREL50\CUSTOM subdirectory on your hard disk. When you want to switch back to PHOTO-PAINT's color palette, choose Load Palette and choose CORELPNT.CPL from the same COREL50\CUSTOM subdirectory on your hard disk.

Defining Subtractive Color Models

The color models available on the Color roll-up discussed so far belong to the family of *additive* color models; the light you "paint" within PHOTO-PAINT creates areas of progressively lighter areas where different colors overlap. Painting with light has no real-world equivalency, however, and if you intend to give your designs a life outside of the PC, you must express your color specifications for artwork with equivalent subtractive values.

Using CMY and CMYK Color Models

The pigments, dyes, and inks that commercial presses use cannot express the *gamut* of colors available to you in PHOTO-PAINT due to inherent impurities in physical pigments. A different, subtractive model for color specification, therefore, is commonly used—CMYK, or **C**yan, **M**agenta, **Y**ellow, and Bla**c**k. These four color pigments are used to express the RGB values in designs, and PHOTO-PAINT offers a color model in the Color roll-up for addressing the need to create camera-ready color art, or for last-minute retouching of 32-bit CMYK image scans.

Notice that the Color roll-up does not offer a CMYK color model, but instead has a CMY model. This is because the black plate of four-color process separations is added to the other three to "punch up" areas of black in a printed image. The black plate for four-color process printing is actually a composite, weighted average of the RGB color channels in an image, expressed as grayscale values. No black-color value is offered when you want to choose from CMY colors while editing an RGB color-mode image.

Figure 27.10 is a split screen of the RGB color model and the CMY. Notice that the center of the CMY wireframe is white, while the RGB's center is black, which reflects each model's respective property of subtractive and additive color. The higher the primary subtractive CMY color value, the darker the resulting color.

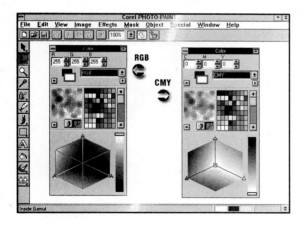

Figure 27.10

RGB and CMYK color models reflect the additive and subtractive properties of their color components.

You only have the option of working with a CMYK color model when an active image is a 32-bit/pixel CMYK image type. CMYK separations are discussed later in this chapter in the section, "Using PHOTO-PAINT's Color-Separation Options."

Using Process and Spot Colors

Process color is the method of specifying all the shades of reproducible color in an original image by using cyan, magenta, yellow, and black inks on printing plates that have been output to reflect the corresponding image areas. By successively covering a surface with percentages of these four pigments, you can get a fairly broad range of color expression. The colors that can be expressed with process color might not match a color transparency or your monitor. Process color can be used with spot color separations, however, to achieve more stunning visual looks on the printed page.

Spot colors are unique mixtures of values that often fall outside the range of printable colors achieved by process color printing, such as a fluorescent detergent bottle in a Sunday supplement. Because spot colors are a special mixture of pigments, a separate, additional pass is required in process-color printing to add the unique color (or colors) to the other CMYK values. Like CMYK values, an equivalent color is displayed in PHOTO-PAINT for spot colors to give the user a fairly accurate idea of how a spot color will be reproduced. There are several spot-color specifications available to choose from on the Color roll-up, but a 32-bit/pixel CMYK image must be active in order for the PANTONE, FOCOLTONE, and TRUMATCH color models to display.

Working with PANTONE, TRUMATCH, and FOCOLTONE Colors

PANTONE is a color-specification model that commercial printers work with on a daily basis for both spot and process color matching. PANTONE swatch books are available at most commercial art stores for around $90, and this is a good investment if you have clients whose corporate and product colors exactly match PANTONE standards. Basically, Corel and other graphics applications companies have licensed electronic versions of PANTONE and other color print specifiers, and the names of specific colors found in PHOTO-PAINT for PANTONE colors match those printed to paper about as closely as electronic and printed media can display.

Like PANTONE, the TRUMATCH and FOCOLTONE color standard systems can be used to specify spot and process colors. As mentioned earlier, the use of spot colors in a printed piece can help reproduce a color that is out of the gamut of process color by adding another printing plate, but PANTONE, TRUMATCH, and FOCOLTONE colors also can be used to specify a process (four-color) value, and this is useful when you need to add a specific value to a CMYK image before printing camera-ready color separations.

When you convert an RGB image to CMYK, PHOTO-PAINT must translate one color model to another, transforming images colors from a broader gamut to a narrower gamut. For this reason, PHOTO-PAINT makes a copy of an RGB image; converting between color modes more than once degrades image quality, and what is lost converting RGB colors to CMYK cannot be retrieved.

When printing digital color separations of CMYK images, separate spot-color plates can be defined only in the vector modules of Corel. You can define and use PANTONE spot colors in a PHOTO-PAINT design, but the spot-color values are converted to CMYK *equivalents* when you print color separations from PHOTO-PAINT. Using a CMYK equivalent of a spot color usually results in a mismatched color.

The PANTONE, FOCOLTONE, and TRUMATCH color models are available in PHOTO-PAINT to provide a method for translating spot color to the closest CMYK color match, and to supply you or your client with an on-screen approximation of what a design will look like when printed.

The next exercise shows how to access the PANTONE spot colors to use for display and for process printing. The MEGABURG.TIF image on the *CorelDRAW! The Professional Reference* companion CDs is used in this exercise. MEGABURG.TIF is a mock advertisement that needs a corporate logo in the lower right corner of the design. The corporate logo for the MegaBurger company uses PANTONE colors 211 and 312 on all corporate signage, and your task is to add the logo using the PANTONE digital spot-color equivalents to the design.

The first part of the assignment has been created for you; PHOTO-PAINT masks have been defined for the MEGABURG image using CorelDRAW, and the mask files are saved as PT211.TIF and PT312.TIF on the *CorelDRAW! The Professional Reference* Companion CDs. The masks are loaded on top of the MEGABURG image to isolate image areas that will be painted in with the PANTONE spot colors used in the logo. Again, these techniques are used for approximating PANTONE color matching on your monitor and for printing the four process-color separation plates, and *not* for creating additional spot-color separation plates.

After this exercise, you learn about a methodology that uses CorelDRAW to produce CMYK separations and additional spot-color separations.

Follow these steps to define two different PANTONE color values for use with any of PHOTO-PAINT's paint tools in a design:

1. Open the MEGABURG.TIF image from the CHAP27 subdirectory of the *CorelDRAW! The Professional Reference* companion CDs.

2. Choose Convert To from the **I**mage menu, and then select **C**MYK Color (32-bit). PHOTO-PAINT makes a copy of the MEGABURG image as NEW-1.CPT until you save it. You might want to compare the color quality of the two images side by side before closing the MEGABURG.TIF image without saving it. PHOTO-PAINT is displaying the NEW-1 image with a close approximation to how it will print to paper.

3. Choose **L**oad from the **M**ask menu, and then choose the PT312.TIF image from the CHAP27 subdirectory on the *CorelDRAW! The Professional Reference* companion CDs. PT312 is one of two masks created for this image using CorelDRAW. See Chapter 23 for information on using CorelDRAW to create PHOTO-PAINT masks. The PT312.TIF image defines an area in the MEGABURG image in the bottom right corner. Zoom to a 200-percent

viewing resolution to get a better look at the area the mask defines and where the spot color will be added.

4. Choose PANTONE Spot from the list of color models on the Color roll-up and click on the Show Color Names check box.

5. Scroll down until you find PANTONE 312CV—the first of two colors used to specify MegaBurger's corporate logo colors. Click on the color swatch.

6. Click on the Paint Brush tool on the toolbox, and then make sure that you have at least a 50-pixel-diameter brush size specified in the Tool Settings roll-up.

7. Click-and-drag within the marquee area, as shown in figure 27.11. Cover the entire marquee interior at least twice, or until you see a flat color within the marquee.

Figure 27.11

Specify a PANTONE spot color to fill a selection area within the image.

8. Choose **L**oad from the Mask menu, and then select the PT211.TIF image from the CHAP27 directory on the *CorelDRAW! The Professional Reference* companion CDs. PHOTO-PAINT enables only one mask of any type to be loaded at a time within an active image, so there is no need to use the Remove command to replace the present mask.

9. Choose PANTONE 211CV from the list of colors on the Color roll-up, and repeat step 7 for the second spot color for the advertisement, as shown in figure 27.12.

Figure 27.12
Use masks to add spot colors to an area within a CMYK color mode image.

10. Click on the Mask tool on the toolbox, and then click on the Remove button on the ribbon bar (or choose **R**emove from the **M**ask menu). Zoom out to a 50-percent viewing resolution to better see your handiwork, as shown in figure

27.13. You can save the finished image in CPT, TIF, SCITEX, or placeable EPS format. 32-bit/pixel images cannot be saved to file formats containing structures that cannot handle color-channel information. Tagged Image File Format generally is the safest bet when your final output is to an image setter at a commercial printer.

Figure 27.13
The finished CMYK image will be printed with colors as you see them in PHOTO-PAINT.

The color components of the PANTONE spot (and process) colors you chose in the last exercise correspond to percentages of cyan, magenta, yellow, and black inks a commercial printer uses on an offset press.

Using CorelDRAW to Reproduce Spot-Color Separations

As mentioned earlier, the ink colors represented on-screen when a subtractive color model is used for a digital image are as close as an entirely different medium can come to color matching. The accurate calibration of your monitor, scanner, and any other devices as well as the kind of press, ink, and paper all play important roles in how closely what you see on your monitor matches the printed output. The digital color-matching standards that PANTONE, FOCOLTONE, and TRUMATCH offer add to the accuracy that can be achieved and their use has gained widespread acceptance.

The PANTONE-filled MEGABURG logo produces as accurate an *on-screen* color match to a properly separated version of the printed version of the image as you can get. Short of seeing a color proof, you and your client can be reasonably assured that the corporate colors will be consistent when printed.

However, if you need to print color separations with accurate spot-color overlays (as fifth, sixth, and other extra separations), PHOTO-PAINT is not the program to use to create them. CorelDRAW can recognize and render PANTONE and other color-specification spot colors in a design, and the design doesn't have to be composed solely of native CorelDRAW vector objects. You can import a TIF image into CorelDRAW, create objects that go on top of the bitmap, assign the objects spot-color values, and then print the graphical "sandwich" to an image setter as color separations with additional spot-color overlays.

In the next example, the MEGABURG.TIF image has been imported into the MEGABURG.CDR file, which is located in the CHAP27 subdirectory of the *CorelDRAW! The Professional Reference* companion CDs. This file contains the

MegaBurger logo used to create the masks used in the last PHOTO-PAINT exercise.

The exercise that follows demonstrates how to create the same effect as you performed in the last exercise, except that when CorelDRAW objects are filled with PANTONE spot fills, you can generate as many spot-color separations as you need. CorelDRAW provides the trapping for vector objects placed on top of a bitmap, and because Corel's color specifications are built on the CMYK color model, converting a bitmap PHOTO-PAINT RGB image to CMYK color mode is not necessary when you print the design from CorelDRAW.

To generate proper CMYK color separations with spot-color overlays from CorelDRAW, follow these steps:

1. Close any Corel applications that are running. You need to change a default in a Corel INI file that enables spot-color separations to be printed.

2. Open a text editor such as Windows Notepad and open the CORELPRN.INI. This file is located in the CONFIG subdirectory of the COREL50 directory (or whatever you chose to call the Corel directory when you ran CorelDRAW 5 Setup).

3. In the [Config] section, find the PSSpotFountainsAsProcess=1 line and change the 1 to 0 (zero). This enables CorelDRAW and the other vector-oriented Corel modules to print spot color as spot color, and stops Corel's default conversion of spot color to CMYK equivalents.

4. Save the CORELPRN.INI file and close the text editor.

5. Launch CorelDRAW 5 and open the MEGABURG.CDR file from the CHAP27 subdirectory of the *CorelDRAW! The Professional Reference* companion CDs. This file contains an RGB copy of the MEGABURG.TIF image and the MegaBurger logo designed as two separate objects: one for the PANTONE 211 color and one for the PANTONE 312 spot-color area, as shown in figure 27.14.

Figure 27.14
CorelDRAW can import bitmap images and print a mixture of bitmaps and vector designs as color separations.

6. Choose the Pick tool and click on the MegaBurger lettering in the black vector logo. This selection includes the M drop-shadow area, and both these areas will be assigned PANTONE 211 spot color.

7. Click on the Fill tool and select the Uniform Fill tool from the fly-out menu.

8. Choose PANTONE Spot color from the Sho**w** drop-down list box.

9. Type **211** in the S**e**arch For field. CorelDRAW's search engine makes quick work of finding a specific color within the PANTONE, TRUMATCH, or FOCOLTONE color model. Click on the PANTONE 211CV color swatch in the Sho**w** window to select it, and then click on OK, as shown in figure 27.15.

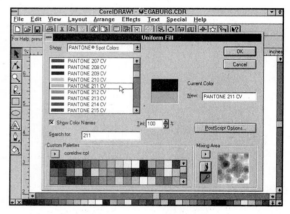

Figure 27.15
Choose a PANTONE spot color to assign to a selection.

N O T E

Although you can assign any color you want to a vector object in CorelDRAW, you cannot assign a color to a bitmap imported into CorelDRAW that has a bit-depth greater than 1 bit/per pixel. CorelDRAW can, however, fill a vector design drawn in CorelDRAW or imported from CGM, EPS, or other vector graphics.

10. Repeat steps 6 through 9, clicking on the M part of the logo design, and assign it PANTONE 312 from the Uniform Fill menu. Then click on OK. As you can see in figure 27.16, the selected object has its new fill indicated on the status line.

Figure 27.17
Reposition and resize the logo using the same techniques you would in PHOTO-PAINT.

Figure 27.16
Use CorelDRAW's status line to confirm the colors you have assigned to an object.

11. Marquee-select both objects and click on the Group button on the ribbon bar. Choose **G**roup from the **A**rrange menu, or press Ctrl+G if you don't have CorelDRAW 5 set up to display the ribbon bar.

12. Click-and-drag the grouped objects to the lower right of the bitmap, and then click-and-drag a corner selection handle to resize the logo to fit in the area shown in figure 27.17.

You're done editing the MEGABURG.CDR file, and it's time to print color separations. Color-separation printing is covered in more detail later in this chapter, but the exercise at present is intended to show you how to print spot-color separations. You don't actually have to print the file now, but the following are the steps to get four-color separations for process (CMYK) printing, and the additional two separations for spot colors in the design.

13. You really want to use a PostScript image setter to reproduce color separations, but any defined printer will do here for the purposes of this example. Choose **P**rint from the **F**ile menu. Click on the **O**ptions button and then click on the Separations tab.

14. Click on the Print **S**eparations check box, and then click on the specific colors you want to print on the colors box. When a color separation is chosen, the selection is highlighted, as shown in figure 27.18.

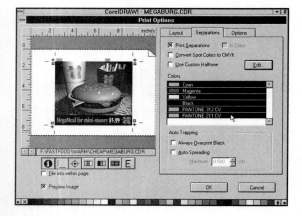

Figure 27.18
CorelDRAW offers options for printing all color separations, or only the ones you might need for an assignment.

15. Click on the OK button on the bottom of the screen. CorelDRAW prints a grayscale image for each of the CMYK color plates and the two you specified as color overlays. The camera-ready separations you just printed can be copied to press plates, and each plate made from the separations will be rendered with its corresponding pigment to paper or other material.

Although the preceding exercise is the only way Corel offers to produce spot-color overlays, there are many considerations and options to choose from when creating a print

from PHOTO-PAINT or DRAW. PHOTO-PAINT printing output options and considerations are covered next.

Output

There are many avenues the PHOTO-PAINT user can take to turn a design or photograph into hard copy. From laser print to 35-mm slide, there are a number of preprint considerations you can address though PHOTO-PAINT's Print command that will ensure that your output is faithful to the original image.

Because bitmap images are different fundamentally in structure from vector graphics, you might find that a laser print of your PHOTO-PAINT work doesn't contain refined blends, fills, and outlines. This lack of refinement can be quite a disappointment, particularly if your output is to a common 300-dpi, non-PostScript printer. RGB and grayscale images depend on Adobe System's PostScript technology to accurately reproduce halftones needed to express shades of gray on paper. The following section is a description of the halftone process, which produces the best results when used to print bitmap images.

Using the PostScript Language for Halftoning

There are two types of laser printers commonly available today: ones that use a graphics-descriptor language, and ones that don't. Of the two most popularly accepted standards, Adobe PostScript is practically the *de facto* descriptor language for graphics printing, and Hewlett-Packard's PCL language and variations of it are used in non-PostScript machines.

The difference between PCL language and PostScript is that PostScript technology is capable of rendering digital-halftone cells. Digital-halftone cells are a pattern of ink dots that are identical in nature and arrangement to those produced by using a physical halftone screen on a photographic print. Printer Command Language, on the other hand, produces pleasant-looking, black-and-white images from grayscale files, but the dots are not arranged in a pattern, or a series of lines, that commercial printers are accustomed to using to make printing plates.

The decision on whether to use a PostScript or PCL-based printer to create camera-ready halftones is problematic—you'll get noticeably poorer results and perhaps some criticism from a commercial printer if you submit a PCL laser print of your work for reproduction.

Using the Digital Halftone Cell

The following sections address the role of halftoning when applied to grayscale images. Color prints use halftones to represent a digital image; the technique for color-process printing is similar and is covered as a separate discussion in the section, "Using PHOTO-PAINT's Advanced Screening Options," later in this chapter.

Halftoning traditionally has been performed on *continuous tone* images to represent the shades of gray found in an original photograph. The physical process of halftoning is accomplished through the use of a film screen that contains lines. The term *lines per inch* is a description of the resolution of an image when rendered to paper, and the dots per inch a laser printer renders becomes a component of a image's resolution when printed. Halftone dots (arranged in lines) correspond to darker and lighter shades in an original image. The human eye integrates the collection of dots created by the line screen into continuous tones that make a printed image recognizable.

Figure 27.19 is a stylized illustration of rows of halftone dots. If you stand about 10 feet away from this page (and possibly squint), you can see that the larger dots simulate a darker shade than the smaller ones. The shade of gray that each line of dots is intended to represent is indicated at the top of figure 27.19.

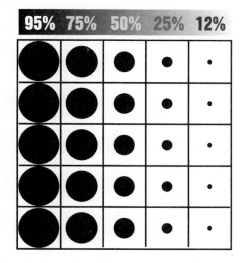

Figure 27.19
Halftone dots are arranged in a line to simulate shades in a continuous-tone photograph.

Presently, halftoning is the only means for laser printers and commercial print presses to express the intermingling shades found in chemical photographs.

The *digital halftone cell* is the computer equivalent of a physical halftone dot created by screening a photographic image; like the physical halftone, the digital halftone is composed of dots arranged in rows. You can control two qualities when creating a laser print halftone—*screen angle* and *screen frequency*. Depending on the resolution of your output hardware, it's possible in 1994 to create a camera-ready halftone that a commercial printer can use to produce magazine-quality prints. The following two controllable aspects of a computer-generated halftone are the same as those used to physically screen a physical photo:

- **Screen Angle.** Lines of dots need to be organized at an angle to the edges of an image, and the screen angle is this measurement. Typically, a grayscale image is screened at 45 degrees, although this can vary from manufacturer to manufacturer. If you're preparing a laser print to be published, it's a good idea to ask the press operator at the commercial printer at what angle they require the image to be screened. Then match the angle using PHOTO-PAINT's **P**rint, **S**etup, **O**ptions, Advanced settings.

Often, commercial presses use custom physical screens to produce the film negatives for offset printing, and their screen angles are optimized to work best with their presses. You always should strive to match your camera-ready laser print to the results a printer is accustomed to producing with its physical screen work.

- **Screen Frequency.** Screen frequency refers to how many lines-per-inch halftone dots represent the shaded areas in an original image. There is a mathematical relationship between *lines per inch* (lpi) and the *dots per inch* (dpi) a laser printer can render. How many lines per inch a laser printer can render is based on the resolution of the printer mechanisms (300, 600, 1200, 1800 dpi), user preference, and physical composition of the toner. Screen frequency also is set through the Advanced settings of PHOTO-PAINT's Print command.

A commercial printer chooses an optimal screen frequency for a job based on experience gained using the specific paper and ink you have specified on a specific printing press. Ask the commercial printer what screen frequency they would use for your job if *they* were to do the screening. If your laser printer is capable of producing good results with that screen frequency, only then should you consider printing camera-ready artwork from your laser printer.

Determining Line Frequency and Image Resolution

The higher the screen frequency defined for a printed image, the less capable the print will be at expressing the range of grayscale values found in the original image. It's an inverse function—the higher the screen frequency, the smaller the number of grayscale values represented by halftone dots. The best printer screen frequency for a grayscale image is one-half the image resolution measured in pixels/inch. The following is a mathematical formula for calculating the optimal lpi value based on any given image:

Printer Screen Frequency × 2 = Image Resolution

Suppose that you create a PHOTO-PAINT TIF file at 150 pixels per inch; the optimal screen frequency to define for a laser print of the image would be 75 lines per inch. It is best, then, to begin a design (or to acquire a scanned image) with a happy balance struck between image resolution and your machine's capability to handle a large image file.

Looking At Image Resolution and Shades of Gray

Unfortunately, today's high end laser printers have a threshold of dots-per-inch capability of about 1200 to 1800, depending on the manufacturer. Most office laser printers are only able to produce 300 or 600 dpi. Several types of add-in boards are available from manufacturers to increase the resolution of some brands of 300 or 600 laser printers, and some manufacturers, such as Laser Master, even offer stand-alone, high-resolution printers they bill as plain-paper image setters.

What level of visible quality can a plain-paper laser printer achieve, and at what point

do you want to forgo "home brew" camera-ready prints in favor of image setting your work? The answer lies largely with the intended purpose of your finished product. Here, a second mathematical formula can be used to determine the number of unique shades of gray a laser printer can render as halftone dots:

$$\frac{\textbf{Printer Resolution}}{\textbf{Printer Screen Frequency}} = \textbf{n (squared)}$$

= Shades of Grey

To make this equation a little more meaning-ful, here's an example of how you can evaluate the number of shades a laser printer will print versus how many shades you have in an original design at a specific printer dpi capability.

The grayscale-image mode in PHOTO-PAINT is 8 bits/pixel, which means that it has the capability of 256 unique tonal values. Suppose that you create a grayscale design at a resolution of 150 pixels/inch, and you have access to a 300-dpi laser printer. Remembering that the best line frequency for printing is half the image resolution, the line-per-inch value for this example is 75. Given these parameters, here's what you'll get on a good day:

$$\frac{\textbf{300 dpi}}{\textbf{75 lpi}} = \textbf{4 (squared) = 16 shades of gray}$$

A simple qualitative analysis of this scenario suggests that most of the possible tonal values in the grayscale image will not reproduce.

The visual result of this scenario would be a poor image—almost posterized in its appearance.

Decreasing the lines-per-inch value in this situation is not really the solution for increasing the printed image's quality; fewer lines per inch would create visible lines similar to rotogravure etchings common to the turn of the century. The answer to creating prints that reflect accurate image detail is by rendering the image to hardware that has greater dot-per-inch capability such as a Linotronic or another brand of image setter. Image setters aren't constrained to rendering dots of toner on plain paper; instead, they use film. When film is used, resolutions of greater than 1500 halftone dots per inch can be recorded accurately from original image information. The Lino model 630, for example, is capable of rendering 1693 dots per inch to film. Given the same set of parameters as those in the last example, here's how faithfully you can expect the same grayscale design to go to camera-ready, halftone artwork:

$$\frac{\textbf{1693 dpi}}{\textbf{75 lpi}} = \textbf{22.57 (squared)} = \frac{\textbf{509.4 shades}}{\textbf{of grey}}$$

As you can see, an image setter can provide more than an adequate amount of halftone values to represent a 256-color grayscale image. In reality, a printer would use a screen with a higher screen frequency in this situation. A higher screen frequency would produce a printed image with much greater printed resolution and would decrease the amount of gray shades expressed as halftone dots to within the color capability of the original image.

At some point in your imaging career, you will need higher resolution prints of your work, and this means necessarily trusting some of your output to someone else—unless, of course, you own a commercial print press. There are a number of possibilities beyond the conventional laser printer for outputting your work, and the next section describes how you can have some input on your final output.

Printing to Disk

PHOTO-PAINT offers the Print to Disk option from the Print dialog box, and this creates an opportunity to use a printer driver belonging to a machine you might not own to specify printing options. Many service bureaus own image setters, but might not own PHOTO-PAINT version 5. Your own pre-press work and workaround in an instance like this is to set the output options you need from within PHOTO-PAINT on your own PC, and then print the image to a printer-instruction file. You take the printer-instruction file to the service bureau, they print the image to film, and you have a high-resolution color or black-and-white image ready for the commercial printer to work from.

The next series of steps in the following example are hypothetical, but if you have a little time, this is a valuable exercise. The first step in printing to disk is to get a copy of the specific printer driver works with the service bureau's image setter. Be sure to ask for a Windows version of the printer driver. Service bureaus are happy to provide drivers; it causes them less work, and they have absolutely no creative calls to make with your work. Printer-instruction files are unlike image files in that they contain *machine code*—instructions that tell an image setter specifically how to render an image.

For this exercise, suppose that your service bureau uses a Linotronic model 630 image setter to record halftones to film. Windows 3.1*x* ships with a Linotronic 630 print driver, so if you want to follow along in this Print to File experiment, you need to find the Setup disks for Windows 3.1 or higher before beginning. If your service bureau actually uses a Linotronic model 630, be sure to ask it for the most recent Windows version of the driver. Drivers are updated constantly, and the ones found on your Windows disks are fine for experimenting with, but should *not* be used if a newer driver is available.

T I P

The Microsoft PostScript printer drivers 3.56 and 3.58 are current as of the writing, and you should replace versions below these. The version number of the currently installed PS driver can be found in the Control Panel, Printers, Setup, About dialog box.

Here's how to print an image to disk that a service bureau then can render to high resolution:

1. In Windows Program Manager, double-click on the Control Panel icon and then double-click on the Printers icon. This is the Windows utility for installing printer drivers.

2. Choose **A**dd, and then choose Install Unlisted or Updated Printer from the **L**ist of Printers if you actually have a printer driver from a service bureau on disk. If you're simply following this

example for hands-on experience, choose Linotronic 630 from **L**ist of Printers.

3. Click on **I**nstall, and then insert the Windows disk that the Install Driver dialog box requests; or simply type **A:** or **B:**, depending on which media the service bureau gave you to store its printer driver.

4. Click on OK, and then choose the driver from the **L**ist of Printers list in the Add Unlisted or Updated Printer dialog box.

5. Click on OK, and then click on S**e**t As Default Printer. Click on **C**lose to exit the Printers dialog box. Double-click on the control menu button to close the Control Panel. Restart PHOTO-PAINT.

6. Open the B&W_WOOD.TIF image from the CHAP27 subdirectory of the *CorelDRAW! The Professional Reference* companion CDs. This is a very small grayscale test image you will print to file.

7. Choose **P**rint from the **F**ile menu or click on the Print button on the ribbon bar.

8. Click on the Print to **F**ile check box from the Print dialog box. If your service bureau is Macintosh-based, you might decide to check the For **M**ac check box. The For **M**ac option copies Macintosh-specific printer instructions to a file. Macintosh front ends for image setters need minor variations on instruction sets to handle IBM/PC-based image files. Click on OK.

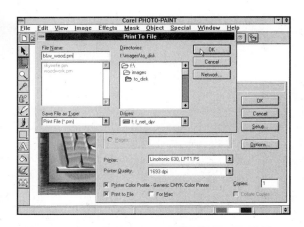

Unlike the Macintosh operating system standard for writing images as printer instructions, an IBM/PC PRN file contains a character command, Ctrl+D, at the beginning and end of the printer code instructions. Checking PHOTO-PAINT's For **M**ac check box creates a PRN file without the Ctrl+D characters at the beginning and end of the file—it simply strips the characters from the file, without altering any other information.

These characters cause problems with AppleTalk connections, and will crash a Macintosh front end for an image setter. Most PC-savvy service bureaus have utilities to strip out the characters from a PRN file, but many Macintosh bureaus who have yet to come around to understanding IBM/PC operating characterisitics will have problems if the characters are present.

9. Choose a directory and drive on your hard drive for the location of the file. Print-to-file information takes up more space than an image file, and it definitely would be a mistake to specify a floppy drive for the file; a floppy drive not only has a small capacity, but its write time is slower than hard disks.

10. Name your file and give it the PRN file extension. As you can see in figure 27.20, the file was given the same name as the TIF image, and the PRN file was pathed to a location that is easy to find later and transfer to removable media.

11. Click on OK and PHOTO-PAINT prints the image to file.

Figure 27.20
A PRN file contains all the instructions an image setter needs to render your file to high resolution.

There is more to this exercise, but basically you've accomplished the hard part! Again, images printed to file contain printer-specific information about how to render the image, and not the actual image *per se*, so a service bureau cannot perform after-the-fact corrections with only the print-to-file information. To print the information file to the Linotronic 630 (or another image setter, depending on the driver you installed), copy the PRN file to the PC's drive that is the front end for the image setter, and type the following at the DOS prompt:

```
COPY [filename].PRN PRN
```

If you performed the last exercise, you now have a file of almost 300KB on your hard disk. Compared to the original image, the PRN file is almost three times the size; you should anticipate this magnitude of file increase and plan accordingly for a good way to transport the PRN file for larger native images.

Using Removable Media

Whether you print an image to file, or simply want to transport a design in its native saved file format, disks aren't a solution for transporting image files larger than 1.44MB. You'll find that you exceed this figure constantly due to high-quality scans, RGB color mode, and large image resolutions. The solution for porting your PRN files can be removable, large-format media. SyQuest manufactures drives and removable cartridges that can hold anywhere from 44MB to more than 200MB. Removable media drives using the SyQuest standard commonly are found at service bureaus. Bernoulli cartridges operate along a similar principal to SyQuests, but the drives aren't as commonly found at service bureaus. If you're considering purchasing a large-format, removable media drive, find out which model the service bureaus in your area use and get the same type. Removable media cartridges are very sensitive to the make and model drive they're written to, and are not interchangeable, as disks are.

You also can use a tape backup cartridge for transporting an image, or number of images, to a service bureau or commercial printer. As with removable media, you should match the type of tape cartridge and the backup software used to the drive and your service bureau.

Using Compression Utilities

PHOTO-PAINT supports JPEG compression for both grayscale and RGB images. You can achieve near-perfect copies of original files at a compression rate of from 5 to 100 times an original image's file size.

JPEG is a scheme of *lossey compression*, where almost imperceptible colors in an image are

averaged to dramatically reduce file sizes as they are stored on disk. When a JPEG image is re-opened in an imaging program like PHOTO-PAINT, or other programs that recognize the JPG format, the file expands again to nearly its original size. JPEG is a product of the Joint Photographers Expert Group, an organization of imaging professionals who recognized the need to conserve hard disk space when digital imaging was barely more than a concept in the PC community. JPEG images are not exact duplicates of original image information, but most people kid themselves when they claim that they can tell a JPEG image from an original digital image. The difference between a JPEG image and an original image is nominal at best, and this standard was agreed on by experts in the photographic field as an acceptable means of compression through extremely minor color reduction.

To create a JPEG file, first make a copy of the image if you don't have total confidence in JPEG technology. Then choose JPEG bitmap (JPG) from the Save File as **T**ype drop-down list box. PHOTO-PAINT offers you three compression formats. It is a good idea to not aim for "fancy" compression schemes when working with a commercial printer or service bureau; JPEG, JFIF-compliant is the JPEG format that is most in use professionally, and the CMP format is almost proprietary to Corel products. Bear in mind that PHOTO-PAINT 5 is a new product with new features and options, and end users generally upgrade before service bureaus.

Choose a Quality factor for JPEG compression in the Export JPEG dialog box. JPEG compression amount is inversely proportional to resulting image quality; the higher

the compression, the more unique colors are averaged in an image. You might want to experiment with various degrees of compression before sending a JPEG image to a service bureau. At the maximum setting of 255, you might notice loss of color quality. Lossey compression is different for each image; the resulting image quality and compression ratio you achieve depends on the visual content of an image.

Using PKZIP

PKZIP, the standard for PC compression utilities, stores a PRN or regular image file in more space than a JPEG file, but its method of compression is lossless; you don't lose any original image information when you make a ZIP copy of a design.

PKZIP is not included with PHOTO-PAINT, and it does not compress and decompress images on the fly like the JPEG format does. Instead, PKZIP is a shareware program manufactured by PKWARE, Inc., and unregistered copies of the program can be found on every electronic bulletin board (BBS) around the world. Shareware is not freeware, and if you find PKZIP to be useful in your profession, you're required to register it by tendering a small fee to PKWARE.

PKZIP version 204G has the capability to span disks. *Spanning* is a method for copying a single file to multiple floppy disks. If you have the patience, you can copy a file that is 18MB to several floppy disks, and then reassemble the file on the host PC at a service bureau. PKZIP writes a kernel of its own program to the disks you span, and all the information for "splicing" a spanned file is contained on the disks.

Additionally, you can save a little more file space if you PKZIP an image that has been

JPEG-compressed, but don't expect a dramatic reduction in file size because compressed file formats almost never respond to a second compression. PhotoCD images in the PCD format, for example, don't compress at all using PKZIP because part of the compression technology used to store PCD images is the same as that used in PKZIP.

ARJ and LZH are two other popular compression programs similar to PKZIP, and although their features are not identical to PKZIP, some service bureaus and commercial printers use the programs.

Before you compress a file, be sure to talk to your service bureau to find out whether they have the software and the hardware to decompress the file. Some Macintosh-only service bureaus refuse to deal with files compressed in a PC format. If you run into this situation, your money will gladly be accepted elsewhere.

Transporting via Modem

Occasionally, you might want to call in your order. Many service bureaus and commercial printers offer dedicated data lines that you can use to send an image by way of modem. Today's modems are capable of fast speeds and speedy data transfers; however, this option should be reserved for situations when you cannot physically transport an image on disk or other media. Modem transfers of exceptionally large image files can take quite a while and can tie up a data line for several hours. If a compressed image is less than 1MB and you are handcuffed to your PC or something, consider using a modem to make a file transfer; otherwise, use any of the other alternative means listed in this section to get your work out to the bureau.

Working with Color Printing and Color Separations

Because you see the world in color, you instinctively design in color; color printing is a PHOTO-PAINT option if you have the right hardware and understand a few things about color printing requirements and what to expect from a color print of your original image.

Using a Personal Color Printer

The cost of color printers has decreased dramatically from a few years ago, and will continue to become more affordable as new technology pushes present technology's sticker price down. If you already own a color printer, your first step to printing from PHOTO-PAINT is to check the **C**olor Manager menu in search of the corresponding profile for your printer in the **P**rinter drop-down list box. Corel supplies a profile for the top 15 color printers from manufacturers such as Hewlett-Packard, Canon, and Tektronix. If your printer is not listed here, click on Other in the **P**rinter drop-down list box to see a Printer Calibration menu in which you can specify models of ink your printer uses, the amount of *Undercolor Removal* (UCR) you want PHOTO-PAINT to calculate for the image and send as information to the printer, and the curve for the amount of black you want to use in the CMYK printing.

It's important that you take advantage of every option PHOTO-PAINT offers to calibrate your color printer to correspond to your monitor. Color accuracy is a very relative quality with printers that cost less than $8,000, and your best chance of avoiding blue image areas that print purple, for example, is to let PHOTO-PAINT's Color Manager build a profile of all your peripherals. See Chapter 21 for more details on PHOTO-PAINT's Color Manager.

Color printers vary in technology and the materials used to render color onto paper or other materials. Color printers that most individuals consider reasonable output at a reasonable price consist of inkjet, thermal wax transfer, color ribbons, and dye sublimation. The use of a personal color printer should be limited to presentations and documented hard copy, and should *not* be used to evaluate colors as they would be printed as process-color inks at a commercial printer or for use as color proofing. Personal color printers simply are inaccurate and fail to render a high enough resolution to be seen as acceptable substitutes for photographic prints or dye transfers. Additionally, personal color printers use a different medium than commercial printers to render an image, so different pigments react to light differently.

Personal color printers are the digital equivalent of Polaroid cameras in 1994; they are marvelous machines for producing physical output you can tack on a wall and mail to a client, but they don't accurately reflect the color values found in an original.

Using PHOTO-PAINT's Color-Separation Options

PHOTO-PAINT offers advanced color separation options that are of the most use by a commercial printing facility. Color separations are four passes of grayscale halftones that correspond to the C, M, Y, and K color channels of the same digital image type. The technique of producing four-color process color prints from CMYK separations is an art in the same sense that creating digital images is. To create color separations that will result in magazine-quality images requires patience, skill, an education in commercial printing, and an image setter.

The following is a walkthrough of PHOTO-PAINT's options for producing four-color separations, and this is intended to acquaint you with the four-color printing process; if the bulk of your work is in creating and retouching images, your spare time is better spent developing a good relationship with a commercial print house than attempting to render accurate color separations!

In figure 27.21, an RGB image has been converted to CMYK color mode, and the **P**rint command has been chosen from the **F**ile menu, then the **O**ptions button has been clicked to display the Print Options dialog box. A Linotronic image setter is defined as the output source. This is the same menu you get with a personal color printer defined, and if you're using a color printer, the option buttons beneath the image preview window play a substantially less important role in printing.

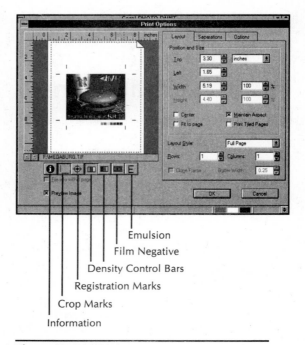

Emulsion
Film Negative
Density Control Bars
Registration Marks
Crop Marks
Information

Figure 27.21
The Print Options dialog box in PHOTO-PAINT.

The options beneath the preview window follow from left to right, as follows:

- **Information.** If you click on the Information button, the printer sets the name of the image, the process color plate (C, M, Y, or K), and the date and time. Generally, it's a good idea to make the image size smaller than the paper or film size you're using to allow extra printing information to fall outside the image area. When the Information option is active, the **F**ile Info within Page option check box becomes active. This option is a tad misleading: by *within page*, Corel means *within the image window*. If you're printing an image that has no border within the image window, do not check this box—PHOTO-PAINT will print *inside* the image.

- **Crop Marks.** When you choose this option button, Corel places crop marks outside the image area on color separations or color prints.

- **Registration Marks.** Because it is critical for all four color separations to be aligned as they are printed to one page, registration marks are an indicator to the press operator where each separation should meet the printed page. Although you can choose this option for your separations, a lot of commercial printers ignore registration marks placed by designers and substitute their own before printing. They do this because film and paper separations can stretch when rendered, and the registration marks can come out of alignment. So unless you're a commercial printer, don't sweat this option.

- **Density-Control Bars.** These options place solid and percentages of color and grayscale densities next to an image for use in checking with a densitometer at printing time. Commercial printers use these bars to ensure that a cyan separation, for example, has printed the correct amount of cyan, and so on. This is a feature for a commercial printer's use, and can affect your image's quality if a commercial printer has no means by which to test a solid color or grayscale halftone value apart from the live image area.

- **Film Negative.** This option reverses the chroma in the color print to create negative values. Occasionally, you may want to make a film negative, from which a commercial printer makes a plate positive; you should definitely ask a commercial printer for their preference if you're bringing homemade separations to them to reproduce. You also want to choose Film Negative if you want a 35mm negative from a Service Bureau's film recorder, a topic covered later in this chapter.

- **Emulsion.** Image setters can use paper or film, depending on the nature of your design and the cost-effectiveness in producing it. When using film to render high-resolution color separations, the film has an emulsion on one side. Which side of your separations are to be printed on the emulsion side is entirely up to the commercial printer and its printing methods, so again, consult with the people who use your color separations before deciding on this option.

Using PHOTO-PAINT's Separations Options

PHOTO-PAINT offers user-defined controls for creating custom halftones and auto-trapping in the Separations tab from the Print Options command. It is here that you decide to print separations; four prints from which the CMYK color composite is rendered as dots of ink to paper. You must have the Print **S**eparations check box checked to generate these four copies.

The Use Custom Halftones check box also must be checked in order to respecify the halftone angle and frequency of any of the four-color separations. Additionally, you can choose to print only one or more of the color separations in one session. Click on the color names in the Colors field to select which color separations you want to print. When a process color is highlighted, this separation prints to the image setter.

The Auto-Trapping controls toward the bottom of the Separations menu are useful in situations where you have two adjacent solid-color fields in a design. The MEGABURG image in this chapter features a PANTONE color inside a large black field, for example. In this situation, trapping is required to prevent bleeding between colors as the image is printed. When the Auto-Spreading option is checked, PHOTO-PAINT provides you with an overprinting option—you specify how many points you want PHOTO-PAINT to enlarge an image area so that a choke or spread is created between color values.

A *choke* is when a darker color is overprinted on a light color to confine the bleed of the lighter color, as is the situation with the MEGABURG image. A *spread* is the converse effect; a lighter color is overprinted on a darker color, and PHOTO-PAINT creates an enlarged outline of solid light color to fill in areas surrounding the darker value.

Trapping is a science like commercial printing, and although you gain a little more control over the finished print by checking the Auto-Trapping option, it often is best to consult with the commercial printer about problem areas in a design that require trapping. The commercial printers might have a better solution for their presses, and at

the very least, they can provide you with a value for the Auto-Spreading option.

When the Always Overprint black option is checked, any image area that is equal to or greater than 95-percent black will be trapped with a spread. If the Auto-Spreading option also is checked, any black (regardless of its *percentage* of black) in the image prints on top of all the other colors. This is an expedient way to create traps, but an experienced pre-press person can build much more elegant and refined traps than Corel's Auto-Trapping option can. If you need to create high quality output, let an experienced human perform this service.

Using PHOTO-PAINT's Advanced Screening Options

If you check the Use Custom Halftone check box, the Edit button appears, and you can move to the Advanced Settings menu. PHOTO-PAINT gives you hands-on control over halftone screening options for color separations. The defaults for screen angle and line frequency are set according to the printer you have defined, but these can be overridden if your commercial printer has different optimal settings for the screens used on their presses.

Unless you're trying to achieve a special effect, it's generally not a good idea to respecify color-separation output settings. Traditional, physical line screens have been calculated carefully to avoid moiré patterning in a process color print. *Moiré patterning* is the unwanted resonating of line screens within an image. Certain angles are complementary for overlaying cyan, magenta, yellow, and black lines of halftone dots; the *rosette* effect (a good effect) is achieved by specifying different, oblique angles for each component color separation to simulate a continuous color image.

Traditional printing screens have been set at C=105°, M=75°, Y=90°, and B=45°. You'll notice that PHOTO-PAINT uses slightly different values than traditional, physical line screens because image setters don't render 105-degree and 75-degree angles as well as they can be reproduced photographically due to the right angle, bitmap nature of digital reproduction. Instead, Linotronic and other image setter manufacturers have come up with optimal combinations of screen angles and frequencies that address the problem digital image setters have matching traditional values.

Using RT Screening

If you have a Linotronic image setter defined as your output device in PHOTO-PAINT, the **S**creening Technology drop-down list in the Advanced Screening menu contains different options for *Rational Tangent* (RT) screening. As shown in figure 27.22, different models of Linotronic image setters are listed, and when one is chosen, the optimal screen frequency and angle is defined in the Screen Frequencies and Angles area of the Advanced Screening menu. You would be ill-advised to manually enter data different than the optimal settings, unless your commercial printer specifically asked you to change a setting to work better with its print presses, or if you are trying to achieve an artistic effect with your process color print.

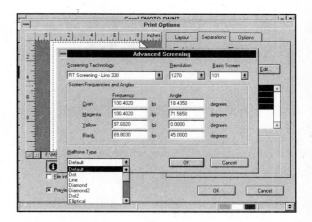

Figure 27.22

The RT Screening Technology selections in the Advanced Screening menu.

Using HQS and RIPS

Most image setters at commercial printers and service bureaus use the Adobe PostScript descriptor language or an emulation such as TrueImage. A *Raster Image Processor* (RIP) is needed to translate PostScript descriptions to the binary code the image setter uses to render an image to film or paper. Every model of image setter requires a unique RIP. Manufacturers of image setters and RIPs have developed different sets of optimized screens and have implemented various technologies to improve the output from each model of image setter. These optimized screens are specific to a make and model of an image setter and cannot be used interchangeably or on a creative whim. Only if the image setter used to output your work supports optimized

screens (ask your service bureau) should you specify their use, because they are more accurate than the default RT screens.

The HQS screening technology also is offered by PHOTO-PAINT when you have a Linotronic image setter defined, and HQS is a more accurate screening technology for digital screening than RT screening. Like RT screening, HQS consists of a preset combination of line frequencies and screen angles that are optimized for a specific image-setting device. HQS screening is closer in values to traditional, physical screens, and therefore produces better process color results. HQS screening is proprietary to Linotronic image setters and specific RIPs used with Linotronic image setters. If you aren't rendering to a Linotronic image setter, HQS options are not available to use when printing from PHOTO-PAINT.

Additionally, other image setter manufacturers offer their own, proprietary deployment of screening technology, all designed to bring a digital halftone screen closer to the angles and frequencies used in physical halftone screens for color separations. AGFA, for example, offers BST screening technology. Check the documentation of a specific image setter to see whether it offers a screening technology that can be used with PHOTO-PAINT. Otherwise, you should ask the service bureau to override the Corel screen settings to take advantage of the image setter's optimized screens. If you are sending your work to a commercial printer as a PRN file, this might not be possible.

Using Halftone Dot Types

In addition to the traditional round shape, halftone dots can be rendered in the shape of

diamonds, ellipses, and a variety of other shapes. In the Advance Screening menu, the Halftone **T**ype drop-down list offers different types of dots to be used in screening.

You can achieve some artistic effects in a color process print by specifying different dot shapes for your separations, but as always, you should talk to your commercial printer about the best halftone dot shape before going through the effort and expense of generating nonstandard color separations. Occasionally, a commercial printer requests a specific dot shape to better render the final four-color print. A diamond shape sometimes is used for halftone dots because the edges of the diamonds produce clean edges within the print. Ellipses sometimes are used as halftone dots to better fill color areas within the print and to prevent unpleasant halftone patterns. Always bear in mind that a color print is composed of slightly overlapping CMYK colors, and that the closer they are bought together in a pattern without creating oversaturated, muddy image areas, the more convincingly the halftone dots represent a continuous tone color image.

Working with Color Transparencies

Process color printing plays an important role in visual communications today, but 35-mm slides and other color transparency formats are still big business, and are used in boardrooms and motion picture studios daily.

Using a Film Recorder

A color transparency of a bitmap image can be made through the use of a film recorder. Unlike process-color printing, a film recorder exposes film to the RGB values contained in a TIF or other digital image format to produce slides, not prints. Because of the nature of color transparencies, halftone dots are not used, but instead emulsion areas are created with three primary layers of dyes that accurately reflect image characteristics almost identical to those viewed on your monitor.

Film recorders vary in price range, but a professional quality film recorder can cost about as much as an image setter, which basically puts it out of the budget of most designers.

Fortunately, many service bureaus across the country offer film-recorder services or actually have a film recorder on premises, and you can have PHOTO-PAINT images rendered to a number of color transparency formats for less than the cost of a process-color proof.

Setting Up a PHOTO-PAINT Image for Film Recording

Because film recorders produce images to a photographic medium, you should observe a number of conventions unlike those for color printing. Convention number one is that *the quality of a color transparency is dependent on image file size, not image resolution.* Film recorders take a quantitative look at image information, not at how many pixels per inch are represented in an image. This works

because image resolution is relative to an image's overall dimensions (in height and width).

Determining Image File Size and Partial Image Areas

It therefore is a good idea to create a PHOTO-PAINT image as large as possible in file size, and this means having as much RAM installed on your PC as your budget allows. Unfortunately, PHOTO-PAINT only accesses 18MB of image; if you want to load a large PhotoCD image, for example, PHOTO-PAINT offers you the option of loading a partial image area. If you want to edit an image that is larger than PHOTO-PAINT or larger than your system RAM permits, you need to work with partial image areas. The following section tells you how to edit a partial image area.

Unlike the other images used in exercises in this chapter, the SEASONS.TIF image is not on the *CorelDRAW! The Professional Reference* companion CDs. You should follow the steps in this exercise if you have an image that's too large to load in its entirety. The image you intend to edit must be stored on read-write media such as your hard drive, but here's how to retouch a small area of a 12MB image that would be an ideal candidate for imaging to a film recorder:

1. Choose **O**pen from the **F**ile menu, and then select the image in which you want to edit a partial area. In figure 27.23, you can see the preview of SEASONS.TIF. The **O**ptions button provides information on the creation date of the file, as well as the size of the image.

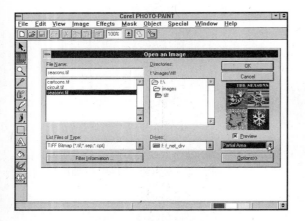

Figure 27.23

*The **O**ptions button provides details of the file you want to open before loading it.*

2. Choose Partial Area from the drop-down list to the right of the Dri**v**es list, and then click on OK.

3. PHOTO-PAINT displays a grid around a thumbnail image of the picture you want to open a partial copy of. If you click on Custom Size in the Grid Size drop-down list and then click on the Edit Grid check box, you can place your cursor inside the preview window and click-and-drag to define the area you want to load, as shown in figure 27.24. You can see that the partial area defined in the image "weighs in" at almost 3MB.

4. Click on OK. PHOTO-PAINT opens the partial area of the image.

5. Edit the part of the image you want. As you can see in figure 27.25, the sun portion of the SEASONS.TIF image is getting a tinted pair of shades by using the Tint tool. The status line icon at

the far right shows that a partial area of a larger image is the active image, and the name of the file is displayed on the title bar.

Figure 27.24

Click-and-drag on the grid in the preview window to define the partial area of an image you want to open.

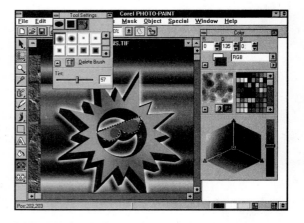

Figure 27.25

Editing a partial image area is less resource-intensive than having an entire file loaded.

6. When you're done editing, choose **S**ave from the **F**ile menu. PHOTO-PAINT applies your edits to the entire image. In addition to the **S**ave command, you can use Sa**v**e Partial Area As to save only the area you've worked on. If you've made a mistake and don't want to apply your changes to a large image, there's a "chicken switch" in PHOTO-PAINT you can use after choosing **S**ave; press Esc to abort a save back to the image, but press it *immediately* after choosing the **S**ave command.

Determining Image Dimensions

 A film recorder doesn't care about file resolution or inches, but the *proportion* of your image must be 2:3. Most film recorders record to 35-mm film, and the proportions of 35-mm negatives and transparencies is always 2 to 3. This reality can play an important factor every time you create a new image if your final output is to a slide.

Unfortunately, the 2:3 proportion is not very "artistic," and a lot of designers already have proportions for an image in mind, or have created a number of images that simply don't match this specification. In instances such as these, you have two options before submitting your work to the service bureau: you crop the image to 2:3 dimensions or you add a background. Service bureaus don't get paid to be art critics, and the best service bureaus leave the call to crop up to the designer. As a designer, it's your right to specify a crop or a color background, so it's sort of counterproductive to leave guesswork up to a service bureau. Because cropping usually destroys

part of a design, the following example walks you through your other alternative for making an image film-recorder compliant.

Follow these steps to create a border for an existing digital image to make its proportions 2:3, using an image from the *CorelDRAW! The Professional Reference* companion CDs:

1. Open the VIRGISLE.TIF image from the CHAP27 subdirectory of the *CorelDRAW! The Professional Reference* companion CD.

2. Choose **I**mage Info from the **I**mage menu.

   As you can see in figure 27.26, the VIRGISLE's dimensions are 458 × 343 pixels—close, but not exactly the 2:3 ratio needed by a film recorder that renders 35-mm slides. If this was an image of your own, your next step would be to fetch a pocket calculator or to open the Windows calculator (CALC.EXE in the Windows subdirectory).

Figure 27.26

PHOTO-PAINT's Image Info dialog box tells you image size and resolution.

Simple math in this example tells you that if the total image dimensions were 600 × 400 pixels, you would meet the aspect ration for the film recorder. It's usually best to create a frame along all sides of an image; adding background color to only two of an image's four sides creates an unappealing composition.

3. Evaluate the image content. In this example, the VIRGISLE image contains many dark greens, and you can adopt the traditional framemaker's approach of using a color matte for the border of the image that matches one of the colors found in the image. Choose one of the greens in the image by choosing the Eyedropper tool, and then press Ctrl while left-clicking on a green image area. This action sets the background (paper color) for the active image.

N O T E

Actually, even if you have a light composition or a white paper color for your design, you might want to stick with a dark color for the background of your image when proportioning it to 35-mm dimensions. Slides generally are shown in dimly lit conference areas, and a slide featuring a light or white border is bound to get a reaction out of the audience when popped onto the screen. This is known as *blasting the audience* in the same way that an empty carousel slot in a projector slams the viewer with a blinding transition from color images to absolute white. Plan your presentations carefully, and don't use white borders if your slide is going to be projected.

4. Choose **N**ew from the **F**ile menu, and then specify 24 Bit Color as the **C**olor Mode, type **600** pixels for New Image **W**idth and **400** pixels for Image **H**eight, specify 150 dpi as Resolution (because **I**mage Info has told you the VIRGISLE image is also 150 dpi), and then click on OK. You already have determined the **P**aper Color as a shade from the VIRGISLE image.

Alternatively, you can reset the paper size in the Image menu to perform an equivalent technique with an image, but by creating a background as a new image for the VIRGISLE image to be copied to, you can reposition the copy later, which the Paper Size command cannot do.

5. Reposition and resize both image windows so that they are clearly in view, and then click on the VIRGISLE title bar to make it the active image window.

6. Click on a Mask tool (any Mask tool will do) and click on the Select All button on the ribbon bar.

7. Click on the Copy button on the ribbon bar (or either choose **C**opy from the **E**dit menu or press Ctrl+C).

8. Click on the NEW-1.CPT title bar to make it the active image window.

9. Press Ctrl+V (or click on the Paste button, or choose **P**aste from the **E**dit menu and choose As New **O**bject).

10. Click-and-drag the copy of the VIRGISLE image until it's positioned where you want it, as shown in figure 27.27. Then press Ctrl+G or choose

Merge from the **O**bject menu to composite the floating selection to the NEW-1.CPT image background.

Figure 27.27

Position the copy of an image within a new background that is proportioned to film-recorder specs.

11. Service bureaus tend to display a strong preference for one file format over the other, and because you now have a copy of the original design, you're free to help the service bureau do its work on your slide. Save the NEW-1.CPT file to TIF, TGA, or even Corel's CPT format if your service bureau prefers to work with images in this format.

Service Bureau Checklist

The bulk of the work submitted to a service bureau's film recorder for rendering is presentation slide material. Business presentation material almost always is created in a landscape format, and film recorders are set up to expose images in landscape mode. Artwork, on the other hand, often is created with a printed page's portrait dimensions in

mind. If you send your work to the service in portrait orientation, there is a good chance your slide will come back with the top and bottom cut off and larger-than-life clear margins for left and right borders. If you chose a service-minded service bureau, you will receive a call asking if you would like to pay to have the slide rotated.

Save yourself a load of grief—always send your work to a slide service bureau in the 2:3 image ratio and always send the image in landscape orientation. This doesn't mean that you must design your images with landscape orientation. If you have a tall, narrow image, use **R**otate from the **I**mage menu on the copy you send to the service bureau so that it's landscape-oriented; it won't make any difference to you when you receive the 35-mm slide (you rotate it manually to its portrait position), but landscape orientation is important to a film-recorder operator.

Do yourself a favor before using a service bureau to turn your work into slides. Look at the following brief checklist before hitting the door:

- **Is your image in a digital format the service bureau prefers to use?** The CPT format is proprietary to Corel PHOTO-PAINT; if the bureau doesn't own PHOTO-PAINT 5, you're out of luck. TIFs and TGAs commonly are accepted formats for service bureaus, and PHOTO-PAINT saves to these formats.

- **How much will the imaging cost?** This too, is an important question to ask, and it might be negotiated before you give the go-ahead on slide-making. Try to have several image files ready to

be film recorded at once; doing this might qualify you for a bulk discount.

- **Does the service bureau clearly understand your directions?** The only way to make certain of this is to ask to speak with the film recorder *operator*. Don't trust that instructions given to whoever happens to answer your call will be reliably passed on. Better still, put all your instructions in writing and include laser printouts of how your images should look.

- **Does the service bureau own compatible large-format media?** Your images are going nowhere if you own a Bernoulli and the service bureau owns a SyQuest drive. Ask what formats of large-media storage the service bureau supports, and then find a compatible format to transport your images.

- **Are your images saved to the proper aspect ratio?** In addition to 35-mm slides, many bureaus offer 4-by-5-inch and 8-by-10-inch color transparency service. Like the 2:3 ratio for 35-mm slides, larger format transparencies made from film recorders require the same image aspect ratio as the frame of film to which they record.

who know as much about production as you do about design, and ultimately it's a fair deal to leave an arrangement that way.

Production houses can give your ideas a physical shape if you meet them half-way, and if you build solid working relationships with good personnel. But the only way to weed the pros from the minor leaguers in digital-image production is to work with several of them; through time spent communicating, you will understand their capabilities and unique needs.

In turn, a good service bureau or commercial printer will come to better understand your needs as a designer, and before you know it, you'll have a conduit for bringing CorelDRAW, PHOTO-PAINT, and other computer graphics into the real world.

Summary

Unless you live in a vacuum and are independently wealthy, your imaging experience in PHOTO-PAINT is a shared experience if you want to turn the pixels that make an image into something that can be passed around. Commercial printers and service bureaus are staffed by imaging professionals

Part

CorelCHART

Understanding and Building Charts in CorelCHART

*N*ot too long ago if you wanted to "take a look at the figures," you actually had to read real numbers. Today, when someone examines the figures, they don't see actual numbers; instead, they see charts and graphs. For years, charts and graphs were the domain of engineers, mathematicians, and accountants who toiled for ways to make their complex data comprehensible to nontechnical types. When the business world discovered graphics as a powerful way to show trends and statistics, charts exploded in popularity.

This chapter covers:

- Designing charts with CorelCHART
- Identifying basic chart elements
- Choosing the right chart type
- Understanding CHART
- Adjusting program settings and preferences
- Creating a new chart
- Working with CorelCHART templates

In the past few years, charts and graphs have gone through an evolution of sorts. What used to be called charts are now called info-graphics or presentation graphics. The key word is graphics, and that is where you come in. No longer are charts just visual representations of numbers. Charting has become an art form in its own right. As an example, consider the little charts appearing each day on the front page of *USA Today*. These quick, concise little graphs provide readers with interesting tidbits in a visually entertaining way. Whether you're learning about the First Ladies' cookie recipes or how much time people spend with their dogs, these graphs catch your eye and make you think. This is your charge as a developer of presentation graphics—first capture the viewer's attention, and then quickly convey a message.

Designing Charts with CorelCHART

As a graphics professional, you are in the business of creating stimulating, attention-grabbing designs. You understand how to use color and style to influence how data is interpreted, and how to create visually impressive charts with the professional look so important in competitive business environments. CorelCHART has a broad range of charting options and attention to detail that even the pickiest of number crunchers will admire. As you will see, CorelCHART thinks and works from an artist's point of view. This advantage gives you the power to manipulate, adjust, tweak, and fine-tune almost every chart element in the pursuit of creating a chart that communicates and inspires.

CorelCHART also has powerful allies in CorelDRAW, CorelPHOTO-PAINT, CorelMOVE, CorelSHOW, and CorelVENTURA, some of the other applications provided with Corel 5.0. In many cases, if you can't create the graphic you need in CorelCHART, you can produce it in CorelDRAW or CorelPAINT and then bring it into CorelCHART. The movement and animation features of CorelMOVE let you add energy to your presentations. And the wonderful transition effects in CorelSHOW provide an excellent showcase for your presentation masterpieces.

This chapter introduces you to some of the charting terminology used in CorelCHART. For instance, when creating a bar chart, it helps to know what a data series and a category axis are. An overview of each of the chart types available in CorelCHART is provided to help you select the right chart type. Basic file mechanics such as opening and saving files are also covered. The chapter ends with the steps for creating new charts. Here, you will find the steps for using sample data and working with CorelCHART templates.

Identifying Basic Chart Elements

The whole objective of your chart is to communicate an idea. Many charts fail to do this by using the wrong chart type or overloading the chart with too much information. It is important to learn not just how to create charts, but how to create effective charts. Therefore, to create effective charts and graphs in CorelCHART, it is essential that you have an understanding of how CorelCHART identifies and labels these chart elements.

Working with Chart Titles

The chart titles are the first thing your audience sees. As displayed in figure 28.1, titles are normally displayed at the top of the chart and are usually the largest text element on the chart. Titles set the visual tone for your chart, so you want to be sure they state the point of each chart as vividly as possible. As with all chart text, your title should be confined to three to five words and limited in punctuation and in the use of words such as "and," "the," and "of."

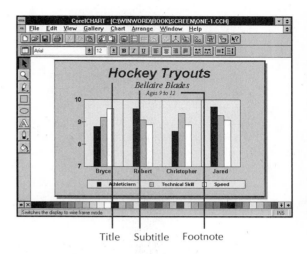

Figure 28.1
Titles, subtitles, and footnotes enhance the readability of your chart.

The subtitle is used to describe the chart beyond what is revealed in the title. Subtitles should include something that encourages your reader into further inspection of the chart. They are normally displayed just beneath the chart title and are usually the second largest text element on the chart.

Many of the charts you create will be filled with statistical data. It is frequently important that you provide support information about those statistics in a footnote. For instance, a footnote might tell us when the chart data was compiled or what organization originally published the statistics. Keep in mind that footnotes should tell us something that we don't already know from viewing the chart.

Understanding Category and Data Axes

Many of the popular chart types are XY graphics in that they are composed of an X axis and a Y axis. Included in this group are bar graphs, area graphs, and line graphs. An axis is a line that serves as a reference point for plotting data in a graph. The X axis, which CorelCHART refers to as the *category axis*, shows the different groups of data that you want to graph. The Y axis, which CorelCHART refers to as the *data axis*, serves as a reference point for you to gauge the numerical value of what you are graphing. For instance, in figure 28.2, the category axis displays months, and the data axis displays numerical values. CorelCHART refers to the vertical bars that represent the data as *risers*.

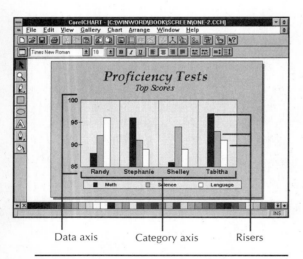

Data axis   Category axis   Risers

Figure 28.2
XY charts use two axes to plot chart data.

Understanding Data Groups and Data Series

The classifications along the category axis are called *data groups*. In figure 28.3, the data groups are years. Notice that for each data group there are three risers: one for Coupes, one for Sedans, and one for MPVs. Collectively, a set of similarly colored risers is called a *data series*. A data series enables you to gauge the quantity or value of an item over a specific period of time. For instance, the data series for Sedans enables you to gauge the number of sedans sold each year.

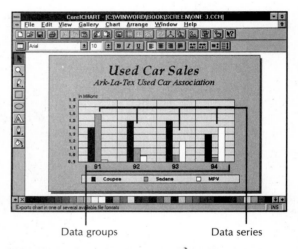

Data groups   Data series

Figure 28.3
The categories of data along the category axis are called data groups. The values for each set of data per category are data series.

In some cases, you may want to include titles for the category and data axes. For instance, you might add a *data axis title* to inform the viewer that the values along the data axis represent currency. You could add a *category axis title* to inform the viewer how the data on the category axis should be interpreted. For instance, if you're using fiscal quarters along the category axis, you could enter "1995 Quarters" as the axis title.

Understanding Legends and Legend Markers

A *legend* identifies each data series, much like a road map provides a guide to the colors and symbols on a map. As displayed in figure 28.4, the legend is generally at the bottom of the screen and contains *legend markers*, which are generally colored boxes that identify which color is used to represent each data series. Legends can be turned on or off in CorelCHART and formatted to display in a variety of ways.

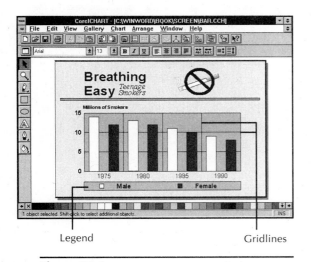

Legend   Gridlines

Figure 28.4
Legends play an integral part in communicating the chart data.

Understanding Gridlines

The horizontal lines adjacent to each number on the data axis are the *data axis gridlines*. Running vertically on the category axis are the *category axis gridlines*. These lines help guide the eye from each series marker to the corresponding value or category on the axis. Gridlines help make a graph more readable, especially if the graph is very large. Be wary of too many gridlines, however, since they can really clutter up your chart. In CorelCHART, you can turn gridlines on or off and adjust the width and style of the lines.

Choosing the Right Chart Type

Choosing the right chart type is the key to communicating a message. Data presented in the wrong chart type can become convoluted and even project the wrong message. Before creating a chart, give serious thought to the best chart type for communicating your data. CorelCHART can create 16 basic chart types, with most of the chart types available in a variety of formats. The chart type that best presents your data will depend upon the kinds of relationships you are illustrating. The main chart type is selected when you first create the chart in CorelCHART. From there, you can select one of the chart variations from the Gallery menu. Later in this chapter, you will find the steps for creating new chart files.

Using Bar Charts

Bar charts are excellent for illustrating a comparison between numerical values. In figure 28.5, for instance, comparing the bars makes it easy to see that Alaska was the most popular cruise location for the past three years. Bar charts can be divided into two distinct groups: horizontal bars and vertical bars. Vertical bar charts better illustrate how values change over time (see fig. 28.5).

Horizontal bar charts are scaled along the horizontal axis and are the most simple of the XY chart types. Optimally, horizontal bar charts are used in situations with limited number of data series per data group. For instance, in figure 28.6, the horizontal bars document only one series or bar per data group. Table 28.1 covers the available templates for bar charts.

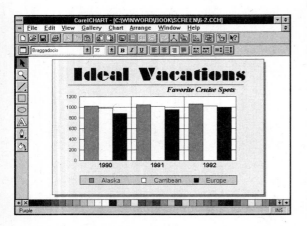

Figure 28.5

Bar charts facilitate comparisons among series of data.

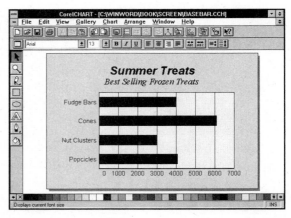

Figure 28.6

Horizontal bar charts work well when expressing a limited number of data series per data group.

Table 28.1
Types of Bar Charts

Chart Type	Description
Side-by-Side	Standard bar chart, where bars are placed side by side along the category axis.
Stacked Bar	The bars in a data group are stacked on top of each other to represent the total value for a data group.
Dual-Axis Side-by-Side	A second value or Y axis is placed on the chart. Some bars are plotted against a second data axis to compare series that use different units of measure or exhibit a large disparity in magnitude.
Dual-Axis Stacked	Similar to Dual-Axis Side-by-Side, except bars are stacked on top of each other to represent the total value for a data group.
Bipolar Side-by-Side	Chart has two data axes, each starting at the center of the chart and increasing in value as they move outward, away from the center.
Bipolar Stacked	Similar to Bipolar Side-by-Side chart, except that the bars are placed on top of each other to represent the total value for a data group.
Percent	The percent chart displays values as a percentage of the total for a specific data group. The total value is represented as 100 percent, and the values in a given data group are shown as a percentage of the whole.

Using Line Charts

Select a line chart when you want to show trends or a change in data over a longer period of time. For instance, in figure 28.7, the line chart examines how men's neckwear sales increase in June, due to Father's Day. Each point on the line marks a known occurrence, and the connection of these marks forms a line that emphasizes time flow and rate of change. Line charts are great when you need to plot multiple sets of data. For example, if you have to plot the sales of VCRs over the last twenty years, a line chart would be your best bet. However, line charts are not a good choice for a graph with multiple series. For example, if you have to plot the sales of VCRs, TVs, CD Players, and camcorders over the last two years, you would have better luck using a bar chart. Table 28.2 covers the available line chart templates.

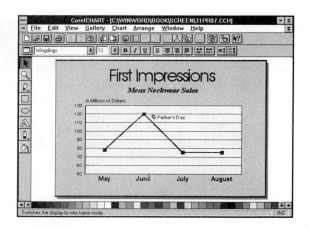

NOTE

Though CorelCHART doesn't specifically state that it does a 3D line chart, the 3D Connect Series and the 3D Connect Group options in the Gallery menu provide variations on 3D line charts with a third axis for depth.

Figure 28.7

Line charts help the viewer analyze trends.

Table 28.2
Types of Line Charts

Chart Type	Description
Absolute	A basic line chart. The data points are connected by a line that stresses change between data groups.
Stacked	The lines for each data group are stacked to represent the total value for a data group. Stacked lines communicate the same basic information as traditional lines, plus the contribution of the parts to a whole.
Bipolar Absolute	This chart has two data axes, each starting at the center of the chart and increasing in value as they move outward, away from the center.
Bipolar Stacked	The lines in each data group are treated cumulatively to represent the total value for a data group, but in a bipolar format.
Dual-Axis Absolute	A second value or Y axis is placed on the chart. Some lines are plotted against a second data axis to compare series that use different units of measure or exhibit a large disparity in magnitude.
Dual-Axis Stacked	Similar to Dual-Axis Side-by-Side, except lines are stacked on top of each other to represent the total value for a data group.
Percent	The percent chart displays values as a percentage of the total for a specific data group. The total value is represented as 100 percent, and the values in a given data group are shown as a percentage of the whole.

Using Area Charts

Area Charts are similar to line charts with one addition: the space defined by the line and the horizontal axis is filled in. The filled-in area suggests volume or quantity. The area chart in figure 28.8 documents the dramatic increase in women voters. Similar to bar charts, area charts can be either horizontal or vertical. You can place greater emphasis on the volume of the data by using 3D area charts. Table 28.3 covers the available area chart templates.

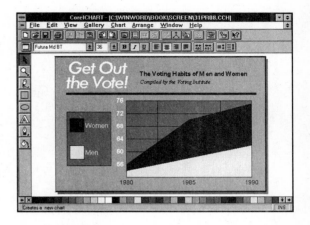

Figure 28.8

Area charts dramatize changes over time.

Table 28.3
Types of Area Charts

Chart Type	Description
Absolute	Basic area chart. The data points are connected by a line that stresses change between data groups.
Stacked	The areas for each data group are stacked to represent the total value for a data group. Stacked areas communicate the contribution of the parts to a whole.
Bipolar Absolute	Chart has two data axes, each starting at the center of the chart and increasing in value as they move outward, away from the center.
Bipolar Stacked	The areas in each data group are treated cumulatively to represent the total value for a data group, but in a bipolar format.
Dual-Axis Absolute	A second value or Y axis is placed on the chart. Some areas are plotted against a second data axis to compare series that use different units of measure or exhibit a large disparity in magnitude.
Dual-Axis Stacked	Similar to Dual-Axis Side-by-Side, except areas are stacked on top of each other to represent the total value for a data group.
Percent	The percent chart displays values as a percentage of the total for a specific data group. The total value is represented as 100 percent, and the values in a given data group are shown as a percentage of the whole.

N O T E

Though CorelCHART doesn't specifically state that it does 3D area charts, the 3D Connect Series and the 3D Connect Group options in the Gallery menu provide variations on 3D area charts with a third axis for depth.

Using Pie Charts

Pie charts represent the simplest form of charting. Pies show proportions in relation to a whole. Pie charts are easily comprehended and are good for highlighting a significant element for comparison. In figure 28.9, for example, the pie chart quickly informs the viewer of the way monetary donations are spent. By default, CorelCHART creates three-dimensional pies. You can change the tilt and thickness of the pie to simulate a

greater 3D effect, or no dimension at all. 3D pies put more emphasis on the values on the front of the pie by simulating depth and volume. Table 28.4 covers the available pie chart templates.

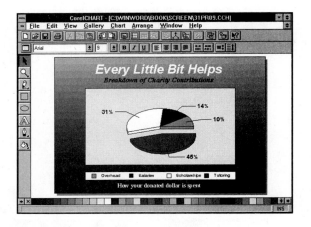

Figure 28.9
Pies show proportions in relation to a whole.

Table 28.4
Types of Pie Charts

Chart Type	Description
Pie	This is the single pie format.
Ring Pie	Pie is shaped like a ring with a hole in the center. The pie total is generally placed in the center of the ring.
Multiple Pie	Multiple pie charts to plot several data groups. Multiple pies can demonstrate several related ideas at once.
Multiple Ring Pie	Multiple pie format, but with ring-shaped pies.
Multiple Proportional Pie	Multiple pie charts with all figures sized in relation to the other pies based on numerical volume. This option enables you to emphasize how pie totals (group data) have changed over time.
Multiple Proportional Ring Pie	Multiple proportional pies, but with ring shapes.

Using Scatter Charts

Scatter charts have two data axes, thus enabling you to show the correlation or relationship between two sets of data. They are particularly useful for showing patterns or trends and determining how variables might show a relationship to one another. For example, as illustrated in figure 28.10, a scatter chart might be preferable to a line chart to compare new home vs. old home sales. Scatter charts are frequently accompanied by a regression line. The slope and placement of the line are calculated from the data to identify the trend of the data set. Table 28.5 covers the available scatter chart templates.

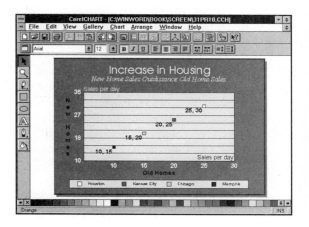

Figure 28.10

Scatter charts show the correlations or relationships between the two sets of data.

Table 28.5

Types of Scatter Charts

Chart Type	Description
Scatter	This is the fundamental scatter chart.
X-Y Dual-Axis	A second value or Y axis is placed on the chart. Some areas are plotted against a second data axis to compare series that use different units of measure or exhibit a large disparity in magnitude.
X-Y with Labels	Basic scatter chart, except each data point is accompanied by a label.
X-Y Dual-Axis with Labels	Dual-axis scatter chart, but with labels for each data point.

Using High/Low/Open/ Close Charts

High/Low/Open/Close charts are used to express a range of values for a single item in a particular time period. As displayed in figure 28.11, these charts are most often used to display stock market information. High/ Low/Open/Close charts are excellent for showing data that regularly fluctuates in a given time period, such as weather or currency exchange rates. Table 28.6 covers the available High/Low/Open/Close templates.

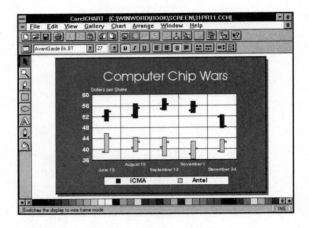

Figure 28.11
High/Low/Open/Close charts express a range of values in a particular time period.

Table 28.6
Types of High/Low/Open/Close Charts

Chart Type	Description
High/Low	Plots the high and the low values for a specific data group.
High/Low Dual-Axis	High/Low chart with two data axes. Some values will be plotted against a second data axis, enabling you to compare series that use different units of measure, or that exhibit a large disparity in magnitude.
High/Low/Open	Identical to the High/Low chart, but with a third data point added to display the starting value for a specific data group.
High/Low/Open Dual	High/Low/Open chart, but with two data axes.
High/Low/Open/Close	Identical to the High/Low/Open chart, but with a fourth data point added to display the closing value for a specific data group.
High/Low/Open/Close Dual-Axis	High/Low/Open/Close chart, but with two data axes.

Using Spectral Maps

Spectral maps are best used to demonstrate the occurrence of an item with regard to a specific spatial relationship. As displayed in figure 28.12, a common use of a spectral map is to show population density. Spectral maps are unique in that they exhibit value based on color intensity rather than numerical quantities. Spectral maps have only one template.

Using Histograms

Histograms show the frequency of values in a data group. The shape of a histogram exhibits a pattern of measurements in a way that reveals the individual values of each item. A good example of a histogram is a bell curve displaying group scores or results (see fig. 28.13). The curve plots the number of values that fall in a particular range of scores. Table 28.7 covers the available histogram chart templates.

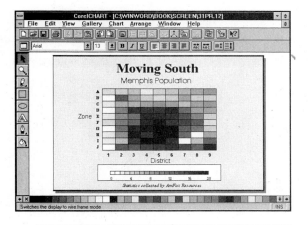

Figure 28.12

Spectral Maps demonstrate occurrences in a specific spatial relationship.

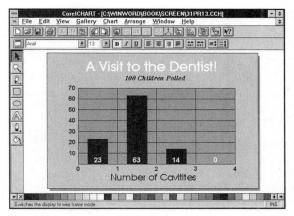

Figure 28.13

Histograms show the frequency of values in a data group.

Table 28.7
Types of Histogram Charts

Chart Type	Description
Vertical Histogram	A histogram in which the bars are vertically oriented.
Horizontal Histogram	A histogram in which the bars are horizontally oriented.

Using Table Charts

Table charts show the actual numbers in a ledger form with columns and rows, rather than in a graph. Though tables are visually less exciting, they are useful for communicating text-oriented data. Tables are also used when the disparity between series numbers is great or with particularly detailed data (see fig. 28.14). Table charts can be tedious when they contain too much numerical data. In cases where you have more than five data groups or data series, you should consider a graph instead. Table 28.8 covers the available table chart templates.

Using 3D Riser Charts

In CorelCHART, *risers* are bars that extend vertically from the category axis. As such, 3D riser charts are another name for 3D bar charts. Essentially, all parameters pertaining to bar charts are relevant here. The main difference between 3D riser charts and the typical bar chart is the addition of the third axis that eliminates the need for a legend to identify each series of data. As displayed in figure 28.15, 3D risers let you add the illusion of depth to your charts. Table 28.9 covers the available 3D riser chart templates.

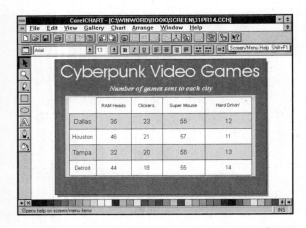

Figure 28.14
Table charts are great for text-oriented data.

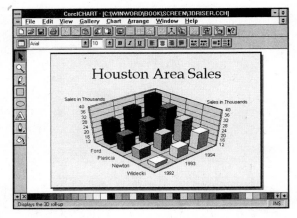

Figure 28.15
3D risers are similar to bar charts, adding the illusion of depth to your charts.

Table 28.8
Types of Table Charts

Chart Type	Description
Rows	This option enables you to alternate color by rows.
Columns	This option enables you to alternate color by columns.
None	This option has no color division.

Table 28.9
Types of 3D Riser Charts

Chart Type	Description
3D Riser	Basic 3D bar chart. You can choose from four different riser shapes: Bars, Pyramids, Octagons, or Cut-Corner bars—rectangular bars with cut corners.
3D Connected Group	Points in a data group are connected to form floating lines or anchored 3D areas. The floating-line types—"Ribbon" and "Step"—are suspended above the chart floor, enabling you to view the area beneath the data points. The "Area" option is essentially a 3D area chart.
3D Floating Bars	3D riser chart with data depicted as floating objects, rather than bars that extend upward from the baseline. You can choose from Floating Cubes or the multisided Floating Spheres.
3D Connected Series; Area	Points in a data series are connected to form 3D areas. The "Area" option displays as a 3D area chart.
3D Connected Series; Ribbon	Points in a data series are connected to form 3D lines. The floating-line types—"Ribbon" and "Step"—are suspended above the chart floor, enabling you to view the area beneath the data points.

Using 3D Scatter Charts

Three-dimensional scatter charts are basically scatter charts with an added axis. As shown in figure 28.16, the third dimension enables you to show the correlation between three variables rather than two, as in a traditional scatter chart. Table 28.10 covers the available 3D scatter chart templates.

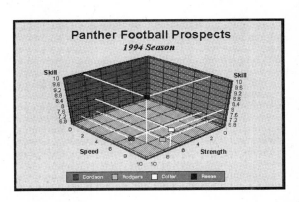

Figure 28.16
3D scatter charts show the correlations among three variables.

Table 28.10
Types of 3D Scatter Charts

Chart Type	Description
XYZ Scatter	Basic 3D scatter chart with three values per data point.
XYZ Scatter With Labels	3D scatter chart with labels for the data points.

Using Pictographs

You can use pictographs to replace the bars in bar charts and histograms with graphic images. For example, as displayed in figure 28.17, the bars are replaced with stacked images of disks illustrating computer sales. This effect obviously increases visual interest in your charts, but should be confined to charts with a limited number of data groups. Table 28.11 covers the available pictograph chart templates.

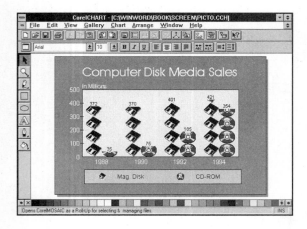

Figure 28.17
Pictographs use graphic images to plot the data values.

Using Bubble Charts

Bubble charts are similar to scatter charts with a third data set added. The first two sets of data are represented on the horizontal and vertical axes, with the third data set represented by the size of the bubble. For example, in figure 28.18, the horizontal axis gauges the test score, while the vertical axis measures the tenure of the teachers. CorelCHART includes bubble charts with labels and with dual axes. Table 28.12 covers the available bubble chart templates.

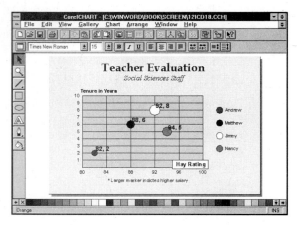

Figure 28.18
Bubble charts are an effective way to compare two sets of data.

Table 28.11
Types of Pictograph Charts

Chart Type	Description
Horizontal	Horizontal bar chart with the bars displayed as pictographs.
Horizontal Bipolar Side-by-Side	Horizontal bipolar bar chart with the bars displayed as pictographs. This chart will exhibit two data axes, each starting at the center of the chart and increasing in value as it moves outward, away from the center.
Vertical Side-by-Side	Vertical bar chart with the bars displayed as pictographs. The pictograph bars representing each data point are placed side by side along the category axis.
Vertical Bar Dual Y Axis	Dual Y axis chart with the bars are displayed as pictographs. Some pictograph bars will be plotted against a second data axis to compare series that use different units of measure or that exhibit a large disparity in magnitude.

Table 28.12
Types of Bubble Charts

Chart Type	Description
Bubble	Basic Bubble chart with three values per data point.
Dual-Axis Bubble	Bubble chart with a second value or Y axis placed on the chart. Some areas are plotted against a second data axis to compare series that use different units of measure or exhibit a large disparity in magnitude.
Bubble with Labels	Bubble chart with label identifiers next to each bubble marker.
Dual-Axis Bubble with Labels	Bubble chart with a second value or Y axis placed on the chart and label identifiers for each bubble marker.

Using Radar Charts

Radar charts are used to display the variations of a series of data in relation to other data series. Use radar charts to demonstrate the relationship between each series of data and the correlation between a specific series of data and the whole of the other series. For example, figure 28.19 illustrates how much time is spent on each phase of the production of three print projects. Table 28.13 outlines the available radar chart templates.

Using Polar Charts

This chart type uses circular and radial axes to plot chart values (see fig. 28.20). The effect is to illustrate the distance and angle of how each data point sits from other data points and the chart's center. CorelCHART offers a single and dual axis polar chart.

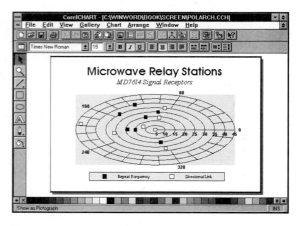

Figure 28.20
Polar charts use circular and radial axes to plot data.

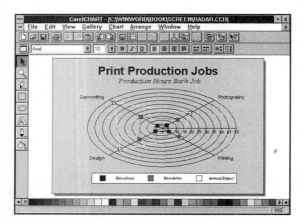

Figure 28.19
Radar charts demonstrate the relationship between series of data and their relation to the whole.

Table 28.13
Types of Radar Charts

Chart Type	Description
Radar	Basic radar chart.
Stacked Radar	The areas for each data group are stacked to represent the total value for a data group.
Dual Axis Radar	Radar chart in which some areas are plotted against a second data axis to compare series that use different units of measure or exhibit a large disparity in magnitude.

Using Gantt Charts

Gantt charts diagram a schedule of activities relating to a specific project or series of projects. Figure 28.21, for example, diagrams two multimedia projects. The projects begin October 4 and are completed November 19. Each step in the production process is represented by a horizontal bar that shows the projected starting date and ending date. Thus, each bar illustrates the time required to perform a specific activity. The cumulative of all activity bars adds up to the total intended time span for the project(s).

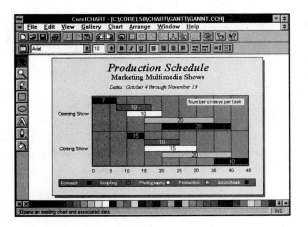

Figure 28.21

Gantt charts diagram project activities.

Obviously, CorelCHART provides a wide assortment of chart types to give you tremendous flexibility in creating and designing charts. You will find that most sets of data can be expressed in a number of different chart formats, but usually one will stand out as being superior to others. The more you know about the various chart types available in CorelCHART, the easier your job of producing effective, professional charts and graphs will become.

Understanding CorelCHART

As an artist, you may be accustomed to drawing charts mechanically, using rectangles to create bars and wedges to create pie slices. Though this method works, it is time-consuming, and even the slightest change in data forces you to start all over again. CorelCHART uses a more powerful way of creating charts by composing the chart based on numerical data. For example, imagine you needed a pie chart illustrating your monthly expenditures. With CorelCHART, you simply enter the actual dollar figures, and CorelCHART composes a pie chart with slices representing each expenditure. When there is a change, just enter the new data and the pie slices grow or shrink accordingly. Since last-minute changes are a way of life for most people in the graphics biz, this powerful concept is a lifesaver.

Becoming proficient with CorelCHART is easier if you understand how the program "thinks." Thus, this section begins with an examination of the two main components of CorelCHART—the Data Manager and the Chart View. These two modules are used for entering data and designing charts. Also covered in this chapter are the steps for opening and saving chart files. This section focuses on creating charts, such as selecting a chart type and using sample data. You will find in-depth coverage of working with templates to streamline your charting efforts in CorelCHART. Finishing up this chapter is information about chart setup, such as paper size and orientation. With all this information, you will be ready for Chapter 29, "Working in the Data Manager."

Starting CorelCHART

CorelCHART is a separate program included with CorelDRAW. It is installed in the Windows Program Manager Corel 5.0 group along with CorelDRAW. To start CorelCHART, open the Corel 5.0 group window and double-click on the CorelCHART icon. The initial CorelCHART screen appears, with all of the elements grayed out except for the File and Help menus. All the operational functions become available when you open or begin a new file. The steps for opening a chart file are covered next, so you can open a sample file and examine the different components of the screen. As displayed in figure 28.22, the CorelCHART screen has many of the same tools found on the CorelDRAW screen.

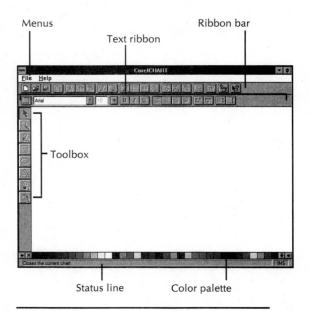

Figure 28.22
The initial CorelCHART screen.

CorelCHART's screen includes a tool palette for annotating charts with graphic shapes and text on the left. The ribbon bar under the menu bar provides quick access to several menu commands. For example, the first button creates a new chart file, while the eighth and ninth buttons import and export data. The text ribbon bar located immediately above the chart area includes buttons and list boxes for formatting text objects. The status line at the bottom of the screen displays information about selected commands and tools.

To determine the function of a button, press and hold on it. A description of the button appears in the status line. Pull away from the button before releasing the mouse to avoid activating the command

Opening Chart Files

With CorelCHART, you can have several files open at one time. This capability makes it easy to share data between charts and check for consistency when necessary. The actual number of files you can have open at one time is limited only by the size of the chart data and your computer's memory.

To open an existing CorelCHART file, select **O**pen from the **F**ile menu or click on the Open button in the ribbon bar (the file folder). When the Open Chart dialog box appears, as shown in figure 28.23, change to the appropriate drive and directory to locate the CorelCHART file you want to open. The CorelCHART files located in the specified directory appear in the File **N**ame box. CorelCHART files have the file extension .CCH. Click once on a file name to display a preview and description of the chart. (You will see a description only if you entered one when you originally saved the chart.) Click on OK or double-click on the file name to

open the chart. If you have previously opened other files, the last chart file you open will be displayed and active in Chart View. As with other Windows applications, use the **W**indow menu to switch to other open chart files.

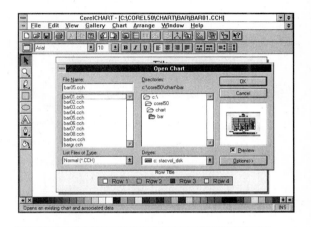

Figure 28.23
The Open Chart dialog box.

Saving Chart Files

Sometime during the creation of your chart file, you will, of course, need to save it. The first time you save the chart, select **S**ave or Save **A**s from the **F**ile menu, or click on the Save button in the ribbon bar (the small computer disk). The Save Chart dialog box appears, as shown in figure 28.24. Change to the drive and directory to which you want to save the file, and then enter a file name in the File **N**ame box.

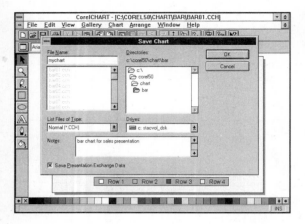

Figure 28.24
The Save Chart dialog box.

To display a description of the chart in the Open Chart dialog box, enter it in the Description box. You might use a description when you have several bar charts with the same background and basic layout and find it difficult to determine one from the other by looking at the preview. The description helps you identify the exact chart you want to open. You can use as many characters for the description as you need. After specifying the file name, directory, and description, click on OK to save the file. The new file name will appear at the top in the title bar.

If you make any other changes to the chart, you will need to save the file again before closing it. Select **S**ave from the **F**ile menu, or click on the Save button, and the chart is updated with the latest changes. Select Save **A**s from the **F**ile menu if you need to change the directory, file name, or description of the chart you want to update.

It's wise to save often when working with any application, but this is particularly important in chart files with big blocks of numbers and text. Get into the habit of using the Save button or the keyboard shortcut, Ctrl+S, to save.

Switching between the Data Manager and Chart View

As mentioned earlier, numerical data is entered and used to compose a chart. The data is entered in the Data Manager, and the chart is composed in the Chart View. After you have opened a chart file, you can view the Data Manager and Chart View. You will find yourself moving back and forth between the Data Manager and the Chart View frequently, especially when you first begin creating a chart. While some users may enter all of the data at one time, others will enter part of the chart data, switch to the Chart View to see how it looks, and then switch back to the Data Manager to enter more data. In this way, you can watch as the chart is being built.

To switch from the Data Manager to the Chart View, click on the top button in the toolbox. (The rest of the tools are grayed out in the Data Manager.) This button is called the Chart View button and looks like a tiny bar chart (see fig. 28.25). Once in Chart View, notice that the button changes to a tiny spreadsheet; clicking on this button will take you back to Data Manager.

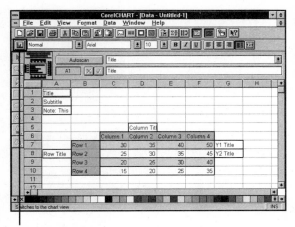

Chart View button

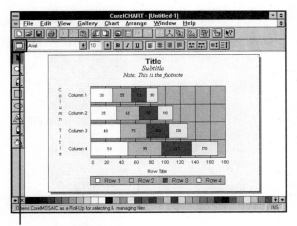

Data Manager button

Figure 28.25

The Chart View and Data Manager buttons enable you to move between the windows.

Exploring the Data Manager

The Data Manager is where you will begin producing your charts. Here, you will enter the text and numbers that comprise your chart. You enter data into an electronic ledger, or spreadsheet (see fig. 28.26). The data can be entered manually or imported from another application, such as Excel or Word for Windows.

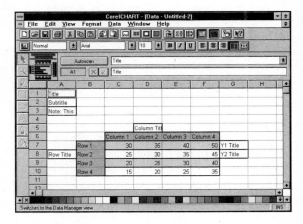

Figure 28.26

The Data Manager screen.

The Data Manager includes many of the tools found in spreadsheet programs such as Excel or Lotus 1-2-3. In fact, if you are a spreadsheet user, you'll be surprised how quickly you'll feel comfortable working in the Data Manager.

Exploring the Chart View

After entering data in the Data Manager, you'll switch to the Chart View to see your chart (see fig. 28.27). The Chart View is where you format the various chart elements. You can enlarge the title text, explode a pie slice, or change the color of the gridlines. The text ribbon at the top of the screen makes formatting text elements a breeze. The Chart View also contains a toolbox, similar to the one used in CorelDRAW. These tools can be used to enhance your charts with graphic shapes and text.

Tiling

You can see both the Data Manager and the Chart View at the same time by tiling the windows (see fig. 28.28). The tiling options are in CorelCHART's **W**indow menu. You can choose to tile the windows vertically or horizontally. The following steps illustrate tiling the Data Manager and the Chart View windows horizontally:

1. Open the file you want to tile. Tiling works better if there is only one chart file open.

2. From the **W**indow menu, select Tile Horizontally. The Data Manager and Chart View windows are tiled.

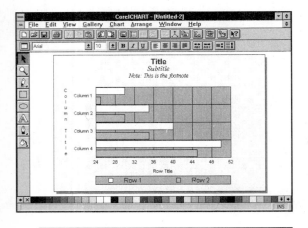

Figure 28.27
The Chart View screen.

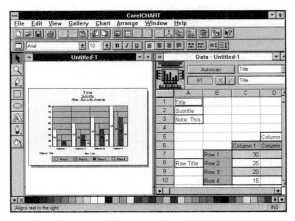

Figure 28.28
The Data Manager and Chart View screens tiled.

The menu titles and screen tools will change, depending on which window is currently active. For instance, if you click in the Chart View, you see the Gallery and Chart menus on the menu bar. If you click in the Data Manager, you see the Format and Data menus. When tiled, it may be difficult to work in the Chart View because the chart is significantly reduced in size. Use the Zoom tool to magnify the chart and see the data more clearly. (The Zoom tool works just as it does in CorelDRAW.)

Adjusting Program Settings and Preferences

CorelCHART gives you control over the settings that affect how the program displays objects on the screen and how it performs certain operations. You can change these settings at any time.

To adjust the program settings, select **P**references from the **F**ile menu. The Preferences dialog box appears, as displayed in figure 28.29. An X in the check box beside an option indicates that the feature is turned on. The Show **R**ibbon Bar option displays the button bar, located immediately below the menu bar. The Show **T**ext Ribbon Bar option displays the ribbon, located right above the chart area. The Show **S**tatus Line

displays the status line at the bottom of the screen. The Show Pop-Up **H**elp command instructs CorelCHART to display the function of a button when you press and hold the mouse on it. The **I**nterruptible Display option enables you to stop a screen redraw by clicking the mouse or pressing a key. This command is invaluable if you are working on a slower computer.

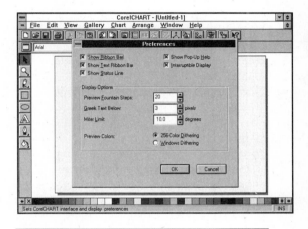

Figure 28.29
The Preferences dialog box.

Other options include the Preview **F**ountain Steps, **G**reek Text Below, and Miter **L**imit. Because these commands work the same as they do in CorelDRAW, this section provides only a brief overview of these options. Refer to the CorelDRAW section of this book for more detailed information.

The Preview **F**ountain Steps command determines the number of bands used to represent fountain fills on the screen. Selecting a lower value (less than 20) speeds up screen redraws, but produces noticeable banding in your printed product. The **G**reek Text Below command simplifies the appearance of text below the size specified. Selecting a high value (maximum 500) causes the text to display as small blocks, resulting in faster screen redrawing. This option does not affect the appearance of text when printed. The Miter **L**imit command affects the appearance of corner joints. Any corner that is less than the Miter Limit will have a beveled point. Corners above the limit will come to a sharp point. The Preview Colors command controls how CorelCHART displays colors on your screen, and has no effect on the printed output. Selecting the 256-Color **D**ithering option will result in smoother colors on-screen. However, unless you have a monitor or graphics adapter that can display 256 simultaneous colors, the **W**indows Dithering option is your only choice.

Creating a New Chart

CorelCHART requires that you select one of 16 main chart types as you create a chart file. Keep in mind that after creating the file, it is possible to switch to another chart type if desired. For instance, if you initially selected a bar chart and then decide to use a line chart, it's easy to change.

When you select a chart type, you also are selecting a template. The templates establish the chart type and formatting, such as colors and fonts. Templates are actually CorelCHART files from which you are "borrowing" the chart type, style, and formatting for your new chart file. Think of the template as a starting point. After selecting a template, you can embellish and enhance your chart with your own personal design style.

To create a new chart, select **F**ile, **N**ew, or click on the New button in the ribbon bar. The New dialog box appears, with the main chart types displayed in the **G**allery list box on the left. Notice that Bar is currently selected. On the right is the **C**hart Types list box, where you see a visual display of the available bar chart templates. When you select a new chart type, the templates change to reflect the newly selected chart type. For instance, in figure 28.30, area is the selected chart type and the templates show area charts. A description of the template and its file location also appear in the bottom of the dialog box. Select the desired chart type and template.

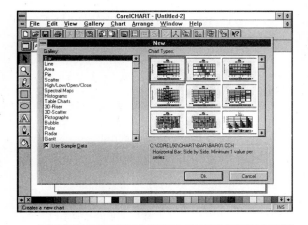

Figure 28.30
The New dialog box.

Using Sample Data

Before clicking on OK to create your chart, consider the Use Sample **D**ata option under the list of chart types. The sample data option is turned on by default. If it is on when you click on OK, sample numbers and text are placed into the new chart. The sample data appears in the Data Manager and is used to generate the chart you see in Chart View. As detailed in the next chapter, "Working in the Data Manager," CorelCHART requires that chart data be entered in a specific manner so it can correctly identify all chart elements. Since the sample data is properly entered, all you have to do is replace the sample data with your own data.

Turning off the sample data option gives you the ability to enter data in a blank spreadsheet. As you become more adept at using CorelCHART, you may find turning off the sample data feature preferable. But take care to match the overall data layout structure used by the sample data. If you don't follow the structure, you could very easily get some unexpected results. For instance, CorelCHART expects titles to be entered in cells A1 and A2. If you enter a title in another cell, it may be ignored or appear on the chart as another chart element, such as a footnote or an axis title.

After selecting the desired chart type and template, click on OK to create a new chart. If the sample data option was left on, you are taken to the Chart View, where the sample data composes the chart. If you turned off the sample data option, you are taken directly to the Data Manager, which displays a blank spreadsheet.

As an example, the following steps illustrate creating a line chart using sample data:

1. Select **N**ew from the **F**ile menu, or click on the New button. The New dialog box appears.

2. Select Line from the Gallery list box. Select a line chart template from the Chart Type box.

3. Make sure the Use Sample Data is enabled and click on OK. As displayed in figure 28.31, a line chart created with the sample data appears in Chart View. (If the sample data was turned off, the Data Manager appears, displaying a blank spreadsheet.)

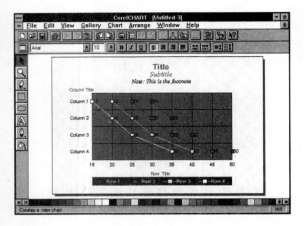

Figure 28.31
A new line chart with the sample data option left on.

Working with CorelCHART Templates

As previously discussed, templates are simply regular CorelCHART files from which you borrow the chart type and formatting. When you create a new chart file, you are using a copy of the template, so any changes you make will not affect the original template. This section discusses how you can speed up your chart creation time by designing your own templates and applying new templates to chart files.

Creating Chart Templates

While the templates help you get started, in many cases they will not fit your needs exactly. For example, you may need to add a company logo, change colors, or adjust font sizes. It's important to know that any chart you design can be used as a template for future charts. This means that once you've designed a chart that captures a "look" you like, you can use it as a template. Using your custom-designed chart file as a template can be a tremendous time-saver. Since you will have arranged the chart style and formatting in advance, all you'll have to do is create a new chart using your customized template and enter any new data. The formatting will already be done.

Creating a chart template is simply a matter of saving your chart file in one of the directories where CorelCHART stores its template files. As mentioned earlier, when you select a chart type in the New dialog box, the template's file name and directory appear in the lower-right corner. CorelCHART stores the templates in the C:\Corel50\Chart directory path. For example, the bar chart template is stored in C:\Corel50\Chart\Bar, and the area chart template is stored in C:\Corel50\Chart\Area. By placing your chart files in one of these directories, you are creating a template that can be previewed and selected when you create a new chart file.

When you select **N**ew from the **F**ile menu, your chart file will be one of the available templates. For instance, in figure 28.32, several custom templates have been added to the Bar chart category. Select the chart type and the desired template, then click on OK to create a chart file with the customized formatting.

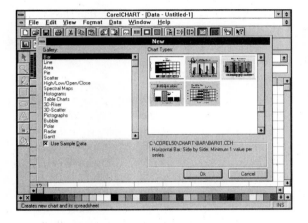

Figure 28.32
You can create your own templates and preview them in the New dialog box.

N O T E

The path for storing template files is automatically created when you install Corel 5.0. During installation, however, you do have the option to alter this path.

Your chart file can be used as a template, regardless of what directory it is stored in. However, you won't be able to preview it in the New dialog box unless you store it in one of the specific directories mentioned previously. The Apply Template command covered in the next section enables you to use any chart file like a template.

Applying Templates to Existing Files

The Apply Template command enables you to apply a different template to a chart after it has already been created. For instance, maybe you created a bar chart using the CorelCHART template. After entering the data, you could use the Apply Template command to apply the formatting from a bar chart you designed earlier. Every time you create a new bar chart, you could simply apply that template. Imagine the time saved when you don't have to format every chart! When you use the Apply Template command, any data that you had previously entered is preserved; only the chart type and formatting from the template is applied to the current chart.

You can use one of your own chart files as a template or a CorelCHART template file. The following steps illustrate applying the CorelCHART line chart template to a bar chart:

1. Open the bar chart file. From the **F**ile menu, choose Apply **T**emplate to display the Open dialog box.

2. Change to the drive and directory where the line chart is stored. The CorelCHART line chart template is stored in C:\Corel50\Chart\Line.

3. Select the file name of the file you want to use as a template. The line chart template is called hline01.cch. A preview and description of the template appear on the left. Click on OK to apply the template.

Remember, when you apply a template to an existing chart, only the formatting and graphic information are applied, not the data. The data you entered before applying the template is retained and applied to the new chart type. For instance, if you entered quarterly sales in the bar chart, the quarterly sales data would still be there after applying a line chart template. However, the data would be displayed in the line chart format.

Selecting Additional Chart Types

The **G**allery menu provides access to all of the chart types available in CorelCHART. You can use the **G**allery menu to change a vertical bar chart to a horizontal bar chart, or a line chart into an area chart. The **G**allery menu is also where you find the more complicated chart types, such as Dual Y Axis, Bipolar, and Percent. The **G**allery menu and the Apply Template command are similar in that they both retain the previously entered chart data while changing the chart type. However, when you apply a template, it changes the chart type and any formatting modifications you may have made, such as new colors or fonts and repositioning of the text. Changing the chart type through the **G**allery menu applies a new chart type, but retains all formatting attributes you had previously made to the chart.

Using the **G**allery menu enables you to quickly experiment with different ways of presenting your data. After entering data into a line chart, you can use the **G**allery menu to display your data in an area chart format. If an area chart isn't quite right either, you can easily take it right back to a line chart, or perhaps try a scatter chart. You also can use this technique to create several different examples of a chart, and then let the end user of the chart—the presenter—decide which one best suits his or her needs.

To use the **G**allery menu, select **G**allery, and choose a main chart type. A fly-out menu (see fig. 28.33) appears, listing the available formats for that chart type. Move to the first choice and press and hold the mouse button to see a preview of the chart format. Drag down to the other chart format choices to preview them. Release the mouse on the desired chart format to apply it to your chart. There are many options available in the **G**allery menu. For more information on using these chart types, refer to the previous section, "Choosing the Right Chart Type."

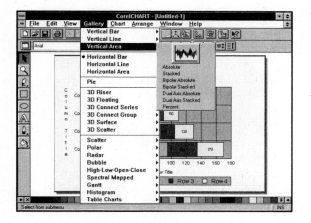

Figure 28.33
*The **G**allery menu uses fly-out menus to offer a wide selection of chart types.*

Setting Up Charts

CorelCHART gives you the flexibility to change the paper size and orientation at any time during the creation of your chart file. A chart file created on a 35mm slide format can be quickly changed to letter-size paper. CorelCHART examines the chart elements and places them in a similar location on the new page setup. This means you can take a chart designed for a 35mm slide and change its page setup to Portrait, legal-sized paper with only minor adjustments in object placement. The ability to change the paper size and orientation after creating your chart makes it easy to transfer a chart originally used in a slide presentation to 4 × 5 film for publication in an annual report.

Generally, you will want to set up the correct paper size and orientation before you begin entering data and formatting the chart. Selecting the final paper size and orientation lets you place objects exactly where you want them. However, bear in mind, if you do change the page setup after composing your chart, you may have to reposition or readjust some chart elements. To control the paper size and orientation for a chart file, select File, Page Setup. The Page Setup dialog box appears, as shown in figure 28.34.

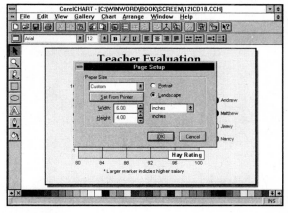

Figure 28.34
The Page Setup dialog box.

Adjusting the Paper Size and Orientation

Click on the down arrow by Paper Size to reveal the available sizes. These are the same page sizes available in CorelDRAW. Select the desired size. The size of the paper appears in the **W**idth and **H**eight boxes. Since you cannot alter a specific paper size, the **W**idth and **H**eight boxes are grayed out. To set up a custom-size page, select Custom from the list of paper sizes and enter the desired measurements in the **W**idth and **H**eight boxes.

N O T E

With the exception of the envelope and slide paper sizes, most of the paper size options can be set up in landscape or portrait orientation. Click on the desired orientation.

CorelCHART's extensive selection of chart types makes it one of the most powerful charting applications available. Regardless of the kind of data you want to present, CorelCHART's wide selection of chart types ensures that you will find the perfect way to express your information. Now that you have a better understanding of some of CorelCHART's fundamentals, you are ready to begin creating a chart. The focus of the next chapter is entering the text and numerical values used to compose your chart and creating formulas to help you calculate your data.

Summary

Charting has truly changed the way you read and interpret data. The power to inform, motivate, and persuade has made presentation graphics an important part of contemporary culture. Due to its flexibility and attention to detail, CorelCHART is an excellent choice for developing presentation graphics. Because graphics professionals like you are charged with the responsibility of developing charts and graphs, you should understand how CorelCHART approaches these tasks.

Working in the Data Manager

*U*nderstanding how the Data Manager works is an important part of learning and using CorelCHART. As discussed in Chapter 1, "Features of CorelDRAW," CorelCHART uses the text and numerical data entered in the Data Manager to calculate the size and placement of the bars, slices, or other graphing elements that make up your chart. You can enter the chart data manually, or import it from another application, such as Lotus 1-2-3 or Excel. As you will see, the Data Manager is much more than a place for entering and labeling data. Indeed, the Data Manager can handle many of the functions you might perform in spreadsheet applications like Lotus and Excel.

This chapter covers:

- Examining the Data Manager screen tools

- Calculating data with formulas & functions

- Importing and exporting chart data

- Tagging and formatting data in the Data Manager

- Formatting, printing, and numerous other topics

Introducing the Data Manager

This chapter focuses on entering and tagging chart data in the Data Manager. Some basic spreadsheet mechanics are discussed to aid in entering and replacing data quickly and correctly. In this chapter, you will also find the steps to format and print the chart data in the Data Manager spreadsheet as a separate document. You can spruce up the data with color, borders, and patterns, and then print it to support and confirm your chart visuals. The steps and features covered here are intended to prepare you for designing charts in Chart View.

When you begin a new chart using the sample data, CorelCHART starts by displaying the chart in the Chart View. If you chose not to use the sample data when beginning your chart, CorelCHART instead displays a blank spreadsheet in the Data Manager. This section focuses on working with the Data Manager, so if you are in the chart view, you should move to the Data Manager by clicking on the Data Manager button—the tiny spreadsheet at the top of the toolbox. If the Sample Data Option was turned on when you began the new chart, the Data Manager will display the sample data.

The Data Manager screen, displayed in figure 29.1, has many tools to help you enter the data that will generate your chart. Starting at the top of the screen is the *Data Manager ribbon bar*, which provides quick access to commands such as opening, saving, and printing files. The *Text Ribbon* provides buttons for formatting data, such as applying bold and italic. Below the Text Ribbon is the *Tag List*, which contains a list of the tags

you'll use to identify the various types of chart data. The *Autoscan* button is used to search through the data and tag it automatically. To the left of the Autoscan button is the *Chart Preview box*, which displays a small picture of a chart. The *Contents* box displays the contents of the selected cell.

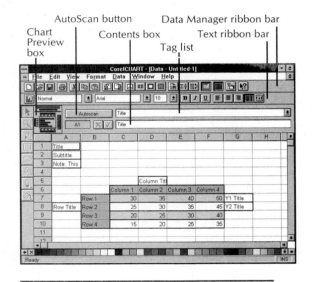

Figure 29.1
The Data Manager screen.

Examining the Data Manager Spreadsheet

A very important part of the Data Manager is the spreadsheet window. This is where you will enter the text and numbers that will generate your chart. The spreadsheet consists of 240 vertical columns, denoted by column letters along the top, and 16,384 horizontal rows, marked by row numbers on the left. At the intersection of each column and row is a *cell*. Each cell has a cell address that includes the column letter and row number. For instance, the first cell is addressed as A1. Text and numbers are entered into the cells of the spreadsheet.

Selecting Cells

Before you can enter data into a cell, you must first select it. When you initially open the Data Manager, the selected cell will be A1. The selected cell address appears at the top of the screen, right below the AutoScan button, and the selected cell is surrounded by a black border. To select another cell with the mouse, position your mouse on the cell and click. To select with the keyboard, simply use your arrow keys to move to the cell you want to select. To select a group or *range* of cells, drag with the mouse from the first cell to the last cell in the range. For example, as shown in figure 29.2, the cells from B2 to F10 are selected. The selected range in this case would be expressed as B2:F10. The colon between the cell references is interpreted as meaning *through*, as in cells B2 *through* F10. You can also select a range of cells with the keyboard. Click in the first cell, and then hold the Shift key as you use the arrow keys to move to other cells. All of the cells in between are selected.

T I P

Click on the column letter to select an entire column of cells and the row number to select an entire row of cells.

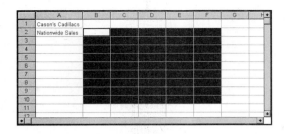

Figure 29.2
Selecting a range of cells in the Data Manager.

If there is data in the selected cell, you will see the cell contents in the Contents box at the top of the screen. The sample data has also been tagged for placement in the chart. The tag name of the selected cell appears in the Tag List. For instance, in figure 29.3, A1 is the selected cell, the Contents box displays the title text, "Boomers Focus on Quality, not Quantity," and the Tag List displays "Title."

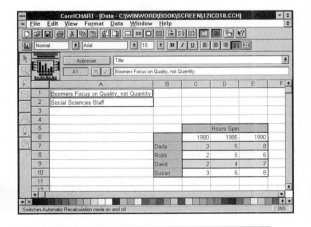

Figure 29.3
When a cell is selected, you can view the cell contents and tag name.

Moving in the Spreadsheet

You can move through the spreadsheet using the scroll bars. However, as featured in table 29.1, there are some keyboard shortcuts for moving through the spreadsheet.

Table 29.1

Keyboard Shortcuts for Moving through the Spreadsheet

Key	Spreadsheet Movement
Arrow keys	One cell in the selected direction.
Ctrl+Home	Move to cell A1.
Ctrl+End	Move to the end of your data.
Page Down	Move down one screen.
Page Up	Move up one screen.
Ctrl+Page Down	Move to the right one screen.
Ctrl+Page Up	Move to the left one screen.

TIP

You can use the Go To button in the Text Ribbon to quickly move to a specific cell. Click on the Go To button, enter a cell address in the GoTo dialog box, and click on OK.

Entering Data in the Data Manager

To enter data in the spreadsheet, select the cell where you want the data to appear. Once the appropriate cell is selected, you can simply start typing. Your typed data appears in both the cell and the Contents box directly above the spreadsheet. When you're finished typing, press the Enter key to accept the data in the cell.

NOTE

If you enter a long text string into a cell, the text may appear to be "cut off" in the cell. In such cases, the cell is not wide enough to display the text. This has no effect on how the data appears on your chart in Chart View. Widening columns is discussed later in this chapter.

Alternatively, you can use the arrow keys to accept the data and move to another cell in one step. If you decide not to accept the data after typing it, press the Escape key to cancel the entry.

You can use the Enter Data button (the check mark) in place of the Enter key when entering data. Likewise, the Cancel Entry key (the X) can be used in place of the Escape key to clear data.

Replacing Data

When you type data in a cell that already contains data, the old data is replaced by the new data. Replacing data is the basic principle behind using sample data. Essentially, you are replacing the sample data with your own. Figure 29.4 shows the sample data CorelCHART places when you create a new bar chart. The sample data is already tagged for placement in the chart. Therefore, all you need to do is select the cell containing the data you want to replace, and type in the new data. For instance, when using sample data, cell A1 is tagged as the chart title and A2 as the subtitle. You can replace the sample titles with your titles by simply typing on top of them.

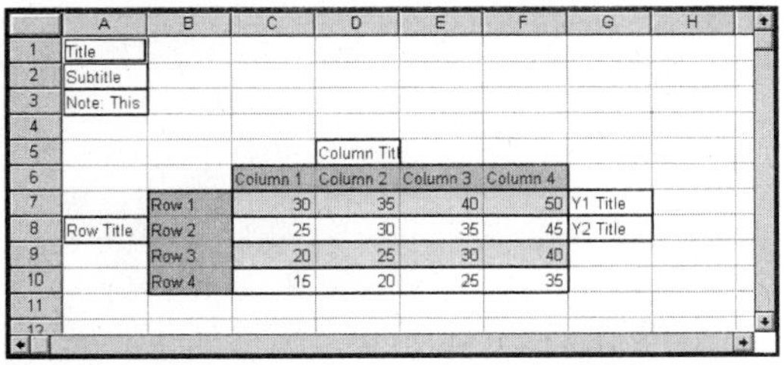

Speeding Up Data Entry

The numbers used to generate your chart must be placed in a contiguous range of cells without any blank columns or rows. In figure 29.5, for instance, the numbers and headings appear in the cells B7 through F10. The following steps can speed up your data entry time:

1. Select the range of cells in which you want to enter the data. The top left cell within the selected range is white. This is the active cell.

2. Type in the data for the active cell and press Enter. The active cell moves down to the next cell in the selected range.

3. Type in the next set of data and press Enter again. When you get to the bottom of a column within the selected range, pressing Enter will take you to the top of the next column. This shortcut prevents you from having to use the arrow keys to return to the top of each column.

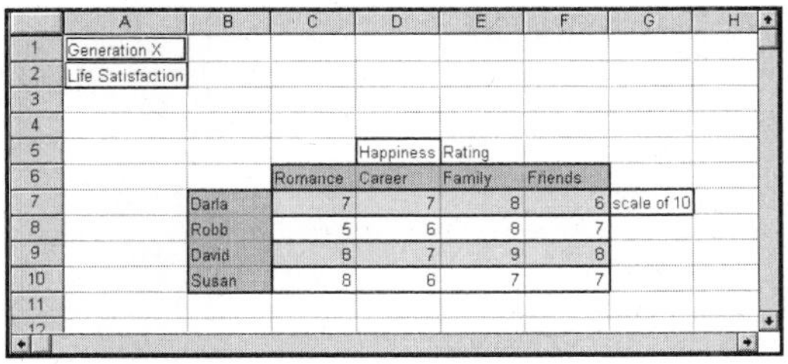

Figure 29.4

The sample data placed in the Data Manager screen.

Figure 29.5

Chart text and values are often placed in a contiguous range of cells in the Data Manager.

Editing Data

In many cases, the best way to edit cell contents is to retype the data in the cell and press Enter. For instance, if a cell currently shows a value of 100 and you want to change it to 525, just type in the new data over the old and press Enter to accept the new data in the cell. There may be times, however, when you want to keep what is already in the cell and simply amend it. For instance, if the cell containing the chart title currently says "ABC Company" and you need it to say "ABC Company Incorporated," rather than retyping the entire headline, select the cell you want to edit and click on the cell data in the Contents box. When an insertion point appears in the data, you can edit the data as necessary. When you are finished editing, press Enter and the updated data appears in the cell.

N O T E

You can also edit the cell contents by pressing the F2 key. This method enables you to edit the contents in the formula bar or in the cell itself. After pressing F2, click in the cell or formula bar to place the insertion point and begin editing.

Calculating Data with Formulas and Functions

CorelCHART provides tools to help you write formulas and functions for calculating chart data. For instance, you may need to determine an average of your company's entertainment expenses for the past five years, or project the number of cars sold in the coming year. If you have experience with spreadsheet applications such as Lotus 1-2-3 or Excel, you will find the formulas and functions in CorelCHART quite familiar. If you are new to spreadsheet formulas and functions, the Formula Editor dialog box also contains a calculator where you can perform some quick number crunching. The next section discusses writing formulas and functions, including some pointers for novice spreadsheet users.

Entering Formulas

On the spreadsheet, formulas begin with an equal sign and are written using cell addresses instead of the actual number values. In figure 29.6, for example, the formula =C7+C8 was entered into cell C9 to sum up the contents of cells C7 and C8. The formula appears in the Contents box, while the summed value appears in the cell. The formula adds up the contents of the specified cells. If the content of either cell changes, the formula recalculates to display the new value. For instance, if the number in cell C7 were changed to 100, the summed value in cell C9 would automatically recalculate to display 200.

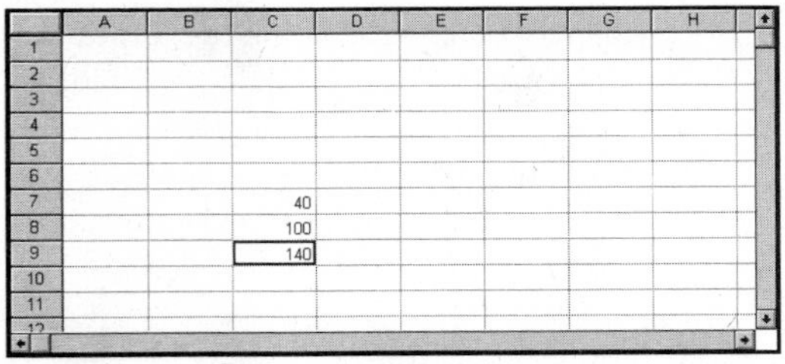

Figure 29.6

A formula using cell addresses.

When writing formulas, you will employ basic math functions such as addition, subtraction, multiplication, and division to perform calculations. CorelCHART requires that you place an "operator" between each of the cell addresses in your formula. The operators you will use are + for addition, – for subtraction, * for multiplication, and / for division. For example, the formula =C7+C8– C9 instructs CorelCHART to add the contents of cells C7 and C8, and then subtract the contents of C9. Keep in mind when you are writing formulas that the operations will be performed in a specific sequence. The * multiplication and / division operators take precedence over the + addition and – subtraction operators. That makes a big difference in the formula =D7+D8/E8, where the division takes place first, and then the addition. You can override this by inserting parentheses around the part of the formula you want to calculate first. For instance, =(D7+D8)/E8 instructs CorelCHART to perform the addition first, and then the division.

Entering Formulas Directly

Formulas can be entered directly into the cell. After selecting a cell, type in the formula and press Enter. The formula is displayed in the Contents box, and the calculated value is displayed in the cell. In figure 29.7, the sales figures for two months are entered in cells C5 through D8, and the commission rate appears in D2. The following steps illustrate how you might write a formula calculating the commission rate earned by each sales representative:

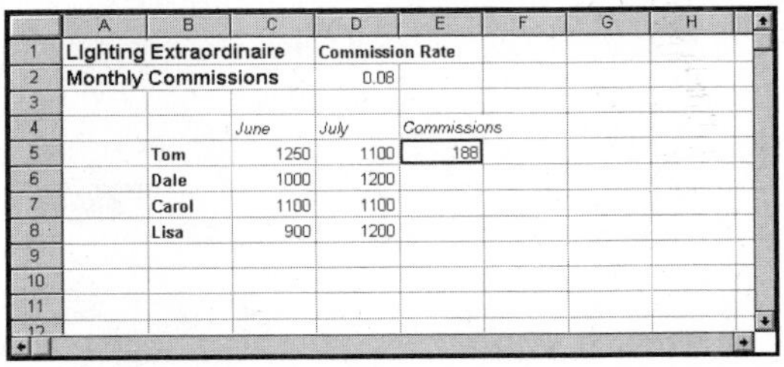

Figure 29.7

Entering formulas to calculate sales commissions.

1. Select the cell where you want the first commission rate to appear. Select E5 to start with the first salesperson, Tom.

2. Type =(C5+D5)*D2 to instruct CorelCHART to add the two months' sales figures first, and then multiply that total by the commission rate in cell D2. Press Enter to compute the formula.

3. Move down to the next cell and repeat the preceding steps for the remaining sales representatives. Make sure you are using the correct cell references when entering the formulas.

Creating Formulas with the Enter Formula Dialog Box

Formulas can also be created in the Enter Formula dialog box, and then placed in the spreadsheet. The Enter Formula dialog box works much like a standard calculator. As shown in figure 29.8, the dialog box contains a numeric keypad and buttons to calculate formulas. You can either click with the mouse on the desired numbers or operator buttons, or type the formula into the text box at the top of the dialog box. Also contained within the dialog box are buttons to Cut, Copy, and Paste formulas from one cell into another cell or group of cells. The following steps use the Enter Formula dialog box to calculate the commission rate for each sales representative in figure 29.7:

1. Select the cell where you want the first commission rate to appear. Select E5 to start with the first salesperson, Tom.

2. From the **D**ata menu, choose Enter For**m**ula or click on the Enter Formula button in the ribbon bar. The Enter Formula dialog box appears, as shown in figure 29.8. All formulas are entered in the Editor box at the top of the dialog box.

3. Enter the formula (C5+D5)*D2. When finished, click on the Enter button to place the formula into the cell. The result is displayed in cell E5. Notice that the formula is displayed in the Contents box.

4. Repeat the preceding steps for the remaining sales representatives. Make sure you are using the correct cell

references when entering the formulas. If the Enter Formula dialog box blocks your view of the cells you want to calculate, drag on the title bar of the Enter Formula dialog box to move it aside.

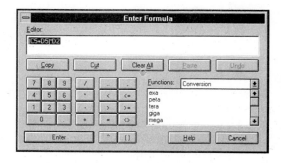

Figure 29.8

The Enter Formula dialog box.

Entering Functions

The Enter Formula dialog box gives you access to prebuilt worksheet functions to perform mathematical calculations. Think of functions as "shorthand" formulas. For example, to add up 8 cells of data, you could enter the rather lengthy formula, =B4+B5+B6+B7+B8+B9+B10+B11, or the shorter sum function, =SUM(B4:B11). The SUM function tells the Data Manager to total up the number values specified in the parentheses.

CorelCHART includes over 300 functions to help you perform all sorts of number crunching. You can do everything from summing and averaging monthly sales, finding the future and present values of annuities, to determining the monthly payment on your car loan. CorelCHART includes functions for the following types of data manipulation:

- Conversion functions
- Date and time functions
- DDE/External functions
- Engineering functions
- Financial functions
- Information functions
- Logical functions
- Lookup and reference functions
- Math and trig functions
- Statistical functions
- Text functions

N O T E

CorelCHART's functions work exactly like those found in the popular spreadsheet applications. For more information on using individual functions, refer to CorelCHART's online help topic, "Spreadsheet Functions."

All functions are utilized in the same basic way. First, you select the function, and then enter the cell addresses of the numbers you want calculated. As an example, this section will discuss using two frequently used functions, SUM and AVG (for averages). In figure 29.9, the goal is to total all company sales figures and then determine the average

sales for all sales representatives. Both of these can be accomplished quickly by using functions. The following steps illustrate the process for placing a sum function in cell D9 and an average function in D10.

1. Select cell D9 to create the formula to total the sales. From the **D**ata menu, select Enter For**m**ula, or click on the Enter Formula button in the Ribbon bar to display the Enter Formula dialog box.

2. Choose the type of function you need by clicking on the down arrow by Functions. The SUM is in the Math & Trig category. Scroll through the **F**unctions list to locate SUM(list). Double-click on the function to place it in the Editor box.

3. An insertion point is blinking between the parentheses in the function. Enter D4:D8 as the cells to be summed. Click on the Enter button to display the result in the spreadsheet. The formula appears in the Contents box.

4. Select cell D10 and press the F12 key—this is a shortcut for the Enter For**m**ula command. Choose the Statistical function category and double-click on the AVG (list) function to place it in the Editor box.

5. Enter D4:D8 and click on the Enter button to place the sales average into the spreadsheet.

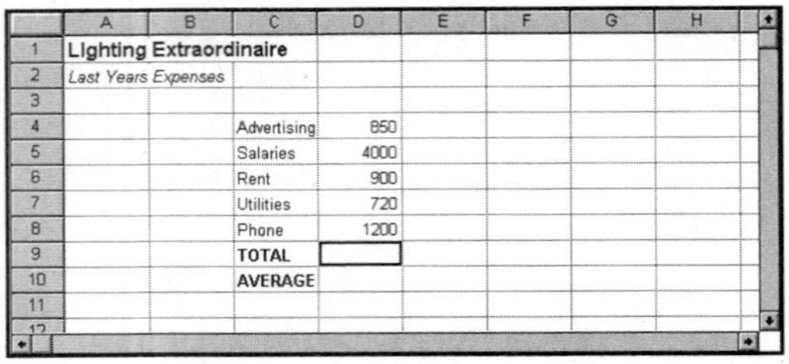

Figure 29.9
Data using SUM and Average functions.

Recalculating Formulas and Functions

As mentioned earlier, formulas and functions are written using cell references so that if the number values change, the formula or function is automatically recalculated for the new data. The automatic recalculation feature can be turned on and off with the **A**uto Recalculate command in the Data menu, or by clicking on the Auto Recalculate button in the Ribbon bar. If automatic recalculation has been disabled, formulas and functions will not automatically recalculate until you select **R**ecalculate Now from the Data menu.

Importing and Exporting Chart Data

The ability to transfer data between CorelCHART and other applications can be a big time-saver. For instance, if the chart data has already been entered in another

spreadsheet application, such as Excel or Word for Windows, you can import the data into the Data Manager; or, after entering the departmental sales figures in the Data Manager, suppose you are asked to place the figures in a Word for Windows table. CorelCHART can export the data in a format Word for Windows can accept.

N O T E

If your chart data is entered in a Windows application, such as Word for Windows, you can also transfer it into the Data Manager by copying and pasting the data through the Windows Clipboard. For more information regarding transferring data from one Windows application to another, you may want to refer to your application reference manual. You will also find more about the Copy and Paste process in later sections of this chapter.

Importing Data

The imported data will fill the cells of the spreadsheet in the Data Manager. Importing clears all existing data in the spreadsheet and replaces it with the new data. If the existing data is important, save it before importing any new data. It is important to consider this before importing because the Undo command is not available to revoke the importing step. Table 29.2 lists the file formats that can be imported into the Data Manager.

Table 29.2
File Formats that Can Be Imported into the Data Manager

Format	File Extension	Notes
Corel Sheet	.CDS	The chart data in the Data Manager can be exported to this format.
Corel Sheet v. 4.0	.TBL	Same as preceding, except for version 4.0.
Import from Text	.TXT	Many applications, such as Word for Windows and Word Perfect, can export to this format.
Import from CSV	.CSV	Many database programs, such as dBASE and Paradox, can export to this format.
Import from RTF	.RTF	Many Windows applications, such as Ami Pro and Lotus for Windows, can export to this format.
Excel 3 & 4	.XLS	Excel 3.0 and 4.0 spreadsheet files. (You can save version 5.0 files in the 4.0 format.)

Keep in mind that after importing, you may need to rearrange the data to meet the requirements of the Data Manager for tagging and Autoscan. The data arrangement needed for CorelCHART to correctly tag or "place" the data is covered later in this chapter. To import a data file into the Data Manager, follow these steps:

1. Select **F**ile, **I**mport or click on the Import button in the ribbon bar. The Import Data dialog box appears, as shown in figure 29.10.

2. Click on the down arrow by List File of Type and select the file format to be imported, such as Excel 3 & 4.

3. Change to the drive and directory where the file to be imported is located. Double-click on the desired file name to import the data. The data is imported into the Data Manager spreadsheet.

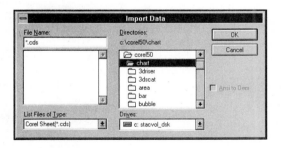

Figure 29.10
The Import Data dialog box.

Exporting Data

Exporting saves the chart data in a format other applications can read. Table 29.3 lists the available formats for exporting the data in the Data Manager.

To export a data file, follow these steps:

1. Select **F**ile, **E**xport or click on the Export button on the ribbon bar. The Export Data dialog box appears, as shown in figure 29.11.

2. Click on the down arrow by List Files of **T**ype and select the file format to be exported, such as Excel 4.0.

3. Change to the drive and directory where you want to save the exported file. Enter a file name and click on OK. The file is saved in the new export format.

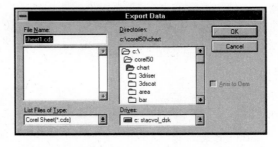

Figure 29.11
The Export Data dialog box.

Table 29.3
Available Export File Formats

Format	File Extension	Applications that Accept Format
Corel Sheet	.CDS	This data can be imported into another CorelCHART file.
Tab-separated text	.TXT	Most word processing and spreadsheet applications can import text files.
Comma-separated files	.CSV	Many spreadsheet and database applications can import the "Comma Separated Value" format.
Export to RTF	.RTF	Most Windows applications can import the "Rich Text Format."
Excel 3.0	.XLS	Excel 3.0.
Excel 4.0	.XLS	Excel 4.0.

Tagging and Formatting Data in the Data Manager

After entering the chart text and numbers, you are almost ready to switch to Chart View. Remember, Chart View is where you see the chart data transformed into a visual representation of your data. But before switching to Chart View, you must "tag" the chart data. Tagging lets CorelCHART know which cells contain the elements used to compose the chart in Chart View. For example, tagging tells CorelCHART which cells contain the subtitle and data sets so they can be placed correctly on the chart. You must tag every cell of data that you want to appear on the chart. However, not all data in the spreadsheet must be tagged. For instance, if you have included a note or comment on the spreadsheet, this data does not need to be tagged.

There are basically two ways to tag chart data: Autoscanning and manual tagging. The Autoscan method quickly scans your chart data and tags it automatically. With the manual method, you select the cell(s) for each individual chart element, and then apply a chart tag. The next section will cover how to tag chart data with both the Autoscan and manual methods.

Identifying CorelCHART Tag Names

Tagging requires that you assign tag names to the cells containing the data needed to compose the chart. Most of the tag names are relatively straightforward. For example, the Title tag is for the title data, and the Subtitle tag is for subtitles. Some tags, however, may require some clarification. Table 29.4 identifies the tag name for each chart element. Figure 29.12 shows how each tagged element displays on the chart.

Table 29.4
Tag Names and Corresponding Chart Elements

Tag Name	Chart Element
Title	Chart Title
Subtitle	Chart Subtitle
Footnote	Chart Footnote
Column Title	Category Axis Title
Column Headers	Category Axis Labels
Row Title	Series/Legend Title
Row Headers	Series Labels
Y1 Title	Data Axis Title
Y2 Title	Second Data Axis Title
Data Range	Number Values

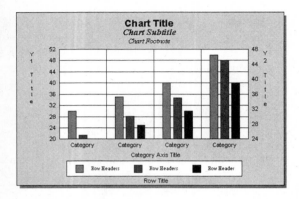

Figure 29.12

Identifying chart elements.

Examining the Effect of Sample Data on the Tagging Process

The sample data feature available when you first create a chart can make the entire tagging process easier. As discussed in Chapter 2, "Using Graphic Tools," the New dialog box includes an option for placing sample data in the chart. If the sample data feature is turned on when the chart is created, sample data is placed in the Data Manager that generates the chart displayed in Chart View. If the sample data feature is turned off when creating a new chart, a blank spreadsheet appears, ready for you to enter the chart data. If you switch to Chart View without entering and tagging data, a large red null sign appears because there is no data to generate a chart. This section examines how sample data affects the tagging process.

Using Sample Data

Using the sample data option simplifies the chart creation process because the sample data is already tagged for placement in the chart. To see the tags, select the cell(s) and refer to the Tag List at the top of the screen. In figure 29.13, for instance, cells C6 through F6 are selected, and the Tag List will identify these cells as "column headers." Notice also that the Preview box signals how the cell has been tagged by highlighting that element in the chart picture.

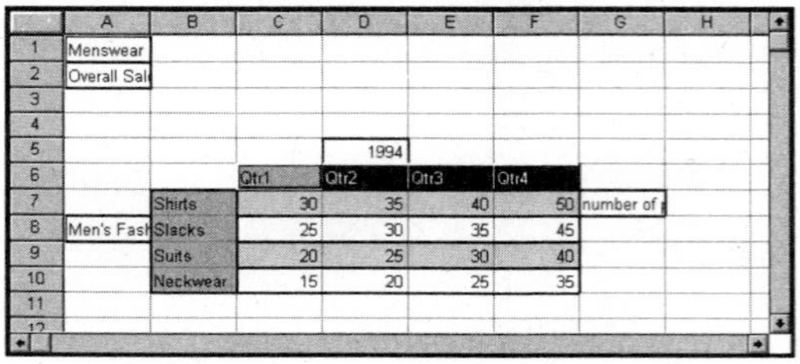

Figure 29.13

The Tag List displays the selected tag name.

The sample data for most chart types will look the same. Some chart types, such as spectral maps and tables, use slightly different sample data. The data itself is not particularly important; however, the way data is arranged and tagged is highly important. Sample data is arranged in the order and orientation necessary for Autoscanning to tag chart elements. (Autoscanning is discussed in the next section.) When Autoscan searches through the spreadsheet, it looks for a specific arrangement of the chart data. If the data is arranged according to the Autoscan requirements, your data is tagged correctly. If the data is not arranged according to the Autoscan requirements, your data may be tagged incorrectly. Using sample data ensures that you are arranging the chart data in the manner specified by Autoscan. The sample data in figure 29.14 was replaced with chart data to illustrate the arrangement required by Autoscan.

	A	B	C	D	E	F	G	
1	TOP 5 Radio Dee Jays							
2	Monthly Ratings							
3	compiled by WG99							
4								
5				1992				
6			January	February	March	April		
7		Bryce	21	23	22	21	listeners in	
8	Favorite DJS	Cason	24	23	22	24		
9		Kelly	21	24	23	21		
10		Parker	20	19	22	20		
11								
12								

Figure 29.14

Chart data using the Autoscan data arrangement.

Since the sample data is already tagged, when you replace it with your own data, your data will be automatically tagged. Then, when you switch to Chart View, *your* data composes the chart. It all works very smoothly, until you need to add more categories of data than the sample data provides or delete the categories you don't need. Whenever you deviate from the sample data, you will need to perform some retagging. Tagging with Autoscan and manual tagging is discussed in the next section.

In summary, there are two strong reasons for using sample data. First, sample data aids you in creating charts because the data is already tagged—you just replace the sample data with your data. Second, the sample data is

arranged in the order required by Autoscan, which makes any retagging easier.

Not Using Sample Data

Creating a new chart without the sample data enables you to enter chart data into a blank spreadsheet. You can enter chart data to match the arrangement needed to Autoscan, or you can enter the data in whatever cells you choose and use the manual tagging method to identify the chart elements. However, even with manual tagging, you must still follow a few rules regarding where certain chart elements must be placed. For instance, all chart data must be entered with row headers (series labels) to the left of the number values, and the column headers (category labels) above the data range. In general, it is recommended that you use the sample data to avoid any confusion about data arrangement and tagging.

Using Autoscan

Autoscanning searches through the data in the spreadsheet and tags it for placement in the chart. Whether you replaced the sample data or entered data into a blank spreadsheet, you can use Autoscan to quickly tag the data. In fact, it's a good idea to click on the Autoscan button whenever you are ready to switch to Chart View. This way, any changes to the data are automatically recognized. However, as previously discussed, the Autoscan feature only works if your data is arranged in a specific order. Figure 29.15 depicts a typical Autoscan data arrangement for most charts types. Matching your chart data to this layout lets you take advantage of the speed of Autoscan.

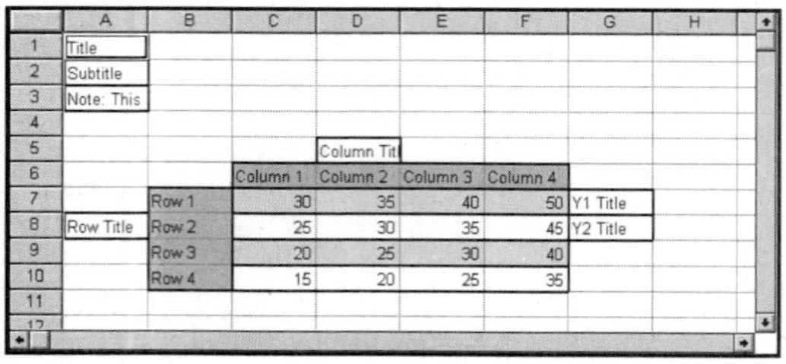

Figure 29.15

Autoscan chart data arrangement.

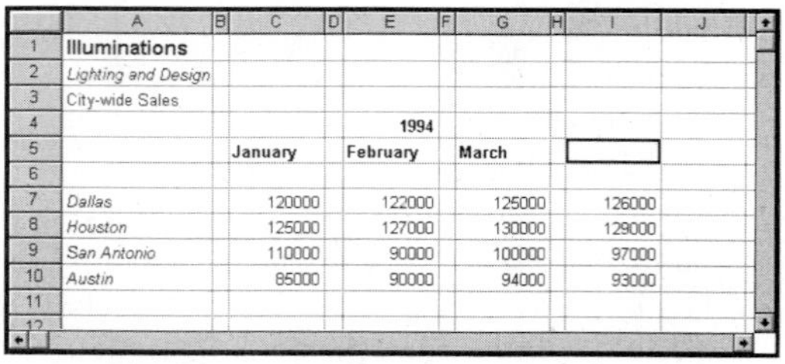

Figure 29.16

Autoscan will not work if empty columns are placed between the chart data.

Autoscan searches the spreadsheet for a large block of cells comprised of numbers. It assumes that the top row of cells in that block are the column headers, and the left-most column in the block are row headers. The rest of the block is scanned as the data range. You will encounter problems if you leave blank columns or rows in the data range. For example, the data in figure 29.16 would not compose an accurate chart because of the empty column. In addition, Autoscan requires that you have a column header for every column of numbers and a row header for every row of numbers. Again, problems would occur with the data in figure 29.16 because the last column of numbers has no header. The row title must be to the left of the row headers and the column title must be to the left of the column headers. The chart title, subtitle, and footnote should be placed in A1, A2, and A3, so Autoscan will tag them correctly.

If you enter data into a blank spreadsheet or import it from another program, it may not match the arrangement required by Autoscan. In such cases, you can cut and paste the data to the proper location. In this way, the data will match the required arrangement so that you can take advantage of Autoscan.

To use Autoscan, select a single cell anywhere in the spreadsheet and click on the Autoscan button. If you select more than one cell, Autoscan will not scan properly. CorelCHART scans through the data and tags it accordingly. After Autoscanning, the Data Range, Column, and Row Headers are highlighted. To preview the tag names, click on a cell and refer to the Tag List at the top of the screen. After Autoscanning, if your data is tagged incorrectly, it is probably arranged in the wrong order. To remedy this problem, try arranging it in the order specified in figure 29.15, and then click on the Autoscan button again. Once your data is properly tagged, switch to Chart View to preview your new chart.

Manual Tagging

Though Autoscanning requires that your data be arranged in a specific order, you can vary from this order as long as you manually tag the data to identify each chart element. Figures 29.17 and 29.18 illustrate two ways you might enter data for manual tagging. As illustrated in both figures, manual tagging has a few requirements regarding how the data should be arranged. Manual tagging requires that column headers be placed above the data range and row headers be placed to the left of the data range.

To manually tag chart data, select the cell(s) that contain the data and then apply a tag from the Tag List. Though manual tagging is an easy process, you must tag every chart element. To help you select the appropriate tag, refer back to the previous section "Identifying CorelCHART Tag Names." The following steps illustrate how to tag the data range in figure 29.18:

1. Select the cell(s) containing the data you want to tag. For instance, select D5 to G8 to tag the data range in figure 29.18.

2. Click on the down arrow by the Tag List to reveal a listing of the tag names. You will have to scroll to see all the names.

3. Click on the desired tag name. Tag the cells D5 through G8 as the Data Range. After the selected cell(s) are tagged, the Tag List displays the selected tag name.

Repeat this procedure until all chart elements have been tagged. When you finish tagging each element, switch to the Chart View to see if your data was placed correctly. If the chart elements do not appear correctly in the chart, you may have to return to the Data Manager and retag the data.

	A	B	C	D	E	F	
1			Illuminations				
2			Lighting and Desi				
3			City-wide Sales				
4				1994			
5			January	February	March	April	
6							
7	Dallas		120000	122000	125000	126000	
8	Houston		125000	127000	130000	129000	
9	San Antonio		110000	90000	100000	97000	
10	Austin		85000	90000	94000	93000	
11							
12							

Figure 29.17
Arrangement of data for manual tagging.

	A	B	C	D	E	F	G	H	
1									
2					1994				
3				January	February	March	April		
4									
5	Illuminations		Dallas	120000	122000	125000	126000		
6			Houston	125000	127000	130000	129000		
7	Lighting and Design		San Anton	110000	90000	100000	97000		
8			Austin	85000	90000	94000	93000		
9	City-wide Sales								
10									
11									
12									

Figure 29.18
Another data arrangement for manual tagging.

Rearranging and Manipulating Data

As you enter text and numbers to build a chart, you may need to rearrange and manipulate the data. For instance, you may need to delete data, move it to another row, or insert a column for new data. Rearranging data becomes especially important in the tagging process. As discussed in the previous section, tagging requires that the chart data is entered in a specific order. For instance, CorelCHART expects you to place the category axis titles above the number values. To meet the arrangement of data required for tagging, you may occasionally have to rearrange your data so that it will be tagged appropriately. This section discusses deleting, moving, copying, pasting, and filling chart data in the Data Manager.

NOTE

Many of the commands for rearranging data covered in the next sections are also available from CorelCHART's *cell menu*. To use the cell menu, position the mouse pointer in the cell(s) you want to edit, and click on the right mouse button. The cell menu pops up with choices for clearing, cutting, copying, and pasting data. Though these are the same commands found in the Edit and Format menus, the cell menu is designed to put these frequently used commands right at your fingertips.

Deleting Data and Formatting

The Clear command is used to delete or clear the contents of a cell or group of cells. Use this command when you want to eliminate any data from the spreadsheet. For instance, when you create a bar chart, CorelCHART places four sets of sample series data. If your chart only requires three sets, you will need to delete the fourth set of data. The Clear command also lets you delete cell formatting. This is useful, for instance, when you want to keep the data but delete the bold and italic formatting.

To clear all data or formatting, select the cell or cells containing the data you want to delete and select **E**dit, **C**lear or press the Delete key. (You can also use the cell menu.) The Cut and Clear Options dialog box appears, as shown in figure 29.19. The X's by each item indicate what types of data and formatting will be deleted. By default, each of the options is marked to be deleted. You can customize what is deleted by clicking on the data type or features you do not want deleted. For instance, to delete all data but formulas, uncheck the Formulas option. To delete all formatting information except for the font, uncheck the **F**ont option. After selecting the data and formatting you want deleted, click on OK to delete the specified data or formatting.

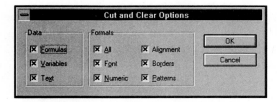

Figure 29.19
The Cut and Clear Options dialog box.

Cutting, Copying, and Pasting Data in the Data Manager

You can use the Cut and Paste commands to move data from one cell to another. The Cut command differs from the Clear command in that you can paste "cut" data elsewhere on the spreadsheet. Cleared data cannot be pasted elsewhere in the spreadsheet. The Copy and Paste commands enable you to copy data between cells.

Using Cut and Paste

The Cut command removes the selected cell data and sends the data to the Windows Clipboard. The Paste command is then used to place the data from the Windows Clipboard back into the spreadsheet at a new location. Use the following steps to cut and paste data in the Data Manager:

1. Select the cell(s) containing the data you want to move, and select **E**dit, Cu**t** or click on the Cut button in the Ribbon bar. (You can also use the cell menu.)

2. The Cut and Clear Options dialog box appears. This is the same dialog box used with the Clear command. In the dialog box, select the desired data and formatting options you want cut and click on OK. The data is removed from the spreadsheet.

3. Select the cell where you want to place the data and select **E**dit, **P**aste or click on the Paste button in the Ribbon bar. (You can also use the cell menu.) You only need to select the top left cell of the range in which you want the data pasted, even if you are pasting multiple cells of data. The pasted data will use the selected cell as a starting point, and then fill down and to the right with the rest of data.

Using Copy and Paste

The Copy and Paste commands enable you to copy the contents of one cell to another. To copy and paste data, follow the same steps for cutting and pasting, except use the Copy command instead of Cut. Keep in mind that copying and pasting is a great way to copy data from one chart spreadsheet to another—it saves you the time of having to reenter data such as titles, category axis, or headings.

Copying and Pasting Formulas and Functions

Building multiple formulas on a spreadsheet can be time-consuming. Imagine if you had to total the monthly sales of a hundred products. This would amount to one hundred formulas! Instead of writing all

those formulas and functions individually, you can save a lot of time by copying and pasting them to other cells. Each time you copy and paste a formula, the pasted formula is essentially rewritten for the new cell location. For instance, in figure 29.20, the formula in cell C8 reads =C4 + C5 + C6. When this formula is copied and pasted in cell D8, it is automatically adjusted to read as =D4 + D5 + D6. The change in the pasted formula occurs because of a process known as *relative cell referencing.*

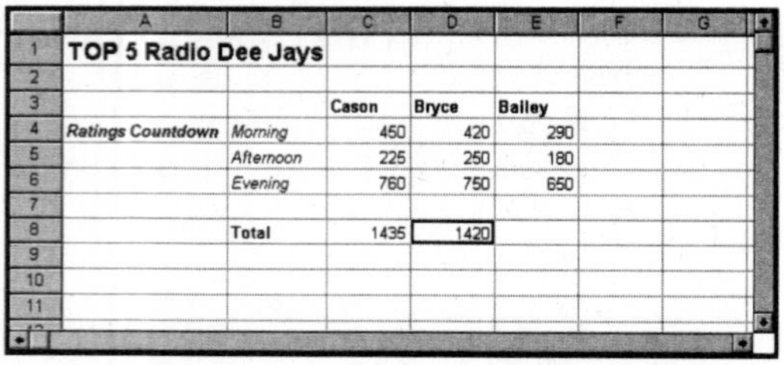

Figure 29.20
When you copy and paste a formula, the pasted formula adjusts for its new cell location.

Filling Data

The Fill commands provide you with another, often quicker way to copy data between cells. With the Fill commands, you can "fill" adjacent cells with data and formulas. You simply select a range of cells that includes the data you want to fill and the cells you want the data to fill into. The Fill Down command enables you to fill data from the top of the selected area down into the cells below. In figure 29.21, for example, you could select cells C4 through C7, and fill

the formula in C4 down into the other cells. Remember, the formulas adjust to calculate for the data relative to the new cell location. The Fill Right command enables you to fill data from the left of the selected area to the right.

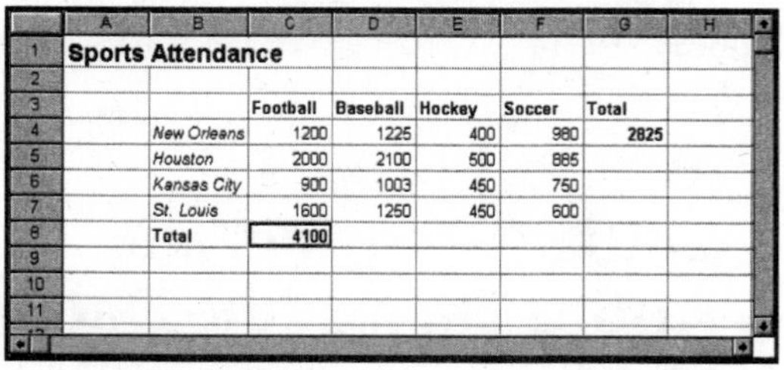

Figure 29.21
The Fill command makes it easy to copy data or formulas to other cells.

The Fill commands work only when you want to copy data to adjacent or "touching" cells. For instance, you cannot fill from cell B10 to D10, and then skip to C10. If you want to copy data to nonadjacent cells, use the Copy and Paste commands. The following steps illustrate using the Fill Down command:

1. Select the cells containing the formula you want to repeat, and the cells where the formulas will be filled.

2. From the Edit menu, select Fill **D**own, to fill the data from G4 to the other selected cells on the right.

Inserting Columns and Rows

In the charting business, it is not at all uncommon to update charts with a new series of data. For instance, you may be asked to update a sales chart by inserting a row for a new sales representative. When you insert a column or row, any existing data moves over to make room for the new column or row.

To insert a new column or row, follow these steps:

1. Select the column(s) or row(s) where you want the new columns or rows inserted. To select a column, click on the column letter. To select a row, click on the row number. To select more than one column or row, drag across several column letters or row numbers.

2. Select **E**dit, **I**nsert to add the new column(s) or row(s). When you insert a new column, any existing data is shifted to the right. When you insert a new row, any existing data is shifted down.

N O T E

Your formulas and functions will adjust to the new location when you insert columns and rows. For instance, the formula C4 * C5 in column C would change to D4 * D5 when a new column C is inserted. However, even though formulas and functions will adjust when you insert columns and rows, it's still a good idea to double-check them for accuracy.

Deleting Columns and Rows

You can remove data from a spreadsheet by deleting entire columns and rows. For instance, you could delete a row containing last year's sales figures. It's important to remember that deleting a column or row also deletes any data in the column or row.

To delete a column or row, use the following steps:

1. Select the column(s) or row(s) you want to delete. To select a column, click on the column letter. To select a row, click on the row number. To select more than one column or row, drag across several column letters or row numbers.

2. Select **E**dit, **D**elete. The column(s), row(s), and/or any selected data are deleted.

Adjusting Column Width and Row Height

When entering chart data, you will find that longer text strings do not completely fit into a cell. By default, columns in the Data Manager spreadsheet are 50 points or about 3/4 inches wide, and rows in the spreadsheet are 15 points tall. If your text strings exceed these boundaries, the text will appear to be cut off. Actually, all of the text is still there; it just appears cut off because the column is not wide enough. You can adjust the column width and row height to accommodate the

text. For instance, the title "Working Safely" in figure 29.22 is cut off because the column is not wide enough to display all of the text. The top and bottom of the text are also clipped off because the row is not tall enough.

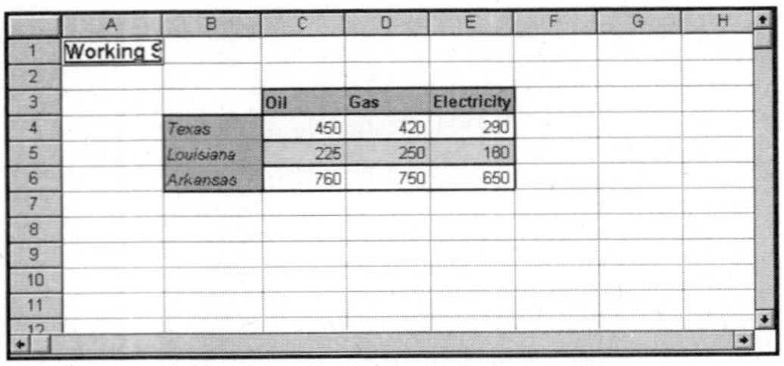

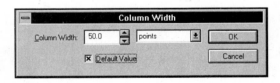

	A	B	C	D	E	F	G	H
1	Working S							
2								
3			Oil	Gas	Electricity			
4		Texas	450	420	290			
5		Louisiana	225	250	160			
6		Arkansas	760	750	650			
7								
8								
9								
10								
11								
12								

Figure 29.22
Examining data that is too large for the cell.

You can adjust the column width and row height to fit longer text strings. However, the column width and row height affects only what you see in the Data Manager, not what you see in the Chart View. Even if your title is cut off in the Data Manager, the title will still appear completely in the Chart View. You really only have to worry about column width and row height when formatting the spreadsheet to be printed.

Adjusting Column Width and Row Height by Dragging

The easiest way to adjust the column width is to drag on the dividing line between the column letters. For instance, to widen column A, place the mouse on the dividing line between columns A and B. The mouse shape changes to a double-sided arrow. Drag the mouse to the left or right to adjust the

width of the column. When the column is at the desired width, let go of the mouse button, and the column width is adjusted. To adjust the width of several columns at one time, select all of them before dragging the width of one column.

The same process is used to adjust row height. Place the mouse on the dividing line between any two row numbers. Again, the mouse shape will change to a double-sided arrow. Drag up or down to increase or decrease the row height. Release the mouse button at the desired height.

Adjusting with the Column Width and Row Height Commands

The Column Width command lets you enter a precise measurement for the column width. Select a cell in the column you want to adjust and choose Column **W**idth from the Fo**r**mat menu. The Column Width dialog box appears, as displayed in figure 29.23. Type in a new width and click on OK.

Figure 29.23
The Column Width dialog box.

The Row Height command functions similar to the Column Width command. Select a cell in the row you want to adjust and choose Row **H**eight from the Fo**r**mat menu. The

Row Height dialog box appears, as displayed in figure 29.24. Type in a new height and click on OK.

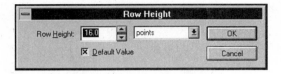

Figure 29.24
The Row Height dialog box.

A value of 0 (zero) in the Column Width or Row Height dialog box hides the row completely. This is a great way to hide sensitive data.

Using the Best Fit Command

The Best Fit command automatically adjusts the column width and row height to match the largest entry in the selected column or row. To use Best Fit, select the column containing the data you want fit and choose Best Fit from the Format menu. All cells in the column are adjusted to the width necessary to display the longest text string.

Sorting Data

CorelCHART's sorting feature helps you organize chart data in alphabetic or numeric order. For instance, you may need to sort a list of sales representatives alphabetically by last name. Information is sorted by a *key*.

The key tells CorelCHART which element of the data to use as a guide for the sort. To sort by city names in figure 29.25, for example, you would use column B as the sort key. To sort by attendance totals, you would use column F as the sort key. The key is simply the category by which you want the data sorted.

	A	B	C	D	E	F	G	H
1	Sports Attendance							
2								
3			Football	Baseball	Hockey	Total		
4		New Orleans	1200	1225	400	2825		
5		Houston	2000	2100	500	4600		
6		Kansas City	900	1003	450	2353		
7		St. Louis	1600	1250	450	3300		
8		Dallas	3100	3200	2700	9000		
9		Total	8800	8778	4500	22078		
10								
11								

Figure 29.25
Examining data to be sorted.

You can choose to sort the data by columns or rows. For instance, in figure 29.25, the cities and attendance figures are lined up in rows. To arrange the city names in alphabetical order, you would choose to sort by rows. However, the sports categories are lined up in columns. To arrange the sports categories in alphabetical order, you would choose to sort by columns. CorelCHART assumes you want to sort by rows unless you specify otherwise.

Before sorting, it is important to select all the data you want sorted. In figure 29.25, you would not want the cities sorted without the corresponding attendance figures, so both the city names and the attendance figures must be selected. The following steps illustrate sorting the data in figure 29.25 alphabetically by city name:

1. Select the cells you want sorted.

2. Select **D**ata, **S**ort or click on the Sort button in the Ribbon bar to display the Sort dialog box, as shown in figure 29.26. Make sure **R**ow is selected as the orientation for sorting the data.

3. Enter B4 in the **K**ey box, instructing CorelCHART to use column B as the sorting key. You must type in a whole cell address, even though only the column letter will be used when sorting by rows, and only the row number will be used when sorting by columns.

4. **A**scending is the default sort order. Ascending sorts alphabetically A to Z, and numerically from the lowest to the highest number. Descending sorts alphabetically Z to A, and numerically, highest to lowest.

5. Leave the **M**ove Formats option on so that all cell formatting is sorted along with the cell data. Click on OK and the data is sorted alphabetically by city name.

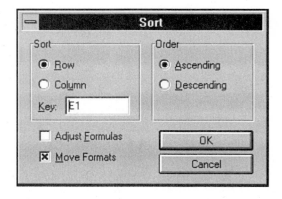

Figure 29.26
The Sort dialog box.

Formatting in the Data Manager

Charts and graphs can instantly communicate a value-based concept. One glance at a bar chart and you can tell if sales are going up or down. One look at a pie chart and you can see what department has the highest expenditures. However, there is no disputing that real numbers provide more precise, concrete facts. The chart data in the Data Manager can be formatted to create visually impressive documents that are easier to understand. The formatting options let you apply different fonts and type styles to titles, add currency symbols to number values, and embellish data with borders and shading. However, keep in mind that any formatting changes you make to the chart data in the Data Manager affect only the data in the spreadsheet—they have no effect on the chart itself.

Text Formatting

Formatting text in the Data Manager is similar to formatting text in other popular Windows applications, such as Excel or Word for Windows. To change text attributes, you simply select the cell or group of cells you want to change, and then choose the appropriate menu command or click on the desired button on the text ribbon bar. Figure 29.27 displays the text ribbon bar and identifies each of the text formatting tools.

Changing Type Styles

To apply bold, italic, or underline to the chart data, select the cell(s) containing the data you want to format and click on the B button for bold, the I button for italic, and the U button for underline. You can apply more than one type style to the selected cell(s). For instance, clicking on the bold and italic buttons creates bold-italic text.

Changing the Typeface and Typesize (Font)

To apply a new font, select the cells containing the data you want to change, and then click on the Font (*Ff*) Button, or select **F**onts from the Fo**r**mat Menu. The Font dialog box appears, as displayed in figure 29.28. In the Font list box, choose the desired font. In Font St**y**le and **S**ize list boxes, select the desired attributes. In the Effects section, click in the appropriate checkboxes to apply Stri**k**eout and **U**nderline attributes. Click on the down arrow beside the **C**olor option to select another color for the data. As you make changes, notice that the text in the sample box provides a preview. Click on OK to apply the selected font information.

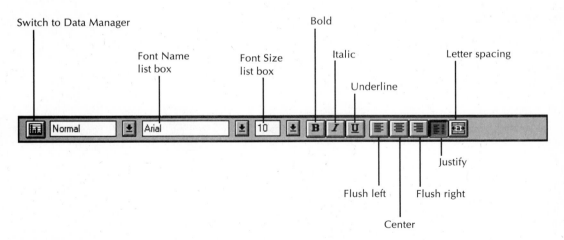

Switch to Data Manager — Font Name list box — Font Size list box — Bold — Italic — Underline — Letter spacing — Justify — Flush left — Flush right — Center

Figure 29.27
The text ribbon bar.

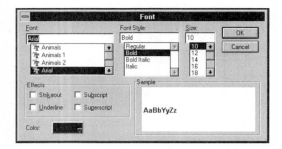

Figure 29.28
The Font dialog box.

You can also access the Font dialog box by clicking on the right mouse button on the selected cell(s). When the cell menu appears, select the Font option.

Aligning Cell Data

You can adjust the alignment of the data within the cells with the Alignment buttons on the text ribbon. There are four alignment buttons; from left to right, they are Left align, Right align, Center align, and Auto align. To use the alignment buttons, select the cells containing the data you want to align and click on the desired button.

Numeric Formats

The numbers in the Data Manager spreadsheet can be formatted to display commas, currency, percentage signs, and decimal places. For example, the number 5000 can be formatted to display as $5,000.00, 5,000, or 5000.00%.

Understanding Numeric Formats

CorelCHART uses basic numeric formats and codes to apply numeric formatting. General is the default format, displaying up to 12 decimal places with no commas or currency. The Percentage format displays numbers with a percent sign (%). The Scientific format displays numbers in exponential (scientific) notation.

The numeric codes are similar to those found in Microsoft Excel. The codes are created with digit placeholders, such number signs (#) and zeros (0), which represent your numbers. For instance, the format code #,##0 would format 3000 as 3,000. When choosing the desired format, look for the code that displays the attributes you need, such as currency, and the number of decimal places. If you select a format that does not display decimal places, CorelCHART will round any decimal numbers. For instance, if you enter 3000.80 and apply the format #,##0, the number will display as 3,001. However, the actual number value is not changed. For example, even though the number 3000.80 is displayed as 3,001, formulas calculating that value use 3000.80, not the displayed value of 3,001. Table 29.5 lists the available numeric format codes in CorelCHART.

Table 29.5
CorelCHART Format Codes

Code	Data Entered	Data Displayed
###0	3000.80	3001
###0.0	3000.80	3000.8
###0.00	3000.80	3000.80
###0.000	3000.80	3000.800
###0.0000	3000.80	3000.8000
$###0.00	3000.80	$3000.80
#,##0.00	3000.80	3,000.80
#,##0.00DM	3000.80	3,000.80DM
$#,##0	3000.80	$3,001
#,##0	3000.80	3,001
#,##0DM	3000.80	3,001DM

As you can see, the zeros force the display of a specified number of decimal places. For instance, the code ###0.0000 forced the display of four decimal places, even though only two were entered.

CorelCHART also provides formats for displaying the time and date. The formatting symbols are *d* for date, *m* for month, and *y* for year. For example, m-d-y will display the date September 1, 1993, as 9-1-93, while d-mmm-yy displays as 1-Sep-93.

Applying Numeric Formatting

To apply numeric formatting, select the cell or group of cells to be formatted, and then click on the Numbers button (#) in the Text Ribbon or select **N**umeric from the Fo**r**mat Menu. The Numeric Format dialog box displayed in figure 29.29 appears. Scroll through the list of formats to select the desired numeric format style. The Sample box at the bottom of the dialog box previews how the data will appear with the selected format style. When ready, click on OK to apply the numeric formatting to the selected cell data.

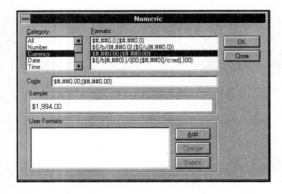

Figure 29.29
The Numeric Format dialog box.

You can also access the Numeric Format dialog box by clicking on the right mouse button on the selected cell(s). When the cell menu appears, select the Numeric Format option.

Borders and Shading

You can embellish chart data with borders and lines to separate data and to mark subtotals and totals. For instance, it is common practice to add lines under subtotals and totals. Shading cells is another way to add emphasis and flair to your chart data. For example, the column headings can be shaded to make them stand out on the page.

Applying Borders

Borders can be placed on all four sides of a cell or in combinations, such as top and bottom, or left and bottom. Figure 29.30 shows a bottom border placed on cells B6 through E6, and an outline border around cells A10 through E11.

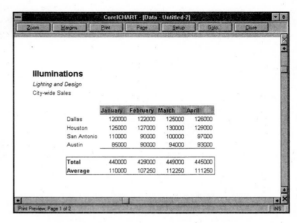

Figure 29.30
Print preview of chart data illustrating the use of borders and shading.

To place borders, select the cells where you want the borders to appear, and click on the Border button or choose **B**orders from the Fo**r**mat menu. The Borders dialog box appears, as displayed in figure 29.31. Choose **O**utline to place a border around the exterior of the selected cell(s). Choose **T**op, **B**ottom, **L**eft, or **R**ight to place borders on the different sides of the selected cell(s). To select a line style, click in the desired **S**tyle box. To choose a color, click on the down arrow by **C**olor and select a color. When you are finished making selections, click on OK to apply the border.

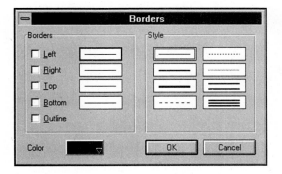

Figure 29.31
The Borders dialog box.

Figure 29.32
The Patterns dialog box.

Applying Shading to Cells

Shading is often used to set off titles and column headings. You can select from several backgrounds and colors to shade cells. To apply shading, select the cells you want shaded and click on the Patterns button, or choose Patterns from the Format menu. The Patterns dialog box, displayed in figure 29.32, appears. Select the desired brush pattern, and click on the color buttons to create a colored pattern. Click on OK to apply the shading to the selected cell(s). The Data Manager always displays the sample data with some shading already applied. In order to view and print your own shading choices, you must turn off the default shading by selecting Chart Tags from the View menu.

Printing in the Data Manager

After sprucing up the chart data with fonts, borders, and shading, you're ready to print. The printed copies of your data can be used to verify the figures for your resident number crunchers or as audience hand-outs supplementing the charts. Although printing in the Chart View is very similar to printing in CorelDRAW, printing in the Data Manager is more like printing in a spreadsheet program such as Excel. For instance, you can print cell grid lines and create headers and footers. This section documents the special options of printing your chart data. Printing in Chart View is covered in the next chapter.

Previewing Your Document

CorelCHART provides the Print Preview command to let you check the appearance of your printed chart data before sending it to the printer. To see how your chart data will look on the page, choose Print Preview from the File menu. The preview screen appears, displaying a full page view of your document, as shown in figure 29.33. The buttons at the top of the screen control certain aspects of the Print Preview screen and the printed page. To exit Print Preview and return to the Data Manager, click on the Close button. Print Preview is introduced first, so you can view any changes made to the chart data, such as adjusting margins and building headers and footers.

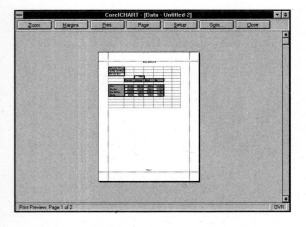

Figure 29.33
The Print Preview screen.

The Zoom button magnifies the page to the 100 percent view, or the approximate size your document will appear when printed. Click on the Zoom button to view the chart data at 100 percent. Click again on the Zoom button to return to the full page view. The mouse provides another way to zoom into the page. Position the mouse cursor on the part of the page you want to zoom into. Notice the mouse shape changes to a magnifying glass. Click on the left mouse button to zoom into that part of the page. Click again to zoom back out to the full page view.

The Margins button enables you to visually adjust the page margins in the preview window. Click on the Margins button to display dotted lines representing the margins. (These will not print.) Place your mouse on the margin you want to adjust, and it will change to a two-sided arrow. Click and drag the margin line to the desired position, and release the mouse. The chart data is redrawn on the screen, showing your new margins.

Click on the Page button at the top of the preview window to open the Page Setup dialog box. The options in the Page Setup dialog box are covered in the next section "Controlling Page Setup." If you have more than one page of chart data, click on the Go to button. Enter the page number you want to preview in the Go to Page dialog box, and click on OK. You can also use the Page Up or Page Down keys to move to the next or previous page in your document.

If you want to select a new printer or change printer parameters, click on the **S**etup button to display the Printer Setup dialog box. Setting up your printer is covered later in this section. When you are ready to print, click on the Print button to display options for printing the chart data. These options are also discussed later in this section. The Print dialog box is discussed in the next section. To exit Print Preview and return to the spreadsheet window, click on the **C**lose button.

Controlling Page Setup

The Page Setup dialog box provides several options for creating professional-looking documents. If you are in the Print Preview window, click on the Page button. If you are in the Data Manager window, select Page Set**u**p from the **F**ile menu. The Page Setup dialog box appears, as displayed in figure 29.34. By default, CorelCHART uses 72 points or one inch as the top, bottom, left, and right margins for printed chart data. Enter the desired margin settings in the **L**eft, **T**op, **R**ight, and **B**ottom boxes. You can also click on the arrows to select a desired measurement. To use another measurement system such as inches, simply click on the down arrow by points and select the desired system.

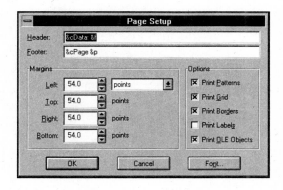

Figure 29.34

The Page Setup dialog box.

Creating Headers and Footers

Headers and footers are text such as company names, dates, and page numbers that can be placed at the top or bottom of each printed page. You can enter any text as header and footer text, but CorelCHART provides codes for displaying the date, time, file name, and page number in the header or footer text. You can also enter codes to control the alignment of the header and footer text. Table 29.6 lists the header and footer codes available in the Data Manager.

Table 29.6
Header and Footer codes

Code	Effect
&L	Aligns text against left margin.
&C	Centers text between margins.
&R	Aligns text against right margin.
&D	Inserts the current date.
&T	Inserts the current time.
&F	Inserts the file name of the spreadsheet or chart.
&P	Inserts the page number.

Header and footer codes can be combined for specific results. For instance, the header code &C&T would center the time at the top of the page. The footer code &R&D would right-align the date at the bottom of the page. The alignment codes must appear before the data codes; otherwise, the data will be left-aligned. You can also combine the codes with your own text to create custom headers and footers. For instance, the code &D&C John Smith &R &P would left-align the date, center the author name, and right-align the number.

To create headers and footers, enter the desired codes in the Header and Footer boxes in the Page Setup dialog box. Headers and footers can only be previewed in the Print Preview window; you cannot see header and footer text in the Data Manager.

Using Print Options

The Page Setup dialog box includes several other printing options unique to spreadsheet applications. For instance, you can print the cell grid lines and row and column headings

The Print Shado**w** and Print Bor**d**ers are turned on, instructing CorelCHART to print any shading or borders you have added to data. To print the data without any shading or borders, click on the X's by the commands to turn these options off. The Print **G**rid option prints the cell grid lines displayed in the Data Manager. Figure 29.35 shows chart data with the Print Grid option turned on. Turn this option off to print cell contents only.

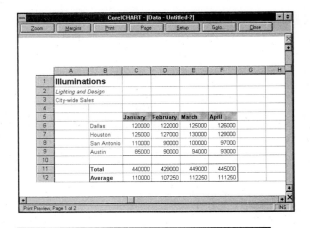

Figure 29.35
Print Preview of chart data with the Grid Lines and Print Labels options selected.

To print the row numbers and column letters with your chart data, click on the Print Label**s** command. Figure 29.35 displays printed chart data with the row numbers and column letters. Turn on the Print **O**LE Objects command to print embedded or linked objects created in another OLE server, such as a graphic from CorelDRAW.

Printer Setup

After determining the margins, and setting up any headers and footers, the next step is setting the parameters for your printer. From the **F**ile menu, choose P**r**int Setup. The Printer Setup dialog box displayed in figure 29.36 appears. Here, you can choose a printing device and set up printing parameters such as paper size and orientation. Under **P**rinters, click on the desired printing device, and then click on the **S**etup button. A dialog box with information about the selected print device appears. Although the options available in the dialog box will differ based on the print device you have chosen, the basic output options—resolution, paper size, paper source, paper orientation, and number of copies—appear for every type of print device. For more information about setting up printers and the settings appropriate for your printer, refer to Chapter 14, "Printed Output," and your printer manual. After selecting the desired options, click on OK to return to the spreadsheet.

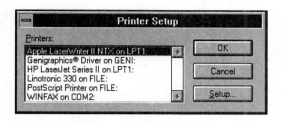

Figure 29.36
The Printer Setup dialog box.

Printing Your Chart Data

With the page and printer setup complete, you are ready to print. If you are in the Print Preview window, click on the Print button. If you are in the Data Manager window, select **P**rint from the **F**ile menu. The Print Data dialog box appears, as displayed in figure 29.37. Enter the number of copies you want printed in the **C**opies box. The First Page **N**umber option lets you specify the number to be assigned to the first page of your document. For instance, entering the number 10 would instruct CorelCHART to start numbering the pages of your chart data at 10. This option is handy if you want the page numbers of your chart data to match up with documents created in another application.

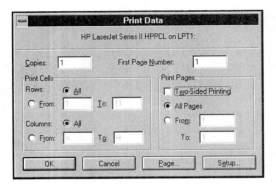

Figure 29.37
The Print Data dialog box.

The Print Cells section lets you print only specific columns and rows of your data. Printing only part of your chart data is great when you have added comments or notes on the spreadsheet that you don't want to appear on the printed document. By default, the **A**ll option is selected, indicating all columns and rows with cell data will print. To print only certain parts of the spreadsheet data, click in the **F**rom box. Enter the first column or row you want to print, and then move to the **T**o box and enter the last column or row you want to print. For instance, you could print from column A to column F and from row 10 to row 30.

When chart data is more than a single page in size, you can use the Print Pages section of the dialog box to control which pages you want to print. The options in the Print Pages section are available only if the **A**ll option is selected for both columns and rows in the Print Cells section. Select the T**w**o-Sided

Printing option to print the odd and even pages separately. By default, the All Pa**g**es option is selected, indicating that all the pages of the spreadsheet data will print. To print only specific pages, click in the Fro**m** box and enter the first page you want printed. Then, click in the To box and enter the last page you want printed. When finished selecting the desired print options, click on OK to print your document. A message box appears, displaying the status of your print job as it is sent to the printer.

Summary

The Data Manager is an integral part of creating charts in CorelCHART. As you have seen, the Data Manager makes it easy to enter and edit your chart data. The tools for writing formulas and functions gives the Data Manager power on par with the major spreadsheet applications. The ease of working with chart data, combined with the ability to format and print the chart, makes the Data Manager a powerful ally in communicating and presenting data. In the next chapter, you will see the results of your efforts in the Data Manager as you switch to the Chart View to format and design your chart.

Chapter 30

Building Pie, Bar, Line, and Area Charts

*T*he previous chapter discussed entering and tagging data in the Data Manager. In this chapter, you are ready to view and format your chart. To view the chart, click on the Chart View button in the Data Manager window.

There could be a number of changes and adjustments you want to make to the chart. You may want to change chart colors, adjust the thickness of a bar, or explode a pie slice. Every chart requires a unique look and style that best conveys the information. Whatever the optimal style may be, CorelCHART has all the tools you need to produce attractive charts.

This chapter covers the options for formatting pie, bar, line, and area charts. For instance, it covers the steps for adjusting the spacing between bars, or modifying the thickness of a pie chart. The options for the remaining specialized chart types, such as spectral maps and hi/lo/open/close charts are covered in the next chapter.

This chapter covers:

- Formatting charts
- Charting options for pie charts
- Building bar charts
- Building line charts
- Building area charts

Formatting Charts

The last chapter on CorelCHART is where you find information on formatting chart titles, legends, and backgrounds. After reading the options for formatting your chart, switch to Chapter 32 for ideas on changing fonts and adding color. Chapter 32 also examines using the toolbox to annotate charts with graphic shapes.

Charts and graphs create powerful first impressions that can make or break a sale, influence an investment, or win over a competitor. A well designed chart grabs your attention and leads your eye through an examination of the data. CorelCHART provides tremendous flexibility to help you design charts that communicate facts and figures in a visually appealing way. With the right chart, you can transform numerical data and abstract concepts into an instantly comprehendable visual format.

Understanding Templates

The template you choose to create the chart determines the placement of elements in your chart. Remember, the template is just the starting point. From there you can manipulate and modify almost every chart element to suit your needs. For instance, the template predetermines the spacing between bars in a chart and the thickness of a pie chart. In this section you discover the features available for adjusting and modifying these, and other elements in a chart.

Selecting Chart Commands

There are several ways to select commands for changing chart attributes. This chapter makes use of the menus to access commands. For example, to adjust pie thickness, this chapter instructs you to select Pie Thickness from the **C**hart menu. However, CorelCHART also provides "pop-up menus" to quickly access certain commands. The Pop-Up Menu tool is the third tool in the toolbar. Select the tool and click on a chart element, such as a slice, bar, title, or legend. A context-sensitive pop-up menu appears displaying options for that particular chart element. Clicking on a pie slice displays a pop-up menu for formatting the slice, for example (see fig. 30.1). These commands are identical to those covered in the sections on formatting charts. You can also click on a chart element with the right mouse button to reveal the pop-up menus.

Figure 30.1

The pop-up menu for pie slices.

Charting Options for Pie Charts

Due to their simple, flexible structure, pie charts make interesting and expressive charts. Many designers enjoy working with the pie shape because the uncomplicated form makes it easy to adorn the chart with shadowing, tilting and dimension. Pie charts give an immediate, intuitive sense of the proportions of the whole. For example, as displayed in figure 30.2, a pie chart can show you quickly which restaurant makes the most milkshakes, or which vacation resort has the most beaches.

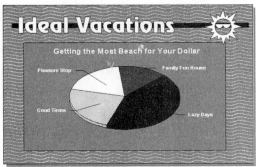

Figure 30.2
Examples of two pie charts.

Changing Slice Colors

The slice colors in a pie chart help to visually create a mood for the presentation of your data. For instance, greens and browns work well in a pie chart detailing the adventures of forest rangers. Pinks, reds, and peaches work well in a pie chart examining lipstick sales. To change the color of a pie slice, select the slice. An outline appears around the slice to confirm its selection. Click on the desired color in the Color Palette to apply the new color choice.

In a Multiple Pie chart, when you change a pie slice on one pie, that slice color changes in each pie. This is because multiple pies are structured to show how a particular item relates to the whole over a period of time. In order to gauge the change in a data series, you want to keep the slice color consistent from pie to pie.

N O T E

For added texture, you also can apply fountain and patterned fills to pie slices. If you are familiar with CorelDRAW, you will find the Fill tool in CorelCHART to be very similar.

Adjusting the Pie Tilt

A pie chart can be tilted slightly backward to add the illusion of depth. You can control the degree of tilt with the Pie Tilt command in the Chart menu. Keep in mind that a slight tilt can add visual appeal, while too much tilt can distort the shape of the slices and actually misrepresent your data. To modify the tilt of a pie, select Pie Tilt from the **C**hart menu to reveal the sub-menu.

You can preview each of the tilt choices by pressing and holding the mouse button and dragging down the list of choices. Release on the desired selection and your pie chart assumes the specified tilt.

Adjusting the Pie Thickness

Controlling pie thickness is another way to add dimension and visual style to pie charts. As illustrated in figure 30.3, a thicker pie with just the right amount of tilt makes the chart appear as though you could reach out and touch it. However, just as with tilting, be careful not to overdo your pie thickness. A thick pie with a pronounced tilt can be difficult to examine and comprehend.

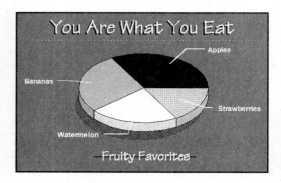

Figure 30.3
Adjusting the Pie Thickness and Tilt can increase the visual appeal of pie charts.

To control the pie thickness, select Pie Thickness from the **C**hart menu to reveal the sub-menu. You can preview each of the thickness choices by pressing and holding the mouse button and dragging down the list of

choices. Release on the desired selection and your pie chart assumes the specified thickness.

If you adjust the pie tilt or thickness on any pie in a Multiple Pie chart, it affects all pies on the chart accordingly.

Rotating the Pie

CorelCHART places the slice for the first set of data at the top of the pie chart. If you think about the pie chart as a clock, CorelCHART places the first set of data at 12:00. For instance, rock music was entered as the first set of data in the Data Manager (see fig. 30.4). As a result, CorelCHART places the rock music slice at the top of the pie chart. The remaining sets of data wrap around the pie in a counter-clockwise fashion.

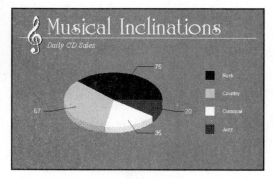

Figure 30.4
The first set of data is displayed as the slice at the top of the pie chart.

With CorelCHART, you can change the position of the pie slices by rotating the pie. Rotating the pie is convenient when you want to emphasize a slice by rotating it to appear in the front of the chart, or to re-position an exploded slice that crowds the pie title. To rotate the pie, select Pie Rotation from the **C**hart menu to reveal the sub-menu. A small pie chart appears at the top of the sub-menu, with the rotation choices listed beneath. As you drag down through the rotation choices, watch the black arrow at the top of the sub-menu to indicate the amount of rotation. Release on the desired degree of rotation to rotate the slices of your pie chart.

Sizing the Pie

You can manipulate the size of the pie with the Pie Size command in the Chart menu. Decreasing the pie size may be necessary when you have lengthy slice labels as illustrated in figure 30.5. On the other hand, with short slice labels, you can often increase the size of the pie to add more impact to your chart.

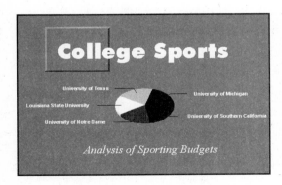

Figure 30.5

Consider the length of the slice labels when adjusting the pie size.

To size the pie, select Pie Size from the **C**hart menu to reveal the sub-menu. A small pie chart appears at the top of the sub-menu with the size choices listed beneath. As you drag down through the size choices, the size of the pie chart at the top of the sub-menu changes representing the different sizes. Release on the desired pie size and your pie chart assumes the specified size.

N O T E

Another way to adjust the pie size is to size the chart frame. The size of the frame directly affects the size of the chart. Refer to Chapter 32 for more information about sizing and formatting the chart frame.

Adjusting the Pies per Row

CorelCHART includes a template to help you create charts with multiple pies. Multiple pies can be used to compare how a set of data changes over different periods of time. For example, the chart in figure 30.6 provides a quick look at how advertising expenses have increased over the last four years. Keep in mind that it can be difficult to compare the size of slices in different pies unless they are extremely simple. For more complex data, a bar chart can express comparisons between groups more effectively.

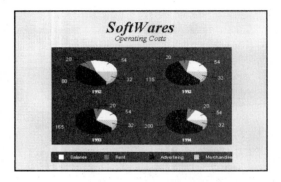

Figure 30.6

A multiple pie chart examining operating expenses over four-year period.

When working with multiple pie charts, you can control the number of pies that display on each row. For instance, with six pies you could place three in the top and three in the bottom. To control the number of pies per row, select Pies Per Row from the **C**hart menu. The Pies Per Row dialog box appears. Enter the amount of pies you want displayed per row and click OK.

For charts with an uneven number of pies you cannot place more pies in the bottom row. For instance, you cannot place two pies in the top row and three in the bottom row, you must place three at the top and two at the bottom. Further, regardless of the number of pies on the bottom row, they always left-align.

Detaching Pie Slices

Detaching or exploding a pie slice is a popular way to emphasize one set of data.

The detached slice quickly becomes a dominant element as you examine and analyze the data. There should be a reason for detaching a slice. For example in figure 30.7, the detached slice showcases the increase in video movie rentals. Detaching several slices lessens the impact and sends a confusing message as to which slice is the most important.

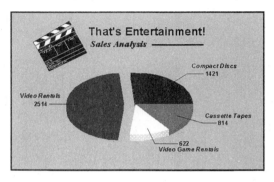

Figure 30.7

Detached slices draw attention to certain sets of data.

To detach a slice, select the slice you want detached. Next, choose Detach Slice from the **C**hart menu to reveal the sub-menu. A small pie chart appears at the top of the sub-menu, with a list of the detaching choices. As you drag down through the choices, a slice in the pie chart at the top of the sub-menu moves away from the pie to illustrate the different detaching options. Release on the desired detachment option and the selected slice is detached. To re-join the slice in the pie, select the detached slice and choose No Detachment from the Detach Slice sub-menu in the **C**hart menu.

Deleting Pie Slices

You can add impact to a presentation by building pie charts one slice at a time. For instance, in a presentation on the company budget, the first chart could display a single slice for the salary data. In the next chart, the slice for rent and utilities could be added; then the third chart adds a slice for equipment. By building the chart one slice at a time, you keep the audience interested and involved in the presentation. To create a chart build, delete a slice and then save the chart file. Next, delete another slice and save the file again under a different name. Repeat this procedure for each slice in the pie to create a build of pie slices for your presentation. For instance, in figure 30.8, the first chart with all slices displayed was saved as Chart4.CCH. Then the second, with one slice deleted, was saved as Chart3.CCH. The third, with two slices deleted, was saved as Chart2.CCH, and the fourth with three slices deleted was saved as Chart1.CCH. When these four charts are shown in order, Chart1 through Chart4, the pie slices build to a pie chart.

To delete a pie slice, select the slice you want deleted and choose Delete Slice from the Chart menu. The slice is removed from the Chart View but the data still appears in the Data Manager. To display the slice again, select Restore All Slices from the Chart menu.

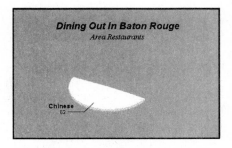
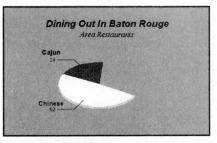
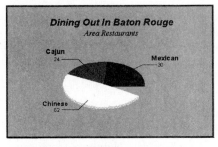
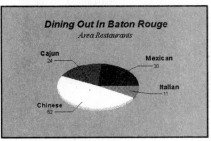

Figure 30.8

Creating a build of pie slices by deleting slices.

Controlling the Slice Number Format

The slice values around the pie can be formatted to display currency, commas, and decimals places. For example, in figure 30.9 the values around the pie are formatted to show currency. The values can also be formatted to display the percentage each slice represents of the whole.

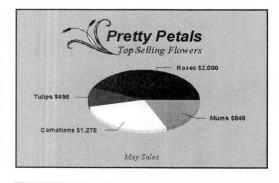

Figure 30.9
Formatting slice values to display currency.

To add numeric formatting to the slice values, select Slice Number Format from the Chart menu. The Numeric Format dialog box appears as displayed in figure 30.10. The Numeric Format dialog box is the same one used to apply numeric formatting to data in the Data Manager. Remember, any numeric formatting created in the Data Manager has no affect on the chart in Chart View. Select the desired formatting option from the list of choices and click OK. For example, select Percentage to display percentages for each of the slice values and $#,##0 to add currency symbols to the slice values.

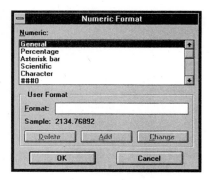

Figure 30.10
The Numeric Format dialog box.

In a multiple pie chart, all slice values must use the same numeric formatting. However, you can use the Text tool to add any special formatting to a specific pie slice or single pie.

Controlling Slice Feeler Size

Slice Feelers are the lines connecting the slice and the slice labels. CorelCHART gives you control over the position, color and line width of the feelers. For example, as displayed in figure 30.11, the feelers are thick. They are also modified to begin deeper into the slice and end right outside of the slice to make more room for the slice labels.

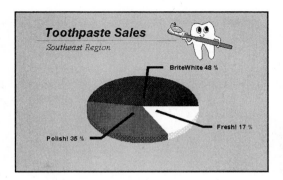

Figure 30.11
CorelCHART gives you control over the style and location and style of the slice feelers.

In a single pie chart you can adjust the position of all feelers at one time, or each feeler individually. To adjust the position of one feeler it must be selected prior to choosing the Slice Feeler command, otherwise the changes affect all slice feelers. In a multiple chart, your adjustments apply to all feelers in the same data series. To adjust the position of the slice feelers, select Slice Feeler Size from the **C**hart menu. The Slice Feeler Size dialog box appears as displayed in figure 30.12. The three black dots represent the points to which you can move to reposition the feeler. Drag the dots to change the length of each segment of the slice feelers. As you adjust the size of the feeler segments, the dialog box provides the horizontal orientation, feeler length, and center distribution of the feeler.

You can change the color of the slice feelers by selecting one of the feelers, and clicking with the right mouse button on the selected color in the Color Palette. To adjust the line width of the feelers, use the Outline tool.

When you select the Outline tool a fly-out appears with several preset line widths. To apply one of the preset widths, select a slice feeler and choose the desired thickness. All slice feelers must use the same line width and color.

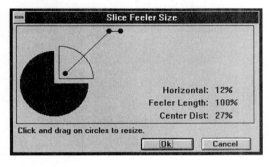

Figure 30.12
The Slice Feeler Size dialog box.

Additional Options for Ring Pies

Ring pies are used to add a unique look to the standard pie chart. In addition, ring pie charts enables you to place the total of all slices in the center of the ring. As illustrated in figure 30.13, the ring pie is formatted to resemble a life-ring in a chart examining aquatic equipment sales. CorelCHART provides a template for creating single and multiple ring pies. Ring pies use the same formatting commands as normal pie charts with special commands for adjusting the size of the ring and applying a numeric format to the total.

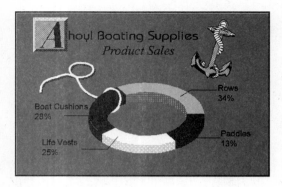

Figure 30.13

An example of a ring pie chart.

Adjusting the Hole Size in a Ring Pie Chart

To adjust the size of the ring or hole, select Hole Size from the **C**hart menu to reveal the sub-menu. A small ring pie chart appears at the top of the sub-menu with a list of hole sizes. As you drag down through the choices, the hole in the pie chart at the top of the sub-menu changes reflecting the available hole sizes. Release on the desired hole size and the selected hole is applied to your ring pie.

Controlling the Total Format in a Ring Pie Chart

A total of all the slice values can be placed in the center of a ring pie chart. To apply numeric formatting to this total, select Ring Total Format from the **C**hart menu. The Numeric Format dialog box is the same one used to apply numeric formatting to the slice values and data in the Data Manager. Refer

to the section titled "Controlling Slice Number Formats" earlier in this section for more information.

Reversing the Data Orientation

By default, the first row of data entered in the Data Sheet appears as the top slice in the pie. The remaining data produces the slices that run counter-clockwise around the pie. There may be times when this order is exactly opposite of the way you want your pie to display. Rather than rotating the pie, you can reverse the order so that the first slice is positioned last on the pie, and the last slice is positioned first. The Data Reversal feature reverses or flips the order of your data. To reverse your pie data, select Data Reversal from the **C**hart Menu. The sub-menu appears with two options. On a single pie, Reverse Series puts the slices in the exact opposite order. On a Multiple Pie chart, Reverse Groups reverses the order of the pies so that the last pie is first and the first pie is last in the group. On a Multiple Pie chart, the Reverse Series command changes the order of the pie slices for each pie on the chart.

Displaying Pie Chart Titles, Legends, and Slice Labels

Titles and headings are important chart elements that assist the viewer in understanding your chart data. Titles announce company names, dates, and resources, in addition to the type of data being examined. CorelCHART lets you control which titles and other text elements are displayed in pie charts. For instance, some pie charts look better with the slice names displayed by the slices as labels, while other charts look better with the data displayed in a legend. This section discusses displaying pie chart text elements, such as titles and legends. Refer to Chapter 32 for information on changing the font and colors of text elements.

To manage the display of your pie chart text elements, choose Display Status from the **C**hart menu. The Pie Chart Display Status dialog box appears and enables you to choose which text elements, such as pie titles, legends, slice names, and values, are displayed.

The dialog box includes a series of display features you can turn on or off by clicking in the desired checkboxes. For example, to turn on the pie title, click to place a checkmark in the Pie Title checkbox. To eliminate the chart's footnote, click to clear the checkmark. To display the slice names around the pie slices, click by the slice names option. At the top of the dialog box are buttons for All Text and No Text. These buttons make each of the display status features active or inactive. After making the desired selections, click OK to display the chart.

N O T E

Another way to turn off the display of titles and footnotes is to delete the data from the cell in the Data Manager.

Building Bar, Line, and Area Charts

Bar, line, and area charts demonstrate relationships and trends, and facilitate comparisons. As an example, the bar chart in figure 30.14 illustrates the decline in cigarette smoking by teen-age girls and boys. Bar, line, and area charts come in several variations, including side-by-side, stacked, bipolar, and dual Y axis. Each of these chart styles is designed for specific sets of chart data. For instance, in a stacked bar chart, the bars are placed on top of each other to represent the total value for a data group. CorelCHART provides templates for creating these specific chart types. Refer to Chapter 31 for more information on selecting the right chart type.

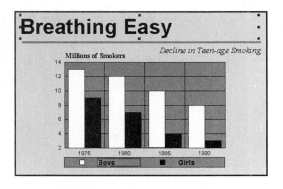

Figure 30.14
An example of a bar chart.

Bar, line, and area charts all work with an XY axis format. The XY axis format uses two axes against which the data is compared.

The X axis or category axis breaks the data down into different groups such as years or quarters. The Y axis or data axis provides a reference to determine the quantity of the data. For example, the data axis indicates how much money was spent or how many gallons of oil were pumped. Since many of the commands for manipulating the three chart types—bar, line and, area—are similar, they are covered together in this section. In most cases, a bar chart is used to illustrate a feature. Unless noted, the feature also is available with line and area charts. For instance, when discussing grid lines, the figure may show a bar chart, but the same grid lines could apply to line and area charts. The features specific to certain chart types, such as line markers and area fills, are covered in the section "Special Options." For example, for more information specific to Line Charts, refer to the section "Special Options for Line Charts."

Creating Vertical or Horizontal Bar, Line, and Area Charts

The data in bar, line and area charts can be displayed vertically or horizontally. In figure 30.15, the same data is presented in both a horizontally and vertically oriented bar chart. Horizontal bars are used primarily in situations where you want to compare just a few items with one series of data. For multiple series of data, vertical bar charts are preferable.

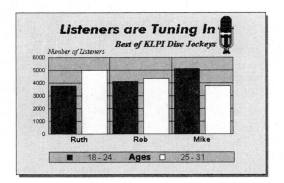

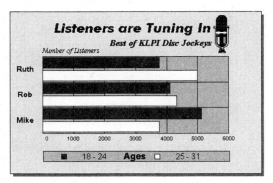

Figure 30.15

Examples of horizontal and vertical bar charts.

Use the Gallery menu to change the orientation of your chart. To create a vertical bar chart, select Vertical Bar from the **G**allery menu. A sub-menu appears listing the available vertical bar chart types. As you drag down through the choices, a preview of each option appears at the top of the sub-menu. Release on the desired option and your chart is re-drawn in the selected vertical style. To create a horizontal bar chart, select Horizontal Bar from the **G**allery menu.

The same basic steps apply when creating vertical or horizontal line and area charts. For line charts, select either Vertical Line or Horizontal Line from the **G**allery menu. For area charts, select either Vertical Area or Horizontal Area from the **G**allery menu.

Changing Fill Colors and Outlines

Color is an integral part of designing charts. For instance, many companies prefer to avoid using the color red because of the negative connotation of being financially "in the red." This section details changing the color of the bars, areas, and lines in charts. Refer to Chapter 32 for changing the color of other chart elements, such as backgrounds, titles, and legends.

To change the fill color of the bars or areas in your chart, select a bar or area (also called riser), and click on the desired color in the Color Palette. In a bar chart, notice that all bar risers in the series are changed. To change the line color in a line chart or the outline color around bars or areas, select the line, bar, or area and click on the desired color with the right mouse button. Again, all risers in a series are changed.

T I P

You can change the color of just one bar when you want to draw special attention to it. To change the color of one bar, select the bar and choose Emphasize Bar from the **C**hart menu. The emphasized bar is filled with gray. If desired, you can select a different color from the Color Palette.

To apply a new line width to the lines in a line chart, or the outlines around bar and area risers, select the element (line, bar, or area) and click on the Outline tool. As displayed in figure 30.16, when you select the Outline tool a fly-out appears with several preset line widths. Select the desired thickness. Refer to Chapter 32 for more information on creating custom line widths.

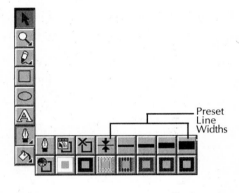

Preset Line Widths

Figure 30.16
Use the Outline tool to set line widths.

T I P

For added texture, you also can apply fountain and patterned fills to bars and areas. If you are familiar with CorelDRAW, you will find the Fill tool in CorelCHART to be very similar. For more information on using the Fill tool, refer to Chapter 32.

Placement of Category and Data Axes

In a vertically oriented chart, the category axis is displayed on the left side of the chart and the data axis is displayed on the bottom. CorelCHART gives you the flexibility to alter the display of the axes by placing them on different sides or on both sides. As an example, in figure 30.17 the category axis is placed at the top of the chart, and the data axis appears on both the left and right sides. You may find displaying the data axis on both sides of the chart helps the viewer interpret the data by providing another axis against which data is compared.

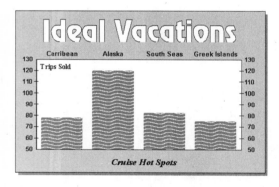

Figure 30.17

A chart with the Category axis placed at the top of the chart and the Data axis placed on both sides of the chart.

To adjust the placement of the category axis, select Category Axis from the **C**hart menu. A sub-menu appears with a checkmark indicating the current position of the category axis. In a vertically oriented chart, your options are Display on Top and Display on Bottom. In a horizontally oriented chart, your options are Display on Left and Display on Right.

Select the desired placement and the chart is re-drawn with the axis in the selected location. Turning both options off removes the Category axis from the display altogether.

Adjusting the placement of the Data axis works much the same way. From the **C**hart menu, select Data Axis to reveal the sub-menu. Select the desired axis placement and the chart is redrawn with the specified axis placement.

N O T E

Options for changing the type face and size of the data on the category and data axes are covered in Chapter 32.

Displaying Grid Lines

Grid lines help lead the viewers eye from a data set to the data axis. With CorelCHART, you can display grid lines for both the category and data axis. Be careful to avoid going overboard with grid lines. Lines coming from both the category and data axis can add a lot of clutter to a chart. You can eliminate some of the clutter by using subtle colors and thin line widths for the grid lines. Tick marks, the small lines placed along the data axis, are another alternative to using grid lines.

Category Axis Gridlines

To adjust the display of grid lines on the category axis, select Category Axis from the **C**hart menu. Click on the Show Grid Lines command to display or remove the grid lines from your chart. CorelCHART does not provide options for placing tick marks on the category axis.

Data Axis Gridlines

You have several options for displaying grid lines on the data axis. From the **C**hart menu, select Data Axis. In the sub-menu, select Grid Lines to display the Grid Lines dialog box as shown in figure 30.18. The dialog box controls the display of major and minor gridlines. Major divisions are the units between each numerical value along the data axis. Minor divisions are the units between the major divisions. CorelCHART gives you control over the number of major and minor divisions.

Figure 30.18
The Grid Lines dialog box.

The first option, Show Major Grid Lines, controls the display of grid lines along the major divisions. When Show Major Grid Lines is selected, options for displaying the grid lines become available. Select Normal to display the grid line without tick marks. Select Normal with Ticks to display the grid lines with tick marks outside the data axis. The three remaining options turn off the display of grid lines and place tick marks instead. Select Inside Ticks to display tick marks inside the data axis. Select Outside

Ticks to display tick marks outside the data axis. As illustrated in figure 30.19, select Spanning Ticks to display tick marks on both sides of the data axis. The options for controlling minor divisions are the same as those for major divisions. It is important to note that lines for minor divisions display in white by default and will not appear if your chart background is also white.

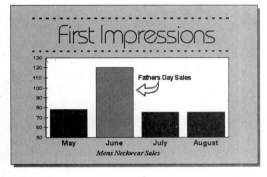

Figure 30.19
A chart with a data axis displaying spanning tick marks.

CorelCHART automatically sets the number of major and minor divisions. To enter a different amount of major divisions, click on the Manual feature at the bottom of the Grid Lines dialog box and type in the desired number of major divisions. When minor grid lines are turned on, you also can enter the number of minor divisions. When you are finished selecting options for the grid lines, click on OK.

You can change the color of the minor grid lines by selecting one with the Pick tool and then clicking on a color in the on-screen palette with the right mouse button. To adjust the line width of the grid lines, select

one and choose a thickness from the top row of buttons on the Outline fly-out toolbar. All grid lines must use the same line width and color.

Scaling the Data Axis

The data axis scale provides a reference point to gauge the amount of a specific item. The scale is defined by a minimum and a maximum value with data points incrementally spaced. CorelCHART uses your chart data to determine the scale of numbers appearing on the data axis. For instance, if all of your chart values are under 50, the data axis might scale from a minimum of 0 to a maximum of 50. If your chart values range from 150,000 to 350,000, the data axis might scale from 120,000 to 360,000. You can adjust the scale on the data range to begin and end at the values you specify. For example, in figure 30.20 the data axis was scaled from 1,000 to 8,000.

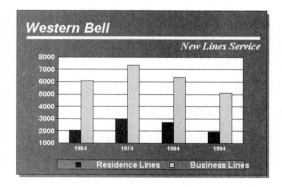

Figure 30.20
A chart with Data Axis Scale adjusted.

To adjust the scale of the data axis, select Data Axis from the **C**hart menu. From the

sub-menu, select Scale Range to display the Scale Range dialog box as shown in figure 30.21. By default, the Automatic option is selected. To enter different values for the data axis scale, click on the Manual option. Enter the desired number values in the From and To boxes to create a customized scale. At the top of the dialog box, click on Exclude Minimum to turn off the display of the lowest value in the data axis scale. Click on Exclude Maximum to turn off the display of the highest value in the data axis scale. Click on OK, when finished making your selections.

Figure 30.21
The Scale Range dialog box.

Working with Linear and Logarithmic Scaling

CorelCHART provides two types of scaling options—Linear and Logarithmic. The default option, Linear, is a standard scale representing an amount or quantity in evenly spaced increments. For example, on a linear scale, one division on a chart may represent 100 gallons; two divisions represents 200 gallons; six divisions to 600 gallons; and so on.

Logarithmic scales compress or expand the data values in powers of 10 as they ascend the Y axis so that the distance between each unit along the data axis decreases as you go up the scale. A logarithmic scale is generally used when there are large disparities in data values. For example, in figure 30.22 some of the data values are as little as $20, while others are as much as $100,000. On a linear scale, the difference between those value points would render the bar for $20 so small it would scarcely be visible. With the logarithmic scale illustrated, the numbers are more easily comprehended. To change to a logarithmic scale, select Data Axis from the **C**hart menu. From the sub-menu, click on Log Scale. The Data Axis on the chart is re-drawn to display as a logarithmic scale.

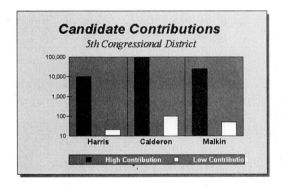

Figure 30.22
A chart with logarithmic scaling.

Applying Numeric Formatting to the Data Axis

You can apply numeric formatting, such as commas and decimal places, to the numbers along the data axis. For instance, in figure 30.23 currency symbols are added to the data axis to inform the viewer that the axis is scaled in currency. To format the data axis, select Data Axis from the **C**hart menu. From the sub-menu, select Number Format to display the Numeric Format dialog box. The Numeric Format dialog box is the same one used to apply numeric formatting to data in the Data Manager. Remember the numeric formatting applied to data in the Data Manager has no effect on data in the Chart View. Select the desired formatting option from the list of choices and click OK. For example, select $#,##0 to add currency symbols to the data axis.

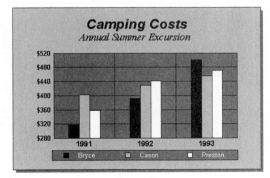

Figure 30.23
Applying Numeric Formatting to the Data Axis helps the viewer intrepret the data.

N O T E

On a logarithmic scale, you cannot display any minor grid attributes or manually adjust the scale range.

Working with the Second Data Axis in Dual Y Axis

CorelCHART includes templates for creating dual Y axis and bipolar bar, line, and area charts. A dual Y axis chart adds another data axis for comparing data that cannot be effectively plotted against the same scale of measurement. For example, in figure 30.24 the data axis on the left plots the number of books sold, while the axis on the right plots the revenue from book sales. Examined together, this chart illustrates how book sales influence revenue.

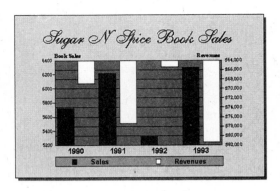

Figure 30.25

A dual Y axis bar chart with descending scale.

To display the second data axis in ascending scale, select 2nd Data Axis from the **C**hart menu. From the sub-menu, select Ascending. Notice that with a descending scale, it is easy to visualize which bar sets refer to which data axis. However, things may get confusing when the second data axis is changed to ascending because all bars or data sets build from the bottom axis. Therefore, it is important to inform the viewer which bars refer to which data axis, with titles and colors.

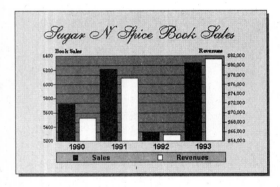

Figure 30.24

An example of a dual Y axis chart.

With dual Y axis charts, the second data axis can be displayed in descending or ascending scale. As displayed in figure 30.25, CorelCHART assigns the first and third sets of bars to the ascending data axis on the left. The second and fourth sets of data are assigned to the descending data axis on the right.

Reversing Data Sets

By default, chart data is displayed in the order it is entered in the Data Manager. CorelCHART gives you the option to reverse this order. To reverse the data in your chart, select Data Reversal from the **C**hart menu. The Data Reversal feature offers two options for reversing your data; Reverse Series, and Reverse Groups. Choose Reverse Groups to swap the order of the data groups so that data from last category appears first on the chart, and the first category appears last. Choose Reverse Series to flip the order of the bars, lines, or areas on your chart. For example, the first chart in figure 30.26 shows the data in the order it is entered in the Data Manager. The second chart has both the series and group data reversed so the years appear chronologically backward and the order of the legend data is swapped.

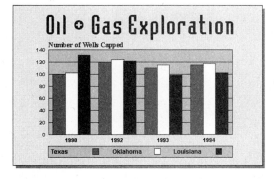

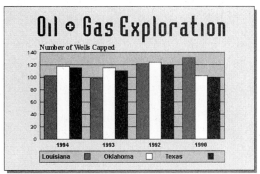

Figure 30.26
The Data Reversal command reverses the order of data on the Category axis.

Using the Data Analysis Feature

CorelCHART has tools to help you calculate and analyze statistical data in your chart. With the Data Analysis feature, you can determine quickly the mean, standard deviation, or averages for a set of data and then plot the figures as a line on your chart. The data analysis is done to one set of data at a time. In figure 30.27, the black line in the bar chart represents the mean sales for king-size beds. The white curved line represents the upward trend of queen-size bed sales throughout the year. Using the Data Analysis feature is much easier than using the calculator to figure these values yourself.

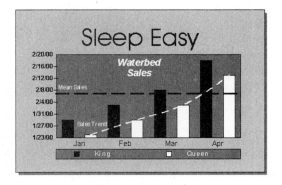

Figure 30.27
The Data Analysis command lets you add lines representing means and trends to your charts.

To display lines representing different types of data analysis, select the bar, line or area representing the series of data you wish to analyze. Then, select Data Analysis from the **C**hart menu. The Data Analysis dialog box as displayed in figure 30.28 appears. After selecting the desired type of data analysis, click on OK. Table 30.1 details the options for statistical analysis.

Figure 30.28
The Data Analysis dialog box.

N O T E

Least Square is a method of creating a best guess straight line; one that best reflects a collection of data points. See CorelCHART's On line Help for information on how CorelCHART calculates the least square.

You can change the color of the data analysis lines by selecting the line, and clicking with the right mouse button on the selected color in the Color Palette. To adjust the line width, select the line and choose a thickness from the top row of buttons on the Outline fly-out toolbar.

Displaying Titles, Data Values, and Other Text Elements

In all charting, it is important to include chart titles, footnotes, axis titles and legends that help convey your chart's message. Chart titles inform the viewer of company names and dates. Axis titles and legends explain how data is organized and presented. With CorelCHART, you can control which titles and other text elements are displayed in your bar, line, and area charts. For instance, if you want to use an image created in CorelDRAW instead of the chart title, you could choose not to display the chart title. In addition, in bar, line, and area charts, it is popular to display the actual data values on the chart. This section discusses *displaying* chart text elements, such as axis titles and data values. Refer to Chapter 32 for information on changing the font and colors of text elements.

To manage the display of your bar, line, and area chart text elements, choose Display Status from the **C**hart Menu. The Display Status dialog box appears as shown in figure 30.29. This dialog box provides a series of display features you can turn on or off by clicking in the desired checkboxes. For example, to turn on the chart title, click to place a checkmark in the Title checkbox. To eliminate the category axis and title, click to clear the checkmark. At the top of the dialog box are buttons for All Text and No Text. These buttons make each of the display status features active or inactive.

Table 30.1
Statistical Analysis Options

Function	Explanation
Mean	The "mean" equals the sum of the values divided by the number of the values. For instance, 100+200+300 divided by three equals a mean of 200.
Standard Deviation	Lines are placed at each standard deviation distance from the mean line along the data axis. CorelCHART determines the standard deviation distance and places lines at this interval above and below the mean line. For instance, if the mean equals 100, and the standard deviation equals 6, deviation lines will appear at 106 (100+6) and 94 (100-6).
Connected Line	CorelCHART draws a line connecting the top of the selected group of data sets to place a line connecting the top of a series of bars in a bar chart.
Smooth	This option draws a line through or near each data point in a series. A smooth curve is created where the line connects points that have been evenly distributed between data points. The more points added, the smoother the curve becomes.
Moving Average	Select this option to draw a line at the moving average of the data points. You must specify whether the average is Financial or Scientific, and enter the number of periods used to calculate each moving average point. By using moving averages with the appropriate number of periods you can eliminate cyclical, seasonal, or irregular patterns, thus clearly illustrating the moving trend.
Linear Regression	This option instructs CorelCHART to draw a line approximating the sum of least squares for the selected series. Linear Regression uses the formula $y = a0+a1$. This formula is equal to a polynomial fit with the Order set to 1.
Common Log Regression	Select this option to draw a curved line that fits the data points concurring with the log regression formula $y = (\log x)+ b$. The line is a sum of least squares approximation of data for a selected series.

continues

Table 30.1, Continued
Statistical Analysis Options

Function	Explanation
Natural Log Regression	This is the same as a common log regression, but with a base of e.
Exponential Regression	Use this option to instruct CorelCHART to draw a line approximating the sum of least squares for the selected series. Exponential regression uses the formula y = a(b).
Polynomial Fit	When this option is selected, CorelCHART draws a line that curves to fit the data points following the polynomial regression formula y = a0 + a1 + a2x + ...+ anx where n = the order of the polynomial. Note that the order "0" draws a line at the mean of the data. This curved line is a "least squares" approximation of data for a selected series.

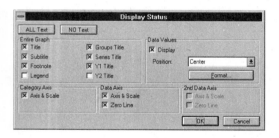

Figure 30.29
The Display Status dialog box.

To display the data values on your chart, click on the Display checkbox under Data Values. You can control where the data values are placed by clicking on the down arrow by the Position list box. Click to select a position. For instance, choose Inside Maximum to display the values inside the bars at the maximum value. In figure 30.30, the data values are placed in the center of each bar informing the viewer of the exact amount of video games sold. Click on the Format button to modify the formatting of the data values. After making the desired

selections, choose OK to display the specified titles and text elements.

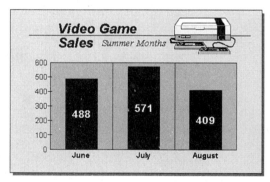

Figure 30.30
CorelCHART lets you control the placement of data values.

Another way to turn off the display of titles and footnotes is to delete the data from the cell in the Data Manager.

Special Options for Bar Charts

CorelCHART provides many options for controlling the appearance of bar charts. CorelCHART refers to the bars as "bar risers." Depending on the number of bar risers your chart uses, you may want to adjust the bar thickness and spacing to enhance the chart. In addition, you can substitute a triangle or diamond shape for the standard bar shape. These options can make bar charts a lot of fun to create and design. This section covers commands specific to bar charts.

Using the Base of Bars Command

The Base of Bars command lets you control whether the data axis begins scaling with zero or the lowest number entered in your chart data. For instance, if 25 was the lowest number in your chart data, you could adjust the data axis to begin scaling at 25.

To adjust the data axis to scale from the lowest number in your data, select Base of Bars from the **C**hart menu. From the sub-menu, select From Scale Minimum. The bar representing the lowest number does not show on your chart. To adjust the data axis to scale from zero, select Base of Bars from the **C**hart menu and choose From Zero Line.

Adjusting the Bar Thickness

Add extra flair to your bar charts by adjusting the thickness of the bars. Especially when working with two or three sets of data, widening the bars gives them more prominence on the chart. To control the bar thickness, select Bar Thickness from the

Chart menu to reveal the sub-menu. You can preview each of the thickness options by pressing and holding the mouse button and dragging down the list of choices. Release on the desired selection and your bars assume the specified thickness (see fig. 30.31).

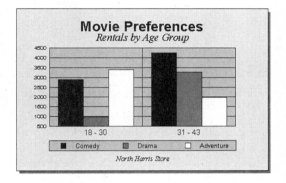

Figure 30.31
Adjusting the Bar Thickness can draw attention to your data.

Adjusting the Bar to Bar Spacing

The Bar to Bar Spacing command lets you control the amount of space between bars in the same category. Controlling the amount of space between bars can make charts much easier to read and interpret. As displayed in figure 30.32, "clustering" bars together helps the viewer distinguish between the categories of skaters. To control the bar spacing, select Bar to Bar Spacing from the **C**hart menu to reveal the sub-menu. You can preview each of the spacing options by pressing and holding the mouse button and dragging down the list of choices. Release on the desired selection and your bars assume the specified spacing.

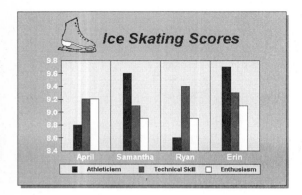

Figure 30.32
Adjusting the spacing between bars helps the viewer separate and understand the chart data.

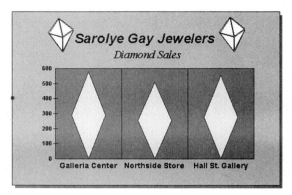

Figure 30.33
CorelCHART lets you change the marker shape in bar charts.

Changing the Marker Shape

By default, bar charts use rectangular bars as the marker shapes. For special effects in your chart design, you may want to change marker shape to circles, stars or some other graphic shape. For instance, in figure 30.33 a diamond shape is used to illustrate jewelry sales. Make sure that the selected marker shape does not detract from the readability of your chart. Depending on the chart, you may find it best to stick with a rectangular bar shape and add clip art or symbols to embellish your chart.

To choose another marker shape, select a bar riser from the data set you want change. From the **C**hart menu, select Marker Shape. A sub-menu appears displaying the available graphic shapes. You can preview each of the shapes by pressing and holding the mouse button and dragging down the choices. Release on the desired shape and the bars in the selected data set are changed.

Creating Pictographs

When you select a different marker shape, one shape is used to represent the height of the data. Instead of distorting one shape to illustrate the different chart values, you can instruct CorelCHART to stack the shapes as illustrated in figure 30.34. To stack the selected marker shapes, choose Show Pictograph from the **C**hart menu.

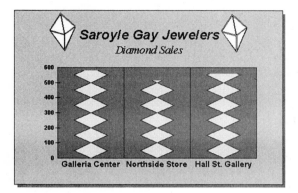

Figure 30.34
Stacking Marker Shapes with the Show Pictograph command.

In addition to stacking markers, you also can stack CorelDRAW .CDR files to create special effects. The .CDR files or "pictographs" replace the markers in a bar chart. For instance, in a chart documenting food sales at ball parks you could use hamburgers and hot-dogs as pictographs to represent favorite fast-food munchies. CorelCHART includes templates for Pictographs. They work basically the same as bar charts, except that the Show Pictograph command is already selected.

To create a chart with pictographs, turn on the Show Pictograph command in the **C**hart menu. Next, click on the Fill Tool to display the fly-out. Click again on the last button in the fly-out to display the Pictograph roll-up as shown in figure 30.35. CorelCHART provides a few built-in images for placing as

pictographs. Click on the big white area marked with an X to display the images. To select an image, click on it once and click OK. The image displays in the roll-up. To display the image on your chart as a pictograph, select a bar riser from the data series you want displayed as a pictograph and click on the Apply button. The bars are re-drawn with the selected pictograph.

Figure 30.35
The Pictograph roll-up.

To import a .CDR file as a pictograph, click on the Import button in the Pictograph roll-up. The Import Files dialog box appears, change to the drive and directory where the file you want to import is located. Select the file name and click on OK. A preview of the file appears in the Pictograph roll-up. To display the image as a pictograph, select a bar riser from the data set you want changed and click on the Apply button. The bars are re-drawn with the selected .CDR image.

For frequently used images, you may want to add the image to the Pictograph roll-up. Click on the white X area to reveal the Pictograph menu commands. Select Import Pattern from the File menu to display the Import File dialog box. Select the desired file and click on OK. The images are added to the available images in the roll-up.

Displaying Data as a Line

In a bar chart, you can display one set of bars as a line to differentiate it from other chart data. For instance, in figure 30.36 the last set of data represents the average 200 meter sprint time. The average is displayed as a line to distinguish it from the other bars which represent individual sprint times. To display a series as a line, select a bar riser and, choose Display as Line from the Chart menu.

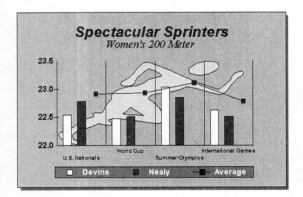

Figure 30.36

Displaying one series of data in a bar chart as a line.

Special Options for Line Charts

When designing line charts, CorelCHART gives you options to adjust the shape and size of the markers. This section covers commands specific to line charts.

Showing Markers

CorelCHART creates line charts with "markers" or small squares at the data point on each line. To turn off the display of the markers, select a line and choose Show Markers from the Chart menu. The markers for the selected line disappear.

Changing the Marker Shape

By default, line charts use small squares as the marker shapes. You can change the marker shape to circles, stars, or another graphic shape. For instance, in figure 30.37 a triangle shape is used in the line chart.

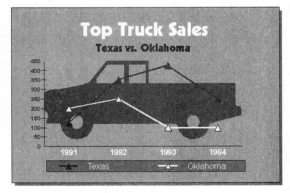

Figure 30.37

CorelCHART lets you change the marker shape in line charts.

To choose another marker shape, select a line and choose Marker Shape from the **C**hart menu. A sub-menu appears displaying the available graphic shapes. You can preview each of the shapes by pressing and holding the mouse button and dragging down the choices. Release on the desired shape and the markers in the selected line are changed.

Controlling Marker Size

The size of the marker can also be adjusted. A larger marker shape can draw more attention to the lines in your chart. However, if your chart has many lines, you may want to make the markers smaller to reduce clutter.

To control the size of the markers, select a line and choose Marker Size from the **C**hart menu. A sub-menu appears displaying the available sizes. You can preview each of the sizes by pressing and holding the mouse button and dragging down the choices. Release on the desired size and the markers in the selected line are changed.

Displaying Data as a Bar

In a line chart, you can display one set of data as a bar to differentiate it from other chart data. For instance, in a line chart illustrating cruise sales, the lines may represent the number of cruises sold, while the bars represent the revenue from the sales. To display a series as a bar, select a line and choose Display as Bar from the **C**hart menu.

Special Options for Area Charts

Area charts are colorful graphs designed to show volume. The only command specific to area charts is the Base of Areas command. This is similar to the Base of Bars command covered in the section, "Special Options for Bar Charts."

The Base of Areas command lets you control whether the data axis begins scaling with zero or the lowest number entered in your chart data. To adjust the data axis to scale from the lowest number in your data, select Base of Areas from the **C**hart menu. From the sub-menu, select From Scale Minimum. To adjust the data axis to scale from zero, select From Zero Line.

Summary

This chapter covered the options for formatting pie, bar, line, and area charts. It covered the steps for adjusting the spacing between bars, modifying the thickness of a pie chart, changing colors, and developing many other options for displaying your chart data.

The options for the remaining specialized chart types, such as spectral maps and hi/lo/open/close charts are covered in the next chapter, "Building Specialized Charts."

Building Specialized Charts

*Y*ou will find that some data requires a more complex, specialized chart type to effectively communicate a message. Medical professionals, for example, use histograms to plot the frequency of adverse reactions to a particular medicine. Demographers employ spectral maps to convey the increasing population growth in suburban areas. Dietitians use scatter charts to illustrate how excess body fat affects the rate of heart disease. Certain messages require specialized charts designed to accentuate frequency and correlation, or to demonstrate cause and effect relationships that cannot be accurately communicated in pie, bar, line, and area charts.

As discussed in Chapter 30, selecting the correct chart type is critical to effectively communicating your message. This fact becomes even more important when you move into the realm of using specialized charts, such as scatter charts and histograms. The information for these types of charts must fit the selected chart type and be properly displayed so the viewer can correctly analyze and understand the message.

This chapter covers:

- Charting options for specialized chart types

- Charting options for bubble, gantt, hi/lo, histograms, and scatter charts

- Charting options for spectral maps

- Charting options for table charts

- Charting options for polar and radar charts

- Building 3D riser charts

Charting Options for Specialized Chart Types

Data that calls for a unique type of analysis requires a unique chart form. CorelCHART provides templates for creating these specialized chart types. As discussed in Chapter 30, the template utilized to create your chart determines the position of chart elements. The template determines the chart colors, grid lines, numeric formatting, and much more. As you venture into this more specialized field of charting, make use of the sample data in the template to simplify the data entry process in the Data Manager. Refer to Chapter 29 for more information on working with sample data and the Data Manager.

This chapter covers the options for manipulating hi/lo, histograms, scatter, 3D riser, 3D scatter, spectral maps, polar, radar, bubble, gantt, and table charts. The features for each chart type are covered in the following sections.

Selecting Chart Commands

There are several ways to select commands for changing chart attributes. This chapter makes use of the menus to access commands. For instance, to control the display of titles and text on a chart, you can select Display Status from the **C**hart menu. However, CorelCHART also provides pop-up menus to quickly access certain commands. The Pop-up Menu tool is the third tool in the toolbox. Select the tool and click on a chart element, such as a line, bar, title, or legend. A pop-up menu appears displaying options for that particular chart element. For example, clicking on a grid line displays a pop-up menu for formatting the grids (see fig. 31.1). You also can click on a chart element with the right mouse button to reveal the context-sensitive pop-up menus.

Figure 31.1
The pop-up menu for formatting grid lines.

Charting Options for Bubble, Gantt, Hi/Lo, Histograms, and Scatter Charts

Similar to the XY charts (bar, line, and area) covered in the previous chapter, bubble, gantt, hi/lo, histograms, and scatter charts all work with an XY-axis format. As shown in figure 31.2, the histogram uses two axes to illustrate that most children have two cavities, and the two axes in the scatter chart describe how new homes sales are outdistancing old home sales. The chart types are also similar in that a bar or marker is used to plot the chart data. In gantt, histograms, and hi/lo charts, bars are used. In scatter and bubble charts, markers are used.

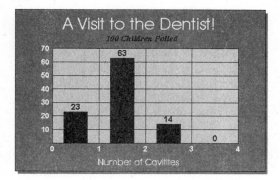

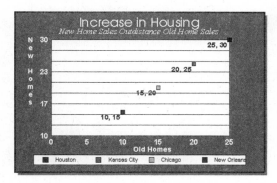

Figure 31.2

An example of histogram and scatter charts.

Because these chart types all use two axes, the options for formatting them are relatively similar. Therefore, bubble, gantt, hi/lo, histograms, and scatter charts are covered together in this section. Features that are specific to certain chart types are covered in the "Special Options" sections. For example, the Histogram Intervals command, which pertains solely to Histograms, is covered in the section "Special Options for Histograms."

Changing Fill Colors and Outlines

Color is an important aspect of designing charts. For instance, studies have shown that many audiences react negatively to certain shades of green in presentation graphics. This section details changing the color of bars and markers in bubble, gantt, histograms, hi/lo, and scatter charts.

> **N O T E**
>
> Refer to Chapter 32 for changing the color of other chart elements, such as backgrounds, titles, and legends.

To change the fill color of the bars and markers, select a bar or marker and click on the desired color in the color palette. The chart type determines how the color is applied. For instance, in a histogram all of the bars assume the new color; in a hi/lo, only the bars in that series change. To change the outline colors around the bars or markers, select the bar or marker, and click on the desired color with the right mouse button.

To apply a new outline width to the bars and markers, select a bar or marker and choose a thickness from the Outline tool. As displayed in figure 31.3, when you select the Outline tool, a fly-out appears with several preset line widths. Click on the desired line width. Refer to Chapter 32 for information on creating custom line widths with the Outline tool.

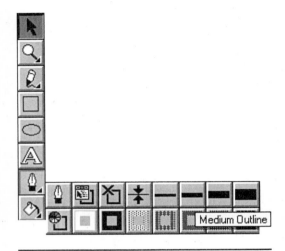

Figure 31.3
The Outline tool offers several preset line thicknesses.

For added texture, you can also apply fountain and patterned fills to bars and markers. If you are familiar with CorelDRAW, you will find the Fill tool in CorelCHART to be very similar. For more information on using the Fill tool, refer to Chapter 32.

Working with the Chart Axes

Whether you are producing a bubble, gantt, histogram, hi/lo, or scatter chart, you are working with a basic XY-axes structure. Your chart has an axis running vertically up the side of the chart, and another running horizontally across the bottom of the chart.

If your chart is vertically oriented, the Y axis appears on the left and the X axis appears along the bottom. In a horizontally oriented chart, the axes are switched to display the Y axis running along the bottom, and the X axis on the left. (Use the **G**allery menu to flip the orientation of a chart.) Figure 31.4 illustrates how the axes are flipped when the histogram changes from vertical to horizontal orientation.

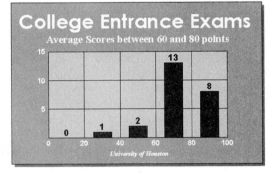

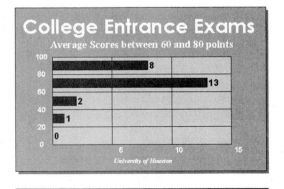

Figure 31.4
In a vertical chart, the Y axis is on the left and the X axis along the bottom. In a horizontal chart, the Y axis is along the bottom and the X axis is on the left.

Because bubble, gantt, histograms, hi/lo, and scatter charts each plot different types of data on their two axes, CorelCHART uses different terminology to identify them. However, the options for formatting the axes are very similar regardless of how they are named. Table 31.1 identifies the name CorelCHART assigns to the axes in the different chart types.

Table 31.1
Identifying Axis Names

Chart Type	X Axis Name	Y Axis Name
Bubble	X-Axis	Y1-Axis
Gantt	Category	Data
Histogram	Interval	Data
Hi/Lo	Category	Data
Scatter	X-Axis	Y1-Axis

Displaying Chart Axes

CorelCHART gives you the flexibility to alter the display of the axes by placing them on different sides, or on both sides of your chart. For instance, the data axis appears on both the left and right sides of the hi/lo chart (see fig. 31.5). You may find that displaying the data axis on both sides of the chart helps the viewer interpret the data by providing another axis against which data can be compared.

To adjust the placement of the axes, select the appropriate axis name from the **C**hart menu. For instance, if you are creating a histogram, select Interval or Data Axis from the **C**hart menu. (Refer to table 31.1 for the axis names.) A submenu appears with a check mark indicating the current position of the axis. Your options include Display on Top and Display on Bottom, *or* Display on Left and Display on Right. Select the desired placement. As an example, in a vertically oriented scatter chart, you can choose to display the X-Axis along the top and/or bottom and the Y1-Axis at the left and/or right of the chart. Turning both options off removes the axis from the display altogether.

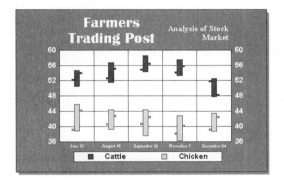

Figure 31.5
A hi/lo chart with the data axis placed on both sides of the chart.

Options for changing the type face and size of the data on the axes is covered in Chapter 32.

Displaying Axis Grid Lines

Grid lines help lead the viewer's eye from a data set to the data axis. With CorelCHART, you can display grid lines for all axes. The control you have when displaying grid lines depends on the chart type and the axis. Though you may not be able to control all elements of some grid lines, you do have the option to turn on or turn off their display. As detailed in table 31.2, you have full control over the display of one or both of the chart axes.

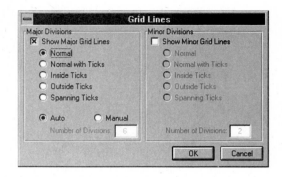

Figure 31.6
The Grid Lines dialog box.

Table 31.2
Control Over Grid lines

Chart Type	Full Control of Grid lines	Only turn on and off
Bubble	X-Axis & Y1-Axis	
Histogram	Data	Interval
Hi/Lo	Data	Category
Scatter	X-Axis & Y1-Axis	
Gantt	Data	Category

To format the grid lines, select the name of the axis containing the gridlines you want to adjust from the **C**hart menu. For instance, in a hi/lo chart select Data Axis. From the submenu, select Grid Lines to display the Grid Lines dialog box as shown in figure 31.6. The dialog box controls the display of major and minor grid lines. Major divisions are the units between each numerical value along the data axis. Minor divisions are the units between the major divisions. CorelCHART gives you control over the number of major and minor divisions.

The first option, Show Major Grid Lines, controls the display of grid lines along the major divisions. When Show Major Grid Lines is selected, options for displaying the grid lines become available. Select Normal to display the grid line without tick marks. As shown in figure 31.7, selecting Normal with Ticks displays the grid lines with tick marks outside the data axis. The three remaining options turn off the display of grid lines and place tick marks instead. Select Inside Ticks to display tick marks inside the data axis. Select Outside Ticks to display tick marks outside the data axis. Select Spanning Ticks to display tick marks on both sides of the data axis. The options for controlling minor divisions are the same as those for major divisions. It is important to note that lines for minor divisions display in white by default and do not appear if your chart background is also white.

CorelCHART automatically sets the number of major and minor divisions. To enter a different amount of major divisions, click on the Manual feature at the bottom of the Grid

Lines dialog box and type in the desired number of major divisions. When minor grid lines are turned on you can also enter the number of minor divisions. When you are finished selecting options for the grid lines, click on OK.

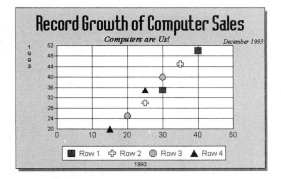

Figure 31.7

A chart displaying gridlines with tick marks.

You can change the color of grid lines by selecting one with the Pick tool and then clicking on a color in the on-screen palette with the right mouse button. To adjust the line width of the grid lines, select one and choose a thickness from the top row of buttons on the Outline toolbar. All grid lines must have the same line width and color. Refer to Chapter 32 for information on creating custom line widths with the Outline tool.

As mentioned earlier, some axis grid lines only can be turned on and off. To control the display of these grid lines, select the name of the axis from the Chart menu. On the submenu, a check mark by the Show Grid lines command indicates the grid lines are currently displayed. Select the Show Grid

lines command to remove the check mark and therefore remove the axis grid lines from the chart.

Scaling the Axis

Gantt, histograms, hi/lo, scatter, and bubble charts all use some type of reference axis to gauge data values. In a histogram, the frequency data is measured against the data axis. In gantt and hi/lo charts, the data is also gauged against the data axis. Bubble and scatter charts are different in that the data is measured against two axes.

The axis against which the data is measured displays a scale with a minimum and maximum value. CorelCHART automatically determines the minimum and maximum from the values you enter in the Data Manager. For instance, if all of your chart values are under 50, the data axis might scale from a minimum of 0 to a maximum of 50. CorelCHART gives you the flexibility to adjust the scale to begin and end at the values you specify.

To customize the scaling, select the name of the axis you want to scale from the Chart menu. For instance, in a histogram or hi/lo chart, select Data Axis. From the submenu, select Scale Range to display the Scale Range dialog box as shown in figure 31.8. By default, the Automatic Scale option is selected. This option automatically sets the upper and lower scale limits according to the chart data you entered. To enter different values for the data axis scale, click on the Manual Scale option. Enter the desired number values in the From and To boxes to create a customized scale.

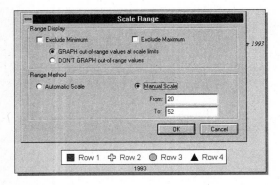

Figure 31.8

The Scale Range dialog box.

Additional options for adjusting the axis scaling appear at the top of the Scale Range dialog box. Click on Exclude Minimum to turn off the display of the lowest value on the data axis scale. Click on Exclude Maximum to turn off the display of the highest value on the data axis scale. Click on OK when you are finished making selections.

Selecting Linear and Logarithmic Data Axis Scaling

CorelCHART provides two types of scaling options—linear and logarithmic. The default option, Linear Scale, is a standard scale representing an amount or quantity in evenly spaced increments. For instance, the axis might measure currency with every increment increasing by $100. Logarithmic scales compress or expand the data values in powers of 10 as they ascend the Y axis so that the distance between each unit along the data axis decreases as you go up the scale. You can apply logarithmic scaling to the data axes in

histograms and hi/lo charts, and both axes in bubble and scatter charts. To change to logarithmic scaling, select the name of the axis you want to change to logarithmic from the **C**hart menu. From the submenu, click on Log Scale. The chart is redrawn with the specified axis displayed in logarithmic scaling.

Formatting the Axes

You can apply numeric formatting such as percent signs, commas, and decimal places to the numbers along the chart axes. For instance, the bubble chart in figure 31.9 shows currency symbols added to the vertical axis. In histograms, bubble, and scatter charts, you can apply numeric formatting to both axes. In gantt and hi/lo charts, numeric formatting only can be applied to the data axis.

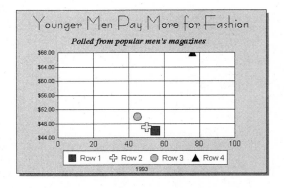

Figure 31.9

Applying numeric formatting to the axes makes the data easier to examine and understand.

To apply numeric formatting, select the name of the axis you want to format from the

Chart menu. From the submenu, select Number Format to display the Numeric dialog box as shown in figure 31.10. The Numeric dialog box is the same one used to apply numeric formatting to data in the Data Manager. Select the desired formatting option from the list of choices and click on OK. For example, select $#,##0 to add currency symbols to the axis numbers.

not know that the Y axis defines the hours slept, and the X axis defines the sleeper's age. With CorelCHART, you can control which titles and other text elements are displayed in the charts. In addition, with complex charts it is common to display the actual data values on the chart. Again, this helps the viewer interpret the data. This section discusses displaying chart text elements such as axis titles and data values.

Figure 31.10

The Numeric dialog box.

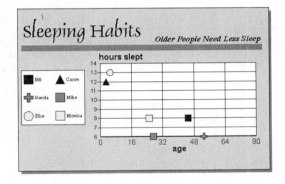

Figure 31.11

Chart titles and other text elements help the viewer analyze the chart.

Displaying Titles, Data Values, and Other Text Elements

It is important to include chart titles, axis titles, and legends to help convey your chart's message. With more complicated chart types such as histograms, hi/lo, bubble, and scatter charts, chart titles and other text elements play an important role in helping the viewer understand the chart. This is demonstrated in figure 31.11, where the chart and axis titles helps the viewer process the information. Without the titles, the viewer would

To control the display of chart text elements, choose Display Status from the **C**hart Menu. The Display Status dialog box appears (this dialog box varies slightly depending on the chart type). Figure 31.12 shows the Chart Display Status dialog box for scatter charts. Each dialog box provides a series of display features you can turn on or off by clicking in the desired checkboxes. For example, to turn on the chart title, click to place a check mark in the Title checkbox. To eliminate an axis title, click to remove the check mark. At the

top of the dialog box are buttons for All Text and No Text. These buttons make each of the display status features active or inactive.

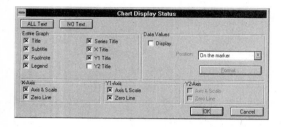

Figure 31.12
The Chart Display Status dialog box.

N O T E

Another way to turn off the display of titles and footnotes is to delete the data from the cell in the Data Manager.

To turn on the display of the data values, click on the checkbox by Data Values (it may already be turned on). You can control the placement of the data values by clicking on the down arrow by the Position list box. For instance, in a histogram, choose Inside Maximum to display the values inside the bars at the maximum value. Click on the Format button to modify the formatting of the data values. After making the desired selections, choose OK, and the specified titles and text elements appear on the chart.

Special Options for Histograms

CorelCHART provides several options for controlling the appearance of histograms. You can create horizontally or vertically oriented histograms with CorelCHART templates. CorelCHART also gives you the options to change the shape of the bars or stack graphic pictures in place of the bars to create a pictographic histogram.

Adjusting the Interval Axis

A histogram plots the frequency of values within specified intervals. For instance, the histogram in figure 31.13 demonstrates how 100 people scored on a driving test. The interval axis at the bottom is scaled in four intervals from 0 to 25, from 25 to 50, from 50 to 75, and from 75 to 100. The CorelCHART templates for creating histograms place five intervals in the axis. You can customize the number of intervals to correspond with your chart data.

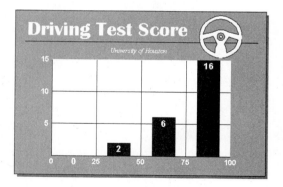

Figure 31.13
The Interval Axis can be adjusted to display the number of intervals you specify.

To customize the number of intervals in a histogram, select Intervals from the Chart menu. The Histogram Intervals dialog box appears as displayed in figure 31.14. By default, the Manual option is selected, and the number of intervals is set at 5. Enter the desired number in the text box. You can select the Automatic option to let CorelCHART set the number of intervals; however, you will find that setting your own number of intervals produces the best results.

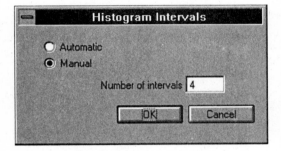

Figure 31.14
The Histogram Interval dialog box.

Changing the Marker Shape

By default, histograms use rectangular bars for the marker shapes. You can change the marker shapes to triangles or some other graphic shape for a special effect. Make sure that the selected marker shape does not detract from the readability of your chart.

To choose another marker shape, select a bar in the histogram and select Marker Shape from the Chart menu. A submenu appears displaying the available graphic shapes. To preview the choices, press and hold the left

mouse button, then drag down the list of choices. Release on the desired shape, and the histogram bars are changed.

Creating Pictographs

When you select a different marker shape, only one shape is used to represent the height of the data. Instead of distorting the one shape to illustrate the different chart values, you can instruct CorelCHART to stack the shapes. To stack the selected marker shapes, choose Show Pictograph from the Chart menu. In addition to stacking markers, you can also stack .CDR files to create special effects. The .CDR files or "pictographs" replace the markers in a bar chart.

Special Options for Hi/Lo Charts

Hi/lo charts are typically associated with showing stock market buying trends. When initially creating a hi/lo chart, you can select a chart that displays just the high and low values and a chart that displays the open and close values as well. You have several options for formatting hi/lo charts, including the ability to adjust the size of the main bars, and the open and close markers.

Reversing Data Sets

You can reverse the display order of the data in a hi/lo chart. For instance, in figure 31.15 the first chart shows wheat as the first series in the legend, while the second chart is reversed, showing corn first. The data on the category axis also can be reversed to display

the dates backwards. To reverse the data in your chart, select Data Reversal from the **C**hart menu. The Data Reversal feature offers two options for reversing your data—Reverse Series and Reverse Groups. Choose Reverse Series to invert the order of the data series (wheat and corn), and choose Reverse Groups to swap the order of the data groups (category axis).

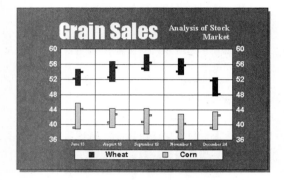

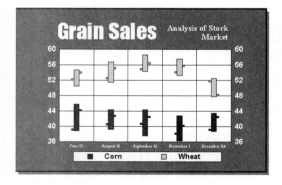

Figure 31.15

The Data Reversal command lets you reverse the order of how chart data appears in the chart.

Using the Data Analysis Feature

CorelCHART has tools to help you calculate and analyze statistical data in a hi/lo chart. With the Data Analysis feature, you quickly can determine the mean, standard deviation, or averages for a set of data and then plot the figure as a line on your chart. The data analysis is done to one set of data at a time. To use the data analysis feature, select one of the bar markers representing the series of data you wish to analyze and select Data Analysis from the **C**hart menu. Select the desired type of data analysis and click OK.

Adjusting the Bar Thickness

You can widen the bars in hi/lo charts to give them extra prominence. To control the bar thickness, select Bar Thickness from the **C**hart menu to reveal the submenu. To preview the choices, press and hold the left mouse button, then drag down the list of choices. Release on the desired selection and your bars assume the specified thickness.

Adjusting the Width of the Open and Close Markers

You can adjust the width or size of the open and close markers on a hi/lo chart. From the Chart menu, select Open & Close Width to reveal the submenu. To preview the choices, press and hold the left mouse button, then drag down the list of choices. Release on the desired selection and the markers assume the specified thickness. This command is available only if your chart shows the open and close values as well as the high and low values.

Special Options for Gantt Charts

Gantt charts are used to represent the duration, and the start and end times of particular events. For instance, in figure 31.16 the chart shows the length of time needed to complete a multimedia show. The chart informs the viewer that 10 days are needed to complete the photography for the opening show.

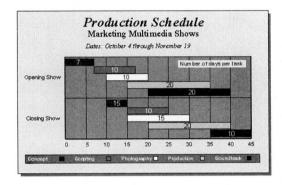

Figure 31.16

Gantt charts inform the viewer how much time is needed to complete certain tasks.

Reversing Data Sets

The order the data is entered in the Data Manager determines how it appears on the chart. CorelCHART gives you the option to reverse the display order of the data. To reverse the data in your chart, select Data Reversal from the **C**hart menu. From the submenu, choose Reverse Series to invert the order of the data series. Choose Reverse Groups to invert the order of the groups.

Adjusting the Bar Thickness

You can widen the bars in a gantt chart to give them extra prominence. To control the bar thickness, select Bar Thickness from the **C**hart menu to reveal the sub-menu. To preview the choices, press and hold the left mouse button, then drag down the list of choices. Release on the desired selection and your bars assume the specified thickness.

Special Options for Scatter Charts

You have several options for controlling the appearance of scatter charts. There are features for performing data analysis and for adjusting the marker shape and size.

Using the Data Analysis Feature

With the data analysis feature, you can quickly determine the mean, standard deviation, or averages for a set of data and then plot the figure as a line on your chart. The analysis is done to one set of data at a time. To use the data analysis feature, select one of the markers representing the series of data you wish to analyze. Then, select Data Analysis from the **C**hart menu to display the Data Analysis dialog box. Select the desired type of data analysis and click OK.

Changing the Marker Shape

By default, scatter charts use rectangular bars as the marker shapes. For special effects in your chart design, you may want to change marker shape to circles, stars, or some other

graphic shape (see fig. 31.17). To choose another marker shape, select a marker from the data set you want to change. From the **C**hart menu, select Marker Shape. A submenu appears displaying the available graphic shapes. To preview the choices, press and hold the left mouse button, then drag down the list of choices. Release on the desired shape and the markers in the selected data set are changed.

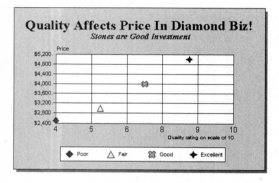

Figure 31.17

You can change the marker shape used in scatter charts.

Sizing the Markers

You can manipulate the size of the markers to draw more attention to the markers on your chart. To size the markers, select Marker Size from the **C**hart menu. A submenu appears displaying the available marker sizes. To preview the choices, press and hold the left mouse button, then drag down the

list of choices. Release on the desired size and the markers in the selected data set are changed.

Special Options for Bubble Charts

Bubble charts are similar to scatter charts in many respects. However, there are a few options that are specific to building and designing bubble charts. You can control the size of the bubble and show the quadrant lines.

Sizing the Markers

You can manipulate the size of the bubbles to increase their promenience on the chart. To size the markers, select Marker Size from the **C**hart menu. A submenu appears displaying the available marker sizes. To preview the choices, press and hold the left mouse button, then drag down the list of choices. Release on the desired size and the markers in the selected data set are changed.

Showing Quadrant Lines

In figure 31.18, the gridlines for the horizontal axis are turned off and "quadrant lines" are displayed to divide the bubble chart into sections. To turn on the quadrant lines, select Show Quadrant Lines from the **C**hart menu. The quadrant lines are formatted the same as gridlines.

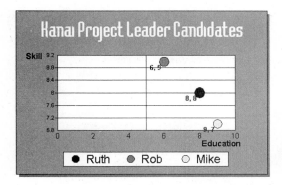

Figure 31.18
Quadrant lines divide bubble charts into sections.

Charting Options for Spectral Maps

Spectral maps are specialized charts that indicate how a variable changes over an area. CorelCHART gives you several options for controlling the appearance of spectral maps. You can change the shape of the markers and specify which colors to use in the spectrum.

Displaying the Series and Groups Headers

As shown in figure 31.19, spectral maps display the Series header information on the left and the Groups header at the bottom. You can change the header information to display on different sides of the chart, or on both sides of the chart. To adjust the placement of the series header, select Series Header from the **C**hart menu. From the submenu, select Display on Left, Display on

Right or both. Turning both options off removes the header information from the display altogether. The placement of the Groups header works the same way. Select Groups Header from the **C**hart menu, and choose Display on Top, Display on Bottom or both.

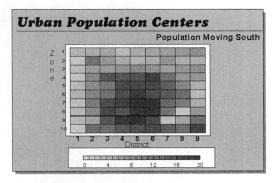

Figure 31.19
Spectral maps use Series Headers and Groups Headers to explain chart information.

Working with the Spectrum Label

The Spectrum label placed at the bottom of the chart is similar to a legend in other chart types. The spectrum label identifies the values assigned to each color range. Select Spectrum label from the **C**hart menu to reveal a submenu with formatting options. Select Display on Top or Display on Bottom to control the placement of the spectrum label. You also can choose from linear or logarithmic scaling, work with gridlines, and apply numeric formatting. For more information on these features, refer to the section

"Charting Options for Hi/Lo, Histograms, Bubble, and Scatter Charts."

Reversing Data Sets

By default, the first row and column of data entered in the Data Manager appear as the first markers in a spectral map. CorelCHART gives you the option to reverse the display order of the data. To reverse the data in your chart, select Data Reversal from the Chart menu. From the submenu, choose Reverse Series to flip the order of the data series so that the first row of data is last, and the last, first. Choose Reverse Groups to flip the order of the data groups so that the first column of data is last, and the last, first.

Setting the Color Range

In a spectral map, you may want the colors to gradually change to illustrate the relationship between the values. The viewer understands that a great change in color denotes a great change in the chart values. To specify the colors used in the spectral map, select Spectrum from the Chart menu. From the submenu, select Spectrum again to display the Color Range dialog box as shown in figure 31.20. This box lets you select the starting and ending colors for the blend in the spectrum. Click on the Start button to reveal the Select Color dialog box. Pick the desired color, and click OK. Repeat the same steps with the End button. The number of divisions is 20, enter a different amount to create a rougher (fewer divisions) or smoother (more divisions) blend. When finished, click on OK to change the colors used in the spectral map.

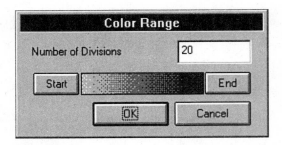

Figure 31.20
The Color Range dialog box.

Changing the Marker Shape

By default, spectral maps use rectangular bars as the marker shapes. You can change the marker shapes to circles or some other graphic shape for a special effect. To choose another marker shape, select a marker in the spectral map and choose Marker Shape from the Chart menu. A submenu appears displaying the available graphic shapes. To preview the choices, press and hold the left mouse button, then drag down the list of choices. Release on the desired shape and the spectral map markers are changed.

Charting Options for Table Charts

Table charts are best used when you have data that cannot be sufficiently expressed in a chart. For instance, in figure 31.23 the table explains the month each new product was released. This data is more text-oriented and would not fit well into a bar or other chart type. Table charts also can be used when you need to provide the viewer with actual numerical values.

column header   row header

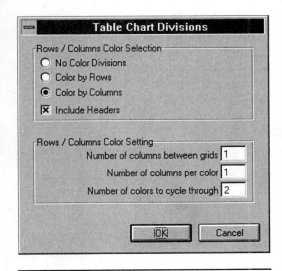

Cyberpunk Video Games
Number of games sent to each city

	RAM Heads	Clickers	Super Mouse	Hard Drivin'
Dallas	35	23	55	12
Houston	46	21	57	11
Tampa	32	20	56	13
Detroit	44	18	55	14

Figure 31.21
Table charts are a great way to present textual data.

Table charts consist of columns and rows. At the intersection of a column and row is a cell. As shown in figure 31.21, every table chart has column headers in the top row and row headers in the first column. Headers are generally used for table titles and headings. Keep in mind that all tables should be designed with a flow of motion that directs the eye to absorb the data in some logical sequence.

Adjusting the Table Divisions

CorelCHART lets you design your table charts with color divisions by row, column, or with no color divisions at all. Figure 31.21 shows a table chart with color division by rows. Notice how the alternating shades of

gray on the rows assist the viewer in reading the table. To control the color divisions in a table chart, select Divisions from the **C**hart menu. The Table Chart Divisions dialog box as shown in figure 31.22 appears.

Figure 31.22
The Table Chart Divisions dialog box.

Click in the first checkbox, No Color Divisions, to use the same color in all of the columns and rows except the column and row headers. Click in the Color by Rows option to alternate colors from row to row. Click the Color by Columns option to alternate colors from column to column. By default, the header cells appear in a different color than the row or column data. You can control this aspect of your chart with the Include Headers feature. For instance, if you are using Color by Rows, turn on the Include Headers to make the row headers the same colors as the rows.

You can control the repeat of the colors on the table. In the Number of rows/columns per color text box, the default is one, meaning that the colors alternate every other row. You can enter a different amount to control the number of continuous rows or columns you want to have the same color. As displayed in figure 31.23, the number of rows per color option is set at 2, so that color alternates between every two rows.

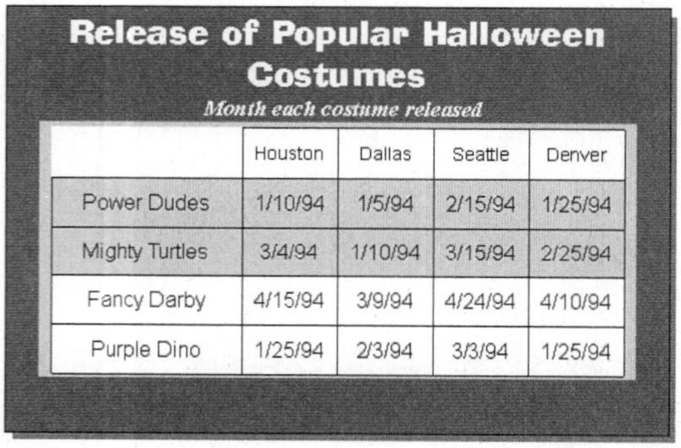
Release of Popular Halloween Costumes

Month each costume released

	Houston	Dallas	Seattle	Denver
Power Dudes	1/10/94	1/5/94	2/15/94	1/25/94
Mighty Turtles	3/4/94	1/10/94	3/15/94	2/25/94
Fancy Darby	4/15/94	3/9/94	4/24/94	4/10/94
Purple Dino	1/25/94	2/3/94	3/3/94	1/25/94

Figure 31.23
Example of row colors alternating every two rows.

In the Number of colors to cycle through text box, enter the number of colors you want to cycle between for your rows or columns. For example, the default number is 2, meaning that the table alternates colors every other row or column. To change color for every third row or column, enter the number 3. After making the desired color division selections, click OK to view your changes. If you changed the number of colors to cycle through, it still displays only two colors. You have to manually select the additional colors. For example, if you choose to alternate between three colors, you have to select a cell from that row or column, and apply a new color from the color palette. The new color is applied to every third column or row in your table.

Changing Row or Column Colors

You can change the colors used in a table chart. If your table is set up with color divisions by rows, changing the color of any cell in a row changes the colors for all rows within that color division. Likewise, if the table is set up with color divisions by columns, changing the color of any cell in a column changes the colors for all columns of that color division.

To change a row or column color, select a cell in the row or column you want to change. The cell displays a white border when selected. Click on the desired color in the color palette and the corresponding row or column colors are changed. Make sure you have the cell selected, not the text inside the cell. If you have the text selected, you change the color of all the text, not the cell background.

Changing Grid and Border Attributes

You can modify the color and line width of the table grids and borders. To change the line color, select any grid line and click the right mouse button on the desired color in the color palette. Changing the color of any grid line changes the grids and borders for the entire table. In other words, you cannot choose to display thick red lines on the horizontal lines, and thin blue lines on the vertical lines.

To change the line width of the table grid, select any grid line and apply a line width with the Outline tool. When you select the Outline tool, a submenu appears with several pre-set line widths. Select the desired thickness. To remove the grid lines, click on the X in the Outline tool. Refer to Chapter 35 for more information on creating custom lines widths with the Outline tool.

Formatting Table Text

You can change the color and size of the table text. To change the text color, select a text string and click on the desired color in the color palette. If your table is set up with color divisions by rows, changing the color of any text string in a row changes the color of all text in the rows within that color division. Likewise, if the table is set up with color divisions by columns, changing the color of any text string in a column changes the colors of all text in the columns within that color division.

CorelCHART's Autofit Table command automatically sizes the table text according to the data you enter. You need to turn the Autofit Table option off before changing the size of table text. To turn off the Autofit Text feature, select Autofit Table from the **C**hart menu. The feature is turned off when there is no check mark by the command. Now, select a text string and choose a new type size from the type size list box at the top of the screen.

Adjusting Column Width and Row Height

The Autofit Table command introduced in the previous section also adjusts automatically the width of the columns in your table. When the Autofit Table feature is on, CorelCHART adjusts the column widths to fit the data. For instance, in figure 31.24 the width of the "Cats" column is narrow, while the next column is wider to contain the word Hamster. The Autofit Text option also forces each row to be the same height, regardless of the amount of text entered in the Data Manager.

Wildwood Elementary Favorite Pets
First through Fourth Grade Students

	Dogs	Cats	Hamsters	Fish
First	30	16	11	8
Second	31	19	13	11
Third	37	17	9	16
Fourth	35	21	6	19

Figure 31.24
The Autofit Table feature adjusts the column width based on the text entered.

To make all of the columns the same width, turn off the Autofit Text command by selecting it from the Chart menu. The feature is turned off when there is no check mark by the command. The Uniform Cell Width, and Uniform Cell Height commands become available when Autofit Text is turned off.

The way your table reacts to the Uniform Cell Width and Uniform Cell Height commands depends on whether your table has been set up with color divisions by row or by column. If you have set up your table with color division by columns, the width of the columns is controlled by the size of the text in the columns. The smaller the text, the narrower the columns. When the size of the text is changed, the column width adjusts to fit. You can choose to make all columns the same width as the largest column header, by selecting Uniform Cell Width from the Chart menu.

The height of the rows is based on the size of the text in the rows. The smaller the text, the shorter the row needs to be. As you enlarge the text, the row height is increased to accommodate the text. Select Uniform Cell Height to instruct all rows to conform to the height of the tallest row.

Displaying Table Titles, Subtitles, and Footnotes

The Display Status command in the Chart menu enables you to control the display of the table chart text. From the Chart menu, select Display Status to open the Table Status dialog box. The three checkboxes enable you to turn on or off the display of the Title, the Subtitle, or the Footnote. Click in the appropriate checkboxes to make your display choices then click OK to view the chart.

Charting Options for Polar and Radar Charts

Polar and radar charts work with two axes—a circular axis, and a radial axis (see fig. 31.25). The commands for modifying these axes are similar those found in any XY-axis chart. An overview of the features is provided here, for more information refer to the earlier section "Charting Options for Bubble, Hi/Lo, Histograms, and Scatter Charts."

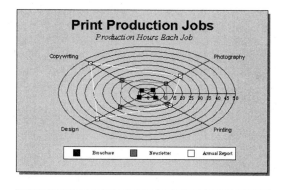

Figure 31.25

Example of radar chart with circular and radial axis.

Working with the Circular Axis

For polar charts, from the Chart menu choose the Circular Axis command to display a submenu which lets you show or hide the scale labels, choose a linear or logarithmic scale, set an ascending or descending scale, and autofit the the axis text. From this sub-menu, you also can access dialog boxes to set the Scale Range, Number Format, and Grid Lines options for the circular axis. For radar charts, the circular axis options let you show or hide the axis headers and grid lines. You also can choose to autofit the header text.

Working with the Radial Axis

The options for formatting the radial axis on polar and radar charts are identical. Select Radial Axis from the **C**hart menu, to reveal the sub-menu. The first options, Display on Top and Display on Bottom, let you specify whether the axis data is placed above or below the radial axis line. The submenu also gives you the capability to select from linear or logarithmic scaling, and setting an ascending or descending scale. From this sub-menu, you can access dialog boxes to set the Scale Range, Number Format, and Grid Lines options for the radial axis. Refer to the earlier section "Charting Options for Bubble, Hi/Lo, Histograms, and Scatter Charts" for more information.

Using the Data Analysis Feature

The data analysis feature detailed in earlier sections also is available with polar and radar charts. The analysis is done to one set of data at a time. To use the data analysis feature, select one of the markers representing the series of data you wish to analyze. Then, select Data Analysis from the **C**hart menu to

display the Data Analysis dialog box. Select the desired type of data analysis and click OK.

Changing the Shape and Size of the Marker

You can choose from a variety of shapes to represent the data points in polar and radar charts. To choose another marker shape, select a marker from the data set you want changed. From the **C**hart menu, select Marker Shape. A submenu appears displaying the available graphic shapes. To preview the choices, press and hold the left mouse button, then drag down the list of choices. Release on the desired shape and the markers in the selected data set are changed.

To size the markers, select Marker Size from the **C**hart menu. A submenu appears displaying the available marker sizes. To preview the choices, press and hold the left mouse button, then drag down the list of choices. Release on the desired size and the markers in the selected data set are changed.

Displaying Table Titles, Subtitles, and Footnotes

The Display Status command in the **C**hart menu enables you to control the display of the chart text. From the **C**hart menu, select Display Status to open the Chart Display Status dialog box (see fig. 31.26). Click in the appropriate checkboxes to make your display choices then click on OK to view the chart. Refer to the section "Charting Options for Bubble, Gantt, Hi/Lo, Histograms, and Scatter Charts" for more information.

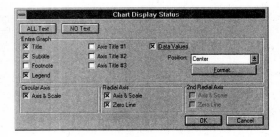

Figure 31.26
The Chart Display Status dialog box.

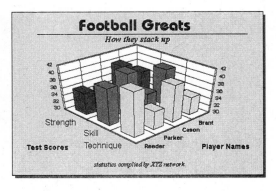

Figure 31.27
A legend is not necessary with 3D riser charts since the series data is displayed on the chart axis.

Building 3D Riser Charts

3D riser charts are essentially bar charts with a third dimension, a Z axis, added to give the chart the illusion of depth. As shown in figure 31.27, 3D charts use an X, Y, and Z axis to plot the chart data. With 3D Riser charts, it is not necessary to use a legend because the Z axis identifes the series data. CorelCHART calls the bars that extend vertically from the category axis, risers. Though many of the options for formatting bar charts apply to 3D Riser charts, CorelCHART provides extensive flexibility for modifying the dimensional aspect of 3D charts.

Adjusting the Viewing Angle

To adjust the viewing angle of your chart, choose Preset Viewing Angles from the **C**hart menu. From the sub-menu, you can choose from 16 different viewing aspects. To preview the choices, press and hold the left mouse button, then drag down the list of choices. Release on the desired selection, and your chart is redrawn accordingly.

Manipulating Riser Sizing

You can also adjust the size of the riser by selecting the Riser Sizing command from the **C**hart menu. When you select this command, a submenu with 17 sizing options is displayed. To preview the choices, press and hold the left mouse button, then drag down the list of choices. Release on the desired selection, and your chart is redrawn accordingly.

Using the 3D Roll-up

You can use the 3D roll-up to alter the size, scale and perspective of 3D charts, and to modify length of axes and thickness of walls. The 3D roll-up also includes a tool to rotate the chart. Choose 3D Roll-up from the **C**hart menu to access the roll-up as shown in figure 31.28. Click on the first button of the roll-up to display a tool for moving the chart. Press and hold your mouse on one of the red arrow tips to move the chart in the specified direction. As you adjust the chart's display, an outline of the chart illustrates how much the chart has moved. Release the mouse button when you have positioned the chart outline where you want it to be. Click on the Redraw button to display your changes, or the Undo button to return the chart to its original position.

The second button in the 3D roll-up displays three tools for manipulating the chart. You can make the chart bigger or smaller by pressing on the red arrow tips on the large diagonal arrow. Press and hold on the arrow tips in the four-sided arrow to pan, or move the chart vertically or horizontally, without affecting the size of the chart. Press and hold on the arrow tips in the small 3D chart to adjust the perspective of your chart. The perspective tool controls the chart's appearance by making one part of the chart appear closer and larger, and the other parts farther away and smaller. Increasing or decreasing the perspective can give the chart a dramatic look by making certain data appear closer to the viewer. As you adjust the chart's display, an outline of the chart is shown as a reference point. Release the mouse button when you have positioned the chart outline where you

want it. Click on the Redraw button to display your changes, or the Undo button to return the chart to its original position.

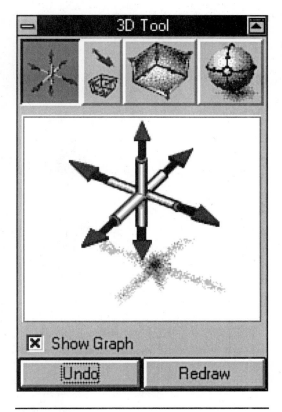

Figure 31.28
The 3D roll-up tool .

The third button in the 3D roll-up displays a tool to change the length of any axis, or to modify the thickness of chart floor or walls. Press and hold the mouse button on any of the red arrow tips inside the chart to shorten or lengthen the axes. Press and hold on the

red arrow tips outside the chart to add thickness to the chart floor or walls. As you adjust the chart's display, an outline of the chart is shown as a movement reference point. Release the mouse button when you have positioned the chart outline where you want. Click on the Redraw button to display your changes, or the Undo button to return the chart to its original position.

The fourth button in the 3D roll-up displays a tool for rotating the chart. Rotating lets you change the viewing angle of the chart. For instance, you can rotate up for more of a bird's-eye view. Press and hold on the left and right red arrow tips to move around the chart, and the diagonal arrows to rotate the chart clockwise or counter-clockwise. As you adjust the chart's display, an outline of the chart is shown as a reference point. Release the mouse button when you have positioned the chart outline where you want. Click on the Redraw button to display your changes, or the Undo button to return the chart to its original position.

At the bottom left of the 3D roll-up is the Show Graph checkbox. When checked, CorelCHART displays your chart as you use the 3D roll-up tools. Uncheck this box to hide the chart and display only the chart outline. The chart reappears when you click on the Redraw button.

Adjusting Riser Colors

The Riser Color command enables you to make color modifications to the bar risers in your chart. Select Riser Color from the **C**hart menu to display a submenu. Choose Color by Face to make all risers the same color. All

risers assume the color of the first bar in the first group.

To emphasize the series data, choose Color by Series. This option forces all risers in a series to use the same color so trends for series data can be easily identified. To place greater emphasis on the group data, choose Color by Group. This selection forces all risers in a group to have the same color to make trends for group data easily recognizable.

The Color by Height option enables you to emphasize growth by making risers different colors depending on their relative height. Once you've chosen Color by Height, you can control the range of colors by selecting Color Range from the Riser Color submenu. The Color Range dialog box, as shown in figure 31.29, appears. Choose a color range by selecting the Start and End colors. In the Number of Divisions text box, enter a number up to 32 to specify the number of color divisions used to blend between your two color choices. When finished with your selections, click OK. The shorter bars are displayed in the start color, graduating toward larger bars in the end color.

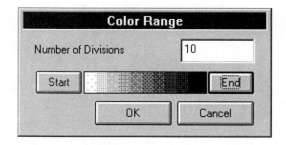

Figure 31.29
The Color Range dialog box.

The Color by Angle option is most often used for surface charts (covered later in this chapter) to color the relief surfaces according to the position of the light source, and the perspective of the viewer. To set the start and end colors, choose Color Range, and select a start and end color in the dialog box.

Surface charts are not available as a chart template by selecting File, New. They are, however, available as a chart option in the Gallery menu.

Applying Shading Effects

Much of the illusion of dimension with 3D charts can be attributed to shading effects. Think of shading as a light source hitting the chart, making some parts of the object appear lighter, and other parts darker. CorelCHART gives you control over the shading on your chart. Choose AutoShade Cube from the Chart menu to make it look as though light is striking the chart floor and walls. Choose AutoShade Risers to create the effect of a light source illuminating the riser bars in a 3D chart. Click to remove the check marks and disable these features if you wish to apply fountain or patterned fills to the risers or walls on the chart.

Displaying Grid Lines

Grid lines help lead the viewers eye from a data set to the data axis. With CorelCHART, you can control the display of grid lines for

the X, Y, and Z axes. To adjust the display of grid lines, select 3D grid lines from the Chart menu to display the Grid Lines dialog box as shown in figure 31.30. The dialog box controls the display of grid lines on the floor and walls of the chart, as well as on the risers themselves. The check marks indicate which grid lines are currently showing. Click in the check boxes by Show X-, Y-, or Z-Axis Grid Lines under Walls & Floors to turn off the display of the grid lines. You can also place Z axis grid lines directly on the bars, to help gauge the value of your risers. Under Risers, click to place a check mark in the Show Z-Axis Grid Lines check box.

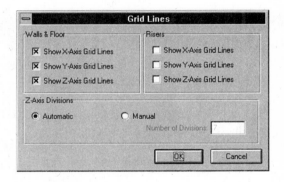

Figure 31.30
The Grid Lines dialog box.

CorelCHART lets you control display grid lines on only the 3D Connect Series, and the 3D Connect Groups chart types.

CorelCHART automatically sets the number of grid divisions for the Z-axis scale. To enter a different amount, click on the Manual feature at the bottom of the Grid Lines dialog box, and type in the desired number of divisions. After making your grid line selections, click OK to view your chart.

You can change the color of the grid lines by selecting a grid line with the Pick tool and then clicking on a color in the on-screen palette with the right mouse button. To adjust the line width of the grid lines, select one and choose a thickness from the top row of buttons on the Outline fly-out toolbar. All grid lines must use the same line width and color.

Scaling the Vertical Axis

The Z (vertical) axis provides a reference point to gauge the values of the chart risers and markers. This axis uses a scale which is defined by a minimum and a maximum value with value points incrementally spaced between. You can adjust the scale on the data range to begin and end at the values you specify. To adjust the scale of the data axis, select Vertical (Z) Axis from the **C**hart menu. From the submenu, select Scale Range to display the Scale Range dialog box, this is the same dialog box used to scale all chart axes. Refer to the section "Scaling the Axes" covered earlier in this chapter for more information on scaling axes.

Selecting Linear and Logarithmic Data Axis Scaling

As with XY-chart types, 3D riser charts provides linear or logarithmic scaling. To change to a logarithmic scale, select Vertical (X) Axis from the Chart menu. From the sub-menu, click on Log Scale. The Data Axis on the chart is re-drawn to display as a logarithmic scale. For more information on logarithmic and linear scaling refer to the section "Selecting Linear and Logarithmic Scaling" earlier in this chapter.

Formatting the Data Axis

You can apply numeric formatting, such as commas and decimal places, to the numbers along the Z (vertical) axis. Select Data Axis from the **C**hart menu. From the submenu, select Number Format to display the Numeric Format dialog box.

Reversing Data Sets

As with XY charts, you can reverse the order of how data appears in 3D charts. Select Data Reversal from the **C**hart menu. From the sub-menu, choose Reverse Series to invert the order of the series or Reverse Groups to invert the order of the groups.

Controlling 3D Text Options

To control the appearance of the text on your 3D chart, select the text you want to change, then choose Text View Options from the Chart menu. The Text View Options dialog box appears as shown in figure 31.31. Use this dialog box to specify how you want text in 3D charts to appear. Select the Autofitted Text option to resize text automatically as you scale the chart with the 3D Tool. Remember you cannot change the font size of autofitted text using the text ribbon. For example, as you change the size of your chart, the text changes proportionate to the new chart size. Select the All Headers Same Size option to make all text in the selected series the same size. Select the Headers Change Size with Perspective option to resize text so that it corresponds to the chart's perspective.

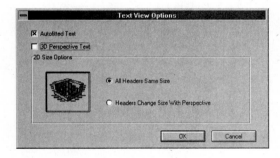

Figure 31.31
The Text View Options dialog box.

N O T E

To specify options for multiple series headers, hold down the Shift key and click at least one header in each series.

Turn on the 3D Perspective Text option to display 3D Placement Options as displayed in figure 31.32. The options are represented visually. You can place your text parallel or perpendicular to the chart floor or walls, or align it towards or away from the chart's implied vanishing point. Under Align To, select Inside Edge to align the text to the inside edge of the chart wall. Select Outside Edge to align the text to the outside edge of the chart wall.

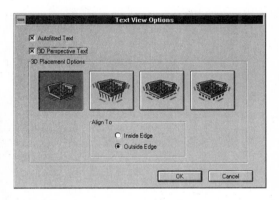

Figure 31.32
The Text View Options dialog box with 3D Placement Options.

Displaying Titles, Data Values, and Other Text Elements

In all charting, it is important to include chart titles, footnotes, axis titles, and legends that help convey your chart's message. To manage the display of your chart text elements, choose Display Status from the

Chart Menu. The Display Status dialog box appears. This dialog box provides a series of display features you can turn on or off by clicking in the desired checkboxes. For example, to turn on the chart title, click to place a check mark in the Title checkbox. To eliminate the category axis and title, click to clear the check mark.

Special Options for 3D Risers

CorelCHART offers several display options for 3D charts including 3D Floating, 3D Connect Series, 3D Connect Group, 3D Surface, and 3D Scatter Charts. Since these charts are all variations of the standard three axis chart, many of the commands for modifying these charts are similar to those discussed in the sections covering 3D Riser charts.

Using 3D Floating Charts

Choose 3D Floating from the **G**allery menu to change the bar risers to dimensional objects that float above the chart floor as shown in figure 31.33. Select 3D Floating from the **C**hart menu to reveal a submenu with options to display the data points as Cubes, or Spheres. To preview the choices, press and hold the left mouse button, then drag down the list of choices. Release on the desired option to redraw the chart.

Figure 31.33
Example of floating riser chart.

Using 3D Connect Group or 3D Connect Series Charts

From the Gallery menu, choose 3D Connect Group or 3D Connect Series for more ways to display your 3D charts. Select 3D Connect Series to connect the data points in a data series to form 3D areas. As shown in figure 31.34, the emphasis is on noting how the values in a series of data change over a period of time. The 3D Connect Group option emphasizes the changes in group data by connecting the data points in a data group to form 3D areas. When you select 3D Connect Series or 3D Connect Groups, submenus appears with options to represent the data points as Areas, Ribbons, or Steps. To preview the choices, press and hold the left mouse button, then drag down the list of choices. Release on the desired option to redraw the chart.

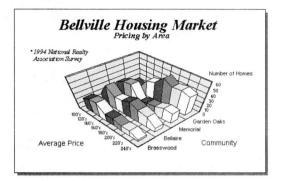

Figure 31.34
Example of 3D Connect Group.

CorelCHART provides several different riser shapes to choose from with the 3D Connect Series and 3D Connect Groups options. To apply a riser shape different from the other chart risers, select the riser you want to change, then choose Riser Type from the **C**hart menu. The submenu appears with several riser options. To preview the choices, press and hold the left mouse button, then drag down the list of choices. Release on the desired option to redraw the chart.

Using 3D Surface charts

For charts with large amounts of data, 3D Surface charts are often quite useful. As shown in figure 31.35, a surface chart connects the data points to form a relief surface. This type of chart is particularly good for identifying specific high and low values over a broad range of data points. When you select 3D Surface from the **C**hart menu, a submenu appears with options to draw the chart as the traditional Surface,

Surface With Sides, or Honeycomb Surface with sculpted honeycomb appearance on the floor of the chart's interior.

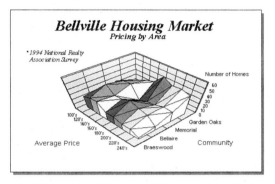

Figure 31.35
Example of 3D surface chart.

Using 3D Scatter charts

3D Scatter Charts exhibit a third axis to show the correlation between three variables rather than two. Unlike the other 3D charts, the data is not spaced evenly along the floor (X and Y axes). Since the data points are floating in space along three dimensions, CorelCHART provides several options for helping gauge the value of any point along the three axes. Tie lines assist your audience in recognizing the value of a data point by drawing a tie line from the marker to reference positions on the data axes.

To control the display of the tie lines, select Tie Lines from the **C**hart menu. From the sub-menu, select to tie the data point to the floor, the left wall, or the right wall on the chart. You can adjust the color of tie lines to any shade on the chart by selecting the tie line and clicking the right mouse button on the color palette. To adjust the line thickness of tie lines, select one of the preset line widths from the Outline Tool fly-out.

Choose Data Point Size from the **C**hart menu to adjust the size of the data markers. From the sub-menu, you can choose from five different sizes. To preview the choices, press and hold the left mouse button, then drag down the list of choices. Release on the desired selection, and the markers are re-drawn accordingly.

To change the marker shape, choose Data Point Shape from the **C**hart menu. From the sub-menu, you can choose from 15 different shapes. To preview the choices, press and hold the left mouse button, then drag down the list of choices. Release on the desired selection, and your markers are redrawn accordingly.

The colors of the data markers can be adjusted by selecting Data Point Color from the **C**hart menu. From the sub-menu, choose Color by Face to make all risers the same color. All risers assume the color of the first marker in the first group. To emphasize the series data, choose Color by Series. To place greater emphasis on the group data, choose Color by Group. You also can choose to color the data points by their distance from either the left wall, the right wall, or the floor of the chart.

Summary

This chapter explored charting options for specialized chart types; charting options for bubble, gantt, hi/lo, histograms and scatter charts charting options for spectral maps; charting options for table charts; charting options for polar and radar charts; and building 3D riser charts. The final chapter on CorelCHART covers formatting, enhancing, and printing charts with CorelCHART.

Chapter 32

Formatting, Enhancing, and Printing Charts

*W*hen designing charts, your goal is to increase the readability and effectiveness of the chart data. The design should enhance the chart's message and make it easy to understand. Every new set of data and each new chart presents a new design challenge.

Use the graphic elements at your disposal—type face, size, style and alignment, design elements such as rule lines and boxes, illustrations, and color choices—to engage the viewer's eye and invite further examination of the chart. As a designer, you know simplicity is best. It's important not to let decoration get in the way of communication. Clean, simple design enhancements give charts integrity and credibility.

This chapter covers:

- Formatting and enhancing charts
- Selecting chart colors
- Special options for formatting axis text
- Special options for formatting legend text
- Annotating with graphic and text objects
- Transferring data between applications
- Printing charts

Formatting and Enhancing Charts

The template used to initially create the chart determines not only the chart type, but many elements of the chart design. CorelCHART's templates specify the size and placement of titles and chart frames, the colors used in the background, the fonts used in the legend, and much more. Of course, you can use the default style established by the templates, but it's more fun to play with colors, lines, and type as you design a charting masterpiece.

This chapter discusses the techniques for formatting chart elements such as titles, backgrounds, and legends. You also find steps for annotating your chart with graphic lines, artwork, and extra blocks of text. If you are familiar with CorelDRAW, you will find many of the commands very similar. The various options for importing and exporting data with CorelCHART are examined to help you transfer graphics and data between CorelCHART and other applications. The chapter concludes with a look at the options and features for previewing and printing your chart files.

Selecting Chart Elements

As with CorelDRAW and other graphic applications, you must select an element before moving, sizing, or formatting it. When you click on the element—title, chart frame, background, legend—a selection box or a series of selection buttons appear around the outside edges. For instance, as displayed in figure 32.1, eight small buttons, called

handles, surround the chart title when selected, while a box surrounds the selected legend text. By default, only one object is selected at a time. To select more than one object, press and hold the Shift key as you click on the other objects.

N O T E

The marquee-select feature found in CorelDRAW is not available in CorelCHART.

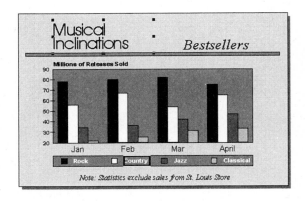

Figure 32.1
Selected objects, such as the "Musical Inclinations" chart title here, appear with a box or handles surrounding the object.

Working with the Chart Frame

CorelCHART places charts in a frame or box. The chart frame controls the size of the chart and axis titles or slice labels. Though you cannot delete this frame, you can adjust the frame size and apply different fill colors and outlines. When you click in the frame, handles appear around the outside of the frame indicating it is selected.

You can enlarge the chart frame to give the chart more dominance, or reduce the frame to make room for another chart or graphics. To size the chart frame, select the frame and then drag one of the handles. Just as with CorelDRAW, drag one of the four corner handles to scale the frame, thereby sizing it proportionally. Dragging one of the middle handles to stretch the frame distorts the original shape. After sizing the frame, chart elements, such as bars and slices, are reduced or enlarged along with any axis titles or slice labels. To move the chart frame, simply press and hold the mouse button on the frame and drag to the desired position. Release the mouse to redraw the frame in its new location.

N O T E

You cannot delete the chart frame; however, you can remove the fill and the outline with the button marked X in the Color Palette to create the same effect visually.

Selecting Chart Colors

As a designer, you know the impact of color cannot be overstated. Red conjures up images of financial danger; blues work to keep the viewer calm; while rich, metallic colors

portray stability and strength. CorelCHART gives you control over the fill and outline color of every chart element. In addition, all of the wonderful fountain and patterned fills found in CorelDRAW are also available in CorelCHART.

Applying Fill and Outline Colors with the Color Palette

The color palette at the bottom of the CorelCHART screen provides quick access to a wide range of colors. To display all of the colors in the palette, click on the button on the right side of the palette marked with an up arrow. Click on the button again to restore the palette to one row of colors.

N O T E

CorelCHART displays the Custom Palette by default. You can select another color model to display in the color palette by choosing Color Palette from the **V**iew menu.

To choose a new fill color for a chart element, select the element and click on the desired color in the color palette. Click on the button marked with an X in the palette to remove the fill of the selected object. To choose a new outline color, select the element and click with the right mouse button on the color in the color palette. Click with the right mouse button on the X button in the palette to remove the outline.

Applying Fills with the Fill Tool

CorelCHART's Fill tool is identical to the one found in CorelDRAW. When you click on the Fill tool (the last tool in the toolbox), the fly-out toolbar appears as shown in figure 32.2. The fill tools are the same as those available in CorelDRAW, with the exception of the Pictograph roll-up tool. The Pictograph tool enables you to select images to be stacked in Pictograph charts. Since the fill tools work just as they do in CorelDRAW, this section provides an overview of using the tools.

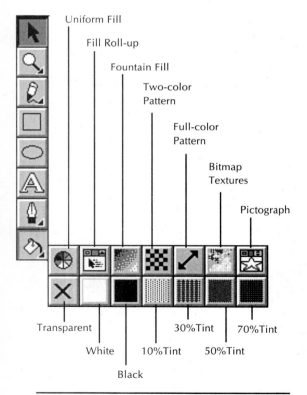

Uniform Fill

Fill Roll-up

Fountain Fill

Two-color Pattern

Full-color Pattern

Bitmap Textures

Pictograph

Transparent

White

Black

10%Tint

30%Tint

50%Tint

70%Tint

Figure 32.2
The Fill Tool fly-out.

CorelDRAW's PostScript Fill tool is not available in CorelCHART.

Applying Solid Fill Colors

When the Color Palette does not offer the specific color you need, use the Fill tool to access more color choices. CorelCHART uses the same color models, such as Pantone and Grayscale, found in CorelDRAW. To apply a solid or uniform fill color, select the object you want to fill and click on the Fill tool. Select the Uniform Fill Color tool (the color wheel on the top row) to display the Uniform Fill dialog box as shown in figure 32.3. Click the down arrow by the Sho<u>w</u> list box and select the desired color model. Click on the desired color in the palette and click OK. The color is applied to the selected object. Use the tools on the bottom row of the Fill Tool fly-out to apply no fill (X), white, black, 10% black, 30% black, 50% black, or 70% black fill.

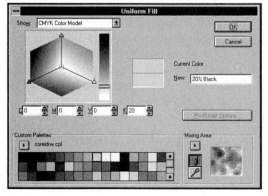

Figure 32.3
The Uniform Fill dialog box.

Applying Fountain Fills

Fountain fills are a great way to enhance chart backgrounds (see fig. 32.4). You can apply fountain fills to almost every chart element including titles, legend text, chart frames, bars, and pie slices. To apply a fountain fill, select the object you wish to fill, and click on the Fill tool. From the fly-out, select the Fountain Fill tool (third on top row) to reveal the Fountain Fill dialog box. Select the fountain type: Linear, Radial, Conical, or Square. Click on the From and To buttons to choose the colors for the fountain fill. Click OK to apply the fill.

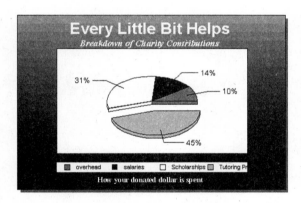

Figure 32.4
Fountain fills create interesting chart backgrounds.

Applying Pattern Fills

Black-and-white pattern fills are useful in bar, area, and pie charts when you don't have access to color (see fig. 32.5). Just as in CorelDRAW, CorelCHART offers two types of pattern fills—two-color and full color. Pattern fills can be applied to most chart elements, such as titles, frames, bars, and pie slices. To apply a pattern fill, select the object you wish to fill and click on the Fill tool. From the fly-out, click on the Two-Color Fill tool (fourth on top row), or the Full Color Fill tool (fifth on top row), to reveal the Pattern Fill dialog boxes. Click on the preview window in the middle of the dialog box to display the available patterns. Select a pattern and click OK to apply the fill.

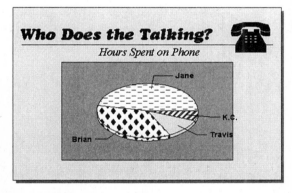

Figure 32.5
Using patterns in black-and-white charts.

Applying Texture Fills

Texture fills add an interesting design touch in charts. Like pattern fills, texture fills can be applied to most chart elements, with the exception of chart text. To apply a texture fill, select the object you wish to fill, and click on the Fill tool. From the fly-out, click on the Bitmap Texture Fill button (sixth on top row) to reveal the Texture Fill dialog box as shown in figure 32.6. Select a texture from the **T**exture List and click on OK.

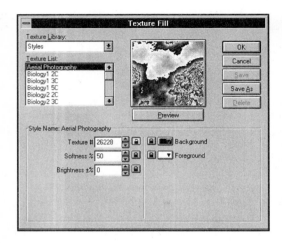

Figure 32.6
The Texture Fill dialog box.

Formatting Outlines with the Outline Tool

CorelCHART places black outlines around many chart elements, such as bars, frames, and legends. You can change the line color, thickness, or remove the line with the Outline tool. CorelCHART's Outline tool works just as it does in CorelDRAW. Click on the Outline tool (the seventh tool in the toolbox), to display the fly-out toolbar as shown in figure 32.7. Because many of the commands for formatting outlines are the same in CorelDRAW, this section provides a basic overview of using the Outline tool.

You cannot apply outlines to chart titles and text in CorelCHART.

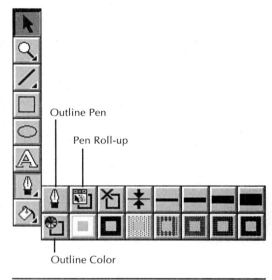

Figure 32.7
The Outline Tool fly-out.

Changing Outline Color

Though you also can apply outline colors with the color palette, the Outline tool offers many more color choices. Click on the Outline Color tool (the color wheel on the top row) in the fly-out to display the Outline Color dialog box. Click the down arrow by the **S**how list box and select the desired color model. Select the color you want in the palette and click OK to apply the outline color to the selected object. The tools in the bottom row of the Outline tool fly-out let you apply white, black, and percentages of black to the outlines.

Changing Outline Thickness

The tools on the top row of the Outline tool fly-out control line thickness. Click on one of the last six tools to apply a pre-set line thickness. You can press and hold the tools to preview the line thickness in the status line at the bottom of the screen. To set a custom line thickness, click on the Outline Pen tool (first tool on top row) in the fly-out. The Outline Pen dialog box as shown in figure 32.8 appears. Enter the desired line thickness in the **W**idth box. Also available in this dialog box are options to change the line colors and dashed line styles. When finished making your line selections, click on OK to apply the outline formatting.

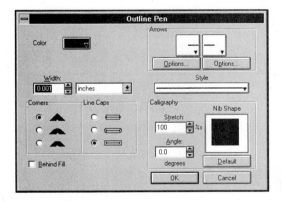

Figure 32.8
The Outline Pen dialog box.

Formatting Chart Text

The placement, size, and style attributes of chart text elements are some of your most important design considerations. Chart titles should catch the viewer's eye, axis titles should facilitate understanding, and legends should clarify chart data. In addition, there will be times when you want to annotate your chart with extra text to really emphasize your message. The tools for formatting text are in the Text Ribbon at the top of the screen (see fig. 32.9).

Two types of text are used in CorelCHART. The main text type is chart text, which is placed on the chart through the Data Manager. Chart text includes chart titles, subtitles, axis titles, and so on. Chart text is created in the Data Manager and tagged for placement in the chart. The second type, annotated text, is placed directly on the chart with the Text tool. Both types can be sized and formatted; however, some chart text, such as the axis scales and titles, cannot be moved. This section details the options for formatting both types of text. Any differences between formatting chart text and annotated text are noted.

N O T E

Applying color to text objects is covered in the previous section, "Selecting Chart Colors." Refer to the next section for steps on creating annotated text.

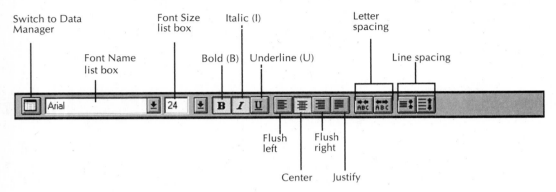

Figure 32.9
Use the text ribbon at the top of the screen to control text attributes such as font and style.

Moving Text Elements

Moving or repositioning text elements enables you to create attractive design effects. For instance, you may want the chart title and subtitle to the left of the chart and the footnote at the bottom. CorelCHART lets you move most chart titles and annotated text; however, you cannot move axes or legend text. To move a text element, select it and then drag the text to the desired location. A four-sided arrow and an outline of the text appears as a reference point as you move text. When you have positioned the outline where you want the text to appear, release the mouse to redraw the text at its new location.

Applying Type Attributes

You can use all of your favorite fonts from CorelDRAW in CorelCHART. To apply a new type face, select the text you want to change, and click the down arrow by the Font list box at the top of the screen. Click on the desired font, and the selected text displays in the new font. To change the type size, select the text, click the down arrow by the Font Size list box and click on the desired size. The maximum font size is 72 points in CorelCHART. If you need larger type, create it in CorelDRAW, then copy and paste it into CorelCHART through the Clipboard. Pasting graphics into CorelCHART is covered later in this chapter.

N O T E

CorelCHART uses an autofit feature that automatically controls the size of axis and legend text. While you can change the type face and style, you cannot adjust the type size until the autofit feature is turned off. Refer to the following section, "Formatting Options for Axis and Legend Text," for more information.

You can add emphasis to text elements by applying type styles such as bold, italics, and underline to text. In the text ribbon, the B button creates bold text, the I button creates italic, and the U creates underlined text. To apply a type style, select the text and click on the appropriate button in the text ribbon. If the button appears "pushed in," the style has already been applied. To remove the style, select the text and click to "pop out" the desired style button.

It is important to note that changing the type face, size or style of any axis text will affect all data on the axis. For example, in figure 32.10, changing the font of the first city on the category axis changes the font of all category data. The same is true for pie slice labels and values; changing the attributes of one affects all others.

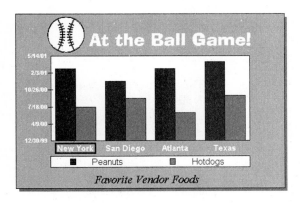

Figure 32.10

Any formatting changes made to axis data affects all data on that axis.

Adjusting Text Alignment

The CorelCHART templates center-align most text elements on the chart. The text alignment can be adjusted to fit your particular chart design needs. For instance, in

figure 32.11, the chart title is left-aligned, the subtitle is right-aligned, and the footnote is centered at the bottom of the chart. The text ribbon includes four buttons for controlling text alignment (see fig. 32.9). Use the first button to set left-aligned text, the second for center-aligned, the third for right-aligned and the last button for justified or "right & left aligned" text.

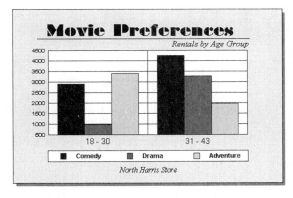

Figure 32.11

The alignment of chart text can be manipulated to suit your needs.

When you select a text element, the button representing the current alignment of the text is "pushed in." For instance, if a center-aligned chart title is selected, the Center Alignment button is pushed in. To change the text alignment, simply click on the desired alignment button to change the alignment of the selected text.

Chart titles are aligned within the area surrounded by the gray selection buttons. Pie slice labels, axis, and legend text are aligned

within the gray selection box. For example, when axis or legend text is selected, a gray box appears. The text can be left-, center-, or right-aligned within this gray box. If you change the alignment of any axis or legend text, all other axis or legend text also is changed.

At times you may find it necessary to resize the text block that contains your text. For instance, if you decrease the width of the title text block, the text will wrap around to create a multiple-line or stacked heading. You can stretch a multiple line text block into a single line by widening the text block. To size a text block, select it and then drag on one of the selection buttons. Use the corner buttons to scale the text block proportionally, and the inside buttons to stretch the text block into a different shape. The text wraps into the newly sized box.

Adjusting Letter Spacing

You can create unique text styles by adjusting the spacing between the letters or characters in your text elements. To decrease letter spacing, select the text element you want to adjust, and click on the Decrease Spacing button in the text ribbon (see fig 32.9). Each time you click on the button, the space between the characters is decreased, bringing the characters closer together. To increase letter spacing, select the text element and click on the Increase Spacing button. Again, each click increases the space between characters spreading them out across the chart. You cannot adjust the letter spacing in axis text, pie labels, or legend text.

Adjusting Line Spacing

When text blocks include several lines of text, you can adjust the spacing between the lines. To decrease the line spacing, select the text you want to adjust, and click on the Decrease Line Spacing button (see fig. 32.9). Each time you click on the button, the line spacing is reduced slightly. To increase the line spacing, select the text and click on the Increase Line Spacing button. Each click increases the line spacing slightly.

Special Options for Formatting Axis Text

CorelCHART provides two unique options for formatting the axis text in XY charts. These options, Autofit and Stagger, can be applied to the axis text in XY charts such as bar, line, area, scatter, histograms, and spectral maps. Many of the chart types refer to the XY axes by different names. For example, in bar, line, and area charts, the axes are called Category and Data. In histograms, the axes are called Interval and Data. Refer to the Chapters 30 and 31 for more information about axis names.

Working with Autofit

CorelCHART uses a feature called Autofit to control the size of axis text. The Autofit feature determines the "best size" for the text to prevent any overlapping. The size of axis text is proportional to the length of the axis text block. For example, longer axis text appears in smaller type to avoid overlap. The size of the chart frame also affects the size of the axis text. If you enlarge the chart frame, the axis text is also enlarged. You must turn off the Autofit feature if you want to adjust the size of the axis text without sizing the chart frame. For example, in figure 32.12, Autofit is turned off so the text on the category axis can be enlarged, making it more prominent on the chart.

Staggering Axis Text

CorelCHART lets you stagger axis text to alternate the text as shown in figure 32.13. Staggering axis text is particularly useful with longer axis text blocks because you can increase the type size to emphasize the data, and stagger them to prevent any text overlap.

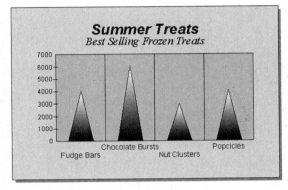

Figure 32.13

Staggering axis text prevents text overlap.

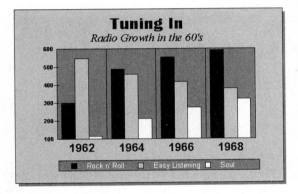

Figure 32.12

You must turn off Autofit before manually sizing axis text.

To turn off Autofit, select the name of the axis text you want to size from the Chart menu. From the sub-menu, select Autofitted Scale or Autofitted Text. Clicking on the Autofit command removes the check mark and turns off the feature. Click again to turn Autofit back on. For example, in a bar chart, you could choose Category Axis from the Chart menu and turn Autofit off to manually size the text on the category axis.

To stagger axis text, select the name of the axis text you want to stagger from the Chart menu. From the sub-menu, click on Staggered Scale or Staggered Text. As an example, in a line chart you could choose Data Axis from the Chart menu and select Staggered Scale to stagger the data on the Data axis.

Special Options for Formatting Legend Text

A descriptive, easy-to-read legend goes a long way in effectively communicating a chart's message. In figure 32.14, the legend is stacked vertically and used as a graphic element, adding some pizzazz to the chart. By default, the CorelCHART templates place the legend at the bottom of the chart and automatically size the legend text to prevent any text overlap. When the default placement and sizing are not quite what you want, you can move, size, and adjust the legend to create the effect you need. Keep in mind it may take several steps to get the legend exactly as you want it.

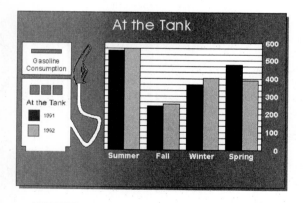

Figure 32.14

You have many options for formatting the legend in CorelCHART.

Moving and Sizing the Legend

The legend box can be moved and sized just like any other graphic object. When you select the legend box, make sure you select the box and not the legend text. Selection buttons appear around the box when it is selected. To move the legend, place your mouse inside the legend box and drag it to the desired location. Size the legend by dragging on one of the corner handles until you reach the desired size. Sizing the legend can change the orientation of the legend text and markers. For instance, increasing the height and decreasing the width of the legend box causes the markers to line up vertically (see fig. 32.14) instead of horizontally.

Removing the Legend

Pie charts and some simple bar, line, and area charts may not need a legend to explain the chart data. For instance, in figure 32.15, there is only one series of bars, and the chart titles explain and inform the viewer of all the necessary details. Pie charts are another example where legends might not be used. Instead of a legend, the labels and values are placed around the pie. Refer to Chapter 30 for information on displaying pie labels and bar values.

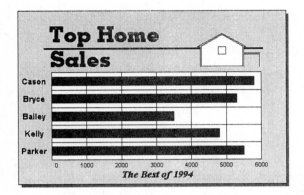

Figure 32.15
Simple charts may not require a legend.

To turn off the legend display, select Legend from the **C**hart menu or click on the Legend button in the ribbon bar. The Legend dialog box appears as displayed in figure 32.16. Click on the Display Legend option to remove the X. Click on OK and the legend is removed from the chart display.

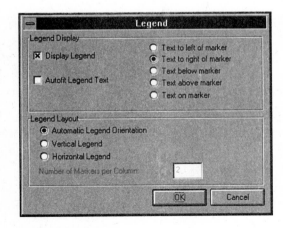

Figure 32.16
The Legend dialog box.

Working with Autofit

CorelCHART's autofit feature automatically sizes the legend text and prevents any overlap. If you wish to enlarge or reduce the text size, you first need to turn Autofit off. For example, in figure 32.17, Autofit was turned off so that the legend text could be enlarged, adding to the overall design of the chart.

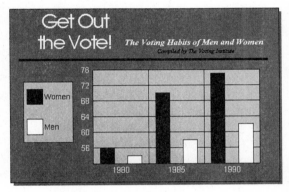

Figure 32.17
You must turn off Autofit before manually sizing legend text.

To turn Autofit off, select Legend from the **C**hart menu or click on the Legend button. In the Legend dialog box, click on the Autofit Legend Text option to remove the X in the text box. Click on OK and now you can adjust the size of the legend text with the Font Size list box on the text ribbon.

Adjusting Legend Text Placement and Legend Layout

CorelCHART gives you control over the orientation of the legend and placement of the legend text and markers. In figure 32.17, the legend is vertically aligned with the text placed to the right of the legend markers. By default, CorelCHART horizontally aligns legends, placing text to the right of the marker. However, you can place the text to the left, above, or below the markers. After adjusting the placement, you can use the alignment buttons to position the text exactly where you want it.

To change the legend orientation, select Legend from the **C**hart menu or click on the Legend button. Under Legend Layout at the bottom of the dialog box, select Horizontal or Vertical Legend. Enter a number in the Number of Markers per column text box to determine how many markers are stacked in the legend. For instance, in a chart with four data series, you could enter 2 to create two columns of legend markers. You could also enter 4 to stack all four legend markers in one column.

To adjust the placement of the legend text, click on one of the options for positioning legend text around the markers on the right side of the dialog box. For instance, click on Text below Marker to place the legend text below the legend marker. When you are finished modifying legend options, click on OK to observe the changes.

Annotating with Graphic and Text Objects

Once you have established the basic structure and appearance of your chart, you can personalize your chart by adding graphics and extra text. For example, you may want to add a company logo, or a string of text that highlights an increase in sales. Added text and graphics, such as boxes, circles, and arrows are called *annotations*. Annotated graphics and text are created on top of your chart, rather than in the chart's Data Manager. Figure 32.18 shows a chart about power usage embellished with added text and artwork.

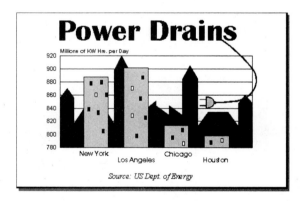

Figure 32.18
Use graphic objects to further explain and emphasize chart data when needed.

You create annotations using the Pencil tool, the Rectangle tool, the Circle tool, and the Text tool, all located on the toolbar (see fig. 32.19). You can also bring in graphic elements from CorelDRAW and other graphic programs to annotate your chart. Sharing data between applications and importing and exporting data is later in this chapter.

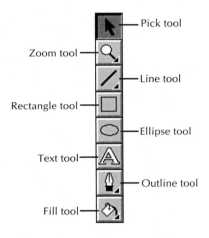

Pick tool

Zoom tool

Line tool

Rectangle tool

Ellipse tool

Text tool

Outline tool

Fill tool

Figure 32.19
The CorelCHART toolbox.

Adding Annotated Text

The Text tool (the letter A) is used to add text annotations to your chart. Unlike other chart text such as titles or axis text, annotated text is not linked to the Data Manager. Annotated text is added as an independent element on top of the chart, and is free to be manipulated separately from all other chart elements. Annotated text is created and edited in the Chart View.

To add annotated text to a chart, select the Text tool (see fig. 32.19). When you bring the cursor onto the chart, it will change to a crosshair. Press and hold the mouse to draw a box representing the width of the text block you want to add. When you release the mouse, you can begin typing at the insertion point at the top of the text box. The box establishes the left and right boundaries of the annotated text. As you continue to type, the box depth grows to accommodate all of your text. When you are finished typing, select the Pointer tool to move the text string. Annotated text appears in the most recently selected type face and type size. For instance, if you format the title to display in 24-point Times New Roman, and then add annotated text, it appears in 24-point Times New Roman. Use the formatting commands described in the previous sections to change the type face, size, and style.

N O T E

Instead of dragging a box to create the boundaries for annotated text, you can select the Text tool and just click where you want to begin typing on the chart. However, since there are no defined left and right boundaries, you have to press enter to wrap the text to the next line.

Adding Annotated Graphic Objects

Using CorelCHART's drawing tools you can enhance your charts with lines, curves, rectangles, and ellipses. These annotated

objects can be cut, copied, and pasted from one chart file to another. Any graphic object you draw automatically is assigned the current default fill and outline attributes such as color and line thickness. Refer to the sections on changing fills and outline for information on formatting annotated graphic objects.

Drawing Lines and Curves

To use the Pencil (or Line) tool, click and hold the mouse to reveal a flyout toolbar with three drawing options (see fig. 32.20). The first tool, the default, is used for freehand drawing. To draw freehand curves, select the Freehand drawing tool (the pencil), and position the crosshair where you want to begin the line. Click and hold the left mouse button down while you drag. Release the mouse button to end the freehand line.

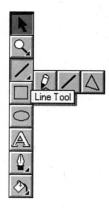

Figure 32.20
The Pencil (or Line) Tool fly-out.

The second drawing tool draws straight and diagonal lines. To draw lines, select the Straight Line tool, and place the crosshair where you want to begin the line. Press and hold with the left mouse button, drag to where you want to end the line, and release the mouse. Hold the Ctrl key while drawing a line to create perfectly vertical or horizontal lines. Be sure to release the mouse *before* the Ctrl key.

The third drawing tool draws closed polygon shapes. To draw a polygon, select the Polygon tool, and move to where you want to begin the polygon. Click and release the mouse button, move to another location and click again. Continue this process to establish the desired outline for your polygon, then double-click to finish the shape. When you double-click, a line connects the beginning and the ending point to create a closed shape.

Drawing Rectangles and Ellipses

Use the Rectangle and Ellipse tools to add rectangles, squares, ellipses, and circles to your charts. To draw a rectangle or ellipse, select the desired tool, then click and drag the mouse at an angle. When you have defined the desired shape, release the mouse. To draw perfect squares or circles, hold down the Ctrl key while you draw with the Rectangle or Ellipse tool. Be sure to release the mouse *before* the Ctrl key. Hold down the Shift key while you draw with the Rectangle or Ellipse tool to draw your shape from the inside out rather than from one anchor point to another. You can draw perfect squares or circles from the inside out by holding down the Ctrl and Shift keys while you draw.

Moving, Scaling, and Stretching Graphic Annotations

CorelCHART gives you control over the size, shape, and position of all annotated graphic objects. To move an object, select the line, rectangle, or ellipse you want to move, and drag to the desired position. When you hold down the Ctrl key while moving objects, CorelCHART constrains the movement to horizontal or vertical, based on the direction you move first. Be sure to release the mouse *before* the Ctrl key.

To size an object, select the object and drag on one of the selection buttons. Use an object's corner selection buttons to scale the object proportionally. If you hold down the Shift key while you scale, the object scales from the inside out, or in all directions at once. To change an object's proportions or "stretch" an object to a new shape, drag on any of the four interior selection handles and drag. When the object's outline is the desired shape, release the mouse to redraw the object. You can also use the Shift key while dragging to stretch the object from the inside out.

Transferring Data between Applications

You can place charts designed in CorelCHART in other applications, such as a desktop publishing or a word processing program. For instance, when designing an annual report, you can include charts depicting the company profits and losses. In addition, bringing graphics created in other applications (such as CorelDRAW) into CorelCHART is a great way to enhance a chart. CorelCHART provides several methods for sharing data with other applications—drag-and-drop, copying and pasting through the Windows Clipboard, and importing and exporting files. The following sections explore the different ways of transferring data between CorelCHART and other applications.

Copying Charts to Other Applications

To copy a chart into another Windows application, select Copy Chart from the Edit menu. This command copies all chart elements including the background to the Windows Clipboard so you can paste the chart into another Windows application. The Copy Chart command is a great way to place a chart file into another Corel application, such as MOVE or SHOW. CorelCHART supports Object Linking and Embedding (OLE) which provides options for updating the chart after you have pasted it into another program.

> **NOTE**
>
> Object Linking and Embedding is a powerful way to share data between all Corel applications. For more information on OLE, refer to your Corel software manual.

Drag-and-Drop

The quickest way to place a CorelCHART file into another program is to drag-and-drop. This feature lets you drag a chart from the CorelCHART application window and drop it into another application window. You can drag and drop a whole chart but not its individual parts into other applications. Drag-and-drop creates an embedded object in the receiving or client application. Not all Windows applications can receive charts in this manner. Check the applications documentation for information on OLE. The following steps illustrate how to drag and drop a chart from CorelCHART into CorelDRAW.

1. Size the CorelCHART Chart View window and the CorelDRAW window so that you can see both on your computer screen (see fig. 32.21).

2. Click and hold the mouse button anywhere in the chart in the Chart View.

3. Move or "drag" the pointer from the Chart View window to the CorelDRAW window.

4. When the cursor becomes a blinking white arrow with a small rectangle underneath, release the mouse button to "drop" the data into the CorelDRAW window.

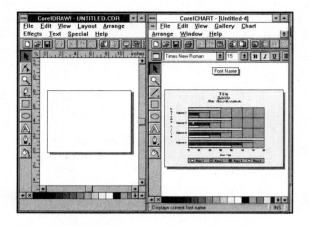

Figure 32.21
Use the drag-and-drop method to quickly transfer a chart into CorelDRAW.

Using Cut, Copy, and Paste to Transfer Data

One of the advantages of working in the Windows environment is the capability to share data between applications. Think of sharing or transferring data between applications as a two-way street. You can transfer charts from CorelCHART in other applications, such as Corel Ventura or CorelSHOW. You can also transfer graphics from CorelDRAW or CorelPHOTO-PAINT into CorelCHART through the Clipboard.

The Cut, Copy, and Paste commands work almost like they do in other Windows applications. The Cut or Copy command is used to place selected object(s) on the Windows Clipboard. The Paste command is used to place the Clipboard objects into another chart or different Windows application. As displayed in figure 32.22, the CorelCHART ribbon bar provides buttons for cutting, copying, and pasting data. There is one difference with CorelCHART. Only annotated text and objects can be cut or copied to the Clipboard. This means you cannot select the chart frame or chart title and copy it. However, you can cut or copy objects drawn with the graphic tools or text entered with the Text tool.

N . O . T . E

Data can be copied from the Data Manager in one chart file to the Data Manager in another. Refer to Chapter 29 for more information on working with the Data Manager.

To copy annotated text or objects from one CorelCHART file to another, select the object and choose **C**opy from the **E**dit menu or click on the Copy button. Switch to the file in which you want to place the objects and choose **P**aste from the **E**dit menu or click on the Paste button. This same process

is used to transfer graphics or data from another Windows application such as CorelDRAW. After creating and selecting the objects in CorelDRAW, use the Cu**t** or **C**opy command to send it to the Clipboard. Switch to CorelCHART and open the file in which you want the objects pasted. From the **E**dit menu, select **P**aste to place the objects into a chart file. Pasted objects can be moved and sized. However, you cannot change any object attributes, such as colors or fonts. If you need to alter an object after it has been pasted in CorelCHART, return to the program in which you originally created the object, make the changes, and then repeat the steps for copying and pasting the object back into CorelCHART.

For special effects, you might try the Paste Inside command to paste graphics into the chart frame as shown in figure 32.23. After copying the desired graphic to the Clipboard, select the chart frame and choose Paste **I**nside from the **E**dit menu. The Paste Inside command replaces the chart frame with the pasted graphic. It's important to note the pasted graphic will be distorted to fit the frame size.

Cut   Paste

Copy

Figure 32.22
The Cut, Copy, and Paste buttons in the ribbon bar.

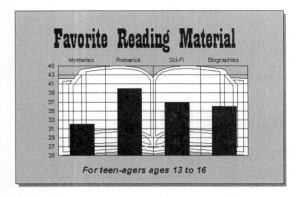

Figure 32.23

The Paste Inside command lets you paste graphics inside the chart frame.

Importing Graphics

CorelCHART's import function in Chart View gives you access to graphics created by other illustration and presentation programs, as well as clip art and scanned images. CorelCHART has the capability to import most popular graphic formats, such as CGM and EPS. As an example, you could import a scanned map into a CorelCHART file. The following steps illustrate importing a .TIF scanned image.

1. Select **I**mport from the **F**ile menu or click on the Import Data button on the ribbon bar. The Import dialog box appears as displayed in figure 32.24.

2. Click on the down arrow by List Files of **T**ype and choose TIFF Bitmap.

3. Change to the drive and directory where the file you want to import is located.

4. In the File **N**ame box, select the file you want to import and click on OK. The imported TIF file can be moved as desired.

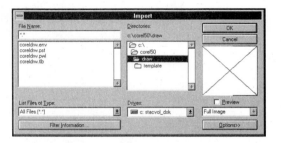

Figure 32.24

The Import dialog box.

CorelCHART's Import and Export feature works the same as in CorelDRAW. Refer to the section on exporting in the CorelDRAW section of this book for more information.

Exporting Charts

CorelCHART's Export feature saves the chart file in a file format that other programs can read. *File format* refers to the way in which a graphic is stored in a computer file. CorelCHART exports to all popular graphic file formats. Refer to the documentation for the application into which you want to import the chart for a listing of available import formats. For instance, you can export the chart to a Windows Metafile (.WMF) file and then import the WMF into another application such as Aldus PageMaker or Quark XPress. The following list illustrates the steps for exporting a CorelCHART file into the Windows Metafile format.

1. Select **E**xport from the **F**ile menu or click on the Export Data button on the ribbon bar. The Export dialog box as displayed in figure 32.25 appears.

2. Click on the down arrow by List Files of **T**ype and choose Windows Metafile.

3. Change to the drive and directory where you want to save the exported file.

4. In the File **N**ame box, enter a file name for the exported data. CorelCHART automatically adds the correct file extension, such as WMF for Windows Metafiles. Click on OK and the export file is created.

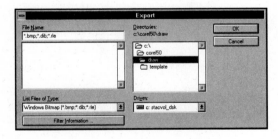

Figure 32.25
The Export dialog box.

Printing Charts

Graphic designers know the hard work put into designing graphics doesn't amount to much until it's printed and all the world can stand in awe of your talent. Printing, of course, is the culmination of all your creative labors. There are two things that direct the process of printing your charts. The first consideration is the type of media for your finished piece. Are you creating a 35mm slide, 4 × 5 film, or a black-and-white overhead transparency? Second, is the printing being done in-house, or are the chart files being sent to a service bureau for high-resolution output? The answers to these questions determine how you proceed through the printing process. For example, if your final output is an overhead transparency printed on the Laserwriter at your desk, you manage the whole print job yourself. If the final output is a 35mm slide, you might send the file to a service bureau where they direct the printing.

This section covers the basic printing features and options for printing charts in CorelCHART. The options for printing chart data in the Data Manager are detailed in Chapter 29. Because most of the printing features in CorelCHART are identical to CorelDRAW, they are also discussed in the CorelDRAW section of this book. Refer to that chapter for more detailed information on topics such as color calibration and creating color separations.

Designing in color when the output device is black-and-white can be frustrating because the conversion from color to black and white is unpredictable. You are better off working with shades of gray when designing your charts to ensure that "what you see is really what you get."

Setting Up the Printer

It's always smart to check the printer setup before printing to determine if the right printer, orientation, and paper size are selected. Like all Windows applications, CorelCHART uses the printer drivers installed when you loaded Windows. To select a printer, choose P**r**int **S**etup from the **F**ile menu. The Print Setup dialog box appears as shown in figure 32.26 displaying the current printer. If you want to print to another device, click on the down arrow by the printer name. Select the desired printing device from the list of available printers. Click on the Setup button to display a dialog box with options for controlling page orientation and paper size. Click on OK in the setup dialog box to return to the Printer Setup dialog box. Click on OK again to set up the specified printer.

Figure 32.26
The Print Setup dialog box.

Printing Charts

To print a chart, open the file you want to print in the Chart View and select **P**rint from the **F**ile menu or click on the Print button. The Print dialog box appears as shown in figure 32.27. You only can print one chart file at a time in CorelCHART, so the options, **A**ll, C**u**rrent Page and S**e**lected Objects, produces the same output—one printed chart. You cannot print selected objects only in CorelCHART.

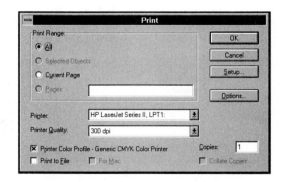

Figure 32.27
The Print dialog box.

N O T E

Because you can only print one file at a time in CorelCHART, you might find it easier to insert the charts into a CorelSHOW presentation, and then print the presentation.

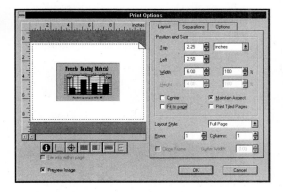

Figure 32.28
The Print Options dialog box.

CorelCHART can print up to 999 copies of your file. To change the number of copies, simply enter the desired number of copies in the **C**opies text box. If you are sending the chart file to be output at a service bureau, you may need to click on the Print to **F**ile option to create a print file.

To preview the chart before printing, click on the **O**ptions button. The Print Options dialog box, as shown in figure 32.28, appears with a preview of your chart file. This dialog box contains the options for adjusting the print image, such as Center and Fit to Page. At the top of the dialog box, click on the tabs marked Separations and Options to create color separations and control. Click on OK to return to the Print dialog box. After selecting the desired print options, click on OK to print the chart file. A status bar indicates the progress of the print job. Click on the Cancel button to terminate the print job.

Summary

This chapter examined formatting and enhancing charts; selecting chart colors; formatting chart text; special options for formatting axis text; special options for formatting legend text; annotating with graphic and text objects; transferring data between applications; and printing charts.

The next section covers creating animations and presentations with CorelSHOW and CorelMOVE.

Part

Creating
Presentations

Understanding CorelMOVE Basics

CorelMOVE is an application designed to create animation movies with movement and sound. Don't let the perception of cartoon animation fool you; animation is much more than singing chipmunks. In a business environment, animation is integral to powerful sales and marketing presentations. CorelMOVE animation files are built from graphics designed in CorelDRAW, photographs spruced up in CorelPHOTO-PAINT and charts created in CorelCHART.

For example, your presentation could include logos and technical illustrations, photographs of new products, and bar charts documenting the latest sales increase. With CorelMOVE, you can even throw in some videotaped footage with sound effects to really blow them away! Your multimedia extravaganza can then be projected onto a big screen for presentation, or transferred to videotape for mass distribution.

This chapter covers:

- Understanding how animation works in CorelMOVE

- Working with actors and props

- CorelMOVE basics—opening and playing animation files

- Creating new animation files

Understanding How Animation Works in CorelMOVE

With CorelMOVE, you can bring your graphics to life! Instead of just drawing a bird in the sky, you can have the bird *fly* across the sky. With CorelMOVE, an eight-ball can roll across the pool table and spurts of oil can gush out of a well. In addition, you can add sound to your animated graphics. Imagine a pop just as a balloon bursts, or the roar of a saxophone as the instrument rocks on the screen. The animation capability of CorelMOVE places you in the arena of multimedia, where you can illustrate, animate, and add sound to your graphic designs.

CorelMOVE simulates the traditional frame-by-frame animation process. Remember the old cartoon books where you would thumb quickly through the pages to make the cartoon figure move and dance around? On each page, the figure is moved slightly so that when the pages are flipped through rapidly, the images create the illusion of movement.

Basically, this same concept is used to create animations in CorelMOVE. Instead of placing figures on pages, CorelMOVE places actors and props on frames. On each frame, the "actors" and "props" are manipulated so that when the frames are displayed in rapid succession, the objects appear to move. The changes can be subtle to produce fluid and

smooth movement. For instance, you can place a drawing of a boat on the left side of the first frame of the animation. The boat can then be moved slightly to the right on each of the next twenty frames. When the frames are played back quickly, the boat appears to sail across the screen.

This chapter examines how animation works in CorelMOVE. Animation objects—actors, props, and sounds—are discussed to help you understand their role in the animation process. The steps for opening and playing animation files are covered here. You will also find the steps for creating and defining new animation files, such as sizing the animation area, adjusting the number of frames, and controlling the animation playback speed. After learning the basics of playing and setting up animation movies covered in this chapter, refer to the next chapters for the steps to build animation movies with props, actors, video, and sound effects.

Working with Actors and Props

It's not surprising that the terms "actors" and "props" are borrowed from the theater. In stage productions, actors move across the stage while the props create an environment with scenery and backdrop elements. In CorelMOVE, actors also move across the screen, while props remain stationary to establish the scene and provide a reference point for the actors to move against. For instance, in figure 33.1, the fish is an actor, and the water, rocks, and plants are the props. The fish can be animated to "swim" in the water past the rocks and plants. You might even bring in another actor, such as a worm, for the fish to chase.

Figure 33.1
Placing the fish as an actor allows you to move the fish across the screen. The "water" background can be placed as a prop since it remains stationary in the animation.

Understanding Actors

Actors "move" in the animation. For instance, an actor might be a kangaroo jumping across the screen, or a chair that rocks back and forth. There are basically two ways to animate actors. The first way is to add *movement* in the form of a "path." An actor's path is a route the actor follows to get from point A to point B. For instance, a path can direct a car to pull up to a gas station or, as displayed in figure 33.2, the path leads the airplane's flight across the screen.

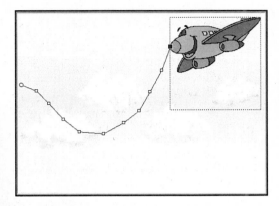

Figure 33.2
Creating a "path" for an actor lets you add movement to your animation.

The second way to animate an actor is through *motion*, where the shape or size of the actor is changed. For instance, you might want a bird to flap its wings up and down, or a car's hood to pop open. Generally, you will want to combine actor movement on a path with actor motion for the best effect.

For instance, a bird flapping its wings would illustrate actor motion, while the path the bird follows across the screen would be the actor's movement. Thus, combining movement and motion would create a bird that flaps its wings as it flies across the screen.

In a business presentation, an actor might be a briefcase opening to reveal a cellular telephone or an electrical current that moves along power lines. Creating actors and paths is covered in Chapter 34, "Animating with Props and Actors."

Understanding Props

Props cannot move along a path or change shape and size from one frame to the next in your animation. Because props are essentially motionless objects, they are often used to represent background elements, such as furniture, trees, and horizons in your animations. For instance, in an animation of a car race, the race track could be the prop. In a business presentation, objects that you do not want to move, such as charts, maps, and photographs, can be placed as props.

Although props cannot have movement or motion, they can "appear" on-screen in a variety of transition effects, such as zooms, scrolls, and fades. For instance, you might have a pie chart zoom in from the bottom of the screen and zoom out at the top of the screen. Prop transitions are also great for designing opening sequences with company logos that fly and dance across the screen. Creating props is covered in Chapter 34.

Opening and Playing Animation Files

Before designing a new animation, it is a good idea to preview and tinker with an existing animation, such as one of the sample animations supplied with Corel. Playing and previewing a finished animation gives you a feel for how the whole animation process

comes together. This section covers some basics of using CorelMOVE, such as starting the application, as well as opening and playing animation movies.

Starting CorelMOVE

CorelMOVE is a separate program included with CorelDRAW. To start CorelMOVE, open the Corel 5 group window and double-click on the CorelMOVE icon. The initial MOVE screen appears with all of the elements grayed out except for the File and Help menus. From this blank screen, you can start a new animation or open an existing animation.

Opening an Existing Animation File

To open an existing animation file, select **O**pen from the **F**ile menu. The Open Animation File dialog box appears, as displayed in figure 33.3. If necessary, change to the drive and directory where the animation files are stored. If you installed CorelMOVE's sample files, you will find a sample animation file in the COREL50\MOVE\SAMPLES directory. If you cannot locate the SAMPLE directory, you will have to reinstall Corel 5.0, and choose to install CorelMOVE's sample files. Refer to your Corel documentation for more information on installing Corel. If you installed Corel from the CD-ROM, you will find several other animation files available on Disc 2.

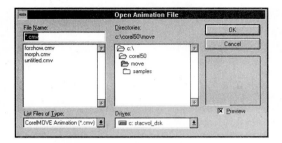

Figure 33.3
The Open Animation File dialog box.

The CorelMOVE files located in the specified directory appear in the File **N**ame box. CorelMOVE files have the file extension .CMV. Click once on a file name to display a preview of the first frame in the animation. (The preview box displays the first frame of the animation.) Click on OK or double-click on the file name to open the animation.

N O T E

If there are no objects placed on the first frame of the animation, the preview box in the Open dialog box will appear empty.

T I P

You can use the keyboard shortcut Ctrl+O to display the Open Animation File dialog box. In addition, CorelMOVE places the name of the four most recently opened animation files in a list at the bottom of the File menu. Clicking on the file name is a quick way to open a file.

Exploring the CorelMOVE Screen

After opening an animation file, the center of the CorelMOVE screen displays the first frame of the animation. The frame is called the *window area*—this is where you design the animation by placing actors and props and defining paths. As displayed in figure 33.4, the CorelMOVE screen includes various tools and roll-ups for creating and designing animations. Table 33.1 provides a description of the tools along the left side of the screen.

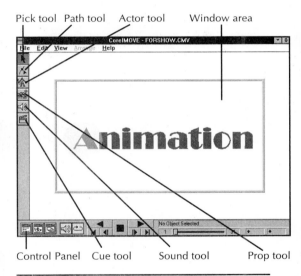

Figure 33.4
The CorelMOVE main screen.

Table 33.1
CorelMOVE's Toolbox

Tool	Used For
Pick tool	Selecting objects, similar to the Pick tool in CorelDRAW.
Path tool	Opening the Path Edit roll-up; used to create, shape, and delete actor paths.
Actor tool	Creating new actors for the animation.
Prop tool	Creating new props for the animation.
Sound tool	Creating new sounds.
Cue tool	Creating new cues.

T I P

To create a "floating" toolbox that you can move around on the screen, select **F**loating from the Toolbox command in the **V**iew menu. For an even quicker response, double-click on the bottom of the toolbox while holding down the Shift key.

Located at the bottom of the screen is CorelMOVE's Control Panel. Here, you will find controls for playing the animation, as well as access to several important functions such as the Timeline, Library, and Cel Sequencer roll-ups (refer to Chapter 35, "Advanced Animation Features," for information on working with these features).

The Sound and Loop buttons, along with the Frame counter, also appear on the Control Panel. The Sound button turns on or off any sound you may have added to the animation.

You can use the Loop button to repeat the entire application over and over again. The Frame counter displays the number of the frame currently being viewed on the left and the total number of frames on the right. You can view other frames in the animation by dragging the slide control to the left or right in the Frame counter. Release when the number of the frame you want to view appears on the left.

Playing Animation Files

The Control Panel includes playback controls that resemble those on a CD player (see fig. 33.5). Click on the Play Forward button to play the animation. If the Loop button is pushed in, the animation will continue to repeat itself until you click on the Stop Animation button. Disable the loop feature to play the animation and stop. Click on the Play Reverse button to play the animation in reverse.

To quickly return to the first frame of the animation, click on the Rewind to Start button. To jump to the last frame of the animation, click on the Fast Forward to End button. Use the Step Frame Forward and Step Frame Reverse buttons to move forward or backward in the animation one frame at a time. If the animation includes sound, you can turn the sound on and off by clicking on the Sound button.

Rewind to Start Play Review   End Frame
Library button   Play Forward   Start Frame
        Sound   Fast Forward to End
        button   Stop   Status Line

Timelines   Step Frame   Frame counter
button   Forward
Cel Sequencer   Step Frame   Slide control
button   Reverse
              Loop button

Figure 33.5
The Animation Playback controls in the Control Panel.

N O T E

Animation files can be quite large. Playing lengthy, complex animation files requires a lot of memory. A minimum of 16MB is suggested when working with CorelMOVE, and more is even better!

To see all of the animation objects and tools in action, open the sample animation file supplied with the Corel software. If you included the sample CorelMOVE files during installation, there is a sample CorelMOVE file named "Sample.CMV" in

the C:\COREL50\MOVE\SAMPLES directory. After opening the file, the first frame appears in the animation window, as shown in figure 33.6. Click on the Play button to play the animation. The Dollar Bill man is the actor, with the desk and picture as the background props.

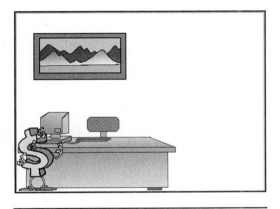

Figure 33.6
The first frame of the Sample.CMV file.

Notice the bullets and text are also props that enter the animation at different times. A quick look at the frame counter indicates there are 80 frames. If the animation keeps playing, click on the Stop button and click on the Loop button to disable the repeat feature. Click on the Rewind to Start button to return to frame one. This time, click several times on the Step Forward button to watch the actor move slightly in each frame.

Notice in frame nine, the first bullet prop enters the animation. Click on the Fast Forward to End button to display frame 80. Another way to move through the frames is to drag on the slider in the Frame counter. Place the mouse pointer on the slider and drag to the left or right until the number of

the frame you want to display appears on the left. Its amazing how it all comes together, isnt it? Next, you'll find the steps for creating your own animation.

Creating New Animation Files

When designing new animations, there are several things to consider before you begin transitioning props, creating paths, and adding sound. For instance, you need to establish the frame size, frame speed, and number of frames. This section discusses the steps for starting a new animation file and then "setting it up" so you are ready to proceed with the art of animating.

Starting a New Animation File

To start a new animation file, select **N**ew from the **F**ile menu. The Select Name For New File dialog box appears, as displayed in figure 33.7. CorelMOVE asks you to name and save the file before beginning to design the animation. This is not a bad idea—animation files can become quite complex, and you certainly do not want to lose anything because you forgot to save.

Enter a name for the animation file in the File **N**ame box, and change to the drive and directory where you want to save the file. If you do not enter a name, CorelMOVE will

assign the name Untitled.CMV. Click on OK to save the file. CorelMOVE displays the animation area with the file name in the title bar across the top. The file name extension .CMV is automatically added.

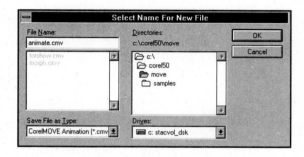

Figure 33.7
The Select Name For New File dialog box.

Setting Up the Animation

New animations contain 100 frames in the default frame size (see fig. 33.8). In addition, the Sound and Loop features in the Control Panel are enabled. While you can change these defaults at any time, it's a good idea to establish some parameters for your new animation in the beginning. For instance, there's no need to continually play through 100 frames if you are designing a "quickie" animation that only requires 25 frames. The frame size is also important because it determines how much room you have to place actors and props.

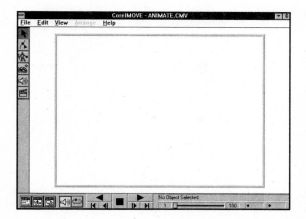

Figure 33.8

A new animation frame with the default frame window size and number of frames.

To set up the animation, select Animation Info... from the **E**dit menu. The Animation Information dialog box appears, as displayed in figure 33.9. The values at the top of the dialog box indicate how many actors, props, sounds, and cues are currently in the animation. These values will change as you add and delete objects in your animation.

Sizing the Animation Window

Especially important in the initial setup of any animation is the animation window size. The animation window is measured in pixels. *Pixel* is short for *picture element*, a unit of measurement that literally means picture cell. Your visual display is made up of rows and columns of tiny dots, or cells, each of which is a pixel. The resolution of the picture is expressed by the number of pixels in the display. For example, 1,024 pixels in width by 768 pixels in height is a much sharper picture than 640 × 480 because it has more

pixels to display any given image. The default window size is 480 × 360, though you can enlarge the animation window to any size up to 1,500 pixels horizontally and vertically.

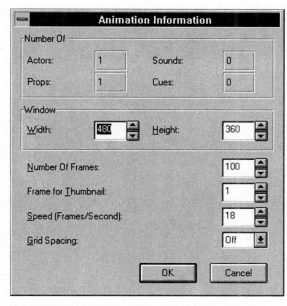

Figure 33.9

The Animation Information dialog box.

You should consider two major things when sizing the animation window. First, what type of unit is the animation intended to be played upon? For example, if you intend to play back the animation on a display that has a maximum display resolution of 640 × 480, then you should not set up the original animation window for 800 × 600. Doing so would give you a sharper image, but much of the window would be cut off because the animation display area exceeds the display unit's capacity. The bottom line is you should always exercise caution when you are designing the animation on one computer,

but playing it back on another. The second major consideration when setting up the size of the animation window is file size. The larger the animation window, the larger the file. CorelMOVE's animation window size is purposely kept small to reduce file size.

Most electronic display units, including your monitor, data display panels, and CRT projection devices, display in a standard 4 (horizontal width) to 3 (vertical height) ratio. The following resolutions meet this 4 to 3 ratio:

- 320 × 200
- 480 × 360
- 640 × 480
- 800 × 600
- 1024 × 768

Your monitor and video graphics display board determine which of these resolutions are available on your system. You should refer to your equipment documentation for more information about your display capabilities. Further, it is a good idea to experiment with different screen resolutions to get a better understanding of how they ultimately will display.

Setting the Number of Frames and the Frame Speed

At the beginning of this chapter, animation in CorelMOVE was compared to the old cartoon books where a character is illustrated in a slightly different position on each page. When you use your thumb to fan through the pages, the characters appear to move. The faster you thumbed through the pages, the faster the character moved, and the shorter the duration of the animation.

For example, if you fanned quickly through the booklet, you might be flipping through 30 pages per second, thus making the movement seem very smooth and ending the animation quickly. If you thumbed through at a rate of 15 pages per second, the animation would take longer to complete and movement would appear less fluid. In this scenario, the number of pages in the book is analogous to the number of frames used in the animation. The speed at which you thumb through the book is much like the animation speed or frames per second in CorelMOVE.

The frame speed and number of frames are set in the Animation Information dialog box (see fig. 33.9). The frame speed is measured in *frames per second* (fps)—the available speeds range from 1 to 18 fps, and the default frame speed is 18 fps. To change the frame speed, simply enter the desired value in the Speed text box. The default number of frames is 100, with a maximum of 9,999 frames. To change the number of frames, enter the desired number in the Number of Frames text box.

T I P

The total length of an animation can be determined by dividing the number of frames for the animation by the number of frames per second. For example, if you have an animation that totals 54 frames, and your number of frames per second is set at 12, the total length of the animation will be 4.5 seconds. At 18 frames per second, the same animation will exhibit smoother motion, but will last only 3 seconds.

The final consideration for animation speed and duration is the speed of your equipment. Your computer and video card processes information at a specific rate. The slower your equipment, the more shaky your motion may appear. Full motion video, like you see on television, moves at 30 frames per second. Most commercial computer hardware and software can't effectively process information at such a rate. Thus, the top animation speed of CorelMOVE is 18 frames per second. Remember, the fewer the number of frames per second, the longer the total animation, and the more jerky the movement. More frames per second create a smoother movement effect, and a shorter total animation time.

Frame Thumbnail and Grid Spacing

The value entered in the Frame for **T**humbnail box indicates which frame of the animation is to be used as the thumbnail in Preview window in the Open Animation dialog box. The default is Frame 1. You will want to change this if the first frame in your animation is empty and you want your thumbnail to include the objects on a later frame.

The Grid Spacing pop-up menu sets up an invisible grid. If the grid is turned on, when you move actors or props on the screen, they are placed to the nearest point on the grid. If you choose 5 from the pop-up menu, the points are placed to the nearest fifth pixel from the top left of the window. The grid is invisible and has a range of every 5 pixels to every 200 pixels. If you want to turn off the grid, choose OFF from the pop-up menu.

Changing Default Animation Settings

To change the default settings for new animations, choose P**r**eferences from the **F**ile menu. Click on the New Animation tab sheet to display the options, as shown in figure 33.10. The settings work like those in the Animation Information dialog box covered in the previous sections. Any changes made here affect all future animation files. Any previously created animation files, including the file currently open, are not affected by changes made in the New Animation tab sheet.

For instance, entering 1000 for the number of frames means that all future animation files will default to 1000 instead of 100 frames. However, the number of frames used in previously created files is not affected. Changing the defaults for new animation will come in especially handy after you have determined the exact frame size for your presentation output. You can enter it here and all future animation will default to this frame size.

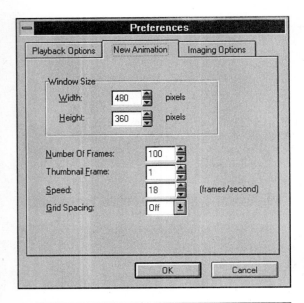

Figure 33.10
The New Animation tab sheet in the Preferences dialog box.

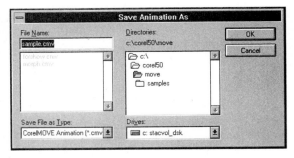

Figure 33.11
The Save Animation As dialog box.

Get into the habit of saving frequently with CorelMOVE by using the keyboard shortcut Ctrl+S.

Saving Animation Files

Choose **S**ave from the **F**ile menu to save the animation file using the file name and file location specified when the file was first created. Choose Save **A**s from the **F**ile menu when you need to change the file name or location of the animation file. The Save Animation As dialog box appears (see fig. 33.11); enter the desired file name and specify the drive and directories where you want to save the file.

Summary

Now the stage is set, and you are ready to begin working with the more exciting elements of your production—actors and props. In the next chapter you learn how to control the movement and motion of your actors, and how to create incredible special effects so that objects sweep onto the screen with dramatic flair. The process is simple, and you will be amazed at how quickly you can transform yourself into a full-fledged multimedia artist!

Animating with Props and Actors

*D*irecting an animation in CorelMOVE is a little like directing a play on stage. Think of the stage as the animation window in CorelMOVE, and you are the director. Your job is to assemble the actors and props, and determine when and how they enter the scene, and what they do while on stage.

While this chapter focuses on using CorelDRAW to create props and actors, you will also find the steps for placing charts and photos from CorelCHART and CorelPHOTO-PAINT into CorelMOVE. The tools and features for creating props and actors in the CorelMOVE paint program are discussed at length in Chapter 35, "Advanced Animation Features."

This chapter covers:

- Adding props to your animation

- Moving and editing props and actors

- Working with prop entry and exit frames

- Working with actor entry and exit frames

- Using the cell sequencer

- Duplicating and cloning props and actors

Adding Props to Your Animation

With all of their whiz-bang special effects and curve-editing capabilities, CorelDRAW and CorelPHOTO-PAINT are ideal tools for quickly designing props and actors. In addition, all of the symbols and clip art included with CorelDRAW provides a treasure-trove of predesigned props and actors. CorelMOVE also includes a basic paint (bitmapped) program for illustrating actors and props.

Creating props and actors and controlling when they enter and exit the animation are important parts of building animation files. This chapter covers adding props to animations, with a close look at applying transition effects for a little extra zing in your animations.

This section covers adding and designing actors for your animations. Here, you will learn how to illustrate actor movement and create the paths that set your actors in motion. The chapter concludes with information on using the Timelines roll-up and duplicating actors and props.

As discussed in Chapter 33, props are stationary objects that do not change shape or move in an animation. In an animation illustrating traffic on highways in major cities, the highways would be placed as props. Figure 34.1 illustrates an animation of oil well sites. The land and oil wells, which remain fixed in the same shape and location throughout the animation, are placed as props. In a business presentation, a background displaying the company logo could be placed as a prop. Charts and photos that do not need to move during the animation can also be placed as props.

Figure 34.1
In this animation frame, props are background elements such as the land, sky, and oil wells.

As a general rule, you will use props to place objects that do not need to move during the animation. However, as discussed later in this section, you can apply transition effects to props. Transition effects allow props to reveal themselves on-screen in a variety of ways.

You can create a slick opening for your animation with text placed as props that zoom, scroll, and wipe across the screen. Understanding how to apply prop transition effects dramatically broadens the scope of your animations.

Creating and Naming Props

Clicking on the New Prop button (the fourth button in the toolbox) opens the New Prop dialog box, as displayed in figure 34.2. Enter a name (up to 32 characters) for your new prop in the Object **N**ame text box. It is important that you take the time to enter an identifying name for your new prop. Using specific names makes it easier to differentiate between several props when you begin working with timelines and assigning transition effects.

Figure 34.2
The New Prop dialog box offers several options for placing props into your animation.

The New Prop dialog box offers two ways to place props into animations. The default option, **C**reate New, lets you create and illustrate the prop from scratch. The second option, Create from **F**ile, lets you create the prop from an existing file. Both of these methods are discussed in the following sections.

T I P

For props created in CorelDRAW, avoid the use of white fills. These will turn transparent when transferred to CorelMOVE. Instead, substitute a light shade of gray.

Creating Props from Scratch

Though CorelMOVE provides the ability to create props, you will find that the tools available in CorelDRAW, CorelCHART, and CorelPHOTO-PAINT are far superior. The **C**reate New option allows CorelMOVE to temporarily open another Corel application, where you can design and illustrate the prop, and then return to CorelMOVE's animation window. As displayed in figure 34.2, you can create and illustrate new props in CorelMOVE, CorelDRAW, CorelCHART, and CorelPHOTO-PAINT.

To create a prop in an application other than CorelMOVE, select the application where you want to create the prop, and click on OK. The selected application is then opened

and the toolbox displays the file name of your animation and the prop name. You can then use the tools in the program to illustrate and design the prop. When your prop is complete, select E**x**it from the **F**ile menu. A message box similar to the one shown in figure 34.3 appears, asking you to update the object in the CorelMOVE animation—click on **Y**es. The newly designed prop is then placed in CorelMOVE's animation window.

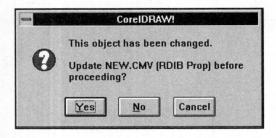

Figure 34.3
Select Yes to update your animation with the newly created prop, or No to disregard it.

As an example of the process, imagine that you need to create some clouds for a prop in an animation on weather forecasting. First, click on the New Prop button and enter **Clouds** as the prop name. Because the clouds will be easier to create in CorelDRAW, select CorelDRAW 5.0 Graphic as the Object **T**ype and click on OK. After a few moments, the CorelDRAW screen appears. Now create the clouds as you normally would with CorelDRAW's illustration tools. When you've finished coloring and arranging the clouds, select E**x**it from the **F**ile menu.

In the message box that follows, click on **Y**es to update the prop in CorelMOVE. CorelDRAW then closes down, and the clouds are placed as props in CorelMOVE's animation window.

T I P

All objects displayed on CorelDRAW's printable page are brought into CorelMOVE as one prop. Objects you do not want to appear in CorelMOVE as part of the prop should be deleted before selecting E**x**it from the **F**ile menu.

Creating Props from Existing Files

The Create from **F**ile option enables you to access existing CorelDRAW, CorelCHART, and CorelPHOTO-PAINT files, and place props into your animation. For instance, if you had previously illustrated a city skyline in CorelDRAW and saved it as a .CDR file, it could be placed as a prop in CorelMOVE. It is important to note that only Corel files saved in their native file format can be placed as props in CorelMOVE. For example, CorelDRAW files must use the file extension .CDR, CorelCHART files must use .CCH, and CorelPHOTO-PAINT files must use the .CPP extension. Thus, CorelMOVE will not place other popular file formats such as .CGM, .WMF, .TIF, or .BMP as prop objects. You can however, *import* a variety of bitmapped formats into CorelMOVE. This process will be discussed in Chapter 35.

To place an existing Corel file in CorelMOVE, select the Create from **F**ile option in the New Prop dialog box to display the screen shown in figure 34.4. In the File text box, enter the drive, directory, and file name of the file you want to place as a prop. For instance, you might enter C:\Corel50\clip art\lincoln.cdr to place a clip art picture of Abraham Lincoln in your animation. Click on the **B**rowse… button if you are unsure about the exact file location. You can then search through the drives and directories until you locate the desired file. When you find the file you want, select it and click on OK. The path and file name are entered in the File text box. Once you have specified the name of the file, click on OK. After a few moments, the contents of the file appear as a prop in the animation window.

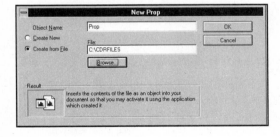

Figure 34.4
*Select the Create from **F**ile option to place a previously created object from another application in your animation.*

T I P

When using an existing Corel file, CorelMOVE places all objects in the file as a single prop. You cannot separate the elements into individual props. If you want to use only part of an existing file as a prop, delete any objects you do not want placed as part of the prop and resave the image under another name.

Moving and Editing Props

After props are placed into CorelMOVE, they appear in the center of the animation window. You will probably want to move the prop and maybe even resize and edit it. It takes a little practice to get used to sizing props to fit correctly in the animation window with other actors and props.

As with other graphic applications, your prop must be selected before you can modify it. To select a prop, click on the prop object. A blinking marquee square appears around the prop. To select multiple props, hold the Shift key while you click on the other props. To move a prop, place the mouse cursor on the prop, and drag the prop to a new location. You can position props partially outside of the animation window. For instance, in figure 34.5, the prop is a street that is positioned so it appears to run off the animation window.

Figure 34.5

A blinking marquee square appears around selected props. You can drag props to the desired location in the animation window.

Editing Props

To edit a prop, you must return to the Corel application where you originally created the object and utilize the tools available in that application. As an example, assume that you want to modify a prop originally created in CorelDRAW. From CorelMOVE, you will launch CorelDRAW, make the desired changes to the prop, and then return to CorelMOVE. Props created outside of CorelMOVE are actually "embedded objects." Embedded means the prop object contains information that links it to the source application—the application used to initially create the prop. In essence, the

embedded prop "remembers" where it was created (CorelDRAW, CorelCHART, or CorelPHOTO-PAINT). When editing changes are required, the embedded prop restores the connection to the application where the prop was created, and launches that application.

To edit a prop, select it and choose **O**bject from the **E**dit menu. After a few moments, the application in which the prop was created appears with the prop in the drawing area. Now, you can make the desired editing changes. When you are finished with your edits, select E**x**it from the **F**ile menu (just as you did when initially creating the prop). A message appears, asking you to update the changes. Click on **Y**es if you want the edited prop to be placed in CorelMOVE; click on **N**o if you want to return to CorelMOVE without the editing changes.

TIP

You can also double-click on the prop to open the Prop Information dialog box. Click on the **E**dit Prop... button in the lower left corner to open the Corel application where the prop was created.

Working with Prop Entry and Exit Frames

As discussed in Chapter 33, an animation consists of a number of frames on which you place props and actors. (Remember that you can move through the frames by dragging on the frame counter or by clicking on the Step Frame Forward button.) When adding props to your animation files, you can control the *entry frame*—the frame where the prop first appears in the animation—and the *exit frame*—the frame where the prop leaves the animation. For example, in an animation documenting hotel reconstruction, you might want trees and other landscaping props to appear in later frames, illustrating changes made during the reconstruction. If the animation consists of 100 frames, you may want trees to appear in frame 36, and flowers to appear in frame 58.

> **NOTE**
>
> Specifying the number of frames for an animation was covered in Chapter 33.

By default, the entry frame is the frame displayed when the prop is first placed into the animation, and the exit frame is set as the last frame of the animation. This means if

frame one is displayed when the prop is placed, frame one is the entry frame. If frame 36 is displayed when the prop is placed, then frame 36 is the entry frame. To quickly determine a prop's entry and exit frames, select the prop and refer to the bottom right corner of the Control Panel by the frame counter. The Enters at Frame Number box (the up arrow) indicates the entry frame, and the Exits at Frame Number box (the down arrow) indicates the exit frame. As displayed in figure 34.6, the selected props entry frame is 12 and the exit frame is 50.

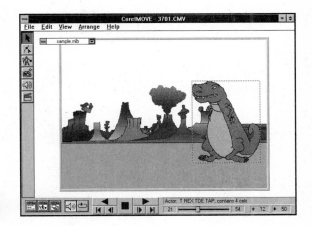

Figure 34.6

The Enters at Frame Number and Exits at Frame Number boxes let you instantly see how the selected prop appears in the animation.

To adjust a prop's entry and exit frames, select the prop and choose Object Info from the Edit menu, or double-click on the prop. The Prop Information dialog box appears, as displayed in figure 34.7. In the Enters At Frame and Exits At Frame boxes, type in the frame numbers you want the prop to enter and exit the animation, and then click on OK. The new entry and exit frames appear in the Control Panel. Don't be surprised if your prop disappears from the current frame. You may be viewing a frame in the animation that is before the prop entry, or after the prop exit frames. In such a case, you will simply move to a frame within the entry and exit frames to view the prop.

N O T E

The Timelines roll-up can also establish the entry and exit frames for props. Refer to the section "Using the Timelines Roll-up" later in this chapter for more information.

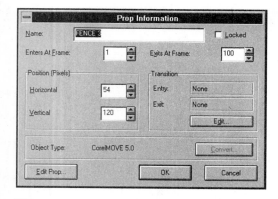

Figure 34.7

The Prop Information dialog box.

Applying Prop Transitions

Prop transitions are special effects that enhance how a prop enters and exits the animation. Without transitions, props just pop in and out at the specified frames. For example, a company logo placed as a prop entering at frame 10 would abruptly appear on the screen. With transitions, props can enter and exit the animation in a smoother, more appealing manner. For instance, you might have the company logo enter the animation with a zoom transition from the bottom right corner of the screen, and exit the animation with a transition that makes it appear to fade off the screen. Prop transitions include scrolling, iris effects, and circular wipes. As you can imagine, transitions often increase the visual appeal of an animation by adding another element of movement and style.

N O T E

Transitions can only be applied to props. Actors cannot use transitions.

To apply a transition, select a prop and choose Object Info from the Edit menu. The Prop Information dialog box is displayed, as shown in figure 34.7. Click on the Edit button in the Transitions section of the dialog box. The Transitions dialog box appears, as displayed in figure 34.8. Select the desired transitions in the Entry or Exit

Transition list boxes. For instance, you could select TL to BR Wipe (top left to bottom right wipe) as the entry transition and BL to TR (bottom left to top right wipe) as the exit transition. Click on the Preview button to see a sample of how the selected transitions will look in the Preview window. The Preview window will not display your prop. Instead, the Corel balloon logo is used to demonstrate the chosen effect.

When the Scroll, Zoom, or Zoom Rectangles transitions are selected, an Edit Zoom button appears instead of a steps box (see fig. 34.8). Click on the Edit Zoom button to display the Edit Scroll dialog box (or Edit Zoom… /Zoom Rectangles… dialog box). As displayed in figure 34.9, a small thumbnail of your animation frame appears in the dialog box.

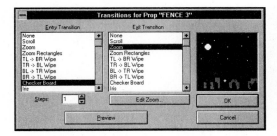

Figure 34.8

The Transitions dialog box with the Checker Board effect selected as the entry transition, and the Zoom effect selected as the exit transition.

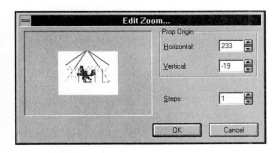

Figure 34.9

The Edit Zoom… dialog box enables you to control the appearance of your prop transitions.

After selecting a transition, notice the **S**teps box or Edit Zoom… button appearing below the list of transitions. For instance, in figure 34.8, the Checker Board effect is selected to make the prop appear and disappear in a pattern of checker board squares. The **S**teps box lets you control how many steps are used to complete the Checker Board effect. The Checker Board effect becomes slower and more fluid as you increase the number of steps. Each transition effect has a steps setting you can adjust to your liking.

Use the Edit Zoom… dialog box to specify the steps used to complete the transition. You can also adjust the point of origin, which is where the transition begins. For Zoom transitions, four perspective lines indicate the point of origin. You can drag these lines to a new position to change the point of origin. For instance, the lines are positioned so the zoom starts from the top center of the screen (see fig. 34.9). In Scroll transitions, a rectangle indicates the point of origin. You can drag the point of origin and place it as desired.

After selecting the transitions and adjusting the steps, click on OK. You can now rewind to frame one and play the animation. There are a few points to consider as you build the transitions. First, if you have applied a transition to a prop that enters in frame one and exits at frame 100 (the last frame), you will not see the transition. The entry and exit frames need to occur somewhere between the second frame of the animation and the second to last frame of the animation for the prop transition to occur. For instance, in an animation with 100 frames, you could specify frame three for the entry frame and frame twenty for the exit frame.

It is also important to be aware that the prop transitions effect takes place in one frame. The entry transition is performed during the specified entry frame, and the exit transition is completed during the specified exit frame. Thus, a zoom entry transition with 11 steps does not take place over 11 frames—the complete transition occurs within the specified entry or frame. This is an important point to remember if you want to have a prop transition enter the screen while an actor is animating. Because transitions occur as a series of steps in a single frame, all other animation will stop until the frame containing the transition has completed its steps.

For example, assume you have an actor that enters the left of the animation screen in frame 6, and then "dances" across the screen and exits at frame 36. Now, assume you place the words "Boot Scootin!" as a prop in frame twenty, with a Checker Board transition

effect in 15 steps. In this scenario, at frame 20, the dancing actor will freeze mid-step until the 15 step prop transition is completed. Then, at frame 21, the actor will continue his dancing motion until he exits the animation at frame 36.

T I P

Adding transitions to text placed as props is a quick way to design an opening sequence. The company name might zoom in from the top, the company logo could "iris" on screen, and the presentation title might scroll up from the bottom.

Adding Actors to Your Animation

Actors are objects you want to "move" in your animations. As discussed in Chapter 33, there are two ways to move actors. First, you create *movement* by building a path for the actor to follow around the screen. Second, you create *motion* by changing the color, shape, or size of the actor. For instance, in figure 34.10, actor movement is created with the path the fish uses to "swim" around the screen. Actor motion is the change in shape of the fish's mouth from frame to frame. This section begins with a thorough look at actor motion, explaining the concept of single-cel and multiple-cel actors. Creating actor movement by building paths is covered later in this section.

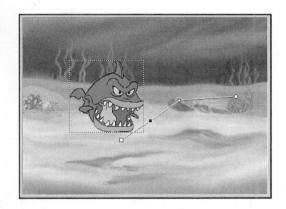

Figure 34.10

Clockwise from upper left: Actors can exhibit movement, as well as inherent motion, as they move around the screen.

Understanding Single-Cel and Multiple-Cel Actors

A *cel* is one unit or a single step in an actor's motion. A simple illustration of a two-cel actor would be the wink of an eye. In one cel, the eye is open; in the other cel, the eye is closed. A more complex example would be a frog jumping. There would be multiple cels

of motion as the frog's body and legs leaned backward while bracing for the jump, more cels for the actual push off, and landing with the frog's legs collapsing underneath.

Not all actors require multiple cels of motion. Some actors require only a single cel of motion. These *single-cel actors* have only one shape and size, and therefore do not

Figure 34.11
Clockwise from upper left: The cheetah requires four distinct cels to illustrate a range of running motions.

change form during the animation. The fixed form of a single-cel actor makes it comparable to a prop. Unlike props, however, single-cel actors can move along a specifically designed path. As an example, imagine that you want to animate a hot-air balloon floating across the sky. A path would make the balloon move across the screen. If the shape and size of the balloon do not need to change as it floats across the screen, the balloon could be a single-cel actor.

Actors that change color, shape, and size during the animation are *multiple-cel actors*. The number of cels depends on the number of steps the actor takes to complete the desired changes. For instance, in the animation of the hot-air balloon, you might use six cels to illustrate the balloon swaying back and forth as it moves across the screen. As an example, consider the image of a cheetah running in figure 34.11. This animation requires four different cels to fully illustrate the different positions the cheetah's body goes through to complete a full cycle of running motion.

Each cel of an actor's movement is played on a separate frame in the animation. For example, the four cels of motion of the cheetah running appear on four frames of the animation. If the actor enters the animation at frame one, the four cels of movement are played on frames one through four. At frame five, the cels of motion begin repeating.

In the animation of the cheetah displayed in figure 34.11, frame five displays cel one,

frame six displays cel two, and so on. The cels of motion are repeated again and again until the last frame of the animation. In the case of the cheetah, the four cels simulate a full range of running motions. As long as those four cels are repeated over and over, the cheetah will appear to run.

N O T E

The order and arrangement that cells are played can be adjusted with the Cell Sequencer. Refer to the section, "Using the Cel Sequencer," later in this chapter for more information.

Creating and Naming Actors

The initial process for creating actors is very similar to creating props (see "Creating and Naming Props" earlier in this chapter). As stated earlier, the focus in this chapter is using CorelDRAW to create props and actors. Therefore, this chapter looks at the steps for creating multiple-cel actors in CorelDRAW. You will follow the same basic steps for creating actors in CorelPHOTO-PAINT and CorelCHART.

Click on the New Actor button (the third button in the toolbox) to open the New Actor dialog box, displayed in figure 34.12. Enter a name of up to 32 characters for your new actor in the Object Name dialog box. Just as with creating props, select the **C**reate New option to design and illustrate the actor

from scratch. Select the Create from **F**ile option to create the actor from an existing file. The process of creating a single-cel actor is similar to creating a prop. Once inside the Corel application where you want to create the actor, you will design the actor and choose E**x**it from the File menu. However, as you will see, creating multiple-cel actors is a little more complex.

Figure 34.12
The New Actor dialog box.

Creating Multiple-Cel Actors in CorelDRAW

To create a multiple-cel actor in CorelDRAW, select **C**reate New and CorelDRAW 5.0 as the object type in the New Actor dialog box. Click on OK to start CorelDRAW. The CorelDRAW screen appears, displaying the Frame Select roll-up shown in figure 34.13. The Frame Select roll-up includes special features for creating multiple-cel actors.

Figure 34.13
The Frame Select roll-up is used to create the cels of motion for multiple-cel actors in CorelDRAW.

For a better understanding of how the Frame Select roll-up manages a multiple-cel actor, refer to figure 34.14. The roll-up indicates that four frames were used to animate the clinking of the champagne classes. When you select the frame in the roll-up, that frame (or cell of motion) is displayed. In the example, the frames are selected in consecutive order, which illustrates each step of motion as the glasses come closer together.

It is important to note that the frames used in the Frame Select roll-up are equivalent to the cels in CorelMOVE. Don't let this incongruity fool you. As you recall, frames and cels are two very different things in CorelMOVE. Frames are like the pages in a cartoon flip book. A flip book with 30 pages has 30 frames. Remember, cels make up each individual unit of motion for an actor.

When you are creating frames with
CorelDRAW's Frame Select roll-up, think of
each frame you create as an animation cel.
For example, the clinking champagne glasses
use five frames in CorelDRAW's Frame
Select roll-up. When this sequence is placed
in CorelMOVE, however, the five frames are
actually five cels that can be played over and
over again throughout a 100-frame animation.

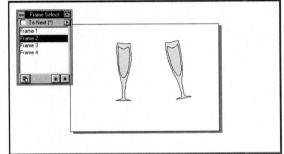

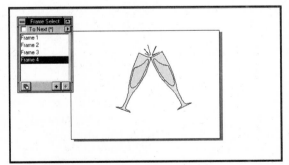

Figure 34.14

*Selecting each frame in the Frame Select roll-up displays
a cel of motion for a multiple-cel actor.*

Using the To Next Feature

The easiest way to create a multiple-cel actor is to insert frames using the To Next feature. Here's how it works.

1. Create the actor while frame one is selected in the roll-up.

2. Click to place an X by the To Next option at the top of the Frame Select roll-up.

3. Change the form of the actor by altering the shape, size, or color. A new frame two is automatically created, displaying the change in the actor form.

The To Next feature remains enabled, so every subsequent change made to the actor automatically creates a new frame. Using this method, you can very quickly create a multiple-cel actor.

When the To Next option is enabled, a new frame is created after every single change is made to the actor. This can be frustrating if, for example, you need several changes in form to occur in one frame. In such a case, you can disable the To Next feature until you have made all the desired changes to that frame. For instance, to animate a dinosaur walking, you might want his tail to wag as his legs change position in the same frame. In this case, you would disable the To Next feature and make all modifications. Because the To Next feature is disabled, a new frame is not created. Continue designing the movements for that frame, and then turn on the To Next feature. Now, when you make the final modification, the next frame will automatically be created. You can repeat the whole process as necessary from frame to frame.

N O T E

When using the To Next feature, objects that are not modified are not carried over to the next frame. For instance, if there was a circle and a square on frame one and you enlarged the circle, the bigger circle appears on frame two, but the square does not. Refer to the section on "Using the Frame Select Roll-up" to address this issue.

Previewing Your Animation

At any time in the creation of your animation, you can preview your work. Until you are comfortable with the process of multiple-cel actors, it is a good idea to preview often to gauge your progress. Click on the button at the bottom left corner of the Frame select dialog box to open the Preview Frame dialog box, as shown in figure 34.15. Upon opening, the Preview Frame dialog box steps through your animation. To examine the motion again, click on the Preview button. The arrows on the bottom left of the dialog box enable you to step through your animation frame by frame. Click on the up arrow to move backward, and the down arrow to move forward a frame at a time. After previewing, click on OK to continue working with your animation.

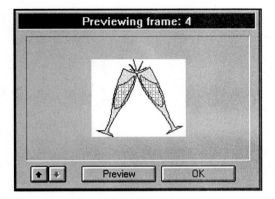

Figure 34.15
The Preview Frame dialog box enables you to examine your animation.

Editing Your Animation

After previewing the animation, you may decide that you need to edit a particular frame. For instance, if you have animated a woman walking over 16 frames, you might determine that the position of the arm in frame eight is awkwardly placed. To remedy the problem, simply select frame eight from the Frame Select roll-up. The image on frame eight is then displayed. Now you can modify the position of the arm as needed.

The node-editing capabilities in CorelDRAW make it an ideal tool for illustrating the subtle changes in form of a multiple-cel actor. Imagine you need to animate a man bending over to touch his toes in four cels. With the Node tool, you could drag and rotate the nodes and curves of the man's shape to create the cels of motion.

Using the Frame Select Roll-Up

The Frame Select roll-up has additional options for creating multiple-cel actors in a fly-out menu. Click on the Expand Arrow on the Frame Select roll-up to display the fly-out. As displayed in figure 34.16, the fly-out includes commands for adding, deleting, and moving objects. These features are discussed in the following sections.

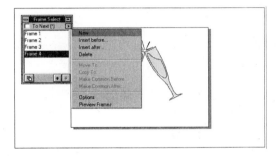

Figure 34.16
The Frame Select roll-up with the fly-out menu displayed.

Normally, the Frame Select roll-up will not appear unless you accessed CorelDRAW from within CorelMOVE. However, with a slight adjustment, you can create multiple-cel actors without running CorelMOVE. In the Windows Program Manager, change the command line of the CorelDRAW icon to read "CORELDRW.EXE(insert a space here)-MOVE." You can do this by clicking on the icon and then choosing **P**roperties from the **F**ile menu.

Inserting and Deleting Frames

As you build an actor, you might decide to insert or delete frames. For instance, if you used four frames to animate a bouncing ball, you might discover that it moves too fast. To slow down the animation, you can insert additional frames. Actors with fewer frames exhibit more abrupt motion and progress at a faster rate. Likewise, actors with many frames exhibit more fluid motion, and progress at a slower rate.

There are basically two ways to insert frames. Select New in the Frame Select fly-out to open a dialog box, which enables you to add a number of frames to the end of the frame list. You can also insert frames before or after the currently selected frame in the roll-up.

For example, if frame three is selected on the roll-up, select Insert Before to insert new frames before frame three. The Insert new frames dialog box appears, as shown in figure 34.17. Enter the number of desired frames and click on OK. If you had selected Insert After, the new frames would be inserted after frame three. Select Delete from the fly-out to delete frames. In the Delete Frames dialog box, enter the number of frames to be deleted and click on OK.

Moving and Copying Elements

The frames you insert with the roll-up will be empty. In other words, they will display as blank white frames in your animation. To construct your animation properly, you will want to place the animation images on these empty frames. You can use the Copy To and

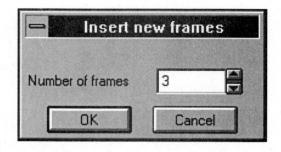

Figure 34.17
The Insert new frames dialog box.

Move To commands in the Frame Select fly-out to place your animation objects on the inserted frames. For instance, if you had inserted two frames after frame one, you could use the Copy To command to copy the contents of frame one to the blank frames two and three. Once in place, you can modify the contents of the new frames according to the way you want the animation to progress.

To copy an object from one frame to another, select the frame containing the object you want copied. Select the object and click on the expand arrow to reveal the fly-out. Click on the Copy To option. A black arrow appears (see fig. 34.18); click on the arrow on the frame in the roll-up where you want the object copied. The Move To command works in the same way, except the selected object is moved to the selected frame.

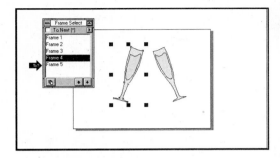

Figure 34.18

The Copy To option enables you to copy the contents of one frame to another.

Using Common Frames

As described earlier, the To Next feature automatically creates a new frame every time the actor is modified. However, only the objects that are modified are placed on the new frame. For instance, if you placed a circle and a square on frame one, and then enlarged the circle three times, three frames would be added. Those three frames would show the expanding circle, but not the square.

Because the square was not modified, it was not placed on the new frames. By using the Make Common command on the Frame Select fly-out, you could make the square a "common" object across all the frames. Common objects are actually "clones," meaning that any changes made to the original object will affect all other clones or common objects. For example, changing the color of the square on frame one changes the color of all of the squares.

N O T E

Refer to the CorelDRAW section of this book for more information about working with cloned objects.

To make objects common across several frames, select the object and choose Make Common Before or Make Common After on the Frame Select fly-out. To make the square in the previous example appear on all four frames, you would select the square on frame one and choose Make Common After. Entering three in the Make common object dialog box would make the square common (or appear) on the next three frames (see fig. 34.19). The Make Common Before option works similarly, except the object is made common on frames "before," not "after," the selected frame.

Figure 34.19

The Make common object dialog box.

Using the Frame Options

When designing one frame of an actor's motion, you may want to see the shape of the actor on the previous frame as a "guide" for shaping the current frame. CorelMOVE includes the Onion Skin feature that lets you do exactly that. As displayed in figure 34.20, the *onion skin* is a dotted outline indicating the actor position in the previous or next frame. In figure 34.20, for example, the Onion Skin feature was used to show the shape of the sun in the first frame. As viewed from frame two, the onion skin lets you see the size of the sun in the previous frame so you can gauge the changes made between frame one and frame two.

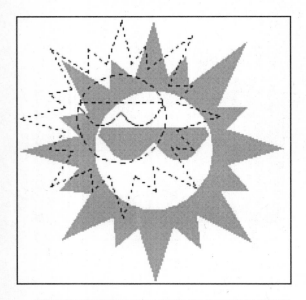

Figure 34.20
Onion skin is the dotted outline showing an actor's position on the previous or next frame.

Select Options from the fly-out to display the Frame Options dialog box, as displayed in figure 34.21. Select Next Frame or Previous Frame to display the transparent onion skins when you are editing an actor. You can select the color of the onion skin with the color buttons by each option. The Selection Wire Color feature displays an outline of the selected object. For instance, if you select an object on frame two, and then switch to frame four, an outline of the selected object from frame two appears in frame four. Use the color button to control the outline color.

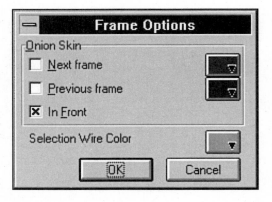

Figure 34.21
The Frame Options dialog box.

Placing Actors in CorelMOVE

After designing your single- or multiple-cel actor in CorelDRAW, select E**x**it from the **F**ile menu. (Select this same command if you are creating an actor in CorelCHART or CorelPHOTO-PAINT.) Just as with creating props, a message appears, asking you to update the changes in CorelMOVE—click on Yes. The actor is then placed in CorelMOVE. Remember, the *frames* you assigned to actors in CorelDRAW are now *cels* in CorelMOVE.

Moving and Editing Actors

The steps for editing actors are similar to those found in the section "Editing Props." You can position or move the actor around the animation window by selecting the actor and dragging to the desired location. All other editing changes require that you return to the Corel application where you originally created the actor. For instance, to edit the colors on the actor created in CorelDRAW, you will need to return to CorelDRAW. Just as with props, actors created outside of CorelMOVE are "embedded objects." When you edit an embedded object, you are returned to the Corel application where the object was originally created.

To edit an actor, select it and choose **O**bject from the **E**dit menu. After a few moments, the Corel application where the actor was created appears with the actor in the drawing area. Now you can make the desired editing changes. When finished editing, select E**x**it

and return from the File menu. A message appears, asking you to update the changes. Click on Yes if you want the edited actor to be placed in CorelMOVE. Click on No if you want to return to CorelMOVE without the editing changes.

T I P

You can also double-click on the actor to open the Actor Information dialog box. Click on the Edit Actor button in the lower left corner to open the Corel application where the prop was created.

Working with Actor Entry and Exit Frames

You control when the actor appears in the animation with entry and exit frames. For example, when animating a farm scene, you may want the rooster to enter the animation after the sun rises. As discussed in the previous section "Working with Props Entry and Exit Frames," entry frames specify in which frame the actor first appears in the animation, and exit frames specify in which frame the actor leaves the animation.

By default, an actor's entry frame is the frame displayed when the actor was placed into the animation. The default exit frame is the last frame of the animation. To determine an actor's entry and exit frames, select the actor and refer to the bottom right corner of the Control Panel by the frame counter. The

Enters at Frame Number box (the up arrow) indicates the entry frame, and the Exits at Frame Number box (the down arrow) indicates the exit frame.

To control an actor's entry and exit frames, select the actor and choose O**b**ject Info from the **E**dit menu, or double-click on the actor. The Actor Information dialog box appears. In the **E**nters at Frame and E**x**its at Frame boxes, type in the frame numbers that indicate where in the animation you want the actor to enter and exit, and click on OK. The new entry and exit frames appear in the Control Panel. As covered later in this chapter, you can also use the Timelines roll-up to set entry and exit frames.

Creating Actor Paths

Creating actor paths lets you add real movement to your animations. With actor paths, you can animate birds flying across the sky, dolphins jumping out of water, and babies crawling across the floor. The paths guide the actor's movement around the animation window. As displayed in figure 34.22, paths are comprised of a series of steps or points. The points determine where the actor moves from frame to frame. Each point of a path takes place during one frame in the animation, so a path with five steps requires five frames to complete.

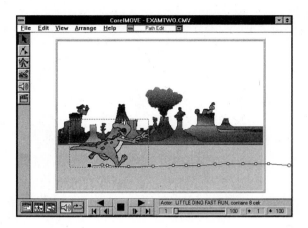

Figure 34.22
Paths are comprised of a series of steps or points, which resemble the nodes in CorelDRAW.

Plotting and adjusting the points along a path is similar to working with the Node tool in CorelDRAW. You basically click to place the points, and then play the animation to see how it looks. Here are a few tips to help you create the perfect path for your actor:

- For slow movement, place the points of the path close together. This way, the actor does not move much from frame to frame.

- For more rapid movement, spread out the points.

- For even movement, use a consistent amount of spacing between the points. When animating a swimming fish, an evenly spaced path makes it appear to float.

■ For erratic movement, such as a bouncing ball, use varying spacing between the points of the path. Finally, keep in mind that the actor remains on the last step of the path until the actor's exit frame or the end of the animation, whichever comes first.

Building a Path

To create a path, select the actor you want to move and click on the Path tool (second in the toolbox). The Path Edit roll-up appears. Make sure an X appears by the Allow Adding Points option in the roll-up. This feature must be enabled before you can begin plotting the points of the path. A black dot called the *registration point* appears along the edge of the selected actor. The location of the registration point determines which part of the actor is used to guide the path. For example, in figure 34.23, the registration point appears at the top left of the actor, so the path stems from the top left of the actor.

N O T E

You can adjust the position of the registration point for actors created in CorelMOVE, or those converted from CorelDRAW, CorelPHOTO-PAINT, or CorelDRAW to CorelMOVE objects. Refer to Chapter 35, in the section titled "Using the CorelMOVE Paint Editor," for more information.

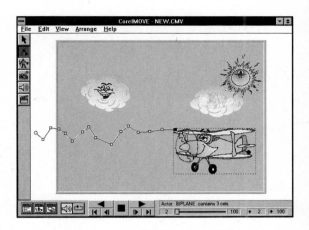

Figure 34.23

The Path Edit roll-up. Notice the registration point, which determines the part of the actor that aligns with the path points.

Use the registration point as a guide for adding additional points. To place a new point on the path, click where you want the point to appear, and the point is added. Continue clicking to build the points along the path. The active or selected point is displayed as a small black rectangle. All other points in the path are displayed as small white rectangles.

While building the path, you can reposition an earlier point by dragging the point to a new location. Be aware that the newly positioned point will then be selected, so if you click to place a new point, it will build from this selected point forward. Before resuming the path from its endpoint, you will need to click on the last point of the path.

You may find it easier to create paths if you can see the actor stepping along the path as you create it. The Move Frame with Point option covered in the next section helps you do this.

When you're finished building the path, select the Pick tool (the first tool in the toolbox). The Path Edit roll-up and the path disappear. Play the animation to preview the actor moving along the points of the new path. Remember, each point along the path represents a frame in the animation. If the actor enters at frame 20 and follows a ten-point path, the last movement along the path occurs in frame 30.

Editing Paths with the Path Edit Roll-Up

Creating the right kind of path is essential to animating objects in a believable way. A kangaroo that looks like it's "baby-stepping" across the screen won't look convincing. Whether your path needs to be smooth and slow or erratic and jumpy, you will find the tools in the Path Edit roll-up to be very useful.

Some of the options in the Path Edit roll-up require that you have a range of points selected (see fig. 34.24). As previously mentioned, the selected point appears in black. To select multiple points, hold the

Shift key and click on the last point of the range you want to select. For instance, if point two in your path is selected, holding the Shift key and clicking on point five selects points two, three, four, and five.

Figure 34.24
The Path Edit roll-up.

Scaling, Smoothing, Distributing, and Mirroring Points

Click on the Scale Path button to reveal the Scale Path dialog box, displayed in figure 34.25. You can increase or decrease the number of points on the entire path or over a selected range of points. The current number of points is displayed; enter the desired number of points and click on OK.

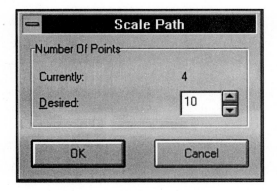

Figure 34.25
The Scale Path dialog box.

Click on the Smooth Path button to make the path less angular and more fluid. Each time you click on the button, the path becomes smoother. Click on the Distribute Path button to equalize the distance between the points on the path. For example, if you have six points between the beginning and end point of the path, the Distribute Path button will place each of the points an equal distance apart.

Click on the Mirror Horizontal or Mirror Vertical buttons to flip the path horizontally or vertically. For example, by using the Mirror Horizontal command, you could flip the path of an actor so it moves from right to left across the screen instead of left to right.

Looping Path Points

Normally, actors follow the path from beginning to end and then just stop. The Looping feature causes your actors to return to a specified point of the path and keep

cycling from that point through the end point. The loop point appears as a circle instead of a rectangle on the path. In figure 34.26, the path leads the airplane into the screen. After the path is completed, the airplane returns to the looped point on the path (the circle) to start flying in circles.

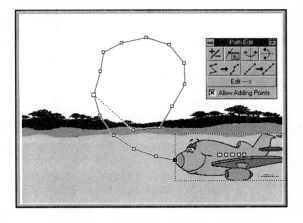

Figure 34.26
An actor with a looped path.

To create a loop point on a path, select the point and click on the Point Information button. Click on the Loop To Here option at the bottom on the Point Information dialog box (see fig. 34.27). You can also reposition the selected point by entering new **H**orizontal and **V**ertical coordinates. When finished with your selections, click on OK.

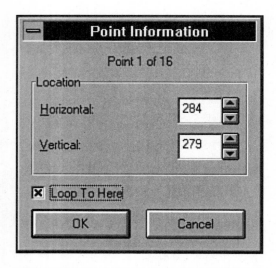

Figure 34.27
The Point Information dialog box.

Using the Path Edit Fly-out

Click on the Edit button in the Path Edit roll-up to display a fly-out with commands for clearing, cutting, and pasting points. The first command, Undo Path Operation, reverses any operations that are done to the path. This is invaluable when you first learn how to create paths.

The Cut and Paste commands let you move entire sections of a path to different locations on the path. Select the point you want to cut, and choose Cut Points from the Path Edit fly-out. Next, select the point where you want to place the "cut" points and choose Paste Points from the Path Edit fly-out. The points are placed after the selected point. The Copy and Paste commands work basically the same as Cut and Paste. However, the Copy command lets you repeat sections of the path—for example, a few of the points in your path may work perfectly, and you want to copy these to use again in the path.

Select the Clear Whole Path command to remove the whole path. This is useful when you want to remove the current path and build a new one. The Select All Points command is a quick way to select all of the points in the path.

Select the Move Frame with Point option before building the points of your path to "move" the actor along the path as you build it. This is a great way to preview how each step of the path looks. This feature is off by default—you will have to select it each time you begin creating paths.

Using the Cel Sequencer

The Cel Sequencer controls the order in which an actor's cel of motion is displayed during the animation. The following overview of cel sequencing is designed to prepare you for working with some of the complex features of the Cel Sequencer.

In the section, "Understanding Single-Cel and Multiple-Cel Actors," a cel is defined as one unit or step in an actor's motion. A single-cel actor has just one cel, or unit of movement. As illustrated in the following example, this one cel is displayed on every frame in which the actor is active in the animation. For instance, an arrow placed as a single-cel actor appears in the same shape, size, and color from its specified entry frame to its specified exit frame.

Frame	1	2	3	4	5
Cel	1	1	1	1	1

Multiple-cel actors consist of several cels of motion where the actor changes color, shape, and size. Each cel is displayed on a separate frame in the animation. By default, the cels are played in order—first to last. The example illustrates how the five cels of motion are played for an actor that enters the animation in frame 10. The first cel of motion appears on frame 10, the second cel appears on frame 11, the third on frame 12, and so on.

Frame	10	11	12	13	14
Cel	1	2	3	4	5

If the actor is still active in the animation after the last cel of motion is played, the actor plays through all the cels again. This causes the actor to repeat his or her motion over and over. For instance, you could use four cels of motion to animate a man answering a phone. First, the phone rings; second, the man picks up the phone. In the third cel, the man talks on the phone, and in the fourth cel, he puts the phone back on the receiver. As illustrated in the following example, the movement of this four-cel actor is repeated three times during twelve animation frames.

Frame	1	2	3	4	5
	6	7	8	9	10
	11	12			
Cel	1	2	3	4	1
	2	3	4	1	2
	3	4			

CorelMOVE provides the Cel Sequencer to control the order in which the cels of motion are displayed. Using the Cel Sequencer, you could manipulate the order of the cels in the previous example so that the third cel of motion—the man talking—would hold for several frames, and then move on to putting down the phone. The following example indicates how this new cel sequence might appear:

Frame	1	2	3	4	5
	6	7	8	9	10
	11	12			
Cel	1	2	3	3	4
	1	2	3	3	3
	3	4			

You can also modify the size of the cel displayed in the frame. For instance, in figure 34.28, the size of the cels increase in 25 percent increments across the four frames. As a result, the actor appears to enter the animation from a distance.

Adjusting the Cel Sequence

Select the actor whose cel sequence you want to adjust and click on the Cel Sequencer button (the third button in the bottom left corner of the Control Panel). The Cel Sequencer appears, displaying information about the selected actor (see fig. 34.29).

The title bar displays the actor name.

The top row, Frame, displays the frames in which the actor is active in the animation. The first frame number in the Cel Sequencer corresponds with the actor's entry frame; the last frame number corresponds with the actor's exit frame.

The second row indicates which cel is played on each frame.

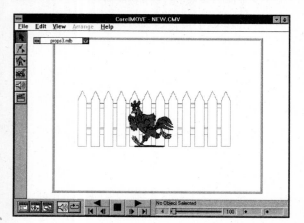

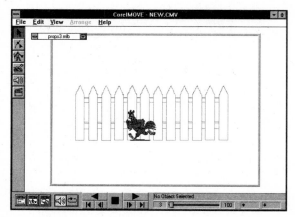

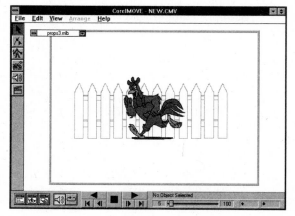

Figure 34.28

Using the Cel Sequencer to adjust cel size can create interesting effects.

The third row displays the size of the cel appearing on each frame. Double-click on the Control Box to close the Cel Sequencer roll-up.

Frame	2	3	4	5	6	7	8	9	
Cel	1	2	3	4	5	6	7	8	▶
Size%	100	100	100	100	100	100	100	100	▶

Actor: ROOSTER RUNNING

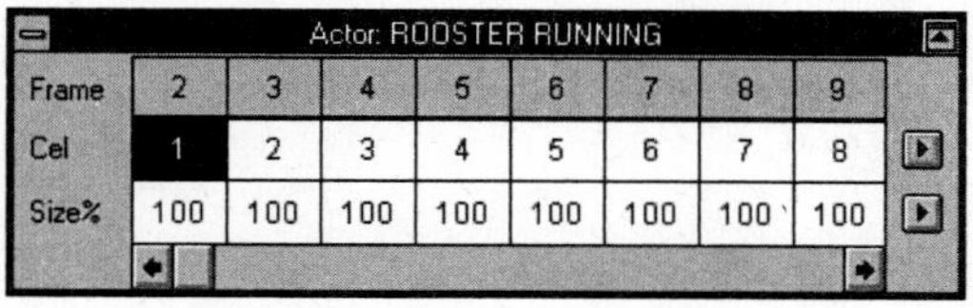

Figure 34.29
The Cel Sequencer roll-up.

Manually Adjusting the Cel Sequence

You can change the order of the cel sequence manually by typing the desired sequence in the Cel row of the roll-up. Just double-click on the cel number you want to change, and type in the new cel number. For instance, in figure 34.30, the cel numbers were changed so that some cels were held across a series of frames.

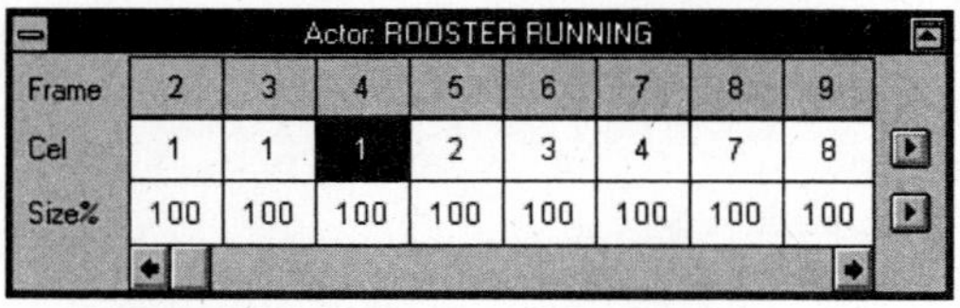

Frame	2	3	4	5	6	7	8	9	
Cel	1	1	1	2	3	4	7	8	▶
Size%	100	100	100	100	100	100	100	100	▶

Actor: ROOSTER RUNNING

Figure 34.30
Double-click on the cel numbers in the roll-up to manually enter a new cel sequence.

Using Special Sequence Effects

Before entering a sequence manually, check out the sequence effects included with the Cel Sequencer. Using one of these sequences is much faster than entering the sequence by hand. To use a sequence, click on the Sequence Effects fly-out button and choose Select All to select all of the cels. Click again on the Sequence Effects button and choose the desired effect. Table 34.1 explains each effect.

Sizing Cels

All cels display at 100 percent unless a new cel size is entered. You can enter a new size manually by double-clicking on the cel size in the Cel Sequencer roll-up and entering a new value. You can also choose from several sizing effects included in the roll-up. To modify the cel sizes with a sizing effect, click on the Sequence Sizing Options button and choose Select All. Click again on the Sequence Sizing Options button and choose the sizing effect. Table 34.2 explains each effect.

Using the Timelines Roll-Up

Timing is key to designing effective, believable animations. All the elements in your animation—props, actors, sounds, and cues—must work together to create realistic movement and motion. For example, in an animation of a bomb exploding, the sound for the explosion must be timed to precisely coincide with the image of the exploding

bomb. The entry frames, exit frames, and duration of each object in your animation, can be collectively viewed as a "timeline."

As discussed earlier, entry and exit frames can be set in the Prop or Actor Information dialog box. Using this method, however, you can only set the entry and exit frames for one object at a time. With the Timelines roll-up, you can adjust the timelines of several animation objects and see how they work in relation to each other. For instance, you can adjust the entry frame of the sound explosion using the timeline of the exploding bomb actor as a guide.

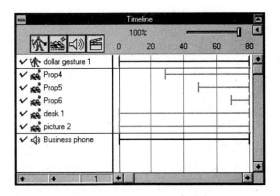

Figure 34.31
The Expanded Timeline roll-up.

N O T E

Adding sound and cues to animations is covered in Chapter 35.

The Timelines roll-up provides a visual representation of each object's timeline. Click on the Timelines button in the lower left corner of the Control Panel to display the Timelines roll-up. Click on the expand arrow on the roll-up to reveal the timelines for the objects in your animation, as displayed in figure 34.31. At the top of the roll-up are buttons representing actors, props, sounds, and cues. When these buttons are "pushed in," the timelines for those objects are displayed. When the buttons are not pushed in, the timelines for those objects do not appear. Displaying the timelines for only actors and sounds might be useful when you want to focus exclusively on the timings for these elements.

Along the left side of the roll-up are names for the actors, props, sounds, and cues in your animation. They are grouped according to object type. For instance, all the props appear at the top of the list in figure 34.31. An icon representing the type of object also appears. The "running man" icon indicates the object is an actor, the "horizon" icon symbolizes a prop, the "horn" icon represents sounds, and the "clapboard" icon represents cues. The timelines for each object indicate when the object enters and exits the animation. The color of the timeline depends on the object type. Actor timelines appear in red, props in green, sounds in blue, and cues in pink.

You can select an object in the Timelines roll-up by clicking somewhere on the name or timeline. When the object is selected, the Status Area in the lower left corner of the roll-up displays the entry and exit frames. The up arrow indicates the entry frame, and the down arrow indicates the exit frame.

Table 34.1
Special Sequence Effects

Effect	Cel Sequence
Normal Cycle	This is the default. All of the cels are displayed in consecutive order.
Reverse Cycle	The order of the cels is reversed. For instance, cels that normally display as 1, 2, 3, 4, 1, 2, 3 would be reversed to display 4, 3, 2, 1, 4, 3, 2, 1.
Ping Pong	The sequence of cels "flip flops" between forward and reverse. For example, the sequence might be 1, 2, 3, 4, 3, 2, 1.
Slow Forward	The cels are shown in the original order; however, the same cel is repeated over two consecutive frames. This effect slows the actor's motion. For example, a sequence might appear as 1, 1, 2, 2, 3, 3.
Slow Reverse	Same as Slow Forward, except the cels are shown in reverse order, with the same cel repeated over two frames.
Random	This effect uses no particular order; the cels are displayed in a randomly selected sequence.

Table 34.2
Sizing Effects

Effect	Cel Sizing
Normal Size	This is the default. All of the cels are displayed at 100 percent.
Small to Large	The first cel is displayed at 1 percent of normal size; each subsequent cel is gradually increased in size until the last frame is displayed at 200 percent.
Large to Small	This is opposite of Small to Large. The first frame is displayed at 200 percent normal size; each subsequent cel is gradually decreased in size until the last frame is displayed at 1 percent.
Normal to Large	The cel size starts at 100 percent, then each cel is gradually increased in size until the last frame appears at 200 percent.
Large to Normal	The cel size starts at 200 percent, then each cel is gradually decreased in size until the last frame appears at 100 percent.
Small to Normal	The cel size starts at 1 percent, then each cel is gradually increased in size until the last frame appears at 100 percent.
Normal to Small	The cel size starts at 100 percent, then each cel is gradually decreased in size until the last frame appears at 1 percent.

You can delete an object from the timeline by first selecting it and then pressing Delete.

Adjusting Entry and Exit Frames with the Timelines Roll-Up

Each timeline has a start frame and end frame handle. You can move these handles to adjust the entry and exit frames for each object. To change the entry frame, place the mouse cursor on the start frame handle. The cursor shape changes to a single left arrow. Now, drag the handle to the left or right to set the new entry frame. As you drag, watch the Status Area to determine to which frame you have moved. When you're ready, release the mouse, and the timeline is changed. To adjust the exit frame, point to the end frame handle. The cursor shape changes to a single right-facing arrow. Drag this handle to the desired exit frame, and release.

Moving Timelines

You can move the whole timeline for an object to a new position in the roll-up. Moving timelines is handy when you want the object to appear for the same length of time, but just enter and exit later or earlier in the animation. To move a timeline, place the mouse cursor in the middle of the timeline—the cursor shape will change to a double-sided arrow. Now, drag the whole timeline to another location and release.

Duplicating and Cloning Props and Actors

At various times, you may need another copy of an actor or prop already placed in the animation. Rather than creating the object all over again, you can simply duplicate or clone the object using the commands in the **E**dit menu.

To duplicate an actor or prop, select the object and choose **D**uplicate from the **E**dit menu. The Duplicate Actor/Prop dialog box appears, as displayed in figure 34.32. By default, CorelMOVE adds a "2" to the actor or prop name. You can enter a new name, if desired, and then click on OK. The duplicate is placed near the original object and is automatically selected.

It is important to note that when you duplicate an object, you are duplicating all the information about that object as well. For instance, when you duplicate an actor, you are duplicating not just the cel you are viewing, but every cel in the actor's animation as well as the path. Likewise, when you duplicate a prop, you are also reproducing any transitions that may be assigned to it. You can select any duplicate and modify its attributes, including actor paths and prop transitions.

Figure 34.32
The Duplicate Actor dialog box.

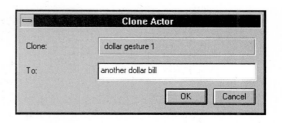

Figure 34.33
The Clone Actor dialog box.

The Clone command works like the Duplicate command in that a copy is made of the selected object. However, cloning establishes a connection between the original object and any clones. This connection means that changes made to the original are automatically applied to the copy (called the clone). For example, if you change the color of the original object, the color of the clone is changed as well. Unlike cloning in CorelDRAW, the reverse is also true—changes made to a clone will be applied to the master. Just as with duplicating objects, cloning an object also reproduces any paths or transitions associated with it. Likewise, the prop or actor information cloned from an original can be independently modified.

To clone an object, select it and choose Clo**n**e from the **E**dit menu. The Clone Actor/Prop dialog box appears (see fig. 34.33). You can enter a new name for the object if you want. Click on OK to place the clone in the animation. As with duplicates, the clone is selected and ready to be moved.

Summary

As you have seen, animating actors and props can produce exciting visual effects. It takes a little practice to become proficient, but the results are well worth the effort. Until you become adept with animating actors, you can take comfort in the fact that CorelMOVE comes with libraries stocked with fully animated actors. In the next chapter, you will learn how to access and utilize these libraries in your presentations. You will also learn the more advanced features of building an animated presentation, such as importing sound and video into your animation.

Advanced Animation Features

*I*n previous chapters, you learned how to set up a new animation and fill it with actors and props. This chapter focuses on several features of advanced animation, such as working with sound, importing objects, and adding cues to your animations. The first section covers the Paint Editor. The next section covers working with the CorelMOVE animation libraries. These libraries are full of actors, props, and sounds you can insert into your animations. Your knowledge of the Paint Editor will be useful in the section on the CorelMOVE libraries, because those actors and props can be edited in the Paint Editor.

Inserting sound and video into your animations creates powerful presentations. In this chapter, you will learn how to add and edit sound effects. The steps for importing sound and video clips are also covered. The chapter ends with a look at creating interactive presentations with cues. Here, you will discover how to stop or pause the animation, wait for a viewer response, such as a mouse click or keystroke, and then continue the animation. These advanced features will take you to a whole new level of producing and designing animations.

This chapter covers:

- Using the CorelMOVE Paint Editor

- Using special effects

- Using CorelMOVE libraries

- Adding sound to your animations

- Creating interactive animations by adding cues

- Importing and exporting files

Using the CorelMOVE Paint Editor

The *Paint Editor* enables you to create new actors and props within CorelMOVE and is also where you find special effects such as morphing and tinting.

With the Paint Editor, you can create new actors and props without ever leaving CorelMOVE. When you need to design simple props and actors, such as plain backgrounds and short text strings, creating the objects in the Paint Editor is often quicker than using another Corel application. However, the Paint Editor is not a full-featured drawing application, like CorelDRAW. The Paint Editor is a bitmapped graphics application, which means it operates more like CorelPHOTO-PAINT.

A major difference between designing in the Paint Editor and CorelDRAW is apparent when drawing shapes. After the shape is drawn in CorelDRAW, you can reshape it with the Node tool. In the Paint Editor, you must draw the shape correctly the first time, or you will have to erase it and start all over. In addition, you cannot send objects to the back or to the front in the Paint Editor—you must draw the bottom object first, and then draw other objects on top of it. Although the Paint Editor is useful for creating simple graphics and text, it is rather cumbersome for

designing complex multiple-cel actors. For this reason, designing actors and props in CorelDRAW was emphasized in Chapter 34, "Animating with Props and Actors."

There are several reasons why you should become familiar with the Paint Editor. First, the libraries containing actors, props, and sounds found on the Corel 5 CD-ROM are CorelMOVE objects that can only be edited in CorelMOVE. Second, the Paint Editor includes some special effects that can enhance your animations. For instance, *morphing* (a new effect that blends one actor shape into another) can only be performed in the Paint Editor.

Actors and props created in other Corel applications can be converted to CorelMOVE objects and then edited in the Paint Editor. For example, if you want to morph an actor created in CorelDRAW, you will have to convert the actor to a CorelMOVE object before you can access the Paint Editor where morphs are created.

N O T E

The steps for converting objects to CorelMOVE objects are covered later in this section.

Creating Actors and Props with the Paint Editor

To create a new actor or prop in the Paint Editor, select the New Actor or New Prop button. Next, select the **C**reate New option, choose CorelMOVE 5.0 as the Object **T**ype and click OK. The Paint Editor window opens. The *painting window* is the canvas or area where you create the actors or props. By default, the Paint toolbox appears on the left side of the window, though you can drag the toolbox title bar to reposition it (see fig. 35.1).

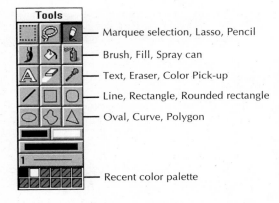

Figure 35.1
The Paint Editor toolbox.

- Marquee selection, Lasso, Pencil
- Brush, Fill, Spray can
- Text, Eraser, Color Pick-up
- Line, Rectangle, Rounded rectangle
- Oval, Curve, Polygon
- Recent color palette

Changing the Size of the Painting Window

The size of the painting window can be adjusted to accommodate larger objects. The painting window is sized in pixels, just like the animation window. You will find it useful to size the painting window to match the sizing of the animation window. When both windows are the same size you can better judge the relative sizing of objects created in the painting window. For instance, when the painting window is the size of the animation window, you can easily draw a background in the painting window that will perfectly fit the animation window.

To adjust the size of the painting window, select **P**age Setup from the **F**ile menu. The Set Size dialog box appears, as displayed in figure 35.2. Enter the desired page size in pixels and click on OK. Refer to Chapter 33, "Understanding CorelMOVE Basics," for more information on sizing with pixels in CorelMOVE.

Figure 35.2
The Set Size dialog box.

Using the Paint Editor Tools

The *Paint toolbox*, also called the Paint Tool Palette, consists of a palette of paint tools, such as pencils, brushes, spray tools, fill tools, and lines and shapes drawing tools. Also available are buttons for selecting foreground and background colors. The following sections explain how each tool is used.

Selecting in the Paint Editor

Selecting in the Paint Editor is different than selecting in CorelDRAW. You are not selecting objects as in CorelDRAW; instead, you are selecting a portion of the painting window. For instance, in figure 35.3, only half of a circle and part of a text string are selected. When selecting, make sure you've selected all that you intended to select. If you do not get the intended images the first time, simply start again and reselect the desired area.

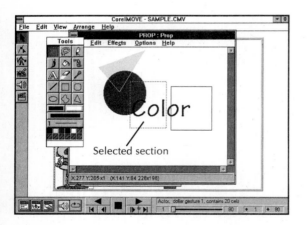

Figure 35.3

In the Paint Editor, the selection tools select a portion of the painting window.

There are two tools for selecting in the Paint Editor. First, the _Marquee tool_ selects rectangular-shaped areas. Drag diagonally across the images to be selected. A blinking marquee square defines the area you are

selecting. When you release the mouse, the images inside the square are selected. The _Lasso tool_ selects irregular-shaped areas. Select the Lasso tool and drag around the area you want. The line that trails the lasso's tip shows what you are lassoing. When you release the mouse button, the area drawn by the lasso's line is the selected area.

N O T E

A quick way to select the entire image area is to use the Select All command in the **E**dit menu. A blinking marquee outline appears around the entire painting window, indicating any images in that area that are selected.

Selecting in the Paint Editor is used for deleting, moving, and applying special effects to the selected area. Unlike with CorelDRAW, you cannot select an area and change its patterns, colors, or line widths in the Paint Editor. These attributes must be set before the object is drawn.

Selecting Patterns and Line Widths

The Pattern Selector button lets you choose from several patterns for your paint and fill operations to reveal the Pattern Fill pop-up as shown in figure 35.4. As previously mentioned, these attributes must be selected before you draw an object. To select a pattern, press and hold on the Pattern Selector button, drag to the desired pattern, and release. The pattern is displayed on the Pattern Selector button. The look and feel of a particular pattern on the Pattern pop-up is directly influenced by the currently selected foreground and background colors. Experiment by changing these colors to get the desired pattern effects.

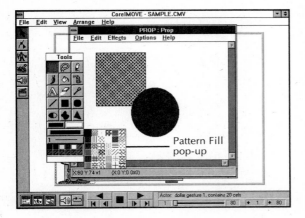

Figure 35.4
The Pattern Fill pop-up.

Use the Line Width Selector button to adjust the width of lines and the outlines of rectangles and ovals. Press and hold on the Line Width Selector button to display the Line Width pop-up, drag to the desired width, and release. The line widths are measured in pixels.

Selecting Foreground and Background Colors

You can select the foreground and background colors used to fill shapes and text. Foreground colors are the "front" colors in patterns, while background colors are the "back" colors in patterns. In figure 35.4, the square is filled with a pattern in which black is the foreground color and white is the background color. If the selected pattern is solid, only the foreground color is used, as with the circle in figure 35.4.

To select a foreground color, press and hold on the Foreground Color Selection button to display a palette of available colors. Drag to the desired color and release the mouse to make it the current foreground color. The color is displayed on the Foreground Selection button. To select a background color, press and hold on the Background Color Selection button. Drag to the desired color on the palette, and release to make it the current background color. The colors you select are added to the Recent Color Palette at the bottom of the toolbox.

When you want to use a color that is not available in the Paint Editor's Color palette, but is part of a previously created image, use the Color Pick-up tool. For instance, using the Color Pick-up tool, you can select a color displayed in a prop from one of the CorelMOVE libraries. Select the Color Pick-up tool and click on the part of the image displaying the color you want. The color is added to the Recent Colors palette.

The Recent Color palette makes it easy to access the 12 most recently used colors. You can select one of these as your foreground or background color, rather than selecting it from the palette. To select a foreground color, click the left mouse button on the desired color. To select a background color, click on the color with the right mouse button. The selected colors are displayed on the Foreground and Background color buttons.

Drawing Lines, Curves, Rectangles, and Ovals

Several tools exist for drawing shapes in CorelMOVE. Remember—if the shape is not drawn correctly the first time, you will need to erase it or choose Undo from the Edit menu. Use the Line Width pop-up to set the line thickness before drawing your objects.

Select the Pencil tool to draw thin freeform curves, and select the Line tool to draw straight lines. The Brush tool lets you "paint" lines much as if you dipped a brush in a can of paint, and then dragged the brush on a canvas. To select another brush shape and thickness, double-click on the Brush tool button. As displayed in figure 35.5, a brush-shape selection pop-up will appear; click on the desired brush shape. Select the Spraycan tool to "spray" color on the painting window similar to an airbrush. To control the width and pressure of the spray, double-click on the Spray Can tool. Enter the desired options in the Air Brush Settings dialog box. The higher the Aperature Width, the thicker the spray. A higher pressure setting makes the spray more concentrated.

The Tool palette includes tools for drawing several different shapes, including rectangles, rounded edge rectangles, ovals, free-form shapes, and polygons (see fig. 35.6). Remember, before drawing any shape, first select the desired line width. The color of the line is determined by the current foreground color. You can also select a color or pattern for the new shape before you draw it. By default, these tools draw empty shapes. To draw shapes that are filled with the currently selected pattern and color, double-click on the desired tool. The drawing tools will turn black or display the current pattern, as displayed in figure 35.6. Now, each new shape you draw will be filled with the current colors and patterns.

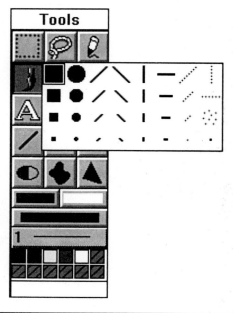

Figure 35.5
Double-clicking on the Brush tool displays a pop-up for selecting a brush shape.

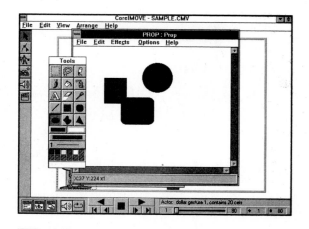

Figure 35.6
Double-clicking on the drawing tools lets you draw filled objects.

Drawing shapes in the Paint Editor is similar to drawing in other Corel applications. Select the Rectangle tool to draw rectangles, the Rounded Rectangle tool to draw rectangles with rounded corners, and the Oval tool to draw oval shapes. Hold the shift key while drawing rectangles and ovals to create perfect squares and circles. When you want to draw a closed free-form object, select the Curve tool. Position the pointer where you want to start, then drag out your shape. CorelMOVE will draw a straight line connecting the start and end points of the shape when you release the mouse button. Select the Polygon tool to draw closed polygons with irregular sides. To draw a polygon, position the mouse where you want to begin, and then click and release. Move the mouse to the second point and click, then to the third point and click, and so on. To finish the polygon, double-click on your last point. The last and first point are automatically joined.

T I P

Use the Zoom option in the Options menu to zoom in closer to your drawings. The 1x command means you are editing the actual size of the bitmap. Select the 2x option to magnify each pixel in the drawing to twice its normal width and height. Select the 4x option to magnify each pixel in the drawing to four times its normal width and height. Select the 8x option to magnify each pixel in the drawing to eight times its normal width and height.

Filling Objects

The Paint Bucket tool fills "closed" shapes with the selected color and pattern. Click on

the Paint Bucket tool (the shape of the mouse cursor changes to a paint can) place the cursor inside the closed object, and click again. The "paint" is poured into the shape. If the shape is not completely closed, paint will spill out to fill the surrounding area of the image. Choose <u>U</u>ndo from the <u>E</u>dit menu to fix this problem, and redraw the object as a closed shape. Use the Foreground Color Select and the Pattern Selector buttons to choose the color and pattern with which shapes are filled.

T I P

Filling an object using the Paint Bucket tool is the only way to get an object with an outline color that differs from the fill. First, draw an empty object with the desired outline color and width, then use the tool to fill the object with another color.

Entering Text

The Text tool lets you enter text for labels and titles in your animations. Select the tool, and click painting window where you want the text to appear in the painting window. Type in the text, pressing Enter to wrap the text to the next line. Immediately after typing the text and before clicking anywhere else on the screen, change the text's font, size, and style by double-clicking on the Text tool to display the Font dialog box (see fig. 35.7). Select the desired options and click on OK. Before clicking elsewhere on the screen, use the Foreground Color Selection button to change the color of the text. Clicking anywhere else on the screen effectively causes the paint to "dry," rendering the text unable

to be changed. You must make attributal changes either before you type the text string or immediately after typing it, and prior to clicking anywhere else.

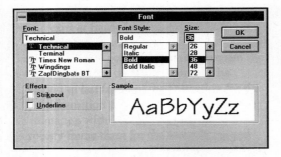

Figure 35.7
The Font dialog box.

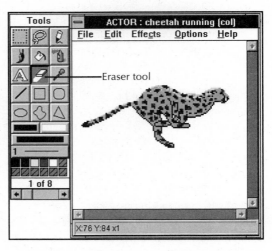

Eraser tool

Figure 35.8
Press Ctrl while erasing with the Eraser tool to remove only the current foreground color.

Erasing Images

The Eraser tool lets you erase or remove part of an image. Select the Eraser tool and drag over the images in the Paint area you want to erase. The Eraser tool erases all colors, displaying the white background underneath. To erase only the selected foreground color, hold down the Ctrl key to turn the Eraser tool into a Color Eraser. Now, when you drag the eraser over the image, only the selected foreground color is removed. Any other color on the image remains. As displayed in figure 35.8, you could remove the spots on the cheetah and leave the background fur color using the Color Eraser.

Correcting Mistakes in the Paint Editor

As with other Corel applications, the Paint Editor includes the Undo command for "undoing" the last action. For instance, if you add a red circle to your drawing and then decide you don't want it, you can choose **U**ndo from the **E**dit menu to remove the circle. As another example, if you accidentally erased over part of an image, you can choose **U**ndo to undo the erasing and restore the image. **U**ndo is limited to the last action performed. For example, if you drew a red circle and a blue square, only the square would be removed when the **U**ndo command was chosen.

The **K**eep Paint and **R**evert Paint commands in the **E**dit menu provide a powerful way to undo several actions. Basically, the **K**eep Paint command saves or "stores" how the

image currently appears. If, after making
several changes, you want to return to the
latest stored image, just select the **R**evert
Paint command. For example, imagine you
had created a perfectly shaped flower with
just the right colors. Before experimenting
with a few special effects, you could select the
Keep Paint command to store the image of
your flower. Now you can try out the special
effects, knowing if you really mess things up,
you can always select the Revert Paint
command to return to the version of the
flower created just prior to your experimentation.

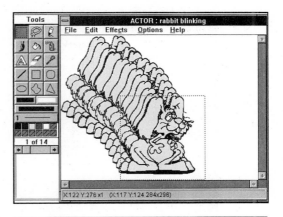

Figure 35.9

*Hold down the Ctrl key while dragging the selection area
to create multiple copies of the image.*

Selecting the Revert Paint command without
previously selecting the Keep Paint command
reverts to the original blank canvas, and
removes all objects from the painting window.

Moving and Copying Objects

After selecting images in the painting
window, you can move or copy them to a
new location. To move a selection, position
the cursor inside the selected area until the
pointer changes to a four-sided arrow, then
drag to the new location. To copy a selected
area, hold the Ctrl key down when you
initially select the image. Now when you
drag the image, the original is left behind,
and a duplicate appears in the new location.
To make multiple copies of the images inside
the selection area, hold the Ctrl key as you
drag (see fig. 35.9). This creates a series of
copies, relative to how fast you moved the
mouse—slower movement creates many
copies; faster movement creates fewer copies.

Moving and Copying Transparent and Opaque Images

The **T**ransparent and **O**paque options in the
Options menu affect how images appear
when they are moved or copied. **T**ransparent,
the default option, makes the background of
the selected area transparent. With the
Opaque command, the background of the
selection area becomes opaque and you
cannot see through it.

For example, in figure 35.10, both frames
show a selection area moved close to other
images. In the first frame, the transparent
option is selected—notice you can see
through the background of the selection area
to the objects underneath. In the second
frame, because opaque is selected, the
background is opaque and you cannot see the
objects underneath the selection area.

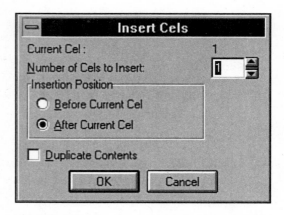

Figure 35.10

The Transparent and Opaque options affect how objects appear when moved or copied.

Inserting Cels for Multiple-Cel Actors

When creating actors in the Paint Editor, you can insert additional cels to create multiple-cel actors. By default, one cel is created for a new actor. To insert additional cels, select **I**nsert Cel from the **E**dit menu. The Insert Cels dialog box appears, as displayed in figure 35.11. Type in the number of cels you want to insert. Select **B**efore Current Cel to insert the cels before the currently displayed cel. Select **A**fter Current Cel to insert the cels after the currently displayed cel.

Figure 35.11

The Insert Cels dialog box.

The newly inserted cels will be blank unless you choose the **D**uplicate Contents option. This option can be quite a timesaver because it copies the contents of the current cel to all new cels. For instance, imagine your multiple-cel actor was a text string that rotated slightly from cel to cel. Turning on the Duplicate Contents option would place a copy of the text string on each inserted cel. From there you would only have to rotate the text, not recreate it on each cel. Click OK in the Insert Cels dialog box to add the cels. Use the arrows on the Cel Cycle Scroll bar to scroll through the cels and display the one you want to edit.

N O T E

For more information about multiple-cel actors, refer to the section, "Animating with Props and Actors," in Chapter 34.

Using Special Effects

With the special effects available in the Paint Editor, you can increase the visual appeal of your actors and props. Some of the effects, such as rotating and scaling, can be done in other Corel applications, but only the Paint Editor can tint, anti-alias, and morph images. These special effects can be applied to objects created in the Paint Editor, or objects converted to CorelMOVE objects.

All of the effects, with the exception of morphing, can be applied to actors and props. Morphing, covered later in this section, is only available with multiple-cel actors. You can apply the effect to the whole image area, or just selected parts. To select the whole image area, choose Select **A**ll from the **E**dit menu. To select a portion of the image, use the Marquee or Lasso tools described in the previous section, "Selecting in the Paint Editor."

Tinting Objects

The Tinting effect adds small increments of the current foreground or background color to the images selected in the Paint Editor. You can repeat the process until the desired tinting level is achieved. For example, if the currently selected foreground color is red, the Tint Towards Foreground command would add a red tint of color to the image. If you performed the command again, more red would be added to the image.

If nothing is selected in the image area, the tinting is applied to the whole image. To apply tinting to just part of the image area, select the area first. The Tint command is in

the Effects menu. If images are selected, the command will read **T**int Selection. If nothing is selected, the command will read **T**int Prop or **T**int All Cels, depending on whether you are creating a prop or actor. As shown in figure 35.12, the Tint submenu lets you choose Towards **F**oreground to add the foreground color to the image or Towards **B**ackground to add the background color to the image.

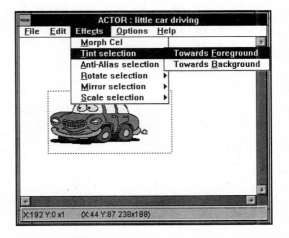

Figure 35.12

Tinting lets you add increments of the foreground or background color to your images.

Using the Anti-Alias Effect

The Anti-Alias effect can help to remove jagged edges from color images. Another set of pixels is added between the edge of the image and the background. This set of pixels creates a smoother blend between the edge color and background color. Anti-aliasing does not work particularly well with white backgrounds because the blending pixels

appear as gray. The effect works better with colored backgrounds. For example, in an image of a yellow bird on a blue background, the anti-alias effect would use yellow and blue as the colors for the blending pixels.

You may find anti-aliasing to be especially useful if you are transporting the animation to video or displaying it on a video screen. Anti-aliasing creates softer edges that may look better in video.

If nothing is selected in the image area, the anti-aliasing is applied to the whole image area. To apply anti-aliasing to just part of the image area, select the area first. The **A**nti-Alias command is in the Effe**c**ts menu. If images are selected, the command will read **A**nti-Alias Selection. If nothing is selected, the command will read **A**nti-Alias Prop or **A**nti-Alias All Cels, depending on whether you are creating a prop or actor. You can perform the command several times to reach the desired effect.

Rotating Images

The Rotate command lets you rotate images by degrees or manually by dragging rotation handles. If nothing is selected when you choose the Rotate command, the whole image is rotated. To rotate just part of the image area, select the area first. The **R**otate command is in the Effe**c**ts menu. If images are selected, the command will read **R**otate Selection. If nothing is selected, the command will read **R**otate Prop or **R**otate All Cels depending on whether you are creating a prop or actor.

As displayed in figure 35.13, the Rotate submenu offers several choices for rotating the image. Choose **C**ustom to display a dialog box where you can enter the desired rotation angle. Choose **F**ree to rotate the image manually. The Free command, only available when you have part of the image selected, displays rotation handles around the image area. Drag the handles to the desired rotation.

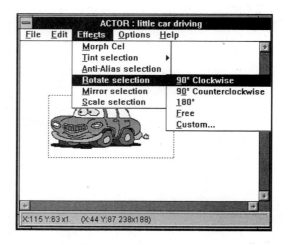

Figure 35.13
The Rotate submenu offers several options for rotating images in the Paint Editor.

Mirroring Images

You can mirror or flip objects vertically or horizontally from their center point. If nothing is selected when you choose the Mirror command, the whole image is mirrored. To mirror just part of the image area, select the area first. The **M**irror command is in the Effe**c**ts menu. If images are selected, the command will read **M**irror Selection. If nothing is selected, the command will read **M**irror Prop or **M**irror All

Cels, depending on whether you are creating a prop or actor. From the Mirror submenu, choose **V**ertically or **H**orizontally to flip the image.

Scaling Images

You can scale or size images in the Paint Editor. However, keep in mind that any jagged edges will only become more pronounced if the image is enlarged. If nothing is selected when you choose the **S**cale command, the whole image is scaled. To scale just part of the image area, select the area first. The **S**cale command is in the Effe**c**ts menu. If images are selected, the command will read **S**cale Selection. If nothing is selected, the command will read **S**cale Prop or **S**cale All Cels, depending on whether you are creating a prop or actor.

From the Scale submenu, choose Free or Custom. Choose **C**ustom to display the Scale By dialog box, shown in figure 35.14. Enter the percentage you want to scale the image up to 200 percent and click on OK. The **F**ree command, only available when you have part of the image selected, displays handles around the image area. Drag the handles to the desired size, and hold the Shift key to restrain the scaling to proportional scaling.

Figure 35.14
The Scale By dialog box.

Morphing Actors

The Morphing effect creates multiple-cel actors in which one image gradually transforms into another over a specified number of cels. As displayed in figure 35.15, morphing creates an interesting metamorphosis between images. You can create the two images in CorelMOVE, import them from the libraries, or create them in another Corel application and then convert them to CorelMOVE objects. Converting to CorelMOVE objects is discussed in the next section. As you will see, morphing can only be applied to multiple-cel actors.

Figure 35.15
Morphing enables you to create a transformation between two images.

Creating New Morphing Actors

The following steps illustrate how to create a new actor that morphs from one image to another:

1. Select the New Actor button and choose to create the actor in CorelMOVE's Paint Editor.

2. In the Paint Editor, create the first image on cel one. For instance, you could draw a blue sad face on cel one.

3. Next, insert a new cel with the Insert Cels command in the **E**dit menu. Do not duplicate the contents.

4. In cel two, create the second image, the image the first image will morph into. For instance, the second image might be a red happy face. The image on cel one will morph or transform into the image on cel two.

5. Return to cel one and select **M**orph Cel from the Effe**c**ts menu. The Morph dialog box appears, as displayed in figure 35.16.

The image on the first cel appears in the From window and the image on the second cel appears in the To window. The Pick and Zoom tools are available in the middle of the dialog box. The next step is to plot the points that control how the first image morphs into the second.

6. With the Pick tool, click in the From window to place a point. Notice a corresponding point is placed in the To window.

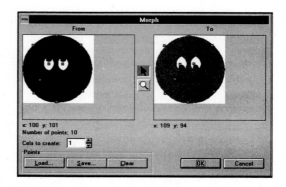

Figure 35.16
The Morph dialog box.

Placing points is an important part of creating an attractive morph. The point in the From window morphs to the corresponding point in the To window. Points should be placed in critical areas of the images. For instance, in figure 35.16, points are placed around the edges of the objects and on the eyes and mouth. You can use up to 1,000 points.

7. Use the Zoom tool to reduce or enlarge the images. When the Zoom tool is selected, the shape of the mouse cursor changes to a hand. Click on the image with the left mouse button to zoom in and with the right mouse button to zoom out.

After positioning all the points, it is a good idea to save the points by clicking on the **S**ave button.

8. In the Save Control Points dialog box, enter a file name and click on OK.

N O T E

Saving the position of the points enables you to reload them at a later time. This is important because after you have viewed the morphed actor into the animation area, you may determine that a few control points need to be modified for a better morphing effect.

Unless you have saved the control points, you will be unable to go back and edit them. Now you are ready to enter the number of cels to be used in the morph in the Cels to Create box. The more cels used, the slower the morphing effect. Generally, 10 cels is good to start with. Remember, you are specifying cels here—if you enter more cels than the total number of frames in your animation, the morphing will get cut off. The maximum number of cels in a morph is 200.

9. Once all your points are set and saved, and the number of cels is specified, click on OK. A status bar appears, displaying the progress of the morph. Be aware that this may take several minutes. When the morph is finished, you are returned to the Paint Editor.

10. Select Exit from the File menu to place the actor in the animation window, where you can play the animation to view your new morphing effect.

Morphing Between Two Existing Actors

With a slight variation to the previous steps, you can morph between two actors already created and placed in the animation area. For instance, you may want to morph between two images found in the CorelMOVE libraries. Basically, the Cut and Paste commands are used to send the second actor to the Clipboard. This actor is then pasted into a cel in the Paint Editor.

The following scenario demonstrates how to morph between two single-cel actors from the CorelMOVE libraries:

1. Place both actors in the animation window. (Refer to the next section for the steps on placing actors from the libraries.)

2. Select the second actor—the one the first image will morph into—and choose Cu**t** from the **E**dit menu. This removes the actor from the animation and stores it in the Windows Clipboard.

3. Select the first actor and choose **O**bject from the **E**dit menu to open the Paint Editor. The first actor appears in cel one of the painting window.

4. Insert a new cel with the **I**nsert Cels command in the **E**dit menu.

5. Move to cel two, and select **P**aste from the **E**dit menu to place the second actor, which was stored in the clipboard, in cel two.

6. Return to cel one and select **M**orph from the Effe**c**ts menu. You can now plot the points and set up the morph as described previously.

N O T E

To morph between multiple-cel actors, you will have to move to the last cell of the first actor, insert a new cel, and then paste the second actor. Return back to the last cel of the first actor and choose Morph from the Effects menu.

Editing Morphed Actors

After playing the morph in the animation window, you may decide you need to add or adjust a few points, or increase the number of cels used to complete the morph. To edit a morphed actor, complete the following steps:

1. Select the actor and choose **O**bject from the **E**dit menu. The actor appears in the Paint Editor. You can use the Cel Scroll bar at the bottom of the toolbox to preview each step of the morph.

It works best if you delete all of the transition cels, leaving only the two cels displaying the first and second actors. For instance, if the morphed actor has a total of 12 cels, you could delete cels two through eleven, which are the cels displaying the morph transition. This would leave the first actor on cel one and the second actor on cel two.

2. To delete the transitional cels, move to cel two and select Delete Cels from the **E**dit menu.

3. Enter the number of cels you want deleted in the Delete Cels dialog box.

4. After deleting the cels, make sure cel one displays the first actor and cel two displays the second actor.

5. Return to cel one and choose **M**orph Cels from the Effe**c**ts menu. The two actors appear in the Morph dialog box. If you saved the control points from the first time you morphed the images, click on the **L**oad button.

6. Select the file name used to save the points and click on OK. The points appear on the two images. Now you can add and modify the points as necessary. You may want to save them again, in case you need to edit the morph a third time.

7. Enter the desired number of cels used to complete the morph and click on OK. The morph effect is created again.

8. Choose E**x**it from the **F**ile menu to place the edited morphed actor into the animation window.

Placing Actors and Props in the Animation Window

When you have finished creating and editing the actor or prop, select E**x**it from the **F**ile menu. A message appears, asking you to update the changes to the Actor before closing—select Yes to place the actor or prop into the animation window. You can move the object, assign entry and exit frames, and play the animation. If you created a new actor, you can add the actor path. If you created a new prop, you can add transitions. Refer to Chapter 34, "Animating with Props and Actors," for more information on working with props and actors.

Editing Actors and Props in the Paint Editor

After creating actors and props, you may want to edit them at a later time. You can edit actors and props created in the Paint Editor or "converted" to CorelMOVE objects. The actors and props included on the CD-ROM are CorelMOVE objects that can be edited with the Paint Editor. These clip art animation objects are great to play with as you're learning, and may be just what you need in your next presentation.

To edit a Using Special Effects object, select it and choose **O**bject from the **E**dit menu. The Paint Editor window appears, with the object displayed in the painting window. The tools and effects discussed in the previous sections can be used to modify the object. To return the edited object to the animation, select E**x**it from the **F**ile menu. Select Yes from the Update message box, and the object appears in the animation window.

Converting to CorelMOVE Objects

You can convert actors and props created in other Corel applications to CorelMOVE objects. This enables you to edit the object in the Paint Editor, giving you access to some of the special effects, such as morphing. Make sure you are happy with how the object looks before converting it to a CorelMOVE object—once the object is converted, you can no longer edit it in the application where it was originally created.

To convert an object created in another Corel application to a CorelMOVE object, select the actor in the animation window. Next, choose O**b**ject Info from the **E**dit menu to display the Information dialog box for the actor or prop (see fig. 35.17). Click on the Convert button in the middle of the dialog box and click on OK. Now the object is a CorelMOVE object that can be edited in the Paint Editor. Select the object and choose **O**bject from the **E**dit menu to open up the Paint Editor.

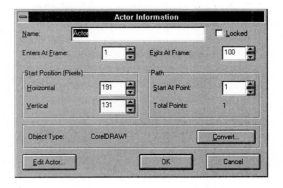

Figure 35.17
Click on the Convert button in the Actor Information dialog box to convert actors to CorelMOVE objects.

Changing the Registration Point for Actor Paths

When creating actor paths, a registration point appears on the actor that determines which part of the actor is following the path. For instance, the registration point may appear at the top left of the actor, which means the path originates from the top left

corner. The Paint Editor enables you to change the placement of the registration point. Since this option is in the Paint Editor, you will have to convert any actors not created in the Paint Editor to CorelMOVE objects.

Select the actor and choose **O**bject from the **E**dit menu to open the Paint Editor. Select **R**egistration from the **E**dit menu to display a small blinking line, which indicates the current position of the registration point. Move the mouse, which is shaped like a registration point, to the desired position for the registration point and click (see fig. 35.18). Select **R**egistration from the **E**dit menu again to set the new registration point. The newly positioned registration point appears when you begin building the actor's path.

Figure 35.18

Click to reposition an actor's registration point.

Refer to Chapter 34 for more information on actor paths.

Using CorelMOVE Libraries

CorelMOVE provides an extensive collection of predesigned actors, props, and sounds for use in your presentations. The objects are stored in libraries that are accessed through the Library roll-up. To display the Library roll-up, click on the library button on the Control Panel. As displayed in figure 35.19, the roll-up opens. If the sample files for CorelMOVE were installed, a sample library appears in the roll-up. The file name Sample.MLB appears in the roll-up title bar. This file is located in the COREL50\MOVE\ SAMPLES directory. If you have a CD-ROM, you have access to many libraries of animation objects. The steps for accessing other libraries will be discussed later in this section.

The SAMPLE.MLB library contains several images relating to dinosaurs. When the library first opens, the first actor in the collection, BABY DINO ROAR, should be animating in the Preview Window. If it is not, click on the Play button. This button toggles between Play and Stop Playing. Click on Stop Playing to halt the animation preview. Use the scroll bar above the Play/ Stop Playing button to view the other actors and props in the library. The Play button is available for actors and grayed out for props. You can use the Object Type buttons above the image to assist in locating the appropriate object. When a button is pushed in, all objects of that type are shown in the Preview Window. For example, if the Prop button is pushed in, all the props in the current library can be viewed and are available for selection.

When you find an object you want to place in the animation, click on the Place button. All library objects are placed in the animation as CorelMOVE objects, and can be edited in CorelMOVE's Paint editor. Once an object is placed into the animation, you can position it as you would any other animation object.

Figure 35.19
The SAMPLE.MLB library.

Opening Libraries

As previously mentioned, Corel's CD-ROM gives you access to many other libraries of actors, props, and sounds. These libraries are located on CD-ROM Disk Two. For a complete listing of the objects available on the CD, refer to section F of your Corel Clipart/Font book.

To open a library, click on the fly-out button at the top right of the Library roll-up. From the fly-out menu, select Open Library to reveal the Open Library dialog box, as shown in figure 35.20. Navigate to the MOVE\ LIBRARY directory on your CD-ROM. Select the desired library file, then click on OK to load it into the Library roll-up. Although the roll-up allows access to only one library at a time, you can have up to ten Library roll-ups open simultaneously.

Figure 35.20
The Open Library dialog box.

Creating a New Library

CorelMOVE enables you to make your own libraries and fill them with actors, props, and sounds that you have created or imported from other applications. For example, after spending hours perfecting the company logo, you can save it for use in other presentations. To create a new library, open the Library roll-up, and then click on the fly-out button. From the fly-out menu, select New Library to open the New Library dialog box, as shown in figure 35.21. Give the new library a distinctive name. The file extension .MLB will be added automatically.

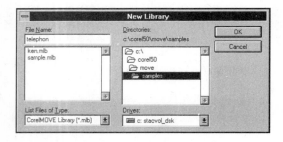

Figure 35.21
The New Library dialog box.

You cannot place any objects in a library on the CD-ROM drive. These drives are intended for READ ONLY, and cannot be written to with new data. Instead, save your new libraries to your computer's hard drive.

Be aware, however, that a library containing several animations can be quite large in size. You may want to find alternative storage options to loading your hard disk with large libraries of actors, props, and sounds.

Adding and Removing Objects in Libraries

You can add objects, delete objects, and rename objects in your libraries. To add a new object to a library, select the object in the animation window and then select Add Member to Library from the fly-out menu. The object is included in the library and listed in alphabetical order. To delete an object from a library, scroll to display it in the library Preview Window, and choose Delete Member from the fly-out menu. To rename an object, display it in the Preview Window, and select Rename Member from the fly-out menu. The Rename Member dialog box appears, as shown in figure 35.22. The current name appears at the top of the dialog. Type in a new name and click on OK.

Figure 35.22
The Rename Member dialog box.

The last command in the Library roll-up fly-out toggles between the Visual Mode and the Text Mode listing of library objects. By default, this command is active so that each member in a library is shown visually in the Preview Window. Click on the Visual Mode button to switch to the text mode listing of each object in the current library.

Adding Sound to Your Animations

If you have ever tried watching your favorite movie or television show without sound, you know how important sound can be. Imagine seeing *Jaws* without that ominous thumping soundtrack—it just wouldn't be the same.

Sound can be an integral part of your animations as well. Sound can emphasize movement, underscore action, dramatize content, and add emotional support to your animations.

CorelMOVE provides utilities for recording, editing, and controlling the playback of sound. In order to add, hear, and edit sound in your animations, you must have the proper sound capture and playback equipment, such as a SoundBlaster, or some other similar sound-capturing hardware/software configuration. If you have a microphone, you can record your own sounds for use in animations. Even if you don't plan on recording sound files, there are plenty of sound files in the CorelMOVE libraries with which you can experiment.

Adding Sounds from CorelMOVE Libraries

Before delving into creating and editing new sounds, this section starts with the steps for placing an existing sound file into your animation. A sound file from one of the CorelMOVE libraries will be used as an example.

1. Click on the Library button on the control panel to open the library roll-up, and open the library file called ALIENS.MLB from the CD-ROM.

N O T E

For more information on working with the Library roll-up, refer to the section, "Using CorelMOVE Libraries," found earlier in this chapter.

2. Use the scroll bar to move to the last entry in the aliens library called SKRONK.WAV. The file extension .WAV is shorthand for *Windows Audio Visual*—this is the most common sound file format for CorelMOVE and other Windows applications. The library will display the file name SKRONK.WAV, as shown in figure 35.23.

3. The dotted pattern in the preview window is a visual representation of a .WAV file. Click on the Play/Stop Playing button to hear the sound file.

4. After hearing it, place the file into the animation by clicking on the Place button. Once you have placed the sound file in your animation, you can play it along with other animation objects by clicking on the Play button on the Control Panel.

For sound to work well in your animations, it should coincide with the actors or props "making" the sound. For instance, it would look silly for the sound of a car starting to appear before the car is on-screen. The following section discusses editing sound effects after they are placed in the animation.

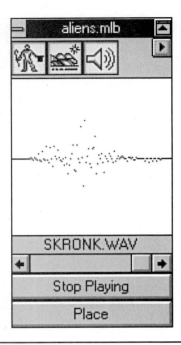

Figure 35.23
The Aliens library with the file SKRONK.WAV selected.

Editing a Sound File

Because sound files are not visible in the animation, you will have to open the Timelines roll-up to "see" them. Sound files are represented in the roll-up with blue timelines. To edit a sound file, double-click on the sound file name to open the Sound Information dialog box, as displayed in figure 35.24. Enter the desired entry and exit frames for the sound file in the Starts at Frame and Ends at Frame textboxes. You can adjust the sound level of the file with the Volume fader.

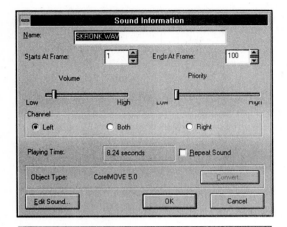

Figure 35.24

The Sound Information dialog box.

The Priority fader enables you to assign a preference to the file with regard to other sound files. When more than one sound file is scheduled to play at the same time, the sound file with the higher priority is assigned playing precedence. For example, if you have scheduled three sounds to play at the same time, and your system provides only two channels, the sound with the lowest priority will be overidden by the sounds with higher priority. Lower priority sounds may not play at all, or may play after the higher priority sound is completed. This option enables you to have control over the most important sound synch aspects of your animation.

If you are designing a sophisticated production with stereo sound, you can use the Channel radio buttons to control the projection of the sound. Stereo sounds are designed with some sound assigned to the left

channel, and others to the right channel. If you check only the Left button, the stereo sound will come only from the left speaker. If you are using mono sounds, both speakers will play the mono sound, regardless of the selection.

The Playing Time box displays the length of the selected sound file in seconds. Use the **R**epeat Sound function to instruct the file to repeat itself over and over until it exits the animation. The **C**onvert button will convert a foreign sound file to a CorelMOVE object.

If the sound was created in CorelMOVE, the **E**dit Sound button opens CorelMOVE's Wave Editor, a facility for changing the characteristics of .WAV sound files.

If the sound file was imported, clicking on the **E**dit Sound button will open the application where the sound was created. The Wave Editor is covered in detail in the next section. After you have finished making the desired adjustments to the sound file, click on OK.

Using the Wave Editor

The Wave Editor provides you with tools to modify sound files to fit your specific needs. To select a sound for editing, you will have to use the Timelines roll-up, since sounds are not visible in the animation. After selecting the sound file, select **O**bject from the **E**dit menu to open the Wave Editor dialog box, as shown in figure 35.25. Depicted in the box is a graphic representation of a sound called a *waveform.*

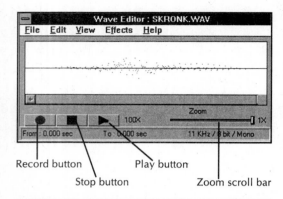

Figure 35.25

The Wave Editor dialog box.

The control panel on the bottom of the dialog box is much like those on a standard VCR. Click on the Play button to play the selected sound. If you have a microphone, you can record your own sounds by clicking on the Record button. The Stop button stops the playback or recording of a sound file. The Zoom scroll bar lets you zoom in on a particular section of a sound file. Dragging the scroll bar button left increases the magnification level of the portion of the sound wave you are viewing. You can zoom in up to 100 times the normal full view. Zooming in provides a more detailed view of the characteristics of the sound file. Drag the Zoom scroll bar back to the right to return to normal view.

On the right side of the status bar are three references that pertain to the reproduction quality of currently open sound file. The first

is the sample rate of the file. *Sample rates* are a means of determining sound quality. Basically, the higher the sample rate, the more accurate the sound reproduction. A unit of measure called Kilohertz (KHz) is utilized to measure sampling rates. CorelMOVE makes use of three popular soundwave sampling rates: 11KHz, 22KHz, and 44KHz.

The second reference applies to the bit width or volume resolution of the sound file. The available bit widths are 8 and 16. The higher the bit width, the greater the dynamic range of the sound. The last reference on the Status Bar indicates whether the sound file is a one channel (mono) sound, or two channel (stereo) sound. The next section discusses the tools available for editing waveform.

Editing in the Wave Editor

The commands in the Wave Editor's Effects menu lets you fade, amplify, and echo your sounds. Before editing the sound, you need to select the portion of the waveform you want to modify. To select a section, click on the waveform to create an insertion point and drag to highlight a portion of a file. The selected portion will turn black. Remember that you can zoom in for more precise selecting. Double-click on the waveform to select the entire sound. For audible confirmation that you have selected the correct portion, click on the play button. Only the selected portion will play.

The status bar along the bottom of the Wave Editor dialog box displays the beginning and endpoints of the current selection. The From and To fields are displayed in seconds. For example, in figure 35.26, the From and To fields display the part of the waveform that is selected.

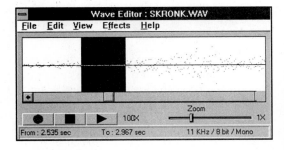

Figure 35.26
You can use the Status Bar to determine how much of the waveform is selected.

N O T E

Although you can change these sound quality options in the Change Wave Characteristics dialog box, the sound equipment you are using determines, in part, whether or not some of these options are available on your system. Check the documentation of your sound capture and playback equipment for more information about your sound capabilities.

To change the reproduction aspects of a sound file, choose **C**hange Characteristics from the E**f**fects menu. The Change Wave Characteristics dialog box appears, as shown in figure 35.27. Select the desired sample rate, sample size, and channel characteristics, and click on OK. It is important to recognize that these characteristics will have bearing on the size of your sound file. Stereo sound files with higher bit widths and sampling rates will certainly produce larger files.

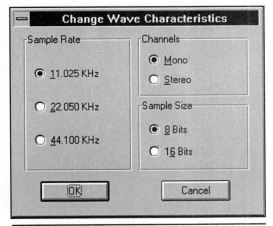

Figure 35.27
The Change Wave Characteristics dialog box.

The Effects menu provides several other options for modifying the attributes of a sound file. Choose **S**ilence to insert periods of silence into selected portions of a sound file. The Fade **U**p command enables you to gradually increase the volume of a selected portion of a file. When you choose this option, the Fade Selection Up dialog box appears, as shown in figure 35.28.

Use the numerical text box to adjust the maximum volume level of the sound file. For example, you might select the first four seconds of a sound file, and choose to create a four second fade from silence into the full 100 percent volume level. The Fade **D**own option works similarly, except that the volume controls enable you to fade down from the full volume level to whatever level you choose.

Figure 35.28
The Fade Selection Up dialog box.

The **A**mplify function works much like the Fade **U**p and Fade **D**own feature. Simply select the section where you want to increase or decrease the volume, and adjust the amplification values. Amplification options range down from 100 percent to 1 percent to decrease volume, and up from 100 percent to 9999 percent to increase volume. Choose the

Reverse option to make a sound file, or a selected section to play backward. The **E**cho option can be used to produce an echo or reverb effect on the file or portion of the sound file. If you do not select a portion of the file, the entire sound file is modified with the specified changes.

N O T E

You can use the Clipboard tools available in the **E**dit menu to further manipulate your sound files. You can delete, copy, and paste portions of the waveform to affect the sound playback.

After you have finished editing and modifying your sound file, choose E**x**it from the **F**ile menu of the Wave Editor. You will be asked if you want to save any changes you have made to the file. Choose Yes to save the changes and apply them to the sound object in the animation. Choose No to negate any changes.

Creating New Sounds

If you have a microphone, you can record your own sounds in CorelMOVE. To record a new sound, click on the Sound button to display the New Wave dialog box, as shown in figure 35.29.

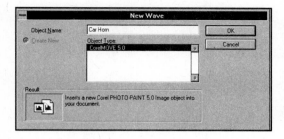

Figure 35.29
The New Wave dialog box.

In the Object **N**ame textbox, enter a distinctive name for the new sound. If you have other Wave Editor applications on your system, they will be listed in the Object **T**ype list, and a Create from File button will be available. Otherwise, the **C**reate New button will be automatically selected. Click on OK and the Wave Editor opens with the new file name displayed in the title bar. Click on the record button to begin recording your sound. Click on the Stop button to stop recording.

After recording the new sound file, you can play it by clicking on the Play button. You can also modify it as you would any sound file with the tools available in the Edit Menu. When you are satisfied with the new sound file, select E**x**it from the File menu.

Creating Interactive Animations by Adding Cues

Cues are signals in the animation file that instruct the animation to pause, wait for a response, and then resume. By adding cues, viewers can interact with your animations. For example, you might set up a cue that waits for the viewer to press Y for yes if he or she wants to continue viewing the animation. In figure 35.30, an animation on space exploration, a cue is set up so the viewer can click on the alien ship to learn more about extraterrestrial life.

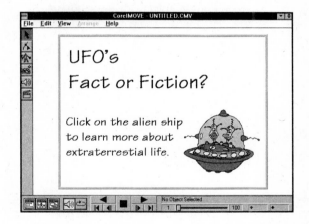

Figure 35.30
Cues let viewers interact with your animations.

When placing cues in your animations, consider whether you need to include on-screen instructions so the viewer knows what steps to perform.

Working with cues is similar to working with actors and props. You name the cue and place it in the animation with set entry and exit frames. Cues differ from actors and props in that they include a *condition* or prerequisite that must be met, such as a mouse click, or pressing a certain key. After the condition is met, an *action* is performed. The action might be ending the animation or jumping to a certain frame number.

Every cue must have a condition and an action. For example, in an animation on CPR, the condition might be pressing the C key. The action could be to jump to frame 10 and continue playing the animation. Once the condition of pressing the C key is met, the action, jumping to frame 10, is performed.

To add a cue to your animation, do the following:

1. Click on the New Cue button (the clapboard, also called a slate) in the toolbox. The Cue Information dialog box appears, as displayed in figure 35.31.

2. Enter a name for the cue that reminds you of its purpose. For instance, you might name a cue "Pause for 30 secs" to indicate the function of the cue.

3. Type in the desired entry frame in the Enters at Frame box. The cue will then be activated in the specified entry frame.

All other action in the animation stops as the conditions and actions of the cue are completed. For example, an entry frame of 7 means the cue takes place in frame 7.

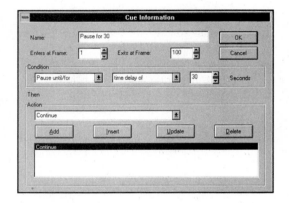

Figure 35.31
The Cue Information dialog box.

The next part in creating a cue is setting the condition to be met.

As displayed in figure 35.32, click on the arrow by the drop-down list in the Condition section of the dialog box to reveal the three available conditions—Always, Pause until/for, and If/After. The following paragraphs examine the conditions available in CorelMOVE.

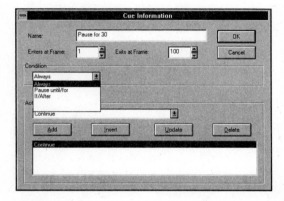

Figure 35.32
Use the drop-down menus to display the available conditions.

■ **The Always condition** is the default setting. There are no conditions to be met with Always—the specified action is always executed. For instance, a cue at frame 50 with the condition "Always" and the action "End Animation" would always stop the animation at frame 50. A cue at frame 18 with the condition "Always" and the action "Change Frame Rate to 10" would always change the frame rate (or playback speed) to 10 frames per second at frame 18.

■ **The Pause until/for condition** pauses the animation until one of three conditions is met. Notice when the Pause until/for condition is selected, another drop-down list appears. Click on the arrow by the second list to reveal three options.

The first, **Time Delay of**, pauses for a time delay of up to 600 seconds. As displayed in figure 35.33, enter the desired time delay in the Seconds box. For example, a cue at frame 5 with the condition "Pause until/for 30 seconds" would pause the animation at frame 5, perhaps giving the viewer time to read a frame. The action could then be "Continue" to resume playing the animation.

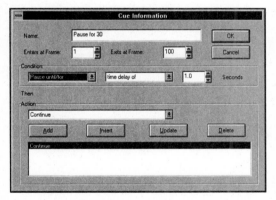

Figure 35.33
With a Time Delay cue, you can enter exactly how much time you want the animation paused.

The second option for Pause until/for conditions is **Mouse Click On**. This option pauses the animation until the mouse is clicked. As displayed in figure 35.34, click on the arrow in the third list box to specify whether the mouse can be clicked anywhere on the screen or if it must be clicked on a certain actor or prop. For example, a cue with the condition "Pause until/for Mouse Click on Anything," and the action "End Animation," stops the animation when the viewer clicks on the mouse.

(see fig 35.35), where you can select another key to be pressed. As an example , you might add a cue with the condition "Pause until/for Key Down 1," and the action "Go To Frame 1" that enables the viewer to press 1 to return to the beginning of the animation.

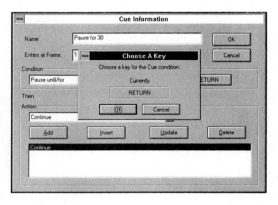

Figure 35.35
The Choose a Key dialog box.

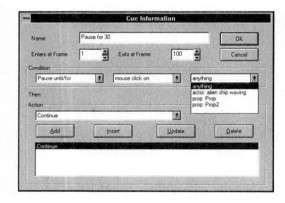

Figure 35.34
Use the third list box to specify what the viewer must click on—anything, or specific actors or props.

The third option for Pause until/for conditions is **Key Down**, which pauses the animation until a key is pressed on the keyboard. Unless specified otherwise, the cue waits for the Enter key to be pressed. Click on the button to display the Choose a Key dialog box

■ **The If/After condition** is similar to the Pause until/for condition in that you must specify a time delay, mouse click, or key down. However, a cue with the If/After condition does not pause until the condition is met. The condition can be met at any time the cue is active in the animation. If the condition is not met, the cue is ignored and the animation continues playing. For example, a cue with the condition "If/After Mouse Click on Anything" and the action "End Animation" would enable viewers to click on the mouse whenever they wanted to end the animation.

As another example, a cue with the condition "If/After Key Down B" and the action "Goto Frame 1" enables viewers to press B if they want to return to the beginning of the animation. Since If/After conditions can be executed over a stretch of time, exit frames for these cues are important. In the previous example, if the cue exited the animation at frame 50 and the viewer pressed B in frame 51, the action would not be performed because the cue was no longer active in the animation.

After establishing the conditions, you need to specify what action will take place when the conditions are successfully met. Follow these steps:

1. As displayed in figure 35.36, click on the arrow by the drop-down list in the Action section of the dialog box to reveal the available actions.

2. Select the desired action and click on the **I**nsert button to add it to the action list.

3. If you want to remove an action, select it and click on **D**elete.

4. Click on OK to add the cue to your animation.

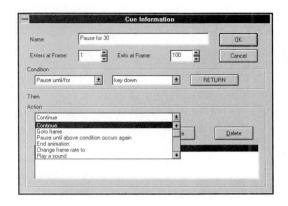

Figure 35.36

Use the drop-down menus to display the available actions.

The following paragraphs examine the actions available in CorelMOVE.

- Continue, the default action, simply continues playing the animation. For example, the condition "Time Delay 15" followed by the action "Continue" would simply pause the animation for 15 seconds and then continue playing.

- The Goto Frame action causes the animation to jump to a specific frame number. For instance, a cue with the condition "Pause until/for Mouse Click on Anything" and the action "Go To 14" would pause until the viewer clicked the mouse, and then jump to frame 14 and continue playing. As displayed in figure 35.37, enter the frame number to which you want to jump in the list box.

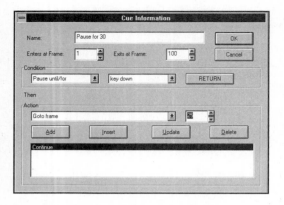

Figure 35.37
*When the Go To action is selected, enter the frame
number in the list box.*

■ With "Pause until above condition
occurs again," the animation pauses
until the condition statement becomes
true again. For example, you could
create a cue that pauses the animation
until you click on a prop. If the prop is
not clicked, the animation remains
paused.

■ The End animation action stops the
animation. For example, you could
create a cue that enables viewers to
press Enter if they want the animation
to stop.

■ The Change frame rate to action lets

you specify a different playback speed
for the animation from that point
forward. This action displays a field
where you enter a new frame rate for
the rest of the animation. This action
enables you to make different parts of
your animation play at different
speeds.

■ The Execute cue action lets you create
a cue that starts up another cue. When
you select this action, a drop-down list
appears, enabling you to select any of
the cues that are currently part of the
animation. The selected cue will
execute when the conditions of the first
cue are met. You can use this cue
action when you want to repeat a cue
that is already in the animation.
Repeating the cue might be easier than
adding another cue that does the same
thing. For example, you could create a
cue with the condition Always and the
action Execute Cue2 to repeat the cue.

Editing Cues

Because cues are not visible in the animation,
you will have to open the Timelines roll-up
to "see" them. As displayed in figure 35.38,
cues are represented in the roll-up with pink
timelines. To edit a cue, double-click on the
cue name to open the Cue Information
dialog box. Here, you can adjust the entry
and exit frames, and modify the conditions
and actions if necessary.

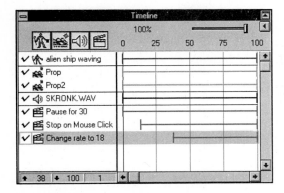

Figure 35.38
Use the TimeLines roll-up to access cues for editing.

Importing and Exporting Files

You can import actors, props, and sounds created in other applications into your CorelMOVE animations. This option becomes particularly important with regard to video and 3D animations created in programs such as Video for Windows and Autodesk Animator Pro. Imagine the impact you can make with a CorelMOVE presentation that includes actual video footage of your company's product line, or a photorealistic 3D animation of your company's logo.

Importing Actors into CorelMOVE

You can import a variety of different image formats as actors, including simple still images or complex animations. Perhaps the most exciting import option is the ability to import movie files, such as video and 3D animations.

To import a movie file into CorelMOVE, select **I**mport from the **F**ile menu. From the fly-out, choose **A**ctor from Animation File. The Import Actor dialog box appears, as shown in figure 35.39. In the List Files of **T**ype textbox, select the desired import format. Table 35.1 lists the movie formats accepted by CorelMOVE.

Figure 35.39
The Import Actor dialog box.

Table 35.1
Movie Import Formats

Application Format	File Extension
Video for Windows	.AVI
Autodesk Animator Pro	.FLI, .FLC
CorelMOVE	.CMV
QuickTime for Windows	.MOV
MPEG Movie	.MPG
Motion Works	.MWF
Macintosh PICS Animation	.PCS
Macintosh PICT images	.PCT

Navigate to the directory where the file is located, and select the desired file. Check the **P**review checkbox to view a low resolution sample of the first frame of the file. Click on OK to place the file in the animation window.

Large movie files may take several minutes to import. Once the file has been imported, you can position it on the animation window just as you would any animation object. Imported movie files can be sized in CorelMOVE's Paint Editor. However, enlarging the movie file window may increase file size and cause the animation to slow down dramatically, resulting in jerky, stilted motion.

N O T E

If you have the appropriate *Media Control Interface* (MCI) drivers, you can use Microsoft Windows Media Player to quickly preview an animation file prior to importing it. You can access the Media Player in the accessories Group in the Program Manager.

After you have imported a movie file, it can be manipulated like any other animation object. You can control the entry and exit frames in the Actor Information dialog box, or by adjusting the object's timeline. Imported movie files can be edited in CorelMOVE's Paint Editor. To edit the movie file, select it, and then choose **O**bject from the **E**dit menu to open the Paint Editor. Use caution in scaling or stretching a movie file's window. Imported animations are bitmapped files—distorting the size and shape of the window even slightly can distort the image.

Importing Bitmapped Images

Bitmapped images can also be imported into CorelMOVE as actors. If you have created a series of images in a paint program such as CorelPHOTO-PAINT or Adobe Photoshop, you can import them into CorelMOVE and put them in sequence to create a multiple-cel actor. This option enables you to have greater range to create complex bitmap actors, since the tools available in these high-level paint programs are much more sophisticated than those in CorelMOVE's Paint Editor.

As a Group of Cells

You can import bitmapped images into CorelMOVE as a group of cels that are strung together as multiple-cel actor. For instance, if you have created three images in CorelPHOTO-PAINT of a balloon bursting, you could select all three images at once and import them as an actor with three cels.

In order to import bitmaps to create multiple-cel actors, your images must meet certain criteria. First, the images must all be the same file format. For example, they must all be .PCX files or all .TIF files. In addition, all the files must be in the same directory.

It is also extremely important that the files are named in the order you want them to appear as cels for the actor you are creating. For example, to animate the balloon files, you will need to name each file in the order it will appear in the animation. Thus, you would name the image intended for the first cel, Balloon1.PCX. The image for the second cel should be Balloon2.PCX, and the third, Balloon3.PCX. The order in which you select them is insignificant. Upon import, the files will be arranged chronologically in the multiple-cel actor.

As an Actor

To import a bitmap as an actor, choose **I**mport from the **F**ile menu. From the fly-out, choose Actor from **B**itmap Files. The Import Actor dialog box appears, as shown in figure 35.39. Choose the desired file format from the List files of **T**ype textbox, then navigate to the appropriate directory. Select the desired file, and then click on the **P**checkbox to view a low resolution copy of the file.

If you are importing several images for a multiple-cel actor, use the Shift key to select contiguous, or touching, files. Use the Ctrl key to select non-contiguous files. Click on OK to place the image(s) in the animation window. Imported bitmapped images can be manipulated and edited just as any other animation object. However, keep in mind that these are bitmapped files that may distort if you change the size and shape of the image. Table 35.2 lists bitmapped formats accepted by CorelMOVE.

Table 35.2
Bitmap Actor Import Formats

Application Format	File Extension
Windows	.BMP, .DIB, . RLE
Compuserve	.GIF
JPEG	.JPG
Kodak PhotoCD	.PCD
Paintbrush	.PCX
Targa	.TGA, .VDA, .ICB, .VST
TIFF	.TIF, .CEP, .CPT

N O T E

Importing is recommended rather than Create from File if you intend to morph two complex bitmapped images. To create a morph, both morphing images must be actors, and they must be CorelMOVE objects. Importing bitmapped images meets this criteria.

Importing Props into CorelMOVE

You can import props created in other programs into your animation. To import a prop into your animation, choose **I**mport from the **F**ile menu. From the Import fly-out, choose **P**rop. The Import Prop dialog box appears, as shown in figure 35.40. Choose the desired file format from the List files of **T**ype textbox. Table 35.3 lists bitmapped formats accepted by CorelMOVE.

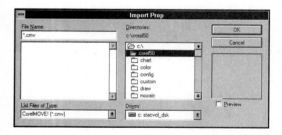

Figure 35.40
The Import Prop dialog box.

Table 35.3
Bitmap Prop Import Formats

Application Format	File Extension
Windows	.BMP, .DIB, .RLE
Compuserve	.GIF
JPEG	.JPG
Kodak PhotoCD	.PCD
Paintbrush	.PCX
Targa	.TGA, .VDA, .ICB, .VST
TIFF	.TIF, .CEP, .CPT

Navigate to the appropriate directory and select the file you want. The **P**review checkbox enables you to view a low resolution copy of the file. Click on OK to place the image in the animation window.

Imported bitmapped images can be edited just as any other animation object. Remember, these are bitmapped files that may distort if you change the size and shape of the image.

Importing Sound into CorelMOVE

If you have the appropriate sound capture and creation equipment, you can import sound files created in other sound generating applications into CorelMOVE. To import a sound file into CorelMOVE, choose **I**mport from the **F**ile menu. From the Import fly-out, choose **S**ound. The Import Sound dialog box appears, as shown in figure 35.41.

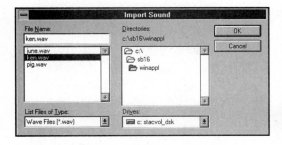

Figure 35.41
The Import Sound dialog box.

Choose the desired file format from the List Files of **T**ype textbox. Table 35.4 lists the sound file formats accepted by CorelMOVE.

Table 35.4
Sound Import Formats

Application Format	File Extension
AIFF Audio	.AIF
Video for Windows	.AVI
CorelMOVE	.CMV
QuickTime for Windows	.MOV
Motion Works	.MWF
Mac SND binary	.SND
Amiga SVX Audio	.SVX
SoundBlaster Audio	.VOC
Windows Sound File	.WAV

Navigate to the appropriate directory, and select the file you want to place in the animation. Imported sound files become CorelMOVE objects and can be manipulated just as any CorelMOVE sound file.

N O T E

You can also drag and drop files into CorelMOVE from CorelMOSAIC. You can access the Mosaic roll-up from the File menu. For more information on this option, refer to the section of this book on CorelMOSAIC.

Export Options

CorelMOVE enables you to export your animations to a number of different movie formats for playback in other popular animation applications. Animations can also be exported frame-by-frame, where each frame of the animation is an individual file. This option provides you with the ability to critically examine each frame of the animation. Sound files created in CorelMOVE can also be exported to a file for use in creating a more detailed soundtrack file for your animation.

To export an animation, select **E**xport from the **F**ile menu, and **M**ovie from the submenu. The Export To Movie dialog box appears, as shown in figure 35.42. Choose the desired export format from the List Files of **T**ype textbox. Table 35.5 lists the available export formats.

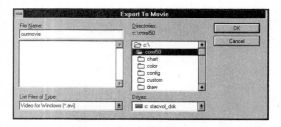

Figure 35.42
The Export To Movie dialog box.

Table 35.5
Movie Export Formats

Application Format	File Extension
Video for Windows	.AVI
Quick Time for Windows	.MOV
MPEG Movie	.MPG
PICS Animation	.PCS
Macintosh PCIT Images	.PCI

- If you choose the Video for Windows format, a dialog box will follow that enables you to choose a compression method to reduce the file size. It is recommended that you choose

the Corel RLE compression standard since it does not require additional software to perform the decompression.

The MPEG format also has a dialog box associated with it that provides options for you to compress the file. In addition to compression, you can also choose to emphasize the speed of the compression process over the quality of the compressed animation file. The MPEG Options dialog box also enables you to export only the audio portion of the file, only the video portion, or the entire file including both audio and video.

Exporting to Individual Files

You can export your animation as a series of individual files. In this case, each frame of the animation becomes a separate file. This option is particularly useful when an examination of each frame is important. After you have exported to individual files, each file can then be printed as a separate image.

Select Export from the **F**ile menu. From the fly-out, choose To **I**ndividual Files. The Export To Individual Files dialog box appears, as shown in figure 35.43. Choose the desired export format from the List Files of **T**ype textbox. Each individual file will be exported with the same file format. Table 35.6 lists the available export formats.

Figure 35.43
The Export To Individual Files dialog box.

Table 35.6
Individual File Export Formats

Application Format	File Extension
Windows Bitmap	.BMP
OS/2 Bitmap	.BMP
CompuServe Bitmap	.GIF
JPEG Bitmap	.JPG, .JFF, .JTF, .CMP
CorelPHOTO-PAINT	.PCX
TIFF 6.0 4-color Bitmap	.SEP
Targa	.TGA, .VDA, .ICB, .VST
TIFF 5.0 Bitmap	.TIF

Enter a name for the files in the File Name textbox. CorelMOVE will need up to three characters of the file name to designate a specific number for each file generated by an exported animation frame. Since you are limited to only eight characters for a file name, this means that most of your files should be named with no more than five characters. For example, in an animation called SEMINAR.CMV that contains 288 frames, you might name the export file SEM. In this way, CorelMOVE will name each file of the exported animation, SEM001, SEM002, ...SEM288.

You can export just a portion of the animation. The Export Options enables you to specify a starting and ending frame for the section you want to export. If you do choose to export in sections, the First File Number textbox enables you to assign a file number to the first exported frame so you won't be confused about which frames of the animation you are working with.

Choose the destination directory for the export file, then click on OK to begin exporting. This process can take many minutes to complete. It is important to recognize that depending on the size and complexity of the animation you are exporting, the exported files may require a great deal of your hard disk space.

Exporting Sound Files

To enhance the sound of your animation, you may want to export your sound files to a sound editing program that provides more sophisticated wave editing tools. With the

proper hardware and software, you can transform your sound files into elaborate multitrack productions, and then import the enhanced sound files back into CorelMOVE.

To export a sound file, select Export from the File menu. Choose Sound from the fly-out, and the Export To Sound dialog box appears, as shown in figure 35.44. In the List Files of Type textbox, choose the desired export format. Table 35.7 lists the available export formats.

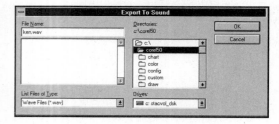

Figure 35.44
The Export To Sound dialog box..

Table 35.7
Sound Export Formats

Application Format	File Extension
AIFF Audio	.AIF
Mac Sound MacBinary	.MB2
Amiga SVX Audio	.SVX
SoundBlaster Audio	.VOC
Windows Sound File	.WAV

Enter a distinctive name for the exported sound file, choose a destination directory, and click on OK to export the file.

Using CorelMOVE's MCI Player

CorelMOVE comes with a facility called CorelMOVE MCI Player, which enables you to play your CorelMOVE animations from Windows Program Manager without opening CorelMOVE. Even more, you can even use the MCI Player to run CorelMOVE animations on a computer that does not have Corel installed. This is a huge advantage for those times when you want to hit the road with your animation. With the MCI Player, you don't have to worry about whether Corel is loaded on the computer you will use to play back your animation.

To load CorelMOVE's MCI Player on a computer that has Corel installed, simply run the installation program and choose to do a custom install. Proceed with the custom installation, then choose to Customize the options for CorelMOVE. Click in the checkbox to install the MCI Player, and then continue with the installation. The CorelMOVE MCI Player will become an icon in the Corel 5.0 Program Group. To play a file with the MCI player, double-click on the MCI Player icon, and open the file you want to play.

To play a CorelMOVE animation on a system without Corel installed, you must load two files onto the playback computer. The two files you will need are: COREL5.0\MOVE\OEMSETUP.INF and COREL50\PROGRAMS\MCICMV50.DRV.

Copy these two files onto the playback system in the following way. From Program Manager, open the Main Program Group, and launch the Control Panel. Double click on the Drivers Icon to open the Drivers dialog box. Click on the Add button. From the Add dialog box, choose the option Unlisted or Updated Driver to open the Install Driver dialog box. Type in the floppy drive where the MCI driver is stored. Choose the CorelMOVE Player as the file to install and click on OK.

Once the appropriate files are installed, you can use Window Media Player to play your CorelMOVE animations. To play an animation from the Media Player, open the Accessories Program Group, then double-click to launch the Media Player. Select Open from the File menu; the Open dialog box will appear. Navigate to the directory where your animation file is stored, select it, and click on OK. You may have to size the

Media Player window to cover the Program Manager in the background.

N O T E

Do not play your animation from a floppy drive. The speed limitation of the floppy drive will slow your animation down drastically.

Summary

With CorelMOVE, you now have all the tools necessary to become a multimedia artist—animations, sound files, video—it's all here. Take some time and explore. You may be suprised at how quickly you will be constructing your own multimedia presentations.

When you combine the power of CorelMOVE with the impact of charts created in CorelCHART, and graphics developed in DRAW and PHOTO-PAINT, you have all the tools you need to present effective productions. The next chapter, "Building Presentations in CorelSHOW," will help you do just that. With CorelSHOW, you can consolidate a graphic created in DRAW with animations created in MOVE, images manipulated in PHOTO-PAINT, and charts created in CorelCHART—all to create a presentation that is persuasive and memorable.

Building Presentations in CorelSHOW

*W*ith CorelSHOW, you can build visually appealing presentations with graphics, charts, and animation. CorelSHOW works as an assembling program, meaning presentations are built or assembled from data created in other applications. For instance, in a presentation on the city zoo, you could use CorelDRAW to draw blueprints of the new elephant grounds. CorelCHART could contribute charts analyzing how building costs would be handled. With CorelPHOTO-PAINT, beautiful photos of the animals in their new facilities could become part of the animation. The presentation could end with fun animation created in CorelMOVE depicting the animals throwing a party to celebrate their new home. Imagine the presentations you can create when you have the power of CorelDRAW, CorelCHART, CorelPHOTO-PAINT and CorelMOVE at your fingertips.

This chapter covers:

- Understanding CorelSHOW basics

- Examining CorelSHOW's presentation views

- Creating a new presentation

- Saving a presentation

- Understanding object linking and embedding

- Adding and formatting text in CorelSHOW

Understanding CorelSHOW Basics

CorelSHOW is a presentation program designed to assemble graphics, charts, and data from other applications and to display them in a slide show or presentation.

The presentations you create in CorelSHOW can be output to slides, overhead transparencies, or videotape. With CorelSHOW, you can also create desktop presentations, where the presentation is shown from a computer monitor. Or you may be connected to a data display or video player. When your presentations will be shown from a computer, you can add special effects such as wipes, zooms, and fades to perk up the show.

Although CorelSHOW can enter and format text, it has no other tools for generating data such as graphics and charts. CorelSHOW uses a process called *Object Linking and Embedding* (OLE) to access graphics, charts, photos, and animations generated in CorelDRAW, CorelCHART, CorelPHOTO-PAINT, and CorelMOVE. In fact, OLE provides CorelSHOW the power to access data from any Windows application that supports Object Linking and Embedding. For instance, you could build presentations that include spreadsheets from Excel, text documents from WordPerfect or Word for Windows, and charts from Freelance Graphics for Windows. An overview of Object Linking and Embedding is provided later in this chapter.

This book includes two chapters on CorelSHOW: this chapter and Chapter 37, "Presenting with CorelSHOW." This

chapter focuses on building presentations in CorelSHOW. You will learn how to set up a new presentation file, specify the number of slides, and set up the page. Next, you'll find all the information you need for inserting into your presentation objects created in other applications; here you will also discover how to import graphics from CorelDRAW and charts from CorelCHART. Finally, the chapter looks at the steps for adding text, such as titles and bulleted lists, to your presentation slides. The next chapter concentrates on displaying the presentation in CorelSHOW; you'll find information for applying slide transitions, adjusting slide timings, and creating interactive presentations by adding cues.

Starting CorelSHOW

CorelSHOW is a separate program included with CorelDRAW. To start CorelSHOW, open the Corel 5 group window and double-click on the CorelSHOW icon. The initial CorelSHOW screen appears with all of the elements grayed out except for the **F**ile and **H**elp menus. From this blank screen, you can start a new presentation or open an existing one. How to open a presentation is covered first so that an introduction to the CorelSHOW screen may be provided.

Opening an Existing CorelSHOW File

To open an existing presentation file, select **O**pen from the **F**ile menu. The Open File dialog box, as displayed in figure 36.1, appears. If necessary, change to the drive and directory where the presentation files are stored. The CorelSHOW files located in the specified directory appear in the File **N**ame box. CorelSHOW files have the file extension .SHW. After selecting the file name, you can click in the **P**review checkbox to see a low resolution copy of the file. Use the scroll bar beneath the preview image to view other slides in the presentation file. Click on the **O**ptions button to gain access to Keyword searches and Notes about the file. When you are ready to open the presentation file, click on OK. To get a feel for how a presentation in CorelSHOW is set up, you might open the sample presentation file called SAMPLE.SHW. The sample presentation is found in the COREL50\SHOW\SAMPLES directory.

N O T E

You can open more than one presentation at a time in CorelSHOW. When you have more than one file open, use the Window menu to switch between presentations. However, some presentations can be quite large and might require a great deal of your system's resources, so having multiple presentations open can slow you down significantly.

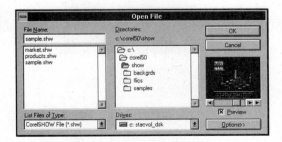

Figure 36.1
The Open File dialog box.

T I P

You can use a keyboard shortcut, Ctrl+O, to display the Open Animation File dialog box. In addition, CorelMOVE places the name of the four most recently opened animation files in a list at the bottom of the **F**ile menu. Clicking on the file name is a quick way to open a file.

Exploring the CorelSHOW Screen

As illustrated in figure 36.2, the CorelSHOW screen has the same basic look as other Corel applications. The title bar appears at the very top of the screen, displaying the name of the currently opened file. Beneath the title bar is the menu bar. Just under the menu bar is the ribbon bar, which provides quick access to frequently used features such as saving, printing, and running the screen show. The text ribbon bar appears directly beneath the ribbon bar and provides tools for formatting text created in CorelSHOW.

toolbox   ribbon bar

   rulers   text ribbon bar

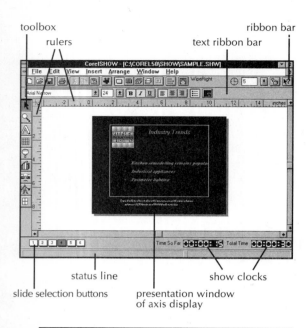

status line

slide selection buttons   presentation window   show clocks
                           of axis display

Figure 36.2
The CorelSHOW screen.

N O T E

You can turn off the display of the ribbon bar, the text ribbon bar, the status line, and other screen display options by selecting **F**ile, Pre**f**erences. From the Preferences dialog box, select the View tab, then click in the appropriate check boxes to turn on or off the chosen screen display options.

In the center of the screen is the Presentation Window. You will design and assemble the slides in your presentation here. To the left and above the presentation area are rulers. You can remove the rulers from the screen display by selecting **R**ulers from the **E**dit

menu. Along the bottom of the screen is the status line. The status bar is an indispensable tool for helping to familiarize you with CorelSHOW. When you hover the cursor over any tool or command on the screen, the status line provides a description of that tool or command. Just above the status line are two clocks for helping you manage the slides in your presentations.

To the left are the Slide Selection buttons. Click on these buttons to display a particular slide. For example, clicking on number 10 displays slide 10 of the presentation. The Slide selector displays up to ten slides. As displayed in figure 36.3, if you have more than ten slides, arrows appear to the left and right of the buttons. Click on these arrows with the left mouse button to scroll forward and backward one slide at a time. If you click the right mouse button on the scroll bar, the display jumps forward or backward ten slides at a time.

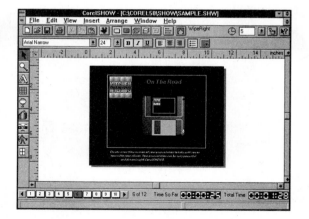

Figure 36.3
Use the Slide Selection buttons to move through your presentation. Use the Show clocks to determine the length of your presentation.

To the right of the Slide Selection buttons are the Show clocks. These clocks are used to time screen shows for presentation playback. The clock on the left indicates the length of the show up to the currently selected slide. The clock on the right indicates the entire length of the show. In figure 36.3, the clock on the left indicates the show is scheduled to play for 25 seconds up to slide 6, and the clock on the right indicates the length of the whole show is 1 minute, 28 seconds.

The toolbox along the left provides access to the tools necessary to build your presentations. Table 36.1 provides a description of the tools.

Table 36.1
CorelSHOW's toolbox

Tool	Used For
Pick tool	Selecting objects, similar to the Pick tool in CorelDRAW.
Zoom tool	Used to adjust the view of your presentation. Similar to the Zoom tool in CorelDRAW, you can zoom in when you want a closer look at a slide and out when you want to see the overall picture.
Text tool	The Text tool enables you to type text directly into CorelSHOW. Clicking on the Text tool displays a fly-out menu that includes two options: Artistic and Paragraph text. Working with text is covered later in this chapter.
Background Libraries tool	Displays a dialog box for applying predesigned backgrounds to your presentation.
OLE to CorelDRAW tool	Used to add embedded objects created in CorelDRAW.
OLE to CorelCHART tool	Used to add to your presentation embedded objects created in CorelCHART.
OLE to PHOTO-PAINT tool	Used to add embedded objects created in CorelPHOTO-PAINT.
Insert Animation tool	Displays a dialog box for inserting an animation into the current slide.
OLE to Other	Opens a fly-out Applications tool menu with icons representing applications that you can use to create embedded objects for your presentation.

To create a "floating" toolbox, which you can move around on the screen, select Floating from the Toolbox command in the View menu.

Examining CorelSHOW's Presentation Views

CorelSHOW provides several "views" or ways for you to look at and work with your presentation files. The first, Slide view (see fig. 36.3), lets you view one slide at a time. Slide view is where you'll probably spend most of your time because this is where you design and build each slide in your presentation. In Slide view, you can edit and manipulate text and insert objects from other applications, such as CorelDRAW, CorelCHART, or CorelPHOTO-PAINT. Click on the Slide View button in the ribbon bar or choose Slide from the View menu to work in Slide view.

CorelSHOW often refers to the images on your screen as slides, although they might not be output to slides at all. For example, although you might create a presentation that you show from the computer, CorelSHOW frequently refers to each individual page in the show as a slide.

The Slide Sorter view is extremely useful. As shown in figure 36.4, the Slide Sorter enables you to view several slides of your presentation at one time. Each slide is displayed in miniature. In the Slide Sorter, you can delete and move slides to adjust their order in the presentation. For instance, you can change slide 3 to slide 10. To move a slide, drag the miniature slide to the new location. A dotted outline with a vertical black bar serves as a guide as you drag. Position the black bar at the new location for the slide and release the mouse. To display the Slide Sorter view, click on the Slide Sorter button on the ribbon bar or choose Slide Sorter from the View menu.

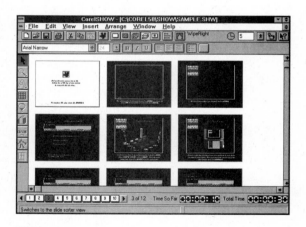

Figure 36.4
The Slide Sorter view enables you to view several slides at once.

The Speaker Notes view (fig. 36.5) displays a page with a thumbnail image of the slide at the top of the page, reserving the bottom for related text. For example, you can add text to this page and use it as reference notes for the presentation; the speaker can then use the notes during the presentation to recall certain points and remember which slide comes next. Speaker notes are automatically created for each slide in the presentation, are saved along with the presentation file, and can also be used for audience handouts. You can use the Slide Selector buttons to move between speaker note pages for each slide in your presentation. To access the Speaker **N**otes view, click on the Speaker Notes button or choose Speaker **N**otes from the **V**iew menu.

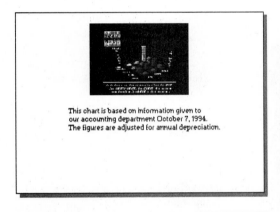

Figure 36.5

The Speaker Notes view.

The Slide **B**ackground view (see fig. 36.6) displays a slide in which you design the background for all of the slides. For instance, if you create a blue background in the Slide **B**ackground view, all of the slides display the blue background. The Slide **B**ackground view serves as a kind of master view for the overall appearance of a presentation. Any object that you want to appear on every slide should be placed in the Slide **B**ackground view. As shown in figure 36.6, for example, you could place the company logo and any decorative lines in the Slide **B**ackground view.

Figure 36.6

Elements placed on the Slide Background view appear on every slide of the presentation.

N O T E

Speaker note pages assume the same page orientation as the presentation images do in a show. You can, however, temporarily change the page orientation for printing speaker notes, then return to an orientation suitable for your presentation images.

You cannot make changes to the presentation background in any view except the Slide **B**ackground view; if you were to place a red ball on the background layer, it would appear on each slide in the show and cannot be modified except from the Slide **B**ackground view. You can access the Slide **B**ackground

view by clicking on the Slide Background View button or by choosing Slide **B**ackground from the **V**iew menu.

Creating a New Presentation

To begin a new presentation, select **N**ew from the **F**ile menu. The New Presentation dialog box appears, as shown in figure 36.7. By default, CorelSHOW places five slides in your presentation. If you want more or less, enter the desired number of slides in the **S**tarts with text box. The maximum is 999. Don't worry about creating the correct number of slides here because you can always add and delete slides later.

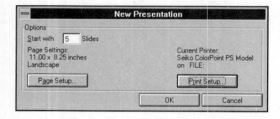

Figure 36.7
The New Presentation dialog box.

The New Presentations dialog box also displays the current page settings and printer information, and buttons are supplied to make changes to both of these settings.

1. Click on the P**a**ge Setup button to open the Page Setup dialog box, as displayed in figure 36.8.

Figure 36.8
The Page Setup dialog box.

2. Select the desired page orientation and size.

3. Click on the Custom page size to enter your own horizontal and vertical page measurements. You can enter any dimension up to 17×17 inches.

4. Click on the down arrows in the list boxes by "inches" to select another system of measurement.

5. When ready, click on OK to accept the page setup changes and return to the New Presentation dialog box.

T I P

You can also access the Page Setup dialog box by clicking the right mouse button on the slide and choosing Page Setup from the pop-up menu.

If you intend to print your presentation rather than show it from the computer screen, you should select your target print device *before* building the presentation. Because printers often use different page command languages, some images might shift position if you try to print a show from a print device different than the device for which it was originally built. For example, suppose you design the presentation with a setup for a desktop laser printer, but you intend to ultimately print to an inkjet printer. When you change the print device to the inkjet to print the presentation, some objects might shift to accommodate the print command language of the new printer.

> **N O T E**
>
> If you are working with PostScript printers, you don't need to worry about items shifting as a result of changing print devices. PostScript language is consistent on all PostScript print devices.

1. Click on the P**r**int Setup button to open the Print Setup dialog box, shown in figure 36.9.

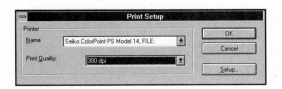

Figure 36.9
The Print Setup dialog box.

2. Choose the desired printer from the **N**ame drop-down list box and select the appropriate resolution.

3. Click on the Setup button to access information about the selected printer.

4. Click on OK to return to the New Presentations dialog box.

5. When the settings in the New Presentations dialog box are correct, click on OK to begin building your new presentation.

> **N O T E**
>
> If you decide to change the page or printer setup after creating the new presentation, select Pa**g**e Setup (or P**r**int Setup) from the **F**ile menu.

Saving a Presentation

To save a new presentation, choose Save **A**s from the **F**ile menu. The Save Presentation As dialog box appears (see fig. 36.10). In the File **N**ame text box, enter the name of your file. Use the Directories List box to navigate to the desired directory to store your file. The **K**eywords and Not**e**s boxes can be used to attach additional reference information to the saved file.

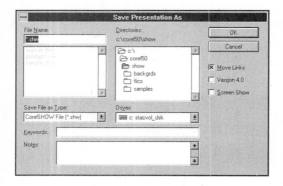

Figure 36.10
The Save Presentation As dialog box.

The check boxes beneath the OK button enable you to save your presentation file so that it can be edited and run in version 4.0 of CorelSHOW. You want to check the Move Links option if you plan to save your presentation to run from another computer. This way, any linked files are saved along with the presentation file so that when the presentation file runs, the linked files are accessible. You should activate the Screen Show option to save your presentation as a non-editable file that can only be run as a screen show. Refer to chapter 37, "Presenting with CorelSHOW," for more information on building screen shows.

Selecting a Presentation Background

Backgrounds add visual appeal and continuity to your presentations. A similar background on each slide ties a presentation together, adding professionalism to your work. You can use one of the backgrounds provided by CorelSHOW or build your own.

Before applying a background, be sure you switch to the Background view. To use one of the many attractive backgrounds provided by CorelSHOW, click on the Background Library button on the tool bar. A sample library of predesigned backgrounds appears (see fig. 36.11). Use the scroll arrows on the right to scroll through the images stored in the sample library. Select a background and click on the Done button to set the image as the backdrop for every slide in your presentation.

Figure 36.11
The Sample Background Library provided with CorelSHOW.

Creating a Customized Background

You can use CorelDRAW's graphics tools to create your own customized background. After switching to the Slide **B**ackground view, click on the OLE to CorelDRAW button. CorelSHOW launches CorelDRAW where you can design your background.

When the background design is complete, choose **F**ile, E**x**it, and press Enter. In the subsequent dialog box, choose **Y**es to Update CorelSHOW. You are returned to CorelSHOW with the new object in place.

To ensure that the new background object fits the current slide dimensions in CorelSHOW, select the background object and choose Fit Object to **S**lide from the **A**rrange menu.

After creating a backdrop for your presentation, you might want to add additional background elements, such as a company logo or a series of colored bars. Once these elements are brought into CorelSHOW, you can use the commands in the **A**rrange menu to adjust the stacking order of the objects. The commands work similar to those in CorelDRAW, enabling you to bring objects to the front and send them to the back. In addition, you can use guidelines in CorelSHOW to align objects for precise placement. As with CorelDRAW, drag the guidelines from the rulers. You can also use the **G**uidelines Setup command in the **A**rrange menu to add, delete, and edit guidelines.

You can keep the background for future use by saving it in a background library. To save the background, choose Save **B**ackground from the **F**ile menu. The Save Background dialog box appears (see fig. 36.12). To save the new background to an existing library, select the library name in the list box below the File **N**ame text box. Be sure to click on the Insert in **L**ibrary check box before saving to an existing library. Otherwise, your new

background will not be inserted in the existing library, but it will replace the existing library—the library would only contain the most recently added background. Click on OK to insert your background into the selected library.

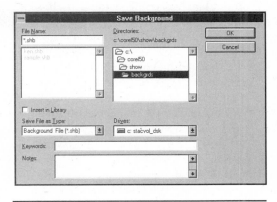

Figure 36.12
The Save Background dialog box.

To create a new background library file, type a new name in the File **N**ame text box and click on OK. The new library will then contain only the single new background. When you have several background libraries, use the Change Library button to view other libraries.

Backgrounds that you create and save might not display properly in the sample box and might appear black instead. Click on the background you want and it will apply itself to the presentation background where you can view it. If it is the desired choice, simply click on OK to apply it.

Understanding Object Linking and Embedding

Object Linking and Embedding or OLE (pronounced olé) is an integral part of CorelSHOW. OLE is a feature in many Windows applications that enables you to work in one Windows application and access data created in other Windows applications. OLE provides the power that allows CorelSHOW to include in your presentation information or objects created in CorelDRAW and other applications. As previously discussed, CorelSHOW has few tools for actually creating anything—the tools in CorelSHOW are instead aimed at assembling and manipulating objects created in other applications. By using CorelSHOW's OLE capabilities, you have the advantages and power of several pro-grams available while you assemble your presentation.

N O T E

For more information on OLE, refer to your Microsoft Windows documentation or to *Inside Windows, Platinum Edition*, by New Riders Publishing.

Much more than a way to access information or objects created in other applications, OLE establishes a connection between the application the object was created in and the application the object is displayed in. This connection provides to you the capability to edit and modify the object even after it is placed in another application.

For instance, imagine you placed a graphic created in CorelDRAW in a CorelSHOW presentation. If you needed to edit the graphic, OLE provides CorelSHOW with the power to launch CorelDRAW, edit the graphic, and then return to CorelSHOW with the edited graphic. In this example, CorelDRAW would be the *source application*, the application that originally created the object. CorelSHOW would be the *destination application*, the application where the object is ultimately placed.

As the name implies, Object Linking and Embedding provides two methods—linking and embedding—for consolidating objects into your CorelSHOW presentations. The following section provides an overview of both methods. Following that, you will find the steps for creating linked and embedded images in CorelSHOW.

Understanding Linking

Linking enables you to associate to another application a file created in a different application. For example, you could link a file of the company logo created in CorelDRAW into a CorelSHOW presenta-tion file. CorelDRAW, where the file is originally located, would be the source, and CorelSHOW, the receiver of the data, would be the destination. The link establishes a special connection between the source and destination files. This connection alerts the destination file to reflect any changes in the source file.

For instance, imagine that you have created the company logo in CorelDRAW and linked it to an animation in CorelMOVE, a photo in CorelPHOTO-PAINT, and a presentation in CorelSHOW. After some consideration, you decide that the color of the logo is slightly off. You could easily remedy this problem by opening the original file in CorelDRAW and making the necessary changes. But changes made to the CorelDRAW file are reflected in *all* of the other three locations because the original file is linked to CorelMOVE, CorelPHOTO-PAINT, and CorelSHOW. Thus, if you were to open CorelMOVE, CorelPHOTO-PAINT, and CorelSHOW, the latest changes to the original CorelDRAW file would be displayed.

Understanding Embedding

Embedding lets you work in one application, but gives you access to tools in other applications. For instance, while working in CorelSHOW, you can launch CorelDRAW and design a graphic. When you exit CorelDRAW, the graphic is embedded in CorelSHOW. The embedded object retains information about the source application (CorelDRAW) so that you can easily edit it. To edit the embedded object from within CorelSHOW (the destination application), simply double-click on it. This opens the source application where you can perform any modifications.

Unlike linked objects, embedded objects do not exist as separate files. An embedded

object appears only in the destination application and thus becomes part of the destination document. Therefore, even though an embedded object is created in another application, it exists only in the destination document.

For example, if you are in CorelSHOW and decide you need a blue box for a slide, you could launch CorelDRAW, create the box, then exit CorelDRAW and go back to CorelSHOW where the embedded blue box now appears. In this scenario, the blue box does not exist in CorelDRAW. It has no file name and has never been saved in CorelDRAW. The box exists only within CorelSHOW as an object embedded from CorelDRAW.

Creating Linked Objects in CorelSHOW

As previously discussed, linking lets you insert and display files created in CorelDRAW, CorelCHART, and CorelPHOTO-PAINT into your CorelSHOW presentation files. CorelSHOW can also link data from other Windows applications, such as Excel or Word for Windows. As you can imagine, this gives you a lot of flexibility in assembling your presentation. Before linking a file, display the slide where you want the object to appear. To link a file, select **O**bject from the **I**nsert menu to display the Insert Object dialog box, then select the Create from **F**ile option on the left of the dialog box, shown in figure 36.13.

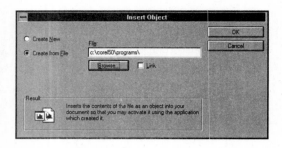

Figure 36.13
The Insert Object dialog box.

In the Fil**e** name text box, enter the path and name of the file to be inserted into CorelSHOW. You can also click on the **B**rowse button to open the Browse dialog box, shown in figure 36.14. Navigate to the location of the file you want to insert. If you want to establish a linked connection to the original file, check the **L**ink check box. In this way, any edits you make to the original file are reflected everywhere else the file is linked, so that all links will display any changes made to the original. After making the appropriate selections, click on OK to link the object in CorelSHOW.

Figure 36.14
The Browse dialog box.

You can continue to edit the linked object after it is placed in CorelSHOW. To edit the linked file, double-click on the linked image. When the source application opens, make the desired edits, then choose **F**ile, E**x**it. When asked if you want to save changes to the file, choose Yes. The application where the file was created closes, and CorelSHOW appears with the edited linked object. Remember that if you edit a linked file in this way, you are changing the original file, as well as all of its links. When you edit a linked file in this manner, the file no longer exists in its original state.

As an example, imagine that you have linked to your presentation a chart file created in CorelCHART. After linking, assume that you discover some errors in the chart. To edit the linked chart, simply double-click on it to launch CorelCHART. The linked chart appears in CorelCHART's display area. Now you can make the necessary changes to the chart. When finished with your modifications, click on E**x**it in the **F**ile menu. A dialog box appears asking you to save the changes; click on Yes. CorelCHART then closes, and you are returned to CorelSHOW where the latest changes to the chart appear in the presentation.

If the latest changes do not appear in CorelSHOW after editing a linked object, you might have to update the link manually. To manually update a link, choose Lin**k**s from the **E**dit menu. The Links dialog box appears (see fig. 36.15). Select the linked object you want to update, then click on the **U**pdate Now button.

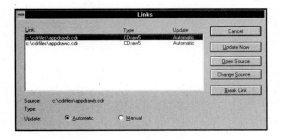

Figure 36.15

The Links dialog box.

Click on the Change Link button to open the Change Link dialog box in which you can change the present link to establish a new link to another file or application.

The Break Link button severs the selected link so there is no longer a connection between the CorelSHOW file and the object's source application. You might want to use this option to decrease the size of a CorelSHOW file because OLE connections create larger files. Break the connection only if you do not think you will need to edit the object again. After making the appropriate selections, click on Close to return to your presentation.

N O T E

If you want linked files to be updated automatically, go to the Links dialog box, select the linked file and click on the **A**utomatic Update radio button.

Creating Embedded Objects in CorelSHOW

In earlier discussions, embedding was described as the capability to launch an application from within another application. While working in CorelSHOW, for instance, you can open CorelDRAW and create a graphic object. The object created in the source application, CorelDRAW, is then embedded in the destination application, CorelSHOW. Before embedding, display the slide in which you want the embedded object to appear.

By using the OLE buttons on the toolbox, you can embed into CorelSHOW objects created in other Corel applications. Click on the OLE to CorelDRAW button (the CorelDRAW balloon) to open CorelDRAW. Click on the OLE to CorelCHART button (the small bar chart) to open CorelCHART. When you click on the OLE to CorelPHOTO-PAINT button (the camera), CorelPHOTO-PAINT opens. When the Corel application opens, design your graphic, chart, or photo, then choose E**x**it from the **F**ile menu. A message appears asking you to update the image in CorelSHOW; click on Yes. The object is then embedded in your CorelSHOW presentation.

CorelSHOW can embed data from other Windows applications, such as Excel or Word for Windows. Click on the OLE to Other Applications button to display the Insert Object dialog box (see fig. 36.16). By default, the Create **N**ew option is selected.

All objects on your system that are capable of embedding an OLE object into CorelSHOW are listed in the **O**bject Type list box. To proceed with creating a new OLE object, select the application you want to create the object in and click on OK. The chosen application opens, and you can begin creating the new object. When you finish with the new object, selec**t F**ile, E**x**it, then choose Yes to update CorelSHOW with the new object. The application closes, and CorelSHOW appears with the newly created object in place.

Figure 36.16
The Insert Object dialog box.

To edit an embedded object, simply double-click on the embedded image to open the source application. Make the desired edits in the source application, then choose **F**ile, E**x**it. Choose Yes to update the file in CorelSHOW. The source application closes and the newly edited embedded object appears in your CorelSHOW presentation.

Adding and Formatting Text in CorelSHOW

Because titles and bulleted lists are an important part of most presentations,

CorelSHOW includes tools for adding text to your presentations. Once the text is in place, you can format it with the tools available on the text ribbon bar. Like CorelDRAW, CorelSHOW's text tool is a fly-out menu that gives you access to Artistic and Paragraph text.

Adding Artistic Text

Artistic text is designed for short text strings, such as titles and captions. You have to press Enter to create a new line when using Artistic text. In addition, Artistic text can be scaled with the selection buttons, just as you can scale text in CorelDRAW.

To add Artistic text to your presentation, press and hold the mouse on the text tool to reveal the text fly-out. Click on the Artistic text tool (the A) and bring your cursor onto the page. Place the crosshair where you want to enter text and click the mouse to create an insertion point. Type the desired text. After typing the text, click on the Pick tool to select the text block. Selection handles appear around the text so you can size or move the text block. To move a text block, click on the text block and drag to the desired location. To size text proportionally, click and drag on any corner sizing handle. Release the mouse when the dashed box is the size you want the text to be.

T I P

You can select multiple text blocks by holding down the Shift key as you select.

Adding Paragraph Text

Paragraph text is designed for longer text blocks such as multiple paragraphs or bulleted lists. Paragraph text is placed in a frame, which determines the width of the text block. The text wraps inside the frame so you do not have to press the Enter key to create a new line of text.

To add Paragraph text to a slide, press and hold on the Text tool to reveal the fly-out menu. Select the Paragraph text tool and move to the slide where you want the text. Use the crosshair to drag and create a paragraph frame. You can enter your paragraph text just as you would in CorelDRAW. After entering the text, select it with the Pick tool. To move a paragraph frame, click in the text block and drag to the desired location. You can size a paragraph frame by using the sizing handles. Sizing a paragraph frame modifies how the text wraps at the end of each line, not the size of the text itself.

Formatting Artistic and Paragraph Text

You can format Artistic and Paragraph text by selecting **F**ont from the **E**dit menu or by using the text ribbon (see fig. 36.17). The text ribbon provides quick access to many editing functions. The text must be selected before it may be formatted. On the far left of the ribbon is the Font list box where you can select a new font. Immediately to the right is the Point size box. The three Text style buttons enable you to make the text **bold**, *italic*, or <u>underlined</u>. You can use the

Justification buttons to make text left, right, or center aligned. The Bullet button enables you to create bulleted text, and the Color button lets you change the color of the text.

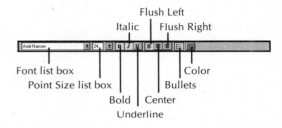

Figure 36.17
The text ribbon bar.

NOTE

CorelSHOW's formatting tools apply only to text created in CorelSHOW. You cannot format text brought in from other applications.

Adding Bullets to Text

One of the most popular types of presentation slides is the bullet slide. You can assign bullets in CorelSHOW to both Artistic and Paragraph text. To apply bullets, select the text block to be bulleted with the Pick tool, then click on the Bullet button on the text ribbon. Each line of text preceded by a hard return will be bulleted. Likewise, to remove bullets, click on the bullet button to turn the bullets off. You can also add or remove bullets from a specific line of bulleted text by selecting the appropriate text tool (Artistic or Paragraph) and placing the cursor anywhere on the line you want to add or remove a bullet.

To format the bullet style and color, choose **B**ullet Style from the **E**dit menu. The Bullets dialog box appears, as shown in figure 36.18. Choose the desired bullet font from the Font text box at the top left. You can make the entire character set bold or italic with the accompanying buttons. Choose the desired bullet from the set, and, after selecting the bullet you want, select the size you want the bullet to appear relative to the text it will precede. Selecting 100 percent makes the bullet the same point size as the accompanying text. The color button at the top right enables you to choose a color for the bullet. After making the appropriate selections, click on OK to apply the bullets. To control the amount of space between bullets, add or delete spaces with the spacebar.

Summary

CorelSHOW has some of the finest tools available for assembling and showing presentations. You can compound these tools with other Corel applications by using embedding and linking techniques to build your presentations. With CorelSHOW, you have quick access to literally any object created in CorelDRAW, CorelPHOTO-PAINT, CorelMOVE, or CorelCHART.

Once you assemble your presentation in CorelSHOW, you will find extensive tools for controlling the presentation. In the next chapter you will learn how to manipulate slide timings, develop cues for interactive presentations, and create freestanding screen shows that can be run from virtually any PC.

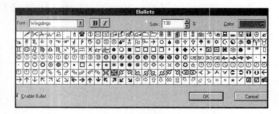

Figure 36.18
The Bullets dialog box.

CorelSHOW's text capabilities are very similar to working with Artistic and Paragraph text in CorelDRAW. For more information about working with text, refer to Chapter 4, "Working with Text and Symbols."

Chapter 37

Presenting with CorelSHOW

*T*his chapter focuses on the features available
for creating desktop presentations. Here, you
will find the steps for controlling the presentation timing, inserting cues, and adding transitions. First, the chapter discusses how to build
manual or auto-advancing presentations. Next,
the chapter examines how to direct the timing of
each slide and each object on the slide. As you
will see, the timing of each element in the
presentation is controlled with a timeline much
like the Timeline roll-up in CorelMOVE.

This chapter also discusses how to create
interactive presentations with cues, giving the
presenter full control over how the show
progresses. Applying transitions effects to slides is
also examined. By adding transitions, you can
direct how each slide appears and leaves the
screen by choosing from a variety of transition
effects. The chapter ends with a look at creating
a portable screen show using CorelSHOW's
Runtime Player. With a portable screen show,
you can present your show from almost any
computer, even if CorelSHOW isn't installed.

This chapter covers:

- Displaying a
  presentation

- Timing your slide show

- Creating interactive
  presentations by adding
  cues

- Creating screen shows

Displaying a Presentation

CorelSHOW lets you impress an audience by providing tools that spruce up the display of your presentation. If you are creating a desktop presentation, which means the CorelSHOW presentation will be presented from a computer monitor, you're in luck. CorelSHOW has some of the finest tools available for adding transitions, controlling the timing, and establishing cues.

You have two ways to control how your presentation progresses through the slides—manual advance and automatic advance. *Manual advance* means the speaker controls how the presentation progresses. The speaker clicks on the mouse or presses a specific key on the keyboard to move forward or backward through the slides. Manual advance is designed for presentations where the speaker is not sure how much time will be spent on each slide, and therefore wants to manually control when the show progresses from one slide to another.

Shows that advance automatically are timed so that the presentation progresses at a predetermined rate. For instance, slide 10 may be timed to display for 20 seconds and then transition to slide 11. By default, CorelSHOW uses automatic advance with new presentations. To specify Manual or Automatic advance, choose Preferences from the File menu. The Preferences dialog box appears, as displayed in figure 37.1.

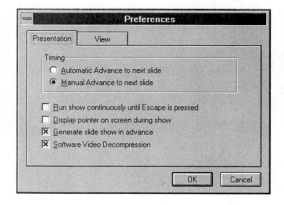

Figure 37.1
The Preferences dialog box.

Working with Manual Advance

In the Presentation tab sheet, select Manual Advance to enable the presenter to control how long each slide is on-screen. Now, when the presentation is running, the speaker can double-click the left mouse button to display the next slide, and double-click the right mouse button to display the previous slide. Table 37.1 lists the keyboard shortcuts used to move through the presentation.

Table 37.1
Running Manual Slide Shows

Press (Hotkey)	To (Function)
Right or Down arrow next PgDn, F6, Enter, Spacebar	Advance to slide.
Left or Up arrow PgUp, F5	Go back to previous slide.

Press (Hotkey)	To (Function)
Home or F9	Return to first slide.
End or F10	Advance to last slide.
Escape	Stop screen show and return to main screen.

Press (Hotkey)	To (Function)
Home or F9	Return to the first slide.
End or F10	Advance to the last slide.
Escape	Stop the screen show and return to the main screen.

Working with Automatic Advance

In the Presentation tab sheet, choose "Automatic Advance to next slide" to instruct CorelSHOW to run without prompting. You will use the Timelines dialog box to establish the specific times for each slide. Refer to the following section on "Timing Your Slide Show" for more information. Table 37.2 lists the keyboard shortcuts used to move through an automatically advancing presentation.

Table 37.2
Running Automatic Slide Shows

Press (Hotkey)	To (Function)
F2	Pause the presentation. Press F2 a second time to continue the presentation.
F3	Play the screen show backward.
F4	Play the screen show forward.

The Preferences dialog box offers several other features for controlling the playback of your presentation. Select the "Run show continuously until Escape" option to loop your presentation. This instructs the presentation to play continuously, beginning again after the end. Select the Display pointer on-screen during show option to display a white arrow (the Pick tool) on-screen during the presentation. This enables the speaker to point at various elements on the screen during the presentation.

Select the "Generate slide show in advance" option to load the slide show into your computer's memory. This will allow smoother movement from slide to slide because the system will not have to retrieve subsequent slides from the hard disk. If you have checked this option, the slides will reside in your system's memory until you exit CorelSHOW or switch to another slide show. Select the final option, "Software video decompression," to improve the display of your slides when using CorelSHOW's Runtime Player. Refer to the section, "Running A Screen Show," at the end of this chapter for more information. After making the desired selections, click on OK to return to the Slide View.

Timing Your Slide Show

The timing of each slide in your presentation is integral to producing a presentation that communicates effectively. When a presentation automatically advances from one slide to another, it is up to you to determine how long each slide is displayed. There are several things to consider when setting slide timings. For instance, will the reader need time to read the slide? Does the slide include a chart that requires some time to analyze? If the slide displays an animation file, how long does it take the animation to play? CorelSHOW provides a lot of flexibility and power when it comes to timing your presentation. Not only can you control the length of time each slide is displayed, you also can control the length of time each object on the slide is displayed.

Controlling Slide Timings with the Time On Screen Box

Use the Time On Screen box located in the top-right corner of the CorelSHOW window to set the length of time a slide or object is displayed during the presentation (see fig. 37.2). CorelSHOW sets a default time of five seconds for each slide. To set a slide time, switch to Slide View and display the slide you want to time. Click on the Time On Screen box and type the time you want, or select the time from the list revealed by clicking the arrow on the right. For instance, in figure 37.2, the slide timing is set for 12 seconds.

Time On Screen box

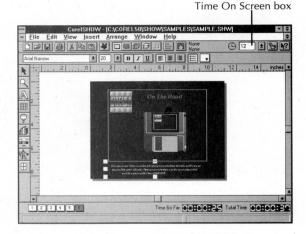

Figure 37.2

Use the Time On Screen box to set timings for each slide and the objects on each slide.

CorelSHOW also lets you control the timing of individual objects or "frames" on each slide. For instance, you may want a chart on your slide to disappear a few seconds before the slide disappears. In this case, you could set up the slide to display for ten seconds and the chart to display for eight seconds. The chart would then leave the presentation two seconds earlier than the slide. To control the timing for individual objects on the slide, select the object and enter a time in the Time On Screen box.

The timing for objects must be shorter than the timing for the whole slide. This is logical because it wouldn't work if a chart was set up to display for 12 seconds on a slide set up to display for 10 seconds. If you do enter an amount for an object that is longer than the slide, the slide timing will be increased to correspond with the timing you assigned the object. Use this method to set up the timing for each slide in your presentation; when you're ready, run the screen show to test the slide timings.

T I P

You also can set timings in the Slide Sorter view by selecting each slide, and then assigning a time from the Time On-Screen list.

Controlling Slide Timings with Timelines

Timelines offers a more precise way to control the timing of your presentation. With Timelines, you can adjust the timings of all slides and objects at one time and see how they work in relation to each other. Timelines work with the slide timings as they pertain to the duration of the entire show. Instead of directing the slide to display for twenty seconds, you decide when the slide is to appear and when it is to disappear. For instance, a slide might appear at 35 seconds into the presentation and disappear at 55 seconds into the presentation.

Select Timelines from the **V**iew menu, or click on the Timelines button to display the Timelines window, as shown in figure 37.3. The Timelines window provides a visual representation of how long each slide and each object is displayed during the presentation.

At the top of the window are buttons representing slides, sounds, and timelines. When the first two buttons are "pushed in,"

the timelines for slides and sounds are displayed. When the buttons are not pushed in, the timelines for those elements do not appear. Displaying the timelines for only slides or sounds might be useful when you want to focus exclusively on the timings for one element. The third button, the Time Scale button, enables you to compress the timeline scaling so that timelines for all slides fit in the current timelines window. You can use the scroll bars at the bottom of the dialog box to move throughout your presentation and view slide timings that are not currently visible in the timelines window.

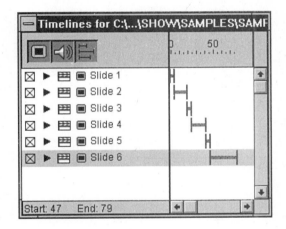

Figure 37.3
The Timelines window.

T I P

You can enlarge the Timelines window by dragging on its borders. This will expand the scale so that slide timelines are easier to manipulate.

Along the left side of the Timelines window are the slide numbers, and on the right are the timelines for each slide. The timelines indicate when the slide enters and exits the presentation. To see the timelines for the objects on each slide, click on the down arrow by the slide number. As displayed in figure 37.4, this expands the timeline to show the objects on the selected slide. The timelines for slides appear in green, and the timelines for objects appear in red.

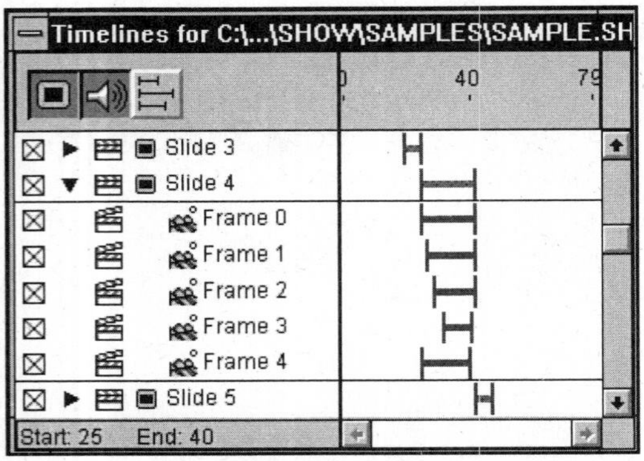

Figure 37.4
The Timelines window expanded to show slides and slide objects.

Click on the Toggle Slide/Frame Checkbox to turn a slide or frame on or off. When a slide or frame is off, it cannot be selected, and will not appear in the show if you run the presentation. This makes work on complex slides easier by enabling you to temporarily remove objects from the slide. Click on the Display Cue Information icon to display the Cue Information dialog box. Adding cues to your slides is discussed later in this chapter.

The Object Type icon indicates what type of object appears on the slide. The icons provide a quick visual reminder of the contents of each slide. Table 37.3 lists what the icons represent.

Table 37.3
Timeline Object Types

Icon	Definition
	Is a CorelMOVE animation.
	Is a CorelDRAW graphic.
	Is a CorelPHOTO-PAINT image.
	Is a CorelCHART object.
	Is text created in CorelSHOW.
	Is a sound.
	Is an embedded object.

You can select a specific slide by clicking somewhere on the name or timeline. When the object is selected, the Information Bar in the lower left corner of the dialog box displays the start and end times for the selected slide or object.

Each timeline has a start frame and an end frame handle. You can move these handles to adjust the start and end times of the selected slide or object. To change the start time, place the mouse cursor on the start frame handle. The cursor shape changes to a single left arrow. Now, drag the handle to the left or right to set the new start time. As you drag, watch the Information Bar to determine the desired start time. To adjust the end time, point to the end frame handle. The cursor shape changes to a single right-facing arrow. Drag this handle to the desired end time, and release.

Notice that if you adjust the time on a slide in your presentation, the other slide timings adjust to the new timing. For instance, if you set the end time for slide 3 at 25 seconds, then the start time for slide 4 is set to 25. If you alter slide 4 to end at 45 seconds, then slide 5 is adjusted to start at 45 seconds. When timing objects, keep in mind that the timelines for the objects must fit within the timeline for the slide. You cannot have an object appear in the presentation longer than a slide. For instance, if the end frame for the slide is 55 seconds, you cannot drag the timeline for one of the objects on the slide to 60 seconds.

Working with timelines enables you to create eye-catching presentations with objects appearing and disappearing on the slides at different times. For instance, on the title slide, you could have the company name appear with the slide, followed by the company logo two seconds later. The topic of the presentation could pop on three seconds after that. On a chart slide, the title could appear first, followed by the chart, and finally, a synopsis of the chart. Giving your presentations movement makes them all the more exciting to watch and comprehend.

Creating Interactive Presentations by Adding Cues

Cues are signals in the presentation that instruct the presentation to pause, wait for a response, and then resume. Cues can be added to each slide in your presentation. On slide 2, for example, you could set up a cue that enabled the presenter to jump to slide 5 if the Enter key were pressed. In figure 37.5, a cue was set up on slide 20 that enabled the presenter to press Y for yes to end the presentation; if Y is not pressed, then the presentation continues. It's important to note that when placing cues in your presentation, you need to consider whether to include on-screen instructions for operating the cue.

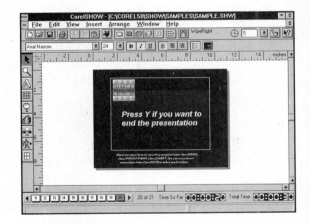

Figure 37.5

Cues let you add tools for controlling the display and progress of your presentation.

Cues are made up of a *condition* and an *action*. Think of the condition as a prerequisite that must be met before the action can be performed. For instance, a condition might be pressing the Enter key, or clicking the mouse. After the condition is met, the action is performed. The action might be ending the presentation or moving to a specific slide in the presentation. As an example, in a sales presentation, a cue could be created on slide 5 with the condition of pressing the number 3 on the keyboard, and the action of displaying slide 3. If the condition (pressing 3) is met, the action (displaying slide 3) is performed.

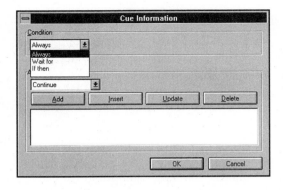

Figure 37.6

The Cue Information dialog box with the Condition list displayed.

Adding Cues

To add a cue to a slide in your presentation, display the slide in the Slide View, and select Edit Cue from the Cue menu. The Cue Information dialog box appears, as displayed in figure 37.6. The first part in creating a cue is setting the condition to be met. As displayed in figure 37.6, click on the drop-down list in the Condition section of the dialog box to reveal the three available conditions—Always, Wait for, and If then.

The following paragraphs examine the conditions available in CorelSHOW:

■ The Always condition is the default setting. There are no conditions to be met with Always—the specified action is always executed. For instance, a cue in slide 30 with the condition "Always" and the action "End Presentation" would always end the presentation at slide 30.

■ The Wait for condition pauses the presentation and waits until one of three conditions is met. Notice that when the Wait for condition is selected, another drop-down list appears. Click on the arrow by the second list to reveal the three options.

The first, Time Delay Of, pauses for a time delay of up to 1000 seconds. As displayed in figure 37.7, enter the desired time delay in the Seconds box. For example, a cue on slide 12 with the condition "Wait For 30 seconds" would pause the presentation at slide 12, perhaps giving the audience time to examine the slide. The action could then be "Continue" to resume playing the presentation.

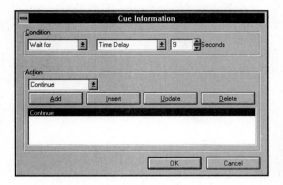

Figure 37.7
With a Time Delay cue, you can enter exactly how much time you want the presentation to pause.

The second option for the Wait for condition is "Mouse Click on." This option pauses the presentation until the mouse is clicked. As displayed in figure 37.8, click on the arrow in the third list box to specify whether the mouse can be clicked anywhere on the screen, or if it must be clicked on a certain slide object. For example, a cue on slide 3 with the condition "Wait For Mouse Click on Anything" and the action "GoTo Slide 10," pauses the presentation on slide 3. When the mouse is clicked, the presentation moves forward to display slide 10.

The third option for the Wait for condition is "Key Down," which pauses the presentation until a key is pressed on the keyboard. Click on the Key button to display the Choose a Key dialog box (see fig. 37.9). Press the key you want used in the condition, and click on OK. As an example, you

could add a cue to the last slide in your presentation with the condition, "Wait For Key Down 1" and the action "GoTo Slide 1." This would enable the speaker to press 1 to return to the first slide in the presentation.

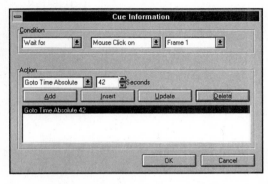

Figure 37.8
Use the third list box to specify what the mouse must click on for the condition to be complete—anything, or a specific object on the slide.

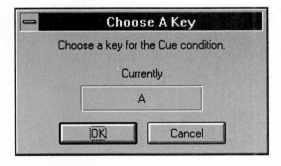

Figure 37.9
The Choose A Key dialog box.

■ The If then condition is similar to the Wait for condition in that you must specify a time delay, mouse click, or key down. However, a cue with the If then condition does not pause the presentation until the condition is met. The condition can be met at any time the slide is displayed in the presentation. If the condition is not met, the cue is ignored and the presentation continues. For example, a cue on slide 20 with the condition "If Then Mouse Click on Anything" and the action "End Presentation" would enable the speaker to click the mouse and end the presentation sometime during the display of slide 20. If the mouse is not clicked during slide 20, the presentation resumes as normal.

After establishing the conditions, you need to specify what action will take place when the conditions are successfully met. As displayed in figure 37.10, click on the drop-down list in the Action section of the dialog box to reveal the available actions. Select the desired action and click on the Insert button to add it to the action list. If you want to remove an action, select it and click the Delete button. Click on OK to add the cue to the slide. The following paragraphs examine the actions available in CorelSHOW.

■ Continue, the default action, continues playing the presentation. For example, the condition, "Wait For Time Delay of 15 seconds" followed by the action, "Continue" would simply pause the slide for 15 seconds and then continue to the next slide.

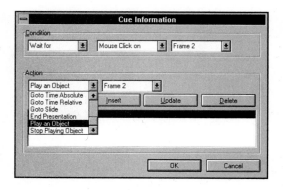

Figure 37.10
Use the drop-down menus to display the available actions.

■ The Goto Time Absolute action skips to a specified point in the screen show. As displayed in figure 37.11, enter the time to skip to in the Seconds box. As an example, on slide 2, you could place a cue with the condition "If Then Mouse Click on Anything" and the action "Goto Time Absolute 45 seconds." This cue would take the presentation to the 45 second mark if the mouse was clicked in slide 2.

■ The action "Goto Time Relative" skips to a point in the screen show relative to the current slide. As displayed in figure 37.12, enter the time to skip to in the Seconds box. As an example, you could place a cue on slide 5 with the condition "Wait For Key Down Enter" and the action "Goto Time Relative 10 seconds." This cue would pause on slide 5; when Enter was pressed, the presentation would jump forward 10 seconds into the presentation.

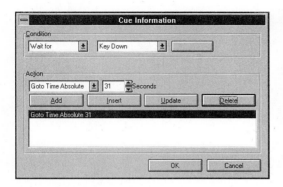

Figure 37.11

The Goto Time Absolute action lets you enter the exact time to which you want to move in a presentation.

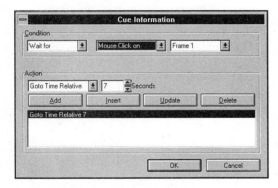

Figure 37.12

The Goto Time Relative action lets you enter a relative time to which you want to move in a presentation.

- The Goto Slide action causes the presentation to jump to a specific slide number. As displayed in figure 37.13, enter the slide number you want to jump to in the list box. For instance, you could place a cue on slide 3 that jumped to slide 14 if the mouse was clicked.

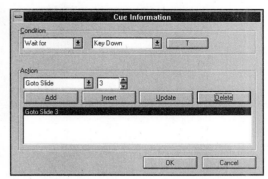

Figure 37.13

When the Goto Slide action is selected, you can enter the number of the slide to which you want to jump in the list box.

- The End Presentation action stops the presentation. For example, you could create a cue on slide 50 with the condition "If Then Key Down Enter" and the action the "End Presentation." If the speaker pressed Enter during the display of slide 50, the presentation would end.

- The Play an Object action plays a dynamic object (sound or animation) in the specified frame. As displayed in figure 37.14, click the second drop-down list to select the frame number of the object you want to play. For example, on slide 10, you could create a cue that waits for the speaker to click the mouse and then begins playing a sound object.

- The Stop playing Object action stops the play of a dynamic object (sound or animation) when the specified

condition is met. As displayed in figure 37.14, click the second drop-down list to select the frame number of the object you want to stop playing.

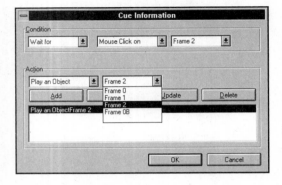

Figure 37.14

The drop-down list enables you to specify a frame number for an action to take place.

Editing Cues

It may take several attempts to get your cues set up and timed perfectly. When you need to adjust a condition or edit the cue in any way, display the slide containing the cue and select Edit Cue from the Edit menu. You also can click on the Display Cue Information icon in the Timelines dialog box. The Cue Information dialog box appears where you can make all the necessary changes.

Working with Screen Transitions

After compiling all the elements of your presentation, charts, graphics, animations, and sounds, it is time to add some personality to the show. Transitions are a perfect way to put character into what otherwise might appear to be a fairly pedestrian display. For example, instead of just cutting from one slide to the next, why not dissolve or fade into the next image? The effect can be quite impressive, and only takes a moment to master. In addition to transitioning between slides, you also can control the way individual objects appear on the slide. For instance, you might schedule the slide title to wipe on the screen, and bullet text to zoom in. Once you have assigned slide transitions, they are saved to show so that each time the presentation is played back, it will display exactly as you designed.

Slide transitions are most evident when applied to slide elements such as charts, text, and graphics. You also can transition between slides, but only if you have assigned independent backgrounds on consecutive slides. If you use a common background for your presentation, you cannot assign transitions between slides. To assign a transition effect to a slide, either select the slide in the Slide Sorter View, or make it the current slide in the Slide View. Select the object to which you want to assign a transition effect. Click on the Transition Effect button to open the Transition Effects dialog box, as shown in figure 37.15

N O T E

If you have nothing selected on the slide, the transition effect applies to the entire slide, provided that the two slides have independent backgrounds. Contrary to applying transition effects to objects, where you can implement both opening and closing effects, you can only apply opening transition effects between entire slides.

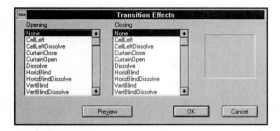

Figure 37.15

The Transition Effects dialog box.

Scroll in the Opening list box and select an opening effect. Scroll and select a closing effect from the Closing list box. Click on the Preview button to display the chosen transition effects, then click on OK. To confirm the effect assigned to an object, select the object, then look at the caption just to the right of the Transition Effect button. The top reference is the opening effect, and the bottom one is the closing effect.

T I P

When an object is selected for assigning a transition effect, this is a good time to assign a screen time or duration to the object. See "Controlling Slide Timings with the Time on Screen Box" in this chapter for more information on assigning times to objects.

When applying transition effects to screen objects, it is important that you order them appropriately. For example, you probably wouldn't want a slide subtitle to fade on before the slide title. You can use timelines to select objects and adjust their entry and exit points for appropriate screen display. For more information on using timelines, see the section titled, "Controlling Slide Timings with Timelines," in this chapter.

Previewing Your Screen Shows

Once you have assigned transition effects to your show, you are ready to take a look at your finished presentation. Chances are that after previewing, you will want to make some adjustments to the show. For example, you may find that you need to re-order the slides. Or you may want to spend some time experimenting with the various transition effects and timings to discover the on-screen results.

To preview your presentation, choose Run Screen Sho**w** from the **F**ile menu, or click on the Run Screen Show button. The show will begin assembling with all the transitions, timings, and cues you have established. The Status bar at the bottom right of the screen displays the progress of the show as it generates. After the show is assembled, the Start Screen dialog box appears, as shown in figure 37.16. Click on OK to start the show. If the show is set up for manual display, you will have to prompt with the keyboard to continue with the presentation. Otherwise, you can sit back and enjoy the show as it

progresses automatically. When the show is complete, you will be returned to CorelSHOW. If you want to stop the show at any time, press the Escape key.

You also can press F5 to start a screen show.

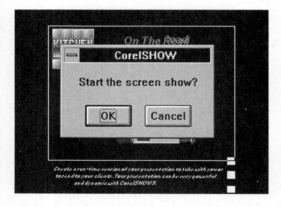

Figure 37.16
The Start Screen dialog box.

Creating Screen Shows

After you have created your masterpiece, you are ready to share your genius with the rest of the world. For playback convenience, you can save your presentation as a screen show that can be run without CorelSHOW being open. In fact, you can even save the show to a disk and run it from a computer that

doesn't have CorelSHOW installed. This is the best way to distribute your presentation so others can view it without being able to edit it in any way.

To create a screen show, select Save as from the **F**ile menu. The Save Presentation As dialog box appears, as shown in figure 37.17. Saving as a screen show is similar to saving any CorelSHOW file, as discussed earlier in this chapter. Enter a name for the screen show file, and navigate to the desired directory to store the file.

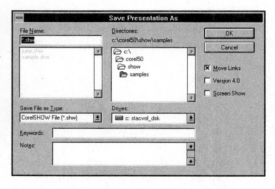

Figure 37.17
The Save Presentation As dialog box.

Place a check in the **S**creen Show checkbox to reveal two other options, as shown in figure 37.18. Select Render in low resolution to save the screen show in a lower resolution. This will create a smaller file size and cause the show to render faster on screen, but may result in "jaggies" on slides and objects. Check the option Use Device Dependent Bitmaps if your presentation includes video and animation clips, and you want them as device dependent bitmaps optimized for your computer. This increases the overall speed of the screen show, but can only run on a computer that has the same video card, video driver, and resolution settings as the PC used to build and save it. After choosing the desired options, click on OK to generate and save the screen show.

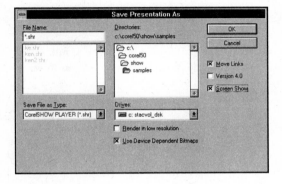

Figure 37.18
Options for saving a screen show.

When you choose to save a file as a screen show, it is assigned the extension .SHR. It is important that you recognize that .SHR files are not editable. Before you save a file as a screen show, you should always first save it as a CorelSHOW .SHW file. In this way, if you later find you need to make any changes to the presentation, you can go back to the SHW file, edit it as necessary, and then save it again as a .SHR screen show file.

Running a Screen Show

As previously discussed, you can run screen shows without having to open CorelSHOW. Opening CorelSHOW just to view a

presentation can be a cumbersome and unnecessary effort. You can run any screen show directly from Windows Program Manager with CorelSHOW's Runtime Player. In order to use this option, you must have installed the Runtime Player when you loaded Corel 5.0 on your system. If you chose not to install the Runtime Player during the original installation, you can add it at any time by reinstalling Corel.

To use the Runtime Player to display a screen show, double-click on the CorelSHOW Runtime Player Icon from Program Manager. The CorelSHOW PLAYER dialog box appears, as shown in figure 37.19. This dialog box works nearly identically to CorelSHOW's Open dialog box. Refer to Chapter 36, "Assembling Presentations in CorelSHOW," for more detail on CorelSHOW's Open dialog box.

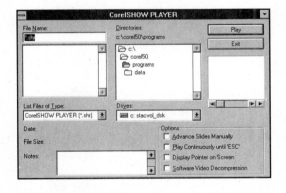

Figure 37.19
The CorelSHOW PLAYER dialog box.

Navigate to the directory where the screen show is stored, and select the desired .SHR file. You can use the Preview box to display a

copy of the chosen .SHR file. The bottom left of the CorelSHOW Player dialog box displays the date the file was created, the file size, and any notes attached when the file was originally saved. The options on the bottom right of the dialog box enable you to control how the slide show is played. Choose Advance Slides Manually to run the show manually with the slide advancement keys detailed earlier in this chapter. The show runs automatically if the option is not selected. Choose Play Continuously until "ESC" instructs the show to insert a loop command at the end of the screen show, making it go back to the first slide and run continuously. The option Display Pointer On Screen makes the pointer visible during the presentation so that you can visually refer to certain points.

The Software Video Decompression option is used when problems are experienced in displaying bitmapped images in a .SHR file. When you originally saved the file as a screen show, you had the choice to save bitmapped images using the Device Dependent Bitmaps option in the Save As screen show dialog box. If you selected this option, you may experience some display problems when playing them back in a .SHR screen show, particularly if you play them on a computer that has a different video display and video card than the system upon which it was originally created. If this is the case, select this option to decompress the *Device Independent Bitmaps* (.DIB) files that are included in a .SHR screen show.

After making the desired selections, click on OK to begin the screen show. The show will display full screen. If you choose to run the

show manually, you can use the manual advance keys detailed earlier to move through the show. Press Escape at any time to end the show and return to the CorelSHOW Player dialog box. Click on the Exit button to close the Runtime Player.

Creating a Portable Screen Show

In a perfect world, perhaps everyone would have Corel 5.0 loaded on their computer. If this were the case, taking your screen show on the road and presenting it on any computer would be no problem. But alas, all things are not as they should be. This won't stop you from taking your show on the road, however, since CorelSHOW enables you to make portable shows that can be displayed on any personal computer.

To create a portable screen show, you simply have to include CorelSHOW's Runtime Player on the floppy disk with your presentation. First, save your presentation file as you normally would. Next, in Windows File Manager, navigate to the directory where Corel 5.0 is stored, and then open the subdirectory or folder called Programs. Select and copy the file CORELPLR.EXE to the floppy disk, along with the screen show file.

Now the disk contains everything you need to play your screen show on any PC. To play the file, insert the disk into the disk drive. In Windows Program Manager, choose **R**un from the **F**ile menu to open the Run dialog box, as shown in figure 37.20. In the command-line textbox, enter the floppy drive and CORELPLR.EXE. For example, if the disk with the screen show and the Runtime Player is in the A drive, enter A:\CORELPLR.EXE. When the CorelSHOW Player dialog box appears, select the screen show file on the floppy, choose the appropriate options, and click on the Play button. The show will play full screen.

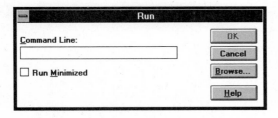

Figure 37.20
The Run dialog box.

N O T E

If you have included any animation files in the presentation, the playback computer must have installed the animation program on which the animation was designed, such as CorelMOVE, Autodesk Animator Pro, or Quicktime for Windows. Otherwise, the screen show will skip the animation slide and proceed to the next slide in the show.

Summary

Multimedia has forever changed the nature of presentations. With a program like CorelSHOW, you can consolidate work done in many different mediums for a production that will engage your audience with brilliant images, moving animations, purposeful graphs, and enhancing sound effects.

More than ever it is incumbent upon you to dazzle your audience. Your viewers are more sophisticated today than even a few short years ago. No longer will mundane static images get the job done. Every day we are inundated with glitz television, spectacular movie effects, and other forms of multimedia wizardry. CorelSHOW has all the tools you need to create presentations that will indeed impress any audience.

As you become more adept at creating presentations in CorelSHOW, you will grow to appreciate its vast flexibility. The ability to create interactive shows with cues enables you to build in control to your presentation; in turn, this control allows you to reflect your foresight, preparation, and precipitation of audience reaction.

Part VI

Advanced Topics

Chapter 38

Color Management

*C*hapter 6, *"Working with Fills,"* introduced
the issue of color by detailing the color models and
color matching systems, available when you apply
color to objects. This chapter considers more advanced
color topics.

This chapter covers:

- PostScript halftone effects

- Dot gain

- Gamut

- Dynamic range

- Transformation

- Color management

Understanding the Interconnectivity Problem

The graphics community has a long-standing problem: no two groups of people have ever spoken the same language. Copywriters speak one language, layout artists another, and artists, photographers, and printers indeed speak other languages. Then, computers joined the graphics industry, and more languages were born. Today's graphics professional has to be a linguist to ensure successful output of even the most simplistic design.

Your printer, monitor, scanner, and CPU may all be parts of one system, but when it comes to color, they do not always speak the same language, either. Add your favorite graphics software package and a network, and you have a prescription for a color disaster, as figure 38.1 demonstrates.

Figure 38.1

One author's view of computer interconnectivity problems.

The rest of this chapter helps you explore solutions for getting the highest possible color and output quality, no matter what languages your equipment speaks.

Using Halftone Effects

Using halftone effects can add interest to bitmapped and vector images. A halftone screen is a pattern of dots, lines, or other shapes that you can apply to PostScript objects and images (see fig. 38.2). These screens are useful for creating special effects, and for minimizing moirés and rosettes in your output. CorelDRAW enables you to assign halftone screens to specific objects, monochrome bitmaps, or entire images. These screens are added at print time and are not visible in the drawing window.

There are two ways to add halftone screens to your images. If you are printing separations, you can apply halftone screens to the films of the individual channels. Separation halftone screening controls are located on the Separations property sheet in the **P**rint dialog box. The second method of applying halftone screens is to apply them to individual objects, using the spot color PostScript options found in the Fill and Outline dialog boxes. Using spot color halftone screening enables you to have a large amount of control over the angle and frequency of the screen. With either method, you can choose from a variety of screen styles.

Figure 38.2
The effect of a diamond screen.

Four variables control the appearance of a halftone screen: frequency, angle, the style of screen, and the paper stock on which the image is being printed.

Frequency

Screen frequency is measured in lines per inch (lpi). The frequency you choose should take into consideration the resolution of the output device, and the effect you are trying to achieve. To choose a screen frequency, first consider the effect you want. If you want a more dramatic effect, choose a coarse screen of 10–30 lpi. To achieve a finer, more dense effect, choose a higher screen frequency of 100 or more.

N O T E

A balanced image contains a range of grays that span the spectrum. The ideal is 256 levels of gray. In Chapter 14, "Printed Output," figure 14.1 displays a chart to guide you in choosing the optimum lpi for a given resolution, in order to maintain an ideal gray level.

Rule of Sixteen

PostScript output has a limitation of 256 levels of gray. To find the optimum screen frequency for your printing job, you can consult the screening chart, or you can perform a little calculation. The Rule of Sixteen enables you to quickly determine the optimum screen frequency to obtain 256 levels of gray. The following formula is applied:

Output Resolution =
Screen Frequency × 16

or

Maximum Screen Frequency =
Output Resolution / 16

For example, if you were printing a halftone screen on a 300 dpi PostScript printer, the maximum screen frequency you could have to get 256 levels of gray would be 18.

If your job required a 120 lpi screen, you would need a minimum of 1920 dpi to gain 256 levels of gray. Because 1920 is an unusual number, you would want to use 2540 dpi output.

Choosing Screen Angles

The default screen angle available with spot color halftones is 45 degrees. Generally, this angle produces the best results with the least amount of moiré. This is important when applying halftone screens to monochrome photo bitmaps. A *moiré* is a splotchy pattern that appears when two or more halftone screens are not overlaid properly. When applying single halftone screens to an object, choose the screen angle for the amount of dramatic impact you want. The orientation of the object influences the screen angle you select. Use oblique angles to create more dramatic effects. Screen angles are more apparent at lower frequencies.

N O T E

Screen angles are constant and do not change when you transform an object by rotating, skewing, scaling, or stretching the object. You may need to adjust the screen angle after performing one of these operations on an object.

Screen Styles

CorelDRAW provides a set of screen shapes you can use when applying spot color halftone screens to objects and bitmaps. To apply a halftone screen, select the object and access the Fill dialog box. Choose a Pantone Spot color and click on PostScript Options to display the PostScript Options dialog box. Select a halftone screen style, and enter the frequency and angle you want. Click on OK to return to the Fill dialog box; click on OK once more to return to the drawing window. You can also apply a halftone screen to the outline of an object, using the same method in the Outline color dialog box. PostScript halftones can be applied to fountain fills, if both anchor colors of the fill are tints of the same spot color.

N O T E

Each halftone screen style has points that recommend it. Some create screens that appear darker, since each screen responds to the frequency and angle differently (see fig. 38.3). You may have to experiment to achieve the results you want.

Halftones and Paper Stock

The paper stock you use can affect the appearance of a halftone screen. This is the result of dot gain. If you select a screen frequency that is too high for the output resolution, the effect of the screen can be lost. The image will appear to have blobs of color. This is especially true for more porous stock, such as newsprint.

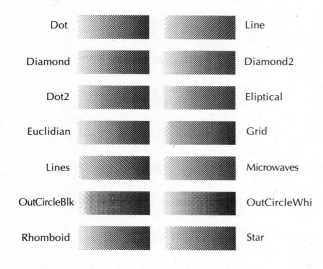

Dot	Line
Diamond	Diamond2
Dot2	Eliptical
Euclidian	Grid
Lines	Microwaves
OutCircleBlk	OutCircleWhi
Rhomboid	Star

Figure 38.3
Screen styles.

Applying Screens to Separations

The controls for applying halftone screens to separations is on the Separations sheet of the **P**rint dialog box. Enable Separations and select **C**ustom, then **E**dit, to access the Advanced Screening dialog box. Note that the angles for the four CMYK channels are already staggered to help prevent moiré effects. If moiré effects still occur, try swapping the screen angles for the black and yellow, making Black 0 degrees.

Select the output device you want from the list, and enter the corresponding resolution. If you want to change the frequency of all of the channels, enter a new value in the Basic Screen box. You can also change the

frequency of the individual channels by entering new values in the corresponding frequency entry boxes. Select a screen style, and then click on OK to continue making your printing choices.

Moirés and Rosettes

Any time two or more halftone screens are superimposed, you run into a potential moiré problem. A digitized photo is represented as a halftone screen. If you add a screen to a photo image, the risk of a moiré or rosette occurring is good. You cannot eliminate moirés completely, but you can minimize their impact on your image. Evenly staggering the angles of superimposed screens between 0 degrees and 90 degrees helps limit moiré effects.

Rosettes are patterns that can help minimize moiré effects at higher screen frequencies. Rosettes can either have open or closed centers. While no rosette selection is available in CorelDRAW, you can simulate a rosette by setting your screens at the following angles: Cyan = 15 degrees, Black = 45 degrees, Magenta = 75 degrees, and Yellow = 0 degrees.

T I P

You can create a duotone effect in CorelDRAW when working with monochrome bitmapped images by setting the dominant color at 45 degrees and the secondary color at 0 degrees.

Understanding Dot Gain

Dot gain is an effect where colors appear darker than desired. There are a number of factors to consider when dealing with dot gain. The output device and the paper stock on which a document is being printed are two of the most important issues. Dot gain becomes more noticeable when the line frequency is greater than the optimum at a given resolution. Dot gain is the difference between the desired color and the actual output.

For example, if you selected a 40-percent gray for a fill, but when the image was printed the gray was measured at 60 percent, the dot gain would be 20 percent. Generally, this is the result of the porosity of the paper stock (see fig. 38.4). Some software programs enable you to compensate for this effect by increasing the dot gain setting. CorelDRAW automatically calculates the dot gain when you calibrate your printer, using the Color Manager, found under the File menu.

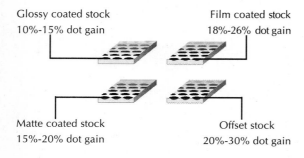

Glossy coated stock
10%-15% dot gain

Film coated stock
18%-26% dot gain

Matte coated stock
15%-20% dot gain

Offset stock
20%-30% dot gain

Figure 38.4
Dot gain and paper stock.

Transformation

When colors are translated and converted between color palettes or between devices, it is called *transformation*. For example, when you specify a Pantone spot color, CorelDRAW must convert the color to RGB for the display on your monitor. Since most printers are CMYK, the color must be converted again for output. Although there is no substitute for using a swatch book to designate printed colors, ideally the color as it is displayed on your monitor should match the color of the output.

Gamut and Dynamic Range

Color gamut is the range of displayable colors on a given device. Your monitor is capable of displaying a far greater gamut than printers using CMYK output can print. Color correction must take this into account, and calculate the closest possible match for a given color.

The dynamic range is the possible color or tonal range between pure black and pure white on a given device. CorelDRAW takes the gamut and dynamic range of devices into account, using a color mapping system to perform color correction.

Summary

An understanding of color, color management, and the printing process can help to minimize or eliminate output problems. By varying paper selection and halftone screening you can add interest to your documents. This chapter addressed advanced color issues. Chapter 39, "Color Calibration," continues this effort by illustrating the use of CorelDRAW's Color Manager.

Color Calibration

CorelDRAW's color management system enables you to create a system profile for color correction. Each system file contains transformation information regarding the components of your system. This system file enables you to view colors on your monitor, whether from an image you are creating or from a scanned source, and ensures that the output matches those colors as closely as possible.

This chapter covers:

- Basic color correction
- Advanced color calibration
- Calibrating your monitor
- Calibrating your printer
- Calibrating your scanner

Basic Color Correction

Each component of your system has an associated characterization that identifies how it displays color. The system profile consists of three characterization files: Monitor, Printer, and Scanner (optional). The system profile is custom-tailored to your system. Therefore if you change a component, you need to update the system profile. Similarly, if you output to a service bureau, you want to build a system profile that corresponds to each of the devices they use. CorelDRAW includes a set of device characterizations for each of the three types of components. By selecting your brand and model of components from the lists, you can generate a system profile that closely matches your equipment.

After you generate a system profile, you can load the file that corresponds to your job and hardware. Enabling **C**olor Correction in the **V**iew menu activates the color correction and alters the color palettes appropriately.

To generate a system profile, follow these steps:

1. Select **C**olor Manager from the **F**ile menu to display the System Color Profile dialog box (see fig. 39.1).

2. Click on the down arrow beside **M**onitor to display the monitor list, and select the monitor that matches yours.

3. Repeat step two for your printer and scanner.

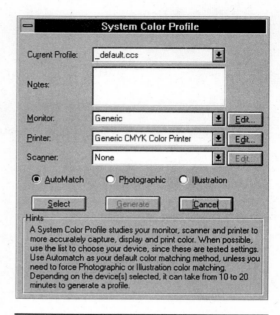

Figure 39.1
The System Color Profile dialog box.

4. Enable the color matching system you want to use. **A**utoMatch is the default color-matching system, and the best for overall use. If you primarily need to match photographic images or illustrations, select the corresponding option. Edit any of the three characterizations as needed.

5. Click on **G**enerate to display the Generate Profile dialog box. Enter a name for your system profile in the entry box and click on OK to continue. CorelDRAW automatically adds the appropriate CCS extension.

Depending on your system, it can take up to 30 minutes for CorelDRAW to complete the system profile after you click on **G**enerate.

WARNING

Overwriting the default.ccs file is not a good idea. Make a backup copy of your system profile so that you can recopy the file back to the Corel5\Color directory if you need to reinstall the program at a later date.

Advanced Color Calibration

Advanced color calibration enables you to create system profiles for devices that do not have pretested characterization files. If you have an unlisted device, you can either calibrate for color correction visually or by entering numeric values for that device in the configuration entry boxes. Because visual calibration is not as accurate as entering numeric values, you should check the user manual for the device to obtain the information required by CorelDRAW's Color Manager. If the user manual does not have the required information, contact the manufacturer.

Calibrating Your Monitor

When you select Other from the monitor list, the Monitor Calibration dialog box appears (see fig. 39.2). This opening dialog box enables you to calibrate your monitor.

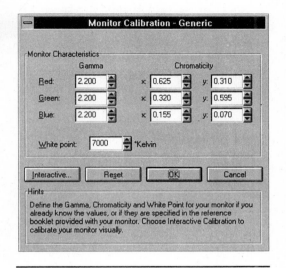

Figure 39.2

The Monitor Calibration dialog box.

To calibrate your monitor numerically, follow these steps:

1. Enter the name of your monitor in the entry box.

2. Enter the monitor Gamma and Chromaticity listed in your monitor user's manual for each of the RGB channels.

3. Enter the **W**hite point for your monitor, and click on OK to return to the System Color Profile dialog box.

If the values for your monitor are not available, you need to make the adjustments visually. To visually calibrate your monitor, follow these steps:

1. Click on **I**nteractive in the Monitor Calibration dialog box to display the

Interactive Monitor Calibration dialog box (see fig. 39.3).

Figure 39.3
The Interactive Monitor Calibration dialog box.

2. Adjust the Gamma settings for the three channels so that the colors on both sides match.

   ■ Adjust one channel, and click on Identical to change the other channels to match.

   ■ Then adjust each channel individually.

3. Drag the slider in the Chromaticity box to select a cooler or warmer white point. Cooler white points introduce more blue into an image; warmer white points introduce more yellow. CorelDRAW packages the photo shown in the dialog box with the software. Use this photo as a reference to adjust the white point.

4. The chromaticity settings should never need adjusting because they are determined by an industry standard. Monitors generally display identical chromaticity values, regardless of brand or model. If you need to adjust the chromaticity, move the markers in the channel view boxes to achieve the results you want.

5. Click on Preview to check the adjustments you made. When you are satisfied with the results, click on OK to return to the System Color Profile dialog box.

Calibrating Your Printer

If your printer is not on the Printer list in the System Color Profile dialog box, select Other to access the Printer Calibration dialog box (see fig. 39.4). Enter the name of your printer in the Printer type entry box. Most printers are CMYK printers. If you choose RGB you will be prompted for the path and file name for the RHN file that corresponds to your RGB printer. Enter the name and follow the prompts.

N O T E

To create an IM, RHN, or GRY file, you need a spectrophotometer or colorimeter.

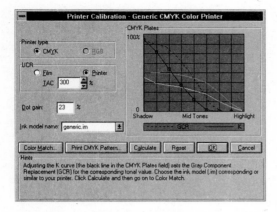

Figure 39.4
The Printer Calibration dialog box.

To calibrate a CMYK printer, follow these steps:

1. Select CMYK as the printer type and paper as the output, unless the device is an imagesetter. Choose Film for imagesetters.

2. Enter the percentage of Total Area Coverage (TAC) that corresponds with your printer. TAC refers to the sum of the percentages of cyan, yellow, and magenta inks required to make black.

3. Enter the dot gain for your printer, and adjust the K curve by dragging the markers in the CMYK Plates view box.

4. Choose Print CMYK Pattern and select a printer. The CMYK320 file is output to the printer you select.

5. Use the spectrophotometer or colorimeter to measure the CIE XYZ values for each of the color squares from 1 to

320. Enter these values in a three-column ASCII file. Name the file to correspond to the printer, with an IM extension.

6. Return to the Printer Calibration dialog box and choose the IM file you created. Click on Calculate to continue. The Printer Characterization dialog box should appear, as in figure 39.5.

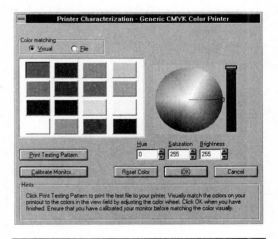

Figure 39.5
The Printer Characterization dialog box.

7. Choose Calibrate Monitor and select the monitor circuit you created. If you have not created a monitor circuit, you can do so at this time.

8. Select Color matching and enter the method you want to use to match color. If you choose File, you're prompted to enter the RHN file for your printer. If you choose Visual,

select **P**rint Testing Pattern to print the page of 16 colors you must match.

9. Adjust the colors to match the printout you have or enter the corresponding HSB numbers in the entry boxes. Click on OK to continue.

10. Click on OK once more to return to the System Color Profile dialog box.

Calibrating Your Scanner

You can calibrate your scanner from an image or a file by using the Scanner Calibration dialog box (see fig. 39.6). Start from the System Color Profile dialog box and go to the Scanner list box. If your scanner is not listed, choose Other. Otherwise enter the name of your scanner in the entry box. If you are calibrating from a file, enter the SCN file name that corresponds to your scanner and click on OK to continue.

Follow these steps to calibrate your scanner from an image:

1. Disable the Scanner Calibration option in the Preferences dialog box of CorelPHOTO-PAINT if you are scanning from inside that program.

2. Scan the target photo packaged with CorelDRAW, or an IT8 target if one is available. Save the scan as a TIFF file.

3. Choose **I**mage from the Scanner Calibration dialog box, and load the TIFF file you created.

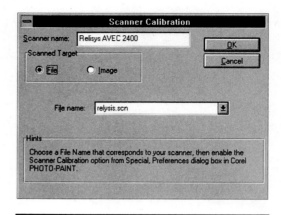

Figure 39.6
The Scanner Calibration dialog box.

4. Select a reference file. You can use the REF file that CorelDRAW installs or one that comes with your scanner.

5. Click on Scanned Target to display the Scanned Target dialog box.

6. Drag the corner markers to create a bounding box around the color grid. Be sure they match the fiducial marks.

7. Click on OK and enter a file name for your scanner calibration. Click on OK again to return to the System Color Profile dialog box.

Summary

Generating a system profile can take some time, but the results are worth the time invested. Using color correction enables you to match the display of your monitor to the output from your printer, so that you can create images with greater ease.

Chapter 40

Importing and Exporting

CorelDRAW enables you to import and export files from a number of different formats. The broad range of Windows and MAC formats that are supported provide you with connectivity to almost any application. You can import and export bitmapped and vector images, as well as text, into your documents. The Windows Clipboard and OLE2 compatibility expand these abilities even further.

This chapter covers:

- Importing from other applications

- Exporting to other applications

- Saving CorelDRAW documents for other versions

- Using the Clipboard

- OLE considerations

Importing from Other Applications

The general instructions for importing files into CorelDRAW are the same for any format (see fig. 40.1). To import a file from another program, perform the following steps:

1. Select **I**mport from the **F**ile menu.

2. From the List Files of **T**ype list box, select the file format you want to import.

3. Enter the path and file name of the file you want to import. Enable **P**review to see a thumbnail of the image you are importing. Selecting Options allows you to view information about the file. It also allows you to specify **A**uto-Reduce when importing vector images.

4. If you are importing a bitmap, you can choose to crop, resize, or resample an image during the import by clicking the down arrow beside Full Image. This can reduce the file size and the time it takes to load the image.

5. Click on OK to return to the drawing window. The file you are importing will appear in the drawing window.

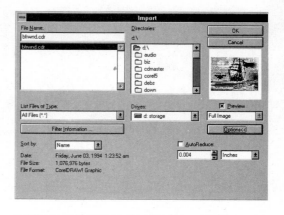

Figure 40.1
The Import dialog box.

N O T E

Extremely large or complex files place an enormous demand on system resources, and can take a while to import.

Supported Formats

Though CorelDRAW supports a number of different file formats with import and export filters, there are technical notes and restrictions that apply to some formats. CorelDRAW imports and exports the following formats:

■ **.AI Adobe Illustrator.** Full support is provided for all Adobe Illustrator formats, including 3.0, Illustrator 88, and 1.1. vector graphics, whether created for Windows or Macintosh.

The graphics are imported as a group of objects. Ungroup the objects to manipulate them individually.

- **.AI Arts & Letters.** See .AI Adobe Illustrator.

- **.AI Micrografx Designer, Graph Plus.** See .AI Adobe Illustrator.

- **.AI Macintosh-based vector packages.** See .AI Adobe Illustrator.

- **.BMP.** CorelDRAW supports monochrome, grayscale, and color .BMP files. Both Windows and OS/2 BMP bitmapped images are supported.

- **.CCH CorelCHART.** This filter enables you to import graphics from Corel's charting program.

- **.CDR CorelDRAW.** Imports graphics in CorelDRAW's native format. This enables you to add images created in one CorelDRAW document to another document. Images appear as grouped in the drawing window. Ungroup the objects to manipulate the objects individually. When importing text from an earlier version of CorelDRAW, the inter-character spacing may be different. To correct spacing, use the shape tool to interactively kern the text.

- **.CGM Harvard Graphics.** CorelDRAW supports this vector format, with the following restrictions. CorelDRAW's .CGM import filter only allows markers to be supported. Imported text is editable, provided the file was exported, using the correct text

options. In Harvard Graphics 3.0, you must select the .CGM font for the text to be editable. CorelDRAW provides no support for bitmapped images or fills.

- **.CGM Lotus 1-2-3.** See .CGM Harvard Graphics.

- **.CGM Lotus Freelance Plus.** See .CGM Harvard Graphics.

- **.CMP.** See .JPG.

- **.CPT.** You can import files from Corel PHOTO-PAINT. .CPT files are a RGB TIFF 6.0 format. CorelDRAW does not support objects placed in Corel PHOTO-PAINT.

- **.CT.** CorelDRAW can only import 32-bit color SCITEX bitmaps. There is no grayscale support for this format.

- **.DOC.** This filter supports Microsoft Word for Windows 1.*x*–6.*x* files. CorelDRAW attempts to match all the fonts in your document with the same or similar fonts. The default text attributes are applied to text that was created in Word, using the Normal text style. The import filter supports indexes created with the embedded field method. The current page size settings in CorelDRAW determine the placement and size of the paragraph text frame. This may affect the positioning of the text. Endnotes and footnotes are not supported.

CorelDRAW supports the import of Microsoft Word for Macintosh 4.0 and 5.0. Imported text is fit to the current

CorelDRAW page size. Text is imported into a paragraph frame. Point size and font information are maintained. CorelDRAW does not support footnotes or endnotes created in Microsoft Word for Macintosh 4.0 or 5.0.

CorelDRAW can interpret .EPS, .PS, and .AI files. This filter is primarily for importing print files. The .EPS information that is used when the image is printed to a PostScript printer can be imported into CorelDRAW.

Importing a file with large or complex objects or fills generates a large file. The import may fail due to memory limitations. If the import fails, you can increase the Virtual Memory that the interpreter allocates when it initializes. This may help you import larger or more complex files. Set VMSize=n (where n is megabytes of allocated memory and 2 is the default) to a larger number.

■ **.DRW Micrografx Designer, Graph Plus.** This filter supports Micrograpx 2.*x* and 3.*x* files. It does not support the following: clip regions, raster operations, and fountain fills.

■ **.DXF AutoCAD.** Vector format. CorelDRAW only supports a single view. If the image is 3D, save the view you want to import into CorelDRAW. If the file fails to import, reduce the complexity of the drawing by plotting the image to file, using an HP7475 as the selected device. Use a curve resolution of .004" to further reduce

the complexity of the file. Then use the HPGL import filter to open the file in CorelDRAW. The import filter does not support .SHX files or files that contain 3D extrusions of shapes, polylines, or text. CorelDRAW does support text with no text justification; however, it may not support the font or point size. The text will be resized to meet CorelDRAW's limitations.

■ **.EPS CorelTRACE.** This filter enables you to import the .EPS output from CorelTRACE.

■ **.EPS Micrografx Designer, Graph Plus.** See .AI Adobe Illustrator.

■ **.EPS Placeable.** CorelDRAW can import .EPS, .PS, and .AI in a Placeable format. CorelDRAW displays the thumbnail, or placeable header, in the drawing window. The .EPS information remains attached to the header, and is used when the image is printed to a PostScript printer. The .EPS file itself is not editable, nor can text in the .EPS file be edited. Imported placeable graphics come into the program as a group of objects.

■ **.GDF IBM PIF and IBM Mainframe files.** Vector format.

■ **.GEM Artline.** Enables you to import files from Artline with the following restrictions. Symbols are treated as text objects in CorelDRAW, and are imported as curves. There is no support for endcap styles. Text is also imported as curves, and cannot be edited as text.

■ **.GEM Draw Plus.** This filter enables you to import files from Draw Plus. CorelDRAW supports solid filled and tinted objects. Specialty fills, such as grids, hatching, and so on, are not supported, and will be replaced with a corresponding colored fill in CorelDRAW. This filter also supports rounded, endcap styles. Text is imported as editable text, using the character attributes of the default text in CorelDRAW, if the font is not available. There is no support for underlined text.

■ **.GEM Graph.** Enables you to import files from Graph. Text is placed as editable text, using the same font, if it is available. If it is not currently on the system, CorelDRAW's default font and attributes are applied.

■ **.GIF.** CorelDRAW enables you to import version 87A and 89A version .GIF files.

■ **.HPGL.** Vector format. Images are restricted to CorelDRAW's maximum image size. Use the resize feature in the import dialog box to resize the image. The curve resolution can be any value between .001" and 1.0"; however, a curve of .004 is recommended because of the complexity of the curve at smaller sizes. .HPGL files use pen numbers, rather than fills associated with them. You can specify any of the 256 colors in the pen list to a pen. CorelDRAW supports a variety of dotted, dashed, and solid pen styles. The import filter supports the import of text, with the specific restrictions.

Text strings are imported as an editable monospaced font. Set Background Mix, Set Foreground Mix, Call Segment, Set Paper Color, and Set Pattern Symbol are not supported.

■ **.JFF.** See .JPG.

■ **.JFT.** See .JPG.

■ **.JPG.** Provides import support for JPEG bitmapped images. JPEG is a standard format developed by the Joint Photographers Experts Group that allows the transfer of files between a wide variety of platforms, using superior compression techniques.

■ **.PCC.** See .PCX.

■ **.PCD.** This filter provides import support for Kodak Photo CD and Corel Photo CD images into CorelDRAW. Photo CD images are created from 35mm film negatives or slides. These images are converted to digital format and stored on a compact disc (CD).

■ **.PCX.** This filter supports version 2.5, 2.8, and 3.0 .PCX files.

■ **.PIC Lotus.** This filter enables you to import graphs from Lotus 1-2-3. Colors are converted to a set of eight colors. Text imported using this filter is editable. Times Roman is used for title text; non-title text becomes monospaced.

■ **.PICT Macintosh-based vector packages.** This filter enables you to import graphics created on a Macintosh, using a program such as

MacDraw. The images can be vector- or bitmapped. Any objects that contain both a fill and an outline are imported as two objects. CorelDRAW attempts to maintain attributes such as bitmap pattern fills, outlines, arrowheads, and dashed lines; however, the appearance of these objects may not have the desired appearance. The objects may contain extraneous nodes, or have attributes that have no direct equivalent in CorelDRAW. The program does not support the following MacDraw II features: accurate text alignment, font selection, and text styles.

■ **.PLT AutoCAD.** See .HPGL AutoCAD.

■ **.RLE.** CorelDRAW enables you to import .RLE files. These files are compressed .BMP files. If the RLE was created in CorelDRAW 3, or if the file bands, you can edit the CORELFLT.INI. In the [CorelBMPImport] section of the CORELFLT.INI, add the following line: Import Corel30RLE=1.

■ **.RTF Microsoft Rich Text Format.** This filter supports RTF files with the following restrictions. The page size will be resized to fit the current page size in CorelDRAW. This may affect the positioning of the text. Tables of contents and indexing are not supported.

■ **.SAM Ami Professional.** Supports text files created in Ami Professional 2.0 or 3.0. In CorelDRAW, the text is fitted

to the current page size. This may affect the placement of the text.

■ **.TGA.** CorelDRAW enables you to import 16- and 24-bit Targa files. It also imports uncompressed color-mapped images, uncompressed RGB images, RLE compressed color-mapped images, and RLE compressed RGB images. This filter may strip the last 8-bits from some 32-bit Targa files.

■ **.TIF.** CorelDRAW enables you to import monochrome, color, and grayscale TIFF files up to and including version 5. You can also import TIFF files using the CCITT, Packbits 32773, or LZW compression. This import filter provides support for TIFF 6.0 files, using JPEG compression or with CMYK data. TIFF is a bitmap file format used by many digital scanners. No support is provided for YCbCr.

■ **.TXT ASCII text.** Paragraph text import.

■ **.WMF Windows Metafile.** This filter supports files created in Aldus Persuasion, Lotus Freelance Graphics, and Harvard Draw. CorelDRAW uses Panose font substitution to select fonts.

■ **.WPG WordPerfect.** CorelDRAW supports graphic imports from WordPerfect applications, with the following exceptions: Graphics Text Type 2, .WPG version 6, and .WPG version 2.

CorelDRAW also supports WordPerfect 5.0 and later text files, in both DOS and Windows format. Text is placed in the current page size in the CorelDRAW drawing window, and the positioning of the text may differ. The following text features are not supported: Table of Contents, Indexes, Style Sheets, Hline, and Vline.

- **.XLS Excel for Windows.** Supports files from versions 3 and 4. Spreadsheets are imported into a frame, with tab stops matching cell widths.

Considerations when Importing Bitmapped Images

Bitmapped images do not respond well to resizing. They should be printed as close to the creation size as possible. When a bitmapped image is resized in the drawing window of CorelDRAW or printed, the result can be an image with a jagged appearance. Resizing and resampling an image when you import it helps minimize this problem.

All bitmapped formats create large files. When you import a bitmapped image into CorelDRAW, the size of the image file affects the loading time, refresh time in the window, and the size of the CorelDRAW file. This can put a drain on resources, as well as take up hard disk space. To minimize this problem, do not choose a resolution that exceeds your printing requirements. Also, cropping an image upon import can help keep the file size within acceptable limits.

Importing Text

Imported text is always treated as paragraph text. The text can either fill an existing paragraph text frame, or create a new text frame when it is imported. The text frame appears centered on the printable page. Generally, the text is imported with the font and character attributes of the originating application, if they are supported. If you are creating a text file in another application that you know will be imported into CorelDRAW, avoid using too much formatting. The text is easier to edit in CorelDRAW.

Importing CorelDRAW Clip Art

CorelDRAW's vast library of clip art is on the CD-ROM. Previous versions allowed the clip art to be opened, as you would any other file. To use the clip art in version 5, you must import the clip art using the .CMX import filter.

Exporting to Other Applications

The general instructions for exporting files from CorelDRAW are the same for any format (see fig. 40.2). To export a file for use in another program, perform the following steps:

1. Select **E**xport from the **F**ile menu to display the Export dialog box.

2. You can export a selection of objects by themselves without exporting the rest of the image, by choosing **S**elected Only. Make sure the objects are selected before accessing the Export dialog box.

3. Choose an export format from the list.

4. Enter a file name for the exported file. You can also accept the name in the window, or select a name from the list box. CorelDRAW automatically adds the appropriate extension to the file.

5. Select a different path if you want, and click on OK to begin the export.

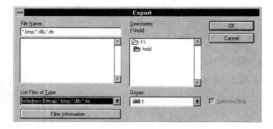

Figure 40.2
The Export dialog box.

N O T E

Exporting places extraordinary demands on system resources and can take a while, depending upon the format chosen and the file size.

Supported Formats

CorelDRAW's export filters enable you to export files for use in a number of different applications. Some formats are more suitable for some applications than others.

CorelDRAW supports the following export formats:

- **.AI Adobe Illustrator 88 and 3.0.** .AI is a type of .EPS format. It should not be used as a direct substitute, however—some of the features you incorporate into your image may not be supported in .AI. Choose .EPS, unless you specifically require .AI format. If the document is to be imported into a publishing package, .EPS is the recommended format.

  Fountain fills are exported as bands of color. The number of bands corresponds with the number set for Preview Fountain Steps in the **P**references dialog box. Arrowheads are exported as separate from the line with which they are associated. Bitmapped images are not supported. Texture fills are exported as a solid gray.

  If a text object has had attributes applied to individual characters, such as vertical shift or font changes, then each character in the text is exported as a separate text sting. Similarly, each character of a text string that has been fitted to a path is exported as a separate text string.

Calligraphic Text must be enabled in the **P**references dialog box, in order for calligraphic outlines to be supported. Export text as curves, if Illustrator does not have the font in your image (see fig. 40.3).

Figure 40.3
The Export Adobe Illustrator dialog box.

Memory considerations: combining objects in your CorelDRAW document makes exporting more difficult. EPS exports create complex objects that can cause editing problems, whether edited in CorelDRAW or in another application. To minimize this problem, keep a copy of the original CorelDRAW document, and use it for all editing.

■ **.BMP Windows and OS/2.** Scales images to size prior to exporting. This is especially helpful if the bitmapped image will be used in a publishing package—it prevents the bitmapped image from disproportionately increasing the file size, while maintaining a quality appearance (see fig. 40.4).

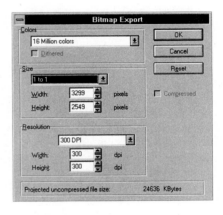

Figure 40.4
The Bitmap Export dialog box.

■ **.CGM.** This filter supports most features in CorelDRAW, with the exception of the following limitations. The number of steps in a fountain fill is determined by the setting for the Preview Fountain Steps in the **P**references dialog box. There is no support for bitmaps or PostScript texture fills. Objects filled with a PostScript texture fill will be converted to solid gray filled objects (see fig. 40.5).

Figure 40.5
The CGM Export dialog box.

■ **.CMP.** See .BMP.

■ **.CT Matrix/Imapro SCODL.** See .SCD Matrix/Imapro SCODL.

■ **.DXF AutoCAD.** This export filter creates files that can be rather large. A complex drawing could easily export to a file in excess of 500KB. The following CorelDRAW features are not supported by this export filter: calligraphic pen effects, bitmaps, layer information, texture fills, and objects with no outline. It is recommended that you select standard colors. The export filter supports 255 full colors, but may yield unpredictable results (see fig. 40.6). Text is exported as curves and is not editable.

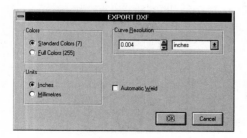

Figure 40.6
The DXF Export dialog box.

■ **.EPS Placeable.** The EPS placeable export filter uses a header format of TIFF 4.2, with a selectable resolution range from 1 to 72 dpi (see fig. 40.7). If the application to which you are exporting the file has a header size limitation, use a monochrome header to prevent import failure. The export filter includes the file name, program name, and date in the file. The program automatically sizes the bounding box. Choose Include Fonts if you are not certain the output device will have the fonts available. Check with your service bureau for a list of available fonts. Be certain that fonts are downloaded to your in-house printer, if necessary. If the font is not found, the file will either print in Courier or printing will fail.

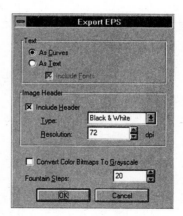

Figure 40.7
The Export EPS dialog box.

■ **.GEM Draw Plus.** The GEM filter exports objects as two components: an outline and a fill. Arrowheads—dotted and dashed lines—are exported as individual polygons. Any colors are reduced to the 16 colors supported by .GEM, which can yield undesirable results when exporting fountain fills. Text is exported as curves, and is not editable.

.GEM limits the number of objects per file. If the file is complex and exceeds the limit, the image is truncated and parts of the image will be incomplete. To minimize this problem, simplify images as much as possible. Texture fills, bitmaps, and corner styles are not supported. Bezier curves are converted to line segments, which may not exceed 128 points. If the object exceeds that limit, the object will be broken into smaller objects. If the application to which you are importing the .GEM file does not understand the Bezier information, select polylines during the export (see fig. 40.8).

Figure 40.8
The Export GEM dialog box.

■ **.JFF.** See .BMP.

■ **.JTF.** See .BMP.

■ **.JPG.** See .BMP.

■ **.GIF CompuServe version 89A.** See .BMP.

■ **.PCT MACINTOSH Picture.** This export filter supports most outline effects, including calligraphic and line caps. Calligraphic Text must be enabled in the **P**references dialog box, and the line caps appear as a group of separate objects. Bitmap fills are not supported. PostScript texture fills are converted to gray. Filled objects with outlines are exported as a group of two objects. The number of bands used in fountain fills is determined by the Preview Fountain Steps, in the **P**references dialog box. Colors are device dependent. If the display of the Macintosh is 8-bit, the colors will be converted to 256. To maintain colors closely matching those in CorelDRAW, the Macintosh must have 24-bit color capability. Outlines on text will not appear, unless the text is converted to curves prior to exporting. Text is converted to curves on export, and is uneditable (see fig. 40.9).

Figure 40.9
The Export PICT dialog box.

■ **.PCX Paintbrush Version 3.0.** See .BMP.

■ **.PFB Adobe Type 1.** All text exports are unhinted. Text characters must be a single object. Combine multiple objects before exporting. Avoid intersecting lines; combined objects must lie entirely within one another. Fills and outlines are not supported (see fig. 40.10).

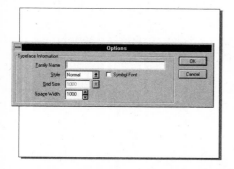

Figure 40.10
The Options dialog box.

■ **.PIF IBM.** Colors are reduced to a 16-color palette. This may give fountain fills an unacceptable appearance. Texture fills are not supported and are converted to gray. If the application to which you are exporting does not support Bézier curves, export curves as polylines. Enable Calligraphic **T**ext in the **P**references dialog box to export calligraphic pen effects, line caps, and custom outline widths. Text may be exported as text or curves. When text is exported as text, the file is smaller, and the text is editable; however, fonts and spacing may not be maintained. When text is exported as curves, the appearance is maintained; however, the text is not editable. This export filter does not support bitmaps or PostScript textures (see fig. 40.11).

Figure 40.11
The Export PIF dialog box.

■ **.PLT HP Plotter HPGL.** This filter allows export to HPGL applications. It has a number of limitations, however. With exception of solid uniform fills, most fill types are not supported.

Texture fills are converted to gray, and solid fills only are simulated. All lines are mapped to HPGL standards, which means that all lines have a maximum width of one pen width, and Bézier curves are converted to line segments. Calligraphic pen styles are not supported. All colors are matched to the current pen library. Although 256 pens can be defined, you may be restricted to eight or fewer pens. Page size and orientation of the CorelDRAW image must match that of the plotter for a successful export. Any objects without outlines will be assigned an outline during the export process. All text is exported as curves and is not editable (see fig. 40.12).

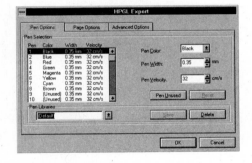

Figure 40.12
The HPGL Export dialog box.

■ **.RLE Windows.** .RLE is a Windows .BMP format that supports compression. Very few applications support compressed .BMP files, and will generate error messages or display the bitmap improperly. Only 4- or 8-bit .BMP files can be compressed.

■ **.SCD Matrix/Imapro SCODL.** This export filter supports most outline effects, including corner styles, calligraphic, and line caps, provided CalligraphicText is enabled in the **P**references dialog box. Fountain fills are supported; however, there is no support for bitmap fills or PostScript textures. These limitations can be eliminated if you use a service bureau that has Adobe PostScript RIP for their Agfa-Matrix film recorders. Use the page layout for Slide and be sure to maintain the aspect ratio. Objects may not fall outside the printable page, or the export will fail. Try to create the file in landscape orientation. If you must create the file in portrait orientation, switch the page layout back to landscape and rotate the image appropriately. You may only export images in landscape orientation (see fig. 40.13).

Figure 40.13
The Export SCODL dialog box.

■ **.TGA.** This filter supports either RLE-compressed color-mapped images, or RLE-compressed RGB images. The type of file produced depends on the number of colors exported: 24-bit color .TGA files will be exported as RLE-compressed RGB bitmaps. There is currently very little support for compressed .TGA files.

■ **.TIF.** This export filter supports TIFF 6.0, LZW version 4.2, and LZW version 5.0. See .BMP.

■ **.TTF TrueType Fonts.** All text exports are unhinted. Text characters must be a single object. Combine multiple objects before exporting. Avoid intersecting lines; combined objects must lie entirely within one another. Fills and outlines are not supported (see fig. 40.14).

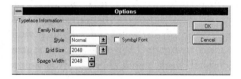

Figure 40.14
The Options dialog box.

■ **.LZW CompuServe.** See .BMP.

■ **.WMF Windows Metafile.** .WMF files may not import correctly into publishing packages—.WMF files can be very large, and some publishing packages place limitations on file size. You can include an image header,

which will make it easier to place and view the image in publishing packages (see fig. 40.15); however, some applications do not support image headers in .WMF files. If the application does not support image headers, the import will fail. The number of steps used for a fountain fill is determined by the value for Preview Fountain steps in the **P**references dialog box. This export filter does not support PostScript features, including texture fills and halftone screens. There is also no support for two-color, four-color, or texture fills. Objects containing these fills will be exported as having gray fills.

Figure 40.15
The Export WMF dialog box.

■ **.WPG WordPerfect.** This export filter supports most outline effects, including corner styles, calligraphic, and line caps, provided CalligraphicText is enabled in the **P**references dialog box. The outlines will export as a group of polygons that match the appearance of the outlines in CorelDRAW, but add significantly to the size of the exported file. Fountain fills appear banded unless the 256 color option is enabled (see fig. 40.16). There is no support for PostScript fills or bitmaps. Objects filled with texture fills are exported filled with gray. WordPerfect supports a standard set of 16 colors. Exporting with the 256-color option enabled may yield truer colors; however, some colors may be represented as gray. Text is exported as curves and is not editable.

Figure 40.16
The Export WPG dialog box.

Recommended Export Formats

Some export formats are more suitable for one application than another. A few applications require a proprietary format. Other applications, such as publishing packages, will import multiple formats, but you may find that one format provides better output than another.

When exporting to layout and publishing applications without graphics editing support, .EPS is the preferred export format, if the application has .EPS import capability. If .EPS support is not available, make your selection based upon the application and the output device, as follows:

- For export to Ami Professional, use .EPS for PostScript output and .WMF for non-PostScript output.

- For export to Delrina Perform, use .GEM for PostScript output and .GEM for non-PostScript output.

- For export to PageMaker, use .EPS for PostScript output and .WMF for non-PostScript output.

- For export to CorelVENTURA, use .EPS for PostScript output and .CMX for non-PostScript output.

- For export to WordPerfect, use .EPS for PostScript output and .WPG for non-PostScript output.

When exporting to layout and publishing applications with graphics editing support, make your selection based upon the application and the output device, as follows:

- For export to Adobe Illustrator, use .AI for PostScript output and .AI for non-PostScript output.

- For export to Arts & Letters, use .EPS (using Decipher) for PostScript output and .WMF for non-PostScript output.

- For export to AutoCAD, use .DXF for PostScript output and .DXF for non-PostScript output.

- For export to GEM Artline, use .GEM for PostScript output and .GEM for non-PostScript output.

- For export to Macintosh-based vector applications, use .AI for PostScript output and .PICT for non-PostScript output.

- For export to Micrografx Designer, use .CGM for PostScript output and .CGM for non-PostScript output.

- For export to PC Paintbrush, use .PCX for PostScript output and .PCX for non-PostScript output.

Saving CorelDRAW Documents for Other Versions

You can save CorelDRAW documents for use in other versions of CorelDRAW. This is helpful if you support more than one version, or need to share files with others. Some special features may be ignored when the file is saved, because the versions are not backward-compatible.

To save a version 5.0 file as version 3.0 or 4.0, follow these steps:

1. Select Save **A**s from the **F**ile menu to access the Save **A**s dialog box.

2. Select the version for which you want to save the file.

3. Enter a path and file name. Click on OK to complete the operation and return to the drawing window.

T I P

It is a good idea to give the file a name that differentiates it from the version 5.0 file, rather than overwriting the 5.0 file. This allows you to maintain a document complete with any special effects you might have created. It also helps prevent confusion when hunting for a file, if you add a note in the Note entry box regarding the version of the file.

Using the Clipboard

Data can be transferred using the Windows Clipboard between CorelDRAW and other applications. If you want to preserve calligraphic features and text, CalligraphicText and TextInMetafile should be enabled in the **P**references dialog box. CorelDRAW can places data on the Clipboard as a .CMX or .WMF. You can paste objects into CorelDRAW that support .WMF, .BMP, .RTF, and ASCII text on the Windows Clipboard. The Clipboard provides no support for PostScript textures or pattern fills.

Some Windows Metafile features cannot be pasted into CorelDRAW. Those features include the following:

- Background commands, such as SetBkMode and SetBkColor.

- Pattern fills.

- Clipping regions.

- Flood fills.

- Individual pixel manipulations.

- ROP2 modes other than R2-COPYPEN.

- Text in excess of 8000 characters. Text under 250 characters is treated as artistic text. Text in excess of 250 characters is treated as paragraph text. RTF text is always pasted as paragraph text, and retains any formatting attributes.

OLE Considerations

CorelDRAW provides some support for OLE Automation commands available with Visual Basic for Applications. Using these commands, you can write scripts that allow you to automate some of the routine work you do. The commands CorelDRAW supports include the following:

- `Open"filename"`: This command loads the file into CorelDRAW.

- `Print"filename"`: Opens the file in CorelDRAW, and accesses the **P**rint dialog box to print the file. The **P**rint dialog box only appears the first time. The selected options are applied to subsequent calls for printing.

- `Export"filename"`: Opens the file in CorelDRAW and exports it. When performing batch exports, the **E**xport dialog box appears the first time. Export options selected the first time are applied to subsequent calls.

- `Import"filename"`: Imports the file into the current document.

- `SaveAs"filename"`: Saves the current document to the specified file name.

- `Quit`: Closes CorelDRAW.

T I P

Sample Visual Basic automation files can be found in the Samples directory on the CD-ROM.

CorelDRAW supports the Visible property. If Visible=TRUE, windows and dialog boxes will be visible during OLE Automation events. If Visible=FALSE, windows and dialog boxes will not be visible, and the event will occur in the background.

Summary

CorelDRAW provides connectivity to a broad assortment of Windows, DOS, and Macintosh applications using its import and export capabilities. The Windows Clipboard enables you to transfer data between applications, without importing or exporting files. This is useful for transferring small amounts of data. OLE2 supports drag-and-drop-embedding and linking to interconnect OLE2 compliant applications from a variety of sources.

Chapter 41

Working with Service Bureaus

CorelDRAW has consistently been the favored graphics tool for Windows users since its release. CorelDRAW's success has been due, in large part, to the ease with which new users are able to start creating great-looking designs. Finishing the graphics process, however, is equally important. This is where you may need to work with a service bureau. This chapter explores what service bureaus are, what they can do for you, what they need from you in order to best serve your work, and discusses image setters, slides, color, imaging, choosing fonts, understanding Windows PostScript drives, transporting files, and tips and hints.

This chapter covers:

- Why do you need a service bureau?

- What are the different types of service bureaus?

- Finding a service bureau

- What equipment is needed to image your files?

Understanding CorelDRAW 5's Capabilities

After five major revisions, CorelDRAW is not only a fantastic tool for the masses who need computer graphics capabilities, but it is also able to meet the standards of the most demanding professional illustrators, graphic designers, and production artists.

The capability of CorelDRAW to meet such a wide variety of professional needs is really a combination of factors that have merged over recent years. One of the most important is that a great assortment of devices exist that are able to image computer files. Some of the most common include color printers that can handle a wide variety of papers, film recorders for imaging photographic slide material, and high resolution imagesetters that can make positive or negative materials specifically geared for making commercial printing plates.

Another factor is that Microsoft and the device manufacturers have collaborated to enable Windows applications to communicate with these imaging devices by way of a piece of software called a device driver. The *device driver* merely takes data from a source (in this case, Windows), and converts it into the necessary instructions to physically make a device carry out all the steps necessary to create an image on a piece of media.

A third factor is that Corel engineers have added stunning special effects features to CorelDRAW 5.0, and they have gone to great lengths to ensure that these can be imaged on the huge array of output devices available. To their credit, they have studied the world of publishing and have added advanced features to CorelDRAW's printing functions so that the professional user has the needed flexibility and control over many exacting output processes.

All the previously mentioned factors have helped fuel an emerging (and ever-changing) service industry: the service bureau.

What *Is* a Service Bureau?

In the graphics world, the term would be applied to any organization that takes in computer files and outputs them on the devices that they have available. Because of the many types of printing devices, these organizations usually specialize in one type of imaging.

Why Do You Need a Service Bureau?

The biggest reason why every service bureau does not have all types of imaging is cost; the same reason why you, more than likely, don't have "one of everything" connected to your computer. High-resolution imagesetters, suitable for making negatives for printing presses, cost in the tens to hundreds of thousands of dollars. Film recorders can be purchased for less than one thousand dollars;

however, professional-level machines can cost 10 to 50 times more. The same can be said for color printers. Costs go up considerably as you increase paper size, resolution, and speed.

The need for service bureaus now becomes quite clear. The *service* they provide is output to a device to which you don't normally have access. The working concept is simple: you give them computer files and they give you physical images back.

What Are the Different Types of Service Bureaus?

Although there are service bureaus that provide many different kinds of imaging, the types can be classified by the nature of the material being imaged. The most common are the following:

- High-resolution imagesetting
- Photographic slides
- Color imaging

High-Resolution Imagesetting

High resolution is generally considered to start at 1200 dots per inch (dpi). Newer-generation imagesetters can achieve well over 3000 dpi. These imagesetters typically image onto photosensitive paper or film by exposing it with light from a laser. The resulting

materials are supplied to commercial printers to continue a process that ends in making printing plates for their presses.

To produce good-quality printed materials, such as brochures containing four-color, process photographs, the imagesetter must be very accurate. Less demanding printing projects won't need the services of a state-of-the-art imagesetter.

Photographic Slides

Slide presentations, such as those given by seminar speakers, are generally displayed from 35mm slides. A slide service bureau has very different equipment than the first type of service bureau because the end product is a piece of photographic material, just like the film you put into your 35mm camera. The basic manufacturing process comes down to taking a picture—no separating of colors onto individual printing plates, no ink, no paper.

What this type of service bureau uses is called a *film recorder*. Inside the film recorder is a small CRT display, something like your computer monitor. The image stored on the computer file is reconstructed and displayed on this CRT, and then a camera takes a picture of it. The film is then developed and placed in slide mounts. Presto! Your presentation is ready to be projected.

The quality of a slide is not measured in dpi like other devices. It is measured by how many lines of pixels are displayed on the CRT. The lines are expressed in "k." It is similar to computer memory, where 1KB equals 1,024 bytes. A slide with a resolution

of 2k means that CRT imaged it using 2,048 pixels per line. The higher the k number, the better the slide will look. Slides generally come in 2, 4, or 8k. Many slide service bureaus offer formats larger than 35mm. Ask whether they provide 4×5 and 8×10.

Color Imaging Services

The last type of service bureau covers a wide variety of devices. The common denominator is that they produce full-color, composite images. The variety here is in sizes of output. Some imaging centers have printers, called *plotters*, which produce large color printouts suitable for signs and posters. Others might offer fast, high-quantity color photocopy quality duplicating.

Color prints can be used to proof jobs that are destined to end up on printing presses, to create color overhead transparencies for presentations, or to turnout a small run of posters that would be too costly to produce with traditional printing presses.

Finding a Service Bureau

How do you find service bureaus? Ask colleagues whom they use. If you are working with a printer, ask whom they have experience with. Look in the back of trade magazines and newsletters. User groups are also a great place to get recommendations.

Bear in mind that there are many bureaus that do business all over the nation. They take in files sent to them on disks or modem, image the jobs, then send out the finished work by overnight courier, mail, or UPS. If you are not experienced with working with service bureaus, this can be complicated. It would be better to get some experience with local organizations. Having people nearby to answer questions and get you over some of the first hurdles makes a difference.

If you need to find someone local, look in the phone book. Depending on what type of imaging you need, look under Graphic Arts, Printing, Typesetting, Photographic Services, Copying, or Signs.

Finding service bureaus is like shopping for shoes. There generally isn't a problem locating them, but finding a nice pair that's comfortable and affordable—that takes some time and effort. And time and effort you invest in finding good service bureaus is worth it.

After you find some likely candidates, talk to them. If they are located close enough, make an appointment to see their establishment and meet the people. If they are a small shop, they might not have a full-time salesperson who will explain the company's equipment and services. However, somebody needs to convey that information to you. If no one has the time for you now, there's a good chance that you will receive this same low level of service later. Look at your next candidate.

There are many questions to ask a prospective service bureau. You can talk equipment, software, pricing, and turnaround times, but try to discover more about the organization to which you are trusting your files. Try to find out what they did before they got into the service bureau business.

What Kind of Background Do They Have?

"Why should it matter where they came from?" you ask. Remember that service bureaus are a relatively new phenomenon, but the industry of graphic arts is not. There are many persons who got their start in a specific area of the graphic arts who now find themselves in the service bureau business. Depending on what type of service you need, this can be very helpful.

For example, some materials imaged for the printing industry have additional factors that need to be anticipated at the time the "Print" button is pushed. So the specialized training and experience of service bureau employees in other disciplines, such as printing, photography, and computer operations, can make a big difference between a successful or frustrating experience when imaging your files at a service bureau. Then too, the devices to which they are outputting are often much more complicated to operate correctly than is the humble desktop laser printer.

Typographers

Long before you had your personal computer and formatted your first word in 12-point Helvetica regular, typesetting was being done by people who spent many years learning their craft. Several decades ago, this group, known as *typographers*, were led kicking and screaming into the computer age. The pros and cons of the consequence of switching to digital type would fill several volumes. The

relevant point for you is the fact that typographers became experienced with computers, digital data, and high-resolution photographic imagesetters.

Rolls of photographic paper infested with columns of black type streamed out of their processors everyday. Rule lines could be drawn, but that was the extent of graphics capabilities. Also, the computers used to input the information were not your standard PCs, and the software that controlled the whole process was nowhere near what you would call "friendly."

Then the personal computer, with its desktop publishing software, came along and helped to kill off the typesetting industry. Struggling typesetting companies needed to apply their experience somewhere. Today, many service bureaus have been built on the foundations of once thriving photo-typesetting businesses.

What does that mean for you? If they are good, these organizations probably know computers and graphic files. They probably know more about the MAC than PC/Windows, but this is changing rapidly.

But if you are working on a project that will eventually run on a printing press, will they know about the specifics of the printing industry? Can they tell you what amount of trap to add and to what objects? Can they advise you on allowance for dot gain? Or what is the best linescreen frequency to use for a particular type of printing project? Probably not. These are answers you need to find out for yourself, from other sources.

Pre-Press Specialists

There are organizations that have serviced the needs of the graphic arts industry for almost as many years as there have been printing presses. They have provided printing companies with negatives, color separations, photo scanning, page imposition, and just about any service that was needed to make printing plates. These shops know everything there is to know about producing images destined to roll off a printing press. They work hand-in-hand with many different printing companies.

Could they tell you what type style and size a particular word was set in? Probably not. But, when you need to know about trapping and dot gain, you need the expertise of a shop with pre-press knowledge.

Photographers and Photographic Labs

Who would know more about color film and negatives, photo retouching, or processing film than a photographer or a photographic lab? They are both naturals to offer digital slide imaging.

Suppose you wanted a photographic enlargement of one of your CorelDRAW designs. You could image it directly to an 8×10 negative and have it photographically blown up to make beautiful color posters. These types of services are right up the alley of professionals who have previous photographic experience.

Duplicators

High speed document duplicating (xeroxing) has been around for a long time. It's the color laser copier and the necessary equipment to connect it to a computer that has only recently found its way into the copier shops. Today's digital color duplicating machines can image at medium resolution (300 to 600 dpi) on both sides of an 11×17 piece of paper at a cost of only a few dollars.

In the past, a closely related field was blueprint duplicating. This field has evolved so that plotters have replaced much of the work of running out large schematics and drafting work. The plotters have advanced to act more like printing presses, using small dots of four ink colors—cyan, magenta, yellow, and black—to simulate most of the colors that a human eye can perceive.

Again, these devices are in the medium resolution range and are not meant to replace printing or photography. But there are a number of applications where these devices have found niches.

By the way, many of the traditional forms of these services overlap. Just because a former photographer is running a high resolution imagesetter doesn't necessarily mean that he is not capable. He may have worked at a pre-press shop as an in-house photographer and photo retoucher. While there, he could have picked up much real-life experience regarding the printing industry. So, while it is helpful to know the history of a service bureau, don't make hasty judgments about their competency to do a job. You should look at their overall abilities and even give them a test job to determine what they are capable of doing for you.

Is Their "Front-End" Mac or PC?

For many years now the debate invariably comes up in the graphics arts world: Which is better, Mac or PC? Well, the DTP revolution did start and get a large foothold with the Mac. More graphics software and technology was developed for the Mac. When you start a race first, it is hard not to have the advantage.

Macs are entrenched in the graphics world. That's a fact. On the other hand, PCs have come a long way in the last few years. The gap between Mac and PC hardware and software capabilities is becoming indistinguishable. So, which is better doesn't really matter. The fact is you are using a PC running Windows and CorelDRAW and you need someone to image your files. If a service bureau is running their devices from a Mac (right now, the majority do), can you work with them?

The answer is yes—maybe. It depends on a few key questions as follows:

- Do they have experience with PC/Windows files?

- Do they have any PCs running Windows applications in the shop?

- Do they have software that can access and read PC files?

- Do they express a predisposition to dislike PC files?

These are few of the essentials to consider before getting involved with a service bureau that is running on a different computer platform than your own. None of the preceding considerations are really a major obstacle for the service bureau to overcome; therefore, it shouldn't be an obstacle that a service bureau is Mac-based.

But consider that the remote imaging process is easier if the service bureau is run by PCs. This is a less common, but growing circumstance.

It is more common that service bureaus have both types of computers, and the best arrangement is that they are all connected by a network. Perhaps they will have more Macs with higher power than the PCs, but the fact that they can take your files and read them directly from PCs overcomes some technical difficulties that could get in the way of a smooth working arrangement.

A good-natured wisecrack about the superiority of one platform over another is certainly an acceptable comment, especially if things are going well. However, if your jobs are always running into problems and you keep hearing, "You wouldn't have problems if you had a Mac," get out your list of service bureau candidates and start making calls.

What Equipment Is Needed to Image Your Files?

Besides a computer, the actual imaging equipment a service bureau uses is often extremely complicated and very expensive to purchase and maintain. For the CorelDRAW

user, however, it is more important to understand the process that goes into imaging files than it is to know the exact way a certain brand and model of machinery works.

From a purely technical viewpoint, the imaging process is very complicated. The concepts that underlie this process can be distilled down to common steps, however.

First, the bytes that make up your CorelDRAW file are sent to the Windows device driver of the device you have targeted in the Control Panel. (Optionally, you can change the targeted device from CorelDRAW's Print dialog box.) Next, the device driver processes the incoming data and converts it into specific instructions that can be carried out by the physical printing device. This continuing flow of instructions is then sent, by way of your computer's serial or parallel port, through a cable and "down" to your printer.

The flow of instruction data is often called the *print stream*. CorelDRAW makes it very easy to capture this print stream by redirecting it to a computer file instead of to a computer port. This capability, called *printing to disk*, is one of the main reasons that you can use outside services to image your files. It also is what allows your CorelDRAW files, which are created on an IBM PC-compatible computer, to be imaged on machines that are being run by Apple Macintosh computers.

It is important to note that printer instruction data for each type, brand, or model of imaging device is different in some way or another. Care must be taken to get the

correct and most recent version of the Windows device driver for the specific device(s) your service bureau uses. Do not trust the Windows drivers that came with your Windows software. Check with your service bureau to see if there is a more recent version.

The next two steps in the printing process go on outside of your computer—*Raster Image Processing* (RIP) and Imaging.

On a desktop printer, you might not notice the distinction between these two processes because the RIP is built in to your printer, which also takes care of marking the image on whatever media you have in the paper tray. However, with larger, more expensive output devices, the delineation of these functions is more discernible because the processes often take place on two different machines.

The RIP

The RIP must take the print stream mentioned earlier, interpret whatever instructions are received, and turn that into on and off signals used by the imager to mark the media. With color imaging devices, the on signal may be accompanied by detailed color information. This is a simplistic explanation of a very complex job.

The RIP can be hardware- or software-based. In a hardware-based system, a dedicated computer with specific software and chips has been assembled by the manufacturer. This computer does only one thing: RIPs incoming data and sends it on its way to an imager.

Some common RIP models sold by the Linotronic company for their high resolution imagesetters are RIP2, RIP4, RIP40, and RIP50. The first few are older and less powerful than the latter ones. When a hardware RIP is in need of upgrading, it is generally a very expensive proposition for the service bureau.

A software-based RIP doesn't rely on a dedicated computer system, although one computer is often used exclusively for this process. Any computer that is powerful enough to run the software will do the job. A software RIP is much like a device driver you use in Windows. It takes in the instruction stream, performs the interpretation/ rasterization, then sends the resulting image data on its way, either directly to an imager or to a file. The advantage of saving the data to a file is it can be sent to the imaging device when it is convenient.

The advantage of a software RIP is that upgrading is like any other piece of software—if you buy a bigger, faster, more powerful computer, the RIP will also reflect this improvement. Common software RIPs are Freedom of Press and RipIt.

The Imaging Engine

Sometimes called a *recorder*, *plotter*, or *marking engine*, the imaging device takes the rasterized information and applies it to the media that is loaded in the machine. Depending on the device, the rasterized data may be turning a laser on and off to expose a piece of photosensitive paper, doing something similar to a photosensitive drum, or making cyan or magenta ink spit out of a nozzle.

Because there are hundreds of types of devices, it is very hard to simplify the various imaging processes. However, there are two technical points of information about any imager that you should try to determine. The first is the resolution of the device. The resolution capability of a device is expressed in *dots per inch* (dpi). For example, there are some large format plotters that can lay down dots of ink at 200, 300, or even better, 400 dpi. The higher the resolution, the better your images will look.

The second specification that should interest you is the default linescreen frequency, which refers to the number of lines per inch (lpi) that the device uses to image halftones (scanned photos) and screen tints (percentages of pure ink colors). Again, the higher the number, the smoother the image will look. This number is very useful in determining how you should set the resolution of scanned photos, and helps determine if you will get banding in graduated fountain fills. *Banding* is a term used to describe the effect that one sees if the steps in a graduated fill are discernible by the eye.

Resolution and lpi have a direct relation to each other. Some devices, such as low resolution (200 to 400 dpi) plotters and printers, offer only a small variation in lpi settings. High resolution devices enable you to choose several dpi and lpi settings. Therefore, high resolution devices offer a wider variety of flexibility that enables the CorelDRAW user to get the best quality reproduction possible.

PostScript

All images that are sent to a device driver are defined by some form of *page description language* (PDL). The RIP's interpreter is programmed to understand this language—if it does not come along as expected, the device will signal an error.

The most comprehensive and high-level graphics PDL is PostScript. PostScript is actually a programming language that is well suited for describing graphics-intensive images. It is the imaging description language of the professional graphics world. Not only does it support bitmap images, but it excels at describing vector-based images like those made with CorelDRAW's drawing tools. When it comes to fonts and typographic support, there is no technology that is superior.

N O T E

Unless otherwise stated, subsequent information in this chapter is based on using PostScript devices in conjunction with a Windows PostScript Driver.

What Do You Need from a Service Bureau?

Working with outside services to output your files can be either quite rewarding or extremely frustrating. You need to interview

a potential vendor and see if they are capable of delivering the service you require.

You know you need accurate and clean output, and you need it delivered on time. Most service bureaus want work and will readily reply, "Fast, accurate, and top quality—yup, that's us. Send the files." Don't be so fast to jump at their invitation. You really don't want to get involved with the hassle and lost time (which means lost profit) that will occur because an inexperienced and overzealous service bureau got a hold of your files.

Questions That Need Answering

The only way to make an informed decision about the experience level of a service bureau is to ask questions. Start with the following:

- Can they accept your Corel CDR files?

- Do they have the same fonts as you?

- Have they had problems with TrueType fonts?

- Can you send them test files at no charge?

- What brand and model of RIP and recorder do they have?

- What is the maximum paper size?

- What is maximum imaging area?

- How much Virtual Memory is available in the RIP?

- Any special drivers needed?

- What are the resolution choices?

- What kind of special screening technology is available on their equipment?

- Can they override resolution, linescreen frequency, and angle, negative, and emulsion settings at their end?

- What is their standard turnaround time?

- What are their charges for faster turnaround and troubleshooting files that won't image?

- Do they offer trapping services if you need it?

- What kind of proofing systems do they have, especially for negatives and color separations?

- Do they accept files by modem?

- What forms of removable storage devices do they have?

- Can they accept PKZip files?

- What delivery services do they offer?

Most of the information you need to qualify a service bureau and to prepare files to send to them are included in the preceding list. Bear in mind that these are not the only questions that come up. In fact, one question often leads to another. It always takes some time to get things running smoothly. Also, technology and equipment in the computer and graphics world keep changing. Never assume that what worked last year will work today. Call your service bureau and ask.

Service

You need a portion of the service bureau's time to discuss your system, software, and project specifications. If possible, visit the service bureau. Get to know the people that you will be dealing with over the phone. Try to get to know the people who will be doing the actual imaging; they are valuable advisors when you need questions answered accurately and quickly.

If the people are too busy to explain their organization or even suggest how you can get the most from their equipment, this is not a good sign. Some service bureaus just want to push output, whether correct or not, through the front door. If you get the impression that billable work takes precedence over good customer relations, you should look for another bureau.

On the positive side, there are service bureaus that want files to image as the customer expects. These firms feel that customers should be educated and made to understand what is happening if something doesn't work right. The word "service" is the credo in their customer relations efforts. These kinds of service bureaus do exist. Sometimes it takes a few jobs to evaluate which type of bureau you are dealing with.

Good, Clean Equipment

There are many service bureaus that regularly work with customers from all over the country by sending files by modem and faxing orders and proofs. Final output can be sent through the mail or by overnight courier. This is a reasonable way to do business if it meets your needs.

The advantage of working with a local service bureau, however, is it will be easy to visit their establishment and see what type of operation they run. If the shop is untidy and disorganized, there is the possibility that this could effect your work.

Complex imaging devices need clean and stable environments to perform consistently day in and day out. Imagesetters need to be calibrated and film developer processors need to be meticulously maintained. It's a very good indicator if the shop is clean and organized. Think of the many times you have lost a floppy disk in your own work area, then try to imagine the flow of floppies, Syquest removable drives, paper proofs, order forms, and other matter that works its way through a busy service bureau. Being neat, clean, and organized makes sense.

Technical Help

The computer world is, at times, very fragile. It often seems that this fragility is evident when some job that you need completed decides to indiscriminately fail.

This happens a lot with remote imaging scenarios. The exact reasons are numerous. The short story is there are so many variables introduced in moving files around from one computer to another and there are so many conversions and interpretations in the imaging process, that anything which goes wrong in a previous step could cause a problem that eventually keeps another process from working. And don't forget that all software has bugs. Many are not detected until a very specific set of circumstances are

met, then—crash time. Maybe your job happened to set up one of those special circumstances.

Imaging failure could also mean that you are doing something wrong. How will you know how to fix it? How will you know if you have the right device drivers or have set them up properly in Windows? What is going on when your fonts come out as Courier?

These questions should be answerable by the service bureau. If they can't give you the answers that will help you get your files imaged, look for a new service bureau.

Special Services

What other services might you need? It depends on the nature of your projects. Are you making signs for retail stores, trade shows, and seminars? Then you likely need laminating and mounting facilities.

Are you supplying negatives and color separations to commercial printers? Then you may need to have trapping or color correction services performed. You will also need proofing, whether the proofs are color prints made from the digital files or matchprints made from the finished color separated film. Many of the technical issues regarding trapping amounts, film emulsion side, and dot gain can be handled by the service bureau. This would be one area where a service bureau's past experience in pre-press services to the printing industry would be beneficial to you.

If your needs are high-speed color duplicating of documents, perhaps the imaging is only the first part in the making of your finished product. Do you need collating and bindery services? How about mailing your completed product out to many different locations? Your bureau may be able to supply these services also.

What Does a Service Bureau Need from You?

For the service bureau to give you what you want, they need everything necessary to reproduce the your image on their devices. Basically, they need the same *resources* you needed to assemble the design or document in the first place.

A resource can be a graphics file, such as a scanned photo or a typeface that was installed on your computer, which you used in your file. Just because these resources were available on your computer as you created your CorelDRAW file doesn't mean that they are present on the remote computer. If they are not present, then the file will either not image or will come out with substitutions made for the missing resources.

A Properly Prepared File

There are several ways to deliver computer files to a remote imaging service. They all depend on your knowing how to properly prepare the files.

Several of the most common file formats that are accepted by service bureaus are discussed in the next section. Each format has its own

advantages and disadvantages. You will need to ask your service bureau whether they have a preference for which type of files they image from.

One point cannot be stressed enough: It is never wise to take files to be imaged unless you have already discussed with the service bureau the best way to set up and deliver them. Preparing files without knowledge of the service bureau's requirements will likely waste your time and that of the service bureau. Even if you do get your job done, it might end up costing more than you anticipated.

CorelDRAW Files

Supplying a copy of your CorelDRAW file has many advantages. The greatest advantage becomes apparent when a problem occurs at the service bureau. Should something not be prepared properly or not image correctly, the service bureau can try to fix the problem from inside CorelDRAW.

Another attraction of the CDR route is that the file size will be the smallest of all your alternatives. If you do not have large capacity, removable storage devices such as SyQuest, Bernoulli, or Magneto Optical drives, then the size of files will become a concern for you.

There are four distinct disadvantages to supplying CorelDRAW native files. The first is that the service bureau must be able to run CorelDRAW, which eliminates many service bureaus that use Mac computers to run their imagers.

The second disadvantage is font availability. Not having the same fonts as the user is the largest problem that service bureaus encounter. Are you using a variety of Type1 and TrueType fonts? Have some come from bundled software deals or have they been downloaded from bulletin boards? These are some factors that make it very difficult for a service bureau to successfully image your files, unless you take proper precautions. Font management is discussed later in this chapter.

Another disadvantage is that the Corel file can be opened at the service bureau and inadvertently changed. It sounds like an unlikely situation, but it happens.

Finally, there are some jobs that need very tight security. Electronic files can be copied and reused anywhere, so if you are concerned that some or all of your Corel artwork will be copied and used by an unscrupulous service bureau for other purposes, then you won't want to send them native Corel files.

Print-to-Disk Files

Print-to-Disk (PRN) files differ from native Corel files in that they have already been processed by the Windows PostScript driver and now contain only the information that the PostScript RIP needs to image the page.

You have tremendous control over the printing settings of a PRN. Among other advanced settings, you control the resolution, lpi, screen angles, special screening technologies, and even emulsion side. You can also set whether the job is imaged, color separated, or composite.

You also control the font resources. If the fonts you used are not available on the imagesetter's hard disk, you can choose to embed them in the PRN or convert them to curves. Exactly what these strategies mean is discussed later in this chapter.

Some service bureaus prefer PRNs; if the fonts used in the original Corel file have been handled properly, the PRN is a self-contained package that is ready to be downloaded and imaged. There is no need for the imaging operator to start Windows and CorelDRAW, open the file, set printer settings, or anything. In fact, the service bureau doesn't even need Windows, CorelDRAW, or an IBM-compatible PC. Mac-based service bureaus are most familiar with this file format.

The issue of security isn't a problem because this file cannot be opened up and fiddled with. This is not to say that some enterprising PostScript hacker won't be able to read the file and extract data from it somehow. To do this, however, would be such a serious endeavor it would likely discourage most would-be "file thieves."

Now for the disadvantages—font resources rears its ugly head once again. The advantage of controlling whether a font resource is included in the PRN file can easily become a disadvantage. If you forget to set up the Windows PostScript driver to embed your font, that beautiful headline you set in one of the 825 fonts that Corel supplies may come out as Courier. CorelDRAW 5.0, in conjunction with FontMinder 2.0, has made it much easier to manage fonts for remote imaging.

Another negative concern is file size. A PRN is a verbose description of the pages in your Corel drawing. As an example, examine the test file shown in figure 41.1. The test image contains a 4×4-inch square filled with Pantone Red 032. The type is artistic text, set at 70 points in the Brochure (Normal) Type1 font. This image creates a CDR file size of 8,108 bytes. When you print this image to disk, targeted to a Lino 330 at 1,270 and with the Type1 font embedded in the file and set to image as color separations, the resulting file is approximately 109,000 bytes. As the amount of objects created, fonts used and colors assigned increases, as does your PRN file size.

Figure 41.1
The test file image.

A final consideration is that if something should go wrong with imaging the file, there is not much that your service bureau can do. They may have a clue as to what is wrong with the file, but they can only call you and ask you to make it over with the necessary modifications. If you were on a tight deadline, you may have blown it.

EPS Files

Encapsulated PostScript (EPS) files are a form of PostScript file. It is mostly the same information that is contained in a PRN. The exception is that it is meant to be imported into other programs; therefore, certain printing-specific commands are not included. Specifically, disabled printing capabilities would be separations and multiple pages.

An EPS file can be imported into another computer program, such as Quark Express or PageMaker, and printed from this application. In this case, the printing capabilities of the host application would be used to affect the printing of the EPS file contents.

EPS files are created in CorelDRAW 5.0 using the Export function. The proper filter to use is EPS(Placeable),*.EPS. The EPS Export dialog box offers several options that control how resources are embedded in your EPS file (see fig. 41.2). The most important setting regards how text is handled. Text can be converted to curves, which means that the letterforms are no longer dependent on font files; they have been transformed into drawing shapes. Alternatively, the fonts used for your text can be embedded into the file, the same as with a PRN file. To enable this functionality, make sure the As **T**ext and Include **F**onts options are checked.

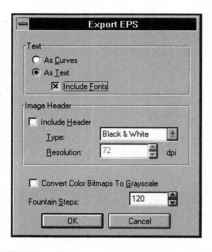

Figure 41.2
The Export EPS dialog box.

An EPS that does not have a TIF header for screen previewing can usually be imported into a Mac application with relative ease. To turn off the screen preview header when making an EPS file, uncheck the Include **H**eader option in the EPS Export dialog box.

File size differences are negligible. The same test image used in the previous Print-to-Disk section produced a file size of 104,000 versus the 109,000 for the PRN version. This EPS had the Type1 Brochure font embedded in the file, so everything is comparable.

There aren't many advantages to this way of transporting a Corel image. It is really a factor to the service bureau. The device that they are imaging to may be controlled by special software that is geared toward accepting EPS files.

There are other file formats that can be used to convey files to other platforms and devices, such as Adobe AI and Scitex CT.

Adobe Illustrator (AI EPS)

This is another subset of the PostScript language. The AI format can be read by Adobe Illustrator on the Mac and printed from that application to the imaging device. The advantage of this strategy is that the file can be opened by a Mac-based service bureau and edited if there are any imaging problems.

The procedure for making an AI file is very much like that of the EPS mentioned previously. Choose Export, and then use the Adobe Illustrator,*.AI,*.EPS filter. As shown in figure 41.3, the Export Adobe Illustrator dialog box offers a choice of three different Illustrator file versions. Consult with your service bureau to see which will work the best.

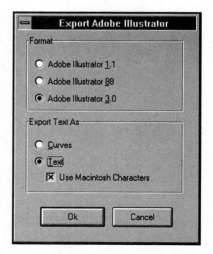

Figure 41.3
The Export Adobe Illustrator dialog box.

The disadvantage to using the AI EPS export filter is that some special effects that CorelDRAW 5.0 offers have no equivalent in the Illustrator program. These effects will be lost.

The good news is that the file size is fairly compact when compared to the PostScript file formats. The example image exported in Illustrator 3.0 format, with the text converted to curves, weighed in at 14,500 bytes.

Scitex CT

If your service bureau or printer has a Scitex imaging system, this may be another way to transport files. The Scitex company makes high-end imaging systems. What makes their systems different from the more common imagesetters found in service bureaus is they incorporate photo retouching, automatic trapping, and photo replacement, along with many other printing industry specific controls, into their line of equipment and software.

The Scitex system takes your PostScript file, interprets it, and then converts it into one of two intermediate file formats that can be manipulated by Scitex's proprietary software. One of these intermediate file formats is called a *CT*. Corel can export to a Scitex compatible CT file. The file extension it uses is .SCT. This file format is a bitmap, not vector, and is limited to 300 dpi. It offers 32 bits of information, however, making it perfect for 4-color process jobs.

The advantage to this strategy is that Scitex systems that use Macs for their front end will be able to work with the file.

A disadvantage is the many steps that need to be taken and the sizes of files created. Because the .SCT format contains 32 bits of information, it is much larger than most bitmaps. Our test file, exported at 300 dpi, created a SCT file in excess of 10MB! It is sufficient to say that one would need to have very special circumstances to warrant this approach to convey images to a service bureau.

An example of such a "special circumstance" is to image Corel files larger than the 32×32-inch limit that Corel imposes. The CDR is exported as large as possible, brought into PhotoShop resized, color corrected if necessary, and resampled to 300 dpi. Separations can be run from Photoshop, or the file can be exported to a .SCT file and taken into the Scitex system.

Notification of Fonts

Fonts are the biggest problem that service bureaus and users face in the imaging world because fonts are considered resources, to be called on only when needed by the host computer system. This means that they must be available when an application makes a request to use them.

Usually, the service bureau has an order form that you fill out. This form has a place to list all fonts used, by font name and manufacturer. Even if they don't have such a form, you should explicitly tell them what fonts you have used.

If you are sending a PRN file in which you have embedded the fonts, it is not necessary to worry about font files. In this case, the

font resources are available because they are stored in the PostScript file. You should, however, make it clear to the service bureau that you have prepared the PRN file with all the fonts embedded.

Written Instructions

"Never assume anything that isn't written down." "Never transmit important information verbally without sending written confirmation." These are two standard operating procedures that should never be violated, no matter how much you trust your services bureau or they trust you.

Usually, a service bureau has an order form that needs to be filled out entirely before starting to work on your job. Be skeptical of service bureaus that do not require some type of written confirmation of your job's details and specification.

At the least, you will need to convey the following information:

- What media you want your file imaged on: RC paper, film negative, slide film, transparency material, colored paper, or card stock

- Resolution, expressed in dpi for printers or k for film recorders (only necessary if more than one resolution setting is supported by the output device)

- Linescreen, expressed in lpi (only necessary if more than one lpi setting is supported by the output device)

- Size of page used in CorelDRAW, and if crop marks or other page information is needed

- Fonts used, listed by name and manufacturer

- Date needed back in your shop

- Delivery information

It is best to give as much information as possible to the service bureau, even if you think it might not be needed. Remember the two "standard operating procedures" mentioned earlier.

Proofs

Good service bureaus want to deliver what the customer expects. It is not unreasonable to assume that a service bureau should check what they have imaged for problems. They cannot check the output thoroughly, however, unless they have a proof of what you created on your system.

The service bureau did not create the file and it is not always clear that substitution or conversion problems have occurred. Don't assume that because Courier came out in your image, the service bureau should have "known better" and called you rather than just deliver the job. Courier is a valid font and some people do use it on purpose.

The best procedure is to send some type of proof with your order. Black and white laser proofs should be adequate for most jobs. If you have a complicated color job, then send color printouts, if possible. For jobs that you want color separated, send separate black and white proofs of each color you expect to receive back.

If you can, try to send proofs at the same size as the finished images. One exception would be if you are sending out for slides. Proofing 35mm slides at actual size would be ridiculous. Print them out large enough so that the service bureau operator can see them clearly to determine whether fonts and line endings are the same.

Do not skip sending proofs just because you are "modeming" your files to the service bureau. It is best to deal with a bureau that has a fax machine. This way, you can fax your order form and proofs to them.

LaserCheck

If you are sending out for expensive high-resolution imaging, it is worth it to check out what is in your PRN files before you send them. Did you remember to include crop marks, grayscale calibration bars, or register marks? If you are not sure, then a utility like LaserCheck is extremely handy to have around.

After LaserCheck has been "downloaded" to your laser printer, your printer will simulate an imagesetter. Your file can now be sent to the printer to be imaged on whatever size paper is loaded—the image is automatically scaled down to fit. Besides being able to visually check what is in the file, there is plenty of important information regarding the file printed around the outside perimeter of the page—information like what fonts were "called" for and what fonts were

successfully found. LaserCheck also displays information on how much virtual memory was used or how much time transpired in imaging the page.

If you use service bureaus regularly, LaserCheck pays for itself very quickly. It is the final checking step that could save you bundles by heading off costly mistakes. LaserCheck is available from the following address:

> Systems of Merritt
> 2551 Old Dobbin Dr. E.
> Mobile, AL 36695
> 205-660-1240.

Communication

Good communication always makes a difference. Discuss your job with the service bureau before you get ready to finish the job. It is a good idea to talk to your service bureau at the design stage, even before you start the job on the computer. There may be tips and hints that they can provide that will make a difference in how you construct your CorelDRAW image.

Things are always changing in the computer graphics world, and your service bureau is in the same boat as you. If there is a new driver, production technique, or bug found, you will want to know about it. It is even plausible that you will have information that they will not be aware of.

Remember that good communication is not nagging. It's imparting information and listening. If your service bureau tells you that they cannot do something, don't try to force

them to do it. Make friends at the bureau. Be a good, reasonable customer, and the service bureau will likely treat you well. If they don't, you can always go elsewhere.

Using High-Resolution Imagesetters

High-resolution imagesetters are commonly used to provide positive or negative materials that will be used to make printing plates for commercial printing presses. If you are purchasing imagesetter output for this purpose, it is noteworthy to reflect on the added responsibility of supplying what the printer needs to complete his job successfully.

This means you must communicate with the printer about specific technical aspects with which you may not have had previous experience. You should, however, endeavor to learn as much as possible about these areas. Technical concerns such as trapping, dot gain, film emulsion, and linescreen options matter to the printer a great deal. If you ignore these aspects when creating your CorelDRAW files and ordering resulting output, you might be jeopardizing the quality of the printer's work. This will not make you, your client, or the printer happy.

After you talk to the printer about the job for which you are supplying materials, discuss the job with the service bureau. Talk about your design goals and the technical specifications of the printer. Almost all difficulties can be overcome if planned for in advance.

However, trying to overcome problems after output has been imaged—or even worse, at the press—is costly and time-consuming.

Some basic knowledge of imagesetters is important because there are some factors involved that can impact the printing process. The next sections provide a simple overview of imagesetter technology.

Kinds of Imagesetters

There are two basic classifications of high-resolution imagesetters: capstan and drum. Capstan is the older of the two designs, but is probably the most common found in service bureaus today.

Capstan imagesetters move photosensitive material by way of a system of rollers. As the material is moving, a laser beam exposes the rasterized image onto the material. The accuracy level of this type of imagesetter is very good, but it depends greatly on the precision of the roller transport system. This type of transport system allows for media to be loaded in rolls rather than precut sheets, which is why some capstan-type imagesetters can output images that are much longer than they are wide.

Drum-type imagesetters have the same two basic components: a laser and photosensitive material. The main differences are that the material is a precut sheet that is wrapped around a drum, and instead of the photosensitive material moving, it is the laser that does all the traveling. This technology increases the accuracy of exposing the rasterized image on the material.

Why do you need to care about this? If you are working on images that will be printed under very demanding circumstances, you will want to have your files output on a drum-type imagesetter. Because this is not the most commonly found machine in service bureaus, you may have to look harder to find a service bureau that will meet your needs. If you are working on a project that will be printed under less demanding conditions, then a service bureau with a capstan-type machine will do fine.

What is considered demanding? The first area of demarcation would be four-color process jobs, but not all four-color process work is beyond the capabilities of capstan-type imagesetters. If you or your printer's requirements fall into any of the following, look for a service bureau with a drum-type imagesetter:

- Resolution higher than 2,540 dpi

- Linescreen frequency higher than 175 lpi

- Stochastic screening

The reason for the preceding recommendations is that a very small dot size is needed to meet any of these requirements. Add to this the fact that four-color process work requires four pieces of film with different version of the same image to make up the finished image. These four images must register exactly to create the best quality reproduction on press. A capstan roller imagesetter may be able to produce a small enough dot, but its transport system does not allow for all the negatives to be generated with the images

repeated accurately enough. The colors will not register properly, and this will produce a lower quality image on the printing press.

Resolution and Linescreen Frequency

The smallest element that an imagesetter can mark on a piece of media is called a *pixel*. Resolution is a way to express the number of pixels that a device can image in the span of one linear inch. The more pixels or dots that make up an image, the smoother it will look. Imagesetter resolution will have an effect on the quality of your images.

The general rule is the higher the resolution, the better the image will look. So, 2540 is better than 1270, and 3387 is better yet. However, the highest resolutions are overkill for simple printing projects that contain only line art or one color photographs. For these jobs, 2540 dpi should be more than enough. Considering that materials imaged at higher resolutions are always more expensive, you should also weigh pricing into your decision on what resolution setting you will need.

When your printed projects incorporate 4-color process photographs, large fountain-fills, or bitmap textures, higher resolutions will definitely provide a better quality image. Different brands and models of imagesetters offer different resolution options, so check with your service bureau on what resolution settings are available.

Another specification that you must supply to your service bureau is very important to your printer is linescreen frequency. The

printer should supply this figure. The linescreen frequency is the amount of dots used, per inch, to make up a halftone image or screened tint of any solid color ink.

The printer supplies this number because only they know how close together the dots can be before they become indistinguishable. Once this happens, they just become one mass of solid ink. Every press is different; even paper stock will effect how well a press can "hold" a certain size dot. For smaller, inexpensive presses, the printer may specify 120 lpi. Higher quality presses likely can handle 150 lpi. Really great presses can reach well beyond 300 dot per inch.

The linescreen frequency effects the smoothness of fountain fills and screen tints and the sharpness of photos. You should be working at 133 lpi and higher for any decent-quality four-color process projects. The linescreen frequency should be determined early in your project schedule because it effects the dpi setting at which you should scan photos, and helps you to determine if you are going to get banding in large graduated fills.

Photos, whether they will be one color, duotones, or four-color process, should be scanned at a dpi setting of 1.5 to 2 times the linescreen frequency used by the imagesetter. Note that the dpi setting should be determined at the size the photos will be used in your finished CorelDRAW file so don't scan an image at 266 dpi and then enlarge it 200 percent in CorelDRAW. You will have an image that is effectively 133 dpi and will only look good at a linescreen setting of 85 lpi; this is the lpi setting that newspapers generally use to print halftone images.

Banding is the term for the noticeable effect of changing from one tint value to another in a fountain fill or graduated screen. This is certainly not desirable if you intended the fill to be very smooth. Banding occurs when a fill has too few numbers of bands. The number of available bands is a direct result of your resolution and linescreen settings. When an imagesetter fills an object with a fountain fill, it takes the available number of tint values and divides them up to fill the object. As an object increases in size, the width of the bands are increased. The bands become noticeable to the human eye when their width exceeds 1/32 of an inch (0.03).

Under the best circumstances, the PostScript language has a limit of imaging 256 screen tints (bands) of any one color. This is what is meant by "levels of gray." So as the length of a fill expands, the width of the steps (even using the maximum 256 steps) can easily exceed 0.03. To see this, multiply 0.03 times 256. This calculation shows that under optimum conditions, the maximum length of a graduated fountain fill is 7.68.

There are two other factors that can mar your "optimum conditions." One is lowering the percentage of change in your fountain fills. For example, a fill that starts at 100 percent of a color and ends at 0 percent has 100 levels of change, but a fill that goes from 50 percent to 10 percent has only 40 levels of change. This is not the final determination for the level of grays that will be used to image your postscript file, however. To determine that, you must add another factor: What levels of gray are available. This is calculated as follows:

$$\text{dpi}/\text{lpi}^2 \times (\% \text{ of change})/100.$$

By taking some real-world numbers and applying the preceding formula, you can see the effects of linescreen, resolution, and percentage of fill change. Note that PostScript does not use any more than 256 levels, so any answer that goes higher should be rounded down to 256.

Example A

Fill: 100% to 0%; Resolution = 1270; Linescreen = 120

$(1270/120)^2 \times (100)/100 = 112$ levels of gray (bands)

Example B

Fill: 50% to 10%; Resolution = 1270; Linescreen = 120

$(1270/120)^2 \times (40)/100 = 44$ levels of gray (bands)

Example C

Fill: 100% to 10%; Resolution = 2540; Linescreen = 150

$(2540/150)^2 \times (100)/100 = 286$ (rounded down to 256) levels of gray (bands)

Example D

Fill: 40% to 10%; Resolution = 2540; Linescreen = 150

$(2540/150)^2 \times (40)/100 = 115$ levels of gray (bands)

You can see that as linescreen frequency increases at any particular resolution, banding is more likely to be noticed because the number of bands decreases. With a lower number of bands available, they have to be made wider to fill the object. The ways to reduce banding are to either lower resolution, shorten the physical length of the fill, or increase the difference between the starting and ending percentages of the fill.

You can also see from Example C that another way to reduce banding is to increase resolution. This way, higher linescreen values do not have to be sacrificed, and halftones and process photos can look their best. Remember to multiply any answer you get by 0.03 to determine the maximum length of any fountain fill. As Example D shows, even with the same resolution and linescreen settings as Example C, banding occurs if the length of the fill goes beyond 3.45 inches.

Trying to determine whether you will have banding in your graduated fills might seem like a lot of work, but it will be worth it if you head off the problem before it occurs at the imagesetter. Not only will you save the cost of redoing the job, but you will stay on schedule, which will make everyone down the production line happy.

When you make a PRN file, you can set the resolution and linescreen from CorelDRAW, but some imagesetters can override one or both of these settings. Make sure you communicate with your service bureau what they can do and what you expect back in the way of linescreen frequency and resolution for your files.

Screening Technologies

Along with the linescreen frequency comes another related issue—screen angle. This effects halftones that are printed on top of each other like four-color process photographs. If all the dots that are on the cyan,

magenta, yellow, and black plates were set to exactly the same frequency and angle, they would fall directly on top of each other. This would result in a very dark brown, "mushy"-looking photo.

Printers long ago established that the best angle for each of the four process colors should be as follows: cyan at 15 degrees, magenta at 75 degrees, yellow at 0 degrees, and black at 45 degrees. Because an imagesetter doesn't really make halftone dots in the traditional manner, the screen angles and frequencies have been further "optimized" by imagesetter manufacturers.

Two options that are available from CorelDRAW's Print dialog box are RT and HQS. To gain access to these special settings, choose Options. On the Print Options dialog box, select the Separations tab. Enable the Print **S**eparations and the **U**se Custom Halftone check boxes. Next, press the **E**dit button to the right of the **U**se Custom Halftones check box. The Advanced Screening dialog box enables you to choose a screen setting from the Screening Technology drop-down list (see fig. 41.4).

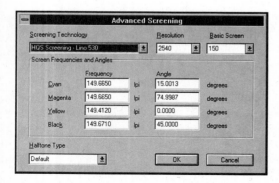

Figure 41.4
The Advanced Screening dialog box.

The advantages of using these optimizations are that they further enhance the quality of process photos and reduce the chance of undesirable moiré patterns. The thing to remember is that RT and HQS screening technologies are built in to specific RIPs and recorders, so ask your service bureau before using these custom halftone settings.

Using Slides

Color slides are another form of output that is commonly purchased from service bureaus. The imaging technology is very different from the imagesetters used to make printing industry output. The slide service bureau is exposing film much like the high res shop, but the image that is captured on the slide film is composite. Where a printing press lays down four colors to make its color photos, the slide recorder uses only three.

The color model that is used to image slides is called *RGB*, which stands for red, green, and blue. It is the same color model used by your computer monitor to display your CorelDRAW images on-screen. The slide service's film recorder is actually making a full color image of your CorelDRAW file on a small monitor inside. It then takes three exposures on the same frame of the film—one exposure captures the red components, another exposes the green, and finally the blue portions are captured. When the film is processed, you will have a full color image of your CorelDRAW creation.

For the film recorder to display the image on its internal CRT, it must receive rasterized information from a RIP. The RIP is fed the source material from a file you supply. This is the same interpreting/rasterization process as occurs in the high resolution imagesetters. However, the data is specifically designed to display a composite image rather than one color at a time. Again, the RIP can be hardware- or software-based. There isn't a lot of difference from the Corel user's standpoint; it is really a matter of what works best for the service bureau and the equipment that they have installed.

Resolution is an area of concern for slides also. The same general rule applies: The higher the resolution, the better the quality of the finished image. Resolution is expressed differently for slides than for other output types. Rather than dots per inch, resolution indicates the number of pixels used to paint one row on the internal CRT. The most common resolutions are 2k and 4k, although you can also get 8k resolution, which is considered very good quality.

The letter "k," as mentioned previously, stands for one thousand—in the computer world, that's 1,024. This means that a slide with a resolution of 2k has 2,048 pixels in each row of the image. A 4k resolution slide has 4,096 pixels in each row. With twice the amount of pixels, a 4k slide will look better; the fountain fills will be smoother and type will look sharper. A 4k slide will also cost more. Remember that the number of pixels referes to the image displayed on the film recorder's internal CRT. The film that is being exposed has no bearing on resolution.

Many slide bureaus offer several different formats of film size: 35mm and 4×5 are common, with 8×10 available at some.

Although 35mm is most useful for slide shows and presentations, the larger formats can be used to make photographic enlargements for posters and trade show displays. Also, larger formats are better for scanning and being used in traditional printing situations.

Your slide service bureau may even offer negative film output, which is useful if you need many photographic copies of your CorelDRAW image. If you start out with a positive image, a negative called an *inter-neg* would have to be made. This would need to be done by traditional means, and adds another copying step to the process of producing your bulk order of photos. With every generation of copying, quality is lost. By starting out with a negative image, you cut down the number of generations and steps needed to supply your final order of photographic copies. It is recommended that you have a positive slide made at the same time as your negative image because there is great latitude available in the exposure process when making photographic copies— colors will shift dramatically, depending on how the new copies are exposed. The positive slide will give the photo lab a target image to shoot for.

How To Set Up Your Files

Slides are easy to prepare in CorelDRAW. Simply choose **P**age Setup from the **L**ayout menu and pick Slide from the drop-down list of page sizes. Don't worry that the page size is set up for 11.00×7.33 and not 35mm×23mm. The slide service's RIP will handle scaling the image down to fit on the

film. (It is worth mentioning that, although not common, some slide RIPs might expect a page size other than the default to which CorelDRAW is set up. As usual, check these details with your service bureau.) If you are setting up for a 4×5 slide, use a page size of 10×7.5 inches.

You will want any background to completely fill the page size. This way, there will be no clear area of film showing around the edges of the slide. Do not use the Paper Color setting found on the Display tab of the **P**age Setup dialog box to produce your background color. This color only displays on your monitor and will not image on a slide. A good way to make a background is to select Add Page Frame on the Display tab, and then fill this frame with your background color.

You will want to create margins for any live material on your slide. This will ensure that nothing is cut off and that your slides don't look crowded. A margin of .5 inches all around is sufficient.

When you are happy with your slides, you can make composite (not color separated) PRNs or export them as EPS files. Some service bureaus have a preference, so make sure you ask. If you make PRNs, you should install and target the QMS ColorScript 100 printer. In the Print dialog box, set up to print to a Letter or A4 paper size.

It is good practice to limit the number of slide images in a PRN file. It might be convenient for you to work on a 30-slide presentation by adding 30 pages to one CorelDRAW file, but if you print-to-file with all those pages activated, the file might

become too large to handle. An added danger is that the file might not image properly at the service bureau. If the imaging has only gotten to page five of your presentation and causes an error, you cannot get the other 25 slides. Try to split many images into smaller "packets." In the 30-slide scenario, perhaps 10 images per PRN file would be better; if one "packet" fails, it will be easier to send replacement files to the service bureau for reimaging. This "packet" strategy does not apply to EPSs because you cannot save more than one image to an EPS file.

Of course, there are service bureaus that can take your CDR files and work directly from them; this may be an easier route than adding drivers and making PRNs. Regardless of what strategy used, you will still need to be concerned with fonts. Check with your service bureau about the fonts they have. If they do not have the ones you are using, you will have to send EPSs or PRNs with the text converted to curves. The other course is to make PRNs with the fonts embedded in the file.

At times, using bitmaps in your slide images is necessary; they also add more considerations to your list of "things to think about" when constructing your CorelDRAW files. The "resolution rule" of 1.5 to 2 times the linescreen of your output device does not apply. There is no linescreen in slide imaging. It is considered that 100 to 150 dpi, 24-bit color, or grayscale bitmaps can reproduce well on a 35mm slide. This dpi setting is determined at actual size when working on a CorelDRAW page of 11×7.33 inches. Any higher dpi setting just adds data to the file that will not be used. Twenty-four-bit and grayscale bitmap images can get very big, very fast. It is important, therefore, to manage them well, right from the start.

Remember that CorelDRAW's Texture fills are bitmaps. CorelDRAW 5.0 offers new options in choosing higher resolutions and tile sizes for these fills. When you are in the Texture Fills dialog box, choose **O**ptions; the Texture Options dialog box appears (see fig. 41.5). You can choose one of many Bitmap **R**esolution settings, ranging from 75 to 400 DPI. Also, the Maximum **T**ile Width size can be changed from 65 to 2,049. Both of these settings affect your image quality and impact your file sizes. Boosting resolution to a dpi setting higher than 160 does not affect your fill's image quality on a slide as much as increasing the Maximum Tile Size to 513 or higher does. You need to experiment and run tests to determine what quality level you need.

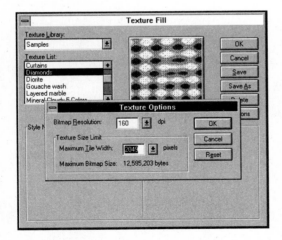

Figure 41.5

The Texture Fill Options dialog box.

There is another alternative to getting slide output from service bureaus other than supplying postscript files. You can export an image using the SCODL filter. The proper filter to select in the type of filter drop-down list is Matrix/Imapro SCODL,*.scd.

SCODL support is not as common as it once was—it is much more limited than the PostScript language. This alternative is not available in some service bureaus and, because of the limitations of the language, might not be able to handle your needs. The limitations include lack of support for PostScript textures, bitmaps, and two-color and full-color pattern fills.

Using Color Imaging

Color imaging is a broad and varied category. The resurgence of color printers and imagers into the service bureau world has been phenomenal over the past few years. Large color plotters which can image 36 inch-wide media can now be purchased for less than $10,000. Color digital copiers connected to computers and RIPs are becoming very common sites in duplicating centers. Prints imaged on thermal wax, crayon-based, inkjet, and dye sublimation color printers are bought from service bureaus for use as client proofs, comps, color overhead transparencies, and photographic quality reproductions.

In most cases, the RIP and printer are part of the same machine. An exception to this general rule is the digital copier, which

usually has a dedicated computer and RIP that is separate from the imaging device itself.

The following sections explain the basics of several color devices commonly found in service bureaus.

Thermal Wax Printers

Thermal wax printers have been around for quite awhile. They are the grandaddies of color printing technology. The raster image is sent to the imaging engine in color separated form. Some machines are based on the RGB model, so the color-separated data corresponds to the red, green, and blue portions of the image. Other devices are based on the CMYK model. In this case, the separated data is broken down into four colors. Then again, some printers can image in both forms.

Inside the printer is a ribbon that is coated with wax-based color material. For three-color printers, this ribbon is, alternately, yellow, magenta, and cyan. For four-color devices, the ribbon adds black as the last color in the sequence. As a piece of paper is fed to the printer, the first color is applied, the paper is pulled back out, and the next color portion of the ribbon is moved into place. The paper moves back into printer, receiving the next coating of color. This happens for three or four passes; when the paper is finally ejected, your image is presented in full color.

As far as resolution is concerned, thermal wax printers are generally in the 300 to 600 dpi range. The older generation machines can

only print on special "glossy" paper that is expensive; newer models offer a little more flexibility in paper selection. Many newer models can handle 11×17 inch paper; however, it is far more common to find letter-size printers in circulation.

You can use thermal wax printers in a variety of ways, from making proofs for client approval to color overheads and even iron-on transfers.

Dye Sublimation Printers

Dye sublimation printers are very similar to thermal wax devices. The difference is in the ribbon material and the paper. Rather than a wax color being transferred to the media, there is a dye transferred to special paper. The dye permeates the stock and spreads out. Even though these devices have a resolution of 300 dpi, their output looks photographic because the dots have spread slightly into each other, thus diffusing any noticeable dot.

These printers are very new technology and are very expensive, not only to buy, but also to buy materials for. Expect to pay much more for a dye sublimation print than a thermal wax print. For proofing photographs or scanned artwork, however, there is nothing better. Be aware that the special paper used in these printers is the only option available.

The price on one particular printer has been dropping dramatically, however. The Primera Pro from Fargo Electronics, is priced well below $2,000. The output produced by this printer is remarkable and comparable to more expensive printers. The reason why the

Primera Pro has a very low price tag is because it is only made by a printer engine, without RAM or a processor. The computer connected to this printer will do the job.

Crayon-Based or Phase Change Printers

These types of printers don't use a ribbon of wax or dye to create images on a page. They take hard "crayons" of colored material, melt them down, and spray dots of color on the paper. These types of printers are usually using four colors of crayons and work on the CMYK color model. They are naturals for proofing work that is going to be reproduced on printing presses.

Because of the unique way that these devices adhere "ink" to paper, they can printout on a number of different kinds of stock. Some can image on anything from tissue paper to card stock. This means you will be able to load custom colored stock to get a better idea of what your creation will look like when it is actually printed by a commercial printer.

These printers are not usually good for overhead transparencies because the crayon-based "ink" is opaque and interferes with the transmission of light from an overhead projector. However, the opaque ink produces very vibrant-looking images on almost any paper stocks.

Digital Color Copiers

Color copiers have been around for quite a few years, but the digital color copier has changed things considerably in the copier world. When hooked up to a computer interface, rasterized data is imaged by way of four colors of toner.

Many color copiers can accept 11×17-inch paper; some newer models can even print on both sides of the sheet. These machines are very finicky when it comes to paper stock. You won't get much choice in paper quality when you use them.

When it comes to resolution, the term "continuous tone" is often used. This is slightly misleading. There are no "dots" perceptible, but the image might appear to be made of "lines." Compared with the quality of true, photographic continuous tone or dye sublimation prints, the color copies come up short.

One of the most common color copiers found in service bureaus is the Canon CLC 500. When controlled by a computer interface that includes a RIP, these copiers can output a computer file. The price per copy has come down considerably in the past few years, making it very reasonable to produce good-quality proofs of full color CorelDRAW files.

How To Set Up for Color Output

The simple answer is to ask your service bureau. If the bureau cannot take your CDR files directly, you will have to make a PRN file. The service bureau can tell you what color printer driver to load into Windows and what page sizes are available.

Make sure that you ask the service bureau about the maximum image area. Almost every output device needs some margins; they just can't image all the way to the edge of the paper.

Choosing Fonts

Fonts are the number-one headache for service bureaus. You may not think they are for you—you have 825 of them in TrueType and Type1 format from Corel. That's a fantastic deal! You know which ones you had installed in CorelDRAW 5.0, and you used just the ones you wanted to create your graphics masterpieces. What could be simpler?

The problem is that not every service bureau has CorelDRAW 5.0, let alone all 825 fonts, in both font formats, installed. Further, how do they know which ones you used? How do they know if you used the TrueType version of Charter or the Type1 version? It really does become a problem for you. If you want your files to image successfully, you have to manage what fonts you use, how you use them in your files, and how you communicate what fonts are used to your service bureau.

TrueType Fonts

Just in case you have not run across it yet, some service bureaus don't like TrueType fonts. Some have had so much trouble with them that they refuse files that have used them. A lot of this prejudice has come as a backlash to some bad TrueType fonts that

were distributed with CorelDRAW 3. If you are upgrading straight from version 3 to 5, replace all the version 3 TrueType fonts with the version 5 equivalents. And if it were up to the service bureaus, they would have you replace all the TT versions with the Type1 equivalents. This may not make you happy, but you will have to deal with the problem if it becomes an issue with your service bureau.

Even though TrueType fonts can be converted to Type1 format at print time by CorelDRAW 5.0, standardizing on Type1 fonts would be a very practical strategy if you are dealing with service bureaus regularly. If problems occur with imaging your files, the service bureau will likely suspect a TrueType to Type1 font conversion as a possible culprit.

Type1 Fonts

As stated earlier, PostScript is a programming language, and the files are really mini-programs. These programs call on resources such as Type1 fonts, which meet Adobe's specifications. If the file cannot gain access to the font for any reason, the job images with a substituted font. This default substitution is usually Courier.

The most common reason why a font would be substituted is that it is not installed on the computer imaging the job or is not embedded in the postscript file itself. This applies to PRN and EPS files. This is also why you must notify your service bureau of all the fonts you use in your CorelDRAW file.

Service bureaus must know the font name so that they can install it prior to running your files. The manufacturer of the font is needed because several fonts with the same font name may be available from different font makers, but the character outlines and spacing information may be different. If your output comes back and the letter or word spacing is off, you probably have come across this situation.

It is not uncommon for Macintosh computers to have the same font as a PC, but with a different font name. If the font name, as seen by the computer, is not exactly the same, the PS interpreter makes a substitution.

A reliable way to get your fonts to the service bureau, even if they don't have the font themselves, is to embed the font files in your PRNs. You accomplish this by selecting the **D**ownload Type1 Fonts on the Options tab of the Print Options dialog box (see fig. 41.6). When you do this, you add the necessary font information right into the postscript data. It is a very special set of circumstances that causes an error to occur that would make the imaging device substitute Courier. It could be that your service bureau's device just cannot handle the overall complexity of the file, or that so many fonts were downloaded, they overran the allotted memory storage space. However, anything is possible with a computer, so don't be surprised if it just happens one day.

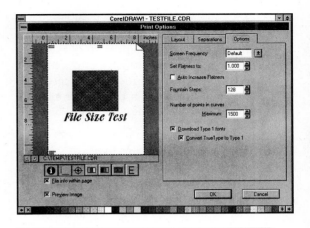

Figure 41.6

The Options tab on the Print Options dialog box.

For your fonts to be downloaded, they must be registered properly by Windows, meaning that the proper lines are present in the WIN.INI file for each printer to which you will be printing. This includes any drivers you are using for printing files on remote devices at service bureaus. The following lines from the WIN.INI file show the correct information needed to download the Type1 font Brochure:

```
[PostScript,LPT1]
softfonts=15
softfont1=c:\psfonts\pfm\b013000t.
➡pfm,c:\psfonts\b013000t.pfb
softfont2=c:\psfonts\pfm\com_____.pfm
```

The first part of the softfont1 entry shows Windows and CorelDRAW 5 where the font metrics file is located. This file contains spacing and kerning information. The second part of the entry (after the comma) is the

location of the PFB file, which contains the font outline information that is needed by the printing device to image a font. Note that the entry for softfont2 has no PFB section following the PFM portion; this occurs because that entry is for the Courier font that is resident in the printer. Sending redundant font data would be a waste.

Corel makes printing to a file easier than with many other applications because the option can be set right in CorelDRAW's Print dialog box (see fig. 41.7). This also makes it possible to set up all your remote printer drivers to print to the same port, and therefore only install softfonts on that port. This keeps your font management efforts to a minimum and your WIN.INI file slim and trim. In the previous WIN.INI example, any PostScript device that is set up to print on the LPT1 port will have the proper softfonts included in the PRN file.

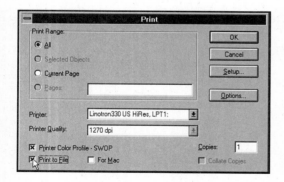

Figure 41.7
The Print to file check box on CorelDRAW's Print dialog box.

Converting-to-Curves

A surefire way of knowing that your fonts will image is to convert the text to curves. This has the effect of changing all the letterforms to drawing shapes. One disadvantage of this strategy is that your text is no longer editable; therefore, it is wise to wait until the last minute before converting text to curves. Also, make a copy of the original text into a different hidden layer, enabling you to go back to the original in case last minute changes are made after your original output has been made.

Another downside to this is that a file with great amounts of type gets very large. You must weigh what is the best strategy to take on a file-by-file basis.

Understanding the Windows PostScript Driver

Because the PostScript language really is the key link in successfully integrating with service bureaus, it is important to have a working knowledge of the Windows PostScript Driver and its basic components.

The driver strategy itself consists of two parts. The first part is the file PSCRIPT.DRV. This is the core of the driver. This file is placed into the SYSTEM subdirectory of the directory in which you have installed Windows. For example, if the Windows files are installed in a subdirectory named WIN31, the PSCRIPT.DRV file would be in the WIN31/SYSTEM subdirectory. This file is always accompanied by its Help file, PSCRIPT.HLP. If, for any reason, you need help with installing or configuring a PostScript Printer, you can press the **H**elp button and you are brought to the appropriate location in the Help file that pertains to the area you need assistance with.

The second part of the driver strategy is the WPD file, which stands for Windows Printer Description. This file "hooks" into the driver and allows it to "see" what features and options are available for a specific model of printer. These files are "compiled," meaning there is no way that a user can modify them. A WPD is furnished by the maker of the PostScript driver or the manufacturer of the printer. The WPD file contains information regarding paper sizes, resolution, and the fonts that are built-in (resident) to the printer's RIP.

The WPD strategy is a good one—it allows for specific printers to be introduced in the market well after the Windows 3.1 driver was written, yet still be able to hook into it. It also allows for WPDs to be updated when necessary, to fix bugs or add features.

If you want to install the Windows PostScript driver, after you installed Windows, follow these steps:

1. In the Control Panel window, double-click on the Printers icon.

2. Select the Add button in the Printer dialog box.

3. In the List Of Printers box, select the printer you want to install. If your

printer is not listed or does not emulate a printer that Windows supports, but you have a printer driver for it, select Install Unlisted or Updated Printer.

4. Choose the Install button. The following two steps do not apply if the printer you are installing uses the same printer driver as another printer already installed on your system.

5. In drive A, insert the disk containing the printer driver, or type a drive letter and directory path in the text box. (If you are adding a printer and WPD that comes from a disk other than Windows driver, type the drive letter and directory path to the disk supplied by the manufacturer.) You can also use the Browse button to find and select the drive and directory where the printer driver is located. When you are finished using the Browse dialog box, click on the OK button to return to the Install Printer dialog box.

6. In the Install Printer dialog box, click on the OK button. If you are installing a driver not included with Windows, a dialog box appears, listing several printers. Select the printer you want, then click on the Install button.

7. Assign a port to the printer.

8. Choose the **C**onnect button.

9. From the **P**orts list, select the port you want to assign to the printer. If you select a COM port, you might need to change the communications settings.

10. If you want to change communications settings, click on the **S**ettings button, complete the Settings dialog box, and click on the OK button.

11. Click on the OK button in the Connect dialog box, then the Close button in the Printers dialog box.

This is all there is to setting up the Windows PostScript driver on your computer. Now you are ready to make files that can be transported to a service bureau and run out on their PostScript devices.

It is important to have the latest copy of the PostScript driver. The current Microsoft version is 3.58. To check and see what version you have installed, click on the **S**etup button in the Printers dialog box, then select the About button. A screen appears that shows the driver version information.

Alternative Drivers

There are alternatives to the Windows PostScript driver for printing to PostScript devices. Some printer manufacturers have taken the Windows PostScript driver and modified it to offer very specific printer options. There is a potential problem if the manufacturer names the special driver PSCRIPT.DRV because only one file by that name may reside in the SYSTEM subdirectory. This leads to a problem when an application needs the Microsoft version PostScript driver. One such popular application is PageMaker 5.0.

There are alternatives to the standard Microsoft PostScript driver. Some printer vendors have taken the code for that driver

and modified it to offer printer-specific options relevant to their own models. Generally, these vendors have named their variant other than PSCRIPT.DRV—for example, AGFAPS.DRV, COMPAQPS.DRV, and HPWINPS.DRV. This does give rise to some potential problems, as follows:

■ ATM, when adding or removing fonts, only writes or removes the correct entries in the WIN.INI [PostScript,<PORT>] sections if the <PORT> is linked to require a PostScript driver called PSCRIPT. This linking can be seen in the [devices] and [PrinterPorts] sections of WIN.INI.

■ PageMaker 5.0, which writes its own PostScript, requires access to the Microsoft PSCRIPT.DRV (or third-party equivalent differently named) at version 3.56 or later. Third-party variants based on versions earlier than 3.56 do not work correctly with PageMaker 5.0.

Some vendors have retained the name PSCRIPT.DRV and extended that driver to provide their own printer specific options. Generally, these are backward compatible with issued Microsoft printer drivers, but you are advised to check this before installing.

Before you add a printer driver supplied by a printer manufacturer, ascertain whether it is printer-specific and is replacing the PSCRIPT.DRV file, or if it is just a WPD file that is being hooked into the standard Windows driver.

There is one exception to this rule—the Persimmon driver. This driver is a direct replacement for the Microsoft driver. It fixes several problems with the Microsoft driver and supplies many updated WPD files written for most popular desktop printers. There are also WPDs available for high-resolution imagesetters.

It is worth mentioning that the current Scitex driver is the Persimmon driver with specific Scitex WPD files. For a high-end imagesetting system like Scitex to endorse this driver is very praiseworthy. If a service bureau has special needs and desires a custom WPD file to be built, Persimmon can handle this task.

Because this driver is named PSCRIPT.DRV, it overwrites the Microsoft PSCRIPT.DRV file, but is completely compatible with applications like PageMaker 5.0. The only catch is that the associated WPD files are compiled to work only with the Persimmon driver. If you need a WPD file for a new printer, you must contact Persimmon directly and have it written. This process is not a real problem, more of a minor inconvenience, and Persimmon will charge only a nominal fee to cover their costs.

The Persimmon PostScript driver in its basic configuration is available directly from Persimmon or can be downloaded from the CompuServe Ventura Forum Library. The file is named PSMDRV.EXE and is a self-extracting, compressed file.

Complete install instructions and copious notes are included in several accompanying ASCII text files. Persimmon can be reached by CompuServe mail at 100113,514 or at the following address:

> Persimmon Software
> 10, Back Street,
> Ashton Keynes
> Wilts SN6 6PD
> England.
> Tel/Fax UK (0)285-860790

Transporting Your Files

Once you have your CorelDRAW PRN, or EPS files ready to be imaged, you must get them off your computer and to the service bureau. There are quite a few options available. Some are hardware dependent; others are software solutions.

Floppy Disks

Most computers have floppy drives. The 5 1/4-inch disks are becoming less common than the 3 1/2-inch ones. A PC-based service bureau will likely have a 5 1/4-inch floppy drive, if that is what you have to supply files on. Be aware that Mac-based service bureaus will more likely be able to read 3 1/2-inch disks than 5 1/4-inch disks.

The maximum file size that can fit on a 3 1/2 inch floppy disk is 1.38 megabytes. This limit is very easy to hit with CorelDRAW 5.0 files, especially if you use bitmap objects such as texture fills and scans in your images. The only way to pack more on a floppy disk is to shrink your files with a compression utility such as PKZip.

PKZip is available on most bulletin boards or directly from the following address:

PKWARE, Inc.
9025 N. Deerwood Dr.
Brown Deer, WI 53223-2437

The current version is 2.04g and it can shrink files to 50 percent of their original size. Because it is a DOS program with a very unfriendly interface, it is best also to obtain a Zip Manager. One such Windows program is WinZip 5.5. It is available on most bulletin boards or by contacting the following address:

Nico Mak Computing, Inc.
P.O. Box 919
Bristol, CT 06011

WinZip offers many features that make working with Zip files a breeze.

If you are working with a Mac-based service bureau, you should ask them if they can handle zipped files. There are programs like Stuff-It that will handle expanding the files compressed using PKZip on the Mac.

Removable Storage Devices

When you have to move very large files (over 5MB), the only practical way is in some form of removable mass storage. Two of the most prevalent in service bureaus are SyQuest and Bernoulli drives.

SyQuest is the most common. The removable cartridges can hold 44, 88, or up to 200MB of information. To take this route, you and your service bureau must install a

SyQuest drive. If you are working with a service bureau that has its SyQuest hooked up to a Mac, they may have a preference about how the cartridges are formatted. Contact the service bureau and ask before you assume that their machine will read your disks.

The Bernoulli drives are much like the SyQuest. They are generally regarded as more reliable, though not as prevalent. The Bernoulli drives can currently store a maximum of 150MB of information on a cartridge. Bernoulli offers a model called the Transportable which is just that—a self-contained drive that can be taken to your service so that they don't even need to own their own Bernoulli drive. The catch is that they must have the right interface card and software driver loaded on one of their machines. If you can work this out with the service bureau, you will have a great method of transporting your large CorelDRAW files to the bureau.

By Modem

If you have a modem, the world is at your fingertips. If your service bureau has a modem, you can connect to them and send your files directly to one of their computers. For this to work, you must have communications software to handle connecting and transferring the data files.

You must set up your modem and software to "talk" to the bureau's communications software. Beside the phone number of the modem, you need to know the data bits, stop bits, and parity setting of the bureau's modem. A common setting is 8,N,1, which means 8 data bits, no parity, and 1 stop bit. After this, you need to choose a protocol, which helps ensure that your transmission is being checked for accuracy as it is sent over the phone line. Common protocols are XModem and ZModem. Remember that although you might have many protocol choices available in your communications program, you must pick one that your service bureau also has.

If you intend to buy a modem, get one with a baud rate of at least 9,600 baud. The higher the baud rating, the faster the modem sends the information. If you can afford one, a 14.4 modem is better and automatically slows down to a lower baud rate if it connects with a modem that is only capable of a lower speed; if you buy a faster modem than your service bureau, you are not running the risk of being incompatible.

It is a good idea to zip your files with a compression program before sending them. This cuts down on transmission times and makes sending many files in one zip file much easier to handle for all involved.

Tips and Hints on Making Files

The following are some points that make getting reliable output from service bureaus easier. Some points apply to all types of imaging, and others are specific to a particular kind of output. Before you start your next job, take a look at the list; it might help you avoid needless problems.

For High-Resolution Imagesetters

The following tips apply to those users who want to use a high-resolution imagesetter:

■ Don't crop bitmaps extensively using the Node tool in CorelDRAW; do your cropping in a bitmap editing program such as CorelPHOTO-PAINT. The best way to do this is to crop the image before it is imported into CorelDRAW. In the Import dialog box, select Crop from the drop-down menu below the preview box, and click on OK. You are prompted to go to the Crop Image dialog box. Crop your bitmap and click on OK. The reason you should not overcrop bitmaps is that CorelDRAW is still saving the entire bitmap in the file and the PostScript RIP is still processing all of it and masking the portions that will not show on the printed image.

■ Do set your target printer and resolution from the Control Panel before you start CorelDRAW. This way, CorelDRAW is ready to print with all the right settings. If you need to change target printers during a CorelDRAW session, you can do this from CorelDRAW's Print dialog box.

■ Do set your resolution properly (there is one exception—see the following tip). If the PostScript driver and resolution is set for a lower dpi than desired, change it—TrueType fonts are sent as bitmaps at the selected resolution.

- Do set the resolution to a setting lower than you intend to output at if you are trying to get large User Defined page sizes out of CorelDRAW. The reason for this is there is a limit imposed by the Windows PostScript driver. For example, if you are using the Lino 330 driver, you cannot print a 30×30-inch image (the maximum page size that CorelDRAW allows) out of CorelDRAW unless you lower the resolution to 635 dpi. If you take this strategy and are using small TrueType fonts, be sure to read the next point.

- Do set `PSBitmapFontLimit=0` in CORELPRN.INI so that no TrueType fonts will be rasterized. This is necessary to get good quality TT fonts when you are forced to use a lower resolutions to accommodate a large page size (see the preceding point).

- Do try to find out the available *Virtual Memory* (VM) figure from your service bureau. You can enter this in the correct place on the Advanced screen of the PostScript driver Setup screen.

- Do change the Flatness setting on the Options tab of CorelDRAW's Print Options dialog box to .25, and send your files to your laser printer. This will more closely simulate the "difficulty factor" that a high-resolution RIP will have interpreting your file at 1,200 dpi. If you are going to output at 2,400 dpi, change the flatness setting to .12. If the file fails to print, it is a good candidate to fail on the high-resolution device also. Remember to change the setting back to 1 after your testing is complete.

- Don't rotate or scale bitmaps in CorelDRAW unless absolutely necessary. It is better to figure out the size and rotation first and do this in a bitmap editing program such CorelPHOTO-PAINT. This speeds up printing files because the PostScript interpreter does not have to perform all the calculations at print time.

- Don't set negative or emulsion settings in CorelDRAW or Windows setup dialog boxes. It is safer to inform the service bureau of exactly what you want. They will set their machines to do the job.

- Don't use CorelDRAW's RT or HQS settings in the Advanced Screening dialog box unless you check with your service bureau to see if they can use this information. For the most part, the Default screen settings are fine and service bureaus can override them if they want to apply any special screening technologies available to their particular RIP and recorder.

- Don't use CorelDRAW's Auto Spreading function on the Separations tab of the Print Options dialog box. This is not really producing the proper spreads and chokes with which a commercial printer will be happy.

For Color Slides

The following points apply to users who want to image to color slides:

- Do get samples of Pantone colors frequently used in slides. This enables you to see if the colors that the film recorder produces match your swatch book. If not, you need to modify your colors to get a closer match. Remember that you are imaging on an RGB device and that there are great differences between service bureaus. Get tests done at all the service bureaus you will use.

- Do use .5-inch margins on your slides. Keep all "live" material inside the margins. Backgrounds should extend all the way to the extremity of the page.

- Don't use too many radial or conical fountain fills in your slides. This leads to very excessive RIP and imaging times.

- Don't make slides with no background color. This is extremely unpleasant on the audience's eyes. Light colors on dark backgrounds and dark colors on medium-colored backgrounds work well.

- Don't target a black-and-white laser printer when making PRNs. If not, the necessary color data might not be included in the print file. Pick a color printer such as the QMS Colorscript 100.

For All Kinds of Imaging

The following tips apply to all users planning to use a service bureau:

- Do talk to your service bureau about all jobs *before* you start them.

- Do run proofs of your PRN files through your local laser printer. To do this, type **Copy** *filename*.**PRN LPT**x at the DOS prompt, where *filename*.PRN is replaced by the name of the PRN file you want to test and LPTx is the name of the port to which your laser printer is connected.

- Do try to get accurate error messages from the service bureau when your files fail. These messages can provide clues to what is failing.

Summary

The key ingredient in having successful experiences using outside vendors like service bureaus is communication. What you have read in this chapter is a sizable chunk of the information that you need to work with remote imaging devices. But the graphics and computer worlds are changing so much, so fast that service bureaus are always adding new equipment, software, and services. As a result, you constantly learn new things. By communicating with your service bureau(s) frequently, or at least before you start your CorelDRAW files, you are able to head off problems and save time and money. Everyone can then accomplish their parts in the production chain, and your clients will be happy.

Chapter 42

Creating Your Own Fonts

*T*his chapter is first meant to provide a general description of how writing and different styles of lettering have evolved. The first section of this chapter is devoted to a concise, narrated history of letters and the design and meaning of those letters.

The second section of this chapter is a practical course in lettering. The entire chapter, of course, has the purpose of inspiring the graphic artist to work and create with CorelDRAW 5.0 letters, type, and page layout as creative design.

This chapter covers:

- History and technique of lettering

- Principles and design of fonts

- TrueType and Adobe Type 1 fonts

- Creating a font from handwriting

- Converting letters into TrueType characters

- Modifying and Installing fonts

History and Technique of Lettering

In the beginning, people communicated orally, but they soon found out that spoken communication was not enough to transmit the message. A visual representation was needed so that important messages could be recorded. At the same time, people had to send a message farther than they could shout.

Man's first attempt at writing, to our knowledge, came from the need to record events—pieces of their history. Take, for example, all the cave paintings, also known as *pictographs*. These drawings tell stories ranging from hunting to everyday events.

Pictographs were not enough to describe every thought, though. Cavemen could draw a picture of a Mammoth hunt to record the event, but they could not convey the feelings of excitement and fear they experienced when going on the hunt or the smells of the feasting afterward.

Thus, *symbols* were created to assign meanings to feelings such as smells, wishes, and fears—things that cannot be seen. Symbols are quick and easy to recognize and understand (a good example is the skull and crossbones symbolizing danger). They are close to a universal language.

As the need to simplify the enormous number of symbols developed, writing evolved. Today only the Chinese and Japanese still use symbols in their writing.

These languages use more than 15,000 characters to represent everyday things and more complex ideas.

The First Alphabet

According to our history books, Egyptians were the first population to write with pictures or *hieroglyphs*. They started to write *pronounceable phonograms*—pictures with sound. They would string together the symbols (or sounds) to construct syllables, thus building words. This was the first attempt to create an alphabet.

The (Roman) alphabet in the Western hemisphere actually is based on the Greek alphabet, although some paleographers dispute this fact.

With their 24 characters, the Greeks established the core of Western culture. Keep in mind that each one of our letters in the alphabet today can be traced back through various stylizations of pictures. The Greeks also are credited for creating defined symbols for vowels. The word *alphabet* comes from the first two letters of the Greek alphabet, *alpha beta*, for example.

Later, the Romans borrowed from their ancestors—reading left to right like the Greeks, and in columns like the Egyptians and Chinese.

The connection between the writing styles and the architecture of a specific period of history is very fine. The Romans, for example, employed curves in shaping their text just as they did in the designs of arches and cathedrals. Later in this chapter you can examine the relationship between Gothic writing and Gothic architecture.

In the beginning, there were only capital letters, which were rigid and concise. The style was shaped by the tools used. As writing tools evolved, the appearance and form of the letters became more defined. With the introduction of the reed pen, for example, writing became easier; the hand movement flowed in a more natural way. Thus, each letter became smaller and eventually was joined with the letters surrounding it, creating what is now known as *script writing*. Script actually follows the motion of the hand, joining all letters in a freer, rounded shape.

Culture, including communication in the form of writing, all but disappeared with the fall of the Roman Empire. It was not until Carl the Great, more than 300 years later, that writing progressed once again. Carl the Great is also remembered for his minuscule letters (*Carlovingian minuscules*). These letters are very familiar to us today as lowercase letters.

The style known as Gothic replaced the round, plain-quality shape of Carlovingian. Again, the connection between writing style and architecture is very fine. *Gothic* letters are characterized by the pointed, rising vertical of each letter (known as a *madorla*). Gothic architecture is characterized by the high windowed walls, ribbed vaulting, flying buttresses, pointed arches, and steep, high roofs.

The Renaissance

With the birth of the Renaissance, Gothic times faded away and were replaced with a new wave of thought. New interests brought a natural appreciation of the Earth and human values, as well as a vigorous desire for information.

Books, letters, and other means of writing still were reproduced individually by hand and owned only by an elite few who could pay for such service. There was a need to broadcast ideas, of making ideas available through mass distribution.

Johannes Gutenburg was the first person to accomplish and find a solution to this need. He developed a system with which he was able to set characters into big, lead plates, ink them, and press them onto paper. His method is very similar to today's printers. This was the beginning of the art of printing.

Modern-Day Writing Instruments

With the advent of the industrial revolution in the nineteenth century, handwriting was replaced almost completely by a noisy machine called the typewriter. As the rise of businesses brought a need for faster writing, handwriting—although beautiful and very artistic—became too slow and typewriters took over. At that time, typists could generate about 30 words per minute.

By the middle of this century, computers began to influence all aspects of the written word, from business communications to personal communications. Computers have been integrated into almost all aspects of our lives. They have replaced many methods of communication and probably will replace more someday. The widespread use of computers is shaping our lives—from picture telephones to fax machines, from paying bills via modem to correspondence by e-mail.

We are becoming a very accessible society. Anytime, anywhere. In doing so, however,

we have lost some of the artistry of the written word. Hence the importance of creating your own fonts.

Principles and Design of Fonts

The first thing to keep in mind in designing a font is readability. A brief description of the most common styles follows.

Sans-Serif Letters

Sans-serif fonts may not be as decorative as some other letters, but they are very legible. Very simple and essential, these fonts derive from the Roman alphabet but lack decorative qualities. You can alter sans-serif fonts by boldfacing them for more emphasis or making them thinner to give them a touch of delicacy. Of course, it all depends on the application of these letters.

The first thing to notice is that letters come in different widths. This is not by chance; instead, it is the result of several centuries of development to achieve the highest degree of legibility.

Sans-serif, italic fonts derived from upright letters that gradually sloped to the right because of the natural inclination of the hand to lean forward. Italic retains the essential form of the upright version, but in a few letters, the proportion of the letter is modified slightly.

Italics can be drawn in any weight, and the remarks applied to upright letters apply equally to italics. Italics should never be used for the main body of any message, but used rather sparingly for emphasis or for leading the eye into an important passage.

Serif Letters

Serif, or shoulder, is a style to consider when the letters need to be beautified and finished off to encourage the eye to pass along the line. Serifs are based on a circle. Notice that the ends of the strokes are not flat, but are arched slightly. Do not exaggerate these serifs, because this might give the letters an unattractive appearance. They should merge gracefully into the body of the letter. Straight, even lines to the thin stroke seldom are used. These thin strokes are curved slightly on either side, giving a sense of movement to the letter and making it obviously drawn.

Categories of Letters

You can divide the letters of the alphabet into different groups that have similar characteristics. You safely can say that *E, F,* and *L* belong to the same group. They are the least difficult letters to design, because they are based on half squares occupied by a vertical stroke, with one or more strokes branching off to the right.

The letters *A, V,* and *W* also represent a group letters that have much in common. *A* is the first and oldest letter of the alphabet. It has a triangular shape formed by two diagonal strokes intercepted by a horizontal stroke right below the middle height.

While letters with sloping sides are under consideration, you can continue logically by studying another group formed by *X, Y, Z,* and *K.* In *X,* the upper and lower triangles are balanced and defined by the crossing strokes a little above the center. The triangle in *Y*, however, falls just below the center to prevent a spindly effect. *Z* occupies a square, but the upper horizontal stroke is slightly shorter than the bottom stroke.

The Roman alphabet did not contain the letter *K*. It is therefore free ground for controversy. From the middle of the vertical stroke, two diagonals are drawn that form two triangles. The lower triangle is slightly wider than the top triangle to avoid a caved appearance.

The remaining letters of the alphabet become progressively more difficult to master because curves and loops are featured. The letters *D*, *P*, and *R* are related distinctly; they have as common features the vertical stroke and an upper loop. Another group formed by round shapes contains *C*, *O*, *G*, and *Q*. These letters are self-explanatory. They all start with a circle drawn inside a square.

The letter *S* is a letter on its own and is the most difficult to design. This letter starts with two circles, one on top of the other, which are drawn within half squares.

Having established the very basics for designing letters and subsequently, fonts, we finally can focus on the real subject of this chapter: creating your own fonts in CorelDRAW.

TrueType and Adobe Type 1 Fonts

CorelDRAW 5.0 bundles a very generous number of high-quality fonts in its program's suite. More than 820 fonts are included and each comes in two formats: TrueType and Type 1.

TrueType fonts, developed by a joint venture of Apple computers and software giant Microsoft, are *scalable* fonts, which means that each character is defined by an outline mathematically created. Every time you select a typeface and point size, the vectors that make the character are customized to the specified size.

Type 1 fonts, developed by Adobe systems, also are scalable and act much like TrueType fonts, but the mathematical computation is different. These fonts are based on a language called PostScript. *PostScript* is a programming language that describes the characteristics of a font: its shape, size, and geographical location relative to a printed page.

Advantages and Disadvantages

If you had to select between TrueType and Type 1 fonts, it would be a very difficult choice, because each of those technologies has its advantages and disadvantages.

The only disadvantage with Type 1 fonts is that they are not supported in the Windows environment. You need to interact with a font-manager program such as Adobe Type manager, which is included in CorelDRAW 5.0, to use Type 1 fonts in Windows. This can be a problem if the computer system in which the manager will be used has low Windows resources. The Windows resources decrease further if the font manager is loaded.

TrueType fonts are built into Windows and can be used in any Windows application without the use of a font manager. Another advantage of TrueType fonts is that the cost of these fonts is reasonable compared to Type 1 fonts. Not everything is in favor of TrueType fonts, however.

Adobe Type 1 fonts are much cleaner and sharper when printed, especially if the printer is PostScript compatible. If a service bureau is going to output your files, Type 1 fonts are the way to go. Almost every service bureau bases its output on Type 1 fonts. If you use TrueType fonts, a service bureau may not be able to output the file without a substitution of an equivalent Type 1 font.

PostScript is not limited to describing only font specifications; it also can help to create halftones and other tricks with a laser printer.

Another way to make sure that your file can be outputted by a service bureau is to convert to curves all the text in your file.

Notice that, when the word `TEST` is selected, the status bar does not say `Artistic Text`

anymore, but `Curve on Layer 1`. The text is now a graphic entity and can be treated and printed as such.

T   I   P

Make sure that you make a copy of your text by placing it in a different frozen layer of your file before you convert the text into curves. After the text is converted, it cannot be edited anymore.

Why Create a Font?

Although CorelDRAW contains more than 820 fonts, you might want to give a personalized accent to your work, or you might tire of using the same fonts. With CorelDRAW, you can create our own fonts. Corel's export filters enable you to convert graphics into Adobe Type 1 (PFB) or TrueType (TTF)

Exercise: Converting Fonts into Curves

1. Click on the Text tool, then click an insertion point on your printable.

Selects the Text tool and turns the page pointer into a cross. The cursor becomes an I bar.

*2. Type **TEST**, press Ctrl+space bar.*

Adds the test word and selects the entire text string.

3. Press Ctrl+T.

The Character Attributes dialog box appears.

*4. From the **F**onts list, select Arial or any other font you prefer. Type **300** in the Point **S**ize field, then click on OK.*

Specifies the typeface and the point size.

*5. Choose Con**v**ert to Curves from the **A**rrange pull-down menu or press Ctrl+O.*

Converts text into curves.

fonts. These filters convert your graphics characters into text characters, enabling you to use them in CorelDRAW 5.0 or any Windows application.

You can use different methods to create fonts. You can use any existing font and customize it to your liking. You can create totally new fonts by starting from scratch. With the help of a scanner, you also can create an alphabet of your own handwriting. You learn how to do this in the following section.

Creating a Font from Handwriting

First write your handwritten letters individually on 8 1/2-by-11-inch sheets of paper. Generally, the larger your letter, the more precise and accurate the final result is. Write one letter per sheet of paper. Although the file size of the scanned images will be large, don't worry about it now.

After you complete your handwritten alphabet, scan the letters individually and save the files in PCX or TIFF format. After you create the files for each letter, you can convert them into vector-based images by using CorelTRACE. Of course, if you have a TWAIN-compatible scanner, you can scan your images directly into CorelTRACE (see fig. 42.1).

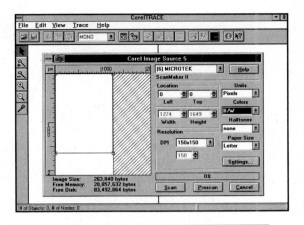

Figure 42.1

The TWAIN interface enables you to scan your images directly into CorelTRACE.

T   I   P

If you are using CorelTRACE to electronically trace your scanned image, make sure that the image size does not exceed 3,000×3,000 pixels. You might have a problem tracing your image if the file is too large. Set your resolution to 150×150 dpi and the color to black and white.

The following exercise provides step-by-step instructions for creating an electronic font of your handwriting.

Exercise: Creating a Handwritten Font

1. Double-click on the CorelTRACE icon in the CorelDRAW 5.0 group in the Program Manager.	Launches CorelTRACE in program.
*2. Choose **O**pen from the **F**ile pull-down menu.*	Opens the Open File dialog box.
*3. Select the file to open. Change **D**irectory, File **T**ype, and Dri**v**e, if necessary, to locate the file. Then click on OK.*	Opens the file and displays it on the left side of the screen.
*4. Choose **E**dit Options from the **T**race pull-down menu.*	Displays the Tracing Options dialog box.
*5. In the Setting group of the Image folder, select MONO from the **F**ileName drop-down list box (see fig. 42.2).*	Sets the tracing default to monochrome.
*6. In the Lines folder, set **C**urve Precision to Good, **L**ine Precision to Good, **T**arget Curve Length to Medium, **S**ample Rate to Fine, **M**inimum Object Size to 3, **O**utline Filtering to None. Then click on OK (see fig. 42.3).*	Optimizes program to trace the letter. Settings may vary, depending on the quality of the scanned image.
7. Click on the trace edges in the source image on the ribbon bar (the one with the pencil over the line segment).	Displays the traced letter on the left side of your screen (see fig. 42.4).
*8. Choose **S**ave from the **F**ile menu, then choose Trace As.*	Displays the Save Trace As dialog box.
9. Name the file and click on OK.	Creates and saves the vector-based image.

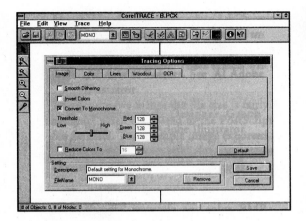

Figure 42.2
The Image folder in the Tracing Options dialog box.

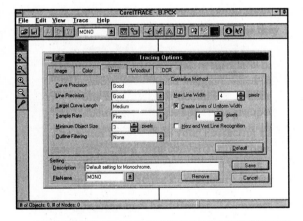

Figure 42.3
The Lines folder in the Tracing Options dialog box.

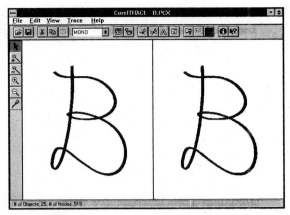

Figure 42.4
The bitmapped B on the left and the vector-based B on the right.

You now have a series of handwritten letters ready to be converted into a typeface that can be used in Windows or any other Windows application.

Converting Letters into TTF Format

Begin the conversion process by launching CorelDRAW. You will convert the letters to TrueType (TTF) format so that you will not need a font-manager program to use them. The conversion process is the same for each letter.

Although all capital letters are the same height, this is not the case for lowercase letters. You must take into consideration the length of the ascenders and descenders of lowercase letters. Letters with *ascenders* (long strokes that project above the main body of the letters such as *d*, *l*, *k*, *h*, and so on) will be the same overall height as the capitals. The

main body will be slightly more than half this size. Letters containing *descenders* (such as *p*, *q*, *y*, and so on) project down from the baseline of the characters and are the same length as the ascenders. Consequently, more space is necessary between the lines of wording when lowercase is used than when capitals are drawn. Printers call this space between lines the *beard*. Figure 42.5 illustrates the various letter heights.

To achieve this look, it is essential that the area of white between each letter is approximately the same. The eye sees space, not distance. If you look at the *W* in figure 42.6, for example, you see that although the *W* is the same distance from the *A* as the other letters, is too far away from the *A*. How much nearer it must be should not be a function of the ruler, but instead a matter of judgment by the artist.

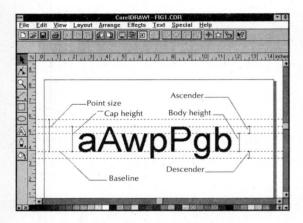

Figure 42.5
Various heights to keep in mind when designing letters.

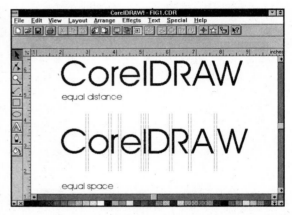

Figure 42.6
Notice the optical difference between the two text strings.

Having arrived at the point where individual letters can be drawn reasonably well, it is time to take the first steps in arranging them to form a word (or words) so that they are easy and pleasant to read. This process is called *spacing*.

Spacing is balance, not distance. The area of white space must harmonize with the density of black—the letters themselves—so that the word does not appear disjointed or difficult to read, and the eye is not attracted to any one letter. The word should look complete and form a pattern or design.

Importing the Letters

Having progressed as far as this, it now is time to fire up CorelDRAW and start creating your own fonts. You begin by importing your first letter.

1. Choose **I**mport from the **F**ile menu. The Import dialog box appears.

2. Locate the file containing the letter previously traced and click on OK.

T I P

The letter probably contains unwanted lines and dots produced by the scan. Clean up the letter by or exploding it first and deleting all the unnecessary objects. Use the Shape tool to refine the shape of the letter if you think it is necessary. You also can use the Auto-Reduce feature to eliminate some of the superfluous nodes forming the letter. With the Shape tool selected, double-click on the object. The Node Edit dialog box appears. Select all the nodes forming the letter, then click on the Auto-Reduce button on the Node Edit roll-up menu. The *B*, for example, had 473 nodes. After applying Auto-Reduce, it now has only 111 nodes.

Keeping in mind what has just been said about the principals of typography, you now need to set the general parameters that will reflect on all the letters.

The first thing to do is to set the page size where every single letter will be placed and proportionally scaled so that you will have consistency between all the letters.

Exercise: Setting up the Page Layout for New Letters

1. *Choose **P**age Setup from the **L**ayout menu.*

   Displays the Page Setup dialog box.

2. *In the Size folder, select Custom. Change the **W**idth and the **H**eight to 750 points, then click on OK.*

   Sets printable page to about 10 1/2-by-10 1/2-inch dimensions.

3. *Double-click on any one of the two rulers.*

   Displays the Grid and Scale Setup dialog box.

4. *Change the horizontal and vertical grid frequency to 1 point, then set the horizontal and vertical grid origin to 30 points; click on OK.*

   Sets a new origin needed for the new character's baseline.

5. *Drag a horizontal and a vertical guideline to intersect the new origin.*

   Makes these two lines the baseline and the left margin of all your letters.

6. *Resize the letter to fit it into the page and move it toward the new origin so that the vertical guideline touches the far left side of the letter and the horizontal guideline touches the bottom of the letter.*

   Positions the letter so that it is almost ready to be converted into a TrueType character.

continues

7. Drag a horizontal guideline to the 540-point mark and then scale down the letter to touch the top of it with the new guideline.

Sets letter to the correct size (see fig. 42.7).

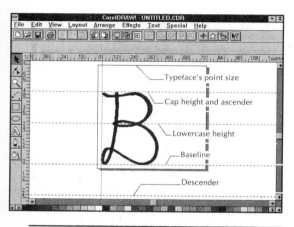

Figure 42.7

The first letter now is completely designed and ready to be exported.

The letter appears to be smaller than the printable page, which is 720 points from the new origin. The letter is smaller because 720 points is the typeface's point size and not the cap height. The space is called *interline spacing of typeface.*

You might have noticed two more horizontal guidelines on figure 42.7. The lowercase guideline is needed when a lowercase letter is drawn. This will be the height of all lowercase letters. The cap height's guidelines also act as the ascender's height. This guideline sets the height of all letters with ascenders like *b*, *d*, and so on.

The bottom horizontal guideline is needed for all the letters with descenders such as *g*, *y*, *p*, *q*, and so on. Don't worry about it if the guideline is out of the printable page; it will not affect the final product.

At this point, before we go on with our final journey, which is the conversion of the graphic letters into TrueType or Type 1 typefaces, you can print the letters you just created and make sure that everything is as expected. Some of the letters will print outside the margins of the page.

W A R N I N G

Do not scale down the letter, because you will lose the proportionality with other letters. To see the entire letter, just print it using the Print to Fit feature found in the Print dialog box. If the printout is satisfactory, you finally are ready for the conversion.

Converting Letters into TrueType Characters

The following exercise uses the TrueType filter so that you will not need to use a font-manager program. Keep in mind though, that the following exercise is exactly the same as if you were converting the graphic letters into Type 1 format.

Exercise: Converting Your Letters into TrueType Format

1. *With your first letter on-screen, choose **E**xport from the **F**ile pulldown menu.*

Displays the Export dialog box.

2. *In the Export dialog box, scroll down list files of **T**ype, select TrueType Font (TTF), then type the name of your font in the FileName text box. Click on OK.*

Displays the Options dialog box (see fig. 42.8).

3. *In the **F**amily Name list box, type the name of your font, then click on OK.*

Displays the TrueType Export box (see fig. 42.9).

4. *Click on Yes in the TrueType Export box.*

Displays the TrueType Export preview window.

5. *Select the character corresponding to your exporting letter by using the scroll bar next to the Character **N**umber list box, check the Auto option, and click on OK.*

Makes the letter a TrueType character ready to be used in CorelDRAW as well as any other Windows applications.

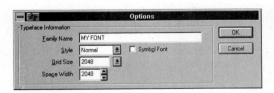

Figure 42.8

The Options dialog box.

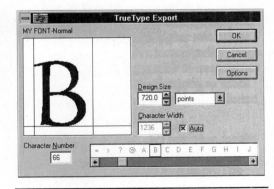

Figure 42.9

The TrueType Export dialog box.

Congratulations! You have just created the first letter of your own calligraphy. Continue with this process until each letter has been exported.

Modifying an Existing Font

With CorelDRAW, you also have the option of modifying an existing font. You might not need an entire alphabet. You might just want to stylize a few letters to create a logo, for example.

The following discussion shows you how to take an existing font and modify it to your liking. With the page set to 750 points horizontal and vertical, and the origin still set to 30 points, use the lowercase letter a of Britannic Bold, a typeface bundled with CorelDRAW 5.0.

With the Text tool selected, click an insertion point on the printable page. Type a lowercase **a** and press Ctrl+space bar. Then press Ctrl+T. The Character Attributes dialog box appears (see fig. 42.10). Select Britannic Bold from the **F**onts list and change the size to 720 points.

Select the Rectangle tool and draw a rectangle next to the letter. Left-click on the white swatch and right-click on the **X**, both located on the color palette at the bottom of the dialog box. The rectangle is now white and without outline.

Click on the Transform roll-up button located on the ribbon bar to activate the Transform roll-up. Click on the Size button

and use the spin controls to change the size to 8 points horizontal and 0 points vertical. Move the rectangle and place it so that its right side touches the right side of the letter, as shown in figure 42.11.

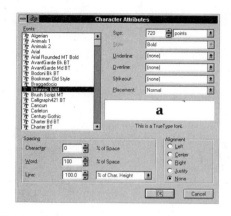

Figure 42.10

The Character Attributes dialog box.

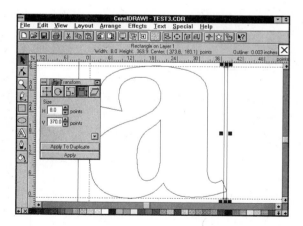

Figure 42.11

Placing the rectangle next to the letter a.

Select the rectangle and change its position by clicking on the Position button in the Transform roll-up and using the spin controls to set the position to 16 points horizontal and 0 points vertical. Then click on the Apply to Duplicate button (see fig. 42.12).

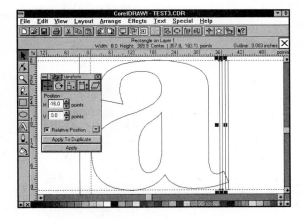

Figure 42.12
You now have two rectangles over the letter a.

Press Ctrl+R 22 times to cover the letter with thin rectangles. Choose Select **A**ll from the **E**dit menu. Then choose **T**rim from the **A**rrange menu. All the objects are trimmed together.

With all the objects still selected, click on the letter as you press and hold down the Shift key. Then press Del. The letter is now ready to be exported into a TrueType character (see fig. 42.13).

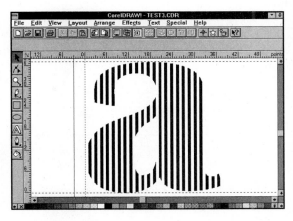

Figure 42.13
The finished letter.

Installing the Font in Windows

After you convert all your characters, you can try using them in any Windows application. Before you do this, however, you need to install the font in Windows.

To install the font, follow these steps:

1. Double-click on the Control Panel icon in the Main group of the Windows Program Manager. The Control Panel appears (see fig. 42.14).

2. Double-click on the Fonts icon to display the Fonts dialog box (see fig. 42.15).

Figure 42.14

The Control Panel.

Figure 42.15

The Fonts dialog box.

3. Click on the **A**dd button in the Fonts dialog box. The Add Fonts dialog box appears (see fig. 42.16).

4. Select the directory in which your font is located, select the name of your font from the list of fonts, and then click on OK. Your font now is installed and ready to use.

Figure 42.16

The Add Fonts dialog box.

Try your new font. Open any Windows application and your font is available for use. Now that you have learned how to create your own font, you should keep in mind a few limitations, which are discussed in the following section. The only other limitation is your imagination.

Limitations

Creating fonts is easy and the limitations are few. Note that you cannot create a character made out of different objects. The character has to be a single object or a combined object. If the character is formed by several objects, they must be combined and each of them must be a closed path.

Intersecting lines are also a restriction. If you have lines or objects that cross over to each other, use tools such as Trim or Weld so that the final object will not have overlapping lines. Also be forewarned that fills of any kind or outline attributes are not accepted. If you use these techniques, the Export procedure is ignored by the program.

Summary

Now that you have an understanding of the philosophy of letters, you should be able to create your own fonts in CorelDRAW 5.0. In this chapter, you learned the history of lettering, the parts of a letter, and the way in which to use this powerful program to create your own fonts.

Using CorelDRAW
with Other Applications

*T*he Corel suite of applications provides powerful solutions to a number of graphic design and layout needs. In today's graphics world, no application can stand alone, however. To meet expanding demands, having a variety of applications makes work both more efficient and faster.

This chapter covers:

- Imaging editing software
- 3D rendering software
- Paint and special effects programs
- Microsoft Word for Windows 6.0
- Desktop publishing
- Winfax Pro
- PinPoint Error Reporter

Image-Editing Software

There are a number of photo image-editing packages on the market today. Imaging packages generally support numerous file formats and scanning devices. CorelPHOTO-PAINT, which is part of the CorelDRAW suite of applications, provides seamless connectivity to other Corel applications. CorelPHOTO-PAINT has a file size limitation, though, that can make it difficult to manage large images over 16MB. Aldus PhotoStyler, Micrographx Picture Publisher, Altamira Composer, Adobe Photoshop, and Ulead ImagePals do not have such limitations. The available packages offer various levels of features and speed. Other packages, such as Photo-Morph by Northcoast Software and Morph by Gryphon Software, enable you to add transitional morphing images to your work.

Photoshop

Photoshop is one of the most popular image-editing packages on the market today. It features scanning support and full image editing ability. By combining Photoshop with CorelDRAW, you can create images with impact. "Harley," by Phillip Williams, shown in figure 43.1 and in the color insert, is an excellent example of combining the abilities of CorelDRAW with an image-editing package such as Photoshop. Williams, an extremely talented graphic artist, is especially adept at combining the power of

computer graphics packages to create spectacular images. In figure 43.1, Williams created the base image in CorelDRAW and then exported it into Photoshop, where he added light enhancements. The difference between the two images, the base image and the Photoshop-enhanced image, shown in the color insert, is dramatic.

Figure 43.1
"Harley," by Phillip Williams.

ImagePals

ImagePals, although it lacks the sophistication of Photoshop, is a workhorse. Its image-editing capabilities combine scanner support and a full compliment of editing tools with ease of use. The program is more than image-editing software. It is a media-management program. ImagePals provides image tracking with its album feature, file conversions, and a capture program that boasts enhanced post-processing. ImagePals created many of the captures for the figures in this book.

Typestry

Typestry enables you to apply 3D effects to TrueType and Type 1 fonts. You can add a variety of finishes, as well as blur, and add patterns, shadows, lighting, embossing, and cutouts to a string of text. The resulting bitmap can be imported back into CorelDRAW to enhance documents. The plaque effect shown in figure 43.2 was created by combining 3D text from Typestry with a PowerClip effect from CorelDRAW.

3D Rendering Software

The face of the graphics software industry is changing constantly. One of the newer applications on the graphics scene is 3D modeling and rendering software, which was once confined to mainframe computers.

Figure 43.2

An image created with Typestry and CorelDRAW.

Visual Reality

Visual Reality is a powerful 3D rendering suite. The suite enables you to create realistic 3D effects, including texture mapping, modeling, animation, font effects, and 2D mapping to a 3D object. The book shown in figure 43.3 was rendered in Visual Reality and imported into CorelDRAW as a Targa image. Lens effects were applied to create the aged look, and the title was added using extruded text.

Figure 43.3
An image created using Visual Reality and CorelDRAW.

Paint and Special-Effects Packages

Paint and special-effects packages enable you to add bitmapped images to your documents. Most paint packages, such as CorelPHOTO-PAINT and Fractal Design Painter, also serve as image-editing packages, providing versatility not found in all image-editing packages. Third-party add-on packages such as Kai's Power Tools and ImageCels have made their way to the marketplace, enabling you to expand packages that support bitmapped effects. ImageCels is a package of high resolution bitmaps that can be used as fills and to apply textures in paint packages that support third-party texture mapping. Kai's Power Tools enables you to apply special-effects filters to bitmapped images.

Fractal Design Painter

Fractal Design Painter is a full-featured paint program offering scanner support as well as a number of image-enhancement tools. The image in figure 43.4 was scanned in CorelPHOTO-PAINT and imported into Fractal Design Painter. Texturing was added to the image, and it was imported into CorelDRAW.

Figure 43.4

An image created using Fractal Design Painter and CorelDRAW.

Kai's Power Tools

Kai's Power Tools is a special effects utility designed to work with a number of paint and image-editing packages, including CorelPHOTO-PAINT. The image in figure 43.5 was scanned in CorelPHOTO-PAINT. Kai's bright glass lens was applied to the image to create the ball effect. The image was then imported into CorelDRAW, and a powerclip was applied to smooth and further define the round shape. A 30-percent cyan color add lens was applied over the ball to achieve the final effect.

Figure 43.5
An image created using Kai's Power Tools with CorelPHOTO-PAINT and CorelDRAW.

Microsoft Word for Windows 6.0

Microsoft Word for Windows 6.0 is an OLE2-compliant word processing package. OLE2 provides interconnectivity between CorelDRAW and MS Word, enabling you to import text with the ease of drag and drop, or export images from CorelDRAW to MS Word documents. Most of the imported text shown in this book was imported from MS Word 6.0.

Publishing Packages

Publishing packages pull everything together into a neat package to send to press. Using style sheets and other formatting options you can include both text and graphics into documents. Publishing packages enable you to create even lengthy documents with ease. CorelVENTURA, PageMaker, and FrameMaker represent some of the most powerful publishing packages on the market today.

CorelVENTURA

CorelVENTURA Publisher has broken new ground by providing seamless integration between text and graphics. This powerful application, currently packaged with CorelDRAW, has a new interface that provides new ease to those familiar with CorelDRAW's interface. CorelVENTURA still maintains the power that previous Ventura Publisher users enjoy. For more information about using CorelDRAW and CorelVENTURA Publisher, see Part II, "CorelVENTURA."

PageMaker and FrameMaker

PageMaker and FrameMaker are two of the largest names in publishing packages. Both provide enormous power in layout and pre-press capabilities for documents of any length and ideally for use in either of these packages. Although these two publishing packages support a number of graphics formats, graphics should be exported as .EPS files from CorelDRAW to achieve the best results.

Winfax Pro

Sending comps to clients in a timely manner can be difficult. You can, however, designate Winfax Pro as a printer, enabling you to send documents directly from your application to a client. Images from CorelDRAW are transferred quickly and easily by this method. Although the quality of the print of an image faxed from CorelDRAW is not equal to the quality produced by other methods of printing, such images do not have the jaggies common to most faxed images.

PinPoint Error Reporter

PinPoint Error Reporter is a highly recommended PostScript error reporter. By downloading PinPoint to your printer prior to printing, you can identify and eliminate potential PostScript errors. CorelDRAW enables you to create rather complex images. Finding an object that creates a PostScript error among thousands of other objects can be a tedious task. PinPoint gives you the precise coordinates of an offending object, enabling you to modify the image to eliminate the problem. PinPoint Error Reporter was used extensively in this book to check for potential postscript output errors.

Summary

The demands placed upon graphic artists are increasing daily. The graphics software industry is changing rapidly, however, to meet those needs by providing a broad assortment of tools. Choosing the right software for a particular job is like choosing the right tools to build a house. You would not use a handsaw in place of a powersaw to cut large quantities of wood. Similarly, image-editing applications are more appropriate for photo-editing than CorelDRAW. The expanded features of publishing packages and 3D applications enable you to produce excellent results. Two of CorelDRAW's strengths are its importing and exporting abilities that provide connectivity to other applications. By using these packages in conjunction with one another and CorelDRAW, the excellent can become spectacular with a minimum amount of effort. CorelDRAW provides an eclectic assortment of tools in its application suite.

Part VII

Managing Your System and Files

Customizing Your Computer for CorelDRAW

*T*here is an ongoing battle between the growth of the software and hardware industries. Each new generation of computers creates the potential for more powerful software; more powerful software requires larger and faster computers. An end to this battle does not appear to be in sight.

CorelDRAW 4.0 and 5.0 are two of the most powerful graphics packages on the market. They require larger computer systems to take full advantage of their capabilities. Version 5.0 has greater requirements than version 4.0. The hardware and software recommendations in this chapter address those requirements, as well as the needs of the rest of the CorelDRAW suite of applications.

This chapter covers:

- System recommendations
- Ancillary hardware and software
- Optimizing memory
- Modifying SMARTDRV.EXE
- Temporary swap files
- Swap files and virtual memory
- Looking at TSRs, networks, and 32-bit access

Examining System Recommendations

The following list shows you the minimum requirements needed to operate CorelDRAW 5.0, along with the *recommended* minimum and optimum requirements that are readily available on the market.

- **Base CPU.** CorelDRAW uses the math coprocessor extensively for various functions within the program. The program will operate on a system without a math coprocessor, but some functions will remain unavailable.

  Minimum: 386DX-40MHz (with math coprocessor)

  Minimum recommended: 486DX2-50MHz

  Optimum: Pentium, any speed

- **Bus type.** Each of these bus types handles data transfer differently. They are listed in order of performance speed with CorelDRAW.

  Minimum: AT-ISA

  Minimum recommended: VESA Local Bus

  Optimum: PCI

- **RAM.** RAM prices fluctuate constantly. The requirements of software continue to go up. Larger amounts of RAM mean more speed.

  Minimum: 4MB

  Minimum recommended: 16MB

  Optimum: 32MB or more

- **Video adapters.** When purchasing a video adapter, be aware that even a new adapter can come bundled with drivers that are out of date. CorelDRAW is very sensitive to video adapters. Some brands currently are known to cause problems.

  Minimum: SVGA accelerator (ISA bus) with 1MB RAM capable of at least 65KB colors at 800×600 pixels/inch (except ATI, Diamond, and Orchid due to nonstandard methods of obtaining acceleration)

  Minimum recommended: STB Pegasus VLB with 2MB RAM (several VLB cards have been reported to have problems with Corel, mostly with outdated drivers)

  Optimum: STB Pegasus PCI with 2MB RAM or Matrox MGA II 2+ (PCI bus)

- **Hard drive.** Graphics files are large. A 5MB file can create a 20MB TEMP file during printing. Photo-CD and bitmap files frequently are larger.

  Minimum: 120MB IDE or SCSI

  Minimum recommended: 540MB IDE or SCSI with SCSI-2 controller (VLB controllers are highly recommended because of increased transfer rates)

  Optimum: 1.5GB or larger IDE or SCSI (VLB or PCI controllers highly recommended because of increased transfer rate)

- **Floppy drives.** Although floppy drives are available in both of the size formats listed below, it is common to see systems today configured with a single 3.5" floppy drive.

Minimum: 1.2MB 5 1/4-inch or 1.44MB 3 1/2-inch drives

Recommended: 1.2MB 5 1/4-inch and 1.44MB 3 1/2-inch drives

- **Pointing devices.** A wide range of pointing devices is available. Digitizer tablets are more attuned to working with graphics applications than other types of devices. CorelDRAW has features that support pressure-sensitive digitizers.

Minimum: Microsoft-compatible mouse

Recommended minimum: Pressure-sensitive digitizer tablet

Never recommended: Trackballs are not recommended devices for use with CorelDRAW, because they lack the precision control desired for optimum use of the program.

- **Display devices.** A number of brands and types of monitors exist in the marketplace today. Prices can vary widely. Flat screen monitors are easier on the eyes if you sit in front of a monitor for extended periods of time.

Minimum: 14-inch VGA

Recommended: 15-inch or 17-inch flat screen SVGA capable of 1024×768×256 colors (or better) with a .28 dot pitch and a 72 Hz refresh

- **CD-ROMs.** Corel 5 ships with either 2 CD-ROM discs or several floppies. Most memory-intensive programs like CorelDRAW will likely ship exclusively on CD-ROM in the future (you'll have to request floppies).

Therefore, a CD-ROM drive is highly recommended.

Minimum: Single speed

Recommended: Double speed

Optimum: Quad speed (4x)

Examining Recommended Ancillary Hardware and Software

The following list shows recommended hardware for running CorelDRAW:

- 2x (or better) CD-ROM (XA and PhotoCD compatible)

- 1,200 dpi (or better) TWAIN-compliant flatbed scanner

- 600 dpi PostScript-2 laser printer

- 14.4 v.32bis fax/modem

- 16-bit or 16-bit DSP (Digital Sound Processor) sound card (sound card for use with SHOW and MOVE)

- Tape backup or SyQuest removable tape drive

The following list shows recommended software for use with CorelDRAW:

- Minimum operating system: MS-DOS 5.0 or later

- Recommended operating system: MS-DOS 6.2 or later

- Minimum operating environment: Microsoft Windows 3.1

- Recommended operating environment: Microsoft Windows 3.11 (Windows for Workgroups should be avoided unless necessary for running on a network, due to poor speed performance. Also, OS/2 has been reported as being incompatible with CorelDRAW 5.0)

- CorelSCSI V2.*x* (or later)

- Defragging utility (Norton)

- WinProbe or WinSleuth Gold (to aid in system optimization)

- WinZip 5.0b

- PKZip 2.04g

Optimizing Memory Exclusion

Note the memory address of peripheral cards that are memory addressable. If this is not possible, run MSD (included with Win31 or later) to find the address ranges where these cards are residing.

Load peripheral cards as high in memory as possible. (Address a SCSI card at E000h, for example.) If there is more than one card, follow this procedure:

1. Install the first card.

2. Run MSD to identify how much memory was used.

3. Set the next card at the next highest address. (When installing a SCSI card and a scanner card in a system, for example, address the SCSI card at E000h. Running MSD shows that it takes up memory from E000 to somewhere past E400. Set the scanner card for E800h.) In the CONFIG.SYS, modify your EMM386.EXE statement to read `DEVICE=C:\DOS\EMM386.EXE X=E000-EFFF NOEMS`.

N O T E

Step three only applies to MS-DOS 5.0. With MS-DOS 6.*x*, run MEMMAKER and have it place your CD-ROM and drivers in the highest-possible memory address. Scan XMS aggressively and reclaim monochrome memory addresses.

You also should modify your Windows SYSTEM.INI `[386Enh]` section, as shown in the following line:

`EMMExclude=E000-E7FF`

N O T E

It is only necessary to make this change to the SYSTEM.INI if you are running MS-DOS 5.0. MS-DOS 6.*x* makes the change if you answer Yes to its question about Windows and provide it with the complete path statement for Windows.

Modifying SMARTDRV.EXE

If you are using MS-DOS 5.0, you can improve Windows' performance significantly by turning off the Write-Behind option. Edit your AUTOEXEC.BAT to reflect the following:

```
C:\DOS\SMARTDRV.EXE C-
```

You also can improve performance by specifying the amount of XMS memory that SMARTDRV.EXE can use for its cache in DOS and in Windows. Modify your SMARTDRV.EXE statement in your AUTOEXEC.BAT:

```
C:\DOS\SMARTDRV.EXE C- 1024 1024
```

The first number is the size of the cache in DOS and the second is the size in Windows. (The default is 1024KB for DOS and 512KB for Windows if you have 4MB of RAM. The cache increases with the amount of RAM available. Tests have shown that a cache of 1024KB of XMS memory is the optimum amount, however, regardless of the amount of RAM on the system. In fact, tests have shown that an increase above that amount degrades performance of disk read/writes in Windows.)

Understanding the Temporary Swap File

MS-DOS 5.0 and later attempt to set up a temporary swap file—also known a TEMP environment statement—in your AUTOEXEC.BAT file. The default location is C:\DOS. If everything was stable and Windows never crashed, this would be fine. However, whenever there is a GPF (general protection fault) or a fatal error in a Windows program, any temporary files that were open are likely to be left behind, cluttering up your hard drive. GPF or other errors can cause a zero-byte TEMP file. These files can cause problems with Windows and should be deleted as soon as possible.

The ideal solution is to have a hard drive or a drive partition reserved for temporary or permanent swap files (this reserved space is known as *virtual memory*). Failing that, the next best solution is to set up a directory for your temporary swap file, and to have it wiped clean each time you boot the computer.

To do this, first create a TEMP directory on your hard drive. Then open your AUTOEXEC.BAT file in an ASCII editor and change the TEMP variable from SET TEMP C:\DOS\TEMP to SET TEMP C:\TEMP.

The next time you boot your computer, any temporary files will be written to this directory. This is true of most programs. Some applications, like Word for Windows, have a habit of opening TEMP files in unusual places.

To get your computer to clean itself each time you boot up, add this line as the last line of your AUTOEXEC.BAT file:

```
ERASE C:\TEMP\*.TMP
```

This line erases any stray TEMP files that still are in your TEMP directory when you boot your computer. If there are no files, you see a File Not Found error message.

Using a Permanent Swap File or Virtual Memory

Windows attempts to create a permanent swap file that it calls *virtual memory*. Windows uses this as a holding area to swap pieces of program code, as needed, in and out of physical memory. This swap file also serves as a buffer, while it performs file conversions, printer spooling, and other memory-intensive chores.

Virtual memory is similar to RAM. Up to a point, the more RAM you have, the faster Windows operates. The formula Windows generally uses to calculate virtual memory is one-half of contiguous hard drive space or (RAM*2)+1/4th RAM—whichever is greater. If a system has 8MB of RAM and 100MB of free hard drive space, for example, Windows tries to reserve 50MB for virtual memory. If you chose a temporary swap file, it only allows 15MB.

Although you might have 50MB of virtual memory, 16–20MB is a more realistic number. Unless you have applications that specifically require more virtual memory, you should not require more than this amount. Higher amounts of virtual memory actually can slow down the Windows environment with excess drive access, depending on what is loaded into memory from the WIN.INI and SYSTEM.INI files.

Using 32-Bit Access

One way to improve Windows performance is to enable 32-bit disk access. Before attempting to enable this option, you need to do the following:

1. Open the Windows Control Panel in the Main Program Group and open 386 Enhanced by double-clicking on it.

2. Click on the Virtual Memory button. If it does not say `Type: Permanent` (using 32-bit access), click on the Change button.

3. Change the type to None and then click on OK. Do not restart Windows at this point. Back out of everything, including Windows, to the DOS prompt.

4. Run CHKDSK (MS-DOS 5.0) or ScanDisk (MS-DOS 6.0) to reclaim any lost clusters. Then run disk-defragger software, such as Norton's Speed Disk or DEFRAG in MS-DOS 6.*x*. Defrag the entire disk, not just the fragmented files, to free as much hard drive space in one contiguous block as possible.

5. After the hard disk is optimized, open Windows and access the Virtual Memory dialog box. Click the 32-Bit Disk Access check box and select Permanent. If you think the size of the swap file is too big, you can change it

to the size you want. RAM*2 is highly recommended, if you have the room for it. Click on OK and restart Windows. You should notice a significant change in disk access.

Some older SCSI controllers will not allow 32-bit disk access because a driver or hardware limitation exists. Contact the manufacturer to see if there is an updated driver or other remedy.

Windows for Workgroups provides 32-bit disk access and 32-bit file access. Problems have been reported with using 32-bit file access, however, so it should be avoided.

N O T E

You cannot use removable media—Bernoullis, flopticals, and so on—as virtual memory, because Windows reserves the space for its exclusive use. Swapping to a disk that did not have those areas marked off in the disk's FAT would crash Windows.

According to Landmark's WinProbe, adding the following two lines increases Windows efficiency and helps minimize Network and TSR conflicts. You should add these lines to the [386enh] section of the Windows SYSTEM.INI file and then restart Windows:

```
Int28Critical=FALSE
UniqueDOSPSP=TRUE
```

Looking at TSRs and Networks

TSRs in both Windows and DOS should be limited to what is essential to run the system's hardware. This includes replacements for the Program Manager (Norton Desktop, PC Tools for Windows, and so on), screen savers, memory-resident personal-information managers, and so on. Screen savers should be disabled prior to installing CorelDRAW.

If you intend to install CorelDRAW on a network, it is recommended that Windows for Workgroups be run on a Novell NetWare network. Even MS-DOS 6.*x* is not capable of truly coping with a network environment.

Summary

Selecting and configuring your hardware and operating environment provides an optimal setup for both CorelDRAW and other Windows applications. This is the first step toward ensuring that CorelDRAW operates properly and efficiently. After you have configured your operating system, you can complete the setup by configuring CorelDRAW, as discussed in the following chapter.

Chapter 45

Customizing CorelDRAW for Optimum Performance

One of the key components to CorelDRAW's immense power is its versatility. You can customize the program for the way you work and the requirements of your business or the job at hand. Not every user has the same needs and it would be impossible to detail all the different ways CorelDRAW can be configured in this book.

Explanations are provided to help you configure CorelDRAW to meet your specific requirements.

This chapter covers:

- Speed, resources, and system capabilities

- Production needs for various applications

- Output for screen, in-house printers, and presswork

- Creative control

Inside CorelDRAW

Chapter 1, "Features of CorelDRAW," provided an overview on options found in the Preferences dialog box and the **V**iew menu. The settings that follow are more detailed, as well as more need- and system-specific.

The Preferences Dialog Box

Look once more at the property sheets in the Preferences dialog box. Most of the settings available in the Preferences dialog box are efficiency settings. These settings can take minutes and hours off design time, enabling you to create, rather than fiddle with, the program.

The General Property Sheet

The General property sheet contains the following settings:

- **Place Duplicates and Clones:** When most artists create an image, the relationship between objects takes priority over the relationship between the object and the page. The latter is reserved for larger sections of the image or the finished drawing. A number of excellent methods are available to position objects on the page. It is generally more efficient to place duplicates and clones one on top of the other by setting the **H**orizontal and Ve**r**tical settings to 0.0". The default for this setting is .25" Horizontal and Vertical. Use the other methods to move the object on the page. Using this setting provides more control over the relationship between the original object and its duplicate or clone.

- **Nudge:** Nu**d**ge was never intended to move objects a significant distance. Its primary purpose is to offset objects slightly or to provide the means for small-step and repeat operations. The setting here should be what you do most often. If you offset objects frequently by small amounts, set Nu**d**ge to .001" or .01". The default setting for Nu**d**ge is .01". The small incremental amounts enable you to fine-tune the placement of objects. Note that if you set nudge for .001", you may find it difficult to see the difference of a single move. If you perform many step and repeat operations, set the value for the amount you most commonly use.

- **Constrain Angle:** The default value for this setting is 15°. Most of the angles one finds in the real world are increments of a 15-degree angle. This is the most convenient and popular angle for the constrain-value setting. The next most popular angle is 5°, but this setting can slow down creation a bit.

- **Miter Limit:** The default value for the miter limit is 45°. This value is probably the optimum setting as well. Settings below this value create more complex objects, which is a consideration at print time. Settings above this value can create some visually unpleasant results. This is most noticeable with artistic text that is set at large point sizes. Sans serif, bold fonts, such as Swiss, can appear to have points jutting out of sharp corners. This is caused by the line extending beyond the corners. At small sizes, the font looks dirty.

■ **Undo Levels:** The default value for Undo is 4. Even if you have significant resources, keep this number as low as possible. In addition to putting an enormous drain on your resources, temp file space, and swap file space, every operation you perform writes to the hard drive. The continuous accessing of the hard drive slows down the operation of the program as it swaps data in and out of memory.

■ **Right Mouse Button:** If you work in a high-production environment, using styles and templates reduces layout and creation time considerably. Selecting the Object menu as the function for the right mouse button enables you to quickly apply styles. The Object menu is the default right mouse function.

The View Property Sheet

The View property sheet contains the following settings:

■ **Auto-Panning:** If you are working with multipage documents, enabling Auto-**P**anning is beneficial. Any object you position off the printable page, in the desktop portion of the drawing window, is placed on the desktop layer. The desktop layer is like a virtual on-screen holding area. Objects placed here are available for all pages of a document. When you enable

Auto-**P**anning, you can place and edit objects held in this area more easily. By default, Auto-**P**anning is enabled.

■ **Interruptible Refresh:** Enabling Interruptible Refresh is invaluable when working with complex files or when creation and layout speed are an issue. This setting enables you to halt the refresh in order to continue editing an object. The drawback is that CorelDRAW refreshes the screen from back to front. If the object being edited has many objects overlapping it, you might have to wait for a partial screen refresh to see the object in Editable Preview.

■ **Manual Refresh:** One way around the problem associated with Interruptible Refresh is to enable **M**anual Refresh when editing a complex image. Although none of the editing will become visible until you force a refresh, you can perform multiple edits without waiting. This feature is especially effective when using the Transformation roll-up to perform operations on several objects. By default this option is disabled.

■ **Cross Hair Cursor:** By default CorelDRAW uses a cursor that appears as an arrow. By enabling Cross H**a**ir Cursor, you can change that cursor to a thin cross hair. This is especially useful when precision placement is important.

■ **Preview Fountain Steps:** The value set here affects SCODL files and the screen appearance. If you are not dealing with SCODL files, it is

recommended that you leave the number of steps at a reasonably low number. The default value is 20 steps. Preview Fountain Steps is an extremely memory-intensive feature. On slower systems, higher values can cause lengthy screen-refresh times. Although 20 steps can cause a banded on-screen appearance, the screen refresh time is more acceptable for most purposes. The ideal method of using this option is to leave the setting at a low number while creating the initial design. Change the setting to a higher value between 90 and 120 for the final tuning of the image. Note that the number of fountain steps you set in the Fill dialog box overrides any setting made here.

■ **Show Status Line:** This setting is enabled by default. You should never disable this feature. The information displayed on the status line is critical to editing and layout. Disabling this feature decreases editing and layout efficiency.

■ **Show Ribbon Bar:** The ribbon bar contains buttons for the most commonly used commands. Using the ribbon bar provides more efficient operation of the program. Several programs are available that enable you to edit this command bar. By default this option is enabled. For more information about these programs, see Chapter 43, "Using CorelDRAW with Other Applications."

■ **Show Menu & Tool Help:** By default this option is enabled. With this option enabled a help message appears in the Status Line regarding features, commands, and so on as your cursor travels over the item. If you want to know quickly the function of a button or command, simply point at it with the cursor to display the associated help message in the Status Line.

■ **Show Pop-Up Help:** Show Pop-Up Help is used as an alternative if you don't want to display the Status Line, but you still want the help messages to appear. By default this option is enabled. To receive help on the function of a command or button, point at it with the cursor to display the associated help message in a balloon. If Show Menu & Tool Help is enabled, it takes precedence and the help message appears in the Status Line.

The Curves Property Sheet

The Curves property sheet contains the following settings:

■ **Freehand Tracking:** The value you enter in Freehand Tracking should reflect the equipment you use and the steadiness of your hand. The default value is 5 pixels, which is not generally suitable for most people. Drawing a smooth curve with a mouse requires a very steady hand. A value of five pixels or less creates a rough curve with a number of nodes. The complexity of an object goes up with the number of nodes. This creates larger files and can cause printing problems. Cleaning up a curve is time consuming. A more realistic setting is eight or nine pixels if you are using a mouse. A stylus and digitizer pad are controlled more easily, but the default value is still high. Consider setting the value at 6 or 7 pixels when using a stylus.

- **Autotrace Tracking:** This setting enables you to determine how closely you want the Bézier curve to follow the edges of a bitmap during on-screen tracing. The default for this setting is 5 pixels, which provides medium tracking. A low setting of 1 to 3 pixels follows the edges more precisely, where a large setting of 8 to 10 pixels loosely follows the edge of the bitmap.

- **Corner Threshold:** This setting enables you to control how corners respond when you are drawing a line with the Freehand Pencil tool or while tracing a bitmap. The default for this setting is 5 pixels. Settings lower than the default tend to result in more cusps on a line; settings greater than the default produce more flowing Bézier curves.

- **Straight Line Threshold:** This setting controls the tolerances that determine whether the program draws a straight line or a curve segment when using the Freehand Pencil tool or performing an autotrace. The default setting is five pixels. Settings greater than the default produce more straight lines, whereas settings lower than the default produce more curves.

- **AutoJoin:** Ends of lines behave like magnets attracting the end point of lines being drawn, causing lines to be joined. This setting determines the radius within which lines are automati-

cally joined when you draw a line with the freehand or Bézier pencil tool. The default for this setting is five pixels. AutoJoin Controls the AutoJoin radius when drawing in Freehand or Bezier mode. If the starting point of a new line falls within the setting you make here, the lines are automatically joined.

- **Auto-Reduce:** Auto-Reduce is especially important when importing traced bitmap images. Tracing frequently creates an unacceptably high number of nodes, which creates an object that can create printing problems. PostScript devices are sensitive to the complexity threshold of an image. If there is an excessive amount of nodes, or two or more complex objects overlap, a PostScript error can occur and the file will not print. The default value for Auto-Reduce is .004". This value might not reduce the nodes sufficiently to avoid printing problems. If the value is too high, however, the image can be distorted. For most uses, a value of .05" reduces the number of nodes sufficiently without compromising the image.

- **Min. Extrude Facet Size:** This setting enables you to control the minimum facet depth the program draws when it creates an extrusion. The facet size is the distance between shades of color in an extrusion. The default setting is .125". You can adjust the setting as desired between .01" and .5". Settings greater than the default setting reduce screen refresh time, but also reduce the quality of the illustration's appearance. Settings lower than the default setting increase the refresh time, but create a

greater quality appearance. If refresh speed is an issue, increase the setting while you are creating an image, then lower the setting before printing the image.

The Text Property Sheet

The Text property sheet contains the following settings:

- **Calligraphic Text:** Calligraphic **T**ext creates large files when exporting using a vector format or when transferring data across the Clipboard. The default for this option is enabled. If speed and file size are an issue, disable this option.

- **Text in Metafile:** This setting is important if you work frequently with other applications. The default for this option is disabled. If you need to edit text in another application, this option should be enabled.

The Advanced Property Sheet

The Advanced property sheet contains the following settings:

- **Make Backup on Save:** It is generally a good idea to enable this option. If system resources drop and cause a GPF, the current file might become corrupted. Having the backup file and saving frequently can minimize the amount of work lost. The backup file is saved in the directory with the original file and has a BAK extension. To open this file, rename it with a CDR extension.

- **AutoBackup:** **A**utoBackup is designed primarily for people who forget to save frequently. The default value saves the file every 10 minutes. If you are working with a complex file, the frequency of the backup can interfere with your work by causing delays while the file is saved. Consider resetting this value for 30 minutes. If you want to disable **A**utoBackup, enter a value of 0 minutes. A backup file is saved in the AUTOBACK directory with an ABK extension. To open this file, rename it as you would a BAK file.

- **Preview Colors:** None of the choices for this option affects printing; however, they do affect screen-refresh speed. These options are device dependent, and may not be available for your video card. Video accelerator cards frequently do not support 256-color dithering, which provides the fastest screen refresh. They have proprietary palettes optimized for Windows use.

- **Full-Screen Preview:** Optimized Palette for Full-Screen Preview is also device dependent, with the same restrictions as Preview Colors. This does not mean that you will not be able to view pure color renderings in full screen preview, however. Most video accelerator cards support 24-bit or true-color displays.

- **High-Resolution Rotated Bitmaps:** Enabling this feature improves the screen appearance of bitmaps, but is memory intensive. The default for this option is enabled. Unless you require a high-resolution display, disable this option. This decreases screen-refresh time. When this option is disabled, CorelDRAW displays a thumbnail of the bitmap. The dots per inch of the bitmap thumbnail is approximately 1/256ᵗʰ of the original bitmap.

The View Menu

The View menu contains the following settings:

- **Color Palette:** Displays the color model or color-matching system you want to use for your image. The default for this option is **U**niform Colors. If you are creating an image for on-screen presentation, use the RGB palette. For four-color spot applications, such as screen printing or halftone screening output, display the Pantone **S**pot Color palette. For other printed output, display one of the process palettes. Choosing the correct palette for your output and using it exclusively within an image allows for more successful output. Mixing palettes within an image can be costly, both in the consistency of the output and in film costs at press time.

- **Bitmaps:** Both the visible and high-resolution options are memory-associated options. By default both the **V**isible and **H**igh Resolution options are enabled. When **V**isible is disabled, it does not affect Editable Preview. The bitmap appears as an empty rectangle in Wireframe view, enabling you to edit your image more easily. When **H**igh Resolution is disabled, CorelDRAW displays bitmaps as

thumbnails in Editable Preview. For maximum resource conservation and speed both of these options should be disabled.

N O T E

When you add presets, styles, or fills, or customize any CorelDRAW feature, you should create a backup of the file as an archive copy. If you need to reinstall, you can copy these files back to their respective directories and data will not be lost.

Editing Configurable Files

There are a number of configurable files you can edit in CorelDRAW to modify the way the program functions. To edit these files, open them in the Windows Notepad.

W A R N I N G

Before editing any configurable files, take the following precautions:

- Make a backup of the file. This minimizes the possibility of having to reinstall the program.

- Make a backup of the new configuration file as an archive after editing it.

- Approach editing a configurable file with EXTREME caution. You should not edit any configuration without being certain of the results.

CORELDRW.DOT

Editing this file enables you to create up to 40 line styles. You can choose from 15 preconfigured lines. All the characters, whether dots or dashes, are described as dots. For example, 4 1 5 1 10 describes a line with 4 basic elements. The first element is 1 dot in length, followed by 5 spaces, followed by an element 1 dot in length, followed by 10 spaces. To add a new line to the file, enter the numeric equivalent on a separate line. Put a single space between each of the numbers. Do not delete the `END OF FILE` statement at the end of the file.

CORELAPP.INI

Only the entries shown should be edited. Some of the entries are configured in the Preferences dialog box or in selections you make during a CorelDRAW session.

`[Config]`
`BigPalette=0`

0 is the default for this option. Selecting 1 toggles a larger display of the palette. This is useful with 1024×768 or higher displays on 17-inch monitors or smaller.

`BigToolbox=0`

0 is the default for this option. Selecting 1 toggles a larger display of the palette. This is useful with 1024×768 or higher displays on 17-inch monitors or smaller.

`FontRasterizer=1`

0 is the default for this option. Selecting 1 enables CorelDRAW to send fonts as bitmaps to non-PostScript printers.

`TTFOptimization=1`

0 is the default for this option. Selecting 1 enables CorelDRAW to optimize TrueType fonts for printing.

`TextureMaxSize=900`

257 is the default for this option. You can enter a value of up to 1280. This improves the appearance of texture bitmap fills on-screen, but does not affect printing. This is memory sensitive. The value you enter here should take system resources into consideration. The higher the value, the slower the refresh time.

`UseClippingForFills=0`

0 is the default value for this option. Select 1 if you are experiencing difficulty printing to inkjet or dot-matrix printers.

Summary

Custom configuring CorelDRAW increases productivity while enabling you to maintain control. In many cases the settings for speed and other requirements, such as creative control, are the same. Most settings are dependent on the type of final output you select for your image. The operation of CorelDRAW, like other high-end graphics packages, relies heavily upon the type of system you are operating, your resources, and your Windows configuration. Font management impacts the operation of Windows and CorelDRAW. The following chapter discusses font management and other font-related concerns.

Font Management

CorelDRAW supports fonts in WFN, TrueType, and Adobe Type 1 formats. WFN was the primary outline font format in earlier versions of CorelDRAW. When you install version 5.0, you are given the option to install a selection from more than 825 fonts in TrueType and Adobe Type 1 format. These formats are the most popular font formats on the market today.

If you install all the fonts in both formats, the number of fonts would exceed 1,600 and would take up a large amount of hard disk space. This also would make it impossible for Windows to operate. Every font you install adds a line to the WIN.INI, which has a maximum size of 64KB. It is a good policy to keep the number of fonts small in order for Windows to operate properly.

This creates a font-management dilemma of having fonts you want readily available, while maintaining optimum Windows operation. CorelDRAW provides a set of font-management and other font utilities for your use. Font-management programs such as FontMinder enable you to maintain fonts in manageable sets and have them available on-the-fly.

This chapter covers:

- Using font-management programs, such as Adobe Type Manager and Fontminder

- Using PANOSE font matching

- Using CorelKERN

Font-Management Programs

Even with the best font management, it is impossible to maintain every font available on the market. CorelDRAW provides PANOSE font matching to meet this need. PANOSE font matching automatically substitutes fonts when a file is opened in CorelDRAW that contains fonts not installed on your system.

CorelKERN also is packaged with the font-management applications in CorelDRAW. This program gives you the capability to control kerning of PostScript fonts.

The CD-ROM that came packaged with CorelDRAW contains all the 825 fonts in Type 1 and TrueType formats. In order to use Type 1 fonts, you must have Adobe Type Manager installed on your system. CorelDRAW's setup program installs and performs the setup for TrueType fonts. Type 1 fonts must be installed manually using Adobe Type Manager or a font manager such as FontMinder.

The Windows Control Panel

If you want to add third-party or custom TrueType fonts, you need to use the Windows TrueType Font procedure or a third-party font manager. To add a font using the Windows Control Panel, follow these steps:

1. Access the Fonts dialog box by double-clicking the font icon.

2. Click on Add and enter the path for the font.

3. Select the font you want to add and click on OK. The font is added to your WINDOWS\SYSTEM directory and a line is added to your WIN.INI.

4. Restart Windows.

Using Adobe Type Manager

To install Type 1 fonts, follow these steps:

1. Run the ATM control panel.

2. Click on Add, and then select the FONTS\TYPE1 directory on CorelDRAW CD-ROM Disk 2. The subdirectories are arranged alphabetically. Choose the subdirectory you want.

3. Select the fonts you want to install and click on Add.

4. Close ATM and restart Windows.

N O T E

For more information about using Adobe Type Manager, consult the manual that came with the program.

Using FontMinder

An introductory version of FontMinder is included with CorelDRAW. FontMinder enables you to install and manage fonts without having to restart Windows. The fonts do not have to be in the WINDOWS\SYSTEM directory unless they are in use, which enables you to trim the font section of the WIN.INI to a manageable size.

FontMinder packages fonts into bundles that you specify. If you have the full package, it enables you to associate these font packs with documents. This means that each time the document is opened, FontMinder makes sure that the necessary fonts are installed and ready to use.

To install FontMinder, follow these steps:

1. Choose **R**un from the **F**ile menu of the Program Manager. Specify the path for your CD-ROM drive. FontMinder is located on Disk 1 in the FONTMINDER directory.

2. In the Command Line text box, type **d:\fontmnder\setup** (where *d* is the letter of your CD-ROM drive) and click on OK.

3. The setup program prompts you for the directory where you want to install FontMinder. Enter the directory and path, and click on Continue.

4. Click on OK to exit from setup after FontMinder is installed.

The FontMinder Master Library

FontMinder maintains a database of all the fonts currently available on your system. When you install FontMinder, you need to create the database by letting FontMinder search your hard disk for fonts. Depending on the size of your hard disk and the number of fonts you have installed, this can take a few minutes. You also can specify directories you want FontMinder to search by clicking on Continue and entering the path.

FontMinder is an intuitive program that uses drag-and-drop functions. Open FontMinder by double-clicking its icon in the Windows Program Manager. To use FontMinder, click on the button in the center of the dialog box that corresponds with the operation you want to perform (see fig. 46.1). A new dialog box appears corresponding to the function you select.

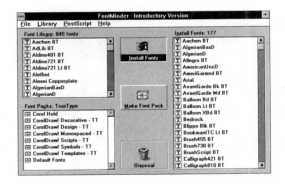

Figure 46.1

FontMinder's opening screen.

To create a font pack, follow these steps:

1. Click on the Make Font Pack button to move all the font families to the list box on the left. Each font family can contain up to four kinds of fonts: normal, bold, italic, and bold italic. Double-click a font name to see what font styles are available for a given font.

2. Select the fonts you want to add to the font pack, by holding down the shift key while clicking on them. If the fonts you want are not consecutive, depress the Ctrl key while selecting the fonts. Drag them to the Install Fonts list box on the right. To remove a font, drag it to the Disposal icon at the bottom of the screen. This only removes the item from the list. It does not delete the file.

3. Add and remove fonts from the Install Fonts list box until you have the fonts listed that you want to include in the font pack.

N O T E

Every font listed in the Install Fonts list box will be included in the font pack. If you only want to include part of a font family, double-click on the font family in the Font Library list box to display the available styles. Drag the font styles you want to the Font Pack Fonts list box. Avoid the temptation of creating large font packs. The concept of FontMinder is to create small, manageable packages of fonts. A package of 20 to 25 font families is ideal.

4. Choose **S**ave Font Pack As from the **F**ile menu. The Save Font Pack dialog box appears.

5. Enter a file name for your font pack. If you are creating a number of font packs, also be sure to enter a name in the Long Name text box (see fig. 46.2). You can enter up to 32 characters in this box. This avoids confusion later regarding the contents of a font pack.

Figure 46.2

The Save Font Pack dialog box.

6. Click on OK to complete the operation and return to the FontMinder screen.

7. Repeat this operation to create all the fonts packs you want.

To install fonts, follow these steps:

1. Choose the font format you want to install from the **L**ibrary menu.

2. Click on the **I**nstall Fonts button.

3. Select and drag the fonts you want to install from the Font Library list box to the Installed Fonts list box. You can drag an individual font, a font family, or an entire font pack to the box.

4. Select the fonts you want to install from the Installed Fonts list box. Press Shift while clicking on fonts to select contiguous fonts; Press Ctrl while clicking on fonts to select noncontiguous fonts. To select all the fonts, right-click on a font or press Ctrl+/.

5. Remove any fonts you do not want on the list by clicking on them and dragging them to the Disposal icon.

N O T E

You can delete font files from your hard disk by dragging fonts from the Font Library to the disposal icon.

6. When the Installed Fonts list contains the fonts you want to install, double-click the Install Fonts button, press F5, or select Install Fonts from the File menu. A message box appears asking you to wait while the fonts are installed.

To display a sample of a font, follow these steps:

1. Double-click a font in any of FontMinder's list boxes (see fig. 46.3). To display TrueType fonts, TrueType must be enabled in the Windows Control Panel. To display Type 1 Fonts, ATM must be active.

Figure 46.3

The font sample display box.

2. To change the sample text, click on the text to set an insertion point. Type the text you want to see in the text display box (see fig. 46.4).

Figure 46.4

Changing the text in the font sample display box.

3. Click on the Font Data button to display the Font Data dialog box. The Font Data dialog box provides technical information about the font, including the TTF file name. This can be helpful in restoring a font, should one become corrupt.

4. Click on the Character Set button to display the Character Set dialog box. The Character Set dialog box lists the extended characters available for that font. If you click on a character, the corresponding character name and ANSI code number appear in the boxes at the bottom of the dialog box.

5. Click on Close to return to FontMinder's main screen.

Using FontMinder with PostScript Printers

PostScript fonts can be downloadable, driver-resident, or printer-resident. Downloadable fonts are sent to the printer's RAM when the printer is initialized for a specific print job. These fonts remain resident until the printer is turned off or reset.

FontMinder tracks driver-resident fonts, which are installed on your hard disk and are specific to each PostScript device. These fonts have associated calls stored on the printer's ROM. The font itself is not on the ROM.

Printer-resident fonts are stored on a printer's hard disk or on a font cartridge attached to the printer. Screen representations of these fonts reside on your hard disk. FontMinder cannot discern which fonts are driver-resident

and which fonts are printer-resident. You must specify manually printer-resident fonts for each PostScript printer.

To specify printer-resident fonts, follow these steps:

1. Consult your printer manual to determine which fonts are provided with the printer.

2. Choose Printer Resident **F**onts from the **P**ostScript menu to display the Printer Resident Fonts dialog box.

3. Remove from the Resident Font list fonts that are not associated with the printer for which you are configuring fonts.

4. Choose the printer from the **P**rinter to Update list box, for which you are designating fonts.

5. Select the fonts you want from the Font Library and drag them to the Printer Resident **F**onts list.

6. Click on OK to complete the operation. These fonts are not downloaded to the designated printer if you are using Windows-based software.

7. Repeat the process for each PostScript device.

To specify printer ports, follow these steps:

1. Choose Setup Printer Ports from the PostScript menu to display the Setup Printer Ports dialog box.

2. Check the port to include its resident-font settings when you install fonts in Windows, and select the associated printer.

3. Click on OK to save the changes and return to the FontMinder screen.

Using PANOSE Font Matching

PANOSE font matching enables you to substitute fonts that are not installed on your system. PANOSE options are set in the Text property sheet of the Preferences dialog box. When you open a file that contains an uninstalled font, you can choose a similar font to take its place (see fig. 46.5).

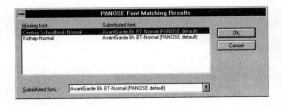

Figure 46.5

The PANOSE Font Matching Results dialog box.

You can accept the suggested font substitution or click the down arrow to access the Substituted Font drop-down list box to choose an alternative.

N O T E

PANOSE font substitution is enabled in the Preferences dialog box. For more information, see Chapter 1, "Features of CorelDRAW."

Using Alternate Spellings

The Alternate Spellings dialog box enables you to modify the substitution table that coordinates Windows and Macintosh font names (see fig. 46.6). You access the dialog box by clicking on PANOSE font matching, then Spellings. You can map a single Windows font name to a single Macintosh font name. To add an alternate spelling to the list, click on Add. The Add Alternate Spelling dialog box is displayed, enabling you to enter alternate spellings for Windows or Macintosh names. Click on OK to complete the operation. To remove an alternate spelling, select it and click on Remove.

Figure 46.6

The Alternate Spellings dialog box.

Font-Matching Exceptions

You can use the PANOSE Font Matching Exceptions dialog box to customize font substitutions—just choose a specific font you want to substitute for another font (see fig. 46.7). By default, this box is empty. To add an exception, click on Add and then select a font from the list box or enter the Missing Font and Substituted Font information in the box. Click on OK to save the entry.

Figure 46.7
The PANOSE Font Matching Exceptions dialog box.

CorelKERN

You edit the kerning of PostScript fonts by using CorelKERN, a new amendment to the CorelDRAW suite of applications. Although this stand-alone package is designed as an enhancement tool for CorelVENTURA Publisher (CVP), its basic function makes it useful for any application that uses PostScript fonts.

PostScript fonts are stored as PFM files, usually in a directory called PSFONTS. When you select automatic kerning from within VENTURA, the programs use the kerning information from these fonts. You can use CorelKERN to add, delete, adjust, and modify kern pairs of any PostScript font. The changes you make become a permanent part of the font information, so the modified font is available for use in any Windows application that supports PostScript fonts.

Using CorelKERN

Before using CorelKERN, it is important to make a backup copy of the current PFM files on your system. To use CorelKERN, follow these steps:

1. Start CorelKERN. The Load PFM File dialog box appears (see fig. 46.8).

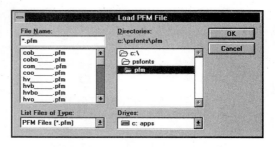

Figure 46.8
The CorelKERN Load PFM File dialog box.

2. Choose a PostScript font by clicking on it and click on OK. A list of the kern pairs appears (see fig. 46.9).

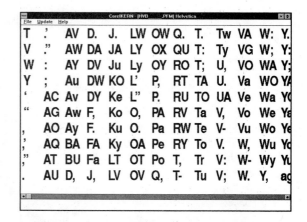

Figure 46.9
Viewing kern pairs.

3. Double-click the kern pair, or click the pair and choose **E**dit from the **U**pdate menu. The Edit Kern Pair dialog box

appears (see fig. 46.10). The kern pair you want to adjust appears in 12-, 18-, 24-, and 72-point type.

Figure 46.10
The Edit Kern Pair dialog box.

4. Adjust the kerning of the pair by entering a value in the Kerning Value box or by using the scroll bar to change the value. Moving the scroll box to the right increases the kerning; moving the scroll box to the left decreases the kerning. Click on OK to return to the main CorelKERN window.

5. Save the PFM file, or choose Save Kern Pair set to save the kern pair sets as an ASCII file. This procedure enables you to append or replace a kern pair set in another PFM file.

It is a good idea to print the kern pair to check the kerning before you save the file. When you save the file, you must overwrite the existing file or save it as one of the existing files in the WIN.INI fonts section. This method enables Windows to recognize the font. CorelKERN cannot create a new font.

The File Menu

The **F**ile menu contains commands for the basic management of the fonts and kern pairs:

- **O**pen: Loads a PFM file.

- **S**ave: Saves the current PFM file.

- **L**oad Kern Pair Set: Imports an ASCII kern pair set. If you choose Replace, the current kerning table is replaced with the ASCII kern pair set. Selecting Append adds the kern pair set to the current kerning table.

- Save **K**ern Pair Set: Saves the kern pair set as an ASCII file. You can open these files to replace other kern pair sets, or append the sets of another PFM file.

To adjust the kerning within an ASCII editor, follow these steps:

1. Load a kerned pair set that has been saved as an ASCII file.

2. Adjust the first line of each set by increasing or decreasing the percentage. The kern pair set becomes looser or tighter, respectively.

- **P**rint: Enables you to print examples of the select kern pair set and any kern pair sets that begin with the same first character. The kern pairs are printed in five sizes. You can enable Include Reference Lines to compare the effect of different kern values (see fig. 46.11). The vertical reference lines are printed six points apart with your examples.
- E**x**it: Exits the program.

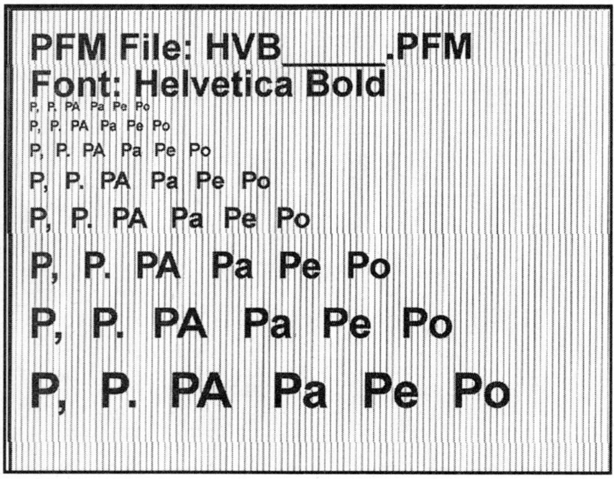

PFM File: HVB_____.PFM
Font: Helvetica Bold
P, P. PA Pa Pe Po
P, P. PA Pa Pe Po
P, P. PA Pa Pe Po
P, P. PA Pa Pe Po
P, P. PA Pa Pe Po
P, P. PA Pa Pe Po
P, P. PA Pa Pe Po
P, P. PA Pa Pe Po

Figure 46.11
Printed kern pairs with reference lines.

The Update Menu

The **U**pdate menu contains the editing commands used in CorelKERN:

- **A**dd: Enables you to add new kern pairs to the open list of kern pairs. You can add new kern pairs by entering ASCII, decimal, or hexadecimal values in their respective entry boxes. Decimal and hexadecimal values must be separated by a comma. You can add extended characters by using the decimal-input mode. Figure 46.12 shows the Add Kern Pair dialog box that appears after you choose **A**dd.

Add Kern Pair
Kern
ST
Ok
Type
Cancel
Asci
Decima
Hex

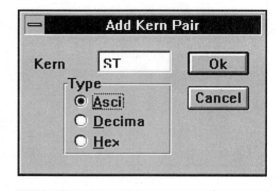

Figure 46.12
The Add Kern Pair dialog box.

- **E**dit: Opens the Edit Kern Pair dialog box, with the selected characters displayed. The Kern Pair dialog box allows you to adjust the kerning between the displayed pair.
- **D**elete: Deletes the selected characters from the current kern pair list.
- Change **S**ize: Changes the point size of the font displayed in the CorelKERN window (see fig. 46.13). The default is 24. The value must be 12 points or greater.

Figure 46.13
The Set Display Size dialog box.

- Change Count **F**actor: Enables you to change the unit radix. The count factor is the number of units to the EM. This is used to match kerned pairs to those available on other systems (see fig. 46.14).

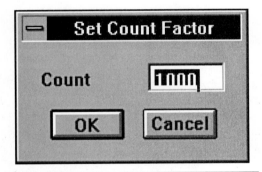

Figure 46.14
The Set Count Factor dialog box.

Summary

Font management is critical to the efficient operation of CorelDRAW and Windows. The font-management tool included with CorelDRAW gives you the flexibility and power to meet most of your font-management needs. Chapter 47, "Troubleshooting," covers basic strategies for solving complications or problems when working with CorelDRAW.

Troubleshooting

*O*ne of the pitfalls to any large program is that things can go wrong that require trouble-shooting. When the "program" is actually a suite of programs, such as the CorelDRAW suite, the potential for problems increases. Some of the problems can be avoided altogether. Others are the result of conflicts between applications, system inadequacies, problems with the program itself, or configuration problems. This chapter discusses some of the problems that might occur as you use CorelDRAW, and provides you with solutions to make your use of CorelDRAW more error-free.

This chapter covers:

- Memory
- Common Windows- and Corel-related GPFs
- OLE errors in the Corel applications
- Printing problems
- PostScript printing errors

Troubleshooting Memory Errors

This section covers unexpected errors, system lockups, and GPFs (general protection faults) that are the result of memory conflicts or insufficient memory.

Unexpected Errors: Choice is Close or Ignore

Try to choose Ignore. You might have to choose Ignore more than once. If choosing Ignore is successful, follow these steps:

1. Resave the file under a new name.

2. Close the Corel application and close Windows.

3. From the DOS prompt, check for TMP files in the TEMP directory. Erase any files found.

4. Restart Windows and continue working.

If selecting Ignore is unsuccessful, follow these steps:

1. Choose Close. This results in a GPF or closes the Corel application.

2. If a GPF message is displayed, record that message by writing it on a piece of paper.

3. Close Windows and erase any TMP files.

4. Restart Windows and continue working.

System Lockups or GPFs

If you experience these problems, follow these steps:

1. Save the file, if possible, under a new name.

2. Exit the Corel application and Windows using the normal method, if possible.

3. Erase any TEMP files and reboot the system.

4. Restart Windows and continue working.

N O T E

If the lockup occurred while working in DRAW, check the \COREL50\DRAW subdirectory for *.ABK files. These are CorelDRAW autobackup files. Rename the file with a CDR file extension to attempt to recover the file. You must rename the file extension to CDR before exiting Windows.

If system lockups or GPFs happen frequently, you might want to check whether your system meets the minimum requirements to run Corel applications. If the answer is yes, follow these steps:

1. Ensure that TMP files and the Windows swap file are not on a stacked or compressed drive.

2. Run CHKDSK/F (DOS5.0) or SCANDISK/ALL (DOS6.x). The total bytes memory line should read 655,360. If it does not, run a virus checker such as MSAV.EXE.

3. Before restarting Windows, open the WIN.INI file in a DOS editor and ensure that there is nothing after the `Load=` and `Run=` statements. If there are entries on those lines, insert a semicolon (;) in front of the L in Load and the R in Run. This prevents the applications from loading. Check to make sure that WIN.INI does not exceed 64KB.

4. Restart Windows. Try adding the following parameters to the WIN command, if necessary, to determine where the problem is:

```
Win /3   /D:FSVX    /B
```

/3	Forces 386 enhanced mode.
/D:F	Turns off 32-bit disk access.
/D:S	Specifies that Windows should not use ROM address space between F000:0000 and 1MB for a break point.
/D:V	Specifies that the ROM routine handles interrupts from the hard drive controller instead of using Windows internal code.
/D:X	Excludes all of the adapter area from the range of memory Windows scans to find unused space.
/B	Starts Windows bootlog to diagnose why Windows will not start. Creates a file called BOOTLOG.TXT in the Windows directory.

5. Disable or uninstall alternative Windows shells to the Program Manager (Norton Desktop, DashBoard, Central Point's PCTools for Windows, and so on).

6. Turn off all TSRs (screen savers, disk-cache displayers, mouse watchers, and so on).

7. Change video to the standard Windows VGA driver (16 colors, 640×480 resolution). Other graphics cards using comparable VGA resolutions might be accessing different memory addresses and might be causing a memory problem (Video or GPF related).

8. Re-create the Windows SWAP file by doing the following:

   Access the Control Panel, click the 386 Enhanced icon, select Virtual Memory, and click on Change.

   Set the SWAP file size to None and then restart Windows.

   Repeat this procedure. Then set the SWAP file size to (RAM*2)+1/4 RAM Permanent. You might have to run an Optimizer (Norton SpeedDisk, PCTools Optimize, and so on) to access a larger contiguous section of disk space. Make sure that the swap file is located on an uncompressed drive.

9. Reload any device, application, or file causing the problem from disks or CD-ROM. This might involve a setup or an unarcing (unarchiving) procedure.

   You might have to read or reload a font file from disk or CD-ROM. To see whether the font is the problem,

use this test: Double-click on the Font icon in the Control Panel. Highlight the font that you think is causing the problem. Check the preview window; if there is no display, the .FOT file that describes the screen appearance for that particular font is probably corrupted. Additionally, if the number of bytes shown is 0, it is likely that the font file is corrupted.

10. Try reloading the printer driver. Verify with Microsoft or the printer manufacturer that you have the most recent PostScript or non-PostScript drivers.

11. Check the properties of the designated program's icon. If the command line or working directory is not correct, try re-establishing the command line or working directory.

12. Try executing the program directly from File Manager.

13. Check the BIOS date:

    The BIOS date and version appear on your monitor when you first boot your system. If the BIOS is not current, consider replacing the BIOS chip in your computer.

    ■ **AMI BIOS:**

    1987 causes the system to reboot when a floppy is accessed through File Manager.

    1989 causes intermittent system hangs.

    1991 causes a serial port problem; your mouse or modem stops working.

■ **PHOENIX:**

Any BIOS dated 1988 or earlier should be upgraded.

■ **AWARD:**

Should be version 3.1 or higher.

Common Windows- and Corel-Related GPF Error Messages

This section covers 1000-Series errors, 2000-Series errors, and 5000-Series errors. These errors are generally the result of insufficient memory. This memory can be physical (insufficient RAM), or virtual (insuffient SWAPFILE or TEMP space).

1000-Series Errors

The following error messages are the results of memory shortages or memory conflicts on your system:

```
1000  Allocate memory failed
1001  Lock memory failed
1002  Reallocate memory failed
1010  Memory block exceeded length
      limits
```

If these errors occur, follow these steps:

1. Save your file immediately, if possible.

2. Exit Windows.

3. Reboot your system.

2000-Series Errors

Errors numbered from 2000–2013 are disk errors and usually the result of insufficient temporary directory space. If these errors occur, follow these steps:

1. Exit Windows.

2. At the DOS prompt, change to the directory where TMP files are stored and delete any files with the TMP extension.

3. Make sure that you have 5MB to 10MB of free disk space to accommodate future TMP files. If you do not have enough disk space, clear space on the hard disk or redirect the SET TEMP statement in AUTOEXEC.BAT to another drive.

5000-Series Errors

5000

This error occurs as a direct result of a memory conflict on your system. The message is file- or object-specific. If the error message returns, follow the instructions in this section to isolate the offending object and delete it. Make certain that you have adequate TEMP space. If not, delete TMP files.

5001 and 5002

These errors occur as a result of two conflicting pieces of data. Exit CorelDRAW and delete CORELDRW.INI. When you restart CorelDRAW, this file is re-created.

If these errors occur, follow these steps:

1. Try to clear the error message. If possible, exit the Corel application and exit and restart Windows. Search for ABK files and rename them before restarting Windows. If it is not possible to clear the message, reboot the system.

2. Try opening the CDR file, if you saved the file. If that is not possible, try importing the file.

3. Search for a TMP file and rename it.

4. Search for a BAK file and rename it.

5. At the DOS prompt, change to the directory where TMP files are stored and delete any remaining TMP files.

CorelDRAW automatically deletes its own TMP files when you restart the application after a crash. You also can specify extra temporary space on other drives. This can be done in the CORELAPP.INI file:

`[TempPaths]`	These two lines already
`Cleanup=1`	exist.
`0=D:\TEMP`	Add statements such as these, starting with 0=
`1=E:\MYSTUFF`	and adding a drive and subdirectory. The drive path statements can point to floppy, net work, Bernoulli drives, and so on.

If none of the solutions listed in this chapter seem to solve the problems, consider reinstalling first the Corel applications, and

then Windows. If the problems persist, check the configuration of your computer (see Chapter 44, "Customizing Your Computer for CorelDRAW").

Troubleshooting OLE Error Messages in the Corel Applications

These messages indicate that the REG.DAT file has become damaged. If this error occurs, follow these steps:

1. Close the Corel application.

2. Open the Windows File Manager. Double-click on REGEDIT.EXE. If you cannot open the Registration Information Editor, rename REG.DAT to REG.OLD, exit and restart Windows, and open and close the Corel application.

3. Select the Corel application that had the OLE problem and delete it from the list by choosing Delete from the Edit menu.

4. Exit the Registration Information Editor and Windows.

5. Restart Windows and the Corel application. It re-registers itself in REG.DAT.

N O T E

Corel and other OLE programs require VSHARE.EXE in order to function properly. Corel 5.0 installs VSHARE.386 in the SYSTEM.INI file. VSHARE.386 replaces SHARE.EXE. It is advisable to REM out the SHARE.EXE statement in the AUTOEXEC.BAT and to use only SHARE.EXE if you have DOS applications that require it.

Examining Printing Problems

If you print a file from Corel and the output is incorrect, follow these steps:

1. Check the print preview. It displays the file exactly as it should print out. If this screen does not look correct, the printout will not be correct.

2. Check cables and connections for potential communication problems. A sign of communication problems is ASCII characters appearing on your page where graphics should appear.

3. If printing in PostScript, make sure that you are using the most up-to-date printer driver.

4. Try changing your video driver to plain VGA.

When you print a file through a Corel application, the following things happen:

■ Corel processes the information. You see a percentage bar increase to 100 percent or a band count.

■ If the process is completed successfully, the print job is passed to the Windows Print Manager. You can watch the job progress by clicking on the Print Manager icon.

■ If everything runs smoothly, the print job is then passed to the printer.

If a printing problem occurs, the first step is to identify the bullet at which printing stopped. If you encounter problems while printing a file, consider the procedures in the following situations.

Printing Stops in the Corel Application

If printing stops in the Corel application, follow these steps:

1. Exit and restart the Corel application.

2. Ensure that the default printer is correct. While working in DRAW, temporary files are created and placed on your system.

3. Exit Windows and delete any TMP files found in the Windows TEMP directory. While there, ensure that you have at least 5MB to 10MB of free disk space.

4. Try disabling the Print Manager.

Printing Stops in the Print Manager

If printing stops in the Print Manager, you can try the following procedure:

1. Open the WIN.INI file. Find the reference to `TransmissionRetryTimeout=45`.

2. Set this value to 999. A value of 999 is equal to an infinite amount of time. Save the file.

3. Exit from Windows and then start it again.

4. Check Load and Run statements in WIN.INI. Programs and utilities can be set to run automatically when Windows is started by adding references to these lines. Type a semicolon (;) in front of either line if there is anything referenced. Save any changes you make to the WIN.INI.

5. Exit and restart Windows if you make changes to the WIN.INI. From the DOS prompt, erase any TMP files.

6. Move any icons found in the Windows Startup group to another icon group.

7. Disable Fast Printing to Port.

8. Make sure that you are using the most recent printer driver.

Printing Stops in the Printer

If printing stops in the printer, follow these steps:

1. Set infinite timeouts on the printer. Refer to your printer documentation for instructions.

2. Check timeouts on the network, if applicable.

3. Check to see how much RAM is resident in the printer. A minimum of 1.5MB is required to print a full page of graphics to a 300-dpi device. To print fairly complex files, you probably should have a minimum of 4MB of RAM in the printer.

4. Disconnect any switch boxes and reconnect the printer directly.

5. If you are using LPT1, try using LPT1.DOS.

6. If you are printing on a PostScript printer, check for PostScript errors, as detailed in a later section, and retry printing the file.

N O T E

Some files might require more than 4MB of printer RAM. Large-format PostScript printers frequently have 24MB RAM minimums, and can have as much as 128MB RAM. Check with the manufacturer of your printer for possible RAM upgrades. Make sure that you have the most recent BIOS and ROM versions for your printer.

Only Part of a File Prints

You might have a corrupted object in the file. The output is created in the same order as the objects were created. Find the offending object; it is the object created after the last printed object. To locate a corrupt object, do one of the following:

- Select the last printed object and press Tab+Shift. The object currently selected is most likely the source of the problem.

- Split the graphic into four quadrants, and print each quadrant with Print Selected Only enabled. By process of elimination, you should be able to find which quadrants do not print. Split the remaining quadrant until only one object is unprintable. If this object does not print by itself, you can delete and re-create it or reduce its complexity as follows:

  Select one object and press Shift+Tab to scroll through the objects on the page. Sometimes a very small object that you didn't notice becomes selected. If your image is complex, you may find it easier to identify the object in Wireframe View. This object might be corrupted. Delete the object or drag it off the page. Save the remaining objects using Selected Only.

- Save the file as a version 4.x file or export it as a CGM if you are having trouble saving, printing, or exporting. Reopen or import the file and try again.

■ Often the error can be reproduced by selecting the offending object and copying it to the Clipboard. To isolate the object, marquee-select half the objects on your page and copy them to the Clipboard. If no error occurs, then marquee-select another area and repeat the process. When the error occurs, select fewer objects from that area and continue with the copying process until you locate the offending object. Delete and re-create the offending object.

■ An open path with a fill frequently causes a printing error. Tab through objects, searching for an open object that has a fill attribute. Eliminate the fill.

The Printing Problem Is Not Object Related

If your printing problem is not object related, reduce the complexity of the graphic. To reduce the single object, try some of these procedures:

■ Reduce the number of nodes.

■ Reduce the number of fountain stripes if the file contains fountain fills.

■ Do not combine text with other objects (to create masks and clipping holes).

■ Break a complex object into smaller, less detailed objects.

■ Remove any extraneous outlines.

■ For PostScript printing problems, try setting the Number of Points in Curves to 300 in the Options section of the Print dialog box. Enable Auto Increase Flatness.

To reduce the overall complexity of a file, try the following:

■ In the Options section of the Print dialog box, set the Number of Points in Curves option to 600 or less.

■ In the Options section of the Print dialog box, select Auto Increase Flatness.

Solving PostScript Printing Errors

You can use the Windows Control Panel to enable a PostScript Error Handler; use Printer Setup in the Advanced Options section. This error handler defines the errors that the PostScript language encounters when processing a file. Some common PostScript error codes, their definitions, and solutions (where applicable) follow:

Offending Command: OB

The likely cause of this error is selecting Negative in the PostScript Driver options in the Control Panel, as well as selecting the Film Negative icon in Corel's Print Options dialog box. Choose only the CorelDRAW Negative option.

Error: Limitcheck. Offending Command=Nametype: EOCLIP

This message indicates a path-implementation error. This usually occurs when PostScript is unable to complete the clipping routine for filled objects. Try these suggestions:

- Enable Auto Increase Flatness on the CorelDRAW print screen in the Options section.

- Set Number of Points in Curves to 300 in the Options section of the Print dialog box.

- Remove any extraneous outlines from objects.

- If you are printing separations, try printing just one separation at a time.

- Consider substituting solid-color fills for gradients or pattern fills in irregularly shaped objects.

Error: Limitcheck. Offending Command=Nametype: EOFILL

This message indicates a path-implementation error when PostScript is completing a fill routine. Set the Number of Points in Curves option to 300 in the Options section of the Print dialog box.

Error: Limitcheck. Offending Command=Nametype: LINETO or CURVETO

An implementation limit has been exceeded, usually indicating too many nodes on a straight or curved path. Use the Auto Reduce Nodes option in the Node Edit roll-up in CorelDRAW, or manually remove extraneous nodes from the objects.

Error: Stack Overflow

The stack limit has been exceeded, which often indicates embedded EPS files, too many nodes on a path, or complex fill patterns and bitmap fill patterns in complex shapes. Try the suggestions for EOCLIP.

Offending Command: Stack Underflow

The stack does not have enough objects for the requested operation. Try the suggestions given for EOCLIP.

Error: Invalid restore

This message might appear after canceling a print job. Try clearing the Print Manager and repeating the printing process.

Error: Invalid font

This error message might appear if the file requires a font that has become corrupted. Try reinstalling the font.

Other Troubleshooting Options

At least two more alternatives exist when it comes to troubleshooting: Consulting with the Corel support personnel and consulting with other CorelDRAW users.

The Corel corporation offers Corel Technical Support Services to all registered CorelDRAW users. Complete information about these services is found at the front of the CorelDRAW doumentation, Volume 1. A brief rundown of Corel's support resources is as follows:

Free Technical Support (limited to one 15-minute call; further calls must be credit-purchased through this number as well):

1-800-818-1848

Non-Credited Technical Support (you pay for the call):

1-900-896-8880

IVAN (Automated/interactive support with answers to common Corel questions):

1-613-728-1990

Fax Support (Technical tips for Corel products; document number for a current list of topics is 2000):

1-613-728-0826, ext. 3080

Corel B.B.S. Download Service (Tech notes, supplementary files, product updates):

1-613-728-4752 (1200, 2400, 9600, 14,400, 28,800 baud; no parity; 8 data bits; 1 stop bit)

Corel Forum on CompuServe (Exchange information with other Corel users, as well as Corel technicians):

Type **GO COREL**.

hesitate to seek out other Corel users for answers. CompuServe's Corel forum is the best source, but by no means the only source—check desktop publishing forums and other graphics forums wherever you can on user networks.

The next and final chapter is a glossary of Corel- and computer graphics-related terminology.

Summary

This chapter has covered useful strategies for troubleshooting CorelDRAW problems, especially with memory, GPF, OLE, and printing errors. Remember to make use of Corel's extensive online Help menu files as well. Corel Corporation offers a wide range of technical support for its users, although most of this support is not free. Finally, don't

Glossary

386 Enhanced mode

Makes the fullest use of Windows capabilities in regard to memory management, task swapping, and disk access.

Align

Lines up objects in relation to one another. Objects can be aligned horizontally (left, center, right), vertically (top, center, bottom), horizontally *and* vertically, or to the center of the active page.

Anchor points

Enables you to change the point of origin around which the object will be transformed. The anchor point acts as a locked pivot for the operation.

Behind Fill

Enables you to place the outline of an object behind the fill of the object so that only half the total line weight is visible.

BIOS

Basic Input/Output System. A BIOS can be found on the computer motherboard, disk controllers, video adapters, and other peripherals that handle complex tasks. The BIOS contains the basic information on how the device handles information that goes into and out of it.

Bit depth

Pertains to the number of colors available for any given bitmap. These normally are 1 (black and white), 2 (four colors, usually black, white, and two grays), 4 (16 colors), 8 (256 colors), 15 (32KB colors), 16 (64KB colors), or 24 (16.7 million colors).

BPT

The file where two-color bitmap fills are stored.

Break Apart

This option enables you to break apart objects that had been combined and contained subpaths into separate objects again.

Brighten (Lens)

Gives the area of an object the appearance of having additional light applied to it. *See also:* Lens

Cache

A means of sending and receiving data in large blocks, rather than one byte at a time.

Catalog

Contains a thumbnail bitmap of the file and the path information for the file, but does not contain the file itself. *See also:* collection, library, MOSAIC

CDR

The native file format for CorelDRAW graphics. *See also:* CMX

Child object

Any object within a group of objects. It is possible to edit the attributes of child objects without changing the overall attribute applied to the group.

Clone

Similar to Duplicate in that it creates a copy of the selected object. Changes made to the original object, or *master object*, are reflected in the cloned object.

CMX (Corel Presentation Exchange)

Corel's file format for use with presentations made with CorelDRAW's companion programs.

Collection

A collection can be a library or a catalog. *See also:* catalog, library, MOSAIC

Color Add (Lens)

Adds a selected color to an object. *See also:* Lens

Color gamut

The range of colors that can be displayed on a given device.

Color limit

Works like a color filter on a camera. Filters out all but the designated color. *See also:* Lens

Color Manager

Enables you to calibrate monitors, scanners, and color printers for optimal use with CorelDRAW and its companion products.

Color Override

Enables you to change temporarily the outline of objects on a selected layer. The objects on a layer that has had Color Override applied will appear with the color of the outline applied and no fill.

Combine

Enables you to combine multiple objects and to treat them as a single object.

Conical fountain fill

Creates a gradient in a clockwise or counter-clockwise direction. *See also:* fountain fill

Control object

The object at the beginning or end of a dynamically linked group. The attributes of a control object are used as the start or end of an effect applied to a dynamically linked group. *See also:* dynamically linked group

Convert (MOSAIC)

Enables you to convert one or more files to another file format.

Cusp node

Used to make radical changes in direction to a curve. A cusp node has two control points that move independently of one another, enabling the segment to be reshaped from either side of the node. *See also:* node

Defragging

Computer jargon for sorting a hard drive and putting all the files in sequential order. When files are created or modified, DOS places them in the first available sectors on the hard drive. If a file is modified and saved, it is not always to the exact same sectors. In time, data is scattered everywhere on the hard drive and DOS has to search for it, thus slowing down disk performance. Defragging moves the blocks of data so that they are clustered one after another, making it easier for DOS to find them.

Desktop layer

The drawing layer that is off the printable page. Objects placed on the desktop layer are available to all pages in a multipage document. *See also:* layers

Digitizer

An input device that looks like a sketch tablet with a puck mouse or stylus pen. The tablet is actually a fine radio receiver grid and the puck or stylus is the transmitter. Digitizers are *virtual*, because where they are placed on the tablet corresponds to where the cursor appears on-screen.

DOT

The configuration file for dashed and dotted lines.

Dot gain

The effect in which the printed colors appear darker than desired.

Dynamic Data Exchange (DDE)

Enables you to share data between OLE applications that do not have a common file format.

Dynamic range

The possible color or tonal range between pure black and pure white on a given device.

Dynamically linked group

Groups of objects with attributes you can change by changing the attributes of one or more of the group's control objects. *See also:* control object

Embedded object

An object that actually is placed in the destination document of the client application. Changes made to the original object in the source document are not reflected in the embedded object in the client application. *See also:* linked object, Object Linking and Embedding

END

The file where arrowheads are stored.

Envelope

Enables you to distort text and graphics objects.

Extract

Enables you to save artistic or paragraph text in a file for editing in a word processor. Can be edited in any word processor that accepts ASCII text format. *See also:* Merge-Back

Extrude

Applies a 3D solid effect to a text or graphics object.

FOCOLTONE process colors

Used primarily in Europe, contains at least 10 percent of a process color in common with any other color.

Fountain fill

Enables you to apply a gradient of one or more colors to an object. *See also:* conical fountain fill, linear fountain fill, radial fountain fill, square fountain fill

Group

Collects a series of selected objects and treats them as one object for the purpose of movement and application of effects. Grouped objects cannot be edited using the Shape tool. *See also:* Ungroup

Heat Map

Creates an infrared appearance. *See also:* Lens

INK

The Pantone color-translation file.

Intersection

Creates a new object from the area of two or more overlapping objects. Intersection cannot be applied to grouped objects.

Invert

Causes the colors of an object to appear to be in negative. *See also:* Lens

Invisible layer

Objects on an invisible layer are not rendered to the screen, but are printable unless otherwise specified. *See also:* Layers, Layers roll-up, locked layer, printable layer

IPL

The Pantone ink file.

ISA bus

The Industry Standard Architecture bus first appeared in the early 1980s with the release of the IBM-AT. The bus featured 16-bit card slots for hard drive controllers, video cards, and so on. Although there are still many computers with this bus, it is considered obsolete and not recommended for graphics applications.

Keyboard shortcuts

A series of key combinations that can be used in place of the menu or ribbon bar. For example, Ctrl+S=Save.

Layers

Enables you to place objects on different planar surface areas. Layers can be thought of as a stack of transparent sheets of paper. You can add or delete layers and edit their control attributes in the Layers roll-up. *See also:* invisible layer, Layers roll-up, locked layer, printable layer

Layers roll-up

A roll-up that enables you to add, delete, and edit layers. *See also:* layers, invisible layer, locked layer, printable layer

Lens

Simulates various filter-style effects.

Library

A series of bitmap, vector, text, or sound files that have been compressed, using file-compression algorithms, for convenient storage. These files can be viewed and uncompressed for use in MOSAIC. *See also:* catalog, collection, MOSAIC

Linear fountain fill

Creates a straight line gradient. *See also:* fountain fill

Linked object

Places a pointer in the client application for the retrieval of information about the object. Changes made to the original object in the source document are reflected in the linked object in the client application. *See also:* embedded object, Object Linking and Embedding

Locked layer

A layer in which the objects cannot be moved or modified. *See also:* invisible layer, layers, Layers roll-up, printable layer

Magnify

Provides a close-up of the area of an object. *See also:* Lens

Master layer

Objects on this layer appear in all pages of the document unless specifically hidden for a given page. There can be more than one master layer.

MEMMAKER

MEMMAKER is a utility that is included with MS-DOS 6.0 and later. This utility examines the CONFIG.SYS and AUTOEXEC.BAT of a computer and makes recommendations on how to optimize it for the most efficient use of available memory.

Merge-Back

Integrates text that has been modified using Extract. *See also:* Extract

MOSAIC

A companion program to CorelDRAW that enables you to visually manage bitmap, vector, text, and sound files. Files are represented as thumbnails. You can view directories, library files, catalogs, and collections. *See also:* catalog, collection, library

MSD

The Microsoft Diagnostic included with Windows. Run from a DOS prompt without Windows running, it can provide significant information that you can use to resolve problems with a computer system.

Node

The control point for a line segment or where two line segments meet. There are three types of nodes: Cusp, Smooth, and Symmetrical. *See also:* cusp node, smooth node, symmetrical node

Object Linking and Embedding (OLE)

A means of placing an object from another Windows application into a CorelDRAW document. *See also:* embedded object, linked object

OE

Operating environment. A software program that is used as a common interface for other applications—for example, Windows.

OLE client

The application that receives the information from the OLE server's original document and places it into the destination document.

OLE server

The application that contains the original information in the source document.

Order

Enables you to adjust how objects are stacked on a layer.

PAL

The custom palette files.

PANOSE Font Matching

Enables you to substitute fonts that appear in a drawing but might not be installed in Windows.

PCI

The Personal Computer Interface was developed by Intel as an alternative to VESA Local Bus (VLB). PCI offers significant performance increases over any other bus currently produced for PCs. This is the recommended bus for graphics applications.

Perspective

Changes the view of an object in relationship to a vanishing point. *See also:* vanishing point

PowerClip

Enables you to place one or more objects inside another object. Can be used to place an imported bitmap into an irregularly shaped object, eliminating the white rectangular bounding box common to imported bitmaps.

PowerLine

Enables you to add pent type effects. Although PowerLines appear as a line, they are actually a dynamically linked group of objects. Objects of varying or tapered widths are calculated and linked to a line.

Presets

A series of pre-established, multistep effects applied through the Presets roll-up. Effects can be added by using the Presets roll-up. Presets can be applied only to a single object. *See also:* Presets roll-up

Print Merge (Mosaic)

Similar to Mail Merge in word processors. Enables you to create a form document and replace selected artistic text with text created in a word processor.

Printable layer

Objects on any layer can be made printable or nonprintable by editing the Printable check box in the Layers roll-up. *See also:* layers, Layers roll-up, invisible layer, locked layer

Property sheet

A subset of a dialog box that offers specific and expanded options.

Radial fountain fill

Creates a gradient of concentric circles. *See also:* fountain fill

RAM

Random Access Memory is the physical memory that computers use for the processing of information.

Ribbon bar

A series of icons across the top of CorelDRAW's workspace window. Enables you to quickly access most of the frequently used commands, such as Save, Print, and so on.

Roll-up

An auxiliary toolbox that can be opened to perform functions controlled by that roll-up. Roll-ups can be minimized or "rolled-up" and reopened as needed.

ROM

Read-Only Memory. ROM is located on chips on peripheral interface cards—video adapters or disk controllers, for example—that contain instructions on how these devices are to interface with the computer system.

ROM address

ROMs usually have fixed memory-address ranges, expressed as hexadecimal numbers, that they use as markers for the computer system to send instructions to. Every peripheral that has a ROM must reside at its own unique address. ROMs trying to access the same range of memory addresses is one cause of system failures and fatal errors. *See also:* ROM

Rule of sixteen

The formulas by which halftone screening is determined.

SCSI

Small Computer System Interface. SCSI controllers can control up to seven devices, including hard drives, CD-ROM drives, scanners, and so on. SCSIs give your computer system greater flexibility and versatility.

Separate

Separates a control object from a dynamically linked group of objects.

SHARE.EXE

Enables you to open multiple copies of the same file without corrupting the original. *See also:* VSHARE.386

SMARTDRV.EXE

Replaced SMARTDRV.SYS in MS-DOS 5.0. Provides DOS with a means of caching or improving reading and writing to storage drives (for example, hard drives, removable drives, and so on).

Smooth node

Makes smooth, transitional curves between segments. A smooth node has two control points that lie on a straight line. When one control point is moved, the other moves proportionally. *See also:* node

Square fountain fill

Creates a gradient of concentric squares. *See also:* fountain fill

Styles roll-up

Enables you to define and apply formatting instructions to text and graphics. *See also:* styles

Swap file

A temporary holding space for file and program information. Windows applications often create temporary swap files that they use to store a copy of the file currently open for use as a reference copy. Windows prefers to use a permanent swap file, known as *virtual memory*. *See also:* virtual memory

Symmetrical node

Used to join two curve segments while maintaining a symmetrical curve at the node. Symmetrical nodes have two control points that lie on a straight line equidistant from the node; these points move as one. *See also:* node

SyQuest

A brand of removable hard drive that commonly is used for file storage and transferring large files.

SYSTEM.INI

The INI, or initialization, file that Windows uses to tell itself how to handle hardware devices and hardware-associated interfacing.

Tape back-up

A unit that records computer information onto a magnetic tape cartridge for archiving and emergency restoral.

TMP

The file extension for temporary files created by Windows applications. These files sometimes are left behind when Windows crashes or an application generates a fatal error.

Total area of coverage (TAC)

The sum of the percentages of cyan, yellow, and magenta inks required to make black.

Transformation

Translation and conversion of colors between color palettes or devices.

Trim

Cuts out the section common to two or more overlapping objects. The last object selected is the one that is trimmed, retaining its fill and outline attributes.

TRUMATCH process colors

Designed specifically for digital output. Using the HSB color model as its base, TRUMATCH colors still rely on CYMK conversion for the final output.

Type Assist

Automatically replaces commonly misspelled words, capitalization errors, or abbreviations.

Ungroup

Returns a group of objects back to individual objects or groups of objects. *See also:* Group

Vanishing point

A point on a horizon, real or imaginary, where a pair of parallel lines would appear to meet. *See also:* perspective

Video adapter

Translates the information sent to it from the video driver software to a signal that can be displayed on a monitor.

Video driver

A software program that translates the information from computer applications about what is to be displayed on the monitor into a instruction set that the video adapter uses to send the signals to display the application's information on-screen. Because computer applications are evolving constantly, video drivers are updated frequently. It is not unknown for a supposedly brand new video adapter to arrive with outdated drivers.

Virtual memory

The permanent swap file that Windows uses to augment a computer system's physical memory. Virtual memory is a section of a hard disk on which Windows places any program and file code not currently in use, in order to free physical memory for program or file code that is called for. Windows retrieves any code placed in virtual memory as it needs it. *See also:* swap file

VLB

VESA Local Bus. This bus, usually based on the ISA-style motherboard, adds a secondary card connector. VLB cards exchange information at an increased rate and enhance performance of applications that are heavily graphics-oriented. VLB video adapters are considered the minimum standard for graphics applications.

VSHARE.386

A Windows replacement for SHARE.EXE that enables Windows to have more than one copy of a document or program open at the same time. *See also:* SHARE.EXE

Weld

Similar to Combine, except that intersecting paths of the objects are removed.

XA

Refers to a CD-ROM being *multisession*, which means that it can play back multiple types of information—computer data, PhotoCDs, and CD-Audio files, for example.

Part VIII

Appendixes

A p p e n d i x A

Installing CorelDRAW 5

*Y*ou have just purchased one of the largest graphics packages on the market today. CorelDRAW is more than just a single application. This suite of applications approaches a total solution for desktop publishing and graphic design. This appendix is a guide for the hardware and software requirements for CorelDRAW 5.0. The software setup offers you a number of software installation choices. Included in this appendix is a description of the choices available, and instructions for implementing them:

This chapter covers:

- Hardware and software requirements

- Hard disk installation

- CD-ROM installation

- Installing fonts

- Upgrading from CorelDRAW version 4.0

- Network installation

Understanding Hardware and Software Requirements

Today's high-end software packages are getting more powerful with each new release. With this power, however, comes the need for a more powerful computer. These packages require a large amount of hard disk space, along with an ever-increasing amount of system memory. You need to keep these requirements in mind, not only when you purchase or upgrade your system, but also when you install these programs.

<hr>

T I P

<hr>

Installing CorelDRAW is not a difficult process, but it does require you to give some thought to your system configuration, and the way in which you plan to use the program. Giving some thought to these considerations now may save you time and trouble later.

There is a large disparity between what constitutes a minimum system to run CorelDRAW, and an optimum system configured for high-end production. While you can run CorelDRAW with the minimum system requirements, the price you will pay in speed and efficiency will be considerable.

Minimum Hardware and Software Requirements

CorelDRAW publishes a recommended minimum hardware and software requirement, but you may find that in reality you need much more to optimize your utilization of the program.

The following requirements represent the bare-bones setup you will need (these are the author's recommendations after working with CorelDRAW):

- 386/4 DX with 8MB of RAM
- 120MB hard disk
- 1.2MB or 1.4MB floppy drive
- VGA monitor
- Microsoft Windows 3.1
- Microsoft-compatible mouse
- Math coprocessor (DX)

When considering system size and resources, the primary issues are speed, storage space on the hard disk, and ease of use. In addition, complex graphics files can easily be in excess of 5 megabytes in size. Loading, saving, and screen refresh times can be enormous on a slow system, such as the preceding minimum system setup.

A full installation of CorelDRAW requires over 50MB of hard disk space. Windows can require another 10MB. Windows also requires hard disk space for temporary files and a swap file. These requirements would leave very little free space on a 120MB hard disk for storage. This could result in out-of-memory-error messages, or restrict your usage of CorelDRAW and its ancillary packages. The size of a drawing and the color mode in PHOTO-PAINT, for example, are memory-dependent, and rely upon the Windows swap file to supplement the available RAM.

A mouse will work for most of CorelDRAW's features; however, in order to take advantage of some of CorelDRAW's more advanced features, you must have a pressure-sensitive pointing device, such as a digitizer pad.

Suggested System Requirements for the Professional

CorelDRAW is just one of a number of graphics packages available for the graphics professional. The ability to incorporate the power of these applications with CorelDRAW enables the graphics professional to custom tailor a highly efficient set of design tools. Because all graphics applications are memory intensive, and the files they create take up large amounts of hard disk space, your computer system should exceed the minimum system requirement. Although your budget is one consideration, trying to run high-end graphics packages like CorelDRAW on an underpowered system can be a time-consuming exercise in frustration.

The following list represents a system that will offer you optimum use of CorelDRAW:

- Pentium 60 with 32MB of RAM: Consider a PCI-based machine

- 540MB or larger hard disk: Consider a SCSI type II drive and caching controller

- Double-speed (or greater) CD-ROM drive: High-capacity removable drives like a Syquest, Bernoulli, or a Magneto Optical (MO) drive are even more convenient

- SVGA monitor: Minimum 1024×768×256 resolution—72 Hz or better refresh rate—.28 dot pitch

- Graphics accelerator card with a minimum of 1MB of RAM on the board

- Pressure-sensitive digitizer pad

- Printer: PostScript Laser—PostScript Level II recommended

- Scanner: Flatbed

- 14.4 Kbps v.32 bis modem

A Pentium 60 PCI motherboard is the foundation for this fast and extremely efficient system. Augmented by 32MB of RAM, a graphics accelerator, and a SCSI II hard disk and caching controller, it has the power necessary to reduce the waiting time

for disk access and screen refresh. The 1MB video card offers the ability to work with pure colors, rather than dithered colors, making the creative process easier.

Unlike most mice, digitizer pads are configurable for an absolute mode of operation. This means that each point on the pad has an equivalent point on the screen, eliminating the need to reorient the pen or stylus on the pad. Using a digitizer pad is much like using a pen and paper. The stylus or pen allows for better control, and makes the creation of smoother shapes and lines effortless.

Printers are the most common output devices. Though your final output might be to film via a service bureau, having the use of a PostScript printer for checking your output can save invaluable amounts of time.

Similarly, a scanner can speed the re-creation of artwork from existing printed art, photos, or slides. It also offers a large range of possibilities when creating custom or special effects.

Modem-based communications and file transfers have become the preferred method of quickly sending data from one location to another. Most service bureaus have file transfer capability. The fax abilities of some of these modems can increase productivity time, enabling you to send drawings and notes to clients for approval.

Your computer represents an investment, not just for today's needs, but hopefully for some of tomorrow's needs as well. Maintaining a level of technology equal to the tasks required of it requires some planning. This ongoing process pays large dividends in productivity and gains the most efficient use of your investment.

Installation Methods

CorelDRAW gives you the choice of either a hard disk installation or running the program from CD-ROM. The hard disk installation offers you two choices—**F**ull Install and Minimum/**C**ustom installation.

N O T E

CorelDRAW version 4 uses much the same installation procedure. Hard disk requirements are less, however.

The full installation requires approximately 50MB of hard disk space. If you choose this option, CorelDRAW will install all of the modules, help files, and samples. You will be able to choose from a selection of filters and fonts, as well as scanner support. The disk version of CorelDRAW does not contain all of the available fonts. The balance of the fonts are on the CD-ROM disks. If you have need for all of CorelDRAW's modules and have adequate hard disk space, you might choose this option.

N O T E

The estimates shown here for hard disk space do not include space required for any fonts beyond those installed by default during the setup procedure. Font space requirements vary greatly, depending upon the quantity and type of fonts installed.

The Custom installation is designed for those who do not require all of CorelDRAW's modules, have somewhat limited hard disk space, or need to split the installation among multiple drives. This option requires a minimum of 18MB of hard disk space and can range up to the amount required for a Full installation.

If you are short of hard disk space, you might consider running CorelDRAW from CD-ROM. Installing CorelDRAW to run from the CD-ROM still requires some hard disk space. The amount of space it requires varies from approximately 7MB–15MB. This has the disadvantage of being slow. It also can make accessing files located on the second CD-ROM disk difficult, because the first disk contains most of the executable program files.

N O T E

Corel's setup requires the installation of VSHARE.386. Setup installs the file automatically, and adds the VSHARE statement to your Windows SYSTEM.INI. A backup of your previous SYSTEM.INI is made and named SYSTEM.COR.

Basic Hard Disk Installation

CorelDRAW 5.0 comes packaged in two ways. The full version comes with either 3 1/2" 1.4MB or 5 1/4" 1.2MB disks and CD-ROMs. The CD-ROM version does not include floppy disks. CorelDRAW can be installed either from floppy or CD-ROM to the hard disk, but the installation procedure is slightly different. The CD-ROM-based installation is faster than the floppy disk installation. This basic installation procedure is also used for some network applications, as indicated later in this appendix.

N O T E

The CD-ROM version of CorelDRAW contains two CD-ROM program disks and also contains clip art and font files not available on floppy disks.

The basic installation process is simple. Start Windows and insert Disk 1 or the CD-ROM in the appropriate drive. From the Windows Program Manager, select **F**ile and choose **R**un to display the Run dialog box. In the Command Line box, type **A:\setup.exe,** making sure to substitute the appropriate drive letter, and click on OK. The Setup screen appears.

After the CorelDRAW Welcome Screen appears, selecting **C**ontinue displays the registration dialog box. Type your name and your serial number, as indicated, and click on **C**ontinue. The serial number for version 5.0 is found in the upper right corner of the Support Services page in Volume One of the User's Manual.

The Installation Options box appears, enabling you to choose Full or Custom installation.

Full Installation

Selecting the **F**ull Install option displays the Destination Directory dialog box (see fig. A.1). The input line shows CorelDRAW's choice as the default installation directory. If this is not the directory location you want, type the correct path information and click on **C**ontinue.

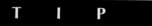

T I P

CorelDRAW can be installed to removable media, such as a Bernoulli® drive, by specifying it as the destination drive during setup.

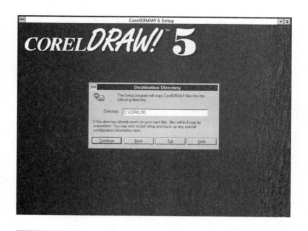

Figure A.1
The Destination Directory dialog box.

CorelDRAW requires up to 50MB of free space for a full installation. If you do not have the required space available, select **B**ack in the Setup box and choose **C**ustom Setup, or E**x**it the program setup at this time. Make more space available on your hard disk before reattempting the setup.

Custom Installation

After you choose **C**ustom Install, the Destination Directory dialog box appears. The default destination is **C:\Corel50**. If this is acceptable, click on **C**ontinue. If you want to change the directory, type the new path in the text entry box and click on **C**ontinue. The Application options box appears, which permits you to choose the modules you want to install (see fig. A.2). You can choose to install all, some, or none of each

CorelDRAW module, except CorelTRACE, CorelMOSAIC, and CorelQUERY. With these modules, you only have the all-or-none options. The amount of disk space needed and the amount of disk space available is recalculated as you make selections, and appears at the bottom of the options box. The far-right column is updated to show the amount needed for each individual selection.

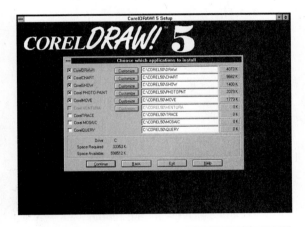

Figure A.2
The CorelDRAW custom installation dialog box.

Deciding which modules to install is a matter of understanding what each one is, and then matching that information to your needs.

CorelDRAW is the headline application of the package. Its power lies partially in its ability to meet a large range of graphic design needs. Utilizing a vector-based format, it allows for precision illustration. If you intend to combine its versatility with other graphics

or publishing packages, you will want to install any import and export filters supported by the other packages you intend to use. The setup procedure automatically installs the filters required by CorelDRAW's other modules. New users with previous Macintosh or other DOS/Windows-based experience should install the help files. These can be a valuable source of information. The sample files serve as examples of some of the uses of the program. CorelDRAW offers an extensive symbols library. By clicking on **Customize,** you can choose which symbol libraries you want to install.

Corel VENTURA is a full-featured publishing package that expands the document layout and typesetting abilities of the CorelDRAW suite. By using style sheets, documents gain a consistent appearance, creating a professional-looking document. OLE2 compatibility enables you to drag-and-drop text and graphics from other compliant packages for enhanced composition control. If you are installing VENTURA, consider installing Zandar TagWrite™, which is included in the package. This utility allows for document tag conversions, augmenting VENTURA's publishing abilities.

CorelPHOTO-PAINT is more than a paint package. It features TWAIN scanner support and allows for sophisticated editing of bitmapped images, such as photos. Image enhancement and special effects filters expand its editing ability. PHOTO-PAINT supports third party PhotoShop-compatible

plug-ins from Kai's Power Tools and other companies to add to your editing ability. Your edited bitmaps can be imported back into CorelDRAW to augment your drawings. Installing the help files and samples assists you in becoming acquainted with the program.

CorelTRACE enables you to convert bitmapped images into vector images that CorelDRAW can edit and manipulate. It also features scanner support, which enables you to trace scanned images and save them in a vector format.

CorelMOSAIC is a visual file manager, which allows you to create libraries and catalogs of your files which are then displayed within MOSAIC as thumbnail drawings. It features file compression, batch operation, sorting, and application linking. If you work with multiple versions of one file, CorelMOSAIC cuts the time spent searching for the correct file.

CorelCHART offers the ability to create visually powerful charts. Featuring OLE support and Dynamic Data Exchange (DDE), you can link your chart to other OLE applications and spreadsheet files created in DDE-compatible applications such as Excel.

CorelMOVE is an animation program. It provides the creation tools necessary to create props, actors, and sounds, and compiles them together in an animated format.

CorelSHOW provides the vehicle for creating powerful multipage presentations, using files from any OLE server application. You can also incorporate animation files from CorelMOVE or Autodesk Animator, as well as others.

CorelQUERY enables you to extract information from popular database applications for use in both CorelVENTURA and CorelCHART.

CorelDRAW has included an assortment of other applications with version 5.0. These third-party packages are discussed in Appendix C, along with their installation instructions. Some of these applications must be installed separately.

As you can see, CorelDRAW is more a suite of powerful applications, rather than just a single application with add-ons. All of these applications are capable of standing alone, but their real power comes from their ability to work in concert with one another.

N O T E

You must install the program files for any of the applications you intend to use. Individual applications can be installed later without reinstalling the whole suite of applications.

Note also that no selection is permanent until you click on **C**ontinue. You need to consider your available hard disk space and how the installation will affect your ability to work.

Selecting the Some option enables you to further customize your installation. When you select Some, an options box appears that details the options available for that application. CorelDRAW comes with extensive online help, as well as a number of sample files. You may choose to install any or all of these at this time.

Installing Drivers and Filters

CorelDRAW enables you to customize filters and add optional drivers. Click on **C**ontinue in the Installation options dialog box to display the file installation dialog box (see fig. A.3).

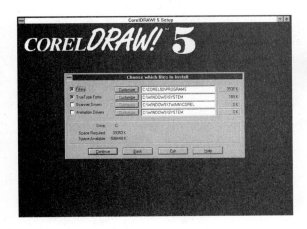

Figure A.3
The file installation dialog box.

Select C**u**stomize for the Filters option. The available filters are displayed in a dialog box. By default, Setup installs all of the available filters. If you don't want to have all the filters

added, select Delete All and add only the filters you want to install by clicking on Add. Click on **C**ontinue to return to the File installation dialog box.

Install any animation drivers you want at this time by selecting the box beside Animation drivers. The available drivers are AVI, Quicktime, and Autodesk Animator runtime players. Click on the box beside each driver you want, and then click on **C**ontinue to proceed with the setup.

You also can select the scanner support at this time. Selecting the box beside Scanner Drivers displays the Scanner Selection dialog box. Click on the down arrow to display the available choices.

N O T E

Just clicking on the check box adjacent to Scanner Drivers displays the Scanner Selection d-box. This is true until you have already selected a scanner. The second time, you have to click on the Customize button.

When you highlight your scanner, a list of the default settings (if applicable) appears in the Options box. The Options box enables you to change the Port address, if needed. Click on OK.

```
N    O    T    E
```

CorelDRAW supports *only* TWAIN scanning modules. Your scanner must already be installed for CorelDRAW to support your scanner. If your scanner is not listed in the setup and has TWAIN drivers, it will still be supported. If you own a non-TWAIN scanner, contact the manufacturer of your scanner to see if TWAIN drivers are available. If they are not, you will need to run your scanner outside of CorelDRAW and import the files.

Click on **C**ustomize beside True Type Fonts to choose extra fonts you want to install. By default, Setup installs a small selection of TrueType fonts. The floppy disk-based installation enables you to select from 24 fonts. CD-ROM Disc 1 contains the complete selection of over 800 available True-Type and Type 1 fonts. Click on **C**ontinue to return to the file installation dialog box.

Note that each font you install adds a line to your WIN.INI file. The maximum allowable file size for the WIN.INI is 64KB. If the file exceeds that size, Windows will not open. Every time you start Windows, the program loads all of the installed fonts into memory. While it might be tempting to install all of the fonts, installing a large quantity of fonts causes Windows to operate slower. Remember that increasing the number of more fonts you install increases the hard disk space required. The amount of hard disk space required for the fonts available with Version 5.0 can be up to 30MB. CorelDRAW gives

you the option between installing fonts to either your hard disk, or accessing them from your CD-ROM. Version 4.0's optional fonts are installed after the basic program installation, as shown later in this appendix.

Another option for maintaining control of your fonts is the use of a font management utility, such as FontMinder™. An introductory version of Ares FontMinder™ is included with version 5.0. It enables you to create custom font packages and install fonts on the fly. This removes extra fonts from the WIN.INI while maintaining their availability, allowing Windows to operate faster and more efficiently. To install FontMinder, insert CD-ROM Disk 1 in your drive. From the Program Manager, select **R**un from the **F**ile menu. Type **F:\Fontmndr\setup** (substitute the drive letter for your CD-ROM) and click on OK. Follow the prompts to complete the installation.

To proceed with the setup, select **C**ontinue. The Temp Drives dialog box appears, enabling you to choose the location for temp files. Setup uses the directory specified for Windows temp files as the default. You can change the location for CorelDRAW temp files by specifying the path in the dialog box. Click on **C**ontinue to proceed with the program setup. A message box appears, telling you that CorelDRAW is ready to install. Click on **I**nstall to continue. If you are using 3 1/2" disks for your installation, Setup prompts you to insert the remainder of the disks.

Running CorelDRAW from CD-ROM

CorelDRAW can be installed to run from your CD-ROM drive. Most of the program files used to run CorelDRAW are read-only, which makes the program ideally suited to run from your CD-ROM. Certain configuration files, however, must be read-write, and must be stored on your hard disk. These configurable files contain information saved from your last CorelDRAW session, as well as preferences you have set, including custom fills, palettes, styles, and templates you have created. With this type of installation, CorelDRAW installs only the configurable files and a small group of data files to your hard disk. While it is slower to run from CD-ROM, it provides enormous savings in hard disk space.

To install CorelDRAW to run from your CD-ROM, start Windows and insert CD-ROM Disk 1 in the appropriate drive. From the Windows Program Manager, select **F**ile and choose **R**un to display the Run dialog box. In the Command Line box, type **F:\setup2.exe,** making sure to substitute the appropriate drive letter, and click on OK.

After the CorelDRAW welcome screen appears, selecting **C**ontinue displays the registration dialog box. Type your name and your serial number, as indicated, and click on **C**ontinue. The serial number for CorelDRAW is located on the Support Services page, in the front of Volume One of

the user's manual. When the Destination Directory box appears, either accept or change the path to a directory on your hard drive for the configuration files, and click on **C**ontinue. The Select applications to install dialog box appears, enabling you to make selections for a hard disk installation as detailed earlier in this appendix. Click on **C**ontinue to proceed with the program setup.

NOTE

Only a full installation is available in version 4.0 if you choose to run CorelDRAW from CD-ROM.

Upgrading From Previous Versions to 5.0

It is possible to keep multiple versions of CorelDRAW on your hard drive.

Before installing 5.0, some files need to be backed up. Create backup copies of any *.IPL, *.BPT, *.INK, *.DOT, *.END, and *.PAL files you have customized. These can be copied back to the appropriate directories after installing version 5.0. Delete PROGMAN.COR, REG.COR, and WIN.COR from your Windows directory to ensure that the version 5.0 setup routine creates backups of the respective .INI files.

If you are deleting version 4.0 from your system:

- Use the Windows File Manager to delete the CorelDRAW 4.0 directory.

- Delete the CorelDRAW 4.0 group icon from the Program Manager.

- Backup the RE.DAT and the WIN.INI files in the Windows directory.

- Run REGEDIT.EXE from the Program Manager to delete CorelCHART Chart, CorelDRAW Graphic, CorelPHOTO-PAINT Picture, and CorelSHOW Presentation.

- Delete the [CorelGraphics4] section from the WIN.INI.

T I P

MicroHelp Uninstaller®, available at most software stores, is an invaluable aid for uninstalling Windows applications. It analyzes the directories and enables you to eliminate all files associated with a given application.

W A R N I N G

Files saved in Corel VENTURA 5.0 cannot be opened in previous versions of VENTURA. You should make backup copies of your existing documents before resaving them in version 5.0. Use the Manage Publication command from the previous version, the Windows File Manager, or Smart Copy in version 5.0, to make a backup copy of your file.

Installing Fonts in Version 4.0

CorelDRAW comes packaged with a large assortment of fonts. Version 4.0 has over 750 fonts. The fonts are TrueType fonts, which allow for Adobe PostScript Type I substitution. CorelDRAW installs a small portion of the available fonts automatically, during the basic installation. Only a limited number of fonts are available with the floppy disk-based installation. The balance of the fonts are contained only on the CD-ROM. The amount of space required to install the optional fonts to your hard disk is in addition to the space required for the program installation. This can be as much as an additional 25MB.

N O T E

Versions 4 and 5 ship with fonts that conform more closely to standard typeface names. For example, the New Brunswick font available in version 3.0 is now Century Schoolbook, and Brooklyn is now Bookman.

To install the desired TrueType fonts with version 4.0, follow these steps:

1. Place Disc 1 in your CD-ROM drive.

2. From the Windows Program Manager, select **F**ile and choose **R**un.

3. Type **F:\fontinst.exe,** substituting the appropriate drive letter of your CD-ROM drive in the command line of the Run dialog box, and click on OK.

4. After the TrueType Font Setup box appears, select **C**ontinue to install fonts, or **E**xit to quit setup.

5. The TrueType Font Directory box appears, listing the path for your CD-ROM as the default. Accessing fonts from your CD-ROM is slower than from your hard disk, but saves space. If you want to install the fonts to your hard disk, type the full path (i.e., C:\FONTS\) on the directory line, and click on **C**ontinue.

6. The Font Selection box appears, enabling you to select fonts by category or customize your font selection by choosing individual fonts. CorelDRAW calculates, and then lists the amount of space available on your hard disk and the space required for the installation.

   To select your fonts by category, click on the boxes beside the desired categories. If you choose Upgrade 3.0, Setup updates your existing fonts.

To select individual fonts, choose Assorted, and then **C**ustomize. A font list appears, permitting you to select the fonts you desire by highlighting them and clicking on **A**dd.

7. Click on **C**ontinue to proceed with the setup. If you select more than 100 fonts, a message box appears, informing you that the installation may affect Windows performance. Click on **C**ontinue to register your fonts, or Back to return to the Font Selection box.

A message box appears, telling you that CorelDRAW is registering your fonts and updating your WIN.INI. This takes a few minutes.

N O T E

Unlike version 4, there is no separate font installation program in CorelDRAW version 5. Installing additional TrueType fonts in version 5 uses the SETUP program on CD-ROM Disk 1. After starting the SETUP program, choose the Minimum/Custom Install button, de-select all applications and click on **C**ontinue. Check the TrueType Fonts box and click on the C**u**stomize button to obtain a choice of TrueType fonts for installation.

Installing PostScript Type 1 Fonts

Corel's fonts are included in both TrueType and PostScript Type 1 formats. Professional illustrators and publishers often prefer to use Type 1 PostScript fonts instead of TrueType to minimize compatibility problems when printing to image setters. These high-end machines are PostScript-based and often have problems when TrueType fonts are used.

To use PostScript Type 1 fonts with CorelDRAW, Adobe Type Manager (ATM) is required. This inexpensive utility program enables Windows to display PostScript fonts on-screen, and also enables the printing of PostScript fonts to non-PostScript printers.

Installing the PostScript versions of the Corel fonts is done through Adobe Type Manager. See the documentation that accompanies Adobe Type Manager for details. Corel version 5.0 Type 1 PostScript fonts are on CD-ROM Disk 2 in the \FONTS\TYPE1 directory. CorelDRAW version 4 includes PostScript fonts on CD-ROM Disc 1, in the \FONTS\TYPE1 directory.

Installing CorelDRAW on a Network

CorelDRAW is designed to operate on both stand-alone systems, as well as network systems. CorelDRAW 5.0 is network-ready. The basic installation is similar to that of a single system. While the setup for CorelDRAW varies according to the type of network being used, some of the setup procedure is universal to most networks.

The instructions in this section refer to Microsoft Windows for Workgroups 3.11 using Ethernet cards. Planning is the key to a successful network installation. Decide which resources and applications you want to share between the individual work stations before starting the installation.

N O T E

The license for use of CorelDRAW extends to a single file server on a local area network and a single user. The number of users at any time cannot exceed the number of licensed copies of CorelDRAW in use on a network. Should you want to add more users, you need to purchase a license for each additional user.

Installing CorelDRAW 5.0 on a Network Server

To install CorelDRAW on the network server, place either floppy disk 1 or CD-ROM Disc 1 into the drive. From the Program Manager, choose **R**un from the **F**ile menu. In the dialog box, type: **A:/Setup /A**. The /A switch designates a network setup. Follow the basic installation instructions given earlier in this appendix. After completing the basic installation, share the drive and directories that hold the CorelDRAW files from within the Windows File Manager.

The Setup program creates a USERDATA.INI on the network server in the CORELDRW\SETUP directory. This file contains the pointers for shared CorelDRAW files, as well as listing the programs available to individual users.

Installing CorelDRAW 5.0 on a Workstation

To install version 5.0 on a workstation, log onto the network. From the Program Manager, choose **R**un from the **F**ile menu. Where F: is the network drive, type **F:\COREL50\SETUP.EXE**. When the CorelDRAW Setup dialog box appears, follow the prompts to complete the setup. Each user's individual CORELAPP.INI file will be updated to identify the network directories where program and data files are stored.

W A R N I N G

Personal files should not be stored in shared directories. This can result in lost files.

Installation to networks may introduce varied troubleshooting problems. See Chapter 47, "Troubleshooting," for more information on consulting troubleshooting information resources.

A p p e n d i x   B

Resource List

Adobe Systems
P.O. Box 7900
Mountain View, CA 94039-7900
(415) 961-4400

Aldus Corp.
411 First Avenue, South Suite 200
Seattle, WA 98104
(206) 343-3277

Chesire Group
321 S. Main Street, Suite 36
Sebastopol, CA 95472
(707) 887-7510

Corel Corporation
1600 Carling Avenue
Ottawa, Ont., Canada K1Z8R7
(613) 728-8200

Delrina Technology, Inc.
895 Don Mills Road 500-2 Park Centre
Toronto, Ont., Canada M3C1W3
(416) 441-3676

Fractal Design Corporation
335 Spreckels Drive
Aptos, CA 95003
(408) 688-8800

Frame Technology Corporation
1010 Rincon Circle
San Jose, CA 95131
(408) 433-3311

HSC Software
1661 Lincoln Boulevard, Suite 101
Santa Monica, CA 90404
(310) 392-8441

Microsoft Corp.
One Microsoft Way
Redmond, WA 98052
(206) 882-8080

Pixar
1001 West Cutting Boulevard
Richmond, CA 94804
(510) 236-4000

ReliSys
320 S. Milipitas Boulevard
Milipitas, CA 95035
(408) 945-9000

Seiko Instruments USA, Inc.
1130 Ringwood Court
San Jose, CA 95131
(408) 922-5949

Summagraphics Corp.
60 Silvermine Road
Seymour, CT 06483
1 (800) 729-7866

U-Lead Systems
970 West 190th Street, Suite 520
Torrance, CA 90502
(310) 523-9393

Visual Software, Inc.
21731 Ventura Blvd Suite
310 Woodland Hills, CA 91364
(818) 883-7900

Using the CorelDRAW! The Professional Reference *CDs*

*T*his appendix explains the contents and installation of the CorelDRAW! The Professional Reference *companion CDs. You will find a wide variety of items that will enhance your use of CorelDRAW, as well as other graphics applications.*

Bonus CD1

The first CD contains demonstration programs of popular graphics programs, shareware, and custom utilities to increase your productivity. CD1 specifically contains the following material:

- **Kai's Power Tools.** The limited version of this popular filters software enables you to apply special effects to your drawings and photographs.

- **Pixar Typestry.** This limited version helps you create colorful 3D images from fonts.

- **Presenting Pixar.** Presenting Pixar introduces you to Pixar and its products. The presentation is based on a gallery of RenderMan images, a tour of Typestry, a Typestry AVI movie, and an introduction to other Pixar products.

- **Pixar 128.** Included on this CD are two Pixar filters that you can use freely in your own work.

- **Simply 3D.** This limited edition of the program shows you how easy it is to create three-dimensional objects by using this software and drawing and illustration programs such as CorelDRAW or Adobe Illustrator.

- **Micrografx Picture Publisher.** This demonstration version shows you this program's strong capabilities in image editing and image enhancement.

- **Design Ware PageWorks.** This limited edition provides users of CorelDRAW and PageMaker with a collection of layout templates, step-by-step tutorials, and technique tips and tricks.

- **5000 Images.** This demonstration version showcases some of this product's stock photographs. You are able to search through particular categories of photographs, such as people or landscapes.

- **Shareware.** The shareware contained on this disc includes Snapgraphics, Units, Where Is, Romcat, and templates and presets to make your work in CorelDRAW more productive.

Bonus CD2

The second CD contains all the artwork that appears in the color signature. The artwork has been placed on the CD so that you can see how the various layers and techniques were used. Note that this artwork is for your viewing and experimentation only. The copyright to the artwork is owned by the artists who created it.

This CD also includes all images that were used in this book's exercises. These images help speed your design work by supplying nearly finished artwork to which you apply version 5 techniques.

Textures are the final component of this CD. The textures are yours to use freely in your work. The textures feature a wide variety of looks and can be used as backgrounds or applied to objects.

Installing the Bonus CDs

Please note that these CDs do not contain automatic installation routines. Rather, you must view the contents of each CD and decide which items to install on your hard drive. Most of the items on CD1 must be installed on your hard drive in order to be used.

Installing Programs

Although the programs do not all follow the same installation procedure, they are similar. To install the product demonstrations and most of the shareware, follow this simple procedure:

1. From the Windows File Manager, create a directory to which you want the files stored.

2. Place the CD in your CD-ROM drive and double-click on the appropriate drive letter.

3. Find the directory or subdirectory that contains the program you want to install.

4. Arrange the two windows by choosing **W**indow, **T**ile in File Manager.

5. Drag the files from the bonus CD window into the directory you created to store the programs on your hard drive.

6. Within File Manager, double-click on either SETUP.EXE or INSTALL.BAT.

Installing Art, Textures, and Exercise Images

Included on the second bonus CD are sample CorelDRAW artwork, exercise images, and textures. The files are stored in separate subdirectories. Because these files are quite large, you might prefer not to install all the images on your hard drive. You might prefer to view the images first and then decide which files to store on your system.

Index

Symbols

CorelDRAW!
Professional Reference
REGISTRATION CARD

Fill out this card to receive information about future OS/2 books and other New Riders titles!

Name _____ **Title** _____

Company _____

Address _____

City/State/ZIP _____

I bought this book because: _____

_____

I purchased this book from:
- ☐ A bookstore (Name _____)
- ☐ A software or electronics store (Name _____)
- ☐ A mail order (Name of Catalog _____)

I purchase this many computer books each year:
- ☐ 1–5   ☐ 6 or more

I currently use these applications: _____

_____

_____

_____

I found these chapters to be the most informative: _____

_____

I found these chapters to be the least informative: _____

_____

Additional comments: _____

_____

☐ I would like to see my name in print! You may use my name and quote me in future New Riders products and promotions. My daytime phone number is:_____

New Riders Publishing 201 West 103rd Street • Indianapolis, Indiana 46290 USA